Footprint

East Africa

The travel guide

Handbook

Michael Hodd

When in Africa in March the long rains begin after four months of hot, dry weather, the richness of growth and the freshness and fragrance everywhere are overwhelming.

Karen Blixen, *Out of Africa*

East Africa Handbook
7th edition
© Footprint Handbooks Ltd 2002

Published by Footprint Handbooks
6 Riverside Court
Lower Bristol Road
Bath BA2 3DZ. England
T +44 (0)1225 469141
F +44 (0)1225 469461
Email discover@footprintbooks.com
Web www.footprintbooks.com

ISBN 1 900949 65 2
CIP DATA: A catalogue record for this
book is available from the British Library

Distributed in the USA by
Publishers Group West

Credits

Series editors
Patrick Dawson and Rachel Fielding

Editorial
Editors: Felicity Laughton and Tim
Jollands
Editorial assistance: Stephanie Lambe
and Claire Boobbyer
Maps: Sarah Sorensen

Production
Page layout: Emma Bryers
Typesetting: Mark Thomas and Leona
Bailey
Maps: Claire Benison, Robert Lunn and
Leona Bailey
Colour maps: Kevin Feeney
Cover: Camilla Ford
Proofreading: Carol Franklin and Jane
Franklin

Design
Mytton Williams

Photography
Front cover: Impact Photos
Back cover: gettyone Stone
Inside colour section: La Belle Aurore,
Eye Ubiquitous, Robert Harding Picture
Library, Dave Saunders

Print
Manufactured in Italy by LEGOPRINT

A foot in the door

Highlights

The snow-capped, tropical mountains of Kilimanjaro, Kenya and the Rwenzoris, views over the great Rift Valley, the Blue Nile Gorge and the Tisissat Falls of Ethiopia; East Africa is all this and more. There are the Indian Ocean islands with their African-Arabic cultures, the magnificent Masai people, and the legacies of Persian, Portuguese, Omani, German, British, French, Italian and Belgian settlements.

Wildlife There is nowhere better than the great National Parks of East Africa to see the 'Big Nine' – elephant, rhino, buffalo, lion, leopard, cheetah, hippo, zebra, and giraffe – and great mountain gorillas, all in their natural surroundings. The birdlife, although less celebrated, is also exceptional and you can see spectacular vultures, marabou storks, cranes, ostriches and swathes of pink flamingos. Reptiles, including crocodiles, abound. Many of the insects have fascinating habits and life-cycles. Flowering trees such as jacarandas, flame trees, corals and flamboyants, colourful and heavy with the scents of the tropics, are everywhere. And then there are the crops: tea plantations, sweet-smelling coffee trees, purple-flowered banana trees, fields of pyrethrum and miles of spiky sisal.

Coast The Indian Ocean shore is one of East Africa's glories. The mainland has glittering palm-fringed beaches of fine white sand and the ancient towns of Malindi, Mombasa, Pangani and Bagamoyo. The coral reefs have brilliant marine life which can be viewed by snorkelling, diving, or in glass-bottomed boats. The wonderful islands of Lamu, Zanzibar, Pemba and Mafia each have their own special charms and culture.

People East Africa is made up of numerous different cultural groups. There are many opportunities to see traditional dances, rituals, festivals and celebrations performed in exotic costume: the magnificent warriors of the Masai, Kamba and Turkana in Kenya; the wood-carving Makonde in Tanzania; Uganda with its traditional Kingdoms; the unique style and customs of the peoples of Ethiopia, Eritrea and Djibouti.

City life It's worth getting to know the capital cities and the major towns. There is the sophistication of Nairobi, with great hotels, exciting nightlife, and a wide range of restaurants, museums and galleries. Kampala is judged by many as the most beautiful city in Africa, green and cool, surrounded by seven hills. Dar es Salaam is in a magnificent harbour setting, and there are the wide boulevards of Addis Ababa, or the charm of Asmara with its Mediterranean architecture spilling over with bougainvillea. Everywhere there are displays of brightly coloured cloth, vegetables, fruits, locally crafted utensils and implements in local markets; the bustle of crowded buses, *dala dala*, *matatus* and *boda boda*; street kiosks with charcoal-grilled food; bands in bars and clubs playing thrilling *lingala* music; and churches packed with singing worshippers.

Art African art is quite unique in its inspiration and in the imagination of its designs. This is particularly true of wood-carvings, with their exaggerated and fantastically conceived figures. Pottery with intricate patterns is made from red clay and fired in open pits. Cloth is woven from cotton and wool, sometimes with batik designs. Traditional leatherwork is sun-dried and cured with clotted milk and linseed oil and horn is carved and polished to make drinking vessels, boxes and ornaments. Jewellery is twisted from silver, copper, brass and amber and basketwork and woven mats are crafted from banana leaves, reeds and sisal.

Previous page Stone Town, Zanzibar, where doors - often elaborately carved or decorated with brass studs - were built to reflect the wealth and social status of their owners

Right Early morning balloon flight over Kenya's Masai Mara

Below The spectacular Tisissat Falls – 'Smoke of the Nile' to the locals – the largest waterfall on the Blue Nile

Bottom left Mombasa's waterfront

Bottom right Mankala is popular throughout East Africa. It is said that the sight of uncut diamonds being used as counters first alerted travellers to the existence of diamonds in Shinyanga, Tanzania

Next page Mount Kilimanjaro, seen from Kenya's Amboseli National Park

6

Right Tree-climbing lion

Below Kenya's bushland, with a group of Masai

Above Lake Magadi, home to thousands of flamingos

Right Bujagali Falls, near Jinja, a short distance from where the Nile begins its journey through Uganda, Sudan and Egypt, and one of the best places in the world for whitewater rafting

Safari

Safari means 'a journey' in Swahili (the language of the coastal people of East Africa), but for the visitor it has a special meaning: going up-country to see the most wondrous display of wildlife to be found anywhere on this earth. For most visitors, a trip to the great parks will be the highlight of their visit. It is a great adventure – in Nairobi and Arusha you can just feel the excitement of groups about to set off. If at all possible, visit the parks as part of a camping safari, or at the very least, stay in one of the tented camps. Such a safari is a memorable experience, the atmosphere is very special and you will be well looked after by the staff.

Just close to Kenya's capital is the Nairobi National Park, and even if you are not able to travel up-country, visit this park in the early morning or at dusk and with a bit of luck, half-an-hour from the city, you will see lions, leopards, cheetahs, zebras, giraffes, buffaloes, hippos and antelopes. **Nairobi National Park**

The Masai Mara has a wealth of game that will take your breath away. Take off at dawn in a hot-air balloon and drift serenely over the landscape as the sun rises. There are many other fine parks in Kenya, including Lake Nakuru where millions of spectacular pink flamingos wade on the lake shore. **Masai Mara, Lake Nakuru**

In Tanzania the Serengeti is very special, particularly at the beginning of the dry season (around the end of June), when a million-and-a-half wildebeest stampede north, plunging through rivers, struggling to keep up with the herd, while fighting off predatory lions and leopards. Nearby Ngorongoro is an extinct volcanic crater about 20 km across. The rim, 500 m above the crater floor, provides glorious views and all the Big Nine are there – even hippos in the small lake on the crater floor. Lake Manyara has a special charm – its abundant birdlife includes swathes of shimmering pink flamingos and it is famous for its tree-climbing lions. **Serengeti, Ngorongoro, Lake Manyara**

Only a few hundred of Africa's mighty mountain gorillas survive. They can be seen close-up in the Virungu Mountains, bordered by Rwanda, RD Congo (formerly Zaire) and Uganda. Visits are once again possible to the colonies in Uganda's Bwindi Forest. And you won't forget a close-up visit to the chimpanzees made famous by Jane Goodall, at Gombe Stream on the shore of Lake Tanganyika. **Gorillas & chimpanzees**

Mount Kilimanjaro (the highest peak in Africa) and Mount Kenya offer special challenges. They are both high enough to be topped by snow and ice all year round, despite being close to the equator. Both can be climbed by the reasonably fit, though they can be demanding and the last section of Mount Kenya can only be managed by experienced climbers. A memorable adventure in Uganda is to go whitewater rafting on the Nile rapids, on one of the well-organized trips from Kampala. **Mountains & rivers**

When you are on safari it can be tough: in the dry weather it is dusty, in the wet the roads can be difficult or impassable; the rain, when it arrives, is like a waterfall and the tracks are rough and bumpy. There is a challenge and a sense of achievement in coming through it all. But having washed off the dust of the day there is nothing quite like a sundowner in the cool of the evening by the campfire, with the aroma of food being prepared, a blood-red sunset, a velvety dusk and the exotic sounds and scents of the African night. **Sundown**

Next page *Looking down from the rim of the Ngorongoro Crater to the 'Garden of Eden' 600 m below*

Zamani

Zamani means 'the past' in Swahili. Africa, seen through the eyes of the great explorers, scholars, writers and adventurers of bygone eras, takes on a new dimension as you conjure up images of the great Dark Continent as they saw it.

Cradle of Mankind Charles Darwin was the first to express the view that human life originated in Africa and since then others, including the famous Leakey family, have made extraordinary discoveries which have established Africa as the 'Cradle of Mankind'. Olduvai Gorge in Tanzania is the site of many of their most famous finds and the museum there puts all the discoveries in the context of man's evolution.

The Mountain Kingdom Ethiopia has a rich history that can be traced back to King Solomon. This long and illustrious past can be admired in the numerous artefacts that survive and in the style and manner of the Ethiopian people, sheltered from the world, as they have been through the centuries, by their mountainous homeland. The country's religion, literature, language, cuisine and spectacular festivals are quite unlike anywhere else on the continent.

Shiraz All along the coast are the ruined cities and settlements of the Shirazi people, who migrated from Persia to Africa. Among these settlements, those at Gedi, Tongoni and Kilwa were extensive and sophisticated. The remains of magnificent stone buildings at Kilwa reveal a once-prosperous 10th-century settlement that grew rich by providing an Indian Ocean terminus for the gold trade to the interior.

Vasco da Gama In 1498 Vasco de Gama rounded the Cape of Good Hope and then voyaged north along the East African coast. The Portuguese left their mark with garrisons, settlements and great forts, most notably those still existing in Mombasa and Zanzibar. Their rule lasted until 1698 when they were vanquished by forces from Oman, heralding two centuries of Arab domination of the coast.

Explorers Livingstone, Stanley, Burton, Speke, Grant and Thompson all made extraordinary journeys into the interior. It is difficult not to be inspired by the site in Uganda where Speke first glimpsed the source of the Nile; or by Ujiji on the shore of Lake Tanganyika, 1,500 km from the coast, where Henry Morton Stanley finally found a sick and ailing David Livingstone; or by Harar in Ethiopia where Sir Richard Burton was the first European to set foot in the Forbidden City.

Colonial railways When Britains, Germans, Italians and French began their periods of rule at the end of the 19th century, they built railways. In Kenya, the British constructed a line that climbs a kilometre as it steadily winds its way from the coast to Kampala. The Germans built a line from Dar es Salaam to Lake Tanganyika and every railway town in Tanzania has a clutch of handsome buildings all constructed nearly a century ago. In Eritrea the Italians built a railway from the coast up to Asmara and beyond, and the French laid down tracks for Emperor Menelik of Ethiopia from Djibouti to Addis Ababa. You can ride on some of these railways, possibly in restored, original steam engines and carriages.

Scribblers Finally there are the great writers: Ernest Hemingway, Evelyn Waugh, Karen Blixen, Elspeth Huxley, Vidia Naipaul. We can retrace their journeys, visit their houses, see the great African continent anew through their eyes and, as Winston Churchill observed in Uganda in 1898, "The more you study the past, the better you understand."

Right Gondar Royal Enclosure, site of five of the city's many castles and palaces built by successive Ethiopian kings from the 17th-19th century

Below Ngome Kongwe, a fort built by Omani Arabs in 1700 to defend Zanzibar against attack by the Portuguese

Bottom left Zanzibar's dhow harbour at its busiest in the morning when the fishermen's catches are landed

Bottom right The maze of streets, palm trees and old stone buildings that characterize Lamu town

Next page Bet Giorgis, a church hewn out of solid rock, Lalibela, Ethiopia

Page 15 Fishermen in their dhows on the torquoise seas of the 'Swahili coast'

Swahili

Swahili is the language and culture of the people of the East African coast. A unique blend of Africa, Islam, the classical world and eastern civilization, it has given rise to distinctive architecture, literature, culture and customs.

Lamu   Lamu is a magical island off Kenya's Indian Ocean coast. Lamu Town is a maze of narrow streets with mosques and traditional, cool stone dwellings with carved, brass-studded doors. There are no vehicles. Donkeys from the island's sanctuary wander through the streets. The centre of town has a large fort dating from 1809, there is a fine collection of Swahili exhibits including the famous Siwa horns at Lamu Museum, the old German Post Office has been reconstructed and the Swahili House Museum gives a fascinating insight into traditional family life. The quayside runs along the water's edge and restaurants and hotels look out over the harbour where dhows sail by. There are few more relaxing places on earth.

Zanzibar   There cannot be many travellers who have not longed to visit Zanzibar, and indeed it is no disappointment. Arriving by sea there is a skyline of the old Customs House, the colonial Hotel d'Afrique Centrale, the former Sultan's Palace, the House of Wonders and the Portuguese Fort. The ancient Stone Town, now being restored, is a World Heritage site. The winding streets are mostly free of cars and there are fine buildings, museums, palaces, mosques, hotels in restored Swahili houses, relics of the slave trade, rooftop restaurants, gardens with alfresco eating, and Persian bath houses. Every evening, from the verandah bar of the old English Club, you can watch a magnificent sunset. Beyond the town, Zanzibar island is strewn with the palaces of the former Sultans, the air is fragrant with the spices of the plantations and there are glorious beaches, such as Jambiani and Nungwe, where you can stay in simple accommodation for a song.

Bagamoyo   Bagamoyo, close to Dar es Salaam, is a small historic town that was the centre of the slave trade on the mainland. From here caravans set out on mighty journeys to the interior. Reminders of the slave trade are everywhere and, as well as a Slave Museum, there are Livingstone's church, German colonial buildings, Shirazi ruins and the Holy Ghost Mission, the first Christian settlement on the mainland.

Beaches,   All along the Indian Ocean coast are splendid beaches and a fine range of places to stay.
fishing, diving   Perhaps the best beaches are Diani, south of Mombasa, and Jambiani in Zanzibar. You can surf at Malindi. The deep-sea fishing in the Pemba Channel is rated among the best in the world. The crystal-clear water makes the marine parks at Watamu and Malindi magnificent places for snorkelling. Diving facilities are good and six sites in Kenya and another six off the islands of Zanzibar, Pemba and Mafia are without rival anywhere. Dive training is offered at all the main sites and taking a PADI course is a popular part of a beach holiday.

Seagoing   Everywhere on the Indian Ocean coast you are aware of the maritime heritage that
history   brought communities together to form the Swahili. Massive ocean-going dhows at the big ports, little coastal outriggers dipping through the shallows, boat-building yards, fishing villages and markets. The coast has always been seen as the place to rest and enjoy the pleasures of life. Weary caravan porters sang to keep up their spirits as they approached the end of their journey from the interior:

> "My spirits lift as the drum-beats roll
> Lay down my heart, and calm my soul
> At last I'm home, Bagamoyo."

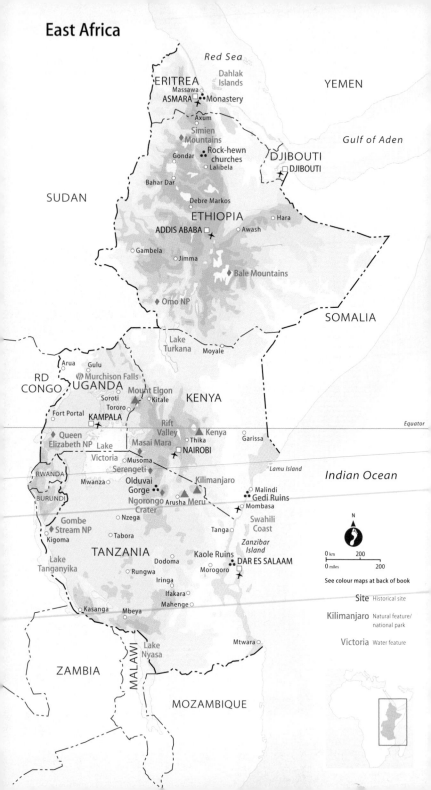

East Africa

Red Sea

Dahlak Islands

YEMEN

ERITREA
Massawa
ASMARA ✈ ● Monastery

○ Axum

Gulf of Aden

Simien ◆ Mountains

Gondar ○ ● ● Rock-hewn churches
● Lalibela

DJIBOUTI
□ DJIBOUTI ✈

Bahar Dar ○

○ Debre Markos

ETHIOPIA

○ Hara

ADDIS ABABA □ ✈ ○ Awash

○ Gambela

○ Jimma

◆ Bale Mountains

SOMALIA

◆ Omo NP

Lake Turkana

○ Moyale

○ Arua
○ Gulu

RD CONGO

〰 Murchison Falls
UGANDA
○ Soroti ▲ Mount Elgon
○ Tororo ○ Kitale

KENYA

○ Fort Portal

KAMPALA □ ✈

Rift Valley ▲ Kenya
○ Thika
○ Garissa

◆ Queen Elizabeth NP
Lake ▲ Masai Mara
Victoria □ **NAIROBI**

Equator

RWANDA
○ Musoma

○ Mwanza

◆ Serengeti

Lamu Island

Indian Ocean

BURUNDI
Olduvai ● ● ● ▲ Kilimanjaro
Gorge ● ● ○ Malindi
Ngorongo ▲ ● ● Gedi Ruins
Crater Arusha Meru ○ Mombasa
✈
◆ Gombe ○ Nzega
Stream NP Swahili
○ Kigoma ○ Tabora Coast

Zanzibar Island

Lake **TANZANIA** ○ Tanga
Tanganyika
○ Dodoma Kaole Ruins
○ Rungwa ● **DAR ES SALAAM**
○ Iringa ○ Morogoro ✈

N ⬆

○ Kasanga
○ Mbeya
MALAWI
Lake Nyasa

◆ Ifakara ○
○ Mahenge

0 km 200
0 miles 200

See colour maps at back of book

○ Mtwara

ZAMBIA

MOZAMBIQUE

────────────

Site Historical site

Kilimanjaro Natural feature/ national park

Victoria Water feature

SUDAN

Contents

Essentials

2

Essentials

Planning your trip

East Africa's great **safarilands** are centred on the three former British territories of Kenya, Tanzania and Uganda. They have broad vistas of grassland, dotted with thorn trees, home to much of the wildlife. They are bordered by the great lakes of the Rift Valley, and Kenya and Tanzania have long coastlines on the Indian Ocean. Each country has highland areas, where the altitude makes for moderate temperatures, and peaks with glaciers and snow all the year round, despite the tropical location. Uganda and Kenya have extensive arid areas to the north.

The territories of the **mountains**, clustering around the Rift Valley lakes in the centre of the continent, make up a second grouping of countries in East Africa. Comprising Burundi, Rwanda and the eastern part of RD Congo (formerly Zaire), they were all at one time administered by Belgium. The terrain is hilly, covered with dense vegetation and cultivation, and the peaks often wreathed in mist. These territories are considered risky for travellers, and are not covered in this book.

To the north are the countries of the **Horn of Africa** comprising Ethiopia, Eritrea, Djibouti and Somalia. Italian influence has been strong here in all the territiories except the port of Djibouti which was a French colony. Great areas of the countries of the Horn are arid. However, Ethiopia and Eritrea have extensive areas of highland with reasonable rainfall and vegetation and are well able to support cultivation. Most of Somalia is desert, with some grassland dotted by scattered bushes and trees in the north and south, and mangroves along the coast. Somalia, another risky country for travellers, is not covered in this book.

Where to go

Quite superb natural attractions offer some very special experiences. In **Kenya** the parks have a range of spectacular lodges, tented camps and ballooning. The big game in the Masai Mara and the flamingos on the Rift Valley lakes are unforgettable. **Tanzania** has perhaps the best wildlife in the region. The Serengeti, Ngorongoro Crater, Lake Manyara and the Selous Reserve are outstanding. The lodges are not as luxurious as in Kenya, but they are improving, and there are some first-rate small establishments. Above all, the great game areas of Tanzania are less crowded than those in Kenya. **Uganda** has two fine parks in Queen Elizabeth and Murchison Falls, and, at the current time, the only viable prospect for viewing mountain gorillas in the Virunga Mountains. (Rwanda and Eastern RD Congo also offer access to mountain gorillas but security remains a problem.) | Wildlife

Both **Kenya** and **Tanzania** have challenging peaks in Mount Kenya and Mount Kilimanjaro. **Uganda** offers the prospect of the Rwenzori Mountains and the Virungas, as well as Mount Elgon, which can also be climbed from Kenya. | Climbing & trekking

Kenya has an excellent range of beach hotels and some really fine places to stay. Diani beach south of Mombasa is miles of white sand, blue seas and palm trees. **Tanzania**'s coast is less developed, but there are good beaches and accommodation at Pangani and Bagamoyo. The two most popular islands, Lamu in Kenya and Zanzibar in Tanzania, have fine tropical coastlines. | Beaches

Olduvai Gorge in **Tanzania** has revealed the evolution of early man from fossils going back 3,000,000 years, and many discoveries there have led to the site being known as the 'Cradle of Mankind'. | Historical interest

Ethiopia has a recorded past going back 2,000 years. There are the ancient cities of Axum, Gondar, and Harar, as well as a wealth of monasteries and early Christian churches.

Remnants of Shirazi settlements on the coast of mainland Africa are thought to date from perhaps as early as the 10th century. The marvellous old town sections of Massawa, Zanzibar, Mombasa, Bagamoyo and Lamu began to be developed somewhat later, from the end of the 14th century. They contain fine houses with balconies and verandahs around courtyards designed to stay cool by catching the ocean breezes, richly carved doors, elaborately decorated mosques, narrow winding streets of cobblestones.

Essentials

The first European impact came with the arrival of the Portuguese in the 15th century. The strategic forts they built to consolidate their trading presence remain, most notably in Mombasa and Zanzibar.

Of the eventual colonizers of the mainland, the Germans left by far the most impressive architecture, a distinctive style adapting European technique to local materials and climatic conditions – examples are scattered throughout what is now mainland Tanzania. Railways were built by the British in Kenya, the Italians in Eritrea, the French in Djibouti and the Germans in Tanzania around the beginning of the 20th century. The stations are still in use, and examples of the early rolling stock and locomotives survive. In the Horn of Africa, Italy has left its mark, with a Mediterranean style of architecture that is most marked in Eritrea but also noticeable in Ethiopia.

Traditional life & culture Many of the mainland people have spectacular traditional lifestyles. The dress, decoration and ceremonies of the Masai are perhaps the best known. However, on mainland East Africa over 300 distinct communities have their own traditional dress, fables and stories, dances, ceremonies, customs and styles of dwelling.

Modern life Urban Africa has a style and excitement all its own: intricately laid out goods at markets; gaudily painted and crowded minibuses covered in slogans with swashbuckling conductors; churches packed to overflowing; weddings with exuberant processions; vibrant local bars, dance halls and discos, with men in dress ranging from silk suits to baseball caps and lycra cycling shorts; girls in second-hand wedding dresses, miniskirts, designer jeans and wide-brimmed hats; hair natural, straightened, plaited; exciting music with sophisticated rhythms and delicate melodies.

Unsafe countries
See page 35 for further advice
At the time of writing, parts of Northern Ethiopia and Eritrea border zones, northern Uganda and northeast Kenya are effectively off limits to all but essential travel and will not therefore be covered in this edition of the handbook . Circumstances can change, however, within a matter of months, and advice should be sought.

Itineraries An itinerary covering the main attractions in East Africa might be:

- Fly in to Addis Ababa and take in the Historic Route of the Blue Nile Gorge, Gondar, Axum, Lalibela and Harar.
- Fly to Kampala, visiting the source of the Nile, Murchison Falls and the mountain gorillas.
- Fly to Arusha and tour Ngorongoro Crater, Lake Manyara and the Serengeti.
- Travel overland from the Serengeti to the Masai Mara in Kenya, from there to Lake Nakuru and Nairobi.
- Take the train from Nairobi to Mombasa, visiting the Old Town.
- Fly to Zanzibar, explore Stone Town and stay in one of the beach resorts.

When to go

There are two rainy seasons in the country, the long rains March-April and the short rains October-December. However, even during the rains there is invariably sunshine each day. January and February are the main months of the wildlife season, as the weather is hot and dry, the vegetation dies down making the animals easier to see, and animals to move to the waterholes where they can be readily located.

Kenya
For very detailed 5-day local weather forecast, go to www.cirrus.sprlu. mich.edu/wxnet/

March-May can be months of heavy rain making travel on unsealed roads difficult. Even in these months, however, there is an average of 4-6 hours of sunshine each day.

Tanzania

The heavy rainy season is March-May with lighter rains in November-December. Generally there is some sunshine each day, even in the rainy seasons.

Uganda

The rainy season is from June-September. The hot and dry months are April-May. However, if you do travel in the rainy season, the countryside is very green and the temperature is cooler.

Ethiopia

Heavy rains fall in July and August, and the dry months of December and February. As roads connecting the main towns are soaked, the rains cause few problems for tourists, and there are usually some hours of sunshine even when it rains. Temperatures are reasonable, around 25°C max all the year round.

Eritrea

Hot June-September, reaching 45°C, October-April cooler. Very little rain with what little there is falling mostly in March and November.

Djibouti

Essentials

Essentials

The history of East Africa

Archaeological sites at Olduvai Gorge in Tanzania and at Lower Awash River in Ethiopia suggest that man began to evolve in the Rift Valley more than 3,000,000 years ago, and hunter-gatherer communities were established.

The area then experienced an influx of people from West Africa, which has become known as the Bantu Expansion, beginning around 500 BC. In the Horn it is thought that Cushitic immigrants came from Mesopotamia (now Iraq) around 300 BC. The newcomers were cultivators and pastoralists, and they began to change the pattern of subsistence away from hunting and gathering.

Contact with other areas began as sea-going traders arrived from the north, sailing down the east coast of Africa and coming from as far as India, China and South East Asia. A sprinkling of settlements by Islamic people from Shiraz in Persia (now Iran) were established along the coast from about 1000 AD.

European contact began with the arrival of the Portuguese who sailed round the southern tip of Africa and passed up the

east coast from 1500 on. They set up fortified settlements to consolidate their trading presence, several of which remain, most notably Fort Jesus in Mombasa.

A struggle for dominance of these coastal strips began between Arab groups drawing support from the Persian Gulf and vying with the Portuguese for the trade in gold, ivory and slaves. By the end of the 17th century the Portuguese found themselves stretched to retain their hold in East Africa, and Fort Jesus fell to the Arabs in 1698. For most of the next two centuries Arab rule prevailed at the coast, and they began to penetrate the interior with caravans to capture slaves and ivory. These set out from Bagamoyo and Kilwa on the coast of present-day Tanzania, following routes that stretched over 1000 kilometres to the Great Lakes and beyond.

In the interior, meanwhile, pockets of centralized rule and formalized social structures emerged, particularly to the west of Lake Victoria. In the Horn of Africa, the dynasty that traces its origins to Biblical times was establishing cities at Axum, Gondar and Harar.

European exploration began in the 18th century. A Scot, James Bruce in 1768-73 travelled from Suskin on the Red Sea up the Abara River to join the Nile. Lacerda, a Portuguese explorer travelled up the Zambesi in 1798-9, and then headed north to reach Lake Tanganyika. Burckhardt in 1809-17 journeyed from Massawa to Lake Tana and down the Blue Nile to Khartoum. The brothers Antoine and Arnaud Abbadie in 1837-48 pressed further south from Gondar in Ethiopia. Kraf and Rebmann, two Germans, in 1848 travelled from the Kenya coast up through the highlands. Richard Burton in 1854-5 managed an excursion from Zaila on the Red Sea coast to Harar in Ethiopia.

The origins of the White Nile (which joins the Blue Nile at Khartoum) began to exercise the imagination in Europe, and the source was eventually traced to Lake Victoria by Burton and Speke in 1860. The two great journeys by David Livingstone in 1858-64 and 1866-73 reached to Lake Tanganyika and beyond, and were followed by Stanley's expedition in 1874-7 which crossed the continent from east to west.

The slave trade

1 Slave trading east or south of line made illegal by Moresby Treaty, 1822
2 All northern slave trading made illegal by Hamerton Treaty, 1845
▲ British anti-slave trade patrol bases

The activities of the explorers were followed by missionary activity and a campaign to end the slave trade. Although slavery was made illegal in 1873, it was some time before it was finally eliminated.

The European nations formalized their presence with the British occupying Kenya, Uganda and Zanzibar, and the Germans established themselves in what is now mainland Tanzania, Rwanda and Burundi. Eastern RD Congo was part of the Belgian Congo. Eritrea and southern Somalia were Italian, and northern Somalia was British. The French held the port of Djibouti. Only Ethiopia retained its Independence, holding off the attentions of Italy.

Economic progress had taken place in the interior as iron implements replaced more primitive stone and wooden tools, and cultivators accumulated farming knowledge. However, droughts, locusts, rinderpest and local conflicts contrived to keep populations fairly stable. Progress accelerated with the advent of European occupation. Diseases were controlled, new crops introduced, roads and railways were built. Death rates fell, birth rates remained high and the population began a steady expansion. Living standards improved and significant sections of the population received basic education.

After the First World War the British took over the part of German East Africa that became Tanganyika, and Belgium absorbed Rwanda and Burundi. Italy occupied Ethiopia for a period from 1936-42. Settler presence increased, particularly in Kenya, and the Asian communities consolidated their positions in commerce and the skilled trades.

Nationalist movements began to emerge as significant political factors after the Second World War. Ethiopia federated with Eritrea in 1952. In Kenya, where there was by now a substantial settler population, there was an armed conflict in the 1950s (the Mau Mau uprising) over land grievances and generally in support of self-determination. Most countries obtained their Independence in the early 1960s, although Djibouti did not break from France until 1977.

Tanzania was created when Tanganyika formed a union with Zanzibar in 1964. The immediate post-Independence period typically saw the establishment of single-party regimes, and in many cases government was unstable (although Tanzanian, Kenya and Djibouti have proved exceptions). In Uganda, Somalia, Rwanda, Burundi, and Ethiopia there have been disastrous collapses of peace and security.

Economic development was pursued by the adoption of socialist development strategies with heavy reliance on the public sector. A deceleration of economic progress followed, and in the 1980s most countries reversed their economic policies and by 1994 had either undertaken, or were planning, multi-party elections.

In 1993, after a referendum, and with the approval of Ethiopia, Eritrea broke away to become an independent state.

The search for the source of the Nile

☞ ## People of East Africa

*The population of the **safarilands** is largely of Bantu origin, comprising several hundred identifiable communities. Most are settled cultivators, but there are many pastoralists, often nomadic. Kenya and Tanzania have Swahili people along the coast, the product of intermarriage between Africans and Arabs. These two countries also have communities from the Indian sub-continent, mostly involved in commercial life and the professions. In Uganda, almost all Asians were expelled under Amin, and it is only now that they are beginning to return. Small communities of Europeans have remained in farming and business.*

*The **mountain** countries of Rwanda and*

Burundi are riven by the division into the majority Hutu (80 %) and the Tutsi (15 %). The Tutsi are tall pastoralists from the north who traded cattle for land and established themselves as a land-owning class, dominating government, the armed forces and access to education. The Hutu are physically smaller, and engaged mostly in cultivation. Eastern RD Congo is a mixture of mostly Bantu people.

*The inhabitants of the **Horn** have distinctive features with a more Arabic appearance and, except in Ethiopia, lighter skin colour. In Somalia there are many pastoralists, following Islam. The Ethiopians have a strong cultivating tradition and their own form of Christianity.*

Tour operators

Truck safari operators in the UK *Acacia Expeditions*, 5 Walm Lane, London, NW2 5SJ, T020-8451 3877, F020-8451 4727. *Dragoman*, Camp Green, Debenham, Stowmarket, Suffolk, IP14 6LA, T01728-861133, F01728-861127, www.dragoman.co.uk *Encounter*, 2001 Camp Green, Debenham, Suffolk, IP14 6LA, T01728-862222, F01728-861127, www.encounter.co.uk *Exodus Travels*, 9 Weir Rd, London, SW12 0LT, T020-8772 3822, www.exodus.co.uk *Explore*, 1 Frederick St, Aldershot, Hants, GU11 1LQ, T01252-39448, F01252-343170. *Guerba*, 101 Eden Vale Rd, Westbury, Wiltshire, BA13 3QX, T01373-826611, F01373-838351, www.guerba.com *Kumuka Expeditions*, 40 Earls Court Rd, London, W8 6EJ, T020-7937 8855, F020-7937 6664, www.kumuka.com *Top Deck Double Decker Bus Safaris*, 131-5 Earls Court Rd, London, SW5 9RH, T020-7370 4555, F7373 6201, *Tracks*, 12 Abingdon St, London, W8 6AF. *Truck Africa*, 37 Ranelagh Mansions, London, SW6 3UQ, T020-7731 6142, F7371 7445.

Specialist tour operators
For further specialist tour operators, see relevant Essentials sections for each country
UK *Africa Travel Centre*, 21 Leigh St, London WC1H 9EW, T020-7387 1211, www.africatravel.co.uk *Bike Tours*, PO Box 75, Bath, Avon, BA 1BX, T01225-480130, F01225-480132. Cycling safaris in Kenya and Tanzania, climbing Mt Kilimajaro. *Encounter*, address above. Trekking, whitewater rafting. *Explore*, address above. Hiking, canoe safaris, gorillas. *Exodus Travels*, address above. Biking, walking, trekking, discovery and adventure. *Leisure Activity Safaris*, PO Box 10190, Mombasa, Kenya, T487326, F485454 or UK:, T01626-775070. Cycling safaris through Rift Valley, Masai Mara, Coast, Mt Kilimanjaro. *Safari Consultants*, Orchard House, Upper Rd, Little Cornan, Suffolk, CO10, T01787-228494, F01787-228949. Old-style tented safaris, walking, climbing, gorillas, chimpanzees, fishing on Rusinga Island, Lake Victoria, Kenya. *Sherpa Expeditions*, 131a Heston Rd, Hounslow, Middlesex, TW5 0RD, T020-8577 2717, F020-8577 9788. Walking tours covering Mt Elgon and Mt Kenya, Mt Kilimanjaro and Kenya, Rwenzori Mts. *Worldwide*, 8 Comeragh Rd, London, W14 9HP, T020-7381 8638, F020-7381 0836. Wildlife, walking, trekking – with emphasis on the environment, conservation and ecology. **Europe** *Jambo Tours*, Langscheider Str. 40C, D-59846 Sundern, Germany, info@jambotours.de Old-style tented safaris, walking, climbing, gorillas, chimpanzees, fishing on Rusinga Island, Lake Victoria, Kenya. **North America** Africa Adventure Company, 5353 N Federal Highway, Suite 300, Fort Lauderdale, FL 33308, T800-8829453, T954-4918877, F954-4919060, www.africa-adventure.com *Distant Horizons*, 350 Elm Av, Long Beach, CA 90802, T800-3331240, T562-9838828, F562-9838833, www.distant-horizons.com *International Expeditions*, One Environs Park, Helena, Al 35080, T800-6334734, T205-4281700, F205-4281714, www.internationalexpeditions.com *Legendary Adventure Co*, 3025 47th St, Suite 1, Boulder, CO 80301, T303-4131182, F303-4131184, www.legendaryadventure.com

Finding out more

There are literally hundreds of websites covering travel in East Africa. In addition to the country-specific sites detailed in the Essentials sections of the individual countries, we would particularly recommend **www.moja.com** whose many useful links include the Kisiju Project's online Swahili dictionary. The *East African* newspaper's coverage of the region can be accessed at **www.nationaudio.com/News/EastAfrican/current**, while the *Boabab Project* at **www.web-dubois.fas.harvard.edu/DuBois/baobab/baobab.html** is a site that provides general cultural information.

Travel Africa, 2 Potland Cottages, Toot Baldon, Oxford, OX44 9NH, T/F01865-434220, www.travelafricamag.com This quarterly publication is a comprehensive source of information for all travellers in Africa.

An excellent source of maps is **Stanfords** at 12-14 Long Acre, London WC2E 9LP, T020-7836 1321, F020-7836 0189, www.stanfords.co.uk **Maps**

Essentials

Language

English is widely used and understood. French is used in Djibouti. Swahili can be helpful in Tanzania, Kenya and to a lesser degree in Uganda. Italian is often understood in Eritrea, particularly by older residents. *See pages 319 and 320 for tips on Swahili*

Disabled travellers

Alas, special facilities for disabled travellers in East Africa are few and far between. Wheelchairs are very difficult to accommodate on public road transport, and private hires will normally need to be made. However, everywhere you will find people will do their level best to help, and being disabled should not deter you from visiting East Africa. The **Royal Association for Disability and Rehabilitation (RADAR)**, 12 City Forum, 250 City Road, London EC1V 8AF, T020-7250 3222, F020-7250 0212, www.RADAR.org.uk, are a good resource in the UK for disabled persons.

Travelability, T0870-2416127, www.travelability.co.uk, *Disability World*, T01383-823420, and *Holiday Care*, T01293-774535, are specialist travel agents who can advise and help arrange holidays for disabled travellers. It is also worth visiting the www.geocities.com site. Their Global Access – Disabled Travel Network site is dedicated to providing information for 'disabled adventurers' and includes a number of reviews and tips for members of the public.

Gay and lesbian travellers

Homosexuality is illegal in all countries except Eritrea and extreme discretion is advocated. However, there is a general toleration by ordinary people of discrete behaviour. There are recognizable gay scenes in Nairobi, Mombasa and Lamu in Kenya, and in Zanzibar in Tanzania. Gay clubs and bars are conspicuous by their absence. If you wish to get updated information try a gay website such as www.afrol.com/Categories/Gay/backgr_legal status.htm

Student travellers

There are generally no discounts for students (apart from international air travel) – student rates advertised for museums and parks will usually only apply to local residents.

Travelling with children

Outside the main towns you will need to take everything with you. Particular attention needs to be given to the risks of malaria, dysentery, sunburn and heat exhaustion (see Health page 58). There is plenty to interest children in the wildlife parks and at the coast. Long dusty road journeys can be a trial, but can be enlivened by wildlife spotting.

Flying with kids
Visit:
www.babygoes2.com

Inform the airline in advance that you are travelling with a baby or toddler and check out the facilities when booking as these vary with each aircraft. *British Airways* now has a special seat for under 2s; check which aircraft have been fitted when booking. Pushchairs can be taken as hand luggage or stored in the hold. Skycots are available on long-haul flights. Take snacks and toys for in-flight entertainment and remember that swallowing food or drinks during take-off and landing will help prevent ear problems.

Women travellers

Normal caution is required. In particular, dress modestly, be wary of unsolicited male company, move around in a group where possible, avoid sunbathing alone on isolated beaches and take taxis at night.

Working in the country

There are virtually no opportunities for travellers to obtain casual work in East Africa. However, it is quite possible to work, paying most of your own expenses, for a volunteer organization. Set this up before you travel. Useful websites are: **www.volunteerafrica.org** and **www.wildnetafrica.co.za**

Before you travel

Getting in

Insurance
For visas and immigration, customs, export restrictions, see relevant Essentials sections for each country

Insurance companies have tightened up considerably over recent years and it is now almost impossible to make a successful claim if you have not followed their procedures correctly. The problem is that these often involve dealing with the country's red tape which can lead to some inconvenience at best and to some quite long delays at worst. There is no substitute for suitable precautions against petty crime. The level of insurance that you carry is often dictated by the level of medical insurance that you require. Also make sure you obtain sports extensions if you are going to go diving, rafting, climbing, etc. Most policies do not cover very high levels of baggage/cash. Don't forget to check whether you can claim on your household insurance. They often have worldwide all-risks extensions. Most policies exclude manual work while away although working in bars or restaurants is usually allowed.

- Take the policy with you (a photocopy will do but make sure it is a complete one).
- Do not travel against medical advice. It will invalidate the medical insurance part of the cover.
- Usually there is a 24-hour medical emergency service Helpline associated with your insurance. You need to contact them if you require in-patient hospital treatment or you need to return home early. The telephone number is printed on the policy. Make sure you note the time of the call, the person you were talking to and get a reference number. Should you need to be airlifted home, this is always arranged through the insurance company's representative and the hospital authorities.
- If you have to cancel your trip for whatever reason, contact your travel agent, tour operator or airline without delay.
- If your property is damaged whilst in the care of an airline, report it immediately and always within three days and get a 'property irregularity report' from them.
- Claims for baggage left unattended are very rarely settled unless they were left in a securely locked hotel room, apartment or locked in the boot of a car and there is evidence of a forced entry. Cash should be carried on your person or left in a locked safe or security box, for which a receipt must be obtained.
- All loss must be reported to the police and/or hotel authorities within 24 hours of discovery and a written report obtained.
- If medical attention is received for injury or sickness, a medical certificate showing its nature must be obtained, although some companies waive this if only out-patient treatment is required. Keep all receipts in a safe place as they will be needed to substantiate the claim.
- Check your policy carefully to see if there is a date before which claims must be submitted. This is often within 30 days of returning home. It is now usual for companies to want your policy document, proof that you actually travelled (airline ticket or travel agent's confirmation of booking), receipts and written reports (in the event of loss). Note that photocopies are not accepted.

Insurance tips

In addition to comprehensive travel insurance, we recommend joining AMREF who will provide emergency air evacuation by the Flying Doctors' Service of Africa if required. Most of the evacuations are from Kenya and Tanzania but they will fly further afield provided they get air clearance. **Flying Doctors' Society of Africa**, AMREF House, Wilson Airport, PO Box 30125, Nairobi, Kenya, T+254-02-501301 (ext. 377), F+254-02-606345, flyingdocs@net2000ke.com

What to take

Travellers tend to take more than they need although requirements vary with the destination and the type of travel that is to be undertaken. Laundry services are generally cheap and speedy. A travelpack, a hybrid backpack/suitcase, rather than a rigid suitcase, covers most eventualities and survives the rigours of a variety of modes of travel well. Serious trekkers will need a framed backpack. A lock for your luggage is strongly advised – there are cases of pilfering by airport baggage handlers. In any case, take valuable items such as cameras and radios as hand baggage on flights. It is also sensible to take bottles of shampoo or other liquids not in a screw top bottle on as hand baggage on aircraft – as the holds are not always pressurized, and the air in a bottle expands, forcing out the liquid, making a mess.

Before you leave, send yourself an email with details of such things as travellers' cheques, passport, driving licence, credit cards and travel insurance numbers. Be sure that someone at home also has access to important details

Clothing of light cotton or cotton/polyester is best, with a fleece or woollen clothing for evenings. Alternatively a jacket with lots of pockets, although not essential, can be useful. Comfortable shoes with socks as feet may swell in hot weather. Modest dress for women including a sunhat and headscarf. *Travelling Light*, Morland, Penrith, Cumbria, CA10 3AZ, UK, T01931-714488 can supply specialized items by mail order.

Essentials

Checklists

Always take half as many clothes as you think you will need and twice the amount of money

See also advice on Safaris, page 49, and medicines, page 59

Most important items are: air tickets; binoculars; camera; cash; chequebook; credit cards; passport including visa; passport photographs; photocopies of main documents (keep separate) and travellers' cheques. Apart from these everybody has their own list. Obviously what you take depends on where you are intending to go and also what your budget is. **Toiletries**: comb; concentrated detergent; contact lens cleaner; deodorant; adhesive bandages; insect repellent; nailbrush; razor and blades; shampoo; soap; sun protection cream; talcum powder; tissues and toilet paper; toothbrush; toothpaste and vaseline/moisturiser. **Other**: ear plugs; electric insecticide vaporizer and tablets; eye mask; folding umbrella; inflatable cushion; lock and chain (securing luggage at night); multiple outlet adaptor; plastic bags; sewing kit; short-wave radio and batteries; small torch plus batteries; sun-glasses; Swiss army knife; traveller's heating jug; universal washbasin plug and water bottle.

Those intending to stay in **budget accommodation** might also include: cotton sheet sleeping bag; money belt; padlock (for hotel room and pack); soap; student card; towel; and universal bath plug.

Money

Traveller's cheques in US dollars are a wise precaution. Almost every country (the exception is Eritrea) has an American Express representative where travellers' cheques can be bought against payment by personal cheque and production of an American Express card. However, this service is usually only available in the capital city.

Some cash is desirable, held in US dollars, with some in small denomination notes for requirements such as payment of airport departure taxes. It is advisable to take dollars issued after 1990 as there have been problems with the acceptability of pre-1990 notes which have been forged.

Discount flight agents

Australia and New Zealand

Africa Travel Centre, *456 Kent St, Sydney, NSW 2000, T02-2673084. In NZ: 21 Remuera Rd, Newmarket, Auckland 3, T09-5245118.*

Flight Centres*, 82 Elizabeth St, Sydney, T13-1600; 205 Queen St, Auckland, T09-3096171. Also branches in other towns and cities.*

STA Travel*, 702 Harris St, Ultimo, Sydney, and 256 Flinders St, Melbourne, T1300-360960, www.statravelaus.com.au In NZ: 10 High St, Auckland, T09-3666673. Also in major towns and university campuses.*

Travel.com.au*, 80 Clarence St, Sydney, T02-92901500, www.travel.com.au*

UK and Ireland

Africa Travel Centre*, 21 Leigh St, London WC1H 9EW, T020-7387 1211, www.africatravel.co.uk*

Council Travel*, 28a Poland St, London W1V 3DB, T020-7437 7767, www.destinations-group.com*

Key Travel*, 92-96 Eversholt St, London NW1 1BP, T020-7387 4933, F020-7387 1090, offer keen prices to and from major African cities from the UK.*

RAJ Air*, 27 Central Chambers, The Broadway, Ealing, London W5 2NR, T020-8840 8881, offer competitive fares to East Africa.*

STA Travel*, Priory House, 6 Wright's Lane, London W8 6TA, T0870-160 6070, www.statravel.co.uk They have other branches in London, as well as Brighton, Bristol, Cambridge, Leeds, Manchester, Newcastle and Oxford and on many university campuses. Specialists in low-cost student/youth flights and tours, also good for student IDs and insurance.*

Trailfinders*, 194 Kensington High St, London W8 7RG, T020-7938 3939, www.trailfinders.com*

North America

Air Brokers International*, 323 Geary St, Suite 411, San Francisco, CA94102, T01-800-8333273, www.airbrokers.com Consolidator and specialist on RTW and Circle Pacific tickets.*

Around the World*, 2241 Polk St, San Fransisco, CA 94109, T415-6739950.*

Council Travel*, 205 E 42nd St, New York, NY 10017, T1-888-COUNCIL, www.counciltravel.com Student/budget agency with branches in many other US cities.*

Discount Airfares Worldwide On-Line*, www.etn.nl/discount.htm A hub of consolidator and discount agent links.*

International Travel Network/ Airlines of the Web*, www.itn.net/airlines Online air travel information and reservations.*

STA Travel*, 5900 Wilshire Blvd, Suite 2110, Los Angeles, CA 90036, T1-800-7770112, www.sta-travel.com Branches in New York, San Francisco, Boston, Miami, Chicago, Seattle and Washington DC.*

Swan Travel*, 400 Madison Av, New York, NY, T212-42111010.*

Travel Cuts*, 187 College St, Toronto, ON, T1-800-6672887, www.travelcuts.com Specialists in student discount fares, IDs and other travel services. Branches in other Canadian cities.*

Travelocity*, www.travelocity.com Online consolidator.*

Essentials

Getting there

Air

It is possible to fly directly to almost all the capitals in the region from Europe. However, many travellers will find it cheaper and often more convenient to fly to one of the well-serviced capitals, and connect from there.

    Nairobi (Kenya) has many regular, cheap flights. There is little advantage in accessing Uganda or Tanzania from here unless you travel on by road or rail.

    Addis Ababa (Ethiopia) is a natural centre for **Djibouti** and **Eritrea**. *Ethiopian Airways* run a frequent network of services. However, internal flights are cancelled without warning, and the fleet is too small to replace aircraft taken out of circulation for maintenance. Travellers have reported lengthy delays, with little information available.

For air links, arrival and departure regulations, airport taxes, customs regulations and security arrangements for air travel, see relevant Essentials sections for each country

Essentials

Road

Overland access is really only feasible from the south – regular tours start in South Africa, and tend to enter Tanzania through Zambia or Malawi. Entry from Sudan and Mozambique is possible, but seldom used. Otherwise the region is surrounded by countries currently off-limits to travellers – RD Congo, Rwanda, Burundi and Somalia.

Sea

The main ports are Massawa and Assab in Eritrea, Djibouti, Mombasa in Kenya, Dar es Salaam and Zanzibar in Tanzania. Access by sea is possible, usually via cargo lines which accept passengers. There are regular sea services for passengers between Dar es Salaam and Zanzibar, and sometimes services linking Zanzibar and Mombasa.

Train

The Tanzania Zambia Railway Authority (TAZARA) railway line links southern Africa to the region via Zambia.

Touching down

Local customs and laws

Bargaining is expected in the street markets. It is often the case that traders will attempt to overcharge tourists who are unaware of local prices. Start lower than you would expect to pay, be polite and good humoured, and if the final price doesn't suit – walk away. Ask about the prices of taxis, excursions, souvenirs, and so on, at your hotel. Once you have gained confidence, try bargaining with taxi drivers and at hotels when negotiating a room. **Bargaining**

A number of physically handicapped persons and destitute mothers with children are present in most large towns. Clearly many are genuine and are heart-rending cases of need. **Begging**
    Street children, however, give pause for thought. In some places they request money to guard vehicles, in others they ask for money for food. Giving to one child usually leads the donor to be surrounded by a throng. A fight may arise as to who should guard a car. Giving a banknote to one child with instructions that it should be shared may result in violence, with the whole sum going to the strongest child. In some places street children are clearly organized by adults.
    A constructive alternative is to make a donation to an organization such as *Save the Children Fund*, Mary Datchelor House, 17 Grove Lane, London, SE5 8RD, T020-7703 5400, F020-7703 2275, which provides subsistence and skill-training programmes in an attempt to provide a long-term solution. There are collection points in the departure lounges of some international airports. They are always grateful for donations of loose coins or notes.

Great store is set everywhere by modesty and courtesy and an effort to dress smartly. Respect toward elderly people is particularly important. In mosques and temples, make sure you follow observances as indicated by attendants. Shoes will need to be taken off, and there may be restriction on visits by women. **Conduct**

In large establishments a service charge is invariably added. Elsewhere it is optional, but a modest tip for courteous and attentive service is greatly appreciated by hotel and restaurant staff, most of whom receive very low pay. **Tipping**

Drugs Illegal in all countries. There are considerable risks in using drugs even where a blind eye is turned to use by local people. In such circumstances you are vulnerable to extortion. **Prohibitions**
    Firearms Cannot be imported or carried, without special permission.

How big is your footprint?

- *Where possible choose a destination, tour operator or hotel with a proven ethical and environmental commitment – if in doubt, ask.*
- *Spend money on locally produced (rather than imported) goods and services and use common sense when bargaining – your few dollars saved may be a week's salary to others.*
- *Use water and electricity carefully – travellers may receive preferential supply while the needs of local communities are overlooked.*
- *Learn about etiquette and culture – consider local norms and behaviour –*
- *and dress appropriately for local cultures and situations.*
- *Protect wildlife and other natural resources – don't buy souvenirs or goods made from wildlife unless they are clearly sustainably produced and are not protected under CITES legislation.*
- *Always ask before taking photographs or videos of people.*
- *Consider staying in local, rather than foreign-owned, accommodation – the economic benefits for host communities are far greater – and there are far greater opportunities to learn about local culture, too.*

Photography in sensitive areas All countries have zones where there are military or communications installations which are off-limits. These are usually well signposted. You must avoid taking photographs, sketching or making notes, however innocent, in these areas. To take risks in this regard invites detention by the police and untold inconvenience. It may not be so obvious that an individual building belongs to the military. Care should be taken before photographing any official people or buildings. Some travellers attempt to circumvent this by photographing their travelling companion in front of the object desired, using a wide-angle lens. This tactic is not encouraged as travellers have been arrested.

Responsible tourism

Without tourism, preserving the glorious attractions of this region would not be possible. People in East Africa are very poor, and the need to keep body and soul together in the immediate future takes priority over everything. Population pressure is inexorable. Wildlife and their habitats are destroyed by poaching and clearance for agriculture; coral reefs are dynamited for fish; traditional ceremonies, decoration, dance and dress fade and die as new generations are brought up in towns; historic buildings are filled with squatters and neglected until they are demolished to build concrete blocks. Protection, regulation and preservation all demand resources and the income from tourism is the only realistic way these measures can be sustained, and local people persuaded that it is worth making the effort. Above all, there is no reason to be apologetic for being a tourist. The income and employment that tourism bring are important everywhere; in Kenya, Tanzania and Zanzibar tourism earns more foreign exchange than any other activity.

Most visitors are well aware of the need to act courteously; behave unobtrusively; dress modestly; ask before photographing or filming; avoid littering, polluting and destroying; conserve water. There is an extensive list of endangered species prepared by the **United Nation Environmental Programme** and the **Wildlife Conservation Monitoring Centre** (UNEP-WCMC) under the **Convention on Trade in Endangered Species (CITES)** which can be accessed through www.cites.org The database lists endangered species by country – the main concerns in East Africa are elephants, black and white rhino, gorillas, Grevy's zebra, chimpanzees, some colobus monkeys, some of the whales, some of the turtles, and quite a lot of molluscs. It is unlikely that you will be offered products made from endangered wildlife if you shop in regular establishments. Casual vendors and small stalls can offer prohibited products – sea-shells can be a particular problem and are best avoided. If you buy something insist on a receipt that displays the address of the seller, and this will help if you run into problems at the airport when you leave – and help the authorities enforce the regulations.

Rare antique objects cannot generally be taken out of the East African countries, but most curios purchased in regular souvenir shops will not fall into this category. Again, ask for a receipt with an address on it.

Safety

Notwithstanding the bombing of the US embassies in Kenya and Tanzania in 1998 by external extremists, the majority of territories in the region can be visited with confidence, although there are areas in most of them where caution is required. Circumstances can change suddenly, however, and if you have any doubts, contact the appropriate country desk of your national external affairs ministry (for the UK, call Foreign and Commonwealth Office, T020-7270 1500).

Check out www.fco.gov.uk for the UK's latest official travelling advice

Nevertheless, some countries have experienced sudden outbreaks of armed conflicts. An example is the border war between Ethiopia and Eritrea in May 1998. The recent violent clashes in Zanzibar in January/February 2001, or the civil unrest in Kisii and other parts of western Kenya in March 2001, have remained localized. Uganda had severe breakdown prior to 1986, and there are ongoing skirmishes in the north close to the Sudanese border. If there is any hint of serious instability, such as a coup attempt with armed supporters of rival factions on the streets, you should immediately leave the country. If necessary you should seek help from your national embassy, or any international agency.

Tanzania has an enviable record of stability, and it has established a consensus among its many peoples that is allowing it to establish a secure multi-party parliamentary democracy.

Safarilands

Kenya had some disturbances following the introduction of a multi-party system in 1993, and there have been occasional incidents involving tourists. With normal precautions, however, it is quite safe to visit.

Uganda has made a remarkable recovery since 1986 from the turmoil of the Amin period and its aftermath. It is not really safe to visit the north of the country, where there is still some unrest. However, the main tourist attractions are mostly in the other, quite secure, regions. The parks bordering RD Congo were subject to a horrific terrorist incident in March 1999 in which tourists and rangers were killed. The Ugandan authorities have improved security and insist that these parks are now safe to visit. Nevertheless, caution is advised.

Ethiopia has made great strides since the fall of the Mengistu regime, and the main groups have all now been included in the political process. There are some remote areas where there is danger, and it is important to take local advice on this. There has been an ongoing dispute with Eritrea over the border, which resulted in the outbreak of hostilities in May 1998. A Peace Accord was signed in December 2000 but the border remains closed, and much of the surrounding area is believed to have been mined.

Horn

Eritrea is now largely peaceful for the first time in many years, having achieved effective independence from Ethiopia. However, the border dispute with Ethiopia has adversely affected large areas to the south and west of the country, with uncleared minefields posing a real hazard to both residents and visitors.

Djibouti has always been very stable, bolstered as it by its links with France and the commercial interests in the port.

Sadly, it is no longer rare for a traveller to have a trip marred by theft or an unpleasant incident. Visitors in supervised parties, on excursions, or staying in large hotels are generally very safe. Otherwise, it is sensible to take reasonable precautions by not walking in deserted, unlit areas at night, and by avoiding places of known risk during the day. Snatch thieves can be a problem, particularly in Kenya, and risks can be minimized by not wearing jewellery, expensive watches, or carrying cameras in busy public places. Waist pouches are very vulnerable as the belt can be cut easily. Carry money and any valuables in a slim belt under clothing. Always lock room doors at night as noisy fans and air-conditioning can provide cover for sneak thieves. Be wary of leaving items by open windows in hotel rooms. **Confidence tricksters** are particularly common in Kenya, but also found elsewhere. Be wary of anyone with a hard-luck story, soliciting sponsorship (particularly educational) or offering a deal to change money at favourable rates.

Security

Police If you have any items stolen, you must report the occurrence to the police, and keep a record of the incident number, the police station, and the name of the officer dealing with it. This is vital if you have lost official documents, or wish to make an insurance claim. The police

👉 ## Hotel price categories

L   Over US$150 a night. International standards and décor, air conditioning, self-contained rooms, swimming pool, restaurants, bars, business services.

A   US$100-150. First-class standards, air-conditioning, attached bathrooms, restaurants and bars, swimming pool.

B   US$50-100. Tourist class, comfortable with air conditioning or fans, attached bathrooms, restaurant, bar, public rooms.

C   US$20-50. Budget, fans, shared bathroom facilities.

D   US$10-20. Guesthouse, no fan, shared bathroom, cold water.

E   Under US$10. Basic guesthouse, simple bed, no soap or towels, no wardrobe, shared bathroom facilities, erratic cold water supply, no fans or mosquito nets.

F   Under US$5. Very basic, although some church, mission or MGO hostels in this price range can be good value, albeit spartan.

will often insist that you report regularly to check on how the investigations are proceeding. These visits can be very time consuming and tedious. Property is almost never recovered, and it is often possible to use your discretion as to whether it is worth following things up.

For petty offences (driving without lights switched on, for example) police will often try to solicit a bribe, masked as an 'on the spot' fine. Establish the amount being requested, and then offer to go to the police station to pay, at which point you will be released with a warning. For any serious charges, immediately contact your embassy or consulate.

Where to stay

Hotels

See also inside front cover for a quick guide to hotel grade prices

Places to stay vary between those used by well-heeled tourists, which are expensive at around US$100 or more a day, self-contained (ie with en-suite bathroom), with air-conditioning, hot water and swimming pools, and those used by locals (and budget travellers) at under US$5 a day, which may comprise a simple bed, shared toilet and washing facilities, local food, plus an irregular water supply. Some of the small beach hotels are in splendid locations and despite having only simple facilities are excellent value. Note that it is not uncommon in Africa for hotels to just have a PO Box number, with no street name recorded. Many hotels provide private security staff – often armed.

Insects Be prepared for mosquitoes in particular, and other insects. Sleep under a net treated with insecticide wherever mosquitoes are a problem; smear exposed skin with insect repellent; use an electric heat-pad insecticide tablet vapourizer at night; buy a can of insecticide to spray your hotel room.

Safari options

Hotels and lodges These vary and may be either typical hotels with rooms and facilities in one building or individual bandas or rondavels (small huts) with a central dining area. Most have been built with great care and imagination and blend very well into the environment.

Tented camps In the parks camping in either a tented camp or a campsite is often more atmospheric and cheaper than staying in one of the lodges. A luxury tented camp is really the best of both worlds. They are usually built with a central dining area. Each tent will have a thatched roof to keep it cool inside, proper beds, and verandah and they will often have a small bathroom at the back with solar-heated hot water. But at the same time you will have the feeling of being in the heart of Africa and at night you will hear animals surprisingly close by.

Campsites There are campsites in most national parks. They are extensively used by camping safari companies (although they often have their own 'permanent' campsites). They are often most attractively sited, perhaps in the elbow of a river course but always with plenty of shade. Birds are plentiful and several hours can be whiled away bird-watching. Some campsites have attached to them a few bandas or huts run by the park where you may be able to shower. Toilet facilities can be primitive – the 'long drop', a basic hole in a concrete slab being very common. Away from the permanent sites, you will be expected to pitch your own tent. Sleeping mats are usually provided but you must bring your own sleeping bag and pillow. Sleeping bags can be hired from most companies for a modest amount. A deposit is required. Check on availability at the time of booking and reserve if necessary.

Most camps are guarded but despite this you should be careful to ensure that valuables are not left unattended. Be careful about leaving items outside your tent. Many campsites have troupes of baboons nearby. They can be a nuisance.

If you are camping on your own, you will almost always need to be totally self-sufficient with all your own equipment. The campsites usually provide running water and firewood. The extent to which you will have to be self-sufficient with food varies from park to park.

Getting around

Air There are quite good regional airlines. However flights can be delayed and sometimes get overbooked. It is essential to reconfirm return flights 48 hours before departure. Allow plenty of time at departure. There is often a considerable amount of bureaucracy to go through involving lots of queuing. Make sure that you have hard currency (preferably dollars) for departure taxes, as local currency, travellers' cheques and credit cards are not accepted. You will usually be able to change travellers' cheques at the airport bank but beware of commission charges – you may have to change more than you thought. Flights are often harder to find on public holidays and the weeks either side of them.

Road Major road networks are serviceable almost everywhere, and improving all the time. However, rain can be torrential, and sealed roads are regularly washed away and unsealed roads rendered impassable. In the wet seasons road travel can be very difficult.

Bus and taxi For long journeys travellers should try to use big buses and coaches as first choice, on grounds of both comfort and safety. Peugeot taxis (station wagons with seats) are fast, comfortable and fairly safe. Small buses and minibuses have very poor safety records, are uncomfortable and are usually terribly overcrowded.

Own vehicle If you are arriving with your own vehicle, you will require a Carnet de Passage issued by a body in your own country (such as the Automobile Association) affiliated to the Alliance International de Tourisme in Geneva. An International Certificate for Motor Vehicles (ICVM) and an International Driving Permit (IDP), again from the appropriate national body, are useful additions to the documentation and can expedite clearance at borders. Before travel, check with the embassy of any country you are planning to visit. In some cases sureties need to be lodged with the authorities on entry, and there may be special regulations relating to insurance.

Car hire In most countries your national driving licence will allow you to drive for a period, usually three months. Nevertheless, it is a wise precaution to obtain an International Driving Permit.

Drivers For motoring in town, a driver is of limited advantage. However for touring or on long journeys a driver can be invaluable in terms of providing local knowledge, experience and resourcefulness. The cost of a driver is very modest, and when touring, the driver will lodge 'swahili' at night – that is, in simple local accommodation that he will find for himself.

Hitchhiking In the western sense (standing beside the road and requesting a free ride) this is not an option. However, truck drivers and many private motorists will often carry you if you pay, and if you are stuck where there is no public transport you should not hesitate to approach likely vehicles on this basis.

Train Where rail systems exist, and haste is not of over-riding importance, travelling by train is thoroughly recommended. It is generally much safer than road, cheap, and comfortable, albeit slow and often subject to delays.

☞ BBC World Service frequencies

Time (GMT)		Frequency (kHz)	Time (GMT)		Frequency (kHz)
0200-0300	Daily	9770	0800-1400	Daily	17885
0300-0400	Daily	12035, 11730	1300-1400	Daily	15420
0500-0700	Daily	17640	1400-1700	Daily	21660
0330-0600	Daily	15420	1500-1530	Daily	11860, 15420, 21490
0500-0600	Daily	17885	1630-1900	Daily	15420
0700-1500	Daily	17640*	1700-1745	Daily	6005, 9630
0600-0800	Sat/Sun	17885	1830-2100	Daily	6005, 9630
0500-1700	Daily	11940			
0800-1300	Daily	21470	* Carries Middle East programmes		

Keeping in touch

Communications

Internet The easiest and cheapest way to keep in touch is by email. If you visit the **hotmail.com** or **yahoo.com** websites you can register a free email address. In East Africa most towns have internet cafés and you can check your messages and send them by visiting the hotmail or yahoo websites.

Telephone Telephoning is generally very expensive, although things are improving as state-owned *Two and three-digit* telecom companies are privatized and the sector is deregulated to allow competition and *phone numbers* internet telephone services. Phoning from a hotel costs three times as much as phoning from *are accessed via* the local telecoms office. It is possible to use your mobile by purchasing a local car, but *the operator* mobiles are particularly expensive and there is no coverage in many areas.

International radio A variety of European and North American countries make short-wave radio broadcasts to East Africa. They are often a more reliable source of news on events in Africa than local radio stations – particularly on major sensitive political items such as coups and outbreaks of hostilities. There is also news of world events that may not be covered by local broadcasts. Finally, for many travellers they offer a welcome contact with home.

Many of the big cities have a relay system which broadcasts international stations such as BBC World Service on a local FM frequency. Details when applicable are given in each country section. As this facility is steadily being extended, it is a good idea to check on **www.bbc.co.uk**

The following points are worth bearing in mind if you wish to listen to international services:

• Buy the best radio receiver you can afford – Sony receivers are well recommended. Unless you are staying in an area with an FM service, it must have **short waveband** reception, and a good radio with this facility will normally cost more than US$100. A radio with a digital display will enable you to key in the exact frequency.

• Frequencies are measured in kilohertz (kHz) or Megahertz (MHz) – 1,000 kHz = 1 MHz. Some radios use metres (M) for frequency, rather than kilohertz. M = 300,000/kHz.

• Reception on each frequency varies as to the atmospheric conditions – if reception is poor on one frequency, try another. In general the shorter wavebands (lower kHz) are more effective during hours of darkness, while the longer wavebands are better during the day.

• Using the radio by a window can improve reception as the steel used in buildings can impair quality. An outside aerial – a length of insulated copper wire – allowed to hang out of the window, or tied up like a washing line, can sometimes improve reception. Some radios include an outside aerial – if not, you can improvise one by using a length of insulated copper wire with the stripped wires of one end wrapped round the base of your telescopic aerial.

• Remember that a short-wave radio is a prime target for thieves. Do not leave it by an open hotel window at night. Keep it with you in hand baggage (with the batteries removed) when you fly – baggage handlers at airports have been known to pilfer luggage, breaking locks on bags to do so.

Restaurant price categories

Given the variations in price of food on any menu our restaurants are divided, where possible, into four simple grades:
Expensive Over US$10 for a meal. A three-course meal in a restaurant with pleasant décor. Beers, wines and spirits available.
Mid-range US$5-10 for a meal. Two courses,

not including alcohol, reasonable surroundings.
Cheap US$2-5 for a meal, probably only a single course, surroundings spartan but adequate.
Seriously cheap Under US$2. Single course, often makeshift surroundings such as a street kiosk with simple benches and tables.

Essentials

BBC World Service Frequencies for reception vary according to the time of day (see table). Highlights (local times) of the BBC World Service (Africa) transmissions are: **News Programmes**: on the hour, every hour; **Sports roundup**: 0145 (not Sunday), 0615, 0915 (not Saturday, Sunday), 1245, 1545 (not Saturday), 2045; **African news and features**: 0630, 0830, 0930, 2030; **Letter from America**: 1345 (Saturday), 0330 (Sunday), 0915 (Sunday), 0130 (Monday) – Alastair Cook on affairs in the United States; **Sportsworld**: 1700-2000 (Saturday) – emphasis on the weekend sport in the UK, usually with a live broadcast, but including good coverage of international events.

Full programme details can be obtained from the following sources: **UK** Bush House, London, WC2B 4PH, T020-7240 3456, F020-7257 8258, www.bbc.co.uk **Ethiopia** PO Box 12619, Addis Ababa. **Kenya** PO Box 46682, Nairobi. **Tanzania** PO Box 9100, Dar es Salaam. **Uganda** PO Box 7620, Kampala. **RD Congo** PO Box 10906, Kinshasha 1.

Voice of America There are many frequencies in use for Africa, but experience indicates that the following frequencies (kHz) are the most reliable for East Africa: 6035 (mornings, 0600–0900 local time); 15410 (evenings and night, 1900–2400 local time). **Highlights** (local times) of the Voice of America transmissions are: (Monday-Friday) **News**: 0630, 0700, 0800, 1900, 2100, 2400; **Africa**: 0600, 0730, 0900, 19.30, 2100, 2200, 2300. (Saturday) **News**: 0600, 0700, 0800, 0900, 2000, 2100, 2200, 22.30, 2400; **Africa**: 1900, 2300.

Food and drink

Bearing in mind the suggestions in the Health section (see page 60) on food best avoided in uncertain conditions, a great choice of African food still remains. For the less adventurous, Western style food is also widely available. The most common drink is tea. Coffee is generally available too. Bottled soft fizzy drinks, often called sodas, are found even in small settlements and are safer than water. **Alcohol** is widely available, though you will be expected to take your own supplies on camping safaris. **Bottled water** is an essential part of every traveller's baggage. However avoid buying the cheapest brand in supermarkets as, although it may be clean, it often doesn't taste so. Safari companies usually stock bottled water for taking on camping safaris – take plenty with you.

See also inside front cover for a quick guide to restaurant grade prices

Holidays and festivals

Islamic holidays and festivals are observed in various parts of East Africa, notably along the coast and in northeast Kenya. Muslim festivals are timed according to local sightings of the various stages of the moon so there is a chance that some of the dates below will move by a day. Note that because the Muslim day begins at sunset, Islamic holidays begin at sunset on the preceding evening. **Hijra** (Islamic New Year): 15 Mar 2002, 5 Mar 2003, 22 Feb 2004; **Ashura** (celebrates martyrdom of Iman Hussein): 24 Mar 2002, 14 Mar 2003, 2 Mar 2004; **Prophet Mohammed's Birthday**: 24 May 2002, 14 May 2003, 2 May 2004; **First day of Ramadan** (fasting begins): 6 Nov 2002, 27 Oct 2003, 15 Oct 2004; **Id-ul-Fitr** (feast to mark end of Ramadan): 6 Dec 2002, 26 Nov 2003, 14 Nov 2004; **Id-ul-Adha** (Festival of Sacrifice – the culmination of the Haj, or holy pilgrimage): 23 Feb 2002, 12 Feb 2003, 2 Feb 2004.

Sport and special interest travel

Diving

Undoubtedly one of East Africa's greatest tourism assets is the vast areas of fringing coral reef that stretch south from the equator hugging the coastline and surrounding islands. These huge living coral formations, which in the past were a mariners' worst nightmare, have now become the playground for the tourist and house at least 3,000 different species of marine animals and plants.

Diving seasons & conditions The best time to dive is between October and April before the long rains and subsequent river outflows affect visibility but check individual locations in this section for more details. Average visibility in the diving season ranges between 10-30 m increasing to 20-40 m around Pemba and Mafia islands. Plankton blooms are reasonably common and can reduce the visibility drastically. The Northeast Monsoon wind (Kaskazi) blows from November to March and can affect diving conditions along the coast of Kenya and Pemba Island during January. The diving conditions surrounding the islands are more reliable and the waters generally clearer. The infamous El Niño has been to blame for much of the coral bleaching and damage to many top reefs of East Africa but the positive signs of regrowth are definitely in place, and for divers the visible damage shouldn't detract from the splendour and abundance of the fish life.

Equipment If you are a qualified diver and have your own kit, take it. All dive centres mentioned in this section have both din and A-Clamp fittings and will give discounts when you bring your own. Prior to departure, check your baggage allowance with the airlines and see if you can come to some arrangement for extra weight.

Water temperature varies between 24°C (September) and 30°C+ (March) depending on time of year. Most dive centres hire 3 mm wetsuits, which are fine, if you are occasional divers and don't get cold quickly. If you do, then bring your own 5 mm one-piece wetsuit.

New divers The warm waters and colourful reefs of East Africa provide an exciting training ground for first-timers wishing to explore the underwater realm. Most dive centres run PADI courses up to Divemaster level. BSAC, NAUI, CMAS and SSI centres also exist but are not as common. Five-day entry level courses include theory, pool sessions and four or five ocean training dives or a one-day 'Discover Scuba' option if you just want to experience diving for fun. Medical questionnaires must be completed prior to a course; medical certificates might be required.

Costs Diving is quite pricey all over East Africa. At time of writing, the cheapest was US$30 and the most expensive was US$46 per dive including all equipment. For two dives a day, the average price was US$75 including lunch and equipment. The beginner's Open Water course takes 4-5 days and costs US$200-500 depending on marine park fees, day excursions including lunch, and whether you get to keep the expensive training manual after the course.

Emergencies The nearest recompression chamber for anywhere in East Africa is the Kenyan Navy Base, Mombasa, T011-451201 ext. 3308 (on 24-hour stand-by). There is now a new, as yet unused, chamber located in Diani Beach at *Diving the Crab* (see page 43 for contact numbers).

Marine hazards Check with your dive centre for local marine hazards. Here are a few of the more common ones and their basic treatments:

· *Venom of the scorpion fish, stonefish and anglerfish* can cause large swelling and intense pain. It is broken down by heat so treat any sting by immersing that part of the body with hot water (50°C) for a couple of hours until the pain eases or stops.

· *Fire coral burns* must be treated immediately with vinegar or acetic acid (lemons/limes) or large blisters may result.

· *Jellyfish (blue bottle or sea wasp) stings* can also be treated with vinegar, alcohol or urine directly on the sting.

Diving jargon and organizations

Coral garden *An area of pristine coral in much variety and concentration. It is allowed to grow like this due to protection from the winds and waves from open sea.*

Drop-offs *Where a coral reef becomes a cliff and drops into the depths. If deep drop-offs, look out for big fish in the blue – sharks, game fish, dolphins, manta rays.*

Fringing reef *This type of reef follows the coastline. Due to the exposure to the winds and tides it forms a patchy reef with individual clusters of coral heads that teem with life. Do not expect carpeting pristine coral off open beaches.*

Liveaboard *A boat on which you live and dive from for the duration of your holiday.*

Two-tank dive *Two dive cylinders per person are taken on the boat to enable two separate dives on the same trip.*

Visibility *How far you can see underwater – measured horizontally and in metres.*

These are all dive organizations with which you can either learn to dive or further your diving career:

PADI *Professional Association of Dive Instructors.*

NAUI *National Association of Underwater Instructors (South African).*

SSI *Scuba Schools International (Italian)*

Essentials

• *The sting in the beautiful stingrays' tails* can cause severe wounds if trodden on or caught. Clean the wound with warm water, give the hot water treatment (50°C for two hours) followed antibiotics and anti-tetanus injection if necessary.

If bitten or stung, immediately notify medic first-aider on board or at the dive centre. Consult a doctor if pain worsens or treatment is ineffective.

An excellent guide to local marine life is *A Guide to the Seashores of East Africa* edited by Matt Richmond, ISBN 91-630-4594, available in local outlets or UK bookshops. Profits benefit SeaTrust, a conservation group interested in East African coastal issues. — **Recommended reading**

The entire coast of Kenya is protected by an extensive fringing coral reef which boasts a dazzling array of tropical fish. The diving season in Kenya is October-April but best visibility is usually November, February and March. During the rainy (May) and windy (June-August) seasons, some dive operators close as the rough conditions and the outflow from the rivers make diving impossible. Malindi is the only exception to this rule and because of its northeast facing bay, July-November are the best months for diving. The water there is murky October-March, when operators will take divers to sites further offshore or south to Watamu. — **Kenya: overview**

Kenyans, seeing the money-making potential of their precious coral reefs, first took the conservation initiative and set up several National Marine Parks and Reserves to protect their sensitive reef habitats. There are four main diving areas, which, thanks to the reserves and parks protecting them, have a high concentration of marine fauna and flora. The **Lamu Archipelago**, near the Somali border, incorporates Lamu, Pate and Manda islands. Watamu, Malindi and Kilifi are classed as the **North Coast**, **Mombasa** and surrounds has its own reserve, and the **South Coast** comprises Tiwi Beach, Diani Beach, Shimoni, Mpunguti Islands and Kisite Island.

At time of writing, a licence to dive or snorkel in the marine parks costs US$5 per person per day. In some areas, booklets have been produced to help with fish and coral identification. Proceeds go to supporting the marine park.

Due to the outflow of the Tana River in the rainy season, the dense smothering mud in the water severely affects the coral growth around the North Islands. Relatively unexplored as far as diving is concerned, there are three main dive sites of note: Jiwe La Mpupu, Jamba la Simba and Kinyika. The visibility averages 8-10 m between October and April, the best diving season. The best of the sites is reputedly Kinyika Island, located off the south coast of Lamu. The coral here is in good condition and the reef is full of life such as yellow and blue snappers, groupers, napoleon wrasse and barracuda. Maximum depth of 20 m this is the second deepest dive site around Lamu. Snorkelling can be as rewarding as diving around these islands, as the fish life in the shallows is spectacular. **Dive centre** *Peponi Hotel*, PO Box 7543, T121-33421, F121-33029, www.peponi-lamu.com PADI course available Nov- Mar. Diving safaris available on request. — **Kenya: North Coast islands: Lamu, Manda, Pate, Kiwayuu**

☞ A lifeline for East Africa's turtles

The marine turtle is over 135,000,000 years old and still fighting for its place in today's oceans in an ongoing battle against the fishing trawlers' nets, the tourist resorts and local tribal traditions. What chance does it have? In Kenya, efforts are being made by a small band of volunteers to save the marine turtle from extinction. Collectively they are known as 'Turtlewatch'.

The female turtles must return to their natal beaches to nest. With increasing coastal tourism, the resulting construction and bright lights of the beach resorts frighten the pregnant female away. She will search all night to find a suitable site, but if she fails she returns to the ocean and aborts her eggs which sometimes number over 100. Another threat awaits her if she is successful in making her nest. The ancient tradition for the Bajuni and Giriana tribes is to kill marine turtles and their eggs for food. The leftovers and resulting

oil are then used for bronchial medicines. The trade in turtle shells continues.

Turtlewatch's methods are simple and will work as long as funding continues. They pay anyone who discovers a nest. They then guard that nest until the eggs hatch. On the occasion that the turtle has laid her eggs below the high-water mark they will painstakingly move the eggs and create an identical nest above it. Successful hatchings from these nests are encouragingly high at 93%.

To help keep Turtlewatch watching turtles, for a few dollars you can adopt a turtle or a nest. Contact Helen Curtis of Watamu Turtlewatch for details, aquav@africaonline.co.ke

Tanzania also has a small turtle conservation project based in Zanzibar and is dependent on voluntary participation of a few individuals and resorts. Look out for the special T-shirts sold around Stone Town and various hotels/resorts.

Kenya: North Coast: Malindi/ Watamu

There is some fantastic diving to be done within the Watamu/Malindi Marine Parks. The area was designated a Biosphere Reserve in 1979 and has since been allowed to flourish. During the rainy season, when river outflow affects visibility in Watamu, *Aquaventures* visit Malindi sites where waters are unaffected (see Kenya overview). Although affected by El Nino in places, there is a wide variety of hard and soft corals and the signs of regrowth are in place. Recommended dives in this area include Canyon, Deep Place and Black Coral. Interesting topography of gullies, canyons and overhangs in which you'll find the all types of eels, bass, rock cod, moorish idols, angel and butterflyfish, lionfish, pufferfish, goldies and schools of yellow tailed fusiliers and blue lined snapper. Watch out for the common titan triggerfish during nesting season. It can get very defensive so keep well out of its nesting zone – a conical area that extends upwards and outwards from the nest. When the visibility is low, fun can still be had seeking the little life such as nudibranchs (pretty sea slugs), leaf fish and mantis shrimps. The life around the Chakwe Wreck is also very pretty. Small acropora (table corals) growing on the mast with little chocolate dipped chromis living amongst their branches. Large groupers and rays also seen at this site.

Should you have the time, a visit to Vuma Caves in Kilifi is a must. This is an awe-inspiring dive site where the fish-filled cave and the series of blowholes along the reef are the attraction. Day trips with a double dive can be arranged through Steve Curtis at *Aquaventures*, Watamu, or Bruce Phillips of *Buccaneer Diving*, Mombasa. There is also a barrakuda dive facility for guests at the *Mnarani* hotel if staying in Kilifi.

Dive centres *Aquaventures*, *Ocean Sports Hotel*, Watamu, T254-122-32420, F32256, aquav@africaonline.co.ke, www.diveinkenya.com   Contact: Steve and Helen Curtis.

Kenya: Mombasa

The fringing reef formations, collectively known as Shanzu Reef, comprise gently sloping outer reef down to a maximum of 25 m with several coral heads teeming with goldies, moray eels, puffer fish, glass fish, and the deadly master of camouflage – the scorpion fish. For novices or photographers wanting calm stable conditions for macro shots, you can dive the shallower inner reef. For advanced divers, one serious attraction but little known dive site, is Birthday Reef. Diveable in calmer weather at low or high slack tide, the reef is spectacular. Converging currents meet at a large oval shaped reef, which rises from below 50 m up to 27 m. Looking up from the depths along the reef's profile is a heavenly sight. Against the small

Tips for responsible diving

Buoyancy Control *through proper weighting and practice, do not allow yourself or any item of your equipment to touch any living organism.*

Skills Review *If you haven't dived for a while, do a review in the pool or on a sandy patch before diving around the reef.*

Control your fins *Deep fin kicks around coral can cause damage.*

Avoid kicking up sand *Sand can smother corals and other reef life.*

Never stand on the reef *Corals can be damaged by the slightest touch.*

If you need to hold on to something *look for a piece of dead coral or rock.*

Know your limits *Don't dive in conditions beyond your skills.*

Avoid the temptation *to disturb or move things around (eg for photography).*

Do not collect or buy shells *or any other marine curios (eg dried pufferfish).*

Do not feed fish

Do not ride turtles or hold onto any marine animal *This behaviour could easily cause severe stress to the creature.*

Choose your operator wisely *Report irresponsible operators to relevant diving authorities (PADI, NAUI, SSI).*

Adapted from the **Marine Conservation Society** *'Coral Code'. Further information at www.mcsuk.org or contact Richard Harrington, Communications Officer, Marine Conservation Society, T01989-566017, F01989-567815.*

Essentials

---

bright ball of white sunlight bathed in dark blue surrounds, black silhouetted clusters of bannerfish, barracuda and bluefin trevally are found in their hundreds. Eagle rays, huge potato bass, tuna and wahoo are often seen out in the blue. Sharks and whalesharks have also been seen (not often) cruising around this reef. Another recommendable reef for advanced divers in this area is Lucky Chance, a drop-off that starts at 22 m down to 40 m housing similar fish life as Birthday Reef.

Dive centres *Buccaneer Diving*, based in *Whitesands* and *Voyager* hotels, Bahari Beach, PO Box 10394, Mombasa, T011-48163, F474587, www.buccaneerdiving.com Kenya's first PADI Instructor Development Centre.

South coast diving encompasses Tiwi, Diani, Wasini Island and Shimoni. The majority of dive sites are above 20 m and are easily accessible by short boat ride from the beach hotels. Visibility averaging 10-15 m is affected by the Kaskazi wind during January. We found five dive sites worth recommending on this stretch. Kinondo and Galu Reefs host a wealth of tropical marine fauna. Look out for the hundreds of territorial red-tooth triggerfish on Kinondo. They'll nip your fins when you're not looking. Tiwi Reef is a very pretty dive but visibility is affected by the Tiwi River on an outgoing tide. Wasini Island houses the Mecca of south coast diving – Nyuuli Reef. For advanced divers only, this bustling coral city starts at 27 m and one dive is simply not enough. Pink Reef, carpeted with plush pink, purple and blue soft corals, is the shallower alternative and by far the most romantic reef in Kenya. Day trips to Wasini including Nyuuli and Pink Reef are organized from Diani or Kisite. **Kenya: South coast**

Dive centres The largest dive operation in East Africa is *Diving The Crab*. Head Office: Nomads Beach Hotel, Diani Beach, T0127-3400, F2372, www.divingthecrab.com Contact: Ralph Winter. Affiliation: PADI & SSI. Nitrox, rebreathers available. Recompression chamber on site. *The Adventure Centre*, Wasini Island, T0127-3055, F3154, www.kisite.co.ke Contact: Sally and Steve Mullens. Affiliation: SSI.

The main diving areas of Tanzania are found on the islands of Pemba, Zanzibar and Mafia. On the mainland, local divers recommend Dar es Salaam and further south towards the Mozambique border there are plans, at the time of writing, for a dive centre in *Ten Degrees South* resort, Mtwara. The diving season is generally from October to March, before the long rains hit in April-May, and many dive centres/resorts close *(Swahili Divers*, Pemba, boast excellent visibility year round and do not close). June-July can get very windy but most centres are open again by this time. **Tanzania: overview**

Tanzania has a wide variety of coastal coral formations from the fringing reef and coral gardens of Zanzibar to spectacular drop-offs around Pemba. Add to this an abundance of tropical fish life around the islands and you have a truly spectacular diving environment. Mainland fringing reefs accessible from Tanga and Dar have been damaged through the illegal practice of dynamite fishing, which, through slack policing, is still a problem today. The Tanzanian authorities are now waking up to the possible consequences if they don't start to protect the marine environment. Several areas have been set aside for marine conservation and are funded through conservation agencies and tourism. These include Misali Island (off Pemba), Chumbe Island (off Stone Town) and the whole of Mafia Island.

Tanzania: Dar es Salaam If you are not visiting Pemba or Zanzibar and need to get wet, there are a number of memorable dive sites around Dar worth a dip or two. Of particular note are Ferns Wall, which is on the seaward side of Fungu Yasin Reef, where you'll find large barrel sponges, gorgonian fans and 2-m long whip corals. Reef sharks are often spotted here. Because of its depth this site is for advanced divers only. Another favourite is Mwamba, a unique reef comprising large fields of pristine brain, rose and plate corals. Although slightly further out, Big T reef is a must dive for the experienced diver but only on a calm day. Latham Island, southwest of Dar, is an area surrounded by deep water where big game fish and elusive schools of hammerheads can be found. It can only be dived with a very experienced skipper who knows the area.

Unfortunately the impoverished coastal communities around Dar have until recently used dynamite fishing to harvest their fish. The government and local tourist offices will tell you that this practice has been stamped out, but while on a dive outside Dar we heard a dynamite explosion underwater. Although this has affected the coral and fish life badly, it seems there are neither the funds nor the inclination to stamp this out properly.

Dive centres *DiveMaxx*, Bahari Beach Hotel/Silver Sands Hotel, PO Box 9312, T051-2650352, T0811-329448 (mob), F051-2650351, info@divemaxx.com Contact: Jens Kruuse.

Zanzibar Zanzibar has a fair amount to offer as far as diving is concerned. October-November are the best diving months with clearer visibility and calm conditions. Diving from Stone Town, there are a number of sites with pristine coral gardens and a proliferation of life. Morogo Reef has probably some of the most beautiful coral on the whole East African coast. Turtles Den is another favourite; this site actually lives up to its name with as many as 10 turtles seen in one 45-minute dive. Boribo Reef is classed as the best by many advanced divers for larger pelagics but is far from shore and minimum numbers are required. On the north coast, Leven Banks is popular with advanced divers as it lies near the deep water of the Pemba Channel and is home to big shoals of jacks and trevally. Famous for remote 'holiday brochure style' beaches and colourful reefs, the east coast diving is the most talked about on Zanzibar. Mnemba Island, reached from Nungwi or Matemwe, has a wide range of sites varying in depth with exciting marine life. Great for snorkelling. Pungu Wall, East Mnemba, is a recommended dive for experienced divers looking for sharks, rays and groupers. This site can only be dived in calm conditions. On the south coast, at Kizimkazi, there is a growing industry springing up around large resident pods of humpbacked and bottlenose dolphins. Marine biologists assess these dolphins as very stressed due to the uncontrolled jostling and chasing of boat operators. They advise that if you snorkel with these dolphins, to exercise respect, restraint and common sense. Splashy water entries and boat drivers in hot pursuit will only drive them away.

Dive centres Stone Town: *Zanzibar Dive Centre*, One Ocean Ltd, PO Box 992, T0242-238374, T0742-750161 (mob), F0242-250496, www.zanzibaroneocean.com **Matemwe:** *Matemwe Bungalows*, PO Box. 3275, Zanzibar, T0242-236535, F236536, www.matemwe.com *Zanzibar Dive Centre*, One Ocean Ltd, opening soon in Matemwe Beach Village (see contact details under Stone Town). **Nungwi:** *Ras Nungwi Beach Hotel*, PO Box 1784, Zanzibar, T0242-32512, F233098, www.rasnungwi.com *Sazani Beach Hotel*, T0242-240014, info@divemaxx.com

Tanzania: Pemba Known as the Emerald Isle for its lush vegetation and idyllic setting, Pemba is most definitely the jewel in East Africa's dive-site portfolio. On the more chartered west coast the deep waters of the Pemba Channel have conspired to create dramatic walls and drop-offs, where glimpses of sharks and encounters with eagle rays, manta rays, napoleon wrasse, great barracuda, tuna and kingfish are the 'norm'. Visibility can range from 6 m in a plankton bloom to 60 m, though 20 m is classed as a bad day and 40 m is average. Some of the coral has been affected by El Nino, but Pemba remains a world-class diving destination.

There are a few dive centres on Pemba – for barefoot luxury try remote *Manta Reef Lodge*. However, to fully appreciate Pemba's magical diversity, take the liveaboard option and dive the east coast, for this is the territory of the schooling hammerheads. It would be impossible to single out the best dive sites; they are all simply breathtaking. On Misali Island and the surrounding reefs, the West Coast is a protected marine park and entrance of US$5 must be paid to dive or snorkel there.

Dive centres *Dive 7/10*, luxury outfit based at Fundu Lagoon, T0242-232926, F32937, fundu@africaonline.co.tz *Manta Reef Lodge* (Barefoot Luxury), PO 22, Wete, Pemba Island, T0811-320025, mantareef@twiga.com Stilted wooden bungalows overlooking crunchy, white sandy beaches. **NB** This property is currently changing hands. *Swahili Divers/Swahili Anglers*, The Old Mission Lodge, PO Box 146, Chake Chake, T024-2452786, F2452768, www.swahilidivers.com Highly recommended for the budget traveller. The kit is well maintained, accommodation basic but comfy, food tasty, their dive-boats are high-powered ribs that can access all sites around the island, all prices are fair and the atmosphere very welcoming. Costs from US$15-60 per night.

Liveaboard boats *'SY Jambo'*, c/o One Earth Safaris, PO Box 82234, Mombasa, Kenya, T011-471771, F473462, onearth@africaonline.co.ke *'Pemba Afloat'*: go to Wete and ask for Pemba Afloat. Costs US$40 per dive, US$100 per day.

The diving around Mafia can be described as a 'shallow Pemba with more fish' – beautiful reefs and spectacular fish life. Jino Pass and Dindini Wall are two sites to the northeast of Chole Bay. Both reefs have flat tops at 8 m dropping vertically in a spectacular wall to 25 m with a sandy bottom. Whip corals 2-3 m long grow out from the walls. There are a couple of interesting (if tight) swim-throughs and a long tunnel cave at 20 m on 'Dindini Wall'. Impressive sightings include huge malabar, potato and honeycomb groupers, giant reef rays, green turtles, great barracuda, kingfish, bonito, shoals of bluefin trevalley and snappers in their thousands. On the eastern entrance to Chole Bay lies Kinasi Pass. There is a recommended drift dive in the Pass but it must be dived on an incoming tide and is for experienced divers only if diving on a spring tide. The Pinnacle in the centre of the mouth of the Pass is a good opportunity to see large rays, groupers, eagle rays and jacks. Best dived on slack or gentle incoming tide and will also need experienced guide to find the site.

Dive centres *Pole Pole*, T0222-601530, F600140, www.polepole.com *Kinasi Lodge*, kinasi@intafrica.com, www.mafiaisland.com

> Tanzania:
> Mafia Island

Safaris

One of the main reasons for going to East Africa is the wonderful wildlife. Seeing the animals – going on safari – can be a most rewarding experience at any time of year. However, for the vast majority of travellers it is something to be prepared for, as it will almost certainly involve a degree of discomfort and long journeys. The roads in East Africa can be very exhausting for travellers. The unsealed roads are bumpy and dusty, and it will be hot. It is also important to remember that despite the expert knowledge of the drivers, they cannot guarantee that you will see any animals. When they do spot one of the rarer animals – a leopard or rhinoceros perhaps – their pleasure is almost as enjoyable as seeing the animal. To get the best from your safari, approach it with humour, look after the driver as well as you are able (a disgruntled driver will quickly ruin your safari), and do your best to get on with, and be considerate to your fellow travellers.

> See Where to stay, page 36, for sleeping options when on safari

Safaris can be booked either at home or in the country concerned – if you go for the latter it may be possible to obtain substantial discounts. If you elect to book in the country avoid companies offering cheap deals on the street – they will almost always turn out to be a disaster and may appear cheap because they do not include national park entrance fees.

Safaris do not run on every day of the week. Trips are often timed to end on a Thursday night. Thus a six-day safari will start on a Saturday, a four-day one on a Monday. In the low

> **Booking safaris**
> There are a huge number of companies offering safaris. These are noted on page 26 and in each country section

Essentials

season you may also find that these will be combined. If you are on a four-day safari you can expect to join another party. This can be awkward as the 'six-dayers' will already have formed into a coherent group and you may feel that you are an outsider.

Unfortunately, there are some 'rogue' operators. At the tourist office in Arusha there is a 'blacklist' of unlicenced operators and people with convictions for cheating tourists.

Food & drink Standards at lodges and tented sites are the same as at normal hotels. Camping safaris usually have a cook. Food is wholesome and surprisingly varied. You can expect eggs, bacon and sausages and toast for breakfast, salads at midday and meat/ pasta in the evening with perhaps a fruit salad for desert. Companies will cater for vegetarians. Tea and coffee are on hand at all times of the day. Insects are a fact of life and despite valiant attempts by the cook it is virtually impossible to avoid flies (as well as moths at night) alighting on plates and uncovered food. Notwithstanding this, hygiene standards are high.

Game drives There are usually two game drives each day. The morning drive sets off at about 0700 and lasts until midday. The afternoon drive starts at about 1600 and lasts until the park closes (roughly 1830-1900). In addition you may have an early morning drive which will mean getting up well before dawn at about 0500.

If you have arrived at the park by public transport, the warden and guides will arrange drives for a moderate charge in the park vehicles.

Specialized safaris & tours Many types of specialized activity can be undertaken in the region. The majority concentrate on the wildlife but other possible pursuits include walking and trekking, ballooning, bird-watching, canoeing, cycling, and fishing. Truck safaris demand a little more fortitude and adventurous spirit from the traveller. The compensation is usually the camaraderie and life-long friendships that result from what is invariably a real adventure, going to places the more luxurious travellers will never visit.

Specialist tour operators are listed on page 26 and in the Essentials section of each country

Papa's safaris

On 8 December 1933 Ernest Hemingway, then 34, and his second wife Pauline disembarked at Mombasa. They took the train up to Nairobi and stayed at the New Stanley Hotel. They engaged the foremost white hunter, Philip Percival, and stayed on the Percival farm near Machakos. Papa began hunting on the Kipiti Plains, shooting gazelles, kongoni impala and guineafowl. On 20 December the safari team motored to Arusha where they stayed at the Athenaeum Hotel (now the New Safari), before heading for the Serengeti where both Pauline and Ernest bagged lions and buffaloes. Ernest contracted amoebic dysentery, and was flown back to Nairobi to recuperate. On 23 January he rejoined the safari just south of Ngorongoro. As they proceeded south to Babati, he shot a rhinoceros and turning east to Kyungu he managed to fell a kudu and a sable. The party continued east to Tanga, then north to Malindi, staying in the Palm Beach Hotel for a few days of deep sea fishing, hooking kingfish, amberjacks, dolphin and sailfish. At the beginning of March they embarked at Mombasa for Europe.

It was another 20 years before Hemingway would visit Africa again, and this was to be an altogether more eventful trip. By now he was with his fourth wife, Mary. August 1953 saw them once again catching the train to stay on the Percival farm. The safari got underway at Kajiado, on the edge of what is now Amboseli National Park, where Ernest shot a big, black-maned lion, zebra and gerenuk. They then moved on to Fig Tree camp in the Masai Mara before returning to the Percivals'.

Here Ernest began getting into the spirit of Africa with some gusto. He shaved his head, dyed his suede jacket and two shirts with Masai red ochre and went leopard-hunting with a spear. He took a liking to an Akamba girl, Debba, purchased her and several friends' dresses for Christmas and brought them back to the camp where the celebrations became so enthusiastic that they broke one of the beds. Some months later Ernest observed that he should now be a father in Africa.

On 21 January Ernest and Mary flew from Nairobi, piloted by Roy Marsh. They stopped at Fig Tree camp then headed for Mwanza where they refuelled, before staying over at Costermanville (now Bukavu). As they circled the glassy waters, dotted with islands and hemmed in by green hills, Mary thought Kivu was the most beautiful lake she had ever seen. They put down at Entebbe. The following day, circling Murchison Falls, the plane hit a telegraph wire and made an emergency landing. The three lit a fire and slept under coats. Next day a boat visiting the falls gave them a lift to Butiaba. They engaged a plane and a pilot to fly them from Butiaba airstrip to Entebbe, but taking off from the bumpy runway, the plane suddenly stopped, and burst into flames. Roy Marsh kicked out a window and managed to drag Mary through. Ernest butted the jammed door open and struggled out. A policeman drove them to Masindi, and they put up in the Railway Hotel before reaching Entebbe and Lake Victoria Hotel. A few days later they flew to Nairobi.

In the meantime, a civilian airliner had reported the plane wreck – the world thought Hemingway had died and newspapers published obituaries. Though alive, he was in poor shape with concussion, ruptured liver, spleen and kidney, a crushed vertebra and burns to his face and arms. There had been plans to conclude the safari with fishing off Mombasa. Although Ernest did fly down to the coast some time later he was not able to take any active part before they sailed from Mombasa.

In 1956 there were plans to make a third trip, but poor health meant that it never materialized. Hemingway's experiences on safari provided the material for many short stories, a fine collection of which are in The Green Hills of Africa.

Essentials

Tipping How much to tip the driver on safari is tricky. It is best to enquire from the company at the time of booking what the going rate is. As a rough guide you should perhaps allow about US$5-7 per adult per night (half this for a child). Always try to come to an agreement with other members of the group and put the tip into a common kitty. Again remember that wages are low and there can be long lay-offs during the low season. If you are on a camping safari and have a cook, give all the money to the driver and leave him to sort out the split.

OFF THE BEATEN TRACK

...way off

It is worth emphasizing that most parks are some way from departure points. If you go on a four-day safari, you will often find that two days are taken up with travelling to and from the park – leaving you with a limited amount of time in the park itself. You will be spending a lot of time in a vehicle. On a more upmarket safari these will almost certainly be of the mini-van variety accommodating about eight people. Leg room can be very limited. They will have a viewing point through the roof (the really upmarket ones will also have a sun shade). In practice this means that only one or two people can view out through the roof at any one time – the view of the others will usually be impeded by legs.

Camping safari companies tend to use converted 10-ton lorries. Although very basic, they are surprisingly comfortable being well sprung (essential on some roads), with good leg room and large windows which fully open. Views of the animals on both sides of the truck are therefore good. They can be a little cramped if there is a full party of about 20 people.

Room is very limited in both mini-vans and lorries. You will be asked to limit the amount you bring with you. There is very little point in taking too much clothing – expect to get dirty, particularly during the dry season when dust can be a problem. Try to have a clean set of clothes to change into at night when it can also get quite cold. Comfortable, loose clothing and sensible footwear is best. Bear in mind that you may well travel through a variety of climates – it can be very cool at the top of the Rift Valley but very hot at the bottom. It is worth having warm clothing to hand in your transport as well as plenty of mineral water. Few safari companies provide drinking water and it is important to buy enough bottles to last your trip before you set off. It is surprising how much you get through and restocking is not easy.

The other important items are binoculars – preferably one pair for each member of your party, a camera with a telephoto lens (you will not get close enough to the animals without one) and plenty of film. Take twice as much as you think you will need. Film can be purchased at the lodges but it will cost you three times as much.

The Wildlife section in this *Handbook* will enable you to identify many animals. However you may wish to take a more detailed field guide. The Collins series is particularly recommended. The drivers are usually a mine of information. Take a notebook and pen as it is good fun to write down the number of species of animals and birds that you have spotted – anything over 100 is thought to be pretty good.

Wildlife and vegetation

Practically everyone travelling around East Africa will come into contact with animals during their stay. To this end you will find the more common animals, birds and reptiles featured in *See also Animal location chart on page 972* the Wildlife of Eastern and Southern Africa colour section in the middle of this book. It is based on an article written by Margaret Carswell, an international expert on the subject. Of course there is much more than the big game to see. You will undoubtedly travel through different habitats from the coast to the tropical rain forests.

Visitors to Africa often comment on the numbers of flowering trees seen in all the major cities. Trees such as the jacaranda and flamboyant are very beautiful when in full flower. The **jacaranda** (*Jacaranda mimosifolia*) is not in itself a beautiful tree being very straggly and rather tall, but when it bears its masses of beautiful mauvish blue tubular-shaped flowers it is very striking. It can be recognized when not in flower by the large divided leaves, each division of which carries very many small leaflets arranged along a central axis.

The **flamboyant tree** (*Delonix rex*) has similar leaves. When not in flower it can be distinguished from the jacaranda by its very different, and more attractive, shape. It does not grow as tall, only up to about 7.5 m, and is spreading and more compact in shape. This makes it an ideal tree to sit under on a hot day. When seen in flower, it is obvious why it is called the flamboyant tree. It is covered in a mass of mainly scarlet flowers. Some of the flowers have yellow tips giving the tree a golden appearance. Both jacaranda and flamboyant trees are often planted in towns.

Another tree with brilliant red flowers, and one which is often confused with the flamboyant, is the indigenous **flame tree** (*Spathodea nilotica*). The two trees really look very different, except

Rhino: black and white

Two species of rhino are found in Africa, the **white rhino** *and the* **black rhino***. These names have no bearing on the colour of the animals as they are both a rather nondescript dark grey. In some guide books the white rhino is described as being paler in colour than the black rhino, but this by no means obvious in the field. The name white rhino is derived from the Dutch word 'weit' which means wide and refers to the shape of the animal's mouth. The white rhino has a large square muzzle and this reflects the fact that it is a grazer and feeds by cropping grass. The black rhino, on the other hand, is a browser, usually feeding on shrubs and bushes. It achieves this by using its long, prehensile upper lip which is well adapted to the purpose. The horn of the rhino is not a true horn, but is made of a material called keratin, which is essentially the same as hair. If you see rhino with their young you will notice that the white rhino tends to follow its young herding them from behind, whereas the black*

rhino usually leads its young from the front.

In East Africa the black rhino originally was found only to the east of the Nile, whereas the white rhino was to be found only to the west of the river. However in 1961 some white rhinos were introduced into Murchison Falls National Park in Uganda from their home in West Nile Province. This was an attempt to establish a breeding population and at one time it was possible to see them there. Unfortunately this fragile population did not survive the many civil wars that raged in Uganda in the 1970s and 1980s. At the same time the original population in West Nile in Uganda was also poached to extinction. The white rhino is now severely endangered in East Africa, and a small population has been introduced into Meru National Park in the hope of reversing this trend. The black rhino is also severely endangered due to poaching, and work continues to rescue both these species from extinction.

for the flowers. The flame tree is very tall, up to 18 m with a straight smooth trunk, and in the wild is found on the forest edge. Particularly fine specimens can be seen in western Kenya. The rather shiny leaves are also divided, but into largish lobes, rather than the tiny leaflets of the flamboyant tree. The flowers are almost tulip shaped and bright scarlet in colour.

Other trees seen in towns and gardens include the **bottle brush** (*Callistemon*), a rather small and slender tree whose branches are thin and tend to droop downwards at the ends. Its flower is shaped just like a bottle brush and is usually red, though white ones occur. The leaf is long and narrow.

Yet another tree with scarlet flowers is the indigenous **coral tree** (*Erythrina*) which grows in rather scrubby land. This has a gnarled appearance with a rough corky bark, often armed with blunt spines. The leaves are rather leathery and divided into three sturdy leaflets. The scarlet flowers appear before the leaves. The seeds are interesting in that they are the familiar red and black 'lucky beans'.

Often planted in or near towns and settlements is the fast growing **gum** or **eucalyptus tree**. It was planted to drain swamps and also to provide firewood. This is readily recognized by its height, its characteristic long, thin leaves and the colourful peeling bark.

In the plains the most characteristic tree is no doubt the **thorn tree** (*Acacia*). There is more than one sort of thorn tree, and though they vary a lot in size and shape, they all have very divided, almost feathery leaves and long sharp thorns. Some have a noticeable yellow bark, and many are characteristically flat topped.

Two other very noticeable trees are the **baobab** (*Adansonia digitata*) and the **candelabra tree** (*Euphorbia candelabrum*). The baobab cannot be mistaken for anything else. It grows particularly on the coast and also inland for some miles. The trunk of a fully grown specimen is enormous in girth and the usually leafless branches stick out of the top of the tree for all the world as if they were roots and the tree was planted upside down. The candelabra tree is often mistaken for a large cactus, as it has succulent branches with ridges or 'wings' running up them. It is widespread in grasslands. These three trees are all indigenous to East Africa.

The **sausage tree** (*Kigelia aethiopica*), which grows on the African grasslands is a rather ordinary looking tree which has extraordinary looking fruit. The name given to it is understandable when you see the long sausage shaped fruit hanging down. These fruit can be nearly 1 m in length and 15 cm wide. They hang down on long thin stalks, giving the tree a remarkable appearance.

Two fruits to be enjoyed are the **mango** (*Mangerifera indica*) and the **pawpaw** (*Carica papaya*), and both the trees are widely grown. The mango tree has very dense dark shiny foliage and grows in a round shape. It is a good shade tree, too. The paw-paw on the other hand has enormous hand-shaped leaves, which are almost invariably tattered in appearance. The trunk is thin and the leaves come off at the top. Only the female tree bears the fruit, which hang down close to the trunk just below the leaves.

Trees that grow in the coastal region include the well known **coconut palms** (*Cocos nucifera*) which are almost everywhere, both in commercial plantations and growing singly. Unlike the coconut with its familiar straight trunk, the trunk of the **doum palm** (*Hyphaene thebaica*) has branches. This palm grows well on abandoned cultivation. The young palm looks like a fan of palm leaves sticking up out of the soil. The **screw pine** (*Pandanus kirkii*), also known as mangrove, whose fruits you will pick up on the beach, is common and noticeable. It grows just above the high water mark, and has remarkable roots. The feathery **casaurina** tree is commonly seen. It has small spiky cones which fall and cover the ground beneath the tree.

Look out for the rounded, sturdy shape of the **cashew nut tree** (*Anancardium occidentale*). This has bright green, shiny, rounded leaves and casts a very dense shade. It is, of course, cultivated and forms an important cash crop. The nuts grow on what are called cashew apples. Be careful of the juice of cashew apples – it makes a stain on clothing that cannot be removed.

Another tree which was introduced for its commercial value is the strange looking **kapok tree** (*Ceiba pentandra*). It is a very tall tree up to about 25 m whose branches grow straight out horizontally, almost at right angles to the trunk. The seed pods produce the fluffy, white kapok which is used to stuff mattresses and pillows.

It is a curious fact that many of the familiar trees and shrubs, which are thought of as quintessentially African, are actually not indigenous at all, but were introduced into Africa by the early European settlers, many of whom were fanatical gardeners. For example the jacaranda comes from Brazil, and the flamboyant from Madagascar. The frangipani (see under shrubs) was introduced from Mexico, both the gum and the bottle brush are Australian in origin, the mango and the hibiscus come from Asia and the pawpaw and the purple wreath (see under shrubs) from the Americas. Anyone interested in trees, both indigenous and introduced should make a point of visiting the Botanical Gardens in Entebbe. This is a beautiful spot on the shores of Lake Victoria.

Flowers & flowering shrubs

Flowers and flowering shrubs are everywhere in East Africa. They are planted in towns and cities and can be seen in the countryside too. One of the most colourful and widely planted in city flower beds is the **canna lily** (*Canna indica*) with large leaves which are either green or bronze, and lots of large bright red or yellow flowers. It can be more than 1 m high.

Flowering shrubs include the well-known **frangipani** (*Plumeria rubra*), which often has a sweet scent. This is a shrub with fat rather stubby branches and long leaves. The flowers are about 3 cm across and usually pink or white in colour and of a waxy appearance. If the bark is cut the sticky sap which oozes out can be very irritating to the skin. The **hibiscus** is another bushy shrub, which, like many other plants, is always known by its scientific name. This is cultivated in many forms, but is basically a trumpet shaped flower as much as 7-8 cm across, which has a very long 'tongue' growing out from the middle of the trumpet. The colours vary from scarlet to orange, yellow and white. The leaves are more or less heart shaped or oval with jagged edges.

One of the commonest cultivated flowering shrubs is the **bougainvillea**. This is a dense bush, or sometimes a climber, with oval leaves and rather long thorns. The flowers often cover the whole bush and can be a wide variety of colours including pinkish-purple, orange, yellow and white. The brightly coloured part is not formed by the petals, which are quite small and undistinguished, but by the large bracts (modified leaves), which, at first glance may be mistaken for petals. Look out too for the **purple wreath** (*Petrea*) which is a semi-climber often used as a hedge. It has strange papery leaves, and the masses of small purple-blue flowers grow densely in long spikes. A plant which is both beautiful and interesting is a form

☞ ## Naming the animals

Several birds and animals in Africa are named after people, reflecting an era of African history when Europeans were exploring and travelling in Africa, and writing home to describe the wonders that were to be found in that continent. Most of African wildlife was not known to science in those days, and classifying and naming species became a preoccupation of these early writers.

Many of the early explorers and travellers are among those honoured in this way. Thomson's gazelle and Grant's gazelle are named after two early European travellers in Africa. Joseph Thomson (1858-95) was a young Scot who travelled widely in Masai land.

He and his companion Chuma, who is better known for having carried the body of David Livingstone to the coast in 1873, undertook many expeditions together in this part of Africa. James Grant (1827-92), another Scottish explorer, is particularly known for his travels in what is now Uganda. Kirk's dikdik is named for Sir John Kirk, a doctor and botanist, who started his African travels as a member of one of David Livingstone's expeditions in 1858 and later became British consul in Zanzibar. Jackson's hartebeest is named for Sir Frederick Jackson (1860-1938) an amateur naturalist. As Governor of Uganda, he is particularly known for his work on the birds of the area.

of morning glory sometimes called the **moon flower** (*Ipomoea*). The moon flower is a creeper with large trumpet-shaped white flowers, very like a large version of the bindweed or convolvulus of Europe. The interesting thing about it is that it opens only after dark, and opens so quickly that you can watch it happening. This is a never-failing source of pleasure.

All the plants mentioned above are mainly to be seen in gardens and city parks, but there are also many interesting or beautiful flowering plants which grow wild. One of these, which is interesting rather than beautiful, is the **touch-me-not** or **sensitive plant** (*Mimosa pudica*). The touch-me-not is a prickly, woody, low growing plant only a few centimetres high which grows in poor soil. The leaves look like that of the mimosa and when touched they immediately fold up. As in the movement of the moonflower, you can see this happening. A very common flowering shrub in grassland and scrub is **lantana**, which comes in various forms. It is rather straggly and has rough, toothed, oval leaves which grow in pairs up the square and prickly stem. The flowers grow together in a flattened head, the ones near the middle of the head being usually yellowish, while those at the rim are pink, pale purple or orange. The fruit is a black shiny berry.

In the mountains of East Africa there are many strange plants. They are the familiar types such as **heather** (*Ericaceae*), **groundsel** (*Senecio*) and **red-hot poker** (*Kniphofia*), but the strange thing about them is that they are giant sized.

Lastly mention must be made of a plant which is very common in all swamps, but does not have very distinguished looking flowers. This is the **papyrus** (*Cyperus papyrus*). Its feathery topped stalks form huge swamps, especially in the region of the large lakes such as Lake Victoria.

Crops Eastern Africa is very much an agricultural part of the world, and many different crops are grown here. Some of them will be very familiar to visitors from Europe and America, but others are quite different. Subsistence farming is still widespread, and most settlements have their small fields of crops planted nearby for the use of the inhabitants. These vary according to the part of the country. In the west of the area, in Uganda, small **banana** plantations surround almost every house. The very large, darkish green, shiny leaves are unlike any other, and the tree often has a tattered appearance. This banana is not the familiar sweet yellow one favoured in Europe, but a large green one which does not turn yellow and is more correctly called a **plantain**, known locally as **matooke**. Matooke is eaten as a staple rather in the way we eat potatoes. It is peeled and cooked by steaming. This is done by wrapping the raw plantain in its own leaves and steaming it, usually over an open fire out of doors, for several hours. It then becomes soft and a little like mashed potatoes in consistency. This matooke is quite local in its distribution being favoured by the Baganda and their neighbours around the shores of Lake Victoria.

Other crops are more widespread. In particular, **maize** (sweet corn) is eaten in many parts and as **posho**, is the staple food in large areas of Tanzania and Kenya. Mostly, but not exclusively, in the drier parts of the region **cassava** is grown. This is a rather straggly bush some 2 m high. The leaves are dark green and divided into thin fingers. The part that is eaten is the root. Cassava is traditionally a famine, or reserve crop, because the root can stay in the ground for long periods without spoiling and be harvested when needed – a sort of living larder. In colonial times planting of cassava was compulsory as an insurance against famine. The plant is doubly useful as the leaves can be used to feed the Tilapia which are raised in fish farms. Cassava is better known in Europe as tapioca.

Tea, coffee and sugar cane are all grown here in the wetter parts, and there are places where all three can be seen growing near each other, for example on the road from the Kenyan border to Kampala. If a herd of cows happens to be passing, you have all you need for a tea or coffee break. **Tea**, though, is mainly a highland crop, and the large tea gardens, with their flat topped, shiny leafed bushes can be seen in western Kenya and western Uganda. The tea gardens are almost all run by large, sometimes international companies. If left to itself tea will grow to a tree 10 m tall. **Sugar cane** is a large grass-like crop standing nearly as high as a man, and is grown in many areas, but not the very dry parts. **Coffee** comes in two forms, **robusta** which used to grow wild in Uganda, and the more highly prized **arabica** which is native to Ethiopia, and is now grown in the highland regions. In East Africa coffee growing is a family enterprise and families grow and tend their own plots or plantations. They sell the coffee beans to the government and it is East Africa's most important cash crop. When the flowers are in bloom, which is mainly in Jan and Feb, the sweet smell is quite overpowering and unforgettable. The unripe coffee berries, or cherries, can be seen as green, and later red, berries clustering along the length of the stems. These three crops are, of course, cash crops and need processing, but a stick of sugar cane is often chewed, especially by children, as a sweet.

Sisal which is grown in the hotter, drier areas of Kenya and Tanzania is another cash crop. It is planted in straight rows in large plantations, and looks rather like the familiar yucca seen growing in pots in Europe. The leaves are straight and have a very spiky tip. From the middle of the leaves grows a very tall stem on the top of which is the flower. The fibre, extracted from the leaves, was a very important cash crop for the making of rope and string, but the advent of synthetic fibres has affected the market. But it can still be seen especially in eastern Kenya and in northern Tanzania between Tanga and Moshi. Another cash crop subject to the whims of fashion is **cotton**. At one time it was the main export but now has been superseded by coffee. It can be seen by the roadside in the rather drier areas growing in rather nondescript knee high bushes. When the cotton is ready for picking the fluffy white bolls are unmistakable. It is processed in factories called ginneries.

Groundnuts are an inconspicuous crop which tend to lie close to the ground. The plant above ground has a leaf which is deeply divided into lobes. The nuts themselves are clustered on the roots and out of sight. Another low growing crop is the **sweet potato**. This is invariably grown on mounds of soil scraped up with the local hoe or *jembe*. The plant is a straggly one with large flat leaves and a very pretty pale purple trumpet-shaped flower.

There are two flowers which are grown in parts of Kenya which are fairly recent cash crops. One of these is **pyrethrum**, which is grown in small plots near houses, especially in the highlands around Nairobi. It has a daisy-like flower and is harvested to make the natural insect killer, pyrethrum. The other flower which is being grown in the cooler parts of the region, especially near Hell's Gate in Kenya, is the **carnation**. This is grown for export and the square fields with the bright green foliage and almost constant irrigation, are conspicuous against the drier natural vegetation.

Origin of crops It may surprise you to know that apart from coffee and perhaps cotton, none of these crops is indigenous to Africa. The plantain probably originated in Asia, as did tea. Sugar cane is from the South Pacific. Cassava, sweet potato, groundnuts and maize are all from the Americas. They were all introduced by early settlers, mostly towards the end of the 19th century or the early part of this century.

Essentials

Freshwater fish The fish in this area are many and those who enjoy fishing can be sure of plenty of opportunity to practice their sport.

The king of the freshwater fish is without doubt the massive **Nile perch** (*Lates albertianus*). This huge predator lives on other fish, and originally came from the Nile below Murchison Falls, but was introduced into Lake Kyoga and the Nile above the Falls in 1955 and 1956. It has now spread to Lake Victoria itself, which has proved to be very much a mixed blessing. Weights of 20 to 40 kg are common and there are several records of over 100 kg. The best place to catch them is in Murchison Falls Park in Uganda, although you can have luck on Lake Victoria. In eastern Zaire, where they are present in Lake Albert, they are known as 'Le Capitan'. Also caught commonly in fresh waters is the **tilapia** (*Tilapia nilotica*), a much smaller, rather bony fish which makes good eating. Unlike the Nile perch this much smaller fish is herbivorous, and is now being farmed in fish ponds, where it is fed largely on the green leaves of the cassava plant.

The beach, To most visitors the East African beaches mean the reef. The fish and coral here are indeed
the reef & wonderful, and can be observed without having to dive to see them. This section concentrates
beachcombing on the many interesting creatures that can be seen by paddling and snorkelling. It is not necessary to be a strong swimmer to do this, nor is expensive equipment needed.

Many of the fish do not have universally recognized English names, but one that does is the very common **scorpion** or **lion fish** (*Pterois*), which is probably the most spectacular fish to be seen without going out in a boat. It is likely to be wherever there is live coral, and sometimes it gets trapped in the deeper pools of the dead reef by the retreating tide. It can be up to 26 cm long and is easily recognized by its peculiar fins and zebra-like stripes. Although it has poisonous dorsal spines it will not attack if left alone.

While most visitors naturally want to spend time snorkelling on the live reef and watching the brilliant fish and many coloured living corals, do not bypass the smaller, humbler creatures which frequent dead as well as living coral. These can be seen on most of the beaches, but one of the best places is Tiwi beach by Twiga Lodge. Here a vast area of dead coral is partly exposed at low tide and you can safely paddle, which is especially good for children. Be sure to wear shoes though, because there are many sea urchins. These sea urchins (*Echinoidea*) are usually found further out towards the edge of the reef, but can be found anywhere. There are two forms, the more common **short-needled sea urchin** and the much less common **long-needled** variety. Their spines are very sharp and treading on them is extremely painful. **Sea urchin skeletons** can be found lying on the sand. These are fragile and beautiful spheres which can be up to the size of a small tangerine. They are sandy coloured with lines and dots running down the sides. Look out also for the common **brittle stars** (*Ophiuroidea*) which frequent sandy hollows. They vary considerably in size, but are usually 10 cm across. They are so called because the arms break off very readily, but they will grow again. These are not sea urchins, though they are related, and can safely be picked up for a closer look, but handle them carefully.

Other living creatures which can be seen crawling along in the shallows include the **sea slug** (*Nudibranchia*) and the **snake eel** (*Ophichthidae*). Both are quite common in sandy places. The sea slug is blackish brown and shaped a bit like the familiar garden slug, though much bigger. It often has grains of sand sticking to it. This is not a beautiful creature. Don't be put off by the name of the snake eel, it is quite harmless. It looks a bit like a snake and has alternating light and dark bands on its body. What are beautiful, without doubt, are the **starfish** (*Asteroidea*) which are best seen by going out in a boat, but some can be seen nearer in shore. *Please don't collect them.* The colours fade in a week or so, and they are far better left to themselves.

Small pieces of broken off coral can also be found on the reef. These can be safely collected, without doing any harm to the reef. In particular there is the **mushroom coral** (*Fungia*) which looks like the underside of a mushroom and can be up to 20 cm across, though it is usually less than that and the **star coral** (*Goniastraea*). The flat **sand dollar** (*Echinoidea*) can also be found lying on the sand. It is rather fragile and is the skeleton of a creature related to sea urchins.

Two rather hard objects which may be a puzzle are the seed of the **mangrove** tree and small pieces of **pumice** which are still being washed up on this shore line, probably from the great explosion of Krakatoa, in Indonesia, in 1883.

The commonest shells are without doubt the **cowries**. Many dead ones can be found on the beach. *Please do not take live ones*. The two most common are the **ringed cowrie** (*Cypraea annulus*) and the **money cowrie** (*Cypraea moneta*). Of these the ringed is especially plentiful and is a pretty grey and white shell with a golden ring. The money cowrie was once used as money in Africa and varies in colour from greenish grey to pink according to its age. The big and beautiful **tiger cowrie** (*Cypraea tigris*) is also seen occasionally. This can be up to 8 cm in length. There is quite a lot of variation in colouring, but it is basically a very shiny shell with many dark round spots on, much more like a leopard than a tiger. There are many varied and beautiful sea creatures to be seen on the coast. The best way of doing this, especially if time is short, is to go to one of the marine parks, where you can go out in a glass bottomed boat with a guide.

There are probably 100,000 different species of insect in Africa, and certainly some not yet known to science. Even the casual visitor to Africa, who never leaves the urban areas and sees only the city streets and insides of houses, and whose only glimpse of animal life is urban dogs and cats, cannot fail to notice the insect life. Inside houses, especially in the kitchen, tiny brown **sugar ants** (*Camponotus maculatus*) can be seen following predetermined paths across the window sill and down the wall before disappearing into a tiny hole or crack in the plaster. They are harmless, but a bit of a nuisance in the kitchen. A good deal more unpleasant are the **cockroaches** which do not usually appear until after dark. The commonest household cockroach is known as the **American cockroach** (*Periplaneta americana*). It is about 30 mm in length, and a dark shiny reddish brown in colour, with long antennae which are constantly waved about. The **German cockroach** (*Blattella germanica*) is smaller and darker. The 'wild' cockroach which occurs in Africa, lives in the bark of trees and under fallen logs. Cockroaches are usually seen scuttling about the floor or up walls and furniture. They rarely fly, but when they do it is peculiarly disconcerting. Cockroaches do not bite or sting and their role in the spread of disease is debated, but nevertheless, they are associated in most people's mind with dirt.

Insects

On safari watch out for insects, and don't be tempted into ignoring everything less obviously impressive than a full grown lion. Termite mounds (or termataria) are a conspicuous feature of many parts of eastern Africa. **Ant hills** as they are also called, when freshly built, are the colour of the underlying soil and, therefore, often reddish. They can be 2 m high or more, and old established ones acquire a covering of herbs and bushes and often small trees. The **termites** (*Termitidae*) which live within these ant hills are commonly (though incorrectly) known as **white ants**.

Stick insects (*Phasmatodea*) and the **praying mantis** (*Mantodea*) are fairly common, but not easy to see. Both of them are masters of cryptic coloration, which means that they resemble their background in the most amazing ways. The incredibly thin, brown body of the stick insect, with its long legs, exactly resembles a piece of dry twig or grass. Similarly, some species of praying mantis grow the most extraordinary appendages on their bodies to mimic flowers and bark. The reproductive habits of some of these insects is rather strange, as it seems that male stick insects are very rare indeed, and, the female praying mantis devours her partner after mating. Neither praying mantises nor stick insects sting or bite, but both can hurt the fingers by the sharp spines on their legs. A praying mantis, so-called because it holds its front legs together in an attitude of prayer, is an attractive insect with an alert and seemingly intelligent way of moving its head from side to side.

Locusts (*Acrididae*) are probably the most famous members of the grasshopper group to be found in Africa. A classical swarm of the Desert Locust is unlikely to be seen, but occasional members of the group, which are recognizable as very large grasshoppers are quite common. When they fly, they reveal colourful wings. There are two important species of locust in Africa. The **desert locust** (*Schistocera gregaria*) which is the one mentioned in the Bible and which occurs mainly in northern Africa including Ethiopia, Somalia and northern Kenya, and the **red locust** (*Nomadacris septemfasciata*) which is found in southern Uganda and western Tanzania. While swarming, locusts fall prey to many birds such as marabous, white storks and various birds of prey which follow the swarms for the abundant food source they provide.

Another member of the grasshopper family very common in Uganda at certain times of the year, is the **nsenene** or edible grasshopper. This is a mainly green or brown grasshopper

Essentials

about 6-8 cm long. It swarms at certain times of the year, and being attracted to light can be seen in hundreds, sometimes thousands around the lights of Kampala after dark. It is much prized as a delicacy and small boys risk death and injury from passing cars by running across the roads in attempts to catch the insects. They are eaten either raw or cooked and taste slightly sweet.

Out-of-doors in Africa the persistent high pitched whine of the **cicada** (*Cicadidae*) is a characteristic sound. There are several species of cicada and they spend their time clinging to the bark of trees where their camouflage is so perfect that even guided by their song they are difficult to see. They are particularly irritating in that as soon as you get near enough to spot them they become silent and immediately invisible. They sing by day, especially in the heat of the day when their song is a quintessential part of the African noon, and also at nightfall.

Another noisy insect is the **cricket** (*Gryllidae*). There are many species found in Africa, and many are nocturnal. If one gets into the room at night it is not possible to get any sleep until it has been captured and put out. Catch it in an upturned glass, then slide something like a postcard under the glass and shake it outside.

If you look on the dry ground under the eaves and overhangs of houses you will notice small smooth conical pits an inch or so wide and deep. These are seen in fine or sandy soil which remains dry all the time. These pits are made by the **antlion** (*Myrmeleontidae*), a strange little creature which is the larval form of a dragonfly-like insect. Take a piece of grass and very gently scratch the side of the pit so that grains of sand tumble down into the bottom. If you do it right you will provoke the antlion, who lives in the pit, to attack. It builds these pits as traps for ants which tumble into the pit, and, because of the soft soil, are unable to climb out. The antlion promptly emerges and with its ferocious jaws, grabs the ant. Have a look at one of them. They are a brownish nondescript little insect perhaps 5-10 mm long, with the most enormous jaws for the size of the animal. When let go it will burrow into the soil at great speed, going backwards. These quaint little creatures seem very different from the adult insect, which is rather like a dragonfly to look at, with large gauzy wings.

Ants seem to get everywhere in Africa and there are many different sorts. Everyone has heard of the so-called **driver ants** (*Dorylinae*). They are more commonly known as **safari ants** or **siafu** in this part of Africa. These are the ants of legend which supposedly can engulf whole households and devour every living thing. In reality it is not quite like that. For a start the column of ants moves quite slowly so most animals have plenty of time to get out of the way. Secondly the marching columns are not as big as the ones in story books. Still it is quite a sight to see these ants on the move. If you are unlucky enough to tread in the middle of a column, you will know all about it as their bite is ferocious. The adult breeding male of these ants is called a **sausage fly**. It is about 3.5 cm long and is a brown, slightly hairy looking insect which bumbles around the lights at night. Although it flies, it seems to spend a lot of its time crashing into objects in the room and falling to the floor where it wriggles about helplessly until it takes off again, only to crash into something else. It is difficult to associate its comic incompetence with the ruthless efficiency of the safari ants.

Perhaps the most photographed insects in Africa are the **dung beetles** (*Scarabaeidae*). Pictures of them rolling their balls of dung across the grasslands are often shown in natural history films. They collect the dung into balls, in which the female then lays her eggs and on which the young feed. They are related to the sacred scarab beetle, which was worshipped by the ancient Egyptians.

The **mosquito** and the **tsetse fly** are two well-known insects in Africa. Not all mosquitoes are malarial, only those belonging to the *Anopheline* group. These can be distinguished from the harmless *Culex* mosquitoes by the way they stand before biting. The malarial ones hold their body at an angle of 45° to the surface, whereas the body of the harmless ones is parallel to the surface. Only the female bites and she can be recognized by her thread-like antennae. The male has feathery antennae, and feeds only on the nectar of flowers. There is more than one species of **tsetse fly** (*Glossina*). They have a bite like a red hot needle and carry various diseases of animals, as well as sleeping sickness in humans. It is about 8 mm long and holds its wings overlapping one on top of the other like the closed blades of a pair of scissors.

Mention must be made of a rather unpleasant insect. This is a *Staphylinid* beetle really called a rove beetle, but commonly known as **Nairobi eye**, after the painful condition it inflicts if you crush it. It is a small, thin, red and black insect which on casual inspection does not appear to have wings. It has a way of wriggling its abdomen about. Typically, the insect alights on your neck, and you instinctively put up your hand to brush it away. In doing this you will crush the insect: its body juices are intensely irritating and cause very painful blistering of the skin. Should you then rub your eyes before washing your hands it will be extremely painful.

Be sure to look out for the beautiful **firefly** (*Lampyridae*). The sight of dozens and dozens of these lovely insects flitting through the trees after dark is one of the sights of Africa never to be forgotten. They are rather local in their distribution, but are worth looking out for especially, but by no means only, in the higher areas.

Butterflies The butterflies of Africa are extremely numerous and in the whole of the continent there are more than 2,500 known species. Many, indeed most, of them, do not have an English name and are known only by their scientific Latin name. Because of this it is not possible to do more than mention a few of the more noticeable ones. However, even if the species cannot be identified, it is usually possible to recognize the family to which a butterfly belongs. In most cases this is not too difficult, but some species are extremely variable in appearance.

Sexual **dimorphism**, that is, when the males and the females of one species look quite different from each other, is very common in the animal kingdom. It is seen in birds, and most people are quite used to the idea. As well as exhibiting sexual dimorphism, butterflies frequently take this a step further, and individuals of the same species *and* the same sex often look quite different. This is known as polymorphism.

There is another interesting phenomenon, to be seen in certain species, known as **mimicry**. Generally speaking, brightly coloured butterflies, such as the **monarchs**, are distasteful to birds and other predators who have learnt, over time, to avoid these insects. Certain other butterflies, which are not inedible, have learnt to mimic the inedible species to such an extent that they look extremely similar. This means that the predators are fooled into believing that they, too, are distasteful, and thus also leave them alone. This mimicry includes copying the way of flying, as well as the appearance.

The different species of butterfly vary in their habits, some being low level fliers and some high fliers. Some are weak fliers and some fast fliers, while some have a buoyant and sailing flight. Many of the more beautiful ones occur in the forests and the popular notion is that they are attracted to flowers. While this is true up to a point, unfortunately it is also true that many more are actually attracted to such things as rotting fruit and animal dung or urine deposited on mud. This does help the observer though, as it means that they can be seen on puddles and on muddy roadsides.

Although there are 10 families of African butterflies, the larger and more obvious ones belong to the following families: **Swallowtails** (*Papilionidae*) These are large and often colourful butterflies, many of which have an obvious 'tail' at the lower outer corner of the hind wing. They are all strong fliers, and some fly very low and readily settle on the ground. **Whites** (*Pieridae*) These are medium sized butterflies which have white or pale yellow as a background colour. **Monarchs** (*Danaidae*) These are large and spectacular butterflies with a characteristic slow and sailing flight. They are distasteful to predators, and thus are mimicked by others. **Browns** (*Satyridae*) This is a rather large family of sombre brown or greyish brown butterflies with a weak flight, often close to the ground. **Nymphalids** (*Nymphalidae*) This is a very large family of stout and colourful butterflies, which, with the Swallowtails are the most beautiful of all. They commonly exhibit the polymorphism described above.

Essentials

Health

See Directory under individual towns for information on local and medical services

It is essential you take every precaution to stay healthy. If you have never been to East Africa before, you should read through this Health section, as a matter of priority. With the following advice and precautions you should keep as healthy as you do at home. Most visitors return home having experienced no problems at all apart from some travellers' diarrhoea.

In East Africa the health risks are different from those encountered in Europe or the USA. It also depends on where and how you travel. There are clear health differences between the countries of East Africa and in risks for the business traveller, who stays in international class hotels in large cities, the backpacker trekking from country to country and the tourist who heads for the beach or game parks. There is huge variation in climate, vegetation and wildlife from desert to tropical beaches, the mountains of Ethiopia to the rainforests of Uganda and to the teeming capital cities. There are no hard and fast rules to follow; you will often have to make your own judgement on the healthiness or otherwise of your surroundings. There are English (or other foreign language) speaking doctors in allt major cities who have particular experience in dealing with locally-occurring diseases. Your Embassy representative will often be able to give you the name of local reputable doctors and most of the better hotels have a doctor on standby.

Local conditions & standards

Because much of the area is economically under-developed, infectious diseases still predominate in the same way as they did in the West some decades ago. Poor living conditions, malnutrition and inadequate medical facilities contribute to poor health in the local population in some of these countries.

Some diseases, however, are no respecters of persons and in some cases, malaria for example, local populations have acquired a degree of immunity which is completely lacking in visitors. It is a myth to suppose that tropical diseases have been largely eradicated from East Africa: mosquito control is nowhere near as good as it used to be during the colonial period with a consequent increase in malaria. River blindness, schistosomiasis (bilharzia) are still common, specific African types of HIV infection are rampant and infections with leprosy and tuberculosis still widespread.

Away from the main centres The quality and range of medical care is extremely variable from country to country and diminishes very rapidly as you move away from cities, although some rural mission hospitals have been able to maintain good standards. In general you can be sure that local medical practitioners have a lot of experience with the particular diseases of their region.

Before you go

Take out medical insurance. Make sure it covers all eventualities especially evacuation to your home country by a medically equipped plane, if necessary. You should have a dental check up, obtain a spare spectacles prescription, a spare oral contraceptive prescription (or enough pills to last) and, if you suffer from a chronic illness (such as diabetes, high blood pressure, ear or sinus troubles, cardio-pulmonary disease or nervous disorder) arrange for a check up with your doctor, who can at the same time provide you with a letter explaining the details of your disability in English and, if necessary, French. Check the current practice in countries you are visiting for malaria prophylaxis (prevention). If you are on regular medication, make sure you have enough to cover the period of your travel.

Children

More preparation is probably necessary for babies and children than for an adult and perhaps a little more care should be taken when travelling to remote areas where health services are primitive. This is because children can be become more rapidly ill than adults (on the other hand they often recover more quickly). Diarrhoea and vomiting are the most common problems, so take the usual precautions, but more intensively. Breastfeeding is best and most convenient for babies, but powdered milk is generally available and so are baby foods in most countries. Papaya, bananas and avocados are all nutritious and can be cleanly prepared. The treatment of diarrhoea is the same for adults, except that it should start earlier and be continued with more persistence. Children get dehydrated very quickly in hot countries and can become drowsy and uncooperative unless cajoled to drink water or juice plus salts. Upper respiratory infections, such as colds, catarrh and middle ear infections are also common and if your child suffers from these normally take some antibiotics against the possibility. Outer ear infections after swimming are also common and antibiotic eardrops will help. Wet wipes are always useful and sometimes difficult to find, as, in some places are disposable nappies.

There is very little control on the sale of drugs and medicines. You will find that many of the drugs that are available have familiar names. This means you do not have to carry a whole chest of medicines with you, but remember that the shelf life of some items, especially vaccines and antibiotics, is markedly reduced in hot conditions. Unfortunately drugs are imported into Africa from many parts of the world where quality control is not good and there have been cases of drugs being supplied with the active agent substituted by inert materials. Buy your supplies at the better outlets where there are refrigerators, even though they are more expensive, and check the expiry date of all preparations you buy.

Medicines & what to take

Self-medication may be forced on you by circumstances so the following text contains the names of drugs and medicines which you may find useful in an emergency or in out-of-the-way places. You may like to take some of the following items with you from home: **Sunglasses**, ones designed for intense sunlight; **earplugs** for sleeping on aeroplanes and in noisy hotels; **suntan cream** with a high protection factor; **insect repellent** containing DEET for preference; **mosquito net**, lightweight, permethrin-impregnated for choice; **tablets** for travel sickness; **tampons** can be expensive in some countries; **condoms** and **contraceptives**; **water sterilizing** tablets; **antimalarial** tablets; **anti-infective** ointment, for example Cetrimide; **fungicidal creams** and **dusting powder** for feet; **antacid tablets** for indigestion; **sachets of rehydration salts** plus anti-diarrhoea preparations; **painkillers** such as Paracetamol or Aspirin; **antibiotics** for bacterial infections or persistent diarrhoea; **first aid kit**: some may be reassured by carrying their own supplies – available from camping shops and airport shops. Get a small pack containing a few sterile syringes and needles and disposable gloves.

Smallpox vaccination is no longer required. A yellow fever vaccination certificate is required if travelling from an affected area, especially Central and West African countries. Cholera vaccination is not officially required, despite the fact that the disease is endemic in a number of East African counties. Although cholera vaccination is not officially required, nor recommended by the WHO because its effectiveness is limited, travellers are occasionally asked to produce vaccination certificates if they have been in other cholera endemic areas such as parts of Asia or South America. If you are concerned this may be a problem but do not want to be given an ineffective vaccine, ask your own doctor for a cholera vaccination exemption certificate. Vaccination against the following diseases are recommended.

Vaccination & immunization

Yellow fever This is a live vaccination not usually to be given to children under nine months of age or persons allergic to eggs. Immunity lasts for 10 years, an International Certificate of Yellow Fever Vaccination will be given and should be kept because it is sometimes asked for. The vaccination is practically without side effects and almost totally protective.

Infectious hepatitis This is less of a problem for travellers than it used to be because of the development of two extremely effective vaccines against the A and B strains of the disease. It remains common. A combined hepatitis A & B vaccine is now available.

Polio Despite its decline in the world this remains a serious disease if caught and is easy to protect against. There are live oral vaccines and in some countries injected inactivated or killed vaccines. Whichever one you choose it is a good idea to have booster every 5-10 years if visiting developing countries regularly.

Tetanus One dose should be given with a booster at six weeks and another at six months and 10 yearly boosters thereafter are recommended (up to a maximum of five doses).

Typhoid A disease spread by the insanitary preparation of food. A number of new vaccines against this condition are now available; the older TAB and monovalent typhoid vaccines have been phased out. The newer, for example Typhim Vi, cause less side effects, but are more expensive. For those who do not like injections, there are now oral vaccines.

Children They should already be properly protected against diphtheria, poliomyelitis and pertussis (whooping cough), measles and HIB all of which can be more serious infections than at home. Measles, mumps and rubella vaccine is also given to children throughout the world, but those teenage girls who have not had rubella (German measles) should be tested and vaccinated. Hepatitis B vaccination for babies is now routine in some countries. Consult your doctor for advice on tuberculosis inoculation: the disease is still common in the region.

Other vaccinations Meningococcal meningitis occurs in epidemic form in a belt extending across Sub-Saharan Africa occurring during most dry seasons. It may be worth being vaccinated against the A and C strains of this disease or indeed if there is an epidemic occurring locally in any of the countries. There is an effective vaccination against rabies which should be considered by all travellers, especially those going through remote areas or if there is a particular occupational risk, for example for zoologists or veterinarians.

Further information

Further information on health risks abroad and vaccinations may be available from a local travel clinic

If you wish to take specific drugs with you such as antibiotics these are best prescribed by your own doctor. Beware, however, that not all doctors can be experts on the health problems of remote countries. More detailed or more up-to-date information than local doctors can provide are available from various sources. In the UK there are hospital departments specializing in tropical diseases in London, Liverpool, Birmingham and Glasgow and the Malaria Reference Laboratory at the London School of Hygiene and Tropical Medicine provides free advice about malaria, T0891-600350. In the USA the local Public Health Services can give such information and information is available centrally from the Centre for Disease Control (CDC) in Atlanta, T404-3324559. The World Health Organisation, www.who.int/ith/ provides malaria and other information for travellers.

There are additional computerized databases which can be assessed for destination-specific, up-to-the-minute information. In the UK there is *MASTA* (Medical Advisory Service to Travellers Abroad), www.masta.org, T020-7631 4408, F020-7436 5389, a private company from whom you can obtain a health brief tailored to your journey by calling T01276-685040 and answering a telephone questionnaire. Be warned that calls are charged at premium rates so this can work out expensive. There is also *Travax* (Glasgow, T0141-9467120, ext 247).

Some excellent travel health websites include www.doh.gov.uk/traveladvice/index.htm; www.fitfortravel.scot.nhs.uk; www.fco.gov.uk/travel and the relevant section of the US Department of Health and Human Services' site, www.cdc.gov/travel/eafrica.html

There are many travel clinics now providing these specialized services; check your local telephone directory for details. In the UK, the **British Airways Travel Clinic** provides inoculation advice and treatment at its clinic in Victoria Place, London SW1, T020-7233 6661. Try also **Trailfinders Travel Clinic**, 194 Kensington Hight Street, London W8, T020-7938 3999.

Other information on medical problems overseas can be obtained from the book by Richard Dawood (Editor), *Travellers' Health: How to Stay Healthy Abroad*, Oxford University Press, 1999, £9.50. We strongly recommend this revised and updated edition, especially to the intrepid traveller heading for the more remote places. General advice is also available in the UK in *Health Information for Overseas Travel* published by the Department of Health and available from HMSO, and *International Travel and Health* published by WHO, Geneva.

On the road

Preparing for long flights

During long haul flights, your blood oxygen saturation level is reduced by 10% and trapped gases may expand by up to 30%, causing severe pain and possible perforation of the eardrum if the Eustachian tubes are blocked. Measures to reduce the risk of developing deep-vein thrombosis include taking pre-flight soluble aspirin, wearing support stockings, avoiding both dehydration and alcohol, and by taking gentle lower-limb exercise in flight as immobility is a known risk factor.

Staying healthy

Intestinal upsets

The thought of catching a stomach bug worries visitors but there have been great improvements in food hygiene and most such infections are preventable. Travellers' diarrhoea and vomiting is due, most of the time, to food poisoning, usually passed on by the unsanitary habits of food handlers. As a general rule the cleaner your surroundings and the smarter the restaurant, the less likely you are to suffer.

Foods to avoid Uncooked, undercooked, partially cooked or reheated meat, fish, eggs, raw vegetables and salads, especially when they have been left out exposed to flies. Stick to fresh food that has been cooked from raw just before eating and make sure you peel fruit yourself. Wash and dry your hands before eating – disposable wet-wipes are useful for this.

Pasteurized or heat-treated milk is widely available in some of the countries as is ice cream or yoghurt produced by the same methods. Unpasteurized milk products, including cheese, are sources of tuberculosis, brucellosis, listeria and food poisoning germs. You can render fresh milk safe by heating it to 62°C for 30 minutes, followed by rapid cooling or by boiling it but this usually makes it taste horrible. Matured or processed cheeses are safer than the fresh varieties.

Tap water is generally held to be unsafe or at least unreliable throughout East Africa. Filtered or bottled water is usually available and safe, although you must make sure that somebody is not filling bottles from the tap and hammering on a new crown cap. Choose carbonated bottled drinking water if there is a choice, as it is less likely to have been topped up with tap water. Ice for drinks should be made from boiled water, but rarely is so stand your glass on the ice cubes, rather than putting them in the drink. The better hotels have water purifying systems.

Travellers' diarrhoea Gastro-intestinal upsets are usually caused by eating food or by drinking water/ice which has been contaminated by food poisoning bacteria, viruses or protozoa. Drinking water is not always the culprit. Sea water or river water is more likely to be contaminated by sewage than swimming pools and so swimming in such dilute effluent can also be a cause.

Infection with various organisms can give rise to travellers' diarrhoea. They may be viruses, bacteria, for example Escherichia coli (probably the most common cause worldwide), protozoal (such as amoebas and giardia), salmonella and cholera. The diarrhoea may come on suddenly or rather slowly. It may or may not be accompanied by vomiting or by severe abdominal pain and the passage of blood or mucus when it is called dysentery.

How do you know which type you have caught and how to treat it?

If you can time the onset of the diarrhoea to the minute ('acute') then it is probably due to a virus or a bacterium and/or the onset of dysentery. The treatment in addition to re-hydration sugar/salt fluid mixures is Ciprofloxacin 500 mg every 12 hours; the drug is now widely available and there are many similar ones.

The symptoms of **cholera** are passing profuse watery diarrhoea 1-5 days after infection which can lead to rapid dehydration. It may be accompanied by vomiting. More than half a litre of fluid may be lost every hour and must be replaced because the dehydration if untreated can be fatal. The cholera vaccine is largely ineffective. Cholera is endemic in parts of East Africa with outbreaks reported every 2-3 years. Transmission is by the faecal-oral route – in other words ingestion of contaminated foods or water/ice. Treatment of cholera is by replacing lost fluids with water containing sugar/salt (see below for proportions). Tetracycline can shorten the period of diarrhoea and infectiousness.

If the diarrhoea comes on slowly or intermittently ('sub-acute') then it is more likely to be protozoal, that is caused by an amoeba or giardia. Antibiotics such a Ciprofloxacin will have little effect. These cases are best treated by a doctor as is any outbreak of diarrhoea continuing for more than three days. Sometimes blood is passed in amoebic dysentery and for this you should certainly seek medical help. If this is not available then the best treatment is probably Tinidazole (Fasigyn) one tablet four times a day for three days. If there are severe stomach cramps, the following drugs may help but are not very useful in the management of acute diarrhoea: Loperamide (Imodium) and Diphenoxylate with Atropine (Lomotil) They should not be given to children.

Any kind of diarrhoea, whether or not accompanied by vomiting, responds well to the replacement of water and salts, taken as frequent small sips, of some kind of re-hydration solution. There are proprietary preparations consisting of sachets of powder which you dissolve in boiled water or you can make your own by adding half a teaspoonful of salt (three and a half grams) and four tablespoons of sugar (40 g) to a litre of boiled water.

Essentials

Essentials

Thus the principles for treatment of diarrhoea are rest, fluid and salt replacement, antibiotics such as Ciprofloxacin for the bacterial types and special diagnostic tests and medical treatment for the amoeba and giardia infections. Salmonella infections and cholera, although rare, can be devastating diseases and it would be wise to get to a hospital as soon as possible if these were suspected.

Fasting, peculiar diets and the consumption of large quantities of yoghurt have not been found useful in calming travellers' diarrhoea or in rehabilitating inflamed bowels. Oral re-hydration has on the other hand, especially in children, been a life-saving technique and should always be practised, whatever other treatment you use. As there is some evidence that alcohol and milk might prolong diarrhoea they should be avoided during and immediately after an attack.

Diarrhoea occurring day after day for long periods of time (chronic diarrhoea) is notoriously resistant to amateur attempts at treatment and again warrants proper diagnostic tests (most towns with reasonable sized hospitals have laboratories for stool samples). There are ways of preventing travellers' diarrhoea for short periods of time by taking antibiotics, but this is not a foolproof technique and should not be used other than in exceptional circumstances. Doxycycline is possibly the best drug. Some preventatives such as Enterovioform can have serious side effects if taken for long periods.

Paradoxically **constipation** is also common, probably induced by dietary change, inadequate fluid intake in hot places and long bus journeys. Simple laxatives are useful in the short-term and bulky foods such as maize, beans and plenty of fruit are also useful.

Purifying water **Boiling** Boiling water for 10 minutes will kill all enteric bacteria, viruses and protozoa. The absolute minimum boiling period should be one minute. Allow an extra minute boiling time for every 1,000 m above sea level. **Chemical disinfection** The most effective agent is 2% tincture of Iodine. Add five drops per litre. Cover and allow the water to stand for 15 hours to kill *Cryptosporidium*. Avoid long term use of iodine, or chose an alternative chemical if pregnant or receiving treatment for thyroid disease. Chlorine is another chemical used to purify water, but is less effective than iodine. Household bleach is frequently chlorine based, and if used at a concentration of two drops per litre, then allowed to stand for 20 minutes, will reduce your risk of acquiring gastro-enteritis. **Filtration** Cloudy water should be filtered before boiling or chemical disinfection. There are a number of filters on the market with varying prices and levels of effectiveness. The most effective are the reverse-osmosis filters that will protect against bacteria, viruses and protozoa.

High altitude East Africa contains two well known mountains, Kilimanjaro and Mount Kenya both of which are over 5,000 m in height. Addis Ababa in Ethiopia is at about 2,400 m. Spending time here is usually a pleasure – it is not so hot, there are no insects and the air is clear and spring like. Travelling to high altitudes, however, can cause medical problems, all of which can be prevented if care is taken.

On reaching heights above about 3,000 m, heart pounding and shortness of breath, especially on exertion are a normal response to the lack of oxygen in the air. A condition called acute mountain sickness can also affect visitors. It is more likely to affect those who ascend rapidly, for example by plane and those who over-exert themselves (teenagers for example). Acute mountain sickness takes a few hours or days to come on and presents with a bad headache, extreme tiredness, sometimes dizziness, loss of appetite and frequently nausea and vomiting. Insomnia is common and is often associated with a suffocating feeling when lying in bed. Keen observers may note their breathing tends to wax and wane at night and their face tends to be puffy in the mornings – this is all part of the syndrome. Anyone can get this condition and past experience is not always a good guide: the author, having spent years in Peru travelling constantly between sea level and very high altitude never suffered symptoms, then was severely affected whilst climbing Kilimanjaro in Tanzania.

The treatment of acute mountain sickness is simple – rest, painkillers (preferably not aspirin based) for the headache and anti sickness pills for vomiting. Oxygen is actually not much help, except at very high altitude.

To **prevent** the condition: on arrival at places over 3,000 m have a few hours rest in a chair and avoid alcohol, cigarettes and heavy food. If the symptoms are severe and prolonged, it is best to descend to a lower altitude and to re-ascend slowly or in stages. If this is impossible because of shortage of time or if you are going so high that acute mountain sickness is very likely, then the drug Acetazolamide (Diamox) can be used as a preventative and continued during the ascent. There is good evidence of the value of this drug but some people do experience peculiar side effects. The usual dose is 500 mg of the slow release preparation each night, starting the night before ascending above 3,000 m.

Watch out for **sunburn** at high altitude. The ultraviolet rays are extremely powerful. The air is also excessively dry at high altitude and you might find that your skin dries out and the inside of your nose becomes crusted. Use a moisturizer for the skin and some vaseline wiped into the nostrils. Some people find contact lenses irritate because of the dry air. It is unwise to ascend to high altitude if you are pregnant, especially in the first three months, or if you have a history of heart, lung or blood disease, including sickle cell.

A more unusual condition can affect mountaineers who ascend rapidly to high altitude – **acute pulmonary oedema**. Residents at altitude sometimes experience this when returning to the mountains from time spent at the coast. This condition is often preceded by acute mountain sickness and comes on quite rapidly with severe breathlessness, noisy breathing, cough, blueness of the lips and frothing at the mouth. Anybody who develops this must be brought down as soon as possible, given oxygen and taken to hospital.

A rapid descent from high places will make sinus problems and middle ear infections worse and might make your teeth ache. Lastly, don't fly to altitude within 24 hours of SCUBA diving. You might suffer from 'the bends'.

Full acclimatization to high temperatures takes about two weeks. During this period it is normal to feel a bit apathetic, especially if the relative humidity is high. Drink plenty of water (up to 15 litres a day are required when working physically hard in the tropics), use salt on your food and avoid extreme exertion. Tepid showers are more cooling than hot or cold ones. Large hats do not cool you down, but do prevent sunburn. Remember that, especially in the highlands, there can be a large and sudden drop in temperature between sun and shade and between night and day, so dress accordingly. Warm jackets, fleeces or woollen clothing are essential after dark at high altitude. Loose cotton is still the best material when the weather is hot.

Heat & cold

Sunburn The burning power of the tropical sun, especially at high altitude, is phenomenal. Always wear a wide brimmed hat and use some form of sunscreen cream or lotion on untanned skin. The sun can cause skin cancer and tanning ages the skin. If you insist on sunbathing then expose yourself gradually to sunlight and use a high factor sun-screen. Normal temperate zone suntan lotions (protection factor up to 7) are not much good; you need to use the types designed specifically for the tropics or for mountaineers or skiers with protection factors of 15 or above. Being in the water offers no protection from sunburn. Glare from the sun can cause conjunctivitis, so wear sunglasses especially on tropical beaches, where high protection factor sunscreen should also be used.

Heat stroke is a potentially life-threatening condition. The function of the sweat glands becomes impaired causing the body's heat-regulating mechanisms to fail, and the body temperature to rise to over 39°C. The person may become disorientated or confused, experiencing weakness or collapse. The person should be placed in the shade, cooled down by fanning and sponging with cool water and given oral fluids if conscious. Without emergency treatment the person may lapse into coma.

Heat stroke is often preceded by **heat exhaustion**, the signs of which are profuse sweating, faintness, cramps, excessive thirst, headache and exhaustion. Unaccustomed strenuous activity, over-eating, drinking too much alcohol and wearing unsuitable clothing are all contributory factors. Older people, if unfit, or in poor general health, may be at greater risk of developing heat exhaustion, which can usually be avoided by gradual acclimatization to hot conditions.

As a general rule it is advisable to try to avoid all insect bites. Some insects such as mosquitoes are, of course, carriers of potentially serious diseases. Sleep off the ground and use a mosquito net or some kind of insecticide. Preparations containing Pyrethrum or synthetic pyrethroids are

Insects

Essentials

safe. They are available as aerosols or pumps and the best way to use these is to spray the room thoroughly in all areas (follow the instructions rather than the insects) and then shut the door for a while, re-entering when the smell has dispersed. Mosquito coils release insecticide as they burn slowly. They are widely available and useful out of doors. Tablets of insecticide, which are placed on a heated mat plugged into a wall socket are probably the most effective. They fill the room with insecticidal fumes in the same way as aerosols or coils.

You can also use insect repellents, most of which are effective against a wide range of pests. The most common and effective is diethyl metatoluamide (DEET). DEET liquid is best for arms and face (care around eyes and with spectacles – DEET dissolves plastic). Aerosol spray is good for clothes and ankles and liquid DEET can be dissolved in water and used to impregnate cotton clothes and mosquito nets. Some repellents now contain DEET and Permethrin, insecticide. Impregnated wrist and ankle bands can also be useful.

If you are bitten or stung, itching may be relieved by cool baths, antihistamine tablets (care with alcohol or driving) or mild corticosteroid creams, for example. hydrocortisone (great care: never use if any hint of infection). Careful scratching of all your bites once a day can be surprisingly effective. Calamine lotion and cream have limited effectiveness and antihistamine creams can cause allergies.

Bites which become infected should be treated with a local antiseptic or antibiotic cream such as Cetrimide, as should any infected sores or scratches. Minor scratches can become rapidly infected, so it is important to clean them scrupulously and take care of them.

Other afflictions **Athletes' foot** This and other fungal skin infections are best treated with Tolnaftate or Clotrimazole.

Jigger fleas In some parts of Africa the jigger flea commonly burrows its way into people's feet causing a painful itchy swelling which finally bursts in a rather disgusting fashion. Avoid these by not going barefoot or wearing sandals and if they do become established have someone experienced winkle them out with a sterile needle.

Lice and scabies When living rough, skin infestations with body lice (crabs) and scabies are easy to pick up. Use whatever local commercial preparation is recommended for lice and scabies.

Crotamiton cream (Eurax) alleviates itching and also kills a number of skin parasites. Malathion lotion 5% (Prioderm) kills lice effectively, but avoid the use of the toxic agricultural preparation of Malathion, more often used to commit suicide.

Prickly heat A very common intensely itchy rash is avoided by frequent washing and by wearing loose clothing. Cured by allowing skin to dry off through use of powder and spending two nights in an air conditioned hotel!

Ticks They attach themselves usually to the lower parts of the body often after walking in areas where cattle have grazed. They take a while to attach themselves strongly, but swell up as they start to suck blood. The important thing is to remove them gently, so that they do not leave their head parts in your skin because this can cause a nasty allergic reaction some days later. Do not use petrol, vaseline, lighted cigarettes to remove the tick, but, with a pair of tweezers remove the beast gently by gripping it at the attached (head) end and rock it out in very much the same way that a tooth is extracted. Certain tropical flies which lay their eggs under the skin of sheep and cattle also occasionally do the same thing to humans with the unpleasant result that a maggot grows under the skin and pops up as a boil or pimple. The best way to remove these is to cover the boil with oil, vaseline or nail varnish so as to stop the maggot breathing, then to squeeze it out gently the next day.

Other risks and more serious diseases

Rabies Remember that rabies is endemic throughout Africa, so avoid dogs that are behaving strangely. If you are bitten by a domestic or wild animal, including bats, do not leave things to chance: scrub the wound with soap and water and/or disinfectant, try to have the animal captured or at least determine its ownership, and seek medical assistance at once. The course of treatment depends on whether you have already been satisfactorily vaccinated against rabies. If you have (this is worthwhile if you are planning to spend lengths of time in developing countries) then some further doses of vaccine are all that is required. Human diploid vaccine is the best, but expensive: other, older kinds of vaccine, such as that derived from duck embryos may be the only types available. These are effective, much cheaper and interchangeable generally with the human derived types. If not already vaccinated then anti-rabies serum (immunoglobulin) may be required in addition. It is important to finish the course of treatment.

AIDS

This has had a devastating effect on the population of East Africa where it is mainly spread by heterosexual intercourse. Men and women are equally affected. Some transmission occurs through infected blood transfusions. Screening for the HIV virus in blood for transfusion is not always accurately performed or even performed at all, so in some East African countries blood transfusion represents a real risk, not only of infection with HIV but with hepatitis, malaria and a few other infections. The main risk to travellers is from casual sex, heterosexual or homosexual. The same precautions should be taken as when encountering any sexually transmitted disease. Female prostitution is common throughout East Africa and an alarmingly high proportion of the prostitute population is HIV positive. The AIDS virus (HIV) can be passed via unsterile needles that have been previously used to inject an HIV-positive patient. Acquiring Hepatitis B is an even greater risk. Risks of acquiring blood-borne viruses need to be emphasized when considering having a tattoo, ear or body piercing. It is sensible to check that needles have been properly sterilized or that disposable needles are used. The risk of HIV transmission in a blood transfusion is greater than from dirty needles because of the amount of fluid exchanged. Studies have shown that tourists most commonly contract HIV from local people or other travellers after having consumed too much alcohol – as this impairs their judgement.

Immuno-compromised travellers should check the medical facilities in the country of destination before departure, and check that their medical insurance covers their requirements. Medication for their whole trip should be obtained before departure and should be clearly labelled.

Catching the AIDS virus (HIV) does not necessarily produce an illness in itself (although it may do). The only way to be sure if you feel you have been put at risk is to have a blood test for HIV antibodies on your return to a place where there are reliable laboratory facilities. The test may not show a positive result for many weeks and during those weeks the person who has caught the virus is likely to be extremely infectious.

Malaria

Malaria remains a serious disease that occurs with varying frequency throughout East Africa, more commonly during the rainy season. Every year travellers die from malaria because they have taken insufficient precautions. Malaria is a serious parasitic disease spread by the bite of an infected female Anopheles mosquito and is the single most important disease hazard for travellers to East Africa. Mosquitoes have developed resistance to insecticides and in several areas to anti-malarial drugs. In some countries – Djibouti, Tanzania and Uganda it is very widespread. Mosquitoes do not usually thrive above 2,500 m, so you are relatively safe above that altitude. However, in 1999 there was an epidemic of malaria *falciparum*, resulting in over 700 deaths in Kenya's Kisii Highlands.

There are different varieties of malaria. The four species that cause disease in man are: *plasmodium falciparum, plasmodium vivax, plasmodium ovale* and *plasmodium malariaea*. Each species spends part of its life cycle in the Anopheles mosquito and part in humans. *Falciparum malaria* infections are most frequently contracted in Africa. The symptoms of malaria include muscle aches and pains, headache, fevers, sweating and chills. They appear when the red blood cells that are affected by the parasite rupture, releasing more parasites into the bloodstream. The period between being bitten by a mosquito and the appearance of symptoms is usually one to two weeks. However, it can be longer if the person has been taking anti-malarial drugs.

In 'classic malaria' the main symptom is fever (malarial ague), described as having three stages – a cold stage with shivering; a hot stage when the body temperature rises, followed by a sweating stage which reduces the temperature. The fever may develop in a cyclical pattern on alternate days.

Plasmodium falciparum differs from other varieties of malaria because it attacks red blood cells of all ages, whereas other forms of malaria only attack young or old red blood cells. As a result *falciparum* malaria affects a greater proportion of blood cells. This form of malaria can prove fatal within a few days of the appearance of symptoms, if it progresses to cerebral malaria. Fever symptoms may resemble severe influenza. Complications of *falciparum* malaria include kidney failure and jaundice. Despite taking anti-malarial drugs and bite avoidance measures it is still possible to contract malaria. Anyone who develops fever and a headache after a trip to the tropics should see their doctor as soon as possible to exclude malaria. Malaria is diagnosed by studying blood samples, where parasites can be identified using a microscope.

Prophylaxis and treatment It is important to undertake a prophylactic (preventative) regime. Start taking the tablets 2-3 weeks before departure and continue to take them for four to six weeks after leaving the malarial zone as advised. Prophylactic (preventative) anti-malarial drugs should be taken by all visitors to the tropics, including pregnant women, children and babies. All the drugs may have some side effects and it is important to balance the risk of catching the disease against the, albeit rare, side-effects of the medication. If your itinerary takes you into a malarial area, seek expert advice before you go on a suitable prophylactic regime. Chloroquine is recommended only for areas where there is no resistance to this drug. There is now widespread resistance to Chloroquine in Tanzania. Proguanil may be preferred for longer term use because it has fewer side effects. Combinations of Chloroquine and Proguanil or Pyrimethamine and Dapsone may be prescribed. Mefloquine (Larium) is the most effective preventative drug against malaria but there are concerns about side-effects. Neuro-psychiatric side effects, such as depression and anxiety, can be quite severe in a small number of cases, estimated to be in the region of one in 200 cases. People with a history of depressive illnesses are advised not to take Mefloquine, but to take alternatives and be stringent in their avoidance of mosquito bite measures. Sub-Saharan Africa, where *falciparum* malaria is most prevalent, is the zone where Mefloquine is the primary recommended anti-malarial medication. Mefloquine should be started two to three weeks before travelling to a malarial zone and continued for four weeks after leaving the zone. Doxycycline may be prescribed if there are contra-indications to Mefloquine.

The increasing complexity of the subject is such that, as the malarial parasite becomes immune to the new generation of drugs, the physical prevention of being bitten by mosquitoes becomes all the more important. In addition to taking preventative medication, all travellers to the tropics should make every possible effort to avoid mosquito bites. The Anopheles mosquito is most active in the evening, emerging at dusk and hunting until dawn. It hunts at ground level and can bite through thin socks. Outdoor precautions include wearing long toursers and sturdy shoes in the evenings. Choose light coloured clothing. Apply an insect repellent containing DEET to exposed skin, but take care when applying it to your face. For longer-lasting protection, wear wrist and ankle bands soaked in DEET. Indoor precautions include choosing a room that has mosquito screens (intact) on all windows and doors. Use an intact mosquito net, preferably soaked in Permethrin, tucking the net under the mattress. Spray the room every evening with an insecticide spray, especially in dark recesses like the wardrobes or under the beds. Use a vaporizing mat for longer protection or burn mosquito smoke coils. Electric buzzers are ineffective.

It is important to complete the course of anti-malarial drugs when leaving the tropics. If you get any flu-like symptoms either during your stay or for three months after leaving a malarial zone, see a doctor immediately and have your blood tested for malaria. Certain people are at higher risk of contracting severe malaria and need to be forewarned. These include children under five years, pregnant women, anyone who is immuno-compromised or has had their spleen removed.

Infectious The main symptoms are pains in the stomach, loss of appetite, lassitude and yellow
hepatitis discolouration of the eyes and skin. Hepatitis A is transmitted via the oral-faecal route, and
(jaundice) avoidance is by careful preparation and storage of food, drinking uncontaminated water/ice and by paying scrupulous attention to toilet hygiene.

Hepatitis B is usually acquired either sexually, by shared use of needles, whilst having body piercing or tattoos, blood contamination during accidents or by blood transfusions. Symptoms vary from none to fulminant hepatitis (sudeen, acute onset of symptoms). The incubation period is much longer (up to six months compared with six weeks) and complications include cirrhosis, chronic hepatitis and liver cancer.

Hepatitis A can be protected against with Hepatitis A vaccine (Havrix) which gives immunity lasting up to 10 years. After that boosters are required.

Hepatitis A and typhoid combined vaccine (Typherix) is also available. The vaccination has negligible side effects and is extremely effective, especially when used in conjunction with avoidance of contaminated food and drink. Gamma globulin injections of pooled serum have been superseded by the vaccine.

Hepatitis B can be effectively prevented by a specific vaccine (Engerix), plus avoidance measures. Three shots are required, ideally given over a six month period before travelling, or the accelerated course of monthly injections with a booster a year later.

A combined vaccine Hepatitis A and B (Twinrix) is now available.

There are several other kinds of viral hepatitis (C, E) but vaccines are not yet available.

Can still occur, carried by ticks. There is usually a reaction at the site of the bite and a fever. Seek medical advice. **Typhus**

These are common and the more serious ones such as hookworm can be contracted from walking barefoot on infested earth or beaches. **Intestinal worms**

This is a rare event for travellers. If you are unlucky enough to be bitten by a venomous snake, spider, scorpion or sea creature, try to identify the creature, but do not put yourself in further danger. Snake bites in particular are very frightening, but in fact rarely poisonous – even venomous snakes can bite without injecting venom. What you might expect if bitten are: fright, swelling, pain and bruising around the bite and soreness of the regional lymph glands, perhaps nausea, vomiting and a fever. Signs of serious poisoning would be the following symptoms: numbness and tingling of the face, muscular spasms, convulsions, shortness of breath and bleeding. Victims should be taken to a hospital or a doctor without delay. Commercial snake bite and scorpion kits are available, but usually only useful for the specific type of snake or scorpion for which they are designed. Most serum has to be given intravenously so it is not much good equipping yourself with it unless skilled at self-injecting. It is best to rely on local practice in these cases, because the particular creatures will be known about locally and appropriate treatment can be given. **Snake, spider & scorpion bites**

Treatment of snake bite Reassure and comfort the victim frequently. Immobilise the limb using a bandage or a splint or by getting the person to lie still. Do not slash the bite area and try to suck out the poison because this sort of heroism does more harm than good. If you know how to use a tourniquet in these circumstances, you will not need this advice. If you are not experienced do not apply a tourniquet.

Precautions Avoid walking in snake territory in bare feet or sandals – wear proper shoes or boots. If you encounter a snake stay put until it slithers away, and do not investigate a wounded snake. Spiders and scorpions may be found in the more basic hotels. If stung, rest and take plenty of fluids and call a doctor. The best precaution is to keep beds away from the walls and look inside your shoes and under the toilet seat every morning. Certain tropical sea fish when trodden upon inject venom into bathers' feet. This can be exceptionally painful. Wear plastic shoes when you go bathing if such creatures are reported. The pain can be relieved by immersing the foot in extremely hot water for as long as the pain persists.

Bilharzia (schistosomiasis) A parasitic disease caused by three species of parasitic flatworms or flukes. It is caught by wading or bathing in infested waters, including fresh water lakes, slow-moving, well-oxygenated rivers or irrigation systems. The fluke spends part of its life cycle inside freshwater snails, where they multiply and are released as cercariae (flukes) into the water. The cercariae penetrate human skin, and migrate via the blood stream to the liver, lungs, bowels and bladder. **Stings, bites & other insects**

Dengue fever This is a common disease in tropical areas where it is sometimes called *Break Bone Fever*, reflecting the severity of the accompanying headache. It can be completely prevented by avoiding mosquito bites in the same way as malaria. No vaccine is available. Dengue is an unpleasant and painful acute viral infection, presenting with a high temperature and generalized aches with joint pains and severe headache. After 4-5 days the symptoms may resolve only to recur a couple of days later accompanied by swollen glands and a widespread rash. The second phase usually abates in another 5-7 days. Visitors are spared the more serious forms (haemorrhagic types) which are more of a problem for local people who have been exposed to the disease more than once. There is no specific treatment for dengue – just pain killers and rest. Transmission is both by day and evening – biting mosquitoes. Avoidance relies on the use of anti-mosquito measures as described in the section on malaria.

Filariasis This causes such diseases as elephantiasis occurs in many East African countries. It is also transmitted by mosquitoes.

Hydatid disease This is common in Ethiopia but can be avoided by keeping well clear of dogs which is good advice in any case.

Leishmaniasis This causes a non-healing skin ulcer which occurs in many East African countries. It is transmitted by sand flies. A more serious form, visceral leishmaniasis or kala-azar affects mainly children, rarely tourists, but occurs all over East Africa.

The severity of the disease reflects the numbers of parasites. The first sign may be an itchy tingling patch where the fluke entered your skin, sometimes called 'swimmers itch'. The next phase called 'Katayama fever' with flu-like symptoms that may manifest after 2-3 weeks. Acute symptoms follow 6-8 weeks after infestation including passing blood in the urine or faeces, and persistent diarrhoea with abdominal or lower back pain. Long-term complications, if the condition is untreated, can include liver enlargement or cirrhosis and kidney failure.

There is no vaccine available against bilharzia. Prevention is the key. Avoid wading or swimming in rivers, lakes, and irrigation systems. Only swim in chlorinated swimming pools. Treatment is by a single dose of Praziquantel which kills the flukes.

Trypanosomiasis (Sleeping sickness) This disease, essentially a brain infection causing drowsiness, is transmitted by a large, greyish-brown tenacious insect, the size of a honey bee – the tsetse fly. This fly is not always repelled by DEET but very susceptible to Pyrethroid fly spray and Permethrin. It can bite through lightweight clothes and is attracted to moving vehicles. The main risk is in game parks where these rather aggressive flies are common. Symptoms include headaches, fever, weakness and aching muscles. If unrecognized and untreated it may progress to cause encephalitis or meningitis (both inflammations of membranes in the brain).

Viral haemorrhagic fevers *Lassa* Fever, *Marburg* disease and *Ebola* virus are classified as viral haemorrhagic fevers. There are intermittent outbreaks in West and less commonly East Africa. Early signs include fever, headache, severe muscle pain progressing to bleeding disorders. All have a high mortality rate.

Dangerous animals Apart from mosquitoes the most dangerous animals are men, be they bandits or behind steering wheels. Think carefully about violent confrontations and wear a seat belt if you are lucky enough to have one available to you.

When you get home

Remember to take your anti-malarial tablets for four to six weeks after leaving the malarial area as advised. If you have had attacks of diarrhoea it is worth having a stool specimen tested in case you have picked up amoebas. If you have been living rough, blood tests may be worthwhile to detect worms and other parasites. If you have been exposed to bilharzia (*schistosomiasis*) by swimming in lakes, check by means of a blood test when you get home, but leave it for six weeks because the test is slow to become positive. Report any untoward symptoms to your doctor and tell the doctor exactly where you have been and, if you know, what the likelihood of disease is to which you were exposed.

Kenya

3

Kenya

Any visit to Kenya will be amply rewarded as there is such a diverse range of things to do and places to see. Kenya's coastline is beautiful, with miles of white sands, and a warm sea protected from sharks by a coral reef just off the coast. The Kenya Highlands are always popular with visitors interested in a more energetic holiday, especially Mount Kenya. However, it is probably the wildlife for which Kenya is most famous, particularly the Big Five (lion, elephant, buffalo, leopard and rhino). Kenya is the most popular tourist vacation spot in East Africa and tourism has become its largest source of foreign exchange. The importance of tourism to the Kenyan economy is reflected in the quality of services; throughout the country there are first-class hotels, and good-quality western-style food is easy to find.

A recent spate of attacks on Europeans has caused worry in people's minds, but with common sense and sensible precautions travellers should be at no more risk than in their own countries. Those touring with the large safari companies are particularly well looked after.

Essentials

Planning your trip

Where to go Kenya has everything to offer the visitor, ranging from watersports, glorious sandy white beaches, deep-sea fishing and opportunities to dive and snorkel among the coral reefs in the warm seas. Plentiful wildlife can be seen in the national parks and reserves including the wildebeest migration in the Masai Mara Game Reserve and the dramatic Rift Valley with its chain of lakes which is haven to thousands of birds including the graceful flamingos. There are also opportunities to climb Mount Elgon and Mount Kenya – Africa's second highest mountain – and to explore Northern Kenya's dramatic desert scenery.

When to go There are two rainy seasons in the country, the long rains in March-April and the short rains in October-December. However, even during the rains there is invariably sunshine each day. January and February are the main months of the tourist season, as the weather is hot and dry, encouraging wild animals to the nearest water-holes.

Tours & tour operators

For specialist operators based in Kenya, see Nairobi, page 106 and Mombasa, page 220

Aardvark Safaris Ltd, RBL House, Ordnance Rd, Tidworth, Hampshire SP9 7QD, T01980-849160, F01980-849161, mail@aardvarksafaris.com Customized safaris. *Abercrombie & Kent*, Sloane Square House, Holbein Place, London SW1W 8NS, T020-77309600, www.abercrombiekent.co.uk Range of packages. *Africa Travel Centre*, 4 Medway Court, Leigh St, London WC1H 9QX, T020-73871211, F020-73837512. Inexpensive package trips. *Art of Travel*, 286 Lavender Hill, London SW11 1LJ, T020-77382038. Customized safaris. *Dragoman*, Camp Green, Kenton Rd, Debenham, Suffolk IP14 9LA, T01728-861133. Overland expedition specialist. *Exodus*, 9 Weir Rd, London SW12 0LT, T020-86757996. Overland expeditions. *Flamingo Tours*, 167 Acton Lane, London W4 5HN, T020-89953505. Inexpensive packages. *Guerba*, 101 Eden Vale Rd, Westbury, Wiltshire BA13 3QX, T01373-827046, F01373-858351. Overland expedition specialist, range of packages. *Hayes & Jarvis*, 152 Kings St, London W6 0QU, T020-87485050. Inexpensive packages. *Hidden Treasure Tours* 162 West Park Av, 2nd Fl., Long Beach, New York 11561, T516-670 9232, F516-432 0544, hiddentour@aol.com *Hoopoe Adventure Tours*, Suite F1 Kebbell House, Carpenders Park, Watford WD1 5BE, T020-84288221, F020-84211396, HoopeeUK@ aol.uk.com *Kumuka Africa*, 42 Westbourne Grove, London W2 5SH, T020-72212348. Inexpensive packages. *Kuoni Travel*, 33 Maddox St, London W1R 9LD, T020-74998636. Range of packages. *Micato Safaris*, 15 West 26th Street, New York, NY10010, T212-545 7111, F212 545 8297, www.africansafari.org/micato Upmarket company, with family based in Nairobi and New York offer a range of safari options. *Rajair Travel & Tours*, 27 Central Chambers, The Broadway, Ealing, London W5 2NR, T020-88408881, F020-88408882. Kenya specialist, a family-run firm who have been in Kenya for 100 years, include safaris, golf, diving, ballooning and fishing. *Select Travel*, 24 Culloden Rd, Enfield EN2 8QD, T020-83638202. *Tracks Africa*, 12 Abingdon Rd, London W8 6AF, T020-79375964. Package and specialist safaris.

Bird-watching, climbing, golf, diving and historical tours can be organized through *Acacia Expeditions*, 5 Walm Lane, London NW2 5SJ, UK, T020-8451 3877. *Discovery Expeditions*, Motcombe, Dorset SP7 9PB, UK, T01747-855050, F85541, organize camel expeditions to Lake Turkana, while lake and deep-sea fishing can be booked by *Lucewater House*, New Luce, Wigstownshire, DG8 0AW, UK, T01581-600271.

Finding out more

For a list of books, see page 312

Tourist information overseas: **France** 5 rue Volnay, Paris 75002, T42606688, F42611884. **Germany** Nue Mainzer Strasse 22, Frankfurt 60311, T69282551. **Hong Kong** 1309 Liu Chong Hing Bak Building, 24 Des Voeux Rd, Central GPO Box 5280, Hong Kong, T236053. **Japan** Room 216, Yurakucho Building, 1-10 Yurakucho, 1-Chome, Chiyoda-Ku, Tokyo, T2144595. **Sweden** Birger Jarsgatan 37, 11145 Stockholm, T212300. **Switzerland** Bleicherweg 30, CH-8039,

Kenya embassies and consulates

Australia, PO Box 1990, 33 Ainslie Av, GPO Canberra, T062-474788.
Canada, Gillia Building, Suite 600, 415 Laurier Av, West Ottawa, Ontario, T613-5631773.
Ethiopia, PO Box 3301, Hiher 16, Kebelle 01, Fikre Mariam Rd, Addis Ababa, T180033.
France, 3 rue Cimarosa, 75116 Paris, T1-45533500.
Germany, Villichgasse 17, 5300 Bonn 2, T0228-356042.
Italy, CP 10755, 00144 Rome.
Nigeria, PO Box 6464, 53 Queens Drive, Ikoyi, Lagos, T01-682768.
Rwanda, Blvd de Nyabugogo, PO Box 1215, Kigali, T772774.
Sudan, Street 3, Amarat, PO Box 8242, Khartoum, T40386/43758.

Tanzania, 4th Floor, NIC Investment House, Samora Av, PO Box 5231, Dar es Salaam, T51-31502.
Uganda, 60 Kira Rd, PO Box 5220, Kampala, T41231861.
United Kingdom, 45 Portland Pl, London W1N 4AS, T020-76362371.
USA, 2249 R St Northwest, Washington DC 20008, T202-3876101; or 9100 Wilshire Blvd, Beverly Hills, CA 90212, T213-2746635.
RD Congo, Plot 5002, ave de l'Ouganda, BP 9667 Zone Gombe, Kinshasa, T12-30117.
Zambia, 5207 United Nations Av, PO Box 50298, Lusaka, T01-212531.
Zimbabwe, 95 Park Lane, PO Box 4069, Harare, T04792901.

Zurich T2022244. **UK** 25 Brooks Mews, London W1Y 1LF, T020-73553145. **USA** 424 Madison Av, New York, NY 10017, T2124861300; 9100 Wilshire Blvd, Doheny Plaza Suite 111, Beverly Hills, CA 90121, T2132746634.

English is widely spoken throughout the country and is the language of all higher education. **Language** Swahili, however, is the official language and it is worth the effort to learn some basic phrases as a courtesy gesture. The more remote the area you visit, the less likely you are to find anyone who speaks anything but their tribal language.

Before you travel

Visas A visa is required for citizens of all Commonwealth Countries with the exception of nationals of Australia, Canada, United Kingdom, New Zealand, India, Pakistan, Nigeria, Sri Lanka, Guyana and Republic of Ireland and citizens of those countries with which Kenya has reciprocal visa abolition Agreement; Ethiopia, San Marino, Turkey, Uruguay, Ghana, Namibia and Eritrea.

So long as your single-entry visa remains valid you are allowed to move freely between Kenya, Tanzania and Uganda without the need for re-entry permits. If you do not need a visa, you will be issued with a visitor's pass on arrival, which allows you to travel freely for up to three months. You will need to negotiate this with the official on arrival. If you want to get an extension you can stay a maximum of six months in the country fairly easily, but at extra cost. In Nairobi this can be done at Nyayo House, corner of Kenyatta Av and Uhuru Highway (Monday-Friday 0830-1230 and 1400-1530); it can also be done at the Provincial Commissioner's Offices in Embu, Garissa, Kisumu, Mombasa and Nakuru. Do check your visitor's pass as it has been known for people who have overstayed their time in the country to be fined quite heavily.

Getting in
It is possible to get a visa on arrival, but this takes ages and if you arrive at night, you may have to wait until the next day

Customs You are expected to pay duty on items bought as gifts or for sale in Kenya, though not if they are for your personal use. You are more likely to be asked if you have anything to declare at airports than at the border crossings from neighbouring countries.

Vaccinations No vaccinations are required by law but if you are entering the country overland, you may be asked for a yellow fever and/or a cholera certificate. You should have these done before arrival as a sensible health precaution anyway. Seek advice from your local doctor about six weeks before your departure. (For health information, see page 89.)

Money

Currency
See inside front cover for exchange rates

The currency in Kenya is the Kenyan shilling (KSh). As it is not a hard currency, it cannot be brought into or taken out of the country. If you have any Kenyan shillings left when leaving the country, do not be tempted to destroy them – people have been arrested for doing this. There are banks and bureaux de change at both Nairobi and Mombasa airports. There are inevitable queues but at Nairobi it is marginally quicker to change your money after you go through customs.

Credit cards
Credit cards are widely accepted around the country, particularly **Diners' Club** and **American Express** with **Visa** a poor third. **Access** and **Mastercard** acceptability is more limited.

Travellers' cheques
You should be able to change money or travellers' cheques throughout the country, particularly British pounds and American dollars. Most large hotels exchange money 24 hours a day, although their rate is usually worse than the bank rate.

Banks
Hours are Monday-Friday 0830-1300. Saturday 0830-1100. Foreign Exchange Bureaux are usually open longer hours. There is a black market in Kenya but it hardly seems worth while. Not only is it risky (you may be treated unpleasantly and deported if caught), but the rate you will achieve is hardly more than bank rates. There are many branches of *Barclays Bank* throughout the country and most have ATMs that accept Visa, Mastercard, Plus and Cirrus cards. *Standard Chartered Bank* has fewer machines, they accept Visa cards.

Cost of living
It is getting cheaper and cheaper for budget visitors as the Kenyan shilling devalues. It is quite possible to eat, sleep and travel by public transport for US$20 a day. Services specifically designed for tourists, such as the safaris, car hire, access to national parks, etc can be expensive, and prices are adjusted as the currency depreciates.

Getting there

Air
Kenya is the cheapest country in East Africa to get to by air and consequently is a good place to start off a tour of the region.

London is by the far the cheapest place in the western world from which to get to Kenya and there are loads of discounted flights and package holidays. In the past, the only discounts were for unsold seats but now there is an enormous range of deals for students, academics or people under a certain age (usually either 26 or 32). Although not all the deals may mean cheaper flights, they usually do mean flexible flight arrangements and flight dates, which is very helpful if you are planning a longish trip and do not know when you want to return. A very good idea is to look for a package deal to Mombasa and travel on from there. All flights either go to Nairobi, the capital (about nine hours from London), or Mombasa on the Indian Ocean coast (about 11 hours).

The cheapest plane tickets are in the 'off-season', from February to June and again from October to early December. If you do have to go during peak times, book as far in advance as you can, particularly if you aim to get there in mid-December when flights get full very quickly. *EgyptAir* offer very good deals and a stopover in Cairo for as long as you like at no extra cost. *Air France*, *KLM*, *Kenya Airways*, *British Airways* all have surprisingly good deals as do *Saudia* and *Ethiopian Airlines*.

If you are short of time, a package holiday could well be a useful option, particularly if you go out of the peak season when you can get excellent deals. Beach holidays are far cheaper than safaris. It is a good idea to find out as much as you can about the hotel in the package deal before going, though you can always stay elsewhere if necessary. It is sometimes the case that a package trip to the coast will be cheaper than a flight alone.

From Africa You can fly to Kenya direct from: **Abidjan** (Ivory Coast); **Accra** (Ghana); **Addis Ababa** (Ethiopia); **Antananarivo** (Madagascar); **Bujumbura** (Burundi); **Cairo** (Egypt); **Dakar** (Senegal); **Dar es Salaam** (Tanzania); **Douala** (Cameroon); **Dzaoudzi** (Comoros); **Entebbe**

(Uganda); **Gaborone** (Botswana); **Harare** (Zimbabwe); **Johannesburg** (South Africa); **Khartoum** (Sudan); **Kigali** (Rwanda); **Kinshasa** (RD Congo); **Lagos** (Nigeria); **Lome** (Togo); **Luanda** (Angola); **Lusaka** (Zambia); **Moroni** (Comoros); **Ouagadougou** (Burkina Faso); **Zanzibar** (Tanzania).

From the rest of the world   There are no direct flights from the USA to Kenya. *Ethiopian Airlines* offer flights to Kilimanjaro (Tanzania) from the States. Americans have to change flights in Europe or the Middle East depending on which carrier they choose. It is usually significantly cheaper to fly via London or Amsterdam if travelling from USA.

Road

Quite a popular option with travellers are the **overland tours** to Kenya from Europe. There are plenty on offer, though itineraries may change, taking account of political and military events around Africa. A popular route is from Western Africa passing through RD Congo around Lake Victoria and cutting through Tanzania to get to Kenya. Another option would be to team up with other people and hire a vehicle or use public transport to cross Africa. This is perfectly feasible but does take some organizing and a lot of time.

Ethiopia   The crossing is at **Moyale**, between Marsabit and Addis Ababa. The restriction that only Kenyans and Ethiopians can make this crossing now apears to have been lifted. It is a matter of hiring lifts from truck drivers on the route.

Somalia   In more tranquil times it has been possible to take a bus from Kismayo to the border at **Liboi**, and then on to Garissa, or from Mogadishu to **Mandera**, and then on to Wajir. These crossings are currently not an option for travellers as a result of the civil war in Somalia.

Sudan   In principle it has in the past been possible to cross from Lodwar to Juba, although there was never any public transport on this route, and it was a matter of hiring rides from truck drivers. This is not currently an option for travellers as a result of civil war in the south of Sudan.

Tanzania   The main road crossing is at **Namanga** (see page 204) on the road between Arusha and Nairobi. This is reasonably quick and efficient and there are through buses and good roads all the way. Other crossings are at **Lunga Lunga** (see page 234) between Mombasa and Dar es Salaam. The road on the Tanzanian side is not as good, but there are overnight through buses between the two cities. There are also crossings at **Taveta** (see page 208) between Moshi and Voi; at **Isebania** (see page 323) between Kisumu, Tanzania (see page 477) and Musoma; and across the border from **Masai Mara Park** into the Serengeti.

Uganda   There are buses that run from Nairobi to Kampala, crossing at **Malaba** and **Tororo**, taking about 15 hours and costing around US$15. Standards of service vary. It is possible to do the journey in stages in minibuses or Peugeot taxis, but buses are more comfortable and safer. There are also border crossings at **Busia**, no through buses, but convenient for Kisumu; and at **Suam** to the north of Mount Elgon.

Boat

In the past there have been boats (hydrofoils) from Mombasa to **Tanga**, **Zanzibar** and **Dar es Salaam** (see page 222). Although these have not been operating for a while, partial resumption of the service has started. *Mega Speed Liners* now run a hydrofoil to **Pemba**, US$30, and Zanzibar US$50, at 0900 Sunday. Book at *Kuldips Touring* on the south end of Mji Mpya Road, or when boarding the boat that leaves from Kilindini Harbour (the cost was about the same as the air fare from Mombasa, US$45).

It is possible to take a *dhow* from Mombasa to **Tanga** and **Dar es Salaam** (see page 360). However you must expect to wait around for a week or more for one to depart. It will take one or two days depending on the weather. Expect to pay about US$15, bring all your own food, and you will sit and sleep on the cargo. At one time it was also possible to get *dhows* to **Kismayo**, **Mogadishu**, **Berbera** and **Djibouti**. These are not currently an option with the civil war in Somalia.

Kenya

Touching down

Business hours Banks: Monday-Friday 0830-1330 and from 0830 -1100 on Saturday. **Embassies**: usually mornings only. **Post offices**: Monday-Friday 0800-1300 and 1400-1630. Some are also open on Saturday. **Shops**: generally from 0800-1700 or 1800, and on Saturday. **Kiosks**: often open all hours, as the owner frequently lives on site.

IDD code T254
Official time Kenya is three hours ahead of GMT.
Voltage 220-240 volts supply. Square three-pin plugs in modern buildings. Great variety in older places. An adapter is advised.
Weights and measures Metric. In country areas items are often sold by the piece.

There are a few companies that will take you by boat from Europe to Kenya, though this is certainly not a budget option. *Strand Cruise Centre*, Charing Cross Shopping Centre, The Strand, London, T020-78366363, specializes in cruises from England through the Mediterranean down the Suez Canal to Djibouti and on to Mombasa. It costs around US$3,000 one way and takes a month.

Touching down

Airport information
Departure tax is frequently incorporated into the air fare in international air tickets. It is advisable to check when purchasing your ticket. If travelling from Kenya to Tanzania there is a US$25 departure tax, payable in cash.

Transport to town Jomo Kenyatta International Airport, **Nairobi**, is located 15 km from the centre to the south of the city. A taxi is roughly US$12. There are set rates to particular hotels – check before getting into the taxi. Moi International Airport, **Mombasa**, is on the mainland about 10 km out of the centre of town. *Kenya Airways* operates a shuttle bus into town, about US$2. Taxi about US$9.

Tourist information
Amazingly there is no tourist information centre in Nairobi. You could try contacting the **Kenya Tourist Board**, T02-604245/6, F501096, instead, or go to the tour companies for information. There is also a free publication called *Tourist's Kenya*, which is published fortnightly and which gives a run down on things going on. There is another publication called *What's On*, which comes out monthly. **Kenya Tourism Federation**, T2604767, Nairobi, safetour@wananchi.com, operate a Safety and Communication Centre which advises tourists on most things including road conditions or emergency help.

Local customs & laws
Conduct Stand for the national anthem and show respect if the national flag is being raised or lowered. Do not take photographs of military or official buildings or personnel, especially the President. Respect the national currency (do not tear it) and the currency laws of the country, and if you have to have any dealings with the police be polite. Comply with the country's drug laws too. The attitude to cannabis (*bhangi* – which is readily available) and *miraa* is ambivalent: both are illegal but appear to be tolerated by the authorities. However, if you are caught your embassy is unlikely to be sympathetic.

Begging is most common in Nairobi and Mombasa. Many Kenyans give money to beggars who are clearly destitute and or disabled and, in a country with no social welfare, have few alternative means of livelihood. A fairly recent phenomenon has been the rise of street children in Nairobi who swarm on tourists who give money. A more constructive approach may be to make a donation to an organization rehabilitating street children (see page 33).

Safety
A general rule seems to be that the more prevalent the tourists, the greater the need to be on your guard. Nairobi and Mombasa have the worst reputations, and the most popular national parks have their fair share of robberies. In early 1998 there were three tourist fatalities, while robberies/muggings were in progress. Since then reports of armed attacks against tourists have increased throughout the country. There is a high rate of street crime not just in Nairobi and Mombasa but also in Kisumu and the coastal beach resorts, most especially

bag-snatching crimes. Basically, you just have to be sensible and not carry expensive cameras, open bags or valuable jewellery and be careful about carrying large sums of money when you are rubbing shoulders with local people. Also, do not automatically expect your belongings to be safe in a tent. In built-up areas, lock your car, and if there is a security guard (*askari*) nearby, pay him a small sum to watch over it, although you should still be careful as con-artists have been known to impersonate hotel employees and even police officers. There is no need to pay street children (see page 33) to guard a vehicle. Avoid walking around after dusk, particularly in the more run-down urban areas – take a taxi – and walking alone at night, even on beaches, is dangerous. The majority of people you will meet are honest and ready to help you so there is no need to get paranoid about your safety. The British High Commission strongly advise against travel in Northeast Kenya (Moyale, Mandera, Wajit and Garissa), because of difficulties with the Somalian unrest. The road from Mombasa to Lamu has also been targeted by Somalian robbers, who have hijacked buses and robbed the passengers. Armed police escorts are now on buses to cope with this problem with the *Shiftas*. If possible leave valuables in Mombasa or Malindi.

Women travellers Women do have to be more wary than men, though Kenya seems to be a more pleasant place for lone women travellers than many other countries. If you are hassled, it is best to ignore the person totally whatever you feel, as expressions of anger are often taken as acts of encouragement. Women in Kenya dress very decorously, and it is wise to follow suit particularly in small towns and rural areas. Kenyan women will generally be very supportive if they see you are being harassed and may well intervene if they think you need help, but the situation is very rarely anything more than a nuisance. You are more likely to be approached at the coast, as the number of women coming for sexual adventure has encouraged this type of pestering. The key is to keep patient and maintain a sense of humour.

Tricksters Suspect anyone who has a hard-luck story. Do not change money on the black market, as this invites a confidence trick. Popular ploys are schoolboys with sponsorship forms, or being bumped into by someone who drops something, you bend to pick it up for them – only to be taken by two men from behind who will relieve you of your possessions.

Where to stay

Kenya has a huge range of hotels from the ultra-luxurious lodges and beach hotels to local board and lodgings. At the cheaper end of the market, a double room should cost you around US$3-5, going up slightly if it is with washing or toilet facilities.

Hotels *For hotel classifications, see page 36*

Almost every town will have some form of accommodation, even if it is a room hired in a local house, so you should rarely be stuck for somewhere to stay.

Prices of hotels are not always a good indication of their quality, and it is sensible to check what you will get before committing yourself to stay. You can expect to pay more in the high season particularly mid-December to mid-February and prices are often negotiable, even in large hotels. Recently the Ministry of Finance announced its intention to impose additional VAT charges on extras like game drives and horse riding at hotels and lodges. If this is confirmed the cost of a stay at hotels and lodges that offer such extras is likely to increase.

This is an increasingly popular option on the coast and is often surprisingly good value if you intend to stay for a while. For more information contact *Kenya Villas*, Westminster House, PO Box 57046, Kenyatta Av, Nairobi, T338072.

Self-catering

The youth hostel in Nairobi is not only an excellent place to stay, but also a good place to meet other travellers. Apart from this one, there are very few hostels around the country, although there are a number of YMCAs and YWCAs, most of which are clean and safe and, of course, very cheap. The ones in Nairobi tend to cater for long-term residents and many people from the university stay at the YMCA, so it is a good place to meet Kenyans. The Naivasha YMCA has a deservedly good reputation. The *Kenya Youth Hostel Association* is on Ralph Bunche Rd, T721765.

Hostels

Camping There are many campsites all over Kenya, they are usually very cheap with basic amenities and some are very good. Camping can be a very useful option as it allows you to stay wherever you want, and is an essential if you are on a tight budget but want to explore the national parks. You should always have your own tent and basic equipment as these cannot always be hired at the sites.

Work camps The *Kenya Voluntary Development Association* set the work camps up in 1962. Their aim is to bring Kenyans and other nationals together to work on local projects such as irrigation ditches, building schools, etc. The work is quite hard, but most people seem to enjoy the camps. The average length of stay is four weeks costing US$170. You will share local conditions, implying pretty basic amenities. The average age is under 25. If you are interested contact *KVDA*, PO Box 48902, Nairobi, Kenya, T225379.

Getting around

Air Internal travel in Kenya is quite cheap and efficient. There are daily flights between Nairobi (the main international airport) and Mombasa and Kisumu on *Kenya Airways*. There are also several flights daily from Wilson Airport, Nairobi to Masai Mara, Malindi, Lamu and other upmarket destinations. There are daily scheduled flights along the coast between Mombasa, Malindi and Lamu. You may also be able to get on to private flights going up to the northeast of Kenya at very reasonable prices (these flights are primarily for carrying *miraa*, a popular herbal drug which is a mild stimulant). **Internal flights incur a departure tax of KSh200 (approximately US$3).**

Boat There is a ferry running between the islands of the Lamu archipelago. Motor ferries from Kisumu on Lake Victoria have been suspended with no discernible restart date. Local fishermen will occasionally take travellers to local destinations but boat maintenance sometimes gives rise to concern.

Road **Bus** There are lots of private bus companies operating in Kenya, and the system is very good on the whole, being reliable, running on time and cheap. Generally, you will be able to reserve a seat a day in advance and they are quite comfortable. If you have problems locating the bus station, or finding the right bus in the bus station, just ask around. The government has recently started its own service called *Nyayo buses*. These are the cheapest buses around and are very good.

Car hire Renting a car has certain advantages over public transport, particularly if you intend visiting any of the national parks or remoter regions of the country, or there are at least four of you to share the costs. One way of keeping the cost down is to link up with other people and share the expense. You should be able to rent either a fixed price per day or by mileage. 4WD Suzuki jeeps are a popular car if going on safari – they do not hold much petrol, so remember to carry a spare can.

To hire a car you generally need to be over 23, have a full driving licence (it does not have to be an international licence, your home country one will do), and will be asked to leave a large deposit (or sign a blank American Express voucher). Always take out the collision damage waiver premium as even the smallest accident can be very expensive.

Driving in Kenya can be alarming. Although driving is on the left, actual practice is dictated by the state of the road to avoid potholes, debris or people and animals. Keeping to any formal 'rules of the road' is further handicapped by many drivers ignoring traffic lights at night (they argue that this is to avoid being robbed while stationary) and the high speed of most motorists. The accident statistics in Kenya are very high, so be warned. If you break down, the common practice throughout Africa is to leave a bundle of leaves some 50 m behind, and in front of, the vehicle.

Taxis *Matatus* are everywhere. Almost any vehicle will be used, but the most common are pick-up vans with wooden benches inside and converted minibuses. They are the fastest and

Buses (schedule and fares)

Please note that fares will be paid in KSh, and the information in this table is for general guidance only, as fares and schedules change frequently.

| Destination | From Nairobi | | To Nairobi | | Fare |
	Dep	Arr	Dep	Arr	US$
Busia	2000	0630	2000	0600	6.00
Eldoret	0830	1430	1030	1630	4.00
	2200	0300	0900	1630	4.00
Homa Bay	0900	1800	0700	1630	5.50
	2030	0500	1930	0500	5.50
Isiolo	0930	1700	0730	1400	4.00
	2030	0300	2000	0100	4.00
Kisii	0900	1600	0900	1630	5.00
	2030	0430	2100	0500	5.00
Kisumu	1000	1600	1000	1600	4.50
	2200	0500	2030	0430	4.50
Kitau	0830	1700	0900	1630	5.00
	2200	0530	2100	1700	5.00
Magadi	1300	1630	0630	0930	2.00
	1500	1830	0730	1100	2.00
Malaba	2000	0530	2000	0630	6.00
Meru	1000	1500	0730	1300	3.00
	2100	0300	2000	0200	3.00
Mombasa	0900	1700	0900	1700	5.50
	2130	0500	2100	0530	5.50
Namanga	1330	1700	0730	1100	2.00
Kampala	0700	1930	0700	1830	11.0
	1900	1100	1500	0400	11.0
Arusha	0730	1230	1400	1930	6.00

	From Mombasa		To Mombasa		
Tanga	0830	1530	1930	0500	6.50
	1800	0200	1830	0400	6.50
Dar es Salaam	0830	1900	1600	0500	6.50
	1800	1500	1500	0400	6.50

most prolific form of transport in the country. They are also the most dangerous, driving terrifyingly fast and often totally overloaded. The drivers often look about 13 years old and are chewing *miraa* to stay awake longer. However, you may have to use them as they are often the only means of travelling in remote areas, and in towns they are the most convenient method of travelling around because there are so many of them. *Matatus* will rarely leave their starting point until full to bursting, so at taxi parks be prepared to wait, perhaps for more than an hour on the less popular routes. **Peugeot taxis** are popular on long routes when you want to travel quickly. They are estate cars with an extra row of seats fitted in the back and are fast, comfortable and reliable. They are also quite expensive compared to *matatus* and buses. If you want to travel in the front by the driver, you will have to pay a premium.

Bicycle There are a number of specialist bicycle tours available. *Paradise Bicycle Tours* in the US (PO Box 1726, Evergreen, Colorado 80439, USA) offers 12-day trips including a ride to the Masai Mara. *Leisure Activity Safaris* in the UK (164 Ellicks Close, Bradley Stoke North, Almondsbury, Bristol BS12 0EU) offers long or short safaris leaving from London.

Hitching Hitching is the easiest way for most people to travel and is common in rural areas of Kenya. It is a simple and safe method of travelling around the country. You will be expected

Kenya

to pay the driver something, though if you cannot afford to, and make this known at the outset, you will rarely be turned away. To gain a driver's attention, put out your arm; a thumb stuck in the air is unlikely to be noticed. On routes not served by much public transport it is invariably possible to hire a ride with truck drivers.

Train The only passenger rail service at present is the Nairobi/Mombasa link. The network suffered extensive damage as a result of the 1997/78 El Niño rains. It is uncertain whether/when the remainder of the network will again offer a passenger rail service.

Taking the **Nairobi-Voi-Mombasa** train is a splendid experience. It runs overnight (supposedly to avoid the heat of the day), although there are plans for a daytime departure to the coast, which will allow some sightseeing through Tsavo National Park. Of the current rolling-stock, the first-class carriages were built in the 1960s in the UK, the second class in the 1920s (UK), and the third-class in 1980s in Sweden. First-class cabins are two-berth with washbasins. Second-class are four-berth, and the wash basins are pretty unreliable as the carriages are around 80 years old. Ear-plugs can be a boon. Bedding is provided in first and second class. Third-class is seated, and can get very crowded. First class is recommended. First and second class should be booked in advance (or through an agent) – it is necessary to go down to the railway station to do this. Sexes are separated in first and second-class sections, unless you book the whole compartment. The compartments cannot be locked from outside, so take your valuables and documents with you if you leave the carriage. Dinner can be taken on the train, and is reasonable. The fare includes dinner (but not drinks), breakfast and the provision of bedding. There is no reduction in cost if you choose not to use these services. Wines, beers and spirits are available.

One train departs each way at 1900 and the journey takes about 13 hours. As it gets dark the train crosses the plains – looking out of the window you can get a real feeling of emptiness with just a glimpse of the occasional pair of glowing eyes. This is a narrow-gauge railway, which enables the train to climb up the steep escarpments. However, it also makes the train more vulnerable to derailments, as happened near Voi in March 1999. It costs US$50 for first class, US$36 for second and US$9 for third.

Prices change and schedules are altered so you are advised to check locally before confirming your travel plans. *Kenya Railways,* PO Box 30121, Nairobi, T02-221211, F340049. Reservations (first class) in Nairobi, T335160, in Mombasa, PO Box 90674, T312221/3. The railway station is situated in Jomo Kenyatta Road.

Maps You should be able to buy most maps you need in Nairobi though you are quite likely to have a better choice of information and maps in your own country than in Kenya itself. A good source is *Stanford's Map and Travel Bookshop,* 12-14 Long Acre, London WC2E 9LP, T020-78361321. The *Survey of Kenya* park maps are well worth getting and are inexpensive in Nairobi (they are double the price if you get them at the park gates). *The Nation*, located on Kenyatta Avenue, next to the *Thorn Tree Café*, has a good selection of maps.

Keeping in touch

Internet Internet cafes and email facilities are plentiful in the major towns, and range from the upmarket hotels, cybercafes with fast connections to small shops and business centres, that may just have a single computer. The cost of access has fallen considerably over the last few years and is available for from about US$1 per 15 minutes, although the use of more modern equipment is likely to cost US$1.25-1.50 per 15 minutes. Receiving emails are cheaper if you do not print them.

Communica-tions **Post** Sending post out of the country is cheap and efficient; it generally takes a week to Europe and about 10 days to Australia and the US. Receiving post is also easy, though not parcels. All parcels need to be checked by officials for import duty and it is not uncommon for them to go astray unless they have been sent by registered post or a similar scheme. If you are sending things out of the country they must be wrapped in brown paper with string. There is no point doing this before getting to the post office as you will be asked to undo it to be checked for export duty. The wrapping charge varies between US$1-1.50. Parcels must not weigh more than 20 kg seamail or 30 kg airmail or be more than 100 cm long.

The **poste restante** service, particularly in Nairobi, Mombasa, Malindi and Lamu, is reliable and free.

Telephone Generally speaking, the telephone system in Kenya is very good. You should be able to make international calls from public call boxes and the easiest way of doing this is if you get a phone card (available from most post offices). If this is not possible, you can book your call through post offices where you get your money back if you fail to get through. The rate is roughly US$4.50 per minute to Europe or North America and if you dial through the operator, there is a three-minute minimum.

IDD for Kenya is T254

For the international operator dial T0196

Local calls are very easy, but the main problem is finding a box. You can generally make phone calls from hotels, though they will usually charge you double the price for the privilege. A new private phone company, *Unique Communications*, Rattansi Educational Trust near the corner of Monrovia/Koinange St, T243302, offers phone, fax and email facilities.

Most parts of Kenya are covered by the ISD system. Telephone calls from Kenya to Tanzania and Uganda are charged at long-distance tariffs rather than international. The public call boxes in Nairobi will only accept the new copper 1 or 5 KSh coins.

Newspapers and magazines There is a range of locally produced papers and magazines. The best of the three English-language papers is *The Nation*, which is the most daring in its editorial. The *Kenya Times* is the government-owned paper, and *The Standard* owned by Lonrho is dull. Of the magazines, *Law* is usually worth reading (if it has not been confiscated) and the *Weekly Review* carries very detailed reports on local political and social issues.

Media

Of the international press, *Time* and *Newsweek* are regularly available, as is the *International Herald Tribune*. UK daily newspapers arrive a day or two late in larger towns.

Radio This is the most common method with which Kenyans keep themselves informed. **Kenya Broadcasting Corporation (KBC)** broadcasts in Kiswahili, English and some local languages. **BBC World Service** is broadcast to Kenya on short wave and also on the FM frequency 93.7 from Nairobi and 93.9 from Mombasa.

Television There are two television channels: **Kenya Broadcasting Corporation (KBC)**, which replaced Voice of Kenya, broadcasts in Swahili and English with a considerable number of imported foreign programmes; and **Kenya Television News**, based on CNN material.

Food and drink

Market liberalization of the Kenyan economy and deregulation of price controls means the price of food has increased over recent years. This has caused hardship on many Kenyans but for tourists the prices are very low, mainly because devaluation of the Kenyan shilling means you get more shillings for your own currency than before. The quality of the food in Kenya is generally excellent. The fruit and vegetables taste very different (invariably better) from produce you get at home (particularly avocados, mangos, pineapples and passion fruit). Kenya's meat is generally very good, although you might get some tough cuts at small restaurants in rural areas. Kenyan buffets sometimes include unusual meats such as zebra, crocodile, ostrich, wart-hog and giraffe. Salads tend to be fairly basic and generally consist of tomatoes, white cabbage and onions with no dressing.

Food

For restaurant price categories, see page 39

Restaurant prices are low; it is quite possible to eat a meal in a basic restaurant for US$2 and even the most expensive places will often not be more than US$20 per person. The quality, standard and variety of food depends on where you are and what you intend to pay. However, even the smallest most remote *hoteli* meal will fill you up. Rice, potatoes, chapatis and *ugali* (maize porridge) eaten with chicken, goat or beef are staple foods and in some restaurants you may be able to get spinach or *sukumawiki* (a type of green vegetable a bit like cabbage). Otherwise, vegetables and salads do not figure highly in cheaper restaurants where there is rarely much choice of dishes. Various western-style fried foods are becoming

Kenya

ever more popular such as chips, hamburgers, sausages and eggs. Roadside stalls selling *mandazi* (a kind of sweet or savoury doughnut), roasted maize, grilled, skewered meat, or samosas are popular and very cheap.

There are a number of Kenyan dishes of note. Swahili cuisine is the most interesting in the country with coconut and tamarind figuring heavily in menus. In Kikuyu areas you will find *irio* of potatoes, peas and corn mashed together. A popular Luo dish is fried tilapia (fish) with a spicy tomato sauce and *ugali*. *Githeri* is a bean stew. Eating out is not common in Kenya (hardly surprisingly as most of the population are so poor), and if people do go out they want to eat something they would not normally have at home – which is meat. Consequently, the most popular places for Kenyans to eat out at are *nyama choma* bars where you order your meat by the half kilo. They are popular places at weekends and very good value. The meat is usually goat or beef and you can choose what you want to eat before it is cooked.

Asian food is extremely good in Kenya and cheap, and an important option for vegetarians travelling in the country. Many Indian restaurants have a lunchtime buffet where you can eat as much as you want for less than US$8 a head. Other cuisines include Italian, French, Chinese, Japanese and even Thai, though only in the larger towns. See restaurant classifications, page 39.

Drink

A survey in Nairobi in the Sunday Standard in 1995 found that 75 out of 78 bottled waters sold contained only Nairobi tap water

Sodas (soft drinks) are available everywhere and are very cheap; bottles are refundable. The other common drink throughout the country is *chai*, milky sweet tea, which is surprisingly refreshing. Fresh fruit juices when they are available are good as they really are freshly squeezed. Bottled water is expensive, around US$1 per 1½ litres and is available in all but the smallest villages. Tap water is reportedly safe in many parts of the country. However it is far more prudent to avoid drinking any tap water, and do not use it to brush your teeth without prior sterilization. Place you glass on ice cubes to cool drinks unless the ice cubes are made of purified water. It is also best to avoid borehole or rainwater unless your stomach is quite hardy.

Kenyan beer is very good; *Tusker*, *White Cap* and *Pilsner* are the main brands sold in half-litre bottles. Fruit wines are also popular; they come in a variety of different flavours but tend to be sweet. Papaya wine is widely available, but is a little harsh.

Spirits tend to be extremely expensive and most local people will buy them in tiny sachets. Local alternatives are *Kenya Cane*, a type of rum, and the sweet *Kenya Gold* coffee liqueur.

Traditional Kenyan drinks include *chang'aa*, a fierce spirit made from maize and sugar and then distilled. Sentences for distilling and possessing *chang'aa* are severe and it is sometimes contaminated. It has been known to kill so think twice before tasting any. Far more pleasant and more common are *pombe* (beer), brewed from sugar and millet or banana depending on the region. It is quite legal, tastes a bit like flat cider and is far more potent than it appears at first. **Palm wine** is drunk at the coast.

Shopping

See the essentials section in individual town listings for further information on local shopping

Kenyan **baskets**, made from sisal and leather, are popular and cheap. They are particularly cheap around Kitui. **Soapstone** sculptures and objets d'art are good value (Kisumu), as are the wooden carvings that are for sale everywhere around the country. **Jewellery** is also popular with beaded necklaces and bracelets of turquoise and garnets or other semi-precious stones being good value.

Many tribal people sell traditional objects including weapons, stools, jewellery and musical instruments. The authentic articles are considerably more expensive than items made for the tourist market. **Antique masks** are very rarely from Kenya, most have been imported from RD Congo or West Africa.

There are many different types of **cloth** peculiar to Kenya. **Kangas** are cotton wraps used by women, designed in hundreds of different styles, often with Kenyan proverbs printed on to them. **Kikois** are men's loincloths and are more sedate prints in wonderful reds, oranges and yellows. They are particularly good value along the coast.

Bargaining

There is an enormous difference between a 'tourist' price and a local price. Until you get a feel for what the local prices might be it is hard to bargain effectively, but you will soon realize most prices are negotiable. As a general rule, you should be able to start by offering half of the price being asked.

Entertainment and nightlife

There are cinemas in the larger towns throughout the country. Some show reasonably current films, but the most popular films appear to be action, martial arts or adventure movies. **Cinemas**

There are displays of dancing put on for the tourists all over the country including the **Bomas of Kenya** just outside Nairobi. The best known are the **Masai** and **Samburu** dances. Traditional Kenyan music is most likely to be performed by the drummers of **Akamba** and the **Mijinkenda**. **Music & dance**

Congolese music (*Lingala*) is extremely popular and the type you are most likely to hear on *matatus*, in the streets, in bars and clubs, in fact anywhere and everywhere. **Western music** has also had its influence here. Many of the more upmarket discos and clubs play western music and there are a few reggae clubs in Nairobi.

A major event in the social calendar is the Agriculture Society of Kenya's **Agricultural Shows**, which are all over the country at different times of the year. As well as the normal animal shows and beer tents, there are women's groups, beekeeping, soil conservation booths and others, and they can be quite interesting. **Social events**

Sport and special interest travel

The biggest event in the year, for the international media at least, is the **Kenya Safari Rally**, which normally takes place over the Easter weekend. It goes all over the country on some of the worst roads and often in appalling weather. The Asian community in particular comes out for this event, though it seems to attract large crowds everywhere. **Sport (spectator)**

Football A popular sport throughout the country and the quality is excellent, Kenya having some of the best teams on the continent. Matches are well attended and are great fun for soaking up the friendly atmosphere, even if you are not a keen football supporter.

Horse racing Regular meetings in Nairobi.

Golf, tennis and squash Annual international tournaments at Nairobi Club.

Riding It is possible to hire horses in the Central Highlands and camels in northern Kenya. **Sport (participant)**

Fishing Not a particularly popular pastime in Kenya's rivers, though it is possible and an interesting trip is to go out with local fishermen, either on the coast or on Lake Victoria. Kenya has excellent deep-sea fishing. For further information, see page 224.

Climbing Extremely popular among visitors, particularly up **Mount Kenya** where you will find many guides to help you. Other good climbing is possible in the **Aberdares**, **Cheranganis Hills**, **Mathews Range**, **Hell's Gate** and **Rift Valley volcanoes**. Each is described in the relevant section. The *Mountain Club of Kenya* (at Wilson Airport T02-501747) is a good source of advice and contacts.

Caving Caving has been growing in popularity and there is enormous potential for it in Kenya. Contact *Kenya Caverns and Lodges*, PO Box 47363, Nairobi, if you want to know more.

Watersports Widely available at the coast.

Running *Hash House Harriers* meet regularly. Contact British Council in Nairobi. The *Safari Marathon* is held towards the end of August each year at Lewa Wildlife Conservancy. The

Kenya

event is promoted by the UK-based charity *Tusk Trust* (T020-79787100) to raise money for wildlife conservation and community projects in Kenya.

Cricket, hockey and rugby   Played regularly by local clubs.

Holidays and festivals

1 January, *New Year's Day*; March/April, *Good Friday and Easter Monday*; 1 May, *International Labour Day*; 1 June, *Madaraka Day* celebrates the granting of self-government; 10 October, *Moi Day*; 20 October, *Kenyatta Day*; 12 December, *Independence Day*; 25 December, *Christmas Day*; 26 December, *Boxing Day*.

The **Islamic calendar** is followed, and **Islamic festivals** are celebrated all along the coast and in the northeast. These include the beginning and end of *Ramadan* (variable); **June**, *Islamic New Year* and **August**, *Prophet's birthday*.

National parks and reserves

A list of most of the parks and reserves is on page 88

Kenya has many national parks and game reserves, which are home to a dazzling array of animals, birds, reptiles and plant species. They rate as among the best parks in the whole of Africa, and are certainly the most accessible in East Africa. Marine life is also excellent and is preserved in the marine national parks off Malindi, Watamu and Kisite. Along with the wildlife, some of the parks have been gazetted to preserve the vegetation and unique locations such as Mount Kenya or the Kakamega Forest.

The Kenyan government has long been aware that the principal attraction of the country to tourists is its wildlife, and since 1989 has been keen to ensure it is available in abundance for tourists to see. Richard Leakey was appointed head of the Ministry of Wildlife in 1989 and put in force some drastic methods to reduce poaching. Poaching patrols are well trained and well equipped with Land Rovers and guns and there are extremely stiff penalties for anyone caught poaching. In 1990, 200 US-trained paramilitary personnel were deployed on shoot-to-kill patrols. The battle against poachers is a hard one. It is easy to see why people faced with poverty would resort to an occupation that appears to have such high risks, but also such high rewards (up to US$3,000 for a kilo of elephant tusk and US$15,000 for a single rhino horn).

The Kenyan government's policies have been controversial, and it has struggled to strike a balance between the demands of conservation and the needs of local people. Notwithstanding these problems Kenya's wildlife is one of its greatest assets and many of the parks and reserves offer a glimpse of a totally unspoilt, peaceful world.

Most of the game parks have to be explored from inside a vehicle, for tourist safety reasons. The exceptions to this are Hell's Gate, parts of Nakuru and Saiwa Swamp National Park near Kitale.

General information

Park classifications

National parks are wildlife and botanical sanctuaries and form the mainstay of Kenya's tourist industry. They are conservation points for educational and recreational enjoyment. **National reserves** are similar to parks but under certain conditions the land may be used for purposes other than nature conservation. Thus, some controlled agriculture may be allowed; in marine reserves there may be monitored fishing. **Biosphere reserves** were set up in 1989 and are protected environments, which contain unique landforms, landscapes and systems of land use. There are four in Kenya, and only 271 in the rest of the world. Specific scientific research projects are attached to them, funded by UNESCO. They are protected under national and international law. **World Heritage Sites** are even more strictly protected under international law. Kenya signed the convention in 1989 but as yet only two sites have been scheduled, Mount Kenya and Sibiloi/Central Island National Parks. Other sites being considered are the Gede ruins, Hell's Gate and the Masai Mara.

National park fees

	Non-residents US$	Residents KSh
Category A		
Aberdares, Amboseli and Lake Nakuru		
Adults	27	500
Children	10	50
Students & organized groups	10	50
Category B		
Tsavo East and Tsavo West		
Adults	23	200
Children	8	50
Students & organized groups	8	50
Category C		
Nairobi, Shimba Hills and Meru		
Adults	20	150
Children	5	50
Students & organized groups	10	50
Category D		
All other parks		
Adults	15	100
Children	5	50
Students & organized groups	5	50
Mountaineering		
Adults	10	100
Children	5	50
Students & organized groups	5	100
Nairobi Animal Orphanage		
Adults	5	50
Children	2	10
Students & organized groups	2	10
Marine parks		
Adults	5	100
Children	2	50
Students & organized groups	2	10

Vehicles, boats and aircraft fees
Aircraft: single landing

	KSh
Gliders & Microlites	100
Less than 3 seats	200
3-6 seats	400
7-14 seats	1,000
15-20 seats	1,500
More than 21 seats	2,500

Vehicles: all parks and visitor groups

	KSh
Less than 6 seats	200
6-12 seats	500
13-24 seats	1,000
25-44 seats	2,000
45 seats or more	3,000

Vehicles: stationed in park

	KSh
PSV's seats & commercial vehicles tonnes	20,000
PSV's 6-12 seats & commercial vehicles 2-5 tonnes	35,000
PSV's 13 seats or more & commercial vehicles 5 tonnes	70,000
Delivery vehicles	500

Boats: single entry

	KSh
All	200
Stationed in park	10,000

	Non-residents US$	Residents KSh
Accommodation and services		
Camping		
Adults: public campsites		
Category A, B, C	8	150
Category D	2	50
Adults: special campsites		
Category A	15	200
Category B	12	200
Category C	10	200
Category D	2	50
Children, students & organized groups	2	50
Public & special campsites (all other parks)	2	50
Booking fee for special campsites per week		5,000
Field study centres		
Non-students	10	500
Students	10	50
Guide service		
Per person per guide per day		500
Per person per guide per half-day (4 hours)		300

Kenya

Kenya national parks

◆ National parks &
   national reserves

1 Sibiloi NP	17 Rahole NR
2 Central Island NP	18 North Kitui NP
3 Southern Island NP	19 Lake Nakuru NP
4 Marsabit NP	20 Aberdares NP
5 Nasolot NR	21 Mount Kenya NP
6 South Turkana NR	22 Ruma NP
7 Losai NR	23 Mwea NR
8 Mount Elgon NP	24 Hell's Gate &
9 Saiwa Swamp NP	Logonot NP
10 Kerio Valley /	25 Masai Mara NR
Kamnarok NR	26 Serengeti NP
11 Maralal Nature	27 Nairobi NP
Sanctuary	28 South Kitui NR
12 Samburu Buffalo	29 Arawale NR
Springs NR	30 Dodori NR
13 Shaba NR	31 Boni NR
14 Lake Bogoria NR	32 Amboseli NP
15 Meru NP	33 Kilimanjaro NP
16 Kora NR	34 Tsavo West NP

35 Tsavo East NP	
36 Tana River Primate	
NR	
37 Kiunga Marine NR	
38 Malindi & Watamu	
Marine NP's	
39 Mkomazi Game R	
40 Shimba Hills NR	
41 Mombasa National	
Marine R	
42 Wasini Marine NP	
43 Kisite Mpunguti	
Marine NP	

Kenya

Costs

The Kenyan park entry fees were revised in 1996, when a differential pricing structure was implemented. Environmentally fragile parks with an overload of visitors will now charge more, while those parks with low tourist volume and not threatened with environmental damage, will charge less, to encourage a wider spread of tourists within the national parks.

Kenya Wildlife Services (KWS) is also re-launching the annual park pass, allowing multiple entry into all the KWS parks and reserves, including any car driven by the pass holder. The only different ones are the Masai Mara and the Samburu-Buffalo Springs-Shaba complex that are administered locally as national reserves and set their own prices.

A recent innovation is the introduction of an electronic entry ticketing system using a Smartcard, soon to be extended to all the national parks and reserves. For further details contact Kenya Wildlife Service, www.kws.org This initiative has curbed corruption by greatly reducing the opportunity for unscrupulous employees to siphon off admission fees, but the disadvantage is that it has caused frustrating delays at the entrance gates of the national parks. Average costs for porters are between KSh 400-500 (US$5.50-6.50) a day and KSh 650-750 (US$8.50-10.00) for a porter/guide per day. These rates can vary, it often depends on how many other tourists are around and how effective your bargaining skills prove to be.

Tips can be based on a cost per person or per group, but it is very important to negotiate exactly what your agreements are prior to departure you set out to prevent misunderstandings later.

When to visit

You are likely to see more animals during the dry season as they will congregate round waterholes. Also, driving during the wet season becomes far harder in deep mud as none of the park roads are paved. However, prices can be up to a third lower in lodges during the rainy seasons.

Where to stay

Accommodation in the parks tends to be of two types, the ultra-expensive lodges or campsites. There is little or nothing in between. If you do not fancy camping and cannot afford the lodges, you may be able to stay in a nearby town and enter your chosen park daily though this is not an option for all parks such as the Masai Mara or Amboseli in the south, given the great distances and poor roads. If you are on a luxury holiday, accommodation is excellent and there are a number of hotels in each of the major parks offering superb facilities. Camping is possible in designated sites (for obvious reasons it is not wise to camp outside these areas in a park full of wild animals). You will need to bring your own tent and other supplies such as a stove, food, water and bedding, as facilities tend to be extremely limited.

Getting around   **Self-drive** is the most convenient method of getting around the parks offering you greater freedom of movement, though it can be quite expensive. You will usually need to have a 4WD vehicle, but it is not absolutely essential in many parks outside the rainy season. If you are driving yourself, it is invariably an advantage to hire a local guide – the habits of the animals change, and the guide will know where to find them. Driving at night in the parks is prohibited.

Tours are arranged by many different companies and can be booked in Europe or in Kenya. There are a number of different types ranging from the luxurious to budget (see Tour Agents, page 72).

Major parks   **Aberdares National Park**, west of Mount Kenya; **Amboseli National Park**, close to the
& reserves   Tanzanian border in the shadow of Mount Kilimanjaro; **Lake Nakuru National Park**, 3 km south of Nakuru town in Kenya's Rift Valley; **Masai Mara Game Reserve**, contiguous with the Serengeti, scene of the wildebeest migration; **Mount Elgon National Park**, in the western Rift Valley on the Ugandan border; **Mount Kenya National Park**, a World Heritage Site containing Africa's second-highest mountain; **Tsavo National Parks East and West**, the largest national park in Kenya; and **Chyulu Hills**, recently incorporated into Tsavo West National Park.

Other parks   **Nairobi region** **Nairobi National Park**, a central location that offers a good chance of see-
& reserves   ing black rhino; **Olorgesailie Prehistoric Site**; **Lake Magadi**, famed for its pink soda pools and graceful flamingos.

Central region Ol Doinyo Sapuk National Park; **Solio Game Ranch**, famed for its rhino conservation; Fourteen Falls National Park

Rift Valley region **Lake Naivasha** and **Hell's Gate** national parks, located to the south of Lake Naivasha in the Rift Valley; **Mount Longonot National Park**; **Lake Bogoria National Reserve**, in the Rift Valley near Baringo, 80 km north of Nakuru; **Lake Baringo National Reserve**.

Western Kenya Impala Sanctuary Kisumu; Kisumu Bird Sanctuary; **Ndere Island National Park**; Thimlich Ohinga Prehistoric Site; Lambwe Valley National Reserve; **Ruma National Park**, 10 km east of Lake Victoria in the South Nyanza district; **Rusinga Island**, rich in fossils; **Mfangano Island**, has rock paintings and offers wonderful fishing; **Kakamega Forest National Reserve**, a remnant of equatorial rainforest; **Saiwa Swamp National Park**, home of the rare sitatunga antelope.

Northern Kenya **Samburu/Buffalo Springs National Park**, 325 km from Nairobi and 50 km from Isiolo town; **Shaba National Reserve**, also in Isiolo District 70 km north of Mount Kenya; **Maralal National Reserve**; **Nasolot and South Turkana** national reserves, in Turkana District in the Rift Valley; **Losai National Reserve**, situated in the northern territory; **Marsabit National Reserve**, in Eastern Province 560 km north of Nairobi. **Mount Kulal Biosphere Reserve**, southeast of Lake Turkana; **Sibiloi/Central Island National Park**, a World Heritage Site adjacent to Lake Turkana.

East of Mount Kenya **Meru National Park**, 85 km east of Meru town is surrounded by several reserves; **Bisanadi National Reserve**, adjacent to the northeast boundary of Meru National Park; **Kora National Park**, on the Tana River, adjacent to Meru National Park; **North Kitui**

National Reserve, southeast of and adjacent to Meru National Park; **Rahole National Reserve**, northeast of Kora National Reserve; **Mwea National Reserve**, southeast of Embu; **South Kitui National Reserve**, located north of Tsavo East National Park.

Shimba Hills National Reserve, a small reserve 30 km southwest of Mombasa; **Mwalunganje Elephant Sanctuary**, adjacent to Shimba Hills National Reserve; **Kisite-Mpunguti Marine National Park**, located close to the Tanzanian border; **Arabuku-Sokoke Forest Reserve**, a remnant of coastal forest close to Kilifi; **Malindi and Watamu Marine** national parks; **Malindi Marine Biosphere Reserve**; **Tana River Primate National Reserve**, 120 km north of Malindi on the Tana River; **Arawale National Reserve**, north of Malindi not far from Tana River Primate National Reserve; **Kiunga Biosphere National Park**, a marine national park in the northeast coastal border district of Lamu; **Boni and Dodori** national reserves, very remote, located in the far northeast of the country close to the Somali border north of Lamu.

Coastal parks, reserves & marine national parks

Kenya

Health

On the whole, Kenya is a healthy country to visit but as with all tropical countries, it is best to take certain precautions. First, **malaria** is a real problem in most areas of the country except way up in the highlands. Do not be fooled into thinking it is not very serious; it is one of the major killers in tropical Africa today. This means you will need to protect against it by taking tablets before, during and after your visit. Ask your doctor for advice on which anti-malaria tablets you should take as the parasite that passes on malaria becomes resistant to tablets from time to time.

See Health, page 58

Secondly, you should avoid the risk of contracting a sexually transmitted disease, **Hepatitis B** or **HIV** by not engaging in unprotected sex.

To be on the safe side, you can get a travel pack from *British Airways Travel Clinic* and other places, which includes syringes. You could also take pain killers, anti-diarrhoea pills, antiseptic cream and swabs, plasters and lipsalve, all of which are very expensive in the country compared to Europe, North America or Australia. If you ever do have a bad stomach upset with diarrhoea and vomiting, weak black tea or water mixed with sugar and salt for 24 hours can help against dehydration.

To avoid **Hepatitis A**, it is best to be careful about water, particularly if you are travelling in areas where a lack of water is a common problem. This may sound easier said than done, but most places will have sodas to drink as an alternative to water. **Bilharzia**, which you usually get from being in stagnant waters, the home of the freshwater snails that harbour the bug, is not a common problem with travellers. To avoid it, keep out of stagnant waters.

Water

The *Sunday Standard*, 28 May 1995, reported that 75 out of 78 brands of bottled water sold in Kenya are in fact Nairobi tap water.

It is important to get medical insurance while travelling as the only hospitals worth going to in Kenya are expensive. If you intend to spend any time in more remote areas, it may be worth subscribing to the flying doctor service at PO Box 30125, Nairobi, T02-501301. They will fly you back to a medical centre if necessary.

Insurance

Nairobi

1° 17' S, 36° 48' E
Phone code: 2
Colour map 3, grid B4
Population: 2,000,000
Altitude: 1,870 m

Capital of Kenya, Nairobi is a lively, cosmopolitan and bustling city. The centre is modern and prosperous, and services are well organized and efficient. Kenya's burgeoning population, however, combined with migration to the towns, has resulted in the size of Nairobi increasing at an enormous rate. Housing and other facilities have failed to keep up and shanty towns in the outskirts are the inevitable result. The population is still officially estimated at 2,000,000, but the realistic estimate as used by the Urban Planning Department is about 3,000,000. The city sits at 1,870 m above sea level – from here it is a long and steady fall to the coast 500 km away.

Ins and outs

Getting there   Nairobi is an important transport hub. International flights for neighbouring East African countries touch down at **Jomo Kenyatta International Airport**, which is located 13 km southeast of Nairobi. There are good road connections into the city. The airport departure has recently risen to US$40, although this is frequently included in the cost of the airline ticket. Transport options to and from the airport are taxis (negotiate the fare first, it should be around US$12) or there is a bus service to and from the airport, board at the new post office or the *Ambassador Hotel*, US$0.50, journey time 40 minutes. Nairobi's second airport is **Wilson Airport**, 6 km south of the city on the Langata Rd. This airport is used for internal, charter and some international flights, as well as being the base for AMREF – the Flying Doctor Service.

The long-distance bus station is on **Landhies Rd** from where there are daily departures to most destinations. The *Akamba Bus* is one of the better organized, safer bus services, travelling long distance within Kenya and to neighbouring countries. The terminus is in Lagos Road.

The railway station is at the southern end of Moi Avenue. There is currently only a passenger rail service from Nairobi-Mombasa, with the train travelling overnight through Tsavo National Park.

Getting around   Central Nairobi is bounded by Uhuru Highway to the west, Nairobi River to the north and east and the railway to the south. Across the Uhuru Highway is Uhuru Park and Central Park. In the southwest of this central triangle of about 5 sq km are most of the government buildings, offices, banks, hotels and shops. In the northern section the buildings are closer together and there are many less expensive shops and restaurants, while to the east of the triangle is the poorer section where there are cheaper hotels and restaurants, shops and markets. This is the area around River Road, which is very lively, full of character and has the authentic atmosphere of the African section of a great city (although it is an area in which visitors should take care over their personal safety).

The best maps of Nairobi are the *City of Nairobi: Map and Guide*, published by the Survey of Kenya in English, German and French. If you want more detail or are staying a while it may be worth getting *A to Z Guide to Nairobi*, by RW Moss (Kenway Publications). Clear and easy to use.

Tourist   There is no tourist information centre in Nairobi, but the tour operators will be able to help
information   (see page 106). Two free publications are available at tour companies and tourist hotels: *Tourist's Kenya*, which is published fortnightly and which gives a rundown on things going on, and *What's On*, which comes out monthly. The **Safety and Communication Centre**, T2604767, safetour@wananchi.com, operated by Kenya Tourism Federation, will advise on most things such as road conditions or emergency help.

Climate   The altitude makes for a marvellous climate with sunny days and cool nights. Sep-Apr are the hottest months, with maximum temperatures averaging 24°C, but falling at nights to around 13°C. May-Aug is cooler, with a maximum average of 21°C, and minimum of 11°C at night. It can be quite chilly in the evenings. The heavy rains are in Mar-May, and smaller rains in Nov

Things to do in and around Nairobi ★

- See the wildlife at the Nairobi National Park (take a taxi); it has all the Big Nine except elephant and rhino. Early morning and just before dusk are the best times.
- Visit the Karen Blixen Museum and evoke the unique Out-of-Africa atmosphere.
- Take a day trip to Lake Naivasha and spend the day at Safarilands where you can swim in the pool, eat well in comfort, and seek out hippo on the lake.
- Discover the marvellous story of the 'Lunatic Express' at the Railway Museum.
- Go horseracing at the weekend at the Ngong Racecourse, scene of some of Beryl Markham's greatest triumphs.
- During the day wander around the National Museum.

Kenya

and Dec, although the timing of the rains has been less regular in recent years. Even on days of heavy rain there will invariably be some hours of sunshine.

Safety Over recent years Nairobi has become one of the poorest, dirtiest and most dangerous cities in Africa. There are increasing reports of muggings, snatchings, car hijackings and robberies in Nairobi. These can certainly be a problem if you are not extremely sensible. If you walk around with a camera around your neck, an obviously expensive watch, jewellery or a money belt showing then you are extremely vulnerable. If you are at all unsure take a taxi that you should lock from the inside if possible, and make it a rule to always do so at night. Places to definitely avoid walking around, especially at night, include River Rd, Uhuru Park, Haile Selassie Av, along Uhuru Highway and the road past the National Museum. Some thieves specialize in jostling, robbing and snatching from new arrivals on buses and *matatus* from the airport. On buses and *matatus* **do not** take items to eat offered by strangers, even by children, as these have frequently been drugged to aid robbery.

History The name Nairobi comes from the Masai words *enkare nyarobe* meaning sweet (or cold) water, for originally this was a watering hole for the Masai and their cattle. As a result of the recent drought you may see Masai grazing their cattle on the grass verges within the confines of the city. Just 100 years ago Nairobi hardly existed at all. It began life in 1896 as a railway camp during the building of the railway from the coast to the highlands. It grew steadily and by 1907 had become a town sufficient in size to take over from Mombasa as capital of British East Africa. Its climate was considered healthier than that of the coast and its position was ideal for developing into a trading centre for the settlers who farmed the White Highlands. Since then the city has continued to grow and is now the largest in East Africa.

Sights

Kenya National Museum Located on Museum Hill this presents an overview of Kenya's history, culture and natural history. The section on prehistory is particularly strong with exhibits of archaeological findings made so famous by the work of the Leakeys. The museum also has an excellent collection of butterfly and bird species found in Kenya. The *Kenya Museum Society* offers guided tours of certain exhibitions and these are recommended. Linked to the museum is an excellent new arts project founded by the *Kuona Trust*. ■ *0930-1800, US$4.* The trust provides studio space in a building next to the museum where artists can walk in off the street and use the space to paint and sculpt. Not only does it offer artists studio space free of charge but it also gives them an opportunity to exhibit (and sell) their work in one of the galleries. This is a great place to meet and talk to young people from Nairobi in a very welcoming atmosphere.

Snake Park & Aquarium The Snake Park and Aquarium is found opposite the National Museum and houses examples of most of the snake species found in Kenya as well as crocodiles and tortoises. Some are in glass tanks and others in open pits. ■ *Opening hours and charges are the same as for the National Museum. Information about these and other museums run by National Museums of Kenya is available from: PO Box 40658, Nairobi, T742131/4, www.museums.or.ke*

Railway Museum

Located next to the railway station on Station Road, visitors should approach from Uhuru Highway, avoiding the two blocks of muddy footpath from the post office. Among the exhibits are a number of the old steam trains. Perhaps the most interesting is the carriage from which a man-eating lion dragged a victim as the line was being constructed through what is now Tsavo National Park. There is also a model of *MV Liemba*, the vessel built by the Germans and which still plies up and down Lake Tanganyika, see page 510. ■ *0800-1645.*

National Archives

This is more interesting than it might sound to the non-historian. The building originally served as the Bank of India and is located on Moi Avenue opposite the *Hilton Hotel*. It contains various exhibitions of arts and crafts as well as photographs and, of course, hundreds of thousands of documents. ■ *Weekdays 0800-1700. Free.*

McMillan Memorial Library

Located close to the Jamia Mosque, the McMillan Memorial Library has an excellent collection of books, newspapers and parliamentary archives. The neoclassical building was erected in 1928 and has huge lions on each side of the main steps. Books can be borrowed from here for a small charge. ■ *Mon-Fri 0900-1700, Sat 0930-1300.*

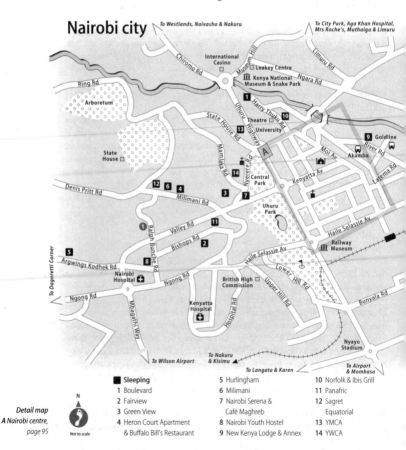

Nairobi city

Detail map
A Nairobi centre,
page 95

Not to scale

■ Sleeping
1 Boulevard
2 Fairview
3 Green View
4 Heron Court Apartment
 & Buffalo Bill's Restaurant

5 Hurlingham
6 Milimani
7 Nairobi Serena &
 Café Maghreb
8 Nairobi Youth Hostel
9 New Kenya Lodge & Annex

10 Norfolk & Ibis Grill
11 Panafric
12 Sagret
 Equatorial
13 YMCA
14 YWCA

Early settlers

On 3 September 1896 a party of new arrivals set off from Mombasa to trek up-country with a view to settling in the Highlands around Nairobi. They were Henry Boedeker (a doctor), Jim McQueen (a blacksmith) and the two Wallace brothers, David (a doctor) and George (a farmer), and their respective wives.

There were porters to carry their belongings and a dozen or so donkeys, which the ladies would ride from time to time – Mary McQueen and Mary Wallace were both pregnant.

The route was through Machakos and then to Fort Smith (now Kabete). It took six weeks, sleeping in tents, and on average they covered about 10 miles each day they were on the trail.

The McQueens settled at Mbagahi about 12 miles west of Nairobi. They built their own house, roofed with makuti thatch, mud and wattle walls, windows without glass with wooden shutters. Lighting was by candle and paraffin hurricane lamps. Water was collected from the Magathi River in four-gallon tins (debes), used to import paraffin. Cooking was done on a wood fire with pots balanced on three stones. A mud shell round a debe with a fire underneath served as an oven. Bird and game were plentiful, and were shot for meat.

The McQueens had six children who went barefoot. The children's clothes were sewn by hand from flour bags and Mary McQueen taught them to read, write and add up.

On the first floor is a collection of furniture from the house of Karen Blixen; several of the pieces can be recognized from descriptions in *Out of Africa*. Sadly many of these pieces are in a bad state of repair, and the library rooms housing this furniture collection have also fallen into disarray.

Parliament House on Parliament Road is recognizable by its clock tower. When Parliament is in session you can watch the proceedings from the public gallery, otherwise you can usually arrange to be shown around the building – ask at the main entrance.

Parliament House

This building is the tallest in the city with 28 floors and was built in 1972. At the top is the revolving restaurant, which functions only periodically. However you can usually go up to the viewing level from where you can take photos – ask at the information desk on the ground floor. There can be stunning views of Mounts Kenya and Kilimanjaro on a clear day. It is free but it is usual to tip the guard.

Kenyatta Conference Centre

The museum is found in the house of Karen Blixen (Isak Dinesen), in the suburb of Karen, about 10 km from the city centre. Many people who have read her books or seen *Out of Africa* will want to savour the unique atmosphere. Most of the original furniture is housed in the McMillan Library (see above) and much of what you see is merely furniture and props used in the film of the same name.

Karen Blixen Museum
See map, page 117

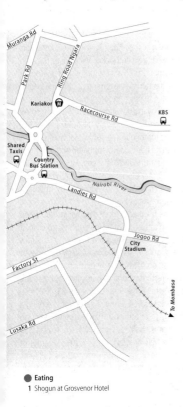

● Eating
1 Shogun at Grosvenor Hotel

Exhibits include many photographs of Karen Blixen, Denys Finch Hatton and various agricultural implements used to grade and roast coffee beans. The house was bought by the Danish government in 1959 and presented to the Kenyan government at Independence, along with the nearby agricultural college. The house is surprisingly small and dark but the gardens are quite special. ■ *Daily 0930-1800, US$2.50, T882779. From Nairobi take the No 111 bus from the front of the Hilton. Journey time 1 hr, cost US$0.50. Change at Karen village to No 24 matatu or walk for half-an-hour . It is best to visit on a weekday, preferably late afternoon, when you are less likely to meet tour groups, and may be able to view the house and contents without a guide.*

Essentials

Sleeping

■ *on maps, pages 92 and 95 Price codes: see inside front cover*

There is an enormous range of hotels from the most expensive to the most basic. Those at the top of the range have all the facilities that you would expect of any international 5-star hotels. Most of the usual establishments are here, such as the *Hilton* (Watali St, T334000, info_Nairobi@Hilton.com), *Holiday Inn* (Parklands Rd, T740906, F748823) and *Inter-Continental* (City Hall Way and Uhuru Highway, T335550, F210675, Nairobi@Interconti.com).

L *Grand Regency*, Loita St, PO Box 57549, T211199, F217120, grandregency@ form-net.com A profusion of marble and gilt. 194 rooms, 3 restaurants, ballroom, gym, swimming pool and a shopping arcade. **L** *Nairobi Safari Club*, PO Box 43564, Lillian Towers, University Way at Koinage St, T330621, F331209. One of the newest of the Nairobi Hotels and probably the most expensive, it was originally known as the *Mount Kenya Safari Club* and is one of the few places where you are expected to wear a tie and jacket. It also does not welcome children under the age of 12. It has been described as palatial, which is not far wrong – marble, fountains and lots of greenery, with two restaurants, a swimming pool, sauna, health centre, hairdresser and meeting rooms; you will have to pay temporary membership to use these facilities. **L** *Nairobi Serena*, PO Box 46302, Kenyatta Av and Nyerere Rd close to All Saints Cathedral, T725111, F725184, central booking PO Box 48690, Nairobi, T711077/8, F718100/2/3, serenanbo@form-net.com Set in beautiful gardens it has plenty of parking space and runs a shuttle service into town. The *Serena* has a good reputation and is popular with business travellers and tourists. There are wonderful views of the city, especially at sunset. It has 183 rooms including 7 suites, and facilities include a swimming pool, health club, meeting rooms, shops and an excellent restaurant. **L** *Norfolk*, PO Box 40064, Harry Thuku Rd, T335422, F212698. Built in 1904, this is a world-famous hotel and as a result many people who cannot afford to actually stay drop in for a drink. It suffered some damage in 1980 when a bomb, believed to be being carried by a terrorist in transit, went off in the hotel. However it was repaired and in 1991 it underwent extensive renovations. There are 129 rooms, 18 suites and 6 luxury cottages. The *Lord Delamare Bar* is a popular drinking spot, which has a series of caricature cartoons of early settlers. You can also sit on the terrace or in the gardens. Other facilities include a swimming pool, shops, 2 restaurants and bars and a ballroom. **L** *Safari Park*, about 15 km, north of Nairobi on the Thika Rd, PO Box 45038, T802493, F802477, safariht@arcc.or.ke Completed in 1990, it has 204 rooms, 7 restaurants serving a variety of culinary options. It has 3 bars, a swimming pool, tennis and squash courts, a casino and meeting rooms. All rooms have 4-poster beds and a balcony with a view. There is a US$5 charge to use the gym. **L** *Stanley* (previously the *New Stanley*), PO Box 30680, corner of Kenyatta Av and Kimathi St, T228830, F229388 (Sarova Group, central reservations, T333248, F211472, reservations@thestanley.sarova.co.ke). This is actually the oldest hotel in Nairobi although originally it was not located here. The celebrated outdoor *Thorn Tree Café* is found here as well as the *Nation Bookshop*. The *Thorn Tree* is famous for its notice board where travellers can leave messages for each other without charge – no advertisements allowed. Has been recently renovated, with a subsequent price increase. The hotel has about 240 rooms and facilities include meeting rooms, shops and a moderate restaurant. **L** *Windsor Golf and*

Country Club, 9 km north of Nairobi on Garden Estate Rd, T862300, F802322, windsor@ users.africaonline.co.ke PO Box No 45587. Built in 1991, it is one of Nairobi's newer hotels, there are about 130 rooms and 15 luxury cottages without a/c. It is modelled on a Victorian-style English country hotel and has extensive facilities including 3 restaurants, meeting rooms, a health club, an 18-hole golf course (located in a forest), squash and tennis courts, and riding facilities.

Nairobi centre

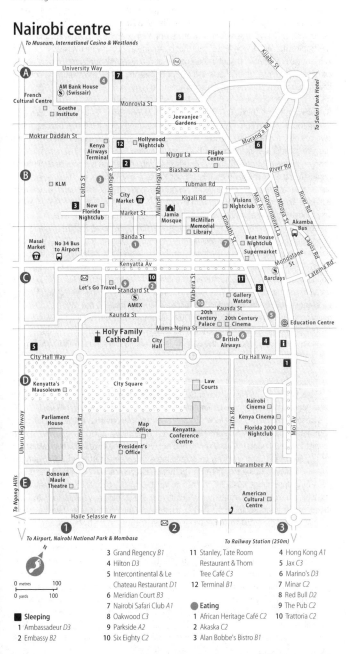

Kenya

3 Grand Regency *B1*
4 Hilton *D3*
5 Intercontinental & Le
  Chateau Restaurant *D1*
6 Meridian Court *B3*
7 Nairobi Safari Club *A1*
8 Oakwood *C3*
9 Parkside *A2*
10 Six Eighty *C2*

11 Stanley, Tate Room
   Restaurant & Thorn
   Tree Café *C3*
12 Terminal *B1*

● **Eating**
1 African Heritage Café *C2*
2 Akaska *C2*
3 Alan Bobbe's Bistro *B1*

4 Hong Kong *A1*
5 Jax *C3*
6 Marino's *D3*
7 Minar *C2*
8 Red Bull *D2*
9 The Pub *C2*
10 Trattoria *C2*

■ **Sleeping**
1 Ambassadeur *D3*
2 Embassy *B2*

A *Landmark*, part of the Block Hotels chain, PO Box 14287, T448714/7, F448977, Waiyaki Way, Westlands, central bookings for Block Hotels, PO Box 40075, Nairobi, T540780, F545948. Has 3 good-quality hotel restaurants, including a balcony/garden pizza restaurant, comfortable rooms, swimming pool, bar, business facilities. **A** *Panafric*, PO Box 30486, Kenyatta Av, T720822 (Sarova Group, central reservations, T717820, F721878). It is a modern practical hotel of 200 rooms, but without an enormous amount of atmosphere. Facilities include a swimming pool, shop, hairdressers and meeting rooms. There is a café by the pool and the *Simba Grill* is popular, with a live band most nights. **A-B** *Fairview*, PO Box 40842, on Bishops Rd, T711321, F721320, reserv@fairviewkenya.com Very peaceful with well-kept and extensive tropical gardens, a wonderful hotel that is extremely popular with overseas visitors and Kenyans alike. It caters both for business people and families. Has conference rooms, and an excellent terrace restaurant, that is also a popular meeting place. New swimming pool and health club recently opened. Highly recommended.

B *Boulevard*, Harry Thuku Rd, PO Box 42831, T227567/8/9, F334071, hotelboulevard@ form-net.com 500 m from city centre, this represents good value. It has 70 rooms, each with own balcony, and facilities include a swimming pool, tennis courts, gardens and restaurant. Has recently added an internet room. **B** *Jacaranda*, PO Box 14287, T448713, about 5 km out of town on Chiromo Rd close to the Westlands shopping centre. This is a popular family hotel, calmer than the city centre hotels, it has about 121 large airy rooms and its facilities include 2 restaurants, an outdoor barbeque, a swimming pool, tennis court, and playground. **B** *Marble Arch*, on the Lagos Rd off Tom Mboya St, PO Box 12224, T245720, F245724. Smart, very modern, friendly and efficient businessman's hotel. Although centrally located, it has an underground car park but no garden or pool. **B** *Meridian Court Hotel*, T333675, Murang'a Rd. Good value, includes breakfast. **B** *Milimani*, PO Box 30715, Milimani Rd, T720760. Large hotel popular with expatriates working in Kenya, prices include breakfast. **B** *Oakwood Hotel*, PO Box 40683, Kimathi St opposite the *New Stanley Hotel*, T220592/3, F332170, www.madahotels.com Good value, there are only 23 rooms and the price includes breakfast. Facilities include a bar, restaurant and a roof terrace. Well furnished single, double and triple rooms with TVs and excellent en suite bathrooms. Laundry service available. **B** *Utalii*, PO Box 31067, located a bit out of town on the Thika Rd, T802540, F803094, utali@form-net.com *Utalii* is the Swahili word for tourism and this is the government-run training centre for hotel and catering students. As a result service is really very good, there are 50 rooms and facilities include a swimming pool, lovely gardens, tennis courts and a restaurant.

C *Ambassadeur*, PO Box 30399, Moi Av, T336803, F336860 (Sarova Group, central reservations, T333248, F211472). This has a good central location, but is nothing special and there are better value hotels in the same range. **C** *Hurlingham*, PO Box 43158, Argwings Kodhek Rd, T721920. This is a small hotel with only 14 rooms, located in western Nairobi. It has a definite charm and is popular with local residents. **C** *Parkside*, PO Box 53104, Monrovia St, T333329, F334681, Reservations T333348. Rooms have bathrooms and hot water and the price includes breakfast. It is friendly and clean but relatively expensive and there is a restaurant attached. **C** *Six Eighty*, PO Box 43436, Muindi Mbingu St, T332680. This hotel has a very central location with an unprepossessing appearance. It has 380 rooms and facilities include a Japanese restaurant, shops and a bar (currently being refurbished with a casino). The staff are very helpful to visitors, and the rooms are clean. Rooms at the back of the hotel are the best option as the noise from a disco across the road can sometimes be heard, even in rooms on the higher floors.

City centre
In this price range the hotels out of town tend to a better standard than those in the centre, which often suffer from noise pollution

D *Africana*, Dubois Rd off Latema Rd, PO Box 47827, T220654. Offers possibly the best value in this category, it is clean, safe and fairly quiet and rooms all have bathrooms with hot water. Café downstairs. **D** *Embassy*, Biashara St/Tubman Rd, T224087. Clean, safe and friendly and rooms have bathrooms with hot water. Has a good restaurant. **D** *Grand Holiday Hotel*, Tsavo Rd, PO Box 69343, T211372, F243851. Noisy, has reasonably clean rooms, hot showers and an acceptable restaurant. **D** *Hermes*, PO Box 62997, T340066, a little way out on the corner of Tom Mboya St and Haile Selassie Av. This is a good value hotel, that is clean and has a fairly good restaurant. **D** *Salama*, corner of Tom Mboya St and Luthuli Av, PO Box 11386, T225898.

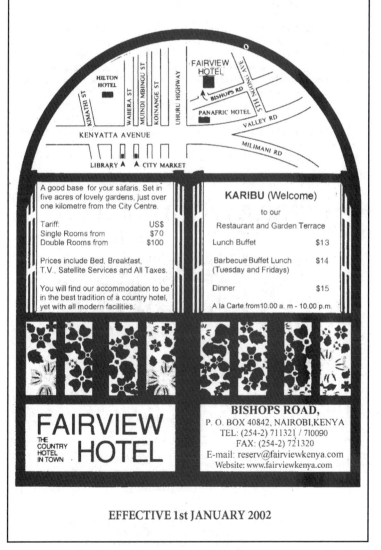

Suffers from the noise, price includes breakfast but it is not terribly good value. **D** *Sirikwa Lodge*, corner of Accra Rd and Munyu St, T26089. Not too noisy. Most rooms have bathrooms with hot water and are clean, and breakfast is included in the price. **D** *Solace Hotel*, PO Box 48867, Tom Mboya St, T331277, F220129. Reasonable value, but best avoided if you can't sleep through noise. **D** *Terminal*, Moktar Daddah St in the northwest of town, T228817, located next door to the *Downtown Hotel*. Popular hotel although it has seen better days. It is, however, clean and safe with friendly, helpful staff. Can be noisy, especially early in the morning and at night. Rooms have bathrooms with hot water, but breakfast is not included. Restaurant next door does good, cheap food. **D** *YMCA*, State House Rd, T724066, kenyaymca@connect.co.ke Dormitories and en-suite rooms on offer. Safe and reasonable value for single rooms but overpriced for shared rooms. It caters mostly for long-term visitors; many of the residents are Kenyan students who live there semi-permanently. It has a swimming pool. No alcohol is allowed on the premises. **D** *YWCA*, Mamlaka Rd, off Nyerere Rd, T724699. Does take couples, good value.

E *Bujumbura Lodge*, Dubois Rd, just off Latema Rd, T221835, near *New Safe Lodging*, this is pretty basic with shared bathrooms and unpredictable hot water supplies. **E** *Orchid Hotel*, previously *Dolat*, Mfangano St, T222797. This hotel is in a great location, very secure, with friendly staff, and is very good value for money. Relatively quiet and friendly, very clean, all rooms have a bath and lots of hot water. Used by *Venture Africa* along with the *Iqbal* (see below) to accommodate Gap Year school leavers. **E** *Evamay Hotel*, River Rd, T216218. Excellent value, cosy s/c rooms with nets, phone and good furniture. Very friendly staff, safe facilities and the price includes breakfast. Recommended. **E** *Gloria*, Ronald Ngala St, T228916. Rather noisy place to stay but as all rooms have bathrooms and hot water and the price includes breakfast it is really quite good value, although the rooms are rather drab and dirty. **E** *Iqbal*, Latema Rd, T220914. One of the most popular places in central Nairobi, so if you

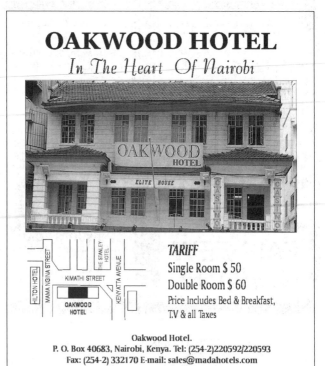

want to stay you will have to arrive early. There is sometimes hot water in the mornings and although it's only basic it is very friendly and you will meet lots of other travellers here. All rooms have shared bathrooms. There are baggage storage facilities and a notice board. However, it is reported to survive mostly on past reputation rather than modern-day service. **E** *New Kenya Lodge and Annex*, River Rd by the junction of Latema St, T222202. The annex is just around the corner in Duruma Rd, T338348. Another very popular budget hotel, again it is very basic, bathrooms are shared and there is only hot water in the evenings, except in the Annex that only has cold water. However, it is reasonably clean and friendly and has baggage storage facilities and a notice board. Travellers have reported that the associated safari company, *Neo-KL Tours and Safaris,* offers very poor service indeed with badly organized tours and refusal to reimburse the costs of failed excursions. **E** *New Safe Life Lodging*, Dubois Rd just off Latema Rd, T221578, is clean and basic with shared bathrooms but has the usual hot water problems. As with many of these places the single rooms are not very good value. **E** *Nyandarwa Lodging*, Dubois Rd, just off Latema Rd. Shared bathrooms and hot water, but can be very noisy. **E** *Somerset Lodge*, Latema Rd, T330362. Another basic but clean place with shared bathrooms that have hot water mornings and evenings. Some of the rooms at the front are rather noisy as it is next door to the lively *Modern 24 Hour Green Bar*, which is, as its name implies, open all day and all night. **E** *Terrace*, Ronald Ngala St, T221636, is close to the *Gloria* and is similar, although it can be rather noisy, and the staff don't appear to make much of an effort.

D *Diplomat Hotel*, Tom Mboya St next to *Ambassadeur*, PO Box 30777, T246114, F220475. Extraordinarily good value and pretty slick for the price, with wall-to-wall carpeting, s/c modern rooms, breakfast included. You can make local calls from the front desk for a minimum of KSh40. The rooms that face the street can be very noisy. **D** *Green View Hotel*, PO Box 42246, Minet ICDC Bldg, situated off Nyerere Rd, T729923. Nice surroundings, there are both private and shared bathrooms, plus a bar and restaurant and prices include breakfast. **D** *Hotel Greton*, Tsavo Rd, PO Box 55909, T242891, F242892. Good value and very secure hotel. Possessions whether left in your room, safe or left luggage are unlikely to go astray. Clean, decent-sized, furnished rooms and breakfast is included in the tariff. Has a relaxed restaurant that is better for drinks than food. **D-E** *Heron Court Apartment Hotel*, PO Box 41848, Milimani Rd, T720740-3, F721698, herco@iconnect.co.ke Popular stopover, it is safe and has a guarded car park. The quality of the rooms vary – all have bathrooms and hot water, and some are s/c with kitchens. Facilities include swimming pool, sauna, shop and laundry service. However, some of the rooms can be noisy as the celebrated *Buffalo Bill's* restaurant and bar is attached.

Beyond city centre

E *Mrs Roche's* is a little way out, situated opposite the Aga Khan Hospital on Third Parklands Av. Legend among travellers and remains popular, campers are also welcome and use the garden, but this can get rather crowded. If you turn up late you will have to sleep on the floor until a bed is free. Friendly atmosphere, although recent travellers have reported thefts on site. Can be reached by *matatu* (which will say Aga Khan on the front) from outside the Odeon Cinema at the junction of Tom Mboya St and Latema Rd. Ask the driver to tell you where to get off. **E** *Nairobi Park Services Campsite*, on Magadi Rd, off Langata Rd, PO Box 54867, T/F890325, shling@net2000ke.com Opened in Aug 1997 this campsite offers good budget facilities, internet and email, pool table, bars and restaurant. Tented accommodation, with 2-storey accommodation and bandas. Hot showers, laundry facilities, western-style toilets are on offer in a secure, fenced compound. Vehicle parks, satellite TV/video, US$3 per night. Can arrange game drives or camel safaris. **E** *Nairobi Youth Hostel*, about 2 km out of town on Ralph Bunche Rd (which runs between Ngong Rd and Valley Rd), T721765. You must be a member of the International Youth Hostels Association to stay here but can join on the spot without any problem. (Costs US$1.25 or KSh100 per day.) The bathrooms are shared but there is hot water all day, and it is clean, friendly and safe. Take the No 8 *matatu* from outside the *Hilton* or at the junction of Kenyatta Av and Uhuru Highway down Ngong Rd and ask to be dropped off at Ralph Bunche Rd. Do not walk back to the youth hostel at night – always take a taxi or *matatu*. The **Kenya Youth Hostel Association** is on Ralph

Bunche Rd, T721765. **E** *Upper Hill Campsite Ltd*, Menengai Rd/Upper Hill, Nairobi, T720290, F723788. Site opened in 1995 with 5 dormitory bedrooms, 2 double and 1 single rooms, plus tent space and tents for hire. Good clean amenities, bar and restaurant, with good security, and is reasonably central, only 30 mins' walk from city centre. The food is cheap but good and the staff are friendly.

Eating

International
● *on maps*
Price codes:
see inside front cover

All the top hotels have good restaurants

Take care, many brands of bottled water sold in Kenya are Nairobi tap water; check the seal

Expensive *Alan Bobbe's Bistro*, small restaurant located on Koinange St, T224945. It is advisable to come here in something more glamorous than shorts and a T-shirt. It specializes in French cuisine and the food and atmosphere are both excellent, and reservations are recommended. *Café Maghreb*, Serena Hotel, T725111, another popular buffet place, this is next to the swimming pool and is particularly busy on Fri evenings. *Carnivore*, Langata Rd about 20 mins out of town past the airport, T501775. This is large complex of bars, restaurants and dance floors that was set up by the owners of the *Tamarind*. As is clear from the name, it specializes in meat dishes including game (wart-hog, giraffe, zebra, gazelle, crocodile, wildebeest and waterbuck) that are grilled over a huge charcoal fire. The waiters bring the skewer of meat to your table and carve until you say stop! It has become very popular with all types of travellers and is often included as part of tours. There is also a vegetarian menu, and in general portions are huge and it works out as fairly good value. It is also a drinking venue and a nightclub. *Ibis Grill*, Norfolk Hotel, T335422. This specializes in nouvelle cuisine and the food is very good. It has a lovely setting and a good atmosphere, jacket and tie recommended. A great (if expensive) Nairobi experience. The *Norfolk* also does a wonderful buffet breakfast that is open to non-residents. *Le Chateau*, *Intercontinental Hotel*, City Hall Way and Uhuru Highway, T335550, F210675, Nairobi@interconti.com Rooftop restaurant is the only one of its kind in Nairobi and serves excellent food, dinner dancing at weekends. *The Pavement*, Westview Centre off the ring road, T441711. Recently reopened, this restaurant has a pavement-café style that is light and bright, reflected in a varied menu of Thai, Japanese and Italian dishes or just steak and chips. A welcome change from the meat and two veg that is more commonly on offer. It has a nightclub attached. *Red Bull*, Silopark House on Mama Ngina St, T224718. This has long been one of Nairobi's most popular restaurants – for residents, business people and tourists alike. The portions are generous and the food is of high quality. *The Tamarind*, National Bank building on Harambee Av, T338959. Probably Nairobi's finest seafood restaurant. Popular with Kenyan business people, this restaurant can get unexpectedly lively. Highly recommended, only open 1830-2130. *The Tate Room*, New Stanley Hotel. Very plush and the food is good, Sunday buffet is very popular here. **Expensive–mid-range** *Horseman*, Ngong Rd in Karen, T882033, is highly recommended for meat lovers. You can also eat burgers and other snacks outside in the garden and at the bar for considerably less than the cost of a meal in the restaurant. Has a rather English ambiance. Intermittent power supply problems. Also has a pre-club disco.

Mid-range *Hard Rock Café*, Barclays Plaza, Loita St, T220802/3. Much more lively in the evenings, with a live band on Thu (usually). *Kengeles*, ABC Shopping Centre, T447944. Lively burger bar with music of the 'Souled Out' with the 'Homboyz and Redds' variety. *Rangers*, Main Gate Nairobi NP, PO Box 63539, T602813. Set on the edge of Nairobi NP on a verandah that overlooks a waterhole (floodlit in the evenings). This is a new restaurant that offers diners the opportunity to spot animals in the NP as they eat. Good *nyama choma* plus western dishes. Free entry offered to the nearby Safari Walk at the Animal Orphanage if you eat here. **Mid-range–cheap** *Java Café*, Adam's Arcade, Ngong Rd. This is a friendly, alcohol-free backpackers' hangout, with a modern bistro atmosphere. Offers generous portions of fairly average chilli con carne or burgers. Does excellent coffee and the breakfasts are good.

Cheap *Buffalo Bill's*, Heron Court Hotel on Milimani Rd, T720740. You can eat here although the main pastime is drinking. It has a lively atmosphere, the food is OK but overall not very good value. *The Jacaranda* is pleasant for a drink and snack and is a favourite with business people. *Jax*, Kimathi St, T228365. This is popular with business people for quick cheap lunches. It is self-service and usually busy and includes a number of Indian dishes. Closed Sun. *Thorn Tree Café*, *New Stanley Hotel*. Very popular place to meet people although the service is notoriously slow. *Pasara Café*, Kaunda St, ground floor of Lonrho House, T338247. Good food, sandwiches, pastries, coffee, very good atmosphere, with newspapers and magazines available. *Railway Restaurant*, at the station, OK food but the setting is everything, décor as it always has been.

Seriously cheap There are lots of cheap places in the River Rd area selling African and Indian food and snacks. The *Iqbal* is particularly popular with travellers. *The Coffee Bar* on Mama Ngina St is busy for lunches and does filling meals. Other places to try are the *Beneve Coffee House* on the corner of Standard and Koinange streets. *Bull Café*, on Ngariama Rd, is cheap and popular. *Malindi Restaurant* on Gaborone Rd. Swahili dishes – tasty, and reasonable price.

Mid-range *Daas*, Lenana Rd, west of centre, off Valley Rd. Possibly the best Ethiopian food, and there is often live music, song and dance. *West African Paradise Restaurant*, T741396. If you fancy something a little different, open daily 0930-2130, in the Westlands district. *Paradiso Hotel*, on 10th St at the edge of Eastleigh. A little out the way for most tourists, in the Somali and Ethiopian part of the city, this is a friendly restaurant that serves authentic Ethiopian meals eaten with the fingers. **African**

Cheap *African Heritage Café*, Banda St, T222010. African food, with Ethiopian cuisine in the evening. Offers a selection of dishes from a buffet, so it is possible to sample the various examples. Highly recommended. There is also a garden. *A La Monde Restaurant* in an office building on Mamlaka just uphill from the *Nairobi Serena Hotel*, in the Utumishi Co-operative House, T721302. Run by a British-educated Kenyan called Kui, serves a different African dish from one of the different ethnic groups each day. The clientele is mostly office workers, prices are very reasonable, the food is good and the atmosphere is lively. For good and cheap African local food the adventurous should try the **Kariokor Market**, Racecourse Rd, turn right as you enter the main gate and at the first corner you come to a *Nyama Choma* will be on your left, with tables to the right. You eat with your hands, although utensils are provided on request. A specimen menu is goats' ribs, *ugali*, chopped spinach, *irio* made with peas, potatoes and sweetcorn, cost around US$1.

Mid-range *China Plate*, Chancery Bldg, Valley Rd, T719194. Expensive, but the food is very good, the décor authentic Chinese and the services attentive. *Dragon Pearl*, Kenyatta Av/Standard St, Ground Floor, in Bruce House, T338863. Deservedly very popular. *Great Chung Wa*, Mwindi Mbingu (opposite *Six Eighty Hotel*). Prominent location with recommended food. *Hong Kong*, Koinange St, T440400. Specializes in Cantonese dishes and has a good reputation. Closed Mon. *Pagoda*, Moi Av, T227036. Very good Szechuan food. One of the best Chinese restaurants in Nairobi, *Panda*, located in Imenti House on Tom Mboya St, T331189. Good food and friendly staff. *Rendezvous*, at Meridian Ct, has a very good buffet of vegetarian, non-vegetarian and local dishes. *Rickshaw*, in the Fehda Towers on Standard and Muindi Mbingu St, T336625. Extensive menu, highly rated. *Tin Tin*, in Kenyatta International Conference Centre, T229093. Reputed to set the standard that the others follow, but is probably overpriced. **Chinese**

Expensive *Haandi*, Westlands Mall, T448294/5/6. Excellent standard. *Minar*, there are 3 *Minars*, one located on Banda St in the city centre, T229999, one in the Sarit Centre in Westlands, T748340, and one in the Yaya Centre, Argwings Kodhek Rd, Hurlingham, T561676. They are popular and reservations are required. They do a buffet lunch and the service is friendly, and their tandoori dishes are especially good. **Indian**

Mid-range *Haveli Restaurant & Coffee House*, Dar es Salaam Rd. Located in an industrial area, T531607. Excellent quality. *Rasoi*, located on Parliament Rd, T25082. Excellent standard. *The Golden Candle*, Ralph Bunche Rd, T720480. Extensive menu, all of which is very good, closed on Monday.

Kenya

Cheap *Al Mamin*, situated on the corner of Banda St and Kimathi. Open plan, airy and bustling, has a limited menu but cheap, filling and tasty biryanis, curry, nan and kebabs. *Dhaba*, Tom Mboya St, T334862. Specializes in North Indian food, it is particularly popular with Nairobi Indians. Their speciality is *taka taka* dishes. *Taka taka* means rubbish in Swahili – although what that has to do with these delicious dishes is not totally clear – maybe they were originally the leftovers. *Durgar*, Ngara St, T742781. Although the décor is certainly not fancy this has good cheap food, with a good range of vegetarian dishes, also lots of Indian snacks that are very popular. *Mayur*, T331586, corner of Tom Mboya St and Keekorok Rd. Specializes in vegetarian Indian food, has seen better days, but the food is still good. *Satkar*, Moi Av, T337197. This restaurant specializes in southern Indian food. *Stavrose*, Post Bank House, Banda St, T210612. Very popular with locals, best to go early or book. Also does a takeaway service. **Sunsweet Restaurant**, back of *New Kenya Lodge*. Serves excellent Indian *thali*. *Supreme*, Kilome Rd, in the River Rd area, T225241. This Indian restaurant is excellent, it also does takeaways and has an extensive dessert menu. Others include **2** *Ambassadeur*, T336803, *Nawab Tandoori*, T740209, *New 3 Bells*, T220628, *Safeer*, *Zam Zam*, T212128, Keekorok Rd, near River Rd. Cheap and cheerful, large portions.

Italian   **Expensive** *Foresta Magnetica*, Mama Ngina St, T728009. With a piano bar, the menu is probably better at lunchtime than in the evenings because the cafeteria does not operate in the evenings. It has a very pleasant atmosphere in the evenings when the pianist is playing, closed Sun.

Mid-range *La Galleria*, International Casino, Westlands Rd, T742600, has good Italian food including some excellent seafood dishes. Closed in the afternoon. *Salumeria*, Valley Arcade. small place with tables outside that serves good pasta and antipasta. *Stop Italia*, Woodfield Grove, in Westlands area, T445234. Wide range of very good pizza, pasta dishes and icecreams. *Trattoria*, T340855, situated on Kaunda St and Wabera St. Rather bustling if somewhat chaotic place, the food is fairly good, but that is more than can be said for the service. It does good cappuccinos and icecream, reservations are recommended especially if you want one of the tables with a view. Open until midnight.

Cheap *Café Latino*, Village Market, Limaru Rd, T522661/2. New restaurant, high quality food, that becomes a Latin music and dance club on Sat nights. *La Scala*, Phoenix House Arcade, Standard St, T332130. Ignore the rather dark and forbidding external appearance. Quiet at lunchtime but gets lively with a local crowd in the evenings. Trendy and friendly, good pizza, pasta, steaks and cakes, also does a good capuccino, expresso and ice cold shakes. *Marino's*, International Life House, Mama Ngina St, T557404. Popular, largely for its desserts, particularly the icecream. *Pomodoro*, Village Market, Limaru Rd, T522058. Fast food, Italian style, offers pizza, calzoni and sandwiches. *The Toona Tree*, International Casino, Westlands Rd, T742600. A cheap outdoor restaurant that is especially good for drinks and snacks. It has live bands about 3 days a week. Closed on Mon and during the afternoon. *Twigs*, Nkrumah Rd, T335864. Menu is part Italian, part French as well as quite a lot of seafood. The food and service are both very good, and downstairs is an ice-cream parlour.

Other nationalities   **Japanese Expensive** *Shogun*, located at the *Grosvener Hotel* on Ralph Bunche St, T720563. This is one of Nairobi's Japanese restaurants, some of which are fairly similar with comparable menus, although the Shogun is not so good for lunches. **Mid-range** *Akaska Hotel*, *680 Hotel*, Ground Floor, Muindi Mbingu St, T220299. Open 1800-2100, very central, with a reasonable standard. **Korean Expensive** *Koreana*, Yaya Centre, Argwings Kodhek Rd, T561578/9. Korean cuisine has become very popular in Nairobi, and this is the leading restaurant. **Lebanese Cheap** *Ali Baba*, Jamia Towers, Muang'a Rd, opposite *Meridian Court Hotel*, T334090. Considered to be the best Lebanese cuisine in the city, although the restaurant is rather spartan. **Mongolian** *The Manchurian*, Brick Court, Mpaka Rd, Westlands, T444263. A rarity indeed. **Thai Mid-range** *Bangkok*, located in Rank Xerox House, T751311/2. It is popular and deservedly so, open every day at lunchtime, and from 1800-2230. Also see *The Pavement* above.

Bars

Eating, drinking and dancing are the most popular evening entertainments in Nairobi. There are a number of popular bars and clubs, and a number of casinos. For most of these clubs entrance for women is cheaper than for men. Single men should expect a lot of attention from girls and prostitutes. As with most establishments in Kenya, dress is casual in all these clubs. The only exceptions to this rule are the *Nairobi Safari Club*, the *Windsor Golf and Country Club Kengeles* and *The Pavement*.

Popular hotel bars include the *Norfolk* and *Fairview*. The *Thorn Tree* is a good meeting place but the service is notoriously slow. If you are there at lunchtime (1100 to 1400) or supper time (1700 to 1900) you will have to order food as well. *Buffalo Bill's* bar in the *Heron Court Hotel* on Milimani Rd is popular and it is certainly one of the liveliest places in town. *The Pub* on Standard St is open from 1100 to 2300 and is also popular. *Shooters Cocktail Restaurant*, Murang'a Rd (opposite Meridian Ct), tastefully modern and spacious cocktail bar. Open day and night with good food, drinks and music. If you want to drink all day and night and are not too fussy about your surroundings you can try the *Modern 24-Hour Green Bar* on Latema Rd. This is the authentic African city side of Nairobi.

Entertainment

Mzizi Cultural Centre, Box 48955, T245364/6, F245366, 6th Floor Sonalux House, Moi Av, very close to *Hilton Hotel* and in same block as the *Zanzibar Curio Shop*, has a gallery and houses works of Kenyan contemporary artists, as well as offering daily performances of music, story telling and poetry reading. They offer rare and reasonably priced souvenirs. At the centre, one can pick up the latest copy of their magazine, *SANAA* (meaning 'art' in Kiswahili), which lists all activities in the city such as theatre performances, shows, film screenings and other activities. Enjoy the relaxed atmosphere, meet Kenyans in the arts, see some great performances for a very reasonable price (shows cost about US$5) and get a real taste of what is going on in the forefront of the arts in the country. The people who run the place are very friendly, and will be delighted to show you around. Programmes are announced in the local press. | **Arts Centres**

Casinos are open until 0300 on weekdays and 0330 at weekends. The oldest is the *International Casino*, T744477, F742620, which also houses *Bubbles* nightclub. The others are found in the *Intercontinental*, located on Uhuru Highway; *Safari Park* located on Thika Rd; *Florida*, corner Uhuru Highway and University Way; *Mayfair*, Parklands Rd; *Esso Plaza*, Muthaiga; and the *680 Hotel*. | **Casinos**

Carnivore Restaurant, Langata Rd, puppet shows, acrobats, face painting and kids' TV every Sat from 1300. | **Children's entertainment**

There are a number of cinemas, including 2 drive-ins the *Fox* and *Belle-Vue* (if you have a vehicle an evening at the drive-in is well worth it). Ticket prices range from about US$1-$3.50. Check the newspapers for programme details. Other good cinemas are the *Nairobi*, *Kenya* on Moi Av, and *20th Century*, the most expensive on Mama Ngina St, T338070, and the *Sarit Centre Cinema*, Westlands. There are other cheaper cinemas on Latema Rd but the quality of the films is not as good. Films on show include British, American and Indian productions and there are often fairly recent releases. | **Cinemas**

Classical Choral concerts are held at All Saints Cathedral by the *Nairobi Music Society*, which also gives evening recitals at the British Council. There are occasional classical concerts held by the *Nairobi Orchestra*. **Popular** The *African Heritage Café* on Banda St has live bands most weekends and *Jabali Africa* and guests on Sat 1400-1700. *Simba Grill*, *Panafric Hotel*, Kenyatta Av, has resident bands playing Thu, Fri and Sat. *Carnivore*, Langata Rd, has a live band, usually rock, every Wed. *Bombax Club*, on Dagoretti Corner on the Ngong Rd, has live bands from Thu to Wed. It is a bit out of town so take a taxi, or else a minibus from outside | **Music**

Kenya

Nyayo House on Kenyatta Av. Quite a few of the hotels also have bands from time to time – see the local press for details.

Nightclubs The *New Florida* and *Florida 2000*, on Koinange St and Moi Av respectively, are both very popular. They have fairly good sound systems and lights and stay open until 0600. *Visions*, Kimathi St, is also popular. It is smaller but otherwise fairly similar and is open from 1200. Other places include *Beat House*, Kimathi St; *Bubbles*, Westlands Rd; *Hillock Inn*, Enterprise Rd; *Hollywood*, Moktar Daddah St; *JKA Resort Club*, located on Mombasa Rd just after the turn-off to the airport, which has an open air-dance floor; *Kenya International*, Murang'a Rd; *Milano Club*, Ronald Ngala Rd; *Carnivore* in Langata Rd, live bands every Wed popular with expats, and Sun draws in the Asian community. Entry US$2.50 open until about 0400. *The Pavement*, Westview Centre, Ring Rd, Westlands is a trendy new club venue, popular with a wide range of ages and groups, predominantly Nairobi residents. Fri and Sat nights are the liveliest. Entry US$3.25.

Spectator sports **Cricket** Main venues are *Gymkhana*, *Premier Simba* and *Aga Khan*, all in Parklands area just to the north of the centre, near City Park. Exciting league games played on Sat and Sun, with good crowds. Take taxi from town centre, about US$4. **Horseracing** The *Ngong Racecourse* holds meetings most Sun from Jan to Jun. It is a wonderful setting as well as being a great place to observe all sections of Nairobi society. **Polo** Weather permitting, polo is played on Sat and Sun at *Jamhuri Club*, Ngong Rd.

Theatre There are 2 main theatres in Nairobi. *The Professional Centre* has performances at the **Phoenix Theatre** on Parliament Rd. Although a small grou,p they are the most active and produce a range of drama of a very high standard. The other is the *Kenya National Theatre* located opposite the *Norfolk Hotel* on Harry Thuku Rd close to the university. Concerts are also held at the **National Theatre**. There are 2 high standard amateur groups, **Lavington Players** and **Nairobi Players**, who present a range of comedies, musicals and pantomimes, all of which are very popular. The local papers have notices of what's on.

Festivals

The big event of the year is the annual *Safari Rally*, which begins and ends in Nairobi. It is held around Easter time and is a great spectacle for local people. The route is over 4,000 km – it used to be the East African Safari but now just covers Kenya. The *Nairobi International Show*, an agricultural fair, is held at the end of **Sep**.

Shopping

Bookshops *The Nation*, on Kenyatta Av next to the *Thorn Tree Café*, has a good selection of fiction and non-fiction, as well as maps and helpful staff. *Select*, on Kimathi St opposite the *New Stanley Hotel*, is larger although rather run-down. There is a good but small antique East African section. Other bookshops that stock a fairly good African selection include the *Book Corner* and *Prestige*, both located on Mama Ngina St, while the *Text Book Centre*, on Kigabe St, has text books as well as fiction. There's also a number of book stalls along **Tom Mboya St** and **Latema Rd** where you may be able to pick up a few bargain second-hand books. There is also a second-hand bookshop on Banda St.

Clothing There is a cluster of shops selling material and cloth squares (kangas and kikois) on Biashara St quite close to the market. Here you can also watch tailors on their foot-propelled machines sewing clothes, cushions, etc and stitching some of the most elaborate embroidery at amazing speed. *Lucky Wear* has a good range of clothes and fabric, as does *Maridadi Fabrics*, which is further out of town on Landhies St. There are lots of places that will kit you out in safari gear. *Colpro* on Kimathi St is recommended as good quality and reliable.

Cycleland and *Kenya Cycle Mart Ltd*, both on Moi Av, close to the main post office, have **Bike shops** bicycles and accessories, but don't expect too much. *Sati's Classic*, T505529, equatrrl@ net.2000.ke.com, repair, buy, sell and hire motorcycles.

There are a huge number of souvenir shops in Nairobi. They vary enormously in terms of **Handicrafts &** price and quality. At stalls you will be able bargain the prices down to between a third and a **souvenirs** half of the original asking price, although not in the more formal shops, which tend to use a fixed price. Shops that are part of hotels are always much more expensive. The best prices on curios are at the *Zanzibar Curio Shop*, on Moi Av, prices are marked and there's no haggling. *Rupas*, PO Box 43698, T224417, have an outstanding selection of gift purchases, good quality, courteous staff and competitve prices. Be sure to have a good look at any purchases – wood that may look like ebony may in fact just have been polished with black shoe polish – it is a popular trick. Also cracks may appear in the wood (particularly when it is placed in a centrally heated room) if it has not been properly seasoned.

Perhaps the best place for baskets is the *Kariakor Market*, on the Ring Rd at Ngara. *Antique Gallery*, Kaunda St, T27759 and *Antique Auction*, Moktar Daddah St, T336383, have antique East African artefact collections. For paintings, batiks carvings and other higher quality crafts try: *African Heritage* on Banda St; *Gallery Watatu* and *Roland Ward*, both on Standard St; *Spinners Web*, on Kijabe St close to the *Norfolk Hotel*, is a good craft shop, in particular for fabrics and baskets. Its merchandise comes from various self-help groups around the country and the staff are very helpful. On Tue the *Masai Market* is held at the hillside site at Muranga Rd below Moi Av. *Blue Market* is opposite the city market between Tubman Rd and Kigah Rd, you are advised to go in late afternoon, as prices are lowest just before they close. Bargain hard! Good for all wooden artefacts, soapstone, jewellery, etc.

For jewellery and semi-precious stones try *Al-Safa Jewellers* at the *New Stanley Hotel* and **Jewellery** *Treasures and Crafts* on Kaunda St.

City Market, Muindi Mbingo St. Around the market and the Jamia Mosque there are numer- **Markets &** ous stalls selling baskets, wooden and soapstone carvings, bracelets and lots of other souve- **supermarkets** nirs. Be prepared to look around and bargain. Other markets worth visiting include the *Masai Market*, near the Globe Cinema, on Tue; and the *Village Market*, Limuru Rd, on Fri.

The *Uchumi* chain of supermarkets offer a reasonable product range. The branch at corner Loita/Monrovia St is very large and opens on Sun. The *Nakumatt* chain of shops is a good source of household goods. There is one on Nanyuki Rd and Uhuru Highway.

Camera Maintenance Centre, located in the Hilton Arcade, Mama Ngina St, T26920 and **Photography** *Camera Experts* on Mama Ngina St, T337750. Get a quote as repairs can be quite expensive. *Elite Camera House*, opposite *New Stanley Hotel*, will hire out lenses (but are expensive).

If you need passport-size photos there are a few booths. One is on the corner of Tom Mboya St and Accra Rd, another is a few doors up from the *Thorn Tree Café* on the corner of Kenyatta Av and Kimathi St. Several photoshops will do passport photographs. Cost US$2.50 for 4.

Sport

Climbing: each Tue evening the *Kenya Mountaineering Club*, PO Box 45741, T501747, meets at its clubhouse at Wilson Airport to arrange expeditions and get high on Kendal Mint Cake. **Go-karting**: close to Wilson Airport, take the Langata Rd turn-off for the *Carnivore Restaurant*, PO Box 56685, T608444, F600557, Fastkart@iconnect.co.ke Recently opened, sprints and practice sessions are available at US$12 for a 10-min sprint or a 20-min practice. **Golf**: there are a number of very well-kept golf courses in the suburbs of Nairobi, although you will need to take out temporary membership. These include: *Karen Country Club*, Karen Rd, T882801; *Muthaiga Golf Club*, Muthaiga Rd, T762414; *Limuru Country Club*, Limuru, T0154-41351(Karuri); *Railway Golf Club*, Ngong Rd, T22116; *Windsor Golf & Country Club*, T862300. **Gym**: *Canyon Health Gymnasium*, R500, 5th Floor, Uniafric House, Koinange St.

Kenya

Aerobics and weight training sessions available. Open 0900-1930 weekdays, 0900-1500 Sat. **Riding**: lessons and safaris can be arranged through the *Arifa Riding School*. Bookings T25255. **Running**: *Hash House Harriers* meet regularly. See notices in British Council, or at British High Commission. **Sailing**: the *Nairobi Sailing Club* sails on Nairobi Dam, found off Langata Rd, T501250. **Swimming**: most of the big hotels have swimming pools that can also be used by non-residents for a daily fee of about US$2. The pool at *YMCA* is particularly good, or try the *Aga Khan's Sports Complex* (next to *Ma Roches*), US$3 for pool. There is a pool with diving board, and lots of other activities. **Tennis and squash**: many of the major hotels have courts. Other clubs include the *Karen Club*, Karen Rd, T882801 and *Limuru Country Club*, Limuru, T40033 (Karuri).

Tour operators and travel agents

The following specialist tour operators are recommended: *Let's Go Travel*, ABC Place, Waiyaki Way, Westlands, PO Box 60342, T447151, F447270 (as well as offices in Tanzania and Uganda) www.letsgosafari.com, offer reasonably priced balloon safaris, camel safaris, horse-back safaris, fishing, gliding, hang-gliding, para-gliding, golf, walking, trekking and climbing, diving, watersports and whitewater rafting. A well-organized company, they act as agents for several other companies, and publish price and information lists of hotels, camps and lodges. *East Africa Ornithological Safaris Ltd*, PO Box 48019, T331684, F216528, eaos@ africaonline.co.ke   Specialize in bird-watching tours. *Best Camping Tours and Safaris Ltd*, Norwich Union House, Mezzanine, Room 212, corner of Kimath/Banda streets, PO Box 40223, T229667/75, F217923, www.kenyaweb.com/bestcampingtours   *Gametrackers*, 1st Floor, Kenya Cinema Plaza, Moi Av, PO Box 62042, T338927, F330903, www.gametrackers.com Well-established company organizing camping safaris with both vehicles and camels to Lake Turkana and the Ndoto Mts, as well as biking and walking safaris. Recommended.

For trekking, camel trekking, mountain-bike safaris, canoe safaris, climbing and gorilla safaris, contact any of the following: *Habib's Tours and Travel*, Agip House, Haile Selassie Av, PO Box 48095, T220463, F220985, habibtours@karibunet.com   Good for car rental. *Savage Camping Tours Ltd*, Soin Arcade, Westlands Rd, Westlands, c/o PO Box 73193, T449467, F449469. *Sunny Safaris*, Portal Place, Banda St, PO Box 74495, T226587, F339809. *Vintage Safaris*, PO Box 59470, Kijabe St, T226547, F211660, and Shimmers Plaza, T742450, F742465. *Wanderlust Safaris Ltd*, 4th Floor, Gilfillan House, Kenyatta Av, PO Box 42578, T212281, F212953. *Bush Homes of East Africa Ltd*, PO Box 56923, T571647, F571665, www.bush-homes.co.ke   *Desert Rose Camels*, PO Box 44801, Barclays Plaza, T228936, F891716, organize walking and camel safaris in the Northern Frontier District of Kenya. They also run the lovely *Desert Rose Lodge*, which is located between Baragoi and South Horr, PO Box 24397, Nairobi, T577374-9, F564945, ras@swiftkenya.com   Lake and deep-sea fishing can be organized by *Finfoot*, PO Box 2434, T891664, F884016. *Bunson Travel Service*, Pan Africa House, PO Box 45456, Standard St, T337712, F214120, bunson@africaonline.co.ke, is a good, reliable, well-established travel and tour agent. Does flight and rail bookings, car hire, safaris and hotel bookings. *Flight Centre*, Lakhamshi House 2nd Floor, Biashara St, T210024, F334207, fcswwat@arcc.or.ke   Recommended travel agent, they also sell overland trips (*Exodus, Encounter*, etc) as well as various safaris. Their one drawback is the 4% fee they charge for using credit cards. *Fly Air Ltd*, T226176, flyair@form-net.com   Efficient travel agency who do not impose credit card fees.

There are numerous other tour operators based in Nairobi where you should be able to get fairly reliable information and book safaris, etc. They include *Abercrombie and Kent*, 6th Floor, Bruce House, Standard St, PO Box 59749, T334955/6/7, F215752, www.abercrombiekent.com   who arrange some of the most luxurious safaris in Kenya. *Acacia Trails Ltd*, PO Box 14249, T446261.   *Express Kenya Co* (*American Express* representative), PO Box 40433, Standard St, T334722. *AA Travel*, Hurlingham Shopping Centre, PO Box 14982, T339700. *Africa Safaris Ltd*, Rehema House, 3rd Floor, Kaunda/Standard St, opposite *New Stanley Hotel*, PO Box 69513, T213186, F213254. *Africa Veldt Safaris Ltd*, Ngong View Rise, Karen, PO Box 35505, T884439.   *Bike Treks*, T446371, F442439, www.angelfire.com/sk/

Kenya

biketreks Organize reasonably priced walking/cycling tours, supported by a back-up vehicle, including a 3-day Masai Mara safari. Excellent value. *Call of Africa Safaris*, Uganda House, 3rd Floor, PO Box 27767, T229729 (T604994 after hours), F604994, callafrica@africaonline.co.ke Recommended for their quality of service. *Dallago Tours and Safaris*, Mercantile House, 1st Floor, Room 133, Koinance St, PO Box 66416, T331562, F245174. New and expanding company receiving good reviews. *East African Wildlife Safaris*, PO Box 43747, T605350, F216528, eaws@form-net.com Very upmarket safaris on offer. *EcoFarm Holidays*, PO Box 3522, T713869, F729572, www.ecofarm.co.ke, specialize in introducing travellers to the local people – walking, biking, tree planting and fishing are some of the activities on offer. *Hiking and Cycling Kenya*, Arrow House, 2nd Floor, Koinange St, PO Box 39439, T218336, F224212, offer a range of cycling trips to the Masai Mara, in addition to trekking. The safaris are vehicle assisted, carrying the baggage and supplies. Reasonably priced, excellent value. *Hotel and Adventure Travel*, PO Box 55182, T/F882774. *Kenia Tours and Safaris*, PO Box 19730, Jubilee Insurance Bldg, Kaunda/ Wabera St, T223699, F217671, also have an office at *Iqbal Hotel*. Good, cheap camping tours. *Lobelia Tours and Safaris Ltd*, Moi Av/Moktar Daddah St, Jct Krisna Mansion, Room 59, PO Box 12459, T211426. Specialize in mountain safaris. Recommended. *Micato Safaris* PO Box 43374, T220743, F336138, www.africansafari.org/micato Long-established Kenyan upmarket safari operators. *Predators Safari Club*, 1st Floor Embassy House, Harambee St, T214369, funtours@swiftkenya.com, specialize in all kinds of tours to Tanzania and Kenya. *Safari Camp Services*, on the corner of Koinange St/Moktar Daddah St, PO Box 44801, T228936, F212160, www.safaricampserv.com This company is famous for their long-established and well-recommended *Turkana Bus* and *Wildlife Bus* services, which offer excellent value to the budget traveller. Camel trekking options are also available in combination with the *Turkana Bus* trip. *Safari Seekers*, 5th Floor, Jubilee Insurance Exchange, Kaunda St, Rm 522/544, PO Box 9165, T226206, F334585, safseekers@form-net.com *Savage Wilderness Safaris Ltd*, whitewater river rafting on several Kenyan rivers, PO Box 44827, Thigiri Rd, T/F521590 (European office: 22 Wilson Av, Henley, Oxon, RG9 1ET, UK, T01491-574752, USA office: 925 31 St Av, Seattle, WA 98122, T206-3231220). *Savuka Tours and Safaris Ltd*, Pan Africa House, 4th Floor, Kenyatta Av, T215256. Offers very good value for budget travellers, including student card reductions. Operate a keenly priced tented camp in the Masai Mara. Open to negotiation on prices. *Sights of Africa Safari Company*, Asili Co-operative Building 4th Floor, Moi Av/Muranga Rd, PO Box 6251, T247439, F242415 (linked to *Tanzannature*, Arusha PO Box 13317). Highly recommended company. *Span African Adventure and Safaris*, PO Box 3288, T/F221112. Promise competitively priced safaris in Kenya and Tanzania, also treks of Mt Kenya and Mt Kilimanjaro. *Special Camping Safaris and Whistling Thorns*, PO Box 51512, T350720, speccampsaf@thorntree.com, organizes safaris in the Ngong Hills, camping safaris to lakes Baringo, Borofia and Nakura, plus the Masai Mara. *SunTrek Tours and Travel Ltd*, PO Box 48146, T443469, suntreksafaris.com *Tobs Golf Safaris*, PO Box 20146, T721722, F722015, www.kenya-golf-safaris.com Golf specialist. *Travel Concepts Tours and Safaris Ltd*, Town House, 3rd Floor, Kaunda St, PO Box 52296, T230049. Offer Mt Kenya and Mt Kilimanjaro treks and game safaris. *United Touring International*, PO Box 42196, Muindi Mbingu St, T331960. *Twiga Tours*, 4th Floor, Victor House, Kimathi St, PO Box 14365, T332364, F337330, www.twiga-tours.com

Tours of Nairobi Most operators will be able to arrange a tour of Nairobi itself and this is a very useful way of familiarizing yourself with the layout of the city, as well as seeing some of the sites that are further out. The tours will usually include a trip to the City Market, which you may well want to return to later, the Parliament buildings, and the National Museum. For a list of safari companies both in Kenya and overseas, see page 45.

Organizing your own safari If you're on a tight budget it requires careful planning. A 4WD is essential; Land Rover, Pajero, or Suzuki for budget travellers. Minimum engine size should be 1300. Anything smaller cannot cope with the mud that forms on rainy days. Make sure that the car is not more than 2 years old. Travellers have reported that *Crossways* (see Car hire below) proved to be very helpful. *Tourist Consultant Kenya*, Beaver House, 1st Floor, Tom Mboya Rd. This agency is highly recommended because they tailor-make the arrangements for the safari to fit your budget, and make the necessary calls to their recommended firms. They are also helpful for other activities like mountaineering.

Transport

There are plenty of buses, *matatus* and taxis, all of which are very cheap by western stan-   **Local** dards. Buses and *matatus* are almost always very crowded and you should beware of pick-pockets when travelling in them. **Matatus**, usually Nissan minibuses, are frequently dangerously overcrowded, poorly maintained and have a very poor safety record. Most *matatu* rides within Nairobi cost US$0.13-0.19. **Bus**: Central Bus Station, T246067. The main city bus terminal is located at the end of River Rd and there are main bus stops outside the *Hilton Hotel* on Moi Av, outside Nation House on Tom Mboya St and outside the General Post Office on Kenyatta Av. **Taxis** are available outside cinemas, restaurants, hotels and at official taxi stands. Your hotel will order one for you. They cannot be hailed in the street. It is recommended that you should always take a taxi if you want to get around at night. A taxi to the airport costs approximately US$12, but you may be charged more on arrival.

Car hire   Cars can be rented easily in Kenya, with or without a driver. You will usually need to be over 25 years of age and have an international drivers' licence. Companies include **Avis Rent a Car**, PO Box 49795, T336794; **Budget**, PO Box 59767, Parliament Lane, Haile Selassie Av, T337154; **Central Hire a Car**, PO Box 49439, Fehda Towers, Standard St, T222888, good value with comprehensive insurance coverage; **Crossways**, on Banda St, T223949, F214372, can arrange hire cars suitable for organizing your own safari; **Europ Car**, PO Box 49420; **Glory Car Hire Ltd**, Diamond Building, Tubman Rd, PO Box 66969, T225024, F331533, also Ground Floor, New Hurlingham Plaza, T722819. A range of 2WD and 4WD vehicles, usually accept national as well as international driving licences; **Habib's Cars Ltd**, PO Box 48095, Agip House, Haile Selassie Av, T220463, F220985; **Hertz**, PO Box 42196, T331960, better value than the multinational companies; **Let's Go Travel**, ABC Place, Waiyaki Way, Westlands, PO Box 60342, T447151, F447270, info@letsgosafari.com **Payless Car Hire and Tours Ltd**, *Hilton Hotel*, Shimba St, PO Box 49713, T223581/2, F223584; **Naz Car Hire**, Clyde House, Kimathi St, T246171, F221296. You can expect to pay between US$20 and US$40 per day plus a mileage charge of about US$0.20 per km and rates are usually negotiable if for a longer period. It is worth asking around to compare prices. 4WD hire will cost between US$30-60 per day plus insurance. Rates obviously vary, but try *Central Hire a Car* for the best deal.

  Driving in Nairobi is a bit of an art and you will have to get used to a large number of round-abouts with rather bizarre lane systems. The right of way is usually (but not always) given to traffic already on the roundabout. Be prepared for a lot of hooting, traffic-light jumping and the odd pothole. Parking is a problem and you will be pestered by parking boys. Policies towards these vary although there is no evidence that it is necessary to pay them to ensure the safety of your vehicle. There is a multi-storey car park at *Intercontinental Hotel* (around US$1 per hr).

Air   The main airport is Jomo Kenyatta International Airport, T822111, located about 15 km   **Long-distance** southeast of the city, connected by a good dual carriageway. There is also Wilson Airport, 6 km south of the city, on Langata Rd, from which smaller planes, including many internal charter flights, leave. If you are travelling on an arranged tour you will probably be met at the airport by your driver who will hold up a notice with your name or the name of the tour company on it. If you are travelling independently you can either take a taxi or bus into Nairobi. Be sure to agree on the price into town (it should be around US$12). You can find a taxi from the airport to town cheaper from outside the airport environs, because some taxis cannot find a return fare to town. Cost is around US$9-11 but you'll need to bargain. Bus No 34 runs every 20 mins from the airport into town. There is a stop opposite the new post office on Kenyatta Av or at the *Ambassador Hotel*. The bus service runs from 0630-2030. Journey time is 30-60 mins. Cost US$0.50. You can change money at the airport 24 hrs a day. For international services into Nairobi see Essentials, page 74.

  Kenya Airways has daily flights to **Kisumu**, **Malindi** and **Mombasa** from Kenyatta Airport. Charter fly to Masai Mara, Malindi, Lamu and other destinations.

👉 ## Beryl Markham

Beryl Markham was a champion horse-trainer, record-breaking aviator, author and celebrated beauty, with two members of the British Royal Family among her many lovers. Her style was formed by a unique childhood which embraced both traditional African and European ways of life.

Beryl was born in Leicestershire in 1902 and, when Beryl was two, the family sold up and sailed for East Africa where her father took a job as dairy manager for Lord Delamere at Equator Ranch near Njoro, Kenya. Home was a rondavel, a mud hut with a thatched roof, and sacking covering the windows.

Beryl grew up with local Nandi house servants and farm workers and their children with whom she formed an enduring bond, going barefoot, eating with her hand and wearing a shulen, an African shirt. Swahili was Beryl's first language.

At nine Beryl was sent to board at Nairobi European School, but she ran away after less than a year, returning to Njoro, the stables and her Kipsigis companions.

Ten years later Beryl began training horses, first for a neighbour, Ben Birkbeck, and then for Delamere at his nearby estate, Soysambu.

In 1928, Kenyan society was in a frenzy of anticipation for the visit of Edward, Prince of Wales, and his younger brother Henry, Duke of Gloucester. Beryl and her then husband, the sophisticated, very well-off but rather frail Mansfield Markham, took up residence for the duration at the Muthaiga Club. In next to no time Beryl had secured both Royal trophies.

When the Royal tour ended at the end of November, cut short by the illness of King George V, Beryl, although six months pregnant travelled to London where the Duke of Gloucester met her on the quay side and installed her in a suite at the Grosvenor Hotel, close to Buckingham Palace. When the Duke was out of town she would tryst with the Prince of Wales. Mansfield Markham came from Kenya for the birth of Gervaise Markham in February.

In the London of 1929 flying became a very fashionable pastime. Both of Beryl's Royal lovers became aviators, and Beryl took some flying lessons before returning to Kenya in 1930. The Prince of Wales revisited. Karen Blixen's coffee farm was failing and about to be sold, and Denys Finch-Hatton, adored lover of both Karen Blixen and Beryl, was killed when his plane crashed at Voi.

This tragedy did not deter Beryl, and under the tutelage of her instructor and lover, Tom Campbell-Black, she gained a pilot's licence in July 1931. In 1933 she got her 'B' licence which allowed her to work as a commercial pilot – the first woman in Kenya to do so.

One evening in the bar of the White Rhino in Nyeri a wealthy local flying enthusiast J C Carberry dared Beryl to fly solo across the Atlantic from east to west, 'against the wind'. Carberry offered to bankroll the flight. The feat had never been achieved in 39 previous attempts. Beryl ordered the recently designed Percival Vega Gull, a single-engined monoplane, from De Havillands at Gravesend. At the end of 1935 she flew to London in her Leopard Moth, hopping across Africa and Europe with Bror Blixen, a former lover and white hunter husband of Karen, as passenger. The Daily Express bought exclusive rights to Beryl's story and the audacity of the attempt allied to Beryl's beauty created a fever of interest as she waited patiently for fair weather. On 4 September the winds had dropped. Beryl, in a white leather flying suit and helmet, squeezed into the cramped cockpit with five

---

Air Kenya, based at Wilson Airport, Nairobi, PO Box 30357, T501601, F602951, resvns@airkenya.com Has scheduled flights to **Amboseli**, **Kilimanjaro**, **Kiwayu**, **Lamu**, **Mombasa**, **Malindi**, **Nanyuki**, **Masai Mara** and **Samburu**. Wilson Airport is 4 km from Nairobi city centre.

Road Bus: the long-distance bus station is on Landhies Rd. There are at least daily departures to almost every destination. The timetable is fairly flexible. For a long journey you will be told to arrive at 0700 or earlier, but the bus will not go until it is full. For information and bookings there are a number of coach company offices along Accra Rd. There are many companies to choose for buses between **Nairobi** and **Mombasa** and they go frequently, taking

flasks of coffee, some cold meat, dried fruit, nuts and fruit pastilles and a hip flask of brandy. There was no room for a life jacket. Edgar Percival, the plane's designer, swung the propeller. With a wave, Beryl rumbled down the runway and climbed slowly into the air. It was close to twilight, just before 1900. Edgar Percival shook his head and observed to onlookers, 'Well, that's the last we shall see of Beryl'.

After a flight of over 21 hours Beryl saw land, but she was on the last tank of fuel and the engine began to splutter. She selected a landing field but ditched in a Nova Scotia bog.

The Atlantic flight made Beryl a sensation in America – a crowd of 5,000 awaited her flight to New York – there were press conferences, radio interviews, banquets and guest spots on comedy shows. This was all cut short when she learned that Tom Campbell-Black, her flying instructor, had been killed in a flying accident. Beryl sailed back to England. She filled in time with an affair with Jack Doyle, the Irish heavyweight boxer.

In 1937 she returned to America to do some screen tests for a film of her epic flight – which were not a success. While in California she met Raoul Schumacher, five years younger than Beryl, tall, born in Minneapolis, comfortably off, and good company, who was working as a writer in Hollywood. They produced West with the Night, *a memoir of Beryl's childhood and transatlantic flight. Although Beryl was credited as author, it seems clear that Raoul provided the structure and style. It was published in 1942 to excellent reviews and was on the bestseller lists. Ernest Hemingway judged it a 'bloody wonderful book'.*

Raoul and Beryl married in 1942 but Beryl took a string of lovers and in 1946 Raoul

moved out. Beryl continued to amuse herself in her accustomed manner, had a farewell fling with the singer Burl Ives, and in 1949 moved back to Kenya.

She stayed in the guest cottage of Forest Farm near Nanyuki, owned by the Norman family. Forest Farm was managed by a Dane, Jorgen Thrane, who became Beryl's lover. Beryl bought a small farm nearby and Jorgen managed that as well.

A trip to see her father in South Africa got her in the mood for training horses again. Back in Kenya she set to with a purpose, and over the next 15 years she was outstandingly successful, training winners for all the Kenyan Classic Races, and winning the Derby four times.

In 1965, the relationship with Jorgen waning, Beryl found a property in South Africa going for a song and she relocated her training stables there, but the move was not a success. Returning to Kenya in 1970, Beryl managed to get her trainer's licence back and she had some triumphs including a fifth Derby win. She carried on training until 1983, although the latter part of this period was marred by continual squabbles with jockeys, owners and the stewards.

The Jockey Club made her an honorary member and allocated her a cottage on the Ngong Racecourse. Interest in her book was revived and a reissue in 1983 sold over 1,000,000 copies. Beryl enjoyed a revival of her fame as a celebrity and she was the subject of considerable television and newspaper interest. Greeting well-wishers with a cigarette in one hand and a tumbler of vodka in the other, however, she could be less than gracious to visitors.

Beryl died in 1986 and her ashes were scattered at Cemetery Corner on Ngong Racecourse.

8-10 hrs, the standard services costing around US$10. Two luxury services operate the Nairobi-Mombasa route. One is called **The Connection**, operated by *Inside Africa Safaris Ltd*. They also operate a courier service. The coach leaves at 0930 from Jubilee House Bldg, Wabera St, T223304, F215448. This very comfortable service costs US$16. **Sav-Line**, bookings c/o Savage Camping Tours, T228236, also offers a/c 18-seater minibus shuttle services between Nairobi and Mombasa costing US$16. The **Akamba Bus**, Lagos Rd, off Latema Rd, T221779, is a private company offering a very good level of service. Buses go from Nairobi to a variety of long-haul destinations both within Kenya and to neighbouring countries. The *Akamba Bus* departs for Kampala at 0700 and 1900. *Akamba* buses are not the cheapest option but are well maintained and have a good safety record. **Tawfiq Bus Services**, T253031, are fairly

Kenya

reliable, but vehicles are less well maintained. *Mombasa Liners*, on Accra Rd, T241564, F332009, offer one of the cheapest services at about US$6.

Since 1983 when the Kenya/Tanzania border was reopened there has been increasing traffic crossing to take advantage of the game parks in Tanzania – in particular the Serengeti and Ngorongoro Crater. There are a number of shuttle buses each day to and from **Arusha**, US$20-25, taking about 5 hrs. There are 0800 and 1400 departures from both Nairobi and Arusha. *Riverside Shuttle,* c/o *Style Travel & Tours*, Koinange St, T219020 (or book through an agent such as *Let's Go*), travel to the Uganda border at **Busia**, about 10 hrs, US$9. Not a journey for the faint-hearted. The buses frequently double-up as cargo carriers and are loaded to over-capacity. The *Akamba Bus* service offers a safer and more reliable alternative to many of the cheaper companies.

Shared taxis and *matatus*: shared taxis, usually Peugeot station wagons, are more expensive than *matatus* (minibuses) but are quicker and safer. They generally take 7 people and leave when full, often early in the morning. Offices in Nairobi are around Accra Rd and River Rd. Some examples of fares and costs are **Kisumu** US$12, 4 hrs; **Nakuru** US$6, 2 hrs; and **Tanzanian border** US$6, 2 hrs.

Train For details of train services, timetables and fares, see page 80.

Directory

Airline offices International: *Air Canada*, Kantaria House, 2nd Fl, Muimdi Nbingu St, T218776. *Air France*, International House, 2nd Floor, Mama Ngina St, T217501/2. *Air India*, Jeevan Bharati Building, Harambee Av, T334788. *Air Madagascar*, *Hilton Hotel*, 1st Floor, City Hall Way, T225286. *Air Malawi*, Hilton Hotel Arcade, City Hall Way, T333683. *Air Mauritius*, International House, Mezz Floor, Mama Ngina St, T229166. *Air Seychelles*, Lonrho House, 6th Floor, Standard St, T229359. *Air Tanzania*, Chester House, Koinange St, T336224. *Air Zaire*, Consolidated House, 1st Floor, Koinange St, T230142. *Air Zimbabwe*, Chester House, Ground Floor, Koinanage St, T339524. *Alitalia*, *Hilton Hotel*, City Hall Way, T224361/3/4. *American Airlines*, 20th Century Plaza, 2nd Floor (Flying Rickshaw Ltd) Mama Ngina St, T242557. *British Airways*, International House, 11th Floor, Mama Ngina St, T244430. *Cameroon Airlines*, Rehani House, 9th Floor, Kenyatta Av, T224743. *EgyptAir*, *Hilton Hotel* Arcade, City Hall Way, T226821. *El Al*, KCS Building, 9th Floor, Mama Ngina St, T228123/4. *Emirates*, Viewpark Towers, 20th Floor, T212990. *Emirates* have been world airline of the year for the past couple of years. If you do not have a return ticket to Europe they offer significantly cheaper fares (via Dubai) than the major carriers. The new aircraft have video cameras mounted outside the aircraft that enable you to have a bird's-eye view on your personal video screen as you taxi along the runway. *Ethiopian Airlines*, Bruce House, Muindi Mbingu St, T330837. *Gulf Air*, Global Travel, International House, Mama Ngina St, T217558. Offer very competitive prices to Europe if you have not got a return ticket, just a little more expensive than *Emirates* but markedly cheaper than the major airlines. *Iberia*, *Hilton Hotel*, Mama Ngina St, T331648. *Kenya Airways*, Barclays Plaza, 5th Floor, Loita St, T210771, F336252. *Olympic Airlines*, *Hilton Hotel*, City Hall Way, T338026. *Pakistan International Airlines*, ICEA Building, Banda St, T333900. *Qantas Airways*, see *British Airways*, *Regional Air*, Mezzanine, *Grand Regency Hotel*, T311623, F311609. *Royal Swazi National Airlines*, KCS House, 4th Floor, Mama Ngina St, T210670. *Saudia Arabian Airlines*, Anniversary Towers, Mezz 11, University Way, T230337. *South African Airways*, Lonrho House, 1st Floor, Kaunda St, T229663, 1st Floor, Standard St, T245520/1. *Swissair*, 11th Floor, A M Bank House, University Way, T250288/9, F331437. *Uganda Airlines*, Uganda House, Kenyatta Av, 1st Floor, T221354. **Domestic and charter:** *Africair*, PO Box 45646, T501210. *Air Kenya*, Wilson Airport, T605745 (reservations), F602951, info@airkenya.com *Eagle Aviation Ltd*, scheduled flights within Kenya, charter flights available, Nairobi T606015/6, F606017. *Equator Airlines*, Wilson Airport, T221177. *Kenya Airways*, Airways Terminal, Koinange St, T332750.

Banks There are numerous branches of *Barclays* and *Standard Chartered* in central Nairobi. They all have ATMs accepting VISA cards. The largest *Barclays* is at the corner of Kenyatta Av and Moi Av, where it is possible to withdraw US dollars on a VISA card. The *Standard Chartered Bank*, half-way along Kenyatta Av, has ATMs protected by guards for anyone feeling nervous.

Communications **Internet** A vast number of places now offer internet access. As well as some of the more expensive hotels, options range from smart internet cafés with fast reliable connections, to tiny corner shops that have just one computer and erratic connections. Here is a selection: *Education Centre*, Union Towers, 3rd Floor, Moi Av, edutrain@nbnet.co.uk, US$1.75 per 15 mins. *Unique Communications* is a new private phone, fax and email facility based at Rattansi Educational Trust near corner of Monrovia/Koinange St, T243302. *The Cyber Centre*, Norwich Union House, 5th Floor, T217406, cybercentre@nbnet.co.ke, public access internet and email services. *Browse Internet Café*, Norwich Union House, 4th Floor, T251947. *Cybersafaris* internet café is located in *Simmers Restaurant* on the corner of Kenyatta Av and Muindi Mbinga St, internet and email services at less than US$6 per hr, ryansnider@hotmail.com *Cybervore*, at the *Carnivore Restaurant*, Langata Rd, T501775, where there are 14 terminals (owned by africaonline, a major internet service provider). *Hard Rock Café*, Barclays Plaza, Loita St, T220802/3. *Vyber Rap Bureau*, Embassy House, 2nd Floor, info@thorntree.com *Chase Cybercafé*, Gilfillon House, Kenyatta Av, info@chasecyber.com *Zenith Interactive*, Room 16, Uganda House, 2nd Floor, Kenyatta Av, KSh100 for 15 mins, KSh300 for 1 hr. Mageso Chambers, 4th Floor, (opposite *Orbit Sportshouse*) Moi Av run by tony_gic@yahoo.com KSh100 for 15 mins, KSh350 for 1 hr.

Post office: Moi Av, half-way between Kenyatta Av and Tubman Rd on the east side, T227401. There is also a post office on Haile Selassie Av, T228441, where you will find the fairly reliable, and free, poste restante. Post offices are open 0800-1230 and 1400-1700.

Telecommunications almost opposite the post office on Haile Selassie Av, is the Extelcoms office from which you can make international phone calls (3 min minimum period of use) or send faxes. You can also make calls from the Kenyatta Conference Centre – the telephone exchange is on the ground floor and it is usually much quieter than the post office. Alternatively go to the 1st floor of the 20th Century Palace, Mama Ngina St, close to the cinema, US$3 per min. Other telephone services include *Danas Communications Centre*, Kaunda St, T223655, F243890; *Philmark Communications*, PO Box 60990, T217505; *Phone Home*, The Mall, Westlands, PO Box 34535, T443866.

You can only buy phonecards from the Extelcoms office

Other places that have films, concerts and talks include the *Alliance Française*, ICEA Building, Kenyatta Av, T340054; *American Cultural Centre*, National Bank Building, Harambee Av, T337877; *British Council*, ICEA Building, Kenyatta Av, T334855; *French Cultural Centre*, Maison Française, Loita St, T336263; *Goethe Institute*, Maendeleo House, Monrovia St, T224640; *Italian Cultural Institute*, Prudential Building, Wabera St, T220278; *Japan Information Centre*, Matungulu House, Mamlaka Rd, T340520; *Mzizi Cultural Centre*, 6th Floor Sonalux House, Moi Av, very close to *Hilton Hotel*, and in same block as the *Zanzibar Curio Shop*. Box 48955, T245364/6, F245366.

Cultural centres

Algerian Embassy, Comcraft House, Haile Selassie Av, T213864. *Australia*, PO Box 30360, ICIPE House, Riverside Drive, T445034/8. *Austria*, PO Box 30560, City House, Wabera St, T228281. *Belgium*, PO Box 30461, Limuru Rd, T741565. *British High Commission*, Upper Hill Rd, PO Box 30133, T714699, F719082, information@nairobi.mail.fco.gov.uk *Burundi*, PO Box 44439, Development House, Moi Av, opposite the Milimani Police Station, T219005. *Canada*, PO Box 30481, Comcraft House, Haile Selassie Av, T214804. *Denmark*, PO Box 40412, HFCK Building, Koinange St, T331088/89/90. *Djibouti*, PO Box 59528, T48089. *Egypt*, PO Box 30285, Harambee Plaza, 7th Floor, T250764, Fourways Towers, 9th Floor, Muindi Mbingu St, T224709. *Eritrea*, PO Box 38651, T443163. *Ethiopia*, PO Box 45198, State House Av, T723027. *France*, PO Box 41784, Barclays Plaza, 9th Floor, Loita St, T339783. Issues visas for Togo, Senegal, Burkina Faso, Mauritania and the Central African Republic. *Germany*, PO Box 30180, Williamson House, Ngong Av, T712527. *Ireland* (consulate), Waumini House 5th Floor, Chiromo Rd, T444367. *Israel*, PO Box 30354, T722182. *Italy*, PO Box 30107, International Life House, Mama Ngina St, T337356. *Japan*, PO Box 60202, Kenyatta Av, T332955. *Malawi*, PO Box 30453, Standard St, T440569. *Morocco*, PO Box 61098, T222264. *Mozambique*, PO Box 66923, T221979. *Netherlands*, PO Box 41537, Uchumi House, Nkrumah Av, T227111, Holland@Form-net.com *Nigeria*, PO Box 30516, Hurlingham, T564116. *Norway*, Royal Norwegian Embassy, PO Box 46363, HFCK Bldg, Rehani House 8th Floor, Kenyatta Av, T337121/2/4. *RD Congo*, PO Box 48106, Electricity House, Harambee Av, T229771. *Rwanda*, PO Box 48579, International Life House, Mama Ngina St, T575977, Mon-Fri 0900-1630. *Saudi Arabia*, PO Box 58297, T762781. *South African High Commission*, PO Box 42441, Lonrho House,17th Floor, Standard St, T215616. *Spain*, PO Box 45503, Bruce House, Standard St, T335711. *Sudan*, PO Box 74059, Minet ICDC House, 7th Floor, T720853. *Sweden*, PO Box 30600, T229043/4/5, F218908. *Switzerland*, PO Box 30752, T228736. *Tanzania*, PO Box 47790, Continental House, T331056. *Zambia*, PO Box 48741, Nyerere Rd, T724796. *Zimbabwe*, PO Box 30806, Minet ICDC House, Mamlaka Rd, T721045/49/71.

Embassies, high commissions & consulates

Kenya

Medical services

Hospitals There are 2 private hospitals which have good facilities and staff: *Nairobi Hospital*, Argwings Kodhek Rd, T722160; and *Aga Khan Hospital*, Limuru Rd, Parklands, T742531. Avoid the *Kenyatta Hospital*, if you can; although it is free it is not worth trying to save the money as the wait can be so long. If you are planning to travel in more isolated areas, consider the *Flying Doctors Society of Africa*, PO Box 30125, T501301, F502699. It provides excellent value should an emergency arise: US$25 for 2 months' membership within a 500-km radius of Wilson Airport, US$50 outside 500 km. **Pharmacies** These are found in all shopping centres but are generally expensive. Try *Jaga Chemists* on Koinange St, T215654, open Mon-Sat. The major hospitals (see above) have 24-hr pharmacies. Vaccinations are available from *City Hall Clinic* on Mama Ngina St, open mornings only.

Places of worship

All Saint's Cathedral is on Kenyatta Av close to Uhuru Park and the *Catholic Holy Family Minor Basilica* is situated on the corner of Parliament Av and City Hall Way. Perhaps the most beautiful of all the places of worship is the *Jamia Mosque*, near the City Market. It was built in 1925 in the Indian style and is set in a lively part of town close to the City Market.

Useful addresses

Police Central Police Station is on University Way, T222222, Nairobi HQ, T717777. Always inform the police of any incidents – you will need a police form for any insurance claims. In emergencies dial 999.

Excursions from Nairobi

Bomas of Kenya

Bomas of Kenya are found in the Nairobi suburb of Langata, 2 km past the main gate of Nairobi National Park (see below). A boma is a traditional homestead. Here programmes based on traditional dances of the different tribes of Kenya are presented. They are not in fact performed by people of the actual tribe but are a professional group called the *Harambee Dancers*. The dancers finish with a lively display of acrobatics and tumbling. The bomas form an open-air museum that shows the different lifestyles of each tribe. There is also a bar and a restaurant that serves a selection of grilled meat specialities. ■ *The shows begin at 1430 and costs US$2. If you are travelling independently you can get here on the matatu from outside Development House on Moi Av which takes about 30 mins.*

Langata Giraffe Centre

Set in 6 ha of indigenous forest, the Langata Giraffe Centre is about 20 km out of the city centre near the Hardy Estate Shopping Centre. It is funded by the African Foundation for Endangered Wildlife and houses a number of Rothschild's giraffes. To date the centre has rescued, hand reared and released about 500 orphaned giraffes back into the wild. The Rothschild's giraffe is no longer threatened with imminent extinction, having tripled in number and been successfully reintroduced to four of Kenya's national parks. Money raised by ticket sales is used to fund an education centre promoting conservation, visited by schoolchildren from all over Kenya. There is information about the giraffes on display, designed to be interesting to children. The young visitors' artistic interpretations of East African wildlife adorn the walls. You can watch and feed the giraffes from a raised wooden structure. The centre is also an excellent spot for bird-watching. ■ *Daily 0900-1730, US$6.50 for adults and US$3.25 for children, T891658, F891698. If you do not have transport you can get there on the No 24 bus.*

Sleeping There is a luxury, on-site sleeping option at the giraffe centre: **L** *Giraffe Manor*, Koitobos Rd, PO Box 15004, T891078, F890949, www.giraffemanor.com Money raised goes to support the centre. The red-brick, ivy-covered house is redolent of an English country manor house, set in beautiful woodland and gardens. Still a family home, there are four double bedrooms with bathrooms on offer, as well as excellent food. A copy of *Bringing up Daisy*, an account of Lady Betty Leslie-Melville's first adopted giraffe and the subsequent successful breeding programme is available for perusal. Intrepid visitors can 'kiss' the giraffes from the conservatory, while feeding these elegant mammals a biscuit clenched between their teeth.

This is a private sanctuary and has a splendid range of birds. You must book in advance, and parties are accompanied by an ornithologist with a well-trained eye. Binoculars are strongly recommended. ■ *US$5, T225255.* **Langata Bird Sanctuary**

This park is just 10 km southeast of Nairobi's city centre and despite its proximity to the city is home to over 100 recorded species of mammals. It is Kenya's oldest national park having been established in 1946. You are very likely to see zebra, giraffe, gazelle, baboons, buffalo, ostrich, vultures, hippos and various antelope. This is one of the best parks for spotting black rhinos – the area is not remote enough for poachers, and Nairobi National Park has proved to be one of the most successful rhino sanctuaries in Kenya. **Nairobi National Park** *1° 18' S, 37° E*

The concentration of wildlife is greatest in the dry season when areas outside the park have dried up. Water sources are greater in the park as a number of small dams have been built along the Mbagathi River. There are also many birds, up to 500 permanent and migratory species in a year. The park is small, only 117 sq km, but is well worth visiting if you are staying in Nairobi.

To the south of the national park is the Kitengela Game Conservation Area and Migration Corridor leading to the Athi and Kaputiei plains. The herbivores disperse over these plains following the rains and return to park during the dry season.

In July 2001, Charles Njonjo, Chairman of the Kenya Wildlife Service, announced plans to introduce tigers into the national parks, requesting the India Wildlife Service to provide a pair for Nairobi National Park.

There are a number of minibus tours for either a morning or an afternoon, arranged by any of the tour companies in Nairobi. The cost can vary if you are lucky you may be able to negotiate a price of less than US$40 per person, although you are more likely to be quoted a price upwards of US$45.

Sleeping *Nairobi Park Services Campsite*, PO Box 54867, Magadi Rd off Langata Rd (past Brook House School), T/F2-890325, shling@net2000ke.com Opened in Aug 1997 this campsite offers budget facilities, bars and restaurant. Tented accommodation with 2-storey dormitory and bandas are expected to be available soon. Hot showers, laundry facilities, western-style toilets, secure fenced compound, vehicle parking, TV/video. US$3 per night. Can arrange game drives and camel safaris. Managed by Brendan Black and Dutch Pete. *For national park costs, see page 85*

Located close to the main entrance of the Nairobi National Park, this is part of the park and was opened in 1963. Orphaned and sick animals are brought from all over **Animal Orphanage**

Kenya

Nairobi National Park

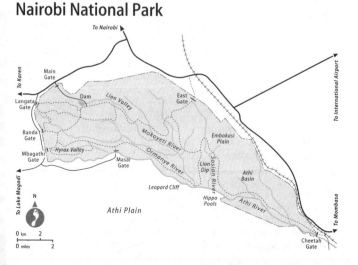

To Nairobi

To Karen

Main Gate

Langata Gate

Dam

Lion Valley

East Gate

To International Airport

Banda Gate

Mbagathi Gate

Hyrax Valley

Masal Gate

Mokoyeti River

Ormanye River

Embakasi Plain

Lion Dip

Sosian River

Athi Basin

Leopard Cliff

Hippo Pools

Athi River

To Lake Magadi

N

Athi Plain

To Mombasa

Cheetah Gate

0 km 2

0 miles 2

Rhino conservation initiatives

Within two decades 1970-90 Kenya lost 98% of its wild rhino population due to poaching. The black rhino, Diceros bicornis, was classified as Critically Endangered in the IUCN 1996 Red List of Threatened Animals. The southern white rhino, Ceratotherium simum, was rescued from virtual extinction 100 years ago when remaining numbers in South Africa were estimated at less than 100. By 1999 the numbers were estimated to be over 10,000. Figures released by the WWF in August 2000 showed that the current conservation measures have proved successful with the total number of rhinos up to 13,000 in 1999 from 8,300 in 1992.

However, these improved figures disguise the fact that two of the six African sub-species remain at critically low numbers. The western black rhino are estimated to be reduced to about 10 animals scattered across northern Cameroon and the remaining northern white rhino are estimated at around 25 animals in the Democratic Republic of Congo. The measures required to conserve rhino habitat are expensive, estimated by IUCN/WWF at US$1,000 per sq km per annum.

The demand for rhino horn used in traditional Chinese medicine, not as is commonly believed as an aphrodisiac, and for making ornately decorated dagger handles for oil-rich wealthy Middle East clients continues to pose a threat to the African rhino. A single horn can earn up to $15,000 on the black market, a major economic incentive for an impoverished people.

There are a number of rhino conservation initiatives in Kenya. The David Sheldrick Trust has played a pivotal role in the reversal of the near extinction of rhinos by financing several conservation initiatives and co-ordinated a joint approach through the Rhino Action Group. The Trust runs a Sanctuary in Nairobi National Park hand-rearing orphaned rhino and elephant calves, later releasing them back into secure sanctuaries. The first high-security rhino sanctuary was set up in

Lake Nakuru National Park, followed by a second electrically enclosed sanctuary at Tsavo West. Nairobi National Park has been successful in providing a safe rhino environment and Tsavo East has the only unfenced sanctuary in the country run by Kenya Wildlife Service, containing an estimated 50 rhino. These animals are provided with armed game rangers for 24-hour protection. Most of Kenya's wildlife lives outside the national parks and the Ngare Sergoi Rhino Sanctuary, now incorporated into the Lewa Wildlife Conservancy near Isiolo, and the Sweet Waters Rhino Sanctuary within Laikipia Ranch near Nanyuki have also developed successful breeding programmes. Solio Game Ranch, a private sanctuary close to Nyeri, contains the highest density of black rhino in the world. Their conservation and breeding programme has been so successful that Solio Game Ranch has provided stock that has been moved to other sanctuaries, such as Nakuru and Tsavo national parks, and it is planned to stock the new Salient sanctuary in Aberdares National Park – currently under construction.

The Rhino Charge off-road four-wheel-drive motor rally is an annual fund-raising event towards the cost of constructing a rhino sanctuary with a solar-powered electrified enclosure fence in the Salient area of the Aberdares NP. The aim of the project is to provide a safe haven for the black rhino as well as other endangered species, while conserving the rainforest that is also under threat by human habitation. The object of the Rhino Charge competition is to complete the challenging course, calling at the 10 control points, while recording the lowest overall mileage within the allocated period of 10 hours. The race is held in rocky terrain and the vehicles are customized, reinforced with steel plates to withstand the rigors of the course. For further details, contact Rhino Ark T02-748750 (in Kenya) or T020-7610 6118 (in UK) www.rhinoark.org.uk

Kenya to be cared for, the aim being release back into the wild. The centre is most popular at about 1430 when it is feeding time. There is also a Wildlife Conservation Education Centre, which has lectures and video shows about wildlife and guided park and orphanage tours, primarily but not exclusively to educate schools and local communities. In response to criticism, the animals are now housed in more spacious accommodation in a more natural environment. The Kenya Wildlife Service has recently created a **Safari Walk**, to highlight the variety of plants and animals in Kenya and how they affect local people.

Daphne Sheldrick lives in the national park on Magadi Road and set up this orphanage following the death of her husband, the anti-poaching warden of Tsavo National Park, with the emphasis on hand-rearing the animals.

David Sheldrick Orphanage for Rhinos & Elephants

The David Sheldrick Trust has taken a primary role in protecting the few remaining rhinos on private land and has co-ordinated a joint approach through the *Rhino Action Group*, comprising all the conservation groups in Kenya. The trust has played a pivotal role in the reversal of the near extinction of rhinos by financing several initiatives such as the construction of holding enclosures, travelling crates and a loading sledge, veterinary costs and equipping KWD with radio communication links. The hand-rearing of orphaned rhinos and the later relocation and release back into secure sanctuaries requires great expertise, which the trust has perfected over the years. The Trust also plays an active role in de-snaring game in the national parks and in treating the injured animals. They have constructed night stockades for orphaned elephants in Tsavo National Park, as part of their programme to reintroduce them to wild herds. ■ *Visiting hours are limited to 1100-1200 and it is essential to phone before visiting. T891996, www.daphnesheldrick.com Access is usually via the Maintenance Gate (normally closed to the public) on Magadi Rd. The Trust is run on a voluntary basis and entry is by donation.*

This village is well known for wood carving and you can come here to see wood carvers learning their trade. It is found a few kilometres to the east of Nairobi toward Thika and is a popular stopping-off point for tours.

Gikomba Village

These undulating hills with four peaks, said to resemble knuckles, commonly numbered one to four – north to south – are located about 25 km to the southwest of Nairobi on the edge of the Great Rift Valley. Masai legend has it that the hills were created from a handful of earth that a giant clutched after falling over Mount Kilimanjaro. Partly wooded, the hills are no longer rich in animals, but zebra, giraffe and bush-buck remain in large numbers. Plan for at least half-a-day for a round trip.

Ngong Hills

Greater Nairobi

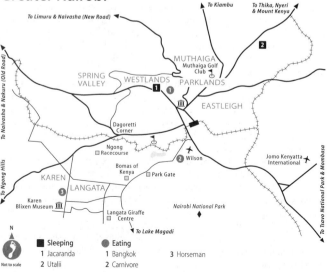

Sleeping
1 Jacaranda
2 Utalii

Eating
1 Bangkok
2 Carnivore
3 Horseman

Not to scale

Born Free

Joy was born in 1910 in Silesia of Austrian parents. In 1937 she came to Kenya to recuperate from a miscarriage. At Christmas 1942, Joy met George Adamson. In 1938 George was appointed Temporary Assistant Game Warden for the Northern Frontier District. In 1944 Joy married George in Nairobi. She was a keen artist and her paintings of flowers had been bought by the Corydon Museum.

Early in 1956, George and his wardens were called to deal with a lion that had killed and eaten a goat-herder. They followed the tracks and came upon an aggressive lioness, which they shot. Nearby were three very young cubs, their eyes still closed, and George took the cubs home where Joy looked after them. Joy kept the smallest, a female she named Elsa.

As Elsa grew up she became more of a handful and the Adamsons started to look for an area where Elsa could be relocated. They found a site near Meru. At the end of 1959 Elsa delivered three cubs, and a few weeks later, in an intensely emotional moment for the Adamsons, she brought them to visit Joy.

Joy and George were not the first to raise a lion cub and release it to the wild. What was unusual was that Elsa remained attached to humans even after being returned to the wild, mating and having a litter of cubs. Joy had taken more than 5,000 photographs and she wrote an account of Elsa's up-bringing, Born Free. *The book sold over five million copies and brought the Adamsons international fame.*

In January 1961 Elsa fell sick and within a few days died from a tick-borne fever. In 1964 work began on the film of Born Free.

It is advisable to go in a group and to take care over security. Take the Langata Road out through the suburbs of Langata and Karen until you reach the town of Ngong. Just after this town turn right up the Panorama Road, which should be well sign-posted. The road winds up fairly steeply in places, and to reach Lamwia, the highest peak (No 4), requires a four-wheel-drive vehicle. The route is about 100 km in all and you climb up 1,000 m. It is possible to walk along the four peaks, allow 2-3 hours for this. From the top you can look back from where you have come to see the skyline of Nairobi. The city centre with its skyscrapers is clearly visible and gradually peters out to the suburbs and farms. On a very clear day you can see Mount Kenya in the distance. Looking over in the other direction, towards the Great Rift Valley, is a view of about 100 km.

Olorgesailie prehistoric site

The area is extremely hot and it is advisable to bring sufficient water supplies

A trip to this important prehistoric site can be combined with a visit to Lake Magadi. The site covers an area of 21 ha, and is the largest archaeological site in Kenya. The site was discovered in 1919 by geologist JW Gregory and later in the 1940s excavated by Kenya's most famous archaeologists, Mary and Louis Leakey. A team from the Smithsonian Institute in the USA continues to work here. In 1947 it was given national park status.

It is believed that a lake covered the present site of the mountain in prehistoric times, and that various mammals, including elephants, hippos, crocodiles and giraffes, lived near or in the lake. The abundant presence of game attracted hunters to this area. These early hunters are believed to have fashioned stone tools and axes.

Fossilized remains of prehistoric animals, some gigantic compared to their descendents, and an abundance of Acheulean hand axes and other stone tools were uncovered here. A small, raised wooden walkway has been built around the display of prehistoric animal remains and tools, enabling the fossils to be exhibited where they were found. At the site is a small **museum**, recently renovated, with a number of exhibits including animal bones and hand axes believed to date from more than one million years ago.

Olorgesailie is located 80 km southwest of Nairobi and is 2 km off the sealed tarmac road to Lake Magadi (C58). The drive here from Nairobi offers spectacular views ascending the Ngong Hills, before the descent down to the Rift Valley floor. It is well signposted.

The Kikuyu, Embu and Meru

The largest tribal group in Kenya, the 6,000,000 Kukuyu make up an estimated 21% of the population. They are believed to have migrated to this area around the 16th century from the east and northeast of Africa as part of the Bantu expansion, and to have intermarried with the groups that occupied the area. These groups were largely hunter-gatherer peoples (unlike the Kikuyu who kept livestock and cultivated the land), and included the Athi and the Gumba.

The Kikuyu belong to age-sets and as they get older they advance in terms of status. One of the most important of the cultural aspects of the Kikuyu is circumcision practised traditionally by both men and women. Circumcision of women, known as clitoridectomy, is now illegal, but there is still evidence that it is practised. For men, the ritual remains an important part of the transition from boyhood to manhood.

The Kikuyu are made up of clans, the two most important being based on Kiambu and Nyeri, and rivalry between them is intense. In the 1992 multiparty elections, the Ford-Asili party, headed by Kenneth Matiba, effectively represented Kiambu interests, while the Democratic Party was led by Mwai Kibaki from Nyeri. Fragmentation of the opposition allowed the incumbent KANU party to retain power.

The Embu and the Meru are two groups, each with their own main town of the same name, which have strong affinities with the Kikuyu. In the 1970s a pressure group called the Gikuyu, Embu and Meru Association (GEMA) was active in advancing the interests of these three peoples.

Kenya

There is a shaded picnic area and limited accommodation at the site (four *bandas*), to which visitors must bring all bedding, food and utensils. ■ *The National Museums of Kenya administer the site and arrange tours. For further information of tours and also for details of accommodation, contact the Nairobi Museum, PO Box 40658, Nairobi, T742131/4.*

Lake Magadi

Located at the base of the Rift Valley at an altitude of 580 m, this is the second lowest of the Rift Valley lakes. It is 32 km long and 3 km wide and is the most alkaline of all the Kenyan Rift Valley lakes. The high rate of evaporation is the only way by which water escapes from the lake. The lakebed consists of semi-solid soda, and the waters have a pink hue, especially in the surrounding shallow pools. Several hot springs, mostly at the southern end of the lake, bring to the surface a continual supply of soda, which evaporates forming a crust of sodium carbonate.

The highly alkaline water, with its accumulated minerals and salts, makes the surrounding soils near the lakes alkaline. This has the knock-on effect of turning ivory and bones into fossils. The lake and surrounding area were first explored by a Captain Smith in 1904.

It is only 110 km from Nairobi but the climate – semi-desert with temperatures around 38°C – is very different to that of the capital . As with many of the other Rift Valley lakes this is a soda lake and, because of the high temperatures, it is particularly rich in the mineral *magadi*, the Masai word for soda. A soda factory has been built on the lakeshore, and the town of Magadi has grown up around this.

It is fairly remote but not inaccessible for those with their own transport. The railway line that serves the factory does not take passengers, but there are twice-daily *matatus* and buses (No 125) that reach Magadi town. To get there take the Langata Road out past Wilson Airport and the Nairobi National Park. Soon after the park entrance take a left fork that leads through the village of Kiserian and then climbs up the southern end of the Ngong Hills. From here you will get some good views of the Rift, and on a clear day both Mount Kenya and Mount Kilimanjaro may be seen. The road (C58) then drops down into the Rift, and as it does the temperature gets hotter and drier. As you approach, the views are splendid and you will probably see Masai grazing their cattle. There is an abundance of birdlife – in particular lesser flamingos, ibis and African spoonbills. The chestnut-banded sand plover is endemic to this area.

Whistling Thorns *Whistling Thorns* is a property of approximately 8 ha, an hour's drive from Nairobi on good tarmac road, and 13 km from Kiserian, on the Kiserian-Isinya Pipeline road. It is off the usual tourist track. To get there, take bus No 111 to Kiserian, then *matatu* to Isinya and get off at *Whistling Thorns*. Apart from food and accommodation, facilities include a swimming pool, horseriding, cycling and bush walks. They also organize safaris.

Sleeping and eating B-C *Whistling Thorns*, PO Box 51512, Nairobi, T350720, www.africaonline.co.ke/campingsafaris, is open daily for lunch and dinner. There are twin-room cottages, camping with hot showers and fabulous views of the Ngong Hills. Booking is essential.

Kiambethu/ Mitchell's Farm An unusual opportunity to tour one of the first tea farms in Kenya. The farm is about 30 km northwest of Nairobi, towards Limuru, and your friendly host will be Mrs Evelyn Mitchell, the daughter of Mr McDonnell who started tea farming in 1918. ■ *The farm is not open all year and visitors must book, usually at least 1 week in advance, T0154-40756. The price of US$20 includes food and drink.*

Central Highlands: Mount Kenya

The Central Highlands of Kenya is the area to the north of Nairobi that used to be known as the 'White Highlands'. This region, which includes two national parks (Mount Kenya and the Aberdares) and forms the eastern boundary to the Rift Valley, is very densely populated. It is the heartland of the Kikuyu people who make up the largest tribal group in Kenya and, as it is fertile and well watered, many of the white settlers chose it for their farmland.

A railway (not currently operational) and a whole network of roads weave their way up into the highlands to Nyeri and on to Nanyuki. There are a number of towns in the Central Highlands – including Nyeri, Embu, Meru, Nanyuki and Isiolo. People come to the Central Highlands to visit the Aberdares National Park (which is home to the famous hotels, the Ark and Treetops), and also to climb Mount Kenya, which is part of another national park.

Climate This area is very high, with peaks in the Aberdares of up to 4,000 m, and Mount Kenya, which is 5,199 m. You should therefore expect it to get fairly chilly, especially at night. The maximum temperatures range from 22-26°C, and the minimum from 10-14°C. It is also very wet here with annual rainfall of up to 3,000 mm not unusual.

History

The settlers The first settlers came to Kenya in search of wealth and adventure and were encouraged by the colonial government, which was desperate to make the colony pay for itself. The White Highland Policy was established in the early 20th century. By 1915 there were 21,400 sq km set aside for about 1,000 settlers. This number was increased after the Second World War with the Soldier Settlement Scheme. Initially the settlers grew crops and raised animals, basing their livelihood on wheat, wool, dairy and meat, but by 1914 it was clear that these had little potential as export goods so they changed to maize and coffee. Perhaps the most famous of the early settlers was Lord Delamere. He was important in early experimental agriculture and it was through his mistakes that many lessons were learnt about agriculture in the tropics. He tried out different wheat varieties until he developed one that was resistant to wheat rust. The 1920s saw the rapid expansion of settler agriculture – in particular coffee, sisal and maize – and the prices for these commodities rose, giving the settlers reason to be optimistic about their future.

However, when the prices plummeted in the Depression of the 1930s the weaknesses of the settler agriculture scheme were revealed. By 1930 over 50% by value of settler export was accounted for by coffee alone, making them very vulnerable when prices fell. Many settlers were heavily mortgaged and could not service their debts. About 20% of the white farmers gave up their farms, while others left farming temporarily. Cultivated land on settler farms fell from 644,000 acres in 1930 to 502,000 acres in 1936, most of the loss being wheat and maize.

About one-third of the colonial government's revenue was from duties on settlers' production and goods imported by the settlers. Therefore the government was also seriously affected by the fall in prices. In earlier years the government had shown its commitment to white agriculture by investment in infrastructure (for example railways and ports) and, because of its dependence on custom duties, it felt it could not simply abandon the settlers. Many of the settlers were saved by the colonial government who pumped about £1 million into white agriculture with subsidies and rebates on exports and loans, and the formation of a *Land Bank*.

Following the Depression and the Second World War the numbers of settlers increased sharply so that by the 1950s the white population had reached about 80,000. As well as dairy farming, the main crops they grew were coffee, tea and maize. However, discontent among the African population over the loss of their traditional land to the settlers was growing. The Africans had been confined to native reserves and, as their population grew, the pressure on these areas increased. Some of the Africans lived as squatters on white land, and many migrated and worked as wage labourers for the settlers.

Political demands by Kenyans accelerated throughout the late 1940s and 1950s and the issue of land was critical (see page 304). Although there are still many white Kenyans in this area, the size and number of their land holdings has been reduced considerably and land has been transferred to the Kikuyu. The allocation of land at and around the time of Independence was a controversial issue – the aim was to distribute land bought by the British government from settlers as equitably as possible. However there is evidence that a few richer Kenyans managed to secure large areas. The issue of the polarization and concentration of land ownership among a privileged few is one that continues today; it is not something that Independence has solved.

Mount Kenya peaks

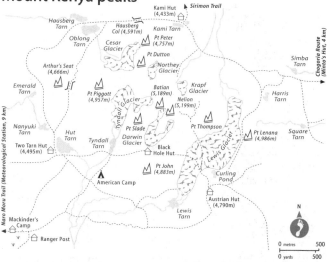

For climbing Mount Kenya, see page 133

Kikuyu in the Up until the 1930s African agriculture had been largely ignored by the government.
colonial period Africans were in fact banned from growing coffee, the most valuable crop. The reason given for this was that production by thousands of small farmers would make it impossible to control coffee berry disease. It had the convenient side-effect of ensuring a cheap labour supply for European farms as Africans could then only pay their hut and poll taxes by working as wage labourers.

When the effects of the Depression reached Kenya it became clear that African producers were better able to survive difficult years and, in particular, were able to produce cereals more cheaply than the settlers. As European agriculture contracted, squatters on white land increased production of food crops and maize in particular, and found they could make a profit despite the low prices of the 1930s. The need to boost exports as prices fell undermined both official and settler opposition to African production, and the East African share of production increased from 9% in 1931 to between 15 and 20% in 1933, as a result of increased maize production and the expansion of the cultivation of wattle by the Kikuyu.

Wattle production, encouraged by the Department of Agriculture, was expanded dramatically and earnings from wattle increased from £35,000 in 1929 to £79,500 in 1932. It was in many ways an ideal crop – it could be used or sold for fuel, or sold to expatriate firms for the extraction of tannin. It needed little attention after the initial planting, and so could be grown without interrupting the normal agricultural cycle.

Mount Kenya region

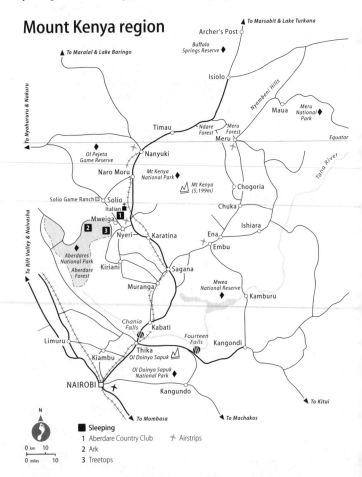

Sleeping
1 Aberdare Country Club
2 Ark
3 Treetops

Airstrips

0 km 10
0 miles 10

The areas most affected were Kiambu, Kikuyuland and Embu, and many small farmers made substantial profits.

Meanwhile, during the late 1920s and early 1930s there were a series of droughts that affected the lowland pastoral areas of the Rift Valley much more severely than Kikuyuland. Livestock prices fell dramatically as the pastoralists sold stock to buy food and Kikuyu agriculturalists took advantage. This was a structural change at the expense of the pastoralists from which they have never recovered. There is little doubt that the Kikuyu acted with great economic acumen. The situation also increased the inequalities within Kikuyu society, as those with secure access to land not only made a comfortable living from maize and wattle, but were also able to increase their wealth through acquiring more livestock, land and wives.

Observers have argued that the Kikuyu not only showed great resilience in the time of the Depression but that they (particularly those with assured access to land) managed to seize the opportunity given to them and benefit greatly. The decline of European production of maize, and the reassessment by the government of the importance of African agriculture, together with the favourable trading conditions with their neighbours, meant that the Kikuyu were given a real opportunity to increase their economic position, and ultimately their political power. The Depression can be seen therefore as a turning point in the fortunes of the Kikuyu – by stimulating production of both food and wattle.

Kiambu
1° 8′ S, 36° 50′ E

This small town, 16 km north of Nairobi, is set in an area of ridges formed by streams flowing southeast from Kinangop (3,900 m). The soil and climate are ideal for growing coffee, which was introduced in 1902. This is an area of great natural beauty on the lower slopes of the Aberdares. The action of water from many streams flowing southeast from Kinangop to join the Athi River has divided the area into sheer ridges and deep valleys. There are several waterfalls in the higher areas.

It is also the centre of one of the main Kikuyu clans (the other is based on Nyeri). The Kiambu Kikuyu were particularly powerful during the presidency of Jomo Kenyatta, who came from this clan. Many displaced Masai refugees settled in this area after the Masai civil wars at the end of the 19th century, and in time intermarried with the Kikuyu people.

Sleeping and eating The **D** *Amani Hotel* near *Barclays Bank* has a bar, reasonable restaurant and simple accommodation.

Thika

1° 1′ S, 37° 5′ E
Phone code: 151
Colour map 3, grid B4

From Muthaiga the road, which has four lanes and a good surface, continues up towards Thika, which is actually off the main road north. This is the town that was made famous by the book (and later the television series) *The Flame Trees of Thika* by Elspeth Huxley. It is about her childhood when her parents came out to Kenya as one of the first families, and their attempts to establish a farm. However, there is little special about Thika – not even many flame trees to brighten the place up – apart from the **Blue Post Hotel**, a famous colonial landmark. A visit to the *Blue Post* is an absolute must if you're in Nairobi for any length of time, and are looking for a day out. It is nestled between Chania and Thika Falls. Thika was known as Ndarugu Heights or Chania Bridge by the early settlers. There are shaded tables within sight of the falls, where all you'll hear is the crashing waters, birdsong and the rustling of leaves. There are also easy trails around the base of the falls, thick with flowers and foliage, teeming with butterflies and dragonflies. Rare birds are occasionally sighted.

Nearby is the **Ol Doinyo Sapuk National Park**, which is located about 25 km from Thika, and 50 km from Nairobi, turn east off the A3, on to the road leading toward Garissa. The name of the park comes from the extinct volcano, which can be climbed, and from which there are views of Nairobi, Mount Kenya and even Mount

Kenya

Kilimanjaro on clear days. Ol Doinyo Sapuk, 2,150 m, means the mountain of the buffalo, and you can drive to the summit in a four-wheel drive where there are examples of flora associated with the Afro-alpine zones of the higher mountains. The top of the volcano is covered in dense forest vegetation including the giant lobelia, and the area is home to large number of birds. There is some game but it is difficult to spot in the heavily wooded terrain.

Sir William Northrup MacMillan, a well-heeled gentleman of St Louis, bought the mountain of Ol Doinyo Sapuk and much of the surrounding land in the early part of the 20th century. This immensely wealthy, 158-kg American came to the protectorate in 1904. He received a knighthood from the British in recognition of his support during the First World War. He was famous among the early settlers for his generous entertainment of most of the people of note who passed through Kenya, including President Roosevelt and Winston Churchill. After his death he bequeathed the mountain to the nation and was buried there at the 7 km mark along the road to the summit. It had been intended that his mortal remains would be interred at the summit, but they proved to be too heavy for the hearse, supported on skis and pulled by a tractor, to complete its ascent. Oak trees were planted by the graveside.

On the way to Ol Doinyo Sapuk, just after the turning off the A3, the **Fourteen Falls** are particularly splendid during the rainy season. Recently declared a national park, this broad plume of water plummets 30 m over a multi-lipped precipice. There is a path leading from the car park to the base of the falls. Thika itself has a fair amount of manufacturing activity, particularly fruit canning for export.

Sleeping
■ *on map*
For price codes:
see inside front cover

C *New Blue Posts*, PO Box 42, Thika, T21086. 30 mins from Nairobi, just north of Thika, on the road to Murang'a, this first opened in 1908 and has been renovated fairly recently. It is still popular, has a very good view over the falls, and is a good place to break a journey. Easily the nicest place to stay in the area, rustic, sprawling, safari-style lodge, with large gardens and ostrich farm, busy at weekends. **D** *12th December*, PO Box 156, T22140. Good value, good-size rooms, some with balconies, price includes breakfast. **D** *Sagret*, T21786. Behind the *matatu* area, it is fairly modern and clean. **D** *White Line*, located on the same road as the post office in the centre of Thika. It is not a bad place to stay, the rooms have bathrooms and there is sometimes hot water, usually in the evenings. Good value for the price, there is also a restaurant. **E** *New Fulilia Hotel*, Kwame, Nkrumah Rd. Good value, clean and basic rooms. **E** *Sky Motel*, Uhuru St. Very clean if a bit basic.

Eating
● *on map*

Cheap *Blue Post*, very good food and wide selection of dishes. *Macvast Executive Restaurant*, good coffee. **Seriously cheap** *Prismos Hotel*, on the 1st floor opposite *New Fulilia* on Kwane Nkrumah. Large popular restaurant with covered balcony and some ambitious dishes.

Transport

Road Murang'a Rd out of Nairobi for the well-signposted *Blue Post*. There are frequent *matatus* from Racecourse Rd and Ronald Ngala Roundabout (45 mins).

North from Thika

From Thika the A2 continues northwards through the lush, verdant countryside. Almost every inch of ground is cultivated and you will see terraces on some of the steeper slopes. You will soon notice that this is pineapple country and many hectares are taken up with

Thika

■ Sleeping
1 12th December
2 New Fulilia
3 Sagret
4 Sky Motel
5 White Line

● Eating
1 Macvast Executive
2 Prismos Hotel

Not to scale

plantations. They look similar to sisal plantations with spiky plants. There are a number of routes to choose from: you can go north to Nyeri and the Aberdares National Park, then clockwise round the mountain via Naro Moru, or anti-clockwise via Embu. The following section will cover the clockwise route around Mount Kenya, taking in Nyeri, Naro Moru, Nanyuki, Meru and then finally Embu.

Murang'a
0° 45' S, 37° 9' E
Colour map 3, grid B4

This is a small, bustling town that is situated just off the main road north. At the turn of the century there was very little here – it was initially established as an administrative centre and, as it was located in the Kikuyu Reserves rather than in the White Highlands, it never became a settler town.

The town has become known as the Kikuyu Heartland because it is close to **Mugeka**, the *Mukuruwe wa Gathanga* (Garden of Eden of the Kikuyu), which has an important place in Kikuyu mythology. The legend is that it was here that N'Gai (God) led Gikuyu to the mountain and told him to build his home there. He was given his wife Mumbi and in time they had several daughters. N'Gai found nine husbands under a fig tree for the nine daughters of Gikuyu and Mumbi, who in mythology are the ancestors of all Kikuyu. These nine became the forefathers of the nine Kikuyu clans – in alphabetical order: Achera, Agachiku, Airimu, Aithaga, Aitherandu, Ambui, Angare, Angui and Anjiru. There was actually also a 10th daughter. However the Kikuyu are very superstitious and one of their beliefs is that the number 10 is unlucky, so the term the 'full 9' is often used instead, and is still in use today especially by older Kikuyus. At one time there was a museum at the site of the original fig tree.

In Murang'a, the **Church of St James and All Martyrs**, also known as CPK Cathedral, is not particularly old but has some interesting decorations painted in 1955 by a Tanzanian artist named Elimo Njau. It shows various scenes from the Bible with an African Christ and in African surroundings. The church was founded in memory of the Kikuyu who died at the hands of the Mau Mau.

Sleeping and eating E *Ngurunga Bar*, close to the bus station, has simple lodging. E *Rwathia Bar and Restaurant*, PO Box 243, opposite the market, T22527, serves reasonable meals.

From Murang'a the main road continues north towards Nyeri, Naro Moru and Nanyuki. It is possible to take a detour into the **Aberdare Forest**. To take the route into the Aberdare Range, follow one of the minor roads from Murang'a, which eventually leads to Othaya and on to Nyeri – the turning for this is to the left just before you get to Murang'a.

Karatina

On the main road travelling north Karatina is the next town you will reach. There are baskets for sale from the Kikuyu women who sit by the road side. It is often the vendors themselves who make the baskets, and they are good value. Worth a visit on market days (Tuesday, Thursday and Saturday), this is one of the biggest fruit and vegetable markets in East Africa, and it attracts buyers from as far away as Mombasa. Also, on either side of the railway line, an extensive market sells second-hand clothes and household goods.

Sleeping and eating D *Tourist Lodge*, Private Bag Karatina, T71522. Reasonable restaurant and accommodation, used as a stop-off point for tourists. E *Star Point Hotel*, Commercial St. Airy, basic but fine rooms. E *3 in 1*, near the bus stand, has restaurant (seriously cheap). **Cheap** *Tourist Lodge* and **Seriously cheap** *Mugi Motherland Hotel*, pleasant balcony overlooking street. *Mokar Annex Restaurant* and *Bethany Café*, behind the market, are other options.

Transport Regular *matatu* to **Nairobi**, **Nyeri** and other Central Province destinations.

Nyeri

0° 23' S, 36° 56' E
Phone code: 171
Colour map 3, grid B4

Nyeri is the administrative capital of the Central Province and is located about 120 km from Nairobi. It is at the base of the Aberdares, close to the boundary of the Aberdares National Park, located west of the town. It is situated a few kilometres off the road that goes around Mount Kenya – the turning is signposted. The town was named by Richard Meinertzhagen in 1902. He had camped at Nyeri Hill nearby during an expedition against the Tetu (a sub-group of the Kikuyu) who had ambushed an Arab caravan.

The surrounding area is fairly densely populated. On a clear morning you can see Mount Kenya in the distance. It is one of the wettest parts of Kenya and has a cool climate, and can even be cold in the evenings.

During the British colonial period Nyeri developed as an army base and then as an important trading centre for farmers from the surrounding countryside. The land is very fertile and as you drive into Nyeri you will see the many shambas (farms) growing maize, bananas and coffee, as well as many varieties of vegetables.

Ins & outs   The town has benefited from recent road resurfacing. The main street, Kimathi Way, is where you will find banks, the post office, the clocktower and several hotels. A little to the south of this cluster is the market and the bus stand. The cemetery, just to the north of the clocktower, bears the grave of Robert Baden-Powell, founder of the international scout movement, who lived in Nyeri until his death (see box opposite).

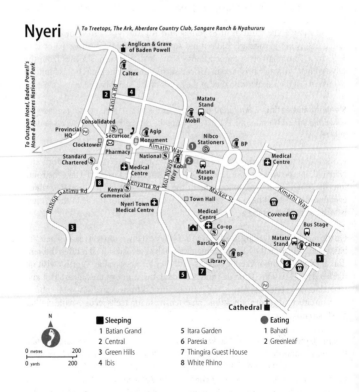

Nyeri

To Treetops, The Ark, Aberdare Country Club, Sangare Ranch & Nyahururu

Sleeping
1 Batian Grand
2 Central
3 Green Hills
4 Ibis
5 Itara Garden
6 Paresia
7 Thingira Guest House
8 White Rhino

Eating
1 Bahati
2 Greenleaf

Baden-Powell

Lord Baden-Powell distinguished himself in the Boer War during the siege of Mafeking. At the time he was 45 years old, the youngest General in the British Army.

Baden-Powell is best known as the founder of the Boy Scout movement. Guides were soon to follow and, for younger children, Cubs and Brownies. The movement was immensely successful, and is still popular around the world with millions of children.

Baden-Powell once visited a small boarding school in the Rift Valley which was popular amongst British settlers and missionaries. Some of the children there were as young as six, and considered to be too small to join the Brownies or the Cubs. Baden-Powell therefore decided to establish something for the youngest children – and so the 'Chippets' were born. The Chippets have continued there to this day and the school (St

Andrew's School, Turi, see page 127) remembers Lord Baden-Powell each year. They also have a flag mounted in one of the corridors which was presented to the school by Baden-Powell's wife after his death.

Nyeri was Baden-Powell's great love and he once wrote that "The nearer to Nyeri the nearer to bliss". In the grounds of the Outspan Hotel is the cottage, Paxtu, built with money collected by guides and scouts from around the world, where Baden Powell spent his final years. He died in 1941 and his obituary states: "No Chief, no Prince, no King, no Saint was ever mourned by so great a company of boys and girls, or men and women, in every land." He is buried in Nyeri cemetery, and his wife's ashes are buried beside him. Lady Baden-Powell was World Chief Guide until her death (in England) at the age of 88 on 25 June 1977.

Sights

On the main road you can see a memorial to those who died during the Mau Mau. It has the inscription: To the Memory of the Members of the Kikuyu Tribe Who Died in the Fight for Freedom 1951-57.

It is possible to visit Lord Baden-Powell's home, which contains a small **museum** with a display of memorabilia. The cottage *Paxtu* lies in the grounds of the *Outspan Hotel*. Baden-Powell's home in England was named *Pax*, and the name of his Kenyan home was a pun on the original (*Pax Two*). Baden-Powell died in Nyeri in 1941 and is buried nearby, at the graveyard of St Peter's Church. His wife Olave, who died in the UK 36 years after her husband, was cremated and her ashes were later buried in the same grave. ■ *US$1.50. Admission is free to Scouts in uniform. Pay at the hotel reception (and make the most of going inside Outspan to see the opulence of the public rooms!).*

After Baden-Powell's death, *Paxtu* was the home of Jim Corbett, famous hunter/destroyer of several man-eating tigers in India in the 1920-30s and author of the books *The Man-Eaters of Kumaon* (1946), *The Man-Eating Leopard of Rudraprayang* (1948) and *The Temple Tiger and More Man-Eaters of Kumaon* (1954). In 1947 Jim Corbett and his sister Maggie moved to Nyeri where he wrote most of his books. In 1952 (when aged 80 years) he received a request to meet Princess Elizabeth and Prince Philip at *Treetops*, where he identified animals for the Royals. His entry for that night into the *Treetops* register records: "For the first time in the history of the world a young girl climbed into a tree a Princess, and after having had what she described as her 'most thrilling experience' she climbed down from the tree the next day a Queen". Jim Corbett was also buried in the St Peter's Church graveyard, Nyeri.

Out of town on the D435 road that leads to the Ruhuruini Gate of the Aberdares National Park is an enormous Italian church built in remembrance of the Italian soldiers who died in East Africa during the Second World War. In front of the main altar lies the grave of Amadeo di Savoia, Duce d'Aosta, the commander of the main Italian armies in Ethiopia, who formally surrendered to the Allied army at Amba Alagi on 20 May 1941, and died in Nairobi in 1942.

Kenya

Essentials

Sleeping
■ on map, page 126
For price codes:
see inside front cover

Kenya

L *Aberdare Country Club*, PO Box 449, Nyeri, T55620. This is located about 12 km to the north of Nyeri itself and is managed by the *Lonrho Group*. Formerly a farmhouse, it is another old colonial-type country hotel, very luxurious with tennis courts and a 9-hole golf course. You can hire self-drive cars here, as well as arrange game drives into the national park. Central bookings, T02-216940, F216796, lonhotsm@form-net.com **L** *Outspan Hotel*, PO Box 24, Nyeri, T2424, booking c/o Block Hotels, PO Box 40075, Nairobi, T02-540780, F545948. This hotel is located a little out of town (about 20 mins' walk or a taxi ride) opposite the golf course. Built in the 1920s and containing within its grounds a cottage that was the last resi-dence of Lord Baden-Powell, the hotel has a wonderful atmosphere, set in the most beautiful gardens (guided walks available) and has the full facilities of a country hotel – swimming, tennis, squash, snooker. There is a range of very spacious rooms, prices depend on the sea-son. This hotel is also used as a safari base for the Aberdares National Park; if you are staying at *Treetops* you will come here to be picked up for the final drive. The *Outspan* is a good place to stop for breakfast or lunch – you can admire the gardens and, as long as the clouds are not down, you will get a good view of Mt Kenya and the Aberdare range behind. There is also a pub on site serving good food. You can rent self-drive vehicles from the *Outspan*, and they also arrange game drives for the day into the Aberdares National Park that are good if you cannot afford the cost of accommodation in the park itself. **L** *Sangare Ranch*, northwest of *Aberdare Country Club*, book through *Bush Homes of East Africa Ltd*, PO Box 56923, Nairobi, T01-571647, F571665, www.bush-homes.co.ke 6 tents, each with 2 beds and en-suite bathrooms. All-inclusive – food and drinks, laundry, game drives in the nearby Solio Game Ranch, and horseriding.

C *Green Hills*, Mumbi Rd, PO Box 313, Nyeri, T30604, 30709, 30710. This hotel is on the top of a hill to the southwest of the town opposite the golf course. It is spread over fairly extensive gardens and lawns and is large with over 100 s/c rooms. Rooms are with balconies or in tradi-tional-style thatched cottages, all with telephone and radio. Friendly staff and excellent facil-ities including 2 restaurants, bar, swimming pool, sauna, laundry service and secure parking. Price includes breakfast. **D** *Batian Grand Hotel,* PO Box 12100, Nyeri, T30783, F2613. Located on the east side of town, near the bus parks, formerly known as the *Crested Eagle*. Large mod-ern block with central courtyard, s/c rooms with hot water, restaurant, bar with pool table, and secure parking. **D** *Central*, Kanisa Rd, PO Box 1229, Nyeri, T4233. This is a modern hotel that is located close to the post office in the north of the town, it is fairly basic but clean, com-fortable and good value. All the rooms have bathrooms with hot water, it has secure parking, a restaurant and a pleasant open-air bar, and a disco at weekends. **D** *White Rhino*, Kenyatta Rd, PO Box 30, Nyeri, T30934. This hotel is located fairly centrally in Nyeri and is one of the old colonial hotels that are found scattered all over the White Highlands. One of the oldest build-ings in the town and starting to feel its age, the facilities are not that extensive, but the atmo-sphere, friendly staff and pleasant gardens make it worth while. It has a bar with a pool table, restaurant, lounge and laundry service.

E *Ibis*, PO Box 184, Nyeri, T4858, F30530. Part of a chain of hotels, with rooms on several floors around a central courtyard, reached through the ground floor restaurant. Good value, clean, fairly large s/c rooms with nets, hot water, wood-panelled bar. **E** *Itara Garden*, PO Box 804, Nyeri, T2537. A new hotel that is close to and similar in price to *Thingira Guest House* (see below) but far superior. Basic but clean s/c rooms in the main modern building or thatched wooden complex. Has a restaurant and good outdoor bar with pool tables. **E** *Paresia*, PO Box 12242, Nyeri, T2765. This is a large block in a run-down area south of the bus station, but clean and bright s/c rooms with hot water, and friendly staff. **E** *Thingira Guest House*, PO Box 221, Nyeri, T4769. Another modern hotel, that looks incomplete and unfinished, near the library. Doubles only, quite shabby rooms have bathrooms with hot water in the evenings, and there is a bar and restaurant attached. **F** *Green Oak Restaurant & Hotel*, Kimathi Way, PO Box 2212, Nyeri, T2726. Very central, sited next to a noisy bar. The restaurant has a covered balcony, clean and secure s/c rooms.

If you are staying in one of the top-range hotels you will probably eat there. Otherwise the **Cheap** *Central* and *White Rhino* have restaurants which are both good value. Many other small restaurants also offer cheap meals, including *Bahati* (chicken dishes) and *Greenleaf*, opposite each other along Kimathi Way.

Eating
● *on map, page 126*

Gliding It is possible to hangglide over the Aberdares National Park with the *Gliding Club of Kenya*, which has its headquarters at Mweiga Air Field, 8 km north of Nyeri, 12 km southwest of Kirinyaga with Petra and Peter Allmendinger, PO Box 926, Nyeri, T/F0171-2748, www.kenyatravel.de This German couple, who live on an old coffee farm, run and manage the *Gliding Club of Kenya* on a commercial basis, in addition to offering farm and riding holidays for families and less adventurous guests. The 'Soaring Safaris' offer a wonderful overview of the Aberdares and are well suited for long high-altitude flights due to the convergence of two differing air masses, the moist cumulus weather at Mweiga and the dry hot desert air just 35 km to the north. There is a runway of 1,300 m length and the Allmendingers also run a gliding school. The gliders are released at an altitude of 1,300 m. The best time to visit is from Sep to Apr; Aug is too wet for gliding.

Sport

Nyeri is the gateway to the Aberdares National Park and you will come here before you go to the park. If you do not already have a trip arranged you can organize one through the *Outspan*. You will need a group of at least 3 people (the more people the cheaper it should work out). They are just for the day and are ideal if you cannot afford the lodges in the park itself. They are also fairly good value and the price varies depending on the season and where you want to go in the park.

Tour operators

Air Nyeri is served by *Kenyan Airways* with daily flights to **Nanyuki** (10 mins), **Samburu** (50 mins) and **Nairobi** (about 1 hr). Flying to Nanyuki is not worth the bother; by the time you have checked in and so on, you could have driven there.

Transport

Road Nyeri is located about 130 km to the north of Nairobi and is on the very good A2 road. From here it is about 60 km to Nanyuki. The bus and *matatu* stand is on Kimathi Way in the centre of town.

Banks Money can be changed at most banks, many of which are found near the post office to the west of town, but *Barclays* and *Co-op* are opposite the library on Kenyatta Rd. *Co-op* offers money transfers, and *Western Union* money transfers are available at the *Post Bank* next to the bus station. **Communications** Internet: (US$2 per email) available from *Nibco* stationers on Kimathi Way but service can be erratic. *Securicor*, near the post office, offer *Omega*, *Pony* and *DHL* delivery services.

Directory

Aberdares National Park

The Aberdares is a range of mountains to the west of Mount Kenya in the Central Highlands region, running roughly in a north-south direction between Nairobi and Nyahururu (Thomson's Falls). The eastern and western slopes in particular are covered with dense forest and tree ferns in places; bamboo and hargenia grow at a higher zone. The national park, established in 1950, encompasses an area of around 715 sq km and is one of Kenya's only virgin forest reserves, situated 10 km northwest of Nyeri town, and approximately 165 km from Nairobi. The Aberdares are the third highest massif in the country, with dramatic peaks, deep valleys, enormous spectacular waterfalls cascading down the rock face, volcanic outcrops of bizarre proportions and undulating moorlands. The Aberdares come to a peak at about 4,000 m and the middle and upper reaches are densely forested with thickets of bamboo, giant heath and tussock grass. The Kikuyu call these mountains *Nyandarua* (drying hide) and they were the home to guerrilla fighters during the struggle for Independence. Nowadays the mountains are home to bongo (elusive forest antelope), buffalo, elephant, giant forest hog, red duiker, and Syke's and colobus monkeys. The rare, handsome bongo is most likely to be spotted near the *Ark*, which is sited close to a

0° 30' S, 36° 50' E

Birdlife is prolific in the park and most obvious are the four species of sunbirds. Among the birds of prey are the crowned hawk eagles, mountain buzzard and the African goshawk

swampy glade, waterhole and salt-lick, or up in bamboo zone. Dawn and the following hour is the optimum time to see these elusive forest antelopes. At about 3,500 m, where the landscape opens up, you may see lions, leopards, serval cats and even bushbucks. Caution is required with the lions as some of them are reportedly habituated to and therefore not frightened of humans. Wildlife is comparatively scarce, but the views in the park are spectacular. Particularly good walks include trekking up the three peaks, **Satima**, 3,998 m, **Kinangop**, 3,906 m and **Kipipiri**, 3,348 m. You can hire a guide if you wish, but an armed guard, costing US$6.50 daily, is obligatory to protect you from the wildlife. There are a few roads traversing the centre of the national park from Nyeri to Naivasha, giving access to most of the waterfalls.

The park is not often visited, either by individual travellers or tour companies, primarily because of the weather. It rains heavily and frequently, making driving difficult and seeing the game and mountain peaks almost impossible. It is usually advisable to set off early in the day, as it frequently clouds over by late morning. The park is often closed during the wet season as the roads turn into mudslides. For this reason vehicles are restricted to four-wheel drive. Trout fishing is very popular, especially high up in the moors. A fishing licence is required, obtainable from the park headquarters for US$5.

Sights The park is split into two sections, the beautiful high moorland and peaks with sub-alpine vegetation, and the lower Salient which is dense rainforest and where much of the wildlife lives. The Aberdare Salient is closed to the public and the animals can only be viewed from *Treetops* or the *Ark* (details below). Access to these lodges is prohibited to private vehicles; visitors are obliged to use the hotel bus.

Aberdares National Park

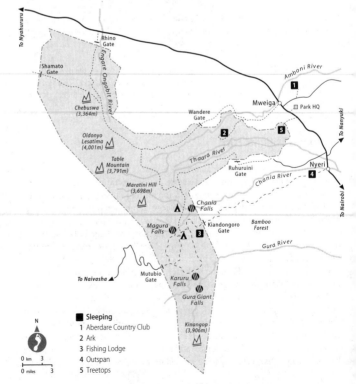

Sleeping
1 Aberdare Country Club
2 Ark
3 Fishing Lodge
4 Outspan
5 Treetops

There are a number of spectacular waterfalls in the park including the **Chania Falls** and the **Karuru Falls** that have a total drop of 273 m in three steps. The more remote and inaccessible **Gura Giant Falls**, to the south, have a higher single drop of over 300 m.

A major project is currently under way to build a **rhino sanctuary** within the Aberdares National Park, funded by the Kenyan Government, the Overseas Aid Agency and conservation organizations. An area of the Salient is being enclosed by a high-security electrified fence, which will extend for 380 km and form a sanctuary for the endangered rhino. Other wildlife will also live in the national park including elephant and various members of the cat family. The electricity for the fence will be generated locally using waterwheels to harness water from within the forest, a project that will also provide power for local people living in the surrounding villages. The local villages support and have also raised money for this project, which will offer protection from the wildlife for their livestock and crops. The rhino for the sanctuary will come initially from the nearby Solio Ranch, situated only a few kilometres away, and which has had an unparalleled success in breeding rhino. Various fund-raising activities in support of the project are being undertaken including the 'Rhino Charge' motor rally (see box, page 116). To date, over 120 km of the fence has been completed.

As accommodation is expensive and limited at the park, a sensible option is to stay at Nyeri (see page 126) and travel to the park from there by *matatu*. *Aberdare Country Club* and *Sangare Ranch*, both outside the park near Mweiga, are also covered in that section.

Sleeping
See page 85 for costs

L *The Ark*, wooden lodge with 46 double, 5 single and 8 triple rooms with en-suite bathrooms, is in the centre of the park. The costs include full board, transfer to the hotel but exclude park entry fees, children under 7 are not allowed. You need to book in advance from *Lonrho Hotels*, Bruce House, Standard St, PO Box 58581, Nairobi, T723776, F216796, lonhotsm@form-net.com **L** *Treetops*, just inside the park entrance. This is a little more basic than the *Ark*, and has small cabin-type rooms with shared bathroom facilities. There is a roof deck from where you can safely view the animals at night. The original tree-house was actually burnt down in 1955, but at that time this was a facility very much for the élite. Princess Elizabeth was staying at *Treetops* when she became Queen Elizabeth II on the death of her father. You will need to book in advance from *Block Hotels*, PO Box 40075 Nairobi, T02-540780, F545948. Access to *Treetops* is from the *Outspan Hotel* in Nyeri, you need to arrive for lunch at 1130, the bus leaves for the park at 1430. **B** *Fishing Lodge*, T24 (Mweiga, via the operator). Offers fully furnished accommodation in the high park, run by the *Kenyan Wildlife Service*. There are 2 stone-built cottages each with 2 bedrooms that have a double and single bed, and a 3rd smaller bedroom that has a single bed. You book your space with the warden at the front gate of the park, or through the KWS Tourism Department, T02-501081/2, F501752, www.kws.org It is usual for a whole cottage to be rented out for US$200 per night, but it is possible to share. Facilities are shared by everyone and include an open-fire for cooking and a communal eating area. You will need to take everything with you except water, including firewood. **Camping** There is a site near the fishing lodge though it is extremely basic.

Transport The nearest bases are at Naivasha or Nyeri and it is easy enough to get a *matatu* to the gates of the park. From **Naivasha** follow the signs along the Upland road until you reach Ndunyu Njeru. From here the road only continues to the park, there are no services (food, petrol etc) from this point onwards. From **Nyeri** there are a number of *matatus* to the park, or you can rent a car (4WD) and drive yourself.

Solio Game Ranch, PO Box 2, Naro Moru, T0171-55271, eparfet@africa online.com, is a private ranch that incorporates the most successful rhino sanctuary in Africa. It contains both white and the even rarer black rhino, *Diceros bicornis*. It is located a little north of Mweiga, between Solio and Naro Moru. Their conservation

Solio Game Ranch

Kenya

and breeding programme has been so successful that Solio Park have provided stock that has been translocated to other sanctuaries, such as Nakuru and Tsavo national parks and will continue to do so for the planned sanctuary in Aberdares National Park Salient Sanctuary – currently under construction. Trips to visit the ranch can be arranged at the *Aberdare Country Club*.

Sleeping L *Solio Camp* operates from Dec-May, run by Patrick Reynolds who specializes in walking safaris (he also runs the *Tiva River Camp* in Tsavo East NP). Bookings through *Bush Homes of East Africa Ltd*, PO Box 56923, Nairobi, T01-571647, F571665, www.bush-homes.co.ke

Mount Kenya Biosphere Reserve

0° 5' S, 37° 20' E This reserve includes the Mount Kenya National Park, 715 sq km, which straddles the equator about 200 km northeast of Nairobi in Central Province. Mount Kenya, or Kirinyaga – the shining mountain, also sometimes referred to as the black and white striped mountain – is the sacred mountain of the Kikuya (Gikuya) people, who believe that it is where their God 'Ngai' lives. The snow-capped peak is rarely visible during the day, being surrounded by clouds, but it is usually clear at dawn and is quite an awesome sight. The upper base of the mountain is nearly 100 km across and has two major peaks, **Nelion** at 5,199 m and **Batian** at 5,189 m. Mount Kenya has a vital role in ecosystems in the area. It is Kenya's most important watershed and its largest forest reserve and the lower slopes make up the country's richest farmlands. The dramatic landscape includes glaciers, moraines, waterfalls, precarious looking rock pinnacles and hanging valleys.

Mountain flora includes a variety of different vegetations over altitudes ranging from 1,600 m to 5,199 m. From bottom to top, it goes from rich alpine and sub-alpine flora to bamboo forests, moorlands with giant heathers and tundra. Over 4,000 m some extraordinary vegetation is found including the giant rosette plants.

In the lower forest and bamboo zones, giant forest hog, tree hyrax, white-tailed mongoose, elephant, suni, duiker and leopard roam. Further up in the moorlands there are hyrax, duiker and Mount Kenya mouse shrews. In higher altitudes still there are the fairly common mole rat and the very rare golden cat.

Mount Kenya

Colour map 3, grid B4 There are a number of towns located along the Kirinyaga Ring Road at the base of
See map, page 121 Mount Kenya, which serve as starting points for the climb up the mountain. The route round the mountain is becoming increasingly popular as a tourist circuit, which is not surprising for it is a really beautiful part of the country, and the mountain and the game parks nearby are an added attraction. The base of the mountain is about 80 km across, making it one of the largest volcanic cones in the world. As you drive along this route you will spend much of the time looking towards the mountain – however, much of the time it is shrouded in cloud. There are some clear days – otherwise very early in the morning or just before nightfall the cloud will often lift suddenly, revealing the two peaks for a few minutes.

Naro Moru The road from Nyeri climbs gradually up to Naro Moru, which is little more than a village located at the base of the mountain. It has a few shops, guesthouses and a post office and is clustered around the railway station that no longer functions as a passenger terminal. Bear in mind before you arrive here that there are no banks in the village. There are no restaurants apart from the one at the *Naro Moru River Lodge*, and if you are cooking your own food you would be advised to stock up before you get here. However, the village does receive quite a few visitors as it serves as the starting point of the Naro Moru Trail, one of the most popular routes up the mountain. Before you set off on this route you have to both book and pay for the mountain huts that you will stay in on the way up. This must be done through the *Naro Moru River Lodge*.

Sleeping **L** *Mount Kenya Mountain Lodge*, Box 123, Kiganjo, Nyeri, T0171-30785, F86011. Situated at 2,194 m on Mt Kenya's slopes overlooking a water hole, 42 double bedrooms with en-suite bathrooms. A close-up viewing bunker is connected to the hotel by a tunnel. **A** *Naro Moru River Lodge*, about 2 km from the village itself off the main road, PO Box 18, T22018, is the most popular place to stay as it organizes climbs up the mountain, the facilities are good including a swimming pool (US$3.50 per person). There is a restaurant, bar and roaring log fire, which is perfect for the chilly evenings. Some cheaper s/c cottages are available. **B** *Sirimon Bandas* (**C** in low season, Jan-Jun), Kenya Wildlife Service managed self-catering accommodation near Sirimon Gate, which is about 9 km along a turning off the road, 16 km north of Nanyuki. It has 2 furnished cottages, each has 1 room with a double bed, 1 room with 2 single beds, fitted kitchen and lounge. Each cottage is normally rented out as a whole, for more information and reservations contact KWS Tourism Department, T02-501081/2, F501752, www.kws.org **B** *Warden's Cottage* (**C** Jan-Jun), as per *Sirimon Bandas* except that there is only 1 cottage, it has 1 bedroom with a double bed and 1 with 2 single beds, and is just inside the park at the main Naro Moru Gate. **B-C** *Mountain Rock Hotel* formerly called *Bantu Lodge*, PO Box 33, T62625 or T22787 (Nanyuki), 8 km north of *Naro Moru Lodge*, on the road to Nanyuki (you will see a signpost off the main road). Lovely surroundings and a range of self-catering cottages with full facilities. They even have fireplaces in each cottage, which is very welcome on a cold evening. The hotel, which arranges a wide range of activities including riding, fishing, bird-watching and evening entertainment, is known for its very well-run treks up the mountain (taking the Naro Moru, Sirimon or Burguret routes), you can choose an itinerary to suit you. **D** *Blueline Hotel*, about 3 km off the main highway along a dirt road towards Mt Kenya. Pleasant rooms with attached bathrooms. Good place to contact *Naro Moru Porters and Guides Association*, hire gear, etc. Recommended. **E** *Mount Kenya Hostel*, about 12 km down the track towards the park entrance off the main Nanyuki road, about 4 km from the park entrance gate, is popular with budget travellers, hot showers and cooking facilities. **E** *Naro Moru Hotel '86*, town centre, has some rooms. **E** *Youth Hostel*, some dormitory accommodation.

Camping (**E**) is possible at *Naro Moru Lodge*, and at the *Youth Hostel*. There is a site attached to *Naro Moru River Lodge*, where you can hire the necessary equipment. You can use all the hotel facilities, and the campsite sometimes has hot showers. There are also bunk beds available in huts, but these are not very good value. Also at *Bantu's Mount Kenya Leisure*, good facilities available, and *Mount Kenya Hostel*, where you can hire a tent.

Point Lenana at 4,986 m is a strenuous hike, but quite manageable if you are reasonably fit and allow sufficient time to acclimatize to the rarefied atmosphere. It is sometimes called the trekker's peak. It is possible to reach **Mackinder's Camp**, about 4,200 m, and back in a day, but it will mean going as far as the Meteorological Station (3,050 m) on the Naro Moru route by four-wheel-drive vehicle. This can be arranged through *Naro Moru River Lodge* (see below) for about US$20 plus park fees. Trekkers should be aware that altitude sickness, sudden storms, heavy cloud cover and fog can predispose to climbers getting lost on the mountain, and guides are recommended unless you are very experienced. The two peaks, **Nelion** and **Batian**, are only possible for experienced mountain climbers with rock climbing experience and equipment. The Kenya Mountain Club owns some of the mountain huts, which are reserved for members only, although there may be reciprocal arrangements with other clubs.

Take great care over equipment and altitude sickness precautions, otherwise the climb can be sheer misery. There are several routes up the mountain. The Mountain Club of Kenya has published an excellent detailed guide to climbing Mount Kenya listing all the routes, edited by Iain Allan. The two most popular routes up the mountain, suitable for trekkers, are described here. They are best taken leisurely in six days, although they can be done in four. It is an interesting variation to ascend by

Climbing Mount Kenya
The relative ease of climbing to 4,200 m in 48 hrs makes altitude sickness a common occurrence on Mt Kenya. Make sure you allow enough time to acclimatize. See Health section, page 62

Snow Mountain on the equator: Halford Mackinder and the first ascent of Mount Kenya

Halford Mackinder was born in 1861 in Lincolnshire, where his father was a doctor. He attended school at Epsom College and then went to Christ Church, Oxford, studying natural sciences and specializing in geology. In 1887 he was appointed the first teacher of geography at Oxford.

When Mackinder learned of the railway under construction in British East Africa which would eliminate the 500-km trek from the coast to Nairobi, he began to plan and prepare for an expedition to climb Mount Kenya.

The core of the expedition was made up of Campbell Hausburg, a relative of Mackinder's wife; Edward Saunders, a biologist; Claude Camburn, a taxidermist; César Ollier, an Italian-Swiss mountain guide; and Joseph Brocheral, an Italian-Swiss porter.

The party sailed to Zanzibar, finalized arrangements with the British administration, and assembled their caravan. They took on 50 Swahili porters, eight Askaris (guards), two cooks, four tent-boys, an interpreter and a headman. Once in Nairobi they recruited another 46 Kikuyu porters before setting out, trekking east along the Nairobi River, then north through Thika, Murango, and Kijango to Naro Moro. Headed by the Blue Ensign flag and winding back for over 200 m down the trail, the whole party, with local guides and hangers-on, numbered about 170. Emergency rations were carried in 40 sealed

tin boxes (iron-rations), but the main source of food was to be game shot along the route and local maize bartered for cloth and beads. The whole of British East Africa was in the grip of a drought, however, and the procurement of food was problematical.

There were many difficulties. Two porters were killed on an expedition foraging for food; others deserted. Floggings were ordered for porters who threw away biological specimens. A report by Hausburg remarks that eight Swahili porters were shot, presumably for indiscipline, but the event, if it did take place, was hushed up. Mackinder kept up his spirits with the occasional bottle of champagne, and by reading Dickens' 'Old Curiosity Shop' at night by candlelight.

After one failed attempt, Mackinder and the two Swiss set off on 12 September. After some stiff climbing, traversing glaciers and axing footholds in the ice, they reached the summit at noon. The peak was named Batian after the legendary heroic chief of the Masai, and the nearby lower peak, Nelion, after his son.

In the days that followed they made a circuit of the peaks and surveyed the glaciers. Once back in Nairobi, a telegram was sent to to the International Geographical Congress, then meeting in Berlin: "Reached Kenia summit. Mountain has fifteen glaciers. Mackinder." Mackinder's portrait hangs in the Mountain Club of Kenya (see page 83). He died in 1947 aged 86.

---

one route and descend by another (but make sure you keep the park fee receipts for the exit).

Naro Moru approach — Naro Moru approaches from the west and is the most direct, popular but least scenic route, and includes trekking through a long vertical bog. Opposite the Naro Moru police station is a signposted road that leads to the park entrance. It is possible to drive as far as the Meteorological Station, although inexperienced climbers are less likely to suffer from altitude sickness if they walk the 26 km.

Day 1 is best spent travelling from Naro Moru to the **Meteorological Station** at 3,050 m. A ride can be hired from *Naro Moru River Lodge* part or all of the way. There are some bandas here or some permanent tents. **Day 2** is to **Mackinder's Camp** (sometimes referred to as *Teleki Valley Lodge*), located at an altitude of 4,200 m, through terrain that is often very wet underfoot. An early departure is recommended as fog and rain is more commonplace during the afternoon. This section includes a very tiring climb through a steep vertical bog, and when you've cleared the bog the route then continues along a ridge on the southern side of the Teleki Valley, gradually descending to the valley floor. This section is much more attractive with

Senecio (giant groundsel), heathers, the broad-leafed *Lobelia keniensis* and the feathery *Lobelia telekii*. The camp, a stone building, has about 40 bunks and some tents. It is possible to visit the Teleki tarn from here, taking about 1-1½ hours, if the weather holds out. **Day 3** it is possible to make the final leg to Point Lenana, although it is more comfortable to spend Day 3 in and around the surrounding area known as Mackinder's, getting acclimatized to the altitude. From here there are some of the best views of the central peaks. **Day 4** climb to **Point Lenana**. Most trekkers leave Mackinder's at between 0200-0400 to ensure that they reach the summit at sunrise, so a powerful torch is an essential piece of equipment, climbing past the Austrian Hut, 4,790 m, owned by the Mountain Club of Kenya. From here it is about half-and-hour to an hour scramble, depending on fitness, to reach Point Lenana. **Day 5** it is possible to descend all the way to Naro Moru (with a lift from the Meteorological Station), but it is more leisurely to return to Mackinder's Camp for a night, and then on to Naro Moru on **Day 6**. From here there are some of the best views of the central peaks.

The Chogoria approach is from the east between Embu (96 km) and Meru (64 km), and is the most scenically attractive of the routes, although it can be wet. Chogoria village is the starting base from where the deeply rutted road (four-wheel drive essential) takes you past small, intensively cultivated shambas within the lowland forest that rises to become bamboo forest. Colobus monkeys can occasionally be seen here. Most trekkers organize the 32-km ride from Chogoria to approximately 6 km beyond the park gate to the roadhead, 3,110 m. However if you walk this stretch you will greatly reduce the possibility of developing altitude sickness.

Day 1 From village to the roadhead by vehicle and camp there. Alternatively it is possible to stay at the bandas near the park gate. The roadhead is about 1 hr from the bandas. **Day 2** From the roadhead cross the stream and follow the path going in a southwesterly direction. The route continues along the west side of the Nithi Gorge and it is about a six-hour hike to **Minto's Hut**, 4,300 m, which has only very basic facilities. En route there are spectacular views of the Gorges Valley. The path leads through dramatic rock fields and later through the heather moors to Vivienne Falls, 3,650 m, where you can swim in the bracing waters. As you progress upwards Lake Michaelson can be seen on the valley floor 300 m below Hall Tarns. **Day 3** It is possible to reach Point Lenana, but it may be more comfortable to spend the day getting acclimatized in and around Minto's Hut, located close to Minto's Tarn, 4,540 m, which is framed by lofty pinnacles, the scree slopes flecked with giant lobelia and senecio. **Day 4** From Minto's Hut it is about a 4-5-hour climb to **Point Lenana**, via the Austrian Hut, close to the Lewis Glacier. **Day 5** It is possible to descend all the way back to Chogoria (with a lift from the park gate), but it is more leisurely to return to Minto's Hut for a night, and then on to Chogoria on **Day 6**.

Chogoria approach
For Chogoria village, see page 144

Camping gear and appropriate warm and waterproof clothing can be hired in Nairobi at *Atul's*, Biashara St, PO Box 43202, T25935. Cost about US$20 per day, with about US$200 in deposits. Alternatively hire at *Naro Moru River Lodge*, PO Box 18, Naro Moru, T0176-22018 (about 50% more expensive than in Nairobi). It is essential to take effective waterproofs, gloves, headgear, spare boots/shoes, as well as warm/windproof clothing (several layers are preferable) as many of the huts have no drying facilities. Also ensure that you have at least a 3-season sleeping bag and a sleeping mat, as above 3,000 m night temperatures can fall to as low as -10°C. Sunglasses are also useful as the glare off the snow and ice can be very uncomfortable. A stove, fuel, food supplies and water must also be carried. You should obtain one of the maps of the mountain showing the trails in some detail (see page 80). Porters and guides cost about US$5-6 a day, and are a sound investment. Make sure that the agreement with any guides or porters is clear before you set off. Lawrence Maina and James Wahome, PO Box 128, Naro Moru, T0176-62265, have been recommended as being friendly, honest and competent. Guides are especially recommended for trekkers with limited high-altitude experience. Guides and porters can be arranged at *Naro Moru River Lodge* or at

Equipment, porters & guides

the *Transit Motel* in Chogoria. *Mount Kenya Map and Guide*, by M Savage and A Wielochowski, is available at The Nation bookshop in Nairobi (see page 104) or from 1 Meadow Close, Goring, Reading, Berks RG89 9AA, England.

Nanyuki

0° 2' N, 37° 4' E
Phone code: 0176
Colour map 3, grid B4

Nanyuki is a small up-country town located to the northwest of the mountain that dates back to about 1907 when it was used by white settlers as a trading centre and for socializing. The town today is home to the Kenyan Air Force as well as a British army base. Despite this it is a fairly sleepy kind of town and retains some of its colonial character. Nanyuki is usually visited by people planning to use the Sirimon or Buguret trails up the mountain. Its good range of shops provides the only interesting diversion in town. On the main road to Nanyuki there are signposts marking the Equator, and more than a few pushy souvenir sellers.

The **Sweet Waters Rhino Sanctuary** on Laikipia Ranch is 15 km west of Nanyuki (see below).

Sleeping
■ *on map*
For price codes:
see inside front cover

L *Mount Kenya Safari Club*, PO Box 35, Nanyuki, T2141. This is Nanyuki's most exclusive hotel, one of the Lonrho chain and extremely luxurious. Central bookings T02-216940, F216796, lonhotsm@form-net.com **B** *Sportsman's Arms*, PO Box 3, Nanyuki, T32347/8, F22895, located across the river, built in the 1930's. Probably the best-value hotel in Nanyuki, surrounded by gardens and in a lovely setting. Rooms are s/c, complete with TVs and fires. Price includes breakfast and full board is also available. It is clean and friendly. Excellent facilities include fitness centre, swimming pool, sauna, tennis, good restaurant and bar with pool tables. **C** *New Silverbeck*, PO Box 79, T2740. This hotel is rather shabby. It offers a range of rooms but the facilities are poor and there are frequently problems with the water supply. However the cottages all have fireplaces and there is an Equator sign in the grounds. Facilities include bar, restaurant and shops. The original *Silverbeck Hotel*, burnt down which was famed as having had a bar that stretched across the Equator. **D** *Joskaki*, Bazaar St, PO Box

Nanyuki

To Nyahururu & Rumuruti

To Police Station (100m), Nanyuki Sports Club (250m), Simba Lodge (250m), Meru & Isiolo

To New Silverbeck Hotel, Airport, Nyeri & Nairobi

To Sportsman's Arms Hotel (200m)

■ **Sleeping**
1 Equator Chalet
2 Ibis
3 Jambo House
4 Joskaki
5 Juba Hotel Boarding & Lodging
6 Nanyuki Riverside Lodge
7 Nyahururu Horizon
8 Sirimon Little Rock
9 Youth Hostel

● **Eating**
1 Marina Grill

0 metres 50
0 yards 50

228, Nanyuki, T22820, located close to the park in the centre of town. Popular, all rooms have bathrooms, and it has a bar and restaurant, and good views around. It has a disco and can be noisy. **D** *Simba Lodge*, PO Box 211, Nanyuki, T22556. Clean, comfortable and secure. Rooms s/c with hot water, hotel has TV, bar with pool tables, parking.

E *Equator Chalet Hotel*, Kenyatta Av. Good s/c rooms, patio, above a cafe. Recommended. **E** *Ibis*, PO Box 286, Nankuyi, T31536. Comfortable s/c rooms with hot water, nets, above its own bar/restaurant. Secure parking, laundry service available, recommended. **E** *Nanyuki Riverside Lodge*, PO Box 101, T32523, located between the park and river. A pleasant, smart hotel, originally set up as an attempt to rival the *Sportsman*, but without the grounds, set within its own compound. Very good value, cottage-like accommodation in pleasant setting. Has clean and comfortable rooms with bathrooms and hot water, laundry service. **E** *Sirimon Little Rock Hotel*, Biashara St, PO Box 516, Nanyuki, T32344. Situated facing the park this hotel is very good value. It has a range of basic but comfortable rooms, each the name of an African country, with bathrooms and hot water in the evening. Secure and friendly, and there is parking space available, laundry facilities available for an additional charge. **F** *Jambo House Hotel*, Bazaar St, PO Box 485, Nanyuki, T22751. Located at west corner of the park, one of several cheap hotels along Bazaar St, and not the worst despite the rather dark, dingy rooms. S/c and has hot water, plus a bar with a pool table. **F** *Juba Hotel Boarding and Lodging*, PO Box 504, Nanyuki, near the park. Almost as cheap as the youth hostel, above a dirty looking restaurant. The shared facilities have hot water, but the rooms are grubby. **F** *Nyahururu Horizon Hotel*, Bazaar St. One of the cheapest hotels and the rooms are s/c with hot water but otherwise basic, small, tacky and dirty. **F** *Youth Hostel* (Anglican Church of Kenya), located on Market Rd, T22112. Very cheap, friendly, but now looking shabby and has shared ablution facilities, frequently dependent on candlelight.

Camping   **E** secure site at *Sportsman's Arms*, US$2.50 per tent.

Apart from the restaurants attached to the hotels there are few places to eat in Nanyuki. **Cheap** *Marina Grill*, opposite the post office, is popular with locals and visiting soldiers, and offers friendly service, an attractive rooftop bar with barbecue and pool table. Convenient for a cold beer and a snack, and has a good selection of desserts. **Seriously cheap** *Maridadi Café*, near bus stand. Good value. *Nanyuki Coffee Shop*, surprisingly modern interior, cheap local meals and snacks. *Nanyuki Riverside Hotel*. Highly recommended fresh food, enormous variety, excellent omelettes.

Eating
● *on map*

Nanyuki Sports Club, east of *Sportsman's Arms*, offers tennis, squash, golf, swimming and snooker for about US$13 a month or US$2.50 each time, but the problem is that you must be sponsored by an existing member. The facilities of the *Sportman's Arms Hotel* can be used for a small fee.

Sports

On main street there is **Settlers Stores**, which is one of the oldest shops in town having been founded in 1938 and selling hardware and groceries. Other shops include the **United Stores** and **Modern Sanitary Stores** where you should be able to stock up on all your supplies. If you are interested in buying hand woven rugs and other items you may want to visit the **Nanyuki Spinners and Weavers Workshop**. This is run by a women's co-operative group, who sell to the Spin and Weave Shop in Nairobi, but you will get a lower price here. Very interesting place to visit, and they are pleased to give you a full guided tour.

Shopping

Flametree Safaris, PO Box 1411, T0176-22053, F32103, flame@healthnet.or.ke Can arrange camel safaris and other trips.

Tour operators

Air *Air Kenya* have daily flights from Wilson Airport, Nairobi, leaving at 0915 and arriving 45 mins later, US$65 one way. Return journey leaves Nanyuki at about 1130, depending on passenger loads. **Road** Nanyuki is located about 60 km from **Nyeri** and 190 km from **Nairobi** – a drive that will take you about 3 hrs. **Bus** Buses leave from behind Ngumba House next to the *Sirimon*. There are frequent buses and *matatus* running between Nanyuki and Nairobi. If you

Transport

Kenya

are heading north to Marsabit and Northern Kenya you can get buses and *matatus* from Nanyuki to **Isiolo** (which is the last town on the good road heading north), and from there continue north. The *matatu* station is located next to the park.

Directory **Banks** On main street there are branches of *Barclays Bank*, *Kenya Commercial Bank* and *Standard Chartered Bank*. *Barclays* has a bureau de change, an ATM and accepts Mastercard and Visa. **Communications** Internet: services are available at *Global Information Centre* next to *Barclays*, PO Box 1502, T31280, F31783, www.mtkenya.org Friendly service, US$0.50 per email or per min internet access. *Internet Café*, near the town hall, charges US$0.25 per min. **Post office**: on the main street. *Securicor*, Kimathi Rd, offer secure delivery services. **Medical services** The **District Hospital** is located about a km out of town to the east.

Nanyuki to Nyahururu From Nanyuki you can take the C76 unmade road west towards **Nyahururu**. This town is closer to Nakuru and more easily reached from there. The road between Nanyuki and Nyahururu is not good – particularly during the wet season. In the rainy season it is advisable to take the A2 road south towards Naro Moru. Then take the unmade gravel road to the right, which is a link road to the B5. This link road provides good opportunities to see a variety of wildlife. The B5 road towards Nyahururu is a sealed road that takes you through the thick green forests of the Aberdare. Later the land opens out into the great Golden Plains, reminiscent of the mid-West American Prairies. The attractions in this Central Highlands region include a number of game ranches, some of which, including the **Laikipia Ranch**, have been important in the battle to save the rhino. The efforts have involved keeping the rhino as part of an integrated grazing system – they seem to do well and do not interfere with the cattle that graze the same land. The **Sweet Waters Rhino Sanctuary** within Laikipia Ranch has developed a successful rhino breeding programme. In July 2001 Kenya Wildlife Service in conjunction with Laikipia Ranch undertook an elephant trans-location initiative, moving 56 predominantly rogue elephants that had been causing havoc in the Laikipia District to Meru National Park. The elephants had been invading local schools and destroying crops. Elephant numbers have been rising in Kenya at a rate of 1,000 per annum, bringing the total number to approximately 30,000 according to Nehemiah Rotich, KWS director. The Laikipia District has many large game ranches where the seasonal migration of elephants can also be observed. The **Ol Pejeta Game Reserve**, which covers an area of about 400 sq km, is open to the public (see Sleeping, below). Much of the reserve is a rhino sanctuary.

Sleeping At the southern edge of the plateau is **L** *Borana Lodge*, book through *Bush Homes of East Africa*, PO Box 56923, Nairobi, T01-571647, F571665, www.bush-homes.co.ke, which has 6 spacious thatched cottages, with en-suite bathrooms, swimming pool, with food some drinks and game drives included. **L** *Loisaba Wilderness*, also book through *Bush Homes of East Africa* (see *Borana Lodge,* above), is a new 150-sq-km private wildlife conservancy on the edge of Laikipia Plateau with a lodge for 14 guests. There are 4 double and 3 twin bedrooms with en-suite bathrooms and verandahs perched over an escarpment, commanding fine views of Mount Kenya. There's a swimming pool and tennis court and also 'skybeds', 4 wooden platforms set against rocky outcrops and partially covered by a thatched roof, with shower and flushing toilet. Costing over US$400 and still the poor relations of the lodge, the skybeds form part of optional walking, horse or camel safaris. **L** *Ol Pejeta Game Reserve*, located about 40 km from Nanyuki, PO Box 58581, Nairobi, T216940, F216796. A stay in the original ranch house costs upwards of US$300 – the facilities include a health spa. Ol Pejeta was formerly one of the holiday homes of the international arms dealer Adnan Kashoggi, and has a luxury lodge called *Sweetwaters Camp* that is more reasonably priced but still in the **L** category. They organize night game-viewing trips and you are likely to see rhino. **B-C** *Tassia Lodge* is a new community lodge located north of *Borana Lodge* on Lekarruki Group Ranch where elephants can be observed. The lodge sleeps 12 adults and has a bunk house for children. For further details contact *Let's Go Travel* , PO Box

60342, Nairobi, T340331, F336890, www.letsgosafari.com   Another ranch that is open to the public is the **D** *El Karama Ranch* (book through *Let's Go Travel*, see above), located about 40 km to the north of Nanyuki. They have a range of good-value accommodation and also organize game-viewing on horseback.

Nyahururu (Thomson's Falls)

Nyahururu is a small town at high altitude (2,360 m) with a splendid climate. Although only a few kilometres north of the equator, it has bracing nights with occasional frosts in the early months of the year. There is good rainfall, the surrounding area is well timbered, and a variety of vegetables and grains are grown. The town served settler farmers in the area during the colonial period, and was boosted when a branch line of the railway reached the town in 1929. It still runs, but only carries freight. In the postwar period the town was prosperous enough to boast a racecourse.

0° 2' N, 36° 27' E
Colour map 3, grid B4

An explorer, Joseph Thomson, came across the waterfall to the north of the town in 1883 which he named **Thomson's Falls** after his father. The cascade plunges 75 m, and is a pretty area to walk around. It's more commonly known as 'T-falls'. Upstream on the Ewaso Narok River is found one of Kenya's highest altitude hippo pools in an area of marshy bogland, approximately 2 km from the falls.

C *Thomson's Falls Lodge*, PO Box 38, T0365-22006. The most popular choice, just off the road out of town toward Nyeri and Nanyuki, set in pleasant gardens adjacent to the waterfall.

Sleeping
■ *on map*
For price codes:
see inside front cover

Very charming colonial atmosphere, there is a choice of rooms in the main building, or cottages, built in 1931, and initially called *Barry's Hotel*. More people visit to see the falls and have a drink at the bar than actually stay but the rooms are well furnished, if a little cheerless, and all have fireplaces, the restaurant is good and the staff are friendly. There's also a campsite on the grounds, with hot showers, US$4. There is free firewood at the campsite but you will need a machete or an axe. Touts at the entrance of the lodge can be a nuisance. **D** *Kawa Falls Hotel*, PO Box 985, T32295, Ol Kalou Rd at southern edge of town. **E** *Baron Hotel*, Ol Kalou Rd, PO Box 423, T32056. Some rooms have bathrooms others have showers, it is clean and comfortable although less than lavish. There is a bar-restaurant, disco at weekends. One disadvantage is that it is very noisy from 0600 when the *matatus* get going. **E** *Equator Lodge*, Sharpe Rd. Rooms s/c, hot water, restaurant, OK, although staff not overly friendly. **E** *Good Shepherd Lodge*, just north of centre. Own bathrooms, good value. **E** *Nyaki Hotel*, T22313. Excellent value in the quieter part of town, clean, s/c rooms with hot water, rooftop shaded tables and chairs. **F** *Aberdare Bar Boarding and Lodging*, Sharp Rd. Very cheap, single rooms only with bathrooms. With restaurant, bar and thatched parasol tables in courtyard, doubtful security. **F** *Amazing Grace Academy Mixed Boarding*, PO Box 1049, T32915, to

Kenya

Miraa

Miraa, also known as qat *and* gatty, *is produced in large quantities around Meru. It is a leaf which is chewed and is a mild stimulant as well as acting as an appetite suppressant. You will see people all over Kenya (but particularly in the north and northeast) holding bunches of these leaves and twigs and chewing them. In the town*

centre there is a street corner that is devoted to the selling of miraa – in case you want to try some. It is a small tree that grows wild here and is also grown commercially. It is produced legally and it is also sold to the northeast of Kenya and exported to Somalia, Yemen and Djibouti.

north of town. Cheap and basic. **F** *Cyrus Lodge*, Ol Kalou Rd. Very cheap single rooms only. Nothing elaborate, but good value as s/c, hot water, clean, light and airy, quiet, secure and friendly staff.

Eating
● *on map*

Cheap *Baron Lodge*, good tasty food. *Cyrus Bar and Restaurant*, Ol Kalou Rd. Attached to *Cyrus Lodge*, mainly serves Nyama Chana (barbecued meats). *Thompsons Fall Lodge*, very good meals and snacks in attractive surroundings at inexpensive prices. Highly recommended, hot showers, lovely setting among tall trees. **Seriously cheap** *Ben's Cakes*, friendly, with good cakes and snacks. *Tropical Bar and Restaurant*, near the *Baron Hotel*. *Nyahururu Budget Store* stocks a few western luxuries like *Cadbury's* chocolate and *Nescafe*.

Entertainment

Bars and nightlife Lively atmosphere at *Muthengera Farmer's Lodge*, just east of Ol Kalou Rd. **Cinema** Just north of clocktower. **Discos** At *Baron Hotel* at weekends.

Transport

Road Bus: regular buses and minibuses linking to **Nakuru** to the west and **Nyeri** to the east. 2-3 departures north each day for **Maralal**, leaving at 0700 and costing US$5.

Directory

Banks *Barclays*, *Kenya Commercial Bank* and *Kenya Co-op Bank* are all in the vicinity of the post office. **Communications** *Securicor*, at Mbaria Centre, PO Box 518, T22576, for delivery services. **Medical services** The *Mbaria Centre* opposite the town hall has a medical centre.

Nanyuki to Meru

Northeast from Nanyuki the road continues around Mount Kenya. The next village that you will reach after Nanyuki is **Timau** – there is very little here. Another 35 km or so down the road is the turning off to the left that goes on up to Marsabit and Northern Kenya. The first town on this road is **Isiolo**, which is located about 30 km off the Nanyuki-Meru road and is where the good road ends (see Northern Kenya section, page 280).

The **Lewa Wildlife Conservancy** is situated approximately 65 km northeast of Nanyuki (see Isiolo, page 287, which is located closer to the main entrance).

Continuing around the mountain about 30 km on after the turning off to Isiolo, you will reach the town of Meru, which is a thriving and bustling trading centre. The journey from Nanyuki to Meru is very beautiful, and shows the diversity of Kenya's landscape. To the south is Mount Kenya, to the north (on a clear, haze-free day) you can see miles and miles of the northern wilderness of Kenya.

Meru

0° 3' N, 37° 40' E
Phone code: 164
Colour map 3, grid B5

Meru is located to the northeast of the Mount Kenya. Although it serves as an important trading centre it does not receive many visits from travellers. As it is not close to any of the trails up the mountain, it has not been developed for this. It is, however, the base for visits to the **Meru National Park** the entrance of which is just over 80 km from the town.

Although Meru National Park is in the Eastern Province it will be described here, as this is the route normally taken by road when visiting the national park.

Kenya

There is a noticeable military presence here and a good range of shops, banks and internet facilities, as well as the celebrated *Pig and Whistle*. There are two **markets** at Meru: one on the main road towards Nanyuki and the other on the opposite side of town. The merchandise on sale is very cheap and includes not just agricultural produce from the farms around Meru, but also baskets and household goods. The prison on the Nanyuki Road produces furniture that is on sale in a shop in town.

Meru stands in a heavily cultivated and forested area at an altitude of about 3,000 m and in the rainy season it is cold and damp. If you are here on a clear day you may get good views.

The **Meru National Museum**, formerly a District Commissioner's Office, and built in 1916, has several small galleries, with displays ranging from local geology, stuffed birds and animals to innovative toys made from scrap materials. The most interesting section of the museum is that related to the customs and culture of the local Meru people: various ethnographic artefacts are exhibited, as well as examples of local timber and stone and tools from the prehistoric site at Lewa Downs. There is a Meru homestead that gives a good idea of how the Meru people live. In the museum shop is a relic of colonial days – a wind-up gramophone made by His Majesty's Voice. This particular model came via Pakistan where the then owner was stationed with the King's African Rifles. There is a small selection of bakelite 78 records which can be played for KSh10. Outside there is a display of various herbs and other medicinal plants, including an example of a *miraa* plant. The museum also has a snake pit and a crocodile pit. A craft shop sells locally produced items. ■ *US$2.50. 0930-1800 Mon-Sat, 1130-1800 Sun. PO Box 592, T0164-20482. Located down the road roughly opposite the Meru County Hotel and in what is the oldest building in town.*

Meru

To Forest Lodge, Greenland Holiday Resort, Rocky Hill Inn, New Milimani & Stansted Hotels, Nanyuki, Isiolo & Meru National Park

Library
Town Hall
Meru Central District HQ
Postal District HQ
4
Meru District Hospital
Meru National Museum & Shop
Samburu Chemist
Paramount
5
Securicor
Co-op   Dentist
British-American
2
2 **3**
Uhuru Monument
Scorpion **5**
Abonyati Traders
Music Store
Clouds Disco **1** National
Chemist
Millennium **6**
Consolidated
African Banking Corporation
Shell
Kenya Commercial
Caltex
Kensilver Bus
3 Barclays
Matatu Stage
Total
Shell
To Embu & Nairobi
MOI AV

0 metres   200
0 yards   200

4 Meru County
5 Meru Safari
6 New Ntugi Lodge
7 Pig & Whistle

● **Eating**
1 Angie's
2 Candy Café
3 Chips Café & Snacks
4 Ivory Springs
5 Julietta Chicken Grill

■ **Sleeping**
1 Brown Rock
2 Castella
3 Continental

Out of town B *Forest Lodge*, about 10 km out to the north of the town, has a range of comfortable cottages, facilities include a bar, restaurant and swimming pool and it is set in fine gardens. C *Greenland Holiday Resort*, PO Box 2065, T0164-20409, about 4 km out of town, also has a swimming pool. C *Rocky Hill Inn*, 8 km north of town, has simple cottages for rent, there is a bar and they have a barbecue which is good value.

In Meru town D *Pig and Whistle*, PO Box 360, T31411, is the most charming hotel in town. It was here that George and Joy Adamson stayed in order for Joy to establish adultery and thus obtain a divorce from her second husband, Peter Bally . There are cottages in the grounds, s/c, hot water, some of those built in the 1930s have period furnishings and fittings. The hotel has a handsome central building from the colonial period with a good restaurant (Mid-range), friendly staff, and excellent security. D *Meru County*, PO Box 1386, T20432, F31264, is situated on the main road and is probably the best hotel in the town centre. It is simple but clean,

Sleeping
■ *on map*
For price codes:
see inside front cover

modern and comfortable, safe and friendly. All rooms are s/c with hot water. It has a very good restaurant (Mid-range) serving huge breakfast for US$4 and dinner for US$6.50. There's also a bar with a patio, video lounge and there are plenty of secure parking spaces. **D** *Meru Safari Hotel*, PO Box 6, T31500, modern, attractive, well-appointed hotel, range of rooms, all s/c with hot water. There is secure parking, laundry services, and a restaurant. **E** *Castella*, simple and good value. **E** *New Milimani*, disco at weekends – plenty of parking space but often has water supply problems. Restaurant (Cheap) serves wide-ranging menu including curries. **E** *Stansted*, PO Box 1337, T0164-20360. All rooms s/c with hot water. This is a very good value hotel – clean, comfortable and friendly. **F** *Brown Rock*, T20247, very central, clean, restaurant. **F** *Continental*, PO Box 1006, T31437. Fairly basic, rooms are rather run-down with shared bathrooms. It has a lively bar on two levels downstairs with a pool table. **F** *New Ntugi Lodge*, PO Box 341, T20551, all rooms s/c, rather gloomy, and not particularly secure.

Eating **Seriously cheap** *Angie's*, on the main road serves mostly grills, also snacks. *Ivory Springs* is very popular with local people. *Candy Café* is busy, small, local food and grills. *Julietta Chicken Grill*, accurately named indeed, and good value. *Chips Café and Snacks*, good variety of meals and snacks. *Castella Hotel*, fairly large with rather dingy décor. Popular with local people, and offers good value. *Supermart* is a well-stocked supermarket on the road out towards Nanyuki.

Entertainment *Clouds* disco on Moi Av, *New Milimani Hotel*, disco at weekends.

Transport **Air** The airstrip serving Meru is in Mitunguru. The road from Mitunguru to Meru becomes very slippery in the wet season. **Road Bus**: the main bus and *matatu* area is behind the Mosque, reached from the road going past Barclays. There are daily buses to Meru from **Nairobi** including the luxury service. The journey to Nairobi takes about 5 hrs, to **Chogoria** about 1½ hrs and to **Embu** about 2½ hrs. The Kensilver & Akamba Bus Services to Nairobi via Embu are cheap and reliable. You can even buy your ticket in advance and have a reserved seat. *Matatus* are not very safe as they are often involved in accidents on this route and the bus is definitely the better option. Meru is located about 70 km from Nanyuki. *Matatus* north to Isiolo take about 45 mins. The scenery quickly changes from healthy banana plantations to looming cacti and dry scrubland. South from Meru the road to Embu is good. The scenery here is well worth spending the time to appreciate. If you can sit on the right you will be able to look out for glimpses of the mountain peaks. About 5 km south of Meru you will again cross the equator.

Directory **Banks** *Barclays*, near the *matatu* station accepts Visa, Mastercard and ATM. *Co-op Bank* will undertake money transfer and has a bureau de change. Money can also be changed at *African Banking Corporation, National Bank of Kenya, Kenya Commercial Bank, British-American Bank*. **Communications** Internet: *Scorpion Internet Café* sends (US$1) and reads emails. *Paramount*, PO Box 125, T30289 sends and reads email and fax. *Abonyati Traders*, T30452, reads and sends emails, prints files and offers word-processing facilities. *Millennium*, T20790, sends and reads emails. **Post office**: near Town Hall, with telephone and fax, and telegraphic money transfer services. *Securicor* (0800-1700 Mon-Fri, 0900-1200 Sat) on main road offers *Omega, Pony* and *DHL* delivery services.

Meru National Park

0° 2' N, 38° 40' E

Check on the security situation before visiting the Meru National Park as there have been some unpleasant incidents between tourists and poachers here

Meru National Park covers an area of 1,810 sq km, and is located northeast of Mount Kenya, 85 km east of Meru town on the northeastern lowlands below the Nyambene Hills. It is approximately 370 km northeast of Nairobi. It straddles the equator and has a road system of over 600 km, much of which has recently been upgraded, which aids game-viewing safaris. As the ground is very stony a four-wheel drive is the preferred option. It is mainly covered with thorny bushland and wooded grasslands to the west. There are 13 rivers and numerous mountain-fed streams that flow into the Tana River from the south.

The late Joy Adamson hand-reared the orphaned lioness Elsa here, later releasing her into the wild. Elsa died of tick-borne fever and was buried in a forest clearing by the Ura River in the south of the park, where her grave is marked by a small plaque.

The national park suffered greatly from lawless poachers during the late 1980s, which resulted in the deaths of several rangers and two French tourists, along with the annihilation of the introduced white rhino population. Following these incidents the option of visiting Meru National Park was effectively withdrawn by all the safari operators. The Kenyan government have now driven out the poachers and restored security. However, much of the wildlife in the park was decimated and it will be some time before numbers are recovered.

In July 2001 the Kenya Wildlife Service embarked on an elephant translocation initiative. They plan to move 56 'rogue' elephants from the Laikipia district of the Rift Valley to Meru National Park. (Human-animal conflicts have included the invasion of schools and the destruction of crops by elephants.)

Dense riverine forests grow along the watercourses surrounded by the prehistoric-looking doum palms. There are hundreds of species of birds including the Somali ostrich, the red-necked falcon and Pel's fishing owl, which can be heard at night by the Tana River. Animals include lion, leopard, cheetah, elephant, Grevy's and plains zebra, gerenuk, reticulated giraffe, hippo, lesser kudu, oryx, hartebeest and Grant's gazelle. There are just a few tourist package tours to this park making it one of the least trampled and unspoiled parks. ■ *Park information from The Warden, PO Box 11, Maua, T0164-20613.*KWS have recently built a three-span Bailey bridge across the Tana River. Funded by the World Bank, the 138-m galvanised steel bridge links Meru National Park to Kora National Park. The bridge has been named the Adamson Bridge in honour of George Adamson who lived nearby with his beloved lions at Kampi-ya-Simba. There are plans to develop an eco-lodge on Tana River Island.

Meru National Park is close to several national reserves including Bisanadi, North Kitui and Rahole. They have no tourist facilities at present. Kora was

Kenya

Meru National Park

N

0 km 3
0 miles 3

■ **Sleeping**
1 Leopard Rock Lodge
2 Elsa's Kopje

Kenya

DC Stone's *Boma*

Many of the early colonial administrators were quite eccentric. Among them was the aptly named Mr Stone, the District Commissioner of Embu. His duties included hearing and give judgement upon local disputes, known in Swahili as shauris. DC required anyone who wished to appear before him to carry a rock on their head up the hill to his office. When enough stones had been accumulated, the boma or district office was constructed.

upgraded from reserve to national park following the death of George Adamson and there are plans to open it up in the near future. For further information about these reserves, see Northern Kenya, page 290.

Sleeping
■ *on map, page 143*
For price codes:
see inside front cover

L *Elsa's Kopje*, 8 thatched stone cottages, either twin or double beds, all with en-suite bathrooms and locally made furniture, 2 of the cottages even have an outside bath with views over the park. Also has a swimming pool and a gift shop. Price (over US$550) includes food, day and night-time game drives, nature walks and fishing. Efforts are made to minimize the impact of the lodge on the environment. Reservations through *Bush Homes of East Africa Ltd*, PO Box 56923, Nairobi, PO Box 56923, T01-571647, F571665, www.bush-homes.co.ke **L** *Leopard Rock Lodge* (**B** Apr-Jun), PO Box 208, Maua, T0873-761929241/2. This is a new lodge offering luxury full-board accommodation, 15 bandas. Has a small museum with library and video room, African-style open-air kitchen, pottery, swimming pool and pool bar. **C** *Bwatherongi Bandas*, 4 self-catering bandas near the park HQ, managed by the Kenya Wildlife Service. 3 of the bandas have a single bed, the other banda has 2 single beds. The bandas are quite basic, and have no kitchen as such, only an outside barbeque area that overlooks the Bwatherongi River. Bring everything you may need. Book through the KWS Tourism Department, T02-501081/2, 602345, F501752, www.kws.org **C** *Murea Bandas*, 4 self-catering bandas just outside Murera Gate, they have 2 bedrooms, each with 1 double and 1 single bed, and en-suite bathroom. Like *Bwatherongi Bandas* these are offered by the Kenya Wildlife Service (contact details as above), have a barbeque area rather than a kitchen and require you to bring everything with you.

Transport

Road You will need your own vehicle. Head from Meru town to Maua, which is the last place to stock up on petrol and supplies. Murera Gate is about 30 km from Maua down an unpaved road, with magnificent views over *shambas*.

Chogoria
For the Chogoria trail,
see page 135

Between Meru and Embu is the village of Chogoria, which is the starting point for the **Chogoria trail**. This is the only eastern approach up the mountain and it is generally considered to be the most beautiful of the routes. It is also supposed to be the easiest as far as gradients are concerned (see Mount Kenya, page 133).

Sleeping **C** *Meru Mount Kenya Lodge*, just inside the park gates, bearing to the right. Reasonable bandas, with showers and log fires. **E** *Transit Motel*, in Chogoria village. Fairly basic but porters and guides can be arranged from here.

Transport The most direct route from **Nairobi** is through Embu. There are plenty of buses and *matatus*. The buses to Embu usually stop off at Chogoria (it takes about an 1½ hrs from Nairobi).

Embu

0° 32' S, 37° 38' E
Phone code: 161
Colour map 3, grid B5

This is the final town in the clockwise circuit around Mount Kenya, before rejoining the road south to Nairobi. The town is strung out along the main road. Named after the Embu people who live in this area, it is the provincial headquarters of the Eastern Province. The surrounding area is densely populated and intensively cultivated. It is a busy town, with the bars staying open late. There's not a great deal to see here although the *Isaac Walton Inn* is a very pleasant place to stay.

C *Isaac Walton Inn*, Embu/Meru Rd, PO Box 1, Embu, T0161-20128/9. This is the best hotel in Embu, situated about 2 km north of town on the road to Meru. It is an old colonial hotel apparently named after an English angler because of the proximity of good fishing spots in the mountain streams nearby. The inn is set in gardens with a comfortable lounge with a log-burning fire, the rooms, in modern cottages, all have bathrooms with hot water and each room has a balcony. The price includes breakfast and there is a good bar and restaurant (Cheap), it is very friendly and the staff are helpful. **D** *Highway Court Hotel*, T20046. Large, modern hotel with excellent views over the town from the roof, rooms s/c, has a restaurant and lively bar, good security, but can be noisy. **F** *Kubu Kubu*, T 0161-20334. Situated down the hill from the centre of town, shops and supermarket, and health centre nearby. Reasonable – basic with small rooms but clean. **F** *Morning Glory*, on main street, is basic but adequate, shared bathrooms, snack bar and takeaway. **F** *Nafuu*, just east of town centre, offers simple accommodation and shared bathrooms. F *New White Rembo Guest House*, Kitui Rd, opposite the bus station, above shops, shared bathrooms. A little dilapidated, but offers reasonable value. **F** *Prime Hotel*, T30692, along a track off the Kenyatta Highway to Nairobi, is fairly central and recommended.

Sleeping
■ *on map*
For price codes:
see inside front cover

Kenya

Seriously cheap *Arkland Hotel*, popular place for Indian snacks and other meals. *Rehana Café*, north part of town, off the main road, up the hill. Good spicy snacks. *Morning Glory Takeaway*. Fish, chips, grilled food and snacks are on the menu. *Unnamed new café* with log-cabin appearance, located next to the BP petrol station. It is very popular and serves a variety of food. There is also plenty of cheap food from kiosks around the market and the bus station.

Eating
● *on map*

Embu

To Provincial Hospital, Isaac Walton Inn & Meru

Town Hall □

Kobil

Chemist

Meru Rd

Beatnet @

Cinema (Closed) □   Co-op Ⓢ

Consolidated Ⓢ

BP

To Mwea National Reserve & Kitui

Barclays Ⓢ   Kenya Commercial Ⓢ

Football Pitch   Mobil

Matatu & Bus Station

To Principality Police Station, Mwea National Reserve

Mugu Shopping Centre, Supermarket & Health Centre □

To Nairobi

Kenyatta Highway

N

0 metres   100
0 yards   100

■ **Sleeping**
1 Highway Court
2 Kubu Kubu
3 Morning Glory & Takeaway
4 Nafuu
5 New White Rembo Guest House
6 Prime

● **Eating**
1 Arkland Hotel
2 Café
3 Rehana Café

Road The road from Nairobi to Embu has a very good surface but is very busy. *Matatus* frequently drive at reckless speeds and are therefore not recommended for this journey. Instead take the *Kensilver* or *Akamba* bus (Nairobi to Meru, via Embu) if possible, which goes everyday and is reasonably safe. Journey to Nairobi takes 1½ hrs.

Transport

Banks *Barclays Bank* is to the south of town; nearby is the *Kenya Commercial Bank*. The *Co-op Bank* is near the old cinema, and *Consolidated Bank* is on Embu-Meru road. **Communications** Internet: *Beatnet Cyber Café*, on the second road left going south from the post office. **Post office**: is located towards the north of town on Embu/Meru Rd. **Libraries** The town library is located on the Meru road that heads north.

Directory

Mwea National Reserve is a small reserve of 68 sq km, gazetted in 1976, located southeast of Embu, approximately 180 km north of Nairobi. The most direct route from Embu is to follow the infrequently used B7 road towards Kangonde, south of *Mount Kaniro*, 1,549 m, and branch off to the right on a small road approximately 10 km before Iriamurai. The small national reserve lies immediately north of the Kamburu Reservoir, constructed at the confluence of the Tana and Thiba rivers, and the

Mwea National Reserve

Kaburu and Masinga hydro-electric dams are sited in the reserve. The vegetation is predominantly thorny bushland with patches of woodland and scattered baobab trees. Mwea Reserve, part of which has recently been enclosed with an electrified fence, contains elephant, buffalo, impala, lesser kudu, baboon, vervet and Sykes' monkeys, hippos and crocodiles in the rivers, and a profusion of birdlife. The adjacent rice-growing paddies and fields have attracted large number of waders and waterbirds and this area is also rich in birds of prey. There are two picnic sites at **Hippo Point** and **Gichuki Island**, but no other visitor facilities. The nearest mid-range accommodation is at Embu.

A dispute between local rice farmers and the National Irrigation Board (NIB), who process and market the crop, but who were accused of exploitation and of leaving the farmers with insufficient rice to feed their families, resulted in the shooting of two of the farmers by police in 2000 at Ngarubani, a local market. The Kenyan Human Rights Commission has expressed concern at the violations of the farmers' human rights. Travellers to this region are unlikely to be aware of, or at risk from, the repercussions of this dispute.

The Rift Valley

The Great Rift Valley is one of the most dramatic features on earth, stretching some 6,000 km from the Dead Sea in Jordan down to Mozambique in the south. In Kenya, the Rift Valley starts at Lake Turkana in the north, and runs right through the centre of the country to Lake Natron just across the southern border in Tanzania. Up to 100 km wide in places, it is a fascinating place of cliffs, escarpments, rivers and arid plains, housing an enormous diversity of wildlife, trees and plants. The valley floor rises from around 200 m at Lake Turkana to about 1,900 m above sea level at Lake Naivasha to the south. The walls rise where the valley floor is at its highest, and reach their peak in the Aberdares, above Naivasha. In the south of the region the Masai Mara, bordering on to the Serengeti in Tanzania, is one of the most exciting game parks in the world, teeming with wildlife and the site of the quite spectacular wildebeest migration. It is also the most likely place to see lions in Kenya. The scenery here is wonderful, with Mount Kilimanjaro in the background acting as the perfect backdrop to miles and miles of arid savannah plains covered with fragile grasslands and scrub bush.

There are some 30 active and semi-active volcanoes in the Rift Valley and countless springs bringing sodium carbonate up to the surface of the earth, forming the soda lakes. Soda lakes are a result of the poor drainage system in the valley, resulting in a number of shallow lakes on the valley floor. Evaporation has left a high concentration of alkaline volcanic deposits in the remaining water. The algae and crustaceans that thrive in the soda lakes are ideal food for flamingos and many of these beautiful birds are attracted here, making a truly spectacular display.

The Rift Valley is one of the few ecosystems that has remained unchanged for centuries, holding a great array of Africa's wildlife. It is the site of two of the most significant digs in palaeontological history, the **Koobi Fora** on the eastern shores of Lake Turkana and **Olduvai Gorge** in the Tanzania section of the Rift. No visit to Kenya is complete without spending some time in the Rift Valley.

Your first glimpse of it is likely to be from the viewpoints along the Nairobi-Naivasha new road just past Limuru, at the top of the escarpments of the Valley. Mount Longonot is directly in front, while the plains seem to sweep on forever to the south. There are a number of tourist stalls along the route selling unremarkable curios. A reasonably good buy, however, are the sheepskins, although they are not particularly well cured.

If you take the old Nairobi-Naivasha road (B3 – the more westerly road) which forks to the left at Rironi, the road continues in a northwesterly direction for approximately 6 km then turns left on a sealed tarmac road in a southwesterly direction around Mount Longonot. The road leads to the small provincial town of **Narok** (see page 166), the main access point to the Masai Mara Reserve, described at the end of this section.

After a drive of about 17 km, a small dirt road leads to the south towards Mount Suswa, 2,356 m, an easily accessed volcano in the heart of Masai country, only 50 km from Nairobi. It is not as well known as Mount Longonot to the north. The outer crater has been breached on the southern and eastern sides by volcanoes, and numerous lava flows are visible. This whole area is honeycombed with lava caves and there are many examples of obsidian pebbles and rocks. One of the caves, over 20 km deep, is believed to be the longest in Kenya. The caves are home to several small mammals and birds including bats, snake owls, rock hyrax and squirrels.

It is possible to drive up to the floor of the outer of the two craters, approximately 10 km in diameter. The outer caldera floor is richly covered with grasses, from which the volcano takes its name. The Masai graze their cattle in this peaceful enclosure,

Mount Suswa

If you visit the caves, take care as there are some concealed drops in the cave floor

Kenya

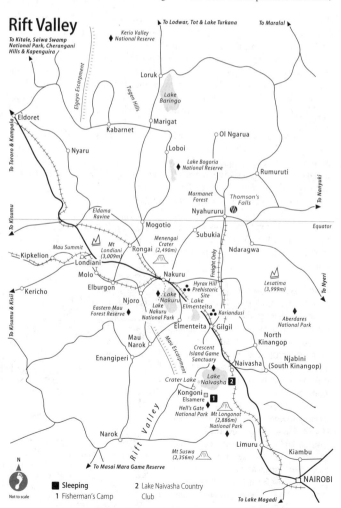

Rift Valley

Sleeping
1 Fisherman's Camp

2 Lake Naivasha Country Club

N
Not to scale

also home to a variety of game. The inner crater, which is ring shaped, has a diameter of approximately 5 km, and is covered with dense vegetation. There is a large central lava plug. The inner crater edge offers a good ridge walk of about 1½ hours to the main summit, **Ol Donyo Onyoke.** Circumnavigation of the crater rim is possible, but can take up to eight hours because of the difficulty going over the sharp lava blocks and fields in the southeast section of the crater. **Camping** It is possible to camp in the caves, but you must bring all supplies, including water, with you.

Transport *Matatus* serve the B3 Narok road, but there is little traffic or hitching opportunities along the last 12 km south on rough unmade roads. The road skirts the northeast flank of the mountain until it reaches a crossroad. Turn right here along a rough track until you reach a group of *manyattas* that extend over a distance of 1½ km. From here a rough track leads up to the caldera. The only identifying marks are the deeply grooved water channels lying to the sides of the track. The distance to the caldera is approximately 7 km. Turn left for the caves or right to reach the inner crater, a distance of another 8 km.

Naivasha

0° 40' S, 36° 30' E
Phone code: 0311
Colour map 3, grid B4

The town of Naivasha is a small trading centre just off the main road from Nairobi to Nakuru. Most famous for its lake, Naivasha was traditionally used as grazing land by Masai, until they were displaced by European settlers at the turn of the 20th century. It used to be more popular with tourists as the old road passed through it, now the best reason to visit is for the excellent *Belle Inn* fruit juices and pastries. It is a stop on the way to **Lake Naivasha**, **Mount Longonot** and the **Hell's Gate National Park**. Naivasha is sufficiently close to Nairobi to be used as a weekend retreat for people working in the capital. There are still a number of White Kenyans farming the land around the lake.

The most likely reason for stopping here is en route to either Lake Naivasha or Hell's Gate. The lack of facilities for budget travellers around the lake makes staying in Naivasha a useful option. However, it may be more rewarding to camp down by the lake, as long as you take your own food and water. **Kamuta Ltd**, T0311-30091 is the base of *Air Naivasha* that offers flights around Lake Naivasha and over Hell's Gate. Of particularly good value is the short flight over Lake Naivasha and Hell's Gate for US$25. It is on the same entrance as *Lakeside House* by Lake Naivasha.

Sleeping
■ *on map*
For price codes:
see inside front cover

There is plenty of accommodation in this popular and expanding weekend retreat for Nairobians, although there is little of attraction in the town itself except for *La Belle Inn*. For budget travellers, it is best to stock up in town and then head for the lake. *Matatus* to and from the lake are among the most packed you will find in Kenya – even the locals complain.

C *Ken-Vash Hotel*, Posta Lane, just up from Moi Av, T30049. Large new building with spacious and comfortable s/c rooms with balconies, and friendly staff. It has a good-value restaurant (Cheap) and a good bar too. **C** *La Belle Inn*, Moi Av, PO Box 532, T21007, F21117. Popular place with

Naivasha

To Petrol Stations, Kilimo Lodge, Sweet Banana Lodge (100m), Securicor (300m), Lakeside View Hotel (500m) & Nakuru

To Municipal Market (50m)

To Nairobi (New Road)

To Railway Station (150m)

To Lake Naivasha (South Lake Road 3 km), Hell's Gate & Nairobi (Old Road)

To Lake View Point

■ **Sleeping**
1 Heshima
2 Kafico Lodge
3 Ken-Vash
4 La Belle Inn
5 Naivasha Silver
6 Othaya Annexe
7 Sam Holiday Inn
8 Wambuku

attentive staff and a selection of comfortable rooms at different prices, all including huge and very good breakfast (fresh fruit juice, croissants, home-made jam, butter, bacon, eggs and lots of coffee). Restaurant (Cheap – the best place to eat in town) and snack bar offer wide range of food. It is also a good place to stop for a drink and a break from driving, it has a selection of pastries (many vegetarian which is unusual for Kenya). The restaurant is closed on Tue. The hotel has quite a lively nightclub with 3 bars, and contains the *Naivasha Business Centre*, with internet access at about US$1.50 per 15 mins or email. **C** *Lakeside View Hotel*, Moi Av, PO Box 894, Naivasha, T30268, 5 mins walk north along Moi Av. Pleasant, large leafy verandah, good modern rooms, some with balconies in the quieter outskirts of town, but by no means beside the lake. Reasonable food in restaurant (Cheap). There's a bar and staff are attentive; prices are cheaper for Kenyan residents. Reservations can be made on a Nairobi number: T02-337103, 248008. **D** *Wambuku Hotel*, Moi Av, T30287. This is very similar to *Ken-Vash* but much better value. Rooms are different sizes, all have basic but clean bathrooms with hot water. Large bar with balcony, price includes breakfast. **E** *Kafico Lodge*, Biashara Rd, T21344. Basic but clean and secure, rooms with bathrooms and hot water. Also has a restaurant and bar and parking. **E** *Naivasha Silver Hotel*, Kenyatta Av, T20580. Above a jolly café, clean and comfortable s/c rooms with hot water, but still relatively expensive. **F** *Heshima*, Kariuki Chotara Rd, T20361. Basic and cheap, with shared facilities, no hot water and the room security is questionable. there is a bar and restaurant on ground floor and parking in central courtyard. **F** *Kilimo Lodge*, Moi Av, PO Box 286, Naivasha, T20416. Basic but friendly, rooms are s/c with hot water, bar at front, food available. Parking in courtyard, bar and restaurant. **F** *Othaya Annexe*, Kariuki Chotara Rd, PO Box 651, Naivasha, T30050. Basic rooms and s/c bathrooms, becoming run-down but is still good value. Restaurant on ground floor, bar with TV and pool table, but with some rather seedy clientele, on 1st floor. **F** *Sam Holiday Inn*, Sokoni Rd, opposite the market. Fairly basic rooms on 3 floors around a central courtyard, a little dirty but rooms are s/c and have hot water. Restaurant and bar that is a popular local darts venue. **F** *Sweet Banana Lodge*, Moi Av, PO Box 1410, Naivasha, T20638, north of the town centre. Cheap single rooms only, s/c, hot water, bar and restaurant.

All the hotels have their own restaurants. **Cheap** *Jim's Corner Dishes* (formerly *Brothers Café*), Station Lane. Relaxed place offers good value, with excellent local food. | **Eating**

Road If you are coming by road from Nairobi there are 2 routes. The first is along the old road that nowadays is the preserve of hundreds of lorries driving between Mombasa and Uganda. The road is poor, though the views are great and you are likely to see herds of zebra and other wildlife roaming the vast valley floors. The other route is along the new A104 road that does not come into Naivasha town itself. It is in good condition and has the added advantage of having the most wonderful views of the Rift Valley, particularly at the equator. **Bus**: Many of the buses head further west to Nakuru or Kisumu. Ask the driver to let you off at the Naivasha turning. You can then walk the few km to Naivasha town or flag down a *matatu*. **Taxi**: Peugeot taxis run to Naivasha throughout the day, taking about 1½ hrs. | **Transport**

Banks *Barclays Bank*, on Moi Av, will change money. **Communications** Internet: from *Naivasha Business Centre* at *La Belle Inn*; *Jophy Computer Centre*, on Mama Ngina Rd (US$5.50 per hr); and *Pewa Computers* (US$2.50 per hr). **Post office** is also on Moi Av. *Securicor*, north along Moi Av, offer *Omega* and *DHL* parcel services. | **Directory**

Lake Naivasha

Lake Naivasha, meaning 'rippling waters', 170 sq km lying at about 1,890 m above sea level, is a lovely place to come for a weekend if you are staying in Nairobi as it is only a 1½-hour drive away. The flying boats used to land here before Nairobi airport was built. It is a freshwater lake on the Rift Valley floor with no apparent outlet, but it is believed to be drained by underground seepage. The lake is dominated by the overshadowing **Mount Longonot** (2,880 m), a partially extinct volcano in the adjacent national park (52 sq km). | *Colour map 3, grid B4*

For a more interesting route to Naivasha, which need not add more than an hour to your overall journey time (if in your own car), Kiambu, a one-way commuter town, and Limuru, a lively market town, could be used as transit points from Nairobi. The drive to Kiambu is hilly, but smooth, through corridors of high trees and past the *Windsor Golf and Country Club*. Although neither town is particularly attractive, the Kiambu-Limuru road provides a quite beautiful half-hour drive through lush, fertile land full of rich tea and coffee plantations, and dotted with the elegant, umbrella-like thorn trees.

It is possible to come to spend a day at one of the lakeside hotels without staying the night (there may be a small charge or it may be free if you eat there). The lake itself is quite picturesque with a mountain in the background and floating islands of papyrus. The water level fluctuates as a result of underwater springs, although the actual mechanism is not clear. There are hippos in the lake that sometimes come out onto the shore at night to graze, and there are many different types of waterbirds.

The lake is best explored by boat (a number of the hotels listed rent vessels out for hire); or alternatively you could work your way around the shore by bicycle. There are a number of activities. A motorboat can be hired for US$20 per hour; a rowing boat for about US$7 an hour. There are fish eagle nests near the Yacht Club. The twin-hulled launch from the country club on its 'ornithological cruise' often tries to entice the birds with fish. The evening cruise at about 1800 is a good time to see them. Morning and evening bird-watching walks can be made to the **Crescent Island Game Sanctuary** via the *Lake Naivasha Country Club*. ■ *US$8-10 entry plus boat across the lake.*

On the way to Fisherman's Camp, the road goes through a major flower-growing area. Owned by Brooke Bond, it is an important exporter and employs thousands of local people. The flowers are cut, chilled and then air freighted to Europe.

A few kilometres past Fisherman's Camp is **Elsamere**, the home of George and Joy Adamson. It is easy to miss, so look out for the sign to the Olkaria Gate of Hell's Gate; it is a few hundred metres further on the right-hand side. There is a small **museum** (not as interesting as the display of her paintings in the National Museum)

Lake Naivasha & Hell's Gate

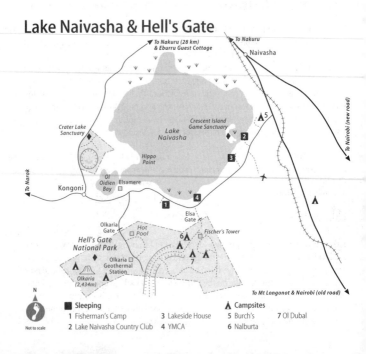

■ Sleeping
1 Fisherman's Camp
2 Lake Naivasha Country Club
3 Lakeside House
4 YMCA

▲ Campsites
5 Burch's
6 Nalburta
7 Ol Dubal

Not to scale

and the gardens are very pleasant with lots of birds flying among the trees. A film shows the life (and death) of Joy. Beware though it lasts well over one hour! ■ *1500-1800 daily. US$3 entry fee includes a copious tea.* See *Sleeping, below.*

West of Lake Naivasha, one hour's walk from Kongoni and approximately 17 km past *Fisherman's Camp* is **Crater Lake**. Its often jade-coloured waters are quite breathtaking. There is an animal sanctuary, but some of the tracks in this area are only manageable by foot or with a four-wheel drive. You are allowed to walk around by yourself and it's easy to see the rare black and white colobus monkey. It is possible to cycle to the game park, although the soft, dusty track after Kongoni is hard going. ■ *Crater Lake has recently become a private game park and there's a US$1.50 entry fee.*

West of the lake are 2 estates which offer exclusive accommodation for wealthy guests: **L** *Mundui Estate*, PO Box 1, T0311-21050, is a conservation area where there are giraffe, zebra, eland, hippo, buffalo and over 250 bird species. Accommodation is in an old hunting lodge, where the Aga Khan, Ernest Hemingway and Evelyn Waugh are said to have stayed. There is a large double bedroom with fireplace, 2 smaller double bedrooms and a large sitting room with fireplace. **L** *Nderit Estate*, is one of the most expensive places to stay in Kenya. There are 2 private homes, the unusual 115-ft-high Dodo's Tower, which has room for up to 9 guests on 4 floors, and *Hippo Point House*, an old colonial house with 8 rooms for up to 14 guests. There is a swimming pool, game drives are included, other activities like horse-riding, sailing, waterskiing and day trips are also available. Stays at both estates should be booked in advance through *Bush Homes of East Africa Ltd*, PO Box 56923, Nairobi, T01-571647, F571665, www.bush-homes.co.ke

Sleeping

L *Crater Lake Camp*. At over US$300 a night, this exclusive hotel has a great position on the shores of the lake. **L** *Lake Naivasha Country Club*, T20013. Run by *Block Hotels,* PO Box 40075, Nairobi, T02-540780, F545948. The best lakeside option, with wonderful gardens which gently lead down to the lake. The rooms are quite good with all amenities including a swimming pool. This hotel welcomes children and has a small adventure playground for them. It serves good food and does an excellent buffet lunch on Sun (on lawns if the weather is good) which is very popular – eat as much as you like for around US$8 – only drawback is it often gets crowded with tour groups from Nairobi. **A** *Elsamere Conservation Centre*, T0311-30079. Joy and George Adamson's house (see above). You can stay here as well, but book in advance as there's only room for about 15 guests. **A** *Lakeside House*, T20908 or T567424 (Nairobi). Package deal includes food and drink in the house of the Anglo-Kenyans who have lived here for many years, they also offer safaris at an extra cost, the prices are considerably less for residents.

C-D *Fish Eagle Inn*, PO Box 1554, Naivasha, T30306. Decent bandas available, as well as small but clean dormitories (with electricity) made with local materials (US$5). Also has camping facilities, but the food and hospitality is not the best. There is an excellent swimming pool but only those staying in the most expensive bandas can use it without extra charge (US$1, US$2 for visitors). Hippos come out of the water at night and graze within view a stone's throw away from the *Fisherman's*. Recommended despite the shortcomings. Hot water available 24 hrs, can get a bit crowded during holiday peak periods. **D** *Eburru Guest Cottage*, North Lake Rd, Naivasha. Bookings through *Let's Go Travel*, Nairobi T340331, F336890. Approximately 30 km from Naivasha town, on Green Park development at an altitude of 2,132 m up Eburru Hill. The cottage comprises 2 small buildings close to the main house, self-catering accommodates 4 adults, and has an electricity supply. **D** *Fisherman's Camp*, T30276, bookings through *Let's Go Travel*, PO Box 60342, T340331, F214713, www.letsgosafari.com Further along the lakeside road, this is set in beautiful surroundings, deeply shaded by huge trees. Motor boat hire is available. There are 2 types of accommodation, bandas are the most comfortable with reasonable facilities including showers and bedlinen, all the bandas have electricity. Cheaper is the spartan youth hostel of dormitory-type bunks, which now has a bar and restaurant, drinks and food available. **D-E** *Candelabra Camp*, up the hill on the opposite side of the road from the entrances of

Kenya

Fisherman's Camp and *Fish Eagle Inn*, run by an English couple. Excellent views of the lake and surrounding area. Has 2 types of banda and camping available, hot showers are available in the evening. **E** *YMCA*, T30396. Cheapest place to stay, it is before *Fisherman's Camp* and the closest accommodation to the main gate of Hell's Gate National Park. A good 15 mins from the lakeside, set in beautiful gardens. It is sometimes possible to buy provisions here.

Camping (**E**) at a site close to the water's edge at *Fisherman's Camp* (need to bring provisions), next door at the *Fish Eagle Inn*, at *Candelabra Camp* or the *YMCA*. Several campsites have opened in Hell's Gate National Park recently – see map for locations.

Eating **Cheap** *Geotherm Club*, ½-hr walk from *Fisherman's Camp* towards Elsamere. Set in lovely gardens with pool at edge of lake, managed by *Belle Inn* so reliably good food. *Yelogreen Bar and Restaurant*, 1st stop on South Lake Rd. Reasonable food but difficult to reach without own transport. **Seriously cheap** A short distance west of *Fisherman's Camp* and across the road is a tiny local restaurant (unnamed), it has a limited choice but the owner is very welcoming.

Transport **Local** **Cycle hire**: there is cycle hire available (US$6 a day) from *Fisherman's Camp*, greatly increasing your options for exploration, particularly to Hell's Gate National Park. The man who runs the small souvenir stalls opposite the entrance to *Fisherman's Camp/Fish Eagle Inn* rents out a mountain bike which is much better than any of those at *Fisherman's Camp* and cheaper too (about US$4 a day; check condition first). **Long-distance** From Nairobi take the A2 to Thika, and then a signposted turning for Kiambu (20 mins' drive). Just before Kiambu town take a left turning for the Limuru Rd (signposted). *Matatus* go regularly to **Kiambu** and **Limuru** from the Tom Mboya end of River Rd. *Matatus* also go regularly between Kiambu and Limuru for the 1-hr drive from Limuru to Naivasha. The lower road to **Naivasha** is in a very poor state. If coming from **Masai Mara** it would be worth taking the longer route round and going back up to the top of the Rift first.

An adventurous way back to Nairobi from Naivasha, which necessitates a very early start, and probably a night in Thika, would be to walk (or cycle) and hitch along the rough road between Njabini and Gatakaini, along the southern edges of the Aberdare mountain range. The forest is wild, noisy with bird and animal sounds (but safe). *Matatus* leave early (0600) for the rural outpost of **North Kinangop** and the journey has dramatic views back to the lake and beyond. You could also go directly from Naivasha to Njadini (if time allows), or else it is another 17 km from North Kinangop.

Hell's Gate National Park

0° 50' S, 36° 20' E Approximately 90 km from Nairobi, and about 14 km southeast of Lake Naivasha, this national park is a major attraction in the Rift Valley and is one of the few parks you are allowed to explore on foot. Both bicycles and motorcycles are allowed too, either offering an excellent way of exploring the park. Access is south of the YMCA at Lake Naivasha, through Elsa Gate and Olkaria Gate, south of *Elsamere*. The park covers an area of 68.25 sq km. The flora is mainly grasslands and shrubland with several species of acacias. It is famous for its water geysers, as well as being a breeding area for Verreaux's eagles and Ruppell's vultures. Lammergeyers have also been spotted hovering over the dramatic cliffs of Hell's Gate Gorge. A feature of this landscape is the lustrous acid-resistent volcanic glass, usually black or banded, called obsidian, formed from cooled molten lava. When fractured it displays curved shiny surfaces.

Two extinct volcanoes are to be found here – **Olkaria** and **Hobley's**. The route through the park is spectacular, leading through a gorge lined with sheer red cliffs and containing two volcanic plugs – **Fischer's Tower** and **Central Tower**. The park is small, and despite there being a wide variety of wildlife, including eland, giraffe, zebra, impala and gazelle, you may not see many of them as they are few in number.

What you will see, though is the incredibly tame hyrax that looks like a type of guinea-pig but is actually more closely related to the elephant, and a host of different birds of prey.

Within the park is the substantial Olkaria Geothermal Station generating power from underground – lots of large pipes and impressive steam vents in the hills. Near Central Tower is a smaller lower gorge that extends out of the park to the south. Here is a ranger post where drinks and sodas can be purchased, and a path that descends steeply into the gorge. The path skirts along the river in the bottom, into which hot springs in the cliffs flow, and then climbs back to the ranger post. While in the gorge branch off into an even smaller gorge that has high, water-eroded walls that are so narrow in places that the sky is almost blocked out. After about 700 m there is a high wall that will force you to turn back, but on your return you will get a great view of Central Tower rising above the gorge.

In the park, close to the ranger post mentioned above, is *Oloor Karia Masai Cultural Centre* where Masai people demonstrate singing, dancing and jewellery making. ■ *No extra charge on top of the park entrance fee, opening times vary. Ask at the information centre at Elsa Gate for details. The information centre sells some food and soft drinks, and also has a good, inexpensive guide to the park.*

There are now several **campsites** within the national park (see map) in addition to the campsites up the road by Lake Naivasha (see page 152) which also have bandas.

To climb Mount Longonot you need to get to Longonot village along the old road; from there it is about 6 km to the base of the mountain. Longonot Park covers an area of 52 sq km, predominantly filled by the mountain. You can be escorted up by Kenya Wildlife Service rangers and the fairly straightforward climb takes about an hour, but be prepared for the last section which is quite steep. A wander round the rim of the mountain takes a further two or three hours. ■ *US$15 fee to climb Mount Longonot (there are student reductions).*

Mount Longonot
See map page 147

Mount Longonot is a dormant volcano standing at 2,886 m. The mountain cone is made up of soft volcanic rock that has eroded into deep clefts, v-shaped valleys and ridges. There is little vegetation on the stony soil. However the crater is very lush and green, with fairly impenetrable trees. There are fine views over the Rift Valley on one side and into the enormous crater on the other.

Sleeping The best places to stay are by the lakeside; there is nowhere in the immediate vicinity of Mount Longonot except the **L** *Longonot Game Ranch*, T332132 (Nairobi), which caters for small groups of up to six people. If you want to see some wildlife on horseback, this would be a good option.

This is a shallow soda lake, similar to Lake Nakuru, though it does not attract such enormous numbers of flamingos. As it is not a national park, you can walk around it and you don't have to pay. Lake Elementeita is between Naivasha and Nakuru, just off the main road, part of the Delamere Estate's Soysambu land. Near the lake are several prehistoric sites, indicating that this area was once densely populated. The best-known archaeological site is **Gambles Cave**, 10 km southwest of the town of Elmenteita. There are few facilities at the lake or in Elmenteita town, but it is an easy day trip from Nakuru with direct *matatus* (one hour) or 30 minutes from Gilgil, a transit point on the Nairobi-Naivasha Road.

Lake Elmenteita
See map page 147

Sleeping **L** *Delamere's Camp*, a luxury tented camp has recently opened here. **L** *Lake Elementeita Lodge*, expensive and somewhat impersonal. Near Elementeita town there is also **L** *Ol Jolai*, an old ranch house with exclusive accommodation arranged through *Bush Homes of East Africa Ltd*, PO Box 56923, Nairobi, PO Box 56923, T01-571647, F571665, www.bush-homes.co.ke

Kenya

Kariandusi is a prehistoric site of the Acheulean period to the right of the Naivasha-Nakuru road (A104) discovered by Dr L Leakey in 1928 and excavated from 1929 to 1947. Studies suggest that it was not an area of permanent habitation and the findings indicate that the people who lived here were of the genus *Homo erectus*. There is a small museum housing obsidian knives, Stone Age hand axes and a molar of the straight-tusked elephant, a variety which roamed in Northern Europe before extinction. The nearby diatomite mine offers a fascinating visit. ■ *0800-1800 daily*.

Nakuru

0° 23' S, 36° 5' E
Phone code: 037
Colour map 3, grid B4

The next major town along from Naivasha, Nakuru is Kenya's fourth largest town and is in the centre of some of the country's best farming land. It is a pleasant, slightly dusty agricultural town with shops mostly selling farming equipment and supplies. Nakuru came into existence in 1900 when the building of the railway opened up access to the surrounding lush countryside attracting hundreds of white settlers to the area. Lord Delamere, one of the most famous figures in colonial times, collected around 600 sq km of land here and developed wheat and dairy farming.

On the corner of Kenyatta Avenue and Mburu Gichua Road is an area where street performers demonstrate their skills, including dancing, music and juggling. An interesting structure is the **Eros Cinema**, an example of functional post-war

Nakuru

Sleeping
1 Amigo's Guest House & Papa Rego's Café
2 Carnation
3 Highlands Boarding & Lodging
4 Le Rhino
5 Midland
6 Mt Sinai Boarding & Lodging
7 Mukoh
8 Nakuru Inn
9 Pekar's Restaurant & Lodging
10 Rift Valley Sports Club
11 Seasons
12 Shirisko High Life
13 Waterbuck

architecture, slender columns and glass walls. **Breaker's Music Centre** on the corner of Kenyatta and Club Road has an unusual cupola room on the corner. **Nyayo Garden** is wellkept and central with a war memorial. **Nakuru Station** is another fine example of post-war architecture. A mural dominates the booking hall. The two artists, M Ginsburg and R McLellan-Sim, depict settlers looking out over the Rift Valley showing the Masai, cattle and rolling wheatfields. A notable Hollywood film-star is said to have been the model for the male settler – he subsequently had a successful career in politics. In the restaurant there are photos of the railway. The station itself has a slender clocktower with slim columns and delicate iron screens. And the clock still keeps time.

The other notable building is the **Rift Valley Sports Club**, PO Box 1, Nakuru, T212086. This was formerly the Nakuru Club, and was first built in 1907, was burnt down in 1924 and then restored. A patio restaurant looks out over the cricket pitch. The cricket pavilion has photos of past teams and the ground is prettily surrounded by jacarandas and mango trees. In the *Men's Bar* (women still not allowed) there are sporting prints and etchings. Tennis, squash and a small swimming pool are available as well as cricket nets on Tuesday and Thursday. It is possible to stay here (see Sleeping, below).

Kenya

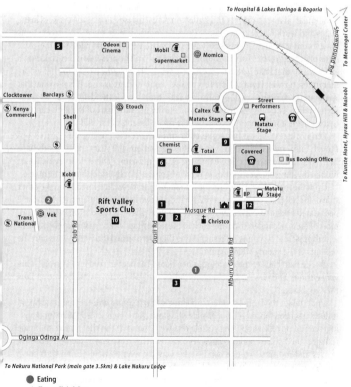

● **Eating**
1 Cheers Club & Bar
2 Coco Savannah
3 Millennium Hotel

Excursions

As you ascend, the views over Lake Nakuru are excellent, although it is not visible from the top

Menengai Crater This extinct volcano on the northern side of town is 2,490 m high and is the second largest surviving volcanic crater in the world, with a surface area of 90 sq km. However it is not easy to see it from the town. A sign erected at the highest point by the Rotary Club shows the distances and general directions of several places world-wide. The crater is 8 km from the main road. If walking, leave from the Crater Climb Road, then Forest Road (it takes a couple of hours but is pleasant enough). However, recent reports of robberies makes this a less safe option, and an alternative is to drive along Menengai Drive out through the suburbs. It is fairly well signposted. There is no public transport from the town to the Menengai Crater, and as few people visit it there is scant hope of hitching a lift. There are a number of kiosks en route to the top where you can get a drink and basic local foods but no refreshments are available at the summit.

In the 19th century the Menengai Crater was the site of a bloody battle between different Masai clans, vying for the pastures of the Rift Valley slopes and Naivasha. The Ilaikipiak Moran (warriors) were defeated by their southern neighbours the Ilpurko Masai, who reputedly threw the former over the crater edge. According to legend the fumaroles rising from the crater bed are the souls of the vanquished seeking to find the way to heaven. The Maa word *Menenga* means 'the dead'.

The views over Lake Nakuru are excellent (although the lake dried up completely in Spring 1994 but has now refilled) as are the views towards Lake Bogoria over the other side. The crater itself is enormous, about 12 km across and 500 m deep. The mountain is surrounded by a nature reserve.

Hyrax Hill Prehistoric Site About 4 km from Nakuru, Hyrax Hill contains neolithic and Iron Age burial pits and settlements, first investigated by the Leakeys in the 1920s and work has been going on there, periodically, ever since. The excavations have found evidence of seasonal settlements from 3,000 years ago, and there are signs of habitation here up until about 300 years ago. The presence of beach sands is an indicator that Lake Nakuru may have extended right to the base of the hill in former times, turning Hyrax Hill into a peninsular or even an island. It is possible that 9,000 years ago this vast prehistoric lake may have extended as far as Lake Elementaita. The hill was given its name during the early part of the 20th century, reflecting the abundance of hyraxes in the rocky fissures of the hill.

The northeast village has some enclosures where the digging was carried out though only one is not overgrown. It dates back about 400 years and the finds have been pieced together and are exhibited in the museum. There is no evidence of human dwellings suggesting this may have been used for livestock but not humans.

Up at the top of Hyrax Hill are the remains of a stone-walled fort and on the other side of the hill it is possible to see the position of two huts in a settlement which have been dated back to the Iron Age. A series of burial pits with 19 skeletons were found, most of them decapitated, dating back to the same time. The remains are all in a heap and all appear to be young men suggesting they were buried in a hurry – possibly the remains of the enemy after a battle.

On the path back to the museum, a bau board has been carved into the rock. One very curious find was six Indian coins dating back 500 years – no-one knows how they got here.

Underneath the Iron Age site, a neolithic site was found and the neolithic burial mound has been fenced off as a display, the stone slab which sealed the mound having been removed. Nine female skeletons were found at the site. Unlike the male remains, the females remains have been buried with grave goods including dishes, pestles and mortars. No one can be sure why the women were buried with grave goods and not the men, but it could indicate that women were more politically powerful in former times. Oral history in the region suggests this may have been the case. Why the Iron Age burial site is directly on top of the neolithic one also remains a mystery. Hyrax Hill was gazetted a National Monument in 1943. The **museum**, that contains artefacts from the site, was previously a farmhouse. ■ *The site is open 0930-1800 daily. There is a small entrance fee.* It is just off the Nairobi road so it is easy to get to. Just take a *matatu* heading for Gilgil and ask to be dropped off at the turning for Hyrax Hill. It is about 1 km from here to the museum. You can camp here if you wish, though there are no facilities except those for the museum staff.

Lake Bogoria, 60 km north of the Menengai Crater (see page 161), and **Lake Baringo** (see page 162) are both within easy reach of Nakuru. Buses leave twice daily to Kampi ya Samaki (*Fisherman's Camp*) on the lake and *matatus* go to the small town of Marigat. From either place you will be able to get a local *matatu* to the lake itself. The journey only takes a couple of hours on good roads. The road is pleasant enough, passing sisal plantations as it goes deeper into the valley. A sign marks the equator where you can be treated to a demonstration: 10 m to the north of the line and water turns clockwise draining from a bowl; 10 m to the south and it turns anti-clockwise; on the line it goes straight down.

Sleeping
■ *on map, page 154*
For price codes:
see inside front cover

L *Lake Nakuru Lodge* (**A** in low seasons), PO Box 561, Nakuru, T85446. Medium-sized lodge situated in the national park near the Ndarit Gate, with pleasant gardens and pool overlooking the park, sister lodges at Lake Elementaita and Lake Naivasha as well as *Sundowner Lodge* can be booked through the booking office in Nairobi (PO Box 70559, T224998, F230962). **B** *Kunste*, T212140, about 2 km out on the Nairobi Rd. **B** *Stem*, about 8 km outside the town itself, close to Nakuru National Park, T85391. **C** *Midland*, on Kamati Rd, PO Box 908, T212125, F44517, midland@africaonline.co.ke Long-established hotel, the most popular place in town for the more upmarket travellers, with restaurant and 2 bars. The comfortable, well-appointed rooms have en-suite bathrooms and a TV, breakfast is included but it is still a bit pricey. **C** *Rift Valley Sports Club*, PO Box 1, T212086/5, Club Rd, very central. You need to become a temporary member, best value in Nakuru.

D *Carnation*, Mosque Rd, T43522. Large hotel with own restaurant in the centre of town. Some of the rooms are a little gloomy, and some bathrooms look dirty, but otherwise fine. **D** *Mau View Lodge*, good cheap hotel, with parking in an enclosed courtyard, on Oginga Odinga Av, 1 km out of town, well served by *matatus*. The closure of the courtyard gates is very noisy, own bar, simple meals. **D** *Waterbuck*, West Rd, T214163. Modern hotel with good facilities, very clean and spacious, the rooms are s/c and have balconies. **E** *Seasons*, Government Av, PO Box 3163, T211896. In part of a converted house, though the best rooms are the additional ones at the back. Large s/c cosy rooms, good value and quiet place except for disco night (Fri). Has a bar and restaurant with an excellent daily buffet lunch. **E** *Carnation Hotel*, PO Box 1620, T43522, Mosque Rd. Good basic hotel. **E** *Hotel le Rhino*, Mburu Gichua Rd, PO Box 14316, T42132. Comfortable and clean, has good rooms with s/c bathrooms. Restaurant and pleasant bar, with helpful staff and good views from roof. The price can be negotiated especially in low season. **E** *Mt Sinai Boarding and Lodging*, Gusii Rd, PO Box 28238, T211779. Large building, very clean in fairly modern rooms, all s/c, hot water, secure. **E** *Mukoh*, corner of Mosque and Gusii Rd. Popular place offering clean, quiet and comfortable accommodation. It has some rooms with baths, hot water in the morning, and the best breakfast in town. It is a little overpriced, and is also good for snacks. Good view of town and Lake Nakuru from the roof. **E** *Pekar's Restaurant and Lodging*, Mburu Gichua Rd, T215455. Well-presented restaurant and large s/c rooms, good security but only warm water available. **E** *Shirisko High Life Hotel*, Mosque Rd, despite the name this is a basic hotel and bar, shared bathrooms, no hot water, and is a little overpriced. **F** *Amigo's Guest House*, Gusii Rd, above *Papa Rego's Café*. Basic, shared bathrooms and small rooms but overall clean and tidy. **F** *Highlands Hotel Boarding and Lodging*, very basic s/c rooms that have seen better days. **F** *Nakuru Inn Hotel*, cheap and clean but is basic and cramped. Has a restaurant and popular bar with an outdoor section.

Eating
● *on map, page 154*

Apart from restaurants attached to hotels are: **Mid-range** *Kabeer Restaurant*, Government Av, on a par with the *Oyster Shell*, offers a choice of Indian or Chinese food, seafood or grills, open daily until 2200. *Oyster Shell Restaurant*, T40946, Kenyatta Av. Considered to be the best restaurant in town with an extensive menu for breakfast, lunch and dinner.

Kenya

☞ ## Flamingo deaths

Recently, an alarming rise in the number of flamingo deaths has been noted at several of the Rift Valley lakes. Approximately 30,000 died within a three-month period in 1993 and two years later in 1995 another 15,000 flamingos perished at Lake Nakuru. In 2000 the number of deaths was estimated at 30,000, and this year there are again a large number of very sick birds. The current deaths have been occurring at lakes Bogoria, Nakuru and Elementeita. Post-mortems appear to show that the flamingos are dying from heavy metal poisoning (cadmium, lead, arsenic and nickel), in addition to pesticide accumulation. However, analysis of the fish stocks show no significant changes in the concentrations of these metals. The water level of Lake Nakuru has decreased by about 60% from its normal level due to recent droughts. The debate continues as to whether the drought has altered the alkalinity of the waters or whether the birds are dying after consuming toxic waste from the nearby sewage plant.

Some of the other lakes, like Magadi and Sonachi, that also have high levels of heavy metal contamination have no surface inflow, a factor that effectively excludes the possibility of man-made pollution in those lakes. As the Rift Valley is volcanic it is possible that the source of these contaminants is natural. Work is currently being undertaken in a Kenyan/Swedish study to determine whether algae toxins may be a co-factor, as many of these deaths have occurred following periods of algae bloom.

The flamingos, a major tourist attraction of Lake Nakuru, have moved to other alkaline lakes including the tiny Lake Simbi Nyaima, 200 km west, close to Lake Victoria. The flamingo has an estimated lifespan of 50 years, and older birds are believed to guide the others. Fortunately, the deaths are not expected to have too great an impact on the overall numbers of flamingos as they are very successful breeders, with 250,000 hatchlings surviving annually.

Cheap *Café Lemon Tart*, Corner of Moi Rd and Kenyatta Av, T213208. Excellent breakfasts and light snacks. *Nakuru Sweet Mart*, Gusii Rd, vegetarian Indian food. *Tipsy Restaurant*, Gusii Rd, T43960. Popular with local people and is good value, they have western dishes as well as good curries and tilapia (fish). *Cheers Club and Bar* and *Coco Savannah*, Club Rd/Government Av, are nightclubs that also offer some food. *Millennium Hotel*, Government Av. Bar/beer garden sells *nyama choma* (barbequed meats). *The Nakuru Coffeehouse*, Kenyatta Av, T214596, serves very good coffee. About 2 km outside Nakura on the road to Nairobi on the left-hand side there is a shopping centre with good snacks for a short stop. *Take a German one* sells grilled German sausages. Recommended.

Entertainment
Apart from the tiresome safari touts, Nakuru is a friendly place with a lively nightlife

Cinemas and theatres There is an *Odeon* cinema on GK Kamau Highway, screenings are twice a night, usually. Just off Oginga Odina Av is the *Nakuru Players Theatre*. **Discos** *Illusions*, Kenyatta Av. *Pivot* (weekends). *Oyster Shell Nightclub*, over the restaurant. MTV all day, young persons club with good sound and light systems. *Coco Savannah*, Club Rd/Government Av corner, PO Box 664, T211426. Large, lively, US$2.

Tour operators
It can be cheaper to book your safari in Nairobi

Blackbird Tours, T45383, at the *Carnation Hotel*, are very helpful with visits to nearby national parks and other safaris. *Crater Travel*, T45409, just off Kenyatta Av, can arrange air tickets. *Leisure Activity Safaris* (cycling), PO Box 7229, T/F37-210325. *PEGA Tours & Travel Agencies*, PO Box 2215, T210379, F45999. Reportedly excellent safari driver/guide called Peter. *Select Travel and Tours*, Kenyatta Av, PO Box 15680, T214030/1, arrange hotel bookings and car hire, and offer *Fed Ex* delivery service. *Taylors Travel*, PO Box 527, Kenyatta Av, near *Standard Bank*.

Transport
Road There are regular *matatus*, buses and Peugeot taxis to Nakuru from **Nairobi** (3 hrs), **Nyahururu**, **Naivasha** (1½ hrs) and all points west including **Kisumu** (4½ hrs), **Eldoret** (4 hrs) and **Busia** (8 hrs). The main bus station is on the eastern edge of town. Buses leave up to midday and *matatus* leave all day from **Mogotio** (1 hr) and **Marigat** (2 hrs).

Directory

Banks Most of the big banks have a bureau de change including *Barclays* and *Standard Chartered* on Kenyatta Av. The *Postbank* on GK Kamau Highway can arrange *Western Union* money transfers. **Communications** Internet: Services are available from two *etouch* centres (US$5.50 per hr), *Vek Computer Bureau*, Government Av (US$5.50 per hr), and *Momica Communication Bureau*, which also offers fax and telephone services. The post office is close to the clocktower on Kenyatta Av. **Courier delivery** can be arranged from *Select Travel and tours* (see below); *Securicor* (Omega and Pony services); and *DHL*, 200 m west of the roundabout near *Waterbuck Hotel*. **Medical services** Chemist: *Fades*, Kenyatta Lane, T212627.

Lake Nakuru National Park

This national park is just 3 km south of Nakuru town in central Kenya, 140 km northwest of Nairobi. It was established in 1960 as the first bird sanctuary in Africa. It is about 199 sq km and the lake is fringed by swamp, and surrounded by dry savannah. The upper areas within the national park are forested. There is a wide variety of wildlife: bat, colobus monkey, spring hare, otter, rock hyrax, hippo, buffalo, waterbuck, leopard, lion, hyena, and giraffe, but the most popular reason for visiting is the wonderful sight of hundreds of thousands of flamingos. At one time there were thought to be around 2,000,000 flamingos here, about one third of the world's entire population, but the numbers have diminished in recent years. The best viewing point is from the Baboon Cliffs on the western shores of the lake. There are also more than 450 other species of birds here.

0° 30' S, 36° E

There is no entry to the park by foot

Lake Nakuru is alkaline and its size fluctuates depending on the time of year from 5.5 sq km in the dry season to 40 sq km during the wet season. The Blue-Green algae *Spirulina Platensis* flourishes in the alkaline waters and is a primary food source for the flamingo population. Recently there have been unexpectedly high death rates of these graceful birds – see box opposite. In 1958 alkaline-tolerant *Tilapia grahami* were introduced to the lake to try to curb the problem of malaria in the nearby town. Fish-eating eagles appeared in this area shortly afterwards.

Take preventative measures against the huge number of malarial-carrying mosquitoes, prevalent in this area and common to all the Rift Valley lakes

The park has also established a special rhino sanctuary and contains 35 black rhino and 10 white rhino in an enclosure, secured by electric fencing to deter poachers. In 1974 the endangered Rothchild giraffes were introduce from the Soy plains of Eldoret where they have bred successfully. Leopards are occasionally spotted.

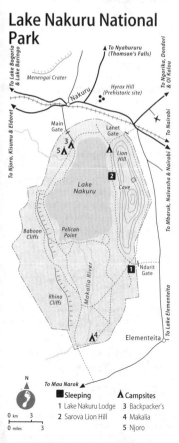

Lake Nakuru National Park

To Nyahururu (Thomson's Falls)
To Lake Bogoria & Lake Baringo
Menengai Crater
Nakuru
Hyrax Hill (Prehistoric site)
To Ngorika, Dondori & Ol Kalou
To Njoro, Kisumu & Eldoret
Main Gate
Lanet Gate
To Nairobi
3
5
Lion Hill
2
Lake Nakuru
Cave
Baboon Cliffs
Pelican Point
To Mbaruk, Naivasha & Nairobi
Makalia River
1
Ndarit Gate
Rhino Cliffs
4
Elementeita
To Lake Elementeita
To Mau Narok
N
0 km 3
0 miles 3

■ **Sleeping**
1 Lake Nakuru Lodge
2 Sarova Lion Hill

▲ **Campsites**
3 Backpacker's
4 Makalia
5 Njoro

L *Lake Nakuru Lodge*, PO Box 70559, Nairobi, T224998, access from Ndarit Gate. Banda accommodation is on offer with a swimming pool, and good views of the lake. House was part of Kenya pioneer Lord Delamere's estate. **L** *Sarova Lion Hill*, PO Box 30680, close to eastern shore of lake, T333248, F211472 (Nairobi), access from Lanet Gate. Each room has a private bathroom and verandah. Swimming pool, sauna

Sleeping
■ *on map*
For price codes: see inside front cover

There is also accommodation at nearby Nakuru (see page 157)

Kenya

and boutique available on site. There are good views, and it is popular with group tours. **B** *Naishi House*, self-catering accommodation offered by the Kenya Wildlife Service in the south of the park, near *Makalia Campsite*. The house is furnished with rugs and paintings by local artists and has a fully equipped kitchen (including fridge), lounge, dining room and 2 bedrooms, each with a double and a single bed. There are also 2 single rooms in an adjacent cottage. Bring all food and drinking water. Escorted game drives can be organized from here. The whole house rents for US$200-US$250, including the cottage, but other arrangements may be possible. Contact the KWS Tourism Department, T02-501081/2, F501752, www.kws.org **E** *Florida Day and Night Club*, close to Main Gate, just beyond the outskirts of Nakuru. Basic but cheerful.

Camping (**E**) *Backpackers' Campsite*, just inside the Main Gate. **E** *Njoro Campsite*, about 1 km into the park on the northwest side of the lake. **E** *Makalia Campsite*, by the southern boundary of the park and close to the waterfall. You will need a vehicle for these last 2 campsites. There are 2 other campsites by the northeast entrance, *Kampi ya Nyati* (Buffalo) and *Kampi ya Nyuki* (Bee). Both lead down to quiet viewpoints on the lakeshore.

Transport This is one of the easiest parks to visit being just outside Nakuru. You will need to be in a vehicle though you are allowed to get out at the lakeside.

From Nakuru southwards, there are regular *matatus* to **Njoro** (30 minutes) and **Mau Narok** (four hours), a small village at the end of the road. There are no *matatus* but it is easy to walk to **Elementeita** and its lake (see page 153) from here, taking about two hours. South of Mau Narok the road leads to a small town called **Enangiperi**, and from here the C57 road runs west of the *Mau Escarpment* 53 km south to **Narok** (see page 166), the closest town to the Masai Mara Game Reserve.

Rongai

Colour map 3, grid B4 This is a small, pretty village about 25 km west of the Nakuru in the valley of the Rongai River, which rises in the Elburgon Hills. Originally the area was inhabited by the Tugen and Njembs tribes, before they were driven out by the Masai. But the Masai never settled and there is no record of of their ever constructing *manyatta* (Masai villages) in the valley.

The land was part of the great tract leased to Lord Delamere, who then rented it out to settlers. In the colonial period Rongai grew to prominence as a maize-growing area. This crop was first introduced to Kenya by the Portuguese, but it did not do well. Then an American variety was used to develop a hybrid known as Kenya White, which flourished. The land was tilled by teams of oxen, maize was being exported by 1910, and by 1917 there were 3,000 ha under maize around Rongai.

The railway arrived in 1926 as part of the line onward from Nairobi to Uganda. A branch line was built from Rongai northeast to Solai, now disused, although you can still see the tracks. The branch went entirely through settler country and, as there was no 'native land' along the route, it was much criticized as an example of the colonial adminstration favouring the interests of the settlers over those of the Africans.

One notable feature of Rongai is the number of churches. The **Africa Inland Church** has arched windows in pairs, glazed in yellow, green and orange, with sunrise airbricks above each pair. The walls are of grey volcanic stone, and it has a tin roof. The **Catholic Church of St Mary** is a modern, neat, functional

Rongai

To Solai (Old Line)

To Rongai Visoi

Mara River

Agricultural College

Catholic Church of St Mary

St Walstan's

Africa Inland

Sports Field

Health Centre

Rongai Bookshop

Heart of Christ Catholic Seminary

Gospel

To Nakuru

N

0 metres 50
0 yards 50

■ **Sleeping**
1 Beach

● **Eating**
1 Blue Café

structure of grey stone with timber panelling. The **Heart of Christ Catholic Seminary**, PO Box 238, dates from 1986, but is cloistered and quiet, with well-tended flower beds, run by Italian Fathers.

The prettiest of the churches, and a testament to the determination of the settlers to reproduce rural England on the equator, is **St Walstan's**, built in 1960. It is an exact replica of an early English (1016) country church at Bawburgh, 6 km east of Norwich in the UK. St Walstan is known as the 'Layman's Saint'. He came from a wealthy land-owning family, was fond of farm animals, and he insisted on working in the fields with the farm labourers. He collapsed and died while working one day, and a spring bubbled up on the very same spot.

The church building has a square tower with battlements, pointed windows, and a shingle (wooden tile) roof. In the vestibule is a piece of flint from the church in Bawburgh. Inside there is a tiny gallery with steps up to it cut into the wall. The saints are depicted in orange, yellow and blue stained-glass windows. The roof is supported by timber beams and there is a small bell, about 30 cm across. The approach to the church is bordered by jacarandas that carpet the path with fallen blue blossoms when the trees are in flower.

Another rather charming building is the **Rongai Railway Station**. It has its name picked out in white cement on the ground. The platform has street lamps, glass panelled, lit by oil. The flowerbeds have frangipani and variegated sisal plants. The rods and wires of the signalling system and the points run over the ground. The station is of wooden weatherboarding in the cream and brick-red livery of Kenya Railways with a small verandah in front. Inside is the original control gear, now about 70 years old, with big brass keys for regulation of the traffic on the single line, and wicker hoops and pouches for collecting mail from non-stopping trains. The original telegraph system is still in place too, now with the addition of some antique black bakelite telephones.

Sleeping & eating

It's probably better to stay in Nakuru, 1 hr away

The exclusive **L** *Deloraine*, is near here, a classic colonial house on the lower slopes of Londianin Mountain. There are 6 double bedrooms with bathrooms and guests are welcomed as temporary members of the host Voorspuy family. Croquet, lawn tennis, horse-riding safaris. Bookings through *Bush Homes of East Africa Ltd*, PO Box 56923, Nairobi, PO Box 56923, T01-571647, F571665, www.bush-homes.co.ke

E *Beach Hotel* but it is very simple. If you wished to stay for a while, it would be possible to stay at the **E** *Heart of Christ Catholic Seminary*. There are several eating places (*hotelis*) of which the *Blue Café* (Seriously cheap) is the best.

Transport

Road 4 or 5 *matatus* each day, leave when full. Take the first *matatu* leaving Rongai as far as the Nakuru-Eldoret road, where it is easy to pick up a *matatu* going in the direction you want. Fare to Nakuru about US$0.50.

Lake Bogoria National Reserve

0° 10' N, 36° 10' E

This reserve, which covers an area of 107 sq km in the Rift Valley, is 40 km south of Lake Baringo and 80 km north of Nakuru, and is mainly bushland with small patches of riverine forest. It is best approached via **Marigat**, a friendly one-street town (often extremely hot), at the northern end. The lake, formerly called Lake Hannington, is a shallow soda lake, between 1m and 9 m in depth. The shoreline of this highly alkaline lake is littered with huge lava boulders, surrounded by grassland, and on the eastern side of the lake are found a number of greater kudu. The antelopes can best be seen in the evening when they come down to the lake to drink. The northern and eastern shoreline is swampy and attracts many waders. Along the eastern end of the lake you can see the northernmost part of the Aberdares. Lake Bogoria has no outlet, water loss is by evaporation and seepage. The rivers feeding the lake are seasonal with the exception of the small Mugun stream at the southern end.

Kenya

Trees including wild fig and acacia grow densely alongside the dry river beds and this is the best place for bird-watching.

The main reason people visit Lake Bogoria is to see the thermal areas with steam jets and geysers (take care, the water is very hot and you can get badly burnt) and the large number of flamingos that live here. There are now thought to be in excess of 2,000,000 flamingos, predominantly the lesser flamingo, that feed on *Spirulina platensis*, the blue-green algae. Many of the flamingos have moved here from Lake Nakuru, possibly because the water level there fell so dramatically.

Lake Bogoria's geysers are located mostly on the western side of the lake. There are pools with rather foul-smelling sulphurous steam bubbles, some of which send up boiling hot water spumes several metres high.

This is the least-visited of all Kenya's Rift lakes, but it can conveniently be included in a visit to Lake Baringo and the Kerio Valley, all of which are in this extremely hot area of the Rift Valley. The lake itself lies at the foot of the Laikipia Escarpment and its bottle-green waters reflect woodlands to the east.

■ *US$15 entrance fee plus US$1.50 per vehicle and US$2 per person for camping.*

Sleeping & eating

Be prepared, it can get extremely hot at night and mosquitoes are very troublesome

In Marigat E *Marigat Inn*. Good value with a variety of rooms, all clean, comfortable and with mosquito nets, well-shaded surroundings. E *Salaam Lodge*. Fenced-off compound behind the *Mtega Bar*. Friendly but tough-looking hostess, very clean rooms with separate drop toilet and shower cubicle. Beware the rooms can get very hot. **Seriously cheap** *Kamco*, good local food. *Marigat Inn*, reasonable food. *Mtega Bar* has amiable staff, warm beer and soft drinks. *Perkirra Hotel*, decent local food.

Camping You can camp by the northern entrance gate at a campsite with a shop selling basic foods, or there is a choice of two campsites at the southern shore of the lake, although with no shop. E *Fig Tree Campsite*, on the southern shore is pleasant and quite quiet. There is a freshwater stream running through the campsite that is just big enough to get into, however baboons can be a problem, so secure your property. Avoid camping directly under the fig trees as the baboons enjoy the fruit enormously, with predictable results. E *Acacia Tree* is on the western shore, no facilities, so you need to bring all equipment, food and drinking water with you.

Transport Road

Buses to **Nakuru** leave at around 0800 every morning. *Matatus* south to Nakuru, north to **Loruk** and west to **Kabarnet** leave earlier in the morning. It is an easy drive from Nakuru taking less than 1 hr along the Baringo road. There are 2 entrances to the reserve: at the southern end Mogotio Gate, which has some difficult

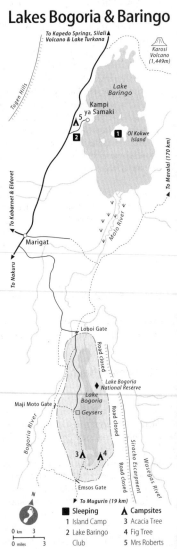

Lakes Bogoria & Baringo

To Kapedo Springs, Silali Volcano & Lake Turkana

Karosi Volcano (1,449m)

Tugen Hills

Lake Baringo

Kampi ya Samaki

Ol Kokwe Island

To Maralal (170 km)

To Kabarnet & Eldoret

Molo River

Marigat

To Nakuru

Loboi Gate

Road closed

Lake Bogoria National Reserve

Maji Moto Gate

Lake Bogoria

Geysers

Bogoria River

Siracho Escarpment

Road closed

Road closed

Wosegos River

Emsos Gate

To Mugurin (19 km)

N

0 km   3
0 miles   3

■ **Sleeping**
1 Island Camp
2 Lake Baringo Club

Λ **Campsites**
3 Acacia Tree
4 Fig Tree
5 Mrs Roberts

roads; at the northern end there is better access via Loboi Gate. Motorbikes are allowed into the park and the road is paved up to the hot springs, after which it becomes very rough. It is not possible to drive all around the lake as the road is closed on the east side between just north of *Fir Tree Camp* to just east of Loboi Gate..

If you continue driving north past Lake Bogoria you will start noticing large sawn-off tree trunks lying horizontally in the higher branches of many of the trees. This odd sight is in fact a method of honey cultivation (the trunks are hollowed out to the bee's taste); the effort to get the branches up there is quite amazing. The result is the delicious Asilah honey on sale at the roadside.

Lake Baringo, 20 km north of Marigat, is a peaceful and beautiful freshwater lake covering about 168 sq km, at an altitude of about 1,000 m. It is a shallow lake with a maximum depth of 12 m. Like Lake Naivaisha, Lake Baringo appears to have no outlet, although it is thought that it is drains to the north through an underground series of rocky fissures, possibly reappearing at Kapedo, 80 km away, where steaming water tumbles over a 10-m cliff, having been heated as a result of subterranean volcanic activity.

It is an extremely attractive lake with small, wooded creeks and little islands white pebble beaches, framed by the mountains to the east and west. It contains large schools of hippo and crocodile, and the delicious fish tilapia is caught here. The lake's greatest attraction is the huge numbers and varieties of birds. There are said to be 450 species of birds here, including the Hemprich's hornbill and Verreaux' eagle. On Gibraltar Island there is a very large colony of the Goliath heron, the largest concentration of these magnificent birds in East Africa. Mammals found locally include Grant's gazelle, waterbuck, mongoose and dikdik. The extended area around the lake is very hot and dry.

Lake Baringo
Colour map 3, grid B4

This part of Kenya used to be heavily populated with game, but rinderpest (see page 726) greatly reduced the wildlife numbers in the early part of the 20th century

L *Island Camp*, T2261, based on Ol Kokwe Island at the centre of Lake Baringo. This is quite an experience, even if only for a day trip. There is a swimming pool at the highest point of the camp. All tents have own bathroom with flush toilet and shower, as well as a shaded verandah. Activities on offer include waterskiing and windsurfing (US$45 per hr). **L** *Lake Baringo Club*, T2259, book through Block Hotels, PO Box 40075, Nairobi, T02-540780, F02-545948. Noted for its colourful gardens, it also has a swimming pool and serves good food. Non-residents are welcome to use facilities on payment of a small fee. A resident ornithologist can accompany you on bird walks. **Boat trips** can be organized here. Boats take 8 people. Cost: US$18 per hr. Allow 2 hrs for a tour to see the lake, islands, crocodiles, hippos and birds. **Camping D** *Mrs Roberts Campsite*, PO Box 1051, Nakuru, T3 (Kampi Ya Samaki), US$4 per person, and bandas are US$25 for 2 people. There is a general store for provisions and a bookshop. Boat hire is available. Recommended. Watch out for hippos in this area and don't approach them; although they seem docile they can be dangerous if startled by lights or noises.

Sleeping
There is also accommodation at nearby Nakuru (see page 157)

This is a malarial zone and mosquitoes are plentiful at the lake; use nets, plenty of repellent and cover up

Northern Rift Valley

Much of the northern part of the Rift Valley remains relatively unexplored by travellers and facilities are few and far between. The landscape is quite different from the central and western parts of the Rift. It is hot and arid, and only sparsely inhabited, but it has a stark beauty and is the home of the spectacular **Cherangani Hills**.

Once past the lakes of Bogoria and Baringo you are heading up into the less-frequented regions of Kabarnet. Marigat to Kabarnet is a torturously slow drive. The extremely steep climb and overloaded *matatus* make for a trotting pace in first gear. The advantage though is of lingering views back over the Rift Valley and the lakes below. The town of Kabarnet is set in the Tugen Hills, which are virtually impenetrable, and looks 1,500 m down into the **Kerio Valley**, designated a national reserve in 1983 in recognition of its bio-diversity. The deep valley covers an area of 66 sq km

Kerio Valley National Reserve

Kenya

and is carpeted with lush, semi-tropical vegetation on the slopes, and thorn bush on the dry valley floor.

Isolated *shambas* (small farms) of the **Kalenjin** are dotted around the mountainous countryside. The Kalenjin people are called the Highland Nilotes, as they live in the highlands of the Rift Valley escarpment of Kenya and are related to the peoples in the Nile area of Sudan and Uganda. There are a related people called the Datooga in northern Tanzania and across the Uganda border they are known as the Sebei. These people are believed to be the descendants of migrants from the west Ethiopian highlands, who migrated approximately 3,000 years ago. The Kalenjins are therefore described as a tribe made up of many clans, which include the Tugen, Kipsigis, Pokot, Keiyo, Saboat and Endo. Their languages although different are linguistically related. One of their customs was ear piercing, with the insertion of sticks to stretch and separate the ear lobes. This is more commonly seen in the tribal elders. The Kalenjin people are very successful in world-class middle- and long-distance running championships (see box on page 165).

Apart from the Kalenjin herders and their livestock, there is little else in the Kerio Valley. The unspoilt beauty and quiet of the place is hardly disturbed by vehicles, though this does make it hard to explore except by hiking. It is best to visit in June, July and August after the long rains, when the land is at its greenest and the temperatures are comfortable.

Kabarnet Kabarnet itself is a quiet, unimposing town despite the fact it is the capital of Baringo district. Its high altitude means it is cool (especially noticeable if you've come from the heat of Marigat), with an Alpine summer feel and there are great views northwards over the Kerio Valley. There is a good supermarket in the same building as the *Sinkoro* restaurant. It is a useful place to shop for food if you intend to go camping later in the hills.

Sleeping **C** Kabarnet, T03282035, is a fine modern hotel, 5 mins' walk from post office, set in well-tended gardens, perched on top of a hill for fine views of the valley. It has a lovely cool pool (non-residents US$2), good food at a price (set lunch US$6; dinner US$8). **D** *Hotel Sinkoro*, PO Box 256, T22245. Central, good-value hotel, all rooms s/c with hot water and breakfast included. The restaurant here is very good for snacks and meals, regardless of budget. **E** *View Point Hotel*, excellent value, with a variety of good rooms.

Transport **Buses** to **Eldoret** (3 hrs) and **Nakuru** (2 hrs) leave early in the morning. There are regular *matatus* to Eldoret, Nakuru and **Marigat**. The journey to Eldoret, especially down to the valley floor is very beautiful.

Kimwarer The largest town in the Kerio Valley is Kimwarer, a company town developed for the fluorspar mine at the head of the Kerio River. Fluorspar, used in the manufacture of steel, aluminium and cement, is an important industry here and the company that extracts it is evident everywhere with its own housing, schools, playgrounds and clinics.

Elgeyo Escarpment Elgeyo Escarpment presents one of the most astonishing panoramic views in the Rift Valley. About 1,000 m below the sheer cliff face south of the village of **Tot**, stretches the hazy scrublands extending as far as the eye can see north to Turkana and Pokot. This region is not easy to access: you'll need a four-wheel drive and calm nerves to drive up the escarpment road. It is probably easier to walk from Tot (about 25 km). If you intend to stay in the area, Tot offers a delightful peaceful atmosphere with small local hotels.

The Elgeyo Escarpment has been inhabited for centuries. The **Marakwet** who live here arrived around 1,000 years ago and claim they took over existing irrigation systems which zigzag all over the escarpment from the Cherangani Hills over 40 km away. The waterways make this area a lush land of agriculture with back-to-back *shambas* (small farms) everywhere.

Kalenjin runners

The Kalenjin people have attracted world-wide attention as they are markedly over-represented in world-class middle- and long-distance running championships. Numbering around 3,000,000, or 10% of Kenya's population, the Kalenjins have won about 75% of Kenya's distance running races, and 40% of international honours in the past 10 years. Kalenjin men are the world champions in more than half the sub-marathon distance races. The first of these amazing athletes from this part of Kenya was Kip Keino, who rose to world prominence in the Mexico Olympics in 1968. Despite suffering severe pain from gallstones he competed in the 10,000-m race. With two laps to go, whilst in the lead pack, he collapsed in pain, staggering off the track, but before the stretcher arrived he returned to the track and completed the race, despite having been disqualified. Just four days later he won the silver medal in the 5,000 m, and beat the American Jim Ryun for the gold in the 1,500 m. In the 1972 Games, Kip Keino won the gold in the steeplechase and silver in the 1,500 m. Nowadays Kip Keino helps to run a

children's home with his wife Phyllis, and they have set up a school as well as the adjacent Baraka Farm with the aim of making these enterprises self sufficient.

Curiously, Kalenjin women have not enjoyed the same level of athletic success, although Joyce Chepchumba did win the London Marathon in 1999. The reason for the Kalenjins success has been ascribed in part to their 'altitude' training as their homesteads and farms are mostly located above 2,000 m, with its known aerobic benefits, plus their normal diet that contains a high percentage of complex carbohydrates. Whether this group of runners have an inherent genetic advantage is currently being studied. They appear to have an enhanced capacity to rapidly increase aerobic efficiency with training. In addition, an important co-factor is that the Kenya Amateur Athletics Association have actively fostered young athletic talent in the past 25 years. In combination with US scholarships, this has enabled many of these promising young Kalenjins to compete at international level.

The Cherangani Hills

These wild, thickly forested hills are miles away from the popular tourist circuit with fine mountain landscapes. The Cherangani range rises to 3,500 m at the northern end of the Elgeyo Marakwet Escarpment and is Kenya's only range of fold mountains. The range offers some of the best walking in Kenya in a pleasant climate, the northern end being particularly attractive. But make sure you are equipped with a decent map. Also see entry on page 283.

You should be able to reach the hills easily enough by public transport as there are a number of *matatus* running between Cheptongei and Chesoi. There are a number of suitable campsites where you can stay. The town of **Kapenguira** is in these hills, the place where the colonial government held the trial of Jomo Kenyatta during the 1950s when he was convicted of being involved in Mau Mau activities.

Western Rift Valley

The main A104 west towards Kisumu is in good condition and quite fast. The more scenic route is the C56 that passes through the towns of Njoro, Elburgon and Molo over the Mau Escarpment, before joining the Kisumu Road. Few tourists travel this route mainly because there is little to visit, but the scenery is lovely and quite varied.

The first town is **Njoro** by the Mau Escarpment about 5 km west of Nakuru. It is home to Egerton University (about 5 km out of town). The main street is an unpaved road lined with jacaranda tees and hotels serving basic Kenyan fare. You will find a post office, bank and petrol station here if you need them.

The road then goes up into conifer country to the town of **Elburgon**, which is bigger than Njoro and quite prosperous as a result of the logging industry. Evidence of logging is everywhere and most buildings are constructed of wood. The railway used to stop here between Nakuru and Kisumu. Again you will find a post office and bank in town as well as a number of small hotels offering extremely cheap accommodation. There is also a very good new hotel here. **C** *Eel*, T0363-3127, set in a lovely garden. Apparently plans are underway to develop an adventure playground and disco here. If you are staying in the area it is worth knowing about the teacher's club at **St Andrew's School**, **Turi**, that is open each Thursday night for meals and a drink. It is also sometimes open at weekends. The school, which was founded in 1932, is still popular with children of farmers, missionaries and aid workers of all nationalities from all over East Africa. During the Second World War it was home to Italian prisoners of war who decorated many of the walls with paintings. The dining room, dormitories, bathrooms and corridors are still covered in their pictures of children's stories and fairytales such as Winnie the Pooh and the Pied Piper.

Just west of Elburgon, you will pass through the **Mau Forest**. This dense forest of huge gum trees has yet to be exploited for tourism, particularly by the Okiek people (hunter-gatherers) who have lived here for generations. The road emerges from the forest among fields of crops, primarily pyrethrum and cereals which border the town of **Molo** which has a post office and bank along the main street. **Sleeping** There are also plenty of places to stay including **D** *Molo Highlands Inn*, T0363-21036, which has lovely wooden rooms with a log fire and a good restaurant, and **D** *Green Garden Lodge,* which is a nice enough place to stay, but very quiet. Just out of town heading south you will find **A** *Juani Farm*, a cosy establishment run by two white Kenyan farmers, with English-style gardens and food. Book through Kesana Ltd, Nairobi, T749062.

West of Molo, between **Londiani** (a small town near the junction of the C56 with the B1 – the main road going into Kisumu) and **Kipkelion**, is the **Cistercian Monastery**. This monastery, stuck in the middle of nowhere, is one of only 18 Cistercian monasteries in Africa. It is a wonderful place to stay if you need a break from the outside world – donations for board and lodging are gratefully received. The monastery was founded in 1956, originally as a Trappist monastery. The monks still only talk when necessary, but the abbot, Reverend Dom Bernard Kaboggdia, is very kind and guests are warmly welcomed. Rooms and dining facilities are available. The monastery provides an important service for the local community through its hospital (the only one in the area) and its school. ■ *If you do wish to stay, you should write to them first: Our Lady of Victoria, PO Box 40, Kipkelion, T0361-21233, F0361-30632.* The monastery is about 11 km from **Baisheli** to the north of Londiani. If approaching from Kipkelion, you need to head off the main highway up the C35 unsurfaced road. Few *matatus* or cars go along this route, but you may be lucky. Coming from Londiana you will need to take a small dirt road on the right-hand side. Unfortunately the road is no longer signposted, so ask for directions if necessary.

Narok Narok is a small provincial town, 141 km west of Nairobi, approximately 100 km north of the Masai Mara Game Reserve. It is the main trading centre for the Masai people in southwestern Kenya. This is the last place you can get a cold drink or refuel if travelling there. The town has become a popular stopping place and abounds with kiosks and hawkers selling Masai shields, spears, batiks, masks and beadwork souvenirs. Narok has two banks (one with an ATM) a post office, and a museum.

The National Museums of Kenya have set up this regional **museum** to promote a better understanding of the Maa-speaking people, a group that includes the Masai, Samburu, Njemps and some of the neighbouring Ndorobo people. The major exhibits are cultural artefacts, that offer insight and information about the traditional lifestyle of these nomadic pastoralist people. The gallery exhibits include 24 reproductions of Joy Adamson's paintings, and 8 photographs taken by her in 1951.

Sleeping There are several budget hotel options (**E** and **F**) close to the market, with little to choose between them. **Camping** is available (basic facilities only) west of the *Agip* petrol station.

Transport From the capital take the old Nairobi-Naivasha road (B3 – the more westerly road) that forks to the left at Rironi, the road continues in a northwesterly direction for approximately 6 km then turns left on a sealed tarmac road in a southwesterly direction south of Mt Longonot. From here it is 82 km to Narok. The route is well served by *matatus* and share-taxis. Narok is also connected to the north by road. The C57 road runs west of the *Mau Escarpment* 53 km north to a small town called **Enangiperi**, from where it is 20 km to **Mau Narok** and a further 38 km to **Njoro** (4 hrs), after which it is just a ½-hr drive north to **Nakuru**.

There is no public transport between Narok and the Masai Mara Game Reserve and the chances of hitching a lift are slim. South to the Masai Mara Reserve there is a choice of roads after 17 km. Left is the C12 road, sealed for 30 km and then murram for 38 km leading to the east of the reserve via the Sekenani Gate, this is the route to the park headquarters. The turning right leads to Ngorengore along the B3 road, the Mara River and the west of the reserve via the Oloololo and the Musiara gates. It is also possible to reach the reserve from the northwest from Kisii via Migori along murram roads (4WD advisable).

Masai Mara National Reserve

The Masai Mara National Reserve covers some 1,510 sq km ranging between 1,500m and 2,100 m above sea level. The Mara receives a high rainfall as a result of the altitude and humidity of nearby Lake Victoria, 160 km west. It lies 275 km southwest of Nairobi, and the journey takes five hours by road. It is an extension of Tanzania's Serengeti National Park, a small part of the Serengeti ecosystem covering some 40,000 sq km between the Rift Valley and Lake Victoria. It is the most popular of Kenya's parks, with very good reason. Almost every species of animal you can think of in relation to East Africa lives on the well-watered plains in this remote part of the country. One of the unique, spectacular and most memorable sights is the annual migration of hundreds of thousands of wildebeest (estimated at 500,000 animals), gazelle and zebra as they move from the Serengeti Plains in January, having exhausted the grazing there, on their way northwards, arriving in the Masai Mara by about July-August. In the Mara, the herbivores are joined by yet another 100,000 wildebeest coming from the Loita Hills, east of the Mara. Once the Mara's new grass has been eaten, the wildebeests, zebra and gazelles retrace their long journey south to Tanzania in October, where their young are born, and where the grasslands have been replenished in their absence. This lengthy trek costs the lives of many old, young, lame and unlucky animals, picked off by predators like lions, leopards, hyenas and crocodiles, or whilst crossing the swirling muddy Mara and Talek rivers. The Masai Mara is teeming with animals from July to September with the migrating wildebeest and zebra, but in addition there are many animals resident here all year round. Among the rarer mammals found here are the Roan antelope in the southwest sector, and the thousands of topi only found here and in the Tsavo National Park. Another shy mammal is the bat-eared fox sometimes seen peering out of their burrows.

Background
0° 20' S, 35° E
Colour map 3, grid B3

The Masai Mara is not a national park but a game reserve, divided into an inner and outer section. The inner section covers an area of 52,000 ha, and the greater conservation area is 181,000 ha. The inner section has no human habitation apart from the lodges. In the outer reserve area the Masai coexist with the game and evidence of their village communities can be seen in the many *manyattas*. The essential difference between a game reserve and a national park is that the indigenous people (the pastoral Masai) have the right to graze their animals on the outer part of the reserve and to shoot animals if they are attacked. However, the game does not recognize the designated boundaries and an even larger area, known as the 'dispersal area' extends north and east contiguous with the reserve, where the Masai people live with their stock.

The landscape is mainly gently rolling grassland with the rainfall in the north being double that of the south. The Mara River runs from north to south through the park and then turns westwards to Lake Victoria. Most of the plains are covered in a type of red-oat grass with acacias and thorn trees.

The reserve is teeming with herbivores – numbering around 2,500,000 including: wildebeest, Thompson's and Grant's gazelle, zebra, buffalo, impala, topi, hartebeest, giraffe, eland, elephant, dik-dik, klipspringer, steinbok, hippo, rhino, warthog and bushpig. There are also large numbers of lion, leopard, cheetah, hyena, wild dog and jackal, as well as smaller mammals and reptiles. In the Mara River hippo and apparently sleepy crocodiles can be seen. The number of animals suited to grasslands living in this area has increased enormously over the last 30 years due to woodland being cleared. In addition to the numerous mammals, over 450 species of birds have been recorded, including 57 species of birds of prey.

The **Oloololo Escarpment** on the western edge of the park is the best place to see the animals, though it is also the hardest part to get around, particularly after heavy rain, when the swampy ground becomes impassable.

There is increasing concern about the impact that the servicing of the requirements of the tourists is having on the finely tuned ecological balance of the reserve. A couple of the identified concerns are the impact that the off-road driving is having on the flora. Many vehicles criss-cross the area causing soil erosion by churning up the grasslands. The animals do not appear to be adversely affected by the huge number of visitors to the reserve. Another concern regards the disposal of waste generated by the tourist industry, as some of the predators like hyenas are discovering an easier food source by rummaging through the garbage.

A community initiative has been established at *Rekero Camp* in the reserve where you are introduced to the cultural side of the Mara as well as seeing the wildlife. Visits to Masai *manyattas* (homes) are on offer as well as game drives. The money generated by this eco-tourism initiative goes directly to the local community. Just outside the Oloolaimutia Gate there is a Masai village, open to the public, which you can wander round taking as many photographs as you wish for US$7 per person.

Masai Mara National Reserve

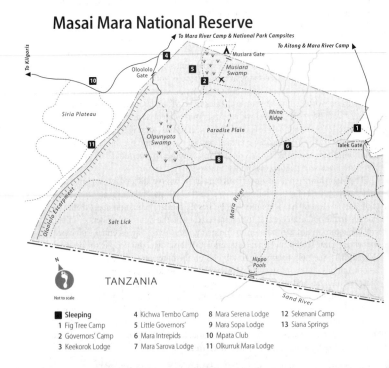

Sleeping	4 Kichwa Tembo Camp	8 Mara Serena Lodge	12 Sekenani Camp
1 Fig Tree Camp	5 Little Governors'	9 Mara Sopa Lodge	13 Siana Springs
2 Governors' Camp	6 Mara Intrepids	10 Mpata Club	
3 Keekorok Lodge	7 Mara Sarova Lodge	11 Olkurruk Mara Lodge	

Lodges L *Mara Serena Lodge*, T711077/8, F718100/3 (Nairobi), serenamk@ **Sleeping**
africaonline.co.ke Well designed, wildlife films, Masai dancing, balloon safaris, superb view
over the Mara River and plains beyond. Two-day packages include return flights from Nairobi
or Mombasa, full-board and 3 or 4 game drives. **L** *Mara Sopa Lodge*, PO Box 72630, Nairobi,
T336724, F223843, mara@sopalodges.com Strategically located near to Oloolaimutia Gate,
this 200-bed lodge, with 77 rooms, 12 suites and 1 presidential suite, is one of the most popular in the reserve. Rondavel rooms with balconies and verandahs, grand African-style public
areas, fine food and friendly staff, excellent swimming pool, conference rooms, balloon safaris and night game drives. **L** *Rekero Farm*, outside reserve to northwest, in Masai Mara Conservation Area, book through *Bush Homes of East Africa Ltd*, PO Box 56923, Nairobi, PO Box
56923, T01-571647, F571665, www.bush-homes.co.ke Expensive – only room for 10
guests, thatched bungalows with en-suite bathrooms for 8 guests, and a twin-bed fully furnished tent, personally conducted safari walks available, game drives, visits to local communities. Also offer 3 nights accommodation for up to 12 people in mobile camps that are sited
according to the position of the wildlife. **L** *Keekorok Lodge* (**A** in low seasons), PO Box 40075,
Nairobi, T02-540780, F545948. Oldest lodge, set in a grassy plain, swimming pool, wildlife
and local culture lectures, shop, will arrange game drives. *Balloon Safaris Ltd* are based at the
lodge, probably the first such company in Africa, T0305-2468. Dawn hot-air balloon trips can
be booked through the head office: PO Box 43747, Nairobi, T02-502850/1, F501424, bal-
loons@africaonline.co.ke **A** *Olkurruk Mara Lodge*, outside reserve, near Oloololo Gate, PO
Box 30471, Nairobi, T336858, F218109. Good views from elevated site, small in comparison
to other lodges, but friendly. **B** *Bush Tops*, outside reserve, nearest to Sekanini Gate, PO Box
44191, Nairobi, T882408. Fairly simple, but quite comfortable, can accommodate 20 guests,
uses solar power.

Tented camps There are 4 'Governors' Camps', all different and all expensive at over *A stay in one of the*
US$500 per night, game drives included. They are unfenced, but patrolled by Masai guards *tented camps, with*
just in case the animals get too curious. All tents have private bathrooms with flush toilets *perhaps a dawn*
and showers. You can even arrange a cham- *hot-air balloon safari*
pagne breakfast! **L** *Governors' Camp*, in area *(around US$375), is an*
to north of park, accessed from Musiara *unforgettable*
Gate, PO Box 48217, Nairobi, T331871, *experience (book well*
F726427. Solid floors for tents, bar lounge, *in advance to avoid*
candlelit dinners, small museum, balloon *disappointment.*
safaris, no swimming pool, beautiful site by *Tented camps often*
the Mara River. **L** *Governors' Il Moran Camp*, *include game drives in*
in area to north of park, accessed from *the price*
Musiara Gate, PO Box 48217, Nairobi,
T331871, F726427, located in bush along
Mara River. Tents not on permanent floors,
high standards. **L** *Governors' Private Camp*,
in area to north of park, accessed from
Musiara Gate, PO Box 48217, Nairobi,
T331871, F726427. Site can be booked for
exclusive use, up to 16 people, minimum of
3 nights. **L** *Little Governors' Camp*, in area to
north of park, accessed from Musiara Gate,
PO Box 48217, Nairobi, T331871, F726427.
Solid floors for tents, access by ferry pulled
across the Mara River, really something special, on a splendid site, very high standards.

Loita Hills

Talek River

To Narok, Naivasha & Nairobi

13

Sekenani Gate

Park HQ

12

7

9

Oloolaimutia Gate

3 ✕

Sand River

Sand River Gate

    L *Bateleur Camp*, PO Box 74957, Nairobi,
T219784, F217498. Within walking distance
of *Kichwa Tembo Camp* below, set privately
in a forest with views from each chalet overlooking Masai Mara. Walking safaris,

Kenya

swimming pool, day/night game drives. Small luxury Hotel of the World. **L** *Fig Tree Camp*, PO Box 40683, Nairobi, T221439, F332170, www.madahotels.com, just outside reserve close to Talek Gate. Quite large, and also has some timber cabins with electricity, swimming pool, shop, balloon safaris. **L** *Kichwa Tembo Camp*, PO Box 74957, Nairobi, T219784, F217498, at the base of the Oloololo Escarpment by the Oloololo Gate. Does have some banda accommodation as well, balloon safaris, nature walks, visits to Masai village, swimming pool. **L** *Mara Explorer*, PO Box 74888, Nairobi, T02-716628, F716547, heritagehotels@ form-net.com   Tented camp opened in 2000, there are 20 beds and expansive views from its location on a bend of the Talek River, downstream of Mara Intrepids, its sister camp. The second of the Heritage Group *Explorer* resorts (the first being *Kipungani Explorer* at Lamu), that are intended to provide ultra-exclusive sophistication and style for couples. A personal attendant will be on hand at all times. **L** *Mara Intrepids*, by the Talek River, PO Box 74888, Nairobi, T02-716628, F716547, heritagehotels@form-net.com, T02-2168/2321 (camp). 30 tents with large 4-poster beds, en-suite bathrooms, balloon safaris, swimming pool, shop, conference room, high standards. **L** *Mara River Camp*, PO Box 48019, Nairobi, outside the reserve, beside river, in pleasant site, T335935, F216528. Specialist ornithologist for tours, game drive, no swimming pool. **L** *Mara Sarova Lodge* (**A** Apr to Jun), PO Box 30680, Nairobi, near the Sekenani Gate, T333248, F211472. Good accommodation, beautiful views, swimming pool, large site, with 75 tents, so rather impersonal. **L** *Sekenani Camp*, close to Sekenani Gate, PO Box 61542, Nairobi, T333285, F228875. Small camp, intimate and luxurious, a place of much charm with polished wooden floors, grand baths, hurricane lamps, excellent food, . **L** *Siana Springs* (formerly *Cottars' Camp*), PO Box 74957, Nairobi, just outside the reserve, T219784, F217498. Unspoilt site, the tents are set out in 3 clusters: Acacia, Palm and Bamboo, but they are well spread out, specialist naturalist for walks and lectures, swimming pool. Another base for *Balloon Safaris Ltd*, see *Keekorok Lodge*. **L** *Voyager Safari Lodge*, PO Box 74888, Nairobi, T02-716628, F716547, heritagehotels@form-net.com Another Heritage

Group resort, the *Voyager* standard is aimed at first-time safari-goers who want a little luxury. **A** *Diners Tented Camp*, PO Box 46466, Nairobi, northeast corner, access from Olemutiak Gate, T333301, F224539. A touch more spartan than some of the other tented camps, excellent food. **A** *Talek River Camp*, inside the reserve, by the river, PO Box 74888, Nairobi, T338084, F217278. Sound facilities (but no pool), good value.

Camping The Masai Mara hardly caters for budget travellers apart from a few campsites. You can camp outside any of the **E** *Park Gates* (there are 5) for a small fee. The best of these locations are **E** *Sand River Gate*, with lavatories, water and a shop. Also **E** *Musiara Gate*, there are no facilities but you should be able to get water from the wardens. The most lively place to stay is the Masai-run **E** *Oloolaimutia Campsite* at the western side of the park where budget safari outfits usually stay. Water here is limited and you will have to buy it if you need it. The nearby *Mara Sopa Lodge* serves food and drink (warm beers) and has a lively atmosphere. There are camping facilities near **E** *Keekorok Lodge* and a place to buy food and drink. This is the only official campsite within the reserve. **E** *National Park Campsites*, without any facilities are at 3 locations outside the reserve beside the Mara River north of Mara River Camp. There are also **E** *Talek River Campsites*, close to the Talek Gate, at 12 locations.

Air *Air Kenya* flights leave twice daily (1000 and 1500) from Wilson Airport in Nairobi and **Transport** take 45 mins. Return flights leave the Masai Mara at 1100 and 1600. The fare is US$105 one-way, US$185 return. *Air Kenya* also have a daily one-way flight from **Nanyuki**, which leaves at 1000 and arrives about 1130, US$175. *Eagle Aviation* fly daily from **Mombasa**, a single fare of US$250 and return of US$300. Flight time is 2 hrs, they leave Mombasa at 0830 and Masai Mara at 1400. Baggage allowance is only 15 kg for *Air Kenya* and 10 kg for *Eagle Aviation*. **Road** The main access to the Mara Reserve is through **Narok** town, 141 km to the west of Nairobi, and the last stop for buying food, water and petrol. The journey to the Masai Mara is fascinating in itself, crossing through the Rift Valley over dry range lands. From Narok to the park is 100 km, part of which is along unsurfaced roads. The other route is from **Kisii**, the road to the park being just about OK in a 4WD outside of the rainy season. Opportunities for hitching are very limited, you will really need transport to explore this park properly.

Western Kenya

Western Kenya is the most fertile and populous part of the country, teeming with market towns and busy fishing villages. For some reason it is not that popular with the big tour operators which is all to the benefit of the independent traveller. In fact, conditions for budget travellers are perfect; over half the population of the whole country lives here so public transport is excellent (though slightly unpredictable) and the road surfaces tend to be above average. There are numerous cheap hotels and restaurants, people are generally helpful and friendly and there is plenty to see and do. Tourists wanting slightly more upmarket services are not so well catered for, their best bet being to stay in one of the better hotels in Kisumu and hire a car to explore other parts of the region.

There are a number of national parks in this region: The Kakamega Forest, the only tract of equatorial rainforest in Kenya, has many animals that are found nowhere else in the country; the Saiwa Swamp, near Kitale, is worth a visit to see the rare sitatunga deer; Mount Elgon has good climbing and is accessed from Kitale; Ruma National Park is in South Nyanza; and, to the south the northeastern section of Lake Victoria, where the climate is far warmer. This is traditionally the area inhabited by the Luo and is quite a poor part of the country. The pace of life is slow and the people are extremely friendly. The northern part of Western Kenya is lush, green and fertile, the climate is more temperate and there are more Europeans around.

Kisumu

0° 35', 34° 45' E
Phone code: 035
Colour map 3, grid B3

Kisumu, on the shore of Lake Victoria, is the principal town in Western Kenya and the third largest in the country. It is a very pleasant place with a slow, gentle pace of life, a relaxed ambience, and the whole town coming to a standstill on Sunday. The sleepy atmosphere is as much due to lack of economic opportunities as to the extremely hot dry weather, which makes doing almost anything in the middle of the day quite hard work.

The town has been by-passed by post-Independence development, and the signs are all too visible. Warehouses by the docks remain empty and the port does not have the bustling atmosphere you would expect in such an important town. Many of the wealthier people have moved out of Kisumu, hence the number of large houses lying empty or run-down.

Ins & outs Kisumu is an excellent base for exploring the region with good bus and matatu links to nearby towns, as well as to Western Kenya and Uganda. Kisumu has a small airfield, but most people come to and go from here by bus or *matatu*. See Transport page 177. Political unrest and rioting in Kisumu in early 2001 generated a tense atmosphere, with many armed police checkpoints. The town of Kisii has also been affected.

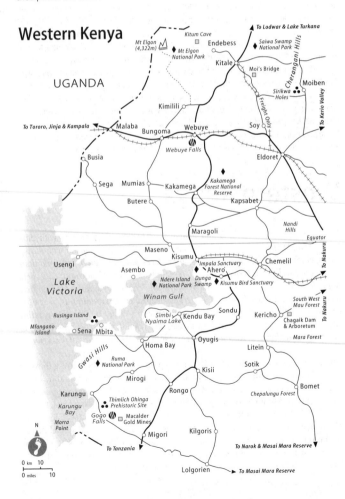

Western Kenya

Kisumu developed during the colonial era into the principal port in the region. The **History**
railway line reached Lake Victoria in 1902, opening up trade opportunities. By the
1930s it had become the hub of administrative and military activities on the lake.
Kisumu was a difficult place at this time, bilharzia was endemic, malaria and sleeping sickness were common and the climate was sweltering. However, the area
attracted investment from many different quarters, including Asians ending their
contracts to work on the railway.

The Luo felt they were neglected immediately after Independence, and that political life was dominated by Kikuyu who centred development on Central province.
The breakdown of trade between Kenya, Uganda and Tanzania and the collapse of
the East African Community in 1977 badly affected Kisumu and there has been no
compensating expansion of manufacturing in the area.

The murder of Robert Ouko, a Luo, in 1990 led to riots where many people died
and much property was destroyed. Later, in the build-up to multi-party elections in
Kenya, the nearby area was the scene of outbreaks of ethnic violence and thousands
of people fled their *shambas*, coming into Kisumu or heading up to Eldoret.

Sights

Kisumu Museum is to the east of the town's lively market. There are a number of
stuffed birds, mammals, reptiles and fish. Most impressive is a lion bringing down a
wildebeest. A 190-kg Nile perch is another of the more noteworthy exhibits. The
ethnographic exhibits centre on the customs and traditions of the tribal groups who
lived in this area: the Luo, Masai, and Kalenjin (see page 309 and page 311). The
curator is both imaginative and energetic, and intends to develop the scope and
range of the museum including the traditional Luo homestead. ■ *0930-1800. Entry
about US$2.50.*

Dunga Swamp is located by following the shoreline road south past the *Sunset
Hotel*. It is home to the rare *Papyrus gonolek*, which faces extinction due to the cutting down of papyrus reeds along the shores of Lake Victoria. Dunga Swamp attracts
birders from all over the world as it is the only habitat of the *Papyrus gonolek*. Ornithologists have expressed concern that the destruction of the environment combined with frequent hunting of the bird is threatening its survival.

Dunga itself is a small village just 3 km outside Kisumu. It is a lovely, peaceful   *Avoid the temptation*
place to visit on the shores of Lake Victoria. *Dunga Refreshments*, where you can get *to swim in the lake*
a cold soda and something to eat whilst watching fishermen bring in their catch, has   *here as bilharzia is rife*
great views over the lake. There are hippos here, but they are elusive. Once night has
fallen they come out of the water to graze on land. You can take a rowing boat, with
guide, to nearby Hippo Point where you can see the hippos in the water. Cost of
excursion US$2. There is a campsite here. Watching the sun set over the lake is a very
pleasant way to end the day. It is possible to negotiate with the fishermen to join a
night fishing trip. On the way up the dirt track to Dunga you pass the compact
Impala Sanctuary. This tiny sanctuary, only 0.4 sq km of marsh, forest and grassland, was created to protect the few remaining impala, decimated over the last century by hunting and for food. The sanctuary was expanded to act as a holding point
for captured animals. Nowadays it has two leopards, a spotted hyena and several
vervet monkeys in addition to several reptiles and birds. Hippos come up to the
sanctuary to graze, and recently there have been sightings of the rare Sitatunga antelope. There are plans afoot to upgrade the sanctuary to a Wildlife Conservation Education Centre, in addition to organizing excursions to Ndere Island National Park.

Kisumu Bird Sanctuary is off the main A1 on the way to Ahero, about 8 km out
of Kisumu. You need to follow the track round the marshy areas along the lake shore
for the best viewing sites. This is a nesting and breeding site for hundreds of birds
including herons, ibises, cormorants, egrets and storks. The best time to visit is from
April to May.

Kenya

Ndere Island National Park

Gazetted in 1986, Ndere Island National Park covers a small idland of just over 4 sq km off the northern shore of Lake Victoria. In the local Luo language Ndere means 'meeting place' and according to legend Kit Mikayi, mother of the tribe, rested up near here following her long journey south down the Nile Valley. The island is home to a large bird population including the fish eagle. Hippos and crocodiles are plentiful on the shoreline, and there is also a small herd of impalas.

The island vegetation is primarily glades in the upland areas, with a shoreline fringe of woodland. However, as with other parts of this area of Kenya, tsetse flies are common, posing a threat to human health, along with the ubiquitous malaria-vector mosquitoes. Access to the island is by boat from Kisumu, although the water hyacinth problem in Lake Victoria has proved to be an impediment. Currently there are no tourist developments on Ndere Island. The Kenya Wildlife Service has recently purchased some land on the mainland where the construction of a park headquarters is planned.

The Lake Victoria Environmental Management Project (LVEMP) has recently begun a major programme to shred 1,500 ha of the **water hyacinth** weed. The project has received funds from the *World Bank*, and two 'Swamp Devils' have been purchased to chop, shred and remove the prolific weed that has formed great mats, inhibiting even large boats from using the ports. The target areas for the project are the Ports of Kisumu and Victoria, Homa Bay, Kendu Bay and Nya Koch Bay (see also box on page 720).

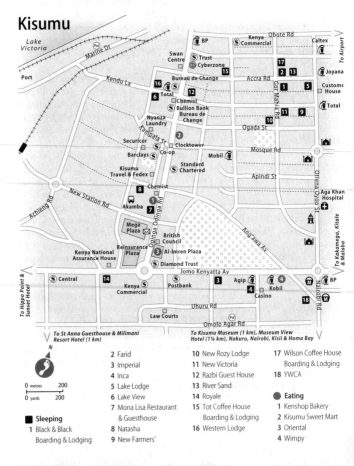

Kisumu

Sleeping
1 Black & Black Boarding & Lodging
2 Farid
3 Imperial
4 Inca
5 Lake Lodge
6 Lake View
7 Mona Lisa Restaurant & Guesthouse
8 Natasha
9 New Farmers'
10 New Rozy Lodge
11 New Victoria
12 Razbi Guest House
13 River Sand
14 Royale
15 Tot Coffee House Boarding & Lodging
16 Western Lodge
17 Wilson Coffee House Boarding & Lodging
18 YWCA

● Eating
1 Kenshop Bakery
2 Kisumu Sweet Mart
3 Oriental
4 Wimpy

Essentials

Kisumu is swarming with mosquitoes, so it is important to look for a room with mosquito nets if you don't have one with you. It is also important to cover up and use repellents. A fan is also a boon.

Sleeping
■ on map
For price codes:
see inside front cover

B *Imperial*, Jomo Kenyatta Av, PO Box 1866, T41455/6/7, F40345, imperial@ africaonline.co.ke The best hotel in this price range. Plush carpets and fittings, a/c, very good swimming pool (visitors can swim for US$1.50) and friendly staff. Two bars (one roof-top), restaurant, coffee shop and internet access. 3 standards of room available, the standard double room is about US$55 a night, although prices are significantly lower Fri to Sun. **B** *Sunset*, to the south of the town, T41100. Verandah looks over beautiful lawns and a good swimming pool. All rooms have views of the lake and sunset, and you can take a good photograph of the lake from the hotel roof. **B-C** *Milimani Resort Hotel*, T23245. Modern hotel with car parking in a quiet situation, a fair distance south of the town centre. Rooms have different prices, are well equipped with fans, nets and TVs but are on the small side whatever the price. Breakfast included.

C *Royale*, Jomo Kenyatta Av, T44240. Average rooms, temperamental hot water supply, the upstairs rooms have netted windows and there are individual mosquito nets for each bed, although some have holes. Casino open 1600-0500, no entry fee, no dress code. Good restaurant on outside terrace, prices reasonable, slow service, good Indian menu, only Indian food available in the evenings. Dingy swimming pool is free for guests (non-residents US$1.50). The oldest hotel in Kisumu, has polished wooden floors and spacious colonial atmosphere, but has seen much better days. There is a nightclub at the back, free to residents (non-residents US$2), sleepy receptionists. Internet access available. **C** *Western Lodge*, Kendu Lane, T42586. New hotel, good cheap rooms and good security, with a safe in each room.

D *Hotel Inca*, near *Imperial*. Clean and comfortable, s/c, hot water, but perhaps overpriced. **D** *Hotel Natasha*, Otuoma St, T43001. Hot water showers and toilet, s/c, very clean, friendly, quiet, though a little gloomy and no mosquito nets but has a fan. Restaurant next door, phone booth outside. **D** *Lake View*, Kendu Lane. PO Box 1216, T45055. Pleasant and friendly hotel from where the lake can only just be seen. **D** *Museum View*, on the same road as the museum, PO Box 544, T21149. Clean, large s/c rooms with hot water and mosquito nets. Comfortable but a bit out of the way, except for the museum. **D** *New Victoria*, Gor Mahia Rd, T21067. Excellent value, clean and large s/c rooms with fans and good protection from mosquitoes. Triple rooms available, second floor rooms have pleasant balconies (rooms 205-207 have views of the lake). Popular TV room, food OK but not to the standard of the rest of the hotel. Muslim-owned, so no alcohol and the rules stress that there should be no 'private meetings' in rooms. **D** *River Sand Hotel*, Accra Rd. All rooms are comfortable and have bathrooms, the double rooms have a balcony, but the water is cold and better value can be had elsewhere. Has a restaurant and bar. **D** *St Anna Guest House*, PO Box 19100, T44617, F23585. Good s/c rooms with hot water, in a pleasant area but is 3 km south of the town centre.

E *Asba Cyber Café*, Ogada St. Internet access is the only redeeming feature. Fairly cheap but the rooms are small and bare, shared bathroom, cold water. **E** *Black & Black Boarding and Lodging*, Gor Mahia Rd, PO Box 282, T42571. Relatively expensive as rooms are very small and basic, no mosquito nets, cold showers and toilets (shared), basins in rooms. **E** *Tot Coffee House Boarding and Lodging*, off Accra Rd. Clean and airy, rooms have bathrooms with bath and shower head, but the water is cold. Restaurant and bar with pool table also available. **E** *Wilson Coffee House Boarding and Lodging*, Gor Mahia Rd. Good clean rooms, s/c with hot water, friendly staff and a good view from the restaurant. Recommended. **F** *Farid*, Accra Rd. Run-down and cheap. Dirty looking mattresses in otherwise clean rooms, only has cold water and shared facilities. Restaurant is not open for breakfast. **F** *Lake Lodge*, Otiena Oyoo St. Clean, basic rooms with nets, secure. The best of the cheapest hotels. **F** *Mona Lisa Restaurant and Guest House*, Oginga Odinga Rd, quite grubby but

Kenya

bearable, s/c and has hot water. **F** *New Farmers' Hotel and Restaurant*, Kendu Rd, PO Box 755, T22351. Small rooms with mosquito nets, cold water and squat toilets in shared bathrooms. **F** *New Rozy Lodge*, Ogada St, PO Box 548, T41990. Very basic, shared facilities, there is no hot water but it is overall fairly clean and cheap. **F** *Razbi Guest House*, Kendu Lane, PO Box 1969, T44771. Cheap, basic and friendly, and has triple rooms available. Laundry facilities, communal shower, no hot water, fan or mosquito nets, and is becoming a little run-down. **F** *YWCA*, off Ang'awa Av, PO Box 1686, T43192. Reasonable, rooms with 3 or 4 sharing, there is not always water. **Camping** There's a **E** *Campsite* near *Dunga Refreshments*. Best place to view the hippos.

Eating
● *on map page 174*

It is quite easy to get good cheap food in Kisumu, except on a Sun, when most places are closed. Of particularly good value are the fish dishes. The large Asian community that has settled here means it is possible to get excellent Indian meals, including vegetarian, very cheaply. There are several very cheap kiosks near the bus station selling grilled meat on skewers or tilapia fish with *ugali* (maize dough). **Mid-range** *Sunset*, out of town to the south. Does a weekend buffet which is plentiful in slightly grand surroundings. **Cheap** *New Farmers' Restaurant*. Has a good, if predictable, menu. *Oriental Restaurant* in the Al-Imren Plaza, Oginga Odinga Rd, excellent value, tasty, generous meals and good service. **Seriously cheap** *Kisumu Sweet Mart*, Oginga Odinga Rd. Sodas, *bhajis* and cheap Indian food. *Mona Lisa*, Oginga Odinga Rd. Good breakfasts. *New Victoria*, Gor Mahia Rd. Does a substantial breakfast from 0700-0900, good Indian menu, owned by a family from Yemem, very quick service and large portions. Can get quite busy, the menu states all food will be served within 15 mins. *Kenshop Bakery*, next door to *Mona Lisa*. Very good pastries, bread, pizza and ice-cream, open 0900-1300, closed 1400-1500 and Sun pm. *Wimpy*, fresh food, best pineapple milkshake ever.

Bars

There are many African bars which play music, mainly Lingala, which are open till late. A particularly popular one is just outside Kisumu to the west near the molasses refinery. It is a bit rough and ready with only warm beers served from behind a metal grille, but the atmosphere on Fri nights is lively and it often has live bands. In town there is the far more sophisticated *Octopus* on Oganda St which plays western music. Good fun. It gets very crowded late in the evening, US$2 entry fee. The *Octopus Restaurant* is often empty, though the dance floor is much more lively. Between the restaurant and disco, there are stairs leading up to the *Pirate's Den Rooftop Bar*, pleasant, has a dartboard and is a good place to have a drink as the sun goes down. *New Rozy*, 100 m down the road to the right, lively, noisy. *Flamingo Casino*, opposite the *Nyanza Supermarket*, PO Box 525, Kisumu, T43701.

Entertainment

Casinos *Royale Hotel* on Jomo Kenyatta Av. Open 1600-0500, no entry fee, no dress code.

Shopping

Handicrafts For curios and crafts it is quite good here as there are many artefacts from other parts of the country also available. Kisii stone is a particularly good buy as are *kikois* (woven cloth). The *Wananchi Crafts* shop is reasonable, selling things made by local women. Street vendors are outside the post office and at stalls on the northern side of Oginga Odinga Rd.

The main matatu/ bus stopping point is just beyond the covered market

Markets Kisumu's main fruit and vegetable market on Nairobi Rd is one of the largest in Western Kenya, and worth a wander to soak up some of the atmosphere. The market bustles every day, although Sun tends to be quieter. You'll find that most things on offer tend to be quite similar. Look out for *kikois*, some real gems are available if you look hard enough. Otherwise it's the-run-of-the-mill stuff: fruit and vegetables, children's clothes, tools, flip-flops, radios, batteries, bags, sheets, etc, but also a surprisingly large number of trainers/sneakers along Jomo Kenyatta Av. The covered part of the market (like a large shed) is the best place to buy cheap fruit, vegetables, pulses, herbs and rice.

Supermarkets *Nyanza Supermarket* at *Mega Plaza* on Oginga Odinga Rd. Ex-pat owned, slightly more expensive, but sells 'reassurables' for those feeling a little homesick!

Rat tales

Around 1916 or 1917 the plague spread across parts of Kenya and Uganda. It was spread by rats, or rather the fleas that live on the rats, and in an effort to curb the problem the medical authorities in Kisumu had a plan. They offered 10 cents for every dozen rats' tails that were brought in to them. About 18 miles from Kisumu, at Maseno, many dozens were collected – but it was a long walk to take them into

Kisumu. So the collectors approached the missionary authorities and asked whether they could give the rats' tails as collection in church. This was agreed on, and provided they were sun-dried, and correctly bundled, there was no objection. Every Sunday the collection tray was passed around, many bundles were collected and on Monday the mission sent someone to Kisumu with them, for payment.

(Heinz beans/ketchup/Marmite/Pringles/Robertson's marmalade). Closes 1245-1400 for lunch. *Big Buys*, Oginga Odinga St, is slightly larger and cheaper and has a wider array of goods. Good spice selection. 3 shopping arcades have opened off Oginga Odinga Rd, near the post office. The largest is *Mega Plaza* which, apart from the well-stocked supermarket, has a bag shop, café bar with pool table and pet shop. The others are *Al-Imren Plaza* and *Reinsurance Plaza*.

Across the road from the *Royale Hotel* there are a number of stalls that sell Kisii stone (soapstone) and wooden ethnic artefacts. Excellent quality and good value. Advised to barter to improve the price. In Kisii stone there are chess boards, bowls, pots, candle holders and sculptures. There are also wooden animals, Masai warriors, drums, spoons/forks, masks and trinkets.

Sport **Golf**: club northeast of the town where you can hire equipment and a caddy. You need to pay a day's membership fee and the whole lot will come to around US$6. **Swimming** use pools rather than the lake as bilharzia is rife. There are 3, the best is at the *Sunset*, there are also pools at *Royale* and the *Imperial*.

Tour operators *Kisumu Travel*, Oginga Odinga Rd, T44122. *Pel Travels Ltd*, Al-Imren Plaza, PO Box 957, Kisumu, T41525, F22495, for transport, hotel bookings and foreign exchange.

Transport **Local Car hire**: *Kisumu Travels*, T44122, only have a limited number of cars available and are more expensive than hiring a car from Nairobi. *Shiva Travels*, T43420.

Long-distance Air *Kenya Airways*, Oginga Odingo Rd, T44055. There are daily flights from **Nairobi** taking 1 hr and costing US$54. **Road** The main *matatu* and bus stopping point is behind the covered section of the main market. here are countless Peugeots, *matatus* and buses travelling between Kisumu and most major towns in Western Kenya leaving from the bus station. There are also many leaving for Nairobi passing through Nakuru and Kericho on the B1. Approximate times: **Nairobi** to Kisumu, express 6 hrs or normal 8 hrs. It takes approximately 2 hrs to **Kericho**, 5 hrs to **Nakuru**, 2 hrs to **Eldoret**, 1 hr to **Kakamega**. The offices of *Akamba Buses* (the safest option) are in the town centre, just off New Station Rd. **Ferries**: Small motor ferries running between Kisumu and a number of lakeshore towns were a very cheap and nice way of seeing around Lake Victoria. However all operations have been suspended until further notice. If the services resume tickets can be bought from Kisumu wharf (it opens at 0800).

Directory **Banks** *Barclays*, Kampala St or *Standard Chartered*, Oginga Odinga Rd are the most efficient for changing money. Both have ATMs as do *Kenya Commercial Bank* and *Co-op Bank*. Banking hrs are Mon-Fri 0900-1500 and Sat 0830-1100. Foreign exchange facilities. There are two **forex bureaux** towards the northern end of Oginga Odinga Rd and one in Reinsurance Plaza. *Western Union* money transfer can be organized at the *Post Bank*. **Communications** Internet access available at *Imperial*, *Hotel Royale*, *MGE Services*, *Cyberzone*, Oginga Odinga Rd, and *etouch* in Reinsurance Plaza, all roughly at US$0.10 per min. **Post office**: Oginga Odinga Rd, Mon-Fri 0800-1700 and Sat 0900-1200, has a reliable **poste restante** service. *DHL*, *Pony* and *Omega* delivery services from *Securicor*, *Fedex* from *Kisumu Travel*, Oginga Odinga Rd. **Telephone:** direct calls from the card phone outside the post office. **Libraries** *British Council*, Oginga Odinga Rd, T45004, Mon-Fri 0930-1700 with 1 hr for lunch, Sat 0830-1245. Papers and magazines, including 3 or 4-day old copies of *The Times*. Here you can watch TV and videos (many films and classic British drama series), and there is very cheap internet access (US$1 per 15 mins). **Places of worship** Majority of people here are Christian (mainly Roman Catholics), but there are a significant number of Muslims. *Jamia Mosque* on Otieno Oyoo St is testament to the long tradition of Islam here. Built in 1919, this green and white building has 2 imams and calls to prayer can be heard in much of the town.

South Nyanza

Homa Bay
0° 50' S, 34° 30' E
Telephone code: 385
Colour map 3, grid B3

This is an easy area to explore by *matatu*, which provide excellent service. Fishing (a male activity) and the smoking of fish (a female activity) are important occupations around here. Homa Bay, the biggest town in the area, is very busy, especially at the end of the month when workers are paid and flock to town. There's no special reason to stay here unless you have to. Homa Bay is the nearest town to **Lambwe Valley National Reserve**, a little-visited reserve established in 1966 to protect the rare roan antelope, and **Ruma National Park** described below.

Sleeping **B** *Homa Bay*, T0385-22070, located on the lake shore. Rarely has many guests here. **D** *Masawa*, simple but good value. **D** *New Brothers*, fairly basic, but has a few mosquito nets. **D** *Nyanza*, offers reasonable value.

Thimlich Ohinga

Quite near Homa Bay (60 km) or 45 km northwest of the town of Migori, Thimlich Ohinga Prehistoric Site is one of the most significant archaeological sites in East Africa. The name means 'thick bush' or 'frightening dense forest' in the local DhoLuo language. It was declared a national monument in 1983, and consists of dry stone enclosures of what appears to be one of the earliest settlements in the Lake Victoria area. It is an impressive example of a style of architecture whose remnants are found all over the district. The main structure consists of a compound about 140 m in diameter with five smaller enclosures in each and at least six house pits. The dry stonewalls were constructed without using mortar, and range from 1-4 m high and from 1-3 m wide. The materials used were collected locally from the nearby hills. Several parts of the enclosing wall have caved in, and conservation work is urgently required. A giant *Euphorbia candelabrum* towers over the site.

The design of these structures would appear to indicate that the dry stone enclosures were built by a cohesive community, thought to date from about the 14th century, believed to be mostly of Bantu origin. It is believed that the Bantu lived here prior to the arrival of the Luo people. Between them, the early Bantu settlers and later Nilotic settlers built about 521 enclosures in over 130 locations in the Lake Victoria region. They are similar to the 17th-century stone ruins in Zimbabwe.

Later settlers appear to have carried out repairs to the stonework between the 15th and 19th century. It is unclear as to why the area was abandoned by the Ohingnis in the early 20th century. A similar style of dwelling is used in some places by Luos today. There is no public transport to get here. You need to follow the Rongo-Homa Bay road as far as Rod Kopany, then head southwest to Miranga where there are signposts to Thimlich Ohinga.

Ruma National Park

The Ruma National Park is 10 km east of Lake Victoria in the South Nyanza district of Western Kenya. Situated in the Lambwe Valley in Suba District, it is approximately 140 km from Kisumu. The park was established to protect the rare roan antelope, found only in this part of Kenya. This area is fascinating with a mixture of small islands and peninsulas and is rarely visited by tourists.

0° 45' S, 34° 10' E

The Lambwe region is infested with tsetse fly that can be fatal to man (sleeping sickness) and domesticated animals, but not to wild animals

The land is a mixture of tall grassland and woodlands of acacia, open savannah and riverine forests interspersed with scenic hills. There are abundant wild flowers, including a varient of the fire lily. In addition to the roan antelope, other mammals found here include the Bohor reedbuck, Jackson's hartebeest, hyena, leopard, buffalo and topi. Rothchild's giraffe, zebra and ostrich have recently been introduced. Birdlife is plentiful and diverse. The diurnal yellow-eared bat is also found in this national park.

The park has unsealed murram roads, which frequently become impassable with black sticky mud. A four-wheel drive is needed especially during the rainy season. Activities include bird-watching, trekking and fishing.

Camping There are two camping sites here, Kamato and Nyati. However, facilities are only basic and given the tsetse fly situation, you may want to give camping a miss. There are no lodges or tented camps. **Access** The main access to the park is from Kisumu via Homa Bay or by Kisii and then take the Migori-Homa Bay. Both these roads are sealed. The park is 22 km from Homa Bay along the unsealed murram road that links Homa Bay to Mbita. Alternatively, the route along the sealed road from Homa Bay to the Karungu road is 42 km. From the Migori Shopping Centre it is 10 km to the park headquarters along a murram road.

Rusinga Island lies in the northeastern corner of Lake Victoria in Kenyan waters. Ferry access from Homa Bay is restricted due to the water hyacinth problem in Lake Victoria, but the island is now linked to the mainland by a causeway. The main town on Rusinga Island, Mbita, is unexceptional. Inland foreigners are rare and you are sure of a welcome. The traditional way of life is threatened here as drought coupled with environmental degradation (mainly tree clearance for fuel or land) has reduced agricultural productivity.

Rusinga Island

See map page 172

The island is rich in fossils, and famed for the discovery by Mary Leakey, the anthropologist, of one of the earliest austrapithecines remains, the skull of *Proconsul Africanus (P. heseloni)*, a sub-group of *Dryopithecus*, said to be 17,500,000 years old. This anthropoid ape lived on the island 3,000,000 years ago, and is believed to be a probable ancestor of the chimpanzee. The skull can be seen in the National Museum.

Rusinga Island was also the birthplace of Tom Mboya, an important Kenyan political figure during the fight for Independence, who was assassinated in 1969 by a Kikuyu policeman, sparking off ethnic violence. There is a school and a health centre named after him, and his mausoleum is at Kasawanga, on the north side of the island.

The island is popular with game fishermen and holds the IGFA all-tackle record for the heaviest Nile perch ever caught. Over 80 species of bird are found here, including fish eagles and bee-eaters. Lake Victoria is renowned for its glorious sunsets, and after dark the Luo fishermen from the villages scattered along the lakeside can be seen out on the lake in their beautifully painted boats, lit by paraffin lamps. Boat trips to visit other nearby islands can be arranged.

On the shores of the island you may see the rare spotted-necked otter, giant monitor lizards or hippo. If you do intend to walk around the island take plenty of water as it is extremely hot and humid here; there is little danger of getting lost, but mosquitoes are plentiful.

Sleeping **L** *Rusinga Island Club*, bookings through *Bush Homes of East Africa Ltd*, PO Box 56923, Nairobi, PO Box 56923, T01-571647, F571665, www.bush-homes.co.ke Thatched cottages overlook the lake. Food specialities include tilapia and Nile perch, some drinks,

Kenya

fishing and laundry included. Game drives at Ruma National Park, waterskiing and watersports are also available. Can collect guests from anywhere in the country with their own light aircraft. Closed April-May.Only 40 mins (130 km) by air from the Masai Mara.

Mfangano Island
See map page 172

Further along Lake Victoria, slightly bigger than Rusinga Island, Mfangano has shade from giant fig trees, and is much more remote and primitive, with few tourist facilities and no roads. Hippos are very much in evidence, as are monitor lizards basking in the sun. There are interesting prehistoric rock paintings here showing signs of centuries of habitation. The rock paintings are in a gently scooped cave on the north coast of the island and are reddish coloured shapes. It is not known who drew them, when or why.

A large wooden boat shuttles people between Mbita and surrounding places. It leaves Mbita at 0900 and takes about 90 minutes to Sena on the east of Mfangano. There is a government rest house (officially free though ask for permission to stay) and local people are usually willing to put up travellers. The island is completely free of vehicles, and has neither electricity nor piped water, so bear this in mind if you intend to stay.

Sleeping **L** *Mfangano Island Camp*, set in beautiful gardens that mostly attracts serious (and wealthy, at US$500 a night) fishermen. Reservations through Governor's Camps, PO Box 48217, International House, 3rd Floor, Mama Ngina St, Nairobi, T331871, F726427.

Kendu Bay

See map page 172

Kendu Bay is a small town in South Nyanza, now Homa Bay District. It is an hour's drive from Kisumu, on the Homa Bay-Katito road, off the Ahero-Sondu-Kisii road. It has become a fairly important lake port, receiving boats from Tanzania and merchandise from the rich Kisii highlands, in the form of coffee and tea, although this has diminished in recent years.

The main reason for coming here is to visit the curious **Simbi Nyaima Lake** a deep volcanic lake, steeped in myths and legends. It has bright green opaque water, and is located only a few kilometres from Lake Victoria. No one knows what the source of the lake is and its size is constantly changing. Local people believe it to be unlucky and the surrounding area is certainly devoid of vegetation. It is not fished and the area is uninhabited. According to one legend, a hungry and tired old woman called Ateku arrived in this area, where she found the villagers celebrating by eating, drinking and dancing. Only one caring female villager gave her food and drink and a bed in which to rest her weary bones. To give thanks, Ateku ordered water to spring from the ground, which later went on to flood the area. Another version of the legend was that the old lady was denied food and lodgings and in wrathful vengeance induced a massive flood that swamped the village.

Recently, however, Lake Simbi Nyaima has seen the widespread migration of flamingos from Lake Nakuru, 200 km away (see page 159). In 1988 many of the birds flew to other soda lakes, including Lake Simbi, for breeding purposes as Lake Nakuru virtually dried up. Another reason for the transposition of the flamingos is believed to be that the level of algae, *Spiruline Platensis*, part of the flamingo's diet, has diminished in Lake Nakuru. Many of the birds that made the lengthy journey are believed to have guided younger birds back to Lake Simbi. As a result, the lake is becoming a tourist attraction. Take the road towards Homa Bay. It takes about two hours to walk around the lake. There are no shops so take your own supplies of food and drink.

Sleeping **D** *South Nyanza* is said to be the best and it has a disco each night. **E** *Kendu Country Hotel*, hot water on request, mosquito nets, good view of lake, drinks/meals provided on request but rather expensive. **E** *Hotel Big 5*, hot water and mosquito nets and coils on request, live bands on Fri and weekends, African music, western music, weekend disco. African and western food available reasonably priced, can be noisy, parking available.

Harbour/Pier Steamers used to dock here, arriving daily from Kisumu. The service also ran to Homa Bay. However, all operations have recently been suspended until further notice.

For Ondago Flamingo Site take the road for Homa Bay, past the Lake Simbi turning. This is a seasonal mudflat frequented by both flamingos and other birds each year. Another **bird sanctuary** has recently been established at Rakewa off the Kisii road at Oyugis, after 23 km on very rough road. It is renowned as a pelican-breeding site – both white-backed and pink-backed. If you are in town, it is worth checking out the beautiful, old **Masjid Tawakal Mosque**. If you are travelling by road, take the newly tarred lakeshore road that meets the A1 Kisumu road going via Katito. The drive is great through countryside that is just opening up.

The main route from western Kenya to Tanzania runs from Kisumu via Oyugis and Kisii, and is in excellent condition, except around Kisii. Mgori is the last town along this stretch, on the Tanzanian border. It is a transit stop for people travelling to Musoma in Tanzania. The town has a rough reputation. If you wish to get to Nairobi quickly, there are a number of buses going direct, at 0600, 0700 and a few in the evening.

Sleeping and eating Basic accommodation and local restaurants are in the town, but if you are staying in the area head for **F** *Migori Mission*, 2 km south of the town centre, PO Box 61, T0387-20447, maramisskenya@net2000.ke.com Run by a Swedish couple, it is very quiet and pleasant, and is excellent value. There are 2 guesthouses, each sleeps 4 and has a kitchen, living room and hot water (US$3 per person). A cook can be arranged. There is also a conference centre and dormitories with a capacity of 44 beds (US$1.50). **Camping** is also possible, as is secure vehicle parking.

West of Migori, approximately half-way to Lake Victoria are two places of interest, located close to one another, the Macalder Gold Mines which were worked out about 60 years ago, and the Gogo Falls. Close to the falls is a **neolithic archaeological site** with evidence in stratified layers of herding, hunting and fishing. Close to Macalder, in this area, with tropical wooded grassland, remains have been found of a number of mammals, including *Equus burchelli*, bushpig, *Alcelaphus*, hippo, bos, and various other ungulates. Gogo Falls has also been harnessed to provide power for the environs.

Northwest out of Kisumu towards the Ugandan border is Siaya District, a heavily populated agricultural region. According to the 1997 District Development Report, Siaya is one of the poorest districts in Kenya, with the vast majority of households living below the poverty line. Economic and social problems include low farm productivity, unemployment and reduced access to health and education services. The district has three distinctive geomorphological areas – dissected uplands, Yala Swamp and Uyoma Peninsula, with a range of altitudes ranging from the lake shore to 1,400 m above sea level. The higher areas have a heavier rainfall and are therefore more suitable for farming.

Busia is a small town on the border with Uganda. It primarily consists of one road lined with shops, kiosks and cafés. The border crossing itself is fairly straightforward, but quite thorough. The best **F** *Hotel* here is about 1 km from the border, on the south side of the road slightly set back, next to a small market. The rooms are clean and have en-suite bathrooms and there is a bar that is popular with local people. The restaurant is very good and cheap and serves mashed potatoes, a rarity in Kenya.

About 20 km out of town is a small hill, **Got Ramogi**. From the top are great views over the lake on one side and of *shambas* on the other. The hill is of great significance to the Luo people as it is the site where their ancestors fought for their right to settle here in the 15th century.

Kisii and the Western Highlands

The Western Highlands are the agricultural heartland of Kenya, separating Kisumu and its environs from the rest of the country. The Highlands stretch from **Kisii** in the south up to the tea plantations around **Kericho**, through to **Kitale**, **Mount Elgon** and **Eldoret**.

Kisii

0° 40' S, 34° 45' E
Phone code: 0381
Colour map 3, grid B3

Set in picturesque undulating hills in some of the most fertile land of the country and with abundant sunshine and rainfall, Kisii is a very lively and fast-growing town. As with so many other towns in agricultural areas, the market here is buzzing and has an excellent array of fresh fruit and vegetables. The town lies on a fault line, so earth tremors are not uncommon. This is the home of the Gusii people, and is famous for its **soapstone**, though you may look to buy some in vain as most of what is locally produced is bought up by traders to stock the tourist shops in Nairobi.

There was some political unrest and rioting in Kisii in the early part of 2001, generating a tense atmosphere, with many armed police checkpoints. The nearby town of Kisumu has also been affected.

Sleeping & eating

Zonic Hotel, PO Box 541, at the corner of Hospital Rd and Ogemba Rd, T30298, is a brand new and very large upmarket hotel. Prices not available at time of writing, phone for details.

D *Kisii Sports Club*, located southwest of the town near *Barclays Bank*. Rooms are within the clubhouse, and are quite spacious, with nets and s/c, but a little gloomy. Has a bar and restaurant. Price includes breakfast, but the use of the facilities (swimming pool, squash, snooker and pool tables) requires an extra small payment. Club membership fee is necessary to play golf. **D** *Storm*, at the southeast edge of town, PO Box 973, T30649. OK, clean rooms, s/c and hot water, but small and somewhat overpriced. Has a bar and restaurant.

E *Kisii*, north of town centre, T20954. Own bathrooms, is probably the best of the slightly more expensive **E**-bracket places, although the rooms are quite basic. There is a comfortable colonial atmosphere, with attractive gardens and OK food. **E** *Mwalimu*, at the far south of town near the town hall, ceiling panelling falling off in places although the rooms are clean, s/c, hot water, bar and restaurant. **E** *Sakawa Towers*, Hospital Rd, by market. PO Box 541, T21218. Secure and clean rooms have own bathrooms and balconies. Newish high-rise

Kisii

To Kendu, Homa Bay, Isebania & Kisumu

To Sotik & Kericho

N

0 metres 100
0 yards 100

■ **Sleeping**
1 Capital
2 Highway Lodge
3 Kisii
4 Kisii Sports Club
5 Kisii Tea Room
  Bed & Lodging
6 Mwalimu
7 Njau Guest House
8 Sabrina Lodge
9 Safe Lodge
10 Sakawa Towers
11 Satellite Bar & Restaurant
12 Silent Lodge
  & White Stone
13 Tip Top Lodge
14 Zonic

● **Eating**
1 New Silver & Bar
2 Obomo

building with own bar and restaurant. Disco held on Fri, Sat and Sun. **F** *Highway Lodge*, PO Box 910, T21213. Cheapest in town and secure but the s/c rooms are dingy and unwelcoming, cold water, get a room at the back if at all possible – the rooms at the front are very noisy as they are over the main road. **F** *Hotel Capital*, somewhat shabby rooms with toilets, no running water, buckets of hot water in the morning on request, noisy. **F** *Kisii Tearoom Bed and Lodging*, Hospital Rd, cheap, clean, secure but very basic, shared bathrooms and cold water. **F** *Njau Guest House*, north along Moi Highway, T21375. S/c rooms, bathrooms have squat toilets, no hot water. **F** *Sabrina Lodge*, just around the corner from the eastern *matatu* park. Friendly and secure place with communal facilities, no hot water. The hotel also has a bar and restaurant. **F** *Safe Lodge*, Sakawa Rd, just to the south of the market, T21375. Own bathrooms, clean and friendly, though a bit run-down and above noisy bar. **F** *Satellite Bar and Restaurant*, Sansora Rd, has just 1 room, it is s/c, clean and secure, available as single or double, and there is a bar and restaurant. **F** *Tip Top Lodge*, flattering name for a place as basic as *Hotel Capital*. **F** *White Stone Hotel/Silent Lodge*, Moi Highway, close to the post office, *Silent Lodge* is directly behind *White Stone*. All rooms have mosquito nets and basic bathrooms (squat toilets) with hot water, good security.

Cheap *Sakawa Towers*, close to market. Good restaurant, probably the best in town. **Seriously cheap** *Obomo*, popular, with good basic food and fresh fruit juices. *Safe Lodge*, reasonable grilled meat skewers and a good breakfast. *New Silver Bar and Restaurant*, Hospital Rd.

Entertainment is centred around bars. *Satellite Bar*, busy drinking den, though not very savoury. There is a disco at *Mwalimu*, southern end of town. Also weekends at *Sakawa Towers*. Kisii's football team, *Shabana FC*, is in the first division and the stadium is just to the west of the main road. **Entertainment**

Kisii Sports Club, behind *Barclays Bank* on the main road, is worth joining if you are here for a few days. It has a friendly atmosphere and facilities for swimming, tennis, squash, pool, darts and bingo. There is a good bar to relax in afterwards. **Sport**

Road *Matatus* for **Kisumu**, takes 3 hrs, leave in front of the market. All others leave from the station, the stand to the east of the main street. **Nairobi** is 8½ hrs away. **Transport**

Uhuru Plaza, located on Moi Highway, contains the offices for *Kenya Bus*, a chemist, photo developer, and *2000 Skytech* on the 3rd floor where it is possible to **email** (US$0.40). On the second floor of *New Sansora Complex* is *Gamma Computers/etouch* where internet access costs US$1.30 for 10 mins. **Directory**

About 25 km from Kisii, this village is the most important producer of soapstone and the centre of carvings in the country. To visit the quarries or the carvers, you need to go past the Tabaka Mission Hospital to the *Kisii Soapstone Carvers Co-operative*. The children are happy to direct you. There are lots of local shops where you can buy soapstone artefacts. The stone comes in a variety of colours from orange (the softest) to deep red (the heaviest). Both *Standard Chartered*, near market, and *Barclays*, on main road, have branches here open Monday-Friday 0830-1300 and Saturday from 0830-1100. **Tabaka**

Kericho

Perched on the top of a hill, the tea plantations stretch for miles on either side of the road, their bright green bushes neatly clipped to the same height with paths running in straight lines in between. At 1,800 m above sea level, the tea plantations stretch along the western edge of the Great Rift Valley. The predictable weather (it rains every afternoon here) and the temperate climate giving a high ground temperature, make this the most important tea-growing region in Africa. Kenya is the world's third largest tea-producing nation, after India and Sri Lanka. This is an orderly part of Kenya, very different from the *shambas* further down the slopes, and very English, *0° 30' S, 35° 15' E*
Phone code: 0361
Colour map 3, grid B3

Kenya

exemplified by the *Tea Hotel* with its lovely gardens that used to be owned by Brooke Bond. Kericho is named after Ole Kericho, a Masai chief who perished in battle at the hands of the Gusii in the 18th century. The town's main purpose is to service the enormous tea plantations, so it has most of the basic amenities on the main road, Moi Highway: branches of the main banks, post office, market, library, village green, the English-style Holy Trinity Church, War Memorial, cemetery, and a Hindu Temple used by Kericho's large Asian population. For **tea plantation tours** where the growing and picking procedures are explained, enquire at the *Tea Hotel*.

Chagaik Dam & Arboretum About 8 km to the northeast of Kericho off the road to Nakuru. Established after the Second World War by a Kericho teaplanter, John Grumbley, now retired to Malindi on the coast. This is an exceptionally attractive arboretum, housing many tropical and sub-tropical trees surrounding by well-tended lawns running down to the lakewater's edge. The lake is covered in water lilies and fringed with stands of bamboo.

Trout fishing This is available in the Kiptariet River. The *Tea Hotel* will arrange for permissions and equipment hire. The river runs close-by the hotel.

Sleeping
■ *on map*
For price codes:
see inside front cover

B-C *Tea Hotel*, PO Box 75, to east of town centre, on Moi Highway, on road to Nakuru, T30004/5, F20576. Set in lush gardens and backing directly onto the tea plantations this is the best hotel in Kericho. Although now looking very slightly drab the old colonial building is spacious, comfortable and well-appointed. It has a swimming pool and very attentive staff make it a very pleasant place to stay. Some of the rooms have TVs. The hotel offers email facilities, and has a reasonable restaurant. Standard and superior rooms available, all have their own bathrooms. Visa and Mastercard accepted. **C** *Midwest*, PO Box 1175, Moi Highway opposite police station, T20611-4, F20615. Own bathroom, relatively modern, central yet with garden, clean, spacious, functional. 2 price categories available. Gym and sauna, good restaurant. **D** *Kericho Garden Lodge Hotel*, Moi Highway, close to *Tea Hotel*, PO Box 164, T20878. Fairly basic but very friendly, s/c, hot water, breakfast included. **E** *Fairview TAS Lodge*, PO Box 304, to northwest of town centre, on Moi Highway, on road to Nakuru, close to *Tea Hotel*, T21112. Own bathroom, loose, hanging wires in rooms but clean, bar, restaurant, attractive garden setting. **E** *Kerico Valley*, north of the *matatu* park, PO Box 637. Very recent construction, looks good, s/c rooms, has bar and restaurant. **E** *Mwalimu*, PO Box 834, Temple Rd, just to north of Chai Sq in town centre, T20601. Corridors are quite dark but the rooms are OK, and clean. Own bathroom, restaurant and bar, price includes breakfast. **E** *New Sunshine*, Tengecha Rd, PO Box 1910,

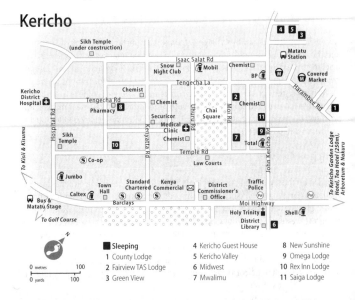

Kericho

Sikh Temple (under construction)

Kericho District Hospital

Snow Night Club

Isaac Salat Rd

Mobil

Chemist

BP

Matatu Station

Covered Market

Harambee Rd

Tengecha La

Chemist

Tengecha Rd

Pharmacy

Chemist

Securicor

Medical Clinic

Chai Square

Chemist

Uhuru Rd

Moi Rd

Sikh Temple

Chemist

Kenyatta Rd

Temple Rd

Total

John Kericho Rd

To Kericho Garden Lodge Hotel, Tea Hotel (250m), Arboretum & Nakuru

To Kisii & Kisumu

Hospital Rd

Co-op

Jumbo

Caltex

Town Hall

Standard Chartered

Kenya Commercial

Law Courts

District Commissioner's Office

Traffic Police

Bus & Matatu Stage

Barclays

Moi Highway

Holy Trinity

Shell

To Golf Course

District Library

0 metres 100
0 yards 100

Sleeping
1 County Lodge
2 Fairview TAS Lodge
3 Green View

4 Kericho Guest House
5 Kericho Valley
6 Midwest
7 Mwalimu

8 New Sunshine
9 Omega Lodge
10 Rex Inn Lodge
11 Saiga Lodge

T21923. Pleasant and clean, friendly staff, restaurant popular with locals. Currently single rooms (with bathrooms and hot water) only, doubles under construction. **F** *County Lodge*, just off Harambee Rd, PO Box 154, T20208. Very basic cell-like rooms with nothing but a bed. Single rooms only. Very cheap. **F** *Green View*, north of the *matatu* park. Large hotel that appears to be unfinished, double rooms with shared bathroom, single rooms available with or without. Has hot water, and a bar with food available. **F** *Kericho Guest House*, near *Kericho Valley*. Large basic hotel, bar and food available, s/c bathrooms have toilets and showers but no basins. **F** *Omega Lodge*, John Kericho Rd, cheap, and rather small and dank, with shared showers, hot water. **F** *Rex Inn Lodge* Temple Rd. Fairly central, friendly, very cheap but no hot water, communal shower and somewhat smelly. **F** *Saiga Lodge*, John Kericho Rd, basic but friendly and fairly cheap. **Camping**   At *Fairview TAS Lodge* on the road to Nakuru.

Eating   **Mid-range** *Tea Hotel*, solid and dependable English-style menu, with some Indian dishes. **Cheap**   *Midwest*, good-value set menu. *Sunshine Hotel*, Kenyatta Rd. Good value, closed Sun.

Entertainment   This is a town with relatively little to see and do, that mostly appears to close down at the end of the business day, and there is not much available in the way of nightlife. *Snow Night Club* on Isaac Salat Rd is about the size of it.

Safety   In May 2001 there was some civil unrest at Kipsegi, Kericho District, that resulted in a couple of fatalities. Government troops restored calm. There have been intermittent problems in this region, with more widespread clashes between ethnic groups in 1992. Travellers have not been targetted.

Transport   The *matatu* station, at the northern end of Isaac Salat Rd, is well organized, and there is plenty of transport, both buses and *matatus*.

Directory   **Bank**   *Western Union* money transfer is available at the post office and post bank. **Communications Internet**: email from *Tea Hotel*. *Omega*, *Pony* and *DHL* delivery services on offer at *Securicor* on Kenyatta Rd.

Maseno

See map, page 172

Maseno is a growing university town, 26 km northwest of Kisumu on the equator. It is a two-hour drive from the Kenya/Uganda border on the B1. It consists of a few hotels and restaurants, but it also has a *Barclays Bank*, a petrol station (Total), a post office with a public phonebox outside and a Mission Hospital. The University is the main focus of the town. The journey to Kisumu takes about 45 minutes by *matatu*.

Sleeping and eating **E** *Land of Majitu Hotel*, basic with unreliable security, cheap, mosquito coil available on request, can get noisy at night. **E** *Maseno Inn*, offers restaurant, bar and lodging, cheap, very basic, lax security, no hot water, jukebox downstairs accounts for the high noise level. **E** *Maseno University College* has a small guesthouse, T035-51011/08 for reservations. They serve generally good-quality food, quick service (Seriously cheap) **Seriously cheap** *Sariba Campus*, 3 km from B1 main road. No guesthouse but food quick and generally good quality, cost US$1.50, lunchtime only.

Maseno

0 metres 800
0 yards 800

N

■ **Sleeping**
1 Land of Majitu
2 Maseno Inn
3 Maseno University
  College Guesthouse

● **Eating**
1 Equator Motel
2 Rock View Hotel
3 Sariba Campus

Rock View Hotel (has a chemist downstairs), the best restaurant in Maseno, deceptive menu as many items are unavailable, clean, good view of Bunyore Hills from upstairs terrace (no accommodation). *Equator Motel*, bar and restaurant, no accommodation, noisy.

Shopping *Maseno General Store*. Small range of basic items on offer, photocopying is available here, also has a furniture shop adjacent. Other than the General Store there is a small market on Tue, which includes most things found in a typical African market: fruit (in season), woven baskets, dried fish, etc.

Directory Banks *Barclays Bank*, 0930-1330 Mon-Sat, has only a minor branch (Agency) that does not handle foreign currency exchange, nor withdrawals exceeding KSh10,000.

Two hours west of Maseno, along an unmade road, is the small village of **Kanbewa**. A further 45 minutes drive takes you to **Kit Mikayi Caves**. ■ *A guided tour through the caves costs US$2.50.*

Kakamega
10° 20' N, 34° 46' E
Phone code: 0331
Colour map 3, grid B3

This pleasant lively place is the main town of the Luhya people. A major attraction is the **Kakamega Forest** (see below), and the town is the place to buy provisions for an excursion there. At the end of November is the **Kakamega Show**, an agricultural festival at the showground just to the north of the town, on the Webuye Road. Most travellers tend to head straight out to the forest reserve and stay there. Kakamega is famous for being the centre of a gold rush in the late 1920s, which attracted huge numbers of hopeful prospectors. The largest nugget found was named the *Elbon Nugget*, so named by reversing the surname of Dan Noble, formerly a postman, who later bought Nairobi's first hotel, the old *Hotel Stanley*.

Sleeping
■ *on map*
For price codes:
see inside front cover

B *Golf*, PO Box 42013, just off main road, behind Sports Club, T30150/1/2, F30155 (T02-330820 Nairobi, for reservations). Own bathrooms, has a swimming pool and facilities for golf, tennis and squash at the Sports Club. The bar is open to non-residents. Modern, very pleasant, excellent service and food, but fairly expensive, especially considering Kenyan residents pay almost half price. **C** *Premier*, well furnished and nicely presented, clean, carpeted rooms with own bathrooms and balconies. **D** *Little Home Resort*, off Amboliba Rd on south edge of town. OK clean rooms, pleasant gardens, bar and good restaurant. **E** *Bendera*, just to the west of the main road. Good value and comfortable accommodation. **E** *Little Home Resort*, just off Amboliba Road, if heading out of town towards Kisumu, has lovely grounds, enabling you to eat out under the stars. Clean rooms, Satellite TV in bar and a restaurant. **F** *Franka*, southwest of the clocktower. Basic and quite small but clean s/c rooms with hot water. Bar and restaurant, overall this hotel is quite reasonable. **F** *Salama*, has very cheap single, double and triple rooms, with shared facilities, cold water, secure parking. **F** *Western*, very cheap, adequate single rooms, communal bathrooms, hot water in mornings.

Eating **Mid-range** *Golf Hotel*, solid fare, English-style cooking with some Indian dishes. **Seriously cheap** *Dreamland Cafe*, formerly offered good service with great-tasting food, but more recently slow service, with only basic food. *Sparkles Cafe*, situated next to the Kenyan Teachers' Union Office, serves very tasty samosas and cheap sodas.

Transport **Road** The town is less than 1 hr from Kisumu (about 50 km) along the excellent though very busy A1 and there are plenty of buses and *matatus* travelling this route. The main bus stand is close to the market. The *Akamba* bus service has its stand opposite the Hindu Temple, off the Mumias Rd.

Kakamega Forest National Reserve

0° 10' N, 35° 15' E This forest is only 45 sq km and is the easternmost corner of the Congo-West African equatorial rainforest. It is the sole remnant of tropical rainforest in Kenya and it has been a protected area since the 1930s. Lying about 17 km north of Kakamega town on the

A snip of the price

Isaac Misigo, the chairman of Lukembe Circumcisers of Kakamega, is dedicated to improving the professional and ethical standards of his members. In a statement to the Standard newspaper in May 1996, Mr Misigo listed the new rules by which his members will now be required to abide:

- No circumcising dead people
- No circumciser to be drunk when operating
- No tools of the trade to be used to:
    threaten other people
    repair motor vehicles
    castrate dogs
Rate for job KSh 3,000 (US$50), although a cow can be accepted in payment.

Kenya

Kisumu-Kitale road, it is an extraordinarily beautiful forest, with at least 125 species of tree, including the Elgon teak. The indigenous trees along the trails are identified with small plaques giving their Latin as well as their local names. There are a number of animals here that are found in no other part of the country, including the grey duiker, bushpig, bush-tailed porcupine, giant water shrew, clawless otter, a few leopards and the hammer-headed fruit bat. There are also several primates including the olive baboon, the red-tailed monkey, the black and white colobus and blue monkey. The forest is also home to the hairy-tailed flying squirrel that can 'fly' as far as 90 m.

The forest is also of great ornithological interest as many birds found here are not seen elsewhere in Kenya. Hornbills, woodpeckers, honeyguides, both Ross's and the great blue turaco, grey parrot and the rare snake-eating bird are among the avian residents. In addition several varieties of barbet including the double-toothed, speckled and grey-throated are found here. Butterflies are abundant, and snakes normally only found in West Africa can be seen too. Look out for the Gabon viper, a particularly nasty, deadly but fortunately very shy snake that lives in the forest.

If you wish to see the flowers at their best, plan you visit during the rainy season from April to July. Exotic orchids grow in the junctions of the tree branches. There are two areas in the forest that cater for tourists, **Isecheno**, towards the south/centre of the forest and **Buyangu** in the north. At Buyangu several walks are possible, the longer of which offers the chance to reach Buyangu Hill, from where there is a good view over the tree canopy or to a small waterfall (Isiukhu Falls). On the banks of the Yala River you can see deep pits, that were dug to extract gold, and occasionally you may see local people panning for the precious metal.

Near to the reserve on the Kakamega-Kisumu road is a curiosity called the **Weeping Stone**. This is an 8-m rock upon which a smaller rock is balanced, and between the rocks a small trickle of water emanates, and continues to flow even during the dry season.

It is advisable to wear waterproofs if you plan to visit, as the rain is heavy, regular and predictable. But it is beautiful walking country. There are 7 km of trails in the forest. ■ *There is no entrance* *charge to the reserve. The guide fee is only US$1.25 per hour and represents excellent value, as the guides are extremely knowledgeable about the forest flora and fauna.*

Sleeping **Isecheno** **E** *Forest Rest House*, PO Box 88, Kakamega. Located within the forest reserve, it is small, with only 4 bedrooms, all with their own bathrooms. Clean and friendly. Book at weekends and at Christmas, Easter and Jul-Aug) . However you will need to bring your own food supplies from town although nearby there is a very small shop/restaurant where you can eat. The only other alternative to the *Rest House* is the **A** *Rondo Retreat Centre*, a religious centre only recently opened up to the public, a serene location. Book through Nairobi, PO Box 14369, or T0331-20145 on Thu.

Buyangu **D** *Udo's Campsite*, just outside the entrance gate. Several bandas, all with 2 beds except 1 that has 3. Bring bedding and food, although there are plans to open a small restaurant. **Camping** US$2.50. There is a small shop that sells a few basic supplies such as bread and soda, and there are small shops and tiny local restaurants in the village beside the main road. It is also sometimes possible to get very basic accommodation in small bandas (**F**) in the local village, ask the officials at the gate if you are interested.

Transport: For **Isecheno** take the Kisumu road south of Kakamega for about 10 km and turn left at Mukumu. Carry on down this road for about 7 km when you will reach the village of Shinyalu where the forest is signposted. Take a right and after about another 5 km you will reach the forest reserve. **Buyangu** is much easier to get to if you do not have your own transport as it is a walk of less than 1 km from the main road, about 20 km north of Kakamega, on the way to Webuye. This route is served by countless *matatus*, but watch out, very few of the drivers or conductors seem to recognize the name Buyangu.

Kapsabet
Colour map 3, grid B3

The journey from Kericho due north to Eldoret passes through the Nandi Hills, some of the most spectacular scenery in this part of the country, and the Kano Plains, bleak mountainous scrubland and ravines. The only town of note on this route is Kapsabet, a small town about 60 km north of Kisumu. **Sleeping** **E** *Bogol Inn*, fairly basic, reasonable restaurant. **E** *Kapsabet*, PO Box 449, T03231-2176. Inexpensive, restaurant and bar. **E** *Keben*, has a restaurant, bar and disco, rather lively.

Eldoret

0° 30' N, 35° 17' E
Phone code: 0321
Colour map 3, grid B3

This pleasant, busy and fairly prosperous highland town is surrounded by fertile countryside growing a mixture of food and cash crops. It is home to **Moi University** and this appears to be benefiting the town and expanding its economic potential. Again, there's no special reason you should stay here, unless you're en route to the Cherangani Hills to the north.

Sleeping
■ *on map*
For price codes:
see inside front cover

B *Sirikwa*, PO Box 3361, Elgeyo Rd, T62499, 63614. Large hotel located in well-tended gardens, it has an impressive entrance hall, and a good swimming pool. Own bathrooms, senior and luxury rooms with TVs available, and the price includes breakfast. **C** *Eldoret Wagon*, Elgeyo Rd, PO Box 2408, T62270/1/2. New and comfortable, has restaurant and bar. **C** *Eldoret White Castle*, Uganda Rd, T62773. Very pleasant clean, s/c rooms and good facilities with own bar, restaurant, health club and disco. **D** *Asis*, Kimathi Av, T61806/7. This is a modern hotel with own bar and restaurant. Clean and tidy s/c rooms are a little on the small size, but comfortable nevertheless. **D** *Highlands*, PO Box 2189, Elgeyo Rd, T22092. Quiet place and good value. **D** *Mountain View Hotel*, on Uganda Rd opposite post office, T32179. Clean, own bathroom, restaurant and bar. Has parking for motorcycles, but gives prison-like feel. **D** *Eldoret New Lincoln*, PO Box 551, Oloo Rd, T22093. Colonial-style hotel, with some character and helpful staff. Easily the best in this price range (but make sure your room is not one of the few with a leaking toilet and without hot water). The restaurant food is good and the bar is a pleasant, but noisy club next door.

E *Aya Inn*, Oginga Odinga St. Good value, rooms are a little small but comfortable, clean and secure, s/c, hot water, friendly staff. **E** *Mahindi*, PO Box 1964, Uganda Rd, T31520. Own bathrooms, hot water, lively atmosphere, close to *matatu* park and so can get very noisy. Bar and restaurant, but breakfasts are at *Honey Drops Hotel* next door. **E** *Sosiani View Hotel*, Nandi Rd, T33215. Basic bright rooms, s/c and has hot water, bar and restaurant. **F** *Cicanda Lodge*, Kimathi Av, PO Box 1080, T22534. Small, spartan rooms, but with mosquito nets, choice of s/c or not, and has hot water in the morning. **F** *Eldoret Valley Board and Lodging*, Uganda Rd,

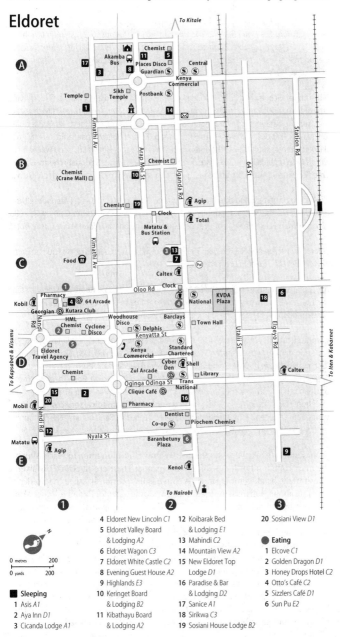

Eldoret

Kenya

Sleeping
1 Asis *A1*
2 Aya Inn *D1*
3 Cicanda Lodge *A1*
4 Eldoret New Lincoln *C1*
5 Eldoret Valley Board & Lodging *A2*
6 Eldoret Wagon *C3*
7 Eldoret White Castle *C2*
8 Evening Guest House *A2*
9 Highlands *E3*
10 Keringet Board & Lodging *B2*
11 Kibathayu Board & Lodging *A2*
12 Koibarak Bed & Lodging *E1*
13 Mahindi *C2*
14 Mountain View *A2*
15 New Eldoret Top Lodge *D1*
16 Paradise & Bar & Lodging *D2*
17 Sanice *A1*
18 Sirikwa *C3*
19 Sosiani House Lodge *B2*
20 Sosiani View *D1*

Eating
1 Elcove *C1*
2 Golden Dragon *D1*
3 Honey Drops Hotel *C2*
4 Otto's Café *C2*
5 Sizzlers Café *D1*
6 Sun Pu *E2*

PO Box 734, T32314. Good value, well-run and quiet, but rather puritanical. Has hot water in mornings. **F** *Evening Guest House*, Arap Moi St. Small, quite dirty rooms, shared bathrooms, hot water in the evening. **F** *Keringet Board and Lodging*, Arap Moi St. OK rooms, shared bathrooms, hot water in the morning, own restaurant and bar. **F** *Kibathayu Board & Lodging*, PO Box 832, Arap Moi St/Tagore Rd, to west side of centre, T0321-22160. Seen better days, single rooms s/c, double rooms not. **F** *Koibarak Bed and Lodging*, corner of Nandi Rd and Nyala St. Quite dirty single rooms (available after 1700) above an often noisy bar, with communal facilities, cold water. **F** *New Eldoret Top Lodge*, corner of Nandi and Oginga Odinga Rd, PO Box 703, T61564. Cheap and secure s/c rooms but not particularly inviting. **F** *Paradise Hotel Bar and Lodging*, Uganda Rd. Secure s/c single rooms with hot water, 'short stays' available. **F** *Sanice*, Kimathi Av. Slighly grubby but OK for the price, s/c single rooms, hot water, own restaurant and bar. **F** *Sosiani House Lodge*, near the *matatu* and bus station, PO Box 1781, T32338. Clean, shared bathrooms, hot water.

Eating **Mid-range** *Elcove*, Oloo Rd. Best food in town, western, Indian and Chinese. Good service,
● *on map, page 189* atmosphere and value, and generous portions. *Golden Dragon*, Kenyatta St, Chinese restaurant. *Sun Pu*, Baranbetuny Plaza, Uganda Rd, T32212. *Sirikwa*, on Elgeyo Rd. Has a buffet lunch at weekends including a barbecue. **Cheap** *Eldoret Valley*, Uganda Rd. Mostly grills, skewered meat, good standard, Somali menu. *New Wagon*, Elgeyo Rd. Good value meals. *Otto's Cafe*, Uganda Rd. Simple, with good range of meat dishes. **Seriously cheap** *Sizzlers Cafe*, Kenyatta St. American diner style, good food, snacks and milkshakes, good service too.

Entertainment **Nightclubs** The best and the newest is *Cyclone Disco*, on Kenyatta St. *Woodhouse Disco* on Oginga Odinga St is also popular and very lively. Others are *Kutara Club* on Oloo Rd, *Places Disco* on Uganda Rd near the post office, and the one at *Eldoret White Castle Hotel*.

Tour operators *Eldoret Travel Agency*, PO Box 888, T33351/2/3, F32588, can book flights including *British Airways*. *EM LEL Travels*, Zul Arcade, T63504/5, F63043.

Transport **Air** There are flights from **Nairobi** departing from Wilson Airport. **Road** The *matatu* stand is in the centre of town just off Uganda Rd and there are a number of Peugeots, *matatus* and buses throughout the day. The journey direct to **Nairobi** takes just 3½ hrs.

Directory **Communications** Internet (all US$1 for 15 mins): *Clique Café*, Oginga Odinga St (also pool table and drinks), *Cyber Chapter*, Mezzanine of KVDA Plaza, *Cyber Den*, Oginga Odinga St (fast access), *Dawn to Dusk Computers*, 10th floor of KVDA Plaza, *Mutakin Enterprises*, Zul Arcade, Oginga Odinga St, also available at *64 Arcade* and *Georgian*. **Post**: The post office is on Uganda Rd, opposite is the *Post Bank* which offers *Western Union* money transfer. *DHL* services from *Eldoret Travel Agency*, Nandi Rd/Kenyatta St corner. **Medical services** Dentist: Dr Wambugu has been recommended by travellers. Based at Baranbetuny Plaza (shopping centre) on the Uganda Rd in the direction of Nakuro.

Eldoret to From Eldoret the A104 passes through **Webuye** and **Bungoma** to reach **Malaba**,
Malaba the most common border crossing into Uganda. These are all geared toward the transit traffic heading for Uganda. **Webuye Falls** (previously called the Broderick Falls) are about 5 km from the road, and provide the water for **Panafric Paper Mills**. It is possible to visit the mills, PO Box 535, T16 (Bungoma, via the operator). **Chetambe's Fort** is a further 8 km from the Webuye Falls, and is the site of the last stand of the Bukusu group of the Luhya people against the British in 1895. The Bukusu had strongly resisted the British incursions into their lands to build the railway during the 1890s. On the lower slopes of Mount Elgon the warriors were grouped together in a fortified stronghold located on the top of a hill. Armed only with spears they proved no match for the British (and sundry other mercenary soldiers) who massacred over 100 of the Bukusu warriors with an early machine gun, known as the Hotchkiss. **Sleeping D** *Hotel*, on the road from Eldoret to Malaba just before the bridge at Malaba. Clean friendly. Safe parking is available for cars and

motorcycles. **Camping** US$3, restaurant. Recommended. Other cheap and basic accommodation in the **F** price range is also to be found locally.kital

Kitale

A pleasant, small town Kitale isin the middle of lush farmland between Mount Elgon and the Cherangani Hills. Originally this was Masai grazing land, but it was taken over by European settlers after the First World War. The town did not really develop until after 1925 and the arrival of a branch line of the railway. The region is known for its fruit and vegetables, including apples that are rare in East Africa. Kitale's main attraction for tourists is as a base from which to explore the Cherangani Hills (see section on Rift Valley, page 165 and information about guides later on in this

1°0'N, 35°0'E
Phone code 0325
Colour map 3, grid B3

Kenya

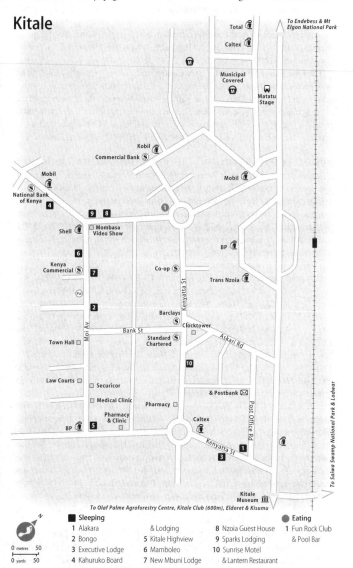

Kitale

To Endebess & Mt Elgon National Park

Total
Caltex

Municipal Covered

Matatu Stage

Kobil
Commercial Bank

Mobil

Mobil

National Bank of Kenya

Shell
Mombasa Video Show

BP

Kenya Commercial

Co-op

Trans Nzoia

Kenyatta St

Barclays
Clocktower

Bank St

Standard Chartered

Askari Rd

Town Hall

Law Courts

Securicor

Medical Clinic

Pharmacy

& Postbank

Pharmacy & Clinic

Caltex

BP

Post Office Rd

Kenyatta St

Kitale Museum

To Olaf Palme Agroforestry Centre, Kitale Club (600m), Eldoret & Kisumu

To Saiwa Swamp National Park & Lodwar

0 metres 50
0 yards 50

■ Sleeping		● Eating
1 Alakara	& Lodging	1 Fun Rock Club
2 Bongo	5 Kitale Highview	& Pool Bar
3 Executive Lodge	6 Mamboleo	
4 Kahuruko Board	7 New Mbuni Lodge	
	8 Nzoia Guest House	
	9 Sparks Lodging	
	10 Sunrise Motel	
	& Lantern Restaurant	

section) or Mount Elgon (see page 194) and the Saiwa Swamp National Park (see, page 193). It's also a stopping-off point on the route to Lake Turkana in the north.

Kitale Museum contains ethnographic displays of the life of the people of Western Kenya with lots of tribal artefacts, and has a section on the evolution of man with special reference to East African and Kenyan discoveries. The museum also contains a very comprehensive insect collection (including butterflies) as well as birds, reptiles and wildlife exhibits. Murals on local life can be viewed in the Museum Hall. The museum buildings are set in spacious gardens, and the indigenous trees are labelled. There is an excellent nature trail through local forest, the remnants of a much larger forest that once clothed this area, that is rich in birdlife and monkeys, terminating at some very pleasant picnic sites. There is also a **Snake Park**, home to both non-venomous and venomous snakes, in addition to an enclosure containing two crocodiles. Another enclosure contains tortoises. Nearby is a display of traditional homesteads of the Luhya, Nandi, Luo and Sabaot peoples. A biogas generation unit to demonstrate the use of animal waste to produce methane is an unusual exhibit. ■ 0800-1800 US$2.50. PO Box 1219, close to the Eldoret Rd, just east of town centre, T20690.

The Kitale Show at the beginning of November is a major agricultural festival

The Olaf Palme (Vi) Agroforestry Centre, next door to the Kitale Museum, has Swedish funding. It was established to assist and educate local farmers in soil conservation and improvement techniques, with advice and support about methods of tree planting and preventing soil erosion. There is an arboretum, an indigenous tree nursery and an agro-forestry demonstration area, in addition to a Conference centre with educational displays. ■ *Free. PO Box 2006, T20139, F31067, viafp@net2000ke.com*

Sleeping & eating

On map page 191

B-C *Kitale Club*, PO Box 30, Eldoret Rd, beyond the Kitale Museum, T31330, F30924, doubles up as a residential establishment for both temporary and permanent residents, in addition to offering sporting facilities. It is said to have been built on the site of the old slave market and has old colonial buildings with a few more modern additions. Range of rooms available, including cottages with own bath and shower, or comfortable single rooms with hot water. Restaurant (Mid-range) serves solid English fare with some Indian dishes. Other facilities include satellite TV, swimming pool, tennis, squash, snooker and an 18-hole golf course set amid clumps of natural forest. It is a very pleasant place but a little overpriced. Temporary membership (US$6) must be paid.

D *Alakara*, Kenyatta St/Post Office Rd corner, PO Box 1984, T20395, F30298. Recommended. Secure, has hot water all day, s/c rooms are pleasant, though the beds are very short. Restaurant (Seriously cheap) serves fairly simple food but good value. **D** *Bongo Hotel*, PO Box 530, Moi Av, T20593. S/c rooms are clean and pleasant, and have hot water and nets, good but just shaded by *Alakara* and *Sunrise Motel*. **D** *Executive Lodge*, Kenyatta St, PO Box 2275. Good rooms, with or without bathrooms (rooms without are in price band **E**), some have mosquito nets. Helpful staff, hot water. **D** *Kitale Highview Hotel*, Moi Av, PO Box 2925, T31570. Pleasant clean, airy rooms, with good veiws, s/c, friendly staff. **E** *Lantern Restaurant and Sunrise Motel*, Kenyatta St. Standard or deluxe (price band **D**) rooms, both are large and comfortable, deluxe have nicer furnishings and balconies. Friendly, recommended. Also has a good restaurant (Mid-range), a close relative of *Elcove Restaurant* in Eldoret and equally good, with a similarly wide menu of western, Chinese and Indian dishes. **E** *New Mbuni Lodge*, clean, hot water. **F** *Hotel Mamboleo*, Moi Av, PO Box 264, T20172. Rooms are a little dark but clean and with bathrooms. The hot water is supplied in a bucket. Cheap and is not at all bad value. **F** *Kahuruko Board and Lodging*, located west of town centre. Quite dark and dingy, s/c, hot water available in buckets, and has a bar and restaurant. **F** *Nzoia Guest House*, clean and basic, shared facilities, cold water. **F** *Sparks Lodging*, close to *Nzoia* and similar, except single rooms only. **Seriously cheap** *Fun Rock Club and Pool Bar*, upstairs, has cheap local food, that is good value, in a friendly atmosphere with live music daily.

Camping There is a campsite about 20 km north of Kitale, at **C-E** *Sirikwa Safaris*. A family concern that has been operating for over 30 years with father and son, Tim and Dick Barnsley, taking clients all over the region, meeting up with the remnants of the Sirikwa people. The enterprise later expanded to include a lodge and campsite in 1978 run by Jane and Julia Barnley. Both indoor and tented facilities are available as well as an all-weather banda. This is a lovely site, with excellent facilities, including a barbeque, flush toilets, hot showers, firewood, electricity and excellent food. Highly recommended. Camping charges US$5 per person. To hire a tent costs US$15 per person, meals US$5. If you don't have a tent you can hire a room in the guesthouse fairly cheaply. A small, family-run place, you need to book through *Barnley's House*, PO Box 322, Kitale. T/F0325-20061. Ornithological tours of the nearby Cherangani Hills to the north can be arranged from here.

On the top of a hill in the garden is a large rock, now broken into sections, that has been carved to form a Bao board, and is estimated to be at least 500 years old. *Sirikwa* is located in an area that contains many depressions called 'Sirikwa Holes'. It is unclear whether these depressions are man-made or naturally occurring, but what appears to be either ancient tools or possibly broken pieces of molten or smelted rock have been found close to these depressions. *Sirikwa* is signposted on the right-hand side of the road a few kilometres past the entrance to **Saiwa Swamp NP**. Alternatively you can camp in the Saiwa Swamp NP. Camp charges are US$2 per person in addition to the NP entry fee.

Guides are available from here for the Cherangani Hills trekking. It can be difficult to obtain good local maps of the hills. The tour includes the villages of Kapsangar-Tapach and Tamcal. Allow 3-4 days for the trip.

Transport Various bus stands and *matatu* stops are at the western end of the road to Mt Elgon. Getting to and from Kitale is relatively easy as it is on the A1 heading for Kakamega and Kisumu in the south, and is the main route to Lake Turkana in the north. There are regular buses and *matatus*. The road north from Eldoret to Marich Pass/Lake Turkana is very good.

Directory **Post** The **post office** is on Post Office Rd and the main banks are pretty close to Bank St, as you might suspect! *Securicor* on Moi Av offer *Pony* and *Omega* delivery services.

Saiwa Swamp National Park Kitale is the nearest town to Saiwa Swamp and Mount Elgon national parks. **Saiwa Swamp National Park**, Kenya's smallest national park, at 2.9 sq km, established to protect the rare semi-aquatic Sitatunga antelope (*Tragelaphus spekei*). The Sitatunga has widely splayed hooves that have evolved, allowing it to walk on the swamp vegetation. Other animals found here include the giant forest squirrel, bushbuck, Bohor reedbuck, bush duiker, the de Brazza monkey and both the spotted-necked and clawless otter. There is prolific birdlife estimated at over 400 species of birds and includes the great blue turaco, several varieties of kingfisher and the wonderfully named bare-faced go-away-bird. The national park is also home to a very large variety of reptiles, amphibians, butterflies and other insects. There are about three nature trails, totalling 10 km, on duckboards traversing the varying habitats, and there are rest areas and picnic areas along the trails. Several tree hides with viewing platforms have been built along the western boundary from where it is possible to view the mammals and birds. The best time to see the Sitatunga is in the early morning or evening, as it rests semi-submerged and very well hidden during the heat of the day. The park has three distinctive vegetation types: wetland vegetation with stands of bullrush, reeds and sedges; wooded grasslands containing shrubs and grasses; indigenous forest as the national park contains remnants of tropical forest including wild fig and banana trees, *Terminalia spp* and *Albizia spp*. ■ *For further information contact the Park Warden, PO Box 4506 Kitale T0325-55022. There are plans to develop an education centre here.* Saiwa Swamp national park is located on the sealed well-signposted road, 22 km east of Kitale on the Kitale-Kapenguria road. There is a 5-km murram road linking Saiwa to the main road. If travelling by air, the airstrip at Kitale is 22 km from the park.

Sleeping Either in Kitale, or at *Sirikwa Safaris* (see under Kitale) on the main Kitale-Kapenguria road 6 km after the Saiwa Swamp NP junction. There is also a small camping ground here at Saiwa NP but you need to bring along all your camping equipment and food.

Mount Elgon National Park

1° N, 34° 30' E
Colour map 3, grid B3

Bring a powerful torch for exploring the caves

Mount Elgon is in the Rift Valley on the western border with Uganda, covering 169 sq km on the Kenyan side. The peak of the extinct volcano reaches 4,322 m, the second highest mountain in Kenya. The Kenya/Uganda border cuts through the caldera of this extinct volcano, giving half the mountain to Uganda, including the highest peak Wagagai (4,320 m), with Lower Elgon Peak (also sometimes called Sudek Peak) (4,307 m) in Kenya. The name Elgon is said to be derived from the Masai *ol doinyo ilgoon* meaning 'the mountain with the contours of the human breast'. The park is approximately 26 km northwest of Kitale, and the roads are clearly signposted. The park's boundaries go down to 2,336 m. This area is known as **Koitoboss** meaning table rock by virtue of its flat-topped basalt columns. Mount Elgon is estimated to be more than 15,000,000 years old. There are a number of **lava-tube caves** formed by the action of water on volcanic ash, some are over 60 m wide and attract elephants and other herbivores in search of salt. Four of these caves can be explored. The El Gonyi people, a Masai tribe, lived in these caves for hundreds of years with their cattle, and the caves were used for many of their ceremonies. The mountain peak is considered to be a sacred place of worship, home to the Gods. **Kitum** is the largest cave extending to over 180 m in depth with a width of 60 m, and overhanging crystalline walls. This is the cave most favoured by the elephants that weave between the bounders and fallen rocks where the cave roof has collapsed. Using their tusks the elephants scrape away at the rock face and pick up the shards with their trunks. Every night it is possible to see long elephant convoys entering the cave to supplement their diet on the rich salt deposits. Kitum is also home to a large population of fruit bats. **Makingeni Cave** is not far from Kitum, and is favoured by buffalo, and both **Chepnyalil** and **Ngwarisha Caves** can also be explored. Three short nature trails lead to Kitum Cave, Makingeni Cave and the Elephant Bluff.

The changes in altitude mean there are a number of ecological zones going from mixed deciduous and evergreen forest, which include wonderful specimens of the *Juniperus procera* more commonly known as the East African cedar as well as the Elgon teak and the great podos. With increasing altitude the vegetation changes to bamboo forest, and then alters to Afro-alpine moorlands. Several rivers rise in these peaks including the Malakis and the Nzoia that feed Lake Victoria, and the Suam

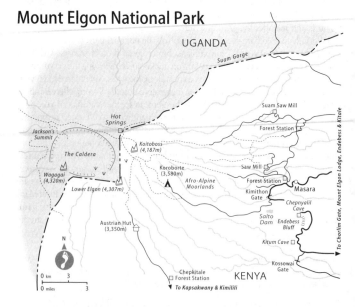

Mount Elgon National Park

and the Turkwell that feed Lake Turkana to the north. The park also contains several beautiful waterfalls, dramatic cliffs and gorges, as well as hot springs. The **Endebess Bluff** offers a panoramic view of the surrounding area. Animals likely to be seen here include black and white colobus monkey, blue monkey, forest elephants (sometimes referred to as cave elephants), leopard, giant forest hog, bushbuck, eland, buffalo, duiker and golden cat.

It is possible to drive up to about 4,000 m – the road passes through forest that is later supplanted by montane bamboo – and then hike over the moorlands with tree heathers up to 6 m tall, to Koitoboss peak. In the Afro-alpine zone are found giant lobelia and groundsels, believed to be survivors from the Ice Age. From there it is possible to climb over the crater rim and descend to the floor of the caldera.

■ *Mount Elgon was reclassified from a forest reserve to a national park in 1993, so standard national park fees are payable.*

Although it is possible to climb Mount Elgon at any time of year, the crater gets very cold and snow and hail are quite common so the best times are between December and March. It is possible to reach the summit and back in a day in dry weather when you are able to drive to within a few hours' hike of the highest point. Make sure that you are suitably equipped with warm and waterproof clothing and appropriate footwear. There is not such a severe problem with altitude sickness as on Mount Kenya, but a night spent en route will lessen any problems that might arise. If you do not have a four-wheel drive, the ascent can be hiked in a fairly leisurely manner, spending three days on the way up and two down.

Climbing Mount Elgon
It is illegal to enter the park zone without a vehicle

The usual entry to the park is through the main Chorlim Gate and then driving through the park to the end of the road track at Koroborte (3,580 m), where there is a campsite and water. From here it is then about 3 hours to the Koitoboss summit.

Kimilili route This runs south of the route through the park. Starting from the village of Kimilili, there is a track to Kapsakwany, 8 km away. Another 2 km on is the turning to the forest gate, which is a further 2½ km. It is then 26 km, which can be driven comfortably in dry weather, to the **Austrian Hut** (3,350 m) where it is possible to stay or camp, with water nearby. There is a further 3 km of driveable track. From here it is about a four-hour hike to Koitoboss summit. There are picnic sites at Elephant Platform and Endebess Bluff. Currently closed for security reasons. The Sasa River route on the Ugandan side is a well-organized alternative (see page 663).

Kimithon route This runs north of the park route. Starting from Enderbess, it is 16 km to Masara village. About 1 km further on take the right fork (not the left to the Kimithon Gate). The middle of three tracks leads to Kimithon Forest Station, where it is possible to camp. Koitoboss is then about six hours hike away. There may be problems with the Forest Station about using this route, but they can usually be negotiated.

Camping gear and appropriate clothing can be hired in Nairobi at *Atul's*, Biashara Street, PO Box 43202, T25935m, at a cost at about US$20 per day, with about US$200 in deposits. You should obtain one of the maps of the mountain showing the trails in some detail (see page 80). Porters for your gear, and guides, cost about US$3 a day, and are a sound investment, and can be recruited at any of the climb departure points. It is wise to ensure that the agreement with any guides or porters is clear. Guides are not obligatory, but if you don't have one, an armed ranger must be hired for the day to take you to the crater rim. *Mount Elgon Map and Guide*, by A Wielochowski, is available at *The Nation* bookshop in Nairobi (see page 104) or from 1 Meadow Close, Goring, Reading, Berks RG8 9AA, England.

Equipment, porters & guides

A *Mount Elgon Lodge*, just outside the main Chorlim Gate, bookings: Msafri Inns, Utali House, Uhuru Highway, Nairobi, PO Box 42013, T330820. It is not certain whether this lodge will remain open as it is somewhat run-down and consequently rather overpriced. A *Lokitela Farm*, PO Box 122 Kitale T/F0345-20695, further away but within driving distance,

Sleeping

Kenya

this farm mainly produces maize and milk. It covers an area of 365 ha, of which 30 ha are riverine forest. 350 different species of birds and mammals have been identified here. It is located 19 km west of Kitale, in the foothills of Mt Elgon, bookings can be made through *Bush Homes of East Africa Ltd*, PO Box 56923, Nairobi, PO Box 56923, T01-571647, F571665, www.bush-homes.co.ke Hosted by the Mills family, it offers nature walks, trips to Saiwa Swamp National Park as well as to Mt Elgon NP, also overnight stays in Cherangani Hide, a shelter built on wooden stilts beside the Suam River. **B** *Delta Crescent Farm*, Endebess PO Box 126, T0325-31462. A family-run enterprise, this farm is situated 28 km from Kitale and 6 km from Chorlim Gate. The farm cover 60 ha and facilities include horse-riding, camping and the rental of camping equipment and 4WDs. Guided mountain safaris can be arranged. **B** *Kapkuro Bandas* (**C** during the low season, Jan-Jun), 2 semi-detached self-catering cottages, the 4 units each have 1 double and 1 single bed, en-suite bathrooms and kitchen. Located in a forest glade near the park HQ near Chorlim Gate, bring everything with you, book through the KWS Tourism Department, T02-501081/2, F501752, www.kws.org **E** *Jasho Lodgings*, in Kimilili. Basic but sound. **E** *Lwala Paradise*, very basic, no water.

Transport The easiest way is from Kitale, the most popular entry to the NP is by Chorlim Gate. This is signposted from a turning off the road to Endebess, about 15 km from Kitale. The other gates can be reached from Kakamega (81 km). You will be able to get a *matatu* from Kimilili.

Southern Kenya

Nairobi

From Nairobi down to the Tanzania border and to Kenya's coastline on the Indian Ocean, Southern Kenya is one of the most visited regions of the country with three of the country's major game parks: Tsavo West and Tsavo East on either side of the Nairobi-Mombasa road make up the largest park in the country, and Amboseli National Park is also very popular. There are many points of interest off the Nairobi-Mombasa road leading to the coast. This is one of the most important thoroughfares in the East Africa region as it runs the length of the country to Nairobi and then to Uganda, where it continues on to Kampala. The Masai Mara Game Reserve in southwest Kenya, contiguous with the Serengeti National Park in Tanzania, is normally accessed via the town of Narok and is therefore included in the Rift Valley section (see page 166).

Mombasa Road

Ensure you have sufficient fuel for your journey as some petrol stations often run out

The Mombasa road starts as a continuation of the Uhuru Highway (A109) in Nairobi, passing one of the city's drive-in cinemas and a number of housing estates. The first small town is **Athi River**, about 3 km from Nairobi. **C** *Small World Country Club*, PO Box 78, T239, is a lively spot open 24 hours. Also **D** *Congress Club*, with accommodation, a restaurant and discos at the weekends. Continuing in a south-easterly direction for 22 km you will reach the turning for Machakos on the left. The town is 19 km from the Mombasa Highway and after Machakos the road continues on to Wamanyu and Kitui. Few tourists make the detour to explore this area.

Machakos
1° 30' S, 37° 15' E
Colour map 3, grid C4

Machakos has a long history as the capital of Ukambani, the home of the Akamba people who have lived in this part of Kenya for around 500 years. The town is named after Masaku, the Akamba chief who predicted the coming of the railway, the iron snake, and the plagues that followed (both smallpox and rinderpest decimated animal and human populations in the region). He died at the turn of the 20th century.

Machakos was also important in colonial times. John Ainsworth, Britain's first upcountry administrator made his headquarters here in 1889, and built a mud-brick fort, the site of which is on the right of the main road just north of town towards Nairobi. Reverend Stuart Watt and his wife arrived soon after and set up a mission that is now the Kenya Orchards Mua Hills Jam Factory. In 1895 the Church Missionary Society arrived and introduced wheat into the area. The importance of this area to the Imperial British East Africa Company made Machakos the ideal place to set up the first inland African Training Centre.

Little sign of its past remains to be seen except the clocktower which was erected in 1956 to mark a visit from the late Princess Margaret, sister of the British Queen. The clock no longer works. However, the tree-lined streets and attractive old buildings make it a pleasant town set in the Mua Hills, and the local people (who are predominantly Kamba) are very friendly. The colourful market, selling locally grown produce as well as sisal baskets (*vyondo*) and other handicrafts, gives the town a bustling atmosphere.

Sleeping & eating

D *Kafoca Club*, T0145-21933, near the market. Pleasant, though quite basic, good restaurant. **D** *Machakos Inn*, just outside the town centre. You can also camp here. **D** *Masaku Motel*, T0145-21745, close to town centre. Inexpensive but adequate. **Cheap** *Ivory Restaurant*, grills and some local dishes.

Shopping

A good place to get a sisal basket is from the *Machakos Handicrafts Centre*, a self-help women's group. There is a small shop full of finished and half-finished baskets. The ones without leather straps are far cheaper, but all are considerably better value than in Nairobi and there is more choice.

Transport

There is no shortage of transport between **Nairobi** and Machakos, you can take your pick from buses, *matatus* or the Peugeot taxis which run from Nairobi's country bus station on Pumwani Rd at the southeast end of River Rd. You should not have to wait more than ½ hr for something. There is also transport from **Mombasa**, though not as frequent.

Wamanyu & Kitui

1° 17' S, 38° 0' E
Colour map 3, grid B5

About 38 km out of Machakos along the road towards Kitui you come across the small village of Wamanyu which is the centre of wood-carving activities in the country. A great grass rectangle in the centre of the village is surrounded by huts sitting in an ocean of wood shavings accumulated from years of work. Most of the wooden carvings end up in Nairobi, but are considerably cheaper if bought here. Kitui itself is in the middle of a semi-arid area which is frequently affected by drought causing malnutrition in this impoverished part of the country. Despite it being so close to Nairobi, it is quite undeveloped, and there is not much here of interest to travellers. Kitui used to be on the trade route of Swahili people in the 19th century, though there are few signs of this now apart from the mango trees planted in the town and the presence of the descendants of the Swahili traders.

Sleeping **E** *Gold Spot*, just to the east of the market. Own bathrooms. **E** *Kithomboani*, close to the market. Quite adequate.

Returning to the Nairobi-Mombasa road, the route passes through the **Kaputiei Plains**. Most of this area is large-scale cattle ranches with herds of gazelle and antelope. It is along here that you turn right for **Kajiado**. The next section of the route is through semi-arid country broken by the **Ukambani Hills**. The road up this long steep slope is poor, as years of heavy trucks making the laborious climb have dug deep ruts into the road. Just south of the road, by the rail line, is **Kima**, meaning 'mincemeat' in Kiswahili. Kima was so named after a British Railway Police Assistant Superintendent who was eaten by a lion. Charles Ryall, using himself as bait, was trying to ambush a lion which had been attacking railway staff and passengers. Unfortunately the ambush went horribly wrong when he fell asleep on the job.

Further on is the town of **Sultan Hamud**. It sprung up during the making of the railway at Mile 250 where it was visited by the then ruler of Zanzibar and named after him. It has hardly changed since that time and is a pleasant enough place to stop off for a soda and snack.

Kenya

South to Amboseli Game Reserve & National Park
(see page 205)

Just to the southeast lie the alluvial **Masai Plains** and the road which leads to the east of the Amboseli Game Reserve and National Park . To get to Amboseli, you can take the C102 road south at Emali towards Makutano where there is a cattle market on Friday visited by hundreds of Masai and Akamba herders. The route continues south to Kimana, after which there is an access road to Amboseli National Park on the right, and then to Oloitokitok on the slopes of Kilimanjaro. However, the more common route to the Amboseli National Park is the A104 south from Nairobi to Namanga, then east along the road that leads in to the west of the national park and game reserve.

The **Kimana Community Wildlife Sanctuary** was the first project of a 'park beyond parks' set up in 1996 to directly benefit the local community. As much of Kenya's wildlife lives outside the national parks, it is not surprising that there are conflicts of interest when game rampages destroy cultivated areas. To overcome this difficulty the Kimana Community Wildlife Sanctuary was established so that the money generated by tourism goes directly to the local people. Next to the sanctuary is the **Kuku Fields Studies Centre**. Situated 225 km south of Nairobi, midway between the Tsavo and Amboseli national parks it offers cultural and environmental education opportunities for all comers. All the money generated directly benefits the local Masai members of the Kuku Group Ranch. On offer are programmes conducted by local Masai people including guided walks to Masai villages, flora and fauna walks and visits to Tsavo and Amboseli national parks.

Back on the Mombasa road, you are now passing through Masai country, which is primarily featureless scrubland. There is a lodge at **Kiboko** that is about a third of the way through the journey (160 km from Nairobi) and a good place to stop off for some refreshment. **C** *Hunter's Lodge*, PO Box 77, Makindu, T2021, named after JA Hunter, a professional hunter with the Game Department in the post-Second-World-War years. The gardens are quite pleasant with hundreds of species of

South to Tanzania

The first coffee growers

Coffee was first planted by John Patterson of the Church of Scotland Mission at Kibwezi, halfway between the coast and Nairobi, in 1891. The Arabica seeds had originally come from Aden and Arabica thrives best at high altitude. Kibwezi was too low for ideal growing conditions, but a crop did mature in 1896, some of which was sold in Europe, the rest used to provide other growers with seed. The French Catholic Street. Austin's Mission at Kitsutu, northeast of Nairobi, was one of the recipients, and set up a nursery to sell seedlings from 1900. Although it takes at least four years for a seedling to produce coffee, coffee growing really took off, so much so that by 1910 over 2,000 bags, each of 120 lbs were harvested.

birds, and there are wonderful views out over the Kiboko River. There is a swimming pool at the lodge though there is rarely any water to go in it.

An excellent place to break your journey is at **Makindu**, about 40 km from Kiboko where a Sikh temple of the Guru Nanak faith offers free accommodation and food for travellers (donations gratefully received). This is particularly handy on the return from Mombasa if you do not want to get back to Nairobi late at night. Slightly further along the road (in the direction of Mombasa) is the *Makindu Handicrafts Co-operative* where around 50 people hand carve figures, mostly of animals, for the tourist market.

The road continues its route passing into more lush pastures with a proliferation of the wonderful and rather grotesque baobabs (see page 242). At this stage the Chyulu Hills are visible to the south. The main trading centre at **Kibwezi** has some cheap places to stay including the **E** *Riverside Lodge*. This is the most important region in the country for sisal growing. Honey production is also much in evidence and you are likely to be offered some from sellers at the side of the road. Try before you buy to check its quality as sometimes it is adulterated with sugar.

From Kibwezi, the road passes through heavily cultivated land to the boundary of Akamba country at **Mtito Andei** – meaning 'vulture forest' – about halfway between Nairobi and Mombasa. There is a petrol station, a few places to eat and a curio shop. It is also the main gate to Tsavo West. Places to stay include the **B** *Tsavo Inn*, and the **D** *Okay Safari Lodge*.

From here the road runs through the centre of the parks Tsavo West and Tsavo East for around 80 km. In the past, herds of elephants could be seen crossing the road in the grasslands making progress along this route slow. Now the grasslands are reverting back to thick bush and scrublands as there are so few elephants left (a combination of hunting and drought). On the right you will pass the Mbololo Hills Prison, formerly Manyani Detention Camp where the colonial forces incarcerated Mau-Mau freedom fighters. Today there is a prison industry showroom with handcrafted furniture and a prison farm shop with a selection of produce.

Galla goats

The traditional Masai goat is comparatively small, males weighing up to 35 kg, females 30 kg. Growth is slow, a yearling seldom weighs more than 20 kg, females have a low rate of milk production, and they cease producing young at five or six years old.

Galla goats from northeast Kenya are bigger, produce more milk, grow more quickly, and the females can produce kids up to the age of 10. Most important is the Galla goat's superior ability to withstand drought, and its rapid rate of recovery in putting on weight, restoring milk yield and starting reproduction when a drought ends. Being taller, they are able to feed on leaves of trees and shrubs that are out of reach of the smaller Masai goats. Galla goats from Isiolo, mostly males, are being introduced to develop both pure bred and cross-bred herds in the area around Kajiado. Some idea of the wealth of Masai goat herders can be gathered from the fact that a female sells at about US$50 and a male at US$75.

Voi
3° 25' S, 38° 32' E
Phone code: 147
Colour map 3, grid C5

The capital of this region, Voi is a rapidly developing industrial and commercial centre. This was the first upcountry railhead where passengers would make an overnight stop. There are a number of bungalows that were built in the early years of the century to accommodate passengers and provide dinner, bed and breakfast, but this is no longer offered as you can dine, sleep and breakfast on the train. Voi is a good place to look for lodgings if you are visiting Tsavo East as it is not far from the park gates and has many excellent cheap places.

Sleeping and eating **C** *Tsavo Park Hotel*, near the bus station, is a new hotel with very good facilities, price includes breakfast. Recommended. **D** *Jumbo Guest House*, T2059, near the bus station, has cheap rooms with bath though it can be a bit noisy. **D** *Sagala View*, T2267, 10 mins from the bus station. Has good rooms. **D** *Voi Restpoint*, T2079. Has 2 restaurants, and cooling fans in the rooms. **D** *Vuria Lodging*, T2269. Fans and mosquito nets in all rooms, and flush toilets. **E** *Distarr Hotel*. Recommended. Very good restaurant, vegetable curry is excellent.

Transport **Train**: This is a major stop on the railway, though the train pulls into Voi from Nairobi at around 0300 and from Mombasa at 1200. **Road**: There are buses coming and going all day long between Mombasa and Nairobi. Buses leave to connect Voi with the border town of **Taveta** at 0930 and 1500.

Directory **Banks**: *Kenya Commercial Bank*, PO Box 137, T2501. **Medical services**: *Voi District Hospital*, PO Box 19, T2016.

Tsavo National Park

3° N, 38° E
Colour map 3, grid B5

This is the largest national park in Kenya at around 21,000 sq km. It lies in the southern part of the country, halfway between Mombasa and Nairobi and is bisected by the Mombasa-Nairobi railway and road link. For administrative purposes it has been split into two sections, **Tsavo East** (11,747 sq km) lying to the east of the Nairobi-Mombasa road/railway is the part of the park made famous by the 'Man Eaters of Tsavo', and **Tsavo West** (9,065 sq km). The Waliangulu and Kamba tribes used to hunt in this area before it was gazetted. The remoteness of much of the park makes it a haven for poachers. As a consequence, much of the northern area (about two thirds of East Tsavo) is off limits to the public in an attempt to halt poaching here which has decimated the rhino population from 8,000 in 1970 to around 100 today. Recent anti-poaching laws have been particularly successful in Tsavo and the number of elephants is increasing again. The first European to visit this part of Kenya was Dr Krapf, who journeyed on foot and crossed the Tsavo River in 1849 on his way to Kitui. Captain Lugards the explorer also passed through this area – the rapids on the Galana River are named after him.

Tsavo West is probably the easiest park to get around if you do not have your own car as there are plenty of buses from Nairobi to Mtito Andei, and your chances of getting a lift are fairly good. To get to the park from Voi, the easiest entrance is at Makatau near the Taita Hills and Salt Lick lodges. This road cuts across the park exiting at the Mbuyuni Gate in the west. It is easy to get to Tanzania from here via Taveta (see page 208). There are no scheduled flights to either Tsavo East or West, although there are several airstrips suitable for chartered light aircraft.

Both Tsavo East and West are fairly easily navigated with a good map as all tracks are clearly defined, and junctions are numbered. Bring all your own provisions into the park including petrol and water. You should be able to eat or drink at any of the lodges if you so desire. There is a shop at Voi Gate in the east selling (warm) beers, sodas, bread and some vegetables and another shop in Tsavo West selling basic provisions.

Tsavo East is the much less-visited side of the park where you will be able to see the wildlife without the usual hordes of other tourists. It mainly consists of vast plains of scrubland home to huge herds of elephants. The landscape is vast, and empty of any sign of humans, dotted with baobab trees (see page 242). The wildlife includes all of the 'Big Five', plus zebra, giraffe, impala, gazelle, eland and cheetah, and there are over 500 bird species. The **Kanderi Swamp**, not far from the main entrance at Voi Gate, has the most wildlife in the area. The main attraction of this part of the park is the **Aruba Dam** built across the Voi River where many animals and bird congregate. **Mudanda Rock**, about 30 km north of Voi, is a 1.6-km long outcrop of rock that towers above a natural dam and at certain times during the dry season draws hundreds of elephants. The **Yatta Plateau**, at about 290 km long the world's largest lava flow, is also found in Tsavo East. The **Lugard Falls** on the Galana River, 40 km northeast of Voi are pretty spectacular. They are a series of rapids rather than true falls. The rocks have been sculpted into fascinating shapes by the rapid water flow that is channelled into a gorge so narrow that it is possible to stand with legs spanning the cleft, overlooking the falls.

As time goes on, Tsavo East is opening itself up to package tourism, particularly the budget camping safaris. The wardens have even started to open up parts of the

Tsavo East National Park

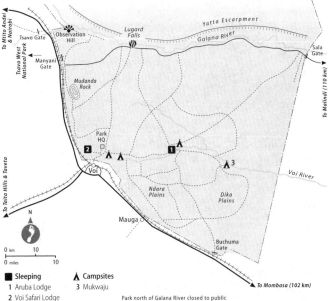

■ Sleeping	▲ Campsites
1 Aruba Lodge	3 Mukwaju
2 Voi Safari Lodge	Park north of Galana River closed to public

northern sector to upmarket low-profile camping and walking parties. This means the overwhelming feeling of solitude is slowly disappearing, though its vast size means you are likely to be alone for most of the time.

South Kitui National Reserve is the second national reserve in Kitui district. It is 1,800 sq km, adjacent to the northern boundary of the Tsavo East National Park, but no tourism is allowed at present.

Tsavo West Tsavo West is the more developed part of the park combining easy access, good facilities and stunning views over the tall grass and woodland scenery. The area is made up from recent volcano lava flows, which absorb rainwater that reappears as the crystal clear Mzima Springs 40 km away. The environment is well watered and this, combined with volcanic soils, supports a vast quantity and diversity of plant and animal life. The main attractions are the watering holes by *Kilaguni* and *Ngulia* lodges that entice a huge array of wildlife particularly in the dry season. During the autumn the areas around *Ngulia Lodge* are a stopover for hundreds of thousands of birds from Europe in their annual migration south.

Not far from the *Kilaguni Lodge* is the **Mzima Springs**, a favourite haunt of hippos and crocodiles. There is an underwater viewing chamber here, but the hippos

Tsavo West National Park

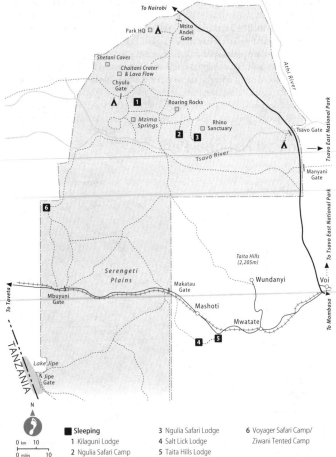

Sleeping
1 Kilaguni Lodge
2 Ngulia Safari Camp
3 Ngulia Safari Lodge
4 Salt Lick Lodge
5 Taita Hills Lodge
6 Voyager Safari Camp/
Ziwani Tented Camp

have obviously decided against being studied too closely by moving to the other side of the pool. Also around the lodges are the spectacular **Shaitani lava flow** and cones, as well as caves that are well worth visiting. You will need to bring a good torch to explore them. **Chaimu Crater** to the south of *Kilaguni Lodge* can be climbed and though there is little danger of animals here, it is best to be careful.

Chyulu Hills National Park was established recently as an extension to Tsavo West. Previously a game conservation area, the park is virtually untouched by man. The long mountain range is home to lion, giraffe, zebra and oryx. Described as being the youngest mountain range in the world, it is made up of intermingled volcanic cones and lava flows. Many of the cones are covered with grass and there are extensive forests, allowing scope for hill walking. There is no permanent water supply in this mountain range except for a small spring at Ngungani. Kilimanjaro is clearly visible from the crest of the Chyulu Hills.

At the extreme southwest of the park, bordering Tanzania, is the beautiful **Lake Jipe** (see page 209), which is fed by underground aquatic flows from Mount Kilimanjaro. Here are found pygmy geese and the black heron along with many other species of birds.

Wildlife you are likely to spot include: hyrax, agama lizards, dwarf mongooses, marabou storks, baboons, antelope, buffalo, zebra, giraffe, jackals and hyenas, crocodiles, hippos, leopards, lions, cheetahs. This part of Tsavo has some black rhino though most have been moved to the Rhino Sanctuary now.

Tsavo East L *Galdessa Camp*, sited 10 km upstream from Lugards Falls on the Galana **Sleeping**
River, has 8 bandas with river frontage. It is situated in the middle of the unfenced black sanctuary in Tsavo East NP, which contains over 50 rhino. Price includes full board, game drives, walking safaris but excludes alcoholic beverages. Book through Galdessa c/o Exclusive Classic Properties, PO Box 714, Nairobi, T892110, F891307, www.galdessa.com
L *Satao Camp* (**A** Apr to Jun), is a permanent 'tented' camp with 10 double tents pitched inside separate wooden roofs, and a bathroom under the same roof but outside the tent. It is very well organized and overlooks a waterhole, where elephant, lions, zebra, etc come down in succession to drink at night. Camel safaris can be arranged from here.
L *Voi Safari Lodge*, PO Box 565, Voi, T0147-30019, F30080. Slightly cheaper than the lodges of equivalent standard in West Tsavo and much less crowded. It is 5 km into the park from Voi Gate, 52 rooms each with 2 beds, swimming pool, and a good location. The animal hide by the waterhole gives very good close-up views at eye level. Baboons and rock hyrax wander freely through the hotel and gardens. There are spectacular panoramic views. From here it is possible to arrange a drive to climb Mudando Rock where, once the area is checked for lions, it is safe to climb. **A** *Patrick's Camp/Tiva River Camp*, traditional tented camp, run by safari guide Patrick Reynolds from Jun to Oct. The camp is beside the seasonal Tiva River in the remote northern area of the park and is the base for game drives as well as Patrick's speciality: walking safaris. Another expensive camp (over US$550 a night) booked through *Bush Homes of East Africa Ltd*, PO Box 56923, Nairobi, PO Box 56923, T01-571647, F571665, www.bush-homes.co.ke **Camping** There are sites (**E**) at Voi Gate, Kanderi Swamp, Aruba Lodge and at the Makwaju Campsite on the Voi River about 50 km from Voi Gate. All have toilets, showers and running water.

Tsavo West L *Kilaguni Lodge*, PO Box 30471, Nairobi, T336858, F218109. Best lodge in the park and also the most expensive, every room faces the waterhole and has a verandah, swimming pool, Mt Kilimanjaro can be seen from the lodge. **L** *Ngulia Safari Lodge*, PO Box 42, Mtito Andei, T0147-30091, F30006. 52-room lodge, is slightly cheaper but still very good with a swimming pool, good location. The waterhole, again, is a big draw both for the animals and tourists. Staff very knowledgeable on the wildlife and extremely helpful. The lodge overlooks the Rhino Sanctuary and the rhinos can be viewed through the binoculars that are set up there. Visits to the sanctuary are restricted to between 4-6 people each day. A leopard visits the lodge's waterhole at dusk most nights to feed. **L** *Ol Donyo Wuas*, in the Chyulu Hills, bookings through *Bush Homes of East Africa Ltd*, PO Box 56923, Nairobi, PO Box 56923,

T01-571647, F571665, www.bush-homes.co.ke 4 cottages for up to 17 guests, all rooms have views of Mt Kilimanjaro. All inclusive of food, drinks and activities including day and night game drives, horse-riding and guided bush walks. **L** *Voyager Safari Camp/ Ziwani Tented Camp* (**A** Apr to Jun), PO Box 74888, Nairobi, T02-716628/710782, F716547, heritagehotels@form-net.com This is one of Heritage Group's 'Voyager' resorts, of good standard. Sited at the western boundary of the park, with full-size permanent tents and excellent food available.

C *Ngulia Safari Camp*, T340331 (Nairobi). Offers self-service accommodation in the park in fully equipped bandas, including bathrooms with hot water. Has a good friendly atmosphere and is popular with Kenyans and tourists alike. It is possible to arrange an early evening visit to one of the lodges from here for dinner and/or drinks. **Camping** There are (**E**) campsites at each of the gates at Tsavo, Mtito Andei and Chyulu.

Transport **Tsavo West** The park headquarters are off the Mombasa-Nairobi road at the northern end of the park through the Mtito Andei Gate. The gate is about 220 km from Nairobi and 255 km from Mombasa. It is 30 km from here to *Kilaguni Lodge* in the park. This is the busiest entrance to the park, and therefore the best one to aim for if you intend to hitch your way through the park. If you drive along the same Mombasa-Nairobi road for 48 km you come to Tsavo Gate.

Tsavo East Follow the same road as for Tsavo West (Nairobi-Mombasa road) and enter at the park HQ at Voi Gate. There is a small educational centre at Voi Gate. If you are coming from Malindi, it is 110 km up to Sala Gate on the eastern side of the park. There is a road cutting across to the Galana River and on up to Manyani Gate on the Mombasa-Nairobi road.

Voi to From Voi the road runs through the **Taru Desert** for another 150 km down to **Mombasa** Mombasa. This area is an arid, scorched wilderness and there is little sign of life. You will see several small quarries. These supply many of the hotels on the coast with natural stone tiles used in bathrooms and patios. The next small settlement is **Mackinnon Road** with the Sayyid Baghali Shah Mosque as its only landmark. 30 km along the route you come to **Samburu** a small town with no tourist facilities.

Another 30 km brings you to the busy market centre of **Mariakani**, a place of palm groves and an atmosphere quite different from upcountry Kenya. If you take the road to the right, the A107, then turn left at the junction with the A106, it leads to the **Shimba Hills**, which can also be reached from the coastal road south of Mombasa. If you are visiting the national reserve here you can either camp on the edge of the range about 3 km from the entrance, or stay at the **L** *Shimba Hills Lodge* or **A** *Travellers Mwaluganje Elephant Camp* (see page 231).

For the next 90 km the scenery becomes progressively more tropical, the heat increases, as does the humidity and the landscape changes to coconut palms, papaya and other coastal vegetation. Eventually you enter the industrial suburbs of Mombasa.

South to Tanzania

Kajiado Directly south of Nairobi is the A104 road to the Namanga border crossing to Tanzania. It is the administrative headquarters of southern Masai-land at the southwestern corner of the Kaputei Plains which run between Machakos and Kajiado. The town is in the middle of bleak grasslands that show little sign of the abundance of zebra, wildebeest and giraffe that used to roam here. The town is typically Masai and there are many indicators of their preoccupation with cattle. Simple accommodation and food and drink are available.

*1° 53' S, 36° 48' E
Colour map 3, grid C4*

Sleeping To the south of Kajiado, on the northern slopes of the Melepo Hills, is a private wildlife estate with a tented camp for up to 10 guests. **L** *Sirata Suruwa*, meaning 'glade of elands', is the home of American naturalists Michael and Judith Rainy, who are working to add wildlife conservation to the traditional pastoral economy of the local community.

Increases in wildlife numbers suggest that the project is working. Game drives, bush walks, bird-watching and visits to Masai villages are offered. Bookings are made through *Bush Homes of East Africa Ltd*, PO Box 56923, Nairobi, PO Box 56923, T01-571647, F571665, www.bush-homes.co.ke

Transport The road to Kajiado (A104) forks right off the Mombasa highway (A109) shortly after the southern boundary of Nairobi National Park, just east of the Athi River crossing the Athi Plains. There are plenty of buses and *matatus* to Kajiado running between Nairobi and Namanga.

Namanga is the Kenya border town on the A104. It is the nearest town to Amboseli National Park, and is a convenient stopover between Arusha and Nairobi. You are advised to take great care when changing money, as there are many scams practiced both here and over the border in Arusha, 130 km to the south. It is important to have a rough idea of the current exchange rates for Kenyan and Tanzanian shillings. Do not allow members of your group to get separated if travelling by *matatu* or bus as coercive techniques are sometimes used to rip off the unsuspecting.

Namanga
2° 30′ S, 36° 45′ E
Colour map 3, grid C4

Kenya

Sleeping **D** *Namanga River Hotel*, set in beautiful gardens with good bars and restaurants. Camping is possible. **E** *Namanga Safari Lodge*, beautiful setting in wonderful gardens. Has excellent bars and restaurants, and camping is possible. Several cheaper guesthouses are also available.

Tour operators *Kentan Travel Agency*, inquire at the *Namanga River Hotel*, can arrange day trips and longer trips to Amboseli at US$60 per person per day (4 people) and less for larger parties.

Transport Bus Namanga-**Nairobi** takes 2½ hours and costs US$3. *Akamba* bus company is recommended. The road to Nairobi (A104) is in good condition and there is a fuel stop here as well as a couple of shops selling Masai crafts. The prices are high but negotiable.

Amboseli National Park

This has long been one of the most visited parks in Kenya. It was first established as a natural reserve in 1948, and in 1961 all 3,260 sq km of it were handed to the Masai elders of Kajiado District Council to run with an annual grant of £8,500. After years of the destructive effects of cattle grazing and tourists on the area, 392 sq km of the reserve were designated as a national park in 1973, after which the Masai were no longer allowed to use the land for grazing.

    Decades of tourism have left well-worn trails, and much off-road driving has made the park look increasingly dusty and rather bleak. The late 1980s saw the start of an environmental conservation programme to halt erosion and Amboseli now has a tough policy on off-road driving. Many new roads are being built which should improve access. The Kenya Wildlife Service has committed US$2 mn to a rehabilitation programme, but this may not materialize.

    Amboseli is in a semi-arid part of the country and is usually hot and dry. The park is comprised of open plains, savannah with areas of beautiful yellow-barked acacia woodland, swamps and marshland and areas containing thornbush growing amidst lava debris. To the west of the reserve close to Namanga is the massif of Oldoinyo Orok at 2524 m. The main wildlife you are likely to see here are herbivores such as buffalo, Thomson's and Grant's gazelle, Coke's hartebeest, warthog, gnu, impala, giraffe, zebra and lots of baboons. One of the most spectacular sites is the large herd of elephants here (some 700 live in the park) and you may be able to see the very rare black rhino that has nearly been poached out of existence. There are a few predators: lions, leopards, cheetahs, hyenas and jackals. Birdlife is also abundant especially near the swamps and seasonal lakes.

2° 30′ S, 37° 30′ E
Colour map 3, grid C4

The best time to visit is just after the long rains in April-May, when the park is lush and green and you should be able to see more wildlife

There have been environmental changes over recent years due to erratic rainfall. Lake Amboseli, which had almost totally dried up, reappeared during 1992-93. The return of water to the lake flooded large parts of the park including the area around the lodges. Since then, flamingos have returned, and the whole park is far greener.

One of the main attractions of Amboseli is its location, with the stunning backdrop of Mount Kilimanjaro, located south just over the border in Tanzania. The whole park is dominated by Africa's highest mountain and at dusk or dawn, the cloud cover breaks to reveal the dazzling spectacle of this snow-capped mountain.

Kimana Wildlife Sanctuary A Masai community 25 km east of Amboseli National Park has set up Kimana Wildlife Sanctuary – the first ever to be owned and run by the Masai. It contains elephants, lions, leopards and other game. Accommodation comprises three tented camps and one tourist lodge. The revenue generated goes to support local schools, and dispensaries and to reimburse the owners whose livestock has been killed by wild animals, or those who are particularly affected during times of drought.

Eselenkei Conservation Area Eselenkei Conservation Area, 17 km north of Amboseli National Park, has also been established with local communities in mind. This 70 sq km area is being developed in a joint venture with a Kenyan company, *Porini Ecotourism Ltd* (PO Box 48010, Nairobi, jake@porini.com) and the Masai people. Roads have been created using local labour and a lodge is being constructed. Again money raised from the entrance fees and rent are paid directly to the Masai. Profits will be used for education and agricultural support. Where once species migrating from Amboseli were killed or driven away by the local people, wildlife conservation is now encouraged.

Near the park is the town of **Isinya** where you will find the *Masai Leatherworking and Handicrafts Centre*. Good buys are the handmade shoes and big leather bags. You will also be able to find some unusual Masai crafts such as marriage necklaces or beaded keyrings..

Sleeping
■ *on map*
For price codes:
see inside front cover

L *Amboseli Lodge*, bookings through *Kilimanjaro Safari Club*, PO Box 30139, Nairobi, T227136, F219982. Good accommodation with pleasant gardens and a swimming pool, offers spectacular views out towards Kilimanjaro, but can get crowded. **L** *Amboseli Serena Safari Lodge*, bookings through *Serena Hotels*, PO Box 48690, Nairobi, T711077/8, F718100/2/3, serenamk@africaonline.co.ke A very attractive design, drawing on elements of Masai traditional dwellings, blending into the landscape. You can even get a lecture on Masai customs, or

Amboseli National Park

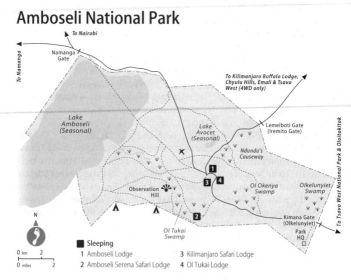

Sleeping
1 Amboseli Lodge
2 Amboseli Serena Safari Lodge
3 Kilimanjaro Safari Lodge
4 Ol Tukai Lodge

watch traditional dancers in the evening, quite the nicest place to stay but expensive. It is near the Enkongo Narok Swamp which means there is always plenty of wildlife to see. **L** *Kilimanjaro Safari Lodge*, bookings through *Kilimanjaro Safari Club*, PO Box 30139, Nairobi, T227136, F219982. Sited in a pleasant setting with white thatched cottages, good views of Mt Kilimanjaro. **L** *Tortilis Camp*, bookings through *Bush Homes of East Africa Ltd*, PO Box 56923, Nairobi, PO Box 56923, T01-571647, F571665, www.bush-homes.co.ke Has 8 twin and 9 double-bed tents with en-suite bathrooms. Full board on offer, also has a package available that also includes game drives and visits to a Masai village. Other excursions are also available. **L** *Ol Kanju*, like *Tortilis* this is a traditional tented camp just outside the park whose bookings are made through *Bush Homes*. **A** *Ol Tukai Lodge*, located near the *Amboseli Serena Lodge*. These bandas have s/c bathrooms, are equipped with electricity and occupy one of the finest viewing points in the park. Swimming pool, good value and good food. Run by Block Hotels, PO Box 40075, Nairobi, T02-540780, F543810, www.blockafrica.com

Camping There are 2 campsites in the park with electric fences encircling them. Wonderful setting, be prepared to be visited by a selection of Masai from the local village trying to sell you artefacts. Facilities are basic, with a hole-in-the-ground toilet and a kiosk selling un-refrigerated drinks. The water supply is unreliable, so bring some with you. Alternatively, it is possible to stay in the border town of **Namanga** and visit Amboseli National Park as a day trip (see page 205, Namanga).

Eating

If you intend to go camping or use the bandas, you will need to bring your own supplies of most things, though there is a kiosk at the campsite selling drinks. The lodges allow non-residents to use their facilities and the *Amboseli Safari Lodge* is a nice place to stop off for a cold drink towards the end of the day.

Transport

Air There is a daily flight from the private aerodrome at Wilson Airport to Amboseli on *Air Kenya*. It costs US$85 one way, US$150 return, and leaves Nairobi at 0730 and Amboseli at 0830. The journey takes 45 mins.

Road From Namanga to the park is 75 km down an appalling road and there are no petrol stations. The whole journey from Nairobi to Amboseli takes about 4 hrs. If travelling by public transport, there is a bus from Nairobi bus station to Namanga. From there on in you will have to hitch. Alternatively, it is possible to get to the northern and eastern gates by driving down the A109 Nairobi/Mombasa road. Take the turning south at Emali along a rough unsurfaced road to Makutamo. From there take the road southwest for the Lemeiboti/Iremito Gate, the total distance is about 230 km. Another possiblity is to drive further south past the town of Kimana until you reach the C103 on the right. This is the road that traverses Amboseli National Park.

Oloitokitok

3° 37' S 30' E
Colour map 3, grid C5

This is a busy Masai town between the parks off the main road that runs from Amboseli in the southeast through to the Kimana Gate of Tsavo West. It is a useful place to stay between the parks, it has a busy thriving atmosphere and the best views of any town in the area of Mount Kilimanjaro. It is also a border crossing leading to the Tanzanian town of Moshi. The town has a bank and a post office, and there are market days on Tuesday and Saturday.

Sleeping As you would expect in a busy market town, there are plenty of cheap and clean lodgings and places to eat and drink. **E** *Mwalimu Lodge* is popular.

Transport Bus: there are buses and *matatus* along the road that links Oloitokitok with **Taveta**, running through Rombo (not marked on some maps), and thence to Voi. Transport is more readily available on Tue and Sat, the market days. There are *matatus* and buses, but less frequent, east to **Tsavo** on the Mombasa Rd; west to **Namanga**; north along the rough road to **Emali** on the Mombasa Rd. A route south runs into **Tanzania**, crossing the border at **Kibouni**, and on to Moshi. However, it is often better to take the road through Kenya to Taveta and cross the border at Himo.

Taveta

3° 23' S, 37° 37' E
Colour map 3, grid C5

Taveta is a small town on the Tanzanian border next to Tsavo West National Park. It is fairly remote and inaccessible, but electricity was recently brought to the town and a bank has opened. It also has a District Hospital, PO Box 31, T06.

The town is near the privately run **Taita Hills Game Sanctuary**, which is actually south of the Taita Hills about 15 km west of Mwatate. Mount Vuria at 2,205 m is the highest point in the Taitas, and from the summit there are excellent views of the plains of Tsavo below. The Chyulu Hills can be seen if it is not misty. The sanctuary is run by the *Hilton Hotel* chain which has three upmarket lodges here for guests on flying safari visits from the coastal resorts. The **Taita Hills** are quite beautiful, densely cultivated and highly populated – in total contrast to the vast empty plains below. The fertile hills have made the Taita-speaking population relatively prosperous compared to other parts of the region.

Sleeping
L *Hilton Safari Camp*, L *Salt Lick Lodge* and L *Taita Hills Lodge* are all are the same price, at over US$300 a night. The *Salt Lick* is noted for its strange design, basically a group of huts on stilts that are connected by open-air bridges over a number of water holes. All rooms in the Taita Hills have a balcony. The lodge is resplendent with African wooden tables and batiks and rugs. Bookings for all 3 should be made through the *Hilton*, Nairobi, PO Box 30624, T332564, F339462. The sanctuary is a pleasant place to visit with a good selection of wildlife for most of the year. Unfortunately it is extremely difficult to get to without your own transport as there is no public transport and it is rather off the regular tourist track and therefore not good hitching territory. There is also a tented camp owned by the *Hilton* chain, alongside the Bura River. **B** *Chala*, T0149-2212. On the right-hand side of the railway level crossing is the most comfortable hotel in town with a good restaurant and bar, staff will be able to help arrange excursions for you to points of interest in the area. **D** *Kuwoka Lodging House*, T0149-228. Clean and pleasant and offers the best value in this price bracket.

Eating
The best places to eat in town are **Cheap** *Taveta*, near the bus station, and the *Taveta Border*, which has good fresh samosas. Food in Taveta is quite good on the whole, and relatively varied.

Tour operators
Balloon Safaris Ltd operate from the *Hilton* lodges, T0147-30076, bookings through the head office: PO Box 43747, Nairobi, T02-502850/1, F501424, balloons@africaonline.co.kecost US$250 per person.

Transport
Road There are irregular *matatus* going to and from **Voi**, public transport being at its best on market days (Wed and Sat). The road passes south of the Taita Hills past Wundanyi through Tsavo West.

Wundanyi
Wundanyi is the district capital here and the best accommodation is just outside town at the **D** *Mwasungia Scenery Guest House*. This is popular with people throughout the hills and consequently has a lively atmosphere and good food. On market days, Tuesday and Friday, it gets particularly busy.

Just outside Wundanyi is the **Cave of Skulls**, where the Taita would put the skulls of their ancestors. Traditionally, people would visit these caves if they needed to contemplate issues that were troubling them. The tradition is dying down as Christianity takes over from older animist beliefs, though the spot is left undisturbed. It's possible to ask someone from Wundanyi to guide you there.

Lake Chala
Lake Chala is just north of Taveta, part of the lake being in Kenya and part being in Tanzania. This deep-water crater lake is about 4 sq km and is totally clear. It is a tranquil, beautiful place to explore by foot and **camping** is possible, though you will need to bring all your own supplies. Getting there is not hard, as there is a bus once a day from Oloitokitok or Taveta. It's also reputed to be safe to swim in.

Grogan's Castle is an extraordinary construction on an isolated hill quite near the main road. It was built by Ewart Grogan as a resort for the sisal estate managers in the area. It has now fallen into disrepair, but retains spectacular views over Kilimanjaro and Lake Jipe.

Lake Jipe straddles Kenya and Tanzania, fed from streams on the Tanzanian side and from Mount Kilimanjaro. There are a number of small fishing villages around the Kenyan side, and its southeast shores lie inside Tsavo West National Park. Again, this is a peaceful place to stop off where you will be able to see hippos and crocodiles, and plenty of birdlife. You can hire a boat to take you round the lake, but there are some vicious mosquitoes in this area, so be warned.

Lake Jipe
Colour map 3, grid C5

E Bandas and **E** Camping are available by the park entrance. The nearest settlement is **Mukwajoni**, a fishing village about 2 km away from Tsavo West National Park. Supplies in the village are limited, except for fish, so bring everything you want from Taveta.

Sleeping

Limited services, basically confined to a few *matatus* on Taveta's market days (Wed and Sat). Leave Taveta 0600 and 1500 and leave Jipe at 0730 and 1630.

Transport

The Coast

Kenya

⬜Nairobi

Mombasa

The town of Mombasa is situated on an island on the southern coast of Kenya. With a history going back 2,000 years, it is the oldest town in Kenya and is the most significant port in the country. It owes its development to its location, for the island forms an ideal natural harbour.

4° 2' S, 39° 43' E
Phone code: 11
Colour map 3, grid C5
Population: 550,000

Mombasa is Kenya's second biggest town and has large communities of Indian and Arabic origin. It has the greatest concentration of Muslims in Kenya and their influence on the culture is strong. The town is centred on an island about 4 km long and 7 km wide, but has now begun to sprawl on to the mainland. It is now linked by causeways to the mainland at three points as well as by the Likoni Ferry.

Ins and outs

Mombasa is easily accessible. There are several direct flights from Europe (see page 74), as well as daily flights from Nairobi on *Kenya Airways* and *Air Kenya*; a daily overnight train from Nairobi (see page 90) and several bus services a day with various different companies. See transport, page 221 below.

Getting there

You can walk around the centre of Mombasa but the heat and humidity will tire you out quickly if you are too energetic. To get from the airport to the centre of town, either take a bus which will cost KSh25 or a taxi which should cost no more than KSh600. A *matatu* (probably easier than waiting for a bus) into town should be about KSh15. If you are heading straight for the beach to the south of Mombasa, you will need to make for the Likoni Ferry (KSh800-1,000 by taxi from the airport or the train station; less if you are a very good bargainer).

Getting around

The tourist office, on Moi Av near the Tusks, T311231, is open 0800-1630 with 2 hrs off for lunch from Mon-Fri and 0800-1200 on Sat. It sells a map of Mombasa as well as detailed guide books of Mombasa Old Town and Fort Jesus.

Tourist information

History

The earliest known reference to Mombasa dates from AD 150 when the Roman geographer Ptolemy placed the town on his map of the world. Roman, Arabic and Far Eastern seafarers took advantage of the port and were regular visitors. The port provided the town with the basis of economic development and it expanded steadily.

By the 16th century Mombasa was the most important town on the east coast of Africa with a population estimated at 10,000. By this time a wealthy settlement, it was captured by the Portuguese who were trying to break the Arab trading monopoly, particularly in the lucrative merchandising of spices. The town first fell to the Portuguese under the command of Dom Francisco in 1505. He ransacked the town and burnt it to the ground. It was rebuilt and returned to its former glory before it was sacked again in 1528. However, the Portuguese did not stay and, having again looted and razed the town, they left.

The building of Fort Jesus in 1593, the stationing of a permanent garrison there, and the installation of their own nominee from Malindi as Sultan, represented the first major attempt to secure Mombasa permanently. However, an uprising by the townspeople in 1631 led to the massacre of all the Portuguese. This led to yet another Portuguese fleet returning to try to recapture the town. In 1632 the leaders of the revolt retreated to the mainland leaving the island to the Europeans. Portuguese rule lasted less than 100 years and they were eventually expelled by the Omanis in 1698. The Omanis also held Zanzibar and were heavily involved in the slave trade. Their rule was in turn supplanted by the British in 1873.

The British efforts to stamp out the slave trade, and anxiety about German presence in what is now Tanzania, led, in 1896, to the beginning of the construction of the railway

Mombasa Island

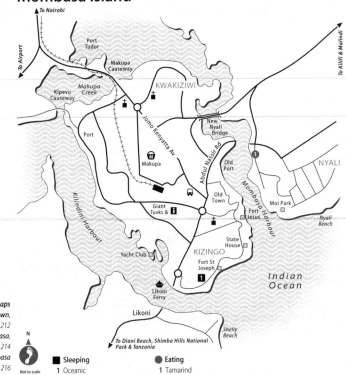

Related maps
Mombasa Old Town,
page 212
Central Mombasa,
page 214
Central Mombasa
detail, *page 216*

N

Not to scale

■ Sleeping
1 Oceanic

● Eating
1 Tamarind

★

Things to do in and around Mombasa

- Visit Fort Jesus, built by the Portuguese in 1593 to an Italian design and now housing a museum devoted to the coast and its history.
- Take a taxi across Nyali Bridge to Bamburi Quarry Nature Reserve and the Kipepo Aquarium.
- Tour Colonial Mombasa from Treasury Gardens past State House along to Fort St Joseph and the Likoni Ferry.
- If it is a weekend, watch some cricket at the delightful Mombasa Sports Club.
- Go on a day trip to the Kisite-Mpunguti Marine Park south of Mombasa for some memorable snorkelling or a trip in a glass-bottomed boat through the coral gardens.
- Go camel-riding or horse-riding at Mamba Village in Nyali, just across the creek to the north.

Kenya

that was to link Uganda to the sea. One of the railway camps that was established before the construction of the line across the Rift Valley was at Nairobi. This town grew rapidly so that by 1907 it was large enough for the administrative quarters to move inland. The climate of Nairobi was considered to be healthier than the coast. Meanwhile, with the railway, the importance of the port of Mombasa increased rapidly and it became known as the Gateway to East Africa, serving Kenya, Uganda, Rwanda and Burundi.

Sights

Fort Jesus, Mombasa Old Town's major attraction, was designed in the 16th century by an Italian architect called Cairati who had also done some work for the Portuguese at Goa on the other side of the Indian Ocean. It dominates the entrance to the Old Harbour and is positioned so that, even when under siege, it was possible to bring supplies in from the sea.

Old Town
It is best to visit early in the morning

Despite this apparently secure position the Portuguese lost possession of the fort in 1698 following an uprising by the townspeople who had formed an alliance with the Omanis. The fort had been under siege for 15 months before it finally fell. During the battle a Portuguese ship named *Santo Antonio de Tanna* sank off the coast and the museum displays some of the relics that were recovered. The British took control of the fort in 1825 and from then it served as a prison until 1958 when it was restored and converted into a museum.

In the late 18th century the Omanis built a house in the northwest corner of the fort in what is known as the **San Felipe Bastion**. Since then this has served various purposes including being the prison warden's house. The Omanis also razed the walls of the fort, built turrets and equipped it with improved guns and other weaponry to increase its defensive capabilities. At the main gate are six cannons from the British ship the *Pegasus* and the German ship the *SS Konigsberg* (see page 389). The walls are particularly impressive being nearly 3 m thick at the base.

Close to the Omani house you'll see one of the trolleys that used to be the mode of transport around town. There is also an excellent view over Fort Jesus and Old Town from here.

The **museum** is situated in the southern part of the fort and has an interesting collection. Exhibits include a fair amount of pottery as well as other archaeological finds from other digs on the coast. The diversity of the exhibits is a good illustration of the wide variety of influences that this coast was subject to over the centuries. Within the Fort are wall paintings and some of the oldest graffiti in Mombasa.

■ *0800-1800 daily. US$2.50 entry for non-residents. Nkrumah Rd. T312839. If you are not part of a tour, local guides will attempt to pick you up. They are very persistent and will expect payment.*

Mackinnon Market This lively, bustling and colourful market on Digo Road was named after Dr W Mackinnon, a colonial administrator, at the turn of the century, who was transport officer for the route between Mombasa and Uganda. The main section of the market is situated in an enormous shed but numerous stalls have spilt out on to the streets. Obviously the number of tourists has affected the prices and the market no longer has the bargains it used to. However, if you are prepared to haggle and bargain in a good-natured manner you can usually bring the price down quite considerably. Apart from fresh fruit and vegetables, you will be able to buy baskets, jewellery and other souvenirs. For *kikois* and *kangas* (brightly coloured cloth squares) the best place is **Biashara Street**. This is also the place to come if you want your clothes repaired quickly and cheaply.

The best way to see Old Mombasa is by walking around, early morning or late afternoon is preferable. The buildings in this part of town clearly reflect the Indian influences. Most of them are not actually more than about 100 years old although there are some exceptions. The finer buildings may have a balcony and one of the elaborate doors that are now so prized. These were once much more numerous than they are now as they were considered a reflection of the wealth and status of the family.

One of the older buildings on the island is **Leven House** located just off the top end of Ndia Kuu. This was built around the beginning of the 19th century and has served many different purposes since then. It was originally occupied by a wealthy trading family and later was the headquarters of the British East Africa Company. It also housed a German Diplomatic Mission and more recently has been used by the Customs Department. Among its most famous visitors were the explorers and missionaries Burton, Jackson and Ludwig Krapf. In front of Leven House are the Leven steps – here a tunnel has been carved through to the water edge where there is a freshwater well. Burton actually mentions climbing up through this tunnel but you do not need to follow his example; there are steps nearby.

The **Old Law Court** is located close to Fort Jesus on Nkrumah Road. The building dates from the beginning of this century. It is now a library and also a gallery of

Photography in the area of the old harbour is forbidden for security reasons, so take care

Kenya

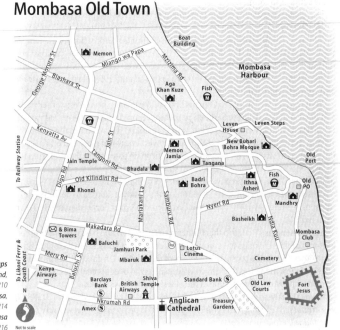

Mombasa Old Town

Related maps
Mombasa Island, page 210
Central Mombasa, page 214
Central Mombasa detail, page 216

Not to scale

Fort Jesus Museum, where there are often historic photograph exhibitions. It also houses the collections of some scholars who have studied the Swahili coast. ■ *Entry costs US$0.40 a day or US$1.25 a month. Well worth a visit.*

Near the Law Courts on Treasury Square is another building of approximately the same age. This was the **District Administration Headquarters**. The roof is tiled and there is a first floor balcony.

The Ndia Kuu (Great Way) which leads from Fort Jesus into the Old Town is one of the oldest roads in Mombasa. It existed during the Portuguese period and formed the main street of their settlement. **Mzizima Road** was the main route between the Portugese town and the original Arab/Shirazi town. **Mlango Wa Papa** marks the wall of the Arab town.

Mzizima

The Old Town is probably not the oldest part of Mombasa – the earliest settlement was probably around what is known as Mzizima to the north of the Old Town. The evidence for this is the discovery of pottery dating from the 11th-16th centuries. There is, however, very little left of this early settlement

Mbaraki Pillar

On the other side of the island at Mbaraki is the Mbaraki Pillar which is believed to have been built largely of coral as a tomb in the 14th century. There was also a mosque next to it which was used by a nearby village. Although this village has long since been abandoned, people still visit the pillar, pray to the spirits of the dead, burn incense and leave offerings.

Colonial Mombasa

The **Kizingo** area in the southern part of the island around the lighthouse has some very fine buildings, whose style has been called Coast Colonial. These buildings are spacious and airy and built to keep the occupants as cool as possible. There are wide balconies and shutters which ensure that the sun's rays do not enter, and the buildings are designed to take advantage of every breeze. Hardwoods were used and many of the building materials were imported from Europe and Asia. Unfortunately many of these buildings have now fallen into disrepair and you will have to look beyond the exterior to appreciate the architecture. Some are now used as public buildings such as the Aliens Office on State House Road.

Along Mama Ngina Drive at the south of the island it is possible to look over the cliffs that rise above Kilindini Channel and out towards the sea. Inland, at the Likoni end of Mama Ngina Drive close to the *Oceanic Hotel*, is the Golf Course. At the other end of the road is State House (this is a sensitive area so do not take photos or you risk being arrested). On the golf course is **Fort St Joseph**, also built by the Portuguese, which can be reached by following the path from the lighthouse that runs between the Mombasa Golf Club and the Police Headquarters.

At the western end of Nkrumah Road is the administrative centre of the British colonial period. The main buildings surround **Treasury Square**, with the handsome **Treasury** itself on the east side which has now been taken over by the City Council. On the southeast corner is another handsome building which currently houses the *Kenya Commercial Bank*. In the square is a bronze statue of **Allidina Visram**, born in 1851 in Cutch in India. In 1863, at the age of 12, he arrived in Mombasa and became a prosperous merchant and planter, encouraging education and prominent in public life. He died in 1916.

On the south side of Nyerere Road, toward the fort is the Old Law Court, now used as offices by the National Museums of Kenya. In the wall nearby is a **Wavell Memorial** commemorating Arthur John Byng Wavell, MC, who organized the local water carriers in Mombasa into the 'Arab Rifles' to defend the town during the First World War. From the same war came the cannons that can be seen, one of them from the *Koenisberg*, and it is daunting to think that it was hauled by hand over rough tracks the length and breadth of East Africa by von Lettow's forces after it was salvaged from a sunken battleship (see page 581).

Proceeding west from Treasury Gardens, on the left is the **Anglican Cathedral**, built in 1903 and with a plaque to mark 150 years of Christianity in Mombasa, celebrated in 1994. The cathedral itself is a mixture of European and Mediterranean influences, whitewashed with Moorish arches, slender windows, a dome reminiscent of an Islamic mosque, with a cross, and two smaller towers topped by crosses.

On the right is the solid and imposing *Barclay's Bank* building, and on the same side, just behind the main road, is the spectacular, modern, **Hindu Lord Shiva Temple**, dazzling white, and in the process of being completed.

Just before the intersection with Moi Avenue is the **Holy Ghost Cathedral**, an elegant structure of concrete rendered in grey cement. Cool and airy inside, it has a fine curved ceiling of three spans in cream and blue, *fleur de lis* designs, and stained-glass windows. The surrounding gardens are somewhat unkempt.

Going west on Haile Selassie Road, on the right-hand side is the **Ismaili Cemetery**, well tended, with frangipani trees and long green concrete benches. Adjacent is the **Islamic Cemetery**, with well-kept gardens, inscribed concrete benches and a small mosque. Finally, there is the **War Memorial** with bronze statues dedicated to the African and Arab soldiers who served with the East African Rifles in the First World War. At the westward end of Haile Selassie, in front of the Railway Station, are the **Jubilee Gardens**, laid out to mark the 60th anniversary of Queen Victoria's reign in 1897. They are rather neglected, and the circular fountains no longer operate.

Near the Tusks are **Uhuru Gardens**. It is difficult to get in from Moi Avenue as curio kiosks block most of the entrance. Inside are some handsome trees, a fountain (not working), a café, and a brass cannon worn smooth from serving as a makeshift seat.

At the eastern end of Moi Av is **Coast House**, a good example of European architecture in the tropics, with a tin roof and two verandahs on the first floor to catch the breeze.

Datoo Auctioneers is located on Makadara Road and **Dodwell House** on Moi Avenue was home to a shipping company. It has a splendid example of a Mangalore

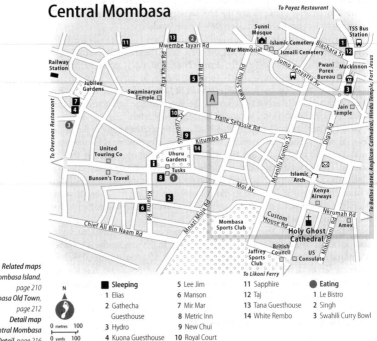

Central Mombasa

■ Sleeping		5 Lee Jim	11 Sapphire	● Eating
1 Elias		6 Manson	12 Taj	1 Le Bistro
2 Gathecha		7 Mir Mar	13 Tana Guesthouse	2 Singh
	Guesthouse	8 Metric Inn	14 White Rembo	3 Swahili Curry Bowl
3 Hydro		9 New Chui		
4 Kuona Guesthouse		10 Royal Court		

0 metres 100
0 yards 100

Ludwig Krapf

Krapf was born in 1810 in the foot hills of the German Black Forest. He was the son of a prosperous farmer and during a period of convalescence he spent many hours reading the Bible. He also showed a keen interest in geography looking at maps of the world and reading travel books. He soon realized that joining the Church was the most feasible, and affordable, way to travel and he set his mind on being a missionary. After his ordination he joined the Church Missionary Society (CMS) and was appointed to a posting in Abyssinia but only stayed there two months. Krapf was married in 1842 to Rosine Dietrich, but not long after tragedy struck in Mombasa when Rosine, who was pregnant, died of a fever three days after giving birth. The child, a girl, lived for just a week.

Krapf continued with his work translating the Bible into the Swahili and Wanyika languages. Two years later he was to be joined by Johann Rebmann and they set off inland and established themselves amongst the Wanyika peoples. Over the next few years the two made trips inland and it was in May 1848 that Rebmann became the first white man to set eyes on Mount Kilimanjaro. His reports of snow on the equator were greeted in Europe with disbelief.

Krapf's basic objective was to improve geographical knowledge of the 'Dark Continent' which would in turn facilitate the stamping out of the slave trade, and allow the spread of Christianity by setting up a string of missions stretching from one side of Africa to the other. He made numerous journeys inland, going further than any white man before, crossing the Tsavo River and setting eyes on Mount Kenya in the distance, then following the coast as far south as Cape Delgado, in the northeast of Mozambique.

In 1851, on what was to be Krapf's last journey into the interior, he was attacked by robbers, most of his porters deserted and he was held prisoner before he escaped and returned to the coast. Although only 43 years old his health was failing him, and in 1853 he was persuaded to return to Europe. He returned to Africa for a brief visit in 1861 but continued his work in Europe. His greatest contribution was perhaps in the field of linguistics: he translated the Scriptures into six vernacular languages, prepared a Swahili dictionary as well as the basic vocabulary of the Maasai, Galla, Pokomo and Ki-Nyika languages. He died at the age of 71 in Nov 1881.

Kenya

tiled roof which would have been imported from India. The large entrance hall has splendid columns and a fantastic hardwood counter.

There are many mosques, over a hundred on the island, some of which date back over 150 years. On Mbarak Ali Hinawy Street, close to the Old Port is **Mandhry Mosque**, with a white minaret. Close to the Leven Steps and the Fish Market is **New Burhani Bohra Mosque** with a tall minaret, built in 1902, and is the third mosque to have been built on this site. On Kuze Road is the **Jamat-khana Mosque** of the Ismaili community. From the upstairs are good views over the Old Harbour where the dhows are docked. The **Bhadala Mosque** is on Samburu Road, with a fine dome and minaret. The Bhadala, a sea-faring people, were among the first settlers. Near the post office on Digo Road is the **Baluchi Mosque**. The Baluchis were a fierce fighting people who served as mercenaries for various sultans. The **Zenzi Mosque** is a small attractive building with a minaret on Digo Street at the intersection with Haile Selassie. The **Jundani Mosque** is on Gusii Street, and was rebuilt in 1958 on the site of a mosque that was established in 1870. Before you enter any of these mosques be sure you are appropriately dressed, ask for permission to enter, and remove your shoes. As well as mosques there are also a number of Hindu Temples.

Mosques & temples
Women will probably not be allowed to enter the mosques

On the corner of Haile Selassie and Aga Khan is the **Swaminaryan Temple** an exotic confection in powder blue and pink. **Siri Guru Singh Saba**, on Haile Selassie, is a cool, elegant and well-maintained Sikh temple built in 1837.

This is Mombasa's main road and is about 4 km long. Along Moi Av there are many shops that the tourist will want to visit including souvenir shops, travel agencies and

Moi Avenue

the tourist information office. The **Tusks** are found on Moi Av and were were built in 1952 to commemorate the visit of Queen Elizabeth (Princess Elizabeth as she was then). They are actually rather disappointing close to. There are curio shops for about 50 yd in both directions – the goods are not very good quality and are rather expensive.

Nyali   One of the wealthier suburbs of Mombasa. There are a number of good restaurants here as well as the Ratna Shopping Centre. It was in this area that newly freed slaves settled, and a belltower is erected in memory. Across the bridge there is a fork in the road. The right goes towards the village of **Kongowea** which is believed to date back to the 11th century. It is a fishing village and the influence of the missionaries in the 19th century remains strong. It is also near here that the graves of the wife and daughter of the missionary Ludwig Krapf are to be found (see box, page 215).

Essentials

Sleeping   Alas, the powers that be have seen fit in recent years to neglect or destroy the two best
■ *on maps,*   places to stay in Mombasa. The historic *Castle Hotel* has lain empty for several years, and in
pages 210, 214   1996 the exquisite *Manor Hotel* was demolished to build a shopping block. There is now no
and below   good reason to stay in Mombasa; much better to lodge at a beach hotel and visit Mombasa
For price codes: Old Town for the day (making sure you don't spend any money in the shops on the old
see inside front cover   Manor Hotel site).

Central Mombasa detail

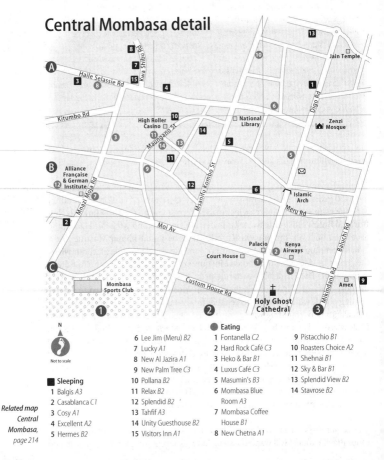

N
Not to scale

■ **Sleeping**
1 Balgis *A3*
2 Casablanca *C1*
3 Cosy *A1*
4 Excellent *A2*
5 Hermes *B2*
6 Lee Jim (Meru) *B2*
7 Lucky *A1*
8 New Al Jazira *A1*
9 New Palm Tree *C3*
10 Pollana *B2*
11 Relax *B2*
12 Splendid *B2*
13 Tahfif *A3*
14 Unity Guesthouse *B2*
15 Visitors Inn *A1*

● **Eating**
1 Fontanella *C2*
2 Hard Rock Café *C3*
3 Heko & Bar *B1*
4 Luxus Café *C3*
5 Masumin's *B3*
6 Mombasa Blue Room *A3*
7 Mombasa Coffee House *B1*
8 New Chetna *A1*
9 Pistacchio *B1*
10 Roasters Choice *A2*
11 Shehnai *B1*
12 Sky & Bar *B1*
13 Splendid View *B2*
14 Stavrose *B2*

Related map Central Mombasa, page 214

A *Oceanic*, PO Box 90371, Mama Ngina Drive, in the south of the island, T311191-3, F314199. Large hotel that has been renovated fairly recently, facilities include 3 restaurants, swimming pool, health centre and meeting rooms. Transport into town is provided. **B** *Royal Court Hotel*, Haile Selassie Rd, PO Box 41247, T223379. Spacious and luxuriant entrance hall decorated in Swahili style, central position, modern hotel with standard rooms, a/c, en-suite bathrooms, hot water and balconies. Good Indian restaurant, excellent curries, rooftop bar/restaurant and a swimming pool. Well-run and offers good value. Recommended.

B-C *Sapphire Hotel*, PO Box 1254, Mwembe Tanjire Rd, T492257, F495280. Has 110 comfortable modern rooms with marble décor, s/c, a/c, balconies. *Mehfil* restaurant, terrace barbecue, buffet lunch, also has a swimming pool and a gym. Relatively expensive for the facilities.

C *Hotel Pollana*, PO Box 41983, Maungano St, T222168, F229181. Large modern functional hotel, 140 rooms, comfortable s/c, a/c, restaurant, good buffet lunch. **C** *Manson Hotel*, Kisumu Rd, PO Box 83565, T222356. Some of the rather dark rooms in this modern hotel have fans, others a/c. Restaurant, massage, reasonable value. **C** *Mombasa Club*, close to Fort Jesus. It is possible to stay if you pay a temporary membership fee, variety of rooms, charming and comfortable, pool jutting into harbour, restaurant and bar. **C-D** *Lotus*, PO Box 90193, Cathedral Lane off Nkrumah Rd, close to Fort Jesus, T313207, F220673. Recently renovated, it has a charming central courtyard and a lovely atmosphere, the rooms all have a/c, and are s/c with hot water. There is a good restaurant that serves buffet lunches. Recommended.

D *Casablanca*, just next to bar and disco on Mnazi Moja, PO Box 88098. Not s/c, noisy, but near the action, rather overpriced. **D** *Hermes*, PO Box 94819, Msanifu Kombo St, T313599. All rooms have bathrooms attached and there is very good restaurant, s/c, a/c, very good value. **D** *New Carlton*, PO Box 86779, Moi Av, T23776. Comfortable, reasonably priced hotel, all rooms have bathrooms and there is a restaurant which is fairly good. **D** *New Palm Tree*, PO Box 90013, Nkrumah Rd, T311756, F222669. One of the better hotels in this price bracket, simple, quiet hotel, fans, s/c, no hot water, rather gloomy atmosphere, there is a restaurant which serves basic dishes. **D** *Splendid*, PO Box 90482, Msanifu Kombo St, T220967. Large modern hotel, it is clean but the rooms are rather small and dark, facilities include a pleasant rooftop restaurant (Mid-range) and bar, a/c, price includes breakfast. **D** *Visitors Inn*, corner of Haile Selassie Rd and Shibu Rd. Price includes bathrooms and breakfast, some rooms are noisy. **D-E** *Excellent Hotel*, Haile Selassie Rd, PO Box 90228, T311744. This is a very popular hotel with a central location, just a short walk from the train station or moderate walk to bus terminals. Advised to arrive early on in the day to secure a room. Rooms (with fans) have bathrooms with lots of hot water. Friendly staff, well run, clean with good security and the price includes breakfast. The restaurant serves good pastas.

E *Al Nasser Lodgings*, Abdel Nasser Rd, T313032. The rooms have their own bathrooms. **E** *Balgis*, Digo Rd, T313358. Very cheap, it has a range of rooms from dorms upwards, some of the rooms are hot and noisy but it is probably one of the cheapest places you will find. however it is not recommended for lone women travellers. Water supply is only rainwater. **E** *Beechani Guest House*, formerly *Kivulini Lodge*, near Haile Selassie Rd and Digo Rd, PO Box 82192, T224106. Fans, first-floor cafeteria, inexpensive and secure. Under new management. **E** *Cosy Guest House*, Haile Selassie Rd, T313064. Popular with budget travellers and all rooms have fans with shared facilities. It is however a bit run-down, no hot water. **E** *Elias*, Abdul Nassir Rd, PO Box 82577. Fans, not s/c, convenient buses, cheap, small. **E** *Gathecha Guesthouse*, Kenya Rd, off Kisumu Rd, PO Box 98642, T224165. Fans, no hot water. **E** *Glory Bed & Breakfast*, just off Digo Rd, PO Box 85527, T228493. Fans, s/c, part of Glory chain. See entry about the **D** *Glory Guest House* above. Not recommended. **E** *Hotel Mir Mar*, Tagana Rd, next to station. Not s/c, fans, breakfast included, restaurant with Indian food. **E** *Hotel Relax*, PO Box 98235, Msanifu Kombo St, T311646. S/c, fans. **E** *Hydro*, PO Box 85360, on Digo Rd at junction with Kenyatta Av, T23784. Well located and inexpensive. **E** *Kuona Guesthouse*, PO Box 98756, Tagana Rd, near station, T220792. Not s/c, fans. **E** *Lee Jim*, Dwana Rd, PO Box 80094, T222867. Massage. **E** *Lee Jim*, Meru Rd, PO Box 60094, T228764. S/c, fans, includes breakfast. **E** *Lucky Hotel*, Shibu Rd, T220895. Fans, hot water, s/c,

Kenya

Bwana Martini

Antonio Martini was born in Malta in 1830. Having no schooling, he was apprenticed to a sailmaker and worked on ships repairing the canvases. While voyaging he picked up the rudiments of helmsmanship and navigation. On a voyage from Calcutta, with the Captain and the other officers below deck and the worse for drink, he found himself at the wheel taking the vessel into Zanzibar, where he ran it aground. Coming ashore he began work as a builder and carpenter for the Central Missionary Society at Freretown (the old Mission Bell is just on the mainland side at Nyali), and changed his name to James Martin. His bad luck at sea continued, and he contrived to sink the Mission's steamer the Highland Lassie near Nyali Bridge.

On land he was more successful. He quickly picked up a series of local languages and was hired by Joseph Thompson to handle the porters for his expedition through Masailand. Expanding his knowledge of the interior and its tongues he began leading regular caravans to Uganda, becoming known to local people along the route as 'Bwana Martini'. Although he could not read or write, Martin kept records with his own private code of symbols in his safari logs. He moved on to become deputy commander of the Sultan of Zanzibar's army, then a Magistrate and District Officer, trading in horses and ivory on the side. When his commercial activities met with official disapproval, he was sent to Buggala, one of the Sese Islands in Lake Victoria, to build a station to be named after Henry Morton Stanley.

In his latter years he lived in the Mombasa Club, and it was his practice to conceal his inability to write by asking a guest to sign his chits on his behalf – explaining that he had forgotten his spectacles. He died in 1925 at the age of 95.

good value. **E** *Metric Inn*, PO Box 98658. In small alleyway behind *Franco's Restaurant*, near Tusks, not s/c but has a patio bar and restaurant. Being improved, well located, good value. **E** *New Al Jazira*, Shibu St, just off Haile Selassie Rd, PO Box 40432, T222127. Double and triple rooms with shared bathrooms but no singles. **E** *New Chui Lodge*, Shimoni St. No hot water, not s/c, fairly basic. **E** *New Peoples Lodge*, PO Box 95342, Abdel Nasser Rd, T312831. Popular budget hotel, however, it has also seen better days and some rooms are rather noisy. There are a variety of rooms some en suite, some not. It is generally safe, reasonably clean and is friendly, and has its own restaurant. **E** *Tahfif Hotel*, Jomo Kenyatta Av, entrance in side street behind café, convenient for buses. "Miraa, gambling, prostitutes and noise not allowed". Tidy, bright and clean, balconies, good value. **E** *Taj*, Digo Rd, PO Box 82021, T223198. Some s/c rooms, well run and inexpensive. **E** *Tana Guesthouse*, PO Box 42200, Mwembe Tayori Rd, T490550. S/c, fans, well run. **E** *Unity Guesthouse*, Rahaleo St, off Digo Rd and Haile Selassie Rd, PO Box 90759, T221298. Fans, s/c, some a/c, nets, includes breakfast, very good value. **E** *White Rembo Lodge*, Kitumbo Rd, near Uhuru Gardens. Simple and small. **E** *YWCA*, corner Kaunda and Kiambu Av, PO Box 96009, T451845. Accepts men as well as women. Reasonable, good value and a safe option at US$3.80 per person per night.

Eating
● on maps
Price codes:
see inside front cover

There are a number of eating places in Mombasa to choose from apart from hotel restaurants. With its large Indian population there is a lot of excellent Indian food as well as fresh fish and shellfish.

African Cheap *Dishes of Africa*, off the Nkrumah Rd behind NSSF building, T222503, cheap, tasty African food in a pleasant atmosphere, popular with local office workers at lunchtime. *Recoda*, Nyeri St in the Old Town and another branch on Moi Av. This serves Indian and African food and is popular with locals as well as budget travellers, the food is basic but cheap with large portions and you should try it if you can, it is only open in the evenings. Closed Ramadan. *Swahili Curry Bowl*, Tangana Rd off Moi Av. Very good for traditional coastal African dishes, closed on Sun, the ice-cream is also very good. **Cheap-Seriously cheap** *Afro Café*, corner of Nkrumah Rd and Mkindani St, lively central café offers Swahali food and burgers. Recommended.

Chinese Mid-range *Overseas*, Moi Av just north of the Tusks, T221585. Popular Chinese and Korean, it is family-run, friendly and the food is pretty good. *Galaxy Chinese Restaurant*, Archbishop Makarios St, T226132. Popular Chinese restaurant and is probably one of the best in town, it has especially good seafood dishes. *Hong Kong*, Moi Av, T226707. Another fairly good Chinese restaurant.

Indian Expensive *Roshani Brasserie*, in the *Royal Court Hotel*, Haile Selassie Rd, PO Box 41247, T223379, F312398. High-quality food in balcony restaurant with pleasant decor with green plants. Also *Tawa Terrace*, on rooftop with wicker furniture and fine views, cool breezes, specializes in tandoori dishes. Recommended. **Mid-range** *Fayaz*, Abdul Nassir Rd, upstairs from café. High-quality Moghul, North Indian cuisine, pleasant, bright décor. *Hermes*, Msanifu Kombo Rd, T313599. A bit shabby and the surroundings are not anything special but it is a/c and the food is good. *Singh*, Mwembe Tayari Rd, T493283. Good a/c restaurant, although the menu is not very extensive the food is freshly prepared and very tasty. **Cheap** *New Chetna*, Haile Selassie Rd. South Indian, vegetarian, all you can eat for US$3, very good value. *Indo Africa*, Haile Selassie Rd, T21430. Reasonable value. *Roasters Choice* restaurant (previously *Geetanjali* and *Indian Ocean*), Msanifu Kombo St. New name and owner. Recommended. *Shehnai*, Fatemi House, Maungano St, T312492. Sound cuisine, pleasant decor. **Seriously cheap** *Splendid View Café* opposite the *Splendid Hotel*, very good, cheap Indian meals – huge portions. Nice variety of dishes for US$2-5.

International Expensive *Tamarind*, Silo Rd at Nyali this is a 15 min drive from central Mombasa, over the Nyali Bridge T471747, F472106. It is well worth the journey for it has marvellous views looking over a creek that flows into the ocean. The Moorish design of the building is well thought out, cool and spacious with high arches, the food and service are both excellent. It specializes in seafood. Try the seafood platter. Phone and reserve a table. They also offer cruises around Tudor Creek on the luxurious *Nawalikher Dhow* (T471948, F471257 to book), where you can sip *dawa* cocktails (vodka, lime, honey and crushed ice) and eat lobster, whilst watching the moon rise over Mombasa Old Town and Fort Jesus, and listening to the strains of a traditional Swahili band. **Mid-range** *Le Bistro*, on Moi Av, T229470. Open all day, and serving a range of food from pizza to seafood – high-quality, imaginative food, but looking decidedly shabby now. Tile-topped tables, wicker lamps covered with red cloth, bar upstairs, tables on pavement. Recommended. **Cheap** *Mombasa Blue Room Restaurant*, Haile Selassie Rd. Excellent bright, clean cafeteria style, tile floor and tables. It serves fish and chips, burgers, chicken and all the usual Indian snacks. Popular with locals and a good place to meet people. *Rozina*, Moi Av, lively and friendly place to stop and have a burger.

Italian Expensive *Capri Restaurant*, Ambalal House, on Nkrumah Rd, T311156. This is one of Mombasa's most sophisticated restaurants, it is a/c, the food is superb – especially the seafood dishes – and it has a wonderful atmosphere. However, service is infamously slow, closed Sun. **Mid-range** *Cinabar*, in Nyali close to the Nyali Bridge, T472373, is good value. **Cheap** *Bella Vista*, Moi Av, near the tourist office after the *Agip* petrol station, offers mainly pasta and pizza, but does a decent seafood curry as well.

Cheap *Afro Take Away*, Moi Av near *Kenya Airways*. Good food, friendly staff. *Arcade Café*, **Cafés** Ambalal House, Nkrumah Rd. Curries and burgers, cheerful modern décor. *Fayaz*, Abdul Nassir Rd. Pastisserie and snacks, clean, bright and modern. *Gemini*, Ambalal House, Nkrumah Rd, in Ambalal Arcade. Fast-food, ice-cream, bright and smart. *Luxus Café*, on Nkrumah Av, just in front of Holy Ghost Cathedral. Grills, sound and sensible, comfortable and clean. *Online Pub*, formerly *Ingo's Snack Bar*, in arcade on Moi Av, west of Tusks. This place has reinvented itself as a cybercafé, but still offers food. Pastas, grills, ice-cream, bar, modern and pleasant décor, with plenty of mirrors and glass. Popular with travellers. *Palacio*, corner of Digo St and Moi Av. Snacks and ice-cream, pleasant modern décor. *Paradise*, at entrance to Fort Jesus, excellent cold juices and snacks. *Pistacchio Ice-Cream and Coffee Bar*, Msanifu Kombo St. Wonderful ice-cream and fruit juices, it serves snacks and you can also have proper meals – including a buffet lunch, pleasant décor, well-run. Thoroughly recommended.

Seriously cheap *Anglo-Swiss Bakery*, on Chembe Rd. Delicious bread and pastries. *Hastee Tastee Ice-Cream Parlour*, Nyerere Av. Another favourite. *Heko Bar and Restaurant*, Kwa Shibu Rd, near Meru Rd. Large lively bar with extensive courtyard area to the rear, charcoal grills. *Mombasa Coffee House*, Moi Av. The best in Kenyan coffee, cold juices.

Bars *Lotus Hotel*, corner of Mvita, comfortable atmosphere. *Sky Bar and Restaurant*, bar and disco, large, central location, has become one of the main social centres of town since the demise of the *Castle Hotel* and its famous terrace, no entrance fee. *Casablanca Club*, Mnazi Moja, bar and disco, not really a club, open courtyard bar on ground floor, disco and bar upstairs, fairly new, pleasant décor, very lively in evenings, no entrance fee. Well recommended.

Entertainment **Cinemas** *Lotus* and the *Kenya*, which are both located fairly central as well as the *Drive In*. See what's on in *Coastweek*, the local paper.

Gambling *International Casino*, *Oceanic Hotel*, Lighthouse Rd, T312838.

Massage *Lee Jim Hotel*, Durana Rd and Meru Rd. *Splendid Hotel*, Msanifu Kombo St. *Kuona Hotel*, Tangana Rd. *Coast Massage*, 2nd Floor, Ambalal House, Nkrumah Rd. *Benita's Massage*, Room 107. *Manson Hotel*, Kisumu Rd.

Nightclubs *Istanbul*, Moi Av. Lively place. *New Florida Club and Casino*, Mama Ngina Drive. Standard 'exotic' floor show. Lots of prostitutes here. Club entry fee US$3.80. *Saba Saba*, Magengo St, free entry, local hangout that plays great African music. *Salembo*, Moi Av, very popular local club in a central location. Busy on Fri and Sat, with a mixture of sounds ranging from Zairian to funk to reggae. *Sunshine*, Moi Av. *Toyz* on Baluchi St. *Tiffany's*, Ambalal House.

Shopping Avoid buying **seashells**. As a result of killing the crabs, molluscs and other sea life that live inside the shells to sell them to tourists, populations have declined dramatically and many are seriously threatened. Vendors may tell you they have a licence, but if you want these species to survive don't encourage this trade.

Souvenirs and curios *Labeka*, Moi Av, east of Tusks, has a good selection of items. The souvenirs that you will find in Mombasa are wooden carvings including Makonde carvings from Tanzania, soapstone carvings and chess sets, baskets, batiks and jewellery. There are lots of stalls in and around the market and around the junction of Digo Rd and Jomo Kenyatta Av. There are also lots along Msanifu Kombo St; along Moi Av from the *Castle Hotel* and down to the roundabout with Nyerere Av; and around Fort Jesus. For *kikois*, *kangas* and other material or fabric go to Biashara St which runs off Digo St parallel to Jomo Kenyatta Av. The bundles of sticks you see for sale on Kenyatta Av are chewed and used to clean teeth. The darker sticks are chewed for stomach upsets.

Sports *Mombasa Sports Club*, Mnazi Mosi Rd, offers a fairly wide range of activities. *Yacht and Rowing Club*, in the southwest of the island close to the *Outrigger Hotel*, have a busy programme (both races and social events). *Mvita Tennis Club*, near *Lotus Hotel*, off Nkrumah Rd.

Tour operators For specialist tours including bird-watching, climbing, diving, golf and historical tours, you can try *Twiga Tours*, Shina Towers, Meru Rd, PO Box 2288, T228-134/222984, F222984. Deep-sea fishing can be organized through *Howard Lawrence-Brown*, Hall Mark Charters, PO Box 10202, Bamburi Mombasa, T11-485680, T/F11-485808, T071-400095 (mob). Other operators include: *Across Africa Safaris*, PO Box 82139, Moi Av, T315360. *African Tours and Hotels*, PO Box 90604, Moi Av, T23509. *Airtour Suisse*, PO Box 84198, Moi Av, T312565. *Archers*, PO Box 84618, Nkrumah Rd, T25362. *Big Five Tours and Safaris*, PO Box 86922, Nkrumah Rd, T311462. *Big Wave Holiday*, Ground Floor, Ambasal House, PO Box 90488, Mombasa, T2288039. *Black Bird Tours & Travel Ltd*, Regal Chamber, Moi Av, PO Box 40003, T225332. *Express Safaris*, PO Box 86031, Moi Av, T25699. *Felix Safaris*, Electricity House, PO

Box 40484, T227836. *Flamingo Tours*, PO Box 83321, Ambalal House, Nkrumah Rd, T315635. *Glory Tours and Safaris*, PO Box 85527, Moi Av, T313561. *Highways*, PO Box 84787, T26886. *Kenya Mystery Tours Ltd*, Canon Tower, Moi Av, Ground Floor, PO Box 41800, T229247, F315927. *Ketty Tours and Camping Safaris*, PO Box 82391, T311355. *Kuldips Touring*, PO Box 82662, Moi Av, T25928. *Leisure Tours and Safaris*, PO Box 84902, Moi Av, T24704. *Lofty Safaris Ltd*, 1st Floor, Hassanali Bldg, Nkrumah Rd, PO Box 81933, T220241, F314397. *Marajani Tours*, PO Box 86103, Moi Av, T314935. *Pollman Tours and Safaris*, PO Box 84198, Taveta Rd/Shimanzi, T316732, F314502. *Private Safaris*, PO Box 85722, Ambalal House, Nkrumah Rd, T316684/5. *Rhino Safaris*, PO Box 83050, Nkrumah Rd, T311755. *Rusco Tours and Safaris*, PO Box 99162, Maungano Rd, T313664. *Savage Camping Tours*, PO Box 561, Diamond Trust House, near *Castle Hotel*, Moi Av, T228236, F315545. *Sawa Sawa Tours*, PO Box 80766, Nkrumah Rd, T313187. *Southern Cross Safaris*, PO Box 90653, Nkrumah Rd, T471960, F471257. *Sunny Safaris*, PO Box 87049, Moi Av, T23578. *Thorn Trees Safaris*, PO Box 81953, Nkrumah Rd. *Tsavo Tours and Safaris*, PO Box 99852, T221600/7. *Transafric Tours and Travel Services*, PO Box 82829, Haile Selassie Rd, T26928. *Turkana Safari*, PO Box 99300, Moi Av, T21065. *United Touring Company*, PO Box 84782, Moi Av, T316333/4, F314549, utcmba@africaonline.co.ke It is possible to do a cruise of the Old Harbour and Kilindini Harbour. They take about 4 hrs and you can either do a lunchtime or evening cruise leaving at 1030 and 1800. They are not cheap, but the price includes food and live music. *Tamarind Restaurant*, T472263, can arrange lunch cruises which are excellent although not cheap (see page 219.)

Transport

Local It is possible to get a *matatu* to the Likoni Ferry even if the taxi touts tell you otherwise. **Car hire** *Avenue Motors*, PO Box 83697, Moi Av, T25162; *Avis*, PO Box 84868, Moi Av, T23048 and at the airport T43321; *Coast Car Hire*, PO Box 99143, Ambalal House, Nkrumah Rd, T311752; *Fredlink Co Ltd*, PO Box 85976, T485335, fredlink@swiftmombasa.com, also hire motorcycles. *Glory Car Hire*, PO Box 85527, next to Tourist Information Centre on Moi Av, T313561, F221196; *Leisure Car Hire*, PO Box 84902, Moi Av, T314935; *Ocean Car Hire*, PO Box 84798, Digo St, T313559. *Tsavo Tours & Safaris Ltd*, PO Box 99852, Moi Av, T221600/7.

Likoni ferry docks at the southeast of the island. The ferries depart about every 15 mins and are free for pedestrians and cyclists (cars US$0.40 and motorbikes US$0.20). There is always a throng of people waiting to board or disembark from the boat – keep an eye on your possessions and beware of pickpockets and thieves. The waters are said to contain sharks. *Matatus* to the ferry leave from outside the post office on Digo Rd – ask for Likoni. When the ferry docks the *matatus* for Diani Beach are located at the top of the slipway from the ferry and turn left.

Long-distance **Air** Moi International Airport is located on the mainland about 10 km out of the centre of town. *Kenya Airways* operates a shuttle bus, about US$2. Taxi about US$9. The airport is also served by public buses and *matatus*. Airport departure tax must be paid – currently US$2.50. Mombasa is served mainly by *Kenya Airways* and **Air Kenya**, as well as by chartered planes for safaris etc. *Kenya Airways*, T221251, does the **Nairobi-Mombasa-Malindi** route once a day in both directions (except Sat). It is a popular route so book well ahead and confirm your seat. The problem of double booking can be serious. Airport tax is around US$2.50. *Air Kenya*, fly between **Nairobi** and Mombasa 2 or 3 times a day, return US$140. They have offices in town, at TSS Towers, Nkrumah Rd, T229777, F224063, and at the airport, PO Box 84700, Mombasa, T433982, F435235. *Air Kenya* serve the route to **Kiwayu** via **Malindi** and **Lamu**, return fares from Mombasa US$300, US$190 and US$50 respectively. *Kenya Airways* flies 4 times a week to **Zanzibar** (US$60 plus US$20 departure tax).

There is an old Swahili saying that Mombasa is very easy to get into but very difficult to leave and this applies as much to the transport system as it does in a metaphorical sense

Road **Bus**: there are lots of bus companies that go to **Nairobi** and their offices are on Jomo Kenyatta Av. They usually leave early morning and evening and take between 8-10 hrs. There are also 2 upmarket a/c shuttle services operating between Mombasa and Nairobi, called *SavLine* and *The Connection*. See Nairobi page 111. Fares vary and are about US$10 for the basic to US$16 for the luxury service. Buses and *matatus* depart for **Malindi** frequently throughout the day and take about 3 hrs, costing US$1.25 by bus and US$1.90 by *matatu*.

Kenya

They leave Mombasa from Abdel Nasser Rd outside the *New People's Hotel*. There is also an express *matatu* that takes about 1½ hrs, less comfortable than the bus but takes only half the journey time. Alternatively you can get together with a group and hire a Peugeot 504 station wagon as a share-taxi. They take 7 people and leave when full so get there early. They work out about the same price as the bus. For **Lamu** by bus (10 hrs, US$8) *Tawfiq*. Booking office on Jomo Kenyatta Av, T494413. Early morning departure. However, *TSS Bus* on Digo St, PO Box 85059, T224541, F223216. Seats can be booked and there is no over-crowding with standing passengers. **NB** Despite travelling in convoys with armed escorts, the bus service to Lamu has been targeted by bandits in recent years, with some fatalities. Not recommended. Heading south to **Tanzania**, *Cat Bus*, runs services on Mon, Wed and Fri. They leave at 1600, and take about 8 hrs to Tanga and 20 hrs to Dar es Salaam. *Hood Buses*, US$3.50 to **Tanga**, US$8 to **Dar es Salaam**, US$9 to **Morogoro**, leave at 0900, driver and conductor listed on daily blackboard for the morrow's departures. Other companies serving the route to Tanga and Dar es Salaam include *Tawfiq* and *Takrim*, both have early morning and overnight services. The **Mombasa-Lunga Lunga** road is reasonable. Note that the border post near Lunga Lunga is very slow, especially at night.

Boat There used to be boats (hydrofoils) from Mombasa to **Tanga**, **Zanzibar** and **Dar es Salaam** although these have been suspended for a while now. It is possible to take a dhow from Mombasa to **Tanga** and **Dar es Salaam** (see page 75). However, you must expect to wait around for a week or more for one to depart. It will take 1 or 2 days depending on the weather. Expect to pay about US$45 to Dar es Salaam, bring all your own food, and you will sit and sleep on the cargo. With the civil war in Somalia, it is no longer possible to get dhows to **Kismayo**, **Mogadishu**, **Berbera** and **Djibouti**.

Train For details of train services, timetables and fares, please see page 80. You can leave luggage at the railway station for a small daily fee.

Directory **Banks** There is a *Barclays Bank* on Moi Av, PO Box 90183, T221952, where you can change TCs from 0900-1630 on weekdays and 0900-1400 on Sat. *Commercial Bank of Africa*, Moi Av, PO Box 90681, T224711, F315274; *Kenya Commercial Bank*, Moi Av, PO Box 90254, T220978. *National Bank of Kenya*, Nkrumah Rd, PO Box 90388, T311508. *Standard Chartered Bank*, Moi Av, PO Box 90670, T224351/2, F316750. **Bureau de change:** *Pwani Bureau de Change*, opposite Mackinnon Market on Digo Rd, fast, efficient, good rates offered. Recommended; *Fort Jesus Forex*, near entrance to Fort Jesus on Nkrumah Rd.

Communications Internet: *Diverse Cybercafé*, New Canon Towers, Upper Ground Floor, Moi Av, T315171. Online access for US$0.09 per min. *Online Pub* formerly *Ingo's Snack Bar*, in arcade on Moi Av, west of *Tusks* operates as a cybercafé, in addition to offering food, There are several other cybercafés or small businesses offering email and internet access in Mombasa. However, access is compromised by frequent interruptions to the power supply. Post office: Digo St, Mon-Fri 0800-1800, Sat 0800-1200.

Consulates **Austria**, Mr T Gaal, PO Box 84045, T313386 (office), T485550 (home). *Belgium*, Mr F Van Burkom, PO Box 90141, T314531 (office), T471315 (home). *Denmark and Finland*, Mr J Nielson, PO Box 99543, T316776 (office), T471616 (home). *France*, Mrs Z Blevins, PO Box 86103, T314935 (office), T485944 (home). *Germany*, Mr G Matthiessen, PO Box 86779, T314732 (office), T0127-20602114 (home). *Italy*, Capt M Esposito, PO Box 80443, T314705/7 (office), T472091 (home). *Netherlands*, Mr LJM Van de Lande, PO Box 80301, T311043 (office), T471250 (home), F315005. *Norway*, Mrs A Sondhi, PO Box 82234, T471771 (office), T490415 (home). *Switzerland*, E Habermachr, PO Box 85722, T316684/5 (office), T485314 (home). *United Kingdom*, Capt Richard GC Diamond, PO Box 80424, T312817 (office), T316502 (home). *United Republic of Tanzania*, Mr Juma A Ali, Deputy Consul-General, PO Box 1422, T228596.

Cultural centres *Alliance Française*, Freed Building, Moi Av. *German Institute*, Freed Building, Moi Av. *British Council*, Sheetal Plaza, off Moi Av just west of the Tusks.

Medical services Hospitals: *Aga Khan Hospital*, PO Box 83013, Vanga Rd, T312953. *Mombasa Hospital*, PO Box 90294, Mama Ngina Rd, T312190. *Pandya Memorial Hospital*, PO Box

90434, Dedan Kimathi Av, T312190. *Coast Provincial General Hospital*, PO Box 90231, T314201/9. **Pharmacies:** *Coast Medical Stores*, Digo Rd, T25600, open 0800-1230 and 1400-1600. *Digo Chemist*, Meru Rd, T316065, open 0800-1900 on weekdays, 0800-1500 on Sat and 0900-1300 on Sun.

Places of worship   For Mosques see page 215. *Jain Temple*, on Langoni Rd, built in 1963, has a splendid pair of lions flanking the entrance. The most important religious centre for Mombasa's Hindus is the **Lord Shiva Temple** on the edge of the Old Town. **The Holy Ghost Cathedral**, on the corner of Nkrumah Rd and Digo Rd, dates from 1918.

Useful addresses   Police station: Makadara Rd, T311401.

South Coast

You are unlikely to visit Mombasa without going to the beach. This is the reason that most people come here as these beaches are some of the best in the world. The sand – coral that has been pounded by the waves over the centuries – is fine and very white. There are a few well-developed areas, but you shouldn't have to go too far to find a quiet spot. Running from Mombasa south, the main beaches are Shelley, Tiwi and Diani. The most popular beach on the south coast is Diani – it is also the most built up and not surprisingly is now the most expensive. However, most of the buildings have been designed well and local materials have been used so the hotels do not intrude too much. The hotels all have their own restaurants and bars and most of them arrange regular evening entertainment such as traditional African dancers and singers.

South Coast

Sleeping
1 Beachcomber Club
2 Black Marlin
3 Capricho Beach Cottages
4 Coral Beach Cottages
5 Coral Cove Cottages
6 Diani Reef Grand
7 Funzi Island Club
8 Indian Ocean
  Beach Club
9 Jadini Beach
10 Robinsons Club
  Baobab
11 Shelley Beach Club
12 Shimoni Reef Fishing
  Lodge

Climate   The coast is hot and humid all the year round although the rainfall varies. April-June is the quietest season when it is often overcast and muggy, but when accommodation is cheaper and there's greater availability of places to stay.

Shelley Beach   This is the closest beach to Mombasa, and is ideal for a day trip if you are staying in the town and are not too bothered by the proximity of the urban sprawl. Swimming here can be problematic due to excessive seaweed.

Sleeping B *Shelley Beach Club*, PO Box 96030, T451001/2/3/4, F451349. Located about 3 km from the Likoni ferry and well signposted. The hotel has over 100 rooms as well as some attractive traditional-style bandas, that are ideal for families. There is a swimming pool very close to the sea, other facilities include tennis courts, watersports, glass-bottomed boat trips, restaurant and coffee shop. The hotel has wheelchair access. C *ACK Guest House*, PO Box 96170, T451048. A church-run place and not very

Deep-sea fishing

Most hotels up and down the coast do not own their own sports fishing boats, with the exception of Hemingways and the Pemba Channel Fishing Club. In order to maintain international standards of fishing such as is governed by the IGFA (International Game Fish Association) and in keeping with the emphasis on conservation in sports fishing, KASA (Kenya Association of Sea Anglers) members support tag and release of billfish. It is a must for visitors to check out the company they are fishing with, and request information about the track record and safety equipment of the fishing boats advertising deep-sea fishing. There are a number of companies that operate with less than satisfactory basic equipment, at cheap rates, with no safety back-up facilities. You are advised to check whether the company are KASA members before making your choice. Kenya has a nine-month deep-sea fishing season which runs from the beginning of August to around late April, although a few boats may sometimes fish through the rainy season as well. August-November is best for tuna and sailfish, and the main billfish run is December-March. However, it is possible to catch big fish throughout the year. Before setting off, it is advisable to find out who owns the fish caught, and how many people the boat can accommodate, since this changes from place to place. Boats vary from luxury 47-ft twin-screw sport-fishing cruisers down through a wide range of lesser craft fishing both for inshore and offshore. The bigger offshore craft boats will be equipped with all the tackle you need, most of it heavy gear in the 80 lb and 50 lb classes. These boats are fitted with VHF radio and are capable of going far out after the biggest fish. Some companies specialize in spin casting and bottom fishing.

near to the beach, but very good value. Rooms vary from rather small with shared bathrooms to more spacious with fans and en-suite bathrooms, which are very good value for money. There is also a swimming pool.

Tiwi Beach

Phone code: 127

The next resort, Tiwi Beach, is about 20 km from Likoni Ferry and 3 km off the main coastal road down a very bumpy track (turn left at the supermarket). It's the least developed of the beaches near Mombasa, so it's not usually swarming with package tourists, there are no beach sellars, and it is therefore the most appealing and relaxed resort south of Mombasa. Avoid walking down the track from the main road to the beach as there have been several muggings, some of which have resulted in fatalities. Instead, arrange transport by taxi ($2.50) to your hotel or campsite as there are no *matatus*. This beach is wider than that at Shelley and it is particularly popular with families and with budget travellers. It is ideal for children, the waves are smaller than those at Diani, and hundreds of rock pools are exposed when the tide is out, all with plenty of marine life in them. There is also some quite good snorkelling here and it is possible to scuba dive too (see below). However, it is prone to large amounts of seaweed in April-May. If you walk up the beach in the direction of Shelley Beach for about 1½ km you come to 'Pool of Africa', a rock pool in the shape of the African continent where you can swim, and even dive through a small tunnel to another pool aptly named Madagascar.

Before you go exploring on the reef check up on the tides (they are published in the local papers) and set out with plenty of time. It is very easy to get cut off when the tide comes in and it turns quite rapidly. Also be sure you have a good pair of thick rubber-soled shoes to protect your feet against the coral and sea urchins. It is possible to walk south to Diani Beach at low tide, but again it is important to ensure you check the times of the tides to avoid getting stranded.

Sleeping & eating

B *Travellers Tiwi Beach Hotel*, PO Box 87649, Mombasa, T51202/6, F51207. Opened in 1997, well designed and in keeping with the local environment. It has an exceptional swimming pool, approximately 250 m long and connected by channels and slides. **C-D** *Coral Cove*

Cottages, PO Box 200, Ukunda, T51295, F51062 (or PO Box 23456, Nairobi, T/F02-582508). Has 9 self-catering bandas that vary in price – the 6 most expensive 2-bedroomed cottages have bathrooms but no a/c, and cost about US$38 per night. Excellent value. The other 4 bandas are cheaper and more basic, with outside toilets and no fans. All are attractively decorated. It is a lovely location, a beautiful white-sand beach, with swaying palm trees in a private cove and is probably the best place to stay on Tiwi Beach. The 2-bedroomed cottages are supplied with a personal cook/house-help/laundry-man at the inclusive rate of US$26 for 4 people per day. **C** *Capricho Beach Cottages*, PO Box 96093, T51231, F51010. Self-contained cottages, in a complex which has a swimming pool. **C** *Graceland Tiwi Sea Castles*, PO Box 96599 Likoni-Mombasa, T51018, F51048. Under the new management of Yadranka, a Croatian doctor, this is a friendly clean relaxed hotel. Very good rooms – some with a/c, others have fans – all with private shower. Good service. Facilities include a swimming pool, bar and restaurant serving very fresh locally caught fish. **C** *Minilets*, PO Box 96242, T51059, next to *Twiga Lodge*. Has a lively bar, and is renowned for barbecues and curry dishes, chalets are set in sloping green garden. Not all the bandas are open. Simple but somewhat overpriced. **D-E** *Tiwi Villas*, T/F51265, T072411795 (mob), PO Box 86775, Mombasa. 2-4 bedroomed villas with s/c bathrooms and mosquito nets, good views as located on small cliff at the north end of the beach, next to campsite. There is a bar and a restaurant with a limited choice of cheap food or you can self cater. Not as good value as *Coral Cove Cottages* – no a/c or fans. Small swimming pool. Suitable for divers. **D** *Twiga Lodge*, PO Box 80820, Mombasa, T51210. This is one of the oldest of the lodges on this beach surviving on past reputation. There are self-contained or shared rooms and bandas or you can camp US$1.40 per night. The rooms are poorly maintained and the service is indifferent. New rooms are being built but will obscure the beach view of the rooms behind them. There is a restaurant, a busy bar (one of the few on the beach) and an overpriced shop with a limited choice. Nice beach at low tide. **E** *Twiga Lodge Camping*, facilities here are fairly basic but it is right on the beach and there is plenty of shade. There have been several reports of security problems recently. **E** *Sand Island Beach Self-Catering Cottages*, PO Box 96006, Likoni via Mombasa, T51233, F51201. Quiet and a little remote.

Tiwi Scuba Divers, Tiwi Beach, PO Box 96242, Kwale, Mombasa. Full beginners' course and open-water dive, 4-day course US$350, first discovery dive US$75. Refresher course and open-water dives and equipment hire US$60, proof of qualifications required. British instructors with PADI/Bsac qualifications. **Diving**

Bus or *matatu* from Likoni and ask to be dropped off at Tiwi Beach. It is about 3 km from the main road to the beach and unless there is a fairly big group of you then it is advisable to wait for a lift as there have been several attacks on people walking down this road. You should not have to wait too long, and it is not worth the risk of going alone. There is also a newly established taxi service doing this route, but be prepared for a bumpy ride. **Transport**

Diani Beach

This is the longest beach in Kenya with about 20 km of dazzling white sand, coconut trees and clear sea. Unfortunately it has acquired a whole string of hotels over the years, rather despoiling the view. It is geared to the big-spending package tourist (usually German or English) and that obviously generates some disadvantages. It is the place to come if you want to do a bit of windsurfing or watersports, including sailing, snorkelling and scuba diving. You can also go waterskiing or parascending, or hire a bike or motor-bike. *Phone code: 127*

It is worth going out to the reef at **low tide** at least once. At Diani you will need to take a boat if you want to go out to the main reef, although you should be able to wade out to the sand bank which is not too far. Of course this depends on the tides. At full moon there are **spring tides** which means high high tides and low low tides, while a fortnight later there will be **neap tides** with low highs and high lows. Wind surfers **The reef & tides** *The timing of the tides changes and are published in local papers*

Lunatic express

Construction of the railway that was to be dubbed the 'Lunatic Express' (see page 304) began in 1896. Until the railway was built the only means of getting inland was on foot and this was how the early explorers and missionaries travelled. It was soon realized that it was not economical for cash crops such as cotton to be grown in Uganda if they then had to face this protracted journey to the coast before they could be exported.

The railway was built using indentured labour from Punjab and Gujarat in India and many of these remained to form the Asian population that is found in East Africa today.

The railway was built through some extremely harsh environments and across some very difficult terrain. A further problem was the wildlife in the area and it was the 'Man-Eating Lions of Tsavo' that really caught the public's imagination. During construction these lions attacked the camps, mauling and killing some of the workers.

Despite the problems – including the engineering difficulties involved in climbing the Rift Valley escarpment – the railway reached Nairobi in 1899 and Kisumu on Lake Victoria in 1901, but did not get to Kampala until 1928.

can go out for longer at neap tides, while those wanting huge waves will do better at high tide.

You will see plenty of notices advertising trips to the marine reserves in glass-bottomed boats. These can be excellent if you go to a good section of reef but on some of the trips you see little more than sand and seaweed.

At the far north of Diani beach just past *Indian Ocean Club*, is the **Kongo Mosque** (also known as the Diani Persian Mosque). It is rather a strange place, very run-down but not really a ruin, that still has some ritual significance. The mosque is believed to date from the 15th century and is the only remaining building from a settlement of the Shirazi people (see page 383) who used to live here. There are a number of entrances and you should be able to push one of the doors open and have a look inside. ■ *Unofficial touts try to charge tourists US$20 each to have a look (they even have their own padlocks); refuse to pay.*

There are now hoards of persistent hawkers who walk up and down the beach selling all sorts of things (mainly dhow trips) as well as offering themselves as models for photos (some of the Masai who come round are not Masai at all but are of other tribes). Most of the goods are of poor quality hugely overpriced, although you can try bargaining the quoted prices down. They may also try to sell you ivory and elephant-hair bracelets which are probably fake but anyway should not be bought if the elephant is not to go the way of the dodo.

Excursions Apart from the beach and the sea the other major attraction on this stretch of coast is the **Shimba Hills National Reserve** (see page 231). Closer to the hotels is the **Jadini Forest** which is a small patch of the forest that used to cover the whole of this coastal area. There are colobus monkeys and porcupine as well as other animals.

There is a really nice 'bushwalk' (about 2 km) from Diani to Ukunda, starting opposite *Trade Winds*, and leading along the airport and Ukunda School. You will end up at a huge baobab tree, said by the locals to be the biggest in Africa, surrounded by several woodcarvers. The carvings are of good quality and are cheaper than at the beach. A colony of black and white vervet monkeys live in the tree. Crossing the village you will see some typical African huts. People are very friendly and don't mind you passing through the village.

Sleeping
Prices vary with the season
Low is Apr-Jun;
Mid is Jul-Oct;
High is Dec-Mar

L *Diani House*, PO Box 19, Ukunda, T3487 F2412, aceltd@africaonline.co.ke This is an extremely exclusive hotel that only takes 8 guests at any one time, in 4 spacious rooms with verandahs and en-suite bathrooms. It was a private house and is set in 5 ha of gardens and forest right on the beach, the price includes all meals and a trip to the Shimba Game Reserve, 1 hr's drive away. *Diani House* has its own private tented camp at Mukurumuji, bordering the

Shimba Game Reserve, enabling an overnight stay. **L** *The Indian Ocean Beach Club*, PO Box 73, Ukunda, T3730, F3557, at the site of the Kongo Mosque, overlooking the Tiwi River estuary at the northernmost point of Diani Beach. Moorish-style arched main building with smaller *makuta* thatched-roof buildings in secluded 10-ha grounds with old coconut and baobab trees. 100 rooms, en-suite bathrooms, a/c, fans, phones, 3 restaurants, 3 bars including the *Bahari Cover Bar*, reputed to have the best view on Diani Beach. Has a 200-m swimming pool and 3 smaller pools. Tennis and marine activities including windsurfing, sailing, snorkelling, scuba diving, glass-bottomed boat trips and deep-sea fishing. Conference facilities, bureau de change, courtesy bus shuttle to Diani shopping centre. Book through Block Hotels, PO Box 40075, Nairobi, T02-540780, F545948, or *Let's Go Travel*, Caxton House, Standard St, PO Box 60342, Nairobi, T02-340331, F336890. **L** *Safari Beach* (**A** in low season), PO Box 90690, Mombasa, T2726, F2357. This is a large hotel with about 220 rooms in round bandas which are grouped into villages set in wonderful gardens. All are a/c and very comfortable, facilities include meeting rooms, tennis courts, squash courts, swimming pool, fitness centre, bar, restaurants and watersports.

A *Africana Sea Lodge*, PO Box 84616, T 2021, F2269. Rooms are in bandas, some of which are sub-divided into 2, set in gardens, each with a little verandah, a/c and bathrooms. Swimming pool. It is linked to the *Jadini Beach Hotel* and you can use the facilities of both; *Africana Sea Lodge* is marginally cheaper than the *Jadini*, and a little more relaxed.
A *Diani Reef Grand Hotel*, PO Box 35, Ukunda, T2723, F2196, dianireef@form-net.com This is a comfortable hotel, all the rooms are a/c and the hotel has all the usual facilities including a craft shop, doctor, bar, restaurant and disco. **A** *Jadini Beach*, PO Box 84616, Mombasa, T2021, F2622. About 170 clean, bright a/c rooms, most have a balcony or terrace. Facilities include swimming pool, squash courts, tennis courts, health club, watersports, business centre, bar, restaurants – serving buffet lunch or dinner, meeting rooms, shops and evening entertainment including live dancing, films and disco. The *Jadini* is linked to the *Africana Sea Lodge*, and you can use the facilities of both of the hotels. **A** *LTI Kaskazi Beach*, PO Box 135, Diani Beach, T3170/3725, F2233, kaskazi@africaonline.co.ke Arabic-style architecture, almost 200 a/c rooms, 2 restaurants, bar, tennis, watersports, all-inclusive resort.
A *Leisure Lodge Club* and *Leisure Lodge Hotel*, PO Box 84383, Mombasa, T2011, F2046, leisure@africaonline.co.ke Adjacent hotels, 113 rooms in the (more expensive) former, 140 in the latter, share facilities including restaurants, casino, several swimming pools, tennis courts and golf course. **A** *Neptune Paradise*, PO Box 696, Ukunda, T3620, F3019, together with its sister hotel Neptune Village the most southerly of the large hotels, more than 2 km south of *Robinsons Club Baobab* and actually on Galu Beach with 110 rooms, restaurant and bar. Watersports available. **A** *Neptune Village*, PO Box 517, Ukunda, T2728, F2354. Almost 170 rooms set in attractive large gardens, all-inclusive watersports, at the far south of Diani, actually on Galu Beach. **A** *Ocean Village Club*, PO Box 88, Ukunda, T2725, F2035, also at the southern end, one of the smaller hotels with about 70 rooms, restaurant, bars, boutique, with lush rainforest-like garden. **A** *Papillon Lagoon Reef*, PO Box 83058, Mombasa, T2215, F2152. Pleasant hotel towards the southern end of Diani, 119 rooms, 2 swimming pools, tennis, watersports. All inclusive or full board available. **A** *Robinsons Club Baobab*, PO Box 32, Ukunda, T2026, F2032. Set up on the cliff at the southern end of Diani this looks out across the sea, to get to the beach you have to climb down the steep steps, it used to be a very popular hotel with package tours who seemed to have their whole day planned out for them. It has about 150 a/c rooms as well as a number of bungalows suitable for families or groups, facilities include a library, restaurant, swimming pool, bar, watersports and diving facilities, shops, hairdresser and lots of organized activities, you can learn Swahili here.
A *Southern Palms* (**B** in low season), PO Box 363, Ukunda, T3721, F3381. Large hotel with 300 rooms, facilities within the hotel compound include boutique, hair and beauty salon, 2 swimming pools and a pool bar, 2 a/c squash courts, outside tennis courts, and gymnasium, watersports including windsurfing, scuba diving (lessons available) and deep-sea fishing.
A *Trade Winds*, PO Box 8, Ukunda, T2016, F2010. One of the most northerly of the big hotels this is also one of the older ones on Diani, it has about 100 rooms all of which are a/c, it was well designed and is one of the most attractive of the hotels, facilities include 2 swimming

■ *on map, page 223*

The better hotels are all good value compared, say, with similar hotels in the Seychelles or Mauritius

Kenya

pools, watersports and very attractive gardens. The hotel has been temporarily closed recently. **A-C** *Nomad Beach Hotel*, PO Box 1, Ukunda, T2155, F2391, nomad@ africaonline.co.ke Banda accommodation, price includes breakfast, good value and probably (with *Diani Sea Lodge*) the cheapest place to stay on Diani if you are not camping. There is a very good seafood restaurant here and a relaxed low key bar that does a good and popular Sunday lunch. Watersports including good diving facilities are available.

B *Diani Sea Lodge*, PO Box 37, Ukunda T2114/5. These are a/c self-catering cottages that are ideal for families and are popular with expatriates. They vary in size and price, but you hire the cottage and can get in as many people as you want. They all have a balcony and are simple but very pleasant and offer excellent value. 1 km north is *Diani Sea Resort* owned by the same group (same contact numbers), with similar facilities but apartments rather than cottages. **B** *Glory Palace Hotel* (**C** in low season), South Coast-Diani, PO Box 85527, T3392, F011-221196, on the road between Ukunda and Diani (not on the beach), has a restaurant, swimming pool, and small, simple rather grubby rooms with s/c bathrooms (the rooms near the road are noisy). They offer taxi service and car rental. **B** *Golden Beach*, PO Box 31, Ukunda, T2625, F3180, is one of the less attractive hotels and the architect would not get any prizes for blending it into the surroundings. It is modern and very large with about 150 rooms all with bathrooms, facilities include meeting rooms, swimming pool, shops, restaurant, bar, tennis courts, gym, watersports facilities and wheelchair access. This is another hotel that has recently been closed on a temporary basis. Reservations through AT&H, Utaili House, Uhuru Highway, PO Box 30471, Nairobi, T02-336858, F02-218109. **B** *Leopard Beach*, PO Box 34, Ukunda, T2721, F3424, leopardb@africaonline.co.ke This is one of the cheaper hotels on this stretch of beach and is not bad value, rooms are comfortable, clean although perhaps a little dark. Buffet restaurant, boutiques, diving, disco and live music. Also has a swimming pool. **B** *Pinewood Village*, PO Box 90521, Mombasa, T3720, F3131. Good accommodation in cottages, on Galu Beach, almost as far south as Chale Island and therefore at one of the quietest stretches of beach, breakfast included, watersports available.

There are many self-catering cottages and apartments in the **C** price category, they include: *Bramingham Chalets*, just south of *Robinsons Club Baobab*, T3303. *Chale Sea Villas*, south of *Neptune Village Hotel*, PO Box 1766, Diani Beach, T2498. *Colliers Centre*, T2538, F2537, opposite *Leopard Beach Hotel*. Luxury s/c apartments, swimming pool, secure parking. *Coral Beach Cottages*, opposite the *Barclays Bank Shopping Centre*, adjacent to *Africa Pot Restaurant*, T2413. *Diani Palm Resort*, near *Golden Beach Hotel*, PO Box 528, Ukunda, T2523, F3291. *Diani Villas*, opposite the *Barclays Bank Shopping Centre*, T2408. *Forest Dream*, near *Robinsons Club Baobab*, PO Box 787, Ukunda, T3517, F3223. *Kanini's Island Cottages*, opposite *Two Fishes*, PO Box 640, Ukunda, T/F3244. *Malibu Cottages*, near the post office, T3324. *Simba Village*, near the post office, PO Box 287, Ukunda, T2334, F3290. *Warandale Cottages*, PO Box 11, Diani Beach, T2186, F2187, near *Leopard Beach Hotel*. *Wayside Beach Apartments*, with swimming pool and bar, near the post office, T3119. *White Rose Villas*, just south of *Robinsons Club Baobab*, PO Box 80, Ukunda, T2236. *Wonder Paradise*, just north of *Diani Reef Grand Hotel*, PO Box 1581, Ukunda, T/F2221.

D *Diani Beachalets*, South Diani, PO Box 26, Ukunda, T2180, also located at the southern end of the beach. Has a range of facilities including camping, some of the bandas have shared facilities while others have their own bathrooms and kitchens, there is a tennis court but no swimming pool or restaurant, there is also no shop so you will have to stock up before you get here. **D** *Larry Peacock's*, close to *Trade Winds* is Larry Peacock's which has 3 rooms, the owner, a real eccentric, has been swanning around Diani for years and has always been known as 'The Peacock', the rooms are comfortable and the security is good, it is clean and friendly. **D** *Vindigo Cottages*, just south of the turning from Diani Beach Road to Ukunda, next to the *Trade Winds Hotel* (now closed), T2192. Self-catering bandas, which work out quite cheap if shared between 4 people. The cottages are set in 4 ha of gardens, a little way away from any other development, which gives them a more secluded feel than many other places in Diani. **Camping** is available at *Diani Beachalets* PO Box 26, Ukunda T2180 (see above).

Apart from the hotel restaurants there are a number of others. All do very good fish and sea-food and you can rely on it being very fresh. Many of the hotels do special buffet lunches and dinners and these are usually very good value.

Expensive *Ali Barbours*, bar and restaurant by *Diani Sea Lodge*, PO Box 3, Diani, T2033, F2257. One of the most popular, you can either eat in the open air or else in a sort of under-ground cave, it does excellent seafood as well as French food. If staying on Diani Beach they will provide free transport. *Legend*, T2302, F2555. Large complex near the post office, origi-nally with casino, but now pared down to restaurant, bar and disco, also with vast swimming pool. Pianist or floor shows accompany the food, rotisserie and ice-cream parlour in the land-scaped grounds.

Mid-range *Brvegel Brasserie*, PO Box 78, Ukunda, T2295, F3318, Diani Shopping Centre. Wide choice of international and local cuisine including seafood, pizzeria, snack bar. *Canoe*, PO Box 5172, Diani, south of *Robinsons Club Baobab*, seafood. *Fisherman's Cave*, T2620, F2046, at Leisure Lodge. Prior reservation necessary for this seafood restaurant. *Forty Thieves*, PO Box 53, Ukunda, T3003, F2257, bar and restaurant which serves some food and snacks. A popular night spot with discos on Wed, Fri and Sat nights. *Galaxy*, T2529, northern end of Diani. Tasty Chinese cuisine. *Maharani*, PO Box 277, Ukunda, T2297, F2439, Indian restaurant. *Maisha Marefu*, T/F3417. International and local dishes, seafood, bar and pub, closed Mon. *Nomads Seafood Restaurant*, PO Box 1, Ukunda, T2155, F2391, at *Nomads Beach Bandas*, just south of *Jadini*. Probably one of the best restaurants on Diani, it does a very popular Sunday buffet lunch, which is good value. *Shan-e-Punjab*, Diani Complex, opposite *Diani Reef Hotel*, PO Box 1086, Ukunda, T3092/3. Good-value Indian dishes, more expensive continental dishes available, also open-air beer garden. *Vulcano*, T2004. Italian food and not too expensive.

Cheap *African Pot*, in front of *Coral Beach Cottages*, good value, tasty local food. *Bush - Baby Restaurant*, opposite the *Two Fishes Hotel* (now closed). Open-air restaurant serving basic Swahili dishes with good fresh fish. Later on in the evening it develops into a disco and usually has quite a lively crowd. *Diani Farm House*, Barclays Bank Shopping Centre, PO Box 5443, Diani Beach, T/F2131. Combination of a restaurant, butchery, bakery, snack bar and pub. *Gallo's Restaurant*, PO Box 84616, T3150, F2145, about 15 mins' walk towards Mombasa. Relatively expensive for the budget traveller but well worth a visit, next to Diani Shopping Centre, eclectic restaurant, run by a graduate of an American hotel school, fusion of local ingredients with international techniques. *Hollywood*, PO Box 85118, Mombasa, T3228, located in the nearby village of Ukunda, opposite the *Total* petrol station. Tasty Ken-yan food available at keen prices. *Kimerimeta*, PO Box 5554, Diani, T3522. Local dishes. *Red Lion*, PO Box 5332, Diani Beach, T3497. Bar and beer garden, also offers grills, pizza and ice-cream. *South Coast Fitness Centre*, has a restaurant which is fairly good value. *Sundowner*, southern part of the Diani Beach road, about 10 mins' walk from the *Diani Beach Chalets*. Serves excellent Kenyan food at low prices. *Tropicana*, Diani Shopping Centre, PO Box 5004, Diani, T2303, F3350. Offers a small selection of seafood, pizza. Mainly functions as a bar, disco in the evening. *Turaco*, PO Box 5157, Diani, T2483, bar and restaurant, also phone, fax and email services. **Seriously cheap** *Jambo Club*, in Ukunda, is opposite the police sta-tion. You can eat a reasonable meal here for about US$1.25 but its real attraction is the bar and music (reggae and funk), popular with locals and the odd tourist.

Most of the hotels arrange evening entertainment, or 'animation' as it is known locally. This includes traditional dancers, usually a group, who do a range of dances from tribes all over Kenya. The hotels will often combine this with an evening barbecue. They also hold films shows. **Nightclubs** Almost all the hotels have nightclubs which are of varying quality. Along the Diani Beach Rd there are also a number of discos not run by hotels. These include *Shakatak*, T3124, across the road from *Two Fishes Hotel*, German-run with a restaurant and beer garden, entrance fee US$2. *Tropicana*, located at the *Agip* gas station, open-air, plays only reggae music, entrance fee US$1. *Casablanca*, located at the very southern end of Diani Beach Rd, run by the *Neptune Paradise Hotel*, shuttle bus will pick up guests at certain times and bus stops, entrance fee US$1. See also *Jambo Club* above for a good night out in Ukunda village.

Shopping If you are self-catering it is worth buying most of your supplies in Mombasa where it is cheaper. There are however a number of places closer to the beach. Firstly there is the small village of **Ukunda** which is on the main road close to the Diani turn off. There is a post office here and a shop. You can get most things here. Off the main road, on the road with all the hotels, are now four shopping centres. Opposite *Diani Reef Grand Hotel* is *Diani Complex*, the smallest of the 4, *Barclays Bank Shopping Centre* is next to the bank of the same name, *Diani Shopping Centre* and *Diani Beach Shopping Centre* are close to each other to the north Diani Beach post office. Each shopping centre has a supermarket and several souvenir shops and boutiques. Diani Beach post office is opposite *Trade Winds Hotel*. For fresh fruit, vegetables and fish you will be able to buy off the vendors who come round all the self-catering places with their stock on their bicycles.

Sport **Deep-sea fishing**: *Blue Marlin Fishing Club*, between *Robinsons Baobab Club* and *Neptune Paradise Hotel*, PO Box 5108, Diani, T/F3478, 5 hrs US$275. *Jet-Point Fishing Club*, PO Box 5455, Diani, T/F3459, 5 hrs US$250, also have boat excursions involving light tackle fishing and snorkelling, US$40. *Nomad Boats*, PO Box 1, Ukunda via Mombasa, T/F2156. *Seahorse Dhow Safaris Kenya*, see Tour operators, below. **Scuba diving**: *Diani Marine*, PO Box 353, Diani, T2285, F3452. *Diving The Crab*, near *Nomad Beach Hotel*, PO Box 5011, Diani, T3400, F2372. *One Earth Diving and Safaris*, PO Box 374, Ukunda, T2400, F2046. There is also the *South Coast Fitness Centre* gym. You can hire go-karts here.

Many of the hotels will help organize dhow trips, safaris and diving

Tour operators There are many tour agencies at Diani Beach, mainly in and around the shopping centres. A few of these specialize in dhow trips. *Dolphin Dhow*, Barclays Centre, PO Box 85636, Mombasa Diani Beach Rd, T2094, do 2-day safaris to the Shimba Hills, canoeing in mangrove forests in search of crocodiles. *Funzi Sea Adventures*, PO Box 1108 Ukunda T2044, F2346. Organize trips to Funzi Island (including food). *Kinazini Funzi Dhow Safaris*, in Diani Shopping Centre, PO Box 37, Msambweni, T3221, F3182. Day-long trips stop at Funzi Island to see a fishing village, snorkelling or swimming off a sand-bar, and then an afternoon on Kinazini Island, including lunch. *Pilli Pipa Dhow Safaris*, PO Box 5185, Diani Beach, T/F2401. All-inclusive day trip from Shimoni, snorkelling or scuba diving in Kisite Marine Park, dinner at Wasini Island, US$80, extra with transport from your hotel. *Seahorse Dhow Safaris Kenya*, in Colliers Centre, opposite *Leopard Beach Hotel*, PO Box 426, Ukunda, T2423, F2421. Dhow trip with snorkelling, lunch and walk on island near Chale Island, US$60. Similar but in power boat to Kisite Marine Park, US$65. Transport from hotel extra. They also offer inshore fishing, 5 hrs including lunch, US$60, deep-sea fishing, 5 hrs including lunch, US$300, and waterskiing, US$30 for 20 mins.

Transport **Local Road**: From Likoni drive south on the A14, the main Kenya-Tanzania coastal road. All the turnings off are well signposted. For Diani, go as far as Ukunda village (about 22 km) where there is the turning off to the smaller road that runs along Diani beach. At the T-junction, some hotels are to the left, while all the others are to the right. By *matatu*, you can have to change at Ukunda village for Diani. The fare from Likoni to **Ukunda** costs US$0.65 and from Ukunda to Diani US$0.25.

    Car hire: *Brandy Bet Safaris Ltd*, PO Box 1600, T/F2241, *Fredlink*, opposite Diani Sea Lodge, T011-230484, *Glory Car Hire*, Diani Beach Shopping Centre, T3076. *Ketty Tours*, T3582. A basic car will cost approximately US$19 a day plus a US$0.20 per km supplement. *Leisure Car Hire*, T3225, *Pitia Africa Tours and Safaris*, Diani Complex Shopping Centre, PO Box 246, Ukunda, T/F3343, and *Roadsters Rent-A-Car Ltd*, also opposite *Diani Sea Lodge*, T3184.

    Most of the hotels at Diani will collect you from the airport or train station for a charge of around US$20.

Ferry: To get to the south coast, take the Likoni ferry from Mombasa Island. There are 2 ferries and they go about every 15 mins throughout the day, although there are fewer late in the evening. Cars cost US$0.40 and motorbikes US$0.20. Pedestrians go free.

Long-distance Air There is a small airfield at Ukunda which is used for small planes – usually charters for safaris.

Banks *Kenya Commercial Bank*, Ukunda Branch, PO Box 90254, T2197 (Mombasa). *Barclays Bank of Kenya*, Diani Beach, PO Box 695, Ukunda-Kenya, at the head of the road to Ukunda, T01261-2375. **Medical services** *Diani Beach Hospital*, just south of Diani Complex Shopping Centre (which is north of the access road from Ukunda), T2435. *South End Pharmacy*, Diani Beach Shopping Centre, T3354.

Directory

Shimba Hills National Reserve

This is a small reserve 56 km southwest of Mombasa and it is quite possible to access it on a day trip from the coast. The area is 300 sq km and is covered with stands of coastal rainforest, rolling grasslands and scrubland. Due to strong sea breezes, the hills are much cooler than the rest of the coast making it a very pleasant climate. The rainforest itself is totally unspoilt and opens out into rolling downs and gentle hills. Two of Kenya's exquisite orchids are found here.

4° 15' S, 39° 30' E
Colour map 3, grid C5

Kenya

There are a number of Roan antelope, buffalo, waterbuck, reedbuck, hyena, warthog, giraffe, elephant, leopard, baboon and bush pig in the reserve. However, it is famed for being the only place in Kenya where you might see the Sable antelope. The best place to see the wildlife is near the spectacular **Sheldrick Falls** and on the **Lango Plains** close to Giriama Point.

There is a nature trail that is pleasant to follow and a picnic area. It is possible to take a half-day trip from Mombasa for US$25 (booking through travel agents, see page 220).

Adjacent is the **Mwalunganje Elephant Sanctuary** set up to provide access for the elephants between the Shimba Hills and the Mwaluganje Forest Reserve. There are approximately 150 elephants, mainly large bulls. Close-range elephant viewing is virtually guaranteed. The sanctuary protects 2,500 ha of the traditional migratory route. The flora ranges from baobab trees on the coast to deciduous forests on the hills and vestigial rainforest along the watercourses. A fee is payable to the local community from every visitor to the reserve.

L *Shimba Rainforest Lodge*, PO Box 40075, Nairobi, T02-540780, F545948. Well designed round a water hole, which is illuminated at night for viewing, shop, children under 7 are not allowed, but there is a bridal suite. **A** *Travellers Mwaluganje Elephant Camp*, PO Box 87649, Mombasa, T011-485121/6, F485674/8. Luxury tented accommodation in the Elephant Sanctuary, a 45 km drive from Mombasa. 20 tents, each with 2 beds, bathroom and private verandah with views over the traditional elephant trail. Includes escorted game drives. **E** *Bandas*, located at a site about 3 km from the main gate to the reserve. Communal showers and lavatories. **Camping E** Camping at the banda site.

Sleeping

Regular buses from Mombasa for Kwale, about 30 km away. From Kwale, the reserve is only 5 km along a murram track.

Transport

South of Diani

At the southern end of Diani is a small bay and Chale Island. This is a popular spot for day trips from Diani – boats take you out for swimming, snorkelling and beach barbecues on the island. Contact *Nomad Safaris* on Diani Beach for more details. Along this route you will not be able to miss the coconut plantations that cover a wide area. Chale Island is also the location of a controversial recent development, the expensive all-inclusive **L** *Chale Paradise Island*, PO Box 4, Ukunda, T0127-3235/6, F3319/20, that went ahead despite wrangles about ownership of the island and objections to destruction of the previously pristine vegetation.

Chale Island

Gazi
Colour map 3, grid B5

A village at the southern end of Diani, once significantly more important than it is now as it was the district's administrative centre. Here you will see the **House of Sheik Mbaruk bin Rashid**. There are said to be the bodies of eight men and eight women buried in the foundations of the house to give the building strength. He was also notorious for torturing people, and suffocating them on the fumes of burning chillies. In the Mazrui Rebellion of 1895 Mbaruk was seen arming his men with German rifles and flying the German flag. British troops did eventually defeat him and he ended his days in exile in German East Africa (mainland Tanzania). However, the rather run-down house is now used as a school. It once had a very finely carved door but this has been moved to the Fort Jesus Museum. You will have to ask directions for Gazi as it is not signposted on the main road.

Msambweni

About 50 km south of Likoni is the village of Msambweni which is home to what is one of the best hospitals on the coast as well as a famous leprosarium. The beach here has recently been developed for tourists and there are some bungalows and a hotel. The beach is really lovely with coral rag-rock cliffs and there are some ruins in this area that are believed to have been a slave detention camp.

Sleeping **L** *Funzi Island Club*, PO Box 1108, Ukunda, on Funzi Island, south of Msambweni, T2044, F2346. Very exclusive tented camp situated on a beautifully secluded island, furnished to a very high standard. Facilities for all watersports are available and are included in the price, as are all meals, drinks and transport. Closed May-Jun. **B** *Beachcomber Club*, c/o *Let's Go Travel*, ABC Place, Waiyaki Way, Westlands, PO Box 60342, Nairobi, T447151. 16 double rooms, en-suite bathrooms, fans, restaurant, 2 bars, swimming pool. **B** *Black Marlin*, PO Box 80, Msambweni, T90 (Msambweni). Being renovated, soon to reopen.

Shimoni
Phone code: 1261
Colour map 3, grid C5

A small fishing village whose name means 'Place of the Hole'. This name is derived from the method of entry to the system of **Slave Caves** located to the west of the village. *Shimo* means cave in Kiswahili. The vast network of caves open directly on to the beach. It is said that the caves were used by slave traders to hide the slaves, before they were sold and shipped out to overseas markets. In the caves there are well-preserved examples of the wooden crates used to transport the slaves.

The other story associated with these caves is that they were used as a secret place of refuge by the Digo people during their intermittent battles with various marauding tribes, including the Masai, through the ages. Archaeological findings indicate that these coral caves, with their lovely stalactites, have been inhabited for several centuries. The caves have a thriving population of bats. A torch is required if you want to explore them.

To reach the caves take the path that begins opposite the jetty and walk up through the forest. When you get to the entrance you take a ladder down through a hole in the ground. The cave system is believed to extend about 20 km underground. ■ *There is a nominal entry fee to the caves, and all funds collected directly benefit the local people, helping to pay for the dispensary and educate the children.*

To the far south is the **Kisite-Mpunguti Marine National Park** which has superb coral gardens and lots of sea life. You can take trips out to the park – this is one of the glass-bottomed boat trips that are very good. (For details contact *Kisite Dhow Tours*, T2331 or T11-311752, Mombasa, see also *Pilli Pipa Dhow Safaris* and *Seahorse Dhow Safaris*, in Diani Beach directory.) At 0900 daily there is a snorkelling tour at Kisite National Park. Apart from the fish, coral and shells you may also see dolphins. This stretch of the coastline is also a bird-watchers paradise. The small islands dotting the coastline have old established trees including baobabs with their thick gnarled trunks. Untroubled by elephants, they dominate the island shelves in abundance. Coral seas of turquoise and dark green stretch away. Mountains rising straight up in the south over the ocean mark the Tanzanian/Kenyan border.

Kisite is a flat little marine park, an atoll, with a dead coral shelf in the middle rising up off it like a table. The rest is worn to rough granular sand that is hot and uncomfortable to walk on. Unremarkable on the surface, what is truly amazing is what is in the waters around Kisite. The little convoy of dhows string out in a line, and drop anchor. The water is pure, warm and turquoise in colour, and is so salt saturated that it is difficult to swim in initially, as it seems to suspend you. There are thousands of fish, in a dazzling array of sizes, shapes and colours just below the surface.

There is no shade or protection from the burning sun and wearing a shirt/long sleeved T-shirt whilst snorkelling is a wise precaution. Masks and snorkels are available but flippers are not always obtainable.

Sleeping L *Pemba Channel Fishing Club*, PO Box 86952, Mombasa, T313749, F316875, Mombasa, T2 (local, Shimoni). Rates include full board, this is very good value. Closed Apr-Jun (after fishing season). L *Shimoni Reef Fishing Lodge*, T2627, south of Msambweni, beyond Funzi Beach, wonderful location, overlooking Wasini Island, c/o *Reef Hotel*, PO Box 82234, Mombasa, T011-471771, F471349. High standards. Caters almost exclusively for keen anglers. Deep-sea fishing also available from *Sea Adventures Ltd*, PO Box 56, Shimoni, T12/13 (via the operator), F011-227675, run by the experienced Pat and Simon Hemphill.

Wasini Island

A wonderful place measuring 1 km across and 6 km along. It is totally undeveloped and there are no cars, no mains electricity, and no running water. There is no reliable freshwater supply on the island, only rainwater. Some of the proceeds of the tourist trade are being used to build large culverts where they can store rainwater. A small village on the island includes the remains of an Arab settlement. There are also the ruins of 18th- and 19th-century houses as well as a pillar tomb with Chinese porcelain insets that have, so far, survived. The beach is worth exploring as you might well find bits of pottery and glass. Also interesting are the dead coral gardens behind the village. They are above the sea although during the spring tide they are covered as they are linked to the sea 30 m below through a series of caverns. Some of the coral formations are said to resemble animal shapes (they call one the elephant).

From Wasini Island you may want to organize a trip to the marine park. Get a group together and ask at the *Mpunguti Restaurant*, who will be able to arrange a trip for you. This is said to be the best snorkelling in Kenya. It is not too expensive – especially as the price includes an excellent lunch. You can also hire a canoe and do it yourself but you will not know the best places to go.

On the east side of Wasini Island are the boat moorings of the wealthy, who tie up here between Hemingwayesque marlin and shark-fishing adventures.

Sleeping and eating C *Mpunguti Lodge*, has a number of bandas and the food here is excellent – it is also very friendly, alternatively you can camp but if you want to be totally self-sufficient be sure to bring plenty of supplies from Mombasa as there is not much here, bring as much drinking water with you as you can carry. There are renovations in progress – a pavilion for meals, salt-water toilets, overhead showers and a generator are planned. There's a restaurant, *Wesini Island Restaurant*, T0127-2331, but it's only open from Jul-Apr. The local people run a *restaurant*, high on the hill in an open, airy dining hall, with a thatch roof where bats sleep high above you in the rafters. There are large rough-hewn tables from which there are glimpses of the sea through the rhododendrons and palmetto. Lunch includes steamed sea crabs with claws the size of your fist, along with fresh lime and baked coconut rinds for dipping in salt. This goes down well with cold Kenya beer, but the wise drink water first. Bottled water is expensive here. There is not much of a beach on Wasini Island, as it gets covered by the incoming tide.

Transport To get to Wasini Island under your own steam either hire a taxi or take a *KBS* bus from Likoni to Shimoni (there are not very many). Alternatively take a *matatu* to Lunga Lunga and ask to be let off at the turning for Shimoni, which is about 15 km off the main road. From here you will have to hitch. From Shimoni, there is a dhow run by the *Mpunguti Restaurant*, otherwise a *matatu* boat. The last *matatu* back to Mombasa leaves between 1500 and 1600. Boats to Wasini Island cost around US$2 per person one way.

Lunga Lunga   About 95 km south of Mombasa Lunga Lunga is the nearest village (5 km) to the border with Tanzania and can be reached by bus from Mombasa. Buses between Mombasa and Dar es Salaam or Tanga go about once a week in both directions taking about 20 hours to Dar and eight to Tanga. The border post is slow so you will have to be patient – it can take up to four hours. If you do not get a through bus you can take *matatus* but this involves a fair bit of walking. Coming from Kenya you cross through the Kenyan formalities and from here, unless you have your own transport, you will have to walk the 6 km to the Tanzanian border at **Horohoro**. From here there are two buses a day to Tanga, but several *dala dala* (Tanzanian *matatus*).

North Coast

There is a whole string of beaches, Nyali, Kenyatta, Bamburi, and Shanzu with lots of hotels on the seashore immediately north of Mombasa. North of Mtwapa Creek are Kikambala and Vipingo beaches. The major attractions of Watamu Marine Park, Malindi and Lamu are further north. At these latter places there is much more choice for the budget traveller and anyone who wants to avoid the package tours. There are major historical sites at Kilifi, Malindi and Lamu.

Nyali Beach   As you head north from Mombasa the road crosses Tudor Creek, then reaches Mamba Village, just south of Nyali Golf Course and the Bombolulu Cultural Centre and Hallar Park (previously Bamburi Nature Reserve). The road then runs parallel to Kenyatta and Bamburi Beaches before coming inland at the level of Shanzu Beach prior to crossing Mtwapa Creek. In this area is the Jumba la Mtwana site and Majengo village. A little further on are the Kurita Cottage Complex and the Vipingo Sisal estates.

The strip of beach just to the north of Mombasa Island is called Nyali Beach. It is well developed and there are lots of hotels. Most of them cater for package tours from Europe and usually each hotel caters for one nationality or another. None of them are cheap. All have facilities such as swimming pools, tennis courts, watersports and they tend to look after their guests very well, organizing all sorts of activities and trips.

Mamba Village   This is a **Crocodile Farm** located to the north of Mombasa, just south of the Nyali Golf Course on Links Road, west of Nyali Beach. There are over 10,000 crocodiles here of all ages and sizes from newborns to huge fully grown adults. Film shows explain some of the conservation efforts as well as the financial side of the venture. You can go for camel and horse rides here around the village and on the beach and it is a day trip in a pleasant setting that children in particular will enjoy. There is also a restaurant serving, among other dishes, crocodile

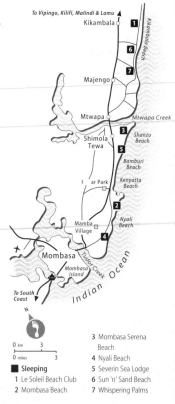

Mombasa North Coast

To Vipingo, Kilifi, Malindi & Lamu

Kikambala **1**

Kikambala Beach

6

7

Majengo

Mtwapa *Mtwapa Creek*

3 *Shanzu Beach*

Shimola Tewa **5**

Bamburi Beach

ar Park *Kenyatta Beach*

2

Mamba Village **4** *Nyali Beach*

Mombasa

Mombasa Island

Tudor Creek

To South Coast

Indian Ocean

0 km   3
0 miles   3

■ **Sleeping**
1 Le Soleil Beach Club
2 Mombasa Beach

3 Mombasa Serena Beach
4 Nyali Beach
5 Severin Sea Lodge
6 Sun 'n' Sand Beach
7 Whispering Palms

meat. It is open all day during the week and on Saturday afternoons. ■ *Adult non-resident US$6. A **Botanical Garden** and **Aquarium** has been added to Mamba Village. It costs an extra US$2 to enter and is a pleasant area but it is small and struggles to justify the additional outlay. For details contact PO Box 85723, Mombasa, T472709, mamba@africaonline.co.ke*

Further north along the main road is the **Bombolulu Workshops and Cultural Centre**, PO Box 83988, Mombasa, T471704, F475325, www.africaonline.co.ke/bombolulu, where you might want to do some souvenir shopping. Founded in 1968, the crafts are produced by local handicapped people and are generally of reasonable quality and good value. A Secondary School for the Physically Disabled is near here. You can also do a tour of the workshops, and a cultural centre, demonstrating traditional dance, music and theatre, was added in 1996. ■ *Mon-Sat, 0800-1700, the shop stays open until 1800.*

The Bamburi cement factory began quarrying coral to make lime for the cement around Mombasa in the 1950s and the disused kilns are visible to the south of the city at Likoni. When quarrying stopped in 1971 an effort was made to reclaim the land by reafforestation and a nature trail (previously called the Bamburi Quarry Nature Park) was created. The reclamation scheme was ahead of its time and it attracted the attention of ecologists from all over the world. The nature park has been renamed Hallar Park after the Swiss agronomist who turned the lunar quarry landscape into luxuriant tropical forest. Part of the process included the introduction of hundreds of thousands of millipedes that helped convert the infertile sand into soil, able to support the forest in which the centre is now situated. Despite this, the whole area is still dominated by the *Simbarite Ltd Quarry.* **Hallar Park**

There are all manner of things to do in this 'Baobab Adventure'. There is a fish farm producing tilapia; a luxuriant palm garden; 3.6-km forest trails along which you can either walk or cycle; a crocodile farm and a butterfly house. There are also various antelope, monkeys, wart hog, buffalo and lots of different birds reared on the farm, some of which find their way in time on to the menu in the *Whistling Pines* restaurant. ■ *You can watch the crocodiles being fed at 2100 on Thu, Fri and Sat. The trail is open 1800-1800 weekdays, 1000-1700 on Sat 1200-1700 Sunday. Adults US$5.75, children US$2.85. For further details contact Bamburi Farm, PO Box 90202, Mombasa, T48901, baobabfarm@swiftmombasa.com* It is signposted on the main road towards Malindi and is 10 km north of Mombasa, easily accessible by bus (bus stop outside).

Kipepee Aquarium Located opposite *Haller Park* this aquarium has about 15 large tanks filled with an estimated 150 different species of colourful fish, including the deadly stonefish. This is an extraordinarily well-camouflaged fish that lies completely motionless on the seabed and is extremely painful if you tread on it. The collection was assembled by Jacques Allard.

Kenyatta Municipal Beach by contrast is where local families go to enjoy the beach. A major attraction is **Pirates**, T011-486020, a popular complex with waterslides, restaurant and a bar. *Sun Line Tennis School and Club*, Kenyatta Beach, has excellent quality courts and you will be able to arrange lessons if you wish.

Set in 6½ ha of a reclaimed quarry in Shanzu, this might be described as a theme park of traditional rural Kenyan lifestyles. There are 10 villages, one for each of the tribes represented, complete with hut, cultivated crops, domestic and wild animals, village witch doctor and villagers. Walk around the site to see anything from subsistence farming methods to Akamba wood carving. There is an emphasis on participation, thus you can plant a tree or try many of the activities yourself, such as maize pounding or harpoon fishing whilst trying to balance on a raft. There is also a market selling jewellery and other ethnic items. *Kienyenji Restaurant*, built in traditional style, serves a range of African dishes and you can sample the local beer. It has a different tribal theme each night (currently Luo on Wed, Kikuyu on Fri, Mijikenda on Sat and **Ngomongo Villages**

Kenya

Masai on Sun, but subject to change), finished off by a display of traditional African music and dance. Highly recommended. Sturdy footwear advised. ■ *PO Box 88478, T486480, F222393, www.ngomongo.com*

Sleeping **Nyali Beach** L *Mombasa Beach Hotel*, PO Box 90414, Mombasa, T471861-5, F472970. Run by *Kenya Safari Lodges and Hotels*, this hotel has about 150 rooms all of which are a/c with balconies. It is set up on a cliff looking over the beach and the sea. It is very well managed and includes conference rooms and business facilities, tennis courts, golf, watersports, bar, restaurant and grill room. The *Palm Beach Annex* is a more recent addition. There are cottages and self-catering apartments, some have a/c, most have balconies. L *Nyali Beach Hotel*, PO Box 90581, Mombasa, T471551/67/68, F472402, central booking through Block Hotels, PO Box 40075, Nairobi, T02-540780, T545948. One of the oldest hotels in the area with a newer and more expensive addition called the *Palm Beach Annex*. All rooms are a/c and most have balconies, there are also some cottages. Facilities include meeting rooms, restaurant and grill room, tennis courts, 2 swimming pools, snack bar and nightclub. L *Voyager Beach Resort* (B Apr to Jun), PO Box 34117, Mombasa, T011-475114, F472544. A new Heritage Group development, 230 modern units, swimming pools, bars, restaurants, sports facilities including watersports centre. This is one of the host resorts for *Family Safari* packages. A *Nyali Reef*, PO Box 82234, Mombasa, T471772. This recently renovated hotel has about 160 rooms, all of which have a/c and balconies. Facilities include meeting rooms, swimming pool, tennis court, sauna, restaurant and bar. A *Voyager Beach Hotel,*formerly the *Silver Beach Hotel*, PO Box 81443, Mombasa, T475114/5/6. This newly renovated hotel is located fairly close to Mombasa. It is popular with package tours and has the usual range of facilities including swimming pool, restaurants and bar. B-C *Kigotho Hotel*, Links Rd, PO Box 86178, T472855 F472677. S/c, a/c, pool, games, not on beach. Also has self-catering apartments which cost US$19 per person if 4 people share. C *Nyali Beach Holiday Resort*, PO Box1874, T472325. All the facilities that you would expect from more expensive places – a/c, swimming pool, games room, restaurant – for considerably less money D *Container Holiday Inn*, PO Box 80762, T486488, 2 km from beach just off the main Mombasa-Malindi road. Cheap but soulless.

D *Moffat Apartments*, T473351 are opposite *Voyager Beach Hotel*. Offers self-catering budget accommodation within striking distance of the beach in Nyali, and is probably the best value in this price bracket. Also try D *Fisherman's Inn*, T471274, next to *Nyali Reef Hotel*, very clean and great value, 5 mins from the beach. Also has a decent restaurant. D *Sokhi Apartments*, T474424, next door to *Nyali Reef Hotel*, only an alternative if *Fisherman's* is full, this place is cheap but not very cheerful.

Bamburi Beach L *Whitesands* (A in low seasons), PO Box 90173, Mombasa, T485926-9, F485652. One of the older and larger hotels with over 300 a/c rooms, this has been refurbished recently. It is set in gardens and has restaurants, meeting rooms, a business centre, 4 swimming pools (1 with water slide), jacuzzi, tennis courts and traditional dancing shows. A watersports centre has facilities for snorkelling, scuba diving, spear fishing, wind-surfing, sailing and deep-sea fishing. A *Nyali Reef*, PO Box 82234, Mombasa, T471771, F471349. This recently renovated hotel has about 160 rooms all of which are a/c and have balconies, facilities include meeting rooms, swimming pool, tennis court, sauna, restaurant and bar. A *Severin Sea Lodge* (B from Apr to Jun), PO Box 82169, Mombasa, T485001/2. This lodge consists of about 180 bungalows all of which are a/c and are very comfortable, facilities include 2 swimming pools, tennis courts, excellent watersports and sailing.

B *Bamburi Beach*, PO Box 83966, Mombasa, T485611, F485900, Another of the older hotels this has recently been renovated, it has about 150 rooms all of which are a/c and have sea-facing balconies. Facilities include a conference centre and extensive sports provision, including squash, gym and various watersports. There is a rooftop bar and nightclub. B *Kenya Beach*, PO Box 95748, Mombasa, T485821. A number of cottages, all a/c, set in gardens with a communal swimming pool, various watersports are available including deep-sea diving. B *Ocean View Beach*, PO Box 81127, Mombasa, T485601-2. A rather old-style hotel, although most of the rooms are a/c they have no phone, however there is a swimming pool, watersports (including deep-sea diving), bar, restaurant and disco. It also has 2-bedroom apartments which represent excellent value if there are 4 people sharing. **B** *Travellers Beach Hotel*, PO Box 87649, Mombasa (North Coast), T011-485121/6, F485674/8, travhtls@africaonline.co.ke New development, spacious a/c rooms, swimming pool, restaurants. **B-C** *Cowrie Shell Beach Apartments*, PO Box 10003, Bamburi, T485971 (**C** in low season). Self-catering apartments in a very unattractive concrete complex. Most rooms have balconies and sea views. Swimming pool but no shop.

C *Giriama Beach Hotel*, PO Box 86291, T 486511, F486191. Located on Bamburi Beach, these 2-bedroom apartments are very comfortable and set in lovely gardens, with a swimming pool and restaurant. Excellent value. **C** *Octopus Apartments*, T485395, opposite *Kenya Beach Hotel*. Basic self-catering apartments, 5 mins' walk from the beach. **C** *Plaza Beach*, PO Box 88299, Mombasa, T485321, F485325. This hotel is reasonably good value, the rooms all have views of the sea and the restaurant, which specializes in Indian food, is especially good. **D** *Baharini Beach Cottages*, T487382, next to *Cowrie Shell Apartments*. These self-catering apartments belong to the owner of the *Ocean View*. On the beach and there is a swimming pool and lively bar. Probably the best value for budget travellers on this stretch of beach.

Shanzu Beach L *Dolphin*, PO Box 81443, Mombasa, T485801. A very pleasant hotel with the full range of facilities. **L** *Mombasa Continental Resort*, PO Box 83492, Mombasa, T485811, F485437, msaconti@africaonline.co.ke A large modern concrete structure, with nearly 200 rooms, all are a/c and have balconies. It has extensive facilities including 2 swimming pools, watersports, 2 tennis courts, 2 squash courts, a health club, and a conference centre. It also has bars, restaurants, nightclub, casino, shopping arcade and car rental service, along with traditional dancing shows and 'animation' tours of the local area. It is set in large grounds and has a long beach front. **L** *Mombasa Serena Beach Hotel*, PO Box 90352, Mombasa T220732, F485453, serenamk@africaonline.co.ke A very pleasant luxury hotel carefully designed to resemble Lamu architecture. About 120 a/c rooms and facilities include meeting rooms, tennis courts, swimming pool, watersports, bar, and restaurant. The *Serena* is superior and slightly more expensive than the other hotels within this price bracket, and represents excellent value in low season, when the price falls to the **B** category.

Eating If you are staying in one of the big hotels then the chances are that you will eat there most evenings. If you wish to try other places, you will usually need to have your own transport or else take a taxi. **Expensive** *Harlequin Restaurant*, T472373. This is an excellent seafood restaurant, it has a wonderful position located overlooking Tudor Creek and the food is guaranteed to be very fresh. **Mid-range** *Galana Steak House*, T485572. A carnivore's delight, it is located near Kenyatta Beach and is good value. *Imani Dhow*, T47572, is a superb grill restaurant at *Severin Sea Lodge* on Bamburi Beach. *Libbas Restaurant*, T471138, Ratna Shopping Mall in Nyali, is a popular family restaurant specializing in Italian food (pizza and pasta). *Rene's Restaurant*, in Nyali on Links Rd, T472986. Another good-value Italian restaurant, with disco in the evenings.

Mtwapa Creek

Mtwapa is a small, bustling, chaotic and extremely friendly town, and is the main service point for Shanzu Beach. The main settlement is just north of the creek, which is busy with boats serving the big-game fishing industry. There is a police station, petrol station, medical clinic, Presbyterian church, a couple of hotels and restaurants and many street stalls selling a diverse range of goods. It is not overrun with tourists as it is a few kilometres from the coastal beaches, but it offers an opportunity to meet with Kenyans rather than other visitors in the bars.

Kenya Marineland, PO Box 15050, Kikambala, T485248, F485265, www.kenyamarineland.com, in Mtwapa Creek, has underwater viewing rooms from where you can see turtles and barracudas, or watch sharks being fed. There are also Masai dancers, wood carvers, a traditional witch doctor and souvenir shops.

There are boats for hire and dhow trips to a coral-fringed sand-bar for swimming and snorkelling.

Jumba la Mtwana

About 13 km from Mombasa is the Jumba la Mtwana site, a national monument located north of the Mtwapa Creek. The name means the 'house of the slave' and may have been a slave-trading settlement in the 15th century, although it was not mentioned in this capacity in either Arab or Portuguese sources. Many of the houses have been rebuilt and undergone frequent changes and it has been suggested that Jumba la Mtwana could have been a meeting place for pilgrims on their way to Mecca. The site is one of Kenya's least-known sites and has only fairly recently been excavated. It is now run by the National Museums of Kenya. Within the site, which is spread over several hectares, there are three mosques, including the **Mosque by the Sea**, a number of tombs and eight houses. You will notice that architecturally they look little different from the houses of today in the area. This was a successful design that there was no need to change. The people of this town appear to have been very concerned with ablutions for there are many remains showing evidence of cisterns, water jars, latrines and other washing and toilet facilities. Building with coral rag (broken pieces of coral) was something reserved for the more privileged members of the community, and it is their houses that have survived. Those that belonged to the poorer people would have been built of mud and thatch. ■ *US$4. At the entrance you can buy a short guidebook to the site, or else hire a guide.*

It is a lovely setting, close to the beach with shade provided by baobabs. To reach the site ask to be dropped off at the sign about a 1 km beyond Mtwapa Bridge and from there it is a walk of about 3 km. However you will probably be offered a lift as you walk down the track.

Kikambala Beach

About 1 km north of the Jumba site there is the *Porini Village Restaurant* which serves local dishes and puts on displays of traditional African dancing (see below). The road continues north with the Kikambala Beach running parallel to the right. There are several beautiful colonial villas belonging to expats on the left-hand side of the main road, as well as the ubiquitous local cement and mud houses reinforced with mangrove poles. Much of this road has been rebuilt following extensive damage sustained during the El Niño rains of 1997-98.

You will then notice the very green, flat, lush-looking fields with hundreds of thousands of spiky plants growing in straight lines. This is sisal and much of what you see is part of the **Vipingo Sisal Estates**. The estate covers an area of about 50,000 ha, and has not just fields, but factories, a railway and housing for the workers. You can do a tour of the estate and will see the spiky leaves being cut by hand and loaded onto a trolley and taken to the factory where the fibre is removed and dried. There are also plantations of cashew nuts, mango trees and coconut trees.

Takaunga

A few kilometres north of the sisal estate is the **Kurwitu Cottage Complex**, an example of a modern Swahili village. It is near to here that Denys Finch-Hatton had a beach cottage. He was the hunter, pilot and lover of Karen Blixen, described in *Out of Africa*. As you get to the end of sisal estates you will reach the village of Takaunga, reputed to be the oldest of the slave ports on the Kenyan coast, located on the banks of a small creek. North of the tiny settlement of Kurwitu, the landscape becomes more undulating and the flat agricultural land gives way to patches of luxuriant, dense tropical forest, before again turning into green pasture land for cattle, just south of Kilifi.

Sleeping

Mtwapa village E *Kanamai Centre*, PO Box 46, T32046, F32048, about a 30-min walk from Kikambala Beach. This centre used to be a youth hostel but you no longer need to be a member of the IYHA to stay here. It has a range of rooms including dormitories, and spacious doubles and singles. There are also a couple of self-catering cottages, they are basic but are good value and the beach is lovely. It is very clean and friendly and there is a dining room serving basic food. There is a rather sparsely stocked shop (better to stocking up on provisions before arrival). It is difficult to get here if you do not have your own transport. You need to take a *matatu* as far as Majengo on the main road, where you will see a sign saying *Camping Kanamai*, from here you will have to walk. Follow the road until you get to a fork. Take the left fork and then it is a little over 3 km down a dusty track.

Kikambala Beach A *Sun 'n' Sand Beach*, PO Box 2, Kikambala, T32008, F32133. A very pleasant hotel, good facilities, all-inclusive, the beach here is particularly fine. **A** *Le Soleil Beach Club*, located 26 km north of Mombasa and 3 km from main Malindi-Mombasa Rd, 100 m north of *Continental Beach Cottages*, PO Box 84737, T0125-32195/6, F32164, lesoleil@users.africaonline.co.ke New development, very clean, TV and phones in rooms, a/c apartments, swimming pool, floating bar restaurant, snooker hall, range of watersports available, tennis courts, friendly staff. Recommended.

C *Continental Beach Cottages*, PO Box 124, Kikambala, T77 (via operator). These are simple cottages that are rather out of the way set in peaceful gardens, some of them have a/c but they have seen better days and are rather grubby. You are charged per cottage, so can cram in as many people as you want. They are difficult to get to unless you have your own transport, however there is a swimming pool and a good beach. Fairly cheap and basic meals are available. **C** *Whispering Palms*, PO Box 5, Kikambala, T0125-32004/5/6, F32029. This is located on a quiet piece of beach and the entrance lobby has been built with a high roof made of palm-leaf thatch known as *makuti*. It has all the usual facilities including a swimming pool, watersports, restaurant, bar and the evening entertainment includes the delightful variations of gospel singers, bingo and snake shows. **D** *Kikambala Beach Cottages*, PO Box 41 T32032, next to the *Whispering Palms*. Self-catering apartments and campsite.

Camping (E), at *Kanamai Centre* and *Kikambala Beach Cottages* (US$2 per person per night).

Eating

Expensive *Le Pichet*, T585923. Another excellent seafood restaurant, this is located overlooking Mtwara Creek in Kikambala. It is very popular, so you are advised to reserve a table. There are lots of craft stalls surrounding the restaurant in response to the tourists who patronize it. They also organize an evening trip on a dhow – you go across the creek to a nearby beach and have your dinner under the stars. The trip includes the evening's entertainment of traditional African music and dancing, and is particularly popular so be sure to book ahead. **Mid-range** *Pembo Bar*, situated between *Le Soleil* and *Sun n' Sand* along the beach. Rooftop dining area overlooking the lagoon. Serves excellent fish and steaks. Also offers C-D self-catering accommodation 6 cottages behind the restaurant. Swimming pool planned.

Deep-sea fishing

Trips can be arranged by *Hall Mark Charters*, based 12 km north of Mombasa on Mtwapa Creek, PO Box 10202, Bamburi, T011-485680, T0-071-400095 (mob), F0-11-475217, *James Adcock Fishing Ltd*, Mtwapa Creek, PO Box 95693, Mombasa, T011-485527, or *Lusitana Magic Ltd*, Mtwapa Creek, PO Box 80364, Mombasa, T011-474517, F474517.

Takaunga

This small, sleepy village located above Takaunga Creek, 10 km south of Kilifi and 5 km off the main road, has whitewashed houses, and a few shops. About 1 km to the east there is a lovely beach that is only revealed at low tide. The swimming here is very good, and even when the beach is covered you can swim off the rocks, the water is beautifully clear. There are also some old ruins, and it is said to be the oldest slave port on the Kenyan coast.

To get to Takaunga you can either take a *matatu* from Mombasa (there are two a day), or else take one to Kilifi and ask to be dropped off at the turning for Takaunga. From here it is a walk of about 5 km – you are unlikely to get a lift as there is little traffic along this road.

Sleeping L *Takaunga House* (book in advance through *Bush Homes of East Africa Ltd*, PO Box 56923, Nairobi, PO Box 56923, T01-571647, F571665, www.bush-homes.co.ke), is an exclusive and expensive option. There is just 1 cottage with 2 rooms, plus a bedroom in the main house, all en suite. There is a small swimming pool and a private sandy bay fringed with old baobab trees. Price is inclusive of food and drinks, provided by your hosts, the Masons. Sailing, snorkelling and bird-watching is also included, and scuba diving, deep-sea fishing and waterskiing can be arranged at extra cost.

There are no other hotels as such, but it is possible to obtain a local room to rent. If you bring your own supplies you can ask the family to cook them for you.

Kilifi

3° 30' S, 39° 40' E
Phone code: 125
Colour map 3, grid C6

Kilifi Creek is located about 60 km north of Mombasa. The town of Kilifi is situated to the north of the creek, while Mnarani village is to the south. In the time of the Portuguese, the main town was located to the south of the creek at Mnarani. This popular boating and sailing centre is in an absolutely glorious location – the shore slopes steeply down to the water's edge and the view from the new bridge is spectacular. Until 1991 you had to cross the creek by ferry; a bridge, complete with street lights, has now been built with Japanese funding.

The town has an interesting mix of people with quite a number of resident expatriates. The main industry in the town is the cashew nut factory which employs about 1,500 people. To the south there are the Mnarani Ruins. It is an easy-going town with an attractive beach, untroubled by the hassle associated with some of the beaches closer to Mombasa.

Mnarani Ruins The Mnarani Ruins were first excavated in the 1950s but renewed interest in the site has led the British Institute in Eastern Africa to work here again. It was the place of one of the ancient Swahili city-states that are found along this coast. It is believed that the town was inhabited from the latter half of the 14th century until about the early 17th century, when it was ransacked and destroyed by a group of Galla tribesmen. The inhabitants of the town are thought to have locked themselves into the Great Mosque as they were attacked.

The ruins include one of the deepest wells (70 m) along the coast, two mosques, part of the town wall and city gates and a group of tombs including a pillar tomb decorated with engravings of a wealthy sharif. Note particularly the tomb of the doctor

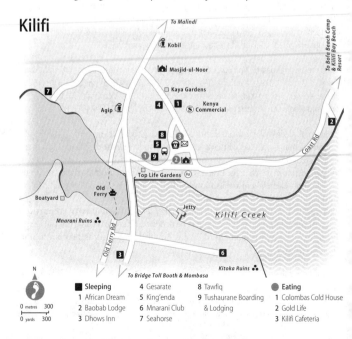

Kilifi

To Malindi
Kobil
Masjid-ul-Noor
Kaya Gardens
Agip
Kenya Commercial
Tawfiq
King'enda
Tushaurane Boarding & Lodging
Top Life Gardens
Old Ferry
Boatyard
Mnarani Ruins
Jetty
Kilifi Creek
Old Ferry Rd
Coast Rd
To Bola Beach Camp & Kilifi Bay Beach Resort
Kitoka Ruins
N
0 metres 300
0 yards 300
To Bridge Toll Booth & Mombasa

■ **Sleeping**
1 African Dream
2 Baobab Lodge
3 Dhows Inn
4 Gesarate
5 King'enda
6 Mnarani Club
7 Seahorse
8 Tawfiq
9 Tushaurane Boarding & Lodging

● **Eating**
1 Colombas Cold House
2 Gold Life
3 Kilifi Cafeteria

Kenya

that is easily the most ornate. At the ruins of the larger or **Great Mosque** can be seen the *mihrab* (which points towards Mecca) surrounded by carved inscriptions. There are many niches in the walls. To the left of the entrance, the smaller mosque is believed to date from the 16th century. There is a huge baobab tree nearby with a circumference of over 15 m. The ruins are best known for the inscriptions carved into them – many of them remaining untranslated. However, in general they are much smaller and less impressive than the ones at Gedi. ■ *0700-1730. US$1.75.*

To get to the ruins, turn left off the main road to the south of the creek (sign-posted Mnarani Ruins) by the toll booth and go through Mnarani village. Turn right when you reach the tarmaced road and stop when you can see the creek. There is a signposted path to the left, and the ruins are a few hundred metres down this path and then a climb of about 100 steps. You also get a wonderful view of the creek from the ruins.

About 3 km south of Kilifi is the smaller site of **Kitoka**, where the ruins include a small mosque and a few houses.

L *Kilifi Bay Beach Resort* (**B** in low season), PO Box 537, on Coast Rd about 5 km out of Kilifi, T22511, F22258, www.madahotels.com Well designed by an Italian, the complex accommodates guests in cottages. It has well-tended surroundings, located on cliffs with path down to beach. Has a pool, scuba diving instruction available. **A** *Mnarani Club*, PO Box 81443, KilifiT22320. Located overlooking Kilifi Creek on Malindi Rd, this hotel is one of the oldest in the country. It has been beautifully rehabilitated, with 84 guest bedrooms, in natural wood finishes. There are smaller creek cottages designed for families. All rooms have a/c, mosquito nets and phones. It is set in marvellous gardens and has wonderful views, facilities include watersports (sailing, windsurfing and waterskiing), a bar, a good-value restaurant overlooking the creek, and evening entertainment such as traditional dancing and music.

Sleeping
■ *on map*
For price codes:
see inside front cover

(side margin) Kenya

☞ ## Baobab trees

These huge trees have enormous girths –
which enable them to survive during very
long dry patches. They live for up to 2,000
years. You will see some extremely large
ones - there is one at Ukunda which has a
girth of 22 m and which has been given
'presidential protection' to safe guard it.

The legend is that when God first
planted them they kept walking around
and would not stay still. So He decided to
replant them up-side-down which is why
they look as if they have the roots sticking
up into the air. During droughts people
open up the pods and grind the seeds to
make what is known as 'hunger flour'.

(Book through *Let's Go Travel*, ABC Place, Waiyaki Way, PO Box 60342 Nairobi T447151, info@letsgosafari.com). **A** *Seahorse*, PO Box 70, Kilifi, T22515 Located looking out across Kilifi Creek on the northern side of the creek this also has good views and is a popular drinking spot for the resident expatriates and is considered to be Kenya's sailing centre.If you are hoping for some crewing this is the place to try your luck.

C *Baobab Lodge*, on cliffs to north, PO Box 537, Kilifi, T22570, F22264. Attractive rondavels, pool, diving, path down to small swimming cove, fringed with mostly coral – the lack of a sandy beach being its biggest disadvantage. An intimate place with a good restaurant. **D** *Dhows Inn*, this small hotel is located on the south side of the creek on the new road leading to the bridge, PO Box 431, Kilifi, T/F22028, Nairobi reservations, PO Box 74698, T/F02-503334. Rooms have bathrooms and mosquito nets, are clean and fairly basic but good value, the hotel has nice gardens and there is a popular bar and restaurant. Can arrange watersports and game safaris. **E** *African Dream*, on road out of town to main road to Malindi, s/c rooms, oil lamps, a little overpriced. **E** *Bofa Beach Camp*, on coast road about 8 km out of Kilifi, PO Box 660, T02-724483, Nairobi. Its distance from town is disadvantageous; otherwise it is good value for a beach break, not terribly clean, water supplies erratic, soft drinks available. **E** *Gesarate*, PO Box 231, between centre and Masjid-ul-Noor Mosque on east side. Small courtyard, simple but comfortable. **E** *King 'enda*, close to bus station, PO Box 188. Fan, nets, good budget value. **E** *Tawfiq Hotel*, behind bus station. Nets, not s/c, basic but cheap. **E** *Tushaurane Boarding and Lodging*, this is a fairly new hotel located in the town centre, facilities are mostly shared, it is simple but it is clean and friendly and mosquito nets are provided.

Eating
● *on map page 240*

Expensive *Mnanari Club*, high standard, superb seafood, excellent atmosphere. **Mid-range** *Baobab Lodge* a good value set menu with delicious seafood. *Seahorse*, reliable international menu. **Cheap** *Dhows Inn*, reasonable food. *Toplife Garden Bar and Restaurant*, PO Box 15, Kilifi, T22234. **Seriously cheap** *Colombas Cold House*, on road into town, near bridge. Mostly freshly squeezed juices. *Gold Life*, at the bus station. Open air, neat, bright patio, excellent fruit juices. *Kilifi Cafeteria*, near bus stand. Grills, snacks and juices, inexpensive.

Entertainment

Top Life Gardens, overlooking creek close to bridge, fine views, live band or disco on Fri, Sat and Sun. *Kaya Gardens*, north of KC Bank, disco Fri and Sat.

Shopping

Bookshops There is a small bookshop, just off the main street.

Tour operators

At *Azzura Tours*, PO Box 2, Kilifi, T22385, you can hire cars, buy bus tickets and organize various trips. *Microlite Kenya*, PO Box 824, T/F22000. *Tuna Travel and Tours*, PO Box 592, Kilifi, T/F23314 (Diani Beach).

Transport

Bus: Kilifi is about 50 km from **Mombasa**, and 45 km from **Malindi**. The buses that go between the 2 towns do pick people up here although they may be full. It might be easier to get a *matatu* ($0.75 from Mombasa). Enquiries and bookings can be made at *Azzura Tours*, T22385, whose office is on the Kilifi's main road. *Tana Express* and *Tawfiq* have booking offices near Bus Station. To get to and from *Nairobi* from Kilifi the Tana Bus Company goes twice a day taking about 9 hrs. The buses leave at 0730 and 1930. The Tana Express and Tawfiq have booking offices near the Bus Station. **Car hire** also at *Azzura Tours* (see above)

Banks The 2 banks in Kilifi are open 0830-1300 on weekdays and 0830-1130 ON Sat. *Kenya Commercial Bank*, PO Box 528, T22034, Kilifi. **Communications** The post office is next to the market. **Medical services** Dr Bomo has a *clinic* on the old Kilifi Rd in Mnarani.

Directory

Kilifi to Malindi

The road from Kilifi continues north running parallel to the coast. As with much of the road from Mombasa it runs straight and true and is in quite good condition. Leaving Kilifi the road passes small villages dotted between lots of cashew nut trees that are surprisingly green-leafed at the end of the dry season. There are occasional stands of eucalyptus trees. Don't expect tropical rainforest as you approach the Arabuko Sokoke Forest Reserve – from the road the only discernible difference is that the scrub disappears and the trees are noticeably closer together. Gazetted as a reserve in 1943 and partly managed by Kenya Wildlife since 1991, it is home to many species of rare birds, and is the most important bird conservation project in Kenya. Clarke's weaver is endemic to this area, and the 16-cm Sokoke Scops owl is only found here and in a small area in eastern Tanzania, in the Usambara Mountains. The reserve also contains rare species of amphibians, butterflies and plants. It is said to be the largest surviving stretch of coastal forest in East Africa and covers an area of 400 sq km. Efforts to prevent the forest being cut down completely are being made, but the constant needs for fuel and land in a country where the population is increasing so rapidly makes this difficult. The forest is home to rare mammals too such as the very small Zanzibar duiker (only 35 cm high and usually seen in pairs), the Sokoke bushy-tailed mongoose and the rare golden-rumped elephant shrew. There are four endemic plants and five endemic butterflies.

The forest is host to a sustainable project where local farmers harvest butterfly pupae, for sale to the Kipepeo project in Gede, and for live export to overseas exhibitions. Bee keeping for honey production is another local initiative under development. The wardens are very well informed about the wildlife and will also be able to advise whether the tracks which join the Tsavo National Park road to the north are passable. From Tsavo East to Malindi the distance is 100 km but a four-wheel drive is necessary during the rainy season. ■ *PO Box 1, Gede, T32102, www.watamu.net The Forest Office is signposted to the left about 1 km from the Watamu turning; obtain permission if you wish to explore the forest. There is a bus stop by the entrance to the forest on the main road.*

Continuing north the road heads inland to skirt around the Mida Creek before coming to the village of Watamu, the location of Watamu Marine Park (see below). A little further on and to the west of the road and south of Malindi you will pass the Gedi National Park. Close to the village of Watamu is the turn-off for the Gedi Ruins (see page 246). Beyond the Watamu turning, the road again passes through scrub with small villages interspersed. At the end of the dry season you will notice, both from the road and from the air, lots of bonfires. This is the villagers clearing their land ahead of the long rains when they will plant their crops. You will also notice termite mounds – some are well over 2 m high and often fantastically shaped. Finally before reaching Malindi you will see signs to the Malindi Marine Park and the Snake Park.

Arabuko Sokoke Forest Reserve
Parts of the coast north towards Lamu are quite difficult to access, although communications have improved recently and some places have been developed for tourism

Kenya

Watamu

Phone code: 122
Colour map 3, grid C6

In recent years this small fishing village has been seeing some fairly rapid tourist development, and is certainly feeling the impact. The atmosphere is mixed, but Watamu still maintains quite a lot of traditional village charm and remains reasonably hassle free, despite the proximity of the tourist hotels. Watamu is known for its spectacular coral reef, and the coast splits into three bays: Watamu, Blue Lagoon, and Turtle Bay.

Apart from the beach and the sea, the attractions of staying here are the nearby Watamu Marine Park and the **Gedi Ruins**. The setting attractive as there are a number of small islands just offshore, and Turtle Bay is quite good for snorkelling (but watch out for speed boats ferrying fishermen to the large game boats. The water is much clearer here than at Malindi during the wet season. The most exciting way to the reef, 2 km offshore, is to go in a glass-bottomed boat, which will cost between US$15-20 but is well worth it. The beach is relatively free of seaweed. Avoid the camel rides along the beach. If you can't afford deep-sea fishing, be at *Hemingways* at 1600-1700 when the days catch is recorded and the fishermen photographed. Tagged fish are apparently returned to the sea. Watamu is also a good place to hire bikes as an alternative way of exploring the surrounding area, including the Gedi Ruins. There are a number of shops in the village, with reasonable rates. Look out for the new village school building that was completed by five unpaid British builders within a fortnight in early 1999; they were rewarded by being appointed as elders of the Giriama tribe and given Swahili names. Other places of interest are the **Snake Farm**, **Midi Creek Swamp**, the **Butterfly Farm** at Gedi Ruins, and **Dhow Building** on the beach.

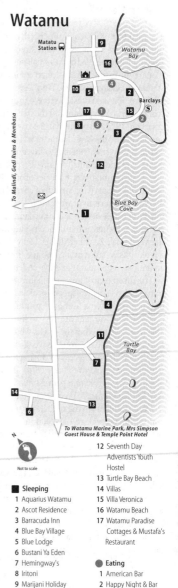

Watamu

Along this coast close to Watamu village there is an excellent marine park which has been made a total exclusion zone. Obviously this change of status met with mixed feelings by some fishermen, but they seem to have adapted well, and the influx of tourists has increased the income of the village. The park headquarters are someway south of Watamu at the end of the peninsula that guards the entrance to the creek. Unfortunately the road goes a little inland, hiding views of the sea. There are approximately 700 species of fish in

**Watamu
Marine Park**

To Watamu Marine Park, Mrs Simpson
Guest House & Temple Point Hotel

Not to scale

■ **Sleeping**
1 Aquarius Watamu
2 Ascot Residence
3 Barracuda Inn
4 Blue Bay Village
5 Blue Lodge
6 Bustani Ya Eden
7 Hemingway's
8 Iritoni
9 Marijani Holiday Resort
10 Nyambene Lodge
11 Ocean Sports
12 Seventh Day Adventists Youth Hostel
13 Turtle Bay Beach
14 Villas
15 Villa Veronica
16 Watamu Beach
17 Watamu Paradise Cottages & Mustafa's Restaurant

● **Eating**
1 American Bar
2 Happy Night & Bar
3 Hotel Dante
4 La Bamba Country Lodge

the marine park and there are estimated to be over a 100 species of stony coral. You go out in a glass-bottomed boat to the protected area and some of the hundreds of fishes come to the boat to be fed. The boats may seem rather expensive but are really well worth it. Trips can be arranged at any of the hotels, or else at the entrance to the actual park. You can also swim or snorkel amongst the fish, which is a wonderful experience. There are lots of shells and live corals that are a splendid range of colours. The water temperature ranges from 20-30°C. If you are short of time, try the islands just offshore from *Hemingways*. ■ *US$5 KWS park fees, plus boat fees of approximately US$4.*

Sleeping

■ *on map*
For price codes:
see inside front cover

There are a number of resort hotels but not much in terms of budget accommodation

L *Blue Bay Village*, PO Box 162, T32626, F32422, about 2 km south of the village in the most southerly of the 3 coves, is also popular with Italians, good facilities. **L** *Hemingway's* (Formerly *Seafarers*), PO Box 267, T32624 (Watamu), T225255 (Nairobi), F32256 (Watamu), hemingways@form-net.com This has more of a mix of clientele although perhaps British, and expatriates living in Kenya dominate. The hotel has been renovated recently, it is to a high standard, but the rooms lack character, being a double-storey concrete block with verandahs. Facilities include 2 swimming pools, bar, an excellent restaurant, and watersports including deep-sea fishing fleet, own dhow. Trips to Tsavo National Park can also be arranged, good value out of season. **A** *Barracuda Inn*, PO Box 402, T32331, F32330, just to the south of the village, is Italian-owned and attracts a large proportion of Italians amongst their clientele. It is a wonderful building with fantastic thatched *makuti* roofs, the gardens are also very pretty and the staff friendly. Closes in May. **A** *Ocean Sports*, PO Box 100, Malindi, T32008 (Watamu), F32266, a little further south, has a series of cottages set in gardens, there is a large bar and restaurant and all the other usual facilities. Sunday lunch is a huge buffet, popular with expatriates and particularly good value. Will arrange big-game fishing (US$140 per person per day), PADI and BASC diving courses, snorkelling, tennis and squash, friendly atmosphere. Well recommended. Good dive shop/school, with British staff. **A** *Turtle Bay Beach Hotel*, PO Box 10, T32003, F32268, turtles@africaonline.co.ke, also has a mixed clientele, it is very relaxed and has all the facilities including watersports. It has a variety of rooms with or without a/c, and will arrange various tours in the area. Organized as a club, encouraging residents to eat all their meals and take all their entertainment at the hotel, it looks after guests very well and is excellently organized. A windsurfing course for beginners costs US$31, a 5-day PADI diving course costs US$250. Offers tennis, basketball, programmes for children, massage, excellent beach and *Cats* restaurant.

B *Aquarius Watamu Hotel* (previously *Watamu Cottages*) PO Box 96, T32069, F32211, aquarius@users.africaonline.co.ke Recently renovated, under Italian ownership. 40 a/c rooms, with pool, gardens and Italian food. Located 100 m from the beach facing Blue Bay Cove. **B** *Ascot Residence Hotel*, PO Box 348, T/F32326. Not on beach, but good central location, bar, tennis, pizzeria, grill, boutique. Civilised Italian management, clientele include many retired Italians. Has spacious grounds and a pool, friendly staff, large rooms. Excellent value. **B** *Watamu Beach*, PO Box 81443, Mombasa T32001, F32367, the northernmost of all the Watamu hotels, is located behind the village on the northern cove. It is a large hotel, popular with German tourists, and set in generous grounds. Facilities include swimming pool, bar, and restaurant. The beach here is lovely and there are lots of fishermen offering to take you out to the reef in their boats. **C** *Hotel Villas*, PO Box 150, T32298, F32487. Not on the beach, but organizes transport to the shore, s/c villas with kitchens, a/c, pool, good value. **C** *Marijani Holiday Resort*, PO Box 282, T/F32448. Beautiful surroundings. Ocean-front resort north of Watamu, near the *African Safari Club*, easily reached by *matatu* as terminus is only 5 mins' walk away. A Kenyan/German enterprise offering a variety of accommodation from basic board to fully furnished s/c cottages available for short and long rental periods. Can arrange pick up from Mombasa Airport. Rooms have nets, fans, hot water, fridge, sun-loungers and room-cleaning service. Fax service available. Bicycle and surfboard rental. **C** *Peponi Cottages*, PO Box 25, T32434 (Res), T32246. Recently built, small but reasonable rooms, with mosquito nets, small swimming pool, breakfast not included.

Kenya

You can usually rent rooms very cheaply in private houses if you ask around

D *Bustani Ya Eden*, PO Box 276, T32262. 6 small, very pleasant rooms available at a very good rate for 2 sharing a room, s/c, fans. 300 m to beach, speciality African and seafood restaurant, friendly Dutch/Kenyan couple run the place. **D** *Villa Veronica (Mwikali Lodge)*, PO Box 57, T32083, is one of the best of the budget hotels in Watamu, rooms have bathrooms attached, mosquito nets provided and rooms are clean. It is a friendly family-run place, and the price includes breakfast. **D** *Watamu Paradise Cottages*, PO Box 249, T32062, F32436, are close to the village near *Mustafa's Restaurant*, there is a swimming pool in the beautiful bougainvillea-filled grounds. **D-E** *Mrs Simpson Guest House*, PO Box 33, T32032, Plot 28. simpson@watamu.net, offers pleasant s/c double rooms, wonderful beach and friendly staff. Has a medium-size **campsite** with a water supply. Can help arrange trips to Arabuko-Sokoke Forest Reserve or to Watamu Marine NP. **E** *Blue Lodge*, in village. Shared bathrooms, inexpensive and basic, has neither mosquito nets nor cool fans, so not comfortable. **E** *Iritoni Lodge*, only has 2 rooms but is clean and friendly. **E** *Nyambene Lodge*, in the village, basic rooms with shared facilities. **E** *Seventh-Day Adventists Youth Hostel*, this is not a proper hostel and you can only stay here occasionally, facilities are basic. **E** *Watamu Cottages*, not to be confused with the *Watamu Paradise Cottages*, are located about 1 km out of town and are very popular, there is a swimming pool in the complex and they are used a lot by expatriate families, the price includes breakfast and they are really excellent value.

Eating

You can eat at all the big hotels which do various set menus and buffets – look around as there are some real bargains

Mid-range *Hotel Dante*, opposite *Mustafa's Restaurant*. Italian cuisine. *La Bamba Country Lodge*, north of village. *Watamu Paradise Restaurant*, part of the cottages of the same name, this serves good food including seafood and is good value. The nearby *Mustafa's Restaurant*, particularly popular at night when it can get quite lively as the *Comeback Club*. **Cheap** *American Bar*, north of village. Hamburgers and grills. *Coco Grill Bar and Restaurant*, north of village. Grills and seafood. **Seriously cheap** *Happy Night Bar and Restaurant*, serves snacks and beers and is good value, occasional live music.

Sports

Deep-sea fishing: *Hemingways Fishing Centre*, PO Box 267, T32052, F32256. *Tega Safaris Ltd*, PO Box 12, T32078. **Scuba diving:** *Malindi Scuba Diving Kenya Ltd*, T32099. *Aqua Ventures*, at Ocean Sports, T32008.

Tour operators

Tuna Travel and Tours, PO Box 26, T322445, near Mustapha's restaurant. *Samurai Tours and Safaris*, PO Box 203, T32306 (office), T32252 (home). *Wildgame Tours and Safaris*, PO Box 131, T32311, near *Barclays Banks*. *Blue Boy Safaris*, PO Box 162, T32626, F32422. *Sambu Tours and Travel*, T32482.

Transport

Local From Malindi to Watamu takes about ½hr, there are plenty of *matatus* and it will cost you about US$0.50. Hotel taxi from **Malindi** US$18; from **Mombasa** US$90. Note these taxis can seat 7, and on this basis cost US$2.50 and US$13 a head. **Bicycle hire**: *Tuna Travel* near *Mustapha's* restaurant.

Directory

Banks There is a small branch of *Barclays* open on Mon, Wed and Fri morning. The big hotels will change money but the rate will not be very good. **Medical services**, Dr Eugene Erulu, T32046.

Gedi Ruins

Colour map 3, grid C6

The Gedi Ruins are about 4 km north of Watamu and are signposted from the village of Gedi. This is one of Kenya's most important archaeological sites and is believed to contain the ruins of a city that once had a population of about 2,500. It was populated in the latter half of the 13th century, and the size of some of the buildings, in particular the mosque, suggest that this was a fairly wealthy town for some time. However, it is not mentioned in any Arabic or Swahili writings and was apparently unknown to the Portuguese although they maintained a strong presence in Malindi just 15 km away. It is believed that this was because it was set away from the sea, deep in the forest. Possibly as a result of an attack from marauding tribesmen of the

Oromo or Galla tribe, the city was abandoned at some time during the 16th century. Lack of water may have also been a contributing factor as wells of over 50 m deep dried out. It was later reinhabited but never regained the economic position that it once had held. It was finally abandoned in the early 17th century and the ruins were rediscovered in 1884. The site was declared a national monument in 1948 and has been excavated since then. It has been well preserved.

There is a beautifully designed new **museum** that opened in late 2000 and includes a restaurant and library. Visitors are made to feel welcome. You can buy a guidebook and map of the site at the entrance gate. There are also informative guides. Ali, the curator for the past 20 years, will show you around personally if available.

The site was originally surrounded by an inner and outer wall (surprisingly thin). The most interesting buildings and features are concentrated around the entrance gate, although there are others. Most that remain are within the inner wall although there are some between the two walls. Coral rag and lime were used in all the buildings and some had decorations carved into the wall plaster. You can still see the remains of the bathrooms – complete with deep bath, basin and squat toilet. There are a large number of wells in the site, some being exceptionally deep. The main buildings that remain are a sultan's palace, a mosque and a number of houses and tombs, a water system and a prison. Other finds include pieces of Chinese porcelain from the Ming Dynasty, beads from India and stoneware from Persia – some are displayed in the musuem, others in Fort Jesus, Mombasa.

The **Palace** can be entered through a rather grand arched doorway which brings you into the reception court and then a hall. This is the most impressive building on the site. Off this hall there are a number of smaller rooms – including the bathrooms. You can also see the remains of the kitchen area that contains a small well.

The **Great Mosque** probably dates from the mid-15th century, and is the largest of the seven on this site. It is believed that substantial rebuilding was undertaken more recently. The *mihrab*, that indicates the direction of Mecca, was built of stone (rather than wood) and has survived well. As you leave note the carved spearhead which is located above the northeast doorway.

A great deal of trade seems to have been established here – silk and porcelain were exchanged for skins and, most importantly, ivory. China was keen to exploit this

Kenya

Gedi Ruins

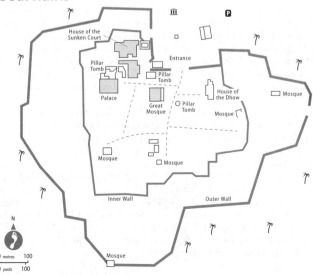

Kenya

☞ Early coastal tourism

In the 1920s a return journey by ship from London to Mombasa through the Suez Canal took four weeks each way and cost £60. A hotel in Mombasa cost six shillings and eight pence.

The first beach hotel was established by a photographer from Goa, Hugo Coutinho, at Bamburi Beach, with thatched rondavels, palm frond beds, and they cost two shillings and ten pence a night. At Malindi, the first

hotel was built by Pat Brady in 1932 and became known as Brady's Palm Beach and was on a site where the present Blue Marlin is located. Ernest Hemingway stayed there in 1934. The next year a retired naval commander, Leo Lawford began a similar enterprise just to the south of Brady's and the hotel, subsequently much developed, still bears his name.

market and in 1414 a giraffe was given to the Chinese Emperor and shipped from Malindi. It apparently survived the trip. There was also trade with European countries and a Venetian glass bead has been found here too.

In all there are 14 houses on the complex which have so far been excavated. Each one is named after something that was found at its site – for example House of Scissors, House of Ivory Box. There is also one named after a picture of a dhow that is on the wall. In the houses you will again be able to see the old-style bathrooms. Deep pits were dug for sewage, capped when full and then used for fertilizer. Such techniques are still used in the Old Town district in Malindi.

The tombs are located to the right of the entrance gate and one of them is of particular interest to archaeologists as it actually has a date engraved on it – the Islamic year 802 which is equal to the year AD 1399. This is known as the Date Tomb and has enabled other parts of the site to be dated with more accuracy. There is also a tomb with a design that is common along the Swahili coast – that of a fluted pillar. Pillar tombs are found all along the coast and were used for men with position and influence.

The site is in very pleasant surroundings – it is green and shady but can get very hot (cool drinks are available at the entrance). There are a spectacular variety of trees including combretum, tamarind, baobab, wild ficus and sterculia, a smooth-barked tree inhabited by palm nut vultures and monkeys because snakes cannot climb up the trunk. You may hear a buzzing noise. This is an insect that lives only for three or four days until it literally blows itself to pieces! There are usually monkeys in the trees above that are filled with the noise of many different types of birds.

It is in fact also a wildlife sanctuary and is home to the magnificent, and now sadly rare, black and white colobus monkey. This monkey has suffered at the hands of poachers for their splendid coats but a few remain and you may see some here. Also in the sanctuary are the golden-rumped elephant shrew (only seen at dawn and dusk) and various birds such as the harrier hawk and palm tree vulture. ■ *0700-1800 daily. Entry about US$3.75, children US$1. If you came by matatu you will have to walk the last 1 km. You can hire a taxi from Malindi for about US$8.*

Kipepeo Project Just inside the entrance to the ruins is a community-based **butterfly farm** that has trained local farmers living on the edge of the Arabuko-Sokoke Forest Reserve (see page 243) to rear butterfly pupae for export overseas. The project aims to link forest conservation with income generation for local communities and at present is the only butterfly farm in Africa of this kind.

At the central breeding unit at Gedi Ruins it is possible to see all stages of butterfly development, learn about their natural history and see a selection of the species of butterflies present in the Arabuko-Sokoke Forest. Half an hour spent in this shady location offers an interesting contrast to the historic site of Gedi Ruins as the emphasis is on providing a secure future for the Arabuko-Sokoke Forest and the communities adjacent to it. ■ *0800-1700. US$2 non-resident adults, US$1 children. To get to the site, take the main Malindi-Mombasa road.*

Malindi

Malindi is the second largest coastal town in Kenya after Mombasa. The beach is excel-
lent and popular and, although seaweed can be a problem (especially before the spring
equinox), it is less so than on the beaches around Mombasa. The surf is good during
July-August but silt from the Galana River can make the water a rather red, muddy col-
our during the rainy season. Although the history of the town dates back to the 12th
century there are few remains of the ancient town.

3° 12′ S, 40° 5′ E
Phone code: 123
Colour map 3, grid C6

   A great attraction is the Malindi Marine Park, with clear water and brilliantly col-
oured fish. It is also one of the few places on the East African coast where the rollers come
crashing into the shore, there is a break in the reef, and it is possible to surf.

Getting there Malindi is well served from Mombasa by air and bus/*matatu* services (there
is no train service). For details, see Transport page 258. **Getting around** You can either
organize day trips through the hotel, or else hire a car or bicycle or else try the public transport. **Safety** Malindi is a friendly place and travellers here are less likely to be hassled than at
the beaches closer to Mombasa.The main parts of town are safe, even at night. Exercise caution elsewhere, however, and take a taxi if you need to go further afield. Travelling north to
Lamu has been fraught with intermittent security problems. People are advised to travel in
convoy accompanied by armed guards. **Tourist offices** The Tourist Office, PO Box 421,
T20747, is located on the Lamu road opposite the shopping centre. The staff are very friendly
and helpful.

Ins & outs

Kenya

History

The earliest known reference to Malindi is found in Chinese geography in a piece
published in 1060 written by a scholar who died in AD 863. The first accurate
description of the town is believed to be written by **Prince Abu al-Fida** who lived
from 1273 to 1331. Archaeological evidence supports the theory that the town of
Malindi was founded by Arabs in the 13th century. In any event, locals claim that
there was a big Chinese trading influence. This belief is supported by the fact that
many of the local people still retain traces of Chinese features.

   In 1498 **Vasco da Gama**, having rounded the Cape of Good Hope stopped off at
various ports along the coast. At Mombasa he was not made welcome – indeed
attempts were made to sink his ships. He quickly left and continued north, stopping
at Malindi, where he found a much warmer reception. Why the response of the two
towns should be so different is unclear – it may have been because of an on-going
feud between the two local leaders as well as the gifts and pyrotechnic display. The
good relations between Malindi and the Portuguese continued throughout the 16th
century. In about 1500 the population of within the town walls was about 3,500, with
another 2,000 Africans living in surrounding plantations. The town was governed
by Arabs, who were the wealthiest group. The wealth came from the trade with India
and the supply of agricultural produce, grown in the surrounding plantations largely
by slaves, for passing ships. One of the visitors in this period was St Francis Xavier
who passed by Malindi in 1542 on his way to India.

   The town went into a period of decline in the 16th century and in 1593 the Portuguese administration was transferred from Malindi to Mombasa. Traders and
labourers followed but the Arabs who remained behind had become too dependent
on the Portuguese to manage without them. The decline was in part a consequence
of the superiority of the harbour facilities at Mombasa. Neighbouring tribes, in particular the Galla, overran the town, and it is believed that Malindi was abandoned in
the late 17th century. It lay in a ruined state for many years and it was not until 1861
that it was rediscovered by the Sultan of Zanzibar and again became prosperous.

   Although Malindi continued to suffer as Mombasa expanded and took more
trade, the town's prosperity did improve during this period and the use of slaves was
undoubtedly an important factor. To get an idea of the scale, in the first year of

resettlement in 1861 there were a 1,000 slaves working for just 50 Arabs. Malindi was not a major exporter of slaves as the demand within the town did not allow it. Malindi had a particularly bad reputation for its treatment of slaves.

The period under the **Imperial British East Africa Company** (IBEAC) began in 1887 when the Company acquired a 50-year lease from the Sultan of Zanzibar for territories in East Africa. The company administered the area, collected taxes and had rights over minerals found. Bell Smith was sent to the town as officer for the Company and he began to lobby for the abolition of the slave trade. From around 1890 slaves who wished and were able to, could buy their freedom. For those who could not, the company offered jobs, or found paid employment. Interestingly relatively few took up the opportunity and the process was a gradual one. It has been estimated that from 1888 to 1892, 2,387 slaves were freed on the coast by the IBEAC and by 1897 there were still 5,442 slaves in the Malindi district.

In 1895 the British government purchased the assets of the IBEAC and established formally the East African Protectorate. The same year the Sultan of Zanzibar transferred the lease of the 10-mile coastal strip to the British Government for the sum of £11,000 per year. The Arabs, who had grown used to having slave labour, found it very difficult to adapt to actually paying workers, and the final blow was dealt in 1907 when the Protectorate government abolished the status of slavery. Merchandise trade developed, and in the early 20th century the most important exports were rubber, grain, ivory, hides and horns. Rubber was grown on European-owned plantations in response to a dramatic increase in the world price around the First World War. However, it was short lived as the world price subsequently fell and most of the plantations were abandoned.

During the second half of the British period the foundations were laid for what is now Malindi's most important industry – that of tourism. During the depression years Malindi's trade and agriculture had suffered not just from low world prices but also from drought. There continued to be a shortage of labour and the only crop that experienced an increase in production was cotton. The 1930s also saw the beginning of the tourist industry with the first hotel *Brady's Palm Beach Hotel* opening in 1932 – famous visitors include Ernest Hemingway who visited in 1934. Most of the tourists at this time were settlers from the White Highlands. Expansion continued after the Second World War

Malindi north

To Lamu

Golf & Country Club

Italian Garden Centre

St Andrew's

Lamu Rd

Tropicana Club 28

Malindi Casino

Sabaki Centre

Falconry

Snake Park   Malindi Complex

Stardust Club

Casino Disco

Galana Centre

Sitawi Shopping Centre

Kenya Commercial

Barclays

Indian Ocean

To Kingfisher Lodge

N

0 metres 100
0 yards 100

Related map
Malindi south, page 252

● **Eating**
1 Carni Africana alla Brace
2 La Malindina
3 Lorenzo's & Iguana Bar
4 Palm Garden
5 Putipu Disco Bar
6 Sportsmans
7 Surahi
8 Vera Cruz

■ **Sleeping**
1 African Pearl
2 Blue Marlin
3 Eden Roc
4 Lutheran Guest House
5 Malindi Cottages
6 Moriema Cottages
7 Palm Tree Club

● **Bars**
9 Hermann's Beer Garden
10 T-T-Bar & Restaurant

Kenya

Fireworks at Malindi

In 1498 Vasco da Gama, sailing north up the East African coast had met with a hostile reception both in Sofala (now in Mozambique) and Mombasa. He needed to establish good relations with a town at the coast so that he could load fresh water and victuals and engage an experienced mariner to guide his fleet to the Indies. The bales of cotton cloth and strings of beads the fleet had brought with them to trade had proved useless – the coastal people had gold from Sofola, ivory from the interior, silk from the east.

Vasco da Gama decided to present some unusual items to the King of Malindi – a jar of marmalade, a set of decorated porcelain dishes and a candied peach in a silver bowl. He then invited the king and his people to witness a firework display on the shore. The king had a brass throne with a scarlet canopy brought down to the shore and with a court of horn players, flautists and drummers gazed out to the San Gabriel and da Gama's fleet. In quick succession the ship's canons fired shells into the air which burst over the King and his townsfolk on the shore. It was spectacular and exciting, and the king was impressed. At last the Portuguese had an ally for their conquest of the mainland.

Kenya

and Malindi became popular as a retirement town for European settlers. With the increase in air travel and affordability of holidays abroad the growth of Malindi as a tourist resort spiralled, spurred on by the popularity of package tours.

Today, Malindi is heavily influenced by the Italians who have been encouraged to invest by the government. Many are attracted by the 'cheapness' of the area and many retirement villas have been built. This has not been altogether welcomed by the local people despite the obvious increase in jobs. A number of shopping malls have sprung up over the last decade that are full of expensive Italian goods and over-priced curios.

Sights

Although there is little left of the ancient walled town of Malindi, there are two remains in the town itself that are worth seeing. In the oldest part of the town, clustered around the jetty, is the **Jami Mosque** and two striking **Pillar Tombs**. These are thought to date from the 14th century. The Malindi Curios Dealers Associations have a huge **market** here. Behind the Jami Mosque lies a maze of small streets that form the Old Town district. The oldest surviving buildings are the mosques of which there are nine (including the Jami Mosque) that date from before 1500. Contemporary accounts from the 14th century remark on two-storeyed houses with carved wooden balconies and flat roofs constructed from mangrove poles, coral and zinc mortar. None of these have survived. The smaller dwellings had timber and latticed walls covered with mud and mortar and woven palm frond roofs, called *makuti*. The density of the housing and the materials made old Malindi very vunerable to fire, and periodic conflagrations (the most recent in 1965) destroyed all the older dwellings. The mosques survived by virtue of having walls of coral blocks and mortar.

For Excursions from Malindi, see page 259

The two buildings of note from the British period are the **District Officers' House** in front of Uhuru Gardens, and the **Customs House** behind the jetty. Both have verandahs, and neither is in particularly good repair, but the District Officers' House is a handsome and imposing structure.

In the centre of town, the **Uhuru Gardens** are being relaid. Close to the bus and *matatu* stand is the **Malindi Wood Carvers** located off Kenyatta Road, which is run as a co-operative. Ask to visit the workshops that are behind the shop. Many of the society's 350 members work in very poor conditions on a variety of wood. You will be able to see how some of the finely carved pieces are manufactured from the most unlikely looking material. Also in this area is the main market where, apart from clothing, vegetables and charcoal, you can see old cars being converted into pots and pans and other hardware.

On Government Road, between Uhuru Gardens and Kenyatta Road is the **Malindi Cotton Ginnery**. If you are in Malindi between September-January, the ginnery will be in operation. Much of the British-made machinery is over 70 years old, but still serviceable. There are some special machines for ginning kapok, used as an upholstery material. If you ask at the office, it is possible to look around.

Walking inland from the jetty, past the Customs House, you will see a **Maize Mill** on the left. Again, the owner will be happy to show you around. There is a British-made Yeoman mill dating from 1920, as well as some modern hammer-mills.

The area between here and Kenyatta Road to the northwest is the trading quarter, a hive of activity. Beyond it are the hotels and modern shopping malls. Access to the beach can be gained by a footpath located just beyond the Tourist Office and Galana shopping centre.

There are a couple of monuments that date from the Portuguese period, in particular the **Vasco da Gama Cross**, which is situated on the promontory at the southern end of the bay. It was erected to assist in navigation. The actual cross is the original and is made of stone from Lisbon, although the pillar on which it stands is constructed of local coral. You can reach it by turning down Mnarani Road.

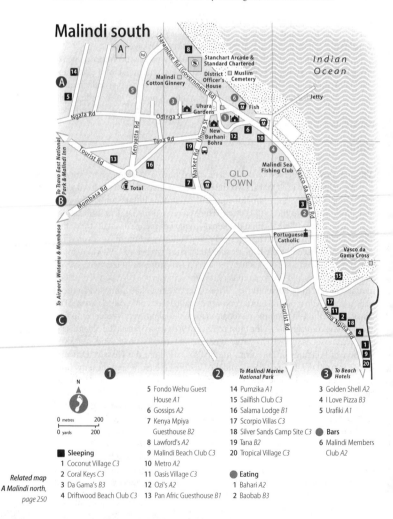

Malindi south

Indian Ocean

Jetty

OLD TOWN

Malindi Sea Fishing Club

Portuguese Catholic

Vasco da Gama Cross

Sleeping
1 Coconut Village *C3*
2 Coral Keys *C3*
3 Da Gama's *B3*
4 Driftwood Beach Club *C3*
5 Fondo Wehu Guest House *A1*
6 Gossips *A2*
7 Kenya Mpiya Guesthouse *B2*
8 Lawford's *A2*
9 Malindi Beach Club *C3*
10 Metro *A2*
11 Oasis Village *C3*
12 Ozi's *A2*
13 Pan Afric Guesthouse *B1*
14 Pumzika *A1*
15 Sailfish Club *C3*
16 Salama Lodge *B1*
17 Scorpio Villas *C3*
18 Silver Sands Camp Site *C3*
19 Tana *B2*
20 Tropical Village *C3*

Eating
1 Bahari *A2*
2 Baobab *B3*
3 Golden Shell *A2*
4 I Love Pizza *B3*
5 Urafiki *A1*

Bars
6 Malindi Members Club *A2*

Related map
A Malindi north,
page 250

The small **Catholic church** close to the cross is also believed to date from the Portuguese period and is thought to be the same one that St Francis Xavier visited in 1542 when he stopped off at Malindi to bury two soldiers on his way to India. It is one of the oldest Catholic churches in Africa still in use today and the walls are original, although the thatched roof has been replaced many times. Nearby are two graves, one of Sir Piers Edward Joseph Mostyn, the twelfth Baron Talacre, and the other of Geoffrey Herbert Locke of Tonbridge, Kent, England.

Both these monuments are about 1 km south of the centre. However, it may be worth hiring a bicycle to visit them. You could then continue along the beach (follow the sign to Vasco da Gama Cross but carry on up the hill – there is a path descending to the beach) and the marine park. The sand is hard and flat – a much better alternative to cycling along the main road.

Essentials

Tourism in Malindi is very seasonal, being packed into Jun-Aug. Outside these months you should bargain and can often pay as little as a third of the high-season rate. Malindi has expanded enormously in the past decade, geared mostly to Italian and German tourists. Some superb restaurants and hotels have been constructed, but there was a great deal of poor development too. Off-season, the large shopping complexes are empty, and about half of the large hotels are shut. The town has suffered from the recent down-turn in tourism in Kenya, and many hotels have closed.

Town Centre   The places in the town centre are mainly for the budget traveller. They often suffer from having more mosquitoes and being hotter as they do not get the sea breezes. They can also be noisy. **E** *Kenya Mpiya Guesthouse*, opposite market, PO Box 209, T31658. Some s/c, fans, no nets. **E** *New Lamu*, Tana Rd, about 50 m from bus station, PO Box 333, T20864. Nets, not s/c, simple but good value. **E** *Pan Afric Guesthouse*, Tana Rd, close to junction with Tourist Rd, PO Box 589, T31148. Small, friendly, not s/c, nets, no fans, cheap. **E** *Salama Lodge*, off Mombasa Rd, in town centre, PO Box 335. Small Swahili building, single storey, no fans, no nets, not s/c, cheap **E** *Tana*, PO Box 766, T20234. Well-run establishment, close to bus station, fans, net, restaurant, recently redecorated. **E** *Wanandil Lodgings*, on corner of intersection of Tana Rd and Mombasa Rd, PO Box 209, T2584. Above a rather lively bar with some splendid murals, no fans, no nets, but cheap.

North of Malindi   **L** *Club Che-Shale*, PO Box 492, T20063, F21257, about 8 km north of Malindi on a remote beach, has 12 thatched bandas with bathrooms and verandahs, they vary, some are a bit run-down. However it is a pleasant atmosphere and is located on a lovely secluded beach. There is plenty to do here sailing, deep-sea fishing and snorkelling, and there is a bar and restaurant which does top-class seafood dishes. **L** *Eden Roc*, PO Box 350, T20480/1/2, F20333, on a clifftop overlooking the bay in generous grounds containing lily ponds. There are over 150 rooms, all a/c with bathrooms as well as some cottages. It tends to cater to European package tours. It has its own beach, though water is 100 m away, and other facilities include swimming pool, tennis courts, watersports, scuba diving, deep-sea fishing, golf, and disco, massage and hair plaiting (US$40 a full head). **L** *Indian Ocean Lodge*, PO Box 171, T20394, F30032, is a very exclusive hotel with just 5 rooms and a private beach, it has been built of local materials in the Lamu Arab style and tastefully decorated, and is set in marvellous colourful gardens, the price includes meals and there are trips arranged, such as fishing, snorkelling and bird-watching, you can also go on a trip to the Gedi Ruins. **L** *Kingfisher Lodge*, some 3 km inland, PO Box 29, T21168, F20459. Thatched cottages round a pool, a/c, fans, small and exclusive, transport to beach, tennis, squash, golf and windsurfing available.

  B *Blue Marlin*, PO Box 54, T20440/1, F20459 (previously *Brady's Palm Beach Hotel*), was the first hotel to open in 1932. It is excellently run, under the same management as *Kingfisher Lodge* and *Lawford's*. Very friendly and has splendid facilities. Ernest Hemingway stayed here in 1934. **B** *Lawford's*, PO Box 20, T20440/1, F20459. This was the second hotel to open in this part of the coast being established in 1934, located very close to the town, under the same

Kenya

Sleeping
■ *on maps pages 250 and 252 For price codes: see inside front cover*

The great advantage that Malindi has over Mombasa is that there are inexpensive hotels located close to the beach. The more expensive hotels clear their section of the beach of seaweed

These hotels are strung out on the Lamu Rd to the north of the town

management as the *Blue Marlin*, except *Lawford's* is slightly cheaper. A new wing was built in the late 1970s and the hotel has singles, doubles and cottages. The rooms are nice although the restaurant only fair. There are 2 swimming pools, meeting rooms and the hotel organizes trips out to the reef in the glass-bottomed boat, water gymnastics, pool, volley ball, beach cricket. **B** *Palm Tree Club*, north end of town, just past Golf and Country Club, PO Box 180, T20397, F20706. Not on beach, but shuttle to the shore, s/c, a/c, excellently furnished, restaurant, pool, horse riding, tennis, golf, bowling.

C *Auberge du Chevalier Hotel and Restaurant Centre* (Kibokoni Hotel and Riding Centre), PO Box 857, T21273, F21030. Cottage-style accommodation, rather charmingly laid out, mostly for riding enthusiasts. **C** *Lutheran Guest House*, T21098, located to the north of the town off the Lamu Rd, PO Box 409, behind Sabaki Centre. This is good value and popular, there are a range of rooms singles and doubles with or without own bathroom, there is also a self-contained cottage, it is clean and the staff are very friendly. **C** *Malindi Cottages*, on Lamu Rd, opposite *Eden Roc Hotel*, PO Box 992, T20304, F21071. These cottages are self-contained and fully furnished with excellent facilities, each sleep 5, and everything is provided, there is a swimming pool in the complex. **C** *Sabaki River Cottage*, PO Box 5289, rodgers@jambo.swiftmalindi.com Cottage on a hill overlooking the mouth of Sabaki River, where thousands of birds, including flamingos, gather, about 8 km north of Malindi. Only 2 rooms, they are large and have en-suite bathrooms, meals can be arranged, camping is also possible. Good value in scenic location. Heading north from Malindi cross the bridge over the river, then immediately turn right to go through the village. Ask here for directions to the home of Rodgers Karabu, which is about 1 km further on. **D** *Fondo Wehu Guest House*, PO Box 5367, T30017, about 10 mins' walk from bus station. Includes excellent breakfast and laundry. Well recommended.

E *African Pearl*, PO Box 5342, on road to Lamu, T/F30917. Courtyard, fans, quite small, not s/c. **E** *Moriema Cottages*, on road to Lamu, PO Box 253, T30822/16, F20302. Includes breakfast, good value. **E** *Pumzika*, small, new guesthouse, on road that runs from *Blue Marlin* past *Surahi Restaurant*, s/c, hot water, good value.

South of Malindi **L** *African Dream Village*, PO Box 939, T20442-4, F20119. Run by the same group that run the *East African Dream Cottages,*further north, this caters for a slightly different type of holiday maker being a top-quality beach resort with full facilities, these include swimming pool, gym, bars and restaurant, all rooms are a/c with bathroom and verandah. **L** *Sailfish Club*, PO Box 243, T20016. This is a very small and exclusive hotel with just 9 rooms, it is very much geared to big-game fishing.

A *Coconut Village*, PO Box 868, T20252, F30103. A popular family hotel with good facilities, the bar has been cleverly built into and around a growing tree, and the disco is under a thatched roof on the beach, but despite all this, it lacks some character. **A** *Coral Keys*, PO Box 556, Mama Ngina Rd, T30717, F30715, about 2 km from town. Very attractive layout, 5 pools, tennis, beach bar, restaurant, videos, boutique. **A** *Kilili Baharini*, on Tourist Rd, about 4 km from town centre toward Casuarina Point, PO Box 1069, T20169, F21264. Pleasant hotel in thatched banda style, pool, restaurants, bars, a/c. **A** *New Kivulini Bay*, 7 km beyond Casuarina Point, on main road south at Leopard's Point, PO Box 5662, T20898, F31396, is a relatively new hotel. Highly recommended. Again it has cottages set in wonderful gardens, and it has it's own private beach, the food is superb and the hotel is very well managed. **A** *Oasis Village*, Mama Ngina Rd, about 2 km from centre, T30953. Well designed, pool, restaurant, bars. **A** *Silversands Villas* (*Blu Club*), PO Box 240, T20739, F20385, has a range of rooms and villas, the cottages are thatched with *makuti* and are set in wonderful gardens, it is tastefully decorated with bits and pieces from across Africa. It is very friendly and well managed, and has a very good restaurant attached. **A** *Tropical Village*, PO Box 68, T20256, F20788. High-standard hotel catering largely for package tours, with good facilities. **A** *White Elephant Sea Lodge*, PO Box 948, T20528, F20528, is a lovely hotel and good value, the cottages are decorated tastefully and are set in magnificent gardens on a beautiful stretch of beach. There is a swimming pool and very good restaurant.

B *Malindi Beach Club*, Mama Ngira Rd, about 3 km from town. Well located. **B** *Scorpio Villas*, PO Box 368, T20194, F21250, Mnarani Rd. This collection of about 17 villas is

A rare catch

A 1.7m long coelacanth weighing 77 kg was caught by fisherman off Malindi in 2001. The specimen has been transferred to the National Museum in Nairobi, where there are plans to display it. Until 1938 when a live specimen was discovered off the coast of South Africa, only fossilized remains of this rare fish dating back 360,000,000 years were known. Described as 'living fossils' coelacanths have fleshy lobes at the base of their paired fins that resemble arms and legs.

set in magnificent gardens. There are 3 swimming pools, a restaurant and bar and the beach is very close. The cottages are all fully furnished and self-sufficient and you even get your own cook, it is an excellently managed complex. **B-C** *Driftwood Beach Club*, PO Box 63, T20155, F30712. One of the older hotels in Malindi, this has managed to retain a clubby, but informal, character. It has a range of rooms including luxury cottages, doubles and singles (with own or shared bathroom), a/c, breakfast is included in the price and some of the rooms work out at very good value. Facilities include what is probably the best restaurant in Malindi (the seafood in particular is spectacular), watersports including fishing, diving and windsurfing, and a squash court. Temporary membership is very cheap, so a lot of people drop in to use the facilities. The service is friendly, often boozy, and ex-pat orientated. Reservations can be made directly through the Manager or through: ABC Place, Waiyaki Way, PO Box 60342, Nairobi, T447151, info@letsgosafari.com **C** *Mayungu*, PO Box 5182, T30437, some 15 km south on main road beyond Casuarina Point at Leopard's Point, restaurant, excellent beach, windsurfing. **C** *Stephanie Sea House*, Casuarina Point, close to marine park, 6 km from Malindi Centre, PO Box 583, T20720, F20613. Pool and restaurant.

D *Gossips*, previously called *Gilinis*, PO Box 380, on shore road near jetty, T20307. Italian owner, price does not include breakfast, fans, comfortable hotel with good restaurant. Well recommended. **D** *Ozi's*, PO Box 60, T20218, F30421. Situated overlooking the beach very close to the jetty, this hotel has a range of rooms. It is simple, but clean and good value and is one of the most popular of the budget hotels, and the price includes a very good breakfast. Tends to be noisy at night because of the proximity of the bus garage.

E *Bandas and Campsite*, at Casuaria, adjacent to Malindi Marine Park. Run by the Kenya Wildlife Service, there are simple bandas with mosquito nets and a camping area. Utensils and crockery are provided but you must bring all food. Very good value. Bandas must be booked in advance, PO Box 109, Malindi, T0123-20845, www.kws.org **E** *Da Gama's*, close to Portuguese Church on Vasco da Gama Rd, PO Box 5073, T30295. Above restaurant, fans, s/c, nets, pleasant atmosphere. **E** *Metro*, PO Box 361, T20400. This is popular and is located close to the *Gilini's*, fans, the rooms are, however, poky and stuffy and the water is unreliable, the people that run it are friendly, fans. **E** *Silver Sands Camp Site*, T20412. Located nearly 2 km out of town this campsite is popular with overlanders and other campers. The facilities are fairly good although there are sea-water showers only and if you do not have a tent you can rent one. There is also a small tented camp (these are tents with a thatched roof over them to keep them cool) and a bathroom and electric lights. There are also bandas with beds and mosquito nets which have shared bathrooms. It is situated on a lovely stretch of beach, and has a friendly atmosphere. There is a snack bar and restaurant, and a well stocked shop, although it's very close to the *Driftwood Club* which does excellent food at a reasonable price. You can also hire bicycles here, for a proper shower and a swim you can join the *Driftwood Club* for the day.

Expensive *Carni Africane alla Brace* (*Braciere*), just south of casino, T20552. Pleasant lay out of tables under awnings in a courtyard, with a big open-air charcoal grill, serving game meats, gazelle, zebra, giraffe, crocodile. *Fermento Bar*, Galana Centre, T31780. Only opens late, but serves Italian food and grills. *La Malindina*, PO Box 5342, T31448, this is located near the *Eden Roc Hotel*. Popular so book ahead in season, Italian food and Romanesque atmosphere by pool, rather special.

Eating
● *on maps*
pages 250 and 252

Most of the restaurants in the hotels are open to non-residents; their set menus and buffets are especially good value

Mid-range *Da Gama's*, just north of Portuguese Church, PO Box 5073, T30295. Omlettes, grills, seafood, fixed price menu, pleasant décor with red table cloths and stone floor. *Driftwood Club*, T20155. This is a nice way to spend a lazy day, you will need to join the Club as a temporary member – you will then be able to eat here as well as use their pool. The excellent restaurant has a set menu, an à la carte menu as well as serving snacks at the bar. *German Beer Garden*, T20533. This bistro, located to the north of the shopping centre, is good for snacks and a beer, it is particularly popular in the evenings. *I Love Pizza*, T20672, located on the Vasco da Gama Rd. This Italian restaurant is good value, it serves pizza, pasta, seafood dishes and other food. *Lorenzo's Restaurant*, Italian Garden Centre, north end of town, T31750. Good standard Italian food, quiet out of season. *Putipu Disco Bar*, opposite Galana Centre, T21132. Italian food, pastas, pizzas, grills. *Sportsmans*, at Falconry behind Malindi complex, T30456. Comfortable atmosphere, sound fare. *Stars and Garters*, opposite *Blue Marlin*. Grills, seafood, good coffee and ice-cream. *Vera Cruz*, opposite Malindi Complex. Grills, seafood.

Cheap *African Pearl*, north end of town. Moderately priced al fresco-style restaurant. *Karen Blixen Café*, Galana Centre, Lamu Rd. Imaginatively designed, sandwiches, juices, coffee, parsols and outside tables, photos of Karen Blixen and Denys Finch-Hatton. *La Gelateria*, T123/20710, located on Lamu Rd. This is the best place in town for ice-creams – they are excellent, good for a coffee and a snack. *Malindi Sea Fishing Club*, PO Box 364, above *Kingfisher Safaris* office, just south of jetty, T30550. Temporary membership available for US$1, and well worth it as the food (grills, seafood) is modestly priced, comfortable club decor, bar, fishing photos, excellent views out over the ocean. *Palm Garden Restaurant*, T20115, also located on Lamu Rd, opposite the *Shell* petrol station. You can sit in the shade of bandas, the food is fine – curries, chicken, seafood and so on – and it is very good value. There is also a lively bar that has live music at the weekends and an ice-cream parlour (rather run down).

Seriously cheap *Baobab Café*, PO Box 5068, T31699. This is located close to the Portuguese church and has a wide ranging menu, you can have breakfast here, snacks and a beer or fruit juice, as well as full meals. *Garden View Café*, by Uhuru Gardens. Pleasant location, simple fare. *Golden Shell*, close to town centre, T30969. Clean and bright, grills and African dishes. *Juice Bar*, in front of Malindi Complex. Excellent juices and local foods. *Malindi Fruit Juice Garden*, is ideal for a break on a hot day, located close to the market, as the name suggests they do very good fruit juice as well as milk shakes. There are a couple of places in the town centre which are good for Indian and traditional African food, such as *ugali* and stew: *Bahari Restaurant*, close to the Juma Mosque. Excellent chapatis, beef stew, good value, and *Urafiki Bar and Restaurant*, on Kenyatta Rd.

Bars *African Pearl*, north end of town. Pleasant gardens, live band on Sun during high season (Jun-Aug). *Fermente Bar*, Galana Centre, T31750. Disco, karaoke and occasional live music, gets under way at about 2300. *Hermann's Beer Garden*, opposite Galana Centre. Open-air bar. *Iguana Bar*, Italian Garden Centre on Lamu Rd, north end of town. Quiet out of season, serves food, mostly grills. *Malindi Members Club*, large open air bar on beach side of Government Rd. It is not necessary to be a member. *Malindi Sea Fishing Club*, on shore road above *Kingfisher Safaris*, south of jetty. Temporary membership US$1, but well worth it as drinks are modestly priced, members congregate for lunch and sundowners, excellent vista over ocean. *Palm Garden*, at intersection of Kenyatta and Government Rd. Very pleasant atmosphere, with several bar areas, live bands at weekends. *Putipu Disco Bar*, opposite Galana Centre. Serves Italian food, pizzas, grills, wicker furniture, dance area. *T-T-Bar and Restaurant*, opposite *Blue Marlin*. Pleasant open air-style with thatched bandas, coffee, ice-cream and grills. *Vera Cruz*, opposite Malindi Complex. Huge concrete replica of the prow of Vasco de Gama's sailing ship, serving as a disco, bar and restaurant. *Wananchi Day and Nightclub*, Tana Rd, town centre. Lively local bar, with huge murals decorating the interior.

Entertainment There is plenty to do in the evenings in Malindi and there are a number of bars and discos. The bigger discos are found at the larger hotels. There is also occasionally live music – ask around at the hotels. **Casino** The *Malindi Casino*, T30878, F30570, is open daily from mid-day, and entrance is free. Blackjack and roulette. **Cinema** *Hero*, near market, mostly Indian films, pleasant building with a little courtyard. The hotels who often have **video shows**. Also the *Malindi Fishing Club* which has regular showings.

Discos *Stardust Club*, T20388, starts fairly late in the evenings but is nevertheless very popular. *Casino Disco*, next to *Stardust Club*, attractive bars with thatched cover and dance area, no entry charge. *Ruputi Disco Bar*, opposite Galana Centre. *Fermento Bar*, T31780, Galana Centre, karaoke and piano bar. *Vera Cruz*, opposite Malindi Complex. The *Tropicana Club 28*, T20480, is situated up near *Eden Roc Hotel* and is small, friendly and popular. *Lawford's*, has a disco, as does *Coconut Village* (open-air on the beach) and a number of the other large hotels. The bar at the *Coconut Village* is well worth seeing – it has been cleverly constructed into and around a tree. *Cacao Club*, at Scorpio Villas, south of centre, PO Box 102, T31198. **Live bands** *Sea Breeze* play at the *Africa Pearl* at the north end of town on Sun during the season (Jun-Aug).

Bookshops There is a bookshop next to *Barclays Bank* at the **Sitawi Shopping Centre**, but with very limited choice. **Handicrafts** Most of the craft shops are close to the beach and the jetty. In general the quality is reasonably good as are the prices – although you must expect to bargain. *Zai Noor Gift Shop*, near Uhuru Gardens, has wicker and basketry items as well as earthenware pieces. *Our Shop*, on the corner of Uhuru St and Government Rd has high-quality handicraft items. *Nafisa Store*, on Government Rd, near Uhuru Gardens, also styled the *Africa Curio Museum*, is quite good, and the prices are reasonable. *Al Noor Gallery*, on Goram Mast Rd, near Uhuru Gardens is a high-class establishment with antique items in wood and metal, including many pieces from Ethiopia. *Shezan*, just north of Galana Centre. Attractive antique items of Indian origin. *Kongonis*, just north of Portuguese Church, PO Box 605, expensive but high-quality t-shirts, bead design sandals, sisal bags.

Shopping

Golf and Country Club, north end of town, right fork off Lamu Rd, T31402. Tennis, 9 hole golf course and squash, inexpensive daily membership available. Daily membership for squash also available at *Driftwood Beach Club*. *Coral Keys* has an artificial climbing wall, supervised by qualified staff. Horse-riding available at *Kibokoni Riding Centre*, T21273.

Sport

Deep-sea fishing: *Baharini Ventures*, PO Box 435, T20879. *Kingfisher*, PO Box 29, Malindi, T21168, F03261. UK agents: *Swahili Connections*, 8 Balls Lane, Thursford, Norfolk NR21 0BX, T01328-878173, F878989. *Malindi Sports Fishing Club*, PO Box 163, T20161; *Malindi Sea Fishing Club*, PO Box 364, T20410, south of jetty. Has notice board for fishermen. *Peter Ready*, PO Box 63, Malindi, T21292, F30032. *Slaters*, PO Box 147, Watamu, T12 (via operator); *Von Menyhart*, PO Box 360, T20840.

Scuba diving *Driftwood Club*, PO Box 63, T20155, at Silver Sands which charges about US$8 per dive, also a diving school; *Guarami Diving Centre*, Kirulini Village, T21267; *Riki Diving*, at Coral Key, T30717; *Talas Diving Centre*, at Blu Club, T20453; *Tropical Diving Club*, at Tropical Village, T20256; *Venta Diving*, Club Jambo, at Casuarina Point by Marine Park, PO Box 444, T21245; *Crab Diving*, at tropical village and *African Dream Hotels*, T20443/4, PADI course US$100 for 5 days.

Windsurfing Arrange through the centre next to the *White Elephant Hotel* at the south end of the beach.

In Malindi: *Prince Safaris*, Silver Sand Road, PO Box 966, T20596, by the main jetty, organize dhow trips. There are several options: safaris, fishing or just sailing and they involve a variety of activities including barbecues on the beach. Prices are around US$60 per person, minimum 4 to 6 people.

Tours & tour operators

Abercrombie & Kent, PO Box 1072, T21169, F30280. *Duna Safaris*, PO Box 1001, T21015, T071-414015 (mob), F30258. *Falcony of Kenya Ltd*, Safari Section: PO Box 1003, T30455, F30455. *Galu Safari Ltd*, PO Box 650, Lamu Rd, T20493, F30032. *Haya Safari Africa Ltd*, PO Box 73, T20374, F20846. *Hewa Tours and Safaris*, PO Box 5322, T21211, F30064. *Hot Sun Safaris*, PO Box 5333, T20190. *Kingfisher Safaris*, south of jetty, PO Box 29, T20123.

Kenya

North Coast Travel Services, centre of town, near *Blue Marlin Hotel*, tours, safaris, car hire, railway and TNT services, PO Box 476, T20531(office), T21294 (home), North Coast, F30313. *Peacock Tours & Travel Ltd*, PO Box 689, T20097, F20097, Uhuru St, opposite DO's office. Arranges adventure diving. *Pollman's Tours and Safaris*, PO Box 384, T20128, F20820. *Private Safaris (East Africa) Ltd*, T30573/4. *Scorpio Tours Ltd*, PO Box 368, T21242, F21250. *Sudi Sudi Safaris*, near jetty, PO Box 966, T20596. Deep-sea fishing, dhow trips, flights to game parks, bike hire. *Sunflower Safaris Ltd*, PO Box 1031, T20822, F30203. *Tusker Safaris Ltd*, PO Box 5348, T30525, F30868, Galana Centre. *United Touring Company*, PO Box 365, T20040, F30443. *WK Ltd*, PO Box 635, T20225, F20226. *Zaitour Kenya Ltd*, PO Box 1059, T31018, F31019, Malindi Complex.

Transport   **Local Bicycle hire**: *Malindi Bike Rental*, near *Stardust Club*, PO Box 1177, T31741, about US$10 a day; *Sudi Sudi Safaris*, on shore road near jetty, PO Box 966, T20596, US$6 a day. If you are using a bike for more than a day, bargain for lower rate. *Silver Sands Camp Site*, *Ozi's Guest House* and a stall just outside the *Tropicana Club 28*. The quality of the bikes varies, so check thoroughly before you choose one. It is possible to buy a new bike on Tana Rd, town centre US$100-120.

Car hire: *Glory Car Hire*, centre of town, close to *Blue Marlin Hotel*, PO Box 994, T123-20065; *Kotsman Car Hire*, PO Box 262, Malindi, T20777; *Avis Car Rental*, opposite *Blue Merlin hotel*. Some hotels also have motorbikes for hire (about US$35 per day). Arrange on a daily basis as there are not many places to visit.

Air The airport at Malindi is served by 3 airlines, as well as by chartered planes for safaris. About 3 km south of the town, a taxi to the centre costs about US$3 and the hotels to the south will be about US$6. *Kenya Airways*, PO Box 634, Malindi, T20237, at the airport: T20192, F20173, does the Nairobi-Mombasa-Malindi route once a day in both directions (except Sat). It is a popular route so be sure to book well ahead and confirm your seat. Some travellers have reported problems with double booking. Serving this route are *Equator Airlines*, T32053 (Malindi), and *Air Kenya*, Galana Centre, on Lamu Rd north of town, PO Box 548, T30808, F21229, who have daily direct flights between Malindi and Nairobi, return US$140. They also serve the Mombasa-Malindi-Lamu-Kiwayu route. Return fares from Malindi to Mombasa, Lamu and Kiwayu are US$50, US$140 and US$250 respectively. Baggage allowance is only 10 kg, and check in time is 30 mins before take off. Airport tax is around US$1.

Train There is no train to Malindi, but your hotel or a travel agent will reserve a sleeper on the Mombasa-Nairobi train for you (they will charge). Just as easy, and about a tenth of the price, is to ring and do it yourself, T011-312221.

Road Bus: there are plenty of buses between **Malindi** and **Mombasa** – there are 4 companies (*Malindi Bus Service*, *Mombasa and Coast Express*, *Garissa Express* and *Tana River Bus Service*) all of which have a number of departures each day. They all have offices in Malindi (around the bus station), Mombasa and Lamu but booking is not usually necessary. They mostly leave early in the morning and take about 2½ to 3 hrs, they cost about US$1. Non-stop *matatus* are faster, and take under 2 hrs. They leave when full throughout the day and cost about US$2.

You can also get the bus to **Lamu** but you should book in advance and check out the current security situation (see below). The trip takes about 5 hrs and costs about US$4. They leave in the morning between 0700 and 0800. If you miss these you might be able to get onto one of the Mombasa buses that get to Malindi about 0830 and go on at 0930 – but there is no guarantee that you will get a seat. The bus will take you to the jetty on the mainland from where you get a ferry across to Lamu (see page 275). The safer, more spectacular and inevitably more expensive option is to fly with *Air Kenya* (US$100 one way). **NB** There have been on-going security problems, including fatalities, with armed bandits known locally as *shifta* on the road to Lamu over the past few years. Vehicles often travel in convoy, accompanied by armed guards. It is advisable to check the situation locally before finalizing your plans.

Swahili culture

The coastal region is the centre of this distinct and ancient civilization. The Swahili are not a tribe as such – they are joined together by culture and language – Ki-Swahili – which is the most widely spoken language in East Africa. It is one of the Bantu languages and was originally most important as a trading language. It contains words derived from Arabic, Indian as well as English and Portuguese.

The Swahili civilization emerged from the meeting of East Africa, Islam, the classical world and eastern civilizations. Traders, as well as immigrants, from Asia and Arabia have had a gradual influence on the coast shaping society, religion, language as well as literature and architecture. These traders arrived at the ports of the east coast by the northeast monsoon winds which occur in March and April (the Kaskazi wind) and left around September on the southerly wind (the Kusi wind). Inevitably some stayed or were left behind and there was intermarriage between the immigrants and the indigenous people. Many families trace their roots back to traders from foreign shores and there is a complex social system.

Slavery was important to the coastal region and was not entirely an alien phenomenon. For long before slaves were being rounded up from the interior and shipped overseas, there was an important although rather different 'slave trade'. This involved a family 'lending' a member of the family (usually a child) to another richer family or trader in exchange for food and other goods. That child would then live with the family and work for them – essentially as a slave – until the debt had been paid off. However, in the same way as with bonded child labourers in India today, the rates of interest demanded often ensured that the debt could never be paid off and the person would remain effectively a slave. Later slavery became an important part of trade and commerce and the old system was replaced with something much more direct. Many slaves were rounded up from the interior (some of them 'sold' by tribal chiefs and village elders) and taken to the coast. Here they would either be sold overseas to Arabia via Zanzibar or put to work on the plantations that were found all along the coast. Successive measures by the British formally ended the slave trade by 1907 although it did continue underground for many years. When slaves were released they were gradually absorbed into the Swahili culture although their antecedents are known it means it is almost impossible to be rid of the stigma associated with being a slave.

Kenya

Taxis: Peugeot 504 share-taxis do the Mombasa-Malindi route. These take 7 passengers and go in the mornings when full. They cost about the same as a *matatu* (US$2).

Banks There are a number of banks in Malindi. *Barclays*, is on the main coastal road (the Lamu road) opposite the *Blue Marlin Hotel* and is open on weekdays 0830-1700 with a break for lunch from 1300-1430, and on Sat from 0830-1200. There is also a *Standard Chartered Bank*, close to the police station and post office. *Kenya Commercial Bank*, PO Box 9, T20148. **Medical services** *Malindi District Hospital*, PO Box 4, T20490. **Dentist**: *Dr Maurizio Lacopo*, T31098. **Optician**: *Vijay Optico*, Lamu Rd, opposite Malindi Complex. **Pharmacy**: *Buhani Pharmacy*, Government Rd, near Uhuru Gardens. **Useful information** Tidal information: posted at Customs and Excise, just near jetty. **Directory**

Excursions from Malindi

You can take a cruise whilst in this part of Kenya. They are usually for two or three nights and are along the delta of the river Tana and tributaries situated to the north of Malindi. It is an expensive excursion – but you will be very well looked after and the food is excellent. The price includes all food, transport and day trips. You can be picked up from the airport or from Malindi, and will be taken by four-wheel drive to the camp on the river bank. While you are there you can swim, do several watersports, go on river trips, bird-watching and animal-tracking. For details and reservations: *Tana Delta*, PO Box 24988, Nairobi (T882826) or through *Bush Homes of East Africa Ltd*, PO Box 56923, Nairobi, PO Box 56923, T01-571647, F571665, www.bush-homes.co.ke **Tana River**

Kenya

Malindi Marine Biosphere Reserve
3° 12′ N, 40° 15′ E
Colour map 3, grid C6

This strip along the coast is 30 km long and 5 km wide and includes Mida Creek. The reserve, gazetted in 1968, covers an area of 213 sq km. It lies about 80 km north of Mombasa, and includes the Malindi Marine National Park and the Watamu Marine National Reserve and National Park. The vegetation includes mangrove, palms, marine plants and various forms of algae that are home to crabs, corals, molluscs, cowrie and marine worms. Coral viewing is popular here, as are boat trips and watersports. **Whale Island** is a nesting ground for roseate and bridled tern, and there are a number of other shore birds here.

Malindi Marine National Park Situated within the Malindi Marine Biosphere Reserve is this small marine national park. Gazetted in 1968 this is an area of only 6 sq km that offers wonderful diving and snorkelling on the coral reefs off Casuarina Point. This park is popular and with good reason. The water is brilliantly clear, and the fish are a dazzling array of colours. There are two main reefs with a sandy section of sea bed dividing them. You can hire all the equipment that you will need and a boat here, but it is advisable to check your mask and snorkel before accepting. The fish are very tame as they have been habituated by being fed on bread provided by the boatman. If you see any shells be sure to leave them there for the next visitor – the shell population has suffered very severely from the increase in tourism. Try and go at low tide as the calmer the sea, the better; also be sure to take some sort of footwear that you can wear in the water. You will also be taken to one of the sand bars just off the reef: take plenty of sun protection. You can organize the trip through your hotel, many of which seem to have arrangements with local boat owners. Be sure to enquire whether the rate includes the national park entrance fee. Nearby is **Crocodile Paradise** with hundreds of crocs as well as snakes and other reptiles. ■ *0900-1750 daily.*

Other excursions

Lake Chem Chem Rhino Reserve This is about 8 km from town on the Tsavo Road. The road is very bad but you can get a *matutu* to Ghardan. Get dropped off at the turning and then walk about 200 m. There is only one rhino at the moment but you can go on a bird-watching tour for about US$25, although it may be possible to negotiate a better rate with the park guards. The lake is dry for most of the year but the birdlife is varied and more plentiful from May to August. **Camel safaris** are also organized for about US$60. Further information from Marcus Russell, Galdesa Office, T31084.

Arabuko-Sokoke Forest is about 20 km south toward Mombasa, with the wildlife service post at the entrance just past Gedi and the road to Watamu. The forest runs for about 40 km south to Kilifi and, at its widest, for 20 km inland. The birds and butterflies are the main attraction as well as some small mammals.

Malindi Falconry This is located a little to the north of the town behind Malindi Complex on the Lamu Road. Said to be the only falconry in the country, there are eagles, hawks, buzzards, kites and owls as well as falcons. ■ *0930-1800. PO Box 1003, T/F31240. Food and refreshments available from bar and restaurant.* Close to the Falconry on Lamu Road is a **Snake Park**. Feeding time (the snakes are fed live mice) is 1600 on Wednesday and Friday. ■ *0900-1800. US$4 adults, US$2 children. PO Box 104, T21084.*

Akambo Village can be visited, T21245. It provides an example of the traditional life of the Kamba people (see page 310). **Gedi Ruins and National Park** are 16 km south of Malindi (see page 246). A visit can be combined with a trip to the **Watamu Marine Park** (see page 244).

Malindi to Lamu

Soon after leaving Malindi you cross the Sabaki River, and then the turning for the village of **Mambrui**. This village is believed to be about 600 years old and all that remains of the ancient Arab City is a mosque, a Koran school and a pillar tomb, which has insets of Ming porcelain. Further on you will eventually pass **Garsen**, a small town at the crossing of the Tana River where you can get petrol and drinks. It also has a health centre, PO Box 42, T35 (Garsen). Just south of Garsen on the Tana River there is a **Birdlife Sanctuary**, home to many herons. From here the road turns back towards the coast and **Witu**, another small old town. As you drive in this area you may see people of the Orma tribe as well as Somalis, for this is getting close to the border. Both groups are pastoralists, and you will see the cattle that represent their wealth. Finally, about five hours after leaving Malindi, you will get to **Mokowe** and you will see the Makanda channel which separates Lamu from the mainland.

By road
The security situation along this route has deteriorated; only travel by road in convoys accompanied by armed protection, as gangs of shiftas still roam the area attacking solitary buses and cars

Flying to Lamu is a fantastic way to get a handle on the geography of Kenya's coast. Just a few kilometres north of Malindi, tarmaced roads become dirt tracks that criss-cross each other and lead to tiny rural settlements shrouded in palmy forest. Sand spits stretch tentacles out into the blue Indian Ocean. After less than an hour you fly over the island of Lamu, a flat mangrove creek paradise with miles of deserted white beach along its south coast. The plane lands on the airstrip on Manda island, just to the north, from where you need to catch a boat across to Lamu. Some of the more expensive hotels will ferry you and your luggage over from the airstrip, otherwise ask around at the jetty and someone will be happy to take you across for a few shillings. (See Lamu transport, page 275.)

By air

Situated 120 km north of Malindi on the Tana River between Hola and Garsen, the Tana River National Primate Reserve (TRNPR) is a highly diversified riverine forest, that has at least seven different types of primate including the Tana River red colobus and crested Mangabay monkeys. This is the sole habitat of these endangered primates. A number of other animals roam here including elephant, hippo, baboon, gazelle, duiker, lesser kudu, oryx, river hog, giraffe, lion, waterbuck, bush squirrel and crocodiles. The TRNPR is located on the lower reaches of the Tana River, covering an area of 169 sq km of which 11 sq km is riverine forest. There is a research station for study of the primates. It is possible to go boating down the swirling Tana River. This reserve has been under threat by human demands for its resources.Clearing and cultivation have been problematic, along with the damage resulting from the pastoralists bringing their animals here for water. A project to reverse this trend with the participation of the local people has been started, supported by international donors including the *World Bank*. A programme of resettlement of the people currently living and farming inside the reserve has begun.

Tana River National Primate Reserve
2° 30′ N, 40° 30′ E

  Planned activites include a bio-diversity inventory, primate monitoring, tree planting and forest restoration of about 60 ha, mapping and developing trails and tourist facilities. Park security will be enhanced and facilities developed to support the projecct. **Camping**   is available at **E** *Mchelelo Camp* in an attractive site.

Transport There are buses running between Lamu and Garissa, and some of them detour to **Mnazini** village just to the south of the reserve, from where it is possible to walk north along the river (there is a small boat ferry just before Baomo Village) to the campsite.

Northeast of the Tana River Primate National Reserve, on the eastern side of the Tana River south of Bura, is the Arawale National Reserve, which covers an area of 1,165 sq km. It is located in Northeastern Province, approximately 78 km south of Garissa. The Tana River marks its western boundary, with a river frontage of 48 km. It is the only area in Kenya where Hunter's hartebeest can be found with their lyre-shaped horns.

Arawale National Reserve
1° S, 40° E

Kenya

The thorny bushland also has zebra, elephant, lesser kudu, buffalo, hippo and crocodiles. Birdlife is abundant and very varied, and include the African golden oriole, the nubian nightjar and the pygmy falcon. There are no tourist facilities and no access roads, so a four-wheel drive vehicle is necessary to visit the reserve. This also means that there is no gate into the reserve, and thus no charge to visit.

Lamu

2° 16' S, 40° 55' E
Phone code: 121
Colour map 3, grid C6

Lamu Island is a laid-back sort of place that makes the quieter spots of Kenya's east coast seem like throbbing metropoli. And yet, at the same time, it is one of the most cosmopolitan few square miles of Kenya, where you are as likely to bump into stockbrokers from Wall Street, Hugh Grant look-alikes from Notting Hill Gate and members of various European royal families as you are Aussie backpackers. The island takes tourism seriously – it is, after all, the main source of income – but does it with a style that is often lacking in other parts of the country. With a fast-growing local population of about 12,000 people – the vast majority of whom are Muslim – and the expansion in tourism, pressure of numbers on the island is becoming a problem. But Lamu really is a paradise; it is so serene and so beautiful that you will want to stay forever.

Ins & outs   **Getting there**   *Air Kenya* and *Kenya Airways* both have flights to the airstrip on Manda Island. From there, you can get a boat taxi or dhow across to Lamu. Despite travelling in

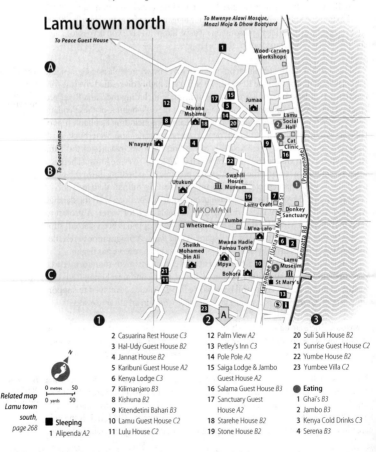

Lamu town north

Related map
Lamu town south,
page 268

Sleeping
1 Alipenda *A2*
2 Casuarina Rest House *C3*
3 Hal-Udy Guest House *B2*
4 Jannat House *B2*
5 Karibuni Guest House *A2*
6 Kenya Lodge *C3*
7 Kilimanjaro *B3*
8 Kishuna *B2*
9 Kitendetini Bahari *B3*
10 Lamu Guest House *C2*
11 Lulu House *C2*
12 Palm View *A2*
13 Petley's Inn *C3*
14 Pole Pole *A2*
15 Saiga Lodge & Jambo Guest House *A2*
16 Salama Guest House *B3*
17 Sanctuary Guest House *A2*
18 Starehe House *B2*
19 Stone House *B2*
20 Suli Suli House *B2*
21 Sunrise Guest House *C2*
22 Yumbe House *B2*
23 Yumbee Villa *C2*

Eating
1 Ghai's *B3*
2 Jambo *B3*
3 Kenya Cold Drinks *C3*
4 Serena *B3*

People of Lamu

The people of Lamu are a mixture of Swahili-speaking people of Arab and African ancestry – with much of the East African blood being brought in by the movement of slaves through this area. Some broad groupings can, however, be distinguished:

Swahili and Bajun Taking advantage of the monsoon winds, traders visited these shores annually in search of ivory, gold and slaves. Arabs, Indians, Persians and Chinese visited the coast and over the years some remained, intermarried with the local people and built up city states. The Afro-Arab peoples, who shared their Islamic faith and way of life became known as the Swahilis. Both the Swahili and the Bajun people claim Arab ancestry, although it is very much mixed with African blood. There is a rural-urban distinction between Bajun and Swahili with the Swahili mainly in the towns. The Bajun people also often claim Somali ancestry as well as Arabic origins.

Oromo or Galla The Oromo people (or Galla as they are also known), are nomadic pastoralists and mainland dwellers who for many years were a great influence on Lamu. While the Arabs and the Swahili speaking people of the islands and mainland were all

Muslims, the Oromo retained their traditional beliefs. They were an aggressive people and a number of towns were abandoned as a result of their incessant pillaging. The ways of the Oromo have changed considerably since the 19th century and at the present they are suffering from pressure on their land.

Omani Arabs At the turn of the 19th century the Swahili and Bajun, including descendants of slaves, formed the majority of the population, with the wangwana (free or nobly born) ruling the communities. During the 19th century Omani Arabs started to arrive until eventually they became the most politically powerful group, despite being outnumbered a thousand to one by the Swahili and Bajun. A governor was appointed to the island who was usually closely related to the Sultan of Zanzibar, and he and other officials settled with their families.

Asians During the 19th century Asians, both Muslims and Hindus, came to Lamu to work as merchants and traders. While the Hindus often came on a more temporary basis and returned to India, many of the Muslim Asians came with their families and formed more permanent communities.

convoys with armed escorts, the bus service to Lamu continues to be targeted by bandits. In recent years there have been some fatalities. Not recommended. **Getting around** There are no vehicles on the island except for the District Commissioner's Land Rover. Even if they were allowed, the narrow streets would make driving impossible in town. Instead there are donkeys and bicycles. **Safety** Safety is not a major problem in Lamu. However, there have been a number of incidents over the last few years. Avoid waking around alone after dark in secluded areas of town and don't go to remote parts of the island unless you are with a group. If you are alone on the beach, stay within shouting distance of other people. **Tourist office** Lama Tourist Information Centre (LATIC) is located on the harbour front to the north of the landing jetty, just south of the German Post Office Museum on Harambee Rd and next to the Swahili Cultural Centre Gift Shop, PO Box 210, T33449, F33251, lamupoly@africaonline.co.ke The staff are friendly, they can organize walking tours of the town and dhow trips for fishing or snorkelling, or trips to surrounding islands. Closed on Sun and public holidays. The increase in tourism has led to an inevitable rise in the number of touts or '**beach boys**'. If they accompany you to your hotel, a substantial 'commission' (33-50%) will be added to u your daily rate. To avoid using their services, carry your own bags to a seafront restaurant first, have a drink and look for accommodation later. You will have no problem finding a room.

Geography The island covers an area of about 3,500 ha. The coral rock is covered with sandy soil, and about a third of the island is covered with sand dunes. Although these render this part uncultivable the dunes serve an important purpose for they act as a filter for the water. Despite this, Lamu does often suffer from severe water shortages and supplies are often limited to certain times of the day. The island also has a fairly

Shela gold

In 1915 a man called Albert Deeming was convicted of the murder of a woman and two children in Melbourne, Australia. He was sentenced to death but before his execution he prepared a document detailing the whereabouts of 50 kilos of gold bars buried on Lamu Island.

In 1901, Deeming had boarded the bullion train from Pretoria to Laurenco-Marques, shot two guards and forced a third to open the bullion compartments. Grabbing as many bars as he could carry he jumped the train and made his way to the coast. At Delgoa Bay, he sailed by dhow to Lamu, but locals were suspicious, and he hid the gold at a small European graveyard at Shela, in the grave of William Searle, a British sailor who died after falling from the rigging of his ship.

Deeming's belongings were eventually returned to his relatives in South Africa, and one of them made a visit to Lamu in 1919, but was unable to locate the grave.

In 1947 the documents passed to a Kenyan farmer, who with a couple of companions travelled to Lamu and found the Shela graveyard. Four graves were marked, but none of them had the name of William Searle. Convinced that this must be the graveyard described by Deeming they began probing the sands. They located a solid object and removed the covering of sand. It was a gravestone with a well-weathered crack. Deeming's instructions were that the gold was in a small wooden box at the head of the grave, at a depth of two feet. Despite extensive excavations they found nothing. They were curious over the fact that an area of sand appeared less compacted than that of its surroundings. Also, when they examined the gravestone it had some cracks that looked quite recent. They made discreet enquiries in Lamu Town. Four weeks earlier a party of three Australians from Melbourne had visited Lamu and had spent two days at the Shela sand-dunes.

extensive area of mangrove swamps, and the only cultivable part of the island lies between the dunes and the marshy swamps. The conditions of Lamu are most suitable for coconut plantations and mango trees.

History

The town of Lamu was founded in the 14th century, although there were people living on the island long before this. Throughout the years, and as recently as the 1960s, the island has been a popular hide-out for refugees fleeing the mainland.

The original settlement of Lamu was located to the south of the town, and is said to be marked by Hidabu hill. There was also another settlement between the 13th and 15th centuries to the north of the present town.

By the 15th century it was a thriving port, one of the many that dotted the coast of East Africa. However in 1505 it surrendered to the Portuguese, began paying tributes, and for the next 150 years was subservient to them, and to the sultanate of the town of Pate on the nearby island, part of the Omani Dynasty that ruled much of the East African coast.

By the end of the 17th century Lamu had become a republic ruled by a council of elders called the Yumbe, who were in principle responsible to Oman. In fact the Yumbe were largely able to determine their own affairs, and this period has been called Lamu's Golden Age. It was the period when many of the buildings were constructed and Lamu's celebrated architectural style evolved. The town became a thriving centre of literature and scholarly study and there were a number of poets who lived here. Arts and crafts flourished and trade expanded. The main products exported through Lamu were mangrove poles, ivory, rhino horn, hippo teeth, shark fins, cowrie shells, coconuts, cotton, mangoes, tamarind, sim sim (oil), charcoal and cashews.

Rivalries between the various trading settlements in the region came to a head when Lamu finally defeated Pate in the battle of Shela in 1813. However, after 1840 Lamu found itself dominated by Zanzibar which had been developed to become the dominant power along the East African coast. At a local level there were factions and splits within the town's population – in particular rivalries between different clans and other interest groups.

New products were developed for export including *beche de mère* (a seafood), mats, bags, turtle shell, leather, rubber and sorghum. Despite this, toward the end of the 19th century Lamu began a slow economic decline as Mombasa and Zanzibar took over in importance as trading centres. The end of the slave trade dealt a blow to Lamu as the production of mangrove poles and grains for export depended on slave labour. Additionally, communications between the interior and Mombasa were infinitely better than those with Lamu, especially after the building of the railway. Many of the traditional exports still pass through Lamu, particularly mangrove poles that contain an extract that resists termites and are used for traditional buildings as roof rafters along the Indian Ocean coast and in the Middle East. Poles can be seen stacked on the Promenade, just south of the main jetty, waiting to catch the dhows sailing north on the September trade winds. In recent decades the tourist trade has helped improve Lamu's economic prospects.

Lamu town

A wonderful old Muslim **stone town** known to locals as *Mkomani*, Lamu town has distinctive architecture, carved doors, narrow streets, an absence of vehicles, donkeys, many mosques, a bustling jetty where fishermen pull up in dhows as well and motorboats and women dressed in black and wearing the *bui bui* who chat in the street. It is the largest (and oldest) stone town on the East African coast, but is still easy to walk around. The town dates back to the 14th century although most of the buildings are actually 18th century, built in Lamu's Golden Age. The streets are very narrow, and the buildings on each side are two or three storeys high. The streets are set in a rough grid pattern running off the main street which is called the Usita wa Mui (formerly Main Street) now known as **Harambee Avenue**. Usita wa Mui runs parallel to the harbour and used to open out to the sea, although building from the mid-1800s onwards has cut it off from the quayside.

Mkomani is a very secluded place where the houses face inwards and privacy is carefully guarded. The families who live in these houses are mainly the patrician *wangwana* who keep themselves to themselves. The non-patricians who reside in Mkomani live there as clients of the patricians, employed or providing services and are often descendants of their patron's slaves. At the edges of the town live people of slave and immigrant ancestry.

Carved doors are one of the attractions for which Lamu has become known. The artesanal skill continues to be taught, and at the north end of the harbour you can see them being made in workshops by craftsmen and apprentices. The maze of streets in the Old Town mean that it is easy to get lost; just bear in mind that Harambee Avenue runs parallel to the waterfront and the all the streets leading into town from the shore slope uphill slightly.

Mosques There are a number of mosques on the island (over 20), but mostly they are usually not very grand affairs and some are little different from other buildings. You will need to seek permission before entering to look around.

The oldest mosque in Lamu is believed to be the **Pwani Mosque**, near the fort, which dates back to 1370. The **Jumaa** (or Friday) **Mosque** is at the north end of town and is the second oldest in Lamu, dating from 1511. Then comes the **M'na Lalo Mosque** (1753), more or less in the centre of town, just a little to the north of the museum and set back from Harambee Avenue. This mosque was built in Lamu's Golden Age, and it was followed by **Muru Mosque** (1821) on Harambee Avenue, **Utukuni Mosque** (1823), well into the interior part of the town, and **Mpya Mosque** (1845), in the town centre. **Mwana Mshamu Mosque** (1855) is in the northwest area of the town; **Sheikh Mohamed bin Ali Mosque** (1875), in the town centre, and the **N'nayaye Mosque** (1880) on the northwest fringe of town. Two mosques have been built in the 20th century, the **Riyadha Mosque** (1901), to the south of the town, and the **Bohora Mosque** (1920), which is fairly central, just inland of Harambee Avenue. The **Mwenye Alawi Mosque** (1850) at the north end of Main Street was originally for women, but it has since been taken over by the men. The small Ismaili community did have their own **Ismaili Mosque**, on the Kenyatta Road at the south end of town, but this is now in ruins.

Adjacent to the Riyadha Mosque is the **Muslim Academy**, funded by Saudi Arabia, and which attracts students from all over the world.

Lamu Museum Lamu Museum, on Kenyatta Road, is run by the National Museums of Kenya, and plays an important role in the conservation of old Lamu. The ground floor has a good bookshop with publications of the National Museum and the entrance has some photographs of Lamu taken by a French photographer, Guillain in the period 1846-49. In a lobby to the right is a Swahili kitchen with pestles and mortars and vermicelli presses. Also on the ground floor are examples of decorative 18th-century *Kidaka* plasterwork, carved Lamu throne chairs with wicker seats and elaborately carved Lamu headboards.

To the rear are displays on the archaeological excavations of the Takwa Ruins (see page 275) on Manda Island, and at Siya and Shanga on Pate Island (see page 277). On the first floor, the balcony has a display of large earthenware pottery. The balcony room has photographs and models of seagoing vessels, mostly dhows, and the various types and styles in use. Just behind the balcony room is a display of musical instruments used in festivals and celebrations, including drums, cymbals, rattles, leg rattles.

The most celebrated exhibits are the two **Siwa horns**. These are in the shape of elephant tusks, with the mouthpiece on the side. The Lamu horn is made of brass, the horn from nearby Pate is of ivory. They date from the 17th century, are elaborately decorated, and are thought to be the oldest surviving musical instruments in

Lamu Museum

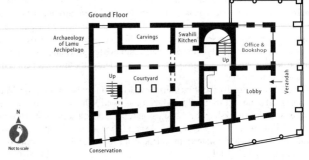

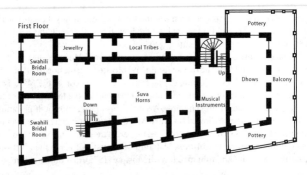

black Africa.

Local tribes are featured in a side-room, and there are displays on the **Oroma** from around Witu, Garsen and southwest of Lamu; the **Pokot** from west of the Tana River, and the **Boni** from the north of Lamu. The jewellery includes nose rings, earrings, anklets and necklaces in bead designs and in silver. There are some illustrations of hand and feet painting, in henna, in black and red. The two end rooms are examples of typical Swahili bridal rooms with furniture and dresses on display. ■ *T1213073.*

Inland from the museum is the small **Swahili House Museum**, a traditional Swahili house, restored, with all the traditional furniture. There are three areas on the main floor. A centre aisle has beds off to the left and right. The beds are wooden with rope and raffia forming the base. The main room has a particularly fine **kikanda** plaster screen on the wall. Furnishings include a clock with an octagonal frame and a pointed pendulum case, a style found all along the East African coast. Outside is a well and a garden with frangipani. ■ *0800-1800 daily, with a small entrance fee.*

Lamu Fort The construction of the fort was begun in 1809 and completed in 1821. The tile awning over the verandah at the front was originally of **makuti**, a thatch made from banana leaves. Inside is a central courtyard surrounded by internal walkways and awnings. The construction is of coral blocks, covered with mortar that has a yellowy-orange hue marked by black patches. It is possible to walk round the battlements, and they afford a good view of the nearby area. The fort initially faced over the quayside, but there are now buildings between it and the sea. In the past it has served as both a fort and as a prison. Now it contains an exhibition on the environment, a shop and a library, plus a pleasant café overlooking the busy square at the entrance. Wedding parties take place inside the fort – women only are allowed to attend the celebration. The invited guests sit downstairs and the town women stand up behind them. The bride sits on a bed, not participating in the dancing. There is a wedding banquet for the guests.

Tombs In the southwest part of town is a fluted **Pillar Tomb**, thought to date from the 14th century. It can be reached by going south, turning inland just after the Halwa Shop, towards the Riyadha Mosque, and continuing beyond the mosque. Alternatively one of the children will be happy to show you the way – just say *nara* and a payment of US$0.25 (KSh20) is reasonable.

Another tomb is the **Mwana Hadie Famau Tomb**, a local woman believed to have lived here in the 15th or 16th century. This is situated a little inland from the museum. The tomb had four pillars at the corners with inset porcelain bowls and probably a central pillar as well. A hermit took up residence in the hollow interior of the tomb, and became a nuisance by grabbing the ankles of passing women at night-time. The solution was to wall up the tomb while the hermit was not at home.

The **Yumbe**, just inland and to the north of the museum was the location of the assembly of Lumu elders that ruled from 1650 to 1830. It is now ruined, but some fragments of the old building remain.

Other sights To the south end of the town, inland from Main Street, is the site of the old **Rope Walk**. Up to 1971, ropes were made here from coconut fibre, twisting the fibres between two wooden frames, for use on dhows. The ropes were thick, about 10 cm in diameter, and became very heavy when wet. Coconut fibre ropes have now been replaced by nylon ropes for use on seagoing vessels.

Behind the fort is the **House of Liwali Sud bin Hamad**, a fine example of Swahili architecture. A Liwali was a governor appointed by the Sultan of Zanzibar. The house has now been subdivided, but it is still possible to appreciate how it looked when it was a single dwelling. Now owned by a Swedish family, it is possible to stay in one of the rooms, US$25.

On Main Street, just next to the *New Star* restaurant is the site of the offices of the

Kenya

German East Africa Company. Originally the Germans thought that Lamu would make a suitable secure base for their expansion into the interior (much in the same way as the British used Zanzibar). The agreement regarding British and German 'spheres of influence' in 1886 caused the Germans to turn their attention to Bagamoya, although they opened a post office in Lamu in 1888. The site is now the **German Post Office Museum**, Towards the rear of the town is the **whetstone** for sharpening knives, said to have been imported from Oman as local stone was not suitable. At the northern end of the town, on the waterfront are **Woodcarving Workshops**, and the proprietors will happily show you around. Further on, on the shore are boats being built and repaired at the **Dhow Boatyard**.

South of the jetty is the **Dhow Harbour**, and mangrove poles are stacked on the waterfront ready for loading on dhows catching the trade winds north to the Gulf.

St Mary's Church, next to the museum on the promenade, is the only church on the island, with walls of coral blocks, small tower, bell, roof of mangrove pole rafters and a fine Swahili door. At the **Oil Mill** on Main Street at the south end of town, the owner will be happy to show you around to observe the antique presses extracting coconut and sesame seed oil. At the extreme south end of town, the doors are always open to let out the heat of the **Generating Station**. There are four huge diesel generators, three working and one stripped down for maintenance. The engineer happy to show you around. **Bakor Studio**, at the southern end of Main Street, has an interesting collection of old photographs of Lamu and of Lamu residents, including the visit of Sultan Khalifa from Zanzibar. The Sultan was too infirm to come ashore, and meetings took place aboard ship. Purchase of any of the photographs requires great patience as the shopkeeper is

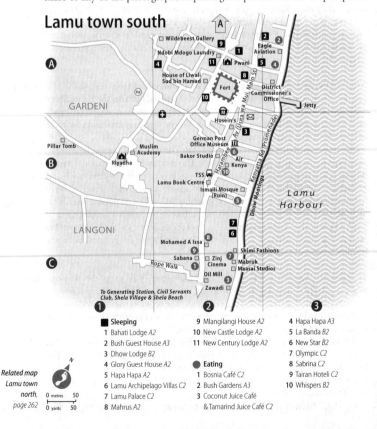

Lamu town south

Sleeping		
1 Bahati Lodge *A2*	9 Mlangilangi House *A2*	4 Hapa Hapa *A3*
2 Bush Guest House *A3*	10 New Castle Lodge *A2*	5 La Banda *B2*
3 Dhow Lodge *B2*	11 New Century Lodge *A2*	6 New Star *B2*
4 Glory Guest House *A2*		7 Olympic *C2*
5 Hapa Hapa *A2*	**Eating**	8 Sabrina *C2*
6 Lamu Archipelago Villas *C2*	1 Bosnia Café *C2*	9 Tairan Hoteli *C2*
7 Lamu Palace *C2*	2 Bush Gardens *A3*	10 Whispers *B2*
8 Mahrus *A2*	3 Coconut Juice Café	
	& Tamarind Juice Café *C2*	

Related map
Lamu town
north,
page 262

0 metres 50
0 yards 50

highly eccentric.

In the northern part of the town close to the waterfront is the **Donkey Sanctuary**, run by the International Donkey Protection Trust, based in the UK. There is a small enclosure where sick donkeys receive care. The remainder of the donkeys roam the town – there is fodder for them at the sanctuary – otherwise the other 50 or so spend much of their time on the rubbish tip at the north of the town, near the abbatoir (which they share with some marabou storks) and on the tip in front of Salama Lodge. **Lamu Social Hall** is a community meeting place at the north end of the promenade, Kenyatta Road. It is a fairly simple building, opened by Jomo Kenyatta in 1971. It has two small brass canons that were captured by the British at Witu, about 70 km from Lamu, a small town on the route to Gersen.

Lamu Island

The southern shores of Lamu Island have the best beach – 12 km of almost deserted **The beach** white sand which back onto the sand dunes. As there is no reef the waves get fairly big. To get there you have to walk through the southern part of the town towards Shela which will take you about 45 minutes and on to the beach. If you do not feel like walking you can take the dhow or motor boat which goes to *Peponi's*. It is possible to strike off directly southwest but, although it is shorter, the walk through the dunes can be hard work.

One-day dhow fishing excursions in the Manda Channel, followed by a barbecue on **Manda Beach** are excellent value at under US$10 per person. These are offered by many of the young men in the town, but check that the dhow offered looks to be in reasonable condition. The larger dhows tend to be better maintained and often have more experienced captains. Deep-sea fishing is also excellent value, especially if you negotiate directly with the dhow captains. Captain Kellie who has a boat called *Taififu* has been recommended. A boat for a full day will cost about US$30. Snorkelling excursions can be at odd hours due to the times of the tide. They frequently take place very early in the morning. The best place is **Manda Toto**, which is a two- or three-hour dhow trip away. Unless you wish to stay overnight it may not be worthwhile. Avoid offers of snorkelling at Manda Island, it's an inferior experience.

Here, on the western side of the island, about 8 km from town, you can see dhows **Matondoni** being built and repaired. The easiest way is to hire a dhow between a group – you will **Village** have to negotiate the price and can expect to pay around US$30-40 for the boat. Alternatively you can hire a donkey – ask at the *Pole Pole Lodge* (up near the Jumaa Mosque – turn inland at the *Pole Pole Restaurant*). A third option is to walk, although you should leave early as it gets very hot. The walk will take a couple of hours and is quite complicated. You want to turn off the main street roughly opposite *Petley's* and keep walking west inland. Ask for directions from there; you want to keep going in the same direction of the telephone wires which go to Matondoni – if you follow these you should get there eventually.

Sticking out on the southeastern tip of Lamu, this village is another of the old stone **Shela** towns south of Lamu town. It is a popular destination for beach lovers and those *This is definitely* slumming it in Lamu Town, as it is just a 40-minute walk from Lamu. In the town are *the upmarket end* a number of old buildings including the **mosque** which is behind *Peponi's* (see *of the island* below) and several wonderfully restored houses that you can rent (at a price).

The people of Shela were originally from the island of Manda and speak a dialect of Swahili that is quite different to that spoken in Lamu. The **Friday Mosque** was built in 1829 and is noted for its slender, conical minaret.

If the tide is low it is an easy walk from Lamu Town, about 3 km: go down to the end of the harbour and then along the beach. There is also a route inland: you need to head southwest and hug the shore. You can always hire a dhow which will take you for about US$0.50 a person, or get a group together and hire a motor boat run by *Peponi's*.

Nearby islands **Manda Island** is quite close, **Pate Island** about 20 km away, and **Kiwayu Island** 50 km off. These islands are described in detail below, see page 275 and page 277. You will see notices advertising trips and will, undoubtedly, be offered trips from various people who usually act as a go-between for the dhow owners. Day trips are popular and because competition is tough the prices are almost standard. For longer trips you will need to be sure that everyone is clear who is arranging the food and drink (you or the dhow owner). Be sure to take lots to drink as it can get very hot. Another thing to remember is that the dhow is dependent on the tides and, if it has no outboard motor, on the winds. So bear in mind that a trip could easily turn into something longer through no fault of the dhow crew. It is unwise to set off with a very tight schedule. You would be advised to bring your own soft drinks or beer, buying the latter at the Kenya Breweries depot on the waterfront. For a party of eight, the price will probably work out at about US$10 per person including food for a three-day trip. You need to know that you will spend the odd night on the boat, so make sure you will be comfortable. Staying in any temporary lodging on one of the islands will be an extra (but nominal) expense.

Other possible excursions (see page 279) are to **Dondori National Reserve**, **Kiunga Marine National Reserve** and **Boni National Reserve**.

Essentials

Sleeping
■ on maps,
pages 262 and 268
For price codes:
see inside front cover

Price varies with the season. The peak periods are Dec and Jan for upmarket travellers, and Jul, Aug and Sep for family visitors and budget travellers. Most of the more expensive hotels are not actually located in the Old Town, but are around the island or on nearby islands. At the lower end of the price range the hotels in Lamu tend to be very hot and suffer from frequent problems with the water supply (expect cold bucket showers much of the time). The worst are those that do not catch the breeze, such as the ones on Harambee Av. Try to get a room as high up as possible or on the waterfront. You may be able to get a cheaper price if you agree to stay for a while. You can often sleep on the roof, which is very cheap. Alternatively, for longer stays, it may be cheaper to rent a house – see page 272.

Lamu Town C *Amu House*, T33420, near the *Paradise Guest House*. This is very central, and a charming place, being a reworked 16th century Swahili house, complete with pretty Swahili furniture and canopy beds. **C** *Jannat House*, inland, north end of town, near Mwana Mshamu mosque, PO Box 195. Good food in pleasant garden atmosphere, serves alcohol, 1 of only 2 hotels with a swimming pool. **C** *Lamu Palace Hotel*, PO Box 421, T33272, F33104. New hotel located on the harbour front at the south end of town, now owned by a German investor. Bar, s/c, a/c, pleasant patio restaurant with the usual average and bland menu, possible to negotiate a better rate off season, Oct-May, one of few places that sells alcohol in Lamu. **C** *Petley's Inn*, PO Box 421, Lamu, T33107, F33378. This is the only top range hotel in town, located on Kenyatta Rd next to the Lamu Museum on the harbour front, it was founded by an Englishman called Percy Petley in 1962 and only has 15 rooms. For a while looking very tired and past-it, it has recently been thoroughly renovated. The rooms are very pleasant, in traditional Swahili style, the 2 front rooms have a private terrace. The restaurant no longer exists, but the bars survive and remain popular, it has a swimming pool and sometimes holds a disco, one of the few places that serves chilled beers. **C** *Stone House Hotel*, inland from the Donkey Sanctuary, PO Box 193, T33544, F33452 (Mombasa: PO Box 81866, T223295, F221926). Well appointed and comfortable, attractive rooms with Swahili canopy beds. It's restaurant on a wonderfully cool, breezy roof-terrace has an unusually imaginative menu. Thoroughly recommended. **C** *Yumbe House*, PO Box 81, Lamu, T/F33101, F33300 (Residence), T33280. This is a wonderful hotel full of atmosphere and excellent value, it is located in the heart of the old town next to the Swahili House Museum and is a traditional house of 4 storeys that has been skilfully converted into a hotel. It has a courtyard, and is airy and spacious, clean, friendly, has a good water supply and the price includes breakfast. Highly recommended. **C** *Yumbe Villa* (see *Yumbe House*), a traditional house with Zidaka niches in the ground floor room, located near the fort, clean, tidy, with traditional Lamu beds, mosquito nets, en-suite shower and toilet, a/c or fan, some have fridges, owned by the same family as *Yumbe House*.

D *Kishuna*, northwest edge of town, PO Box 25, T33001. Quite a modern block, not well located or with a particularly attractive atmosphere, s/c, nets, fans, efficiently run. **D** *Lamu Archipelago Villas*, on waterfront at southern end, PO Box 339, T33368, T33111 (home), F33368. Good location, s/c, includes breakfast, fans, nets, efficiently run, safe. **D** *Lulu House*, inland of town centre, close to Sheikh Mohamed bin Ali Mosque, PO Box 142, T33539. New establishment fashioned from a Swahili house around a charming centre courtyard with bougainvillea and a waterfall, roof restaurant with excellent views, table tennis. Recommended. **D** *Mahrus*, PO Box 25, Lamu, T33001, F33231. This has a range of rooms with and without bathrooms, as well as 1 fully s/c Arab house for rent, it is modern and rather rundown and not very well run, the price includes breakfast. **D** *Starehe House*, inland, north end of town, near Mwana Mshamu Mosque, PO Box 10, T33123. Very charming old house. **D** *Suli Suli House*, inland, north end of town near Jumaa Mosque, PO Box 156, T33119. Handsome house with 8 rooms arranged round a courtyard.

E *Alipenda*, just north of Lamu Town, PO Box 115 and 3119. Some s/c, fans, very comfortable. **E** *Bahati Lodge*, situated to the north of the fort. Some of these rooms are better than others, the ones on the top floor are much cooler because they get the sea breezes and they also have good views, however it is fairly basic and perhaps not the cleanest. **E** *Bush Guest House*, to rear of *Bush Gardens* restaurant, on Main St, PO Box 22. Small, efficiently run and well located, some rooms look out over harbour. **E** *Casuarina Rest House*, PO Box 10, Lamu, T33123. Great location on the waterfront, verandah overlooking harbour, on top of *Kenya Commercial Bank* (due to close), curious bell that sounds like a budgerigar. It is very clean, the rooms are spacious (it used to be the Police station) and it is well run and friendly, also has s/c apartments, there is a large rooftop area. **E** *Glory Guest House* (previously *Dudu's Guest House*), one of the nicest hotels in this range, it is located behind the Fort, and is a wonderful old house, the rooms are spacious and airy, and include bathrooms. There is a kitchen that you can use. **E** *Hal-Udy Guest House*, PO Box 25, T33001. Located in the heart of the old town, back from the harbour, this is a small hotel with 4 s/c suites, each has a bedroom, sitting room, with some lovely furniture, and cooking facilities. There is also a house boy, and this is particularly popular with expatriate families, it is especially good value if you are planning on staying for a few weeks. **E** *Hapa Hapa*, to rear of *Hapa Hapa* restaurant on Main St, PO Box 213, T33226. Fairly simple – some rooms look out over harbour. **E** *Kitendetini Bahari Hotel*, on Main St, to north end, PO Box 293, T33172, F33231. New establishment, pleasant internal courtyard, restaurant, s/c, fans, nets, popular, well run and nice atmosphere. **E** *Lamu Sea Shore Lodging*, on waterfront, next to District Commissioner's Office. Verandah, variety of rooms. **E** *Mlangilangi House*, just by Pwani Mosque, PO Box 260. Comfortable, but a bit utilitarian. **E** *Mtamwini Guest House*, located close to fort. Old Swahili building, large cool rooms, all with bathrooms. **E** *New Century Lodge*, located behind Pwani Mosque, near Fort, PO Box 10. Very simple, not s/c, but comfortable atmosphere with rooms off central courtyard. **E** *New Kenya*, on Main St, close to Museum, PO Box 295. Good central location, simple, not s/c. **E** *New Sabrina*, Main St, south end, PO Box 294, T33552. Dormitory accommodation, but cheap. **E** *Pole Pole*, just inland, north end of town, PO Box 242, T33204. Highest building in Lamu, with good views from roof, s/c, nets, fans, can arrange donkey transport for excursions. **E** *Sanctuary Guest House*, situated in the northern part of town this has a range of self contained rooms and suites. It has good facilities, kitchen, garden and rooftop.

Seasonal: **E** *Dhow Lodge*, on Main St to south of jetty. Closed in off-season, Oct-May. **E** *Jambo Guest House*, inland, north end of town, near Jumaa Mosque. Fans, nets. **E** *Karibuni Guest House*, inland, north end of town, PO Box 209. Quite small. **E** *Kenya Lodge*, located a little inland from the waterfront this is one of the very basic hotels, it is reasonably clean but rather shabby and sometimes has problems with water supply although other times it can be 24 hrs, some of the rooms are hot and stuffy so try and get one with a breeze. **E** *Kilimanjaro*, just inland from Donkey Sanctuary, PO Box 274. Pleasant, s/c, nets, fans, includes breakfast. **E** *Lamu Guest House*, PO Box 240, T33274. Situated at the back of the Lamu Museum and is good value, there are a range of rooms, the general rule is that top ones are usually the best because they catch the sea breezes, it is clean and friendly. **E** *New Castle Lodge*, PO Box

10, Lamu, T33123. This is situated next to the fort, it has a good position and is kept cool by the sea breezes, it has recently been done up so the prices may rise accordingly, it has both a dormitory on the roof and rooms with shared facilities, closed in off-season, Oct-May. **E** *Palm View*, northwest edge of town, PO Box 46, T33172. Quite small, some s/c, not a particularly good location. **E** *Paradise*, inland from Main St, near museum, PO Box 97, T33053. Swahili house, simple facilities. **E** *Saiga Lodge*, north end of town, near Jumaa Mosque. Fairly small and basic. **E** *Salama Guest House*, on Main St, northern end, PO Box 38, T33146. Simple accommodation in a good location. **E** *Sunrise Guest House*, inland of town centre, near Sheikh Mohamed bin Ali Mosque, PO Box 20, T33175. Good value.

House rentals If you are planning to stay here for a longer holiday then it is probably worth getting together with a group to rent a house. Many of the houses are holiday homes of Kenya residents, they can be very good value if you are staying for a while and can fill the house, giving high-quality accommodation at a very modest price. Even if you are not part of a group it is still often possible to rent a room. People post details of houses to rent on notice boards at the museum and *Lamu Archipelago Tours.*

A Dutch woman, Monika Fauth, appears to know the details of virtually every available house and owner, T/F32044, banana@africaonline.co.ke The owners of the *Wildebeest Gallery* can also arrange apartment leasing for long or short-term lettings, for reasonably rates in the region of US$165-255 per month.

Shela Village (about 3 km south of Lamu Town) **L** *Kijani House*, on water's edge between *Peponi's* and Shela beach, PO Box 288, T33235, F33237. Odd Swahili houses, fine gardens, traditional furniture, 2 small pools, excellent standards. Well recommended. **L** *Peponi's*, PO Box 24, Lamu, T33154, F33029. This is located on the beach next to the village of Shela. Highly recommended. It faces the channel that runs between Lamu and Manda and is a really wonderful setting with about 5 km of private beach, the hotel is made up of a series of cottages each with a verandah and full facilities. There is an excellent restaurant which is for residents only, as well a bar and grill for non-residents. The hotel provides full watersports facilities, probably the best and most extensive on the island and organizes various excursions. It is very efficiently run by the Korschen's who are Danish, booking well ahead is definitely advised, it is closed from mid-April to end of Jun. **A** *The Island Hotel Shela*, PO Box 179, Shela, Lamu, T0121-33290, F33588, Nairobi booking; F02-229880. Situated approximately 200 m from the beach, in the centre of Shela village, decorated in traditional Swahili style, 15 rooms with private bathroom, fans and mosquito nets. **A** *Johori House*, house rental, PO Box 48, T33460, F33251. Well restored 18th century house, sleeps up to 6, excellent views.

B *Shela Rest House*, PO Box 199, Malindi, or PO Box 255, Lamu, T20182 (Malindi), or 330951 (Lamu), this small hotel is located in the village of Shela close to *Peponi's*. It is a wonderful converted house and there are rooms as well as several self-contained suites – fine if you want to be self-catering. **C** *Island Hotel*, town location, PO Box 179, T33290. Fans, s/c, rooftop restaurant. **C** *White Rock Pool*, between town and Shela beach, PO Box 296, T33234. Comfortable house with relaxed atmosphere, pool.

D *Shela Pwani Guest House*, PO Box 59, Lamu, Shela, T0121-33540. Very comfortable and friendly. **D** *White House*, on the waterfront, good value. **E** *Samahani Guest House*, PO Box 59, Lamu, T33100. Located in the village of Shela this is particularly popular with budget travellers who want to be close to the beach. It is basic but clean and friendly. **E** *Stop Over*, located right on the beach. Clean and simple but basic, has a good value restaurant.

Rest of Lamu Island **L** *Kipungani Explorer*, Lamu, c/o PO Box 74888, T02-716628, F716547 (Nairobi), heritage@form-net.com The first of Heritage Group's highest standard 'Explorer' resorts. This new lodge, with just 15 *makuti* thatched cottages which are made from local palm leaf mats with coconut thatched roof, is located at the southern tip of Lamu Island. They are all extremely spacious and comfortable and each has a verandah. They organize various excursions and snorkelling trips, sailing, windsurfing, there is a good restaurant and bar outside, and non-residents can visit for lunch, boats leaving from *Peponi's*. **L** *Kipungani Sea Breezes*. Small 24-bed private resort on Lamu Island 30 mins by speed boat from the airport. Built of local materials, sea facing on stilts and offers a full range of watersports. Restaurant serves excellent sea food. Same management as *Kiwayu Safari Village*, PO Box 55343, Nairobi, T503030, F503149. **B** *Gillis Yoga Tower*. Newly built in the dunes in a quiet neighbourhood. There is a great communal atmosphere. Yoga lessons and massage are available. There are excellent meals at table d'hote – one large table shared by all the residents. This complex has 6 rooms. The development attracts lots of interesting people and the owner Mr Gillis is a fascinating well-travelled man. **E** *Peace Guest House*, a bit inland, set in gardens with camping facilities.

There are lots of places to eat in Lamu which has responded magnificently to the demand for tourist menus. You will find lots of yoghurt, pancakes, fruit salads, and milk shakes as well as good value seafood. If you are looking for the traditional food that you find in up-country Kenya, such as *ugali*, beans, curries, chicken and chips, there are also a number of places that do these. They are mainly on Harambee Av – particularly in the southern end of town. Bear in mind that Lamu is a predominantly Muslim society, so during Ramadan – the month of fasting, many of the restaurants and cafes will remain closed all day until after sunset.

Eating
● *on maps, pages 262 and 268*

Stomach upsets are fairly common. Stick to bottled water and avoid ice. See Health, page 89

Lamu Town Expensive *Lamu Palace Hotel*, PO Box 83, T33272, southern end of waterfront. Pleasant restaurant looking out over the harbour, seafood, grills, Indian food, serves alcohol.

Mid-range *Ali Hippy*, plump gentleman who approaches you in the street near Fort and offers traditional Swahili meal in his home with some musical entertainment. *Bush Gardens*, on the waterfront with good view over harbour and is a very good seafood restaurant, it is friendly although can be extremely slow, especially when it gets full. *Ghai's Restaurant* is named after the owner and cook, it is located up in the north of town close to the donkey sanctuary, its speciality is seafood although the quality can vary. *Lamu Palace Restaurant*, south of the town on the waterfront. A very popular restaurant, it has a very nice atmosphere and a good range of food on the menu. Make you sure you pop in and book before you go as it can get very full, the food is good – and there is also excellent ice-cream. *Whispers*, formerly *Rumours*, Main St, toward southern end, opposite *Bakor Studio*. High quality café with juices, cappuccino, ice-cream, spaghetti, pizzas, sandwiches and serves wine. Has a pretty flower-filled courtyard to the rear. *Stone Town Hotel*, inland from Donkey Sanctuary, PO Box 192, T33544. Very good cuisine, crab and lobster, ginger tea, mango flambé, also a snack menu, juices, charming atmosphere with views out over Lamu.

Cheap *Hapa Hapa Restaurant*, on the harbour front. Barracuda is excellent, good fruit juices and snacks, lively place. *La Banda*, on waterfront at south end of town. Good location, verandah overlooks the harbour, comfortable atmosphere, mainly seafoods, grills, but also vegetarian dishes. *Serena* (formerly *Yoghurt*, before that *Coral Inn*), charming garden atmosphere under *makuti* roof, wicker lamps, games (*bai* and dominoes), imaginative menu (pumpkin and ginger soup, seafoods, yoghurts and honey). Recommended.

Seriously cheap *Bosnia Café*, south end of Main St. Set up by soldier who served with the UN forces in Yugoslavia, first rate local food, pilau with chapati's, and cold juices. *Coconut Juice Café*, waterfront, southern end. Specialist juices, freshly made, with combinations of flavours comprising lime, peanut, chocolate, avocado, papaya, mango, coconut, banana. *Jambo Café*, Harambee Av, northern end. Popular with locals and is very cheap, it serves mainly traditional African food and also does good breakfasts. *Kenya Cold Drinks*, located on Harambee Av close to the museum. This is very good for a milkshake and a snack, serves really good spaghetti. *Mangrove*, at the jetty, local menu, pool table at rear. *New Masri*, just around the corner from *Mahrus Hotel*, good cheap Swahili dishes. *New Star Restaurant*, in the southern end of town is reasonable and is very cheap, it has good breakfasts and opens very early – 0530 for the early birds. *Olympic Restaurant* (formerly *Sinbad*), south of the town also on the harbour front. Excellent pancakes and seafood, open, *Makuti* roofed eating area. *Sabrina Restaurant*, southern end of town. Very cheap, has a reasonably wide range of food on the menu, and does breakfasts. *Tairan Hoteli*, south end of Main St. Local café. *Tamarind Juice Café*, southern end of waterfront. Cold, straightforward juices and good milkshakes. *Zinj Juice Café*, Main St. Handy for cinema next door.

Bakery, just to south of *New Star Restaurant* on Main St, pastries and fresh bread.

Shela Village (about 3 km south of Lamu Town) **Mid-range** *Barbecue Grill* at *Peponi's*. Excellent and open to non-residents, the food is very good value and is probably the best on the island. **Cheap** *Stop Over Restaurant*, which serves simple, basic but good value food, it also has a great location right on the beach.

Bars Only 7 places serve alcohol, and one of these, *Whispers* (previously called *Rumours)*, only offers wine to accompany your food. *Petley's*, on the waterfront north of the museum has a rather uninviting bar on the ground floor. There is a very much more attractive bar on the rooftop. *Lamu Palace Hotel*, located at the southern end of the waterfront, also has a bar. The *Police Post*, on the high ground inland from the fort serves beer in the Mess – the guardians of the law are a friendly group, and you will get served if you buy the barman a drink. Has fine views out over the harbour, and there are 2 brass cannons in the front, commanding the bay. The *Civil Servants Club*, south along the waterfront, some distance past the generating station, and then up a steep path, is an unpretentious venue where you will be expected to buy a drink for the clientele, but the compensation, as with the *Police Mess*, is that the beer is cheaper than at either of the hotels with bars. There is also *Jannat House*, where spirits, wine and beer are available. In Shela alcohol is available at *Peponi's*, which you can rely on for an ice-cold beer, and *Kijani House*.

Entertainment **Cinemas** The open-air *Coast Cinema* inland from roughly behind the Museum, on the edge of town. There are films most nights in the peak period, and the programme is posted at the museum. *Zinj Cinema*, excellent small cinema on Main St toward southern end, programme and times posted outside. **Discos** The *Civil Servant's Club* (south end of town) has a disco most weekends.

Sports **Watersports**: organized from *Peponi's*, PO Box 24, Lamu, T0121-33421, F33029. Including windsurfing, surfing, snorkelling, deep sea fishing, sailing, and scuba diving. In Shela is *Upside Down*, T32060, F32061, upside@africaonline.co.ke, a diving shop run by a German PADI instructor. From Nov to Apr diving trips in a dhow are available, US$40.

Shopping **Books** The museum has a very good collection of books on Lamu, its history and culture. There is also the *Lamu Book Centre* which has a reasonable selection as well as the local newspapers. **Gallery** *Wildebeest*, contemporary paintings for sale. **Henna painting** *Mabruk* on waterfront at southern end, traditional Swahili decoration for hands and feet, US$5-10. **Souvenirs** Hand-built model dhows. They are not too easy to carry around so try and get them at the end of the trip. Other woodcarvings are also good value here – chests, siwa horns, Lamu candlesticks, and furniture. Also in Lamu you will be able to get jewellery – silver in particular – as well as curios. You can get things made for you but be prepared to bargain. *Lamu Craft*, behind Donkey Sanctuary, PO Box 56, Lamu. Lamu carving, signs, candlesticks. *Casuarina Gift Shop*, behind *Casuarina Hotel*, on Main St, just north of Museum. Good selection of Lamu crafts and clothing. *Baraka*, Main St, southern end. Expensive, high-quality carvings, Lamu chests, jewellery, clothing. *Shimi Fashions*, on waterfront at southern end, PO Box 18. Good selection of T-shirts and bags. *Maasai Studios*, waterfront, southern end, some very good, original design, clothing. *Zawadi* (Lamu Gift Shop), waterfront, southern end. Excellent, original design clothing and accessories, particularly skirts and patchwork waistcoats and bags. *Husein's*, Fakrudin Gulom Husein and brother, splendid carved door, copperware from Oman, jewellery. **Lamu Polytechnic**, at the southern end of the town, offers traditional carving courses for tourists.

Tour operators *Lamu Archipelago Tours*, south end of waterfront, PO Box 339, T/F33368, T33111 (residence). Efficient operation, will arrange reliable trips to nearby islands. *Tawasal Safaris and Tours*, PO Box 248, T33446, F33533. The 'beach boys' also offer **dhow trips**. Check the vessel for sea-worthiness before parting with your money. The bigger dhows tend to be better maintained and have more competent crews.

Air *Kenya Airways* fly between Lamu and Jomo Kenyatta Airport, **Nairobi**, with a stop in **Transport**
Malindi. Depending on the time of year there may be 1, 2 or 3 flights a week. Total journey
time is just over 2 hrs, return fare US$160. The light aircraft of *Air Kenya* fly daily between
Lamu and Wilson Airport, Nairobi. Depart Nairobi at 1315, arrive 1545; from Lamu departure
time is 1545, arrival 1715, return fare US$270. Both airlines also serve the route between
Mombasa and Lamu, and both stop off at **Malindi**. *Air Kenya* have daily flights, return fare
US$190, journey takes just over 1 hr, return between Malindi and Lamu is US$140. *Kenya Airways* has 1 or 2 flights a week, flight time between 2½ and 5 hrs.

International destinations from Lamu with *Kenya Airways* include **Amsterdam**, **London**,
Bombay and the **Seychelles**. The offices of *Air Kenya* are at Baraka House on Harambe Av,
south of the fort, close to *Whispers* café, PO Box 376, Lamu, T33445, F33063. *Kenya Airways*
have offices on Kenyatta Rd, on the ground floor of *Casuarina Guest House*, PO Box 315,
T32040, F33119. For *Air Kenya* baggage allowance is just 15 kg, check in time is 30 mins
before take off. There is no airport tax when you leave Lamu (although there is from Malindi).

With the current problems with bandits from Somalia, a convoy forms at Garsen and an
armed escort joins the bus.

Bus: to Lamu go fairly regularly but the route is popular so you should book in advance. The   *Because of current*
trip takes about 5 to 6 hrs from Malindi and costs US$4. They leave in the morning at   *problems with bandits*
between 0700 and 0800. You might also be able to take one of the buses from Mombasa that   *from Somalia, a*
stop off at Malindi on the way, but these are often full so you will have to stand all the way   *convoy forms at*
which is not much fun. If possible sit on the left side of the bus (in the shade) and keep your   *Garsen and an armed*
eyes open for wildlife. If you are travelling from Mombasa, *TSS Bus* (in Mombasa on Digo Rd,   *escort joins the bus.*
PO Box 85039, T224541; in Lamu on Main St, PO Box 3, T33059) is recommended. The cost is   *See advice page 261*
about US$8, but seats are reserved and you will not be crushed by extra passengers crowd-
ing the gangway. The trip takes almost all day, arriving about 1700 at Lamu. There is tarmac
to Malindi, a rough track to Garsen then a further 20 km of tarmac after which there is a good
graded coral and sand section to Makowe. The bus will take you as far as the jetty at Makowe
on the mainland from where you get a ferry, about 7 km, taking about 40 mins, across to
Lamu which costs about US$0.50.

Banks Few on the island, *Standard Chartered* on the harbour front has closed. The *Commercial Bank*   **Directory**
of Kenya on the seafront, will change foreign currency and TCs, and accept Visa cards for cash
withdrawals (but not Mastercard), service slow, open 0900-1500 on weekdays. **Communications**
Internet: It is possible to email from the post office and at *Shemanga*, opposite *New Star Restaurant*.
Post office: just to the south of the jetty Mon-Fri 0800-1230 and 1400-1700; Sat 0900-1200. There is a
poste restante service. **Medical services** Hospital: located in the southern end of the town to the
south and inland from the fort, PO Box 45, T3012. **Laundry** *Ndobi Mdogo*, behind Pwani Mosque,
near fort.

Manda Island

This island is just to the north of Lamu and has the air strip on it. It is very easy to get   *Colour map 3, grid C6*
to and is a popular day trip to see the ruins at Takwa. The island is approximately the
size of Lamu but has only a small permanent population – partly because of a shortage of fresh water and also because of the shortage of cultivable land. About a fifth of
the island is made up of sand dunes and sandy flat land with just thorn bushes and
palms. Another three fifths of the island is mangrove swamps and muddy creeks.
Thus only about a fifth of the island's surface area is suitable for agriculture. The
creek that Takwa is located on almost cuts the island in half during high tide. The
main port is **Ras Kilimdini** that is located on the northern side of the island. In the
19th century this deep-water harbour was considered to be superior to Lamu and
was used by ocean-going vessels that would then take dhows across to Lamu.

The **Takwa Ruins** are those of an ancient Swahili town which is believed to have
prospered from the 15th to the 17th centuries, with a population of between
2,000-3,000 people. It was abandoned in favour of the town of Shela on Lamu,

Kenya

probably because salt water contaminated most of the town's supplies of fresh water. The ruins consist of the remains of a wall that surrounded the town, about 100 houses, a mosque and a tomb dated from 1683. As with many of the other sites on the coast, the remains include ablution facilities. The houses face north toward Mecca as does the main street. There is a mosque at the end of the street that is thought to have been built on the site of an old tomb. The other feature of the ruins is the pillar tomb. It is situated just outside the town walls. The ruins have been cleared but little excavation has been done here. Entrance fee of US$2.

There are a number of good **snorkelling** sites off Manda Island. Perhaps the best is actually off the small island to the north of Manda, named **Manda Toto**. You will have to take a dhow to get here.

Sleeping There are 2 hotels on Manda Island: **L** *Blue Safari Hotel*, PO Box 41759, Nairobi, T338838 (Nairobi). A small and exclusive Italian family-run hotel in an idyllic setting, thatched bunga-lows provide extremely comfortable accommodation and the hotel caters for those inter-ested in watersports, scuba diving in particular. It is closed from May to Sep. Has 15 bandas, plus a bar and restaurant, and costs up to US$1,000. **A** *Manda Island Village Resort*, PO Box 78, Lamu, T2751. Looking across to the village of Shela on Lamu, it has self-sufficient cot-tages, a restaurant, bar and shop. The excursions that the hotel organizes include trips to Lamu, deep-sea fishing and snorkelling trips. There is also **E** Camping close to the ruins, few facilities, US$7. Bring a sleeping bag and mosquito net. During the rainy season elephants can be sighted from the campsite.

Transport Access to Manda Island and the towns is by way of motorized ferry as well as by dhow. How-ever dhow is the easiest as it will take you closer to the ruins, otherwise you will have to walk across the island. The dhow will cost you about US$15 for a party of up to 8. Be sure you know what is included in the price. It takes about 1½ hrs and is dependent on the tides. You may have to wade ashore through the mangrove swamp.

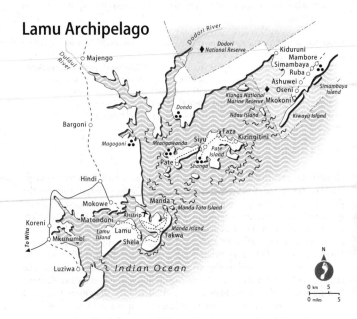

Lamu Archipelago

Pate Island

About three times the size of Lamu and located about 20 km to the northeast. Unlike both Lamu and Manda, it does not have a large area taken up by dunes. The island is divided into two parts – indeed it may have once been two islands but the channel dividing them is so shallow that only the smallest boats can go down it. The land is very low lying and the towns are situated on shallow inlets that can only be reached at high tide. The only deep water landing point is at **Ras Mtangawanda** in the west of the island, but as it is not a sheltered harbour it has never had a major settlement. Although it is fairly easily accessible it does not receive many visitors.

Colour map 3, grid C6

Pate Town

The town of Pate is only accessible from the sea at the right tide – otherwise you will have to walk from the landing place. It is situated in the southwest corner of the island and is one of the old Swahili towns that dot the coast. The town shows strong Arabic and Indian influences, and was once most famous for the silk that was produced here. The old stone houses are crumbling and tobacco has been planted amongst the ruins. The main ruins are those of **Nabahani** which are found just outside the town. Although they have not yet been excavated you should be able to make out the town walls, houses, mosques and tombs.

   The age of the town is disputed – the earliest remains that have been found are from the 13th century – although according to some accounts the town dates back to the eighth century. The town was reasonably prosperous up to 1600, although by the time the Portuguese first arrived it had begun to decline. The Portuguese did not have much success and by the 17th century had withdrawn to Mombasa. The final decline of Pate was the war with Lamu. There had been an ongoing dispute between the two islands. Over the years the port at Pate silted up, so Lamu was used instead by the bigger dhows, and the tensions increased. The situation reached a climax in 1813 when the army from Pate was defeated at Shela and the town went into a decline from which it has never recovered.

Siyu

A stone-built town dating from about the 15th century. It became most well-known as a centre for Islamic scholarship and is believed to have been an important cultural centre during the 17th and 18th centuries. At one time is said to have had 30,000 inhabitants. Today there are probably fewer than 5,000 people living in the town and the inhabited part of the town is slightly apart from the ancient ruined area. A creek separates the residential part of the town from the **fort**, built by Seyyed Said, believed to date from the mid-19th century when the town was occupied by forces of the Sultan of Zanzibar. The fort has some impressive canons and has been partly renovated. The town itself is fairly dilapidated and outside the town are coconut plantations. It is a small fishing village that has a thriving crafts industry – you will be able to see leather goods being made as well as doors, furniture and jewellery.

   About one hour's walk from Siyu there are the **Shanga Ruins**. There have been excavations in recent years and they show signs of unearthing impressive remains. There are buildings from the 13th and 14th century and many artefacts have been found dating back to the eighth and ninth centuries. There is a pillar tomb, a large mosque, a smaller second mosque, about 130 houses and a palace. The whole town was walled with five access gates and outside the wall is a cemetery containing well over 300 tombs. If you are visiting the islands by dhow and would rather not walk you can ask your boatman to take you to Shanga direct.

   The channel which Siyu is sited on is so silted up that only the smallest boats can reach Siyu. It is therefore necessary to approach the town by foot – either from Shanga (about an hour), from Faza (about two hours), or from Pate (about 8 km). In the case of the latter two, unless you are happy to get lost and therefore walk for hours, you would be advised to take a guide, as the route (particularly from Pate) is complicated.

   About a two-hour walk to the northeast of Siyu is the town of **Chundwa** which is situated in the most fertile part of the island. Being agriculturally productive the island is perhaps the most capable of self-sufficiency of all the islands in the archipelago; however, it does suffer from problems with the supply of fresh water.

Sleeping It is possible to rent rooms in local houses – there are no formal guesthouses.

Transport The inlet is very shallow, and sea-going dhows and the motor launch from Lamu by-passes Siyu en route to Faza. It may be possible to persuade a small boat to sail or pole you round from Pate or Faza. Otherwise it is about a 10-km hike to each of these places, and you probably need to hire a guide.

Faza
See map page 276

About 20 km from Pate Town, and 10 km northeast of Siyu. Although the town of Faza is believed to date from the 13th century and possibly as early as the eighth century, there is little in the way of ruins left here. However the town is important in that it is the district headquarters of Pate Island and some of the mainland. It therefore has a number of modern facilities that are not found elsewhere on the island – such as post office, telephone exchange and some shops, restaurants and simple guesthouses.

The town is believed to have been completely destroyed in the 13th century by the nearby town of Pate, rebuilt, and destroyed again in the late 16th century this time by the Portuguese. It was again rebuilt and joined forces with the Portuguese against Pate. However, its significance declined until recently when, being the district headquarters, it resumed its position of importance.

Close to where the ferries anchor are the ruins of the **Kunjanja Mosque**. You can see some the Mihrab which points to Mecca and which is a beautiful example with fine carvings. There are some rather splendid Arabic inscriptions above the entrance. Outside the town there is the tomb of Amir Hamad, the commander of the Sultan of Zanzibar's army who was killed here, in action, in 1844.

Sleeping and eating There are 2 guesthouses in the town: **E** *Lamu House* and **E** *Shela House*, they are simple, basic and family-run. Alternatively you can ask around to stay at a family house. You will probably be offered food at the place that you are staying – otherwise there is a simple restaurant in the village.

Transport To get to Faza from **Lamu** take the motor launch which goes 3 times a week (on Mon, Wed and Fri) and takes about 4 hrs. To get back to Lamu the boat leaves Faza at about 0600 on Tue, Thu and Sat. You have to take a small boat out to the launch so be sure to get there early. The journey to Lamu takes about 4 hrs and will cost you about US$1.50. From Faza to any of the other towns you will probably have to walk – it is advisable to take a guide or ask around to see if anyone else is going who can show you the route. Generally when visiting Pate Island the best thing to do is to start at Pate Town, and walk through Siyu to Faza from where you will be able to get a boat back to Lamu.

To get to Pate from Lamu, you will have to take the motor launch to **Faza** or to **Mtangawanda** and walk from there. To Faza the boat goes 3 times a week, Mon, Wed, and Fri and takes about 4 hrs. To Mtangawanda the trip takes about 3 hrs. Once you get to Mtangawanda the walk will take you about an hour – the track is clear, and you will probably be accompanied by other people from the boat. To get back to Lamu the boat leaves Faza on Tue, Thu and Sat. It does not always call at Mtangawanda so you may have to walk to Faza via Siyu (quite a hike) and catch it from there. You would be advised to take a guide (at least as far as Siyu).

Kiwayu Island

This island is located on the far northeast of the archipelago and is part of the **Kiunga Marine National Reserve**. Unfortunately this area has suffered from the problems to the north in Somalia, and so visitors are fewer than in previous years. The marine national reserve, opened in 1979, has a reputation for having some of the best coral reefs interspersed with limestone islands in Kenya. Sea turtles and nesting migratory sea birds are to be found here.

There is an airstrip which serves the 2 luxury lodges below, as well as a launch which takes an hour to Lamu. **L** *Kiwayu Mlango Wa Chanu Lodge*, on the Island, PO Box 48217, Nairobi, T331878. **L** *Kiwayu Safari Village*, PO Box 55343, PO Box 55343, Nairobi, T503030, F503144. Located to the north of Lamu on the Kiwayu Peninsula, in a beautiful bay on the mainland, opposite the island. Managed by the same people as the *Kipungani Sea Breezes*, and recently refurbished, it consists of 22 luxurious, traditional-style thatched bandas, restaurant, bar and small shop. The hotel has a fleet of deep-sea fishing vessels and is ideal for the enthusiast. The beach is also wonderful, and there is a full range of watersports on offer, and boat trips into the mangrove swamps. The food is excellent, non-seafood dishes available on request. Closes for 2 months from mid-Apr during the low season. **D-E** *Kasim's*, has a number of bandas, located on the western shore of the island, the facilities are good and there is a dining and cooking area. **Camping** If you have a tent you can camp at **E** *Kasim's*.

Sleeping

To get there you can either take a regular boat or (and probably easier) you can get a group of 5 or 6 together and charter a dhow. This should include food and water as well as snorkelling gear and should work out at around US$15 per person. The journey is dependent on the winds and the tides and so be prepared for the journey in each direction to be anything between 8 and 36 hrs.

Air Kenya has daily flights to Kiwayu from Mombasa, via Malindi and Lamu (single US$150, return US$300), and from Wilson Airport, Nairobi via Lamu (single US$200, return US$390).

Transport

The Dodori National Reserve is in Coastal Province and is 877 sq km extending from northeast Lamu District up to Kiunga. The vegetation consists of mangrove swamp, lowland dry forest, marshy glades and groundwater forest and is bisected by the Dodori River. Dodori Reserve was established to protect an antelope called the Lamu Topi, as this area is a major breeding ground. There are also elephant, lions, buffalo, giraffe, duikas and lesser kudu in the reserve. In addition the area is rich in birdlife. Pelicans are particularly common birds here. There is **E** camping for visitors but it is essential to check with the police before choosing to stay as the park is often refuge to armed bandits or desperate Somali refugees. Alternatively tours can be organized through Lamu Tourist Office.

The Boni National Reserve is one of the large, remote parks in the northeast of the country, contiguous with the Somali border down to the coast in Northeastern Province. It is 1,340 sq km, and contains the only coastal lowland groundwater forest in Kenya. It has large concentrations of elephant and Harvey's and Ader's duiker in the dry season. No facilities for tourists at present.

Dodori and Boni National Reserves are located in the far north of the Kenya coast close to the Somali border. Gazetted in 1976 it covers an area of 2,590 sq km. However, because of the recent troubles in Somalia most parts of this national reserve have been out of bounds to tourists for a while. If you want to go up here be sure to check with the local authorities and tour agencies before departure, given its proximity to the Somali border.

Dodori & Boni National Reserves
Colour map 3, grids B6/C6

Located in the far northern part of the Kenyan coast, stretching from Boteler Islands to 20 km north of Kiunga, this marine park suffers from being rather remote. Is 250 sq km from the northeast coastal border of mainland Kenya to the Pate Islands in the Indian Ocean in the district of Lamu. The coastal area is made up of scrublands and mangroves surrounded by microscopic marine plants and dugong grass. The vegetation is home to a wide selection of reef fish. There are also substantial numbers of endangered dugongs and green turtles. Dugongs resemble large sea lions and have been almost hunted to extinction, making them one of the rarest sea mammals. Dugongs give birth to live pups, that suckle on teats situated high on the female's chest wall, and are believed to be the origin of sailor's mermaid sightings. The coral here is extensive. As you would expect, there is a good variety of marine birds with colonies of various gulls and terns. The whole area contains more than 50 offshore islands, some of which house lesser kudu, bushbuck, monkeys, porcupines and wild

Kiunga Marine National Reserve
1° 50′ S, 41° 30′ E
Colour map 3, grid C6

pig. Poaching of the turtles and their eggs has been greatly reduced thanks to the efforts of the game wardens of Lamu.

There are a number of facilities for visitors despite the fact that this is one of the least developed of Kenya's marine reserves. There is swimming, sailing, water-skiing and diving here. There are also some simple places to stay on the mainland in *Kiunga*, the administrative centre of this area about 20 km from the border with Somalia, a village unspoilt by tourism, but troubled by intermittent *Shifta* activity.

Northern Kenya

This is a vast area of forested and barren mountains, deserts and scrubland occasionally broken by oases of vegetation and the huge Lake Turkana. Northern Kenya accounts for almost half of the country and yet only a fraction of the population live here. The people who do inhabit the area, the Samburu, Rendille, Boran, Gabbra, Turkana and Somali, are nomadic peoples crossing the region using ancient migration routes, existing as they have done for generations, hardly affected by the modern world. The main reason tourists come up here is to see the wonders of Lake Turkana – the Jade Sea.

Northern region

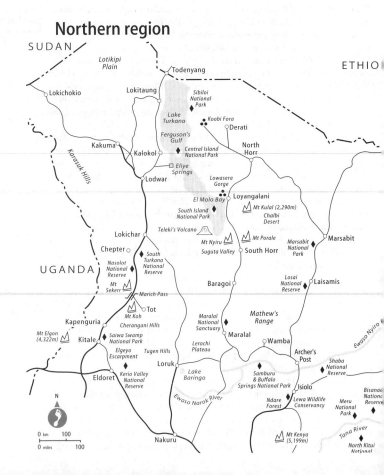

Lake Turkana

The largest lake in the country, Lake Turkana runs about 250 km from the Ethiopian border in a long thin body of water which is never more than 50 km wide. It stretches into the Ethiopian Highlands where the Omo River enters its waters.

3° N, 36° E
Colour map 3, grid A4

Count Sammuel Teleki Von Szek is believed to have been the first white man to see the lake in 1888. In honour of his patron, Von Szek named it Lake Rudolf, after the Austrian Archduke. President Jomo Kenyatta changed the name to Lake Turkana in 1975. This lake used to be far larger than it is today. Around 10,000 years ago it is believed the water level of the lake was about 150 m higher and considered to be one of the sources of the Nile. At that time it supported a far greater number and diversity of plant and animal life. Now a combination of factors including evaporation and major irrigation projects in southern Ethiopia have brought the water level to its lowest in memory. As a result, the water is far more alkaline than in the past. The lake still supports a huge number of hippos and the largest population of Nile crocodiles in the world, estimated to number about 20,000.

Giant Nile perch are reported to grow from 90-180 kg in the lake, but Nile tilapia are a more commercial option as they are more palatable and are either dried or frozen before being marketed all over Kenya. There is also a profusion of birdlife including many European migratory species. Do not be fooled by its calm appearance, the lake's waters are highly unpredictable; storms build up out of nowhere and are not to be dismissed lightly as they are capable of sinking all but the most sturdy craft.

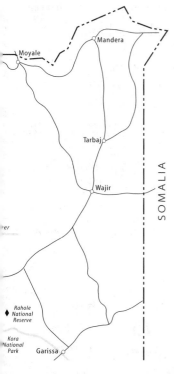

Lake Turkana's **Central Island** is an active volcano which sometimes belches out smoke and sulphur-laden steam. Central Island was established as a national park in 1983, in order to protect the breeding grounds of the Nile crocodile.

The climate up here is extraordinary. It can easily reach 50°C during the day with not a cloud in sight, then out of nowhere a storm will break whipping up a squall on Lake Turkana. For most of the year, the area is dry but when the rains do come, the rivers and ravines become torrential waterways sweeping over the parched plains. It is quite a sight, and it can leave you stranded until the water levels drop.

The environment in Northern Kenya supports many species not seen in other parts of the country such as the Grevy's zebra with saucerlike ears and narrower stripes. There are only about 10,000 left as they are hunted for their skins. The reticulated giraffe is only found here. Lake Turkana's **South Island**, 39 sq km, was established as a national park in 1983 for the protection of the Nile crocodile's breeding ground. South Island is also home to several species of venomous snakes, including vipers, puff adders and cobras. It is also an important breeding ground for hippos.

There are plenty of national parks in Northern Kenya. On the northeastern shores of Lake Turkana is the Sibilois National Park, just north of Isiolo you will find Samburu, Buffalo Spring and Shaba National Reserves, all three along the banks of the Ewaso Nyiro River covering an area of some 300 sq km. Further north still are the parks at Maralal, Losai and Marsabit.

If you're driving in this area you'll need to fill up with plenty of petrol, as it is in particularly short supply

Travelling in Northern Kenya is a real adventure as there is almost no public transport in this desolate region. In fact, there is little traffic of any kind making hitching an unadvisable option. The western approach from Kitale is the simplest way for independent travellers without vehicles as there is transport to Kalokol on the lake on a fairly regular basis. Driving yourself is a possibility (a four-wheel drive is imperative), though this is not exactly trouble free. You will need to bring a number of tools in case of breakdown or getting stuck in the sand: a jack, sand ladders, a shovel and a rope.

An alternative method of exploring Northern Kenya is to go on an organized tour

Most operators offer an eight- to nine-day tour heading up the Rift Valley to stop at Lake Baringo going on to Maralal and then to Lake Turkana via Baragoi and South Horr. The return journey goes via Samburu National Park and Buffalo Springs National Reserve. Some go via the Marsabit National Reserve crossing the Koroli Desert. Most use open-sided four-wheel drive trucks, not built for comfort but sturdy and reliable. If you have a bit more money to spend, some companies arrange flying safaris.

It is essential to take adequate supplies of water as it is not possible to buy water at the lake

Seeing the western side of Lake Turkana by road involves a long rough trip. The desert and lake are beautiful. It is best to spend one or two nights at Marich Pass. *Matatu* touts try to overcharge travellers in Kitale. Expect to pay around US$3 for a ride from Kitale to Marich Pass via Kapenguria. At Marich Pass transport on to Lodwar passes through around midday. In Lodwar the *New Salama Hotel and Restaurant* are cheap and good value. It is possible to get a *matatu* from Lodwar to Kalokol – there are about four daily. Basic food and accommodation is available at *Tours Lodge*. The *Fisherman's Lodge* is scheduled to reopen this year. From Kalokol it is one hour's walk to the lake. You are advised to walk either in the early morning or evening as it gets extremely hot. A guide can be hired at *Tours Lodge*.

Travellers are currently advised against travel into the far northeast of Kenya from Isiolo towards the Somali border because of safety concerns

Another important factor to consider when exploring this region is the time of year. The majority of the inhabitants are Muslim and will adhere to Ramadan, a month of fasting. During Ramadan most stores and hotels are closed through daylight hours, though public transport and official business usually continue as normal. The times of Ramadan vary each year.

The recent problems in Sudan and Somalia, and the subsequent influx of refugees into Kenya from these countries, means there is a high military presence in the north. Vehicles usually travel in convoys, and are escorted by armed guards. Road blocks are common and vehicle searches are a part of everyday life. However, it is rare that this level of precaution is required on the A2 – Trans-East African Highway – that passes through Isiolo, Marsabit and on to Moyale at the Ethiopian border. On the whole this is a safe area to travel, with only the occasional skirmish reported,

Lake Turkana

Sleeping
1 Fisherman's Lodge
2 Oasis Lodge

Campsites
3 El-Molo

and you are assured a warm welcome wherever you go. However, the area north of Isiolo into the far northeast towards the Somali border, including the town of Garissa, has had a number of incidents, resulting in injuries and fatalities.

Marich Pass

If you are coming up into Northern Kenya from Kitale, you travel a glorious route through the highlands, close to the **Saiwa Swamp National Park**, see page 193. Continuing through the northern gorges of the Cherangani Hills, will bring you to the desert plains through the Marich Pass. The views are incredible, looking down onto the plains from the lush highlands. There isn't much happening around here, the only town in these parts is **Ortum** where you should be able to find accommodation though it is pretty basic. If you do intend to stop and explore the area, the best place to stay is the Marich Pass Field Studies Centre (see below). This is an educational facility set up for groups to study various aspects of the environment in this area but it welcomes independent travellers.

1° 50′ N, 35° E
Colour map 3, grid B4

Kenya

In the Trans Nzoia district, Cherangani Hills is a good place to base yourself to explore the area, which offers some of the best walking in Kenya away from other tourists. This is the fourth highest mountain range in Kenya, it includes rolling hills as well as dramatic mountain peaks, and forms the highest, most breathtaking and spectacular escarpments of the Rift Valley. There is plenty of water and it offers some of the best hiking in Kenya. All the main routes cross the 3,000-m contour, with decreased oxygen supplies. Car engine performance may be adversely affected by the altitude, and it is essential to carry extra supplies of fuel as consumption is heavy. The northern ranges are the most dramatic and least populated, but getting to them takes time if hitching, as there is no public transport. There are two approaches, from the Kapenguria-Marich Pass road, past a terrifying deep valley, or through the Kito Pass and up the Tot Escarpment. The main road is known as the Cherangani Highway, and is one of the most terrifying and challenging roads in Kenya. Grave mounds are concealed on top of the Kaisungur range, venerated and closely guarded by the local people. There are occasional sightings of the lammergeyers here, drifting on the thermal currents. The highlands are malaria free, but the lowlands are not. Tours (including ornithological) can be arranged through *Sirilwa Safaris*, PO Box 332, Kitale, TO325-20061.

Cherangani Hills
To visit these hills a good map is required

Mount Sekerr also known as Mtelo Mountain or Sigogowa, is a few kilometres from the Study Centre and is a fairly easy climb over a couple of days. Climbing Mount Sekerr starts from the thornbush covered plains of Turkana to the lush upper reaches inhabited by the Pokot people. As you ascend the flora changes from woodlands to heathland near the summit. The views from the top (3,326 m) are great looking down on to lush green forest glades and in the far distance the open thorn bush-covered plains of Turkana. Mount Sekerr is located to the north of the Cherangani Hills, and is an area where gold-panning is widespread. Mount Koh, 2,608 m, is very steep, with almost vertical rock rising for 300 m from a northerly spur of the Cheranganis. Should you feel inclined to climb it there are footpaths almost all the way, with just a couple of rough areas where scrambling is required. There are wonderful views overlooking the Weiwei Valley. The Marich Pass Field Studies Centre is a good local base and Pokot guides can be arranged from here.

Mount Sekerr

About 1½ hrs from the Marich Pass Field Studies Centre, the **Elgeyo Escarpment** rises to over 1,830 m with spectacular views out over the Kerio Valley. **Nasolot National Reserve** is also close by – see below.

South Turkana National Reserve is just northeast of the Marich Pass Field Studies Centre. Used by Turkana herdsmen as grazing land. Marich Pass is a dramatic deep rocky cleft at an altitude of 3,000 m carved by the Moruny River between the heavily

South Turkana National Reserve

wooded Cherangani Hills, opening out to the arid plains of the Lake Turkana basin below. The **Marich Pass Field Studies Centre**, PO Box 564, Kapenguria, is located 2 km downstream of the pass in a forest clearing. The compound is comprised of 12 ha of virgin forest leased from the Pokot County Country. Four hectares have been used to build the centre on the banks of the Moruny River and there are bush trails through the remaining 8 ha of virgin forest. The centre has been built using local labour and traditional materials and a percentage of its takings are donated to the local development fund. There is a strong eco-tourism ethos. Baboons, vervet monkeys and monitor lizards are permanent residents easily viewed, elephants and antelopes visit occasionally and the forests abound with birds. The centre is primarily an education establishment, catering for school and university groups on academic field study courses, but tourists and independent travellers are also welcome to stay. Pokot guides, many of whom are English speaking, are used for all walks and treks outside reserves. There are a variety of excursions including treks to visit local villages giving travellers an insight into Pokot culture. Further away, three-day trips to climb Mount Sekerr can be organized, or you can explore the Cherangani Hills to the south over several days. There are many caves in the hills, often of great significance to the Pokot people. The area is rich in archaeological findings. Bush walks in the national reserves are organized in conjunction with the Game Department, and require the presence of armed game rangers. The Pokot people, farmers in the hills and semi-nomadic pastoralists on the arid northern plains, have traditionally panned the rivers for gold, and lessons can be arranged.

Sleeping **D-F** *Marich Pass Field Studies Centre*, T0321-31541. Banda accommodation (2 sizes) sleeping 2-3or 5-6 people. There are also larger dormitories housing 5-25 people. The ablution block, about 140 m from the bandas, has toilets and showers (cold). Hot bucket showers can be arranged. Facilities include firewood, a laundry service and fresh, pure drinking water from the well. There is a restaurant offering a buffet of fresh locally grown produce prepared in both African and western style, and a small bar serves beer and cold sodas (no spirits). Some meals like the Abyssinian Special require 12 hrs notice. If preferred guests may eat outside their bandas. Local shops sell provisions, there is a guidebook for sale, but there is no petrol available. **Camping F** Camping is also available at the *Marich Pass Field Studies Centre* (above).

Transport **Road** The Marich Pass is about 70 km from **Kitale** and the most direct route is going north along the spectacular sealed tarmac A1 road, via Kapenguria towards Lodwar.

You can also reach it from **Eldoret** or Kabarnet via Iten and then on through the upper Kerio Valley joining the Kitale-Lodwar road near Kapenguria. The third way is via the unmade road from **Lake Baringo** through the Kito Pass, across the Kerio Valley to Tot, although this route involves travelling a track through the northern face of the Cherangani Hills that becomes impassable after heavy rains, when the streams that cross the track flood the road. This route is only manageable with a 4WD.

The centre itself is off the main Kitale-Lodwar road to the north. It is clearly signposted 1 km north of the Sigor-Tot junction at Marich Pass. There is no public transport.

Nasolot National Reserve The Nasolot National Reserve covers 92 sq km, ranging in altitude from 750-1,500 m, and is located in the West Pokot District, 1 km before the Kainuk centre on the Kitale-Lodwar road. The habitat is predominantly thicket and dry bushland, with many succulents and acacias bordering the seasonal streams and rivers that criss-cross the reserve. There are elephants in the reserve but they are well camouflaged by the flora. Other mammals include the greater and lesser kudu, buffalo, lion, leopard, dikdik, warthog and bushbuck. The birdlife is rich and varied and includes the white-crested turacos, Abyssinian ground hornbills, superb starlings and Abyssinian rollers.

A hydro-electric dam is sited at the head of a gorge harnessing the waters of the Turkwell River. The dammed waters have formed a large artificial lake that stretches westwards between the hills, home to a large variety of birdlife. *Kenya Power and Lighting Company*, the owners of the dam and company town, have cottages for rent. Other facilities include a swimming pool, bar and restaurant. Some of the small birds like starlings and weavers in the compound are unusually tame. ■ *Pre-booking is necessary and there is a small entrance fee to the compound. Contact Turkwell Dam, T0325-20602.*

Situated in the Rift Valley in Turkana District this is remote, rarely visited and has no tourist facilities. It is 100 km north of Kitale and is located between 900-2,720 m. The Kerio River borders the reserve to the southeast. If you do venture up here you are likely to see elephant or greater kudu in the dense thorn bush, riverine forest and scattered forest that make up its 1,000 sq km area. There are two small mountains in the reserve with forests on their summits, home to the larger mammals in the reserve. The local Turkana people have a warlike reputation, and will kill wild animals for food unlike the other groups in this region. There are no tourist facilities in the reserve. The nearest town to the both reserves is **Chepterr**, west of the main road close to Nasolot National Reserve.

South Turkana National Reserve
2° N, 35° 45′ E

Kenya

Lodwar

The only town of any size in the northwest of the region is Lodwar, the administrative centre. Historically it was an important colonial outpost where frequent Ethiopian raids were countered. Jomo Kenyatta was held here briefly whilst in detention. It is not nearly so isolated as in the past due to the opening of a surfaced road from the highlands and air connections to Nairobi, but it is still very much a backwater town with a pleasant enough atmosphere. It is currently the boom town in the region because of the possibility of oil discoveries, the development of the fishing industry at the lake, and the extension of a surfaced road from Kitale. This is a useful base if you intend to explore the lake from the western side. There is both a bank (though do not rely on it taking travellers' cheques) and a post office in town. The local people, predominately Turkana, are persistent in attempts to sell their crafts, but it is generally done in a friendly spirit. You can buy very large, beautiful baskets made by local women. Take good care of your possessions here.

3° 10′ N, 35° 40′ E
Phone code: 0393
Colour map 3, grid A4

At the moment most available accommodation is at the bottom end of the market, though a luxury hotel is planned just outside the town by the Turkwel River, which is frequently just a dry riverbed, lined with dense riverine forests. **D** *Turkwel*, T0393-21201. Best accommodation in town, rooms come with a fan and bathroom, for slightly more you can hire a self-contained cottage with a full breakfast included in the price. The bar is popular with Lingala music playing into the small hours. **E** *Africana Silent Lodge*, basic, no nets, fan, communal showers clean, has a restaurant. **E** *Mombasa*, next to the JM Bus office. The best in this price range. **E** *Nawoitorong Guest House & Conference Centre*, just outside of town to the south. The centre was set up to support single mothers and drought victims but will take travellers. There are mosquito nets, and breakfast is provided. Recommended. Now also do dinners.

Sleeping & eating
You will need a room with both a fan and mosquito protection if you intend to get any sleep

Road **Bus**: buses go between here and **Kitale** daily, taking around 7 hrs. There are also a few *matatus* which work the route though whether they reach their final destination depends on the number of passengers. The bus leaves from Kitale at 1500 and leaves Lodwar for Kitale at 0700. It is wise to take water and food for the trip as breakdowns and delays are common. Book your seat on the return to Kitale the night before as the bus gets very full. The petrol station at Lodwar is the last place to buy fuel and food on the way to Eliye Springs.

Transport

Lake Turkana – West

Kalokol

From this side of the lake it is possible to access Central Island National Park. The main virtue of this approach to the lake is accessibility, as it is only 35 km from Lodwar

This small, simple town 0is just a few kilometres from the lakeshore and the heat is quite oppressive. Getting water supplies in the dry season poses major problems. The women walk 3 km to extract water from the riverbed. Although you can drink the lake water after boiling it, it is brackish and tastes unpleasant.

To get to the lake you will need to walk out to the Italian-sponsored fish processing plant (you can ask for a guide from *Oyavo's Hotel* if you want one). **Ferguson's Gulf**, 64 km northeast of Lodwar, is the most accessible part of the Lake Turkana, but not the most attractive. However, here the lake is fringed with acacias, doum palms and grass, in marked contrast to the moonscape appearance with a mass of volcanic lava around Teleki's Volcano, at the south of the lake. There are loads of birds here particularly flamingos and it is the only place in Kenya where, in the springtime, black-tailed godwits and spotted redshanks can be seen. Birds of prey can also be spotted, and the number of hippos and crocodiles make swimming a fairly exciting activity. If you do intend to swim, ask the local people where to go.

To get on to the wild and beautiful lake you can hire a boat from *Turkana Lodge* at Ferguson's Gulf to take you to the **Central Island National Park**. This is expensive: a cruiser costs around US$100 for eight or a long-boat for four costs US$45, but is well worth the trip. You will also be asked for a national park entrance fee by the park game wardens. The island is just 5 sq km with three small volcanoes on it plus several small crater lakes that are the nesting area of large colonies of water birds, including flamingos. There are many reptiles on the island and if you arrive around April-May, you can witness crocodiles hatching and sprinting off down to one of the crater lakes. The island has black lava sand beaches. It is possible to negotiate with a local fisherman to take you out on his craft, though remember that the lake's unpredictable sudden squalls are a real danger, and there are crocodiles.

En route to or from Kalokol look out for the standing stones of **Namotunga** which have a spiritual meaning to the Turkana who gather here in December.

Sleeping and eating E *Kalokol Tourist Lodge*, very simple, no tap water or mosquito nets, small restaurant. **E** *Oyavo's*, in Kalokol. The rooms are clean and cooler than you would expect, with palm leaf thatch roofs. Food is basic, fish and rice, but sufficient, and there are warm beers and sodas.

Transport Buses go from Lodwar at 0500 (the driver honks his horn to announce his departure) arriving at Kalokol 1½ hrs later.

Eliye Springs

A far more pleasant place to see the lake from and the springs themselves under the palm trees bubble up warm water. However, you will need a vehicle to get here. There is a small village nearby where you can get some food and drink and no doubt some of the local people will want to sell you their handicrafts. The turn-off for Eliye springs is about halfway along the Lodwar to Kalokol road. As it is 70 km from Lodwar, your best bet would be to base yourself there, and travel up to the Springs. The last 10 km is very sandy.

Sleeping   There is one basic place to stay, the *Old Lodge*, but facilities are virtually non-existent. Follow the main sandy road straight to the lake, where the palm leaves are on the road. Basic rooms cost US$10, camping US$5, wonderful showers. Beer and soft drinks intermittently available after a truck delivery. No food.

Lake Turkana – East

Exploring the lake from the east is far more exciting than the west, and you pass through a number of national reserves. Driving here takes skills and steel nerves and you will need a four-wheel-drive vehicle. Few of the roads are surfaced, and the main

A2 road is tricky to say the least. Avoid the rainy season as some routes become impassable. Public transport is available for most of the way, though not as easy as on the west. The following route is taken: north from Isiolo to Archers Post on the A2 road, also known as the Trans-East-African Highway, then looping west along the C79 to Wamba and Maralal National Sanctuary, before travelling north along the secondary road to Baragoi, South Horr and the eastern side of Lake Turkana including the remote Sibiloi National Park. Returning to the Trans-East-African Highway, Losai National Reserve is the starting point for the journey north to Marsabit and points west, and on to Moyale.

Isiolo is an interesting little frontier town, very different from the rest of the Central Province towns around Mount Kenya. Security problems with nomadic bandit groups operating to the north, up to the Ethiopian border have disrupted livestock raising, leading to a fall in prosperity, with the result that various services like the bank and bus services north have closed down. Although Isiolo is safe enough, travel further north requires caution, especially towards the northeast. The town is at the end of the tarmac road heading north, which quickly becomes Samburu country. There's a busy goat, cattle and camel market here, in addition to the fruit and vegetable market. For travelling to Lake Turkana's eastern shores the best route is likely to be from Isiolo, which is 50 km north of Meru, which is why it is included in this section, though strictly speaking it is located in the Central Highlands. The road to Isiolo is sealed and generally in good condition. Petrol is available here, and there is a post office (the last town to have these facilities until you reach either Maralal or Marsabit). It is also the last place to have a good supply of provisions, including an excellent fruit and vegetable market. At the *Frontier Bar and Disco* you can drink and dance with the locals. George Adamson who was later to become internationally famous along with his wife, Joy, for hand-rearing Elsa, the lioness featured in *Born Free*, was a game warden in Isiolo prior to becoming a celebrity.

Isiolo
0° 24' N, 37° 33' E
Colour map 3, grid B5

This is the last place with good facilities on your journey north

Isiolo is the town closest to the entrance of the Lewa Wildlife Conservancy, situated about 15 km to the southwest (see below). It is also the nearest town to explore the national reserves at **Samburu**, **Buffalo Springs** and **Shaba**, all grouped together 40 km to the north. These national parks are the most accessible of the northern wildlife sanctuaries (see page 290).

D *Bomen*, PO Box 67, T0165-2225, F2059. The best hotel in town, a little expensive by Isiolo standards, but it is nevertheless good value. Well furnished with a bar, TV room, pool table and a good restaurant. The staff are friendly, and there is secure parking. Rooms are s/c, with hot water. **E** *Pasoda Lodge*. Good double rooms, s/c, restaurant. **F** *Jamhuri Guest House* is one of the best of the cheap hotels and has been popular with travellers for years, the rooms are clean, have mosquito nets and the communal showers have hot water. You are ensured a warm welcome by the hosts, has undergone recent renovation, and some s/c rooms are still under construction. Has a

Sleeping
■ *on map*
*For price codes:
see inside front cover*

Isiolo

To District Hospital (1 km) & Police
Checkpoint to Marsabit & Moyale

To Post Office & Police Stations

6

7 @ (Closed)

☐ Medical Centre

Total

11   1

Barclays
(Closed)

12   Ⓢ

2

5

1

13

Eastex
Coaches

9   3

8

Frontier
Disco & Bar

14   4

10

N

Not to scale

To Meru & Nanyuki

7 Mashallah
8 Mocharo Lodge
9 Nanyuki Guest House
10 Pasoda Lodge
11 Savannah Inn
12 Silent Inn
13 Silver Bells
14 White House

■ **Sleeping**
1 Bomen
2 Farmers Board
  & Lodging
3 Green Light
4 Highway Lodging
5 Jamhuri Guest House
6 Madina Lodge

● **Eating**
1 Salama

small, clean restaurant attached. **F** *Mashallah*, PO Box 378, T2142. Tallest building in town, good value, very friendly and safe with a variety of rooms, some s/c, hot water in the mornings. Has great roof views – possible to see Mt Kenya summit on a cloudless day, but only limited secure parking. **F** *Mocharo Lodge,* PO Box 106, T0165-2385. Best of the cheaper hotels, obliging staff, rooms functional and clean with mosquito nets, hot water (although the supply can be erratic). Secure parking, and food of moderate quality is available in the restaurant. **F** *Silent Inn*. Quiet location, adequate small rooms based round an open courtyard, hot water in mornings and evenings, shared bathrooms, sign in entrance warns, 'No prostitutes. No alcohol.' **F** *Madina Lodge*. Located behind medical clinic, new and quite smart, hot water, shared bathrooms, basic but comfortable and clean. **F** *Silver Bells*. Good value, safe parking for cars and motorcycles, shared bathrooms, hot water mornings and evenings. **F** *Farmers Board and Lodging*. Basic with shared bathrooms, no hot water. **F** *Savannah Inn*. Fairly simple with shared bathrooms and no hot water **F** *Nanyuki Guest House*, PO Box 211. Spartan, with shared bathrooms, hot water in the mornings, offers a laundry service. **F** *White House*. Built round a courtyard which houses the odd chicken, secure, some s/c rooms, no hot water. **F** *Highway Lodging*. Simple but clean, mosquito nets, shared bathrooms, no hot water. **F** *Green Light*. Secure, shared bathrooms, hot water in mornings and evenings. **Camping** On the way from Isiolo to Marsabit you can stay at the campsite at the Catholic Mission at Laismais, which is approximately halfway to Marsabit.

Eating **Cheap** *The Bomen Restaurant*, has the widest choice and the best food. Excellent place for a beer in the evening. **Seriously cheap** *The Interfast*, at Mashallah. Good basic food. *Salama Restaurant*, T2229, is the best of the cheap restaurants, the simple fare includes Somalian dishes. *The Silver Bells*, decent basic restaurant.

Entertainment The *Frontier Disco and Bar* is a lively place, particularly on Fri and Sat.

Transport **Road** Isiolo is an important transport hub for travel north to **Marsabit** and **Moyale**, and northeast to **Wajir** and the very remote town of **Mandera** close to both the Somali and Ethiopian border in Kenya's far northeast. Travel to northeastern Kenya is currently advised against on grounds of safety.

Transport services are erratic and availability varies **Bus** *Akamba* runs twice daily (0700 and 2000) 6 hrs to **Nairobi**, stopping at Nanyuki, Nyeri and other towns for US$6. *Eastex Coaches*, whose office is near *Salama Restaurant*, run a daily service to Nairobi that leaves at 0700, cost US$3.50.

The *Babie Coach*, a converted Isuzu truck, runs up and down between **Maralal** and Isiolo via Wamba, leaving each town on alternate days. The departure time is 1100-1300 depending on the number of passengers. The trip takes about 5-8 hrs depending on load and road conditions. Cost US$6.

The *Miraj* bus service that ran from Isiolo to **Marsabit** taking about 6 hrs has now closed down. It is possible to arrange a lift on a truck (you may have to travel in the back on top of the cargo) to Marsabit (8 hrs) and Moyale (12 hrs from Marsabit). It is a hot, dusty journey. The people in *Mashallah Lodge* are very helpful with this. Trucks leave in convoy at 0530 from near *Barclays Bank* (closed). There are regular *matatus* to **Meru** and other nearby Central Province towns.

Lewa Wildlife Conservancy The Lewa Wildlife Conservancy is situated about 15 km southwest of Isiolo on the northern foothills of Mount Kenya, approximately 65 km northeast of Nanyuki. The land comprises savannah, wetland, grassland and indigenous forest. It was officially registered as a Non-Profit Organization in 1995. Three quarters of Kenya's wildlife is found on private land outside the national parks and reserves. The conservancy project aims to minimize the conflict between conservation and human settlement and protect and encourage the rhinoceros and other endangered species. The Lewa Downs and later the adjoining state-owned **Ngare Ndare Forest** were fenced to reduce the human/wildlife conflict and loss of smallholders crops to elephants. It also incorporates the **Ngare Sergoi Rhino Sanctuary**, which no longer exists as a separate entity. Numbers of both black and white rhino have increased, with none lost to poachers. It is possible to see the 'Big Five' here (lion, leopard, rhinoceros, elephant and buffalo). Grevy's zebra numbers have risen from 81 to over 400. Lewa Downs also contains an archaeological site where Mary Leakey found prehistoric tools and artefacts, some of which are on display in the Meru Museum.

Tourism is being expanded to help cover the cost on the conservancy, but will be kept within clear limits with a maximum of 60 tourist beds. The original homestead has been converted into a Conservation Centre. As it is a non-profit organization all tourist-generated income goes to pay for security and management of the wildlife.

Sleeping There are 2 lodges on Lewa. **L** *Lerai Tented Camp* is run by *East African Ornithological Safaris Ltd*, and **L** *Wilderness Trails*, on Lewa Downs ranch, is operated through *Bush Homes of East Africa Ltd* (PO Box 56923, Nairobi, PO Box 56923, T01-571647, F571665, www.bush-homes.co.ke). At *Wilderness Trails* there are 16 beds in the house and also 3 thatched cottages with en-suite bathrooms, game drives, horseback expeditions and camel safaris are available. Tourist accommodation is now also available at 2 community wildlife schemes, supported by Lewa. **L** *Il'Ngwesi Lodge*, which has 4 self-catering bandas on Lewa's northwest boundary is the first tourist lodge to be wholly owned and run by the local Samburu people, and *Namunyak Wildlife Conservation Trust* – about 90 km north of Lewa in the Mathews Mountains. Namunyak means 'place of peace' and again the local Samburu community benefit directly from the monies generated from *Sarara Lodge*. To visit the remote wilderness areas of *Il Ngwesi* and *Il Ngwesi Lodge* contact *Let's Go Travel* and for *Namunyak Wildlife Conservation Trust* and *Sarara Safari Camp* contact *Acacia Trails Ltd* – listed under Nairobi tour operators. For further information contact Lewa Wildlife Conservancy, PO Box 49918, Nairobi, T607893, F607197, lewa@swiftkenya.com **Camping** is available through *Abercrombie and Kent Ltd* and includes game drives, full board and laundry facilities – maximum of 16 beds. (For details see page 106).

About one hour's drive north of Isiolo, this is a very small and hot outpost bordered by the Samburu and Buffalo Springs National Reserve to the west and the Shaba National Reserve to the east. There are a couple of places where you can stay, as well as a few small shops and cafés. Curio sellers and tour guides for the parks are also around. It is usually possible to get a lift from here to Marsabit.

Archers Post
Colour map 3, grid B5

The Samburu people inhabit this region. Every 14 years their circumcision rite is enacted when a new group of boys are officially initiated into manhood. For the next 14 years this group become warriers, while the preceding group are elevated to become junior-elders. As the boys are rarely circumcized prior to puberty, the group includes many men. They can be easily identified because they wear goatskins, dyed black and worn draped over one shoulder. These black goatskins are worn prior to and for one month after circumcision.

Sleeping **E** *Acacia Shade Inn*, basic rooms get rather hot, mosquito nets, bucket showers although water supply can be problematic. Has secure parking. Amazingly for such a remote area, credit card payment is possible. You can organize hiking safaris with a local guide from here. **E** *Archers Safari Lodge*, small rooms, a bit rough and smelly. **E** *Kamanga Lodge*, reasonably clean, mosquito nets and paraffin lamps, rooms are likely to heat up during the day as there is little shade around.

Approximately halfway between Archers Post and Loruk, to the west of Samburu National Park is **L** *Ol Malo*, book through *Bush Homes of East Africa Ltd*, PO Box 56923, Nairobi, PO Box 56923, T01-571647, F571665, www.bush-homes.co.ke This is a ranch and game sanctuary with 4 expensive and exclusive guesthouses on a hill near the Ewaso Nyiro River, with en-suite bathrooms and verandahs offering views towards Mt Kenya.

Kenya

Samburu/Buffalo Springs National Park

Samburu
0° 40' N 37°, 30' E
See map page 86

One of the most pleasant national parks in Kenya and not too crowded

This national park was opened in 1965 in the hot, arid lowland area just to the north of Mount Kenya, 325 km from Nairobi and 50 km from Isiolo town on the Isiolo-Marsabit road. *Samburu Lodge* is on the site where the professional hunter Arthur Neumann camped, as described in his book *Elephant Hunting in Equatorial Africa*, published in 1898. The permanent water and forest shade on the banks of the Ewaso Nyiro River attract plentiful wildlife from the region including elephant, cheetah, reticulated giraffe, oryx, vervet monkeys, Grevy's zebra and crocodiles. Leopards are regularly spotted. The birdlife is unusually numerous in this park, and large flocks of guinea-fowl can be seen in the afternoons coming to drink at the river-banks. Doves, sandgrouse and the pygmy falcon are frequently seen. The area north of the Ewaso Nyiro River is very attractive with plains and low hills that are rocky in places. The dry watercourses are fringed with acacias, and the blue-grey mountains fringe the view in silhouette. After a downpour the arid countryside turns green overnight, and a short time later flowers and sweet smelling grasses are abundant.

Buffalo Springs
A bridge over the Ewaso Nyiro River linking the two reserves was built in 1964. Elephant, zebra, giraffe, oryx, cheetah and crocodile can be found in the riverine forest of acacia and doum palm in this reserve 85 km north of Mount Kenya in Eastern Province, adjoining Samburu to the south. In the park is a crater, made when an Italian bomber mistook buffalo for targets in the Second World War. It is now a spring and is reportedly safe to swim in.

Sleeping & eating
Facilities are surprisingly good considering the 2 reserves put together only cover some 400 sq km, catering for both luxury and budget tourists. Many of the more upmarket lodges offer discounts of up to 50% in the off-season between Apr and Jul excluding Easter. **L** *Larsens Tented Camp*, PO Box 40075, Nairobi, T02-540780, F545948, east of *Samburu Lodge*. Located by the river, small, 17 tents with en suite bathrooms. There is an animal-viewing platform in a tree. Highly recommended. Offers game drives and excellent food and the use of *Samburu Lodge* pool. Children under 10 years excluded. **L** *Samburu Intrepids*, T0164-30813, F20022 (camp), or PO Box 74888, Nairobi, T02-716628, F716517, heritagehotels@form-net.com 27 luxurious tents overlooking Ewaso Nyiro River, with large four-poster beds and en-suite bathrooms. Swimming pool, and activities on offer include camel safaris, and rafting when the river level is high enough. *Intrepids* is the mid-range

Samburu/Buffalo Springs National Park

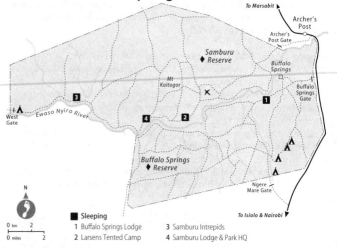

Sleeping
1 Buffalo Springs Lodge
2 Larsens Tented Camp
3 Samburu Intrepids
4 Samburu Lodge & Park HQ

brand of the upmarket *Heritage Hotels Group*. **L** *Samburu Lodge* (**A** in low seasons), T2051 radiocall Nairobi, bookings: PO Box 40075, Nairobi, T540780, F545948. The oldest lodge in the reserve situated in the bend of the river, this is a wonderful place to stop off for a drink at the *Crocodile Bar* even if you do not stay. Relaxed atmosphere in a beautiful setting, swimming pool, shop. **A** *Buffalo Springs Lodge*, T0165 (Isiolo), bookings: PO Box 30471, Nairobi, T336858, F218109. This is a pleasant relaxed lodge with good-value bandas, swimming pool, in an excellent location.

Camping E Camping is possible in Buffalo Springs Reserve, Ngere Mara, Ewaso Nyiro Bridge, and Maji ya Chumvi Stream near Buffalo Springs. The best is the one by Buffalo Springs Reserve that has showers and toilets. Baboons are a real nuisance here, stealing anything not nailed to the ground. It is wise to have a guard provided by the reserve, as there can be problems with theft and unwelcome visitors.

Samburu is a couple of hours north of Nanyuki. Buses run here from Isiolo in the plains below **Transport** on a regular basis. *Air Kenya* have daily flights from Wilson Airport, Nairobi, with a stop at Nanyuki, US$120 one way, US$210 return. They leave Nairobi at 0915 and arrive Samburu at approximately 1030, on the way back they leave Samburu for Nairobi at about 1050.

Shaba National Reserve

Some 70 km north of Mount Kenya, lying to the east of Archers Post is the Shaba   0° 40′ N, 37° 50′ E
National Reserve in Isiolo District of Eastern Province. It lies to the south of the   *See map page 86*
Ewaso Nyiro River. It is home to a number of gerenuk, gazelle, oryx, zebra, giraffe,
cheetah, leopard and lion which roam around acacia woodlands, bushlands and
grasslands. Shaba got its name from the volcanic rock cone in the reserve. The
riverine areas are dominated by stands of acacia and doum palms. There are two luxury lodges and three campsites. This is an extension of Buffalo Springs and Samburu
National Reserve that lies to its west. The martial eagle can often be spotted here,
alert for its prey the guinea-fowl, or the occasional dik-dik. The naturalists Joy and
George Adamson who hand-reared lions and leopards and later returned them to
the wild (the subject of *Born Free*, a book and film) had a campsite in Shaba Reserve.
Joy's last project was the release of Penny the leopard, who subsequently mated and
reared a cub in the eastern part of the reserve, near a swamp. There is a simple
memorial plaque commemorating Joy's life and work erected by Isiolo County
Council at her campsite under the shade of umbrella acacias, adjacent to a swamp in
eastern Shaba.

L *Sambura Serena Safari Lodge*. Well designed, with swimming pool, overlooking the lazy **Sleeping** Uaso Nyuro River that is abundant with birdlife and crocodiles. Central bookings Nairobi, PO Box 48690, T02-711077/8, F718100/3, serenamk@africaonline.co.ke **L** *Sarova Shaba Lodge*, PO Box 30680, Nairobi, T333248, F211472. A luxury lodge, opened in 1989, offering excellent facilities, just to the east of Archers Post. It overlooks the river, is well designed and has a swimming pool that curves around a natural rock formation.

Buses to and from Archers Post to the south and Isiolo are fairly frequent. To the north, **Transport** Marsabit and Moyale, there is no public transport. The *Babie Coach* runs between Maralal and Isiolo via Archers Post and Wamba – see under Isiolo transport for details.

Wamba

A small town 90 km northwest of Isiolo, and 55 km from the Samburu National   0° 58′ N, 37° 19′ E
Reserve. Northeast of Wamba are the Mathew's Mountain Range, where the peaks   *Colour map 3, grid B4*
are covered in cycads and podocarpus forest. The best view of the mountain is to be
seen from the road going up to *Kitich Camp*. The highest peak in the range is Mount
Warges at 2,688 m. Other peaks are Mathew's peak at 2,374 m, Mathew's South Peak
at 2,284 m, Lolokwe at 1,852 m, Lesiolo at 2,475 m and Poror at 2,581 m. These

mountains offer pleasant walking opportunities in the shade but views tend to be restricted by the flora. The Ngeng River has a couple of big rock pools suitable for swimming. Guides and Askaris are needed to visit this area. Wamba is a useful place to stock up on fresh meat and other provisions.

Near Wamba, in lush forest at the southern end of the Mathew's Mountains, is **L** *Kitich Camp*. There are 6 twin-bed tents beside a seasonal river, game walks, bird-watching and a natural pool nearby suitable for swimming. As with all lodges and tented camps organized through *Bush Homes of East Africa Ltd*, PO Box 56923, Nairobi, PO Box 56923, T01-571647, F571665, www.bush-homes.co.ke, the accommodation is exclusive and expensive. **E** *Saudia Lodge*, off the main street where you can get sound food and lodging in a family-run establishment.

Maralal

1° N, 36° 38' E
Colour map 3, grid B4

You can arrange to join a safari to Lake Turkana from here taking about 8 days

The area north of Maralal up to the Ethiopian border has had periodic tribal clashes, with many people killed. Tourists have been robbed. Check it is safe to travel locally

High up in the hills, Maralal looks down onto the Lerochi Plateau, about 240 km from Meru and 160 km from Nyahururu. Long before the British administrators moved in, this was a spiritual site for the Samburu. The route from Isiolo passes though a wildlife haven and from the road you will be able to see zebra, impala, eland, buffalo, hyena and warthog roaming a lovely area of gentle hills and forests. Maralal was until recently home to Wilfred Thesiger, explorer and travel writer.

One of your first meetings with Maralal, if you alight here, will be with 'The Plastic Boys', an unendearing nickname for the local guides and curio sellers, who have been organized into a co-operative. It is not clear whether this has done them any good. If you are polite to them they will happily show you around Maralal. In return you are encouraged to visit their little shop on the town's outskirts and buy a little token. It is through them that excursions within this area can be organized – by camel or donkey. You could even arrange a trek to Lake Turkana from here.

The town itself has all basic amenities, including a number of good cheap hotels as this is the preferred route of safaris going up to Lake Turkana. There is a bank and post office and two petrol stations. Traditionally garbed Samburu are still very much in evidence here, brightening up the surroundings with their skins, blankets, beads and hair styles.

Sleeping & eating

L *Maralal Safari Lodge*, PO Box 45155, Nairobi, T211124, F214261, about 3 km out of town towards Baragoi. A series of cottages with a main bar and restaurant and there is also a souvenir shop. The lodge is by a water hole which attracts a wide range of wildlife, and it is a nice place to go and have a beer (you don't need to be a resident to eat or drink here).

C-E *Maralal Hostel*, about 3 km out of town. Excellent facilities (a library, self-service restaurant and bar, shop and a lounge), it offers comfortable bandas or dormitory accommodation. The bandas and restaurant are relatively expensive. **D** *Buffalo Lodge*, good value, the bar here is a popular, lively place. **D** *Yare Club and Camp*, PO Box 281, Maralal, T/F0368-2295, Nairobi contact: PO Box 63006, Nairobi, T/F213445. 3 km out of town on the road towards Isiolo. If requested the Isiolo-Maralal bus will drop you at their gate, this is a quiet place, although it can get pretty raucous in the evening once the bar gets going, the camping facilities are excellent, with lots of toilets and showers, all a stone's throw away from the bar and restaurant. It costs US$6 a night for the pitch, there are also a dozen charming bandas, all s/c (only cold water) and roomy. Adjacent to the bar is a games room with a couple of dart boards, a table tennis table and a pool table in the making. A token membership is required for their use. Malcolm, the English owner, is always around and is very helpful. His phone and fax can be used. Variety and taste from the kitchen leaves a little to be desired – Malcolm is rumoured to subsist solely on Yorkshire pudding, gravy and beer. With his resident camels, half-day, day and much longer treks are available. Mountain bike trips can also be organized from here.

E *Buffalo*, good basic hotel. **E** *Impala Lodge*, quiet and clean. Recommended. **E** *Jamaru Hotel*, the best place to stay and eat in town with a choice of rooms, walk through the restaurant to reach reception. **E** *Kariara*, cheap and basic for budget traveller. **E** *Kimanik*, good value. **Camping** (**E**) available at the *Maralal Hostel*, with good facilities, and at Yare Club and Camp (see above). **Cheap** *Hard Rock Café*, does excellent food, friendly staff.

Baragoi

This next settlement on the route up to the eastern shores of Lake Turkana marks the end of the Elbarta Plains, climbing into the mountains. Baragoi is very easy to reach from Maralal, with many hitches and *matatus* available. It's an awful road in parts, particularly as there are a fair few steep climbs and descents. It takes from three to six hours depending on conditions. About 40 km before Baragoi you will see what looks like an almost lunar landscape of semi-arid mountains and plains. It is a sight well worth a stop before the descent into the plain that takes you to Baragoi.

1° 40' N, 36° 50' E
Colour map 3, grid B4

Baragoi is an important and expanding centre in this wilderness area. The locals jokingly say that the road is the 'International dividing line' between the Samburu and Turkana, and you will notice the design differences in their homesteads – the dome shape of the Turkana and the flatter wider Samburu *manyattas*.

The nearby Baragoi secondary school produces an amiable bunch of English speakers, knowledgeable about the area. There are a few general stores here and you should be able to get petrol (sold out of barrels). However, at present there is no electricity or running water in Baragoi.

E *Morning Star Hotel*. Paraffin lanterns and comfortable beds in clean rooms, shower and toilet separate – beware the latter because they use an ammonia-based disinfectant which may affect your breathing. This is by far the best place to stay, although a new hotel is planned soon. **Camping** There's a site about 4 km north of town, cross the River Baragoi and take first right, with water, toilets and Samburu warriors who will guard your possessions for US$3 a night.

Sleeping

Al-Mukaram, good, cheap, breakfast of *mandaazi*, eggs and tea, also good samosas. *Morning Star Hotel*, has an in-house butcher and *nyama choma* grill (barbecued meat including game). *Wid Wid Inn Hotel*, tasty meals prepared on demand, on main street. *Zaire Hotel*, new restaurant on the Nachola Rd. Recommended meals.

Eating

Regular *matatus* from **Maralal** cost about US$6. There are irregular lifts to South Horr. Without your own transport, going north to the lake or Marsabit requires putting the word out (and paying) and waiting, possibly for several days. To and from Isiolo – see Isiolo. To **Nyahurura**, the first *matatu* usually leaves around 0300 (making it possible to get to Nairobi by 0900-1000), later *matatus* leave from 0600 onwards.

Transport

South Horr

The nearest village to the southern end of Lake Turkana. The village itself is set in a beautiful canyon and is an oasis of green between two extinct volcanoes (Mount Nyiru and Mount Porale). The Samburu regard Mount Nyiru as being a place sacred to N'kai, their god, at the flat top of the mountain and take their cattle there to graze during the dry season where there is a plentiful supply of water. The shortest approach is via Tum, and an early morning start allows the ascent to be made in the mountain's shadow. On the summit a great pile of rocks marks the grave of a famous *laibon*, and there are excellent views of Lake Turkana and the Sugutu Valley. There are some great walks in the mountain forests all around you and you could either hike through (it's a good idea to take a guide) or go on a camel trek. All the tribes in northern Kenya with the exception of the Samburu own camels, and the Turkana were exceptional insofar as they did not use their camels as beasts of burden. It would appear there is no petrol for sale here.

Colour map 3, grid B4

Kenya

Sleeping & eating	On the southern slopes of Mt Nyiru is **L** *Desert Rose*, PO Box 24397, Nairobi, T577374-9, F564945, ras@swiftkenya.com Located below the tree-covered peaks of Mowongosowon, this is a new and secluded lodge with 5 sympathetically designed luxury guesthouses, a notable feature being the open-air en-suite bathrooms.

There is a Catholic Mission here with a nice site for **camping** nearby. There are a few **hotels** offering accommodation and food, though you will need to order your meal well in advance of actually eating it. There is also a **bar** with plenty of atmosphere, though there are only warm drinks.

Mount Kulal Biosphere Reserve *2° 30' N, 36° E*	This 7,000 sq km of land to the southeast of Lake Turkana in Eastern Province has been made into one of Kenya's four biosphere reserves. The area includes many different types of environments ranging from mountain forest about 2,400 m above sea level to desert with grasslands, dry evergreen forest, woodlands, bushlands and saltbush scrublands in between. It covers most of Lake Turkana, its volcanic southern shores, the Chalbi Desert and the South Island National Park. There are two outstanding volcanoes in the reserve, **Teleki**, that bounds the southern end of the lake, and **Mount Kulal** that stands at 2,285 m high, an extraordinary much-eroded tertiary volcanic mountain, and its ridge runs parallel to Lake Turkana, approximately 24 km to the east. Both mountains are a pretty straightforward climb if you are suitably equipped. Mount Kulal is covered with thick lush green forest in marked contrast to the desolate lava moonscape of the southern shores of Lake Turkana. Its ridge runs in a north-south direction, with deep gorges radiating to the east and west. **El Kajarta**, a great gorge with vertical walls rising over 300 m, located to the southeast of Kulal, appears to almost split the mountain in two. El Kajarta Gorge can be accessed with difficulty around the east side of the mountain.

Animals likely to be found here include giraffe, zebra, dik-dik, gazelle, elephant, cheetah, lion, black rhino, leopard, ostrich and crocodile, as well as less common species such as gerenuk and greater kudu.

This area shows evidence of human occupation from 10,000-12,000 years ago. Today the area is home to Samburu, Turkana and El Molo people around Lake Turkana, all of whom are pastoralists. There are no facilities for visitors to date.

Loyangalani

Colour map 3, grid A4 *There's a post office here, but no bank or garage*	One of the biggest villages on the eastern lake shore, Loyangalani is a collection of traditional huts, with thatched grass and galvanized-iron roofs. This is home to the dwindling numbers of El Molo people, a group of hardy fishermen. Believed to be of Cushitic origin from the northeast, this is Kenya's smallest ethnic group (according to ethnologists the 'pure' El Molo only number about 40, whereas others have traces of Samburu or Turkana ancestery). They are believed to have lived to the north of Lake Turkana, but were driven south by other warring tribesmen, seriously depleting their numbers in the process. They took refuge from their enemies by living on the small offshore islands. However, some of the small communities now live along the shoreline. An El Molo village overlooks the bay, perched above it on a hillside.

The water level of Lake Turkana is declining at a rate of 30 cm per annum, in a region where the annual rainfall is estimated to be only 50-60 mm. The lake is estimated to be 150 m lower than in the last century. This dramatic change in the lake's water level is attributed in part to the increased volume of water withdrawn for irrigation purposes from the River Omo by the Ethiopians.

North of El Molo Bay there is a stretch of metamorphic rocks dating from the pre-Cambrian period, leading to Lowasera Gorge. Excavations here, initially by DW Philipson in 1975, indicate that this is a very important archaeological site, rich in stone tools, weapons, pottery and bones.

The barren lava beds at the southern end of Lake Turkana peter out into the waters of the lake itself. The high salinity and soda mean nothing much grows around the shores.

L *Oasis Lodge*, PO Box 34464, Nairobi, T339025, F750035. Bungalows with electricity, it has a **Sleeping**
beautiful swimming pool and cold beers, non-residents are charged US$9 entrance.
A *El-Molo Camp*, T02-724384, Nairobi. Well equipped with a swimming pool and a bar, there
is also a restaurant that appears to open when you want, bandas with full board available.
Camping E at *El-Molo Camp*, you need to supply your own cooking fuel. Bottled water, 1.5
litres, costs US$5. Take purification tablets or boil the water.

Road The Loyangalini-**North Horr-Marsabit** road is virtually untravelled because the road **Transport**
is so terrible. Loyangalani to **Baragoi** by truck costs around US$8 per person. 1-2 trucks travel
weekly in both directions.

Sibiloi National Park

Sibiloi National Park is one of the less well known of Kenya's national parks, despite *4° N, 36° 25′ E*
its large size of 2,575 sq km It is now designated a World Heritage Site. It does not
have the level of tourist facilities as available in the other national parks. This is probably because of its isolated geographical location on the northeastern shores of Lake
Turkana – the Jade Sea – extending up towards Ethiopia, adjacent to Merille country
just across the border. These formidable tribesmen had a trademark mutilation –
they used to cut out the navels of anybody they killed.

The national park, does not have any water supply apart from the rather brackish
(but drinkable after boiling or chemical sterilization) water from the lake. It is 960
km by road from Nairobi via Marsabit, and about 320 km northwest of from
Marsabit town, in Eastern province. The landscape is relatively verdant lake side terrain with grassy plains with yellow spear grass and doum palms, extending to dry
semi-desert. Within the national park is **Central Island** that contains the world's
largest crocodile population of about 12,000. Other mammals include the reticulated giraffe, Grevy's zebra, Grant's gazelle, oryx, hartebeest, *tiang* (topi), lion and
cheetah. The golden jackal is found near Allia Bay. Birdlife is prolific with over 350
recorded species of bird.

The national park was originally established by the National Museum of Kenya to
protect the unique prehistoric archaeological sites. In 1960-70s the Leakeys made
many remarkable fossil finds of humans from 10,000-12,000 years ago. These finds
included *Homo Habilis* and *Homo Erectus*, which dated man's origin to 3,000,000
years ago. The **Koobi Fora palaeontological site** is located here, as is a museum
near the park's headquarters which houses the remains of prehistoric elephants
among other things. Over 4,000 fossil specimens have been found in this area.
Important finds include the homanid remains; the shell of a giant tortoise believed
to be over 3,000,000 years of age; the fossilized remains of the elephant's forebear –
the behemoth, with massive tusks; and crocodile jaws measuring over 1.5 m, which
equates to an overall length of over 14 m. The discovery of these fossils has resulted
in a greater understanding of the environment one to 3,000,000 years ago.

E There are several campsites in the park but you will need to bring all your own supplies, **Camping**
including petrol.

It is about 120 km from Loyangalani along an unpaved trail through the desert to North Horr **Transport**
and then northwest to Allia Bay, the park HQ. This is only passable by 4WD. It must be stressed
that sufficient supplies of fuel and water must be carried by any travellers who visit this area.
The most practical way of getting here is by air from Nairobi, or by boat from Ferguson's Gulf.

Travelling north on the Trans-East-African Highway from Archers Post the road **Losai National**
travels through the Losai National Reserve, with the majority of reserve located west **Reserve**
of the road. This is 1,800 sq km of thorny bushland situated in the Losai Mountains *1° 30′ N, 37° 30′ E*
southwest of and adjacent to Marsabit National Reserve and about 175 km north of
Mount Kenya, in northern Kenya. The reserve was gazetted in 1976 to give

Kenya

protection to elephant, greater and lesser kudu, lion and a few black rhino. It is a lava plateau with scattered volcanic plugs. There is a landing strip at a missionary post but no tourism is allowed at the moment as the reserve is trying to rehabilitate its elephant and black rhino populations that have been decimated by poachers. It is also unlikely tourism will develop for in the near future as it is virtually impenetrable even with a four-wheel drive.

Marsabit to Moyale

Matthew's Range lies to the west of the Isiolo to Marsabit road, just north of Wamba. This mountain range is thickly forested with its highest peak in the range is Mount Warges at 2,688 m. The area supports elephants, rhino, buffalo and other species and is in the process of being turned into a national reserve for rhino. There is also a spectacular array of butterflies and some unusual vegetation including cycad plants and giant cedars. There is **camping** nearby on the grounds of a derelict research centre, with no facilities, by a river, a beautiful spot. You are likely to be met by Samburu who will offer to guide you around the range for a small fee. The campsite is not easy to find, so ask for directions as there are tracks going all over the place. You will need to be totally self-sufficient here, so bring drinking water, food and fuelwood.

Marsabit

2° 45' N, 37° 45' E
Colour map 3, grid B5

Rising to 1,000 m above the surrounding plains, Marsabit is permanently green. The hills around the town are thickly forested making a nice change to the desert which surrounds the area. The main inhabitants of the town are the Rendille who dress in elaborate beaded necklaces and sport wonderful hairstyles. They are nomadic people keeping to their traditional customs of only visiting the town to trade. **Marsabit National Park** is nearby and houses a wide variety of wildlife though it is difficult to see much through the thick forest.

In Marsabit it is possible to organize a **camel safari** to Lake Turkana (Loyangalani) or to North Horr. Trucks run to North Horr about twice weekly, costing around US$12. The camel safari takes three days from North Horr and is rather gruelling but very worthwhile. The landscape is magnificent and you camp under the stars of the desert sky. The tour is organized by 'Duba' who can be contacted at the *Kenya Lodge* in Marsabit (see below). Duba has run this trip for the past 10 years and is very friendly and the best chapati cook in Kenya. Highly recommended. During periods of drought Marsabit has had no running water.

Marsabit National Reserve
2° 45' N, 37° 45'

Marsabit National Reserve is in Eastern Province 560 km north of Nairobi in the district of Marsabit. The whole area including the smaller national park, is designated a national reserve. It covers 2,088 sq km and contains the cloud-capped Mount Marsabit rising from an empty desert, undoubtedly the most attractive of North Kenya's extinct volcanic mountains. It is a large massif covered with lush, verdant growth that offers a welcome change from the desert that surrounds it. Its altitude stretches from 420 m, where thorny bushland dominates the scenery, to 1,700 m above sea level. There are several craters in the forest. The upper reaches are covered in forest, merging into acacia grasslands. The mountain is covered in a thick morning mist that dissipates by midday, after which it becomes warm and sunny.

Marsabit used to be famous for its large stocks of elephants, but these have sadly become depleted. They included the famous Ahmed, the bull-elephant whose long pointed tusks weighed over 45 kg each. Jomo Kenyatta designated him a national monument, and accorded him 24-hour protection. Ahmed died aged 55 years and his preserved remains can be viewed in Nairobi National Museum.

A number of birds and animals live here, including 52 different types of birds of prey. You are likely to see elephants, greater kudu, various species of monkeys, baboons, hyena, aard-wolf, caracal, cheetah, lion, gazelle, oryx and the reticulated giraffe. The volcanic craters are a special feature of Mount Marsabit, several of which contain freshwater lakes. **Gof Sokorte Guda** (Paradise Lake) is a wonderful spot to observe elephant and buffalo in the late afternoon, when they congregate for water.

To the southeast of the reserve at the so-called 'singing wells', local people are reputed to sing as they draw water from the deep wells.

B *Marsabit Lodge*, PO Box 45, Marsabit, T2044 (book through Msafari Inns, PO Box 42013, Nairobi, T330820, F227815). Wonderfully situated in front of the crater lake, *Gof Sokorte Dik*. *The cheapest place in town is* **E** *Al-Jazeera*, communal showers, bar and restaurant. **E** *Kenya Lodge*, good value, there is a good restaurant attached serving Ethiopian-style food including *ingera* (pancakes made from fermented batter) and stews. **E** *Marsabit Highway Hotel*, basic, simple hotel. There are many other small, cheap and basic hotels, several are built with an attractive courtyard layout, frequently embellished with flowers and offering some welcome shade. **Camping** There is a site (**E**) near the main gate of the NP. However there are no facilities. Also available at the Catholic Mission.

Sleeping & eating

There is a bank and post office here, as well as shops, bars, restaurants, hotels and 3 petrol stations. This is also the administrative capital in the district, and a major trading centre.

Transport

Disco At *Marsabit Highway Hotel* on Fri and Sat nights. Bar stays open every night until 0200. Also has rooms.

Entertainment

Air It is possible to charter a plane from Wilson Airport, Nairobi or take one of the small private airlines directly to Marsabit (see Airlines Domestic and Charter, see page 78).

Transport

Road There is no longer a bus service to Marsabit and Moyale from Isiolo. Trucks and private vehicles travel in convoy, with an armed guard, usually passing through during the afternoon or early evening in either direction. Pick-up to see Marsabit National Park costs about US$45 for a half day. Alternatively try to hitch a ride with the water truck to the lodge in the park. All vehicles travelling around Marsabit, Isiolo and Moyale must travel in convoy to minimize the likelihood of being attacked. The journey to Moyale can take up to 9 hrs passing through the Dida Galgalu Desert. The roads become virtually impassable when it rains.

Maikona is a larger village with shops, but no lodges, though the Catholic Mission here is very friendly and is fairly sure to let you stay (donations gratefully received).

North of Loyangalani you come to **North Horr**. The Catholic Mission here may be able to supply you with petrol (at a price) or lodgings if necessary.

It is possible to strike southwest from North Horr to El Molo Bay on Lake Turkana (see above, page 280).

Marsabit to Lake Turkana

Moyale

About 250 km north of Marsabit, Moyale is on the Kenyan-Ethiopian border. There have been differing reports on the time at which the Kenyan side of the border closes (either at 1800 or 1600 hours, get there before 1600 to make sure). The Ethiopian border (see page 770) is closed all day Sunday, as well as on public and religious holidays. It is possible to cross freely during daytime hours into Ethiopian Moyale to do some shopping, or even stay in the Ethiopian part of the town overnight, leaving the car behind on the Kenyan side, prior to completing the border formalities. This is a small town with a post office, basic shops and a police station that has only recently been supplied with electricity. It is developing slowly and there is now a bank here and two petrol stations.

3° 30′ N, 39° 0 E
Phone code: 0185
Colour map 3, grid A5

D *Medina Hotel*, central but a bit off the main road, clean and friendly hotel, nice balconies, bucket baths, no restaurant. **F** *Barissah*, where you can rent a bed for the night in an unlockable room for less than US$2, there are no showers, but you can have a bucket wash. If this is not available, try the **F** *Bismillahi Boarding and Lodging*, which has the same basic level of facilities but is slightly more expensive at US$2.50 per night.

Sleeping & eating

Seriously cheap *Somali Restaurant*, in *Barissah Hotel*, simple, with good basic food, around the corner from *Medina Hotel*. Has the only bar in town. For alcoholic beverages one must go to the Ethiopian side. **Beer** is available at the police barracks, where the officers are friendly towards visitors.

Transport
Petrol is much cheaper in Ethiopia than in Kenya

Road There is no longer a bus service to Marsabit and Moyale from Isiolo. Convoys leave for the south at around 0800, the lorries tend to congregate near the police station, so staying on the Ethiopian side (definitely the civilized preference), carries the risk of not clearing both immigration posts in time. The bus going north to Addis Ababa leaves at around 0500, so it is not possible to leave Moyale by bus on the day of entry. The bus northwards leaves from *Brothers Hotel* courtyard on the Ethiopian side of this border town.

Northeast Kenya

The most remote part of the country is the northeast, a vast wilderness with almost no sign that humans have ever been here. Part of the attraction is the immense scale and vast emptiness of this remote wilderness. Endless blue skies and flat landscapes produce a sense of solitude that is hard to experience anywhere else. The landscape is made up of tracts of desert and semi-desert barely broken by settlements and with almost no public transport. Its inaccessibility combined with security problems around the Somali border make this area unappealing to even the most intrepid travellers – no tour companies operate in this region. Physically, the area is very flat with two important rivers flowing through, the Tana River and the Ewaso Nyiro. As you would expect, it is around these waterways that settlement is greatest and the national parks are based. The **Tana River Primate National Reserve**, is based near Garsen though it is hard to reach. It was set up to protect the red colobus and crested mangabey monkeys (both endangered species). The reserve is more easily accessed from the coast, north of Malindi, so details are included in the coastal section (see page 261).

Poachers pose a real threat to tourists, being heavily armed and quite willing to attack if they feel it is justified. In recent years the Kenyan Government has had some success in combatting them

The majority of people living in this area are Somali and before the creation of country boundaries pastoralists roamed the area freely. In fact in colonial days, the area was known as Somali country. As countries in the region gained Independence, Somalia unsuccessfully tried to claim this area as part of Somalia. Shortly after, the area was closed to visitors by the Kenyan authorities who wished to drill for oil. Years of neglect and almost no development leave it one of the poorest areas of the country. These problems have been exacerbated more recently by the civil war in Somalia resulting in a huge influx of refugees into northeast Kenya. There are a number of refugee camps now set up for them (and for Somali-Kenyans who can no longer support their way of life in this barren area). Somalis are blamed for most of the poaching in the region.

Grouped together adjacent to Meru National Park (see page 142) are a chain of reserves. Immediately to the east of Meru National Park is Bisanadi National Reserve; next to that is Kora National Park and North Kitui National Reserve. Rahole National Reserve is north of Kora National Park. There are no facilities for visitors in any of these reserves, although there are plans to open up Kora National Park.

Bisanadi National Reserve
0° 10′ N, 38° 30′ E

This is adjacent to the northeast boundary of Meru National Park and is about 600 sq km. The area is mainly thorny bushland and thicket merging into wooded grasslands with dense riverine forests of raffia palm along the watercourses. You are likely to see the same sort of wildlife as in Meru National Park because it acts as a dispersal area during the rains. It is a particularly good place to find elephant and buffalo in the wet season.

On one of Kenya's most important waterways, the Tana River, the Kora National Park is 125 km east of Mount Kenya in Coastal Province and covers 1,787 sq km. It was gazetted in 1973 and was upgraded to a national park following the death of George Adamson. Meru National Park and the Tana River mark its northern boundary for 65 km. The eastern boundary is the Mwitamyisi River. The land is mostly acacia bushland with riverine forests of doum palm and Tana River poplar. On Tana River are the spectacular Adamson's Falls, the Grand Falls and the Kora Rapids.

Kora National Park
0° 10' S, 38° 45° E

Rocky outcrops or inselbergs are a local feature. These are domed hills or hard rocks rising steeply from the surrounding area. Their cracks have filled with soil and a wide variety of shrubs, herbs and small wind-blown trees have become established in the crevices. The highest of the inselbergs is Mansumbi, 488 m, followed by Kumbulanwa, 450 m, and Kora Rock, 442 m. There is also a wide variety of animal species here including elephant, hippo, lion, leopard, cheetah, serval, caracal, wildcat, genet, spotted and striped hyena, and several types of antelope. The rivers hold lizards, snakes, tortoises and crocodiles. This area has had serious problems with poachers in recent years. George Adamson and two of his assistants were murdered here in 1989 by poachers.

Situated to the northeast of Kora National Park, this reserve is an enormous stretch of dry thorny bushland in the Garissa district of Northeastern Province about 150 km northeast of Mount Kenya. It is home to elephant, Grevy's zebra and beisa oryx.

Rahole National Reserve
0° 5 N, 39° E

Adjacent to and southeast of Meru National Park is North Kitui National Reserve in Eastern Province. It measures 745 sq km and is mainly bushland and riverine forest. The Tana River runs through the reserve and you are likely to see crocodiles and hippos.

North Kitui National Reserve
0° 15' S, 38° 30' E

This is the town in the northeast that is closest to Nairobi both geographically and culturally. It is on an alternative route back from Lamu to Nairobi. It is the administrative centre for the district, and there are shops for provisions, petrol and a bank. The heat is fierce and there is high humidity making it an unpleasant climate to stay in for long. The town is mostly populated by Somalis, as well as a few of the original riverine people. The Somalis claim that much of what was then known as the Northern Frontier District (NFD), had originally been part of Somalia following the redrawing of the border between Kenya and Italian Somaliland by the British in 1925, a fact much disputed by the Kenyans. The Laikipiak Masai lived in this area as far north as the Juba River and over the years have fought incessantly with the Somalis. Travellers are advised not to travel east of Garissa towards the Somali border, as there have been many incidents of armed robbery with fatalities by heavily armed *shiftas* (bandits) in recent years.

Garissa
0° 25' S, 39° 40' E
Colour map 3, grid C5

For arriving or leaving Garissa by road, it is advisable to travel in convoy with an armed escort

Sleeping **D** *Garissa Guest House*, just outside of town. Simple but adequate. **E** *Safari*, clean rooms and running water, there is a restaurant attached with reasonable food.

Transport **Air** There is a flight from Nairobi's Wilson Airport direct to Garissa if there is sufficient demand (see page 74). **Bus**: there are 3 bus routes travelling to and from Garissa. A bus goes from Eastleigh, **Nairobi** to Garissa direct on Mon, Wed, Fri and Sun leaving at 0800. The journey takes about 8 hrs. There is a bus from **Lamu** to Garissa leaving at 0700 and taking 8-10 hrs. The other route is between Garissa and **Mandera** at the junction of the Kenya, Ethiopia, Somalia border, going on to **Wajir** on Tue, Thu and Sat and travelling on the next day to Mandera. Returns from Mandera Thu, Sat and Mon, to Wajir, and on to Garissa the next day.

This is 300 km from Isiolo along the most remote route in the country. The area is a vast scrubland that seems to go on forever. Due to security problems in this area following the Somali war, this unappealing journey has become even more difficult. If you are going to try it, check the route has not been closed before setting out.

Wajir
1° 42' N, 40° 5' E
Colour map 3, grid B6

Kenya

The town of Wajir itself is growing. The population and atmosphere of the place has more Arab than African influences and is far more interesting to visit than Garissa. The settlement developed around wells that have been fought over by rival clans for generations, water being such a valuable commodity in this area. In 1984, the rivalry between clans became fiercer than usual, forcing the regional administration to act. An amnesty was announced for all those who surrendered their arms, but thousands of men and boys of one of the clans, the Degodia, did not avail themselves of this opportunity. They were rounded up to be interned by the government authorities in a military airstrip with no facilities, where many died of exposure or dehydration. This tragedy has made the relationship between local people and the administration poor to say the least.

The **market** here is quite different from anything else you are likely to see in Kenya. It consists of a section of grass huts with a wide assortment of produce. Fruit and vegetables are uncommon, but you will find some beautiful pottery. A visit to the wells just outside of town to the north would also be quite interesting. A popular pastime among Somali men is to chew *miraa*, an appetite suppressant and mild stimulant (see page 140).

Sleeping and eating D *Nairobi Hotel*, showers, bar and a restaurant, good value. **E** *Malab*, by the bus station. Has a good reputation, provides fans and mosquito nets.

Transport Air There is an airstrip (see page 74). **Road** Buses from **Garissa** to Wajir on Tue, Thu and Sat and travelling on the next day to **Mandera**. Returns from Mandera Thu, Sat and Mon, and on to Garissa the next day.

Mandera
3° 55′ N, 41° 53′ E
Colour map 3, grid A6

The furthest point in Kenya, 370 km northeast beyond Wajir, on the Ethiopian, Somali and Kenyan border. The war has made this a particularly foolhardy expedition at the moment with marauding rival Somali clans. The main line of contact is on the private aircraft who fly in shipments of *miraa*. In the past, trade and communication with Somalia was more important than with Kenya as Mandera is far closer to Mogadishu, the capital of Somalia, than to Nairobi.

Until recently Mandera was a fairly small border town servicing the local community. Since the Somali civil war, it has become home to literally tens of thousands of Somalians putting an impossible strain on resources. The lack of water, always a problem, has become critical. Also, the stability of the place is severely tested by the prevailing conditions. *Miraa* (see page 140) is the big business in town. There is a post office, police station and bank.

Sleeping D *Mandera County Council Resthouse*, just to east of centre. Fans, showers, own bathrooms. **E** *Jabane*, town centre. Has showers and fans and reasonable restaurant. **E** *Mombasa Inn*, town centre. Simple, basic restaurant.

Transport Air There is an airstrip with several flights a day transporting *miraa* (see page 74). A flight costs US$50-100 to Nairobi, depending on demand, and is negotiated with the *miraa* charterer. **Buses** from *Wajir* on Wed, Fri and Sun. Return to Wajir Thu, Sat and Mon, and on to *Garissa* the next day.

Background

History

There is evidence that the forefathers of *Homo sapiens* lived in this part of East Africa 10,000-12,000 years ago. In the 1960s Louis Leakey, a Kenyan-born European, and his wife Mary, began a series of archaeological expeditions in East Africa, particularly around Lake Turkana in the north. During these excavations they traced man's biological and cultural development back from about 50,000 years to 1,800,000 years ago. They discovered the skull and bones of a 2,000,000 year old fossil which they named *Homo habilis* and who they argued was an ancestor to modern man. Since the 1970s, Richard Leakey, son of Louis and Mary Leakey, has uncovered many more clues as to the origins of mankind and how they lived, unearthing some early Stone Age tools. These findings have increased our knowledge of the beginnings of earth, and establish the Rift Valley as the Cradle of Mankind. Many of the fossils are now in the National Museum of Nairobi. Little evidence exists as to what happened between the periods 1,800,000 and 250,000 years ago except that *Homo erectus* stood upright and moved further afield, spreading out over much of Kenya and Tanzania.

Earliest times

Very recently there have been two significant discoveries. In March 2001 it emerged that a team including Richard Leakey's wife Meave, had found an almost complete skull of a previously unknown creature near Lamekwi River in the north. The skull of *Kenyanthropus platyops* has a flat face, much like modern humans and has been dated at between 3,200,000 and 3,500,000 years old. This is about the same time as the famous 'Lucy' – *Australopithecus afarensis* – found in Ethiopia in 1974 (see page 887), was living, and suggests that modern humans evolved from one of several closely related ape-like ancestors of that period.

A potentially more remarkable find was also announced in 2001. Fourteen fragments of a 6,000,000-year-old 'Millennium Man' were discovered in the remote Tugen Hills west of Lake Baringo. The fossils from four bodies of *Orrorin tugenensis* are among the oldest remains of ape-like ancestors ever found, about twice as old as Lucy. They appear to be more human-like than could have been imagined for a creature that lived so long ago and could be the remains of the oldest known direct ancestor of humans. If this controversial finding is confirmed it could force a major revision in current understanding of the history of human evolution.

In more recent times, from 5,000-3,000 BC Kenya was inhabited by hunter-gatherer groups, the forefathers of the Boni, Wata and Wariangulu people.

Later still began an influx of peoples from all over Africa which lasted right up until about the 19th century. The first wave came from Ethiopia when the tall, lean Cushitic people gradually moved into Kenya over the second millennium BC settling around Lake Turkana in the north. These people practised mixed agriculture, keeping animals and planting crops. There is still evidence of irrigation systems and dams and wells built by them in the arid northern parts of Kenya. As the climate changed, getting hotter and drier, they were forced to move on to the hills above Lake Victoria.

Bantu expansion

The Eastern Cushitics, also pastoralists, moved into central Kenya around 3,000 years ago. This group assimilated with other agricultural communities and spread across the land. The rest of Kenya's ancestors are said to have arrived between 500 BC and AD 500 with Bantu-speaking people arriving from West Africa and Nilotic speakers from Southern Sudan attracted by the rich grazing and plentiful farmland.

The Kenyan coast attracted people from other parts of the world as well as Africa. The first definite evidence of this is a description of Mombasa by the Greek Diogenes in AD 110 on his return to Egypt. He describes trading in cloth, tools, glass, brass, copper, iron, olives,

☞ Ewart Grogan I

Ewart Scott Grogan was born in 1874 in Eaton Square, Chelsea, London, the 14th in a family of 21 children. After being thrown out of Cambridge University and studying art at the Slade School in London Grogan enlisted to fight against the Matabele, travelling up from Cape Town to what is now Zimbabwe.

When hostilities ended Grogan travelled to New Zealand where he fell for Gertrude Watt. Gertrude's stepfather was hostile to the notion of the couple marrying, and pointed out that Grogan had achieved very little in his 22 years. Stung, Grogan suggested a journey from the Cape to Cairo as a suitable test, and Gertrude's stepfather, virtually

certain the expedition would fail, agreed.

Grogan decided to undertake a survey during his journey for the telegraph and railway planned by Cecil Rhodes. He assembled supplies and embarked on the journey. Despite travelling by boat wherever possible, there was plenty of foot-slogging, deserting porters, stolen equipment, bouts of fever, and attacks by cannibals. He arrived in Cairo and returned to England, where he presented the Union Jack he had carried with him to Queen Victoria, finished his book From Cape to Cairo, and married Gertrude on 11 October 1900.

Continued on page opposite).

weapons, ivory and rhinoceros horn at Mombasa. In AD 150 Ptolemy included details of this part of the coast in his Map of the World. It was to be another few centuries before the arrival of Islam on the coast and the beginning of its Golden Age.

Arab and Persian settlers developed trade routes extending across the Indian Ocean into China establishing commercial centres all along the East Africa coast. They greatly contributed to the arts and architecture of the region and built fine mosques, monuments and houses. Evidence of the prosperity of this period can be seen in the architecture in parts of Mombasa, Malindi and Lamu, and particularly in the intricate and elegant balconies outside some of the houses in the old part of Mombasa. All along this part of the coast, intermarriage between Arabs and Africans resulted in a harmonious partnership of African and Islamic influences personified in the Swahili people. This situation continued peacefully until the arrival of the Portuguese in the 16th century.

Portuguese & Arab influence

Mombasa was known to be rich in both gold and ivory, making it a tempting target for the Portuguese. Vasco da Gama, in search of a sea route to India, arrived in Mombasa in 1498. He was unsuccessful in docking there at this time, but two years later ransacked the town. For many years the Portuguese returned to plunder Mombasa until finally they occupied the city. There followed 100 years of harsh colonial rule from their principal base at Fort Jesus overlooking the entrance to the old harbour. Arab resistance to Portuguese control of the Kenyan coast was strong, but they were unable to defeat the Portuguese who managed to keep their foothold in East Africa.

The end of Portuguese control began in 1696 with a siege of Fort Jesus. The struggle lasted for nearly 2½ years when the Arabs finally managed to scale the fortress walls. By 1720, the last Portuguese garrison had left the Kenyan coast. The Arabs remained in control of the East African coast until the arrival of the British and Germans in the late 19th century. In this period the coast did not prosper as there were destructive intrigues amongst rival Arab groups and this hampered commerce and development in their African territories.

The Colonial period

The British influence in Kenya began quite casually in 1823 following negotiations between Captain Owen, a British Officer, and the Mazruis who ruled the island of Mombasa. The Mazruis asked for British protection from attack by other Omani interests in the area. Owen granted British protection in return for the Mazruis abolishing slavery. He sent to London and India for ratification of the treaty, posted his first officer together with an interpreter, four sailors and four marines and thus began the British occupation of Kenya. At this time, interest in Kenya was limited to the coast and then only as part of an evangelical desire to eliminate slavery. However, 50 years later attitudes towards the country changed.

Ewart Grogan II

By 1900 Grogan (see page opposite) was moderately well-off and Gertrude had inherited a considerable fortune. The Empire-builder, Cecil Rhodes, urged Grogan to 'give himself to Africa' and Grogan made huge land purchases in Kenya. He soon became Kenya's largest landowner with around 190,000 acres (Lord Delamere had 115,000), and was elected president of the Colonist Association which represented settlers.

Then in 1911 there occurred an incident that was to blight the memory of Grogan irrevocably. Gertrude was ill and Grogan's sister and a woman friend took a rickshaw to visit her in hospital. The three Kikuyu boys pulling the shafts had been drinking and they careered along, laughing, bouncing the passengers around, before they finally stopped, ran off, and the women were left to walk home. The next day Grogan rounded up the three boys, paraded them through town to the Magistrates' Court on Government Avenue (now Moi Avenue) and then stretched one of the lads on the ground and administered 25 lashes with a kiboko, a hippo-hide whip. Accused of taking the law

into his own hands, he was arrested, tried, fined 800 rupees and sentenced to a month in jail (or rather detention in a small bungalow on Ngong Hill with visitors and meals bought in).

During the First World War Grogan worked in military intelligence. He had become somewhat distanced from Gertrude, with whom he had two daughters, and he went on to have two more daughters from affairs with other women.

In 1928 Grogan financed the building of Torr's Hotel, on the corner of what is now Kenyatta and Kimathi Avenue. The first-floor lounge became the social centre of Nairobi. After the Second World War he developed his huge sisal estates at Taveta, and built a large house, now known as Grogan's Castle, on Girigan Hill. Gertrude died in 1943 and Grogan built a children's hospital, Gertrude's Garden (still in use) on the grounds of their Muthaiga home. In the last year of his life he left Kenya to live in Cape Town, where he died in 1967 at the age of 92. His eldest daughter, Dorothy, was the only relative at his funeral.

In 1887 the Imperial British East Africa Company (IBEAC) founded its headquarters in Mombasa with the purpose of developing trade. From here it sent small groups of officials into the interior to negotiate with local tribesmen. One such officer Frederick Lugard made alliances with the Kikuyu en route to Uganda.

The final stage in British domination over Kenya was the development of the railway. The IBEAC and Lugard believed a railway was essential to keep its posts in the interior of Kenya supplied with essential goods, and also believed it was necessary in order to protect Britain's position in Uganda. Despite much opposition in London, the railway was built, commencing in 1901, at an eventual cost of £5 mn.

Nairobi was created at the centre of operations as a convenient stopping point midway between Mombasa and Lake Victoria where a water supply was available. Despite many problems, the railway reached Nairobi in 1899 and Port Florence (now Kisumu) in 1901, and was the catalyst for British settlers moving into Kenya as well as for African resistance to the loss of their lands.

From 1895 to 1910 the government encouraged white settlers to cultivate land in the Central Highlands of the country around the railway, particularly the fertile Western Highlands. It was regarded as imperative to attract white settlers to increase trade and thus increase the usefulness of the railway. The Masai bitterly opposed being moved from their land but years of war combined with the effects of cholera, smallpox, rinderpest and famine had considerably weakened their resistance. The Masai were moved into two reserves on either side of the railway, but soon had to move out of the one to the north as the white settlers pressed for more land. Kikuyu land was also occupied by white settlers as they moved to occupy the highlands around the western side of Mount Kenya.

The number of Europeans in Kenya steadily increased from only about 3,000 at the beginning of the First World War to 80,000 by the early 1950s. The rise in numbers of people entering Kenya was helped by the British government's decision to offer war veterans land in

☞ ### The Uganda railway

What it will cost no words can express;
What is its object no brain can suppose;
Where it will start from no one can guess;
Where it is going to nobody knows;
What is the use of it none can conjecture;
What it will carry there's none can define;
And in spite of George Curzon's superior lecture,
It clearly is naught but a lunatic line.

London Magazine Truth 1896

the Kenya Highlands. In order to increase the pool of African labour for white settler development (most Africans were unwilling to work for the Europeans voluntarily) taxes and other levies were imposed. Furthermore, Africans were prevented from growing coffee, the most lucrative crop, on the grounds that there was a risk of coffee berry disease with lots of small producers. Thus many Africans were forced to become farm labourers or to migrate to the towns in search of work to pay the taxes. By the 1940s the European farmers had prospered in cash crop production.

As the number of Europeans moving into the country increased, so too did African resistance to the loss of their land and there was organized African political activity against the Europeans as early as 1922. The large number of Africans, particularly Kikuyu, moving into the growing capital Nairobi formed a political community supported by sections of the influential Asian community. This led to the formation of the East African Association, the first pan-Kenyan nationalist movement led by Harry Thuku. His arrest and the subsequent riots were the first challenge to the settlers and the colonial regime.

Jomo Kenyatta, an influential Kikuyu, led a campaign to bring Kikuyu land grievances to British notice. In 1932 he gave evidence to the Carter Land Commission in London which had been set up to adjudicate on land interests in Kenya, but without success. During the war years, all African political associations were banned and there was no voice for the interests of black Kenyans. At the end of the war, thousands of returning African soldiers began to demand rights, and discontent grew. Kenyatta had remained abroad travelling in Europe and the Soviet Union and returned in 1946 as a formidable statesman.

In 1944 an African nationalist organization, the Kenya African Union (KAU) was formed to press for African access to settler occupied land. The KAU was primarily supported by the Kikuyu. In 1947 Kenyatta became president of KAU and was widely supported as the one man who could unite Kenya's various political and ethnic factions.

The Mau Mau era

At the same time as the KAU were looking for political change, a Kikuyu group, Mau Mau, began a campaign of violence. In the early 1950s the Mau Mau began terrorist activities, and several white settlers were killed as well as thousands of Africans thought to have collaborated with the colonial government.

The British authorities declared a state of emergency in 1952 in the face of the Mau Mau campaign and the Kikuyu were herded into 'protected villages' surrounded by barbed wire. People were forbidden to leave during the hours of darkness. From 1952 to 1956 the terrorist campaign waged against the colonial authority resulted in the deaths of 13,000 Africans and 32 European civilians. Over 20,000 Kikuyu were placed in detention camps before the Mau Mau finally were defeated. The British imprisoned Kenyatta in 1953 for seven years for alleged involvement in Mau Mau activities, and banned the KAU, though it is debatable as to whether Kenyatta had any influence over Mau Mau activities.

The cost of suppressing the Mau Mau, the force of the East African case, and world opinion, convinced the British government that preparation for Independence was the wisest course. The settlers were effectively abandoned, and were left with the prospect of making their own way under a majority-rule government. A number did sell up and leave, but many, encouraged by Kenyatta, stayed on to become Kenyan citizens.

The state of emergency was lifted in January 1960 and a transitional constitution was drafted allowing for the existence of political parties and ensuring Africans were in the majority in the Legislative Council. African members of the council subsequently formed the Kenya African National Union (KANU) with James Gichuru, a former president of KAU, as its acting head, and Tom Mboya and Oginga Odinga, two prominent Luos, part of the leadership. KANU won the majority of seats in the Legislative Council but refused to form an administration until the release of Kenyatta.

In 1961 Kenyatta became the president of KANU. KANU won a decisive victory in the 1963 elections, and Kenyatta became prime minister as Kenya gained internal self-government. Kenya became fully independent later that year, the country was declared a republic, and Kenyatta became president. Kenya retained strong links with the UK, particularly in the form of military assistance and financial loans to compensate European settlers for their land, some of which was redistributed among the African landless.

The two parties that had contested the 1963 elections with KANU were persuaded to join KANU and Kenya became a single-party state. In 1966 Odinga left KANU and formed a new party, the Kenya People's Union, with strong Luo support. Tom Mboya, was assassinated by a Kikuyu in 1969. There followed a series of riots in the west of the country by Luos, and Odinga was placed in detention where he remained for the next 15 months. At the next general election in 1969 only KANU members were allowed to contest seats, and two-thirds of the previous national assembly lost their seats.

Kenyatta

The East African Community (EAC) comprising Kenya, Tanzania and Uganda, which ran many services in common such as the railways, the airline, post and telecommunications, began to come under strain. Kenya had pursued economic policies which relied on a strong private sector; Tanzania had adopted a socialist strategy after 1967; Uganda had collapsed into anarchy and turmoil under Amin. In 1977, Kenya unilaterally pulled out of the EAC, and in response Tanzania closed its borders with Kenya.

Kenyatta was able to increase Kenya's prosperity and stability through reassuring the settlers that they would have a future in the country and that they had an important role in its success at the same time as delivering his people limited land reform. Under Kenyatta's presidency, Kenya became one of the more successful newly independent countries.

Kenyatta died in 1978 to be succeeded by Daniel arap Moi, his vice president. Moi began by relaxing some of the political repression of the latter years of Kenyatta's presidency. However, he was badly shaken by a coup attempt in 1982 that was only crushed after several days of mayhem, and a more repressive period was ushered in.

Moi

Relations between Kenya and its neighbours began to improve in the 1980s and the three countries reached agreement on the distribution of assets and liabilities of the EAC by 1983. At this time the border between Kenya and Tanzania was reopened.

In 1992 political parties (other than KANU) were allowed. Moi and KANU were returned (albeit without a majority of the popular vote) in the multiparty elections late in 1992.

In the 1997 presidential elections Moi was again victorious, with an increased share of the vote. In the elections for the National Assembly KANU achieved a slender overall majority with 107 seats out of 210.

Modern Kenya

Politics

Daniel arap Moi was elected to the Presidency in October 1978 following the death of Jomo Kenyatta, and began a programme to reduce Kenya's corruption and release all political detainees. Moi, a Kalenjin, emphasized the need for a new style of government with greater regional representation of tribal groups. However, he did not fully live up to his promises of political freedom and Oginga Odinga (the prominent Luo who had been a voice of discontent in KANU under Kenyatta) and four other former KANU members who were critical of Moi's regime were barred from participating in the 1979 election. This led to an increase in protests against the government, mainly from Luos. Moi began to arrest dissidents, disband tribal societies and close the universities whenever there were demonstrations. This period also saw the strengthening of Kenya's armed forces.

On 1 August 1982 there was a coup attempt supported by a Luo-based section of the Kenyan Air Force supported by university students. Although things initially appeared to be touch-and-go, the coup was eventually crushed, resulting in an official death toll of 159. As a result of the coup attempt, many thousands of people were detained and the universities again closed. The constitution was changed to make Kenya officially a one-party state.

Moi decided to reassert his authority over KANU by calling an early election in which he stood unopposed. Inevitably he was re-elected but less than 50% of the electorate turned out to vote.

Subsequent measures have served to centralize power under the presidency, and to reduce the ability of the opposition to contest elections. The president acquired the power to to dismiss the attorney-general, the auditor-general and judges, while control of the civil service passed to the President's Office. Secret ballots were abandoned, and voters were required to queue behind the candidate of their choice. This severely reduced willingness to be seen voting against the government. Secret ballots were restored in 1990.

In 1990, Dr Robert Ouko, a Luo and Minister for Foreign Affairs and International Cooperation, was murdered. British police were asked to investigate, and named Nicholas Biwott, a Kalenjin and Minister for Energy, as being implicated in the killing. Biwott was dropped from the cabinet, but has subsequently returned.

International pressure in 1991 succeeded in persuading Moi to introduce a multi-party system. The opposition was fatally split, however, and in the 1992 elections Moi was returned as president with 36% of the popular vote. However, the opposition did secure 88 seats of the 188 contested, and the democratic process was significantly strengthened as a result.

The 1997 election was similar, with the opposition again split, and Moi again returned with 40% of the vote. In the Parliament the opposition made gains, with nine opposition parties securing 103 seats between them, while KANU obtained a slender overall majority with 107. Attention now centres on the successor to Moi, who cannot stand again under the present constitution in the next election, expected in December 2002. Within KANU there appear to be two main contenders, the Vice-President, George Saitoti, who styles himself as a Masai, but who is thought to be Kikuyu, and Musalia Mudavadi, a Luhya, who is Minister for Information Transport and Communications.

Moi's relationship with his neighbours has not been an easy one. Although he offered full co-operation with Museveni and the National Resistance Army (NRA) when they came to power in 1986, relations between Kenya and Uganda have often been strained. Moi was at one stage nervous that Uganda might supply arms to dissident elements in Kenya. In 1987 the Kenya/Uganda border was temporarily closed as the two armies clashed, although later they both signed a treaty for co-operation. There have been problems with banditry and cattle raiding across the border with Ethiopia, and traffic has been moving in convoys with armed escorts north of Isiolo on the route to Moyale and Addis Ababa.

There were three incidents in early 1998 where tourists were killed during robberies. Later in 1998 the US Embassy was destroyed by a bomb in an attack mounted by Middle East anti-American terrorists. Although these incidents are very alarming, Kenya overall continues to be a safe holiday destination provided precautions are taken to avoid unnecessary risks.

Economy

Kenya's economic strategy maintains reliance on a strong private sector in manufacturing and services as well as in the farming sector. Foreign investment is encouraged, although the regulations have recently been uncertain, and there are periodic efforts to increase local participation in foreign-owned enterprises. In the East African context, Kenyan economic management has been successful, and has achieved as much as can reasonably be expected of a country with no oil and without any major mineral deposits.

Economic structure Population in 2001 was estimated at 31,000,000, and it continues to grow rapidly at 3.3% a year. This implies an increase in population of just over 1,000,000 each year. Most people live in the rural areas, with only a quarter in the towns. Overall population density is high by African standards, over double the average. Given that a large proportion of the country is arid, the pressure on the land in the fertile areas, particularly in the central highlands and around Lake Victoria, is intense.

Income levels are modest. Converting the value of output to US dollars, indicates Kenya is a low-income economy, and among the 20 or so poorest in the world.

Most families rely on agriculture for their livelihood, and 81% of the labour force is engaged in farming. However, incomes in agriculture are low, and the sector generates only 29% of GDP. Industry contributes 18% of output, but it must be remembered that there is little contribution from mining which boosts industrial output in many other African countries. Services is the largest sector at 53%, and it contains tourism, which is Kenya's largest source of foreign exchange.

Expenditure is reasonably well balanced, with 72% of income going on consumption, a reasonable investment rate of 16%, and a modest level of government spending at 17%.

The economy is very dependent on foreign earnings, and 25% of output is exported. The main sources of export earnings are tourism which generate 27% of receipts, tea 16%, coffee 8% and horticulture 8%. Spending on imports is 30% of all expenditure. The main components of imports are machinery 24%, fuels 21% and vehicles 9%.

Economic performance

Kenya managed to expand output slightly faster than the rate of population increase in the 1980s. However, performance slipped in the 1990s and GDP grew at 2.2% 1991-95 while population expanded at 3.3%. Good coffee prices in 1996 and 1997 boosted performance, but current growth rates have slipped to around 2% a year and living standards are falling.

The main impetus for growth has come from the services sector. Industry, too, has performed well. Agricultural growth has not kept pace with population expansion, and the main constraint is the limited amount of fertile land. Kenya is gradually changing to higher value, intensively cultivated crops such as vegetables and flowers, but the process is slow and limited to areas in the central highlands.

Export volume performance has been good, with a 3.3% rate of annual expansion, but lower world prices have more than offset the increased production and export earnings have fallen. Consequently, import volumes have fallen being limited by the lower export earnings and the need for increasing payments to service external debts. Currently debt service takes up over a quarter of export earnings.

Aid receipts per head are about average for Africa – they would be higher if the international community were more confident about the government's intention to tackle corruption.

Inflation averaged 10% a year in the period 1980-93. This fairly good performance faltered in 1991 and 1992, when prices increased by over 20% thought to be the result of irresponsible spending by the government in the run-up to the 1992 election. Subsequently there has been rather erratic inflation performance, but in 1995 prices seemed more under control with an increase of under 5%. Alas, with the heavy government spending prior to the election in 1997, inflation increased to 12%, but is now averaging around 5% a year.

Recent economic developments

Kenya has been in receipt of structural adjustment loans from the World Bank. Policy changes involve gradual amendments to bring domestic prices in line with world prices. Moves to privatize parastatal enterprises have been resisted (although most agricultural marketing monopolies have now been ended), and the donor community is beginning to lose patience over this issue.

A series of financial scandals led to a suspension of IMF support in 1994, but a new agreement was signed in April 1996. The programme anticipated continued liberalization, more privatization, civil service reform and a campaign against corruption. It subsequently ran into difficulties and payments were suspended pending better performance in controlling inflation and implementing the privatization programme. A new agreement with the IMF and the World Bank was concluded in 2000.

The financial sector has been subject to a series of failures by privately-owned domestic institutions. There have been collapses of five financial groups, where three have shown evidence of irregularities, and two have suffered from the ensuing lack of confidence. Banking regulations have been tightened, and banks with foreign ownership and control, namely Barclays and Standard Chartered, have increased their share of banking business, realizing higher profits.

Efforts are being made to reform and improve the performance of the parastatal sector with changes in management personnel. The grain purchasing body, the National Cereals and Produce Board (NCPB), provides a continuing problem as maize is bought at well above the world price, and in recent years of good harvests, the Board is accumulating stocks and runs at a continual loss. Kenya seems inclined to solve problems in the parastatal sector by reforms rather than privatization, although the monopoly of the NCPB has been terminated by making it a purchaser of last resort.

The government claims that 105 enterprises have been sold under the privatization programme. Two big developments in this area is the reorganization of Kenya Posts and Telecommunications into three units (one to be a regulatory body) prior to privatization. Kenya Power and Lighting is to have the distribution network separated from generation.

Some US$7bn of external debt is estimated outstanding. Debt service takes up just under a third of export earnings and at present this is within Kenya's ability to service, providing export revenues can be maintained.

Kenya's exchange rate policy involves periodic adjustments such that the official rate responds to the market rate. The black market in foreign exchange is not particularly vigorous, but there is evidence of some measure of currency overvaluation. The exchange rate has depreciates each year against the dollar at somewhere between 5% to 10%.

Economic outlook

Despite the good economic performance since Independence, and the avoidance of major stability problems, there are reasons to be cautious about Kenya's prospects. The tourism sector is now the main source of foreign exchange earnings, and this is very vulnerable to perceptions of deterioration of law and order in the country. The political situation has undoubtedly improved with the introduction of a multi-party system and a large contingent of opposition MPs in the national assembly. However, the outbreaks of violence before elections are worrying, and it remains to be seen if the present political system can deliver stability and security on a long-term basis.

Social conditions

Literacy rates are good at 71%, and noticeably better than the African average. There is almost universal primary education with 95% enrolments. Secondary enrolments are also good, with almost 30% of children receiving education at this level. Tertiary education opportunities are limited, despite the fact that Kenya has expanded its university enrolments substantially since 1980.

Life expectancy at 58 years is better than the Africa average. Food availability with 86% of minimum requirements being met, give cause for concern. Population per doctor is high, but medical delivery is good, given the low income level, with the infant mortality rate significantly lower than the African average.

Females have good access to primary education, with the enrolment rate just a little below that of males. Female access is less good at the secondary level, with enrolments a quarter below those of males. Low income levels place heavy demands on women to contribute to family income by working outside the home, and female employment is almost 40% of the total. With such a high population growth rate, the fertility rate is lower than might be expected – at 3.7 children per woman, it is below the Africa average. Contraception usage is high, with a third of women participating, and this will continue to reduce fertility rates and the population growth rate.

Culture

Tribal identity is still important in Kenyan life though this is changing as more people move into towns and tribal groups become scattered. Polygamy is still practised, though it is not officially condoned. The custom of a man taking more than one wife, is only recognized in the traditional systems, and not by official Kenyan family law. There is much resistance to western censure of polygamy. However, the practice is dying under the twin influences of economic realities and social pressure. Few men can now afford to take more than one wife. Among the better off, it is frowned upon for anybody in public life as it causes embarrassment when mixing with the international community. The Christian churches strongly disapprove.

People

Kenya has long been a meeting place of population movements from around the continent. This has resulted in there being as many as 70 different tribes living in Kenya with an estimated overall population of 29,000,000 people. There are three main groupings based on the origins of these groups. The Bantu came from West Africa in a migration, the reasons for which are not clearly understood. The Nilotic peoples came from the northwest, mostly from the area that is now Sudan. They were mainly pastoralists, and moved south in search of better grazing on more fertile land. Finally there is the Hamitic group, made up of a series of relatively small communities such as the Somali, Rendille, Boran, Ogaden and others, all pastoralists, who have spread into Kenya in the north and northeast from Ethiopia and Somalia.

Kikuyu (Bantu)

Primarily based around Mount Kenya, this is the largest ethnic group with 21% of the total population. They are thought to have originated in East and Northeast Africa around the 16th century. Land is the dominant social, political, religious and economic factor of life for Kikuyus and this soon brought them into conflict with colonial interests when settlers occupied their traditional lands.

The administration of the Kikuyu was undertaken by a council of elders based on clans made up of family groups. Other important members of the community were witch doctors, medicine men and the blacksmiths. The Kikuyu god is believed to live on Mount Kenya and all Kikuyus build their homes with the door facing the mountain. In common with most tribes in Kenya, men and women go through a number of stages into adulthood including circumcision to mark the beginning of their adult life. It is not so common for women to be circumcized today.

It is said the Kikuyu have adapted more successfully than any other tribe to the modern world. Kikuyu are prominent in many of Kenya's business and commercial activities. Those still farming in their homelands have adapted modern methods to their needs and benefit from cash crop production for export, particularly coffee and tea. They have a great advantage in that their traditional area is very fertile, and close to the capital, Nairobi.

Meru (Bantu)

Arrived to the northeast of Mount Kenya around the 14th century, following invasions by Somalis in the coast, this group is not homogenous being made up of eight different groups of people, accounting for 5% of Kenya's population. Some of the Meru were led by a chief known as the *mogwe* until 1974 when the chief converted to Christianity and ended the tradition. A group of tribal elders administer traditional justice along with the witch doctor.

The Meru occupy some of the country's richest farmland which is used to produce tea, coffee, pyrethrum, maize and potatoes. Another highly profitable crop grown by the Meru in this region is *miraa*, a mild stimulant particularly popular amongst Islamic communities and Somalis (see box, page 140).

Kalenjin (Nilotic)

Kalenjin is a name used by the British to describe a cluster of tribes, the main being the Kipsigis (4% of total population), Nandi (2%), Tugen (1%), Elgeyo (1%), Keiyo, Pokot, Marakwet, Sabaot, Nyangori, Sebei and Okiek, who speak the same language but different

John Boyes

John Boyes was born in Hull, Yorkshire in 1845, and at the age of thirteen he walked to Liverpool and signed on as a cabin-boy. In 1898 his voyages saw him at Mombasa, where he took the offer and contracted to deliver a caravan of food supplies to the British troops engaged in suppressing the Ugandan mutiny. It was a tough trip for Boyes, he contracted malaria and was semi-conscious for three days, his donkeys fell prey to tsetse flies and his porters abandoned their load and deserted. Nothing daunted Boyes recruited porters who had deserted from other caravans and made the delivery, earning £100.

Boyes reasoned that it ought to be possible to buy supplies of food in Kikuyuland (north of Nairobi) and halve the travelling. Defying officials who tried to stop him, Boyes set off with porters and interpreter and was promptly captured by the Kikuyu warriors of Chief Kawics clan. While the Kiama of Kikuyu elders were deliberating his fate, there was a skirmish with another Kikuyu clan. Boyes dressed the wounds with an antiseptic powder, iodoform, and succeeded in establishing such good relations with the Kiama that he subsequently styled himself 'King of the Kikuyu'.

With his brusque Yorkshire manner, Boyes was never on cordial terms with the other European settlers and administrators, but when he died in 1912, the whole of Nairobi turned out to follow his funeral procession.

---

dialects. They mainly live in the western edge of the central Rift Valley and are thought to have migrated from southern Sudan about 2,000 years ago. Most Kalenjin took up agriculture though they are traditionally pastoralists. Bee-keeping is common with honey being used to brew beer. Administration of the law is carried out at an informal gathering of the clan's elders. Witch doctors are generally women, which is unusual in Africa.

Luyha (Bantu) The Luhya are based on Kakamega town in western Kenya, and make up 14% of the total population. They are Kenya's third largest grouping after the Kikuyu and the Luo. They are cultivators, and small farmers are the mainstay of sugar-cane growing in the west. They occupy a relatively small area, and population densities are the highest anywhere in Kenya's countryside, with plot sizes becoming steadily smaller with the passing of each generation.

Luo (Nilotic) The Luo live in the west of the country on the shores of Lake Victoria. The second largest ethnic group with 14% of the total. They migrated from the Nile region of Sudan in around the 15th century. Originally the Luo were cattle herders but the devastating effects of rinderpest on their herds compelled them to diversify into fishing and subsistence agriculture.

The Luo were also prominent in the struggle for Independence and many of the country's leading politicians, including Tom Mboya and Oginga Odinga, were Luos.

The Luos have a different coming of age ritual to other tribes in the region which involves extracting the bottom four or six teeth, though this practice has fallen into disuse.

Kisii (Bantu) The Kisii are based on the town of the same name in the west, south of Kisumu. Traditional practices have been continued, with soothsayers and medicine men retaining significant influence, despite the nominal allegiance of most Kisii to Christianity. Trepanning, the drilling of a hole in the skull, has been a time-honoured remedy for mental illness and headaches, and is still used occasionally today.

Kamba (Bantu) The Kamba (more correctly the Akamba) traditionally lived in the area now known as Tsavo National Park. They comprise 11% of the total population. Originally hunters, the Kamba soon adopted a more sedentary lifestyle and developed as traders because of the relatively poor quality of their land. Ivory was a major trade item as were beer, honey, ornaments and iron weapons which they traded with neighbouring Masai and Kikuyu for food. Kamba adolescents go through initiation rites at around 12, including male circumcision. In common with most Bantu tribespeople, political power lies with clan elders.

The Kamba were well regarded by the British for their intelligence and fighting ability and they made up a large part of the East African contingent in the British Army during the First World War.

The Swahili dwell along the coast, and make up less than 1% of the total population. Although they do not have a common heritage, they do share a common language, religion and culture. Ancestry is mainly a mixture of Arabic and African. Today the majority of coastal people are Muslims.

Swahili (Bantu)

The Masai are probably the best-known tribe to people outside Kenya with their striking costume and reputation as fierce and proud warriors. They comprise 2% of Kenya's people. The Masai came to central Kenya from the Sudan around 1,000 years ago, where they were the largest and one of the most important tribes. Their customs and practices were developed to reflect their nomadic lifestyle and many are still practised today, though change is beginning to be accepted. The traditional basic Masai diet, is fresh and curdled milk carried in gourds. Blood tapped from the jugular vein of cattle is mixed with cattle urine and this provides a powerful stimulant. Cattle are rarely killed for meat as they represent the owners' wealth.

Masai (Nilotic)

Kenya

Like the Masai, this group has retained its rich and colourful dress and has a reputation as warriors. They comprise 2% of the total population. They are mainly based in the northwest part of Kenya living in the desert near the Ugandan border. This is the most isolated part of the country and as a consequence the Turkana have probably been affected less by the 20th century than any other tribe in Kenya.

Turkana (Nilotic)

The Turkana are pastoralists whose main diet consists of milk and blood. Cattle are important in Turkana culture, being herded by men. Camels, goats and sheep are also important and are looked after by boys and small girls. Recently some Turkana have begun fishing in the dry season.

The traditional dress of the Turkana is very eye-catching and is still fairly commonly worn. Men cover part of their hair with mud which is then painted blue and decorated with ostrich feathers. The main garment is a woollen blanket worn over one shoulder. Women wear a variety of beaded and metal adornments many of which signify different events in a woman's life. Women wear a half skirt of animal skins and a piece of black cloth. Both men and women sometimes insert a plug through the lower lip (see box, page 409). Tattooing is still fairly common. Men are tattooed on the shoulders and upper arm each time they kill an enemy. Witch doctors and prophets are held in high regard.

Land and environment

Kenya is 580,367 sq km in area with the equator running right through the middle. Physically, the country is made up of a number of different zones. It lies between latitude 5° North and 4° 30' South and longitude 34° and 41° East. The Great Rift Valley runs from the north to the south of the country and in places is 65 km across, bounded by escarpments 600-900 m high. This is probably the most spectacularly beautiful part of the country, dotted with soda lakes teeming with flamingos. To the east of the Rift Valley lies the Kenya Highlands with Mount Kenya, an extinct volcano, which at 5,199 m is Africa's second highest mountain. This is the most fertile part of the country, particularly the lower slopes of the mountain range. Nairobi sits at the southern end of the Central Highlands. The north of Kenya is arid, bounded by Sudan and Ethiopia. To the west lies Uganda and the fertile shores around Lake Victoria. Further south, the land turns into savannah, and is mainly used for grazing.

Geography

The Indian Ocean coast to the east of the country runs for 480 km and there is a narrow strip of fertile land all along it. Beyond this, the land becomes scrubland and semi-arid. Somalia borders Kenya in the northeast, and this is also a fairly arid area.

Kenya

Climate Kenya's different altitudes mean that the climate varies enormously around the country. Probably the most pleasant climate is in the Central Highlands and the Rift Valley, though the valley floor can become extremely hot and is relatively arid. Mount Kenya and Mount Elgon both become quite cool above 1,750 m and the top of Mount Kenya is snow-covered. Mount Kenya and the Aberdares are the country's main water catchment areas.

Western Kenya and the area around Lake Victoria is generally hot, around 30-34°C all year with high humidity and rainfall evenly spread throughout the year. Most rain here tends to fall in the early evening.

The country is covered in semi-arid bushland and deserts throughout the north and east of the country. Temperatures can rise to 40°C during the day and fall to 20°C at night in the desert. Rainfall in this area is sparse, between 250 mm and 500 mm per annum.

The coastal belt is hot and humid all year round, though the heat is tempered by sea breezes. Rainfall varies from as little as 20 mm in February to 240 mm in May. The average temperature varies little throughout the year but is hottest in November and December, at about 30°C.

Vegetation Kenya is justifiably famous for its flora and fauna. In areas of abundant rainfall, the country is lush, supporting a huge range of plants, and the wide variety of geographical zones house a corresponding diversity of flora. The majority of the country is covered in savannah-type vegetation characterized by the acacia. The slopes of Mount Elgon and Mount Kenya are covered in thick evergreen temperate forest from about 1,000 m to 2,000 m; then to 3,000 m the mountains are bamboo forest; above this level the mountains are covered with groundsel trees and giant lobelias. Mangroves are prolific in the coastal regions.

Wildlife Kenya's wildlife is as diverse as its flora. On the savannahs you will be able to see the 'Big 5' of lion, leopard, buffalo, elephant and rhino as well as cheetah, gazelle, giraffe, zebra, wildebeest, warthog and a host of other species. Apart from these animals, there are flamingos on the soda lakes and crocodiles in other waterways, many species of monkeys in the forests both by the coast and inland, the amazingly tame rock hyraxes in Hell's Gate and many more. The birdlife is equally as varied including ostriches, vultures and many types of eagle, and even parrots up in Mount Kenya.

Environment Kenya has very little forest, only 2% of the total land area. High rates of population growth place demands on the forested area for cultivation and for fuelwood. Despite these pressures, Kenya has succeeded in preserving its forest area quite well, and over the past decade deforestation has only been at the rate of 0.1% a year.

Kenya has moderate domestic, agricultural and industrial water usage. Each year the usage of renewable fresh water resources is a manageable 7.4%.

Books

History Miller C, *Lunatic Express*, highly readable history of East Africa, centring around the building of the railway. Hibbert C, 1984, *Africa Explored: Europeans in the Dark Continent 1769-1889*, London: Penguin, describes the exploits of the main explorers, including the search for the source of the Nile. Monbiot, G *No Man's Land*, published by Macmillan 1994, tells how the nomadic tribes in Kenya and Tanzanian were forced off their land. Murray Brown J, *Kenyatta*, biography of the man who became the first president of Kenya. Patterson J, *The Man-Eaters of Tsavo*, first-hand account of problems in building the railway.

Reminiscences Blixen K, *Out of Africa*, wonderfully written, impressions of the author's life in Kenya. Huxley E, *Flame Trees of Thika*, stories of the lives of early pioneers. Markham B, *West with the Night*, marvellous autobiography of the woman who made the first solo east to west Atlantic flight.

Fiction Hemingway E, *Green Hills of Africa*, masterly short stories based on the author's African visits in 1933-4. Mwangi M, *Going Down River Road*, grim but entertaining story of African urban life.

Tanzania

4

Tanzania

Tanzania has unrivalled tourist attractions in its glorious game parks, the Indian Ocean coast, and a fascinating history embracing the earliest relics of man's evolution, the exotic influence of Zanzibar, early explorers, and the colonial presence of the Germans and British, which began over a century ago. Tanzanians are friendly, warm-hearted and relaxed, the country is free from any serious tensions between ethnic groups, has an enviable political stability, and is safe for tourists.

Essentials

Planning your trip

Where to go Tanzania is a country of enormous diversity. Four times the size of the United Kingdom, over 25% of its land mass is dedicated to national parks and game reserves. The Selous Game Reserve is the biggest in Africa, supporting large elephant populations, while Serengeti National Park is where the annual wildebeest migration begins. Snow-capped Mount Kilimanjaro is Africa's highest mountain and Lake Victoria to the west is Africa's largest fresh-water lake. Tanzania's coastal attractions include palm-fringed, white sandy beaches and coral reefs surrounding the off-shore islands, some of which drop off forming steep under-water cliffs that plunge to depths of over 600 m, while Zanzibar evokes romantic images of narrow winding streets in Stone Town, fragrant spices and glorious beaches.

The northern circuit This is an extremely popular route as it includes the best known of the national parks in Tanzania. It is a superb resource and the country is obviously very keen that full advantage should be taken of it. It is seeing rapid and increasing tourist develop-ment and while it is not yet as developed as some of the Kenyan parks, nor are there as many visitors, this can be expected to change in the future.

Popular routes take in **Lake Manyara National Park**, **Ngorongoro Crater Conservation Area** (with **Olduvai Gorge**) and the **Serengeti National Park**. However there are a number of other major attractions. In particular, keen climbers and walkers visit the area to climb **Mount Kilimanjaro** and **Mount Meru** in **Arusha National Park**. The **Tarangire National Park**, as a dry season retreat for many animals, is a splendid game viewing opportunity and is also located in the north of the country, as are Mkomazi and Umba game reserves. To see Ngorongoro Crater and Lake Manyara you will need, absolute minimum, 3 days and 2 nights. To see these two plus Serengeti you will need 4 days and 3 nights, and if you add Tarangire to these three you will need 6 days and 5 nights.

Central and southern parks Of the seven parks and reserves in this group, two are reason-ably easy to access from Dar es Salaam. **Mikumi National Park** is popular with residents of Dar, reached from the paved road through Morogoro. **Saadani National Park** is now easier to get to via the paved road to Bagamoyo and then 60 km of sandy track. The main attrac-tions in the southern region – the **Selous Game Reserve** (and adjacent Udzungwa National Park) and **Ruaha National Park** (and adjacent Ruaha and Kizigo game reserves) – have unspoiled atmospheres that reflect their remote locations. Visiting these parks requires long journeys by road from Dar es Salaam. It is possible to go part of the way to Selous by train. The easiest, but most expensive, access is by air to the airstrips at the camps.

Western parks The parks in the west include two famous chimpanzee sanctuaries, **Gombe Stream National Park** and **Mahale Mountains National Park**. Both are difficult to access and have minimal facilities. Nine other parks and reserves – Ibanda, Rumanyika Orugundu, Burigi, Biharamulo, Moyowosi, Kigosi, Ugalla River, Uwanda and Katavi Plains – are all miles from anywhere, with no accommodation to speak of. Travellers to these parks tend to have a specific objective for their visit and make a well-organized, self-sufficient camping trip in their own vehicle, or have an excursion expensively arranged by a safari company.

When to go Situated just south of the equator, Tanzanian temperatures average between 25-30C°. Humidity varies, being high along the coastal strip and on Zanzibar but much lower in the interior highlands. There are long rains, *masika*, from March to May and short rains, *mvuli*, fall from October to December. In addition there are frequently heavy rains in the south of Tan-zania from December until April.

In terms of avoiding the rains, the best time to visit is between May and October, but Tanza-nia has much to offer all year around. The wildebeest migration in the Serengeti occurs in June and July. If you are planning a trekking holiday the best months are May to September. Travelling by road, especially in the more remote areas or through the national parks, is easier

Tanzanian embassies and consulates

Belgium, 363 Av Louise, 1050 Brussels, T26406500.

Burundi, Patrice Lumumba Av, BP 1653, Bujumbura, T24634.

Canada, 50 Range Rd, Ottawa, Ontario KIN 8J4, T613-2321500.

Egypt, 9 Abde Hamid Loufty St, Dokki, Cairo, T7041556.

France, 70 Boulevard Pereire Nord, 75017 Paris, T47762177.

Germany, Theatreplatz 26, 5300 Bonn 2, T0228-353477.

Italy, Via Giambattista Visco 9-00196, Rome, T06-3610898.

Japan, 21-9 Kamiyoga, 4 Chome Setagaya-ku, Tokyo 158, T03-4254531/3.

Kenya, PO Box 47790, Nairobi, T331056.

Mozambique, Ujamaa House, Avenida Marites Da Machava 852, PO Box 4515, Maputo, T744025.

Netherlands, a consulate is open Monday-Friday, 1000-1600, T0180-320939.

Nigeria, 8 Agor Odiyan St, Victoria Island, PO Box 6417, Lagos, T613594.

Rwanda, Av Paul IV, BP 669, Kigali, T6074.

Saudi Arabia, PO Box 94320, Riyadh 11693, T45-42859.

Sudan, PO Box 6080, Khartoum, T78407/9.

Sweden, Oxtorgsgatan 2-4, PO Box 7255, 103-89 Stockholm, T08-244870.

Switzerland, 47 Av Blanc, 1202 Geneva, T318929.

Uganda, 6 Kagera Rd, PO Box 5750, Kampala, T256272.

UK, 43 Hertford St, London W1Y 8DB, T020-7499 8951.

USA, 2139 R St NW, Washington DC 20008, T202-9396128; and 205 East 42nd St, 13th floor, New York, NY 10017, T212-9729160.

RD Congo, 142 Boulevard du 30 Juin, BP 1612, Kinshasha, T32117.

Zambia, Ujamaa House, Plot No 5200, United Nations Av, PO Box 31219, Lusaka, T211422, 211665.

Zimbabwe, Ujamaa House, 23 Baines Av, PO Box 4841, Harare, T721870.

See under Dar es Salaam (page 364) and Kigoma (page 512) for overseas countries' embassies.

during the dry months, as road conditions deteriorate significantly in the rainy seasons. March, April and May can be months of heavy rain making travel on unsealed roads difficult. Even in these months, however, there is an average of 4-6 hours of sunshine each day. Finally, bear in mind that malaria peaks during the rainy seasons, when the mosquitoes are prolific.

Travel and tour agents These are listed under the place of their location: Arusha, page 445; Dar es Salaam, page 358; Zanzibar, page 557. Special interest safari operators, page 318. Specialist hunting tour operators, page 318. **Tours & tour operators**

UK operators *Abercrombie & Kent*, Sloane Square House, Holbein Place, London SW1W 8NS, T020-7730 9600. *Ecosafaris*, 146 Gloucester St, London SW7, T020-7370 5032. *Hoopoe Safaris*, Suite F1, Kebbell House, Carpenders Park, Watford WD1 5BE, T01923-255462, F01923-255452, www.hoopoe.com *Karibu Safari*, Imaginative Traveller, 14 Barley Mow Passage, Chiswick, London W4 4PH, T020-8782 8612, F8742 3045. *Selous Safaris*, 788 Bath St, Cranford, Middlesex, TW5 9UL, T020-8897 9991. *United Touring Company*, Travel House, Spring Villa Park, Spring Villa Rd, Edgware, Middlesex, HA8 7EB, T020-8905 6525, F8905 6945, utc@utcuk.com *Wildlife Safari*, Old Bakery, South Rd, Reigate, Surrey RH2 7LB, T01737-223903, F241102. *World Archipelago Ltd*, 55 Fulham High St, London, T020-7471 8780, F7384 9549, worldarc@compuserve.com *Zanzibar Travel*, Reynards House, Selkirk Gardens, Cheltenham, Gloucestershire GL52 5LY, UK, T/F01242-222027.

Special interest tour operators Balloon safaris: *Serengeti Balloon Safaris*, Unit 9D, Harleston Industrial Estate, Harleston, Norfolk IP20 9EB, T01379-853129, F853127, cost US$375 pp. **Cycling safaris:** PO Box 10190, Mombasa, Kenya, T+254-11-387326, F+254-11-485454. Tours from Kenya to Tanzania with climb of Mt Kilimanjaro. PO Box 75, Bath, BA1 1BX, UK, T01225-480130, F480132. Organizes cycling tours of northern Tanzania, Mt Kilimanjaro and the coast. Some camping, some lodge accommodation. Your luggage carried by vehicle.

Walking *Footprint Adventures*, 5 Malham Dr, Lincoln LN6 OXD, T01522-804929, F804928, www.footprint-adventures.co.uk/tanzania Offer trekking, cycling, canoe and climbing holidays. Based at Lake Manyara & Ngorongoro. *Sherpa Expeditions*, 131a Heston Rd, Hounslow, Middlesex, TW5 0RD, UK, T020-8577 2717, F8572 9788. Organizes tours through Kenya to climb Kilimanjaro. Equipment can be hired if you don't have your own. **Wildlife exploration** *Wildlife Explorer*, 'Manyara', Manpean, Riverside, St Austell, Cornwall, PL26, UK, T01726-824132, F824399. *World Archipelago Ltd*, 6 Redgrave Rd, London SW15 1PX, UK, T020-8780 5838, F020-8780 9482, 100711.3161@compuserve.com

Local safari operators Until 1989 only Tanzanian-registered tour operators were allowed to operate in Tanzania. That has now changed and overseas-based companies have established themselves. There are a large number of safari companies and organized safaris are the most common way of seeing the parks. Safaris to Serengeti National Park, Ngorongoro Conservation Area and Lake Manyara, Tarangire and Arusha national parks are best arranged from Arusha if you have not arranged it before you arrive in Tanzania. For trips to Mikumi and Ruaha national parks and Selous Game Reserve arrangements are best made in Dar es Salaam, while trips to Gombe Stream and Mahale Mountain national parks can be arranged from Kigoma (as well as from Arusha and Dar es Salaam).

More extensive lists of tour and travel companies and contact details of those listed below are given under Dar es Salaam (page 358) and Arusha (page 445). The lists here are of experienced operators. **Balloon safaris** Arusha: *Adventure Centre*. **Camel safaris** Arusha: *Adventure Centre*. **Camping safaris** Arusha: *Arumeru Tours and Safaris, Dove Safaris, Sengo Safaris, Wildlife Safari*. **Hotel and lodge safaris** Arusha: *Abercrombie & Kent, Bushtrekker Safaris, Classic Tours & Safaris, Easy Travel and Tours Ltd, Equatorial Safaris, Hoopoe Safaris, Ker and Downey Safaris, Let's Go Travel, Sandgrouse Adventure Tours & Safaris Ltd, Savannah Tours, Simba Safaris, Sunny Safaris, Takims Holidays Tours and Safaris, The Safari Co, United Touring Company, Wildersun Safaris and Tours, World Archipelago*. **Dar es Salaam**: *Bushtrekker Safaris, Selous Safaris, Takims Holidays Tours and Safaris, Valji & Alibhai*. **Hunting safaris** Arusha: *Bushmen Company, King Tours and Hunting Safaris, Tanzania Wildlife Corporation*. **Dar es Salaam**: *Cordial Tours, Gerald Posanisi Safaris*. **Wildlife exploration** Arusha: *Classic Tours and Safaris, Easy Travel & Tours Ltd, Hoopoe Safaris, Let's Go Travel, Ostrich Tours & Safaris Ltd, The Safari Co, Sandgrouse Adventure Tours & Safaris Ltd, Sunny Safaris, Tanganyika Wildlife Safari, United Touring Company*. **Dar es Salaam**: *Easy Travel & Tours Ltd, Savannah Tours Ltd, Tanganyika Wildlife Safari*. **Moshi**: *Afri Galaxy Tours & Travels Ltd*.

Finding out more Travellers wishing to research and plan their trip prior to departure can obtain brochures and maps from the offices of the **Tanzania Tourist Board** (www.tanzania-web.com, UK address: 80 Borough High St, London SE1, T020-7407 0566). The net is a wonderful resource and the Google web directory **www.google.com/Top/Regional/Africa/Tanzania** lists over 300 sites covering most topics travellers may wish to research. The Baobab Project – Harvard University focuses on cultural and artistic perspectives at **web-dubois.fas.harvard.edu/DuBois/baobab/baobab.html** while the **University of Pennsylvania** has a very comprehensive website, **www.sas.upenn.edu** PC World East Africa maintains the excellent **www.africaonline.com** and the Africa Information Centre's website displays a selection of local newspaper articles at **www.africainformation.co.uk/africa2a.htm**

Language Facility in English is poor. Even well-educated, professional Tanzanians, although perfectly able to make themselves understood, write and express themselves awkwardly. A few words of Swahili are very helpful in dealing with local people. It can be confusing when place names are spelt in various ways in different reference sources. This is a reflection of the oral origin of languages, which have been transliterated into English.

Travelling with children Africans are child friendly. However, many of the accoutrements that are often regarded as necessities in the West – disposable nappies, formula milk powders, puréed foods – are only available in the major cities. It is important to remember that children have an increased risk of gastro-enteritis, malaria and sunburn and are more likely to develop complications, so care must be taken to minimize risks. Few medical facilities are available outside the big

Swahili

Swahili is not a difficult language. In Shadows on the Grass (1960) Karen Blixen called it "a primitive ungrammatical lingua franca," an observation that will infuriate Swahili scholars, particularly in Zanzibar where they take pride in the beautiful and pure form of the language spoken there.

Swahili is the main language of instruction in primary schools, everyone speaks it, and it is continually absorbing new words and concepts (see box, page 320). Those new to Swahili often have difficulty with the use of prefixes for plurals. Thus mzungu *is a European,* wazungu *is Europeans. For those wanting to go further the* Swahili Dictionary *compiled by DV Perrot (Teach Yourself Books, New York: Hodder and Stoughton) contains a concise grammar and a guide to pronunciation.*

Swahili basics

Please	Tafadhali
Thank you	Asante
Sorry	Pole
Hello	Jambo
Goodbye	Kwa heri
Yes	Ndio
No	Hapana
Good	Mzuri
Bad	Mbaya
How much?	Bei gani
Where is?	Wapi
Why?	Kwa nini
Food	Chakula
Water	Maji
Room	Chumba
Bed	Kitanga
Toilet	Choo
One	Moja
Two	Mbili
Three	Tata
Four	Nne
Five	Tano
Ten	Kumi
Hundred	Mia
Thousand	Elfu

Tanzania

towns. Plan entertainment for lengthy road journeys. On a more positive note, there are usually young person's discounts for national park entry fees and some accommodation rates.

Disabled travellers With the exception of the most upmarket hotels there are few designated facilities for disabled travellers. A few of the game park lodges have ground floor bedrooms, in contrast to most hotels where the bedrooms are upstairs and lifts are uncommon.

Working in the country There are few opportunities for travellers to obtain casual paid employment in Tanzania. A number of NGOs and Voluntary Organizations can arrange placements for volunteers, usually for periods ranging from six months to two years, see www.volunteerafrica.org

Before you travel

Visas Visas are required by all visitors except citizens of the Commonwealth (excluding citizens of the UK, Australia, Canada, India and Nigeria who do require visas), Republic of Ireland, and Iceland. Some Republic of Ireland citizens have reportedly experienced difficulties with officials on arrival in Zanzibar, but not on the mainland. This should not happen and Irish citizens who encounter similar problems should firstly protest and, if unsuccessful, pay the visa fee and claim it back from the Tanzanian embassy in Dublin. Citizens of neighbouring countries do not normally require visas.

It is straightforward to get a visa at the point of entry (ie border crossing or airport) and many visitors find this more convenient than going to an Embassy.

Visas obtained from Tanzanian Embassies require two passport photographs and are issued in 24 hours. Visas for citizens of all countries that need one cost US$20, with the following exceptions: Colombia, France, Finland, Greece and Spain US$25; Costa Rica and South Africa US$30; Mexico and Oman US$35; Belgium and India US$40; for Canada, The Netherlands, RD Congo, USA and UK US$50. Visitors who do not need a visa are issued with a visitor's pass on arrival, valid for 1-3 months. Your passport must be valid for a minimum of six months after your planned departure date from Tanzania; this is true whether you need a visa or not.

Tanzania

☞ Swahili slang

Swahili, by origin a Bantu language, has been greatly influenced by Arabic and more recently the language has been further enriched by borrowings from other languages including English. There are examples where two words are in common usage, each with the same meaning but with different origins. For example 'week' – juma or wiki – is derived from Arabic and English; 'handkerchief' – anakachifi or leso – from English and Portuguese; and 'report' – ripoti or taarifa – from English and Arabic.

The origins of some words that have been adopted are very obvious. Modern transport has yielded, for example, basi (bus), treni (train), stesheni (station), teksi (taxi), petroli, tanki, breki. A rich man is mbenzi – he would be expected to drive a Mercedes. A traffic bollard is a kiplefti. Small sweet eating bananas were introduced from the West Indies, and are known as ndizi.

Other adoptions may not seem immediately obvious – for example, 'electricity' is sometimes called elekrii but more commonly stimu because the electricity generating stations used to be run by steam engines. In the same way the word for steamship, meli, derives from the fact that when the word was first used most of the ships would have carried mail. The dockyards are kuli, which is from the dockyard workers who were known as coolies.

The Second World War also produced a number of words that were adopted into the Swahili language, many of them relating to animals: a submarine was papa, the word for shark, a tank was faru, for rhino, an aeroplane is ndege ulaya, which means white-man's bird.

Swahili, like all other languages, also has a large collection of slang words. For example the period shortly before pay day when all the previous month's money has been spent is known as mwambo, which is derived from the word wamba, to stretch tight. This implies that the user is financially stretched.

Coins have also been given a variety of nicknames. Examples include ng'aru, which

derives from the word to shine, ku-ngaa. During the colonial era the shilling, which had a picture of the king's head on it, was known as Usi wa Kinga meaning the king's face. Five and 10 cents pieces, which used to have a hole in the centre, were nicknamed sikio la Mkwavi meaning 'the ear of the Mkwavi', after the Kwavi people who pierce their ear lobes and often used to hang coins from them as decoration. A slang phrase for bribery is kuzunguka mbuyu, which literally translated means to go behind a baobab tree, the implication being that behind such a wide tree as the baobab no one will see the transaction that takes place. The slang term for liquor is mtindi, which actually means skimmed milk – it was probably used to conceal what was really being drunk. A frequently used term for drunk is kupiga mtindi, which translates as 'to beat up the liquor' and is used in the same way that we would use 'to go on a binge'. Someone who is drunk may be described as amevaa miwani, or 'wearing spectacles', suggesting that he can't see well as a result of the alcohol – we might say he was seeing double. A similar phrase is yuko topu, which translates to 'he is full right up to the top'.

Clothes have also attracted various nicknames. Americani was the name given to the cheap cloth imported from America during the colonial era. Drainpipe trousers were known as suruwali ya uchinjo, which means cut-off trousers – because being so narrow they look as if part of them is missing. Many of the names given to items of clothing are derived from English words, such as tai (tie), kala (collar), and soksi (socks). The phrase used by off-duty policemen to describe their clothes also needs little explanation: kuvaa kisivilyan, which means 'to wear civilian clothes', while a fashionable haircut is known as fashun.

Many of the examples here were collected by R H Gower, a colonial administrator, and father of David Gower, the former England cricket captain, who was born in Tanganyika.

Travelling with your own car from Kenya requires leaving the vehicle log book with the Kenyan customs, and keeping a photostat copy for the Tanzanian side.

Tanzania charges US$65 for the car (multiple entry valid for three months) and car insurance US$34 per month.

An agreement between Tanzania, Kenya and Uganda is under negotiation to allow holders of single entry visas to move freely between all three countries countries without the need for re-entry permits. It may be in place when you arrive, so ask, if it is likely to be relevant to you.

Resident status for persons permanently employed in Tanzania can be arranged after arrival. Your employer will need to vouch for you, and the process can take several weeks. Resident status does, however, confer certain privileges (lower rates on air flights, in hotels, game parks).

Customs

There is now no requirement to change currency on entry. A litre of spirits or wine and 200 cigarettes are duty free. There will be no duty on any equipment for your own use (such as a laptop computer). Narcotics, pornography and firearms are prohibited. Duty is payable on fax machines, TVs, video recorders and other household electrical items.

Vaccinations

You will require a valid yellow fever vaccination certificate if you are arriving from a country where yellow fever occurs. Although visitors from Europe are not required to have one, it is strongly advised – you may find you are restricted in visiting neighbouring countries. However, recent travellers have been asked to produce a Yellow Fever certificate on arrival directly from Europe, even though they have not passed through a high risk area.

Money

Currency   Currently in circulation are TSh 200, 500, 1,000, 5,000 and 10,000 notes. Coins are TSh 50, 100: TSh 10 and 20 are little used. The currency has suffered from extensive depreciation since 1983 when the exchange rate was TSh9 = US$1. In current conditions, it will probably continue to depreciate at around 7% a year. Visitors are advised to exercise caution at some of the border crossings. Conmen operate at Namanga, appearing to be 'official' but offering derisory exchange rates.

See inside front cover for exchange rates

It is advisable to bring some foreign currency in small denomination notes and to keep at least one US$20 bill for when you leave. An endless source of annoyance is for a traveller to offer a US$20 travellers' cheque to pay the airport departure tax, only to be told to go to the bureau and obtain dollars. Because of commisssion, the cheque will realize less than the US$20 required. Because of forgery, many banks now refuse to exchange travellers' cheques without showing them the purchase agreement – that is, the slip issued at the point of sale.

Foreign exchange bureaux   The government has authorized bureaux de change to set rates for buying foreign currency from the public. They will also sell foreign currency up to US$3,000 for *bona fide* travellers (you need to produce an international airline ticket).

Foreign exchange payments   In the state-owned and other large private hotels, rates are calculated directly in dollars, and must be paid in foreign currency. Airline fares, game park entrance fees and other odd payments to the government (such as the US$20 airport international departure tax) must be paid in foreign currency. There is pressure from the International Monetary Fund and World Bank for Tanzania to end this requirement, so don't be surprised to find it is no longer the case at the time of your visit. At smaller hotels (B grade possibly, and certainly below) you can pay in local currency. You should pay all hotel bills other than the room rate (such as meals, drinks) in local currency – the rate used to convert the bill into dollars is usually markedly inferior to bureaux rates.

Black market   There is now no temptation to deal on the black market. The genuine street rate is no different from the bureau rate. You will be approached in the main towns, however, with offers of very high rates of exchange. The purpose is to trap you into circumstances where a swindle can be perpetrated. This will most likely take the form of an exchange in a back alley, hurriedly completed on the spurious grounds that the police are coming, only for you to find later that the Tanzanian currency is only a fraction of the sum agreed.

Tanzania

A more sophisticated ploy is to offer a generous rate for US$100, and to hand over the Tanzanian notes for you to count. When you produce the US$100 bill, the contact will express dismay. He says he has raised the Tanzanian shillings from several sources (the contact, in the old days of the thriving black market, always operated as a front for the real financier), and wants smaller denomination dollar notes to pay them off. He will suggest you hold on to the Tanzanian shillings while he goes off to try to break the US$100 bill. In a short while he returns. Alas he explains, he can't do it at the moment, but if you return later, he will have raised enough Tanzanian shillings from one source for the US$100. He hands you back the US$100, and you return the Tanzanian shillings. You are naturally a bit annoyed at the inconvenience. But not as annoyed as when you next try to change the US$100, only to find it is a high-class forgery (but clearly so from the quality of the printing and paper when you look at it closely), printed in Taiwan. Foreign exchange bureaux all have forgery detection machines.

Credit cards These are now accepted by large hotels, airlines, major tour operators and travel agencies. Otherwise you need cash. Travellers' cheques will not be taken by small hotels, restaurants and so on. It is wise to have a selection of small denomination dollar bills for any unforeseen needs.

ATMs The only bank in the country with ATM facilities is *Standard Chartered*, which has machines at its branches in Arusha, Moshi, Mwanza and Dar es Salaam (two branches). The machines accept Visa cards.

It is possible to buy travellers' cheques from *Rickshaw Travel*, the American Express Agents, in Dar es Salaam (see page 359), on presentation of an American Express card, paying with a personal cheque.

Cost of travelling In first rate hotels expect to spend US$150 a day. Careful tourists can live reasonably comfortably on US$60 a day and budget travellers can get by on US$20. However, organized safari costs can exceed US$200 daily and climbing Mount Kilimanjaro is an expensive experience.

Getting there

Air The majority of travellers arrive in Tanzania through Dar es Salaam Airport. There are also direct international flights to Arusha (Kilimanjaro Airport) and to Zanzibar. Carriers will usually make the final leg of the journey from an airport in their own country, but will arrange connecting flights from the other main European cities.

From **Europe** to Dar es Salaam, *British Airways* has three flights a week with a refuelling stop in Nairobi. Passengers in transit are now allowed to disembark, making the total flight time around 11 hours. Airlines with regular flights are *Air France*, *Egypt Air*, *Ethiopian Airlines*, *Gulf Air* and *KLM*. *Air Tanzania* has suspended its service to London. To **Kilimanjaro** (Arusha/Moshi), flights by *Egypt Air*, *Ethiopian Airlines* and *KLM* touch down on the way to Dar es Salaam. To **Zanzibar**, *Gulf Air* has a direct flight.

From other parts of **Africa**, there are regular flights by *Air Botswana*, *Air Tanzania*, *Air Zimbabwe*, *Kenya Airways*, *Royal Swazi*, *Zambia Airways*, *South African Airways*. *Air France* connects from **Comoros**.

For specialist agencies offering discounted fares, see page 31 **Specialist agents** will arrange economical fares from Europe, typically for fixed arrival and departure dates, and for stays of a week or longer. Fares depend on the season. High season is generally July-end March (expect to pay around US$900 return from Europe with a prestige carrier, depending on country of departure), with the low season for April, May, June at around US$750. You may do significantly better by shopping around. Gulf Air have occasionally offered heavily discounted fares of around US$400 return. It is not generally cheaper to arrange a return to Nairobi and a connecting return flight to Dar es Salaam. The connecting flights are not reliable, and delay in Nairobi erodes any cost advantage. For budget travellers, a return to Nairobi and a road connection to Dar es Salaam can result in a saving of perhaps US$100.

Tanzania

Burundi No road access.

Kenya The main road crossing is at Namanga, see page 484, on the road between Arusha and Nairobi. This is reasonably quick and efficient and there are through buses and good roads all the way. Other crossings are at Lunga Lunga, see page 382, between Mombasa and Dar es Salaam. The road on the Tanzanian side is less good, but there are overnight through buses between the two cities. There are also crossings at Taveta, between Moshi and Voi; at Isebania, between Kisuma, and Musoma, see page 323; and across the border from Masai Mara Park into the Serengeti. From Uganda there is crossing at Mutakulu, page 488, between Bukoba and Masaka.

Rwanda There is a good bus link to the border at Rusomo. There is a bus leaving very early each day from Ngara on the Tanzania side and arriving at Mwanza in the evening.

Malawi One bus leaves the border for Mbeya at 1200 daily, takes four hours and costs US$2.50.

Mozambique Ferry near Mtwara but need to arrange formalities in advance in Dar es Salaam.

Zambia There are buses to the border at Nakonde, see page 527. You have to walk between the border posts (or use a bicycle-taxi) to Tunduma where there are buses to Mbeya.

Rail services link Dar es Salaam and Zambia, see page 328 for prices and timetable. Trains used to run across the border to Kenya from Moshi. These were ended with the break-up of the East Africa Community in 1977, but there are discussions on resuming the service.

From Kenya there have been boats from Mombasa to Tanga, Zanzibar and Dar es Salaam. The providers of this service change fairly frequently. The craft in use are usually hydrofoils and catamarans. The cost was about the same as the air fare from Mombasa (US$45).

It is possible to take a dhow from Mombasa, see page 222. However you must expect to wait around for a week or more for one to depart. It will take one or two days depending on the weather. Expect to pay about US$15, bring all your own food, you will sit and sleep on the cargo, and the sea can be unpleasantly rough.

It is reported that passengers on freight ships are not normally allowed to disembark at Dar es Salaam.

Shipping information **Nedlloyd**, PO Box 63361 Dar es Salaam, Mobitel 0811-325222, F46339; **Nasaco Pangani dept**, PO Box 9082, Dar es Salaam, T112574, F44504.

Ferry From Burundi there is a lake ferry to Kigoma from Bujumbura, every Mon. From Mpulungu (Zambia) there is a weekly ferry to Kigoma on Fri (see page 511 for further details). From Nkhata Bay (Malawi) there is a ferry to Mbamba Bay on Wed.

Touching down

Dar es Salaam airport lies 15 km west of the city, T2844211/2. There are foreign exchange bureaux, but limited hotel bookings or car hire facilities. Visitors are advised to proceed directly to a hotel where these things can be arranged. Flight information is virtually impossible to obtain by telephone at the airport. Contact airline direct – airline offices are listed under Dar es Salaam, page 363, and Arusha, page 449.

Airport information
Airport tax on departure US$20 or £15, payable in foreign currency

There used to be a problem with some of the immigration officials at the airport, who would mark your passport on entry with an incomprehensible squiggle. When you left Tanzania you were told you had overstayed and that you would have to pay a fine. However this should no longer happen as the officials now use a rubber stamp to make a clear mark.

Phone cards are available from shops just outside the airport and cost US$3. There are public telephones in the terminal buildings.

Touching down

Electricity 230 volts (50 cycles). However the system is notorious for power surges. Computers are particularly vulnerable and a surge protector plug, obtainable from computer stores, is a vital accessory for the computer-using traveller. Offices will invariably run desk-tops through a voltage regulator. New socket installations are square 3-pin. However, do not be surprised to encounter round 3-pin (large), round 3-pin (small) and 2-pin (small) sockets in old hotels – a multi-socket adaptor (obtainable at travel shops) is essential.

IDD 255. Double ring repeated regularly means it is ringing; short equal tones with short pauses means it is engaged.
Hours of business Most offices will start at 0800, lunch between 1200-1300, finish business at 1700, Monday to Friday; 0900-1200 on Saturday, although the introduction of competition from the private sector will probably lead to longer banking hours.
Official time Three hours ahead of GMT.
Weights and measures Officially metric, but expect to pay for fruit and vegetables by the item.

There are official buses which cost around US$3 and go to the *New Africa Hotel* in the town centre. There are private buses (*dala-dala*), which cost about US$1 but are very crowded, leaving when full. A taxi to town will cost US$10-15 depending on your destination.

Kilimanjaro International Airport, T027-2502223, is halfway between Arusha and Moshi, approximately 40 km from each. Shuttle buses to either town cost up to US$10, taxis US$20.

Zanzibar airport is 7 km southwest of Stone Town, T024-2230213. There is a small bank at the airport immediately before you exit the baggage retrieval area. It does not accept travellers' cheques but will change US dollars, pounds sterling, Euros and some other hard currencies. The rates are OK, but are better at the forex bureaux in Stone Town. Buses to town cost US$0.50, taxis about US$6-10.

Tourist information
Tanzania Tourist Board has offices in Dar es Salaam and Arusha: **Tanzania Tourist Board**, PO Box 2485, Dar es Salaam, 3rd Floor of the IPS Building, at the corner of Samora Av and Azikiwe St, T2111244, F2116420, safari@ud.co.tz, www.tanzania-web.com **Tanzania Tourist Board Information Centre**, PO Box 2348, Arusha, T2503842/3, F2548628, info@yako.habari.co.tz It has been an ineffective organization concerned only in marketing its own state-run hotels, transport services and the national parks. It is now being wound up and a new body is revamping information services but it remains to be seen how effective it will be.

The **National Parks** office in the Arusha International Conference Centre is a good source of information and has such booklets on the individual parks as are currently in print. **Tanzania National Parks (TANAPA)**, PO Box 3134, Arusha, T027-2544082, T/F2548216, tanapa@habari.co.tz

Local customs & laws
Travellers are encouraged to show respect by adhering to a modest dress code in public places, especially in the predominantly Muslim areas like Zanzibar. Respect is accorded to elderly people, usually by the greeting *Shikamoo, mzee* to a man and *Shikamoo, mama* to a woman. At work in offices men will wear slacks, shoes and open neck shirts. If you are visiting a senior official it is safest to wear a tie and a jacket and a suit is desirable (for a man). In the evening at social functions there is no particular dress code although hosts will feel insulted if you arrive for dinner in shorts, sandals or bare feet. Long hair on men makes local people uneasy. Visiting mosques requires removing shoes and modest dress.

Tipping Large hotels will add a service charge. In smaller places tipping is optional. In restaurants most vistors will tip about 10% of the bill.

Prohibitions Photographing any government/military buildings or installations and bridges is forbidden. These restrictions can include old forts built in the colonial period and post offices. Importing or possession of drugs and guns is prohibited and punished severely. Homosexual activity is unlawful so great discretion is advocated.

Tanzania has become less safe for travellers in recent years. The overwhelming majority of **Safety** people are trustworthy, but the following are sensible precautions to observe.

It is unwise to venture into unpopulated areas after dark, particularly alone – always take a taxi. There are notices displayed to the effect that muggers operate on the beaches between the hotels north of Dar es Salaam and this is certainly the case. Stay within the beach areas controlled by the security guards. There are warning signs in Bagamoyo, but you are quite safe if a local person, even a child, accompanies you (they would identify any assailant). Thieves on buses and trains may steal valuables from inattentive riders. Visitors driving in game parks without an experienced driver or game park official accompanying them may be at risk. Crime and hazardous road conditions make travel by night dangerous. Car-jacking has occurred in both rural and urban areas. The majority of these attacks have occurred on the main road from Dar es Salaam to Zambia, between Morogoro and Mikumi National Park. Travellers are advised not to stop between populated areas, and to travel in convoys whenever possible. There has been some banditry against boat travellers on Lake Tanganyika near the port of Kigoma.

Things left lying around may well get stolen. Always lock your hotel door (a noisy air-conditioner can made it easy for a sneak thief). Do not wear expensive jewellery or watches and beware of having a camera or necklace snatched in a crowd. Leave your passport, spare cash, airline ticket and credit cards in the hotel safe unless you will be needing them. When travelling, keep these in a slim money belt worn under clothing, particularly as thieves have recently begun to cut open bags and rucksacks of travellers on buses, trains or while camping and extracting valuables.

Areas of instability After hundreds of thousands of refugees from Rwanda and Burundi entered Tanzania in 1993-94, Tanzania closed its land borders with these countries. Military forces were deployed in the Kigoma and Kagera regions. Although most refugees have now returned home, the border areas, which include several minor game reserves and Gombe Stream National Park, remain tense.

Tricksters These are not common in Tanzania, but always be cautious when approached by a stranger with a sponsorship form.

Begging It is difficult to have a consistent policy towards beggars. Some, particularly women with children, appear so wretched that they cry out for help. On the other hand, it is best not to give to street children – they are often encouraged to skip school or forced to beg by their parents. It is quite unnecessary to pay to have your car 'watched'. If you feel the need to do something constructive about street children, a donation to **Street Kids International (SKI)**, based in Toronto, Canada, can be made using Visa and Mastercard, through their phone number T+416-504-8994. SKI run the *Kuleana* project in Mwanza (see page 444). See also advice on page 33.

Animal safety precautions When you visit game reserves, it is not advisable to leave your tent or banda during the night. Wild animals wander around the camps freely in the hours of darkness. Exercise care during daylight hours too – remember wild animals are dangerous.

Where to stay

Places to stay have been polarized around those used by well-heeled tourists, and are expensive, at around US$200 a day, self-contained with air-conditioning, hot water and swimming pools, and those used by local people (and budget travellers) at under US$10 a day, which may comprise a simple bed, shared toilet and washing facilities, and have an irregular water supply. The expensive establishments used to be run by the monopoly Tanzania Tourist Corporation and the others by the private sector. However, this has now become more liberalized and more private hotels are opening and the competition is giving travellers better choice. There are now some acceptable places to stay (except, alas, in the parks) with fans or air-conditioned, hot water and self-contained at around US$20 a day. In some hotels and

Hotels *For further information on national parks accommodation, see page 334*

Tanzania

airlines a system operates where tourists are charged approximately double the rate for locals – resident and non-resident rates. Insist on the resident rate, and threaten to go elsewhere, if you can, if this is refused. Frequently non-residents are unable to pay in Tanzanian shillings. Insist on paying in TSh if this works out cheaper.

Some of the small beach hotels are in splendid locations and despite having only simple facilities are excellent value.

In the parks, camping in either a tented camp or a campsite is more atmospheric and certainly cheaper than staying in one of the lodges. Many of the camps advertise hot running water for showers. This is accurate when the sun is out, otherwise the water may be cold (see Sleeping classification, page 36).

Getting around

Air *Air Tanzania Corporation* (ATC) has a schedule of domestic flights. The state-owned carrier, ATC has suffered from severe financial and operating difficulties, meaning that flights are cancelled and the schedules changed all the time. Often there are delays of several hours for a flight and a whole day needs to be allocated to a leg of air travel. The line is rather unkindly dubbed 'Air Total Chaos' by local folk. The only sensible procedure is to call in at the ATC office on Ohio St and Garden Av and check what is currently available. ATC generally has daily flights scheduled to Zanzibar and Kilimanjaro and one, two or three times a week to Mwanza, Dodoma, Mtwara, Lindi and Musoma. Several ATC timetabled flights are actually operated by other airlines, particularly Precisionair. This is true for the 1-3 times a week flights to Kigoma, Tabora, Shinyanga, Mafia, Nachingwea, Kilwa and Pemba. Flights are not particularly expensive, a single flight to Zanzibar is about US$45, about US$100 to Kilimanjaro and US$200 to Mwanza, but bear in mind that fares are subject to frequent alteration. There are plans for ATC to be sold to *South African Airways*, who are reportedly eager to take over ATC's international routes, but are less keen on running the domestic network.

Other domestic air services are fairly unstable. Air transport has recently been opened up to private operators, several of whom have started services only to close them when it was apparent that the immediate market was unviable. The best advice is to explore the private carriers through one of the Dar es Salaam travel agents. *Precisionair* have a good reputation to date, and they claim to have an over 98% on-time performance record. However, it is essential to follow the instructions to reconfirm – flight times are frequently at variance with those printed on the tickets. *Precisionair* flights serve Dar es Salaam, Zanzibar, Mafia, Arusha, Kilimanjaro, Shinyanga, Seronera, Mwanza and Bukoba. For popular routes such as between Zanzibar and Arusha it is usually necessary to book in advance, and it has been reported that these routes are occasionally overbooked.

Dar es Salaam-Zanzibar is well served with daily flights by several companies (see page 559). **Dar es Salaam-Pemba** is served on Monday, Wednesday and Friday by Precisionair, with one flight on Tuesday by Eagle Air (see page 392). **Zanzibar-Pemba** has one flight on Wednesday and Friday by Precisionair and one on Friday by Eagle Air (see page 559). **Kilimanjaro-Dar es Salaam** has at least one flight daily by ATC, and less frequent flights by other operators. **Arusha-Dar es Salaam** has several flights a week by Precisionair, Eagle Air and Coastal Travels Ltd (see page 449). **Dar es Salaam- Mafia** has services almost every day, either by Precisionair or Eagle Air (see page 392). Other scheduled flights serve Lindi, Kilwa, Nachingwea, Dodoma, Tabora, Kigoma, Shinyanga, Mwanza, Musoma, Bukoba, and airstrips in Selous Game Reserve and Ruaha, Lake Manyara and Serengeti National Parks. Other towns with airstrips include Moshi, Iringa and Mbeya. Many camps in the national parks and game reserves have their own airstrips suitable for light aircraft charter flights.

Road **Buses** There is now an efficient network of privately run buses across the country. On the main routes (Arusha, Morogoro) there is a choice of 'luxury', 'semi-luxury' and 'regular'. Fares are very reasonable – roughly US$2 per 100 km. On good sealed roads they cover 50 km per hour. On unsealed or poorly maintained roads they will average only 20 km per hour. The roads in Tanzania are of variable quality. The best roads are the tarmac roads from Dar es Salaam to Zambia and Dar es Salaam to Arusha. Most of the remaining roads are unmade gravel with potholes: there are many rough stretches.

Timetable of selected country buses in Tanzania

Daily services from Dar es Salaam to:

	Departure time		Departure time
Arusha		**Moshi**	
Air Msae Tourism Coach	0700	Air Msae Tourist Coach	0700
Bazzu	0900		
Fresh ya Shamba	0800	**Nairobi**	
Master City	0700	Bazzu	0900
Metro Coach	0830	Hood	0900
Royal Sumayi	0700	Tawfiq	1000
Royal Sumayi Luxury	0700		
Tawfiq	0900	**Njombe**	
		Lupelo	1000
Dodoma		Makete	0700
Super Champion	0800 and 1100		
		Singida	
Iringa		Azan Investment	1100
Scandinavia	1030		
		Tanga	
Masasi		AMTCO	0700
Tawaqal	1600	Zafanana	0630
		Atlantic	0600
Mbeya			
Kwacha	1200	**Kyela to Malawi**	
Safina	0900	Magoma Moto	0900
		Stage Coach	1330
Mombasa			
Hood	1100		

Please note that this timetable is subject to change. It is advisable to confirm departure times locally.

Tanzania

On the main routes it is possible to book ahead at a kiosk at the bus stand and this is wise rather than turning up at the departure time on the off-chance. It is sensible to try to avoid being placed on a make-shift gangway seat with only a small seat-back, or sitting over the wheel arch where it's impossible to stretch your legs.

Dala-dala Local private buses and passenger vehicles constructed from small trucks (called *dala-dala*, it is said, because they charged a dollar, although this seems a high sum) are for the adventurous. Tanzania banned these vehicles until 1985, and road transport was a state monopoly. However, inability to provide enough buses (Dar es Salaam required 250 minimum, and was down to 60 in 1980) led to unseemly fights to get on, huge queues, and many commuters were resigned to walking up to 20 km a day. State corporations and private firms tended to provide their own buses for staff. Liberalization of transport is an enormous improvement, but although the *dala-dala* are steadily expanding, they get very crowded and there is often a squeeze to get on. A modifed truck vehicle will carry 50 passengers, of whom 30 will stand and you really need to hang on as it sways around. *Dala-dala* are cheap, US$0.10 for any length of journey, and are frequent on main routes into and out of town. Fellow travellers will be very helpful in directing you to the correct *dala-dala* if you ask (most have a sign indicating their route and destination on the front), will advise on connections, fight on your behalf to try to get you a seat and tell you when to get off at your destination.

Taxis Hotels and town-centre locations are well served by taxis, some good and some very run-down but serviceable. It is wise to sit in the back if there are no front seat belts. Hotel staff, even at the smallest locations, will rustle up a taxi even when there is not one waiting outside. If you visit an out-of-town centre location, it is wise to ask the taxi to wait – it will

Tanzania

Tanzania Zambia Railway Authority (TAZARA) Trains Timetable

Ordinary train service:
Monday, Thursday and Saturday

Express train service:
Tuesday and Friday

Station	Arr	Dep	Station	Arr	Dep
Dar es Salaam		0900	Dar es Salaam		1734
Mzenga	1050	1056	Kisaki	2144	2154
Kisaki	1408	1423	Ifakara	0033	0043
Mang'ula	1648	1657	Mlimba	0257	0317
Ifakara	1745	1759	Makambako	0759	0811
Mlimba	2044	2117	Mbeya	1224	1244
Kiyowela	0051	0053	Tunduma	1529	1548
Makambako	0237	0247	Nakonde*	1454	1554
Chimala	0509	0511	Lugozi*	1724	1744
Igurusi	0536	0538	Kasama*	2056	2116
Mbeya	0750	0810	Mpika*	0023	0043
Idiga	0852	0854	Serenje*	0441	0501
Vwawa	1016	1018	Mkushi*	0651	0659
Tunduma	1120	1145	New Kapiri Mposhi*	0833	
New Kapiri Mposhi*	1500				
New Kapiri Mposhi*		0920	New Kapiri Mposhi*		1345
Tunduma	1305	1322	Mkushi*	1522	1530
Vwawa	1430	1438	Serenje*	1731	1751
Idiga	1608	1613	Mpika*	2152	2212
Mbeya	1655	1720	Kasama*	0122	0142
Igurusi	1954	1950	Lugozi*	0456	0516
Chimala	2024	2032	Nakonde*	0638	0658
Makambako	2300	2317	Tunduma	0804	0824
Kiyowela	0105	0108	Mbeya	1105	1125
Mlimba	0502	0527	Makambako	1611	1621
Ifakara	0803	0809	Mlimba	2113	2133
Mang'ula	0855	0900	Ifakara	2345	2350
Kisaki	1119	1131	Kisaki	0127	0137
Mzenga	1504	1510	Dar es Salaam	0648	
Dar es Salaam	1700				

Denotes Central African Time (CAT), which operates in Zambia. This is one hour earlier than Eastern African Time (EAT), which operates in Tanzania.

Ordinary fares to Mbeya		**Express fares to Mbeya**	
1st class	$45	1st class	$50
2nd class	$30	2nd class	$35
3rd class	$10	3rd class	$25

For further information or clarification, please contact:
General Manager, Tanzania Zambia Railway Authority (Tazara), PO Box 2834,
Dar es Salaam, Tanzania
T2865192/2865187/2864191-9/2862480/2862191/2862479
F2865192/2865187/2862474

NB This timetable is subject to change. It is advisable to check details before travelling.

Tanzania Railway Corporation – trains and marine schedules

Passenger trains

Station	ETD	ETA	Station	ETD	ETA
Dar es Salaam-Morogoro[1]	1700	2030	Morogoro-Dar es Salaam[3]	0215	0850
Morogoro-Dodoma[1]	0015	0735	Dodoma-Morogoro[3]	1840	0135
Dodoma-Tabora[1]	0810	1825	Tabora-Dodoma[3]	0725	1810
Tabora-Mwanza[1]	1930	0535	Mwanza-Tabora[1]	2000	0600
Tabora-Kigoma[1]	1910	0630	Kigoma-Tabora[3]	1900	0630
Tabora-Mpanda[2]	2010	1030	Mpanda-Tabora[4]	1300	0245
			Moshi-Dar es Salaam[5]	1600	0700

[1] = Days of travel are Tuesday, Wednesday, Friday and Sunday
[2] = Days of travel are Monday, Wednesday and Friday
[3] = Days of travel are Tuesday, Thursday, Friday and Sunday
[4] = Days of travel are Tuesday, Thursday and Sunday
[5] = Days of travel are Saturday

Alternative services

There is not direct rail service betwen Mwanza and Kigoma. Change at Tabora.
An additional service on Monday alternates between Dar es Salaam-Mwanza and Dar es Salaam-Kigoma routes.

Marine services

Lake Victoria Services, see page 484. Lake Tanganyika Services, see page 511. Lake Nyasa Services (sometimes called Lake Malawi), see page 531. Zanzibar, see page 560.

Passenger fares: selected stations/ports

Rail	1st class	2nd class	3rd class
		(Sleeping)	
Dar es Salaam-Kigoma	US$60	US$44	US$20.75
Dar es Salaam-Mwanza	US$59	US$43	US$20.50
Dar es Salaam-Tabora	US$43	US$32	US$15
Dar es Salaam-Morogoro	US$17	US$13	US$11

Reservations

These can be done for any class of travel from all over the world at the following telephone and fax numbers: 2112529, 2117833, 2112565 (code: 00 25551).

For further information, please contact:
Director General or the Principal Commercial Manager (Promotion), Tanzania Railways Corporation, PO Box 468, Dar es Salaam.

NB Fares and schedules are subject to change without notice.

---

normally be happy to do so for benefit of the return fare. Up to 1 km should cost US$1. A trip to the outskirts of Dar es Salaam such as the university (13 km) would be US$7.50. There is a bargaining element: none of the cabs have meters, and you should establish the fare (*bei gani?* – how much?) before you set off.

Car hire It is difficult to justify hiring a car for in-town travel in view of the availability, cheapness and willingness-to-wait of local taxis. Drivers may find that hired cars are normally more trouble than they are worth in town. However, if you are planning to visit some of the national parks and don't want to go on an organized safari, hiring a car becomes a necessity.

Car hire is not as well organized in Tanzania as it is in Kenya. There are fewer hire-car companies (although this is changing) and they are more expensive. Also, many of the vehicles are poorly maintained and you may find it difficult to hire a car without a driver. The hire charge for this will depend on where you get the vehicle from. Dar es Salaam is usually cheaper with a Land Rover or VW Combi costing US$20 a day, plus US$1 per km, plus US$5 a day for the driver. A Nissan minibus will cost about US$25 plus US$1 per km. (Both have a minimum mileage of 100 km per day.) In Arusha a Land Rover will cost about US$40 plus US$1 per km. You will have to pay the park entrance fees for the car and the driver and although it will work out expensive this method does allow for greater flexibility than an organized safari. Most of the tour and travel agents listed will be able to arrange vehicle hire (see page 358 for Dar es Salaam; page 445 for Arusha; specialist car hire for Dar es Salaam, page 360).

Sea　**Sea and lake ferries**　The ferries are reliable and pleasant. Between Dar es Salaam and Zanzibar there are several sailings each day, with a choice of hydrofoil or steam ship (see page 362 for details). On **Lake Victoria**, the main sailings are between Mwanza and Bukoba (see pages 484 and 488), though small islands and some other lakeside towns are served. On **Lake Tanganyika** boats go from Kigoma to various small ports south (see page 511). Fares for non-residents greatly exceed those for residents. On **Lake Nyasa** (also known as Lake Malawi) there is a boat going from the northern port of Itungi to Mbamba Bay, the last Tanzanian port on the east shore (see page 531).

The cost of travel varies between US$40 per 100 km for 1st class hydrofoil travel to US$2 per 100 km for 3rd class on a steamer.

Train　Train services are fairly reliable. There are two railway companies operating in Tanzania. **Tazara** is the name of the Tanzania-Zambia Railway Authority and the trains run from Dar es Salaam, southwest to Zambia. The **Tanzania Railway Corporation** operates services between Dar es Salaam and Kigoma with a branch line to Mwanza central line. The Northern line service to Tanga and Moshi has been discontinued.

Keeping in touch

Communica-　**Internet**　Internet cafés and email facilities offered in small business centres have mush-
tions　roomed in all the major towns. The cost of access has fallen considerably and can be found at around US$1 per 15 mins. If using faster, more modern computers the cost rises to US$1.25-1.50 per 15 mins.

Post　Postal system is reliable. Airmail takes about two weeks to destinations in Europe and North America. Buy stamps at the hotel or at a postcard shop. The post offices are crowded and queueing is not observed. **DHL** has offices in the major cities. Packages to Europe take two working days, to North America, three days.

Country code: 255　**Telephone**　**International**　In most towns there is an efficient international service from the
Area codes: see　Telecomms office. Connections are quick and about a third of the price of a call through
individual towns　hotels, which are expensive for phone calls and faxes. **Local**　The recent installation of new telephone exchanges as part of a privatization initiative has led to a radical change of telephone numbers, involving new area codes and the addition of a 2 before most existing numbers, resulting in seven-digit numbers. The upgrading is ongoing: in case of difficulties, the *Tanzania Telecommunications Company Ltd (TTCL)* enquiry number in Dar es Salaam is T022-2116803/4. Zanzibar now has its own telecommunications company, *Zantel*. **Mobile**　Providers of mobile telephone services include *Adesemi* (prefix 0761), TTCL's subsidiary *Cellnet* (0743), *Mobitel* (0741), *Tritel* (0742), *Vodacom* (0744) and *Zantel* (0747).

Media　**Newspapers**　Tanzania has two English dailies, *Daily News* and the *Guardian*, as well as several Swahili dailies, but all are difficult to obtain outside Dar es Salaam. An excellent regional paper, *The East African*, published in Nairobi, comes out weekly and has good Tanzanian coverage. The Kenyan daily, *The Nation*, is available in Arusha, Mwanza and Dar es Salaam from midday, and is a high quality source of regional and international news. There are a number of independent weeklies. The *Business Times* gives excellent coverage of commercial matters, *Family Circle* has served as a vehicle for criticism of the government, as does *The Express*. The Tanzanian press is worth sampling for the bizarre and curious local stories that appear (eg 'Vicar Kicks Worshippers Who Insist on Kneeling' – *Daily News*, December 1992), as well as being the main vehicle for entertainment and sporting announcements.

Radio There are two government operated stations. Radio Tanzania on 1442 KHZ MW broadcasts in Swahili. The External Service at 1204 MW has programmes in English. News bulletins tend to contain a lot of local coverage. Programmes of African music are good, and the discussion programmes tend to be fairly serious, on health, development, education etc. A private station, Radio One, broadcasts mostly music and in Swahili. **BBC World Service** is broadcast to Tanzania and can be received on radios with short waveband reception. See guide, page 38. World Service is now also available via an FM relay in Mwanza (Radio Free Africa 89.8 FM), Arusha (Radio 5 Arusha 105 FM) and Dar es Salaam (BBC/IPP 101.4 FM), and the reception is better than on short-wave.

Television In 1994 ITV began to transmit with a mixture of locally produced Swahili items and international programmes. There are now several local stations, and many hotels will have satellite TV. Zanzibar has had television since the early 1970s, and the larger hotels will have a TV in one of the public rooms. It only operates in the evening, it is difficult to find a programme schedule, and a lot of videos are shown – it is said that if you hand a recent tape into the TV station they will put it out that evening. There is a flourishing video market with hire shops in all towns, though the quality is poor as most tapes are pirated.

Food and drink

Cuisine in Tanzania is not one of the country's main attractions. There is a legacy of uninspired British catering (soups, steaks, grilled chicken, chips, boiled vegetables, puddings, instant coffee). Asian eating places can be better, but are seldom of a high standard. There are a few Chinese and Italian restaurants. Some of the best food is prepared on simple charcoal grills outside in beer gardens .

Food
For restaurant classification, see page 39

A variety of items can be purchased from **street vendors** who prepare and cook over charcoal, which adds considerably to the flavour, at temporary roadside shelters (kiosks). Street cuisine is pretty safe despite hygiene methods being fairly basic. Most of the items are cooked or peeled, which deals with the health hazard. Grapes require careful washing or peeling.

Savoury items include chips, omelettes, barbecued beef on skewers (*mishkaki*), roast maize (corn), samosas, kebabs, hard-boiled eggs and roast cassava (look like white, peeled turnips) with red chili-pepper garnish. Fruits variously in season include oranges (peeled and halved), grapes, pineapples, bananas, mangoes (slices scored and turned inside-out), paw-paw (*papaya*). In the evenings, particularly, but all day at markets, bus and railway stations there are traditional Swahili coffee vendors with large portable conical brass coffee pots with charcoal braziers underneath. The coffee is ground (not instant), is sold black in small porcelain cups fished out of a portable wash-bowl, and is excellent. They also sell peanut crisp bars and sugary cakes made from molasses. These items are very cheap – a skewer of meat is US$0.25, an orange US$0.05, a cup of coffee US$0.05. They are all worth trying, and when travelling, are indispensable.

Local beers (lager) are very sound and cheap (US$1 a litre). There is a wide variety of imported lagers from Kenya and South Africa particularly, but also from Europe at around three times the price of local lagers. Imported **wines** are good value at US$6 a bottle upwards for European and South African labels. Wines from Zimbabwe are quite pleasant. Tanzanian wines produced by the White Fathers at Dodoma, 'Bowani Wine', are reasonable. Wines made by the National Milling Corporation are undrinkable. **Soft drinks** are mainly limited to colas, orange, lemon,

Drink
See also box, page 594

pineapple, ginger beer, tonic and club soda. No diet sodas available. Fresh juices are very rare outside the main tourist areas. Bottled water is widely available and safe. Coffee, when fresh ground, is the local Arabica variety with a distinctive, acidic flavour.

Shopping

Shop opening hours are usually 0830-1300 and 1400-1700 weekdays and 0830-1300 on Saturdays. Tanzania has several unique and interesting craft items for sale including Makonde carvings which are significantly cheaper and of better quality if purchased at source in the far southeast of Tanzania or in Dar es Salaam. Tingatinga paintings, soapstone carvings, wood carvings, musical instruments, basket ware and textiles including *kangas* are widely available. Prices for the latter are keenest in Zanzibar.

Entertainment and nightlife

Dar es Salaam and Arusha have a wide selection of bars, nightclubs, cinemas, live music and traditional dancing venues. Zanzibar has a good selection of bars and music venues. Less visited areas tend to have more basic provision, but even the smallest town will usually have a bar - the exception being some of the Muslim coastal settlements.

Cinemas Found in most large towns, cinemas will show mostly Indian, King Fu and Western films of the action variety.

Music Most musical entertainment is in hotels where traditional dance programmes are staged for tourists, and there are live bands and discos. Hotels and social halls often stage fashion and musical shows where local entertainers impersonate western pop stars. These events are all well publicized in the local press.

Spectator sports In large towns the main activities will be soccer matches. Fixtures tend to be arranged, or postponed, at short notice and details should be checked in the daily press. There are also cricket matches over weekends (predominantly a pursuit of the Asian community), and golf, tennis and squash tournaments are held at clubs but open to the public. Occasional sailing regattas are held at the yacht clubs in Dar es Salaam and Tanga. Hash House Harriers (a paperchase running and social event) meet every Saturday afternoon in Dar es Salaam (details of the location of the meet can be obtained in the British Council offices on Samora Av). Track and field meetings are staged, the Mount Meru marathon is an annual event in June, and there are boxing tournaments. For details see local press.

Holidays and festivals

New Year's Day 1 January; **Zanzibar Revolution Day** (Zanzibar only) 12 January; **CCM Foundation Day** 5 February; **Union Day** 26 April; **Mayday Workers Day** 1 May; **Farmer's Day** 7 July; **Peasant's Day** 8 August; **Prophet's Birthday** 10 September; **Independence Day** 9 December; **Christmas Day** 25 December; **Boxing Day** 26 December.

See also page 39 Good Friday, Easter Monday, Id-ul-Fitr (end of Ramadan), Id-ul-Haji (Festival of Sacrifice), Islamic New Year, and Prophet Mohammad's Birthday are other holidays that vary from year to year. Muslim festivals are timed according to local sightings of the various stages of the moon. Christian holidays will not be observed by all Muslims and vice versa.

Sport and special interest travel

See also Diving on page 40 and Safaris on page 45 Details about diving, snorkelling and deep sea fishing are listed under the local providers. Trekking, cycling or horse or camel riding safaris are popular alternatives to being ferried around in zebra camouflaged vehicles in the national parks. Climbing Mount Kilimanjaro remains a popular challenge.

National parks and game reserves

The parks and game reserves of Tanzania are without rival anywhere in the world. Some are world famous, such as **Serengeti**, **Ngorongoro**, **Kilimanjaro** and **Gombe Stream**, and have excellent facilities and receive many visitors. Many others rarely see tourists and make little or no provision in the way of amenities for them. The differences between a 'national park' and a 'game reserve' depends on the access by local people. In national parks the animals have the parks to themselves. In game reserves the local people, in particular pastoralists such as the Masai, are allowed rights of grazing. Game reserves are often found adjoining national parks and have usually been created as a result of local pressure to return some of the seasonal grazing lands to pastoralists.

It is essential to tour the parks by vehicle. In fact, walking is prohibited in all parks except Arusha (west), Kilimanjaro, Udzungwa, Mts NP, Selous, Gombe Stream and Mahale Mountain are the only parks that can really be enjoyed without a vehicle. However, you will need to employ an armed ranger (US$10 per walk) to accompany you. You will either have to arrange a drive in a park vehicle with a guide (the least expensive option), join an organized tour by a safari company, hire or have your own vehicle. It is a waste not to take a guide – the cost is modest and, without one, you will miss a lot of game, and not go to the promising locations for viewing.

Arrangements are most conveniently made through tour operators who will generally offer a variety of tours of differing durations, luxury and expense. Lists of major operators are given on page 318. If you are making your plans from either Dar es Salaam or Arusha, there are lists of operators with offices in these locations (see page 358 for Dar es Salaam and page 445 for Arusha). For many people a camping safari is the most attractive option, where the conditions are very comfortable but less expensive than staying in lodges. A list of camping safari specialists is on page 318, but most tour operators will offer camping as well as lodge and hotel based touring. Tented camps (see below) are highly recommended, for they combine the adventure of camping with most of the convenience and luxury of the lodges

Balloon safaris, US$375 per person, can be arranged from the *Seronera Wildlife Lodge* in the Serengeti. They are a great experience, with a champagne breakfast afterwards. You can find less expensive balloon safaris through the tour operators.

Hunting safaris are very specialized and expensive operations, and hunting is strictly controlled to ensure conservation. It is possible to hunt all the big game with the exception of rhinoceros, as well as most of the minor species and birds. A hunting safari is usually for a minimum of 7 days. A list of specialist hunting operators is given on page 318.

Rules of the national parks

The rules of the national parks are really just commonsense and are aimed at visitor safety and conservation. The parks are open from 0600-1900 and at other times driving in the parks is not permitted. Walking is prohibited in all parks except Arusha (western section), Kilimanjaro, Udzungwa Mountains, Selous, Gombe Stream and Mahale Mountain national parks, so you must stay in your vehicle at all times. Do not drive off the main track. This causes damage to the vegetation and is strictly banned. Do not ask your driver to do this in order to get closer to game. Blowing your horn is prohibited, as is playing radios or tape recorders. The speed limit is 50 kph but you will probably want to go much slower most of the time as at 50 kph you will miss a lot of game. Chasing the animals is strictly prohibited, as is feeding the animals – this includes animals that gather around the lodges. Take all litter home with you, and be careful when discarding cigarette butts as the fire risk is high, particularly during the dry season.

Safari costs

Safaris vary in cost and duration. On the whole you get what you pay for. Obviously the longer you spend actually in the parks, rather than just driving to and from them, the better. The costs will also vary enormously depending on where you stay and how many of you there are in a group. For a **tented camp** or **lodge safari** the cost will average out at about US$100-200 per person per day. This assumes that there is a group of at least six of you. If you want to go in a smaller group you can expect to pay more, and if you are alone and not prepared to share a room/tent then you will have to pay a single supplement. You will have to pay in foreign currency (usually US$) and the price will include accommodation, park fees, food and transport.

Tanzania

National parks and game reserves

The following is a list of the 13 national parks and 1 conservation area, which together hold a population of over 4,000,000 wild animals.

National parks in Tanzania

Name	Area (sq km)	PO Box	Telephone
Arusha	137	3134 Arusha	3471
Gombe Stream	52	185 Kigoma	–
Katavi	2,253	89 Mpanda	–
Kilimanjaro	756	96 Marangu	50 Marangu
Lake Manyara	320	3134 Arusha	3471
Mahale Mountains	1,613	1053 Kigoma	–
Mikumi	3,230	62 Mikumi	Radio 6037
Ruaha	12,950	369 Iringa	Radio 6037
Rubondo	457	111 Geita	Telex 42130
Saadani	300	–	–
Serengeti	14,763	3134 Arusha	3471
Tarangire	2,600	3134 Arusha	3471
Udzungwa Mountains	1,000	–	–
Ngorongoro Crater	2,288	776 Arusha	3339

In addition, there are 14 game reserves in Tanzania among which the world's largest is the Selous Game Reserve. Few of the reserves have any tourist facilities.

Game reserves in Tanzania

Name	Area (sq km)	Region
Selous	55,000	Coast, Morogoro, Lindi, Mtwara and Ruvuma
Rungwa	9,000	Singida
Kizigo	4,000	Singida
Moyowosi	6,000	Kigoma
Ugalla	5,000	Tabora/Rukwa
Uwanda	5,000	Rukwa
Maswa	2,200	Shinyanga
Burigi	2,200	Kagera
Biharamulo	1,300	Kagera
Rumanyika-Orugundu	800	Kagera
Ibanda	200	Kagera
Umba River	1,500	Tanga
Mkomazi	1,000	Kilimanjaro
Saa Nane Island	0.5	Mwanza

For a **camping safari** you can expect to pay about US$80-100 per person per day including park entrance fees, cost of vehicle and driver, camping fees and costs of food. This assumes you get a group of at least five together. In addition 'tipping' is an extra expense. A guide may expect US$5 a day, and half of this for the porters. Tourists are sometimes intimidated into tipping more than this, but US$5 a day is generous – the average wage of a guide is less than US$2 a day. You are advised not to tip before completion of the trip.

Hunting safaris are extremely expensive and require considerable preparation.

Sleeping **Hotels and lodges** These vary and may be either typical hotels with rooms and facilities in one building or individual bandas or rondavels (small huts) with a central dining area. Most have been built with great care and blend well into the environment.

Fees

Park permit entry fees (non nationals)

Kilimanjaro, Arusha, Tarangire, Lake Manyara and Serengeti National Parks

Adult	US$25
Child 5-16 years	US$5
Child under 5	Free
Vehicle entry:	
Up to 2,000 kg	US$30
Over 2,000 kg	US$150

Katavi, Mikumi, Ruaha, Rubondo and Udzungwa National Parks

Adult	US$15
Child 5-16 years	US$5
Child under 5	Free

Gombe Stream National Park

Adult	US$100
Child 5-16 years	US$20
Child under 5	Free

Mahale National Park

Adult	US$50
Child 5-16	US$20
Child under 5	Free

Permit for camping in any period of 24 hours, or part thereof (non nationals)

Established campsites

Adult	US$20
Child 5-16	US$5
Child under 5	Free

Special campsites

Adult	US$40
Child 5-16	US$10
Child under 5	Free

Guide fees (non nationals)

Fees for the service of official guide	US$10
Fees for the service of official guide who accompanies the Tourist outside his normal working hours	US$15
Walking safaris guides	US$20

Special sport fishing fees

Applicable only to Gombe, Mahale and Rubondo Island National Parks (sport fishing allowed between 0700 and 1700 only)

Adult	US$50
Child 5-16	US$25
Child under 5 years	Free

Huts, hostels, rest houses fees

(rates are payable per head per night)

Kilimanjaro National Park:

Mandara, Horombo and Kibo	US$40
Meru - Miriakamba and Saddle	US$20
Other huts - Manyara, Ruaha, Mikumi etc	US$20
Hostels - Marangu, Manyara, Serengeti, Mikumi, Ruaha and Gombe Stream (strictly for organized groups with permission of park wardens in charge)	US$10
Rest houses - Serengeti, Ruaha, Mikumi, Arusha, Katavi	US$30
Rest house - Gombe Stream	US$20

Rescue fees

Mounts Kilimanjaro and Meru: The park shall be responsible to rescue between the point of incident to the gate in any route. The climber will take care of other expenses from gate to KCMC or other destination as he/she chooses. The rates are payable per person for trip (non-Tanzanian): US$20

Tanzania

Tented camps A luxury tented camp is really the best of both worlds. They are usually built with a central dining area. Each tent will have a grass roof over it to keep it cool inside, a timber floor, proper beds, and verandah and they will usually have a small bathroom at the back with hot water. The atmosphere is unique – you will be extremely comfortable, but you will really feel you are in Africa.

Campsites There are campsites in most national parks. There can be both normal sites, which cost around US$10 per person per night and 'special' campsites, which cost around US$40 per person per night. Both charge US$5 for children per night. You will almost always need to be totally self-sufficient with all your own equipment. Charges for residents can be lower. The campsites usually provide running water and firewood. Some campsites have a few bandas or huts.

Rubondo Island NP, in Lake Victoria, has an airstrip and a luxury lodge.

Marine parks Five marine parks or reserves have been established: **Mafia Island Marine Park**; **Fungu Yasin Marine Reserve** at Barahi Beach, just north of Dar es Salaam; **Mbudya Island Marine Reserve**, near Kunduchi Beach, north of Dar es Salaam; **Bongoyo Island Marine Reserve**, near Kuduchi Beach and **Maziwi Island Marine Reserve** near Pangani. Other possible sites for marine parks include Tanga Coral Gardens, made up of three reefs – Mwamba Wamba, Mwamba Shundo and Fungu Nyama – and located 10-15 km out to sea. Latham Island, about 70 km from Dar es Salaam, has potential as a reserve, being a site of nesting sea birds and the rare green turtle. Around Kilwa, in the south, is another likely site for a marine park as it is one of the few places where the dugong is found.

Health

For further advice see the section on Health, page 58

Provided travellers take adequate precautions their holiday should not be blighted with ill-health. It is not unusual to have a stomach upset on your first visit. Avoid drinking tap water and ice and peel all fruit. Malaria and road traffic accidents pose the greatest risk. **Malaria** Take the tablets, use vapour tablets on heated electrical pads, ask to have your hotel room sprayed each evening. Cover your arms and legs at night and put repellent on your hands and face. If you observe mosquitoes in your hotel room, sleep under a net treated with insecticide. **Water** It is unwise to drink the local water, even when provided in a flask in a hotel. Stick to soft drinks, boil water in a travelling jug, or use water-purifying tablets. Do not add ice to drinks.

Comprehensive travel insurance cover should be arranged prior to departure. It is also worth joining AMREF (see page 29).

Dar es Salaam

Dar es Salaam

6°50'S 39°12'E
Phone code: 022
Colour map 4, grid B6
Altitude: sea level

Dar es Salaam is located at sea level on the Indian Ocean coast and occupies an area of 90 sq km. It is by some measure the largest city in Tanzania, and has grown rapidly since independence in 1961, roughly trebling in size. Almost all administrative, political and business activity is concentrated in the city, although some government bodies and the main parliamentary sittings are in Dodoma, the official capital of Tanzania, 480 km to the west.

The city dates from 1857 and was successively under the control of Zanzibar, Germany and Britain before self-determination, and these influences have all left their mark. The first impression of the city on the journey in from the airport is of very shabby buildings and a dilapidated infrastructure. There is a marked contrast between the conditions of ordinary people (walking long distances, crowded on buses and makeshift transport, living in ramshackle dwellings, operating small businesses from temporary shelters) on the one hand, and the bureaucratic, business and international community, which enjoys much higher standards. On closer acquaintance with Dar es Salaam the visitor is invariably surprised by the wealth of historical interest that has survived, appreciates the splendid coastal location, warms to the friendliness and relaxed manner of the inhabitants, and learns to seek out the special pleasures the city has to offer, which are not always apparent to the casual observer. There is a saying in Dar es Salaam that 'the city has sun, climate, location – everything, in fact, except luck.'

Ins and outs

Getting there
Consider taking a local bus or a dala-dala to the city centre – it's cheaper and often less hassle than a taxi

Air As the main city of Tanzania, Dar es Salaam is the principal terminus for international travel and for the domestic transport network (see page 323). International and domestic flights depart from Dar es Salaam International Airport, along Nyerere (formerly Pugu) Rd, 13 km from the city centre. *Dala-dala* and minibuses run regularly, but are crowded and can be a problem with luggage. There is a shuttle bus service from *New Africa Hotel* on Maktaba St and the fare is about US$2. Taxis to the airport from the centre cost US$8-12, depending on your skill at bargaining. The bus to the airport leaves from opposite the old GPO.

Tanzania

Tanzania

Things to do in Dar es Salaam ★

- Visit the **National Museum** and the nearby **Botanical Gardens**, now restored, and first laid out in the German period.
- Have **lunch at the old Dar es Salaam Club**, now the Hotel and Tourism Training Centre, overlooking the harbour.
- If it is the weekend, take in some **cricket at the Gymkhana Club** off Ocean Road.
- Take a trip to **Kisarawe** and the nearby **Pugu Hills Forest Reserve** some 30 km out of the city, where you can follow the nature trail.
- Visit the **Makumbusho Village Museum**, where there are examples of traditional dwellings and displays of dancing from around Tanzania.
- Take the ferry across the harbour mouth to Kigamboni and **wander along the coast**, where you will find a noticeable lack of bustle, the odd small bar and restaurant, and access to swimming in the sea.

Bus The three small bus stations for up-country travel have been replaced by one large station on Morogoro Rd in the Ubungo area, 6 km to the west of the centre. If you are arriving in Dar es Salaam there will be many taxi drivers plying for your custom. If you are going to a hotel or straight to the ferries for Zanzibar they will probably offer a very cheap fare as they will get commission from the hotel or ferry company. However budget travellers should consider that it may be cheaper in the long run to negotiate accommodation rates or ferry fares yourself, something that is impossible if the taxi driver is getting commission. If you are confident about bargaining get a taxi to the centre of town and then walk the rest of the way. Alternatively avoid this decision and instead take a local bus or *dala-dala* to the centre.

See page 327 for country bus timetable

Rail Central areas run from the Central Railway Station, Sokoine Dr, T2110600. It is convenient for most hotels. Trains for the southwest leave from Tazara station some 5 km from the centre, T2860344. There are plenty of *dala-dala* and a taxi costs about US$4.

See pages 328 and 329 for details of train timetables and fares

Sea Boats to Zanzibar, Tanga, Mafia Island, Lindi and Mtwara leave from the jetty on Sokoine Dr opposite St Joseph's Cathedral. Dhows, sailing and motorized, leave from the wharf just to the south of the boat jetty. The sea services to Mombasa have been suspended, but could resume at any time. Most of the companies request payment in US$.

Getting around
Always negotiate taxi fares before setting off on your journey

Dala-dala (privately run buses, minibuses, pick-ups and lorries converted to carry passengers) are hot and uncomfortable, but cheap at around US$0.20 for any length of journey. The front of the vehicle usually has a sign stating its destination. They leave the start of the route when full, and as that means packed, it is sometimes difficult to get on at intermediate stops, and virtually impossible to get a seat. It is, however, an extremely efficient system providing you can handle the congestion and having to stand. Fellow passengers are unfailingly helpful and will advise on connections. The main terminals in town are at the Central Railway Station (Stesheni) and the Post Office (Posta) on Maktaba St. **Taxis** are readily available in the town centre and cost around US$1-2 per km; they may be new or battered but serviceable. If you are visiting a non-central location, eg Oyster Bay or Msasani Peninsula, and there is no taxi stand at the destination, always ask the driver to wait.

Tourist offices

Tourism has recently come under new management and this is expected to improve services. The Tourist Information Centre is located at the Matasalamat Bldg, Samora Av, T2131555. There are two free publications available from some hotels and travel agencies, the bi-monthly *Dar es Salaam Guide*, and the monthly *What's Happening in Dar es Salaam*. The latter, as suggested by the title, is better for information about upcoming events.

Climate

The hottest months are Dec to the end of Mar, with long rains Mar-May and short rains in Nov and Dec. The best season is Jun-Oct, although there is sun all the year round, even during the rains, which are short and heavy.

History

The name Dar es Salaam means 'Haven of Peace' and was chosen by the founder of the city, Seyyid Majid, Sultan of Zanzibar. The harbour is sheltered, with a narrow inlet channel protecting the water from the Indian Ocean. An early visitor, Frederic Elton in 1873 remarked that "it's healthy, the air clear – the site a beautiful one and the surrounding country green and well-wooded."

Despite the natural advantages it was not chosen as a harbour earlier, due to the difficulties of approaching through the narrow inlet during the monsoon season and there were other sites, protected by the coral reef, along the Indian Ocean coast that were used instead.

Majid decided to construct the city in 1862 as the result of a desire to have a port and settlement on the mainland, which would act as a focus for trade and caravans operating to the south. Bagamoyo (see page 369) was already well established, but local interests there were inclined to oppose direction from Zanzibar, and the new city was a way of ensuring control from the outset.

Construction began in 1865 and the name was chosen in 1866. Streets were laid out, based around what is now Sokoine Drive running along the shoreline to the north of the inner harbour. Water was secured by the sinking of stone wells, and the largest building was the Sultan's palace. An engraving of 1869 shows the palace to have been a substantial two-storey building, stone, with the upper storey having sloping walls and a crenellated parapet, sited close to the shore on the present-day site of Malindi Wharf. In appearance it was similar in style to the fort that survives in Zanzibar (see page 548). To the southwest, along the shore, was a mosque and to the northwest a group of buildings, some of two storeys with flat roofs and some with pitched thatched roofs. Most of these buildings were used in conjunction with trading activities and some of them would have been warehouses. One building that survives is the double-storeyed structure now known as the Old Boma, on the corner of Morogoro Road and Sokoine Drive. The Sultan used it as an official residence for guests, and in 1867 a western-style banquet was given for the British, French, German and American consuls to launch the new city. Craftsmen and slaves were

Greater Dar es Salaam

Related maps
Dar es Salaam centre,
page 348
Dar es Salaam –
Msasani Peninsula,
page 352

brought from Zanzibar for construction work. Coral for the masonry was cut from the reef and nearby islands. A steam tug was ordered from Germany to assist with the tricky harbour entrance and to speed up movements in the wind-sheltered inner waters. Economic life centred on agricultural cultivation (particularly coconut plantations), traders who dealt with the local Zaramo people as well as with the long-distance caravan traffic.

Dar es Salaam suffered its first stroke of ill-luck when Majid died suddenly in 1870, after a fall in his new palace, and he was succeeded as Sultan by his half-brother, Seyyid Barghash. Barghash did not share Majid's enthusiasm for the new settlement, and indeed Majid's death was taken to indicate that carrying on with the project would bring ill-fortune. The court remained in Zanzibar. Bagamoyo and Kilwa predominated as mainland trading centres. The palace and other buildings were abandoned, and the fabric rapidly fell into decay. Nevertheless the foundation of a Zaramo settlement and Indian commercial involvement had been established.

Despite the neglect, Barghash maintained control over Dar es Salaam through an agent (*akida*) and later a governor (*wali*) and Arab and Baluchi troops (see page 369). An Indian customs officer collected duties for use of the harbour and the Sultan's coconut plantations were maintained. Some commercial momentum had been established, and the Zaramo traded gum copal (a residue used in making varnishes that accumulates from the *msandarusi* tree in the soil near its roots), rubber, coconuts, rice and fish for cloth, iron-ware and beads. The population expanded to around 5,000 by 1887, and comprised a cosmopolitan mixture of the Sultan's officials, soldiers, planters, traders, and shipowners, as well as Arabs, Swahilis and Zaramos, Indian Muslims, Hindus and a handful of Europeans.

In 1887 the German East African Company under Hauptmann Leue took up residence in Dar es Salaam. They occupied the residence of the Sultan's governor whom they succeeded in getting recalled to Zanzibar, took over the collection of customs dues and, in return for a payment to the Zaramo, obtained a concession on the land. The Zaramo, Swahili and Arabs opposed this European takeover, and this culminated in the Arab revolt of 1888-89, which involved most of the coastal region as well as Dar es Salaam. The city came under sporadic attack and the buildings of the Berlin Mission, a Lutheran denomination located on a site close to the present Kivokoni ferry, were destroyed. When the revolt was crushed, and the German government took over responsibility from the German East Africa Company in 1891, Dar es Salaam was selected as the main centre for administration and commercial activities.

German period 1887-1916

German development involved the construction of many substantial buildings, and most of these survive today. In the quarter of a century to 1916, several fine buildings were laid out on Wilhelms Ufer (now Kivukoni Front), and these included administrative offices as well as a club and a casino. Landing steps to warehouses, and a hospital, were constructed on the site of the present Malindi Wharf and behind them the railway station. Just to the south of Kurasini Creek was the dockyard where the present deep-water docks are situated. A second hospital was built at the eastern end of Unter den Akazien and Becker Strasse, now Samora Avenue. The Post Office is on what is now Sokoine Drive at the junction with Mkwepu Street. A governor's residence provided the basis for the current State House. The principal hotels were the *Kaiserhof*, which was demolished to build the *New Africa Hotel*, and the *Burger Hotel*, razed to make way for the present Telecoms building. The Roman Catholic cathedral is behind the customs jetty on Sokoine Drive and the Lutheran cathedral is where Kivukoni Front forks away from Sokoine Drive.

The area behind the north harbour shore was laid out with fine acacia-lined streets and residential two-storey buildings with pitched corrugated-iron roofs and first-floor verandahs, and most of these survive. Behind the east waterfront were shop and office buildings, many of which are still standing, and can be recognized by their distinctive architectural style (see page 592).

British period 1916-61

In the 45 years that the British administered Tanganyika, public construction was kept to a minimum on economy grounds, and business was carried on in the old German buildings. The governor's residence was damaged by naval gunfire in 1915, and was remodelled to form the present State House. In the 1920s, the Gymkhana Club was laid out on its present site behind Ocean Road, and Mnazi Moja ('Coconut Grove') established as a park. The Selander Bridge causeway was constructed, and this opened up the Oyster Bay area to residential construction for the European community. The Yacht Club was built on the harbour shore (it is now the customs post) and behind it the Dar es Salaam Club (now the Hotel and Tourism Training Centre), both close to the present *Kilimanjaro Hotel*.

As was to be expected, road names were changed, as well as those of the most prominent buildings. Thus Wilhelms Ufer became Azania Front, Unter den Akazien became Acacia Avenue, Kaiser Strasse became City Drive. Other streets were named after explorers Speke and Burton, and there was a Windsor Street. One departure from the relentless Anglicization of the city was the change of Bismarck Strasse to Versailles Street – perhaps surprising until it is recalled that it was the Treaty of Versailles in 1918 that allocated the former German East Africa to the British.

The settling by the various groups living in the city into distinctive areas was consolidated during the British period. Europeans lived in Oyster Bay to the north of the city centre, in large Mediterranean-style houses with arches, verandahs and gardens surrounded by solid security walls and fences. The Asians lived either in tenement-style blocks in the city centre or in the Upanga area in between the city and Oyster Bay, where they constructed houses and bungalows with small gardens. African families built Swahili-style houses (see page 592), initially in the Kariakoo area to the west of the city. Others were accommodated in government bachelor quarters provided for railway, post office and other government employees. As population increased settlement spread out to Mikocheni and along Morogoro Road, and Mteni to the south. An industrial area developed along the Pugu Road, which was convenient for the port and was served by branch lines from the central and northern railway lines.

Independence 1961-present

For the early years of independence Dar es Salaam managed to sustain its enviable reputation of being a gloriously located city with a fine harbour, generous parklands with tree-lined avenues (particularly in the Botanical Gardens and Gymkhana area), and a tidy central area of shops and services.

New developments saw the construction of high-rise government buildings, most notably the Telecoms building on the present Samora Avenue, the *New Africa Hotel*, the massive cream and brown Standard Bank Building (now National Bank of Commerce) on the corner of Sokoine Drive and Maktaba Street, and the *Kilimanjaro Hotel* on a site next to the Dar es Salaam Club on Kivukoni Front.

With the Arusha Declaration of 1967 (see page 585), many buildings were nationalized and somewhat haphazardly occupied. The new tenants of the houses, shops and commercial buildings were thus inclined to undertake minimal repairs and maintenance. In many cases it was unclear who actually owned a building. The fabric of the city went into steady decline, and it is a testament to the sturdy construction of the buildings from the German period that so many of them survive. Roads fell into disrepair and the harbour became littered with rusting hulks.

The new government changed the names of streets and buildings, to reflect a change away from the colonial period. Thus Acacia became Independence Avenue, the *Prince of Wales Hotel* became the *Splendid*. Later names were chosen to pay tribute to African leaders – Independence Avenue changed to Samora, and Pugu Road became Nkrumah Street. President Nyerere decided that no streets or public buildings could be named after living Tanzanians, and so it was only after his death that City Drive was named after Prime Minister Edward Sokoine.

Old Dar es Salaam was saved by two factors. First, the economic decline that began in the 1970s (see page 590) meant that there were limited resources for building new modern blocks for which some of old colonial buildings would have had to make way. Second, the government in 1973 decided to move the capital to Dodoma. This didn't stop new government construction entirely, but it undoubtedly saved many historic buildings.

In the early 1980s, Dar es Salaam reached a low point, not dissimilar from the one reached almost exactly a century earlier with the death of Sultan Majid. In 1992 things began to improve. The colonial buildings have been classified as of historical interest and are to be preserved. Japanese aid has allowed a comprehensive restoration of the road system. Several historic buildings, most notably the Old Boma on Sokoine Drive, the Ministry of Health building on Luthuli Road and the British Council headquarters on Samora Avenue, have been restored or are undergoing restoration. Civic pride is returning. The Askari Monument has been cleaned up and the flower beds replanted, the Cenotaph Plaza relaid, pavements and walkways repaired and the restoration of the Botanical Gardens has begun.

Sights

The best way to discover the heart of Dar es Salaam is on foot and we have suggested two half-day walks that take in most of the historic buildings. An alternative is to join a guided walking tour. Morning walks through the old town of 2½ hours cost US$30 adult, US$10 children, discounts for groups, including tasting of Swahili, Arab and Indian foods, T2152438, T0741-605109 (mob), loislobo@hotmail.com, or enquire at a tour agency.

A walking tour (about half a day) of the historic parts of old Dar es Salaam might start at the **Askari Monument** at the junction of Samora Avenue and Maktaba Street. Originally on this site was a statue to Major Hermann von Wissmann, the German explorer and soldier, who suppressed the coastal Arab Revolt of 1888-9 (see page 370) and went on to become governor of German East Africa in 1895-6. This first statue erected in 1911 depicted a pith-helmeted Wissmann, one hand on hip, the other on his sword, gazing out over the harbour with an African soldier at the base of the plinth draping a German flag over a reclining lion. It was demolished in 1916 when the British occupied Dar es Salaam, as were statues to Bismarck and Carl Peters. The present bronze statue, in memory of all those who died in the First World War, but principally dedicated to the Africa troops and porters, was unveiled in 1927. The statue was cast by Morris Bronze Founders of Westminster, London, and the sculptor was James Alexander Stevenson (1881-1937), who signed himself 'Myrander'. There are two bronze bas-reliefs on the sides of the plinth by the same sculptor, and the inscription, in English and Swahili, is from Rudyard Kipling.

Walking tour of the old town
See map page 348

Proceeding towards the harbour, on the left is the *New Africa Hotel* on the site where the old *Kaiserhof Hotel* stood. The *New Africa Hotel* was once the finest building in Dar es Salaam, the venue for the expat community to meet for sundowners. The terrace outside overlooked the Lutheran church and the harbour, while a band played in the inner courtyard. Across Sokoine Drive, on the left is the **Lutheran cathedral** with its distinctive red-tiled spire and tiled canopies over the windows to provide shade. Construction began in 1898. Opposite is the **Cenotaph**, again commemorating the 1914-18 war, which was unveiled in 1927 and restored in 1992.

Turning left along Kivukoni Front, there is a fine view through the palm trees across the harbour. Just past Ohio Street, on the shore side, is the **Old Yacht Club**. Prior to the removal of the club to its present site on the west side of Msasani Peninsula in 1967, small boats bobbing at anchor in the bay were a feature of the harbour. The Old Yacht Club buildings now house the harbour police headquarters. In the German period there were several warehouses along this part of the shore.

Opposite the Old Yacht Club is the site of the German Club for civilians, which was expanded to form the **Dar es Salaam (DSM) Club** in the British period and is now the Hotel and Tourism Training Centre. It has a spacious terrace and a handsome bar. On the first floor are rooms that were used for accommodation, with verandahs facing inward and outside stone staircases. It is possible to use the bar, and to have a lunch prepared and served by the trainees. Evelyn Waugh once stayed at the DSM Club.

Passing the *Kilimanjaro Hotel*, on the corner of Mirambo Street is the first of an impressive series of German government buildings. The first two, one now the High Court, and the other the present Magistrates' Court on the corner of Luthuli Road, were for senior officials. These had offices on the ground floor and spacious, high-ceilinged accommodation with verandahs, on the first floor (see Architecture, page 592). In between is the old **Secretariat**, which housed the governor's offices. The first floor is supported by cast-iron brackets that allow the verandah to overhang. The verandah has been enclosed to provide more office space. On the other corner of Luthuli Road is the German Officers' Mess, where some gambling evidently took place as it became known as the **Casino**. These buildings are exceptional, and it is a tribute to the high quality construction of the German period that they have survived, with virtually no maintenance for the past 30 years. Construction was completed in 1893.

On the shore side, just by the entrance to Luthuli Road, was a landing pier in German times. Later, when a passenger pier was constructed opposite St Joseph's Cathedral, some landing steps replaced it, and these can still be seen. Further along Kivukoni Front, beyond the newer high-rise buildings is a group of single-storey government offices constructed in the British period.

On the high ground past these offices is the site of the first European building in Dar es Salaam, the **Berlin Mission**. It was constructed in 1887, and was a fairly functional single-storey rectangular building. Extensively damaged in the 1888-9 uprising it was rebuilt in two storeys with a corrugated-iron roof and an open gap between it and the walls that allowed ventilation. It was demolished in 1959 to make way for a hotel, which, in the event, was not constructed.

The eastern part of the city resembles an eagle's head (it is said the Masasani Peninsula is one of the eagle's wings). At the tip of the eagle's beak was a pier, just where the fishing village stands today, constructed in the British period for the use of the governor. This was just a little further round the promontory from the present ramp for the ferry that goes over to Kigamboni. Past Magogoni Street is the **Swimming Club**, constructed in the British period and now mostly used by the Asian community.

Following Ocean Road, on the left is the present **State House**, with a drive coming down to gates. This was the original German governor's residence. It had tall, Islamic-style arches on the ground floor rather similar to those in the building today, but the upper storey was a verandah with a parapet and the roof was supported on cast-iron columns. The building was bombarded by British warships in 1914 and extensively damaged. In 1922 it was rebuilt and the present scalloped upper-storey arches added, as well as the tower with the crenellated parapet.

The **German Hospital** is further along Ocean Road with its distinctive domed towers topped by a clusters of iron spikes. It is an uneasy mixture of the grand (the towers) and the utilitarian (the corrugated-iron roofing). It was completed in 1897 and was added to during the British period with single-storey, bungalow-style wards to the rear.

Turning left past the baobab tree down Chimera Road and taking the left fork, Luthuli Road leads to the junction with Samora Avenue. Here stood the statue of Bismarck, a replica of the celebrated Regas bust. The area either side of this boulevard, one of the glories of Dar es Salaam in the German era, was laid out as an extensive park. The flamboyant trees and *oreodoxa* (Royal Palms) still border the avenues.

The first Director of Agriculture, Professor Stuhlmann, began laying out the **Botanic Gardens** in 1893. Initially there was also a veterinary station, which was moved when the construction of the hospital began. The building to house the Agriculture Department as well as the Meteorological Station and the Government

Casuarina Cones

A particularly fine set of Casuarina trees are to be seen along Ocean Road in Dar es Salaam. Casuarinas are also found in Australia. The theory is that they originated there – they are quite unlike most other trees in East Africa. It is thought that the seed-bearing cones were carried by the cold tidal currents from the west coast of Australia into the equatorial waters flowing west across the Indian Ocean to the shore of Tanzania and then north along the East African coast in the Somalia current, eventually germinating after a journey of about 10,000 km.

Geographer lies just to the southwest and was completed in 1903. It has recently been restored. By that time the gardens were well established, Stuhlmann using his position as Chief Secretary from 1900-1903 to channel resources to their development. Stuhlmann went on to be Director of the Amani Agricultural Research Station (see page 412). The gardens became the home of the Dar es Salaam Horticultural Society, which still has a building on the site. Recently the gardens have undergone some rehabilitation with most of the exhibits now labelled. It is one of the few places in the world to see the coco-de-mer palm tree apart from the Seychelles. Staff are helpful but relatively few of the plants are labelled.

To the left of the gardens is **Karimjee Hall**, built during the British era and which served as the home of the Legislative Council prior to independence. It then became the home of the National Assembly, the Bunge. In the same area is the original **National Museum** (see page 344), a single-storey stone building with a red-tiled roof and arched windows constructed as the King George V Memorial Museum in 1940, changing its name in 1963. A larger, modern building was constructed later to house exhibits, and the old building used as offices.

Turning left down Shaaban Robert Street, on the other side of Sokoine Drive, in a crescent behind the Speaker's Office is the first school built in Dar es Salaam (1899) by the German government. It was predominantly for Africans, but also had a few Indian pupils, all children of state-employed officials (*akidas*). Walking west down Sokoine Drive we return to the *New Africa Hotel*.

A second half-day walking tour would begin at the *New Africa Hotel* and proceed west along Sokoine Street past the National Bank of Commerce building on the right. On the corner with Mkwepa Street is the German **Post Office** completed in 1893. Although the façade has been remodelled to give it a more modern appearance, the structure is basically unchanged. It was a pleasing two-storey, red-tiled building with a verandah on the first floor and a small tower with a pitched roof behind the main entrance, which made for a more interesting roof-line. The windows were arched, and there was an impressive set of steps up to the main entrance. Just inside the entrance is a plaque to the memory of members of the Signals Corp who lost their lives in the First World War in East Africa. There are some 200 names listed with particularly heavy representation from South Africa and India whose loyalty to the British Empire drew them into the conflict.

On the opposite corner to the Post Office is the site of the old customs headquarters, the **Seyyid Barghash** building, constructed around 1869. The building on the corner with Bridge Street is the modern multi-storey Wizaraya Maji, Nishati na Madim (Ministry of Water, Energy and Minerals), which is on the site of the old Custom House. Next door, sandwiched between the ministry building and Forodhani Secondary School, is the **White Fathers House** – called **Atiman House**. It is named after a heroic and dedicated doctor Adrian Atiman, who was redeemed from slavery in Niger by White Father missionaries, educated in North Africa and Europe, and who worked for decades as a doctor in Tanzania until his death, circa 1924. Atiman House was constructed in the 1860s in the Zanzibar period. In fact the house, including a courtyard, is the oldest surviving house in the city, excluding

Walking tour of the City
See map page 348

Tanzania

administrative buildings. It was built as a residence for the Sultan of Zanzibar's Dar es Salaam wives, and sold by the Sultan to the White Fathers in 1922. In the visitors' parlour of the house are two extremely interesting old photographs of the waterfront at Dar es Salaam, as it was in German colonial times.

Continuing along Sokoine Drive to the west, the next building is **St Joseph's Roman Catholic Cathedral**. Construction began in 1897 and took five years to complete. St Joseph's remains one of the most striking buildings in Dar es Salaam, dominating the harbour front. It has an impressive vaulted interior, shingle spire and a fine arrangement of arches and gables. Next to the cathedral was Akida's Court.

On the corner of Morogoro Road is the earliest surviving building, the **Old Boma** dating from 1867. On the opposite corner is the **City Hall**, a very handsome building with an impressive façade and elaborate decoration. Further along, on the corner of Algeria Street, is a three-storey commercial building with pillars and a verandah at first-floor level. The first two floors are from the Zanzibar period, with the third storey and the verandah being added later.

On the corner of Uhuru Street is the **Railway Station**, a double-storey building with arches and a pitched-tile roof, the construction of which began in 1897. Between the station and the shore was the site of the palace of Sultan Majid and of the hospital for Africans constructed in 1895 by Sewa Haji, but which was demolished in 1959.

Turning right in front of the railway station leads to the **Clock Tower**, a post-war concrete construction erected to celebrate the elevation of Dar es Salaam to city status in 1961. Renovations have recently been carried out on the Clock Tower. A right turn at the Clock Tower leads along Samora Avenue and back to the Askari Monument. There are a number of buildings of stone construction that were erected by the local community, by Goan businessmen and by German commercial interests. The German buildings can be recognized by the two-storey style with a verandah at first-floor level, and by the use of pillars to support the first floor.

National Museum The National Museum has excellent ethnographic, historical and archaeological collections. The old photographs are particularly interesting. Traditional craft items, head-dresses, ornaments, musical instruments and witchcraft accoutrements are on display. Artefacts representing Tanzanian history are on show dating from the slave trade to the post-colonial period. Fossils from Olduvai Gorge kept there include those of Zinjanthropus – sometimes referred to as Zinj or 'nutcracker man' – the first of a new group of hominid remains collectively known as *Australopithecus boisei,* discovered by Mary Leakey. The coastal history is represented by glazed Chinese porcelain pottery and a range of copper coins from Kilwa. The museum also regularly stages exhibitions – see press for details.

■ *0930-1800. Shabaan Robert St next to the Botanical Gardens, between Sokoine Dr and Samora Av. Entry US$3. Student US$2.*

Other sights & museums Other notable buildings in the City area include the present *Mbowe Hotel* on the corner of Mkwepu and Makunganya Streets, which was the *Palace Hotel,* and which dates from about 1920. On Mosque Street is the **Darkhana Jama'at-Khana** of the Ismaili community, three storeys high with a six-storey tower on the corner topped by a clock, a pitched roof and a weathervane. It is in an ornate style with arches and decorated columns, and was constructed in 1930.

There are several other mosques, two (**Ibaddhi Mosque** and **Memon Mosque**) on Mosque Street itself, one on Kitumbini Street (the **Sunni mosque** with an impressive dome), and there are two mosques on Bibi Titi Mohamed Street, the **Ahmadiyya mosque** being near the junction with Pugo Road and the other close by. On Kitsu Street, there are two Hindu temples, and on Upanga Road is a grand Ismaili building decorated with coloured lights during festival periods. This is the main Jama'at Khana.

St Albans Church on the corner of Upanga Road and Maktaba Street was constructed in the interwar period. St Albans is a grand building modelled on the

Tanzania

Anglican church in Zanzibar. This is the Anglican Church of the Province of Tanzania, and was the Governor's church in colonial times. The **Greek Orthodox church**, further along Upanga Street, was constructed in the 1940s. **St Peter's Catholic Church**, off the Bagamoyo Road, was constructed in 1962, and is in modern style with delicate concrete columns and arches.

West towards Kariakoo

The area to the northwest of India Street, on either side of Morogoro Road, was an Asian section of the city in the colonial period, and to a large extent remains so. The typical building would be several storeys high, the ground floor being given over to business premises with the upper storeys being used for residential accommodation. The façades of these buildings are usually ornate, often with the name of the proprietor and the date of construction prominently displayed. Two superb examples on Morogoro Road, near Africa Street, are the premises of M Jessa. One was a cigarette and tobacco factory and the other a rice mill.

Further to the west is the open Mnazi Mmoja (coconut grove) with the **Uhuru Monument** (dedicated to the freedom that came with independence). The original Uhuru monument is a white obelisk with a flame – the Freedom Torch. A second concrete monument, designed by R Ashdown, was erected to commemorate 10 years of independence. This was enlivened with panels by a local artist. On the far side of the space is **Kariakoo**, laid out in a grid pattern and predominantly an African area. It become known as Kariakoo during the latter part of the First World War when African porters (the carrier corps, from which the current name is derived) were billeted there after the British took over the city in 1916. The houses are in Swahili style (see page 592). The colourful market in the centre and the shark market on the junction of Msimbazi and Tandamuti Streets are well worth a visit.

Fish market & Banda Beach

At the point of the eagle's beak, where the ferry leaves for Kivukoni, is the **Mzizima Fish Market**. Fresh fish can be purchased here. Mzizima is the name of the old fishing village that existed somewhere between State House and Ocean Road Hospital before Seyyid Majid founded Dar es Salaam in 1862. This stretch of sand was always known as **Banda Beach**, a well-known place for watching the ships coming in and out. Fishing boats, mostly lateen-sailed *ngalawas*, are beached on the shore. There are some boat-builders on the site and it is interesting to observe the construction techniques, which rely entirely on hand tools.

Gymkhana Club

Further along Ocean Road, past State House, are the grounds of the **Gymkhana Club**, which extend down to the shore. There were various cemeteries on the shore side of the golf course, a European cemetary between the hospital and Ghana Avenue, and a Hindu crematorium beyond.

Nyumba ya Sanaa

This art gallery has displays of paintings in various styles as well as carvings and batiks. It is located by the roundabout on the intersection of Upanga and Ohio streets.

Oyster Bay

At the intersection of Ocean Road and Ufukoni Road on the shore side is a rocky promontory, which was the site of European residential dwellings constructed in the interwar period by the British. These are either side of Labon Drive (previously Seaview Road). Continuing along Ocean Road is Selander Bridge, a causeway over the Msimbazi Creek, a small river edged by marsh that circles back to the south behind the main part of the city. Beyond Selander Bridge, on the ocean side, is **Oyster Bay**, which became the main European residential area in the colonial era, and today is the location of many diplomatic missions. There are many spacious dwellings, particularly along Kenyatta Drive, which looks across the bay. The area in front of the *Oysterbay Hotel* is a favourite place for parking and socializing in the evenings and on weekends, particularly by the Asian community. Ice cream sellers and barbecue kiosks have sprung up on the shore in the last few years.

In spite of the grand houses and embassies, unfortunately Oyster Bay has acquired a reputation for muggings and armed robberies, even in daylight hours

Tanzania

University of Dar es Salaam

The University of Dar es Salaam began life in 1961, in a building on Lumumba Street in the Mnazi Mmoja area of the city, as a college granting London University degrees. Initially it had only a law faculty as, at the time, law was not offered at Makerere in Uganda or at Nairobi in Kenya. In 1964 the college moved to its present site on a hill to the west of the city and in 1970 it became an independent university. The location is very attractive, with views across to the city from Observation Hill. Nkrumah Hall is a fine example of modern architecture and the ravine, crossed by a bridge, which runs from the faculty building to the post office and residential buildings, through trees, is particularly appealing. In the 1980s the fabric of the university buildings deteriorated considerably. In 1992, however, a rehabilitation programme started, and some of the former pride in the institution, buildings and site has begun to be restored. ■ *About 10 km west of the city. Take Ali Hassan Mwinyi Rd, turn left at Mwenge on to Sam Njoma Rd, then right at the petrol station. Bus to Ubungo, then bus to university (both US$0.20).*

Karibu Art Gallery

Located on Bagamoyo Road, beyond the Mwenge turn-off to the university, this gallery has a good selection of carvings, paintings, pottery, jewellery and musical instruments. On Sundays there are traditional dance displays.

Essentials

Sleeping

■ *on maps pages 348 and 352* Price codes: see inside front cover

Hotels in Dar es Salaam have improved in recent years as far as top-grade accommodation is concerned. The *Sea Cliff* and the *Courtyard* are recommended, and the *New Africa* is well located in the town centre. Many deluxe travellers choose to stay at *Bahari Beach* some 25 km north of Dar es Salaam (see page 349). The lower end of the market, however, is good value, although it is always a sensible procedure to check the room and the bathroom facilities and enquire what is provided for breakfast. Ask about phone facilities as often the switchboard does not work. Check on the security of any parked vehicle. Recent travellers have reported that it is possible to negotiate lower rates, especially if you plan to stay a few days. Some upmarket hotels may ask visitors to pay in foreign exchange – this really makes no difference – but just check the rates in TShs and $s against the current exchange rate, and create a fuss if you are charged more than the $ equivalent of the TSh rate. In the middle range it is usually possible to pay in TSh, and this is an advantage if money is changed at the favourable bureau rate. Hotels will often change money at an unfavourable 'official' rate. Even if staying at an upmarket hotel it is advisable to pay for everything (except the room rate) with TSh exchanged at a bureau. It is difficult to get cash against a Visa card in Tanzania. VAT at 20% was officially introduced in 1998 and is added to all service charges.

At the top level are the Hotel Sea Cliff and the New Africa ; in the middle range Motel Afrique and Starlight; at the cheap end, Salvation Army is excellent, while Luther House, and the two YMCAs are also to be recommended

L *Hotel Sea Cliff*, PO Box 3030, northern end of Msasani Peninsula on Toure Dr, T2600380-7, F2600476, seacliff@tz.techno.com *Coral Cliff Bar*, pool and Ngalawa bar, Dhow restaurant, coffee shop, gym, gift shop, casino, bowling alley, a/c, pleasant style, whitewashed walls and thatched *makuti* roofing. Recommended. **L-A** *New Africa*, PO Box 9314, Azikiwe St, T2117136-9, F2116731, newafricahotel@raha.com A/c, satellite TVs, 2 restaurants. The hotel does not provide twin beds. If you want separate beds you have to upgrade to 2 doubles and a sofa bed, called a Queen's Sofa, is put in the room. Recommended. **L** *Oysterbay*, PO Box 2261, Toure Dr, 5 km from city centre, T2600352-4, F2600347, oysterbay-hotel@ twiga.com Beach location, although the beach is poor, a/c, good restaurant with excellent seafood, shopping mall with bureau de change and internet café, bamboo gardens, bar, pool, health club, tennis, squash, par-3 golf course, watersports, diving, offer deep-sea fishing and dhow trips. **L-A** *Protea Hotel Apartments*, Theatre Square on the corner of Haile Selassie Rd and Ali Hassan Mwinyi Rd, PO Box 2158, T2666665, F2667760, proteadar@ cats-net.com 48 a/c, s/c apartments with satellite TV, the hotel has a restaurant, bar, business centre, gym and swimming pool, monthly rates available. **L** *Royal Palm*, Ohio St, PO Box 791, T2112416, F2113532.

Conference and banqueting facilities, shopping arcade and recreation centre with outdoor swimming pool. Rather gloomy, with a sombre brown and cream decor, good standards and service, a/c, has all mod cons except tea/coffee-making facilities in the rooms, best rooms at the rear, smoking and non-smoking rooms available, British Airways office in hotel – useful for reconfirming your flight home, hotel will store luggage for you while on safari. **A** *The Courtyard*, Ocean Rd, PO Box 542, T2130130, F2130100, courtyard@raha.com Standard, superior and deluxe rooms, a/c, with own bathrooms, TV and minibar, business centre, bar, restaurant, swimming pool. **A** *Indian Ocean Hotel* (under construction), Toure Dr, Msasani Peninsula, just past the *Police Canteen*. **A** *Karibu*, Haile Selassie Rd, PO Box 20200, T2602946, F2601426, karibu@afsat.com Oyster Bay area. Well run, good, newly refurbished *Malaika* restaurant with Indian food a speciality, a/c, satellite TVs and fridges in rooms, swimming pool.

B *Ambassador Plaza*, PO Box 2114, Ali Hassan Mwinyi Rd, T2136006, Mx41801, about 4 km from centre. A/c, well run, but now looking decidedly run down, good restaurant, patio bar. **B** *Continental*, Nkrumah St. Some rooms a/c, patio bar, restaurant, shop. **B** *Embassy*, PO Box 3152, 24 Garden Av, T2117082-7, F2112634, embassy@raha.com Well run and comfortable, small pool on first floor with barbecue and bar, a/c, grill, restaurant, bar, hairdressers, chemist, travel agents. **B** *Etienne's*, PO Box 2981, Ocean Rd, T22093. Comfortable with relaxed atmosphere, some rooms a/c, restaurant, bar, garden bar with barbecue. **B** *Kilimanjaro*, PO Box 9574, Kivukoni Front, T2113103/4, T0741-6016673 (mob), F2113304. A little shabby and poor service but comfortable, at present all of the (many) amenities are closed and the hotel is awaiting major redevelopment. **B** *Motel Afrique*, PO Box 9482, Zanaki St, T2131034-6. Recommended. **B** *Oysterbay Executive Inn*, near *Oyster Bay Hotel*, PO Box 23381, T2668518, F2667904. A/c, restaurant, bar. **B** *Peacock Hotel*, Bibi Titi Mohamed St, PO Box 70270, T2120334-40, T0741-327457 (mob), F2117962, mlangila@twiga.com Well run and centrally located, a/c, TV, restaurant, snack bar. **B** *Q Bar and Guest House*, Haile Selassie Rd, Msasani Peninsula, PO Box 4595, T0742-789673 (mob), F2112667, has some comfortable if a little noisy rooms (also offers dormitory accommodation for US$12). **B** *Ricki Hotel*, on the corner of Kipata and Lumumba Sts, west of Mnazi Mmoja Park, PO Box 31673, T2181702-4, F2181705, rikihotel@raha.com, with restaurant, bar and shops. **B** *Smokies Hotel and Guest House*, PO Box 23425, T0742-760567 (mob), F2601077, off Chole Rd, Msasani Peninsula. **B** *Starlight*, PO Box 3199, Bibi Titi Mohamed St, T2119391, F2119389. Well run and good value (a shade over US$50), s/c rooms, a/c, no mosquito nets or screens on the windows, with forex bureau, restaurant and gift shop, near Mnazi Moja. **B** *Swiss Hostel*, Mindu St, in a quiet area northwest of the centre towards Msimbazi Creek, PO Box 75266, T/F2152759, swisshostel@twiga.com

C-D *Econolodge*, corner of Libya St and Band St, PO Box 8658, T2116048-50, F2116053, econolodge@raha.com Clean s/c rooms, the cheaper ones have fans, the more expensive have a/c, price includes breakfast. **C** *Luther House Hotel*, PO Box 389, Sokoine Dr, T2120734, behind the Lutheran church on the waterfront. Excellent value, central and in considerable demand, necessary to book as invariably full, fans in rooms work only slowly. Recommended. **C** *Palm Beach*, Upanga Rd, PO Box 1520, T0741-327015 (mob), F2600151, palmbeach@cctz.com Very run down, with creaky a/c, some rooms with own bathroom and hot water, between-the-wars style, a little away from the centre of town, airy and cool bar and restaurant, serves Greek and Indian cuisine, popular beer garden with barbecue. **C** *Queen of Sheba Hotel*, PO Box 6308, T71780, off Shekilango and Mole Rds. S/c rooms, a/c available, safe parking, bar, restaurant, barbecue. **C** *Valley View Hotel*, on the corner of Congo St and Matumba A St, PO Box 21290, T2184532/56, F2185286. A/c, TVs, fridge, restaurant, a bit out of the way, off Morogoro Rd, a turning opposite United Nations Rd, about 1 km from the intersection with Bibi Titi Mohamed St. **C** *Temboni Regence*, PO Box 33703, T0741-617709 (mob), half board accommodation several km from the city centre, near the university.

D *Deluxe Inn*, PO Box 2583, Uhuru St, T2120873. **D** *Jambo Inn*, PO Box 5588, Libya St, T2110711, F2113149, some a/c, central. Hotel service has deteriorated, no hot water, nets, very noisy fan, no a/c, breakfast very unappetizing, some doors won't lock. However, restaurant serves Indian food and is one of the best in Dar es Salaam. Recommended for its food.

D *Keys*, PO Box 5330, Uhuru St, T2183033, keys-hotel@africaonline.co.tz, near Mnazi Moja.
D *Q-Bar*, PO Box 4595, T2602150, T0744-261919 (mob). Best known as the most popular bar in Dar, serves good food, mostly grills. Has some expensive rooms but also offers dormitory accommodation for US$12. **E** *Kibodya*, PO Box 1091, Nkrumah St, T2117856. Central, straightforward, rooms have fans. **D** *Lion Hotel*, PO Box 33955, T2461808, F2460663. S/c and non-s/c rooms, restaurant and bar, in the Sinza area towards the university. **D** *Mgulani Hostel*, run by the Salvation Army, a Christian Mission, PO Box 1273, Kilwa Rd, T2851467, F2850468, bamartin@maf.org, situated about 3 km along Kilwa Rd to the south of the port area. Well run, outstanding value, includes breakfast, easily accessible by *dala-dala*, single, double and triple rooms with fans, restaurant, swimming pool, but becoming slightly run down, some fans broken, not all rooms have running water. Recommended. **D** *Marana Guest House*, PO Box 15062, Uhuru St, T2121014, near Mnazi Moja. **D** *Mount Msambara*, PO Box 22770, Kango St, T2137422/3, Kariakoo area. **D** *Safari Inn*, PO Box 21113, Band St, T2119104, F2116550, central. Fairly simple, but sound, similar price to the nearby *Jambo Inn* but is significantly better. Continental breakfast included, no restaurant. **D** *Traffic Light Motel*, PO Box 79, Maragwo Rd, T2123438, central. Good value, well run, profits are used to fund a primary school for disabled children and a vocational training centre. **D-E** *YWCA*, PO Box 2086, corner of Azikiwe St and Ghana Av, T2122439, T0741-622707 (mob), and the *YMCA*, PO Box 767, T2110833, F2135457, are one block apart off Maktaba St.

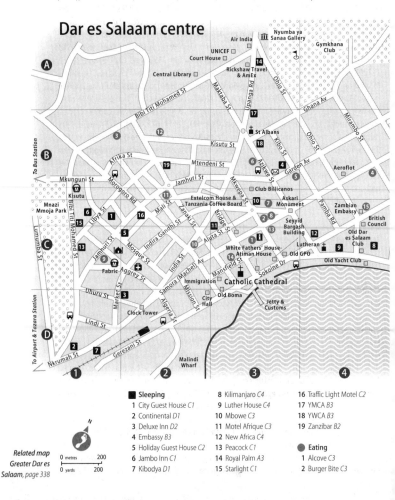

Dar es Salaam centre

Sleeping ■
1 City Guest House *C1*
2 Continental *D1*
3 Deluxe Inn *D2*
4 Embassy *B3*
5 Holiday Guest House *C2*
6 Jambo Inn *C1*
7 Kibodya *D1*
8 Kilimanjaro *C4*
9 Luther House *C4*
10 Mbowe *C3*
11 Motel Afrique *C3*
12 New Africa *C4*
13 Peacock *C1*
14 Royal Palm *A3*
15 Starlight *C1*
16 Traffic Light Motel *C2*
17 YMCA *B3*
18 YWCA *B3*
19 Zanzibar *B2*

Eating ●
1 Alcove *C3*
2 Burger Bite *C3*

Related map
Greater Dar es
Salaam, page 338

0 metres 200
0 yards 200

The former accommodates women and couples, allow a room to be shared by 2 men, central, simple, clean and secure, one traveller reported bed bug infestation, good eating place. The *YMCA* is also basic, no fans and can be hot, care required over belongings. Prices for both include breakfast. Recommended.

E *Al Uruba*, PO Box 8064, opposite Micro Finance Bank on Mkunguni St, just west of Mnazi Mmoja Park. Very strict rules – no alcohol allowed and couples have to show a marriage certificate! **E** *Al Noor*, PO Box 3874, Uhuru St, T2137082, Kariakoo area. **E** *Double Two*, PO Box 22102, Nyati St, T2136027, central. **E** *Holiday Hotel*, PO Box 2975, Jamhuri St, T2112246, holidayhotel@usa.net Basic, clean, good terrace, excellent showers, hot water, well placed for nearby food and internet access, no parking facilities, popular and good value. **E** *Ismail*, Lumumba St, central. **E** *Malapa Inn*, Wmumba St, central. **E** *New Happy*, PO Box 15042, Lumumba St, T2134038, Kariakoo area. **E** *Shirins Inn*, Band St, PO Box 4095, T2124068. **E** *Tamarind Guest House*, Lindi St, west of Mnazi Mmoja Park, PO Box 15076, T2113629. Cheap, some rooms are s/c. **E** *Zanzibar Guest House*, PO Box 20125, Zanaki St, T2121197, central. Cheap, not very clean, communal showers, no hot water.

The beaches are poor near the city centre, with shallow water and rocky shorelines. Although they are an hour's journey (25 km) from Dar es Salaam along poor roads, many visitors choose to stay at one of the beach hotels to the north or south of the city. There is a regular bus shuttle service between the city and the beach hotels to the north leaving from the *New Africa Hotel* on Maktaba St.

Beach hotels
It is unsafe to walk along the beach between the northern hotels

Tanzania

L *Ras Kutani Beach Resort*, bookings through Selous Safari Co Ltd, PO Box 1192, T2135638, F2112794, selous@twiga.com Across Kivukoni ferry and 28 km south of Dar es Salaam, 2-hr road journey or a 14-min flight from Dar es Salaam costing US$50 return, the resort staff meet the flight. This is an excellent place to stay for a rest after a safari, just 12 cottages, some on a hill overlooking the ocean, charming thatched banda accommodation, full board, good beach, freshwater lagoon, windsurfing, sailing, deep-sea fishing and diving can be arranged, some travellers have reported seeing hump-backed whales – visible about 3 times a year. **L** *Protea Hotel Amani Beach*, 30 km south from the ferry, PO Box 2158, T0741-410033 (mob), F2667700/60, proteadar@cat-net.com A/c rooms with TVs, swimming pool, tennis courts, restaurant, bar, conference facilities. **A** *Bahari Beach*, PO Box 9312, Kunduchi, T2650352, T0742-788771/2 (mob), F2650351, bbhbuz@intafrica.com Accommodation in thatched rondavels, a/c, s/c, TV, large bar lounge, restaurant area under high thatched roofing, limited menu but good food, pool bar, swimming pool, band on Sun and public holidays, sandy beach, garden surroundings, gift shop, tour agency, new watersports centre, the most attractive and best run of the northern beach

3 Cedars *B1*
4 Chinese *B4*
5 City Garden *B4*
6 Garden Plaza *B3*
7 Hard Rock Café *C3*
8 Java Café *C3*
9 New Zahir *C1*
10 Planet Bollywood *C2*
11 Purnima *B2*
12 RCL Internet Café *B2*
13 Salamandar *C3*
14 Sno-Cream *C3*
15 Steers & Debonair *C4*

Porters

From the days of the earliest explorers in the 19th century until railways and roads were built, the use of porters was vital to the opening up of East Africa. Anyone planning an expedition inland relied on porters (wapagazi) as the sole means of transport as the use of draught animals was rendered impossible by the prevalence of the tsetse fly.

Porters came from many different tribes but there were two main groups, the Nyamwezi/Sukuma (whose language and culture were similar) and the Zanzibari/Swahili porters (the former usually men who had travelled to the coast on an expedition and were then travelling back, the latter usually Muslim men of the coastal strip). The Nyamwezi/Sukuma were generally considered to be the better porters. They were very musical, singing songs as they walked, and carried their loads on one shoulder, unlike the Zanzibari/Swahili who carried them on their heads. When they arrived at a place for the night the Nyamwezi/Sukuma would build themselves shelters and collect grass for matting while the Zanzibari/Swahili were apparently less bothered about their comfort at the end of the day's walking, which some observers put down to laziness.

Other groups included ex-slaves from around Rabai near Mombasa in Kenya (reputed to be the worst porters) and porters from Uganda, who were supposed to be some of the best – they could carry heavier loads and endure longer marches more cheerfully than the other groups.

When it came to choosing the porters, selection of the head porter was critical to the success of the expedition. He had to oversee the porters and be able to maintain the morale of the caravan at times of difficulty. If one of the porters was ill, it was up to the head porter to carry the extra load. He would often lead the singing and give a marching time to the others. The other porters would be selected, followed by a negotiation of terms. The men were usually given about two months wages in advance depending on the length of the trip.

The routine that most caravans seemed to follow was fairly similar. Before first light a bell would be rung or a bugle sounded to wake up the camp. Sometimes a medical examination was carried out to deal with minor ailments, then the porters would collect up their loads, without having had anything to eat or drink. About two hours after dawn the leader of the expedition would have a light breakfast, but the porters themselves would continue the journey under their huge loads, a remarkable feat of stamina. The caravan would usually stop at around 10.00, as near to water as possible, having covered about 25 km before the main heat of the day. They would then set up camp for the night and the porters would at last get something to eat.

The trade routes would not have functioned without the porters and the impact on the porters' villages was also important – the absence of able-bodied men during the harvest would have been partially offset by their wages and goods that they would have bought. Also, the passing of a large caravan through an area would have increased the demand for food supplies and thus stimulated domestic markets. The necessity for foot safaris did not vanish until the introduction of the railway and the motor vehicle.

---

hotels. **A** *Beachcomber Hotel*, Kunduchi, PO Box 4868, T2647772-4, T0742-782879 (mob), F2647050, beachcomber@afsat.com, www.beachcomber.co.tz New development, a/c rooms with TV, minibar and phone, health club, watersports facilities, shuttle between the hotel and airport. **A** *Jangwani Sea Breeze Lodge*, PO Box 934, Mbezi Beach off Bagamoyo Rd, 20 km north of city, T2647215, T0741-325908 (mob), F0741-320714, jangwani@afsat.com A/c rooms with TVs and en-suite bathrooms, swimming pool, watersports, restaurant, bar. **A** *White Sands*, PO Box 3030, Dar es Salaam, on Jangwani Beach, 20 km north from Dar es Salaam, T2135952, F2118483, whitesandshotel@raha.com Reasonable beach, pool, watersports, restaurants, bars, 88 a/c rooms with TVs.

B *Belinda Ocean Resort*, Kunduchi, off the road to *White Sands*, PO Box 31924, T/F2647551, belinda@africaonline.co.tz Small hotel with only 16 rooms, a/c, en-suite bathrooms, TVs and phones, restaurant, bar, swimming pool. **B** *Kunduchi Beach*, PO Box 361, Kunduchi,

T2127201/2. Modern-style accommodation, Islamic-style architecture for main service areas, bar, pool bar, restaurant, swimming pool, charming beach palms and flowers. Had become somewhat run down before being closed down for major renovations by new owners. Previously had band on Sun and public holidays, watersport facilities and trips to off-shore islands, close to fishing village (hotel restaurant will prepare fresh fish bought there for half menu price). Is due to re-open shortly. **B** *Silver Sands*, Kunduchi, PO Box 60097, T2650231, T0742-781602 (mob), F2650428, silverands@africaonline.co.tz Pleasantly restored restaurant, bar, some rooms have fans and are cheaper than those with a/c, there is also a campsite. **C** *Rungwe Oceanic*, PO Box 35639, Kunduchi, T47185. Good value, bar and restaurant, popular with budget travellers, has camping facilities.

There were camping facilities at **E** *Kunduchi Beach*, and should still be when re-opened, about 1.5 km from where the ferry docks on the Kigamboni side of the harbour. There are also camping facilities at **E** *Silver Sands*, 25 km out of town, see above for contact details, US$3 per person. Managed by Michael, a very helpful South African who will organize tours to Zanzibar or the Marine Reserve. Car parking US$2 per night; you can leave the car/truck here while you make a trip to Zanzibar. Shuttle bus service can be arranged to Dar es Salaam airport. Has a good restaurant and 2 bars. Offers a phone/fax service. Also has good rooms, clean but crowded, theft of property can be a problem. **E** *Kipepo* (meaning butterfly) *Campsite*, T2122981, F2119272, palmbeach@cctz.com, www.go.to\Kipepo Located across the harbour 8 km south of the ferry terminal. Camping $2.50 per person, bandas $10, dormitory $6, showers, bar, restaurant, shuttles to Dar and airport.

Camping

Eating

Variety is improving all the time in Dar es Salaam, with more tourists and new places opening. Particularly recommended are *Casanova's*, *Smokies*, *Karibu* and *Jambo Inn* for Indian food, *Barbeque House* delicious tandoori grills. If you go by taxi to venues in outer areas (*Casanova, Smokies*) it is worth while asking the driver to wait.

● *on maps,
pages 348 and 352
Price codes:
see inside front cover*

99ers Steak House, is a new restaurant at the Sheraton, T2112416, seafood as well as steaks. *Casanova's*, Masaki St, T2600268, F2600269, Msasani Peninsula (30 mins from centre in taxi). *Serengeti Spaghetti*, delightful atmosphere, often with live music, good Italian cuisine, currently one of the smartest Dar es Salaam restaurants. Recently the *Omar El Khayam Restaurant* has been added, with Middle Eastern cuisine and nightly entertainment. *Karibu*, ground floor of *Karibu Hotel*, Haile Selassie Rd, Oyster Bay (20 mins from centre by taxi). Good quality Indian cuisine. *Oyster Bay*, *Oyster Bay Hotel*, Toure Dr (15 mins from centre in taxi), T68631. First floor restaurant with views overlooking Oyster Bay, extensive menu and excellent quality, seafood platter is especially recommended and of daunting dimensions, excellent smoked sailfish. *Serengeti*, at the Sheraton, T2112416. Themed nights every day of the week: Mediterranean on Mon, Italian on Tue, Oriental on Wed, seafood menu on Thu, popular fondue night on Fri, Tex-Mex on Sat and Indian on Sun. *Smokies*, off Chole Rd, Msasani Peninsula (30 mins from centre in taxi), PO Box 23425, Dar es Salaam, T0742 780567. Rooftop, open-air restaurant with views across Msasani Bay, buffet, dinner US$8, live band on Thu evenings, crowded at weekends, superior wine list.

Expensive

Addis in Dar, on Ursino St, off Migombani St/Old Bagamoya Rd in the Oyster Bay area, near the site of the new US Embassy, T0742-786137 (mob). Small but rather charming. Ethiopian cuisine in a traditional setting, closed on Sun. It is wise to drop in and book ahead. *Alcove*, Samora Av. Reasonable Indian food, also some Chinese, usually busy at weekends, one of the best restaurants in town, closes at 1500. *Azuma*, 1st floor at *The Slipway*, Msasani Peninsula, T2600893, T0742-763388 (mob). Japanese and Indonesian restaurant, good views over the bay, closed Mon. *Bali's*, Aly Khan Rd, T0742-784742 (mob), bali@raha.com Mainly Indian cuisine, open evenings only. *Bandari*, in *New Africa Hotel*, Azikwe St, T2117050/1. Uncomplicated international food, live music most evenings. *Budapest Restaurant*, Kimweri Av, T/F2667489, T0742-750989 (mob). First-rate Hungarian food and continental dishes,

Mid-range

Dar es Salaam - Msasani Peninsula

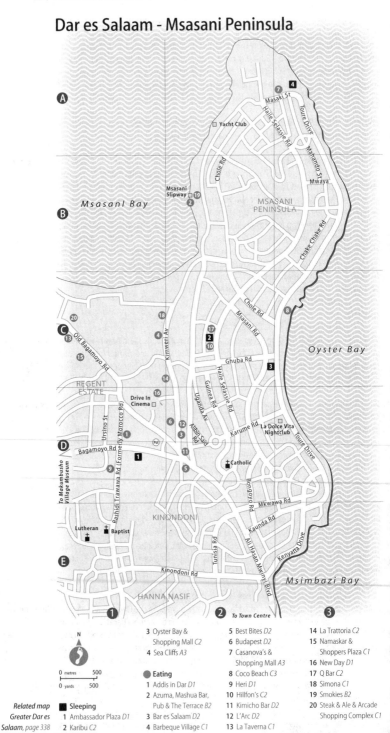

Related map
Greater Dar es
Salaam, *page 338*

■ Sleeping
1 Ambassador Plaza *D1*
2 Karibu *C2*

3 Oyster Bay &
  Shopping Mall *C2*
4 Sea Cliffs *A3*

● Eating
1 Addis in Dar *D1*
2 Azuma, Mashua Bar,
  Pub & The Terrace *B2*
3 Bar es Salaam *D2*
4 Barbeque Village *C1*

5 Best Bites *D2*
6 Budapest *D2*
7 Casanova's &
  Shopping Mall *A3*
8 Coco Beach *C3*
9 Heri *D1*
10 Hillfon's *C2*
11 Kimicho Bar *D2*
12 L'Arc *D2*
13 La Taverna *C1*

14 La Trattoria *C2*
15 Namaskar &
  Shoppers Plaza *C1*
16 New Day *D1*
17 Q Bar *C2*
18 Simona *C1*
19 Smokies *B2*
20 Steak & Ale & Arcade
  Shopping Complex *C1*

generous portions, pleasant atmosphere, outdoor bar to the rear, open Tue-Sun evenings. Well recommended. *Cedars Restaurant*, on Bibi Titi Mohammed Rd, near the junction with Zanaki St. Offers good value Lebanese food, excellent local seafood, takeaway available. *Chef's Pride Restaurant*, virtually opposite *Jambo Inn* hotel, on road between Lubya St and Jamhuri St. Good food at excellent prices, fast service – Italian, Chinese, Indian and local dishes available. *China Restaurant*, near Oyster Bay Hospital, serves authentic and simple Chinese dishes. *Chinese Restaurant*, basement of NIC Bldg, Samora Av. Good standard of cuisine. *City Garden Restaurant*, behind ATC House on Pamba Rd, T2134211. African, Indian and western meals, buffets at lunchtime, excellent juices. Highly recommended. *Dar Shanghai*, behind the Swiss Air office in Luther House, Sokoine Dr, T2134397. Chinese and Tanzanian menus. *Embassy Grill*, T2130006, second floor of *Embassy Hotel* on Garden Av, central. Steaks recommended. *Empire*, in courtyard beside *Empire Cinema*, Maktaba St. Indian cuisine with live Indian music most nights. *Garden Plaza*, T2123520. International menu. *Heri Restaurant*, Morocco Rd. Authentic Chinese food. Highly recommended. *Hillfon's Swedish Restaurant*, next to *Karibu Hotel* on Haile Selassie Rd, Oyster Bay, T2601427, F2602950. Good simple food. Recommended. *Hong Kong*, Bibi Titi Mohamed St and Zanaki St, next to *Cedars*. *Istana*, Ali Hassan Mwinyi Rd, opposite Caltex petrol station, T2650156. Specializes in Malaysian cuisine. *L'Arca di Noe'*, PO Box 2065, Kimweri Av, Msanani Peninsula, T667215, serves Italian pastas, seafood, pizzas, range of desserts, wide selection of wines, pleasant atmosphere. *La Trattoria Jan*, Kimweri Av, Regent Estate, Old Bagamoya Rd, T0741-400753 (mob). Excellent Italian cuisine, ice creams, pleasant atmosphere and good value too. *Lilylike House*, Chinese restaurant on Kimweri Av, T2668998, T0741-333988 (mob). *Mashua Bar & Grill*, at *The Slipway*, Msasani Peninsula, T0741-620003 (mob). Grills, burgers, salads and pizza, open evenings only. *Namaskar*, at Shopper's Plaza, Old Bagamoyo Rd, T0741-338411 (mob). Good selection of Indian cuisine – vegetarian, South Indian, Moughlai and Punjabi. *Paradise*, off Old Bagamoyo Rd, Mikocheni, T72730, T0742-781743 (mob). Ethiopian restaurant. *The Pub*, at *The Slipway*, Msasani Peninsula, T0741-330200 (mob). International food, mainly French and Italian, also serves burgers, sandwiches and grills. *The Rendez-Vous*, Samora Av, near the junction at Morogoro Rd. Eat inside or out, a/c, good service. *Rudy's Farm*, located near the gate of *Bahari Beach Hotel*, T/F2650507, rudyfarm@ud.co.tz Barbecue on Sun afternoons, 1300 until dark, run by a Dutchman, for about US$9 you get to eat as much as you like, good fun. *Sawasdee*, top floor of *New Africa Hotel*, Azikwe St, T21170501-2. Thai food, wonderful harbour views, buffet on Fri, US$15. *Sichuan Restaurant*, Bibi Titi Mohamed Rd, T2150548. *Steak & Ale*, at The Arcade, Old Bagamoyo Rd, T0741-603922 (mob). Grilled steaks, some seafood, live music on Wed, Fri and Sun evenings. *Simona Restaurant* Kimweri Av, Msasani Peninsula, Italian cuisine, rather cavernous interior. *The Terrace*, at *The Slipway*, Msasani Peninsula, T0741-608564 (mob). Italian cuisine and barbecued grills and seafood. Moorish painted arches and outside dining area.

Cheap *Barbeque House*, Vijimweni St, off Upanga Rd (outer central). Specializes in good quality tandoori grills. *Barbeque Village*, Kimweri Av, Msanani Peninsula, outdoor barbeque garden, popular and good value. *Best Bites*, American-style ice cream parlour, pizza – excellent value at A H Mwinyi Rd, Namanga, along the Bagamoyo Rd, T0741-323164. *Burger Bar*, opposite the *Salamandar* on Samora Av. *Burger Bite*, corner of Samora Av and Azikiwe St, T0741-332968 (mob). Burgers, pizza, some curries, snacks, breakfasts. *Café California*, fast food 24 hrs a day, in the *Las Vegas Casino* complex. *Central Fish*, Zaramo St, close to DTV roundabout. Roadside kiosk serving fish and chicken dishes. *Chef's Pride*, just off Jamhuri St near Morogoro Rd, across the road from the *Holiday Hotel*. The food is good, serving local as well as Indian and Chinese dishes. *Chicken King Restaurant*, Jamhuri St. Offers good local breakfasts. *Etienne's*, *Etienne's Hotel*, Ocean Rd, T2120293. Uncomplicated menu. *Hajirah*, India St, next to Alliance Française. Good food but only open at lunchtimes. *Jambo Inn*, Libya St, T35359. Excellent Indian menu, huge inflated chapatis like air-cushions, also Chinese and European dishes, outside and inside dining areas. *Madawa Restaurant*, opposite the Greek Orthodox church on Ali Hassan Mwinyi Rd. *National Bank of Commerce Canteen*, Pamba Rd, off Samora Av. Good charcoal barbecued meats, open lunchtimes only. *New Day*, Kimweri

Av, T0741-604006 (mob). Traditional Ethiopian cuisine. *New Zahir*, Mosque St, off Jamhuri St. Toothsome, inexpensive food, atmospheric, popular with locals, typical coastal dishes. *Palm Beach*, *Palm Beach Hotel*, Upanga Rd, T2128892. Rather uninspired menu of British food, set menu is good value, but runs out early, pleasant verandah atmosphere. *Pizza and Spice*, New Bagamoyo Rd, T71313, T0741-320123 (mob), pizza and Indian dishes. *Planet Bollywood*, Morogoro Rd/Samora Av corner, T2111354. Pizzas, burgers and ice cream. *The Retreat*, Mtendeni/Mrima St, off Jamhuri St. Favourite with the Hindu community, authentic South Indian cuisine, with the *masala dosa* specially recommended. *Ready Food*, Ocean Rd, adjacent to BP petrol station, T2138073, T0742-782392 (mob). Fast food – pizza, burgers and lasagne. *Salamandar*, corner of Samora and Mkwepu (central). Once Dar es Salaam's smartest venue, closed in evening, pleasant ground-floor area opening on to street, snacks and simple grills at lunchtime. *Shalimar*, Mansfield St (central). Sound Indian cuisine, restaurant closes around 1830. *Shari's Dar Bar*, Bibi Titi Mohamed St. Simple charcoal grills, tandoori chicken, salad, fries, good value. *Steers/Debonairs Pizza*, at the corner of Samora Av and Ohio St, T2122855-7. South African fast food chain, burgers and pizza, delivery service available. Not particularly high quality. *Supreme*, Nyerere Rd (outer central in the Genezani area). Vegetarian, reasonable quality, but unbearably grim decor.

Seriously cheap *Husseini's Ice Cream Parlour*, corner of India St and Zanaki St. A Dar institution run by an old coastal family, serving juices, shakes and snacks. *Sno-cream*, Mansfield St. An old-fashioned ice cream parlour serving excellent ice cream, done out in Disney style. *The Subway*, Peugeot House, Ali Hassan Mwinyi Rd, snacks. *Tanzania Coffee Board*, coffee shop on ground floor of Telecoms building on Samora Av (central). Lunchtimes and early evening only, outside patio, rather drab, snacks, disappointingly only serves instant coffee. On corner KLM office, *Eesiq* takeaway is very famous, good food.

Bars and nightclubs

Bars
Specially recommended are the beer gardens at Palm Beach, Etiennes and Oyster Bay for tropical atmosphere and the Zebra for a quiet central meeting place

Ambassador Plaza Inn, Ali Hassan Mwinyi Rd. Outside patio bar has moved upstairs. *Bar es Salaam*, Kimweri Av, Msasani Penisula, superb decor in West African style, excellent barbecued food. Often has live music, highly recommended. *Continental Hotel*, Nkrumah St, has sedate patio bar. *Embassy*, Garden Av. First floor bar, rather dull. *Empire Cinema Bar*, Maktaba St. Nice bar, also does excellent food if you can ask for it. *Etiennes*, Ocean Rd. Pleasant beer garden, rather drab bar inside hotel. *4-Twenty*, Toure Dr, Msasani Peninsula (closed Tue). Sports bar, pool, darts, good food with pizzas, burgers, steaks, Italian and Indian dishes, selection of desserts, first rate cold juices. Kimicho at Mamanga Shopping Centre, just off Ali Hassan Mwinyi Rd. Secluded bar with thatched roofing to open-air area. *New Africa*, Azikiwe St. Secluded bar has moved upstairs.Good place for a beer or two is the *Jolly Club* just outside the centre. On Ali Hassan Mwinyi Rd, next to the *California Dreamer* disco, is a classic Tanzanian outdoor bar/*nyama choma* spot. *New Happy Hotel*, Lumumba/Ungoni Sts, rooftop bar, with views over Mnazi Mmoji. *Oyster Bay*, Toure Dr, pleasant well-appointed bar to rear of hotel overlooking Bamboo Gardens. *Palm Beach*, Upanga Rd. Very popular beer gardens, coloured fairy lights. *Sugar Ray's*, at Palm Beach Hotel on Ali Hassan Mwinyi Rd, is a sports bar/club that will satisfy those with an appetite for English football as matches are shown regularly. For those staying at the Salvation Army there are some good bars nearby in the grounds of the Saba Saba exhibition centre. *Zebra Bar*, Kilimanjaro Hotel, Kirukoni Front, central. Large lounge, quiet.

Nightclubs
Most nightlife gets under way late – things tend not to warm up until the bars close at around 2300. Many venues open (and close) at short notice

California Dreamer disco next to *Las Vegas Casino* on corner of Upanga Rd and Ufokoni Rd. Bright and busy during the week and busier at weekends, girls free before 2300 during the week, rather a lot of strobe lighting, US$4-6. Coco Beach. *Mambo Club*, Haile Selassie Rd, next to *Karibu Hotel*, is open on Fri and Sun. There is a disco at *The Slipway* every Fri night. *La Dolce Vita*, Toure Dr, US$2-4, Fri, Sat. Open-air, pleasant atmosphere with thatched roofing, the smart place with *Bamboo Gardens* closed. *Club Billicanos*, Simu St, US$5-10. Discos most nights, ocasional live band or cabaret entertainment, strobe lighting, smoke machines, revolving glitter balls, expensive, but popular at weekends, though often quiet during the week. *Continental*, Nkrumah Rd, US$2-4. Discos Fri and Sat, popular with locals.

Tazara Hostel, Kilimani Rd, off Bagamoyo Rd, US$4. Bands at weekends. *Bahama Mama's*, Morogoro Rd, US$2-3, 15 km from town centre. Large open-air venue where **Shikamoo**, a legendary jazz and rumba band from the 1960s, play regularly.

Entertainment

Europeans and visitors seldom visit the cinema, which is a pity as the general audience reaction makes for an exciting experience. Programmes are not announced in the *Daily News*, but the *Express*, *Family Mirror* and the Swahili *Uhuru* all carry details. The cinemas show mostly Indian, martial arts or adventure films. Entrance about US$1. The most popular are the *Empire*, Maktaba St, opposite the Post Office; *Empress* on Samora Av; *New Chox* on Nkrumah St; *Odeon* on Zaramo St; *Starlight* on Kisutu St; *Drive-Inn-Cinema* on Old Bagamoyo Rd, just before Morocco Rd. Slightly more up to date is the *Avalon* on Zanaki St.

The British Council on Ohio St has fairly regular film shows on Wed. The Alliance Française on Maktaba St opposite the *New Africa Hotel* shows films from time to time. Announcements in *Daily News*. There are also film shows at *The Slipway* (1930 on Tue), *Mambo Club* (1900 on Sat) and *Sugar Ray's* (1930 on Mon and Tue), all cost about US$2.50.

Cinema

Las Vegas Casino, T2116512, corner of Upanga Rd and Ufukoni Rd. Roulette, poker, blackjack, vingt-et-un and slot machines. *Monte Carlo Casino*, corner of Ohio St and Sokoine Dr, formerly *Skyway Hotel*, claims to have the largest selection of table games in East Africa. *Club Billicanos*, Simu St, is applying for a gambling licence, as is a hotel under construction on Msasani Peninsula. There are also casinos at *New Africa Hotel*, T2119752, and *Hotel Sea Cliff*.

Gambling

Classical music Concerts by touring artists are presented by the **British Council**, the Alliance Française and occasionally other embassies. Announcements in *Daily News*. **Popular music** Special visits by popular African bands and artists and Indian groups occur regularly and are presented at *Diamond Jubilee Hall, Bahama Mama's, Club Billicanos,* Corner Upanga Rd and Ohio St has resident band Tue-Sat. Announcements in *Daily News*. **Zaita** is mainly Congolese, the **Tanzanites** are from the Arusha area, **BICO Stars** are from Dar es Salaam. **Shikamoo** is a famous band of the 1960s with an exceptional saxophonist and lead guitarist. They play regularly at *Bahama Mama's* and at various social clubs such as Langata in Kinondoni, Kawe along the Old Bagamoyo Rd and Mwenge off the Bagamoyo Rd just before Sam Njoma Rd. There are some music announcements in the *Daily News*, but a more comprehensive listing is in the Swahili *Uhuru* – get a local to translate.

Music

See also boxes on page 356 and 557

Athletics Meetings at National Stadium. Details in *Daily News*. **Cricket** Almost entirely a pursuit of the Asian community. There are regular games at the *Gymkhana Club*, off Ghana Av, *Annadil Burhani Cricket Ground*, off Aly Khan Rd, *Leaders Club*, Dahomey Rd, off Ali Hassan Mwinyi Rd and at *Jangwani Playing Fields*, off Morogoro Rd, in the valley of Msimbazi Creek, at weekends. Announcements of forthcoming fixtures are listed in the *Daily News*. **Golf, tennis, squash** Tournaments each year at the Gymkhana Club, off Ghana Av, announcements in *Daily News*. Further information about squash from Col SMA Kashmiri, Chairman, Tanzania SRA, c/o Africonsult Ltd, PO Box 21242, Dar es Salaam, T2132299, F2131842. **Soccer** The main African pursuit, followed by everyone from the President and the Cabinet down. Matches are exciting occasions with radios throughout the city tuned to the commentary. Terrace entrance is around US$1 (more for important matches). It is worth paying extra to sit in the stand. Details of games announced in *Daily News*. There are two main venues, the *National Stadium* on Mandela Rd to the south of the city and *Karume Stadium*, just beyond the Kariakoo area, off Uhuru St. There are two divisions of the National league, and Dar es Salaam has two representatives, *Simba* and *Young Africans* (often called *Yanga*), and there is intense rivalry between them. Simba, the best-known Tanzanian club, have their origins in Kariakoo and are sometimes referred to as the 'Msimbazi Street Boys' – they have a club bar in Msimbazi St. Initially formed in the 1920s as 'Eagles of the Night', they changed their name to 'Sunderland FC' in the 1950s. After independence all teams had to choose African names and they became Simba. The national team *Taifa Stars* play regularly at the National Stadium, mostly against other African teams.

Spectator sports

Tanzania

Popular music in Dar es Salaam

While the central districts of Dar es Salaam quieten down quickly after dark, the outlying districts liven up at this time, especially at weekends. Here, music is an essential part of socializing. There are many venues and many styles of music are available, including distinctly local styles such as Taarab (see box, page 557). Taxi drivers will know the best venues (get the driver to collect you again later) and exercise caution as there is, of course, a lot of beer around at concerts and tempers occasionally become volatile. If you can, go in African company. All the groups mentioned here, and many more, have tapes on sale in the city streets, for instance in Azikiwe Street between the dala-dala stands and the waterfront.

The influence of Congolese pop music on Tanzanian pop is enormous. This style has been developing since the 1950s, inspired, in part, by Cuban influences. The local incarnation is often slightly gentler than the Congolese product. A number of bands in Dar es Salaam formed in the 1970s are still going strong. They include **Milimani Park** *and* **OTTU Jazz Band** *(Organization of Tanzanian Trade Unions). The former can be heard on Sunday nights at DDC Mlimani, behind Kariakoo central market, from about 1900. OTTU Jazz perform regularly at OTTU Social Club in Ilala. Probably the most popular local band in the country is* **African Stars** *, also known as* **Twanga Pepeta** *(pound and husk), a young band who use the same musical idiom. They can often be found in Kinondoni, in a venue adjacent to Vijana Hall.*

Another group coming to prominence is **FM Academy** *. The musicians, of Congolese origin, fell out with their agent, who reported them for working without permits. As a result, they spent some time behind bars.*

Along with the trade unions, the ruling party, CCM, also recognizes the benefits of having a finger in the musical pie. Two widely popular groups, known by the same name (**Tanzania One Theatre** *or* **TOT** *for short)*

but practising different styles, are in the employ of the party. One of them performs a slightly secularized version of 'kwaya' music (choir singing reminiscent of church performances). Led by Captain Komba, an unashamed praise singer for CCM, it provided the music that dominated the streets for weeks after the death of Julius Nyerere in 1999: Nyimbo za Maombolezo. They can be found at Vijana Social Hall, the venue of the party youth organization, or at the CCM offices, both in Kinondoni suburb.

One hugely popular Congolese musician in Dar es Salaam is **Dr Remmy Ongala** *. The titles of his songs give an idea of how directly pop in Dar addresses all that is on peoples' minds, including* That which the heart loves *and* Death has no mercy. *Many songs, as it happens, are about money, and especially the inconvenience of not having any. The other incarnation of TOT meanwhile perform Taarab.*

Of the international styles of music that have become more accessible in recent years, Hip Hop has made the biggest impact. Tanzania's best known rapper is **Mr II** *('Mister Too' – as in 'too' much'). While Gangsta antics are much in evidence among the rappers, as Swahili has a very different rhythm and sound structure from English, Swahili rap has a style all its own. Mr II, the* **Hard Blasted Crew** *and* **Dola Soul** *aka* **Balozi** *are the biggest names, and the places to find them and others include FM Club in Kinondoni on Sunday afternoons, and Mambo Club in Oyster Bay, on Haile Selassie Road.*

Of course, there is also traditional music. Just about the only live venue in the city centre, the Nyumba ya Sanaa near the Sheraton, has 'ngoma' or traditional dance performances on Friday nights. Often performers will come from the 'Chuo Cho Sanaa' or college for the performing arts in Bagamoyo. They are well worth watching. Traditional music, often limited to ritual uses, has a niche existence in this city, but its influence is always there.

Theatre *Little Theatre*, Haile Selassie Rd, off Ali Hassan Mwinyi Rd, presents productions on an occasional basis, perhaps half a dozen a year, usually drama and comedy and one musical a year, very popular, particularly the Christmas pantomime. The **British Council**, Ohio St, occasionally presents productions. *Diamond Jubilee Hall*, Maliki Rd, Upanga. Occasional visits by companies from India performing a bill of variety acts. For all of the above, check announcements in *Daily News*.

Shopping

Woolworth's is the only department store in Dar es Salaam, a South African store located in the New PPF Towers building on Ohio St. Expensive, high quality goods are to be found in *The Slipway*, a new complex of shops and restaurants on Msasani Peninsula, facing Msasani Bay, also housing *The Gallery*. The shopping malls at *Oyster Bay Hotel* and *Casanova's*, both on Msasani Peninsula, have suffered by comparison. Another new mall is *Shopper's Plaza* on Old Bagamoyo Rd, also on the peninsula, where there is a large supermarket. Nearby is *The Arcade*, which has a travel agency, boutiques, hairdresser and restaurants. The shops at *Hotel Sea Cliff* include a jewellers, sports shop, arts and crafts shop, health and beauty spa and a florist. The smaller *Haidery Plaza* is at the corner of Upanga Rd and Kisutu St. Otherwise shops are located along Samora Av (electrical goods, local clothing, footware) and on Libya St (clothing and footwear). Supermarkets with a wide variety of imported foods and wines are on Samora Av between Pamba Av and Azikawe St, on the corner of Kaluta St and Bridge St, opposite Woolworth's on Garden Av, in *Shopper's Plaza* and in the *Oyster Bay Hotel* shopping mall. A popular location for purchase of fruit and vegetables is the market on Kinondoni Rd, just north of Msimbuzi Creek. Fresh fish and seafood can be bought at the market on Ocean Rd just past the ferry to Kivukoni. The shop in the foyer of the *Kilimanjaro Hotel* has a good selection of postcards, and will also sell stamps.

Locally produced tie-dye material can be obtained cheaply about US$2 a metre from the women who congregate at the corner of Aggrey St and Indira Ghandi St. Tie dye also available at one of the craft shops in the complex at Mwenga.

The supermarket next to the *Motel Afrique* is currently the most central available. The selection of goods is a bit limited.

Bookshops Can be bought secondhand at the stalls on Samora Av and on Pamba St (off Samora). The best bookshop by far is *A Novel Idea*, T2601088, which has moved from the *Casanova* shopping mall to *The Slipway* on Msasani Peninsula. This is perhaps the most comprehensive bookshop in East Africa. Others are the **Tanzanian Bookshop**, Indira Gandhi St, leading from the Askari Monument and **Tanzania Publishing House**, Samora Av, but both have only limited selections.

Curios & crafts *Lalji Ramji* has a counter in the *Kilimanjaro Hotel* foyer and he is there 1100-1600 daily, selling old stamps and coins.

Antiques from Africa at the *Casanova Shopping Mall*, at the north end of Toure Dr, has old brass items, antique wood carvings, Zanzibar doors and a fine range of fabrics. Also has some *Kunduchi Ceramics*, oatmeal and blue with traditional designs.

There is also a good curio shop on Mkwepu St between Samora Av and City Dr. This shop is particularly good for antique brass and copper items. Excellent quality modern wood products can be obtained from **Domus**, in the *Slipway* complex, which also houses **The Gallery**, also selling wood products as well as other items such as paintings by local artists; **Acacia**, selling carvings and jewellery; the **Novel Idea** bookshop; a **Tinga Tinga** art workshop; and a variety of eating places. Other curio shops are **Silver Curios** on Asikiwe St, opposite the *New Africa Hotel*. There are 2 curio shops in the *Kilimanjaro Hotel*.

Traditional crafts, particularly wooden carvings, are sold along Samora Av to the south of the Askari Monument. Good value crafts can be purchased from stalls along Ali Hassan Mwinyi Rd near the intersection with Haile Selassie Rd and, in particular, at Mwenge, along Sam Njoma Rd, close to the intersection with Ali Hassan Mwinyi Rd. This is the best place for handicrafts in Dar es Salaam, and for ethnographia from all over Tanzania and further afield (notably the Congo). There are a large number of shops and stalls offering goods at very reasonable prices. The market is about half-an-hour's journey from the town centre, easily reached by *dala-dala* (destination: Mwenge).

Sport

Fishing Marine fishing could be arranged through *Kunduchi Beach Hotel* before closure for refurbishment. This hotel is scheduled to reopen shortly. **Golf, tennis, squash** Although the *Gymkhana Club* on Ghana Av has facilities for all 3 sports, visitors are only permitted to play

For Diving opportunities, see page 44

Tanzania

golf, cost US$12.50. *Upanga Sports Club* on Upanga Rd just past the Greek church has squash facilities. An informal group meets for tennis at the University of Dar es Salaam courts on the campus 15 km to the north of the city at 1700 every day. **Gym** *The Fitness Centre*, off Chole Rd on Msasani Peninsula, has a gym with weights and also runs aerobics and yoga classes. *Millenium Health Club*, Mahando St, at the north end of Msasani Peninsula, T2602609, F2602610, milleniumhealthclub@hotmail.com Gym, aerobics, sauna and beauty parlour. Temporary membership with access to one or all of the facilities is available, full membership for a single visit costs US$10. *BMK*, Ali Hassan Mwinyi Rd, T0742-600720 (mob). **Hash House Harriers** Meet regularly in Dar es Salaam on late Mon afternoons. Details from **British Council**, Ohio St, or **British High Commission**, corner of Samora Av and Azikiwe St. **Sailing** The *Yacht Club* is located on Chole Rd on Msasani Peninsula. Visitors can obtain temporary membership. **Swimming** Can be had at the *Karibu Hotel* (US$4), the *Embassy Hotel*, *Sheraton Hotel*, *New Africa Hotel*, University of Dar es Salaam, and *Salvation Army Hostel* on Kilwa Rd. In the sea, the best location is at the Swimming Club on Ocean Rd near Magogoni St. Otherwise the best sea beaches are some distance to the north and south of the city. Next to *White Sands Hotel* at Jangwani Beach is *Water World*, which has several different water slides and games for children. Open Wed, Fri-Sun, entrance US$3 adults, US$2.50 children. Much larger is *Wet 'n' Wild*, at Kunduchi, 18 km north of Dar es Salaam. This is an enormous new complex largely, though not exclusively, for children. Of the 22 water slides, 2 are very high and one twists and turns for 250 m. There is an area for younger children, tennis and squash courts, go-karting, an internet café, hair and beauty parlour, fast food outlets and a main restaurant, and also facilities for watersports on the open ocean, including windsurfing and fishing trips; there is even a qualified diving instructor. The complex is completed by s/c apartments 1 km away and a furnished camp, with tents for 4-6 people.

Tour operators

A variety of companies offer tours to the game parks, the islands (Zanzibar, Pemba, Mafia) and to locations of historical interest (Kilwa, Bagamoyo). It is well worth shopping around as prices (and degrees of luxury) vary. Among the most experienced companies are: *AMI Travel Bureau*, *Coastal Travels*, *Hippo Tours & Safaris*, *Kearsley Travel and Tours*, *Rickshaw Travel*, *Savannah Tours*, *Sykes*, *Takims Safaris*, *Valji & Alibhai*. *Across Tanzania Safaris*, PO Box 21996, Makunganya St, T219961. *Africa Expeditions*, PO Box 1857, Mindu St, T2134574. *Africa Tours & Travel Bureau*, PO Box 3690, India St, T2117802, F2112846, africant@ud.co.tz *All African Travel Agents*, PO Box 1947, T2120886. *Alone with Nature*, Pamba House St, T2110159, T0741-320913 (mob). *AMI Travel Bureau*, PO Box 9041, AMI Bldg, Samora Av, T2127760. *Azania Tours and Travel*, PO Box 3707, Bibi Titi Mohamed St, T2136959. *Bahari Enterprises & Safaris*, PO Box 15384, T63422/9. *Bon Voyage Travel*, Osman Towers, Zanaki St, T2133080. *Boomerang*, Ohio St, T0741-326008 (mob). *Bushtrekker Safaris*, PO Box 5350, *Bahari Beach Hotel*, T2131957. *Central Tours & Travel*, PO Box 22273, Lumumba St, T/F2184122. *Coastal Travels*, PO Box 3052, 107 Upanga Rd, T2117957-9, coastal@twiga.com *Cordial Tours*, Indira St/Mkwepu St, T2113275. *Cruxton Travel*, PO Box 4973, Extelecom Bldg, 8th Flr, Samora Av, T2133012, cruxton@raha.com *Delvims Travel International*, PO Box 5486, Sukari House, Ground Flr, Ohio St/Sokoine Dr, T2122215, T0741-335813 (mob), F2114185, delvims@cats-net.com *East African Holidays*, PO Box 2895, Samora Av, T2125989. *Easy Travel & Tours Ltd*, Avalon House, 1st Flr, Sokoine Dr/Zanaki St, PO Box 1428, T2123526, F2113842, www.easytravel.co.tz *Emslies Travel Ltd*, NIC Investment House, 3rd Flr, Samora Av, T2117197, T0742-781098 (mob). *Flag Tours and Safaris*, PO Box 16046, T2137075. *Fortune Travels & Tours Ltd*, PO Box 21709, Jamhuri St, T2138288, F2111789. *Four Ways Travel Service*, PO Box 2926, Samora Av, T2122378. *Glide Safaris*, PO Box 4427. *Gogo Safaris*, PO Box 21114, Bagamoyo Rd, T0741-321552. *Hakuna Matata*, PO Box 33259, The Arcade, Old Bagamoyo Rd, T2775001, T0742-784737 (mob), F2700229, hakunamatata@raha.com *Hima Tours & Travel*, Simu St, behind Mavuno House, PO Box 10879, T2126987, T0741-323143 (mob), F2111083, hima@raha.com *Hippotours & Safaris*, PO Box 13824, Ohio St, T2128662, T0744-267706 (mob), F2128661, hippo@twiga.com, www.hippotours.com *Hit Holidays*, PO Box 6666, Bibi Titi Mohamed St (near *Rickshaw*

Travels), T2119024, T0741-781096 (mob), F2112376/2119028, hittrvls@ud.co.tz, www.hittours.co.tz, an excellent travel agency *Holiday Africa Tours & Safaris*, PO Box 2132, TDFL Bldg, Ohio St, T2111357/8. *Hotel Tours & Management*, PO Box 5350, T2124820. *Interline Travel & Tours*, PO Box 6541, NIC Life House, Sokoine Dr/Ohio St, T2112120, F2112345. *Iramba Tours*, PO Box 21856, T44482. *JMT African Heart*, Chagga St, near Libya St, PO Box 21844, T/F2124503, T0744-282251 (mob), info@africanheart.com *J M Tourist*, PO Box 21703, T2122433. *Kearsley Travel and Tours*, PO Box 801, Kearsley House, Indira Gandhi St, T2115026-30, F2115585, kearsley@raha.com *Leisure Tours & Safaris*, PO Box 6100, T2132251, F2862939. leisure@raha.com *Leopard Tours*, Haidery Plaza, Upanga Rd/Kisutu St, T2119750/4-6. *Let's Travel*, PO Box 20194, A H Mwinyi Rd, opposite *Las Vegas Casino*, T/F2112789, T0742-782367 (mob), itravel@intafrica.com *Lions of Tanzania Safari & Tours*, PO Box 967, Peugeot House, Bibi Titi Mohamed Rd, T2128161, F2128162, lions@intafrica.com *Luft Travel & Cargo Ltd*, GAK Patel Bldg, Maktaba St, PO Box 1993, T2138843, F2116613, lufttravel@cats-net.com *Mill Tours & Safaris*, PO Box 19604, T2122114. *Mizat Tours & Travel*, PO Box 65236, Swahili St/Kariakoo St, T2184202, T2185268. *Molenveld Travel Bureau*, PO Box 456, Samora Av, T0741-324609. *Multi Tours and Travel*, PO Box 6940, Zanaki St, Osman Towers, T2111717, F2132138. *Onado Tours*, PO Box 31985, CUT Bldg, Lumumba St, T2183703, T0742-782116 (mob). *Panorama Tours*, PO Box 7534, Bakwat Bldg, corner of Morogoro Rd and Bibi Titi Mohamed St, T2115508. *Paradise Travel & Tours*, PO Box 5896, Pamba Rd, behind ATC Bldg, T2131400, F2134049, paradisetravels@cats-net.com *Parklands Tours*, PO Box 19630, T68586. *Parkway Tours and Safaris*, PO Box 6945, Tanzania Publishing House, Samora Av, T2136731. *Pwani Tours & Safaris*, PO Box 50007, Cnr Kaluta St and Morogoro Rd, T2122433. *Reza Travel & Tours*, Jamhuri St, opposite Caltex Station, T334458. *Rickshaw Travel* (American Express Agents), PO Box 1889, Sheraton Hotel, Ohio St, T2114094/2115110, F2129125/2135456. *Safari Tours*, PO Box 9442, THB Bldg Samora Av, T2128422. *Safeline Travels*, PO Box 10907, Life House, Sokoine Dr, T2111225, F2118543. *Satellite Travel & Tours*, PO Box 5563, Haidery Plaza, 1st Flr,

Tanzania

Suite 19, Upanga Rd/Kisutu St, T2119772/3. *Savannah Tours*, PO Box 20517, Sheraton Hotel, T2112416, T0741-331662 (mob), F2151463, savtour@twiga.com *Searock International*, PO Box 3030, T2132703. *Selous Safaris*, PO Box 1192, DT Dobie Bldg, Nkrumah St, T2134802, F2112794, selous@twiga.com *Shaka Zulu Safaris & Adventures*, PO Box 10678, Msimbazi St/Nyerere Rd, T0742-600430 (mob). *Skylink Travel & Tours*, PO Box 21338, TDFL Bldg, Ohio St, T2115381, T0741-324042 (mob), F2114562, skylink@cats-net.com *Southern Tanganyika Safaris and Tours*, PO Box 2341, TDFL Bldg, Ohio St, T2124897, T0742-782421 (mob), F2116413, stgs@twiga.com *State Travel Service*, PO Box 5023, Bank House, Samora Av, T2112747, F2129295. *Sunshine Safari Tours*, PO Box 5575, T2122700. *Sykes*, PO Box 1947, Indira Ghandi St, T2110552, F2129330. *Takims Holidays Tours and Safaris Ltd*, Sales Office: DTV Bldg, Jamhuri St, Dar es Salaam, T2110346-8, Cable AIRFLY Head Office: Mtendeni St, PO Box 20350, Dar es Salaam, T2110346, F2116659-60, takims@twiga.com, offer an IATA accredited travel agency as well as a bureau de change in Dar es Salaam, long-established company with an office in Arusha (see page 448), London contact: 'Tanzania Experience', T020-7624 5128, F020-7625 8333. *A Tent with a View Safaris*, Muleweld Tours, PO Box 40525, Samora Av Dar, T/F2151106, T0741-323318 (mob), tentview@ intafrica.com *Tourcare Tanzania*, PO Box 22878, T42496. *Trans Africa Guides*, PO Box 853, T2130192. *Vacational*, PO Box 6649, T2134350, F2134160. *Valji & Alibhai*, PO Box 786, Bridge St, T2120522, F2112988. *Vintage Holidays Ltd*, Avalon House, Sokoine Dr/Zanaki St, T2116023, T0742-602150 (mob). *Walji's Travel Bureau*, PO Box 434, Zanaki St/Indira Ghandi St corner, T2110321, T0742-780332 (mob), F2112914, waljis@africaonline.co.tz *Worldlink Travel & Tours Ltd*, Libya St, T2120477.

Hunting safari agents *Cordial Tours*, PO Box 1679, Jamhuri St, T2113275. *Gerald Posanisi Safaris*, PO Box 45640, T47435.

Transport

Local **Car hire** can be arranged through most travel agents (see below). Specialist companies are *Avis*, T2130505, F2137426. *Bugoni Super Auto Garage*, PO Box 25087, T63708. *Evergreen Car Rentals*, corner of Zanaki and Indira Ghandi St, PO Box 1476, T2183345/7, T/F2183348, evergreen@raha.com *Europcar*, 2 Nelson Mandela Express Way, PO Box 40568, Dar es Salaam, 0741-786000 (mob), F2862569, europcar@ raha.com *Hertz*, Savannah Tours, PO Box 20517, at the Sheraton Hotel, T2112416, T0741-331662 (mob), F2151463, hertz.tanzania@twiga.com, rates US$40 daily plus US$0.38 per km for a medium saloon. *Kara Motors*, PO Box 64, T2133549. *Tanzania Rent A Car*, Dar es Salaam International Airport, Shop 2, Terminal 2, PO Box 4347, T2843035, F2843034, trac@africaonline.co.tz *White Cabs*, PO Box 2107, Zanaki St, T2123078. *Yellow Cabs*, Upanga Rd, PO Box 6100, T2135981.

Air *Air Tanzania Corporation (ATC)* generally has daily flights scheduled to Zanzibar and Kilimanjaro and flights 1-3 times a week to Bukoba, Mwanza, Dodoma, Mtwara, Lindi and Musoma. However, *ATC* is not the most reliable airline, see page 326. Most *ATC* timetabled flights are actually operated by other airlines, particularly *Precisionair*. This is true for the 1-3 times a week flights to Kigoma, Tabora, Shinyanga, Mafia, Nachingwea, Kilwa and Pemba. *Aviators Services*, T2546386 (Arusha), has 3 flights a week to Arusha (1100 Mon, Wed, Sat), single US$126; 3 or 4 a week to Mafia (1100 Tue, Wed, Fri, Sun), single US$42.

See Airline offices, page 363, for addresses and telephone numbers

Coastal Travels Ltd and *Sky Tours*, PO Box 2161, T2117730, T0742-770800 (mob), offer flights from DSM to Mafia Island. They all cost about US$85 single. It is possible to charter planes through *Air Tanzania* but that is very expensive. *Coastal Travels Ltd*, Dar es Salaam, T2117959, F2118647; airport T2843033, F2846045. Scheduled daily flights to Zanzibar, Arusha and Selous, and Mon, Thu and Sat flights to Zanzibar, Selous and Ruaha. Can arrange flights to link with Selous airstrips including Mtememe (Rufiji River Camp), Siwandu (Mbuyuni Luxury Tented Camp), Beho Beho and Kiba (Sand Rivers). Some travellers have reported that the service can be chaotic, running hours late.

Eagle Air, PO Box 5794, T2127411, F2127415, eagleair@africaonline.co.tz, serves Zanzibar, Pemba, Mafia, Lindi, Mtwara, Nachingwea, Dodoma, Shinyanga, Mwanza, Musoma, Bukoba, Tabora, Kigoma, Seronera (in the Serengeti), Kilimanjaro and Arusha. *Precisionair* serves Mwanza,

Zanzibar, Arusha, Kilimanjaro, Moshi, Mafia, Mbeya, Iringa, Shinyanga, Seronera and Bukoba, PO Box 70770, Maarifa House, Ohio St, T2130800, T0742-781420 (mob), F2113036, precision-dar@twiga.com **Tanzanian Air Services Ltd (Tanzanair)**. Charter air service, PO Box 364, Dar es Salaam. Airport T2844101; *Sheraton Hotel* office, T2113151 ext 7884, F2112946, T0741-406407 (mob), tanzanair@raha.com *Tanzanair* also have scheduled flights to Arusha, Dodoma, Kilimanjaro, Morogoro, Moshi and Mwanza. For other air charter companies see page 363. **Zanair** links with Zanzibar, Malindi St, PO Box 2113, Zanzibar, T024-2232993, T0742-750478 (mob), F024-2233670, T0741-605230 (mob, Dar es Salaam), zanair@zitec.org

The **Central Railway Station** is located off Sokoine Dr at the wharf end of the city at the corner of Railway St/Gerezani St, T2110600. This station serves the line that runs through the central zone to Kigoma on Lake Tanganyika and Mwanza on Lake Victoria and the line that goes north to Tanga and Moshi. The continuation of the line from Moshi to Taveta, Voi, and the Kenyan rail network has been closed since the break up of the East African Community in 1977. However, there are new initiatives to revive co-operation between Kenya, Tanzania and Uganda.

Train
See pages 328 and 329 for details of train timetables and fares

The **Tazara Railway Station** is located at the junction of Mandela Rd and Nyerere Rd, and is about 5 km from the city centre, T2860344-7. It is well served by *dala-dala* and a taxi from the centre costs about US$4. This line runs southwest to Iringa and Mbeya and on to Tunduma at the Zambia border. It is a broader gauge than the Central and Northern Line.

On the **Tazara** line, Express trains go all the way to New Kapiri Mposhi in Zambia. It takes 40-50 hrs to get to Kapiri Mposhi and for those who are so minded it is possible, with a little luck, to link up with transport, which will get you all the way to Harare on the same day. The local trains, which stop at the Zambian border, are a little slower, and take approximately 23 hrs to get to Mbeya. 1st class cabins on both trains contain 4 berths and 2nd class 6.

There is a 50% discount on Tazara trains for students with ID, although you need to first collect a chit, which you have to take to the Ministry of Education (at Luthuli St/Magogoni St in Kivukoni) to get stamped. In Mbeya they make you go to a school located a couple of kilometres from the station in order to get a letter confirming you are a student.

All cabins on Tanzanian trains are sexually segregated unless you book the whole cabin.

If you are making a long journey you can book a seat at kiosks run by the bus companies at the bus stations. The main bus station has been relocated to Morogoro Rd, at Ubungo, 6 km from the centre, and may be reached by bus, *dala-dala* or taxi. Larger buses give a considerably more comfortable ride and are to be recommended on safety grounds as well. If you are taking a shorter journey (Morogoro or Bagamoyo, say), the bus will leave when full. You can join an almost full bus, and leave promptly for an uncomfortable journey, either standing or on a makeshift gangway seat. Or you can secure a comfortable seat and wait until the bus fills, which can take 1-2 hrs for a less busy route such as that to Bagamoyo. On the larger and more travelled routes (Arusha, Mbeya) there is now a choice of 'luxury', 'semi-luxury' and 'ordinary'. **Arusha**: fare is around US$20 luxury, US$16 semi-luxury and US$12 ordinary and takes about 9 hrs. The road has improved considerably and journey times are getting shorter. **Bagamoyo**: fare is US$1 and takes up to 3 hrs. The road is very poor. **Dodoma**: fare is about US$6 and takes about 6 hrs. Train is really the only feasible option on the Dodoma to Tabora and Kigoma route. **Mbeya**: fare is around US$17 luxury, US$10 semi-luxury and US$7 ordinary and journey takes about 12 hrs. **Tanga**: fare is roughly US$6 and takes about 5 hrs. **Mtwara**: fare is about US$10 and takes up to 24 hrs.

Road
The road is sealed all the way to Malawi, but there are bad stretches especially from Morogoro into the mountains

Recommended for safety and reliability is **Scandinavian Express Services Ltd**, based on Nyerere Rd at the corner of Msimbazi St (taxi from the centre approximately US$2.50), T2184833/4, T0741-325474 (mob), F2182999. There is a small airport style arrival and departure lounge at the station. Buses are speed limited, luggage is securely locked up either under the bus or in overhead compartments, and complimentary drinks, sweets and biscuits are offered. A very professional company. They depart daily for **Arusha** (0730 and 0830, US$14), **Iringa** (0830, 1030 and 1400, journey time 7 hrs, US$9.50), **Mbeya** (0700, US$17) and **Kyela** (0615, journey time 13 hrs, US$17).

Tanzania

The dala-dalas of Dar es Salaam

Ownership of one or more minibuses, or dala-dalas, remains a favourite 'mradi' (income-generating project) for Dar es Salaam's middle class and judging by the numbers squeezed into their interiors and the speed they travel between destinations those returns are handsome. Realizing that they cannot monitor the number of passengers using their buses, the dala-dala owners stipulate how much they expect to receive at the end of the day from the 'crew' they hire to operate the vehicle; the remainder constituting the crew's wages. It is a system that appears to work to everyones' advantage other than that of the passenger, who suffers the consequent overcrowding and the suicidal driving as dala-dala competes with dala-dala to arrive first and leave fullest.

In a forlorn attempt to reduce the number of accidents, the Tanzanian government in early 1997 passed a law requiring all public service vehicles to install governors restricting speeds to under 80 kph. However, dala-dala and coach operators soon worked out ways to override them, or simply disconnected them completely, and within weeks the drivers were proceeding with their old reckless abandon.

The basic crew of each dala-dala is made up of three people: the driver (clearly picked for the ability to drive fast rather than well), the ticket collector, and the turnboy (in Dar slang 'Mgiga debe' – literally 'he who forces things into a tin can"), whose job it is to harangue passengers who fail to make room for one more, as well as to entertain the remainder of the bus with hair-raising acrobatic stunts hanging from the door of the bus (there is at least one Mpiga debe

currently working in Dar who has just one leg – it's not hard to imagine how he lost the other one). Supplementing this basic crew at either end of the journey is a tout, who bawls out the intended destination and route, attempting to attract or, if necessary, intimidate (at times this stretches to actual manhandling of passengers) people into entering his dala-dala. He is paid a fixed amount for each bus that he touts for. In addition, when business is slow, there are people who are paid a small amount to sit on the bus pretending to be passengers in order to give the impression that it is fuller than it actually is to the potential passenger, who will then enter the dala-dala, assuming it will be leaving sooner than the next one along.

*The dala-dala network radiates from three main termini in the town centre, **Posta** at 'Minazi Mirefu' ('Tall palm trees") on the Kivukoni Front opposite the old Post Office; **Stesheni**, close to the Central Railway Station; and **Kariakoo**, around the Uhuru/Msimbazi Street roundabout for destinations south and at the central market for those in the north. From each of these you can catch dala-dalas to destinations throughout Dar es Salaam, although the four main routes are along Ali Hassan Mwinyi to Mwenge (for the Makumbusho Village Museum, Mwenge handicrafts market and the university); along the Kilwa Road to Temeke, Mtoni and Mbagala (these take you to the Salvation Army); to Vingunguti via Kariakoo and Ilala (for the Tazara Railway Station); and along the Morogoro Road to Magomeni, Manzese and Ubongo. For a dala-dala going to the airport ask for Uwanja wa Ndege at Minazi Miretu.*

Sea

See page 560 for Zanzibar ferry timetable

Boat All ticket offices of the ferry companies are on Sokoine Dr adjacent to the jetty. If you arrive with plenty of time to spare (and without touts following to claim credit and take commission) it may be possible to negotiate a fare. This is especially true if Zanzibar is your destination as there are several companies competing against each other, even though the tourist fare for the fast hydrofoil services is supposed to be fixed at US$35 one way (including port tax) for all companies. A good idea is to bargain for an open return ticket – one traveller reports that such a ticket was purchased for about US$45. *Sea Express*, T2137049, F2116723 (Zanzibar: T2233002), operate the *M/S Sepideh* ferry to Zanzibar. This departs Dar es Salaam daily at 0730 and arrives in Zanzibar at 0915, leaving Zanzibar for the return at 1615. On Mon, Wed, Fri and Sun the ferry continues from Zanzibar (departing at 1000) to Pemba where it arrives at 1200, beginning its return from Pemba at 1300. Dar es Salaam to Zanzibar US$30, to Pemba US$65. The cost of transporting a motorcycle to Zanzibar is US$20 plus US$5 charge for the porters to bring it on board. You will need to pay porters to take the bike off the boat in Zanzibar: negotiate a rate beforehand. The ferry *Azam Marine*, T2133013, T0741-334347 (mob) – Zanzibar: T2231655, T0741-334884 (mob) – takes 4 hrs to Zanzibar, costs US$10, departs 1600 daily, on return leaves Zanzibar at 1330. *Azam Marine* also operate Australian-built Seabus catamarans 4 times daily, giving a comfortable and fast service to Zanzibar. Similar services are offered by *Sea Express* (see above) and *Sea Star*, T2139996. *Flying Horse*, T2124504/7, outward journey to Zanzibar departs at 1300, return from Zanzibar departs 2200, takes 130 mins. For some this return journey is inconvenient as passengers are not let off at Dar es Salaam until 0600, the time when Customs open. However, tourists are accommodated in a comfortable, fully carpeted, a/c compartment, and provided with a mattress to sleep on until 0600. Thus it is a good option for budget travellers as the fare is only US$25 and the cost of accommodation for one night is saved. The *Muungano* is the slowest ferry at 4 hrs, US$10. *Zanzibar Sea Ferries* runs a daily ferry to Zanzibar, overnight, 3rd class only, as it is a cargo ship, takes 6 hrs, fare approximately US$6 plus US$5 port tax (which can be negotiated or avoided). *Tanzania Coastal Shipping Company*, PO Box 9461, T2110102, is a cargo service that takes some passengers and serves Tanga, Mombasa, Mafia, Kilwa, Lindi and Mtwara, sailings are irregular, slow and cheap. Mtwara costs US$5 and takes 36 hrs. **Dhows** are irregular, slow and cheap. A motorized dhow will take 12 hrs to Mafia, a sail-powered one up to 24 hrs, cost US$3 to US$6 – you sit or sleep on the cargo and need to take your own food. *Mega Speed Liners* travel to Zanzibar, Pemba and Mombasa, T2110807, T0741-326414 (mob). *Adecon Marine*, located at Sokoine Dr, go to Mafia and Mtwara. *Zanzibar Shipping Corp* travel to Mtwara, Zanzibar and Pemba, T2152870.

Directory

Airline offices

International: *Air France*, PO Box 2661, Upanga Rd, T2116443. *Air India*, PO Box 1709, Bibi Titi Mohamed St, opposite Peugeot House, T2117036. *Air Tanzania*, PO Box 543, ATC Bldg, Ohio St, T2110245-8, F2113114. *Alitalia*, PO Box 9281, AMI Bldg, Samora Av, T23621. *Alliance Air*, corner Bibi Titi Mohamed St and Maktaba St, PO Box 5182, T2117044-8, F2116715, alliance@raha.com *American Airlines*, NEDCO Bldg, Upanga Rd, opposite TDFC Bldg, T2119426/7. *British Airways*, PO Box 2439, based at the Royal Palm Hotel, Ohio St, T2113820-2, F2112629, britishairways@cats-net.com *Egypt Air*, PO Box 1350, Matsalamat Bldg, Samora Av, T2113333. *Emirates*, Haidery Plaza, A H Mwinyi Rd, T2116100-3, F2116273. *Ethiopian Airlines*, PO Box 3187, TDFL Bldg, Ohio St, T2117063-5, F2115875, ethiopiandar@cats-net.com *Gulf Air*, PO Box 9794, Raha Towers, Bibi Titi St/Maktaba St, T2110827, F2111304. *Kenya Airways*, PO Box 8342, Peugeot House, Upanga Rd, T2136826. *KLM*, PO Box 3804, Peugeot House, Upanga Rd, T2113336, F2116492, klmdaressalaam@intafrica.com *Lufthansa*, PO Box 1993, Upanga Rd, T2114461. *Pakistan International Airways*, PO Box 928, IPS Bldg, Samora Av, T2117061. *SAS*, Upanga Rd, PO Box 1114, T22015/22013. *Swiss Air*, PO Box 2109, Luther House, Sokoine Dr, T2118870-3, F2112808. *Yemenia Airways*, TDFL Bldg, Ohio St, PO Box 10761, T2126032, F2126072. *Zambia Airways*, PO Box 21276, IPS Bldg, Samora Av, T46662. *Air Zimbabwe* and *Air Mauritius*, c/o *Easy Travel*, PO Box 1428, Avalon House, 1st Floor, Zanaki St, T2123526, F2113842.

Domestic and charter: *Aviazur*, PO Box 72376, T/F2843075, T0742-321362 (mob), aviazur@africaonline.co.tz *Dar Air Charters*, PO Box 18104, Old Terminal 1, Nyerere Rd, T42332. *Dar Aviation*, c/o Coastal Travel, PO Box 3052, Upanga Rd, T2117957-9, coastal@twiga.com *General Aviation Services Ltd*, PO Box 18166, T2842080, T0742-786671 (mob), F2843313, gas@wilken-dsm.com *Nahalo Air Safaris*, T2843201/2, T0741-320812 (mob), F2844210. *Scan African Aviation Ltd*, PO Box 71919, T/F2667433, T0741-323168 (mob), scanafr@raha.com *Tanzanian Air Services*, PO Box 364, Azikiwe St, T2113151, F2113946, tanzanair@raha.com *Tanzanian Government Flight*, T2124895, F2124887, tgf@ud.com Two Zanzibar based companies with offices at Dar es Salaam airport are *Twin Wings Air Ltd*, T0741-334943 (mob) and *Zan Air Ltd*, T0741-605230 (mob).

Banks

Private sector banks are starting to open for business. *Standard Chartered* is located in the Plaza on Sokoine Dr close to the Askari Monument, and at International House on the corner of Garden Av and Shaaban Robert St. Standard Chartered is currently the only bank in the country that has ATMs that accept Visa cards. The machine at the Garden Av branch is inside the bank so can be used only during banking hours, whereas the Sokoine branch has 24-hr access, however the machines seem to be out of service fairly frequently. *Barclays* is in the TDFL Building, Ohio St, and the central branch of *CitiBank* is in Peugeot House, Upanga Rd. The state-owned banks are improving, but are still notoriously slow and

Tanzania

inefficient – it can take 2 hrs to cash a TC. There are branches of the *National Bank of Commerce* on Samora Av next to the *Twiga Hotel*; and on the corner of Sokoine Dr and Azikiwe St. Hours are 0830-1500 on weekdays and 0830-1130 on Sat.

Foreign Exchange Bureaux

These are to be found in almost every street in the city, and are especially common in the area between Samora Av and Jamhuri St. Hours are usually 0900-1700 Mon-Fri and 0900-1300 on Sat. *National Bureau de Change*, opposite the Extelecom Bldg on Samora Av, offer very favourable rates. 24-hr bureaux are at the airport terminal along Nyerere Rd and in the foyer of the *Kilimanjaro Hotel*. Although these bureaux offer convenience, they offer an unfavourable rate. Rates vary between bureaux and it is worth shopping around. Some hotels, *Starlight* is an example, offer extremely unfavourable rates. *Coastal Travel*, Upanga Rd, offer cash in advance on credit cards at reasonable rates. **American Express**: *Rickshaw Travel*, PO Box 1889, on Upanga Rd, opposite the *Sheraton Hotel*, will issue TCs to card-holders. Western Union money transfer is available at the Tanzanian Postal Bank, on Samora Av, and at the General Post Office on Azikiwe St.

Communications

Internet The cost of access has fallen considerably over the last few years, available for less than US$1 per hour although usually slow and erratic; use of more modern equipment is likely to cost US$1.25-1.50. Try next door to the Zanzibar GH in Zanaki St. Cheap rates with efficient, quiet, friendly staff. Open Mon to Sat 0830-2200. The office has 3 modern machines. *The Internet Café*, near the *Hard Rock Café*. *RCL Internet Café*, PO Box 14324, corner of Zanaki St and Kisutu St, opposite *Buy Best Cash & Carry* supermarket, T2139818, T0741-608937 (mob), F2113862, rcl@rcl.co.tz, open Mon-Sat 0830-2200, Sun 1000-1400 and 1700-2200. Internet access, send and receive emails/faxes. *The Workstation*, Lehmanns Building, at the corner of Samora Av and Mission St, T2114841, internet, email and fax services. *ICS Cobitt*, top floor of Vijana Building, Morogoro Rd, T2152768, F2112752, ics-cobitt.com There are lots of cyber cafés springing up in Jamhuri St offering fast and cheap communication home. *Cyberspot* recommended, T2121425, T0742-785937 (mob), info@cyberspot.co.tz

Post Main post office on Azikiwe St. Other offices on Sokoine Dr, near Cenotaph; behind the bus stand on Morogoro Rd; and Libya St. Post offices are generally crowded. **Courier services**: *DHL* at 12B Nyerere Rd, T2861000/4, T0742-781153 (mob).

Telephone Service on local calls can be variable. The Dar es Salaam exchange is being upgraded, and whole areas of town can be impossible to reach. There are now many private telephone/fax offices all over town where you can make and receive phone calls and faxes. International outgoing calls can be much easier. Hotels will usually charge up to 3 times the actual cost.

Embassies (E), High Commissions (HC) & Consulates (C)

You can usually be sure that diplomatic missions will be open in the mornings between 0900 and 1200. Some have afternoon opening, and some do not open every day. Even when a mission is officially closed, the staff will usually be helpful if something has to be done in an emergency. *Algeria (E)*, PO Box 2963, 34 A H Mwinyi Rd, T2117619, F2117620, algemb@entafrica.com, 0800-1400. *Angola (E)*, PO Box 20793, 78 Lugalo Rd, T2117673/4, 0800-1500. *Australia (HC)*, PO Box 2996, NIC Investment House, Samora Av, T20244/6. *Austria (C)*, PO Box 312, Samora Av, T2112900, 0900-1200. *Belgium (E)*, PO Box 9210, 5 Ocean Rd, T2112688, F2117621, 0800-1400. *Burundi (E)*, PO Box 2752, 1007 Lugalo Rd, T2113710, F2121499. *Canada (HC)*, PO Box 1022, 38 Mirambo St, Garden Av, T2112831-5, F2116896/7, dslam@dfait-maeci.gc.ca, 0715-1515. *Denmark (E)*, PO Box 9171, Ghana Av, T2113887-8, F2116433. *Egypt (E)*, PO Box 1668, 24 Garden Av, T2113591, F2112543. 0830-1430. *France (E)*, PO Box 2349, Ali Hassan Mwinyi Rd, T2666021-3, F2668435. *Germany (E)*, PO Box 9541, NIC Investment House, 10th Flr, Samora Av, T2117409-15, F2112944, german.emb.dar@raha.com, 0700-1545. *Ireland (E)*, PO Box 9612, 1131 Msasani Rd, T2602355, F2602361, iremb@raha.com *Italy (E)*, PO Box 2106, 316 Lugalo Rd, T2115935/6, F2115938, 0800-1430 (1530-1830 Wed). *Japan (E)*, PO Box 2577, 1018 A H Mwinyi Rd, T2115827/9, F2115830, 0830-1500. *Kenya (HC)*, PO Box 5231, NIC Investment House, 14th Flr, Samora Av, T2112955, F2113098, khc@raha.com, 0800-1500. *Madagascar (E)*, PO Box 5254, Malik Rd, T29442. *Malawi (HC)*, PO Box 7616, NIC Life House, Samora Av, T2113238-41, F2113360, 0800-1200 and 1400-1700. *Mozambique (E)*, PO Box 9370, 25 Garden Av, T/F2116502, 0830-1630. *Netherlands (E)*, PO Box 9634, ATC Bldg, Ohio St, 2nd Flr, T2130428, F2112828, nlgovdar@intafrica.com, 0700-1530. *Nigeria (HC)*, PO Box 9214, 83 Haile Selassie Rd, T2667620, F2668947, 0800-1500. *Norway (E)*, PO Box 2646, Mirambo St/Garden Av, T2113366, F2116564, norw/embassy@twiga.com, 0730-1430. *RD Congo (E)*, PO Box 975, 438 Malik St, Upanga, T2150282, 0800-1500. *Rwanda (E)*, PO Box 2918, 32 A H Mwinyi Rd, T2130119, F2115888, 0800-1530. *Saudi Arabia (E)*, PO Box 238, 61 Kimweri Rd, Oyster Bay, T2668203, F2668362. *South Africa (HC)*, PO Box 10723, 1338 Mwaya Rd, Oyster Bay, T2601800, F2600618, 0730-1530. *Spain (E)*, PO Box 842,

99B Kinondoni Rd, T2666936, F2666938, 0830-1430. *Embassy of Sudan*, PO Box 2266, 64 A H Mwinyi Rd, T/F2117641, 0830-1530. *Sweden (E)*, PO Box 9274, Mirambo St/Garden Av, T2111235, F2111340, www.interafrica.com, 0715-1500. *Switzerland (E)*, PO Box 2454, 79 Kinondoni Rd, T2666008/9, F2666736, 0800-1200. *Uganda (HC)*, PO Box 2525, Extelcom Bldg, 7th Flr, Samora Av, T2117646/7, F2112974, 0830-1600. *UK (HC)*, PO Box 9200, Bank House, Samora Av, T2112953, F2116703, bhc.dar@raha.com, 0730-1430. *USA (E)*, PO Box 9123, located at 140 Msese Rd, off Kinondoni Rd, Dar es Salaam, T2666010/5, F2666701, usembassy-dar1@cats-net.com, 0730-1600. *Yemen (E)*, PO Box 4646, 135 United Nations Rd, T2117650, F2115924. *Zambia (HC)*, PO Box 2525, Ohio St/Sokoine Dr, T2116811, F2112974 0800-1200 and 1400-1630. *Zimbabwe*, PO Box 20762, NIC Life House, 6th Flr, Sokoine Dr, T2116789, F2112913, 0830-1300 and 1400-1600.

European Union, 38 Mirambo St, PO Box 9514, T2117473-6, F2113277, eudeltza@twiga.com *Food and Agriculture Organisation*, Tetex building, Pamba Rd, PO Box 2, T2113070-4, F2112401, FAOTZA@FIELD.fao.org *International Labour Organisation*, 40 A H Mwinyi Rd, PO Box 40, T2666029, F2666002-4, ilo-tz@twiga.com, daressalaam@ilo.org *International Monetary Fund*, Sukari House, Ohio St/Sokoine Dr, PO Box 72598, T2112383. *United Nations Development Programme*, Matasalamat Mansion, Zanzki St/Samora Av, PO Box 9182, T2112799, F2113272. *United Nations Education Scientific and Cultural Organisation*, Comtech Bldg, Old Bagamoyo Rd, T2775706, F2775705. *United Nations Fund for Population Activities*, 40 A H Mwinyi Rd, T2666142-5, F2666152, unfpa@raha.com *United Nations High Commission for Refugees*, 18 Kalenga Rd, near MMC, PO Box 2666, T2150075, F2152817. *United Nations Children's Fund (UNICEF)*, Bibi Titi Rd, near the junction with Upanga Rd, PO Box 4076, T2150811-5, F2151593, dar-es-salaam@unicef.org *UNIDO*, Matasalamat Mansion, Zanaki St/Samora Av, PO Box 9182, T2112527, F2118114, felix.ugbor@undp.org *USAID*, 50 Miramo St, PO Box 9130, T2117537, F2116559. *World Bank*, 50 Mirambo St, PO Box 2054, T2114575, F2113039. *World Food Programme*, 82 Kinondoni Rd, PO Box 77778, T2666700, F2667502, wfp.dar@wfp.org.ug *World Health Organisation*, next to Government Chief Chemist, Luthuli Rd, PO Box 9292, T2113005, F2113180, who.tanzania@undp.org, who.tz@twiga.com

International institutions

Alliance Française, behind *Las Vegas Casino*, T2119415, library facilities, French TV news, open Mon-Fri, 1000-1800. The *British Council*, PO Box 9100, on the corner of Ohia St and Samora Av, T2116574-6, F2112669. Has an excellent library, with reference, lending, newspapers and magazines. It is well worth joining the lending section if you are in Dar es Salaam for any length of time. The *US Information Service*, Lufthansa Bldg, at the junction of Bibi Titi Mohammed Rd and Upanga Rd, has good reference facilities, open 1000-1600. *National Central Library* is on Bibi Titi Mohammed Rd near the Maktaba St intersection, T2150048/9. The library at the University of Dar es Salaam currently charges US$50 to use it, even for reference purposes.

Libraries

Hospitals: the main hospital is *Muhimbili Hospital* located off United Nations Rd, northwest of the centre towards Msimbazi Creek, T2150939-46. *Oyster Bay Hospital* is an efficient and accessible small private medical centre (follow the signs along Haile Selassie Rd), T2600015/2600929. *Kilimanjaro Hotel* will recommend a physician in an emergency. The *Aga Khan Hospital* is located on Ocean Rd at the junction with Ufukoni Rd, T2114096/2115151-3. *Ocean Road Hospital* is on Ocean Rd at junction with Chimara Rd. All these hospitals are well equipped and staffed. The *Zenco Clinic*, Samora Av, close to the *Salamander Restaurant* is very good and central, fees US$1 for a consultation, US$1 for a malaria test, which takes about 20 mins. **The Flying Doctors:** Nairobi (emergency), T02-501280, Tanzania office for information on membership, T2116610. **Pharmacies:** are located in all shopping centres. Small **dispensaries** are located in the main residential areas.

Medical services

Churches: *Roman Catholic cathedral* is on Sokoine Dr opposite the Customs jetty. *Lutheran church* is at the junction of Kivukoni Front and Sokoine Dr. *St Alban's Church*, the Anglican church, is situated at junction of Maktaba St and Upanga Rd. *Greek church* is on Upanga Rd. **Mosques:** are located on Zanaki St; there are 3 on Mosque St (one is Ismaili); 2 on Bibi Titi Mohamed St at the Nyerere Rd end; on Bibi Titi Mohamed St near Morogoro Rd; on Kitumbini St; on Ghandi St; on Upanga Rd (Ismaili); off Chole Rd on Msasani Peninsula. **Temples:** there are 2 on Kisuki St, which runs off India St near the Mawenzi roundabout on Maktaba St.

Places of worship

Police: main police station is on Gerazani St near the railway station, T2115507. Also stations on Upanga Rd on the city side of Selander Bridge, T2120818; on Ali Hassan Mwinyi Rd at the junction with Old Bagamoyo Rd (Oyster Bay), T2667322/3.

Useful addresses

Tanzania

Tanzania

Excursions from Dar es Salaam

Makumbusho Village Museum The museum gives a compact view of the main traditional dwelling styles of Tanzania, with examples of artists and craftsmen at work. On Saturday and Sunday afternoons, traditional dancers perform to the accompaniment of drum music.

There are constructions from 13 groups with examples of furnished dwelling huts, cattle pens, meeting huts and, in one case, an iron-smelting kiln. Among the artists and craftsmen resident is Issa Bahari, a Swahili from the coastal area who makes ebony signs (US$7.50), which are better value than in town. Issa will also carve a sign to your individual design. Allow three days for completion.

In one of the rooms of the Swahili banda is Helman Msole, a Fiba from southwest Tanzania whose striking paintings on canvas of village and historical scenes can be bought for US$40-80. Hand-painted postcards are US$2.50. Helman will paint a canvas from his collection (recorded in photographs) in two days. Blassy Kisanga, a Chagga from Kilimangaro, depicts scenes with brown and black banana leaves on wooden panels (US$12.50-40) and postcards (US$1.50). Petre Paulo Mayige, from Tabora, makes clay figures of village scenes and *bao* games for US$7.50-40. Finally, Nyram Hsagula, a Swahili, creates rather garish *tinga tinga* paintings on hardboard, as decorations on tins and bowls (US$2-25). Their works of art are very much a matter of taste – the clay figures and the paintings of Helman Msole are not readily available elsewhere, and most visitors regard these as unusually good.

On Saturday and Sunday, from 1600 to 1800, there are performances from a dance troupe recruited from all over Tanzania. The visitor would benefit from guidance on the origin of the dances, which end with a display of tumbling and acrobatics that is popular with children. There is a café, and an unusual compound, the Makumbusho Social Club, to which the public is welcome, with its small, corrugated-iron, partly open-sided huts, each named after one of Tanzania's game parks. ■ *0930-1800 daily. US$1, Tanzanians and all children free. Still photos US$2.50, video or cine US$10, T700437, village@natmus.or.tz Situated along Bagamoyo Rd, about 9 km from the city centre, on the right-hand side of the road. There is a large sign indicating the entrance. It can be reached by taxi – about TSh 3,500 (US$4) – and it is advisable to ask the taxi to wait for you to return. A dala-dala, destination Mwenge, can be taken from Maktaba St, just opposite the post office, for TSh 150 (US$0.10) and there are frequent returning dala-dala on this route.*

Northern beaches The shore close to Dar es Salaam is not particularly good for swimming. The best beaches are at **Kunduchi**, some 25 km north of the city. A bus leaves from outside the *New Africa Hotel* in the city centre in the mornings and afternoons, and returns in the evening. *Silver Sands Hotel* and *Rungwe Oceanic Hotel* have fairly simple facilities. *Kunduchi Beach Hotel* has an excellent beach, a swimming pool, and offers a variety of excursions to nearby islands and windsurfing. Snorkelling is variable as sometimes the water is not clear, especially during the rainy seasons. *Bahari Beach Hotel* is strikingly constructed from coral with thatched roofing for the main buildings and groups of rooms in similar style, and also has bands on Sunday and public holidays. These hotels make a charge for using their beaches for the day, around US$5-8.

There is a good beach on the uninhabited **Bongoyo Island**, 2 km north of Msasani Peninsula. The island is a Marine Reserve and on it are a few short walking trails, simple seafood meals are also available. A popular destination for a day trip from Dar es Salaam, boats leave from *The Slipway* on Msasani Peninsula at 0930, 1130, 1330 and 1530, each time returning approximately one hour later. A similarly good beach, but no facilities, are to be found on **Mbudya Island**, 4 km north of Bongoyo Island. Boat rides are available from *White Sands Hotel* and *Bahari Beach Hotel*.

Kigamboni The ferry leaves from the harbour mouth, close to the fish market, where Kivukoni Front becomes Ocean Road, at regular intervals during the day, crossing the mouth of the harbour to Kigamboni. The ferry takes vehicles, and this is the best way to reach this area as the approach from the land side circling the harbour inlet is a journey of about 40 km over poor roads. Kigamboni is the site of Kivukoni College, which provided training for CCM party members, but is now being turned into a school and a social science academy. Just before the college, which faces across the harbour to Kivukoni Front, is the Anglican church and a free-standing bell. The Anglican church was formerly a Lutheran church. The Lutheran church, a fine modern building, lies 500 m into Kigamboni. On the Indian Ocean shore side can be seen several small enterprises making lime by burning cairns of coral. The beaches on Kigamboni are the best close to the city, but they have not been developed as the ferry has been out of commission for lengthy periods in the past. A couple of unserviceable ferries can be seen beached on the main harbour shore.

Southern beaches

To the south of Kigamboni there are some very good beaches. To reach the nearest one, catch the ferry from the end of the Kivukoni Front, then it's a 30-minute walk along the coast (do not do this on your own as there are thieves here) or a short taxi ride. The second beach, which is the best one, is 8 km further and requires a car. Carry on directly south and branch off to the left. It is possible to get back to Dar via Mbagala and the Kilwa Road.

Gezauole

A full day at the village, including meals and activities, would cost about US$25

The coastal village of Gezaulole lies 13 km southeast of the ferry at Kigamboni, reachable by *dala dala* or bicycle taxi. This was chosen as one of the first Ujamaa villages, part of an ultimately unsuccessful settlement policy of the early 1970s, in which people from many areas of the country were relocated to form agricultural communes (see page 585). Today the community has an active role in a cultural tourism programme that offers walks through the village and on the beach, short trips on a local dhow, and visits to an old slave depot and a 400-year-old mosque. It is possible to stay with a local family or camp near the beach. Inexpensive and tasty local meals are available and can be taken with one of the families even if you are not staying for the night. Locally made handicrafts are also for sale.

Kisarawe

Colour map 4, grid B5

In the peaceful rural hill town of Kisarawe it is hard to believe that you are just 32 km southwest from the hustle and bustle of Dar es Salaam. During the colonial period Kisarawe was used by European residents of the capital as a kind of hill station to escape from the coastal heat. There is little to see in the town itself but the surrounding countryside is very attractive, in particular the nearby rainforest. Kisarawe can be visited on a day trip from Dar es Salaam. However, the best time for visiting the forest is early or late in the day so you may end up staying overnight. If so, *Zimbabwe Bar & Guest House* is cheap and basic, but it's reasonably clean and anyway you don't have much choice! The *Kigoma Restaurant* serves *ugali* and stew, which is filling and couldn't really be bettered at US$0.75. ■ *Buses to Kisarawe leave from Narungumbe St (next to the Tanzania Postal Bank on Msimbazi St in Kariakoo) about once an hour. The trip takes one hour (plus a further 45 mins or so waiting for the bus to fill up!) and costs US$0.75.*

Pugu Hills Forest Reserve

This reserve is situated about 3-4 km from the centre of Kisarawe town. It constitutes one of the few remaining parts of a coastal forest, which 10,000,000 years ago extended from Mozambique to northern Kenya. It was gazetted as a reserve in 1954, at which time it stretched all the way to the International airport in Dar es Salaam, and was home to many big game animals, including lions, hippos and elephants. Since then the natural growth of the metropolis, as well as the urban demand for charcoal (coupled with the lack of alternative sources of income), has seen a large reduction in the forested area. In the past few years a concerted effort has been made to counter this process and a nature trail has been established in order to encourage people to visit the area. You are unlikely to come across many animals in the forest but it is a very beautiful spot and the perfect tonic for those in need of a break from Dar es Salaam. Pugu Reserve contains flora and fauna which are unique to the forests of this district.

Tanzania

Enquiries about the reserve can be made at the Forest Reserve Office in Kisarawe town. There is no charge at present, but this is likely to change in the near future.

Pugu Kaolin A further 3-4 km on from the Pugu Hills reserve is Pugu kaolin mine, which was
Mine & the established by the Germans in the early 1900s. Kaolin is a type of fine white clay that
Bat Caves is used in the manufacture of porcelain, paper and textiles. The deposits here at Pugu are reputed to be the second largest in the world and should the market for it pick up, the mining of kaolin will clearly constitute a further threat to the survival of the remaining rainforest.

If you continue through the mine compound you come to a disused railway tunnel, 100 m long and German built (the railway was re-routed after the discovery of kaolin). On the other side of this are a series of man-made caves housing a huge colony of bats. At around 1800 or 1900 (depending on the time of year) the bats begin to fly out of the caves for feeding. It is a remarkable experience to stand in the mouth of the caves surrounded by the patter of wings as vast numbers of bats come streaming past you. To do this, however, you must be prepared to walk the 7-8 km back to Kisarawe in the dark, so take a torch.

Dar es Salaam

North Coast:
Bagamoyo and Tanga

Bagamoyo is one of the most fascinating towns in East Africa, with a host of historical associations. Access is only really feasible by road, and although a new surface is being laid, the major part is still very rough. It is quite possible to make a day trip from Dar es Salaam, although an overnight stay is perhaps best. Tanga was an important port in the period up to independence when sisal was Tanzania's main crop, and the main growing area was between Kilimanjaro and the coast. The Usambara Hills are a very attractive detour, and Lushoto and Amani can be visited either on the way to Tanga, or when travelling to Kilimanjaro and Arusha.

Bagamoyo

Ins & outs   **Getting there**   About 70 km north of Dar es Salaam by road, the only feasible way of getting to Bagamayo at present. There are plans for a boat from Dar es Salaam that will avoid the use of the poor road. There is sometimes a weekend shuttle boat from Dar es Salaam – check at the Msasani slipway. **Getting around**   There is not a single taxi at present but all destinations in Bagamoyo are within walking distance. It is a good idea to hire someone (US$0.50) to carry any bags and being with a local person provides security. There are signs warning of muggers, but local residents suggest this is to boost the guide business. It is as well to be careful, however.

History

6°20'S 38°30'E   The coastal area opposite Zanzibar was first settled by fishermen and cultivators.
Phone code: 023   Towards the end of the 18th century, 12 or so Muslim diwans arrived to settle, build
Colour map 4, grid B5   dwellings and establish their families and retinues of slaves. These diwans were all related to Shomvi la Magimba from Oman. They prospered through levying taxes whenever a cow was slaughtered, or a shark or other large fish caught, as well as on all salt produced at Nunge, about 3 km north of Bagamoyo.

The town was threatened by the Kamba around 1800, and an uneasy alliance of the Shomvi, the Zaramo and the Doe was formed to hold them off. In return for their support against the Kamba, the Shomvi agreed to pay a tribute to the Zaramo of a third of the revenues from their commercial activities, mostly the sale of slaves and ivory. In 1868, the diwans granted land to the Holy Ghost Fathers to establish a mission. The Zaramo challenged the right of the diwans to make this concession but, following intervention by the French consul, Zanzibar (first under Sultan Majid, then, after 1870, under Sultan Barghash) put pressure on the Zaramo to accept the settlement.

Bagamoyo's location as a mainland port close to Zanzibar led to its development as a centre for caravans and an expansion of commerce in slaves and ivory soon followed. There was also growing trade in sun-dried fish, gum copal and the salt from Nunge. Copra (from coconuts) was also important, and was used to make soap. A boat-building centre was established, which supplied craft to other coastal settlements.

In 1880 the population of the town was around 5,000 but this was augmented by a substantial transient population in residence after completing a caravan or undertaking preparations prior to departure. The numbers of those temporarily in town could be considerable. In 1889, after the slave trade had been suppressed, reducing the numbers passing through significantly, it was still recorded that 1,305 caravans left for the interior, involving 41,144 people.

The social composition of the town was varied. There were the initial Muslim Shomvi and the local Zaramo and Doe. Among the earliest arrivals were Hindus from India, involving themselves in administration, coconut plantations and boat-building. Muslim Baluchis, a people based in Mombasa and Zanzibar, and following for the most part the profession of mercenary soldiers, also settled and were involved in trade, financing caravans and land-owning. Other Muslim sects were represented, among them the Ismailis who settled in 1840 and by 1870 numbered 137. A handful of Sunni Muslims from Zanzibar established shops in Bagamoyo, some Parsees set up as merchants, and a small group of Catholic Goans was engaged in tailoring and retailing.

North Coast

Caravans from the interior brought with them Nyamwezi, Sukuma and Manyema porters. They might remain in town for six months or so before joining an outgoing caravan, and they resided for the most part in an insalubrious shanty settlement known as *Kampi Mbaya* ('bad camp'), which was just off the main caravan route out of town close to the Caravanserai. Some remained to take up life as fishermen or working the Nunge salt deposits.

In 1888 the German East Africa Company signed a treaty with the Sultan of Zanzibar, Seyyid Khalifa, which allowed the company to collect customs duties along the coast. The Germans rapidly made their presence felt by ordering the Sultan's representative (the Liwali) to lower the Sultan's flag and, on being refused, axed down the flag-pole.

Later in the year a dispute between a member of the company and a townsman culminated in the latter being shot. The Usagara trading house of the

Tanzania

☞ **Mangroves**

Up and down the coast of East Africa you will come across stretches of mangrove forests. Ecologically these can be described as evergreen saline swamp forests and their main constituents are the mangroves Rhizophora, Ceriops and Bruguiera. These are all described as viviparous, that is the seeds germinate or sprout when the fruits are still attached to the parent plant. Mangrove forests support a wide range of other plants and animals including a huge range of birds, insects and fish.

Economically mangrove forests are an important source of building poles, known on the coast as boriti, which were once exported in large quantities to the Arabian Gulf. Their main property is that they are resistant to termite attack. Mangrove bark is also used as a tanning material and charcoal can be obtained from mangrove wood. As with so many natural resources in East Africa care needs to be taken in the use of mangrove forests. Their over-exploitation could lead to the delicate balance that is found in the forests being upset, with serious consequences for these coastal regions.

company was beseiged by irate townspeople, 200 troops landed from the *SS Moewe*, and over 100 local people were killed.

Further resentment was incurred when the Germans set about registering land and property, demanding proof of ownership. As this was impossible for most residents there was widespread fear that property would be confiscated.

One of the diwans, Bomboma, organized local support. They enlisted the help of Bushiri bin Salim al-Harthi who had earlier led Arabs against the Germans in Tabora. Bushiri had initial success. Sections of Bagamoyo were burned and Bushiri formed up in Nzole about 6 km southwest of the town ready for an assault. The German government now felt compelled to help the company and Hermann von Wissmann was appointed to lead an infantry force comprising Sundanese and Zulu troops. Admiral Denhardt, commanding the German naval forces, played for time by initiating negotiations with Bushiri whose demands included being made governor of the region from Dar es Salaam up to Pangani, payment of 4,000 rupees (about US$10,000 in present-day values) a month, and the right to keep troops.

By May 1889 Wissmann had consolidated his forces and built a series of fortified block houses. He attacked Nzole and Bushiri fled. The alliance of the diwans and Bushiri weakened, and in June the Germans retook Saadani and in July, Pangani. Bushiri was captured and executed at Pangani in December. Bomboma, and another of the diwans leading the resistance, Marera, were both executed, and other diwans were deposed and replaced by collaborators who had assisted the Germans.

It was now clear that the German government intended to extend their presence and, in October 1890, rights to the coast were formally purchased from the Sultan of Zanzibar for 4,000,000 German marks.

In early 1891 German East Africa became a formal colony, but in April it was decided to establish Dar es Salaam as the capital. Commercial activity in Bagamoyo revived, and in the last decade of the century rebuilding began with the construction of new stone buildings including a customs house and the Boma, which served as an administrative centre.

The caravan trade resumed and there was a further influx of Indians together with the arrival of Greeks who established a European hotel. Wm O'Swald, the Hamburg trading company, arrived and Hansing established vanilla plantations at Kitopeni and Hurgira. An important Koran school was established in the town.

Despite these developments Bagamoyo was destined for steady decline as its harbour was unsuitable for deep draught steamships and no branch of the railway was built to serve the port. The ending of the German rule further reduced commercial presence in the town, and the last century saw Bagamoyo decline steadily, lacking even a sealed road to link it to Dar es Salaam.

Sights

At the south approach to the town, on the road from Kaole, is the **Old Fort** (sometimes referred to as the Old Prison). It is the oldest surviving building in Bagamoyo having been started by Abdallah Marhabi around 1860, and extended and strengthened by Sultan Baghash after 1870, and then by the German colonialists. It was used as a police post until 1992. Initially one of its functions was to hold slaves until they could be shipped to Zanzibar. It is said there is an underground passage through which the slaves were herded to dhows on the shore, although this passage is not apparent today. The Old Fort is currently being restored and the plan is that it will provide teaching rooms for the nearby **Chuo cha Sanaa** (Art College). The caretaker will allow you to look round, and it is clear that the work will result in a particularly handsome building. The construction is whitewashed, three storeys high, with buttresses and battlements and an enclosed courtyard.

On the path to *Badeco Beach Hotel*, off to the right is the **German cemetery** with some 20 graves dating from 1889/90, and most are of Germans killed during the uprising led by Bushiri in those years (see page 370). A German deed of freedom for a slave is reproduced on a tree. The cemetery is well tended, surrounded by a coral wall. In the ground of the *Badeco Beach Hotel* is the site of the tree reputedly used by the German administration for executions. The site is marked by a plaque.

Continuing along India Street on the left is an old two-storey building, **Liku House**, with an awning supported by slender iron columns and a central double door. This served as the first administrative headquarters for the Germans from 1888 until the Boma was completed in 1897. Emin Pasha stayed there in 1889.

The **Boma** is an impressive two-storey building topped by crenellations, constructed in a U-shape. There are pointed arches on the first floor and rounded arches on the ground floor. This was the German administrative centre from 1897, and it currently serves as the headquarters for the district commissioner. The building is undergoing some restoration, and it is possible to look round. On the inland side of the building is a well constructed by Sewa Haji.

On the shore side is a semi-circular levelled area on which was a monument with brass commemorative plaques erected by the Germans. With the fall of Bagamoyo to the British, the monument was razed and replaced with the present construction which commemorates the departure of Burton and Speke to Lake Tanganyika from nearby Kaole in 1857. The old German plaques have been reset in the walls which support the levelled area, on the shore side. To the left is an Arabic two-storey building fronted by six columns, a fretted verandah and curved arch windows, said to be the **Old Bagamoyo Tea House,** and thought to be one of the oldest buildings in the town, constructed by Abdallah Marhabi in 1860. In front of the Boma is the **Uhuru Monument**, celebrating Tanzania's independence in 1961, and a bandstand.

Continuing north along India Street there is a particularly fine residential house on the right with columns and arched windows just before Customs Road. This leads down to the **Customs House**, built in 1895 by Sewa Haji and rented to the Germans. It is a double-storey building with an open verandah on the first floor, buttresses, arched windows, and lime-washed. It looks on to a walled courtyard and is currently undergoing restoration. Opposite the Customs House are the ruins of the **Usagara Company Store** built in 1888 with the arrival of the German commercial presence. The unusual construction had stone plinths on which were mounted cast-iron supports for the timber floor, raised to keep the stores dry. The cast-iron supports have cups surrounding them in which kerosene was poured to prevent rats climbing up to eat the stored grain. At one end of the building is a tower, held up by a tree growing through it.

Halfway down Customs Road is the covered **Fish Market** with stone tables for gutting fish. When not used for this purpose they are marked out with chalk draughtsboards for informal games with bottle-tops. At the top of Customs Road, just before the intersection with India Street is the **Post Office**, with a fine carved door and a blue-painted upstairs verandah. Further north along India Street are a series of Arabic buildings, one of which, the first on the right after the square to the left, is being restored as a hotel.

Continuing north, on the right, is the **Jama'at Khana**, the Ismaili mosque, which dates from 1880, double-storeyed with a verandah and carved doors. On the right beyond the mosque is the hospital, now part of Muhimbili Teaching Hospital in Dar es Salaam, which is based on the original Sewa Haji Hospital, constructed in 1895. On the death of Sewa Haji in 1896, the hospital was run by the Holy Ghost Mission, and then from 1912 by the Germans. The present hospital has some handsome old buildings and some more modern blocks. It has a rather charming air, with goats lolling on the covered walkways between the wards.

At the northern end of the town on the right is a substantial **Mosque** and Muslim school with curved steps up to the carved door over which is a delicate fretted grill. The building is fronted by six columns and there is a verandah to the rear.

Other buildings of interest in Bagamoyo Town include the **Sewa Jhaji School**, a three-storey construction with filigree ironwork, dating from 1896.

Close to the intersection of Sunda Road and Mongesani Street at the western approach to the town is the white **Block House**, constructed in 1889 by Hermann Wissman during the Bushiri uprising (see page 370). There is a mangrove pole and coral stone roof and an outside ladder, which enabled troops to man the roof behind the battlements. The walls have loopholes through which troops could fire, standing on low internal walls, which doubled as seating, to give them the height to fire down on their adversaries. Behind the Block House is a disused well.

The **slave track** to the interior departed from this point – a 1,500 km trail that terminated at Ujiji on Lake Tanganyika. Off Caravan Street is the **Caravanserai**, a courtyard with single-storey buildings at the front and a square, two-storey building with a verandah at the centre (the corner of which is collapsing). It was here that preparations were made for the fitting out of caravans to the interior.

Chuo cha Sanaa

Chuo cha Sanaa is a school for the arts where music, drama, dance and painting are taught. Most students are Tanzanian, but there are several from Europe, America and the Far East. The main buildings are located along the road to Kaole to the south of Bagamoyo. They are a mixture of a Viking house and a traditional African home, recently constructed, with help from a Swedish Aid Project, and are very impressive. The main building has a Greek-style open amphitheatre, with proscenium stage covered by a 15-m high thatched canopy. The amphitheatre stage backs on to a second theatre area, which is roofed and enclosed. Attached to the stage are workshops and offices. Students can be observed in the area round the dormitories practising their skills. Visitors are welcome to observe the training.

Livingstone's Church

This is a simple construction with a tin roof, curved arch windows and wooden benches. Its formal name is the Anglican Church of the Holy Cross. Above the entrance is the sign 'Through this door Dr David Livingstone passed', referring to the fact that his body was kept in the church prior to it being returned to England.

Cross by the Sea

A monument in green marble surmounted by a cross is located on the path leading to the sea from Livingstone's Church. It marks the spot where, in 1868, Father Antoine Horner of the French Holy Ghost Fathers crossed from Zanzibar (where they had operated a mission since 1860) and stepped ashore to establish the first Christian church on the mainland.

Holy Ghost Mission

Opposite the path to the Cross by the Sea is **Mango Tree Drive**, which was established in 1871 as the approach to the Mission. A statue of the Sacred Heart, erected in 1887, stands in front of the **Fathers' House**, a three-storey stucture with an awning over a verandah on the top floor and arches on the other two floors. It was begun in 1873 and the third storey finally added in 1903. In 1969 the building was taken over by MANTEP as a training centre for educational management.

Behind the Fathers' House is the **First Church**, construction of which started in 1872. It comprises a stone tower topped with arches with a cross at the centre and crosses on the pediments at each corner. The main building is a simple rectangular structure with a tin roof, unusually situated behind and to the side of the tower so that the tower sits at one corner.

It was to here on 24 February 1874 that the body of David Livingstone was brought by the missionary's African followers, Sisi and Chuma, who had carried their master 1,500 km from Ujiji. Speke, Burton, Grant, Stanley, Peters, Emin Pasha and Wissmann all visited the church at one time or another.

Following the path to the right of the First Church is a cemetery where the early missionaries are buried. Further down this path is a small shrine built by freed slaves in 1876 with the sign 'Salamnus Maria' picked out in flowers. A great baobab tree, planted in 1868, stands to the side of the the First Church. At the base can be seen the links of the chain where Mme de Chevalier, a mission nurse, tethered her donkey.

The **New Church**, constructed of coral blocks, begun in 1910 and completed in 1914, stands in front of the First Church. A small iron cross commemorates the centenary, in 1968, of the Holy Ghost Mission in Bagamoyo.

The **Mission Museum** is housed in the **Sisters' Building**. The displays present a history of Bagamoyo and there are relics and photographs from the slave period. One intriguing exhibit is the uniform presented by HA Schmit in 1965, that he wore during the East African Campaign under von Lettow (see page 581). Adjacent to the museum is a craft workshop with *Ufundi* ('craftsmen') picked out in flowers.

One of the main activities of the Holy Ghost Mission was to purchase slaves and present them with their freedom. A certificate of freedom was provided by the German authorities. These freed slaves had originally been captured hundreds of kilometres away in the hinterland, and the Mission undertook to rehabilitate them in **Freedom Village** located just to the north of the main Mission buildings.

Kaole Ruins

Colour map 4, grid B5

It is quite possible to walk to the ruins, but it's a good idea to take a guide for security. At present there are no taxis in Bagamoyo

The Kaole Ruins are located 5 km south of Bagamoyo, along the road past Chuo Cha Sanaa (Bagamoyo Art College). The ruins are on the coastal side of the present-day village of Kaole. The site consists of the ruins of two mosques and a series of about 30 tombs, set among palm trees. Some of the tombs have stone pillars up to 5 m in height. The older of the two mosques ('A' on the site plan) dates from some time between the 3rd and 4th centuries AD and is thought to mark one of the earliest contacts of Islam with Africa, before the main settlement took place. The remains of a vaulted roof constructed from coral with lime mortar can be seen, which formed the *mbirika* at the entrance. Here ceremonial ablutions took place, taking water from the nearby well. There is some buttressing with steps that allowed the muezzin access to the roof to call the faithful to prayer. The recess (*kibula*) on the east side, nearest to Mecca, has faint traces of an inscription on the vaulting.

The stone pillars that mark some of the tombs were each surmounted by a stone 'turban' and the remains of some of these can be seen on the ground. Delicate porcelain bowls with light green glaze were set in the side of the pillars and the indentations can be seen. The bowls, identified as celadon made in China in the 14th century and the main indication of the likely age of the structure, have been removed for safekeeping to the National Museum in Dar es Salaam. Some of the tombs have frames of dressed coral and weathered obituary inscriptions. Bodies would have been laid on the right side, with the face toward Mecca.

Mosque 'B' is of later construction and has been partially restored. It is similar to the triple-domed mosque at Kilwa Kisiwani (see page 394) in style, and it is thought that the builder may well have been the same person.

The community that gave rise to these ruins would have been founded during the Muslim period AD 622-1400. The first Muslim colonies were established from AD 740 by sea-borne migrations from the Persian Gulf down the East African coast as far as Sofala, the area round the Zambezi River. The settlement at Koale would have traded mangrove poles (see page 370), sandalwood, ebony and ivory. It is suggested

Tanzania

that Koale might have had several hundred inhabitants. The dwellings would have used timber in their construction and thus would have been less durable than the all-stone mosques and tombs. Being on more fertile soil inland, as the dwellings collapsed they rapidly became overgrown. The settlement went into gradual decline as the shore became more densely packed with mangroves, making its use by dhows difficult, and commercial activity shifted to Bagamoyo.

Essentials

Sleeping
■ *on map, page 374*
Price codes:
See inside front cover

Several new developments are currently under construction. Bagamoyo is in a glorious location, with a splendid, curved, palm-fringed beach. There are a few beach hotel rooms in town, and it is advisable to book. The currently available hotels are all good value. Enquire through **Coastal Travel**, PO Box 3052, Upanga Rd, T2117959, coastal@twiga.com

L *Lazy Lagoon Island*, private island off the coast, a 20-min boat ride across the water from a jetty close to Mbegani Fisheries (a private airstrip is nearby), 8 km east of Bagamoyo, bookings through *Foxtreks*, PO Box 10270, Dar es Salaam, T2440194, T0741-237422 (mob), F0741-327706, fox@twiga.com 12 bandas with en-suite bathrooms, swimming pool, spacious lounge and restaurant area, price includes all meals. Snorkelling, kayaking, windsurfing and sailing, fishing and boat trips cost extra. **B** *Livingstone Club*, PO Box 105, Bagamoyo, or PO Box 6645, Dar es Salaam, T2440059/80, T0741-324645 (mob), F2440104, www.livingstone-club.com Fairly new complex, a/c rooms with fridge and minibar. The restaurant has

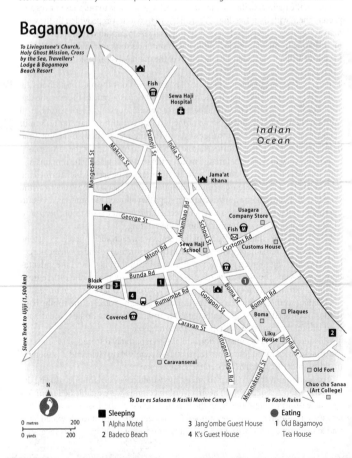

Bagamoyo

To Livingstone's Church,
Holy Ghost Mission, Cross
by the Sea, Travellers'
Lodge & Bagamoyo
Beach Resort

*Indian
Ocean*

Mangesani St
Makran St
Pomeji St
India St
George St
Mnambao Rd
School St
Mtoni Rd
Bunda Rd
Rumumbe Rd
Gongoni St
Caravan St
Kitopeni Soga Rd
Mwanakerezi St
Boma St
Bomani Rd
Customs Rd

Slave Track to Ujiji (1,500 km)

Fish
Sewa Haji
Hospital
Jama'at
Khana
Usagara
Company Store
Fish
Sewa Haji
School
Customs House
Black
House
Covered
Boma
Plaques
Liku
House
Caravanserai
Old Fort
Chuo cha Sanaa
(Art College)

To Dar es Salaam & Kasiki Marine Camp
To Kaole Ruins

N

0 metres 200
0 yards 200

■ **Sleeping**
1 Alpha Motel
2 Badeco Beach
3 Jang'ombe Guest House
4 K's Guest House

● **Eating**
1 Old Bagamoyo
Tea House

an international menu. Facilities include a swimming pool, tennis, watersports and it is possible to arrange local excursions. **B** *Paradise Holiday Resort*, PO Box 119, Bagamoyo, T2440136, T0741-335217 (mob), F2440132, paradise@raha.com Traditional-style thatched bungalows, a/c, with own bathrooms and satellite TV. Restaurant, bar, swimming pool, watersports are available or can arrange trips to Saadani National Park.

C *Badeco Beach Hotel*, PO Box 261, T2440018, F2440075. Glorious location right on the beach at south end of town, small, with 15 rooms, 9 self-contained, thatched bandas along shore. The garden is planted with bougainvillaea. Small restaurant, but does an excellent and imaginative seafood menu. **E** Camping available, includes breakfast. **C** *Bagamoyo Beach Resort*, PO Box 250, Bagamoyo (sometimes referred to as the 'Gogo'), T2440083, F2440154, bbr@ud.co.tz, at the north end of town – continue along India St. French management, a/c or fans, hot water showers, most of the 22 rooms are comfortable but the style is a little uninspired with tin roofs and concrete walls. There are a few traditional-style rooms with thatched roofs, but not facing the ocean. Simple restaurant, plus pleasant open-air bar with thatched roof overlooking beach. Also offers a beach kindergarten, conference facilities up to 45 people for seminars and workshops. Sports facilities include windsurfing, snorkelling, diving, golf, tennis and volleyball, and excursions can be arranged to Zanzibar. The mangrove swamps of the Ruvu River have a wide variety of birdlife, including kingfishers, herons, ibis, bee-eaters and the migratory flamingos. **C** *Kasiki Marine Camp*, approximately 7 km east of Bagamoyo along the road to Dar es Salaam, PO Box 247, Bagamoyo, T0741-340626 (cell), F0741-324707, kasiki@africaonline.co.tz Quiet resort with 6 bungalows, the price includes breakfast, or full board accommodation at twice the cost (US$48 per person). The restaurant specializes in Italian cuisine. Can organize boat trips, watersports and fishing. **C** *Travellers' Lodge*, PO Box 275, T2440077, F2440154, at north end of town on India St. 4 small bungalows and 4 s/c rooms, with a/c or fans, pleasant, traditional thatched style, excellent bar, watersports. Camping is available in the grounds. **E** *Alpha Motel*, PO Box 85, T2440056, in town, on Rumumbe Rd, near covered market. Has a pleasant, shaded outside bar. **E** *Jang'ombe Guest House*, PO Box 268, Mangesani Rd, near intersection with Mtoni Rd. **E** *K's Guest House*, PO Box 15, T2440015, in town centre opposite covered market on Caravan St. **Camping** is also available at *Gogo Beach Resort* and *Travellers Lodge*.

Eating Hotels are the main places. There are some snack bars near the covered market on Caravan St. **Cheap** *Badeco*, excellent seafood, charming small restaurant. *Bagamoyo Beach*, simple food.

Bars Only in hotels and the best are *Travellers' Lodge*, *Badeco Beach* and *Bagamoyo Beach*, all of which overlook the sea.

Entertainment At weekends there are entertainments provided by the **Nyumba ya Sanaa** (Bagamoyo Art College), which include music, dance and drama. They are well attended and the atmosphere is excellent. Ask at the college for times and programmes.

Shopping There are some small general and pharmacy stores on School St. The covered market on Caravan St is excellent for fruit, vegetables, meat and dried fish. Fresh fish at fish market on Customs Rd. There is a curio stall with crafts on sale at the *Badeco Beach Hotel*.

Sport Marine fishing can be arranged through *Badeco Beach Hotel* and there are plans to introduce a range of watersports. **Football matches** at ground on road to Kaole, south of town.

Tour guide Local guide Mr Esa has been fulsomely praised by visitors. He is a young student, very knowledgeable, keen and attentive. Some travellers have reported that they found the local people unwelcoming, and were advised by their guide to keep within close reach of their vehicle. They were also advised locally not to take any photographs.

Transport **Bus** Buses leave from the bus stand opposite the covered market on Caravan St. To Dar es Salaam costs US$2 and takes 2-3 hrs.

👉 ## Krakatoa

In August 1883, a volcano erupted on the island of Krakatoa in the strait of Sundra, just east of Java, in present-day Indonesia. The explosion was enormous, and it is said that it was heard in Rodrigues, 4,800 km away in the Mascarene Islands of the Indian Ocean. Gales of 100 kph were registered for six weeks in the Indian Ocean islands. A huge wave, 20 m high, hit the islands and the East African coast. At Bagamoyo, although the impact was lessened by the fact that it was partly shielded from the direct path of the wave by Zanzibar, local people still reported a sudden 5-m tidal surge that was repeated with gradually diminishing force, six times, during the next 24 hours as the wave was reflected to-and-fro between the west coast of Zanzibar and the mainland. Huge quantities of ash from the eruption floated up into the atmosphere, catching the light to cause the most glorious sunrises and sunsets for several years.

If you are walking on the shore you may find a piece of pumice stone which originates from the foaming volcanic lava after the Krakatoa eruption over 100 years ago and has been brought by the current that sweeps from the South China Seas to Africa.

Directory **Banks** Foreign exchange bureaux: there are none at present in Bagamoyo. *Badeco Beach Hotel* will change money in emergency. National Bank of Commerce is located off road to Dar es Salaam to south of town (follow the sign). **Communications** Post office: Customs Rd. **Medical services** **Hospital:** *Bagamoyo District*, located on India St. **Places of worship** Churches: Holy Ghost Roman Catholic Mission, north of town. There is a small church on Pomji St in town. **Mosques:** India St, north end of town. Small mosque on George St, off Mangesani St. **Useful addresses** Police: at intersection of Caravan St and Boma St at south end of town.

Saadani
National Park
Colour map 4, grid B5

Located opposite Zanzibar on the mainland coast, about 50 km north of Bagamayo, Saadani (300 sq km) has recently been gazetted as a National Park. It has plentiful game including giraffe, hartebeest, waterbuck, wildebeest, eland, buffalo, hippo, crocodile, reedbuck, black and white colobus monkey and warthog. Also present but harder to see are lion, leopard, elephant, sable antelope, greater kudu and the Beisa oryx. Some of the animals come down to the beach, especially at night. To the north of the reserve is a green turtle breeding beach and off the southern shoreline. A particular highlight are the thousands of flamingos found in the salt marshes in the Wami River estuary. There is also an extensive range of bush, river and sea birds.

However, the Saadani National Park has suffered from years of neglect. Anti-poaching patrols have been deployed only in the last few years, and the roads desperately needed the grading work that was due to have started recently. There are various safari options available – walking, boat or game drive – or the Cultural Tour that offers an opportunity to meet the local fishing community in Saadani village. The entrance fee to the reserve is US$20 per day (adult non-residents).

Sleeping *Saadani Safari Camp*, 8 en-suite tented bandas, US$85 per person full board, and a luxury banda, US$125 per person. Restaurant, bar, tree-house overlooking a small water-hole. Game drives cost US$25 per person. Boat safaris along the coast and up Wami River US$30 per person and foot safaris US$15 per person. Bookings can be made through *A Tent with a View Safaris*, PO Box 40525, Dar es Salaam, T/F2151106, T0741-323318, www.saadani.com Alternatively there is a very basic guesthouse (**E**) in Saadani village.

Transport **Air**: charter flights from Zanzibar US$200 for a 5-seater aircraft provided you can fill the plane, or US$320 from Dare es Salaam (DSM). **Road:** The reserve is not really accessible without hired transport. Access by road from DSM takes 4½ hrs – 109 km west to Chalinze, 52 km north to Mandera (2 km north of the large bridge over the Wami River), then 60 km along a dirt track to Saadani via the towns of Miono and Mkange. The reserve entrance is just after the railway line and it is signposted from the Mandera junction. A new road from DSM to Bagamoyo is currently under construction. On completion it will halve the journey time. *A*

Tanzania

Tent with a View Safaris operate a scheduled car service between DSM and Saadani on Wed, Fri and Sun, US$25 per person. **Sea**: a regular dhow service is planned to connect Saadani with Zanzibar and Bagamoyo. **Train**: cheapest access is by train from DSM on Fri and Sun at 1600 arriving at Mvave station at 2030 (the next station after Wami town). A Land Rover from the camp will pick up arriving guests from the station. The return train to DSM comes from Moshi, arriving at Mvave at 1430 on Sun and Tue and reaches DSM at 0700.

Tanga

Tanga is Tanzania's second biggest seaport and third largest town. It has a natural deep water harbour and was briefly the German colonial capital city following the treaty between the Sultan of Zanzibar and the German East Africa Company. Tanga was developed by the Germans in the late 19th century, and much of its wealth came from the sisal plantations in the hinterland. It is an attractive town with a sleepy ambiance, home to many fine German and Asian buildings in the town centre. With the advent of alternative rope-making fibres this industry has fallen into decline, adversely affecting the region. Nearby places of interest include the newly gazetted Saadani National Park, the enormous Amboni limestone caves, the Shirazi ruins at Tongoni dating from the 10th century, and offshore coral gardens. Tanga is within a manageable distance of the beautiful Usambara Mountains to the west.

Getting there Now that passenger rail services between Dar es Salaam and Tanga have been terminated, the only land route to Tanga is by road. Bus services or *dala-dala* take 4-6 hrs from Dar es Salaam and 1-3 hrs from the Kenyan border. An alternative approach is by sea, on a passenger carrying cargo ship or a dhow, but note that these are infrequent and slow. **Getting around** Taxis, buses and *dala-dala* can be obtained in Uhuru Park. However, all of Tanga is within walking distance, although taxis are advisable after dark.

Ins & outs
See page 382 for further details

History

The African groups in the Tanga area, excluding those in the coastal belt, number six. The **Pare** who now live in the Pare Hills came originally from the Taveta area of Kenya in the 18th century. The **Zigua** inhabited the area to the south of Tanga and have a reputation for aggression: Bwana Heri attacked and defeated the force of the sultan of Zanzibar in 1882. The **Nguu** clan to the west occupy the Nguu Hills and the **Ruvu** clan inhabit the Pangani islands. The **Shambaa** are around the Lushoto area and are closely allied with the **Bondei** who occupy the area between Tanga and Pangani. Both these groups have been pushed inland by Swahili and Digo settlement at the coast. The **Digo** originated in Kenya but were forced south by expansion of their neighbours to inhabit the coastal strip between Tanga and the Kenyan border, forcing out the Bondei in their turn. The **Segeju** inhabit part of the coast between Tanga and Kenya. They originated in Kenya from a war party that was cut off by flooding of the Umba River, which meets the sea at the border. They resolved to settle in Digo country. In a rather touching display of male solidarity they decided to avoid any falling out over who should possess the only female in the party by killing her. As a result they have been forced to intermarry with the Digo and the Shirazi.

The coastal people are termed **Swahili** and are descendants of Africans and Arabs following Islam. Among the Arab immigrants are the **Shirazi** who are said to have originated from around Shirazi in Persia (now Iran) and to have come to the East African coast via Muscat in the 10th century. The Shirazis had a hierarchy of rule from the Diwan, centred on Pangani, through Jumbes to Akidas. Tributes were extracted from most domestic events such as marriages and deaths. The role of the Akida was to organize the young men and they acted as headmen for caravans to the interior. With the gradual decline of the caravan trade, being an Akida in the area became little more than a sinecure secured by paying fees to a Jumbe and extracting taxes from the populace.

5°5'S 39°2'E
Phone code: 027
Colour map 4, grid B5

Carl Peters and the German East Africa Company arrived in 1885 and in 1888 leased a 16-km wide strip from the Sultan of Zanzibar along the entire coast of what is now Tanzania, between the Ruvuma and the Umba rivers. The Germans appointed agents (calling them Akidas), though they were often not of the same tribe as the people they administered, to collect taxes and enforce law and order.

With the advent of European settlement and trade, Somalis arrived, trading in cattle but seldom intermarrying. Islanders from the Comoros also settled, but were generally difficult to distinguish in both appearance and speech from the Swahili.

Agriculture in the Usambara area expanded (see page 412), and with the construction of the railway to Moshi Tanga became a flourishing port. Tanga was the site of a substantial reversal for the British during the First World War. Allied troops, including 8,000 Indian soldiers, found it difficult to disembark through the mangrove swamps and were repulsed by the well-organized German defence and some hostile swarms of bees that spread panic among the attackers. Over 800 were killed and 500 wounded, and the British abandoned substantial quantities of arms and supplies on their withdrawal.

After the eventual German withdrawal from Tanga, the German settlement dwindled to be steadily replaced by Greek plantation owners. Tanga's prosperity declined with the collapse in sisal prices in the late 1950s and the large estates were nationalized in 1967. Some have now been privatized, and sisal has made a modest recovery.

Sights

Old Tanga The open space in the centre of town is **Uhuru Park**, originally named Selous Square after the celebrated naturalist and hunter (see box, page 499). At the junction of the square with Eukenforde Street are the German buildings of **Tanga School**, the first educational establishment for Africans in Tanzania.

Tanga

Sleeping	5 Ocean Breeze	Eating	4 Meridian
1 Bandorini	6 Planters	1 Coffee Marketing	5 Patwas
2 Ferns Inn	7 Tanga	Board	6 Princess Nadia
3 Fourways		2 Exotica Fast Foods	Bakery
4 New Upare		3 Food Palace	7 TTS

N

Not to scale

On Market Street to the east of Uhuru Park is **Planters Hotel**. This once grand wooden building is now rather run down, but is reputed to have seen wild times as Greek sisal plantation owners came into town for marathon gambling sessions at which whole estates sometimes changed hands. It is an ornate building with arches, columns and plinths. The first floor has a wooden verandah. The ground floor has a bar with a huge antique corner cabinet full of miniatures.

Proceeding north across Independence Avenue leads to the **Tanga Library,** originally the King George VI Library. The west wing was opened in 1956 and the east wing in 1958 by the then governor, Sir Edward Twining. There is a courtyard behind with cloisters and Moorish arches. To the west is the **Old Boma,** a substantial structure in typical style. Opposite the Boma is a building from the German period with keyhole-style balustrades. Further to the west, in a location leading down to the shore, is **St Anthony's Cathedral,** a modern 1960s octagonal building with a free-standing bell tower, a school and various mission buildings. On Boma Road there is a small, white Greek Orthodox church.

Following Independence Avenue back east one reaches the **Clock Tower** and the **Post Office**. To the west of the Clock Tower is the German Monument in marble, decorated with an eagle and oak leaves, dedicated to the 18 who died in 1889 during the Arab Revolt led by Bushiri (see page 370) and listing the five German naval vessels, under the command of Admiral Denhart, supporting Major Hermann Wissmann on the ground.

Just to the east of the Clock Tower are some ruins thought to be part of the fortifications built during the First World War. On the corner of Independence Avenue and Usambara Street is the **Old Court House**, dating from the German period and still in use today. It is a fine, double-fronted building with a Mangalore tiled roof, offices on the mezzanine level, a fluted façade and fretwork over the windows. A local group, headed by George Weissenstein (PO Box 5924, T2644197), is dedicated to restoring colonial Tanga, and the Old Court House is their first project.

Opposite the Court House is **Tanga Ropeworks** where you can see examples of the ropes and twine made from sisal, known as 'white gold' in the 1950s. The **German Cemetery** is on Swahili Street and contains the graves of 16 Germans and 48 Askaris killed in the action of 4-5 November 1914. One of the Askaris is listed as 'Sakarini' ('crazy drunk'). Also buried here is Mathilde Margarethe Scheel (1902-87), known as 'Mama Askari', who looked after the welfare interests of the African soldiers of the Schutztruppe (see box, page 583) after Tanganyika became a British protectorate. Crossing over the railway line along Hospital Road to Ocean Drive, to the south is Karimjee School and off to the left is the old Tanga Club of the British period. Further east of the centre, the **Bombo Hospital** is a handsome German building, with a three-storey central block, a first-floor verandah overlooking the ocean, a Mangalore tile roof and a gatehouse, now serving as a pharmacy.

Excursions

Formed during the Jurassic Age some 150 million years ago, when reptiles were dominant on land, these natural limestone caves extend over a wide area, lying mostly underground, accessed through openings in the gorges of the Mkilumizi River and the Sisi River. They form the most extensive cave system in East Africa (estimated at over 230 sq km) and there are chambers up to 13 m high with stalactites and stalagmites. A German-Turkish survey in 1994 found that there are 10 separate cave systems, and the longest cave was 900 m. Only one of the caves is used for guided tours.

The location is of great religious significance to local people and offerings to ensure fertility are made in one of the shrines. There are many legends associated with the caves, including beliefs that they form a 400-km underground passage to the foothills of Mt Kilimanjaro. The main cave, known as *Mabavu*, is said to be the home of the Snake God. The Digo people were reputed to dispose of unwanted albino babies in a

Amboni Caves
Colour map 4, grid B5
Warning: take your own powerful torch and go in pairs using a guide. There have been fatalities when people have explored the caves on their own

Bicycle there if you have the time. It's a nice way to meet local people, the birds are numerous and you might spot a dikdik

Tanzania

section of the caves known as the Lake of No Return. The caves were used by the Mau Mau as a refuge during the troubles in Kenya. A guide will escort you round the caves, illuminating the chamber with a burning torch. The caves are home to many thousands of bats (called *popo* in KiSwahili) and a popular attraction is to observe the '*popo* flight', when the bats fly out of the cave entrance at sunset.

■ *0900-1600. The caves are 8 km to the north of Tanga on the road to Lunga Lunga at the Kenyan border. They are badly signposted. A taxi to the caves from town will cost about US$5 (ask the driver to wait). Alternatively you can take a bus or a dala-dala for US$0.50, but these are infrequent. Tours can be arranged through the Amboni Culture & Guiding Promoters, PO Box 1021, Majestic Cinema, Mkwakwani Rd, T/F2643546 – Kassim is a very experienced guide.*

Galamos Sulphur Springs
Colour map 4, grid B5

Discovered by a local Greek sisal planter, Christos Galamos, the springs are hot and sulphurous and are said to relieve arthritis and cure skin ailments. A small spa was erected, but it has now fallen into disrepair. It is still possible to bathe in the springs, however. ■ *About 3 km from Amboni Caves, off the Tanga to Mombasa road.*

Tongoni Ruins
Colour map 4, grid B5

The Tongoni Ruins date from the Shirazi period and the settlement was started at the end of the 10th century. The community would have been similar to that at Kaole (see page 373), but was almost certainly larger and predated it. There are 40 tombs, some with pillars, and the remains of a substantial mosque. The mosque is of the type found along the north part of the East African coast. There is a central *musalla* (prayer room) with arches leading to aisles (*ribati*) at each side. The mosque is constructed of particularly finely dressed, close-grained coral, especially on the lintel of the *kiblah*, the side of the building that faces towards Mecca. The roofs were coral on mangrove rafters. There are depressions in the pillars where there were porcelain bowls, all apparently removed during the German period. It is said that Tongoni was founded by Ali ben Sultan Hasan at much the same time as he established the settlement at Kilwa (see page 393). There are Persian inscriptions at Tongoni that would seem to establish a link with Shiraz. ■ *Located 20 km south of Tanga on the road to Pangani about 1 km off the road. Buses or dala-dala from Tanga cost about US$0.50 and will take up to 1 hr. A taxi will cost about US$12.*

Tanga Coral Gardens

Consisting of three reefs – Mwamba Wamba, Mwamba Shundo and Fungu Nyama – the Tanga Coral Gardens are located 10-15 km offshore. Boat trips to the reefs, or to nearby islands and Pangani, can be arranged locally.

Essentials

Sleeping
■ *on map, page 378*
Price codes:
See inside front cover

In town, the Inn by the Sea is recommended for its location; the Planters Hotel and Tanga Hotel for their colonial atmosphere

C *Mkonge*, PO Box 1544, T2643440, F2642409, located about 1 km from the centre to the east along Hospital Rd, which leads into Ocean Dr. It is set in what was designed as Amboni Park, on grounds by the sea, based on the Sir William Lead Memorial Hall, which became the club for the sisal growers. It is sometimes known as the *Sisal (Mkonge) Hotel*, and there is a mosaic of a sisal plant on the floor of the foyer. It has a/c, bar, restaurant, disco at weekends, swimming pool. A *Bushtrekker* hotel. **C** *Panori Hotel*, east of the centre, south of Hospital Rd, in a quiet area beyond the swimming club and the other hotels, PO Box 672, T/F2646044. Colonial-style building with new wing added in 1997, a/c, Indian and international food in an attractive open banda restaurant. Well run and comfortable, recommended. **C** *Raskazone Hotel*, Fertilizer Rd, east of centre off Hospital Rd, PO Box 5101, T/F2643897, T0741-670790 (mob). Rooms with a/c and minibar are on offer, or slightly cheaper rooms without a/c. It also has a restaurant and a garden bar. **D** *Planters*, on Market St just east of Uhuru Park. Historic hotel from colonial era, but is now dilapidated. It has an extensive verandah overlooking the street, bar, cold water only. **E** *Assad*, PO Box 2004, T2644712, next to *Takrims* office at the bus station, south of centre. Some rooms have a/c, s/c, TV, no alcohol. Very convenient for a late arrival by bus or an early departure. **E** *Fourways*, PO Box 1492, located at intersection of Market St and Guinea St. Some rooms have a/c. Recently constructed bar/restaurant. **E** *Inn by the Sea*, PO Box 2188, T2644614, located close to *Mkonge* on Ocean Dr. A/c or fans, price includes breakfast. Excellent value with a good location on cliffs overlooking the harbour. Rather neglected in recent years. **E** *New Tanga Hotel*, PO Box 6107, T2644631, on Eukenforde Rd at west end. S/c, includes breakfast, bar, good restaurant, fans. **E** *Ocean Breeze*, PO Box 2344, T2643441, just off Independence Av, restaurant with curries, grilled chicken and fish. Good value. **E** *Savanna Inn*, PO Box 330, T2646567, on Mombasa Rd, west of St Anthony's Cathedral, s/c, some a/c, restaurant with curries and grills. **F** *Ferns Inn*, PO Box 391, Usambara St, T2646276, s/c, fans, no hot water, has a small restaurant. **F** *New Upare*, PO Box 940, Usambara St, T2644692, good value.

Eating

Cheap *Avenue*, bar, restaurant, serves good food (close to dhow harbour). *Bandorini Bar & Restaurant*, Independence Av, celebrated hotel in the colonial era, now open for food and drinks in the evening only. Rather dilapidated, serving masala chicken, grilled chicken and fish. *Meridian Restaurant*, corner of Customs Rd and Independence Av. Chinese and international food. Possible to eat outside in the garden. *Patwas Restaurant*, off Market St just south of market. Well run, with snacks of egg-chop (Scotch egg), meat chop, kebabs, samosas. Excellent ice-cold drinks: lemon, mango, pineapple, papaya, lassi, milkshakes, and locally made grapefruit crush, ginger beer and Pippindor Herefordshire appleade. Recommended.

Seriously cheap Local restaurant in front of the *Planters Hotel* is recommended – very popular and cheap. *Coffee Marketing Board*, on corner of Usambara Rd and Eukeberg Rd. Snacks and coffee (alas, instant). *Exotica Fast Foods*, Independence Av, serves chicken, chips, fish and samosas. *Food Palace*, Market St, serves grills, curries, ice cream and fruit juices. Good value and highly recommended. *Kibarua* at the bus station, sound, simple and cheap. *King Fish*, Independence Av, just to the east of *Bandorini*, serves grilled fish, chicken, beeef, chips, rice and steamed bananas. *Market Restaurant*, Market St, behind market. Simple and cheap. *Meridian*, next to Post Office, serves lunch of samosas, grills, African dishes. At night it is a bar, with darts. *Princess Nadia Bakery*, on Market St, recommended for fresh bread and pastries. *Salama Executive Inn*, in the *New Tanga Hotel* on Eukenforde St, good value with prawns and chips. *TTS*, on northwest corner of Uhuru Park, very cheap snacks and local dishes.

Bars

The verandah at the *Planters Hotel* is recommended for atmosphere. The *Yacht Club* along Ocean Dr is a focus for the expatriate population. The *Harbours Club*, on Club Rd off Hospital Rd, is cheap and friendly with good views of the ocean. *Sea-Side Pub* on Ocean Dr past the swimming pool is another budget option.

Entertainment

Cinema Tanga has 4 cinemas: in Ngamiani, the Swahili district, about 1 km on the left along the Pangani Rd; off Pangani Rd behind the station; the *Majestic*, off Market St, near Mkwakwani St; and off Usambara St and Market St. Do not have high expectations that they will be operating. **Disco** There are discos at the weekend at the *Mkonge Hotel*.

Shopping

Tanga Ivory Carvers, Independence Av, PO Box 1135, T43278. Good quality craft work, no ivory on sale these days.

Sports

Cricket At the *Aga Khan Club*, behind the *Aga Khan School* off Swahili St, south of the railway line. **Fishing** Mr Pappa, located on the shore just east of St Anthony's Cathedral, will arrange fishing excursions. **Golf** The *Golf Club* is along the main road running beside the railway as it heads west. **Sailing** At the *Yacht Club* on Ocean Dr. **Soccer** The soccer stadium is on the intersection of Eukenforde St and Mkwakwani St. You will need to consult the *Daily News*, or a local enthusiast, for fixtures. **Swimming** At *Swimming Club*, T2646618, on Ocean Dr before the *Yacht Club*, $0.75, and at *Mkonge Hotel*, US$2. **Tennis and squash** At the *Aga Khan Club* (see Cricket above) and at the *Tanga Club* off Ocean Dr. **Windsurfing** At *Baobab Beach Hotel*, 8 km south of Tanga.

Tour operators

Amboni Culture & Guiding Promoters, Majestic Building, Mkwakwani Rd, PO Box 1021, T2643546, F2643292. *Karimjee Travel Services*, near Post Office on Independence Av, PO Box 1563, T41099.

Transport **Local** **Taxis, buses and** *dala-dala:* can be obtained in Uhuru Park. **Bicycles**: can be hired at several places in town, including *Ali Musso*, PO Box 2344, between 7th and 8th St. **Road** **Bus** and *dala-dala* leave from the bus station south of the town on the other side of the railway track for **Dar es Salaam** from 0800, the trip takes 4-6 hrs and a regular bus costs US$3 and a luxury one US$4. For **Moshi** the bus takes 4-6 hrs and costs US$4. To **Lunga Lunga** at the border with Kenya costs US$1, is slow as the road is poor and can take 1-3 hrs. The roads are unmade dirt roads until the Amboni Sisal Estates, where tarmac begins, although there are some potholes developing. To **Pangani** buses take 3 hrs and cost US$1. **Sea** **Boat**: *Tanzanian Coastal Shipping Line*, a cargo service that takes passengers, runs boats up and down the coast. However, they are irregular, slow and you need to ask at the port. Other shipping companies (*Virgin Butterfly; Canadian Spirit; Sea Horse*) have operated services calling at Tanga at various times. Again, you will need to ask at the port. **Dhows** operate from Tanga. You will need to ask if any are sailing at the port. Routes to and from Tanga are not sailed that frequently.

Directory **Banks** *National Bank of Commerce*, Market St, near *Planters Hotel*, does not change American Express travellers' cheques without sight of purchase agreement. **Communications** Internet: *Globe Net Works* on Market St, T264387, or at *Cyber Joint*, PO Box 10056, on Market St, T5343875, www.tanga.net, $1.00 for 15 mins. **Post:** post office on Independence Av near Msambara St. **Libraries** Tanga library off Independence Av near the Old Boma. **Medical services** Bombo **Hospital:** on Ocean Dr to east of town centre, T2644390. Dr Patel's clinic at the town end of Hospital Rd has been recommended by a traveller. **Places of worship** Churches: *St Anthony's Cathedral*, west of the Old Boma. There is a Roman Catholic church in Ngamiani. **Mosques:** the main mosque is off Independence Av near Uhuru Park, and there are 3 other mosques in Ngamiani. **Temple:** to be found off Ring St, near Guinea St. **Useful addresses** Police: off Independence Av near Tanga library.

Muheza

Phone code: 027
Colour map 4, grid B5

A sprawling, bustling town, 35 km west of Tanga along a good road, Muheza provides a link between the coastal beaches and the lush, cool Usambara Mountains. Muheza district is a relatively cosmopolitan area of Tanzania, a result of the influx of workers for the now defunct sisal industry. The town is being improved under a government urban renewal programme that has already produced a new bus stand and market (market days Thursday and Sunday). There is a post office and bank, but there are no money-changing facilities.

Approximately 6 km to the southwest of Muheza is the small town of **Magila**. From Muheza cross the railway line, head south past the football ground and take the next right. Magila is the original site of the Anglican mission church (1876) and hospital (1884), buildings that survive today. Close by are two waterfalls, fed by a natural reservoir at the top of Margoroto mountain. It takes about two hours to reach the reservoir from Magila (ask around for the best paths to take) and there are excellent views across the plains towards Tanga. There are no guesthouses in Magila.

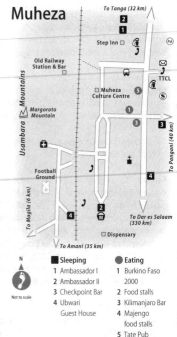

Muheza

To Tanga (32 km)
Step Inn
Old Railway Station & Bar
Muheza Culture Centre
Margoroto Mountain
Usambara Mountains
Football Ground
To Magila (6 km)
To Pangani (40 km)
To Dar es Salaam (330 km)
Dispensary
To Amani (35 km)

N
Not to scale

■ **Sleeping**
1 Ambassador I
2 Ambassador II
3 Checkpoint Bar
4 Ubwari
   Guest House

● **Eating**
1 Burkino Faso
   2000
2 Food stalls
3 Kilimanjaro Bar
4 Majengo
   food stalls
5 Tate Pub

Sleeping **C** *Ubwari Guest House*, at Mbaramo, opposite the football ground on the road to Magila, run by the National Institute of

Tanzania (vertical, left margin)

The legend of the Shirazi migration

Ali ben Sultan Hasan of Shiraz in Persia (now Iran) had a dream in AD 975 in which a rat with jaws of iron devoured the foundations of his house. He took this as a sign that his community was to be destroyed. The court in Shiraz ridiculed the notion but his immediate family and some other followers resolved to migrate. They set

out in seven dhows from the nearby port of Bushehr and sailed through the mouth of the Persian Gulf, into the Indian Ocean. There they were caught in a great storm and separated, making landfalls at seven different points on the East African coast where they established settlements. Among these were Tongoni and Kilwa.

Medical Research, which have a facility next door, very clean, nets, fans, shared bathrooms, price includes all meals. **F** *Ambassador Hotel*, north end of the main road to Tanga, which means it can be noisy. The hotel has 2 blocks, both clean and basic, fans, nets, some rooms s/c, breakfast on request. **F** *Checkpoint Bar*, on top of small hill to the south, a short walk along the road to Pangani, PO Box 221, T2646310, shared facilities, not very clean, very basic although rooms do have mosquito nets and fans.

Eating & bars

After sunset there are many food stalls along the roads and in the market square. They sell very cheap good food including roast cassava, chips and *nyama choma* (grilled meat). **Seriously cheap** *Burkino Faso 2000*, near *Kilimanjaro Bar*, cheap chapatis and snacks, spicy tea. *Checkpoint Bar*, offers fried chicken and chips, popular local bar with satellite TV, pool table and darts. *Kilimanjaro Bar*, on the main road, local fare – *ugali*, rice, beans, tasty *nyama choma*, relaxed atmosphere, has TV and video shows. *Tate Pub*, next to the bus stand, popular spot for locals, plays loud music, good selection of beers, serves chips and fried beef and chicken as well as usual ugali-based meals. There is a disco at least once a week at *Step Inn*, lots of Congolese music is played as well as western pop music. The nights when live music is played vary – enquire locally.

Transport

From the main stand there are several buses throughout the day to Tanga (US$1), Arusha (journey time 6 hrs, US$7.50), and Dar es Salaam (5 hrs, US$6). There are also buses to Pangani (1200 and 1400 daily, taking up to 2 hrs, US$1.25) and Amani (2-3 hrs, US$1.25).

Pangani

Located 52 km south of Tanga on the northern side of the Pangani River, Pangani has good beaches and is a fine location for a quiet beach vacation. There are some handsome old Arab houses, but these are in poor repair.

Phone code: 027
Colour map 4, grid B5

Swahili for 'distribute' or 'arrange', it comes as no surprise that Pangani was one of the earliest ports established by the Arab settlers. A prosperous port during the 19th century, the community was ruled by an Arab Liwali, five Shirazi Jumbes and a network of Akidas. Indian traders financed parties under Akidas to collect ivory and rhinoceros horn in the interior, and there was some trading in slaves. The town prospered as the trade in ivory and slaves flourished. It was at Pangani that Bushiri, leader of the Arab revolt of 1888-89, was finally captured and executed (see page 370).

History
5° 25′ S, 38° 58′ E

The mouth of the Pangani River is crossed by a sand bar. This provided shelter for dhows, and prevented them from being pursued by steam vessels when the slave trade was being suppressed after 1873. However, it also meant that vessels of deeper draught could not use the port. Traffic drifted steadily to the newer facilities at Tanga, subsequently accelerated by the railway linking Tanga to Dar es Salaam and Moshi.

In 1930 the population was around 1,500 but the substantial houses on the north side of the river, built largely by slave labour, have fallen into disrepair. The economy of the town shifted to reliance on the sisal plantations, the Pangani being served by shallow-draught steamers, but sisal declined drastically in price with the advent of synthetic fibres from the mid-1950s. There are still many coco-palms and some fishing.

Tanzania

Sights The old **Customs House**, originally built in 1916 as the post office, and the old **CCM Building** are both fine structures, unfortunately in poor repair. The **Boma** is a handsome building. Built in 1810, it is said that slaves were buried alive to strengthen the foundations. A distinctive roof was added in the German period. It is now the District Commissioner's Office and some of the original carved doors remain. Next to the Customs House is the old slave depot, built around 1850 and still largely intact, with some characteristic carved doors and remnants of whipping posts. It is also thought that there are underground tunnels and pits that lead to the river, along which weak slaves were taken to be washed out to sea. Just by the ferry is a plaque recording the capture of Pangani by the British on 23 July 1916, and the **Uhuru** or **Jamhuri Monument**, celebrating independence.

Across the river by ferry (US$0.10, US$5 cars) is the village of **Bweni**. From the hill behind the village are fine views of Pangani and of the Indian Ocean. The luxurious *Protea Hotel* is located here, but you can buy a soda and enjoy the view without having to stay. It is possible to hire a boat, through *Pangadeco Hotel* or the Pangani Coast Cultural Tourism office (see below), to travel up the river, costing around US$4 per hour for a boat taking up to 10 people. There are many birds, best seen at dusk, and crocodiles further upstream. You will also see local fishermen in dugout canoes and vast coconut plantations beside the river. Men climb the trees to collect coconuts or the sap from cut branches – used to make *mnazi*, an alcoholic drink.

Three offshore islands can be visited (Marve Mdogo, Mwamba Marve and Mazivi) and there is sport fishing and snorkelling, although the quality of the latter can be disappointing in the rainy seasons when the water is not clear. Again, boats can be arranged through *Pangadeco Hotel*.

Along the coral shoreline in the area known as Mkomo and Mwanaunguja, the **fossilized remains of dinosaurs** have been found found, estimated to be 200-300 million years old.

Pangani

Sleeping ■
1 Pangadeco Guest House
2 Protea
3 River View Guest House
4 Safari Lodge

Eating ●
1 Food stalls

Tanzania (side margin)

Rhapta

Around AD 100 an anonymous merchant, born in Egypt, compiled a guide written in Greek for merchants and sailors with details of all the trade routes and ports known in the ancient world. The book was named Periplus maris Erythraei, or 'Voyage around the Red Sea'. In Periplus the lost port of Rhapta is mentioned, but scholars remain divided as to its exact location. Rhapta was described as the most southerly port along the East African coastline, then known as Azania. Details were given of the trade carried out with Azania – the sale of swords, spears, axes and glassware in exchange for cowrie shells, ivory, tortoiseshell and cinnamon. The inhabitants of Rhapta were described as being of great stature, pirates or tillers of the soil, inhabiting the whole coastline, with many local chiefs.

According to Ravenstein (1898), the name 'Rhapta' was believed to have been derived from the Greek or Arab verb 'to sew' – referring to the 'small sewn boats' in use there. The early Portuguese sailors describe Arab boats with the timbers lashed together with coir (rope made from coconut fibre), carrying cargoes of coconuts.

In about AD 50 the Greek merchant Diogenes describes a journey inland from Rhapta to lakes believed to be the source of the Nile and to the 'Mountains of the Moon', which could refer to Mt Kilimanjaro or even the Rwenzori Mountains in Uganda. His findings were marked on the maps of the ancient geographer Ptolemy, considered to be the great authority on the Nile's origin and course until the 15th century. Prior to his death in 1984, archaeologist Neville Chittick argued that Rhapta was in the region of Kilwa or the Rufiji delta, and that the island of Menouthias, mentioned by Ptolemy writing in the 2nd century AD, was the nearby island of Mafia. Other researchers, such as James Kirkman, suggest Rhapta was near Dar es Salaam or Lamu; and several place it at Pangani, with the island Menouthias being either Zanzibar or Pemba.

Rhapta was said to be near the end of the known world. This was because ships were hampered in sailing further south by the Doldrums, a windless zone in the Indian Ocean caused by the collision of the winter monsoon from the north and the trade winds from the south. Ancient Egyptian and Greek trade with Azania was complicated by delays caused by waiting for favourable winds, the return trip taking a minimum of 16 months. By contrast, trading with India was relatively simple as the summer and winter monsoons blow in opposing directions, through 180°, twice a year.

L *Protea Hotel Pangani River*, PO Box 118, Pangani, T0741-324422 (mob), F0741-410099, proteapangani@africaonline.co.tz, www.proteahotels.com Luxury hotel on the hill south of the river ferry, 40 a/c rooms with en-suite bathrooms, swimming pool, offer game drives, inshore and deep water game fishing and guided walking safaris, own private airstrip. **Sleeping**

E *NBC Club*, PO Box 90, T55, near east end of Harbour Rd. Only 5 rooms and often full. **E** *Pangadeco Guest House*, PO Box 76, T2639, near the beach at the east end of town. Very simple, fan but no mosquito net, you need to give notice of meals required well in advance, bar. **E** *Paradise Guest House*, Harbour Rd. **E** *Riverside Inn*, PO Box 4, on the river between the bus stand and the ferry. Simple and cheap. **E** *River View Guest House*, Jamhuri St, just east of the old slave depot, T2650. Very basic, shared bathrooms with cold water, rooms have fans but no nets, food available, nice river view as the name suggests. **E** *Safari Lodge*, on Tanga Rd, straight up the road from the ferry, PO Box 13, T2649031-3 (ext 13), T0741-617561 (mob), 0742-788402. Can be noisy due to integral popular bar, hair salon, tailor and kebab shop, but this is the nicest accommodation within town and good place to meet the locals. Double rooms with en-suite or shared facilities, local and western style food available (typically at least US$5). **E** *Udo Guest House*, close to ferry.

Along the river front are many small food stalls, where you can get items such as chapatti, omelette and rice very cheaply.

The *Pangani Coast Cultural Tourism Programme* has a small office on Jamhuri St (or Harbour Rd), near the post office, PO Box 89, Pangani, T2611, F2644316, tourinfo@habari.co.tz **Tour operator**

Tanzania

The programme is co-ordinated by Mr Sekibaha who has been the district cultural officer for 20 years. On offer are walks through the town, to local farms and homes, river cruises and fishing with local fishermen. Can also arrange bicycle hire, snorkelling and other excursions. The programme is supported by the Dutch development organization, SNV, and profits will be used for development projects, particularly in education.

Transport **Bus** The only regular bus services are from Tanga and Muheza. Buses depart from the main stand at Tanga at around 0800, 1200 and 1400 and cost US$1.50. Although it is only 52 km, the road is very bumpy and buses may take over 3 hrs depending on the season. A bus leaves Muheza daily at 1200, making the return journey at 0630 the next day. This is a graded road in good condition and the 40 km takes a more reasonable 80 mins, cost US$1.25.

The bus stand in Pangani is on Jamhuri St opposite the ferry. There are no buses from Bweni on the other side of the river.

Directory The only bank in Pangani does not change money. Telephone calls may be made from the TTCL shop just west of the Jamhuri Monument.

Mkoma Bay This is a tranquil area about 3 km north of Pangani on the road to Tanga. There are several places to stay, all set in attractive, well-kept gardens with good sea views at the edge of a small cliff. Steps lead down to the beach, which is quiet but a little rocky in places and does not have the brilliant white sands found elsewhere. All resorts will be able to arrange trips in small dhows or dugout canoes. A popular trip is the one to **Maziwe**, an exposed island 4 km from the bay, where you can sit with giant sea turtles and snorkel in the coral reefs (price US$40-60 for the boat and pilot, will take up to 12 people per boat). The resorts also offer sunset boat cruises up Pangani River.

Sleeping **B-C** *Argovia Tented Camp*, PO Box 127, Pangani, T0741-511600 (mob), or through Moshi office, T027-2753531, frey@eoltz.com Recently opened, beautifully furnished tents or cheaper bandas, all have en-suite bathrooms with hot water and flush toilets, mosquito nets, safety deposit box, accept Visa cards. Also camping in own tent, US$5 per person. Swimming pool, well-stocked bar, restaurant offers excellent western food but relatively expensive for budget travellers (US$5-15). **B** *Pangani Lodge*, PO Box 118, T0741-440044, F440045. Good value, excellent site, steps down to cove, offers diving, restaurant, bar.

C *Peponi Holiday Resort*, further north from Mkoma Bay, 15 km north of Pangani at Kigombe village, PO Box 1823, Pangani, T0741-540139 (mob). Thatched bandas with own bathrooms, includes breakfast, advisable to book in advance, good restaurant and pleasant bar. Camping $6. **C** *Tinga Tinga*, PO Box 120, Pangani, T2622, or through Tanga office, T027-2643419. Beautiful rooms inside hexagonal bandas with a spacious, well-appointed bath, fans but no mosquito nets, good food in restaurant (roughly US$5), camping US$2.50 per person, souvenir shop sells locally produced cheese and ice cream.

D *Pangani Beach Resort*, PO Box 13, Pangani, T2649031-3 (ext. 88), T0742-788402, 7 double and 3 triple s/c cottages, a/c, hot water, flush toilets, no nets, includes continental breakfast, other meals also western food (US$5). **E** *YMCA*, PO Box 84, T2644. Very basic, 3 s/c double rooms, extra beds can be added, no hot water, nets and fans. Serve fish or beans with rice, *ugali* or chips, approximately US$2.50.

South of Pangani There are three beach resorts near the village of **Ushomo**, a 40-minute taxi ride from the ferry at Pangani. Here the beaches are excellent and largely free of tourists.

Places to stay include: **B** *Coco Beach Resort*, T0741-333449 (mob). **B** *Emayani Beach Resort*, PO Box 111, Pangani, T2645. **B** *The Tides Beach Resort*, PO Box 46, Pangani, thetides@habari.co.tz, comfortable rooms, bar and restaurant.

South Coast to Mtwara and West to Songea

Dar es Salam

The south coast receives few visitors due to its inaccessibility. However, if you have the patience, or can go by plane, you will be well rewarded. Off the coast is the island of Mafia, which is a proposed marine park. It is an idyllic setting and a paradise for scuba divers and snorkellers. A thoroughly recommended excursion is to hire a sailing dhow at Kisiju (see below) and sail to Mafia, stopping off at little islands en route. Further south is the town of Kilwa, with the small island of Kilwa Kisiwani just off the mainland. This is the location of the Kilwa ruins and although very remote the ruins make the trip worth the trouble. Further south still are the towns of Lindi and Mtwara, best known for being in the area where Makonde carvings are made. However they receive very few visitors due to their isolation.

The coastal village of Kisiju is rather spread out, on a small river, about 80 km south of Dar es Salaam. Its main interest is that dhows leave here on a regular basis for Mafia Island and for small islands on the way. The dhows take household goods and manufactured items to the islands and return with cargoes of fish, cashews, rice, coconuts, charcoal and cassava. There are several small eating places in the village. If you need to stay the night, ask for Mr Shanzi and he will arrange for you to stay in a local house for about US$1.

Kisiju
Colour map 5, grid B6

If you wish to sail around the very pretty islands close to Kisiju, as well as Mafia and the small islands nearby, it is possible to hire a sailing dhow at Kisiju for around US$15 a day. You need to take your own food, water, charcoal, sleeping bags, tent and sea-sickness pills. Plenty of fish can be bought cheaply on the islands, and on the smaller ones there will be no other tourists.

Sleeping L *Amani Beach Club*, T0741-351257, F2667760, abc@twiga.com 10 a/c beach-facing rooms, traditional-style buildings, beach bar restaurant, marine sports, 1½-hr drive from Dar es Salaam or light aircraft, swimming pool, tennis court, opportunity to spot rare birds in the 40 ha of woodland.

Transport Road: minibuses and pick-ups with cargo for the dhows leave from the Esso petrol station on the Kilwa Rd in Mtoni (see map of Greater Dar es Salaam, page 338). The journey to Kisiju takes 4 hrs and costs US$2. **Sea**: about 10-15 dhows sail each day for **Kwali**, **Koma** and **Mafia**. There is a sand bar at the mouth of the river and dhows can only leave at high tide. You need to take your own food and drink, and be prepared to sleep on the cargo. Sea-sickness pills are

South Coast

recommended for inexperienced sailors. **Kwali** is only about 1 km from Kisiju and, depending on the tides and the winds, will be reached in under an hr of sailing for about US$1. **Koma** is about 10 km from Kisiju, will take about 2 hrs of sailing and cost about US$2. A motorized dhow will reach **Mafia** in 12 hrs, a sailing dhow in 24 hrs, and will cost US$3-6.

Kwali Island Very close to Kisiju (about 1 km) with a small fishing village of about 300 families. Perhaps three dhows a day go there from Kisiju. It is possible to walk round the island in about an hour. There are one or two small eating kiosks, providing simple fare, and it is possible to stay in a local house for about US$1. There are onward dhows to **Koma** and **Mafia**.

Koma Island A very pretty island about 10 km from Kisiju and Kwali. There aren't many inhabitants and it is mainly used by dhows as a base on their way south to fish. You will need to be self-sufficient if you decide to stay. Onward dhows to **Mafia**.

Mafia Island

7°45'S 39°50'E
Phone code: 023
Colour map 4, grid B6

There are a number of attractions to Mafia Island, which include historical remains, deep-sea fishing and diving. The population of Mafia are mainly fishermen; the other industries are coconut palms and cashew nut trees. The plantations are left over from those established by the Omanis. The coconut industry is particularly important and the largest coconut factory in East Africa is found on Mafia at Ngombeni Plantation. It produces copra (dried kernels), oil, coir yarn and cattle cake. However the poor soil has meant that the island has never been able to support a very large population. Geological surveys have shown that the Mafia Deep Offshore Basin, an area of 75,000 sq km, contains deposits of oil and gas. Given the extreme poverty of many of the people exploration may be viewed favourably.

Ins & outs
See page 392 for further details

Getting there Flights from Dar es Salaam take 30-40 mins and there are now several operators offering 3-4 flights per week. By sea, there is the choice between irregular services out of Dar or the frequent daily crossings by dhow from Kisiju, further down the coast from Dar.
Getting around The airport is about 20 km from *Mafia Lodge* and a Lodge vehicle will collect you – they charge US$10 if you are not staying at the Lodge. There are no taxis on the island; indeed there are few vehicles of any sort. Mafia has no public transport system. The upmarket tourist hotels arrange for collection and transfer of their guests around the island. Budget travellers have the option of walking, hitchhiking – which can involve lengthy waits – or hiring a bicycle (enquire at *Lizu Hotel* in Kilindoni, the usual point of entry by air or sea).

History

The name Mafia is derived from an Arab word *morfieyeh*, which means a group, and refers to the archipelago. There is evidence of foreign settlers on Mafia from as early as the 9th century. From the 12th to the 14th century it was an important settlement and the remains of a 13th-century mosque have been found at Ras Kismani. By the 16th century, when the Portuguese arrived, it had lost much of its importance and was part of the territory ruled by the king of Kilwa. There is little left of the site of the settlement of the 12th to 14th century, although old coins and pieces of pottery are still found occasionally, particularly to the south of Kilindoni where the sea is eating away at the ruins. On the nearby island of Juani can be found extensive ruins of the town of Kua. The town dates back to the 18th century and the five mosques go back even further to the 14th century. In 1829 the town was sacked by Sakalava cannibals from Madagascar who invaded, destroyed the town and dined on the inhabitants.

Evidence of Chinese visitors to the Mafia Island group comes in the form of Chinese coins dating back to the 8th and 9th centuries, which suggest that the Far East was then trading with these islands.

The legend of Ras Kismani

The town of Ras Kismani was originally settled by the Sakalava from Madagascar. The townspeople built a large ship, and when it was completed they invited the local people of Kua to a feast. During the celebrations, the Sakalava seized several children and laid them on the sand in the path of the ship as it was launched.

The Kua people planned revenge at their leisure. Seven or eight years later they invited the Sakalava of Ras Kismani to attend a wedding at Kua. The celebrations were in a special room beneath a house. Gradually the hosts left, one by one, until only an old man was left to entertain the guests. As he did so, the door was quietly bricked up, and the bodies remain to this day. A message was sent to the headman at Ras Kismani that the account was now squared. Within a month, Ras Kismani was engulfed by the sea.

It is thought that the Shirazi people from Persia may have settled on the islands of **The Shirazi** Juani and Jibondo for strategic reasons. In AD 975 Ali ben Sultan Hasan (see **period** box, page 383) founded the sultanate of Kilwa and it is said that one of his sons, Bashat, settled in Mafia. The Shirazi, under Bashat, found the native Mwera people were settled on the islands – they also inhabited a large stretch of mainland and other islands off the coast. It is thought that the Mwera intermarried with the Shirazi. It was around this time that Islam reached Kilwa and no doubt then spread to these islands. There are believed to be some remains dating from the Shirazi period, including that of a mosque, on Jibondo Island. The Shirazi's influence was at its greatest from the 11th to the 13th centuries and from their headquarters at Kilwa they dominated the coast. Their main income was from gold from inland, and they also commanded huge customs duties on all goods that passed through Kilwa.

The town of Kisimani Mafia is thought to have been founded during the period of Shirazi and Arab domination. There were some suggestions that Kua also dated from this period, but it is now believed that most of these remains are more recent, with just a few dating back further. Kisimani Mafia lies on the west tip of Mafia overlooking the delta. Kua is located on Juani, a much smaller and less hospitable island – very hot with a poor water supply. It is thought possible that some Shirazis from Kisimani Mafia were driven out of the town by Arabs and founded Kua where they would be left alone. The ruins of Kisimani are being eaten away by the sea; the larger part of the town has already been engulfed. However one observer has suggested that the size of the town has been exaggerated and the story that much of the town lies under the sea derives from the rather curious coral reef and ridge in this sea, which could have been mistaken for the remains of a town.

At this time the island was under the control of Kilwa. In April 1498 Vasco da Gama **Portugal's** sighted the island of Mafia as he sailed on his first journey towards Mombasa. Portu- **influence in** gal's influence spread quickly and during the 16th century a number of visits were **the 16th &** made to Mafia and revenues were collected. However it was a period when expedi- **17th centuries** tions were fitful – they would be launched to collect revenue and were then followed by years of neglect. In 1635 a Portuguese commandant, subordinate to the governor of Mozambique, was stationed here and a small fort was erected on the east side of the island with a garrison of 10 to 15 men. The fort is thought to have been at Kirongwe although no trace of it has been found.

The islands of Chole and Juani had to make payments to passing Portuguese ships in the form of coconut fibre and gum copal. The population of the islands was believed to have been concentrated on the island of Jibono and at Kua on Juani, as at some stage (the date is not known) the town of Kisimani had been destroyed. The islands seem to have been used as a port of call for repairs to ships as well as a kind of safe haven when there were troubles on the mainland – as when, in 1570, Kilwa was invaded by the Zimba people and about 1,000 Arabs are thought to have been killed

Tanzania

and eaten. Portuguese influence was waning and by 1697 Portugal had lost control of her East African posts, except for Mozambique.

Arab rule   There followed a difficult period for the inhabitants of the islands with pirates active in the seas around Mafia. The next major event in Mafia's history was an invasion from Madagascar by war canoes. The exact date that this occurred is not known although it is thought to have been during the time of Sultan Said, between 1810 and 1835. According to tradition, the Sakalava came from Madagascar in 80 canoes, each with four men. They sacked Kua and all those who did not escape were killed or carried off as slaves. At this time Kua was the chief town on Mafia and the population was believed to have been large. The news of the raid was sent to Zanzibar and an expedition was sent by the Sultan to chase the invaders. The Sultan's troops found the raiders on a small island nearby and they were taken as prisoners back to Mafia. Kua however was never rebuilt and instead Chole Island, which had until then been home only to a slave population, became the seat of the Sultan's government.

The influence of the Omani Arabs grew although it is not known exactly when the Arabs settled on the Mafia islands. It was not until 1840, after the Sultan moved their headquarters from Muscat to Zanzibar, that his control over the coast reached its zenith. By 1846 he had established garrisons up and down the coast and there is little doubt that his influence on the Mafia group was considerable. Trade grew enormously and Mafia took part in this with gum copal trees being planted in large numbers. The islands were ruled by a series of governors, called *liwalis*, appointed by the Sultan of Zanzibar and after the sacking of Kua the government was moved to Chole. Chole Island is less than 1 sq km and many of the influential Arabs built houses on the island, occupying about half the island. It has been noticed that at least one of these *liwalis* had a eye for orderly town planning for many of the streets ran parallel to one another. This was unusual for Arab towns on the East African coast and comparisons with the narrow and windy streets of other towns show that this was clearly an exception.

From the beginning of the 19th century traders from all over the world had been plying these coastal waters. 'Americani' cloth proved itself to be perhaps the most popular of all the traded goods among the resident population. The trading of goods and of slaves was soon to be followed by the interest of European politics. However it was not until the end of the century that this affected territorial rights. Under the treaty of 1890, Mafia, Zanzibar and Pemba were initially allotted to the British sphere. However it was later agreed that Mafia should go to Germany in exchange for some territory on the southern border, which was allocated to the British Territory of Nyasaland (now Malawi). The island was therefore included in the purchase of the coastal strip from Sultan Seyyid Ali and the German flag was raised in 1890.

Colonial period   The Germans established a headquarters at Chole and in 1892 a resident officer was posted here together with a detachment of Sudanese troops. A large two-storey boma was constructed with various other buildings such as a gaol. The site seemed ideal with good anchorage for dhows, but with the opening of a regular coastal steamship service a deeper harbour was needed and the headquarters were moved to Kilindoni in 1913.

During the First World War it became clear that Mafia represented an extremely useful base from which attacks could be launched. In particular the British needed a base from which to attack the SS *Königsberg*, which was wreaking havoc on her fleet up and down the East African coast. In January 1915 a British expeditionary force under Colonel Ward landed on the island at Kisimani and the islands were captured with little resistance. A garrison of about 200 troops remained on the island.

The *Königsberg* had been damaged and gone into the mouth of the River Rufiji for repairs. The delta, with its many creeks and maze of streams, proved the perfect hiding place. It was important that the British should find and destroy the ship before any further damage could be done. In 1915 a British warplane was assembled on Mafia, took off from there and spotted the ship, and boats went into the delta to destroy it. It was the first example of aerial reconnaissance being used in warfare. A description by a local man of the intense activity of the British fleet at the time was that the searchlights 'turned night into day'. The wrecked remains of the hulk of the crippled boat could be seen until 1979 when it finally sank into the mud out of sight.

For a short period the islands were under military rule, and were later administered under Zanzibar. In 1922 the islands were handed over by the government of Zanzibar to become part of the Tanganyika Territory under the United Nations Mandate.

Sights

On the shore you can watch the construction of boats 20-25 m in length and weighing up to 100 tonnes. Timbers are prepared by hand and the frame of the boat is made from naturally V-shaped forked branches of trees.

Boat-building

Kua is on Juani Island to the south of Mafia Island. The remains are located on the western side of the island covering a large area of about 14 ha. In 1955, when the site was cleared of bush, one observer stated that he believed that these ruins were 'potentially the Pompeii of East Africa'. However, the remains require much work on them to be brought up to anything like this standard. There are several houses, one of which was clearly double-storeyed. Beneath the stairs leading to the upper level is a small room in which slaves could be confined for punishment. Under the building is the *haman* (bathroom), with a vaulted ceiling of curved coral blocks. A soil pipe runs from the remains of an upper room to a pit below. Two mosques and a series of tombs, some with pillars, are nearby. The evidence suggests that the town did not have a protective wall and that the inhabitants were mainly involved in agricultural pursuits on the island rather than in sea-trading.

Ruins at Kua

Kua was famous for the supposed curative properties of milk obtained there. There is a cave on the island formed by the action of the sea. The water streaming out of the cave as the tide turns is reputed to cure *baridi yabis* ('cold stiffness' – rheumatism) and other ailments. The cure is not effective, however, unless the hereditary custodian of the cave is paid a fee and the spirits of the cave appeased by an offering of honey, dates or sugar. Local fishermen will take you to Kua for US$1.

A small island 12 km off the north coast of Mafia with a fishing community of about 50 local boats. There are two small *hotelis* selling rice, *ugali* and fish. It's possible to camp on the beach in a thatched shelter.

Nororo Island

A beautiful small island with fine beaches. Used as a base for fishing dhows. About 12 km off northwest coast of Mafia and an hour's sailing from Nororo. You need to have your own food, water and tent if you want to stay.

Baracuni Island

Activities

Many people will come here to experience some of the best deep-sea diving in Tanzania. There is something here for everyone from the most experienced diver to those who want to snorkel in the shallower pools. The coral gardens off Mafia are marvellous – wonderfully vivid fish, shells, sponges, sea cucumber and spectacular coral reefs. Two of the most beautiful reefs are the Okuto and Tutia reefs around Juani and Jibondo Islands, a short distance from Chole Bay. About 1 km off Mafia's coastline there is a 200-m deep contour along the seabed of the Indian Ocean. The depth contributes to the wide variety of sea life. *Mafia Lodge* will provide equipment, but the quality is variable and you may prefer to bring your own. Note that during April-September the monsoon winds blow too hard, making it impossible to dive outside the lagoon and leading to a deterioration in visibility.

Diving
Best time to dive: Nov-Mar
See also page 45

There is a proposal that Mafia should become a marine park. This has been under discussion for some time now and implementation is imminent. The aim would be to create a series of zones around the island providing areas with differing levels of

Tanzania

protection, while not ruining local fishermen's livelihoods. The preliminary scientific study for this is currently being carried out by **Frontier Tanzania** manned almost entirely by volunteers in collaboration with the University of Dar es Salaam. The Worldwide Fund for Nature has also become involved and if the model is successful it will be used in other marine parks around Tanzania.

Fishing

Best time to fish: Sep–Mar

Fishing is at its best from September to March when the currents and the northeast monsoon (*kaskazi*) give rise to an enormous variety of fish. When the south monsoon (*kusi*) blows during the rest of the year fishing can be rather sparse. 'Big game' fish that can be caught in the area include marlin, shark, kingfish, barracuda and red snapper. There is a fishing club where details are kept of some of the record catches.

Mafia Island and some of the uninhabited islands around are also traditional breeding sites for the green turtle. Sadly you would be very lucky to see these as the local population is now close to being wiped out as a result of man's activities – being killed both as adults for their meat and as eggs. Another threatened species is the dugong, which lives in sea grass such as that found between Mafia and the Rufiji delta, giving rise to the legend of the mermaid. This strange beast is protected by law, but hunting continues.

Sleeping

L *Kinasi Lodge*, kinasi@intafrica.com, is a relatively new complex 100 m up the beach from *Mafia Lodge*. Its beach is not quite as nice as its rivals but it has a beautiful main complex in old coastal traditional style with a small library, bar, patio and dining room. It is furnished tastefully, with attractive pottery, accommodates 20 people, has en-suite bathrooms with hot water, mosquito nets. It has no a/c or phone but does have a swimming pool, can arrange diving and has sailboats. Bookings through PO Box 18033, Dar es Salaam, T2843913/5, F2843495. **L** *Mafia Island Lodge*, PO Box 2, Mafia, or PO Box 2485, Dar es Salaam, T/F022-2116609. 40 rooms, a/c, bar, restaurant, watersports, lovely setting overlooking Chole Bay, recently refurbished, food is good but a bit unvaried (mostly seafood), nice bar, the lodge has its own beach, there are windsurfing boards and Hobicats for rent. There is also a small diving centre at the lodge run by a divemaster, dives US$40 per person with all equipment, plus oxygen facilities with a DAN oxygen provider for safety. **D** *Lizu*, restaurant, bar, simple and tidy, fans, disco at weekends, can be rather noisy when the disco operates.

Transport

See Dar es Salaam transport, page 360, for further advice and contact details

Air *Precisionair* have 30-min flights that leave Dar es Salaam (DSM) at 1520 on Wed, Fri, Sat and Sun, cost US$50 one way. Flights operated jointly with *Air Tanzania*, depart DSM at 0930 on Tue and Thu and take 40 mins. *Eagle Air* fly from DSM at 1050 on Tue, 0900 on Thu and 1600 on Sun, taking 30 mins. All except the Sun flight return to DSM soon after arrival in Mafia. The Sun flight goes on to Zanzibar before returning to DSM. *Aviators Services*, T027-2546386, Arusha, or c/o *Scantan Tours*, PO Box 1054, T2548170, fly from DSM to Mafia at 1100 on Tue, Wed, Fri, Sun, and return the same day at 1200. The fare is US$85 one way. *Dar Aviation*, *Coastal Travels Ltd* and *Sky Tours* are new operators who offer flights from DSM to Mafia. They all cost about US$85 per person one way. **Sea** The crossing from Dar es Salaam to Mafia can be rough, so sea-sickness measures are recommended. *Tanzania Coastal Shipping Line*, PO Box 9461, Dar es Salaam, T26192, operates a service of sorts, but is infrequent and unreliable. **Dhows** can be taken from the dhow harbour in Dar es Salaam. They depart irregularly but there are usually 2-3 a week. From **Kisiju** (page 387), dhows leave every day. A motorized dhow takes 12 hrs, a sailing dhow up to 24 hrs. Passengers sit and sleep on the cargo. Take your own food and drink. Costs US$3-6.

Mbinga Hills

West of Somanga are the Mbinga Hills where there are several extensive **cave systems**, which were explored by German-Turkish and Italian researchers in 1994-5 with support from Tanzanian guides. The best known include Mpatawa Cave, accessed via a sinkhole and extending for over 1.5 km. The Nandembo Cave system nearby may possibly be linked to Mpatawa Cave but this has yet to be confirmed. Namaingo Caves are located in the Matumbi Hills, and include a fossil cave dating from the middle Jurassic period, extending for almost 500 m. In the western Mbinga

Hills are found the Likolongomba Cave and the Mampombo Cave. The village of Kipatimu in the Matumbi Hills is the nearest reference point, a journey of approximately 10 hours from Kilwa.

Kilwa

Kilwa is a group of three settlements, of exceptional historical interest, magnificently situated on a mangrove-fringed bay dotted with numerous small islands. If Kilwa was in Kenya the place would be full of tourists; it is an extraordinarily rewarding place to visit. As it is, it gets just a handful of visitors each week.

9°0'S 39°0'E
Colour map 4, grid B6

Kilwa grew up as a gold trade terminus and when its fortunes faded some magnificent ruins were left behind. These are said to be some of the most spectacular on the East African coast. The town is divided between **Kilwa Kisiwani** (Kilwa on the Island), 2 km offshore; **Kilwa Kivinje** (Kilwa of the Casuarina Trees) on the mainland; and **Kilwa Masoko** (Kilwa of the Market), which was built as an administrative centre on a peninsula and is the site of the main present-day town. There is a superb beach within a stone's throw from Kilwa Masako centre, and another, even better one a few miles north of the town (ask for Masako pwani).

History

Kilwa Kisiwani contains the ruins of a 13th-century city of the Shirazi civilization, which are well preserved and documented. The town was founded at the end of the 10th century by Shirazis (see box, page 383), and flourished with the core of commercial activity based on the trade of gold from Sofala (in present-day Mozambique). It grew to be the largest town on the south coast and prospered to the extent that Kilwa could maintain an independent status with its own sultan and coinage.

The large stone town that grew up thrived and the architecture was striking. The largest pre-European building in equatorial Africa was located here – the Husuni Kubwa. However, Kilwa's fortunes were reversed in the 14th century. Vasco da Gama was said to have been impressed by the buildings of Kilwa and in 1505 a large Portuguese fleet arrived and took the town by force. Their aim was to take control of the Sofala gold trade and they did this by erecting a garrison and establishing a trading post in the town from where they set up a gold trade link with the interior. Without the gold trade the Shirazi merchants were left with little to keep the wealth growing and the town quickly went into decline. Having taken over the gold trade, and thus triggered off the decline of the town, the Portuguese decided there was little point in staying in Kilwa, an outpost that was expensive to maintain. They therefore withdrew from Kilwa and continued the gold trade from further afield.

Deprived of the main source of income, the town continued to decline. In 1589 disaster struck when a nearby tribe, the Zimba, attacked the town,

Kilwa area

To Dar es Salaam

Kilwa Kivinje

Nangurukuru

Indian Ocean

Kilwa Masoko

Kilwa Kisiwani

To Lindi & Mtwara

Sanji ya Kati Island

Songo Mnara Island

Nisas Island

N

0 km 10
0 miles 10

Tanzania

killing and eating many of the inhabitants. In the 17th century, with the arrival of the Oman Arabs, Kilwa began to revive and many of the buildings were taken over by the sultans as palaces. The slave trade (see page 580) made a significant impact on this area and Kilwa Kivinje on the mainland flourished from the caravan route from the interior, which terminated at the port.

Sights

Kilwa Kisiwani
Allow at least half a day for your visit

Small dhows in the harbour at Kilwa Masoko will take you across the 2 km channel for US$7. However, it is necessary first to get a permit to visit the site (approximately US$2) from the Cultural Centre at the district headquarters, which is on the road leading to the harbour. They can also organize a half-day boat trip for US$10 (the boat will take up to six people). There is a guide on the island who will take you through the ruins, giving some background information on the buildings, for a negotiable fee of around US$3.50. For those interested in finding out more about the ruins, *One Thousand Years of East Africa* by John Sutton is highly recommended (available in Dar es Salaam from the museum bookshop).

Gereza Fort The original Gereza was built in the 14th century. The one standing there today was built by the Omani Arabs in the 19th century on the site of the original on the orders of the Imam of Muscat. It is a large square building built of coral set in lime. The walls are very thick with circular towers at the northeast and southwest corners. It has an impressive entrance of fine wood carving and some, although not all, of the inscription is legible.

Great Mosque (Friday Mosque) This mosque is said to have been built in the 12th century and is probably the largest of this period on the east coast. It was excavated between 1958 and 1960 and parts of it have been reconstructed. The oldest parts that remain are outer sections of the side walls and the north wall. The façade of the *mihrab* (the aspect that points towards Mecca) is dated from around 1300. The domed chamber was supposed to have been the sultan's prayer room. The water tanks and the slabs of stone were for rubbing clean the soles of the feet before entering the mosque.

Great House A large single-storey building is said to have been the residence of the sultan and the remains of one of the sultans are said to reside in one of the four graves found within its walls. The building is an illustration of the highly developed state of building and architectural skills in this period with examples of courtyards,

Kilwa Kivinje

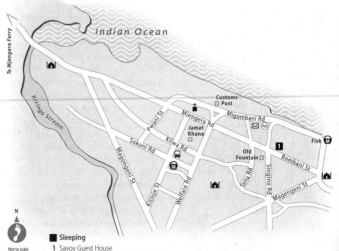

N
Not to scale

■ **Sleeping**
1 Savoy Guest House

reception rooms, an amphitheatre that is unique to this part of the world, latrines, kitchens and cylindrical clay ovens.

Small Domed Mosque This is without a doubt the best preserved of all the buildings in Kilwa. It is an ornamental building with beautiful domes located about 150 m southwest of the Great House. The long narrow room on its east side is thought once to have been a Koran school.

House of Portico Little remains of this once large building. There are portico steps on three of its sides from where it gets its name and its doorway has a decorated stone frame.

Makutini Palace (Palace of Great Walls) This large fortified building is believed to date from the 15th century. It is to the west of the Small Domed Mosque and is shaped in roughly a triangle. Its longest wall, which ran along the coast, is in ruins. Within the complex is the grave of one of the sultans.

Jangwani Mosque The ruins of this stone building are concealed under a series of mounds to the southeast of the Makutini Palace. This mosque was unique for having ablution water jars set into the walls just inside the main entrance.

Malindi Mosque This mosque to the east of the Gereza Fort was said to have been built and used by migrants from Malindi on the Kenya coast.

Husuni Kubwa This building is thought to be the largest pre-European building in equatorial Africa. It is located between 1-2 km to the east of the main collection of ruins on top of a steep cliff. It is certainly an exceptional construction with over 100 rooms and a large conical dome that reaches about 30 m above the ground. The mosque has 18 domes on octagonal piers, separated by high barrel vaults. The piers are decorated with bowls of white porcelain set in the plaster.

Husuni Ndogo This is a smaller version of Husuni Kubwa and they are separated by a small gully. It is said to have been built in the 15th century with walls 1 m thick and towers in the corners.

Excursions

Kilwa Kivinje Located 29 km north of Kilwa Masoko, Kilwa Kivinje is an attractive historical trading centre whose heyday was in the days of the slave trade in the 18th and 19th centuries, but which remained the district headquarters up until 1949. It retains many interesting old buildings dating back to the 19th century as well as the colonial period and is somewhat reminiscent of Bagamoyo. A handsome old boma on the shore dates from the German period, as does the covered market. Several fine though rather dilapidated houses stand along the main street. There is an old mosque in the centre, and to the east of the town is a cemetery with tombs and pillars. The town can be reached by *dala-dala*, heading for Manguruturu, costing about US$1. There are half-a-dozen or so each day.

Sleeping **A** *Kilwa Ruins Vacation Village*, bookings through *Family Travel & Tour Services Ltd*, PO Box 456, Dar es Salaam, T2772215, T0744-280028 (mob), ftts@raha.com Full board, 8 tents and bandas with en-suite bathrooms. **E** *Savoy Guest House*, located near the Old Boma in Kilwa Kivinje, fans, simple and adequate.

Songo Mnara & offshore islands **Songo Songo** is an inhabited island about 25km northeast of Kilwa Kivinje, protected by a reef, lying close to the site of a large natural gas field. The Songo Songo gas field contains unusually dry petrogenic gas, which is 97% methane, in a Lower Cretaceous sandstone reservoir. Songo Songo, Jewe Island and the surrounding smaller islands are an important marine bird breeding site. Access is by dhow, arranged in Kilwas Kivinje

There is a group of islands to the south of Kilwa Kiswani. It is necessary to hire a motorized dhow in Kilwa Masoko to get there, which will cost US$20 for up to six people. If you have the time it is very worthwhile spending a few days visiting some of the more distant islands, camping out on isolated beaches. This is the ideal way to take in all that the islands offer.

The ruined buildings at **Songo Mnara** are exceptional. The settlement is surrounded by the remains of a wall. The main mosque is distinguished by stonework in a herringbone pattern and has a double row of unusually high arches at one end.

The Sultan's Palace is extensive, with high walls, and it was evidently at least two storeys high. The doorways, faced with slender stonework, are particularly fine.

The building to the east of the palace has a room with a vaulted roof and porcelain bowls are set in the stonework. There are three other smaller mosques, two of which abut the surrounding wall. Some of the other ruins leave little to be distinguished, although rectangular windows and door frames are a feature of the group. Fragments of porcelain and earthenware abound, and some relics have been identified as Egyptian, dating from the 14th and 15th centuries.

About 3 km southwest of Songo Mnara is an area known as **Sanje Majoma**, which also contains the ruins of a number of once beautiful houses, complete with courtyards and stone arches. **Sanje ya Kati** is a nearby uninhabited island, which was once settled by the Shanga people who are now extinct. In the 13th century they were considered a force to be reckoned with and strongly resisted foreign control. There are ruins of oblong-shaped houses estimated to date from the 14th to 15th century.

Essentials

Sleeping **E** *Hilton Guest House*, s/c rooms, basic but tends to be noisy. **E** *Kilwa Guest House*, simple but basic. **E** *New Mjaka Guest House*, located on right of road that leads from main Mangurukivu Rd to the market. Fans, only single rooms, clean and tidy. **E** *Pande Guest House*, similar to the others. **E** *Salama Guest House*, on road from Milwa Kirinje and Mangurukuru. Fans, double rooms available, restaurant, bar.

Eating **Cheap** *Masoko by Night*. Charcoal-grilled chicken (*kuku*) and beef (*mishkaki*), breakfast options are especially poor. The restaurant next door to the *Hilton* serves excellent fish sambusas. For lunch or dinner the best bet is the small hotel opposite the bus stand. It is a modest place but the food is better there than at the other restaurants.

Transport **Air** *Air Tanzania* and *Precisionair* are supposed to share the operation of services from Dar es Salaam (DSM). There is a scheduled flight on Mon, leaving DSM at 0800, arriving Kilwa 50 mins later, continuing to Lindi before returning to DSM at 1140. On Fri a flight departs from DSM at 1525 and arrives at 1705, while at about the same time a flight goes in the opposite direction. A charter is a possibility, particularly if you are a party (see Air Charter operators in Dar es Salaam section, page 363).

See Dar es Salaam transport, page 360, for further advice and contact details

Road Bus: direct to Kilwa from **Dar es Salaam**, leaves from Kariakoo, Msimbazi St, at 0500, takes 13 hrs and costs US$6. Confirm exact departure time and book a ticket the day before you travel. Return from Kilwa

Kilwa Masoko

■ **Sleeping**
1 Hilton Guest House & Restaurant
2 Kilwa Guest House
3 New Majaka Guest House
4 Pande Guest House

● **Eating**
1 Masoko By Night

at 0500 daily. Alternatively take one of the numerous buses heading for destinations south of Kilwa, such as Mtwara, Lindi or Nachingwea. These leave Dar between 0700 and 0900 from the Kisutu bus stand on Morogo Rd in Dar. It is advisable to book at least a day in advance. Seats closer to the front are recommended as the going is rough. This bus will drop you off at **Nangurukuru**, a village 35-45 km from Kilwa Masoko, from where you have to transfer to a minibus or pickup to complete the journey (US$1). The cost from Dar to Nangurukura is around US$10. The journey takes 7-9 hrs. There is a simple guesthouse in Nangurukuru if you arrive late. In order to travel south to Lindi, Mtwara or Masasi you have to catch buses coming from Dar es Salaam at Nangurukuru. They start arriving from about 1400 onwards. The journey takes 5 hrs minimum as the road is poor. You'll be lucky to get a seat. There are numerous minibuses/pickups between Kilwa Kivinje and Kilwa Masoko daily.

Sea This stretch of ocean can be rough – travel sickness tablets are recommended. *Tanzania Coastal Shipping Line*, PO Box 9461, T25192, and *Shipping Corporation of Zanzibar*, PO Box 80, Zanzibar, T30300, run irregular freighters taking passengers. Enquire at port in Dar es Salaam or Zanzibar. It is possible to get a **dhow** from Dar es Salaam, but it is a matter of going to the dhow anchorage every day and asking about departure. You may need to go via Mafia. A motorized dhow will take 24 hrs and a sailing dhow 48 hrs. Costs US$6-12. Sleep on the cargo and take your own food and drink.

Lindi

Lindi translates from Ki Mwera (a local language) as 'a pit latrine'. The town is another little-visited place with a great deal of charm, albeit faded. It was an important port for early traders and travellers, and the Arab influence is visible. The centre has many attractive colonial buildings but poor communications, and the collapse of the Groundnut Scheme (see page 584), one site for which was at nearby Nachingwea, have hampered development. Since the opening of the deep-water harbour at Mtwara in 1954, Lindi's harbour, too shallow for modern ships, is only used by local fishing boats, and the quay is slowly crumbling away. Lindi Bay has several attractive beaches fringed with palm trees nearby.

9°58'S 39°38'E
Phone code: 023
Colour map 4, grid C6
Population: 40,000

Getting there There are several direct flights a week to Lindi from Dar es Salaam, or you could charter a plane. Otherwise, unless you have time to wait for boats, the best way is to go by road, perhaps breaking your journey at Kilwa as the daily bus journey from Dar takes anything from 14 to 20 hrs depending on road conditions. **Getting around** The airport is 25 km north of Lindi at Kikwetu. Lindi itself is a very compact town and most of the places of interest are within walking distance. *Dala-dalas* can be caught at the market, the bus stand or along the main streets (Kawawa, Market and Mchinga roads).

Ins & outs

Background

Initial settlement was by Shirazi migrants (see page 383). It was a destination for slave caravans from the interior in the 19th century, being the main seaport for Lake Nyasa (now Lake Malawi). The only remnant of this Omani Arab period is the massive round tower on the beach side of the stadium.

The colonial German powers chose Lindi as the administrative headquarters of the Southern Province, a huge administrative area, which encompassed the whole of the south of Tanganyika right across to Lake Nyasa (renamed Lake Malawi) at the end of the 19th century. A Custom House and store for the German East African Company were constructed close to the remains of the fort, These, and other buildings of the colonial period, are now very dilapidated. One German building is still in use, easily identifiable by its solid build and ornamental finishes – the police station. The German Boma is disappearing behind the trees growing out of it.

Lindi has a long history as a trading port for ivory, beeswax and mangrove poles. Rock salt is extensively mined nearby. Its advantages were the comparatively easy approach along the Lukuledi River valley and the relative proximity of Mozambique, source of much of the produce.

There are fine examples of Asian-inspired architecture along Market and Kawawa roads, dating from when the town used to support an Asian community trading in grain, sisal and cashew nuts.

There are ornamental decorative finishes on some of the buildings, especially the mosques, such as those on Makongoro Street facing the stadium. The modest mosque next to the bus station possesses a wonderful elaborately carved and colourful door. Lindi is now essentially a Muslim town and the Muslim Brotherhoods or *tariqa* are quite active. You are likely to hear, if not see, noisy celebrations at night such as *maulid*, the commemoration of the Prophet's birth. It involves Quran school teachers and their students singing in turn, drumming, lots of incense, and possibly deep-breathing exercises known to Muslim mystics as *dhikr*. If you want to see a *maulid* dress modestly and exercise discretion. Other rather high-pitched drums heard at night are for girls' initiation ceremonies or spirit possession dances – no contradiction for the local brand of Islam.

The present centre of town around the bus stand dates from the British period. The historic centre of the town between Kawawa Road and the beach is now a poor area with a reputation for rampant witchcraft. Here the last descendant of the once-dominant Jamalidini family, of Mombasa origins, lives in a mud hut on a waterlogged compound. Several of the newer houses resemble pillboxes made of cement or breeze-blocks or occasionally mud and wattle.

Many of Lindi's residents come from 'ngambo' (see below) or are from Makonde.

Lindi has a large football stadium and its team is in Tanzania's 1st division, worth watching if you get the opportunity. There is also a branch of the Open University here (PO Box 742, T2202725). The Pentecostal Church just opposite the *Ruya Guesthouse* has a wonderful Gospel choir.

	Sleeping	5 Nankolowa Guest	9 Shiriton Guest House	2 DDC
1	Adela Guest House	House	10 South Honour	3 Green Inn
2	Malaika & Restaurant	6 New Jacky Magongo	Guest House	4 Hidden Treasure Café
3	Gift Guest House	Guest House		5 Maji Mji
4	Machenza Guest	7 Panama Guest House	● Eating	6 NBC Club
	House	8 Ruya Guest House	1 Biashara Club	7 Novelty Y2K Bar

The beach doubles as a boulevard and football pitch in the evenings, and sometimes you can observe the fishermen unloading their catch that includes octopus, kingfish and sharks – caught outside the bay. Their catch of the day is for sale after dark at the bus stand, freshly cooked. The beach by the town is also good for swimming, but you are likely to be closely observed by the townspeople.

Excursions

There are several excellent beaches around Lindi Bay, the best probably at Mitema, 4 km north of the town, just a 10-minute drive from the centre. This is where Lindi's few expatriates go swimming. The long beach, often deserted, is sheltered by palms and closed off at each end by rocks and enormous baobab trees. Occasionally you may meet a herd boy with his goats or a couple of Lindi's Asian traders in their four-wheel drive vehicles. The ground is a bit rocky at low tide and the waves are high in the evening but it makes an enjoyable excursion – if you don't have your own transport make arrangements with *dala-dala* operators at the bus stand.

Mitema

'Ngambo' means 'the other shore' and in Lindi it refers to the peninsula across the bay, Kitunda being the beachside village. For a negligible fare, and at approximately half-hour intervals from Lindi harbour until 1800, you can take a wooden motorboat ferry to Kitunda. Here the water is clearer than at Lindi though mangroves make swimming difficult at low tide. You can hire a dugout very cheaply from a local fisherman to paddle along the shore or across the bay and locals can show you around the hill behind the village. Take the owner along for safety. You will be shown many edible plants and odd animals such as *ndandanda*, a small wedge-shaped fish with large eyes at the top of its head that uses its fins for crawling and jumping in shallow water. The sisal and coconut estates here are in terminal decline and there are the remains of a railway and jetty jutting out over the water, a good vantage point for swims at high tide. Across the hill to the south lie the villages of **Mwitingi**, once the home of Arab plantation owners, and **Shuka**, where locals catch sharks. It may be possible to stay in Kitunda very cheaply.

Kitunda & 'ngambo'

Kikwetu is a breezy promontory 25 km north of Lindi, the location of the town's **airfield** and also of the last sisal estate to close in the area. The estate closed in 1999 after 100 years of production because sisal, used as coarse fibre for sackcloth and ropes, is no longer profitable. Hidden among the large fields is the manager's mansion, from where there are excellent views. There is regular transport to the airport – to see the mansion, a 20-minute walk away from the roadside village, ask for 'kambi' and the locals will show you. There are reports that South Africans may buy the estate, so it could yet have a future.

Kikwetu

This small island in Lindi Bay is famed for its large bat population. Chiropteran fanciers can take a boat trip to the island where the trees are heavy with sleeping bats hanging from the branches during the day. You may also see crocodiles if you take a boat ride south across the Lukuledi River estuary to the other side of Lindi Bay.

Kisiwa cha popo

There are numerous little-known forest reserves dotted throughout Tanzania, including many that exist to help preserve some of the remaining patches of coastal rainforest that millions of years ago covered the whole coastal area. Several of these reserves are in Lindi district, the most accessible of which is west of Litipo. The reserve here consists of a patch of rainforest lying between two small lakes. Litipo Forest Reserve covers an area of 999 ha. It is a beautiful spot and although you are unlikely to see many animals there the area is rich in birdlife, including the red-tailed ant thrush, African pitta and Livingstone's flycatcher. On the nearby Rondo Plateau the spotted ground thrush, the green-headed oriole and green barbet are also found. In order to see the reserve you will need to spend at least one night at the village of **Rutamba** where there is a basic rest house, the *Ali Baba* (a room costs US$1.50).

Litipo Forest Reserve

Tanzania

Tanzania

☞ Cashew nuts

Cashew nuts are the main export product in the Lindi, Mtwara and Kilwa regions of Tanzania. They grow on massive trees, rarely more than 10 m tall, but with sprawling, shady crowns, which line many of the streets in these districts. They supply elephant repellent, poison, furniture varnish, high-voltage liquor, and, of course, nuts. Two properties combine to make the fruit so versatile. First, cashew nuts come attached to cashew apples, a tasty, brightly coloured fruit which is easily fermented. Second, between the shell and the kernel, cashew nuts contain a noxious oil strong enough to cause serious wounds. Hence the use of cashew nuts to drive off elephants: the animals detest the smell of the burning oil.

The oil makes the shelling of cashew nuts difficult and the shelled nuts expensive. The trick is to burn the shells and the oil of the nuts, but not the kernels, by roasting them quickly and then quickly extinguishing the fire. If people do this in their back yards in old gasoline drums, the kernels end up spotty, half raw, half charred. Nuts like these are sold cheaply in the countryside and sometimes in Dar. Better quality ones, shelled in factories, are much more expensive, and a mere handful might cost more than a meal.

Tanzania's cashew shelling industry has not fared very well. Most of the nuts are exported raw and shelled in India. In Tanzania, the state-owned cashew marketing board tried to introduce industrial processing of the nuts. Factories have been opened and closed at various times in Mtwara, Nachingwea and Dar es Salaam. At present, only the one in Dar is working efficiently.

Cashew trees are not indigenous to Africa. They entered Tanzania from Mozambique, where they had arrived from Brazil, a fringe benefit of Portuguese colonialism. For a long time, Mozambique (then Portuguese East Africa) was the only African cashew nut exporter, the nuts being sent to Goa, Portugal's colonial possession in India, for processing. In Tanzania, efforts to build up production only started in the late 1940s, British reluctance to support cashew production being partly due to colonial officials' fear of drunkenness among Africans – cashew apples make a good raw material for distilling illicit spirits.

In the 1940-60s, cashew nuts helped to improve the economic situation of one of the poorest parts of Tanzania where, until then, grains had been the main export crop. It also became a factor in the establishment of inheritable private property in land, and the changeover from inheritance by nephews to inheritance by children in the matrilineal societies of this region. But from the early 1970s, the spread of a tree disease, low producer prices, and the effects of the villagization policy combined to almost destroy cashew production. Villagization separated cultivators from their plots and occasionally even involved the cutting down of trees in order to construct the villages, while disease caused yields to dwindle to almost nothing.

Production was revived only at the end of the 1990s, when people were again free to live where they chose, and it was discovered that if sulphur was sprayed on the leaves, it protected the trees against disease. It has been rising since. In the 1999/2000 season, prices to farmers for Tanzanian cashew nuts hit an all-time high because of a poor harvest in India, the world's largest cashew supplier. The southern regions had a bumper harvest, and for the year 2000 cashew nuts became Tanzania's top foreign-currency earning cash crop.

■ Buses to Rutamba depart from Lindi daily at 1000 or 1200 from opposite the Caltex station on Ghana St. Although only 30 km or so, the journey takes at least 3 hrs. There are daily buses back to Lindi each morning. To get into the reserve, go along the road leading to Tandangogoro village and take one of the paths leading north that go into the reserve. To get more information about Litipo it may be advisable to ask for the forest reserve officer who is usually stationed at Rutamba.

Tendaguru   The richest African deposit of the Late Jurassic strata is found in Tendaguru. The natural history museums in London and Berlin both boast complete dinosaur skeletons from Tendaguru among their exhibits, among the largest ever discovered. Bernhard

Sattler, a German mining engineer who was prospecting in the region for minerals and semi-precious stones, first uncovered fossil remains in 1907. Between 1909 and 1913, W Janensch and E Hennig of the Natural History Museum of Berlin uncovered about 225,000 kg of bones and, using porters, transported them along footpaths – there were no roads – for 70 km to the coast at Lindi and shipped them to Europe. British palaeontologists later continued the research, undertaking excavations from 1925-29. Post-independence, smaller research investigations have been carried out with the permission of the Tanzanian authorities. Many bones remain under the ground and fragments can be seen at the sites of previous digs. The beds consist of three horizons of terrestrial marls alternating with marine sandstone interbeds. Remains of the giant vegetarian, long-necked sauropod, *Brachiosaurus brancai*, named after the museum's director at the time and measuring 22 m long by 12 m high, and the spiny-plated stegosaurus, *Kentrurosaurus aethiopicus*, 4.8 m long by 1.7 m high, both of which were found here, are now on display in Berlin. ■ *The natural resources administration of Lindi (Mali Asili) will be able to help to arrange a visit, something only possible in the dry season. The site is quite remote, so a fossil enthusiast might need at least 3 days for getting there, looking around and getting back. As elephants may be present a game warden will be required. You should also be self-sufficient as there are no facilities, although you may be able to arrange accommodation with local villagers.*

Essentials

D *Malaika Hotel*, Market Av, PO Box 181, T2202717. Good s/c rooms and restaurant, price includes breakfast. **E** *Coast Guest House*, T2202496, located about 500 m north of ferry on beach. Fans and nets. **E** *Gift Guest House*, near *Malaika Hotel* on Market Av, T2202462. New and clean, decent-sized rooms, fans and nets. **E** *Nankolowa Guest House*, Rutamba St, signposted from the clock tower. New and well furnished, good value, s/c double rooms, single rooms have shared toilet, price includes large breakfast, other meals on request, a long wait but good. **E** *Town Guest House*, junction of Eilat St and Makonde St, 5 blocks in from the shore. Fans, nets, clean and simple. **F** *Adela Guest House*, Swahili St, near the corner with Karume St, PO Box 264, Lindi, T2202571. Very cheap, clean and friendly, with nets, but rooms are very small, no fan, shared bathroom. **F** *Machenza Guest House*, very cheap and basic, off Makongoro Rd, near the stadium. **F** *New Jacky Magongo Guest House*, reasonable standard, with nets and fans, but can be noisy as it is on Makongoro Rd, backing on to the bus station. **F** *Panama Guest House*, Jamhuri St, just south of the corner with Amani St, is particularly good value. **F** *Ruya Guest House*, Makongoro Rd, near the corner with Market Av, is of a similar standard to *New Jacky Magongo*. **F** *Shiriton Guest House*, located on the corner of Market Av and Msonobar St close to the bus station. Large rooms with fans, clean and comfortable enough, scruffy shared bathrooms. **F** *South Honour Guest House*, Amani St, 3 blocks back from the ferry. Fans, nets, simple, with agreeable staff – very cheap, costs about $2.50.

Sleeping
■ *on map page 398*

All of the hotels have restaurants, and there are snack bars around the bus station. Fresh fruit and simple fare can be purchased at the market on Jamhuri St. The fishermen's catch of the day is for sale, freshly cooked, at the bus stand after dark.

Eating & bars
● *on map page 398*

Biashara Club, eastern end of Market Av, livelier than *Lindi Club*, good chicken and chips. *The DDC Club*, corner of Makongoro Rd and Amani St, is a bar with some food available, offering excellent *nyama choma* and chips *mayai*. *The Maji Maji Restaurant* does good fish and rice. *Malaika*, Market St, good value menu, best restaurant in town although mainly rice dishes and snacks. *National Bank of Commerce (NBC)*, now called the *Lindi Club*, is a good choice for a drink. A bit dilapidated, but the sea view makes it one of the most pleasant locations.

A cheaper option are the several small 'tea shops' around town that serve sweet, milky tea for about $0.10, as well as *maandazi*, *chapattis* and other snacks. They include the seriously cheap hidden treasure, *Green Inn*, opposite *Malaika Hotel* on Market Av, and a good but unnamed place on Jamhuri St near the corner with Nzunda St. Cheap meals. *Magerezo Social Club*, north of town, near *Coast Guest House*, bar and snacks.

Entertainment The former cinema on Karume St is now the *Novelty Y2K Bar*, which has a small disco of sorts in the evening.

Transport **Air** The airstrip is at Kikwetu about 25 km north of town. *Air Tanzania* have an office in a for-
See Dar es Salaam mer bank on Uhuru Av, PO Box 1084, Lindi, T2202537. Scheduled flights leave **Dar es Salaam**
transport, page 360, (DSM) at 1525 on Thu and Fri, arrive 1 hr later, and return to DSM soon afterwards. The same
for further advice route is served on Tue, but the flight leaves DSM at 1345. *Air Tanzania* and *Precisionair* are
and contact details meant to jointly operate a flight that leaves DSM at 0800 on Mon, passing via **Kilwa** and arriving in Lindi at 0950, and another that leaves DSM on Fri at 1400, arriving in Lindi at 1550.
Eagle Air have 3 flights a week from DSM. On Mon a flight departs DSM at 0830, arriving at
0945, before continuing on to **Nachingwea** and returning to DSM at 1210. On Thu and Sat
the flight leaves DSM at 1500, arriving 1 hr later, before continuing to **Mtwara** and DSM. A
charter is a possibility, particularly if you are a party – see Air Charter operators in Dar es
Salaam section, page 363. Alternatively fly to Mtwara and connect by road.

Bus Buses leave from Kisutu bus stand on Jamhuri St/Morongoro Rd in **Dar es Salaam** at
0600-0900, take 14-20 hrs and cost US$15. Bus to Dar es Salaam leaves at 0500 from bus stand
on Makongaro Rd. The fare to **Kilwa** along the way, approximately US$6. To **Mtwara** buses run
fairly frequently, cost US$1.70 and take about 2 hrs. There are several daily direct buses. The
journey takes about 4 hrs and the fare is US$3. To **Nachingwea** and **Newela** there are daily
buses. The fare to Nachingwea is US$5, the journey time 5-6 hrs, and to Newala it costs US$4
and the journey time is 6 hrs. The road rising up to the Makonde plateau is pretty grim.

Sea *Tanzania Coastal Shipping Line*, PO Box 9461, T25192 and *Shipping Corporation of
Zanzibar*, PO Box 80, Zanzibar, T30300, run irregular freighters taking passengers. Enquire at
port in Dar es Salaam or Zanzibar. It is possible to get a **dhow** from Dar es Salaam, but it is a
matter of going to the dhow anchorage every day and asking about departure. You may
need to go via Mafia. A motorized dhow will take 24 hrs and a sailing dhow 48 hrs. Costs
US$6-12. Sleep on the cargo and take your own food and drink.

Directory There is now only 1 **bank** in town, the *CRDB* near the clocktower, where travellers' cheques command
a 2% commission. The **post office** is on Uhuru Av not far from the ferry. **Medical
services** Sokoine Hospital, T2202027/8.There is a medical clinic at the corner of Amani St and
Msonobar St. **Useful addresses** The police station (T2202505) is housed in an old German building
beside the waterfront, towards the NBC Club.

Lindi to Liwale

Mnazi Mmoja These two small villages, just a 10-minute walk apart, have built up around the junc-
& Mingoyo tion of the roads to Lindi, Masasi and Mtwara. There is nothing of great interest here
Colour map 4, grid C6 but the tired traveller can buy refreshments from the stalls or stay in a guesthouse for
the night. On offer are the usual snacks, drinks, clothes, shoes and watches. There is
a good chips *mayai* vendor outside the *Amana Guest House*. Decent, spacious
rooms with nets and fans are available at **F** *Makala Guest House*, and next door is the
very cheap **F** *Amana Guest House*, whose rooms are more basic and without fans.

Ndanda Ndanda is a nondescript roadside village at first glance, but it has the best hospital in
Approximately 80 km the region, run by German monks, the Missionary Benedictines. The population of
southwest of Lindi on the municipality is 18,000, 2,000 of whom are Christians. The hospital and labora-
the road to Masasi tory have facilities for treating malaria, tuberculosis, malnutrition, leprosy,
waterborne diseases like cholera and typhoid fever as well as worm infestations. The
Mission has many operations including a dairy farm, a tractor ploughing service, a
garage, a printing press and accompanying bookshop.

There are walkways through woods that would not look out of place in southern
Germany and a deep pond where you can swim if you have introduced yourself to

Tanzania

the Mission. There is also a guesthouse, which has hot running water and meals – strictly authentic Bavarian cuisine, including cured pork and sauerkraut – can be arranged. The mission is along the road that heads north opposite the bus stand; to stay you have to ask nicely and make a donation, perhaps US$13 per person, for full board accommodation.

Unfortunately despite all the good works, relationships between the Europeans and the local Africans appear to be a little strained, and local bus drivers and traders are less amicable here than elsewhere.

Sleeping and eating Very basic guesthouses are to be found in the village, the best of which are **F** *Highway* at the eastern end of the village, and **F** *Nuru Guest House* at the bus stand, which is a little run down, has small rooms and a restaurant serving snacks and rice dishes. Other places to eat are the seriously cheap *Miami Bar*, on Aggrey St, north from the market, which does good omelettes, chips, and chicken and beef roasted on a spit, and *Nandope Restaurant*, beside the market, which offers good fruit salad, pilau and snacks.

Born as the headquarters of the fateful Groundnut Scheme, a few incongruously large buildings survive in this town, a sprawling mass of pillbox houses, many unfinished, amid the red dust. There is a sesame oil factory and cashew shelling plant, neither of which are operational. Local people tell stories of amazing machinery buried by the British when closing the groundnut operations, reputed to include ex-American Sherman tanks bought from the Far East after the Second World War and converted into tractors. Here the government still dabbles in cattle rearing and local rumours tell of a prison farm.

Only travellers intrigued by the remnants of a spectacular failure and the pitfalls of technocratic planning will find anything of interest in the area and town itself, which nevertheless has a small airport, lively market and some good value guesthouses.

Nachingwea
Colour map 4, grid C5

Sleeping **F** *Beira Guest House*, PO Box 191, at the roundabout where the roads to Lindi and Masasi meet. Clean and friendly, nets, fans work if there is electricity, shared facilities, no food, recommended. **F** *Rovuma Guest House*, next to *Beira*, and much the same, recommended. **F** *Daraja Guest House* is also on the Lindi Rd, just beyond *Rovuma*. All the guesthouses are very cheap but this is the cheapest – and also seedier. Other small guesthouses like *Daraja* are located near the market, one block north of the Lindi road.

There is one bank in Nachingwea but it does not change money, the nearest facility being in Masasi

Eating **Cheap**: *Hollywood*, just north of the Lindi and Masasi road junction, the best restaurant in town, good choice of food, the TV may provide relief or be a distraction. **Seriously cheap**: *Mwambao*, a short distance north of *Hollywood* towards the market, basic meals. Snacks and fruit can be bought at the market.

Transport **Air**: *Eagle Air* have 1 flight a week from Dar es Salaam (DSM) via Lindi, departing DSM at 0830 on Mon, leaving Lindi by 1005 and arriving in Nachingwea at 1040. The plane then returns to DSM, arriving at 1210. A joint *Air Tanzania/Precisionair* flight leaves DSM around midday on Mon and Thu, journey time 80 mins, then returns to DSM, touching down at about 1500. **Road**: From the bus stand, diagonally opposite the market, buses leave for Lindi, Masasi, Ndanda and Liwale.

See Dar es Salaam transport, page 360, for further advice and contact details

---

Mnero is a large, sprawling village but too isolated to be regularly supplied with items such as soda or newspapers. It lies to the east of the Nachingwea-Liwale road, approximately 30 km north of Nachingwea. If you don't have transport you can try hitching to Mnero, most likely in church or hospital vehicles, or in a Land Rover that runs from Nachingwea every day except Sunday. You could also take the Nachingwea-Lindi bus to Miembeni, and then walk or hitch the last few kilometres to Mnero.

There is an imposing Benedictine Mission at the northeast end of the village, complete with mock Gothic church, and there are excellent views across the valley to Ilulu Mountain. Villagers travel to Mnero for the hospital which is tiny, but as a

Mnero & Ilulu Mountain

Mission facility is relatively well stocked. Mnero Diocesan Hospital is a Voluntary Agency Hospital with 111 beds predominantly supported by overseas donations. The hospital and church are painted red, reflecting the colour of the soil in this region. Mnero stream has bitter water, probably due to manganese in the ground. Obtaining fresh water supplies is a problem here; in dry years people have to go as far as the Mbmkuru River.

The ethnic groups in the Mnero area are almost exclusively Wamwera, with some Wamakua, Wamakonde, Wajao and some Wamagingo. Beside their tribal language most people speak KiSwahali. Most people are Muslim, with a Christian minority, with a few people following traditional animist religions. The area is poor with subsistence farmers eking out a living planting crops.

The mountain is the only real attraction here for a traveller. It is referred to locally as the 'navel' of Mwera country. In the old days it was considered a source of powerful medicine. Although the volcanic soils are very fertile the slopes are populated only in the wet season as permanent homes would apparently be disrespectful to the mountain. When the people do come they live in bamboo huts in defiance of lions. It is said to be the place were the peaceful local Mwera people defeated fierce Ngoni raiders some time before 1900 – there is a shrine to the victorious leader, Nakotyo, at the top. Actually an enormous boulder, a symbolic sacrifice by means of a few coins is required with a prayer in KiMwra. There is a fine view from the top across the plains of Nachingwea and Liwale, and all the way to Masasi. After decades of population growth settlements still appear as islands in a vast expanse of bush.

Climbing the mountain There are several routes. The one from Kipara leads past sites of interest, such as a place where grinding stones are made, but this route undulates for a long time through the foothills of the mountain. The climb is mostly easygoing through bamboo and open woodland until the final rocky ascent, which is a strenuous uphill crawl on rough ground through undergrowth and trees. The quickest way to the top is from Runyu village, a 20-minute drive from Mnero. From here and back, including a long stop at the top, will take about six hours. Ask around for a guide in Mnero if you have your own transport, otherwise try for a church vehicle with driver and get a guide in Runyu. A young man called Abdalla who lives in Runyu has already taken a few groups up the mountain, most of which were prospecting for precious stones. You may be asked to pay a visit to the old woman in charge of the shrine on the mountain. The guide's fee will probably be less than US$5.

Sleeping There are no guesthouses in Mnero, but you can stay at the Mission for about US$3.50 per person including meals. The Mission building is also built in a Gothic style, reflecting the tastes of the missionaries, who left about 20 years ago. You may find a mass chalice is now designated to hold your toothbrush. If you are lucky you may get a room in one of the staff houses of the hospital – ask at the sister's house. This will cost approximately US$6 for a room with 2 beds – you can cook yourself or ask an attendant to cook for you. A canteen in front of the hospital serves tea and rice and fish.

Liwale
Colour map 4, grid C5

Sodas in Liwale are probably the most expensive in Tanzania, an indication of the remoteness of this town. The access roads and town itself are very sandy, something that, together with the palm trees and *taarab* music, give the area an oddly coastal feel. On the way from Nachingwea you will pass through forest where people have erected tall stockades, 3 m or more high, around their homes as protection from lions and elephants. The meat of crop-raiding elephants, shot by government game scouts, is sold in the town. Another Liwale speciality is *'ngende'*, a benign form of witchcraft considered to be very powerful. It is said that if you tell people here that you don't believe in witchcraft, you will wake up in a tree the following morning.

Liwale has a troubled past. The town used to be on the main trading route from Lake Nyasa (now Lake Malawi) to Kilwa. The local people, the Ngindo, had suffered heavily in local wars before German occupation, and struggled to draw benefits from trade passing through. In the Maji Maji uprising they risked everything, seeking the aid of their former enemies, the Ngoni, by attacking the Germans but only incited merciless retaliation.

A German boma stands at the northern end of town, still in use today. Its fortress-like appearance is diminished by a gash in its massive walls. Its predecessor was burnt down by the Maji Maji rebels, the only boma to fall in the uprising. On the first floor, five oval shadows on the wall are said to be portraits of a kind, of the local leaders who were killed in the uprising. Local legend is that their heads were built into the wall.

After the First World War, which depleted the population still further, the trading route was gone and the area was partially evacuated due to the incidence of sleeping sickness. Since the creation of Selous Game Reserve the area has been cut off from the west and Liwale has only experienced decline. "*Mgeni aje, mwenyeji apone*" – "*let visitors come, so the locals may prosper*", says a Swahili proverb. One would wish Liwale, languishing in the shadow of Selous Game Reserve, a share of the proceeds of the tourist trade. Assuming that you have your own transport the local game reserve office can arrange for a guide to take you into Selous. There are several little-used roads, one of which leads to Dar es Salaam, but you will need to be confident that the vehicle, your health and the weather will hold out as no one will be around to help if things go wrong.

Sleeping and eating E *Tumaini Guest House*, near the market, is new and clean, with nets, fans and shared facilities; food is not available. E *Litopite Guest House*, near the fort, has small rooms with nets, fans and shared bathroom. The owner runs the bar next door, which is popular because it has a TV, snacks are sometimes available. *Rainer's Bar*, on the main road to Nachingwea, offers chips, sometimes with chicken or egg. There are many small eateries near the market where simple local meals are offered; close by is also a large bar.

The town's only bank does not change money

Southeast to Mtwara and Mozambique

Mtwara

Mtwara is a sizeable town that came to prominence during the British period. It has been a centre for agricultural processing, and there is a factory for shelling and canning the cashew nuts that are grown extensively in the southeast. The town itself is set a little way from the shore. Mtwara boasts a magnificent sheltered harbour. However the port, built in 1948-54, has never been used to capacity as there is relatively little traffic generated in this economically depressed region. The second deepest port in Africa, it was built as part of the ill-fated scheme to grow and export groundnuts from southern Tanzania, a project that included the construction of a railway from Mtwara to Nachingwea – now dismantled. There are current plans to dredge and widen the port's entrance channel to facilitate the handling of larger modern vessels.

10°20'S 40°20'E Phone code: 023 Colour map 4, grid C6 Population: 80,000

There are some good **beaches** about 2 km from the town centre. Even the more expensive hotels are good value for a beach vacation. The beach here is good for swimming and diving. From here the dhow ferry leaves, and you can cross the peninsula for TSh50, from where you can negotiate travel up and down the coast.

Mtwara is close to the border with Mozambique and there is a launch boat that crosses the Ruvuma River. The boat does not carry vehicles. The fare is US$2-8 depending on the amount of luggage you have. However, visas are available only to Tanzanian nationals at the border; other nationalities need to get one from Dar es Salaam in advance. If you wish to return to Tanzania you will also require a re-entry visa, available from the immigration offices in Mtwara.

Crossing into Mozambique

C *Mtwara Peninsula Hotel*, west of town, T2333965, T/F2333638. Executive rooms have TV and minibar, all rooms a/c with en-suite bathrooms, good restaurant, transport to/from airport provided on request. E *Bondeni*, Tanu Rd, south of police station, spacious, lounge with

Sleeping

Tanzania

satellite TV. **E** *Limo's*, T2333570, rooms with fridge and own toilet, shared shower facilities. **E** *Sea Breeze* (formerly *Shangani Club*), 2 km northwest of town. S/c rooms, good restaurant, bar. **E** *Tingatinga Inn*, between *Sea Breeze* and the headland, T2333146, rooms with own shower and toilet. **F** *Mabatini Inn*, central, T2334025, good, cheap, s/c rooms. **F** *Shukra Inn*, central, signposted from Port Rd, T2333822, also has good, cheap, s/c rooms.

Eating, bars & entertainment

Cheap *Mtwara Peninsula Hotel* is the best restaurant in town, very smart with a good choice of food. *Sea Breeze*, previously the *Shangani Club*, on the beach is also recommended.

All the hotels offer a limited selection of inexpensive simple meals, with little variety – usually rice with chicken or fish. The best cheap street food is at the fish market, beside the beach, where fresh fish and cassava chips are sold.

Limo's is a good place for a drink, there is a nice atmosphere and several open-sided bandas to sit in. *Bondeni Pub* is also pleasant, while the *Bandari Club* on Port Rd is always popular. The club often has live African bands on Fri or Sat nights, entrance fee roughly US$0.60-$3.75 depending on who is playing.

Mtwara

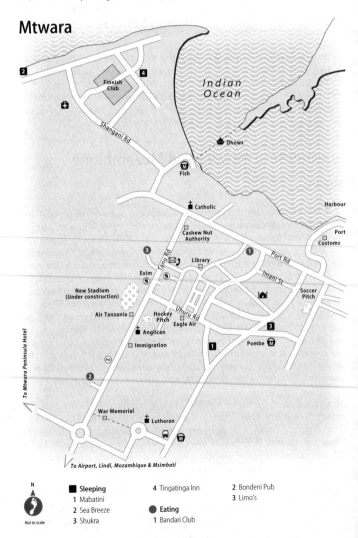

N
Not to scale

■ **Sleeping**
1 Mabatini
2 Sea Breeze
3 Shukra

4 Tingatinga Inn

● **Eating**
1 Bandari Club

2 Bondeni Pub
3 Limo's

Air *Air Tanzania* have an office on Tanu Rd, in front of the stadium currently under construction, PO Box 199, T2333417. They have 3 return flights a week from Dar es Salaam (DSM) – Tue (departs 1255), Fri (0800) and Sun (0800). The fare is around US$100 one-way, US$40 for residents, flights take 45 mins. *Eagle Air* has a flight from DSM via Lindi on Thu and Sat, leaving at 1500 and arriving in Mtwara at 1640. A charter is a possibility, particularly if you are a party – see Air Charter operators in Dar es Salaam section, page 363.

Transport
See Dar es Salaam transport, page 360, for further advice and contact details

Road Bus: from **Dar es Salaam** buses leave early in the morning, take roughly 24 hrs and cost US$8. It's about 400 km from Dar along a rough, unsurfaced road. Buses leave for Dar at 0500 from the bus stand on Market St. Book ticket day before and confirm departure time. Buses to **Masasi** leave fairly frequently, cost US$4. Regular buses to **Lindi** cost US$1. *Dala-dala* to **Mnazi Mmoja** US$1.60, **Mikindani** US$0.25. *Dala-dala* from Mtwara to Lindi will take you for US$0.50. A taxi will cost US$15 for the return trip.

Sea This stretch of ocean can be rough – travel sickness tablets are recommended. *Tanzania Coastal Shipping Line*, PO Box 9461, T25192, and *Shipping Corporation of Zanzibar*, PO Box 80, Zanzibar, T30300, run irregular freighters taking passengers. Enquire at port in Dar es Salaam or Zanzibar. *MV Safari* departs Dar es Salaam at 1200 on Wed, arrives at Mtwara 24 hrs later and returns on Fri, 1st class US$12.50, 2nd class US$8.50 one way, there is an office near the market. It is possible to get a **dhow** from Dar es Salaam, but it is a matter of going to the dhow anchorage every day and asking about departures. You may need to go via Mafia. A motorized dhow will take 24 hrs and a sailing dhow 48 hrs. Costs US$6-12. Sleep on the cargo and take your own food and drink.

Banks You can cash travellers' cheques at the recently opened *Exim Bank* on Tanu Rd, T2334045, F2333871, 1% commission, and *CRDB* T/F2333572, crdb@raha.com **Communications** Internet: email services available inside the *Cashew Nut Authority* building on Tanu Rd, to the seaward side of the post office, US$0.30 to send, US$0.60 to receive. **Post**: post office on Tanu Rd, half-way between *NBC Club* and Port Rd, has phone and fax facilities (US$3.50 per min sending or receiving) services. The post office is also home to the local branch of TTCL. **Useful addresses** The **immigration office** is to the south of the *NBC Club* on Tanu Rd, just past the Anglican church, and the **police station** is across the road from there. *Ligula Hospital*, T32015.

Directory

Mikindani

The small town of Mikindani is 11 km to the northwest of Mtwara on the Mtwara to Lindi road. Unlike most towns in this region, Mikindani has managed to retain much of its traditional Arab charm. It is located beside a sheltered circular lagoon, itself an inlet from the larger Mikindani Bay. The lagoon has made an excellent harbour for the dugout canoes and dhows of local fishermen for centuries and there has been a settlement here for almost 1,000 years. When the Arabs arrived Mikindani grew in prosperity, its importance as a trading centre being greatest in the 15th century. Later, with the arrival of the first Europeans, notably the explorer Dr Livingstone, and with the subsequent ban on slave trade, Mikindani began to decline. There was a revival when the German colonial government briefly made the town the district headquarters in 1890. However, by the 1950s production of groundnuts and oil seed demanded larger ships, for which the port was unsuitable, and Mikindani declined once more.

Colour map 4, grid C6

Much of the traditional character remains. There is an interesting mix of thatched mud houses and Arab-style buildings including several fine two-storey town houses with elaborate fretwork balconies. Arabs, Portuguese, Germans and British have all occupied the town at different times. The 500-year-old Portuguese fort was used as a slave prison, later bombarded by the British in the First World War. There is an old slave market, now a collection of small art shops, and a fort, dating from the German period and built in 1895, which has been renovated to become a hotel. Most of the other old colonial buildings are in a poor state of repair. Mikindani was the port

Sights
Mikindani Bay is not suitable for swimming because the water is contaminated

from which Livingstone departed on his final journey to the interior in 1867 (see page 511) and a house with a fine carved door bears a plaque to mark the site where the explorer is said to have camped.

On the outskirts of the village is a large baobab tree with what appears to have been a small door carved into the trunk. It is said that the Germans who were building the railway through here would lock dissidents inside the tree. A walk up the hill behind the Old Boma will bring you to a very large hole. A witchdoctor saw his lucky chicken scratching in that spot several years ago and ever since has been digging for German gold that he firmly believes is buried there.

Trade Aid Since 1996 this British charity has been working at Mikindani helping the local people to build and develop a sustainable eco-tourist trade and thus alleviate poverty. The old German boma has been rehabilitated and converted to a very comfortable hotel. Trade Aid has had a number of volunteers from the UK working on the project – often gap year students. The Old Boma is the base for the charity, which actively encourages small businesses within the village, and there are plans to restore other buildings for tourist accommodation. They can help organize trips to Msimbati Beach and possibly to other attractions in the future. To find out more about this project or to offer either financial or practical help, contact the UK headquarters of the charity at: *Trade Aid*, Burgate Court, Burgate, Fordingbridge, Hants SP6 1LX, UK, T01425-657774, F656684, www.mikindani.com

Msimbati Msimbati's pristine, white sandy beach fringed with palm trees is about 30 km from Mikindani and only 8 km from Mozambique. Swimming is excellent as the beach shelves steeply. There is a fabulous coral reef lying offshore and turtles are commonly seen. Bring snorkels and flippers to explore the reef.

The self-proclaimed 'Sultan of Msimbati', a British eccentric named Leslie Latham Moore, came to these parts after the First World War. He attempted to declare independence from Tanganyika – a situation that was briefly tolerated before he was arrested. The remains of his dilapidated house can still be seen.

The only accommodation on Msimbati Beach are some **D** bandas owned by a Belgian, Jean Nane, costing US$20 per night. These are not associated with *Trade Aid*. However, *10° South* (see below) has recently acquired permission to build an eco-tourist resort and building should start in 2001-02. PADI courses will be available and a dive school with deep-water entry facilities and a marine education centre are planned.

■ *Access to Msimbati is very difficult, along an unmade road, especially after the rains when parts of the track disintegrate. A 4WD is needed. Trade Aid can arrange a visit at a cost of US$25 per person (minimum 4 people) to include a driver and cook. A shelter and table are set up on the beach and the price includes lunch.*

Geological surveys on Msimbati Island in the Ruvuma Basin have shown several oil seeps, some showing characteristics of true degraded crude oil. There is also a gas seep on the island, believed to be of biogenic origin. This basin lies at the southern end of the large East African Karoo Rift System that extends from Somalia. There are no known plans at present to issue exploration licences to the oil companies.

The newly gazetted **Mnazi Bay Marine Reserve** is only an hour's drive to the south of Mikindani. It offers superb snorkelling and scuba diving.

Sleeping & eating **B** *The Old Boma*, PO Box 993, Mikindani, T023-2333885, tradeaidmtw@afsat.com Converted from the fort (*boma* in Swahili) in 1999, there are standard and superior rooms, the latter having balconies. All have fans, en-suite bathrooms and are furnished with local beautifully style beds and handicrafts. Includes breakfast and dinner, good food and a range of wines. There is a swimming pool for use by guests or diners, email facility for guests only, and they accept payment by travellers' cheques. Note that this is a TV-free zone.

Lip plugs

About 40 years ago it was fairly common to see elderly women wearing lip plugs among the people of south Tanzania. Lip plugs were worn by a variety of ethnic groups and principally among tribes that had originated from what is now Mozambique. The tribes that wore the lip plug most commonly included the Makonde, Mwera, Mukua, Mawiha and Metu.

The procedure that was necessary for the wearing of a lip plug began when a girl was just five or six. One of the older women in the tribe would pierce the girl's upper lip using a thorn and would then thread a blade of grass into it. Three days later another blade of grass would be inserted, this time a little larger. This would be repeated about three times until a millet stalk about the thickness of the little finger would be inserted. A week later a second, thicker stalk would be inserted and would be left in place for about a month. By this time the lip would have healed and from then on a series of lip plugs would be inserted each just a little wider in diameter than the last so that the upper lip would gradually be stretched. The first three plugs usually have a circumference of about 50 mm. The first plug was worn for about two months and the second for about four months. When the third plug was inserted a number of markings would be cut into the girl's face – usually about three vertical lines each side of the eyes. When the girl reached puberty a plug of about 125 mm in circumference would be used and kept in place until the birth of her second child when it would be replaced by a larger one. In Makonde plugs of about 100 mm in diameter were fairly common.

The plugs were mostly made of ebony. They would be hollowed out and often were highly polished. The plugs would be prepared by the older men of the tribe. The wearer of the plug could not remove it at any time in public – in fact it would only have been taken out to be washed. There was also the much rarer practice of having a lip plug in the lower lip. The practice of wearing a lip plug caused problems as the pressure of the plug displaced and distorted the teeth.

The origin of the lip plug is not clear. One suggestion is that they were introduced to stop the women being taken away as slaves in the slave-raiding days. Others suggest that lip plugs were in use long before the slave trade and they were originally used as an ornament. No special rights were associated with the wearing of a plug and there was no religious significance attached to them.

B *Litingi's Hotel*, on a good beach 2 km from the village on the peninsula of Mikindani Bay, s/c banda style accommodation, a/c, well furnished, satellite TV and telephone, large dining area and good food, occasional disco when there's demand. **D** *10° South (Ten Degrees)*, bar plus some accommodation, probably the most atmospheric place to come to for a drink, satellite TV, friendly staff. Large dining area with comfortable chairs and excellent food. Usually a barbecue on Sat evenings. Also sell postcards, stamps and magazines, and you can send mail from here. *10° South* can also offer PADI dive courses up to instructor level (at Msimbati). Contact Martin Guard, T023-2334053 .

Alternatively, if you want somewhere with a more Tanzanian flavour, there is Doa's Container Bar about 2 mins' walk away. Street food including *maandazi*, samosas or bhajis can be bought from the children near the *dala-dala* stand or down towards the market.

Tunduru via the Makonde Plateau

Makonde This area is occupied by the Makonde people who have three claims to distinction.
Plateau The first is their exceptional ebony carvings, groups of exaggerated figures, the tra-
Colour map 4, grid C6 ditional work related to fertility and good fortune. The second is their spectacular
sindimba dancing with the participants on stilts and wearing masks. The third is that
Makonde women are celebrated throughout Tanzania for their sexual expertise. The
best place to experience the atmosphere of the Makonde is to visit **Newala**. The road
passes through dense woodland as it climbs up to the plateau from the coast.

The livelihood of the wood carvers is under threat from excessive sawmill logging
of the *Mpingo* trees in the region. The carvers now have to cycle distances of 20 km or
more to obtain supplies of wood. This tree plays both an economic and socio-cul-
tural role in the lives of the villagers. It is used for its medicinal qualities and, traditionally, new-born babies must be bathed in water containing the leaves to ensure
they grow up to be strong.

Transport Bus: you need to stay at least one night in Newala as there is only one bus a day
to and from **Mtwara**. It leaves Newala at 0500 and Mtwara at noon and costs US$6 one way.
There are several small lodging houses in Newala. There is a daily bus from Masasi at 1200,
leaving from Newala at 0500.

Masasi The other main Makonde town is Masasi, surrounded by granite hills, some 140 km
Phone code: 023 southwest of Lindi and 190 km west of Mtwara. In 1875 Masasi was selected by
Colour map 4, grid C5 Bishop Steere of the Universities Mission to Central Africa as a place to settle freed
Altitude: 440 m slaves and it has been an important mission centre since then. Nowadays it is a pretty
undistinguished town, although it is strikingly located in between a series of large
gneiss kopjes (hills). It acts as an important junction for Nachingwea,
Tunduru/Songea, Lindi, Mtwara and Newala and the Makonde Plateau. There are
some pleasant walks around town (head towards the kopjes) and there is a cave that
contains rock paintings nearby.

The Lukwika-Lumesule Game Reserve is one of the least visited wilderness areas
in Africa. Located 100 km south of Masasi on the Ruvuvi River, which marks the
border with Mozambique, the reserve covers an area of approximately 600 sq km.
Herds of elephant migrate across the Ruvuma River on the southern edge of the
reserve in September. The reserve is also home to lion, leopard, crocodile, hippo,
antelope and numerous bird species. Less well known is that this is one of the
reserves in which a Spanish tour company arranges safaris where professional game
hunters bring clients for trophy shooting holidays.

Plans that *Trade Aid* at Mikindani (see page 408) may organize excursions here
have not yet come to fruition. There are simple lodge or camping facilities available.

Sleeping All in main road: **E** *Chilumba Guest House*, slightly better than the other accommodation in
& eating Masasi. **E** *Katami Guest House*, simple but clean. **E** *Mahenge Guest House*, basic accommodation. **E** *Masasi Hotel*, on the road to Lindi from the town centre. Has nets and fans, bar and
restaurant. **E** *Muruwa Guest House*, basic, clean rooms. **E** *New 4 Ways Guest House*, closest
to the bus stop but slightly more expensive than the others. There are several basic **F** hotels,
including the unnamed *Guest House*, south of the bus stand, the *Npokela* and the
New Taufic Hoteli which serve food, none of which are outstanding.

Transport Road Bus: there are several buses from Masasi to Lindi and to Mtwara daily; to **Lindi** it costs
US$3 and takes about 4 hrs, to **Mtwara** US$3.50 and 5-6 hrs. Buses to **Newala** (US$1.50 and 2-3
hrs) and to **Nachingwea** (US$1.50 and an hour or so) are twice daily. Several buses go to **Dar es
Salaam** each day, these cost US$13 and the journey takes 18-22 hrs. There is usually one bus
per day going to **Tunduru**, which costs US$6 and takes 7-8 hrs. There are no direct buses to
Songea, you have to go to Tunduru and overnight there. Be prepared for breakdowns or

Tanzania

Man-eating lions

The sparsely populated district of 20,000 sq km surrounding Tunduru has achieved a certain notoriety for man-eating lions. There are extensive forests and savannah that offer the big cats good cover. In 1986-87 lions, believed to have come into the region from Mozambique, were reported to have killed 30 people in Tunduru District within one year. Because all of the victims were male, women were sent out to work in the fields.

The attacks may have resulted from the shortage of natural prey due to overhunting that has decimated most of the larger wild mammals in the area. People have been reported to be killing game as they have so few remaining cattle or domestic animals. There has also been speculation that lions acquired the taste for human flesh from eating the victims of the war in nearby Mozambique. Among the victims was a game warden sent to deal with the problem.

Over 250 lions were killed in retaliation within a two-year period. However it is thought that some of the human deaths were in fact paid killings carried out by 'lion men'.

In 1998 a local district commissioner reported the year's human death toll as eight killed by crocodiles and five killed by elephants, and a further two people killed by lions in 1997.

punctures on journeys between Masasi-Tunduru and Tunduru-Songea. The buses are in a sorry state and the roads are atrocious (impassable without a 4WD during the rainy season). For those travelling across the south it is worth knowing that the average speeds of the buses plying the awful roads between Masasi and Mbamba Bay are around 25 kph or less!

Tunduru

From Masasi to Tunduru you pass through mile after mile of miombo scrub whose monotony is only spared by some impressive gneiss kopjes scattered about the countryside for the first few hours after leaving Masasi.

11°5'S 37°22'E
Colour map 4, grid C5
Altitude: 701 m

After the journey from Masasi or Songea – over 340 km distance – you'll be pleased to reach Tunduru. It's a pleasant enough town in its own modest way, attractively situated with fine views over the surrounding undulating countryside, but there's little to keep you here for more than one night – unless you are a gem dealer, for the surrounding area is rich in gemstones, including amethyst, diamonds and sapphires. The population is poor, mostly subsistence farmers growing maize and cashew nuts. Extensive damage is frequently done to crops by wild animals, especially boars, monkeys and elephants.

D *Hunter II Guest House*, rooms with toilets and showers but very overpriced. **E** *Ngaunje Guest House*, clean, simple accommodation. **E** *Yakiti Guest House*, **E** *Mnazi Mmoja Guest House* and **E** *The Hunter Guest House*, are all simple, clean, basic accommodation. The best place to eat is the *Al Jazira* restaurant, which is owned and run by a friendly Zanzibari man living in Tunduru. Be prepared to pay more for your drinks in Tunduru. The state of the road you came in on today (along with the state of the one you'll probably be leaving on tomorrow) leads to sodas being around twice the normal price.

Sleeping & eating

Road Bus: there are daily buses from **Masasi** to Tunduru leaving in the morning (US$6, 7-8 hrs). There is at least one bus leaving for **Songea** early every other morning (US$10, 10-12 hrs). Try to book a seat in front of the back axle, as this can make a big difference considering the state of the road. There are also **Land Rovers** (ask for *ëgari ndogo*) that do this trip carrying passengers. You will pay more for these – up to US$16.50. They are quicker although more uncomfortable than a bus – unless you happen to get a front seat – but they may be the only thing going on a particular day. There are also **lorries** taking passengers in the back.

Transport

Tanzania

Dar es Salaam

North to Kilimanjaro, Moshi and Arusha

Most visitors to Tanzania are likely to see at least part of the northern circuit. There is so much packed into what is, by African standards, a small area. Here you will find the Serengeti National Park, Mount Kilimanjaro National Park, the Ngorongoro Crater Conservation Area and Olduvai Gorge. Each of the national parks is dealt with separately in the region/town closest to their location. The major towns in this area are Arusha and Moshi, but the small towns of Lushoto and Amani are very attractive and well recommended. The road through the well-cultivated Usambara and Pare Mountains is spectacular, and there is good hiking in the hills.

Although listed in this section because of their proximity to the main Dar/Arusha road, the towns of Amani, Korogwe, Mombo and Lushoto are administered from the Tanga Region.

Amani

Colour map 4, grid B5 This delightful small town is based on the agricultural institute and botanical garden established by the Germans in the heart of mountain vegetation.

In 1898, at Amani in the cool Usambara hills, the Germans established an agricultural research institute that was the envy of Africa. With the twin benefits of the north railway from Tanga to Moshi and the Amani Institute, the Usambara area flourished under settler farming. By 1914, 40,000 ha were under sisal, 80,000 ha under rubber and 14,000 ha under cotton, as well as extensive areas of tobacco, sugar, wheat and maize. One of the great lessons of farming in Africa is that crops

Northern region

have to be carefully adapted to local conditions. Amani tested soils, experimented with insecticides and developed new varieties. After 1914, Amani turned its hand to the war effort, developing a local quinine for use against malaria from cinchona bark and manufacturing chocolate, tooth-powder, soap and castor oil.

In May 1997 the **Amani Nature Reserve** was established to protect the biodiversity of the flora and fauna of the sub-montane rainforests of the East Usambara Mountains. This joint venture of the Tanzanian and Finnish governments seeks to protect an area whose biological significance in terms of plant and animal diversity has been compared to the Galapagos Islands. There are, for instance, three endemic bird species, the Usambara alethe, Naduk eagle owl and the Usambara weaver. The rainforests also provide the water supply for 200,000 people in Tanga.

The total area of the Amani Nature Reserve is 8,380 ha, which includes 1,065 ha of forests owned by private tea companies under the management of the East Usambara Tea Company. It also includes the Amani Botanical Garden, established in 1902, which has over 460 plant species and is one of the largest botanical gardens in Africa. Amani also has a medical research centre run by the Tanzanian government. Bird life and small animals such as monkeys abound. It is excellent hiking country.

The reserve's information centre is housed in the recently rehabilitated old German Station Master's house in Sigi, built in 1905. A small resthouse has also been constructed nearby. The East Usambara Catchment Forest Project has made efforts to strengthen the villagers' rights to manage their own forests, and pilot farm forestry activities have been started in a number of villages in an effort to improve local land husbandry. A dozen forest trails have been established, including three driving routes. It is worth trying to buy a copy of the guidebook for the East Usambaras written by Graham Mercer. The development of the tourist services is being co-ordinated at the Old German Resthouse in Amani. For further information contact M Katigula, Project Manager, or Stig Johansson, Chief Technical Adviser, East Usambara Catchment Forest Project, PO Box 5869, Tanga, Tanzania, T/F53-43820, usambara@twiga.com

Sleeping & eating

D *IUCN* (International Union for Conservation of Nature) is recommended. Good food, clean room in a Scandinavian wooden hut, IUCN belongs to a research project of the rainforest. **E** *Rest House*, run by the medical centre, charming colonial atmosphere and really excellent value.

Transport

Road Bus: you will need to make a connection at Muheza on the road linking Tanga to the Dar es Salaam to Moshi highway. There is a bus that leaves Muheza at around 1400 each day for the 25-km trip to Amani, which takes about an hour and costs US$0.50. In the mornings the bus leaves Amani when full, usually around 0800. The bus may not go up to the top and you may have to walk or hitchhike the last 2-3 km.

Korogwe

5°0'S 38°20'E
Colour map 4, grid B5

Korogwe is a small town that you pass through on the way from Tanga or Dar es Salaam north to Moshi. It lies at 52 m, on the north bank of Pangani/Ruvu Rivers, whose fertile valley, with its many settlements, stretches to the west. The local people are of the Zigua and Wasambaa but call themselves Waluvu. It is a local administrative centre due to its position near the local sisal estates, the Dar es Salaam-Nairobi road and railway and its proximity to the Usambara and Pare Mountains. There are a few shops, a market, a hospital and a Christian mission.

Sleeping D *Korogwe Transit Hotel*, on the main road, PO Box 145, T140 (Korogwe). Probably the best hotel in town, mosquito nets, private bath but cold water most of the time, front rooms have a balcony but are very noisy due to the proximity of the main road, ear plugs recommended for front rooms, camping possible. **D** *Korogwe Travellers Inn*, on the main road. Bar, restaurant, fans, basic but quite reasonable, helpful staff. **E** *Miami Guest House*, central, fans, nets, basic. **E** *Mountain View Resort*, PO Box 444, Korogwe, Tanga, T235. Owned and operated by an elderly man and his family who are outstanding hosts. Off the main road,

Tanzania

therefore much quieter than other local accommodation, clean, mosquito nets, private bathrooms, running water, wonderful setting about 1 km from bus stop. Local food outstanding at the attached restaurant/bar, also has a campsite. **E** *Nema* (previously *Safari Park Hotel*), near bus stand. Fans, nets, simple fare.

Transport Road: frequent buses pass through from Dar es Salaam, Tanga and Moshi (see these towns for details).

Mombo
Colour map 4, grid B5

Small town on the Dar es Salaam to Moshi highway. Little of interest – its main activity is the provision of services for travellers. The BP garage offered fabulous service to a recent visitor – four people cleaned the car and three filled it up!

Sleeping and eating D *Midway Express*, PO Box 5, T74, situated on the corner to the turn-off to Lushoto, well-appointed hotel, s/c rooms, hot water, western toilets, pleasant garden. **E** *St Eugene's Hostel*, PO Box 51, T55, Lushoto. Located 30 km along the road to Lushoto, very pleasant, well run and offers very good value. Camping available. *Liverpool Hill Breeze*, PO Box 10, T45, 1.5 km north of Mombo. Menu includes chicken, pilau, kebabs, soft drinks. Has a pleasant band area. Well recommended except for Everton fans, who will not be best pleased to have travelled 5,000 miles to see the Anfield Club's arms embellishing the entrance. *Manchester Executive Inn* on the main highway has excellent barbecued lamb.

Soni
Colour map 4, grid B5

This is a tiny market town half-way up the road from Mombo to Lushoto, close to the capital of the Shambaa people at Vugu. The Shambaa were well organized militarily, and supported Bushiri in the 1888-89 Arab revolt (see page 370). The way up from Mombo is attractive, with glimpses of small waterfalls in Mlalo River. On the edge of town is the pretty, main waterfall. Soni is a good staging-post for hiking in the Usambaras. From *Hotel Falls View* you can hire a guide for walks into the forest and up the peak of Kwa Mongo, a hike of 3-4 hours.

Sleeping E *Hotel Falls View* (formerly *Soni Falls Hotel*), about 1 km from town, a 5-min walk from the bus stand, PO Box 20, Soni, T27 (Soni). Under new management, recently being renovated, the rooms that were finished looked smart. There are 10 double rooms with nets and en-suite bath, shower and flush toilet facilities and hot water. Restaurant has a mixed local and European menu (meals US$2-5), well-stocked bar that offers wine made by the local Benedictine monks. The verandah affords good views of the river and the peak of Kwa Mongo, and there is space for parking. Excellent value, price includes breakfast. Camping in the grounds, from where you can hear the waterfall, US$3.50. In the town are **E** *Kimalube*, PO Box 191, Soni, T10 (Soni), and **E** *Maweni*, both are a little cheaper than *Hotel Falls View*, simple and adequate.

Eating Cheap: *Riverside Café*, good basic food. Has the advantage that you can see the buses arriving while eating. Small local restaurants include **Seriously cheap**: *Maradona*, next to the bus stand, which offers very tasty meals.

Transport Bus: regular buses run from Mombo to Lushoto cost US$0.90.

Lushoto

4°4'S 38°20'E
Phone code: 027
Colour map 4, grid B5
Altitude: 1,500 m

Lushoto is located about 1½ hours off the main Korogwe-Moshi road. The road up to Lushoto via the small town of Soni is spectacular as it twists and turns through the mountains. The town is reminiscent of an Indian hill station and the best places to stay – *Grant's Lodge*, *Mueller's Mountain Lodge*, *Lawn's Hotel* and *Irente Farm*, located just outside the town – have a charming colonial atmosphere.

Sights

Lushoto was the town chosen by early German settlers to escape from the heat and dust of the plains, for vacation residences, when it was called Wilhemstal. The cool, fresh air and lush, green surroundings were greatly appealing and it was once thought that it might develop into the capital of the colonial administration. The Germans planned the site as their version of the ideal colonial town. Many of the surrounding farms and government buildings are originally German. There is a very fine Dutch-style **Governor's House**, just out of town on the road going north. Other reminders of the colonial connection are the horse-riding arenas and the red tiles on some of the roofs of the buildings.

There is a group of **German Alpine-style buildings** with flat red, rounded end tiles, chimney stacks and shutters on the east side of the main road near the Mission Hospital. The British changed the town very little. Their main contribution was to lay out a **cricket ground** just to the west of the town centre. It is still possible to see the old weather-boarded cricket pavilion with a verandah, although it is in poor repair. The ground is now used for football. East of the main road, near the Catholic church, is the **Parade Ground**. Horse-riding was a favourite recreation of the Germans, and this was where the mounted officials were paraded, in front of the timber review stand. The **Lutheran church**, just west of the centre, is an attractive building, with blue window frames, black and white walls, Mangalore tile roof, a front stone arch and a free-standing bell in a wooden tower. The **market** is lively with several small, inexpensive eating places, hair salons, tailors and a maize mill making *posho*.

Set in a valley in the Usambara (sometimes known as Asambara) Mountains it can get quite cold from June to September so take warm clothes. The viewpoints on the southern and western side of the Usambaras are noted for the spectacular vistas of the plains of Mkomazi and Handeni. Kilimanjaro can be seen on the horizon and at the end of the day the sunset turns the area into unforgettable colours.

This area is a place to enjoy the views and countryside. It is fertile and verdant, cultivated with maize, bananas etc, and there are plenty of tracks to **walk** along. One such walk takes about 45 minutes from Lushoto to reach a 'viewpoint' 5 km away, from where the view of the hills and the Masai Plain below really is breathtaking. Take the road out of town towards Irente and head for the children's home. Ask around and you'll be shown the track. On the way is Irente Farm, where fresh fruit, vegetables, preserves, bread and cheese are sold – the large garden is an excellent picnic spot.

The **Usambara Mountains Tourism Programme** is a local tourism initiative advised and supported by SNV, the Netherlands Development Organisation and the Tanzanian Tourism Board. It aims to involve and ultimately benefit the small local communities who organize tourist projects off the usual circuits. These include several one-day walking trips from Lushoto, to the Irente viewpoint overlooking Mazinde village 1,000 m below (see above), a walking tour of Usambara farms and flora, the growing rock tour from Soni and the Bangala River tour, which includes wading through the water. You can also visit and stay in *Carters Camp* at Ndekia. This is a hut precariously perched on a rocky outcrop, built by an American writer as his launch pad for hang-gliding. There are also longer 3-5-day excursions walking into the Western Usambara Mountains via the villages of Lukozi, Manolo and Simga to reach the former German settlement of Mtae, a small village with several guesthouses perched high up on the western rim of the escarpment, and the tour to the Masumbae Forest Reserve.

Most of the guides are former students of the Shambalai secondary school in Lushoto, speaking fair to good English, and can give you information on the history of and daily life in the Usambara Mountains. They also hope to earn some income through their work as guides. The profits from the tourism ventures help fund local irrigation systems, afforestation and soil erosion control measures. The guides are available from the information centre just off the road opposite the bus station, *Friends of Usambara Society*, PO Box 151, Lushoto, T132.

Lushoto is one of only two places in the world where you will find the endangered Usambara/African Violet *Saintpaulia ionantha* (its other habitat is in Mexico). The herbarium on the slope to the north of the town dates from the German colonial period and has thousands of pressed plants from all over Tanzania – ask for Mr

Tanzania

Tanzania

Msangi or Mr Mabula if you would like to see the collection. There are lots of different **churches** and missions in Lushoto that are worth visiting. Missions were established by the Protestant Mission Society; Holy Ghost; Liepzig Mission; Seventh Day Adventists; and African Protestant Union. The town holds a fine **market** (close to the bus station) that is very colourful and lively. Among the many products on sale at Lushoto Market is the locally produced pottery, with a variety of pots for cooking, storage or serving. One of the ancient beliefs of the *Shambaa* people is that *Sheuta*, their God or Supreme Being, made people from a handful of soil in the manner of a potter. In the Usambaras, potters are traditionally women, with the skills passed on from mother to daughter. Men are discouraged from participating in any stage of the potting process, as it is believed that to do so brings great misfortune including sterility. There is good fishing in the mountain streams, one of which runs through the centre of the town.

Sleeping **B** *Grant's Lodge*, Mizambo, Lushoto, PO Box 859, Tanga, T/F027-2642491, tanga4@ tanga.net or grants@lt.sasa.unep.no, www.grantslodge.com 15 km from Lushoto along a road that is rough in places – signposted from Lushoto, start by heading north on the road that passes the post office and district offices. Lovely brick house, 5 rooms, a welcoming atmosphere, open fireplace. Generous helpings of tasty home-cooked food – soups are excellent as is the hot chocolate. Can organize short or long walking safaris with photocopied instructions. Car safaris can also be arranged. Range of bird reference books in the library. Highly recommended. Payment can be made in US$ or TSh. TCs accepted. **C** *Mullers Mountain Lodge*, PO Box 34, Lushoto, T134, on the same road as *Grant's Lodge*, so follow their signs. Built in 1930, it has brick gables, attractive gardens and lovely views, 7 bedrooms with shared dining and living rooms, plus very good food and service; they offer guided walks. **C-D** *Irente Farm*, PO Box 80, located 5 km from town southwest towards Irente viewpoint. Run by a German couple, Anja and Joachim Weber. Has a wonderful cheese factory. **C-D** *Lawns Hotel*, PO Box 33, Lushoto, T5 or 66, or through T027-3445, located about 1 km south of town. Old colonial-style hotel, has wonderful views with fireplaces in the rooms plus a verandah, restaurant and bar and includes very good breakfast. A bit run down, but has running water, and the staff are very accommodating. Some rooms are s/c, the cheaper ones have shared facilities. There are mountain bikes for hire, or you can arrange horse-riding. Run by a Cypriot. Good source of information about Tanzania. From here you can organize hikes to 'Viewpoint'. Camping possible, US$3.50 per person.

Lushoto

Not to scale

N

■ Sleeping
1 Adventure Guesthouse
2 Classic
3 Green Valley Annex
4 Kimyunu Guest House
5 Langoni
6 New Florida
7 New Friends
8 New Milimani
9 New Teachers' Safarini Club
10 Rembo
11 Sun
12 White House

● Eating
1 Action Safari Café
2 Check Point Bar
3 Fadhil
4 Green Valley
5 Hub Club
6 Manyara
7 Mid-Town
8 New Central Bar
9 New Nsumbiji
10 Police Canteen
11 Prison Club
12 Super

Tanzania

E *St Eugene's Hostel*, PO Box 51, T2640055, F2640267, St-ehostel@yahoo.com Run by the Usambara Sisters, 14 s/c rooms, hot water and phones. Serve food including delicious home-made ice cream. **E** *Sun Hotel*, on Boma Rd near the police station, PO Box 104, Lushoto, T82, popular with tourists, has a restaurant. **F** *Adventure Guesthouse*, PO Box 35, just opposite the *Check Point Bar*, good value, s/c rooms, convenient for the bus station. **F** *Green Valley Annex*, PO Box 157, T13/43, on the road to Irente, has s/c rooms, some with double beds and squat WCs. **F** *Kimyunu Guest House*, possibly the cheapest hotel in town. **F** *New Florida*, just off the road to Irente, very inexpensive with shared bathrooms. **F** *New Friends Corner House*, PO Box 157, T43, on the road from the market to the Mission Hospital, has some s/c rooms, hot water, pleasant bar and verandah, and all-year-round Christmas decorations. **F** *New Milimani Guest House*, near bus station. Restaurant and bar facilities available, simple but adequate, has safe parking for cars and motorcycles but there is a charge for a guard. **F** *New Teachers Sarafini Club*, friendly, new, very cheap, opposite *New Milimani*, no parking facilities. **F** *Rembo Hotel*, on the same side of the road as the *Milimani*. Very cheap, but has no single rooms. Small bar serves sodas and beer and they also serve food – chips, omelette and meat. At night Congolese music is played loudly until 2300. Other inexpensive hotels on Irente Rd are **F** *Langoni*, **F** *Classic* and **F** *White House*.

Mid-range *Lawns Hotel*, south of town, see above, serves good Cypriot cuisine as well as international dishes. **Seriously cheap** *Action Safari Café* is central, simple and cheap. *Fadhil Restaurant*, main road opposite market. Basic omelettes, chips, chapattis and soft drinks. *Green Valley Bar & Restaurant*, central location close to the market and bus station, serves reasonable menu of grills and local foods, pleasant atmosphere. *Manyara Restaurant*, close to the market, fairly basic. *Mid Town Restaurant*, just opposite *Check Point Bar*, has simple fare and a garden at the rear. *New Nsumbiji Restaurant*, at the far right-hand corner of the bus stand. Serves fresh bread rolls every day. Food very reasonably priced. *New Central*, on the main road near the market. Grills, rice and local dishes. *New Teachers Sarafini Club*, offers good value local food. *Super Restaurant*, on main road just opposite the cemetery. Fairly simple fare available such as doughnuts, chapattis, eggs and tea.

Eating

Hub Club, sited at the south end of town just off the main road, has a bar, disco and cinema. *Check Point Bar*, lively place with a verandah, near the market. Cheap beer, sodas and barbecued meat can be had at the *Police Canteen* and the *Prison Club*, where, despite any misgivings you may have, you will be made very welcome.

Entertainment

Tourist Information Office, PO Box 151, T132, just off the main road opposite the market, has excellent information on treks and visits to local communities.

Tourist information

Road Lushoto is located off the main Korogwe-Moshi road. The roads are excellent, all sealed, even the 33-km gradual climb up from Mombo, which was resurfaced by the Germans in 1989 and is still in good repair. Hitching may be preferable to using the very overcrowded *matatus* as there are plenty of westerners in 4WDs who will give lifts in this area. **Bus**: bus from **Mombo** takes about 1½ hrs and costs US$1. You can also get a direct bus from **Tanga**, but it is slow, 6 hrs, and costs US$2. There are also slow buses between Lushoto and **Arusha** (6 hrs) and **Moshi** (5½ hrs). Direct buses from **Dar es Salaam** leave the stand on Mafia St in the Kariakoo area throughout the morning and take 6 hrs.

Transport

Banks *National Microfinance Bank*, on the main road opposite the bus station, T0830, 1500 Mon-Fri, 0830-1230 Sat. Offers poor exchange rates. **Communications Post**: post office at the northern end of main street. **Useful addresses** Municipal office beyond the post office on the left where it is possible to get a visa extended.

Directory

With Mt Seguruma (2,218 m) rising just above Mlalo, the Usambaras provide a spectacular backdrop to this small settlement at the junction of two mountain streams, about 25 km north of Lushoto. If you are arranging a football tour, steer clear of the Eleven Killers Football Club, whose premises are just opposite the *A filex*, next to the *Hache Hache Chips Club*.

Mlalo

Look out for the kerosene storage tank, paid for by a group of American high school students to enable local women to buy kerosene in bulk at a lower price. Any profits generated from this business will be spent on local education and medical care.

Sleeping and eating On main road: **F** *Motel Afilex*, PO Box 106, central position, has hot water. Simple accommodation but adequate. **E** *Sambamba Annex*, PO Box 25. Is not s/c, bucket hot water, squat toilets, cheap and good value. **Seriously cheap**: *New Sambamba Restaurant*, opposite the *Afilex*. Serves omelettes, grills, local food, tea – all pretty straightforward. Other small eating places, all fairly basic, can be found on the road out to Lushoto. These include the *Kongoea, Peninsular* and the *Safari Café*, with the *Nyanza* a bit further out on the right-hand side coming into town. There are a couple of **bars** on the Lushoto road as well, the *Bar Kweka* and the first-floor *Chamzingo Bar*.

Transport 1 bus a day to and from **Lushoto**. Leaves Mlalo around 0700 when full, returns at midday, takes 2 hrs and costs US$.50.

Same
Colour map 4, grid A5

A small town on the Moshi-Tanga road, Same is a base for a visit to **Mkomazi Game Reserve**, the Tanzanian extension of the Tsavo National Park (see below). The market has covered and open sections, with a good selection of earthenware pots and bowls, baskets and mats. The Vuasu Co-operative Union is an interesting 1960s building with slender diagonal buttresses, narrow walls and a balcony. The bus station is particularly well organized with bus shelters clearly displaying the destinations of the various bus routes. A feature of the area is the hollowed-out honey-logs hanging from the trees.

Sleeping **D** *Elephant Motel*, simple but adequate. The staff are helpful if arranging to hire a vehicle to get to Mkomazi. Has a small restaurant plus TV. **D** *Amani Lutheran Centre*, close to the market. Clean if a little basic. Facilities include a restaurant. **E** *Tukutane Guest House*, reasonable basic accommodation. **F** *Chanzae Hotel & Lodge*, some s/c rooms, hot water, reasonable value. **F** *Kambeni Guest House*, PO Box 203, T166, s/c rooms, secure parking, very good value. **F** *Sasa Kazi Hotel*, PO Box 156, some of the rooms are s/c, has a verandah bar with food.

Eating **Seriously cheap**: *Parrot Restaurant*, close to main road, has a good selection, including African dishes. *Savannah*, close to the market, serves roasts, beef, bananas, rice

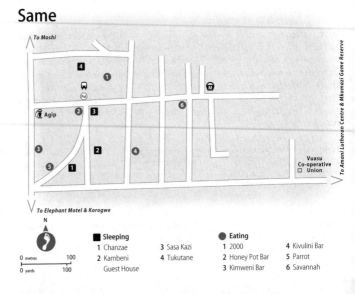

Same

To Moshi

To Amani Lutheran Centre & Mkomazi Game Reserve

Agip

Vuasu
Co-operative
Union

To Elephant Motel & Korogwe

N

0 metres 100
0 yards 100

■ **Sleeping**
1 Chanzae
2 Kambeni
   Guest House
3 Sasa Kazi
4 Tukutane

● **Eating**
1 2000
2 Honey Pot Bar
3 Kimweni Bar
4 Kivulini Bar
5 Parrot
6 Savannah

Tanzania

and beans. Pleasant ambiance. *2000 Restaurant*, at the bus station. Simple grills and local dishes. *Tukutane*, small restaurant attached to the guesthouse, has simple, basic food like grills, plus African dishes. *Sasa Kazi Hotel*, restaurant serves African food and grills.

Bars Include the *Kivulini* with bandas, *Honey Pot* and *Kimweni*, all catering mainly for travellers. Snacks are usually available.

Tourist information Can be obtained from the *Sasa Kazi Hotel*, with details of local excursions and visits.

Mkomazi Game Reserve

This national park of 3,600 sq km lies about 100 km north of Tanga and is contiguous with Kenya's Tsavo National Park (see map, page 412). In the rainy season herds of elephant, zebra and oryx migrate between the parks. The **Mkomazi Rhinos resettlement project**, coordinated by the Tanzania Wildlife Protection fund, has taken a lead role in relocating black rhino from South Africa to Mkomazi Reserve and Ngorongoro. The released rhino are kept in intensive protection zones and it is hoped that they will breed, after which they will be relocated within Tanzania to other traditional natural habitats. It is an expensive programme. The cost of transferring 10 rhinos is put at over US$1 million.

4° S, 38° E
Colour map 4, grid A5

Tanzania

African hunting dogs, the endangered wild dog and other big mammals such as zebra, giraffes and gazelles have also been reintroduced. The reserve is home to about 400 bird species including falcons, eagles, hawks, hornbills, barbets, starlings, weavers and shrikes. There is dense vegetation and an armed guard is needed if hiking.

Sleeping There are no hotel facilities here, although overlooking the reserve is *Hilltop Tona Lodge*, part of the Southern Pare Cultural Tourism Programme. There is a campsite and a banda located at Ibeye, within the reserve, if you are prepared to be self-sufficient. Alternatively there are two campsites around Zange gate.

Transport There are no buses to the reserve, so the options are walking or cycling from Same (5 km), hitchhiking or hiring a car. There is a small airstrip inside the reserve used by chartered planes.

About 150 km southeast of Moshi and a two-hour drive from Same are the **Mbaga Hills** and the Southern Pare Mountains Cultural Tourism Programme, supported by the Dutch Development Organization (SNV). From here local people will take you hiking to **Mghimbi Caves**, hiding places for the people during slave raids in 1860; or **Malameni Rock**, where until 1930, in order to appease evil spirits, children were sacrificed to the gods; and to **Mpepera Hill**, from where there are fine views over the expanse of Mkomazi Game Reserve. Longer treks are possible, to the forest and peak of **Shengena**, the highest point of the Eastern Arc Mountains (Pare and Usambara Mountains), or up the mountains to **Mhero Village** and through **Chome Forest Reserve**.

Southern Pare Mountains Cultural Tourism Programme

Tours begin from D *Hilltop Tona Lodge*, located on a hill just outside Mkomazi Game Reserve. It has five brick cottages, one of which has excellent views over the reserve, with electricity and running water, and meals can be prepared with advance notice. You can swim in a pool in a nearby river. Local homestays are also possible. There are a number of suitable sites for camping along the tour routes but you must bring all your own equipment. The local guides, who have a reasonable standard of English, are well informed about the area's irrigation, soil conservation and afforestation development projects, and will be happy to take you to see them. Monies generated help to support these projects and to subsidize energy-saving stoves and educational scholarships to the local vocational training centre. ■ *Further details of the programme from the Tanzanian tourist information centre in Arusha, T027-2503843, F2548628.*

Nyumba ya Mungu The Nyumba ya Mungu (House of God) dam on the Pangani River is a pleasant place to stop for a picnic. It is located about 30 km west of the main Dar-Moshi road, between Same and Lembeni. If travelling north, the turn-off is about 8 km south of Lembeni. The road travels in a southwesterly direction until it reaches the small town of Kiriya, when it turns due north for another 15 km before reaching the town and reservoir. Nyumba ya Munga is approximately 100 km southeast of Moshi.

Lembeni
Colour map 4, grid A5 Off the beaten track to the south of Lembeni, the rural village of **Ngulu** is set in a beautiful valley between the North and South Pare Mountains. There is not much in the way of tourist facilities, but the E *Ngulu Guest House*, PO Box 85, Mwanga Moshi, T81 (Mwanga), is in a spectacular location. Clean, basic rooms with separate toilet block (*cho*) and washing facilities (*bafu*). The village is approximately 10 km off the main road, well worth a visit if you are looking for cheap accommodation in a wonderful setting.

Kisangara The small town of Kisangara lies off the main Moshi-Dar road, almost half-way between Mwanga and Lembeni, at the foot of the North Pare Mountains. Nearby there is a high school and vocational school located in the village of Chanjale. Here Grace Mngara and her husband Msafiri Banduka run one of the best-kept secrets of rural Tanzania. The couple have both travelled to Europe and the US and have used their experience to create a farm with an education-environmental focus, with tree plantings, water-retention schemes and sustainable food crops. They will help organize local tours, hikes into the mountains or will help you design a unique safari.

There are rooms to rent available in their **C** home, or **E** camping or **D** bandas to let. The Tanzanian food is superb. Contact Grace or Msafiri Hasna – Habari Za Shamba, PO Box 205, Mwanga-Moshi, F027-2751113.

Mwanga & Usangi
Colour map 4, grid A5 Mwanga is the district capital and is situated approximately half-way between Same and Moshi, 50 km southeast of Moshi. Huge palm trees grow abundantly in the water that streams downhill from the Northern Pare Mountains. From Mwanga there is a good sand road that winds upwards to **Usangi**, the centre of the Northern Pare Mountains. The little town is surrounded by 11 mountain peaks and is an important economic centre producing beer, bricks, stoves, pottery and clothing. There is a colourful market held on Mondays and Thursdays, where local farmers come to sell their produce. Two of the stalls reflect a passion for football, *Ronaldo Fashion* and *Maradona Kiosk*. This is one of the most fertile regions in East Africa.

The **Northern Pare Mountains Tourism Programme** is a cultural tourist programme supported by the Tanzanian Tourist Board and the Dutch (SNV) and German (GTZ) Development Organizations. The scheme is co-ordinated at Lomwe Secondary School, in the centre of Usangi, T7, by Mr Kangero. Local people take you on a walking tour of the area, staying in local homes with outstandingly good food. In the mountains there are areas suitable for camping. The guides speak reasonable English; most of them are farmers or local craftsmen. Profits from these tourist projects are used to buy energy-saving stoves to reduce deforestation (they use only one third of the firewood) and to help to reduce the workload of women. The walking tours from Usangi include the Mangata view tour, from where you have excellent views of Lake Jipe and Mount Kilimanjaro. The **Goma Caves** can be visited, where a century ago the Pare chiefs dug deep caves to hide from rival tribes, and later the colonial rulers. Here the skulls of former chieftains killed in battle are preserved. The 2,000-m high table mountain **Kindoroko** and its forest reserve at the top can be reached from the Goma Caves. On the other side of the forest stone terraces and irrigation systems in the village of Kisangara Juu can be seen before returning to Usangi via a route across the moorland. Another one-day tour is a steep climb up the moorland of **Kamwala Mountain** for the views of the surrounding plains. Longer hikes through the forests and mountains can be organized on request.

Old churches and graves of the first missionaries are a reminder of the early German influence at the village of **Shigatini**, which is accessed through a forest. Farmers have established irrigation systems, soil-conservation measures and tree nurseries and are happy to show you around. A recent traveller reported that the tour guides were extremely well informed, proud of their culture and knew a lot about the pre-colonial era. Their vivid stories and knowledge of the local flora and the medicinal uses of the plants greatly enhanced the experience. The facilities were superb and food was delicious.

Sleeping and eating A place to stay is the **F** *Changi Green Inn*, not s/c, but has hot water, restaurant and bar, with cold passion fruit a speciality. **Seriously cheap** The *Shabaha Restaurant*, south of the turn-off to Usangi, is a pleasant place to eat, and the nearby *Kirumo Bar* is comfortable if you are waiting for abus.

Transport Buses from Mwanga take around 1½ hours to Moshi. The bus *'Sahara Beach'* goes directly to Usangi from Arusha – leaves main bus station early in morning and takes 5 hrs.

Moshi

Moshi is the first staging post on the way to climbing Mount Kilimanjaro, a pleasant place to spend a few days organizing your trip. The two peaks of this shimmering snow-capped mountain can be seen from all over the town and it dominates the skyline except when the cloud descends and hides it from view. The town is set at the base of the mountain, about 580 km from Dar es Salaam, 79 km from Arusha and 349 km from Nairobi.

3°22'S 37°18'E
Phone code: 027
Colour map 4, grid A5
Population: 180,000
Altitude: 890 m

Background

Moshi is an unusual African town in that it has very few European or Asian residents, unlike nearby Arusha

The area around Moshi is particularly fertile due to the volcanic soils and there are lots of melt-water streams fed by the snow. This is where Arabica coffee, the premium quality of the two coffee varieties, is grown by the Chagga people, helping them to become one of the wealthiest of the Tanzanian groups. The first coffee grown in Tanzania was planted at the nearby Kilema Roman Catholic Mission in 1898. Growth was steady and, by 1925, 100 tons were being produced each year. The Chagga people are particularly enterprising and formed the Kijimanjaro Native Cooperative Union (KNCH) to collect and market the crop themselves.

Moshi is the centre of Tanzania's coffee industry; the Coffee Board is located here and coffee from all over Tanzania is sold at auction to international buyers. However, apart from the cofffee produced in the immediate locality, the crop does not pass through Moshi, it is auctioned on the basis of certified type, quality and grade, and then shipped directly from the growing area to the buyer. Not all of the wealth generated by the sale of coffee makes its way back to the growing community. Local small farmers have been known to receive only half the Moshi export price. By the time the coffee is sold in London their purchase price amounts to only one-tenth of the London price. Moshi was the site of the signing of the Moshi Declaration after the war with Uganda in February 1979.

Sights

Moshi is safe by day, but don't go out after dark without a local escort

Moshi is a pleasant town with the former European and administrative areas clustered around the clock tower, and the main commercial area southwest of the market. The **Railway Station** southwest of the clock tower is a two-storey structure from the German period, with pleasing low arches, a gabled roof with Mangalore tiles and arched windows on the first floor. On the corner of Station Road and Ghalla Road is a fine Indian shop building dating from the colonial period, with wide curved steps leading up to the verandah, tapering fluted stone columns and a cupola adorning the roof. Also on Station Road is **Da Silva's Garden**, which has intricate arrangements of bottles, batteries, giant snail shells and broken crockery. At the north end of Kuanda Street is **Moshi Ginnery**, which processes cotton using very old machinery. It is usually possible to arrange a trip around the factory.

Many visitors do not stay long in Moshi, but go on to Marangu, the village at the entrance to Kilimanjaro National Park, and arrange the trip up the mountain from

Tanzania

there. There are, however, some places worth visiting in Moshi itself. These include the **Mwariko Art Gallery** on Mufutu Street, which exhibits local arts and crafts, and the **Mweka Wildlife Museum**, part of the College of Wildlife Management, the major centre for training in conservation and wildlife management in Africa.

A leathercraft workshop, which also makes pressed flower cards and jewellery, batik and carvings, is situated in southeast Moshi. *Shah Industries Ltd,* PO Box 86, Moshi, T2752414, F2751010, employ many disabled workers producing high-quality goods, which are available at *Our Heritage*, Hill St, PO Box 86, Moshi.

Excursions **West Kilimanjaro** The road running in a northerly direction from Boma ya Ngombe on the Moshi-Arusha road passes through Sanya Juu and Engare Nairobi to reach Olmolog. This was the main area for European farming in northern Tanzania prior to independence. The boundaries of the old estates are marked on the existing Kilimanjaro Ordnance Survey map. After independence most estates were nationalized. However, lack of capital and management skills has now forced the Tanzanian government to invite foreign commercial interests back, in the hope of increasing production of cereals, seed beans, beef and dairy products.

A drive in this area can include estate visits and a trip through the **Londorossi forest** glades. Most estate managers are happy to receive visitors. Of particular interest is the parastatal owned Rongai ranch, where African 'cowboys', mounted on horseback, herd Boran cattle and Persian black-headed sheep in Texas style.

A valuable source of information in this area is retired forestry officer Stanislavs Malya, PO Box 76, Sanya Juu, who owns a small bar on the roadside at Sanya Juu.

Sleeping **B** *Keys*, Uru Rd, PO Box 933, T2752250, F2183086, keys@form-net.com, just to the north of the town centre. Restaurant and bar, special rate for residents, food and rooms OK, but some rooms over the rear entrance can be noisy at night because of late returners or early starters

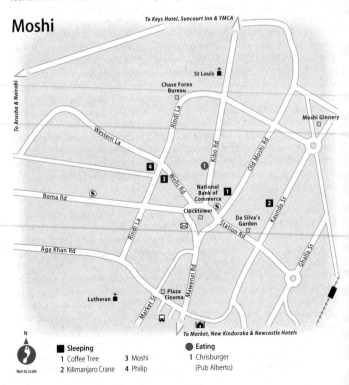

Moshi

To Keys Hotel, Suncourt Inn & YMCA

St Louis

Chase Forex Bureau

To Arusha & Nairobi

Moshi Ginnery

Western La

Rindi La

Kibo Rd

Old Moshi Rd

4

3

Wells Rd

National Bank of Commerce

1

Kaunda St

Boma Rd

Clocktower

Da Silva's Garden

2

Rindi La

Station Rd

Ghalla St

Aga Khan Rd

Market St

Mawenzi Rd

Plaza Cinema

Lutheran

To Market, New Kindoroka & Newcastle Hotels

N
Not to scale

■ **Sleeping**
1 Coffee Tree   3 Moshi
2 Kilimanjaro Crane 4 Philip

● **Eating**
1 Chrisburger
  (Pub Alberto)

Cultivation on the slopes of Mount Kilimanjaro

Mount Kilimanjaro rises high above the East African plateau and for this reason is considerably better watered than the land surrounding it. In particular, the lower southeast slopes of the mountain on the Tanzania side are very fertile with two rainy seasons, in March-May and November-December. The southeast slopes receive the most rain while the northwest slopes also have two rainy seasons but at different times from the southeast. The southwest and northeast sides are drier.

Rain is brought in on the rain-bearing winds that come across the Indian Ocean – the higher the land, the higher the rainfall. On the tropical grassland savannah at the base of the mountain the annual rainfall is approximately 380-510 mm, while halfway up the mountain at the forest zone the rainfall is about 1,500 mm. Above about 3,000 m the temperatures fall to below zero and vegetation ceases.

The Chagga people who live on the slopes of Kilimanjaro take advantage of these differences in rainfall. They cultivate between about 900 and 1,400 m and in some places up to 2,440 m. On the lower slopes just above the tropical grassland savannah they raise annual crops such as millet, maize and beans, while higher up, on the kihamba land, they plant coffee and bananas and keep livestock.

A variety of bananas are grown. Some, savoury, known as matoke, are cooked by steaming for a few hours, others are used for making traditional beer. A banana garden takes three years to establish, but then needs relatively little maintenance. The stems and leaves of a banana tree are also used, as fodder for cattle and mulch for coffee trees.

Coffee is the main cash crop in the area. The superior Arabica bean thrives at high altitude and the volcanic soils are ideal for its cultivation. The plants spend their first year in a shaded nursery before being planted out in the fields, where they need to be kept well weeded. They also need careful pruning to ensure good yields.

On a man's death his land is traditionally divided up between his sons. As in many other parts of East Africa, this tradition, combined with the high birth rate, has meant that the average size of holding is divided into three or four plots when it is inherited. Many farms are now smaller than 1 ha.

for climbing. **B** *Moshi*, PO Box 1819, Moshi, T3701, town centre. Restaurant and bar, rather run down and gloomy. **B** *Philip Hotel*, central, located at the corner of Rindi Lane/Rengua St (formerly Chancery Lane and Wells Rd respectively), PO Box 1775, T2754746, F2750456. **C** *Kilimanjaro Crane*, Kaunda St, PO Box 1496, T2751114, F2754876, kilicrane@eoltz.com Swimming pool, gardens, good views, pizza kitchen, several bars. Well recommended. **C** *Kindoroka*, Mawenzi Rd, close to market, PO Box 1341, T2754054, F2754062, kindoroko@raha.com Restaurant, bar, well-run hotel. **C** *Leopard Hotel*, Market St, PO Box 232, T2750884, F2751261, leopardhotel@eoltz.com **C** *Moshi View Hotel*, Kiusa St, PO Box 13, Moshi, T2750993/4, F2750994, has 16 self-contained rooms, en-suite bath/toilet, hot water, ceiling fans, a/c available, *Cave Bar and Restaurant* offers Tanzanian and international food, rooftop bar with panoramic views including Mt Kilimanjaro, weather permitting, a genuine African experience. **C** *Motel Silva*, Kiadha St, south of market. No hot water, rooms with balconies, good restaurant. **C** *Springlands Hotel*, PO Box 1990, T2753581, sl@twiga.com Set in large, attractive gardens, 37 s/c rooms, restaurant, bar, swimming pool, TV room, massages, conference room, internet and fax services. **C** *YMCA*, PO Box 85, T2752362. Clean, no hot water, shared bathroom facilities, gymnasium, shop, travel office and swimming pool (visitors can use the pool for US$2). **C-D** *New Livingstone Hotel*, centrally located at the corner of Rindi Lane and Rengua St, PO Box 1819, T/F2755212. Suites and cheaper dormitory-style accommodation.

D *Buffalo Inn*, superb value, new, clean budget hotel, sited 2 blocks south and west of the bus station, hot water with/without bathroom. Highly recommended. Good restaurant and bar. Will store luggage for you if you are going on safari. **D** *Newcastle*, PO Box 2000, T3203, close to the market, on Mawenzi St. **E** *Coffee Tree Hostel*, PO Box 184, Moshi, T2787, town centre (2 floors of a large office block). Good views of Kilimanjaro, ideal for the bus station, communal cold showers, wonderful views, will store rucksacks and baggage, restaurant, run down but cheap. **E** *Mlay's Residential Hotel*, Market St, opposite the market, good basic accommodation, restaurant downstairs. **E** *Rombo Cottage*, T2112, off road to Marangu. Hot water, own bathroom, bar and restaurant, good value and atmosphere, safe parking for cars and motorcycles. Charges higher for foreign travellers than local residents. **E** *Suncourt Inn*, off the road to Marangu, restaurant, bar, reasonable. **Camping** There is camping near the *Golden Shower Restaurant*, 2 km from Moshi on the road to Marangu. It is also possible to camp at the *Keys Hotel*.

Eating

All of the hotel restaurants will serve non-residents

Cheap *Chinese Restaurant*, near CCM HQ. Recommended. *Golden Shower*, 2 km from Moshi on the road to Marangu, has a good atmosphere. The owner, John Bennet, is the son of the legendary character 'Chagga' Bennet, ex-First World War Royal Flying Corps ace, and economic adviser to the former Kilimanjaro Native Co-operative Union. He is a wonderful source of local information. There is an excellent cheap restaurant opposite Tambo Cottages. **Seriously cheap** *Chrisburger*, close to the clock tower, has a small verandah at the front.

Entertainment

Chrisburger turns into *Pub Alberto* in the evening, there is good selection of drinks, an outside seating area and a disco. *Golden Shower (GS) Club* is a popular bar with expats.

Tour operators

It is cheaper to book tours for Mt Kilimanjaro from Moshi than from either Arusha or Marangu

African Cultural Tours & Safaris, corner of Boma Rd and Rindi Lane, PO Box 554, T/F2754555. *AfriGalaxy Tours & Travel Ltd*, CCM Regional Building, Taifa Rd (near YMCA), PO Box 8340, T2750268, T0744-309521 (mob), F2753666, www.afrigalaxytours.com *Akaro Tours Co Ltd*, ground floor of NSSF House on Old Moshi Rd, T2752986, F2752249, www.akarotours.com Kilimanjaro climbs with local guides that include visit to small village among the coffee plantations. Specializes in tours to the Masai savanna, grasslands, North and South Pare Mountains and to the foothills of Mt Kilimanjaro, for insights into the way of life of the indigenous peoples and appreciation of the plants and animals. *Come and Go Safari Tours Ltd*, c/o *Moshi View Hotel*, PO Box 13, Moshi, T2750993. Can arrange climbs of Kilimanjaro and tours of all national parks, manager Mr OL Nassari is very helpful. *Emslies Tours*, PO Box 29, Old Moshi Rd, T2752701, F2750236, emslies@eoltz.com *Fortes Safaris*, PO Box 422, Lumumba St, T41764. *Fourways Travel*, PO Box 990, Station Rd, T2620. *Kibo Safari Adventure*, T2750367, F2750609. Led by Mr Athanas Minja. *Kilimanjaro Crown Birds Agency*, based in the *New Kindoroka Hotel*, offers a good, friendly service. Can arrange a 5-day Kilimanjaro climb by the Marangu route for US$450 and a 6-day climb for US$540, all inclusive of guides, fees, transport, food etc. Their guide Mohammed is recommended. Kilimanjaro NP entry fee is US$25 per day and the hut fees are US$40 per day. *Kilimanjaro Guide Tour Safaris*, opposite *Moshi Hotel*, PO Box 210, T/F2751220. *Kilimanjaro Serengeti Tours & Travel Ltd*, Old CCM Building, Mawenzi Rd, PO Box 8213, T2751287, T0741-520106 (mob), F2751056, kstt@eoltz.com *Kilimanjaro Travel Services Ltd*, THB Building, Rengua St, PO Box 1823, T2752124, F2750654. *Laka Tours & Car Hire*, Lutheran Building, 2nd Floor, Market St, PO Box 1331, T/F2751510,

laka@eoltz.com *Matto Mountain Treks*, momotreks@yahoo.com A new company but experienced guides, basic but safe equipment, recommended by recent travellers as a good company for those on a budget. *Mauly Tours & Safaris*, PO Box 1315, Rombo Av, T2787. *MJ Safaris International*, CCM Building, Taifa Rd, PO Box 9593, T/F2751241, mjsafaris@habari.co.tz *Moshi Expedition & Mountaineering*, Granado Building, opposite the central market on Chagga St, PO Box 146, T/F2752451, m.e.m.tours@eoltz.com *Prince Masai Tours & Travel*, Room 201, THB Building, PO Box 8911, T/F2751244. *Shah Tours*, PO Box 1821, Moshi, T2752370, F2751449, www.kilimanjaro-shah.com Specializes in Kili tours, helping to join up groups. *Shidolya Tours & Safaris*, in *New Livingstone Hotel*, Rindi Lane, PO Box 7530, T2752983. *Trans-Kibo Travels Ltd*, PO Box 558, T/F2752017, transkibo@habari.co.tz, located in the *YMCA*. Organizes climbs of Kilimanjaro, recommended by some recent travellers. *Tropicana Safaris*, Old Moshi Rd, PO Box 884, T2752976. *Zara Tanzania Adventure*, located at *New Livingstone Hotel* on Rindi Lane, PO Box 1990, T2754240, T0742-451000 (mob), F2753105, zara@form-net.com, 'Kilimanjaro Climb & Safari', climb US$660 for 5-day 'Coca-Cola route' – sleep in huts, US$720 for 6-day 'whiskey route' – sleep in tents, US$900 for Machame and Umbwe routes, the safari charges are US$90 per person per day for a tour of Serengeti/Ngorongoro. Recommended.

Air **Kilimanjaro International Airport**, Moshi, T027-2502223, is halfway between Moshi **Transport** and Arusha – for flight details, see **Arusha** page 449. The *Air Tanzania* office is next to the *Moshi Hotel* by the clock tower. A shuttle bus leaves from here 2 hrs before the scheduled flight departure, cost US$3. Moshi also has its own small airfield. *Precisionair* operated several services a week to and from Arusha and Dar es Salaam, but this service seems currently to be suspended. **Road**   There are daily buses to and from **Dar es Salaam**. They leave Dar es Salaam from the Morogoro Rd bus station. Fare is around US$20 luxury, US$16 semi-luxury and US$12 ordinary and takes about 9 hrs. The road has improved considerably. For **Tanga** the bus takes 4-6 hrs and costs US$4. To **Marangu** there are lots of *dala-dala* (US$1) or you can share a taxi (US$15). It is possible to get a direct bus to Mombasa, cost approximately US$13, 12 hrs. The *Riverside Shuttle* to Nairobi via Arusha departs at 1030, reaches Arusha at 1300, and arrives in Nairobi at 1830, US$30. Book through the Arusha office, T2639, F3916.

Banks and foreign exchange bureaus   *Standard Chartered Bank* on Rindi Lane (formerly Chancery **Directory** Lane) has ATM facilities, Visa cards are accepted. Foreign exchange bureaus in Moshi include *Chase Forex Bureau* on Rindi Lane, T2755220, F2752242, will advance money on Visa and Mastercard, and *Trust Bureau de Change* on Chagga Rd/Mawenzi Rd, T2751618, F2750096. **Communications** Post: post office can be found in the centre of town near the clock tower. **Telephone**: international calls can be made from the post office. **Medical services** Hospitals: Moshi is home to what is said to be the best hospital in Tanzania, the *Kilimanjaro Christian Medical Centre (KCMC)*, which is located a few km out of town, T2754377. *Maweizi Moshi District Hospital*, located in town. **Places of worship** Church of England: *St Margaret's Church*, English language service at 1030 on most Sun (1 km from town centre). **Useful addresses** Immigration office: where you can renew your visa, is also near the clock tower in Kibo House. The **Library** is on Kibo Rd, just north of *Chrisburger*.

Marangu

This is the closest village to Kilimanjaro National Park, the entrance to which is 5 km *Phone code: 027* away. It is more expensive than Moshi, and budget travellers are advised to plan an assault on the mountain from Moshi. Most people visit Marangu only to attempt the climb to the summit of Mount Kilimanjaro. However, Marangu and nearby **Machame** are excellent centres for hiking, bird-watching and observing rural Africa.

The **Marangu/Mamba Cultural Tourism Programme**, supported by the Dutch **Foothill walks** Development Organisation SNV, arranges guided walks through the attractive scenery of the valleys near Marangu and Mamba. Mamba is a small village 3 km from Marangu. From here you can also visit caves where women and children hid during ancient Masai-Chagga wars or see a blacksmith at work, using traditional methods to make Masai spears and tools. From Marangu there is an easy walk up Ngangu hill, a visit to a traditional Chagga home, or a visit to the home and memorial of the late Yohano Lawro, a local man who accompanied Dr Hans Meyer and Ludwig Purtscheller on the first recorded climb of Mount Kilimanjaro in 1889. He is reputed to have guided Kilimanjaro climbs until he was 70 and lived to the age of 115. Profits from the programme are used to improve local primary schools. Further details of these tours can be obtained from the Tanzanian Tourist Information centre in Arusha, T027-2503842/3, tourinfo@habari.co.tz

The Ordnance Survey map of Kilimanjaro (1:100,000) is an essential guide for walks. The main tracks in the region radiate from the forest boundary, through the cultivated belt of coffee and bananas, to the road that rings the mountain. Other maps are less accurate but widely available at about US$10.

There are many possible choices. One recommended hike is to take the murram road running westwards past the *Kibo* hotel. After about 5 km take the track running northwest up the Mai River valley, past Maua Seminary. From Maua a track winds in a southwest direction to connect with the Kirua road above the Mworoworo Dam. Walkers can either go south to Kirua or proceed via Kidia to Old Moshi, where local transport will be available to take you back to Moshi town.

Sleeping **A** *Capricorn Hotel*, excellent location with great views, approximately 4 km from the park gate, PO Box 938, Marangu, T2751309, F2752442, capricorn@africaonline.co.tz Standard and superior double rooms all with en-suite bathrooms, hotel offers telephone, fax and email services, arranges climbs. **A** *Kibo*, PO Box 137, Moshi, or PO Box 102, Marangu, T/F2751308, about 1 km from Marangu village. Old German building, cool and comfortable, restaurant, bar, fine gardens, well organized, but upmarket – Evelyn Waugh stayed here in 1959, finding it 'so comfortable' with a 'cool verandah'. Kilimanjaro climbs can be organized from here. **A** *Marangu*, PO Box 40, Moshi, T2756594, F2756591, maranguhotel@africaonline.co.tz, www.maranguhotel.com, 40 km from Moshi, 7 km from park gate. Long-established, family owned and run country-style hotel, warm and friendly atmosphere, self-contained cottages with private baths and showers, hot water, set in 12 acres of gardens offering stunning views of Kilimanjaro, swimming pool, croquet lawn, one of the original operators of Kilimanjaro climbs with over 40 years' experience. **B** *Babylon Lodge*, PO Box 227, Marangu, T/F2751315, babylon@form-net.com, 500 m from the post office on the Jarakea Rd. Clean and comfortable, sited in well-kept gardens, built into the hillside, all 18 rooms have private facilities, owner Mr Lgimo is very helpful. **Camping** *Babylon Lodge*, rather less good value at US$10; *Kibo Lodge* charges US$6 and with use of hotel facilities is good value; *Marangu Hotel* charges US$3.

Tour operators *Alpine Tours & Travel Ltd*, PO Box 835, T2754818, F2750096, alpinetrekking@eoltz.com *Kili Climbers & Safaris*, opposite post office, PO Box 610, T2759022/6, F2751113, kudo@eoltz.com Locally owned, professionally run company, reasonably priced camping safaris (about US$90 per day per person depending on size of group) and climbs of Kilimanjaro and Meru.

Transport **Road** Regular *dala-dala* to and from Moshi take 45 mins (US$1). Taxi to Moshi, US$15.

Kilimanjaro National Park

In The Snows of Kilimanjaro, *Ernest Hemingway described the mountain: 'as wide as all the world, great, high, and unbelievably white in the sun, was the square top of Kilimanjaro'. It is one of the most impressive sights in Africa, visible from as far away as Tsavo National Park in Kenya. Just 80 km east of the eastern branch of the Rift Valley, it is Africa's highest mountain with snow-capped peaks rising from a relatively flat plain, the largest freestanding mountain worldwide, measuring 80 x 40 km and one of earth's highest dormant volcanoes. At lower altitudes, the mountain is covered in lush rainforest, which gives way to scrub – there is no bamboo zone on Kilimanjaro – followed by alpine moorland until the icefields are reached. Try to see it in the early morning before the clouds mask it. Despite its altitude even inexperienced climbers can climb it, provided they are reasonably fit and allow themselves sufficient time to acclimatize to the elevation.*

Ins and outs

There are a number of ways of getting to Mt Kilimanjaro (see map, page 412). The easiest is to fly to **Kilimanjaro International Airport** – during your approach you will get a magnificent view of the mountain if it is not covered by cloud. The park entrance is about 90 km from the airport, which takes about 1½ hours by road. Alternative routes are to go to **Moshi** by **road** or **train** and from there to **Marangu** (see map, page 430), the village at the park entrance at the base of the mountain. It is located 11 km north of Himo, which is a village 27 km east of Moshi on the road to the Kenya border. Many *dala-dala* go from Moshi to Marangu each day; they take 45 minutes and cost US$1. It is also cheap and easy to get to Kilimanjaro from Kenya by taking a *matatu* from Nairobi to the border (about 4 hrs) and from there another *matatu* to Marangu Gate.

Getting there
3°7'S 37°20'E
Colour map 4, grid A5
Altitude: 1,829 m at Marangu Gate;
5,895 m at Kibo Peak

Although Mt Kilimanjaro can be climbed throughout the year it is worth avoiding the two rainy seasons (late Mar to mid-Jun and Oct to beginning of Dec) when the routes become slippery. Best time to visit is probably Jan-Feb and Sep-Oct when there is usually no cloud.

Climate

Anyone planning to climb Mt Kilimanjaro is advised to buy the *Kilimanjaro 1:50,000 Map and Guide* (1977) by Mark Savage. This is difficult to obtain in Tanzania but you can get it in Kenya, in England from 32 Seamill Park Crescent, Worthing, BN11 2PN, or from *Kilimanjaro Adventure Trave*l, 1770 Massachusetts Av, Suite 192, Cambridge, MA 02140, USA. It is not currently available from *Amazon*. Another guide that is particularly useful if you want to climb the mountain (rather than walk up like the rest of us) is the *Guide to Mount Kenya and Kilimanjaro* edited by Iain Allan and published by the Mountain Club of Kenya.

Information

Useful websites include *Kilimanjaro Adventure Travel*, www.kilimanjaro.com *Africa Park East*, www.africaparkeast.com *Terra Ferma*, www.terraferma.com

Background

Kilimanjaro was formed about 1 million years ago by a series of volcanic movements along the Great Rift Valley. Until these movements the area was a flat plain lying at about 600-900 m above sea level. About 750,000 years ago volcanic activity forced three points above about 4,800 m – Shira, Kibo and Mawenzi. Some 250,000 years later Shira became inactive and it collapsed into itself forming the crater. Kibo and Mawenzi continued their volcanic activity and it was their lava flow that forms the 11-km saddle between the two peaks. When Mawenzi died out its northeast wall collapsed in a huge explosion creating a massive gorge. The last major eruptions occurred about 200 years ago and Kibo now lies dormant but not extinct. Although Kibo appears to be a snow-clad dome it does in fact contain a caldera 2.5 km across and 180 m deep at the deepest point in the south. Within the depression is an inner ash cone that rises to within 60 m of the summit height and is evidence of former

Formation

Tanzania

volcanic activity. On the southern slopes the glaciers reach down to about 4,200 m, while on the north slopes they only descend a little below the summit.

Vegetation & wildlife Kilimanjaro has well-defined altitudinal vegetation zones. From the base to the summit these are: plateau, semi-arid scrub; cultivated, well-watered southern slopes; dense cloud forest; open moorland; alpine desert; moss and lichen. The slopes are home to elephant, rhino, buffalo, leopard, monkey and eland. Birdlife includes the enormous lammergeyer, the scarlet-tufted malachite sunbird as well as various species of starlings, sunbirds, the silvery-cheeked hornbill and the rufous-breasted sparrowhawk.

History When, in 1848, the first reports by the German missionary Johannes Rebmann of a snow-capped mountain on the equator arrived in Europe, the idea was ridiculed by the Royal Geographical Society of Britain. In 1889 the report was confirmed by the German geographer Hans Meyer and the Austrian alpine mountaineer Ludwig Purtscheller, who climbed Kibo and managed to reach the snows on Kilimanjaro's summit. At the centenary of this climb in 1989, the Tanzania guide was still alive and 118 years old. Mawenzi was first climbed by the German Fritz Klute in 1912.

The mountain was originally located in a part of British East Africa (now Kenya). However, the mountain was 'given' by Queen Victoria as a gift to her cousin, and so the border was moved and the mountain included within German Tanganyika. The national park was established in 1973 and covers an area of 756 sq km.

Climbing Mount Kilimanjaro

Officially anyone aged over 12 may attempt the climb. The youngest person to climb the mountain was an 11 year old, while the oldest was 74. However it is not that easy and estimates of the number of people who attempt the climb and do not make it to the top vary from 50-80%. The important things to remember are to come prepared and take it slowly – if you have the chance, spend an extra day half-way up to give you the chance to acclimatize.

Equipment Being well equipped will increase your chances of succeeding in reaching the summit. In particular be sure you have a warm sleeping bag, insulating mat, thermal underwear, gloves, wool hat, sun-glasses or snow goggles, sun cream, large water bottle and first-aid kit. If you are going on any route apart from Marangu you are advised to take a tent and stove. Although organized climbs will provide food, some people recommend that you should take your own freeze-dried food and cook it yourself. This will decrease the likelihood of getting diarrhoea and thus having to turn back.

Altitude sickness Altitude sickness is often a problem while climbing Kilimanjaro. If you know you are susceptible to it you are advised not to attempt the climb. Symptoms include bad headache, nausea, vomiting and severe fatigue. It can be avoided by ascending slowly – if at all possible, spend an extra day half-way up to help your body to acclimatize. Mountain sickness symptoms can often be allieviated by descending to a lower altitude. The drug Diamox helps if taken before the ascent. Other, more serious conditions include acute pulmonary oedema and/or cerebral oedema. In the former, the sufferer becomes breathless, turns blue in the face and coughs up froth. The latter is even more serious – symptoms are intense headache, hallucinations, confusion and disorientation and staggering gait. It is caused by the accumulation of fluid on the brain and can cause death or serious brain damage. If either of these conditions are suspected the sufferer should immediately be taken down to a lower altitude to receive medical care. It is, however, normal to feel breathless and fatigued at high altitudes and these are not always precursors to the more serious conditions.

The meaning of Kilimanjaro

Since the earliest explorers to East Africa, people have been intrigued by the name Kilimanjaro and its meaning. There is no simple explanation. The Chagga people do not actually have a name for the whole mountain, just the two peaks – Kibo and Mawenzi. Kibo (or kipoo, which is the correct term in Kichagga) means 'spotted' and refers to the rock that can be seen standing out against the snow on this peak. Mawenzi (or Kimawenze) means 'having a broken top' and again describes its appearance.

The origin of the name Kilimanjaro for the mountain as a whole has been much discussed and a number of theories put forward, most of which break the word down into two elements: kilima and njaro. In Swahili the word for mountain is actually mlima while kilima means hill – so it is possible that an early European visitor incorrectly used kilima because of the analogy to the two Chagga words Kibo and Kimawenzi.

The explorer Krapf said that the Swahili of the coast knew it as Kilimanjaro 'mountain of greatness', but he does not explain how he came to this conclusion. He also suggests it could also mean 'mountain of caravans' (kilima = mountain, jaro = caravans), but while kilima is a Swahili word, jaro is a Chagga word. Other observers have suggested that njaro has at some time meant 'whiteness' and therefore this was the 'mountain of whiteness'. Alternatively njaro could be the name of an evil spirit, or a demon, which causes colds. The first-known European to climb Mount Kilimanjaro does make reference to the spirit, mentioning

'Njaro, the guardian spirit of the mountain' and this seems quite a plausible explanation as there are many stories in Chagga folklore about spirits living on the mountain – though there is apparently no evidence of a spirit called Njaro, either by the Chagga or by the coastal peoples.

Another explanation involves the Masai word njore for springs or water. The suggestion is that the mountain was known as Mountain of Water because it was from there that all the rivers in the area rose. The problems with this theory are that it does not explain the use of the Swahili word for 'hill' rather than 'mountain', and also it assumes that a Swahili word has been put together with a Masai word.

The final explanation is from a Kichagga term 'kilelema' meaning 'which has become difficult or impossible' or 'which has defeated'. Njaro can be derived from the Kichagga words njaare, a bird, or else jyaro, a caravan. The suggestion is that attempts to climb the mountain were a failure and thus the mountain became known as kilemanjaare, kilemajyaro or kilelemanjaare, meaning that which defeats or is impossible for the bird or the caravan. The theory has the advantage of being made up of all Chagga parts.

It seems possible either that this was the name given to the mountain by the Chagga themselves, or by people passing through the area, who heard the Chagga say kilemanjaare or kilemajyaro, meaning that the mountain was impossible to climb, associated with their own kilima and so the name caught on and was standardized to Kilimanjaro.

Guides A guide is compulsory on all routes. Marangu is the usual route for tourists and only experienced climbers should use the other routes. If you are going on one of the other routes, although you must take a guide with you, be sure to have a good map and a compass as your guide may not know the route. Do not be tempted to go it alone to avoid paying the park and guide fees – above the tree line the path is not always clear and you will be in big trouble if you are caught. It is also well worth hiring porters – they are not too expensive and will increase your enjoyment enormously.

Costs Climbing Mount Kilimanjaro is an expensive business, though everyone who makes it to the summit agrees that it is well worth it. The costs are much higher than those imposed in the Alps or the Andes. Park fees are US$25 per 24 hours, camping or hut fees US$40 per person per day (whether you use the huts or not). Add to this a rescue fee (insurance) of US$20 per person, guides at US$8-10 per guide per day, and porters at US$5-6 per porter per day, depending on the trail you choose. All the big tour operators have to charge an additional 20% VAT on the total invoice. In addition, an 'arrangement fee' of around 10% may also be charged by the tour operator. On to this you must add getting to the start of the trail, food, hiring equipment and tips for the guide and porters. The cheapest you will probably manage to do it for will be around US$550, but this might well escalate to US$800 or more. Organized climbs do not usually work out much more expensive than doing it yourself and are considerably less hassle, so the most sensible option is to put your faith in a specialist tour operator (see Tour operators, page 436).

Tipping Be aware that on the last day of the tour your guide will request a tip for himself and his porters. The guide may try to negotiate a daily rate of US$15 for the guide, US$10 daily for the assistant guide, US$8 daily for the cook and US$5 for each porter. A reasonable tip for the whole trip is in the region of US$30 for a single guide, and US$10 for each porter. Even this amount is very high in comparison to the local income.

Routes up the mountain

The following descriptions contain insufficient information for unaccompanied climbers

There are a number of different trails. The most popular is the Marangu trail, which is the recommended route for older persons or younger people who are not in peak physical condition. The climbing tends to be much more strenuous than anticipated, which when combined with lower oxygen levels accounts for a 20-50% failure rate to reach the summit.

Kilimanjaro National Park

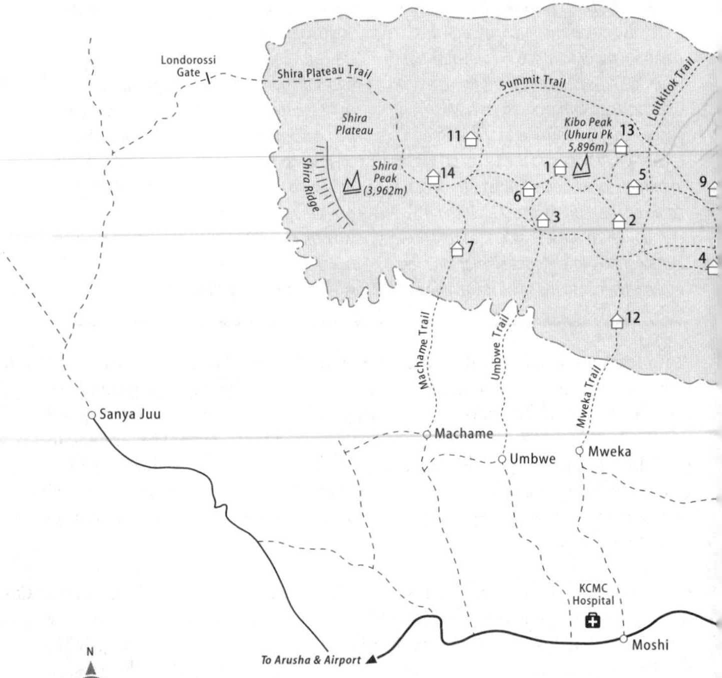
Londorossi Gate
Shira Plateau Trail
Summit Trail
Loitkitok Trail
Shira Plateau
Shira Ridge
Shira Peak (3,962m)
Kibo Peak (Uhuru Pk 5,896m)
11
13
14
1
6
5
9
3
2
7
4
12
Machame Trail
Umbwe Trail
Mweka Trail
Sanya Juu
Machame
Umbwe
Mweka
KCMC Hospital
Moshi
To Arusha & Airport
N
0 km 3

Sleeping huts
1 Arrow Glacier
2 Barafu
4 Horombo
5 Kibo
6 Lava Tower
8 Mandara
9 Mawenzi
10 Mawenzi Tarn

Day 1 The national park gate (1,830 m) is about 8 km from the *Kibo Hotel*. This is as far as vehicles are allowed. From here to the first night's stop at **Mandara Hut** (2,700 m) is a walk of 3-4 hours. It is through *shambas* – small farms – growing coffee as well as some lush rainforest and is an enjoyable walk although it can be quite muddy. On the walk you can admire the moss and lichens, the vines and flowers including orchids. There is an alternative forest trail, which branches left from the main track a few minutes after the gate and follows the side of a stream. It is a little slower than the main track, which it rejoins after a walk of about three hours. The Mandara Hut, near the Maundi Crater, is actually a group of huts that can sleep about 200 people. Mattresses, lamps and stoves are provided but nothing else. The complex was built by the Norwegians as part of an aid programme. There are piped water, flushing toilets and firewood available, and a dining area in the main cabin.

Day 2 The second day will start off as a steep walk through the last of the rainforest and out into tussock grassland, giant heather and then on to the moorlands, crossing several ravines on the way. There are occasional clearings through which you will get wonderful views of Mawenzi and Moshi far below. You can also enjoy the views by making a short detour up to the rim of Maundi Crater. You will probably see some of the exceptional vegetation that is found on Kilimanjaro, including the giant lobelia, Kilimanjaro 'everlasting flowers' and other uncommon alpine plants. The walk to **Horombo Hut** (3,720 m) is about 14 km with an altitude gain of about 1,000 m and will take you 5-7 hours. This hut is again actually a collection of huts that can accommodate up to 200 people. There are flushing toilets and plenty of water but firewood is scarce. Some people spend an extra day here to help get acclimatized and if you are doing this there are a number of short walks in the area. It is a very good idea to spend this extra day here – but there is the extra cost to be considered.

> **Marangu trail**
> *This is probably the least scenic of the routes but being the gentlest climb and having a village at the start and accommodation on the way up means that it is the most popular*
>
> Tanzania

Day 3/4 On the next day of walking you will climb to the **Kibo Hut** (4,703 m), which is 13 km from Horombo. As you climb, the vegetation thins to grass and heather and eventually to bare scree. You will feel the air thinning and will probably start to suffer from altitude sickness. The most direct route is the right fork from Horombo Hut. It is stony and eroded, a climb of 6-7 hours up the valley behind the huts, past **Last Water** and on to the **saddle**. This is the wide, fairly flat, U-shaped desert between the two peaks of Mawenzi and Kibo and from here you will get some awe-inspiring views of the mountain. After **Zebra Rocks** and at the beginning of the saddle, the track forks. To the right, about three hours from Horombo Hut, is Mawenzi Hut and to the left across the saddle is Kibo Hut. The left fork from Horombo Hut is gentler, and comes out on to the saddle 1 km from Kibo Hut. Kibo Hut is where the porters stay and from here on you should just take with you the absolute bare essentials. It is a good idea to bring some biscuits or chocolate with you for the final ascent to

Kikewela River

⌂ 10

▲ Mawenzi Peak (5,149m)

8 ⌂

Park HQ & Marangu Gate

Marangu Trail

Maua Mission

Marangu

Mkiashi

Himo

▲ *To Tanga & Dar es Salaam*

12 Mweka
13 Outward Bound
14 Shira

Tanzania

The snow sepulchre of King Solomon

Legend has it that the last military adventure of King Solomon was an expedition down the eastern side of Africa. Exhausted by his battles the aged king was trekking home with his army when they passed the snow-covered Mount Kilimanjaro. Solomon decided this was to be his resting place. The next day he was carried by bearers until they reached the snows. As they steadily trudged up to the summit they saw a cave glittering in the sunlight, frost sparkling in the interior,

icicles hanging down to close off the entrance. As they watched, two icicles, warmed by the sun, crashed to the ground. They carried the old king inside and placed him on his throne, wrapped in his robes, facing out down the mountain. Solomon raised a frail hand to bid farewell. The bearers left with heavy hearts. The weather began to change and there was a gentle fall of snow. As they looked back they saw that icicles had reformed over the entrance.

the peak, as a lunch pack is not always provided. Kibo Hut sleeps about 120 people. There is a stone-built main block with a small dining room and several dormitory rooms with bunks and mattresses. There is no vegetation in the area and no water unless there has been snow recently, so it has to be carried up from Last Water. Some people decide to try and get as much sleep as possible before the early start, while others decide not to sleep at all. You are unlikely to sleep very well because of the altitude and the temperatures anyway.

Day 4/5 On the final day of the climb, in order to be at the summit at sunrise, and before the cloud comes down, you will have to get up at about midnight. One advantage of beginning at this time is that if you saw what you were about to attempt you would probably give up before you had even begun. You can expect to feel pretty awful during this final five-hour ascent and many climbers are physically sick. You may find that this climb is extremely slippery and hard going. The first part of the climb is over an uneven trail to **Hans Meyer Cave**. As the sun rises you will reach **Gillman's Point** (5,680 m) – it is a wonderful sight. From here you have to decide whether you want to keep going another couple of hours to get to **Kibo Peak** (5,896 m). The walk around the crater rim to Kibo Peak is only an extra 200 m but at this altitude it is a strenuous 200 m. At the peak there is a fair amount of litter left by previous climbers. You will return to **Horombo Hut** the same day and the next day (**day 5/6**) return to Marangu where you will be presented with a certificate.

Mawenzi Peak This peak is accessible from Mawenzi Hut and Mawenzi Tarn Hut, but only experienced rock climbers should attempt any of the difficult routes to the top. **Mawenzi Hut** (4,600 m) sleeps five people. There is a stream nearby, but no toilets. **Mawenzi Tarn Hut** (4,330 m) is a metal and wooden construction with bunk beds and mattresses, and a small dining room, sleeping six. There is a second hut, also for six people.

Umbwe trail The climb is hard, short and steep but is a wonderfully scenic route to take to reach **Uhuru Peak** and as a result is becoming increasingly popular. However it is not recommended for inexperienced climbers. Many climbers descend this way after climbing up by a different route. To get to the start of the trail take the turning off the Arusha road about 2 km down on the right. From there it's 14 km down the Lyamungu road, turn right at the T-junction towards Mango and soon after crossing the Sere River you will get to **Umbwe** village (1,400 m). Ask at the mission school to leave your vehicle here.

Day 1 Umbwe to Bivouac 1, 4-6 hours' walk. From the mission the former forestry track continues through rainforest for about 3 km up to **Kifuni** village. From there it's another 6 km before you get to the start of the trail proper. There is a sign here and the trail branches to the left and climbs quite steeply through the forest along the ridge that is between the Lonzo River to the west and Umbwe River to the east. In several places it is necessary to use branches to pull yourself up. You will reach the first shelter, a cave, about 6-8 hours' walk from Umbwe. This is **Bivouac I** (2,940 m), an all-weather rock shelter formed from the rock overhangs. It will shelter about six or seven people. There is firewood nearby and a spring about 15 m below under a rock face.

If you made an early start and are fit and keen you can continue on to Bivouac II on the same day. However, most climbers take an overnight break here, camping at the forest caves.

Day 2 Bivouac 1 to Barranco Hut, 5 km, 4-5 hours' walk. From the caves, continue up, past the moorland and along the ridge. It is a steep walk with deep valleys on each side of the ridge and this walk is magnificent with the strange 'Old Man's Beard' – a type of moss – covering most of the vegetation. The second set of caves is **Bivouac II** (3,800 m), 3-4 hours from Bivouac I. There are two caves – one about five minutes further down the track – and both sleep 3-4 people. There is a spring down the ravine about 15 minutes to the west.

From the second set of caves the path continues less steeply up the ridge beyond the tree line before reaching **Barranco** or **Umbwe Hut** (3,900 m). Barranco Hut is about five hours away from the first caves or two hours from Bivouac II. The path is well marked. The hut is a metal cabin with a wooden floor, which sleeps 6-8 people. About 200 m beyond the hut is a rock overhang, which can be used if the hut is full. There is one pit latrine, water is available about 250 m to the east and firewood is available in the area.

Some people may choose to spend an extra day at Barrenco Hut to acclimatize to the altitude.

Day 3/4 Barranco Hut to Lava Tower Hut, 3-4 hours' walk. Just before reaching Barranco Hut the hut the path splits in two. To the left, the path goes west towards Shira Hut (5-6 hours) and the northern circuit, or you can climb the west lateral ridge to the **Arrow Glacier Hut** (now defunct after it was buried in an avalanche) towards the new **Lava Tower Hut** (4,600 m) about 3-4 hours away. Up this path the vegetation thins before disappearing completely on reaching the scree slopes. Lava Tower Hut is a round metal hut that sleeps eight. There are no toilets, but water is available in a nearby stream.

Day 4/5 Lava Tower Hut to Uhuru Peak, 4-6 hours. Having spent the night at Lava Tower Hut you will want to leave very early for the final ascent. Head torches are imperative and if there is no moonlight the walk can be quite difficult. Climb up between **Arrow Glacier** (which may have disappeared completely if you are there towards the end of the dry season) and **Little Breach Glacier** until you get to a few small cliffs. At this stage the course follows the Western Breach summit route and turns to the right heading for the lowest part of the crater rim that you can see. This part of the walk is really steep on scree and snow, and parts of it are quite a scramble. From December to February, crampons and ice axes are recommended. Having reached the crater floor, cross the **Furtwangler Glacier** snout to a steep gully that reaches the summit plateau about another 500 m west of **Uhuru Peak** (5,895 m), returning to **Mweka Hut**, among the giant heathers, for an overnight stop.

Day 5/6 Descent from Mweko Hut to Mweko Gate, 14 km, 5-7 hours. The return journey can be achieved in approximately half the ascending time.

Day 3/4 Barranco Hut to Bafaru Hut, 5 km, 4-5 hours. The route is well marked at lower levels but not at higher altitudes. If you take the path to the right from **Barranco Hut** (eastwards on the Southern Circuit) you will cross one small stream and then another, larger one as you contour the mountain to join the **Mweka trail**. The path then climbs steeply through a gap in the **West Breach**. From here you can turn left to join the routes over the south glaciers. Alternatively continue along the marked path across screes, ridges and a valley until you reach the **Karangu**

Umbwe trail – alternative route

Tanzania

Campsite, which is a further 2-3 hours on from the top of the Breach. A further couple of hours up the **Karangu valley** (4,000 m) will come out at the **Mweka-Barafu Hut** path (part of the Mweka trail). If you go left down along this you will get to the **Barafu Hut** after 1-1½ hours. If you go straight on for about three hours you will join the Marangu trail just above the **Horombo Hut**.

Day 4/5 Barafu Hut to Uhuru Peak to Mweka Hut, 5-6 hours' walk to crater rim plus another hour to Uhuru Peak. Parties heading for the summit set off around midnight to 0100, reaching the crater at Stella Point. If the weather conditions are favourable, **Uhuru Peak** (5,895 m) is normally reached by first light. From here it is often possible to see the summit of Mount Meru to the west. Descend to **Mweka Hut** for an overnight stop.

Day 5/6 Descent from Mweko Hut to Mweko Gate, 14 km, 5-7 hours.

Machame trail

This route is not suitable for older people or those of any age who aren't very fit

This trail is considered by some to be the most attractive of the routes up Kilimanjaro. It is located between Umbwe trail and Shira trail and joins the latter route at Shira Hut. The turn-off to the trail is to the west of Umbwe off the main Arusha-Moshi road. Take this road north towards Machame village, and leave your vehicle at the school or hotel there.

Day 1 From the village to the first huts takes about nine hours so be sure to start early. Take the track through the *shambas* and the forest to the park entrance (about 4 km), from where you will see a clear track that climbs gently through the forest and along a ridge that is between the Weru Weru and Makoa streams. It is about 7 km to the edge of the forest, and then 4-5 hours up to the **Machame Huts** (3,000 m). The two round metal huts, on the edge of the forest, will sleep about seven people each. There are pit latrines and plenty of water down in the valley below the huts and firewood available close by.

Day 2 From the Machame Huts go across the valley, over a stream, then up a steep ridge for 3-4 hours. The path then goes west and drops into the river gorge before climbing more gradually up the other side and on to the moorland of the Shira Plateau to join the Shira Plateau trail near the **Shira Hut** (3,800 m). This takes about five hours in total. From the Shira Plateau you will get some magnificent views of Kibo Peak and the Western Breach. The area is home to a variety of game including buffalo. The Shira Hut sleeps about eight people and is used by people on the Shira Plateau trail as well as those on the Machame trail. There is plenty of water available 50 m to the north and firewood nearby, but no toilets.

Day 3 onwards From here there are a number of choices. You can go on to the **Barranco Hut** (5-6 hours, 3,900 m) or the **Lava Tower Hut** (four hours, 4,600 m). The path to **Arrow Glacier Hut** is well marked. The ascent includes scrambling over scree, rocks and snow fields – tough at times and probably only suited to experienced hikers. It goes east from Shira Hut until it reaches a junction where the North Circuit route leads off to the left. The path continues east, crossing a wide valley before turning southeast towards the Lava Tower. Shortly before the tower a route goes off to the right to Barranco Hut and the South Circuit route. To the left the path goes to Arrow Glacier Hut and the Western Breach.

Shira Plateau trail

This route needs a four-wheel-drive vehicle and so for this reason is little used. The road can be impassable during wet periods. However if you do have access to such a vehicle and are acclimatized you can get to the **Arrow Glacier Hut** in one day.

The drive is a complex one and you may need to stop and ask the way frequently. Pass through West Kilimanjaro, drive for 5 km and turn right. At 13 km you will pass a small trading centre on the left. At 16 km you will cross a stream followed by a hard left. At 21 km you will enter a coniferous forest that will soon become a natural forest. The plateau rim is reached at 39 km. Here the track continues upwards gently and crosses the plateau to the roadhead at 55 km. Just before the roadhead, about 19 km from **Londorossi Gate**, is a rock shelter. This site is suitable for camping and there is a stream nearby. From the roadhead you will have to walk. It is about 1½ hours to **Shira Hut** (3,800 m). From here you continue east to join the Umbwe trail to the **Lava Tower Hut**. The walk is fairly gentle and has magnificent views.

Mweka trail

This trail is the most direct route up the mountain. It is the steepest and the fastest. It begins at Mweka village, 13 km north of Moshi, where you can leave your vehicle at the College of Wildlife Management with permission.

Day 1 The first day's walk takes 6-8 hours. The trail follows an old logging road, which you can drive up in good weather, through the *shambas* and the forest, for about 5 km. It is a slippery track that deteriorates into a rough path after a couple of hours. From here it is about 6 km up a ridge to the **Mweka Huts** (3,100 m), which are some 500 m beyond the tree line in the giant heather zone. There are two unfurnished metal huts here that each sleep about eight people. Water is available nearby from a stream in a small valley below the huts five minutes to the southeast and there is plenty of firewood. There are no toilets.

Day 2 From the Mweka Huts follow the ridge east of the Msoo River through heathland, tussock open grassland and then on to the alpine desert to the **Barafu Huts** (4,400 m), a walk of 6-8 hours. These metal shelters sleep about 16 people. There are no toilets, and no water or firewood available – you will need to bring it up from Mweka Huts.

Day 3 From the Barafu Huts the final ascent on a ridge between **Rebmann** and **Ratzel** glaciers takes about six hours up to the rim of the crater between **Stella** and **Hans Meyer Points**. From here it is a further hour to **Uhuru Peak**. At the lower levels the path is clearly marked, but it becomes obscured further up. It is steep, being the most direct non-technical route. Although specialized climbing equipment is not needed, be prepared for a scramble. To catch the sunrise you will have to set off no later than 0200 from Barafu Huts. You return to the huts the same day, and (**Day 4**) make the final descent the next day.

Loitokitok trail

This approach from Kenya is closed to the public and is not recommended. However you may be able to obtain special permission from the park's department to climb it. See the warden who is based in Marangu. You may have problems getting porters to go up this route. This, and the Shira Plateau trail, both come in from the north unlike the other trails.

From the Outward Bound School take the path towards the border road and on reaching it turn left down it. Cross the bridge over the Kikelewa River and go a further 150 m. Here you will see a rough track leading through the plantations. Take this track, along which you will recross the Kikelewa and continue up through the forest, and on to the heather and moorlands until you reach the caves. It is a total of approximately 5-6 hours to the caves.

From these caves follow the path that heads towards a point just to the right of the lowest point on the saddle. You will pass **Bread Rock** after about 1½ hours. The track then divides. To the right is the **Outward Bound Hut** that you will almost certainly find locked. The path continues upwards to the saddle towards the **Kibo Huts** – a climb of 3-4 hours. To the left another path crosses towards the **Mawenzi Hut**.

The Summit Circuit

A route around the base of Kibo, the Summit Circuit links Horombo, Barranco, Shira and Moir Huts. The southern section of the circuit is most spectacular, as it cuts across moorland, in and out of valleys and under the southern glaciers.

Tanzania

Sleeping **A** *Ashanti Lodge*, PO Box 339, Marangu, T2754510. For **A** *Capricorn Hotel*, **A** *Kibo Hotel* and **A** *Marangu Hotel*, see Marangu, page 426. **B** *Aishi Hotel*, PO Box 534, Moshi T/F2754104, south of Machame NP gate near Machame village. 14 rooms with private facilities, set in well-kept gardens, spotlessly clean and very well furnished. **C** *Kilimanjaro National Park Hostel*, PO Box 96, Marangu, T50, located at entrance to park. Bunk beds and bedding supplied; you will need to bring your own food.

Tour operators *Shah Tours*, T2752370, F2751449, kilimanjaro@eoltz.com, www.kilimanjaro-shah.com, specializes in Kili tours, helping to join up groups. *Trans-Kibo Travel*, PO Box 558, Moshi, T/F2752017, transkibo@habari.co.tz, located inside the YMCA. Two operators at Marangu (page 426), the village at the gates of the NP, contactable through *Kibo Hotel* or *Marangu Hotel*. See also Tour operators in Moshi (page 424) and Arusha (page 445). Recent travellers have reported that some of the tour operators' personnel have not given them the best advice about routes up the mountain.

Arusha

Arusha is a pleasant town set at an altitude of 1,380 m above sea level. The drive up from Dar es Salaam to Arusha passes through the semi-arid grass plains, gradually becoming greener, more cultivated and more heavily populated. Mount Meru appears on the right with its fertile, cultivated slopes. It is probably the busiest Tanzanian town after Dar es Salaam. As the starting place for the great safaris in the north of Tanzania – the Serengeti, Ngorongoro, Lake Manyara, Olduvai Gorge and Arusha National Parks – it can be very busy with tourists, mostly either in transit to, or returning from, these attractions. There are lots of good hotels and restaurants, and tourism has made Arusha a very prosperous town.

3°20'S 36°40'E
Phone code: 027
Colour map 4, grid A4
Population: 350,000
Altitude: 1,380 m

Ins and outs

Arusha is 50 km from Kilimanjaro International Airport, which is well served by international flights, 79 km from Moshi, 650 km from Dar es Salaam and 272 km from Nairobi. The road between Dar es Salaam and Arusha is now sealed. The journey by bus takes 6 hrs.

Getting there
See Transport on page 449 for further details

Alas safety is becoming an increasing concern in Arusha. Muggings have become far more common. Sokoine Rd and Moshi Rd towards *Impala Hotel* are unsafe at night, unless you are in a big group. Taxis are advised at night, and extra caution should be taken around the market and bus station.

Getting around

Information for tourists in Arusha, with displays on the surrounding attractions, can be obtained from the following places. **Tanzanian Tourist Board (TTB)**, Information Centre, PO Box 2348, 47E Boma Rd, T2503842/3, F2548628, ttb-info@habari.co.tz, www.tanzania-web.com/home2.htm Does not arrange bookings or hotel reservations but is a useful source of local information, including details of excellent cultural tours run in conjunction with **SNV**, the Netherlands Development Agency (see page 446). In the TTB office there are several leaflets outlining these tours, which directly involve and benefit the local people. For more specialized information, contact the **Cultural Tourism Programme Co-ordination Office**, AICC, Serengeti Wing, Rooms 643-645, PO Box 10455, Arusha, T/F2547515, www.habari.co.tz/culturetours or www.snv.nl The TTB also holds a list of registered tour companies as well as a 'blacklist' of rogue travel agencies (see page 446). **Tanzania National Parks (TANAPA)** has an office in the Arusha International Conference Centre (AICC), PO Box 3134, Arusha, T2501930/9, F2548216, Tanapa@habari.co.tz It stocks booklets on the national parks at much more competitive prices than elsewhere, and is a useful resource if you require specialist information. **Tanzanian Wildlife Corporation**, PO Box 1144, T2548830, has an office near the AICC with information about game reserves. **Bulletin boards** There are also a couple of notice boards with feedback bulletins from travellers at the *Mambo Jazz Café* and the *Outpost Hotel*. There is a superb colour map of Arusha and the road to Moshi by Giovanni Tombazzi, which can be obtained from bookshops or *Hoopoe Safaris* on India St.

Tourist information

Arusha is at the base of Mount Meru and is in the centre of a major farming area producing coffee, wheat, sisal and maize. In 1900 the town was just a small German military garrison but it has expanded and flourished. Many of the wide roads are lined with flame trees, jacaranda and bougainvillaea and if you are lucky enough to be here when they are in bloom it is a splendid sight. It was here, in 1967, that the Arusha Declaration was signed, which marked the beginning of Tanzania's commitment to socialism.

Sights

The centre of town is the **Clock tower**, which was donated in 1945 by a Greek resident, Christos Galanos, to commemorate the Allied victory in the Second World War. The **German Boma** now houses the **National Natural History Museum,** opened in 1987, at the north end of Boma Road. The building was constructed by the Germans in 1886

Centre

and it has an outer wall, with block towers at each corner. Inside the fortifications are a central administrative building, a captain's mess, a soldier's mess, a guard house and a large armoury. A laboratory has been established for paleoanthropological research (the study of man's evolution through the record of fossils).

The museum contains the celebrated **Laetoli Footprints**, dating back 3,500,000 years ago, set in solidified volcanic grey ash. Three hominids walking on two legs have left their tracks. The discovery was made at Laetoli, about 30 km southwest of Olduvai Gorge, by Andrew Hill, who was visiting Mary Leakey's fossil camp in 1978. Another display of interest is the tracing of the evolution of man based on the findings at Olduvai Gorge (see page 465).

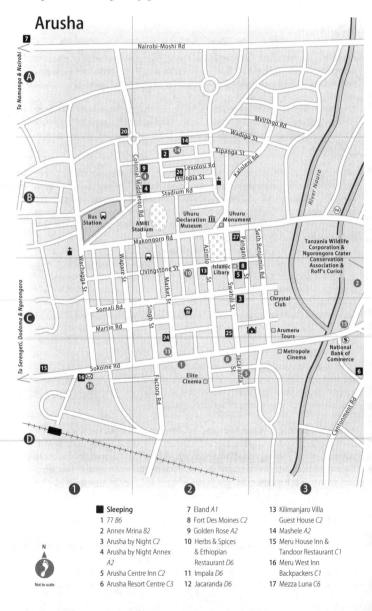

Arusha

Not to scale

Tanzania

North of the museum, the huge **Arusha International Conference Centre (AICC)** is made up of three main blocks – the Kilimanjaro, Ngorongoro and Serengeti wings. It has all the facilities that you would expect of an international conference centre including a hall with seating capacity of 800, an interpretation system, meeting rooms for groups of varying sizes. It has been an important centre for international deliberations, with recent events such as the Rwandan War Crimes Tribunal and the Burundi peace negotiations taking place there. The centre also has within it a bank, post office, foreign exchange bureau and cafeteria as well as various tour operators and travel agents.

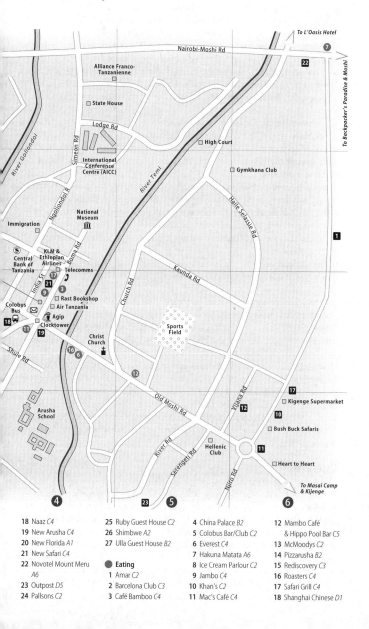

On the east side of Simeon Road, just north of the AICC complex, is **State House**, a small but handsome building with double gables and a green tin roof. This was the residence of the provincial commissioner in the colonial period. Nowadays the president resides there when he is in Arusha. There is no sign announcing that it is State House – and it is best not to take photographs.

Old Moshi Road The layout of the town in the colonial period had the Europeans settled in the area adjacent to the River Temi, along Old Moshi Road, and to the north and south of it. The Asian community lived near their commercial premises, often over their shops in the area between Boma Road and Goliondoi Road. Africans lived further to the west on the far side of the Naura River. On the north side of the Old Moshi Road is **Christ Church Anglican Cathedral**, built in the 1930s in traditional English style of grey stone with a tiled roof and a pleasant interior. The cathedral is surrounded by a vicarage and church offices. Along Old Moshi Road there are several bungalows with red tile roofs and substantial gardens. These housed government servants. There are two buildings that particularly stand out, both with classical porticos. One of these is the **Hellenic Club** on the corner of Old Moshi Road and Njiro Road.

Makongoro Road The **Arusha Declaration Monument** is set on a roundabout past the police station on the Makongoro Road. Also commonly referred to as the Uhuru (Freedom) Monument, it has four concrete legs that support a brass torch at the top of a 10-m column. Around the base are seven uplifting scenes in plaster. The Declaration of 1967 outlined a socialist economic and political strategy for Tanzania. The nearby **Arusha Declaration National Museum** is dedicated to this landmark in Tanzania's history, outlining the evolution of Tanzania's political and economic development. It also has historic photographs of the German period and a display of traditional weapons including clubs, spears and swords. South of the museum is a small park containing the **Askari Monument**, dedicated to African soldiers who died in the Second World War.

On the east side of Azimio Street is an interesting **Temple** with a portico, fretworked masonry and a moulded coping.

Arusha School Arusha School dominates the area on the left bank of the Themi River. It is sited on sloping ground, has huge eucalyptus trees and is surrounded by a large swathe of playing fields. It has a typical low-slung, grey granite colonial-style main building with standard pink *bati* roof and large casement windows, arranged around courtyards with colonnaded loggias. The remaining buildings are run-of-the-mill whitewash and tile classrooms, dormitories and a sanatorium. An exception is the Silver Jubilee Library donated by the Round Table, who met in an old wooden lodge in the grounds. There was always a strong Church of England connection. Nyerere's two sons were taught there. It also hosted the meeting of the Organization of African Unity (OAU) Heads of State in 1966, which included Nyerere, Obote, Kaunda, Moi (as vice president), Haile Selassie and Nasser. Sadly the school and grounds are now very neglected.

Essentials

Sleeping
■ *on map page 438*
Price codes:
see inside front cover

The best hotels in the Arusha area are out of town. They have fine gardens, good standards and charming atmosphere in the foothills of Mt Meru. They are recommended above similar priced hotels in Arusha or its outskirts. They really require that you have your own transport. Recent reports stress security concerns, especially after dark. If using a hotel's 'safe', you are advised to check your money when deposited and on collection. There are reports of false receipts being issued and less money being returned on collection. At the other end of the market there are a number of cheap hotels around Levolosi Rd, north of the stadium. They cost around US$8 and are good value. Recent travellers have advised that it is possible to negotiate lower room rates if you plan to stay a few days.

Mountain hotels (see map, page 412) **A** *Momela Wildlife Lodge*, PO Box 999, Arusha, T2548104, F2548264, about 50 km from Arusha, just outside Arusha NP, 3 km to the north-east of Momela Gate. Made famous by the 1962 movie *Hatari* starring John Wayne, which was filmed in this area, with the hotel acting as the production base – the dining room is named after the film star. The lodge will screen the film on request for guests. The lodge has beautiful gardens, with a swimming pool. There are 55 rondavels with private bathrooms. Excellent views of Mt Meru and Mt Kilimanjaro (when the cloud lifts). The lodge is well placed for visits to the Momela Lakes, and nearby are many plains animals and a huge variety of birds. **A** *Mountain Village, Arusha*, PO Box 376, T2546304, F2544155, out of town, 20 km along Moshi Rd. Thatched bomas, 46 rooms, distinguished by African animal hand carvings on the doors, nestle within a coffee plantation, excellent gardens, splendid location, over-looking the forest-fringed Lake Duluti. Has a very good restaurant. Hotel was taken over by *Serena Hotels* in Oct 2000 (www.serenahotels.com) For further information contact Central Reservations (Kenya), T2542-71-1007/8, mktg@serena.co.ke **A** *Mount Meru Game Lodge*, PO Box 659, T2503303, F2548268, about 20 km off Moshi Rd near Usa River. Small, well-run, high-standard establishment in splendid garden setting, charming atmosphere, very good restaurant. Has an impressive animal sanctuary, which includes baboons, vervet monkeys and probably the only Sanje mangabey, *Cercocebus sanjei*, in captivity. A large paddock is home to zebra, waterbuck and eland, as well as saddle-billed and yellow-billed storks, sacred ibis and ostrich. **A** *Moi Varo*, PO Box 11297, T2548891, T0741-650550 (mob), F2548665, moivaro@habari.co.tz, www.moivaro.com Lovely cottages with verandahs, set in a coffee plantation, swimming pool, good restaurant and bar, internet access available, operated by a Dutch family, recommended by recent travellers. **A** *Ngare Sero Mountain Lodge*, Usa Rive, PO Box 425, T2548689, F2548690, formerly the farm of Hauptmann Leue, a colonial adminis-trator from the German period, is situated in the foothills of Mt Meru. The name means 'sweet waters' and there are magnificent gardens with varied flora and fauna and an esti-mated 200 species of birds. Trout fishing is available in the well-stocked lake. There are 10 rooms including those in the main house and the garden cottages. **A** *Oldonyo Orok Lodge,* T2509305, T0744-312385 (mob), is an old German colonial homestead that is now a small private lodge. Situated in the foothills of Mt Meru, not far from *Momela Wildlife Lodge* just outside Arusha NP Momela Gate, it is ideal as a base to climb either Mt Meru or Mt Kilimanjaro or to observe the game migration. Bookings can be made through *Dorobo Safaris*, T2508336.

All the hotels in this section are well recommended

B *Dik Dik*, PO Box 1499, T/F2548110, about 20 km off Moshi Rd near Usa River. Swimming pool, good restaurant, pleasant grounds, good value, very proficiently run by Swiss owners, no reduction for residents. **B** *Ilboru Safari Lodge*, T7834, T0744-270357 (mob), PO Box 8012, Arusha, ilboru-lodge@habari.co.tz, 2 km west from the centre on Mt Meru itself, a taxi ride from town. Beautiful gardens, very friendly. Highly recommended. **B** *Lake Duluti Mountain Lodge*, PO Box 602, Arusha, T2502699, 11 km from Arusha about 1,500 m off the Moshi Rd. **B** *Tanzanite*, about 22 km along road to Moshi, near Usa River, bookings via *Savannah Tours*: PO Box 3063, T2331662, savtour@twiga.com Popular with locals at the weekend, chalets set in verdant gardens, swimming pool, tennis, restaurant, small animal sanctuary, child friendly, nature trail, bike safaris planned, lovely surroundings, good value.

Town hotels L *Novotel Mount Meru*, Moshi Rd, PO Box 877, T2548804, F2548503. Full facil-ities including swimming pool, set in pleasant gardens, recently renovated, dance shows on Fri and Sat evenings.

B *Impala*, PO Box 7302, T2508448, F2548220, impala@cybernet.co.tz Corner of Moshi Rd and Old Moshi Rd, rooms with TV and phone, pleasant garden and patio, good restaurant, gift shop, bureau de change, arranges tours and safaris through *Classic Tours*. Recom-mended. **B** *Le Jacaranda*, PO Box 11478, T2544624, F2548585, jacaranda@chez.com S/c and slightly cheaper non-s/c rooms, includes breakfast, camping possible for US$5. Recom-mended. **B** *L'Oasis Lodge*, PO Box 14280, Arusha, T/F2507089, T0744-286731/2 (mob), loasis@africaonline.co.tz, 2 km out of town, 800 m down the road opposite the *Mt Meru*

Tanzania

Hotel, in the quiet residential area of Sekei with wonderful views of Mt Meru. Good food, extensive menu including Thai, Indonesian, Greek, seafood and vegetarian dishes. Breakfast included in the price; full and half-board rates also available. Rates are significantly lower Apr-Jun, Masai 'roundhouse' style accommodation each with bedroom and lounge area, construction of volcanic rock with timber frames, ivy covered, thatched roofs, flowers painted on windows, brick walkways, pool with fish and wading birds, a charming dining area, bar, internet services, safe car parking, all 20 rooms have en-suite facilities. Highly recommended. **B** *New Arusha*, PO Box 88, T2548541/3, nah@eoltz,com, well located near Clocktower, formerly the site of the old German hotel, of which the splendid restaurant is the only surviving feature. Behind the hotel is a beautiful garden running down to the Themi River. Facilities include a swimming pool, snack bar, restaurant serving international food, Italian and Indian dishes and the bar downstairs leads to the garden. Also a good bookshop, gift/craft shop and a foreign exchange bureau. **B** *Pallson's*, PO Box 773, T2542485, F7263, off Sokoine Rd, near market. Restaurant overpriced, service terribly slow, has seen better times, East Indian/Chinese food. S/c, hot water.

C *Arusha Naaz Hotel*, PO Box 1060, T272087, F2548893, arushanaaz@cybernet.co.tz, central, near Clocktower on Sokoine Rd. Restaurant with good food (closed in evening), hot water, nets, fans, secure, clean and good value, double rooms s/c, single rooms have shared facilities. **C** *Eland Motel*, north of centre on main road to Nairobi, PO Box 7226, T2507967, F2548468. Bar, restaurant, conference facilities. **C** *Golden Rose*, PO Box 361, Colonel Middleton Rd, Arusha, T2507959, T0741-510696 (mob), F2508862, goldenrose@habari.co.tz Self contained, hot water, telephones, balconies, bar and restaurant, includes English breakfast, accept Visa and Mastercard, reported to have rather noisy generator at back, can arrange car hire. **C** *Mezza Luna Hotel*, PO Box 14365, Arusha, T/F2544381. Recommended Italian family-run hotel with an outdoors restaurant under thatched roofs, excellent furnishings and high quality service and food, local African band plays most evenings. **C** *New Safari*, PO Box 303, T2548545, central, on Boma Rd. Restaurant and outdoor bar, weekend disco. **C** *Outpost*, PO Box 11520, T/F2548405, Serengeti Rd, off the Old Moshi Rd, near *Impala Hotel*. Run by a Zimbabwe couple, Kathy and Steve Atwell, who are wonderful hosts, staff superb, very welcoming. Popular with expats. Accommodation either in the main house, spacious rooms, or in bandas. Within walking distance of the *Mezza Luna* and the *Mambo Jazz Café*. Highly recommended. **C** *Seventy Seven*, PO Box 1184, T2548054, F2548407, off Moshi Rd, about 2 km to the east of the centre. Pleasant bar and restaurant, disco, prefabricated rooms, efficient but a bit utilitarian, substantial discount for residents.

D *Arusha by Night*, PO Box 360, Swahili St, T2542836/7. Top 2 floors of the Urafiki Hospital, s/c, hot water, no restaurant or bar, well maintained but not particularly good value. **D** *Backpackers' Paradise*, a new annex to *L'Oasis Lodge* (see above for contact details), with access to all facilities at the lodge including restaurant, bar, laundry, telephone services, internet access and satellite TV. 12 rooms with twin beds, price includes breakfast. Recommended. **D** *Herbs & Spices*, next to *Impala Hotel* on Old Moshi Rd, PO Box 2732, T2542279, F2548801.Well appointed with a garden and verandah in front leading to the restaurant.The rooms are set around a courtyard to the rear, with a good selection, some with a/c, shared facilities except for 3 s/c double rooms. Very well run and highly recommended. **D** *Hotel Fort des Moines*, PO Box 7321, Livingstone St, T2507406, F2548523, bimel@habari.co.tz Modern, a little gloomy, well maintained, restaurant, s/c, hot water, price includes continental breakfast. Good value. **D** *Midway*, near stadium on Colonel Middleton Rd, PO Box 674, T2502790. Restaurant, good value. **D** *Williams Inn*, PO Box 11710, next to *Midway Hotel*, just off Colonel Middleton Rd. Clean and friendly, s/c rooms, recommended. **D** *YMCA*, PO Box 118, India St, centre. No hot water, shared bathrooms.

E *Amazon*, PO Box 528, T2507005, Sarammo St north of market, not s/c, hot water, restaurant and verandah bar, sited in a lively local area. **E** *Arusha by Night Annexe*, PO Box 360, on corner of Colonel Middleton Rd and Makongaro Rd, T6894. Basic, good value, s/c, hot water, restaurant and courtyard bar. Recommended. **E** *Arusha Centre Inn*, Livingstone St, s/c, hot water, no restaurant or bar. Reasonable value. **E** *Continental*, Swahili St. Very basic, but cheap. **E** *Friends Corner*, corner of Sokoine Rd and Factory Rd. Simple but reasonably good value. **E** *Kilimanjaro Villa*, Azimio St, shared bathrooms, western toilets, hot water, very pleasant and well maintained. Price includes breakfast, has a walkway on 1st floor around courtyard. Recommended. **E** *Kitundo Guest House*, behind the *Golden Rose Hotel*. Reports of theft from locked rooms, so leave no valuables in your room. Good, cheap local bars and restaurants in the vicinity. **E** *Mashele Guest House*, very cheap, popular with backpackers, reasonably clean rooms, nets and fans available, communal facilities include squat toilets, one of the showers has hot water, close to the football stadium, has a small restaurant, OK food. Recommended. **E** *Meru House Inn*, western end of Sokoine Rd just past Wachagga St, PO Box 1530, T2544388, T0744-288740 (mob). With attached restaurant and café, clean, friendly staff, hot water, nets, some rooms s/c, own generator, can help arrange car hire and safaris including walking safaris into local farmland areas, shuttle buses to the airport. Recommended. **E** *Prima Guest House*, Colonel Middleton Rd towards Moshi and Nairobi Rd, rather basic. **E** *Rahaleo Guest House*, north of the stadium. Basic, clean and cheap. Recommended. **E** *Shimbwe Guest House*, Ethiopia St. Clean, hot water in the mornings, communal showers, nets, bar but relatively quiet.

F *Ruby Guest House*, Swahili St, shared bathrooms, central location but otherwise little to recommend it. **F** *Safari Guest House*, PO Box 1284, T2507819, Ethiopia St, north of stadium, shared bathrooms, hot water, no restaurant or bar. Camping. **F** *Shimbwe*, Ethiopia St, shared bathrooms, squat WCs, bar, no restaurant. **F** *Sombrero*, Levalosi St, north of stadium, restaurant, bar with a pool table, satellite TV and has a lively atmosphere. **F** *Ulla Guest House*, PO Box 1053, T2546832, Pangani St, not s/c, bucket hot water, not particularly recommended but it is cheap.

Camping

Safari Hotel, Ethiopia St, north of the stadium, offers camping on a grass strip beside the hotel at US$1 per night. *Kinyoro Campsite*, 1 km along Old Moshi Rd. *Masai Camp*, 3 km along Old Moshi Rd, hot water, restaurant, US$3. Recommended. *Lake Duluti camping ground*, about 11 km from town toward Moshi, restaurant, US$3. *Meserani Snake Park*, PO Box 13669, T/F00743-682087337 (mob), 25 km out of town. Very popular site for tourists looking for something different, basic toilets and showers, interesting snake park. Barry Bale from South Africa offers a fun atmosphere, and trekkers are welcome. The bar serves very cold beers and sodas. Has hot showers. If camping you get free entry to the snake park. Local crafts people sell their goods. There is a small zoo in addition to the snake park. Camel rides and treks can be arranged and ox treks into the bush are planned. Recommended. *Club Africa*, 1 km beyond *Novotel Mt Meru*. Excellent security, camping US$3 per person per night. Camping also possible at the *Tanzanite Hotel* and *Le Jacaranda*.

Eating
● *on map page 438*
Price codes:
see inside front cover

Expensive *Hotel Seventy Seven*, comfortable atmosphere, live band plays for diners most nights. *Mount Meru Hotel*, international menu, very pleasant coffee shop. *Redds African Grill House*, a converted lodge on Burka Coffee Estate, near the airport, Bodoma Rd, T2544521, F2544374, sales@halcyontz.com Owned by the same company that runs *Blues Restaurant* in Zanzibar, which should give a good indication of the quality. Recommended.

Mid-range *Amor*, PO Box 14563, T2503463, just off Sokoine St near *Elite* cinema, serves good north Indian cuisine. Extensive menu. *Dragon Pearl*, just off the roundabout near *Impala Hotel*, newer sister restaurant of *Shanghai*, different menu, good food and pleasant outdoor setting. *Everest*, T2548419, Old Moshi Rd, extensive Chinese (Szechuan) menu, fondues, good drinks list, business lunches, set on the verandah of the house with the restaurant indoors. Well run and recommended. *Hippo Pool Café & Mambo Cafe*, on Old Moshi Rd, 5 mins walk from the Clocktower, verandah with thatched dining area, pleasant gardens, serves good Italian food, including pizzas and sandwiches, buffet lunch daily, brunch at weekends. Recommended. *Mezza Luna*, T2504381, on Old Moshi Rd near the *Impala Hotel*. Generous glasses of South African wine, good cappuccino, terrific Italian food, live African band, often acrobat floor shows. Recommended. *Pallsons*, Market St. Good quality Indian food, very slow service. *Pita Pizzeria*,

Tanzania

Masai St, down from the centre of the market. Serves pizza, pasta, steaks, hamburgers and salads, clean and cool inside. *Safari Grill*, next to the *New Safari Hotel*. Good standard. *Shanghai Chinese Restaurant*, on Sokoine Rd near the bridge, beside the new post office, T2503224. Extensive menu, the hot and sour soup is highly recommended. *Stiggy's*, Old Moshi Rd near *Impala Hotel*, T2544381. Wide range of food, good quality meals and cheaper snacks including grilled meat, run by a talkative Australian.

Cheap *Big Bites* on Swahili St. Serves good tandooris and curries. *Café Bamboo*, T2506451, Boma Rd, near the main post office, very pleasant, bright and airy atmosphere, light pine tables and chairs, blue tablecloths, wicker-shaded lights over each table. Serves good value tasty food, including excellent salads, burgers, juices, fruit salad and ice cream. Fairly busy. Well recommended. *Chick King*, on the ground floor of Serengeti Wing, AICC, offers fast food and grills. *Colobus*, pleasant rooftop bar, offers burgers and good Mexican food. Off Sokoine Rd opposite Swahili St. Recommended. *Golden Rose Hotel*, good standard and sound value. *Hakuna Matata*, northwest of town centre on main Nairobi-Moshi road, has good local and western food and a good atmosphere. *Khans*, Mosque St (1 block north of the central market), sells car parts by day and good cheap grills in the evenings! *Kuleana*, next to the *New Mwanza Hotel*, is a pizza parlour, open 1100-2000. Excellent pizzas, bread and espresso, this is a project run by the Centre for Children's Rights, employing street children as waiters. A visit is strongly recommended. *McMoody's*, on the corner of Sokoine and Market St, T2503791/2. Serves McDonald's-inspired fast food, not quite as good as the original, also serve fries and shakes. Has an interesting circular staircase and mirrored walkway. *Masai Camp*, 3 km west on the old Moshi Rd, T2548299. Good food and bar, excellent place to meet people, serves hamburgers, chips, pizzas and Mexican food. Recommended. *New Safari Hotel Garden Bar*. Recommended for traditional meat barbecues. *Picknick Restaurant*, behind the *Golden Rose Hotel*. Serves good and cheap meals, local food and fish/chicken/egg with chips, friendly and has a bar that sells beer. *PizzArusha*, opposite *Mashele Guest House* on Levolosi Rd, has excellent food and service. Recommended. *Roasters*, Old Moshi Rd, beer garden atmosphere with barbecues but also with an African buffet and Chinese and Indian dishes. Relaxed atmosphere and good value. *Roots Café*, at *Meru House Inn*, Sokoine Rd. Serves good, cheap meals. *Sher-E-Punjab Bar and Restaurant* (previously *Meenar Restaurant*) on Goliondoi Rd. Serves excellent tandoori food, T2503688. *Sherry Bar*, pleasant African outdoor bar on Arusha/Nairobi Rd, 1 km west of Simeon Rd. Clean and comfortable. *Spices & Herbs Ethiopian Restaurant* (formerly *Axum*), approx 1 km from Clocktower next to *Impala Hotel* on Old Moshi Rd, Kijenge district, T2502279. Simple Ethiopian dishes, full bar and jazz club. Recommended.

Seriously cheap *Ark Grill*, on Swahili St. Friendly place serving European food. *Dolly's Patisserie*, Sokoine Rd, smart decor, serves bread, cakes, fruit, yoghurt. Also has an internet café. Recommended. *Ice Cream Parlour*, south side of Sokoine Rd, serves snacks, samosas, extremely cold orange jiuce, and excellent home-made ice cream. Recommended. *Jambo Diner*, Boma Rd just south of the *New Safari Hotel*, has reasonable snacks and grills. *Mac's Café*, near the Clocktower on Sokoine Rd. Fresh bread and pastries, coffee and fruit juice, also an internet café. Recommended. *Naaz*, Sokoine Rd, near Clocktower, celebrated snack bar at the end of an arcade serves meat chop, egg chop, samosas, kebabs and excellent juices. Recommended. *Naura Yard Bar*, on Sokoine Rd near the bridge. Simple but sound. *Silver City Bar*, attached to the YMCA. Good value.

Entertainment **Bars** There are a number of popular bars including the *Re-Discovery*, just on the junction of Sokoine Rd and Goliondoi Rd. Sports bar with a big screen, also serves meals. *Barcelona Club*, off Sokoine Rd, overlooking Goliondoi River, bar, sprawling ramshackle thatched bandas, serves cheap omelettes and barbecues. Popular with local people. *Naura Yard Bar*, next to the Chinese restaurant on Sokoine Rd near the bridge. On Sun this holds a free, very loud, disco. Another popular spot is the *Silver City Bar* attached to the *YMCA*. *Mambo Jazz Café* near the *Mezza Luna*, great atmosphere. Along the Nairobi-Moshi Road is a string of inexpensive bars, all with outside areas and barbecues. Among the most popular are *La Prima, Sunset,*

Moonlight, Swiss, JM, Check Point, Chini ya Mtini ('under the fig tree') and *Miami*. Near the centre of town, *Roasters*, on Old Moshi Rd, overlooking the Temi River, is a beer garden serving barbecued food.

Cinemas *Metropole Cinema* is on Sokoine Rd (formerly Uhuru Rd); *Elite Cinema*, off Sokoine Rd, south of the market. The *Metropole* shows mostly Asian films, martial arts and adventure movies. The *Elite*, a rather fine building, is now used as a functions hall.

Discos *Heart to Heart* on Old Moshi Rd just past the *Impala* is currently the most popular disco in town, open every night. *Chrystal Club & Disco*, Seth Benjamin Rd, open every day from 2200. Large basement area, pool table and darts, very lively at weekends. The rooftop bar at *Colobus* has a wide selection of drinks, also some food, beneath is a disco open Fri and Sat. Another disco is *Crystal* on Seth Benjamin St. There is another good and popular disco held at the **New Safari Hotel** each weekend called the **Cave Disco**. If you want to dance during the week there are nightly discos at the *Hotel Arusha by Night*. *Club 21*, over the *Ethiopian Restaurant* off Ngiro Rd, gets very lively at times. *Seventy Seven* has discos on Fri and often live music at weekends, which attract mostly locals, good music including Congolese *soca*.

Shopping

Bookshops There is a bookshop at the *New Arusha Hotel* that sells international newspapers and magazines as well as books. *Kase Stores* on Boma Rd has a good selection of books, stationery and postcards. There is a new bookshop on Colonel Middleton Rd, just before the roundabout, when leaving town. However, the best bookshop by far is situated in the *Hippo Pool & Mambo Café*, a 5-min walk down Old Moshi Rd, set in a lovely old colonial villa and incorporating a café, bookshop and craft shop.

Crafts There are some good craft shops on Goliondoi Rd and near the Clocktower with some very good examples of carvings. They are probably cheaper here than elsewhere. On Moshi Rd, half-way between *Impala Hotel* and *Hotel Seventy Seven*, is *Art d'Afrique*, T2548126, an art gallery with a small arts and crafts shop. *Roff's Curios*, PO Box 14711, Boma Rd, T0741-652628.

Markets and shops The main market is behind the bus station along Market St and Somali Rd. It is very good for fruit, locally made basketware, wooden kitchenware and spices and is very colourful. There are lots of shops along Sokoine Rd. Small supermarkets are found along Sokoine Rd, Moshi Rd and Swahili St.

Sports

The Mount Meru Marathon is held yearly in Arusha and attracts competitors from all around the world. **Golf** *Gymkhana Club*, on Haile Selassie Rd out towards the High Court. 9-hole golf course at $12 a day. Temporary membership available. Also has facilities for tennis and squash at US$1.50. **Horse-riding** At Usa River, about 15 km out of Arusha, and at Lake Duluti, 11 km out of Arusha on the Moshi road. **Swimming** Available at the pool at the *Novotel Mount Meru*, open to non-residents for a temporary membership fee. **Tennis** and **Squash** *AICC Club*, opposite the *Impala Hotel* on Old Moshi Rd.

Tour operators
Note that climbing Kilimanjaro is cheaper from Moshi

There are a number of tour operators based in Arusha who organize safaris to the different national parks in the north. Some are based in the AICC, others along India St, Sokoine Rd and Boma Rd. When choosing a safari company and before handing over any money on a 'share vehicle' basis, it is advisable to try to meet your driver/guide and to examine the vehicle in order to check out the former's command of English and the roadworthiness of the vehicle. Travellers have reported that rival tour companies sometimes double up, with 2 or 3 groups sharing the same cars and other facilities – all paying different amounts. As a result, itineraries are changed without agreement. It is advisable to draw up a comprehensive written contract of exactly what is included in the price agreed before handing over any money. Sometimes agents for rival tour companies are very persistent and may follow travellers to promote their company. It is also prudent to state that unused park fees will be refunded as the park fees are for 24-hr periods.

Tanzania

Blacklist At the tourist office there is a blacklist of rogue travel agencies, unlicensed agents and the names of people who have convictions for cheating tourists. It is recommended that you cross-check before paying for a safari. In addition, when going on safari you are advised to check at the park gate if all the fees have been paid, especially if you plan to stay for more than a day in the park. Also check that the name of the tour company is written on the permit. Sadly there is a lot of cheating going on at present, and many tourists have fallen victim to well-organized scams. The tourist office also has a list of accredited tour companies in Arusha. The *Tanzania National Park (TANAPA)* office is on the 6th floor of the Kilimanjaro wing of the AICC, Room 610, PO Box 3134, Arusha, T2544088, F2548216, tanapa@habari.co.tz It has a range of park guides as well as the National Parks quarterly reports.

Cultural tourism programmes These programmes are an excellent way to experience traditional customs, music and dance, and modern ways of life in rural areas. They tend to be run by local entrepreneurs, involving and profiting the local communities, and are off the beaten track, giving a very different tourist experience. An example is the Usambara Mountains tourism programme (see page 415) or the Northern Pare mountains walking tours (see page 420). The tours offered by each programme have been described by one traveller as relatively expensive but worth the cost. Further information about the programmes is available at the tourist office and also from the office of SNV, the Dutch development aid organization, based in the AICC building: Tanzanian Cultural Tourism Programmes Co-ordination Office, Room 643-5, Serengeti Wing, AICC building, PO Box 10455, Arusha, T/F2507515, www.habari.co.tz/culturetours

The cost of taking foreign registered cars into the national parks in Tanzania means that it is usually cheaper to hire a driver/guide and cook with their own vehicle to go on safari

Abercrombie & Kent, PO Box 427, T2508347, F2508273. Recommended. *Acacia Travels*, PO Box 12776, T2420113, Boma Rd. *Adventure Centre*, Goliondoi Rd, PO Box 12116, T2508578, F2508997, balloons@arusha.co.tz Recommended, can book balloon safaris in the Serengeti from here. *Adventure Tours and Safaris*, Goliondoi Rd, PO Box 1014, T2507600, F2508195, adventure@habari.co.tz *African Gametrackers*, PO Box 535, T2502913. *African Trails Ltd*, AICC, Kilimanjaro Wing, Ground Floor, PO Box 2130, T/F2544406. *AfricanTravel Bureau Ltd*, Uchumi House, PO Box 1440, T2503849, F2548401, afritravel@cybernet.co.tz *AICC Tours*, PO Box 3801, T2503181 (ext 23). Recommended. *Angoni Safaris* (in the AICC complex). Recommended. *Arumeru Tours and Safaris*, PO Box 730, T7637. *Blue Bird Tours*, PO Box 1054, T2503934. *Black Mamba Travels*, AICC, Serengeti Wing, 2nd Floor, Room 201, PO Box 2674, T/F2544363, blackmamba@cybernet.co.tz *Bobby Tours*, PO Box 716, T2503490. *Bushtrekker Safaris*, PO Box 3173, Arusha, T2503727. *Classic Tours and Safaris*, located at *Impala Hotel*, PO Box 7302, T2508449, F2548220, impala@cybernet.co.tz Recommended. *Come to Africa Safaris*, AICC, Serengeti Wing, 5th Floor, Room 511, PO Box 2562, T2544530, F2544601, T0741-650420 (mob). *Dorobo Tours and Safaris*, PO Box 2534, T2503699. *Eagle Tours and Safaris*, PO Box 343, T2502909. *Easy Travel & Tours Ltd*, Clock Tower Centre, Joel Maeda Rd, 2nd Floor, PO Box 1912, T2503929, T0741-510654 (mob), F7322, easytravel@habari.co.tz *East West Travel & Tours Ltd*, Boma Rd, PO Box 12027, T2508220, T0741-653951 (mob), F2504342, ewtravel@cybernet.co.tz *Equatorial Safaris*, PO Box 2156, Arusha, T/F2502617. Located in Serengeti Block, AICC. *Executive Travel Services*, PO Box 7462, T2502472. *Flamingo Tours*, PO Box 2660, T6976. *Fly-Catcher Safaris*, PO Box 591, T2503622. *Hoopoe Safaris*, India St, PO Box 2047, T2507011, F2508226, hoopoesafari@africaonline.co.tz, www.hoopoe.com UK address: Suite F1, Kebbell House, Carpenders Pk, Watford WD1 5BE, T01923-255462, F255452, hoopoeuk@aol.com This company has been consistently well recommended by a number of travellers. *JMT African Heart*, Makongoro Rd, opposite CCM building, PO Box 12155, T/F2548414, T0744-283990 (mob), info@africanheart.com Luxury and 'budget' (at least US$100 per person per day) safaris, 3-5 day trekking safaris from US$255, and 2-8 day horseback safaris from US$200. *JM Tours Ltd*, Old Moshi Rd, PO Box 392, T/F2548801, jmtours@habari.co.tz *K and S Enterprises*, PO Box 1318, T6465. *Kearsley Travel & Tours*, PO Box 142, T2548043, T0741-338469 (mob), kearsley@raha.com *Ker and Downey Safaris*, PO Box 2782, T7755. Recommended. *King Safari Club*, PO Box 7201, T2503958. *Laitolya Tours and Safaris*, PO Box 7319, T2502422. *Let's Go Marve Holidays*, PO Box 2660, T2503613. *Let's Go Travel*, The Adventure Centre, Goliondoi Rd, PO

Box 12799, T2502814, F2548997. *Lions Safari International*, Sakina/Nairobi Rd, PO Box 999, T2506426, F2508264, lions-safari@safariestal.com *Lost Horizons*, PO Box 425, F2502123. *Mashado, Tanzania*, PO Box 14823, T6585, T0741-510101 (mob), F2548020, Mashado@ habari.co.tz *Nature Discovery*, T2548406, F2544063, for alternative routes and trekking safaris. *Ostrich Tours & Safaris Ltd*, PO Box 12752, T/F2544140. *Peacock Tours and Safaris*, Regional CCM Bldg, Makongoro Rd, PO Box 554, Arusha, T2508103, F2548256, pea-cock@habari.co.tz Previously highly recommended, but most recent comments have been negative. Some travellers who had booked in advance were very happy with the service, including the drivers and cooks but problems seem to arise if tours are arranged at short notice. It seems that tours may then be subcontracted to other (poor) operators without your knowledge, and some travellers have been very dissatisfied with the final product. *Predators Safari Club*, 2nd Floor, Golden Rose Hotel, Middleton St, PO Box 2302, T/F2506471, T0744-562254 (mob), intoarusha@yahoo.com, www.predators-Safaris.com UK office: 277 Sydney Rd, London N10 2NT, T/F020-8365 2215, T07961-392224 (mob). Sister company of *Fun Tours & Safaris Ltd*, Kenya. *Ranger Safaris*, PO Box 9, T3074, F2548205. *Roy Safaris Ltd*, centre of town, PO Box 50, T2502115, F2548892, RoySafaris@intafrica.com Recommended as offering an excellent service. *The Safari Co*, PO Box 207, T2548424, F2548272, mia@marie.gn.apc.org Can organize private safaris. Highly recommended. *The Safari Company*, T7932, F6620, paulmatthysen@yako.habari.co.tz Do the Kili climb as well as Lake Tanganyika trips. *Safari Images Ltd*, ACU building, 3rd Floor, Uhuru Rd, PO Box 407, T6313. *Sandgrouse Adventure Tours & Safaris Ltd*, PO Box 11661, T2503485, F2544095. *Savannah Tours*, PO Box 3038, T2331662, savtour@twiga.com Recommended. *Serengeti Select Safaris*, PO Box 2703, T7182, T0741-401199 (mob), F7182, sss@habari.co.tz *Shallom Tours and Safaris*, PO Box 217, T2503181. *Shidolya Safaris*, AICC, PO Box 1436, T2548506, F2544160, shidolya@yako.habari.co.tz Drivers/cooks/guides are excellent, rec-ommended for lodge/camping safaris but not the Kilimanjaro climb. *Silver Spear Safaris*, PO Box 706, T/F2548885, Boma Rd. *Simba Safaris*, located between Goliondoi Rd and India St,

Tanzania

PO Box 1207, T2503509. *State Travel Service*, PO Box 1369, T2503300. *Star Tours*, PO Box 1099, T2502553. Recent travellers have advised against this tour company, as the new owner Clemence Muta has been unreliable. Check with the tourist office blacklist for an update on the situation. *Sunny Safaris Ltd*, PO Box 7267, T2508184, F2548037, www.sunnysafaris.com Recent travellers report excellent service. *Takims Holidays Tours and Safaris*, Room 422, Ngorongoro Wing, AICC, PO Box 6023, T2508026, F2508211, takims@twiga.com Recommended. *Tanzania Game Trails*, PO Box 535. *Tanzania Guides*, PO Box 2031, T2503625. *Tanzania Serengeti Adventure*, Sokoine Rd, PO Box 1742, T2544609, T0741-651124 (mob), F2548475, tsa@habari.co.tz *Tanzania Wildlife Corporation*, PO Box 1144, T2503501. *Tanzanite Wildlife Tours*, PO Box 1277, T2502239. *Tarangire*, PO Box 1182, T2503090. *Tracks Travel*, PO Box 142, T2503145. *Tropical Tours Tanzania* at Moshi Rd, near the Clocktower. German Swiss managed, offer excellent tours but are not one of the cheapest. *Tropical Trails*, PO Box 223, T2500358, F2548299, www.tropicaltrails.com *TV Burudani Ltd*, Old Moshi Rd, PO Box 1528, T2500400, F2500399, tvb@habari.co.tz *United Touring Company*, PO Box 2211, T2504068, F2508222. *Wapa Tours and Safaris*, PO Box 6165, T2503181. *Wildebeest Migration Safaris*, AICC, 6th Floor, Room 650-2, PO Box 13964, T2503364, F2548497, T0741-510349 (mob), wildebeest@form-net.com Feedback about this company has been mixed. *Wildersun Safaris and Tours*, Sokoine Rd, PO Box 930, T6471. *WS Safaris Ltd*, India St, PO Box 2288, T/F2544004, www.wssafari.com French/Tanzanian team offering a range of safaris, offer good tours for a fair price of US$80 per day per person camping safari to Serengeti and Ngorongoro Crater. *Wildtrack Safaris*, PO Box 1059, T2503547. *W J Travel Service*, PO Box 88, T6444. *World Archipelago*, PO Box 2174, Arusha, T6079, F6475.

For details of other safari companies, both within Tanzania and overseas, see pages 45 and 317. We have been asked to mention that *Paradise Safaris*, also known as *Paradies Safaris Ltd*, located at the Elite Cinema Building, 2nd Floor, Jacaranda St, managed by Ms H Kiel, has offered

poor quality service to some of our contributors, and that the office is particularly disorganized when Ms Kiel is absent. *Paradise Safaris* is on the 'blacklist' – see above.

Horse and camel-riding safaris Increasingly popular and can be arranged from Arusha. Most of these begin from Usa River, which is 22 km from Arusha on the Moshi road. *Adventure Centre* arranges such safaris. See also page 452 for camel safaris guided by local Masai.

Hunting safaris *Bushmen Company*, PO Box 235, T6210. *King Tours and Hunting Safaris*, PO Box 7000, T2503688.

Air Kilimanjaro International Airport, T027-2502223, is half-way between Arusha and Moshi. It is served by international flights as well as by *Air Tanzania*, office on Boma Rd, T3201, who fly to Dar es Salaam (DSM) and back once or twice (booking in advance is essential). *Aviators Services*, T2546386, has 3 flights a week to DSM, 1400 Mon, Wed, and Sat, cost one-way US$126. *Eagle Aviation*, at the Adventure Centre, T7111, F2548997, offers a coach service to Kilimanjaro Airport, flights to Mombasa 3 times weekly, Mon, Wed and Sun. *Ethiopian Airlines*, T2504231, and *KLM*, T6063, also have offices on Boma Rd. The *Gulf Air* office is on Old Moshi Rd, T2504152. *Precisionair*, AICC, Ngorongoro Wing, PO Box 1636, T2506903, F2548204, T0751-510888 (mob), precision@cybernet.co.tz Have flights to and from Mombasa on Wed, Fri and Sat, depart Mombasa 1020, depart Kilimanjaro 1145, take 1 hr. On Sun a flight leaves Shinyanga at 1230, and starts the return from Kilimanjaro at 1425. *Eagle Air* operate a route on Mon and Fri from DSM (depart 0830) to Kilimanjaro (70 mins), then depart 1010 to Musoma (70 mins) and Mwanza. The return leaves Mwanza for Kilimanjaro at 1240, and leaves Kilimanjaro for DSM at 1420. To get to the airport you can get the STS shuttle bus, which costs US$3 and leaves about 2 hrs before flight departure. It stops at the *Air Tanzania* office, *Mount Meru Hotel* and *Hotel Seventy Seven*. A shuttle bus from *Novotel Mount Meru* costs about US$10. Taxi to the airport is about US$20.

Transport

Closer to town is **Arusha airport**, 10 km west along the road to Dodoma, from where there are domestic flights. *Precisionair* (see above) operate a shuttle bus from town, US$1.25. They fly between here and Kilimanjaro airport on Fri and Sat, and have services to Zanzibar, DSM and also to Mwanza and Shinyanga. On Mon and Thu, flights leave at 1325 for Zanzibar, and take just over 1 hr, while flights depart Zanzibar for Arusha at 1350 on the same days. On Tue and Fri, a flight leaves Zanzibar at 1040. From Arusha this service then departs at 1215 for Mwanza, starting back from here at 1350, and then departing Arusha for Zanzibar at 1525. On Wed and Sun there are flights from DSM (taking 75 mins), they leave at 1345, and later depart Arusha at 1525 for Zanzibar. A flight departs Zanzibar at 1350 on Sat, leaving Arusha at 1525 for the return journey. The one-way fare between Arusha and Zanzibar or DSM is US$170. There is 1 flight a week to Shinyanga, leaving at 1515 on Thu and taking 90 mins. *Precisionair* have had scheduled flights to Lake Manyara and Seronera, departing at 0730 or 1530 several times a week, and also to Moshi, but these may no longer be operating. Some *Precisionair* routes, such as those to Zanzibar, are popular and require advance booking, occasionally they are overbooked. *Precisionair* are reputed to offer an excellent service so far. However, it is essential to follow the instructions to reconfirm – flight times are frequently at variance with the times printed on the tickets.
   Coastal Travels Ltd (Dar es Salaam: T/F2233112), have daily flights to Arusha, which depart Zanzibar at 0930 (originally leaving DSM at 0900), and leave Arusha at 1215 for the return, take approximately 2 hrs and cost US$175 one way.
   Regional Air, Nairobi Rd, PO Box 14755, T2502541, F2544164, T0741-510713 (mob), regional@africaonline.co.tz, have daily flights between Arusha and Kilimanjaro, US$30 one way; they take 15 mins and leave Arusha at 1230 and Kilimanjaro at 1330. There are services from Arusha to Lake Manyara (US$50 one way), and to the airstrips at Seronera (US$135 one way) and Grumeti River Camp (US$165 one way) in the Serengeti, returning to Arusha by the same route. These flights leave Arusha every day at 0845 and 1400.
   Air Excel, PO Box 12731, T2501597, F2548429, T0741-510857 (mob), airexcel@ark.eoltz.com, have daily flights to Zanzibar that leave Arusha at 1330, and continue to DSM. From Zanzibar they leave for Arusha at 1625. There are daily flights to Musoma via Lake Manyara, Seronera and

Tanzania

Grumeti, leaving Arusha at 0800, and leaving Musoma at 1040 for the return. On Mon and Thu a flight leaves at 1400 for Dodoma (70 mins) and Ruaha, on the return to Arusha it leaves Dodoma at 1725. On Tue, Fri and Sat there is a return flight that leaves Arusha at 1400 for Lake Manyara, and the airstrips at *Lobo Wildlife Lodge* and *Klein's Camp* in the Serengeti.

Eagle Air (see above) fly from Arusha to Zanzibar (taking 90 mins) at 1630 on Thu, 1445 Fri, 1615 Sat and 1300 Sun, all continue to DSM. From Zanzibar a flight leaves at 1245 on Fri. From DSM there are flights on Thu (depart 1430) and Sat (depart 1415).

Charter air services from *Air Excel*, *Eagle Air* and *Precisionair* (see above), and *Fleet Air* on Sokoine Rd, T2548126, fleetair@africaonline.co.tz, and *Northern Air* on Goliondoi Rd, T2548059, F2548060, northernair@habari.co.tz

Road The bus station is located in Zaramo St just to the north of the market. There are reported to be thieves operating around the Arusha bus station and there are certainly many persistent touts. Go directly to the bus companies' offices and make sure there is the company's stamp on the ticket. For local buses to places like Moshi and Mto wa Mbu buy your ticket from the driver on the day of travel. There are regular buses and *dala-dala* to and from **Moshi**. Trip costs US$1 and takes 1½ hrs. You can also get a shared taxi, which will be more expensive.

Dar es Salaam: fare is around US$20 luxury, US$16 semi-luxury and US$14 ordinary and takes about 9 hrs. The road has improved considerably and journey times are shortening. Large buses are safer than minibuses. *Taqwa* offer a fast, reliable service, *Fresh ya Shamba* and *Royale* are also very good, while *Scandinavian Express Services Ltd* are recommended for reliablility and safety, T2500153, T0741-323131 (mob). *Dar Express* has 3 services to Dar each day. The journey takes about 6 hrs, non-stop.

Tanga: daily buses (Tanga African Motor Transport), US$7 (luxury) and US$4 (ordinary). You can also get buses from here up to Mwanza.

Mwanza: public transport from Musoma to Arusha now goes via Nairobi. It is possible to get to Mwanza via Singida and Shinyanga, although you may need to change buses, and the trip will take the best part of 2 days.

Nairobi: *dala-dala* only take 4 or 5 hrs from here, depart, regularly through the day, and the border crossing is efficient. There are several through shuttle services to Nairobi US$20-25. *Colobus Bus*, located near the Clocktower, goes to Nairobi 3 days a week and offers a through service to Mombasa *Riverside Shuttle*, c/o Riverside Car Hire, Sokoine Rd, near Chinese Restaurant, PO Box 1734, Arusha, T2502639, F2503916, departs at 0800 and 1400 daily from *Novotel Mount Meru Hotel*.

Directory **Banks** *Standard Chartered*, on Goliondoi Rd, is the only bank with ATM facilities, available 24 hrs, accepts Visa cards. The *Central Bank of Tanzania* has a branch on Makongoro Rd near the roundabout with Goliondoi Rd. There is an AmEx office on Sokoine Rd near Friends Corner, and there are now many Forex offices in town. The *National Bank of Commerce* is on Sokoine Rd down towards the bridge, it is open on Sat mornings. *Stanbic Bank* is next to the National Bank of Commerce and *CRDB* is further west along Sokoine Rd, on the corner with Singh St. The *Impala Hotel* will give cash advances but there is a large fee – approximately 25%. Good exchange rates are given at the bank *National Bureau de Change* opposite the post office at the Clocktower. **Car hire** Available from most tour companies and also *Serena Car Hire* on India St, T/F2506593, serenacarhire@habari.co.tz and *Riverside Car Hire*, Sokoine Rd, T2502639, F2503916. **Communications** Internet: *Mac's Café*, close to the main post office. *Arusha Node Marie*, Room 422E, AICC building, T/F2544220. *Colobus Club* and *Cyberspot*, opposite *Colobus Club*, T0742-602160 (mob), cyberspot@arusha.com Other places also offer access, including *Dolly's Patisserie*, Sokoine Rd, and an internet café next to *Meru House Inn* on Sokoine Rd – typical cost US$1.25 per hr, it can be worth looking around as there are differences in charges. **Post**: the main post office is by the clocktower opposite the *New Arusha Hotel*. **Telephone**: recent travellers have reported that the cheapest place to make calls or send faxes from is the TTCL on Boma Rd, opposite the tourist office. Very efficient service. **Cultural centres**: the Alliance Franco-Tanzanienne d'Arusha has a library with magazines, videos, French lessons, films and art displays. The **Islamic Library**, Livingstone St, has a good reference section and is open to all. There are separate tables for Gentlemen and Ladies, and a sign 'Please maintain modesty'. **Medical services** Hospitals: *Mount Meru Hospital* is opposite the AICC on Goliondi Rd, T3351. **Useful addresses** Arusha International Conference Centre (AICC), PO Box 3081, Arusha, T2503161, F6630, aicc@habari.co.tz *Immigration office* is on Simon Rd.

Excursions from Arusha

Meserani houses mostly local snake species with the non-venomous snakes housed in open pits and the spitting cobras, green and black mambas and boomslangs kept behind glass. There are other reptiles in the zoo including monitor lizards, chameleons, tortoises and crocodiles. There are gardens and a restaurant. ■ *About 25 km from Arusha, west and off to the right on the road to Makuyuni (see camping, page 443).*

Meserani Snake Park

This unusual zoo includes a hair-dressing salon on the premises. The animals are not rare but are infrequently seen in zoos, numbering almost 50 vertebrates. The animals are arranged around a neatly tended garden where greater and lesser flamingos and crested crowns wander around freely. There are also primates, the African palm civet, *Nandinia binatata arborea,* the greater galago (the zoo's symbol), spotted hyenas, black and white colobus monkeys, giant pouched rat, and – sharing a paddock – a Thomson's gazelle and a bush duiker. There are also mongooses and squirrels, porcupines, genets, baboons and vervet monkeys. There is an extensive collection of birds including Hartlaub's turaco, blue-naped mousebird, green pigeon, the vulturine and helmeted guinea-fowl and several birds of prey. ■ *On the outskirts of Arusha, through unsalubrious suburbs, accessed by taxi.*

Engosheraton Zoological Gardens

Located just south of *Mountain Village, Arusha* hotel, about 15 km along the Moshi road, this small crater lake, fringed by forest, provides a sanctuary for approximately 130 species of birds, including pied and pygmy kingfishers, anhinga, osprey, and several species of buzzards, eagles, sandpipers, doves, herons, cormorants, storks, kingfishers and barbets. 'Ethno-botanical' walks are available, starting from the hotel through the coffee plantation and circumnavigating the lake. The walks are accompanied by guards – there have reportedly been attacks on tourists in the locality. Reptiles including snakes and lizards are plentiful too. The pathway around the lake starts off broad and level, but later on it narrows and becomes more difficult to negotiate. There are wonderful views of Mount Meru and occasionally the cloud breaks to reveal Mount Kilimanjaro. The guides are knowledgeable about the flora and birds.

Lake Duluti

Several villages on the lower slopes of Mount Meru, north of Arusha, have started cultural tourism programmes with help from the Dutch development organization, SNV, and the Tanzanian Tourist Board. Further details of the four programmes described below can be obtained from the Tanzanian tourist information centre in Arusha.

Cultural tourism programmes
See also page 446

Ng'iresi village Offers half-day guided tours of farms and local development projects such as irrigation, soil terracing, cross breeding, bio gas and fish nurseries. Longer tours can involve camping at a farm and a climb of **Kivesi**, a small volcano with forests where baboons and gazelle live. The Wa-arusha women will prepare traditional meals or a limited choice of western food. ■ *7 km from Arusha. The co-ordinator of Ng'iresi Cultural Tourism Programme, Mr Loti, can be contacted directly on T0742-401043 (mob).*

Ilkiding'a village You will be welcomed in a traditional boma by Mama Anna, can visit craftsmen and a traditional healer, and walk through farms to one of several viewpoints or into **Njeche** canyon. The guides of both this and the Ng'iresi programme are knowledgeable and have a reasonable standard of English. Profits from each are used to improve the local primary schools. ■ *10 km north of Arusha along the road signposted to Ilboru Safari Lodge from Moshi road.*

Mulala village This programme is organized by the Agape women's group. There are walks through the coffee and banana farms to Marisha River, or to the top of Lemeka hill for views of Mounts Meru and Kilimanjaro, and on to the home of the village's traditional healer. You can visit farms where cheese and bread making and flower growing activities have been initiated. The women speak only a little English, interpreters can be arranged. Fees are used to start new development projects and to help Mulala primary school. ■ *Set at 1,450 m above sea level about 30 km from Arusha.*

Mkuru camel safari The Masai of this area began keeping camels in the early 1990s and there are now over 100 animals. Camel safaris of half a day or up to one week, towards Kilimanjaro, further to Mount Longido, or even further to Lake Natron can be arranged. Alternatively there are walks through the acacia woodland looking for birds, or up the pyramid-shaped peak of Ol Doinyo Landaree. The guides are local Masai who have limited knowledge of English, communicating largely by hand signals – another guide to act as translator can be arranged with advance notice. There are three cottages at the camel camp, meals can be prepared if notice is given. Profits are used to support the village kindergarten, which was established because the nearest schools are too far for young children to walk to. ■ *On the north side of Mt Meru, close to the Momela gate of Arusha NP.*

Mountain Birds & Trophies (MBT) Located just outside the boundary of Arusha National Park this snake park has a breeding and exporting programme. It houses both local snake species and 'exotics' like the Usambara bush viper, *Atheris ceratophora*, the East African egg-eating snake, *Dasypeltis medici*, black-tailed rattlesnake and the king cobra. Other reptiles including several species and subspecies of chameleons, red-eared terrapins and chelonians are also on view. There are few visitors and guided tours can be arranged.

Arusha National Park

The compact Arusha National Park is remarkable for its range of habitats. It encompasses three varied zones: the highland montane forest of Mount Meru to the west, where black and white colobus and blue monkeys can be spotted; Ngurdoto Crater, a small volcanic crater inhabited by a variety of mammals in the southeast of the park; and, to the northeast, Momela Lakes, a series of seven alkaline crater lakes, home to a large number of water birds. On a clear day it is possible to see the summits of both Mount Kilimanjaro and Mount Meru from Ngurdoto Crater rim. There are numerous hides and picnic sites throughout the park, giving travellers an opportunity to leave their vehicles.

Ins and outs

Getting there
4°0'S 36°30'E
Colour map 4, grid A4

Arusha NP is situated about 25 km east of Arusha and 58 km from Moshi (see map, page 412). The road is a good one and the turning off the main road, about 35 km from Kilimanjaro International Airport, is at Usa River and is clearly signposted. There are two lodges at Usa River. From the airport the landscape changes from the flat dry and dusty Sanya Plain, which gradually becomes greener, more fertile and more cultivated. Take the turning (on the right if you are heading towards Arusha) and follow the gravel road for about 10 km until you reach the Ngurdoto Gate. This is coffee country and you will see the farms on each side of the road. On reaching the park entrance this changes to dense forest.

A second gate, **Momela Gate**, from which Mt Meru is accessed, is located to the north of the park. There are two routes leading to Momela Gate, starting near the village of Usa River, close by the Arusha/Moshi road. From here it is 8 km to Ngurdoto Gate. A single road enters the park, dividing near Serengeti Ndogo. The road to the northwest is known as the Outer Road (25 km) and NP fees are not payable if in transit. The only available transport are pick-up trucks, which take a few passengers and go the village of Ngare Nanyuki, beyond the Momela Gate. It is permissible to walk this route too. The right fork takes you to the road that runs northeast towards Ngurdoto Crater, before turning north (18 km) beside the Momela Crater Lakes, and this route attracts the NP fee. These roads through the park meet up again at the Momela Gate. If you do not have your own vehicle many of the safari companies offer day trips to Arusha NP.

At the main entrance a small museum provides information for the visitor on the bird, animal and plant life of the park. Park accommodation (see page 456) can be booked in advance through the Warden, Arusha National Park, PO Box 3134, Arusha, T/F027-2548216, tanapa@habari.co.tz

Tourist information
The best time to visit is Oct-Feb

Background

The Arusha National Park, which contains within its boundaries Mount Meru, was established in 1960. The film *Hatari* was made here in 1962 by Howard Hawks, starring John Wayne, Elsa Martinelli, Red Buttons and Hardy Kruger. The vehicle used by John Wayne in the film *Hatari* was at one time on view in Arusha National Park. It had a metal seat over the inside front mudguard from which the 'Duke' lassoed rhino in Ngorongoro. The park has actually changed its name a number of times from *Ngurdoto Crater National Park* to *Mount Meru National Park* and finally to *Arusha National Park*. It covers an area of 137 sq km and rises from 1,524 m at the Momela Lakes (also spelt Momella) to 4,572 m at the peak of Mount Meru. Although it is only small, because of this gradation there is a variety of landscapes, a variety of ecosystems and therefore a wide variety of flora and fauna. Within the park are the Ngurdoto Crater and the Momela Lakes.

Mount Meru is believed to have been **formed** at around the time of the great earth movements that created the Rift Valley, about 20,000,000 years ago. The crater was formed about 250,000 years ago when a massive explosion blew away the eastern side of the volcano. A subsidiary vent produced the volcano of Ngurdoto, which built up over thousands of years. In a way similar to Ngorongoro, when the cone collapsed the caldera was left as it is today. Ngurdoto is now extinct, while Meru is only dormant, having last erupted about 100 years ago. The lava flow from this eruption can be seen on the northwest side of the mountain. It was at around this time in 1872 that the first European, Count Teleki, a Hungarian, saw the mountain.

Arusha National Park contains many **animals** including giraffe, elephant, hippo, buffalo, rhino (if you're lucky), colobus monkey, bush buck, red forest duiker, reed buck, waterbuck and wart-hog. In fact Arusha is supposed to contain the highest density of giraffes in the world. There are no lions in the park although you may see leopard. Birds found in the national park include cormorants, pelicans, ibis, flamingos and grebes.

Routes

Within the park there are over 50 km of tracks. However no road has been built into the Ngurdoto Crater in order to protect and preserve it. From the Ngurdoto Gate a road leads off towards the Ngurdoto Crater. This area is known as the 'connoisseur's park' – rightly so. The road climbs up through the forest until it reaches the rim. At the top you can go left or right, either going around the crater clockwise or anti-clockwise. The track does not go all the way round the rim of the crater so you will have to turn round and retrace your tracks back to the main road. You will be able to look down on to the animals in the crater below but will not be able to drive down. The crater is about 3 km in diameter and there are a number of viewing points around the rim from which you can view the crater floor, known as the 'park within the park'. These include Leitong Point (the highest at 1,850 m), Glades Point, Rock Point, Leopard Hill, Rhino Crest and Mikindani Point. From this latter point you will be able to see Mount Kilimanjaro in the distance.

Ngurdoto Crater

From Ngurdoto Gate, if you take the left track you will reach the Momela Lakes. This track goes past the Ngongongare Springs, Lokie Swamp, the Senato Pools and the two lakes, Jembamba and Longil. At the peak of the dry season they may dry up but otherwise they are a good place to watch the animals and in particular the birdlife. At various spots there are observation hides. At **Lake Longil** there is a camping and picnic site in a lovely setting.

From here the track continues through the forest, which gradually thins out and through the more open vegetation you will be able to see Mount Meru. The Hyena

Momela Lakes route

Tanzania

Camp (Kambi ya Fisi) is reached where you will probably see a pack of spotted hyenas. Beyond this there is a small track leading off the main track to **Bomo la Mengi** – a lovely place from which to view the lakes. Unless the cloud is down you will also be able to see Kilimanjaro from here. The main track continues past two more lakes – Lake El Kekhotoito and Lake Kusare – before reaching the Momela Lakes.

The **Momela Lakes** are shallow alkaline lakes fed by underground streams. Because they have different mineral contents and different algae their colours are also different. They contain few fish but the algae attracts lots of birdlife. What you see will vary with the time of year. Flamingos tend to move in huge flocks around the lakes of East Africa and are a fairly common sight at Momela Lakes. Between October and April the lakes are also home to the migrating waterfowl, which are spending the European winter in these warmer climes.

The track goes around the lakes reaching the **Small Momela Lake** first. This lake often has a group of hippos wallowing in it. Follow the road anti-clockwise and you will pass **Lake Rishetani**, which is a fantastic emerald green colour. Along this route you will be able to stop off at the various observation sites. The next lake that you will get to is the **Great Momela Lake**, which has a huge variety of birdlife and is a lovely spot. The last two lakes are **Tulusia** and **Lekandiro** where you may see animals grazing.

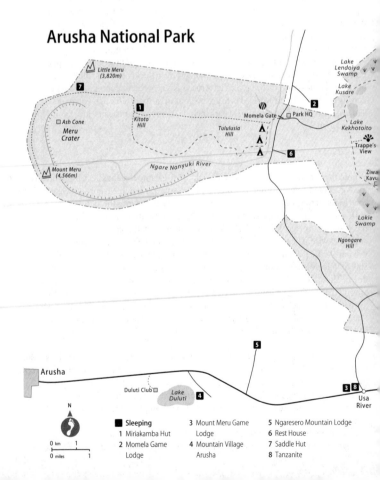

Arusha National Park

Lake Lendoiya Swamp

Lake Kusare

Little Meru (3,820m)

7

1

Kitoto Hill

☐ Ash Cone
Meru Crater

Momela Gate ☐ Park HQ **2**

Tululusia Hill

Lake Kekhotoito

△ Mount Meru (4,566m)

Ngare Nanyuki River

Trappe's View

6

Ziwa Kavu

Lokie Swamp

Ngongare Hill

5

Arusha

Duluti Club ☐ Lake Duluti **4**

3 **8**
Usa River

N

0 km   1
0 miles 1

■ **Sleeping**
1 Miriakamba Hut
2 Momela Game Lodge
3 Mount Meru Game Lodge
4 Mountain Village Arusha
5 Ngaresero Mountain Lodge
6 Rest House
7 Saddle Hut
8 Tanzanite

Mount Meru

The other major attraction of Arusha National Park is Mount Meru (4,565 m), the second highest mountain in Tanzania and also the fifth highest in all Africa. The mountain lies to the west of the Ngare Nanyuki road in the western half of the park. There is a road that leads up the mountain to about 2,439 m from the **Momela Gate**, passing through an open space called **Kitoto** from where there are good views of the mountain, but vehicles are no longer alllowed to pass this way.

Colour map 4, grid A4

The walk up Mount Meru involves a 3,500-m altitude hike, frequently climbed up and down within three days. The last section of the walk to the summit is very steep. It is easy to underestimate the problems associated with this walk – altitude sickness and frostbite. Snow is not unknown at the summit. Nobody checks if you have appropriate equipment for your climb, so go well prepared. During the wet season be sure to have a good pair of walking boots. You will also need to provide all your own food. Although you will not need to hire porters, you will have to take a guide/ranger with you. These can be hired for US$10 per day from the park head-quarters in Momela, as can porters if you decide you want them. Booking a guide and accommodation from the warden in advance is recommended.

Climbing Mount Meru
See Altitude sickness section, page 62, for advice

Tanzania

On the ascent you will pass through the changing vegetation. The first change is to lower montane forest at about 2,000 m, then to higher montane forest. The road climbs up the mountain up to the heath zone at about 2,439 m from where you can climb to the peak. Follow the track from the roadhead until you reach the first hut. Alternatively if you do not have transport you can walk from the park headquarters to **Miriakamba Hut**, which takes about three hours. The first mountain hut sleeps about 48 people, while the second, **Saddle Hut**, sleeps about 24 people. Both huts provide firewood. It is a three-hour walk between the two huts and having reached Saddle Hut you can spend the afternoon climbing **Little Meru** (3,820 m), which takes about 1½ hours. From Saddle Hut climb up to the rim of the mountain and around to the **summit** (4,572 m) before returning to the Momela park headquarters. The final ascent from Saddle Hut is difficult, cold and can be dangerous.

Be prepared for a steep climb, and take plenty of warm clothes as the temperatures fall dramatically at night

Sleeping

L *Mashado Arusha Mountain Lodge*, low-impact 40 bedroom lodge within the park boundaries. **A** *Momela Game Lodge*, PO Box 418, Arusha, T2503798, F2548264. Accommodates 40 people, located just outside the park near the Momela Gate, wonderful views. **A** *Mount Meru Game Lodge*, PO Box 427, Arusha, T2503303, F2548268, located along turn-off from Usa River, 20 km from Arusha, see page 441. **B** *Ngaresero Mountain Lodge*, PO

Box 425, Arusha, T3629, F2548690. Located 16 km from Arusha at Tengeru in the Mt Meru foothills. **B** *Tanzanite*, located along turn-off from Usa River 22 km from Arusha, see page 441. **C** *Rest House*, sleeps 5, self-catering, located near the Momela Gate, bookings through the warden (see page 453). **D** *Campsites*, there are 4 sites in the park, 3 are at the base of Tululusia Hill, the other in the forest near Ngurdoto Gate; another is proposed at the edge of Lake Kusare. All sites have water and toilets and provide firewood, book through the park warden (see page 453).

Mount Longido

Colour map 4, grid A4
Altitude: 2,629 m

Mount Longido is situated 100 km north of Arusha on the road to Namanga. The town of Longido lies on the main road, at the foot of the mountain. To get here by public transport from Arusha take one of the buses that goes to the border town of Namanga or on to Nairobi; the journey to Longido should take about 1½ hours. The mountain rises up steeply from the plains and forms an important point of orientation over a wide area. To climb Mount Longido is an excellent preparation for Mount Meru or Mount Kilimanjaro. The Masai guides will point out lots of wildlife and this area is rich in birdlife.

The **Longido Cultural Tourism programme**, supported by the Tanzanian Tourist Board and SNV, the Netherlands Development Organization, is an excellent way of supporting the local Masai people and learning about their lifestyle and culture. There are several walking tours of the environs, including a half-day 'bird walk' from the town of Longido across the Masai plains to the bomas of Ol Tepesi, the Masai word for acacia tree. On your return to Longido you can enjoy a meal cooked by the FARAJA women's group. The one-day walking tour extends from Ol Tepesi to Kimokonwa along a narrow Masai cattle trail that winds over the slopes of Mount Longido. On clear days there are views of Kilimanjaro and Mount Meru and from the north side there are extensive views of the plains into Kenya. The tour includes a visit to a historic German grave. There is also a more strenuous two-day tour climbing to the top of the steep Longido peak, following buffalo trails guarded by Masai warriors armed with knives and spears to protect you. Accommodation is in local guesthouses or camping. The programme operates a basic campsite in Longido, with pit latrines and bucket showers, friendly and helpful staff, US$2.50 per person. Part of the money generated by this cultural tourism project goes to rehabilitate the cattle dip in Longido. The Masai lose about 1,500 head of cattle per annum, mainly because of tick-borne disease. Since Masai life is centred around their livestock this creates serious problems as reduced herd size means less work, income and food. Regular cattle dipping eradicates tick-borne diseases and the renovated cattle dip will be available to all local Masai families at low cost. ■ *Further details of these tours can be obtained from the Tanzanian Tourist Information centre in Arusha, T027-2503843, tourinfo@ habari.co.tz The tours are co-ordinated locally by Mzee Mollel, a local Masai who studied in Zambia and Australia, who is partially paralysed following an accident. Mzee is happy to answer any enquiries about the Masai way of life.*

Monduli

Monduli is a small town off the main road from Arusha to the Northern Circuit. It is not commonly used by tourists, so it remains very cheap. **E** *The Blue Annex* in the centre of town offers a simple room, opening out on to a courtyard, separate toilet and bucket shower block. Space to park a vehicle, local meals available next door.

Mto wa Mbu

Colour map 4, grid A4

Mto wa Mbu (meaning Mosquito Creek) is a small, busy market town selling fruit and vegetables grown by the fertile surrounding farms. It is located on the route from Arusha to the northern safari circuit of Ngorongoro and Serengeti and only 3 km away from the gate of Lake Manyara National Park (see below). Tourists are likely to be welcomed to the town by being surrounded by people trying to sell arts and crafts. Many of the children tend to be aggressive. There is also Masai central market, a cooperative of about 20 curio sellers. However all items offered in Mto wa Mbu seem to be more expensive than in Arusha. There are many buses to the town from Arusha, taking three hours and costing US$2.

The **Mto wa Mbu Cultural Tourism programme**, supported by the Tanzanian Tourist Board and SNV, the Dutch Development Organization, offers an opportunity to support the local inhabitants and learn about their lifestyle. Walking safaris with Masai guides through the farms in the verdant oasis at the foot of the Rift Valley can be arranged. There are walks to Miwaleni Lake and waterfall where papyrus plants grow in abundance, or an opportunity to climb Balaa hill, which overlooks the whole town. The Belgian Development Organization ACT have enabled locals to grow flowers commercially for export and there are colourful flower fields, with the wonderful backdrop of the Rift Valley. Alternatively you can rent a bicycle and cycle through the banana plantations to see the papyrus lake. The landscape is awe inspiring with the escarpment rising vertically up into the sky on the one side and the semi-desert stretching away to the horizon on the other.

The area around Mto wa Mbu was dry and sparsely populated prior to the irrigation programmes that began in the 1950s and transformed the area into an important location where fruits and vegetables are grown on a large scale. The accompanying population growth turned Mto wa Mbu into a melting pot of cultures. There is greater cultural diversity in this area than elsewhere in Tanzania, so in one day you can sample Chagga banana beer, or see a farmer from the Kigoma region make palm oil. The Rangi use papyrus from the lakes to make beautiful baskets and mats, and the Sandawe continue to make bows and arrows, which are used to hunt small game. On the surrounding plains the Masai tend their cattle.

■ *The cultural tours are organized at the Red Banana Restaurant in Mto wa Mbu on the main road, or at the TTB information centre in Arusha, Boma Rd, T027-2503842/3, tourinfo@habari.co.tz The guides are all former students of Manyara secondary school and they have a reasonable standard of English. Profits from the tours are invested in development projects and for the promotion of energy-saving stoves.*

Sleeping and eating **C** *Twiga Campsite and Lodge*, situated 1 km from Mto wa Mbu towards the gate of Lake Manyara NP, PO Box 16, Mto wa Mbu. Beautiful s/c rooms, hot showers, restaurant, camping US$10, safe parking, curio shop. **E** *Kudu Guest House*, basic but friendly, including breakfast and dinner. **E** *Starehe Bar and Hotel*, about 100 m down a left turning off the road from Mto wa Mbu to Ngorongoro. Clean and friendly, cold water only, good food.

North to Lake Natron

Engaruka is 63 km north of Mto wa Mbu on the road to Oldoinyo Lengai and Lake Natron. The village of Engaruka lies at the foot of the Rift Valley escarpment. The Masai cattle graze on the surrounding plains. Dust cyclones often arise at the horizon. They are feared as the 'devil fingers' that can bring bad luck when they touch people.

Engaruka is one of Tanzania's most important historical sites. In the 15th and 16th centuries the farming community developed an ingenious irrigation system made of stone-block canals with terraced retaining walls enclosing parcels of land. The site included seven large villages. Water from the rift escarpment was channelled into the canals that led to the terraces. For some unknown reason the farmers left Engaruka around 1700. Several prominent archaeologists, including Louis Leakey, have investigated these ruins but to date there are many questions left unanswered about the people who built these irrigation channels, and why they abandoned the area.

The **Engaruka Cultural Tourism Programme** is supported by the Tanzanian Tourist Board and SNV, the Dutch Development Organization. In half a day you can tour the ruins or visit local farms to see current farming and irrigation methods. A Masai warrior can also guide you up the escarpment, from where there are views over the ruins and surrounding plains, along the way pointing out trees and plants the Masai use as food and medicine. In one day you can climb the peak of Kerimasi to the north of the village and there is a two-day hike up Kerimasi and then Oldoinyo

Engaruka
Colour map 4, grid A4

The ruins are deteriorating because, with the eradication of the tsetse fly, Masai cattle now come to graze in this area during the dry season, causing extensive damage

Tanzania

Lengai where you can see inside the crater of the only active volcano in Tanzania. The volcano is erupting continuously, sometimes explosively. The sodium-rich ashes turn the water caustic, sometimes causing burns to the skin of the local Masai's livestock. Monies generated are used to exclude cattle from the ruins and start conservation work, and also to improve the village primary school. ■ *Further details of these tours can be obtained from the Tanzanian Tourist Information centre in Arusha, T027-2503842/3, tourinfo@habari.co.tz*

Ol Doinyo
Lengai
Altitude: 2,886 m

Ol Doinyo Lengai, the 'mountain of God', is Tanzania's only active volcano, located in the African Rift Valley. It is situated north of and outside the Ngorongoro Conservation area in the heart of Masailand, to the west of the road to Lake Natron. This active volcano is continuously erupting, sometimes explosively but more commonly just subsurface bubbling of lava. It is the only volcano in the world that erupts natrocarbonatite lava, a highly fluid lava that contains almost no silicon, and is also much cooler and less viscous than basaltic lavas.

The white deposits are weathered natrocarbonatite ash and lava and these white-capped rocks near the summit are interpreted by the Masai as symbolizing the white beard of God. The last violent eruption was in 1993 and lava has occasionally flowed out of the crater since late 1998. The summit is frequently wreathed in clouds.

It is possible to climb the mountain but the trek up to the crater is an exceptionally demanding one. In parts of the crater that have been inactive for several months the ground is so soft that one sinks into it when walking. In rainy weather the light brown powdery surface turns white again because of chemical reactions that occur when the lava absorbs water. As the mountain lies outside the conservation area no National Park fees are payable.

Climbs are frequently done at night as there is no shelter on the mountain and it gets extremely hot. The gradient is very steep towards the crater rim. A guide is required (cost US$35) and climbers are strongly advised to wear sturdy leather hiking boots to protect against burns should you inadvertently step into liquid lava. Boots made of other fibres have been known to melt. Another safety precaution is to wear glasses to avoid lava splatter burns to the eyes. Only suitable for very fit persons. The Engaruka Cultural Tourism Programme offer guided climbs.

Lake Natron
Colour map 4, grid A4

This alkaline lake is at the bottom of the Gregory Rift part of the Great Rift Valley, which is contiguous with the Kenyan border, about 250 km from Arusha. It is surrounded by escarpments and volcanic mountains, with a small volcano at the north end of the lake in Kenya, and a much larger volcano, Ol Doinyo Lengai, to the southeast of the lake. The lake measures approximately 56 km long (in a north/south axis) by 24 km wide but its size varies according to the rainfall.

The lake has an exceptionally high concentration of salts and derives its pink colour from the billions of cyano-bacteria, the flamingos' staple diet. There are hundreds of thousands of lesser flamingos, as this lake is their only regular breeding ground in East Africa, with many times more of these birds found here than at either Lake Magadi in Kenya or Lake Manyara. Lake Natron is also an important site for many other waterbird species, including palearctic migrants. A few kilometres away there are two waterfalls in the Ngare Sero River. If you follow the river upstream from the campsite, with the occasional bit of wading, it is a hike of about an hour.

The lake is infrequently visited because of its remoteness and you are unlikely to see many other tourists. The route from Arusha is through an area rich with wildlife, depending on the season, particularly ostriches, zebra and giraffe. Numerous Masai herd cattle in this region. During the late 1990s there were security concerns in this region following sporadic incursions by Somali *shiftas* (bandits). There have been no recent reports of civil unrest, but it would be prudent to check the current situation in Arusha.

Sleeping There are community initiatives using the local Masai people as guides who can arrange a visit here, for example the Mkuru Camel Safari Cultural Tourism Programme or the Engaruka Cultural Tourism Programme. For contact details see page 457. Independent travellers report that it is possible to camp reasonably close to the lake, or near the waterfalls on the Ngare Sero River, if fully self-sufficient, although it should be remembered that lions may visit the area to drink. Further downstream of this river, overlooking the lake, is **B-C** *Lake Natron Camp* to the southwest of the lake, the only local accommodation. Climbing **Ol Doinyo Lengai** can be organized from here, including hiring a guide. The cost is US$35 for the first climber and US$20 per additional climber. Contact *Swala Safaris*, PO Box 207, Arusha, T2503935, www.swalasafaris.com/lake_natron_camp.htm Alternatively several other companies, eg *Hoopoe*, *Roy Safaris* or *Takim Holidays*, include Lake Natron in their tour itineraries. Horseback treks can be arranged with www.safaririding.com/natron or walking treks with www.ewpnet.com/ngorongoro-natron

Transport Road: access is really only feasible by 4WD. The turn-off from the Arusha-Ngorongoro road is just before Mto wa Mbu. The drive from Arusha to the lake takes about 6 hrs and is fairly straightforward. 4WDs head this way from Mto wa Mbu in the late afternoon. From the lake it is possible to drive northwest to *Lobo Lodge* in the Serengeti through Sonjo and Wasso, or southwest to *Ndutu Safari Lodge* in the Ngorongoro Crater but you will need a guide, as the tracks are not clear in parts.

Lake Manyara National Park

Many visitors go to Lake Manyara National Park on a safari circuit that includes Ngorongoro and Serengeti. It is small enough to be ideal for a day visit.

3° 40' S, 35° 50' E
Colour map 4, grid A4

Getting there Air: there is an airstrip near the park gate, and *Regional Air* and *Air Excel* have daily flights from Arusha. *Precisionair* did operate scheduled flights from Arusha but these appear to have ended. You could also charter a plane from Arusha. See Arusha, page 450 for further details. **Road**: the park is located 130 km west of Arusha and is reached via the Arusha-Serengeti road (see maps, pages 412 and 462). The drive from Arusha takes about 2½ hrs, the road is good tarmac for the first 80 km, then the road is rough: however it is an enjoyable journey. The entrance to the park is off the left of the Great North Rd at Makuyuni. From here there is a track, reportedly in very poor condition, that goes past the lake and through the village of Mto wa Mbu (see page 456) to the park entrance at the foot of the Great Rift Escarpment. **Getting around** The main road through the park is good enough for most vehicles although some of the tracks may be closed during the wet season. Taking a guide with you is recommended as they will be much better at spotting the game – in particular the lions – than you.

Ins & outs
Best times to visit are Dec-Feb and May-Jul

Lake Manyara National Park

Marere River
To Arusha
Gate
Simba River
1
Picnic Spot
To Serengeti
Msasa River
Chemchem River
Picnic Spot
Ndala River
Bagayo River
Rift Escarpment
Lake Manyara
Maji Moto Ndogo
Endat River
4 WD Only
N
0 km   3
0 miles   3

■ **Sleeping**
1 Lake Manyara   ● Ranger post

The word 'Manyara' is derived from *emanyara*, the name of a plant (*Euphorbia tirucalli*) used by the Masai in the building of their kraals. Set in the Great Rift Valley, Lake Manyara

Background
See page 333 for further information on Tanzania's national parks, including fees

Tanzania

National Park was established in 1960 and covers an area of 325 sq km, of which 229 sq km is the lake. However, within this small area there is a diversity of habitats including open grasslands with rocky outcrops, forests and swamps, as well as the lake itself. In contrast to Kenya, here there is no eastern wall to the Rift Valley which flattens out as the fault continues south.

The lake is believed to have been formed two to three million years ago when, after the formation of the Rift Valley, streams poured over the valley wall. In the depression below, the water accumulated and so the lake was formed. It has shrunk significantly and was probably at its largest about 250,000 years ago. In recent years it has been noted that lake levels are falling in several of the lakes in the region, among them Lake Manyara. This trend often co-exists with the development of salt brines, the rise of which are anticipated.

Recommended reading: Ian Douglas-Hamilton's account of the conservation of the elephant population in Among the Elephants, *1978, London, Collins*

A major attraction of the Lake Manyara National Park are the tree-climbing lions. Unfortunately there is no guarantee that you will spot them. However there are other things to see – elephants, hippo, plains animals as well as a huge variety of birdlife, both resident and migratory. At certain times of the year Lake Manyara is home to thousands of flamingos, which form a shimmering pink zone around the lake shore. Other birds found here include ostrich, egrets, herons, pelicans and storks. Also seen are African spoonbills, various species of ibis, ducks and the rare pygmy goose. As with all the other parks poaching is a problem and it affects elephants in particular. It was a shock when the census of 1987 found that their population had halved to under 200 in just a decade. At the gate of the national park is a small museum displaying some of the bird and rodent life found in the park.

Routes A road from the park gate goes through the ground water forest before crossing the Marere River Bridge. This forest, as its name suggests, is fed not by rainfall, but by ground water from the high water table fed by seepage from the volcanic rock of the rift wall. The first animals you will see on entering the park will undoubtedly be baboons. About 500 m after this bridge the road forks. To the left the track leads to a plain known as **Mahali pa Nyati** (Place of the Buffalo), which has a herd of mainly old bulls cast out from their former herds. There are also zebra and impala in this area. This is also the track to take to the Hippo Pool. The pool is formed by the Simba River on its way to the lake and is home to hippos, flamingos and many other water birds. Some of these tracks may be impassable in the wet season and you may have to turn round and go back the way you came.

Back on the main track the forest thins out to bush and the road crosses the Mchanga River (Sand River) and Msasa River. Shortly after this latter bridge there is a turning off to the left that leads down to the lakeshore where there is a peaceful picnic spot. Soon after this bridge the surroundings change to acacia woodland. This is where the famous tree-climbing lions are found, so drive through very slowly and look out for a tail dangling down through the branches.

Continue down the main road crossing the Chemchem River and on to the Ndala River. Here you will probably see elephants although their numbers have been reduced severely in recent years as a result of poaching. As the park is small they tend to stray across into the surrounding farmland where great damage is done to crops. Outside the park boundaries there is little to stop them being attacked and occasionally killed by villagers. During the dry season the elephants may be seen digging in the dry riverbed for water. At the peak of the wet season the river may flood and the road is sometimes impassable as a result. Beyond the Ndala River the track runs closer to the Rift Valley Escarpment wall that rises steeply to the right of the road. On this slope are many different trees to those on the plain and as a result they provide a different habitat for various animals. The most noticeable are the very impressive baobab trees with their huge trunks.

The first of the two sets of hot springs in the park are located where the track runs along the wall of the escarpment. These are the smaller of the two and so are called simply **Maji Moto Ndogo** (Small Hot Water). The temperature is about 40°C, heated to this temperature as it circulates to great depths in fractures that run through the rock that were formed during the formation of the Rift Valley. The second set of hot springs is located further down the track over the Endabash River. These, known as **Maji Moto**, are both larger and hotter, reaching a temperature of 60°C. You are supposed to be able to cook an egg here in about 30 minutes. The main track ends at Maji Moto and you have to turn round and go back the same way. In total the track is between 35 and 40 km long.

L *Maji Moto Camp*, the only tourist resort inside Lake Manyara NP, sited among acacia trees **Sleeping** on the southern shore of the lake. Accommodation is a luxury permanent camp, affording a panoramic view of millions of flamingos, pelicans and waders. Nearby are the hot sulphuric springs. UK Agents: *World Archipelago*, 6 Redgrave Rd, London SW15 1PX, T020-8780 5838, F020-8780 9482, worldarc@compuserve.com Arusha agent: PO Box 2174, Arusha T027-2546079, F6475. Nairobi agent: PO Box 40097, Nairobi T2-331825, F2-212656, or *Conservation Corporation Africa* – a South African company – Nairobi Office: PO Box 74957, T2-750928, F2-746826. **L** *Lake Manyara Serena Lodge*, PO Box 2551, Arusha, T2546304, F2544155, lakemanyara@serena.co.tz Set on the edge of the eastern Rift Valley's Mto Wa Mbu escarpment overlooking the lake. Offers 'soft adventures' – mountain biking, hiking, nature and village walks, abseiling and rock climbing, canoe safaris and children's programmes. Available to everyone, not just staying guests, but not cheap. Included in *The Times*'s 1999 list of the world's top 100 hotels. **A** *Lake Manyara Hotel (TAHI)*, PO Box 3100, Arusha, T2548802, 100 rooms, swimming pool and shop, located 10 km from the park gate, 300 m above the park on the escarpment overlooking the lake and park – wonderful views.

Tented Camp A *Kirurumu Tented Lodge*, T027-7011, F2548226, or through *Hoopoe*, see page 446, built on the Gregorian Escarpment of the Great Rift Valley, stunning location overlooking Lake Manyara and over towards Mt Losimongori, well appointed (tents on solid platforms under thatched roofs), with splendid views, located close to park. Recommended. Excellent service. Accommodation and meals free for children aged up to 6 years. From 7-12 years the cost is 50% of full board shared rates. **National Parks accommodation** 10 bandas located just before park entrance. Youth hostel at park headquarters, sleeps 48 people, facilities basic. Booking for both through Tanzania National Parks Headquarters (see page 324) or Chief Park Warden, Lake Manyara NP, PO Box 12, Mto wa Mbu. **Camping** Two campsites are located at the entrance to the park. Both have water, toilets and showers. Mosquito nets are essential. Bring sufficient food and drinking water. The campsite in the park is expensive and facilities are minimal. See also Mto wa Mbu (page 457) for **C** *Twiga Campsite and Lodge* and simple guesthouses for the budget traveller.

Ngorongoro Conservation Area

The Conservation area encompasses Ngorongoro Crater, Embagai Crater, Olduvai   *3°11'S 35°32'E* *Gorge – famous for its palaeontological relics – and Lake Masek. Lake Eyasi marks part*   *Colour map 4, grid A4* *of the southern boundary and the Serengeti National Park lies to the west.*

Ngorongoro Crater is one of the largest unbroken and unflooded calderas worldwide. The crater diameter measures 16-19 km and the floor of the crater lies 400-610 m below the rim. Unlike many other African ecological systems, the crater habitat has year-round water supplies that enables it to sustain a large population of mammals and birds. There are several distinct habitats. Scrub heath and remnants of montane forests cloak the steep slopes. The crater floor is mainly grassy plains, with both freshwater and brackish lakes, and there are also patches of forests and acacia woodland. It is home to a small number of black rhino, sustains a huge population of ungulates and has the most concentrated numbers of lions known.

Ins and outs

Getting there
See page 333 for further information on Tanzania's national parks, including fees

Ngorongoro is 190 km west of Arusha, 60 km from Lake Manyara and 145 km from Serengeti and is reached via the Arusha-Serengeti road (see map, page 412). The drive from Arusha takes about 4 hrs and is a splendid journey with a view of Mt Kilimanjaro all the way, arching over the right shoulder of Mt Meru. You will go across the bottom of the Rift Valley and pass the entrance to the Lake Manyara National Park on the left of the Great North Rd at the foot of the Great Rift Escarpment. Just beyond the entrance to the park the road climbs very steeply up the escarpment and at the top the turning to the *Lake Manyara Hotel* is off to the left. From here the country is hilly and fertile and you will climb up to the Mbulu Plateau that is farmed with wheat, maize and coffee. At Karatu (known as Safari Junction), 25 km from Manyara, is the turning off to *Gibbs Farm*, which is 5 km off the main road. You turn right towards the park entrance and on the approach to **Lodware Gate** as the altitude increases the temperature starts to fall. Your first view of the crater comes at Heroes Point (2,286 m). The road continues to climb through the forest to the crater rim.

Getting around

If you have your own transport, you will have to hire an official guide in Karatu. Recent reports suggest that you can drive into the crater without a guide but must pay the US$10 fee anyway. In the crater itself, for most of the year, only 4WDs are allowed. Sometimes in the dry season other vehicles will be allowed but do not rely on this. Whether you have your own vehicle or hire one there you will have to take a park ranger with you at a cost of US$15 per day. Land Rovers can be hired in Crater Village where you pick up the ranger, which is cheaper than hiring through the lodges. There is a US$10 charge to go down into the crater.

Ngorongoro Conservation Area

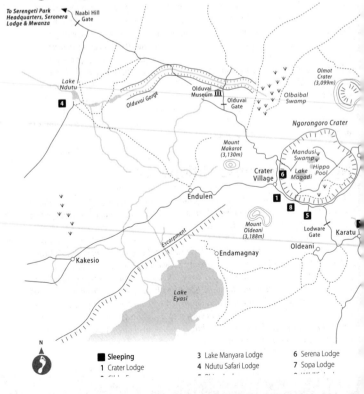

Sleeping
1 Crater Lodge
3 Lake Manyara Lodge
4 Ndutu Safari Lodge
6 Serena Lodge
7 Sopa Lodge

The best times to visit are Dec-Feb and Jun-Jul. During the long rains season (Apr-May) the **Climate**
roads can be almost impassable, so access to the crater floor may be restricted.

Ngorongoro is believed to date from about 2,500,000 years ago – relatively modern **Background**
for this area. It was once a huge active volcano and was probably as large as
Kilimanjaro. After its large major eruption, as the lava subsided its cone collapsed
inwards leaving the caldera. Minor volcanic activity continued and the small cones
that resulted can be seen in the crater floor. To the northeast of Ngorongoro crater
are two smaller craters, Olmot and Embagai. From the crater on a clear day you
should be able to see six mountains over 3,000 m.

The Ngorongoro Conservation Area was established in 1959 and covers an area of
8,288 sq km. In 1951 it was included as part of the Serengeti National Park and contained the headquarters of the park. However in order to accommodate the grazing
needs of the Masai people's livestock it was decided to reclassify it as a conservation
area. In 1978 it was declared a **World Heritage Site** in recognition of its beauty and
importance. The crater has an area of 265 sq km and measures between 16 and 19 km
across. The rim reaches 2,286 m above sea level and the crater floor is 610 m below it.

The name 'Ngorongoro' comes from a Masai word *Ilkorongoro*, which was the
name given to the age group of Masai warriors who defeated the previous occupants
of the area, the Datong, around 1800. The sounds of the bells that the Masai wore
during the battle that were said to have terrified their enemies into submission, was
'*koh-rohng-roh*' and it is from this that Ngorongoro comes. The Masai refer to the
Ngorongoro Southern Highlands as 'O'lhoirobi', which means the cold highlands;
while the Germans also referred to the climate, calling these the 'winter highlands'.

There are an estimated 30,000 **animals** living in the crater. As this is a conservation area rather than a national
park you will also see some of the local
Masai people grazing their cattle here.
Poaching has affected the animal population and in particular the rhino population is believed to be less than 15.
Recent reports indicate that there are
few giraffes left in Ngorongoro.

In early 2001 huge swarms of
Stomoxys flies were harmful to many
animals and particularly the lions, of
which 6 died and 62 were seriously
damaged. The lions apparently left the
crater in an attempt to escape. In a previous outbreak of the flies, in 1962, the
lion population was decimated, with
only 8 lions surviving. Numbers had
slowly increased since that time, but the
Ngorongoro lions, generally bigger and
stronger than lions elsewhere, are in
danger of extinction, not least because
the lack of genetic diversity within the
population leaves it vulnerable to events
such as *Stomoxys* attacks and disease.
There have also been reports that since
the middle of 2000 many other animals
have died of unknown causes, including
over 300 buffalo, 200 wildebeest, over 60
zebra and a few hippo and rhino.

Tanzania

Route Where the road reaches the rim of the crater you will see memorials to Professor Bernhard Grzimek and his son Michael. They were the makers of the film *Serengeti Shall Not Die* and published a book of the same name (1959, London, Collins). They conducted surveys and censuses of the animals in the Serengeti and Ngorongoro Parks and were heavily involved in the fight against poachers. Tragically Michael was killed in an aeroplane accident over the Ngorongoro Crater in 1959 and his father returned to Germany where he set up the Frankfurt Zoological Society. He died in 1987 requesting in his will that he should be buried beside his son in Tanzania. Their memorials remain as a reminder of all the work they did to protect this part of Africa.

Access to the crater is by way of two steep roads, which are both one-way. You enter by the **Windy Gap** road and leave by the **Lerai** road. The Windy Gap branches off the Serengeti road to the right and descends the northeast wall of the crater to the floor of the crater 610 m below. The road is narrow, steep and twists and turns as it enters the crater that is rather like a huge amphitheatre.

Encounters with animals are frequent and there is a wide variety of game in the crater. These include lion, elephant and rhino as well as buffalo, Thompson's gazelle, wildebeest and zebra. You are also likely to see ostrich and Lake Magadi, the soda lake at the floor of the crater, is home to thousands of flamingos.

Lerai Forest is a good place for a picnic lunch. Beware of dive-bombing kites snatching your lunch.

Sleeping **L** *Ngorongoro Crater Lodge*, PO Box 751, Arusha, T7803 (bookings can be made through *Abercrombie & Kent*, Sokoine Rd, PO Box 427, Arusha, T2508347). Very expensive, US$450 per person per night, discount between Easter and end of Jun. The most luxurious lodge on the rim of the crater, individual cottages, good views. Member of Small Luxury Hotels of the World. **L** *Ngorongoro Serena Lodge*, PO Box 2551, Arusha, Tanzania, T2544159, F2548185, ngorongoro@serena.co.tz Luxury development to the highest international standards, built out of wood and pebbles, stunning hotel perched on the rim of the crater. Telescope provided on main balcony to view the crater. Friendly staff, good food, environmentally aware – has its own nursery in the gardens to plant indigenous plant species, offers hiking and shorter nature walks. Local Masai make up 25% of staff. **L** *Ngorongoro Sopa Lodge*, bookings through PO Box 1823, Arusha, T2502332, T0741-510435 (mob), F2508245, info@sopalodges.com Luxury all-suite lodge with 79 suites on the exclusive eastern rim of the crater, all suites enjoying uninterrupted views into the crater, spectacular African rondavel design with magnificent lounges, restaurant and conference and entertainment areas, swimming pool and satellite TV. Most of the lodges are on the southern or western crater rim but the Sopa Lodge, a fabulous place, is located on the unspoilt eastern rim, way off the beaten track. Unfortunately this involves an extra 45-50 km journey (one way) over poor quality roads.

A *Gibb's Farm* (Ngorongoro Safari Lodge), bookings through PO Box 6084, Arusha, T027-2506702, F2508310. Discount between Easter and end June, on the outer slopes of the crater located at the edge of a forest facing the Mbulu Hills to the southeast. Original farm built by German settler in 1930s to cultivate coffee, sold to James Gibb in 1948 after the Second World War, and currently run by his widow, Margaret Gibb. Fine atmosphere, open log fires, excellent gardens. **A** *Ngorongoro Forest Resort* was formerly Dhillons Lodge, owned by a local Sikh family, located on the left side of the approach road from Manyara, well before you get to the other lodges. **A** *Ngorongoro Wildlife Lodge*, PO Box 887, Arusha, T027-2548150, F2548150. Modern building on the rim of the crater with wonderful views, 75 rooms, heated, geared to fast throughput of tours, bar with log fire.

C *Ngorongoro Rhino Lodge*, PO Box 776, Arusha, T3466, on the rim of the crater. Lovely site but does not have the views of some of the other lodges, can sometimes camp here if you have your own tent. **D** *Simba Campsite*, located about 2 km from Crater Village. Facilities include showers, toilets and firewood, but facilities have deteriorated overall and water supplies are irregular; it is important to make sure that you have sufficient water to keep you going for the night and the game drive the next day. **E** *Usiwara Guest House* (Drivers Lodge), located in Crater Village near the post office. Basic, will need sleeping bag, can get food here. **Camping** available in Karatu at the *Safari Junction Camp*, clean, secure, hot water, US$3 per person, also log cabin accommodation – 25 km from Ngorongoro Crater, operated by *Savannah Tours*, PO Box 3063, T2331662, savtour@twiga.com

Ushirika Co-op Restaurant also does cheap, simple food. You can usually buy food in the village but the range and choice are limited so you would be advised to bring supplies with you. You can also eat at *Ngorongoro Wildlife Lodge* even if not staying there; however a 3-course meal costs US$18.

Eating

If you are without transport, you will have to go with an organized safari from Arusha. Buses and trucks head this way from Arusha, but tend to go no further than Karatu, 25 km away. From here you will be lucky to find any transport to the crater.

Transport

Embagai Crater

Embagai Crater (also spelt Empakaai) can be visited in a day from any lodge at the Ngorongoro rim. The caldera is approximately 35 sq km. You can walk down to the 80-m deep, alkaline Lake Emakat, which partly occupies the caldera floor. The vegetation is predominantly highland shrubs and grassland but there are small patches of verdant, evergreen forest in the southern part of the caldera. Buffalo, hyenas and leopards may be seen. Birdlife is prolific and includes the lammergeyer, Egyptian vulture, Verreaux's eagle, various species of bats, pelicans, storks, flamingos, duck, sandpiper, doves, kingfishers and ostrich.This is an isolated, beautiful place, four-wheel drive access only. You need to be accompanied by a ranger because of the buffaloes.

*2°55'S 35°50'E
Colour map 4, grid A4*

Lake Masek is a soda lake located in the Ndutu woodlands in the western part of the Ngorongoro Conservation Area. Rarely visited, it is home to many flamingo, plain game mammals and their attendant predators

Olduvai Gorge

Olduvai Gorge, a water-cut canyon up to 90 m deep, has become famous for being the site of a number of archaeological finds and has been called the 'cradle of mankind'. The gorge lies within the Ngorongoro Conservation Area to the northwest of the crater (see map, page 462). The site is located about 10-15 minutes off the main road between Serengeti and Ngorongoro.The name Olduvai comes from the Masai word *oldupai*, which is the name for the type of wild sisal that grows in the gorge.

Colour map 4, grid A4

Olduvai Gorge first aroused interest in the archaeological world as early as 1911 when a German, Professor Katurinkle, while looking for butterflies in the gorge, found some fossil bones. These caused great interest in Europe and in 1913 an expedition led by Professor Hans Reck was arranged. They stayed at Olduvai for three months and made a number of fossil finds. At a later expedition in 1933 Professor Reck was accompanied by two archaeologists, Dr Louis Leakey and his future wife Mary.

Archaeological finds

The Leakeys continued their work and in July 1959, 26 years later, discovered 400 fragments of the skull *Australopithecus-Zinjanthropus boisei* – the 'nutcracker man' – who lived in the lower Pleistocene Age around 1,750,000 BC. A year later the skull and bones of a young *Homo habilis* were found. The Leakeys assert that around 1.8-2 million years ago there existed in Tanzania two types of man, *Australopithecus-Zinjanthropus boisei* and *Homo habilis'*. The other two, *Australopithecus africanus* and *arobustus*, had died out. *Homo habilis*, with the larger brain, gave rise to modern man. *Habilis* was a small ape-like creature and, although thought to be the first of modern man's ancestors, is quite distinct from modern man. Tools, such as those used by *Homo erectus* (dating from 1-1½ million years ago), have also been found at Olduvai as well as at Isimila near Iringa. Other exciting finds in the area are the

Tanzania

footprints found in 1979 of man, woman and child at Laetoli (this is a site near Oldovai) made by 'creatures' that walked upright, possibly dating from the same period as *Australopithecus afarensis*, popularly known as Lucy, whose remains were discovered near Hadar in Ethiopia in 1974. Dating back 3.6-3.8 million years they pushed back the beginnings of the human race even further. In 1986 a discovery at Olduvai by a team of American and Tanzanian archaeologists unearthed the remains of an adult female dating back 1,800,000 years. In total the fossil remains of about 35 humans have been found in the area at different levels.

Prehistoric animal remains were also found in the area and about 150 species of mammals have been identified. These include the enormous Polorovis with a horn span of 2 m, the Deinotheruium that was a huge, elephant-like creature with tusks that curved downwards and the Hipparion, a three-toed, horse-like creature.

At the site there is a small museum that is open until 1500, entrance US$2.50. The building was built in the 1970s by the Leakeys to house their findings. The museum may, however, be closed during the wet season, April to end June. It holds displays of copies of some of the finds, a cast of the footprints and pictures of what life was like for Olduvai's earliest inhabitants. You can go down into the gorge to see the sites and there will usually be an archaeologist to show you around.

Nearby places of interest include **Nasera Rock**, a 100-m monolith on the edge of the Gol Mountain range – it offers stunning views of the southern Serengeti and is a great vantage point from which to watch the annual wildebeest migration. This is sometimes called the Striped Mountain, so named for the streaks of blue-green algae that have formed on the granite. **Olkarien Gorge**, a deep fissure in the Gol Mountains, is a major breeding ground of the enormous Ruppell's griffon vulture. A geological feature of this area are shifting sand-dunes, or *barchan*, crescent-shaped dunes lying at right angles to the prevailing wind. They usually develop from the accumulation of sand around a minor obstruction, for example a piece of vegetation. The windward face has a gentle slope but the leeward side is steep and slightly concave. The *barchan* moves slowly as more sand is deposited; they range in size from a few metres to a great size, as seen in the Sahara or Saudi Arabia.

Sleeping There is nowhere to stay on the actual site so you will have to make this a day trip. The nearest place to stay, apart from the Ngorongoro lodges and campsites, is **A** *Ndutu Safari Lodge*, bookings through PO Box 6084, Arusha, T027-2506702, F2508310, sleeps 70, bar and restaurant, beautiful setting overlooking Lake Ndutu, located about 90 km from the Ngorongoro Crater near the southern boundary of Serengeti NP.

Serengeti National Park

2°40'S 35°0'E
Colour map 4, grid A4

Serengeti is the most famous of Tanzania's national parks. The name is derived from the Masai word 'siringet' meaning 'extended area' or 'endless plains' and it contains one of the world's greatest concentrations of plains animals. A thick layer of ash blown from volcanoes in the Ngorongoro highlands covered the landscape between 3-4 million years ago, preserved traces of early man, and enriched the soil that supports the southern grass plains. Avoided by the pastoralist Masais because the woodlands had trypanosomiasis (sleeping sickness) carried by tsetse flies, the early European explorers found this area uninhabited and abounding with game.

*Serengeti National Park was established in 1951 and at 14,763 sq km is Tanzania's second largest national park (after Selous). It rises from 920-1,850 m above sea level and its landscape varies from the long and short grass plains in the south, the central savannah, the more hilly wooded areas in the north and the extensive woodland in the western corridor. The **Maswa Game Reserve** adjoins its western border.*

Serengeti is perhaps most well known for the annual migration that takes place across the great savannah plains (see map page 468). This is a phenomenal sight: thousands upon thousands of animals, particularly wildebeest, as far as the eye can see.

Ins and outs

Air There are several airstrips inside the park. *Regional Air* and *Air Excel* both have scheduled daily flights to Seronera and Grumeti River Camp, while *Air Excel* also fly to *Lobo Wildlife Lodge* and *Klein's Camp* on Tue, Fri and Sat. See Arusha, page 449, for further details. *Eagle Air* (Dar es Salaam (DSM): PO Box 5794, T2127411, F2127415, eagleair@africaonline.co.tz) have a flight from DSM via Zanzibar on Sun, leaving DSM at 0700 and Zanzibar at 0800, arriving by 1000. The flight leaves again at 1030 and returns to DSM via Arusha and Zanzibar. **Road** The Serengeti is usually approached from Arusha along a fairly good road (see map, page 412). From Arusha you will pass the entrance to Lake Manyara NP and through the Ngorongoro Conservation Area. Shortly before the park boundary there is the turning off to Olduvai Gorge. Seronera, the village in the heart of the Serengeti, is 335 km from Arusha. Approaching from Mwanza or Musoma on the lake shore take the road east and you will enter the Serengeti through the Ndaraka Gate in the west.

Getting there
See page 333 for further information on Tanzania's national parks, including fees

Most visitors enter the NP at **Naabi Hill Gate** in the southeast, continuing along the road that bisects the Ngorongoro Conservation Area. From here it is 75 km to Seronara village. If coming eastwards the NP can be accessed at **Ndabaka Gate** to the Grumeti Western Corridor. This road requires a 4WD and may be impassable in the rainy season. Options for budget

Getting around

Tanzania

Serengeti National Park

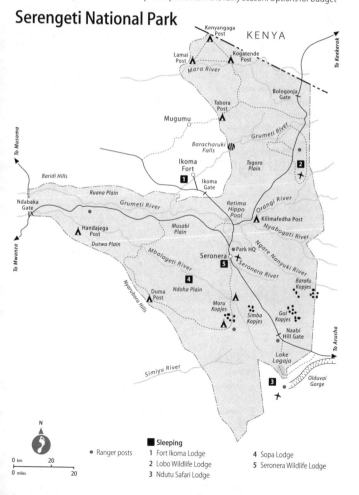

N

0 km   20
0 miles   20

• Ranger posts

■ **Sleeping**
1 Fort Ikoma Lodge
2 Lobo Wildlife Lodge
3 Ndutu Safari Lodge
4 Sopa Lodge
5 Seronera Wildlife Lodge

travellers are few as public transport does not run through the park and hitch-hiking is frequently unsuccessful. Most tourists utilize a safari package or self-drive.

Climate The main rainy season is from November to May.

Wildlife During the rainy season the wildebeest, whose population has been estimated at around 1,500,000, are found in the eastern section of the Serengeti and also the Masai Mara in Kenya to the north. When the dry season begins at the end of June so the annual migration commences as the animals move in search of pasture. They concentrate on the remaining green patches, forming huge herds. It is also around this time that the rutting season starts and territories are established by the males, which then attempt to attract females into their areas. Once mating has occurred, the herds merge together again and the migration to the northwest begins. The migrating animals do not all follow the same route. About half go west, often going outside the park boundaries, and then swing northeast. The other half go directly north. The two groups meet up in the Masai Mara in Kenya. To get to the west section of the Serengeti and the Masai Mara, where they will find pasture in the dry season, the wildebeest must cross a number of large rivers and this proves too much for many of them. Many of the weaker and older animals will die during the migration. Needless to say predators follow the wildebeest on their great trek and easy pickings are to be found. They return to the east at the end of the dry season (November) and calving begins at the start of the wet season.

It was reported in late 2000 that the migration is being threatened by the first ever confirmed outbreak of foot-and-mouth disease, with up to 20% of the wildebeest lame in infected herds.

The Serengeti is also famous for cheetah, leopards and lions, some of which migrate with the wildebeest while others remain in the central plain. Prides of lions are commonly seen, leopards are most frequently detected resting in trees during the daytime along the Seronera River, whereas cheetahs are usually spotted near the Simba Kopjes. The elephant population in Serengeti was decimated by poaching, estimated to have fallen fivefold during the mid 1970-80s, since when the numbers

Serengeti migrations

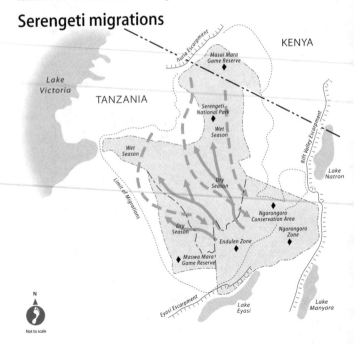

Lions

Lions, Panthero leo, *usually found in open savannah in Africa, are the second largest carnivorous members of the cat family – the largest being tigers.*

Lions are the sole felids to live in prides or permanent family groups, numbering up to around 30 animals. The prides are usually composed of a group of inter-related females and their cubs, led by a dominant male, or occasionally, a group of males. There is no dominant lioness. They communicate with one another with a range of sounds that vary from roaring, grunting and growling to meowing. Roars, more common at night, can reach sound levels of over 110 decibels and be heard from distances of up to 8 km.

A curiosity is that several of the lionesses in the pride will have litters at around the same time, and will suckle cubs belonging to other females. The cubs are playful and affectionate with both adults and other cubs, and their play-fighting, stalking, sparring and chasing helps to hone their hunting skills.

The females do most of the hunting (usually ungulates like zebra and antelopes), while the males are mostly involved in protecting their pride from other lions and predators. Lions are very sociable except when eating, when aggressive fighting can take place. Although the females kill most of the prey the males are first to feed, followed by the lionesses, with the cubs just getting the leftovers. The main cause of cub death is starvation. Lions augment their diet by scavenging prey killed by other predators.

When a pride is taken over by another lion one of the first things he does is to kill, and sometimes consume, all the cubs of the previous male. The resulting sudden termination of lactation brings the females into oestrous, and the new dominant lion is kept busy servicing the pride.

Tanzania

have slowly increased. Birdlife is prolific in the national park and includes various species of kingfishers, sunbirds and rollers, ostrich, egrets, herons, storks, ibis, spoonbills and ducks. Birds of prey include Ruppell's vulture and the hooded vulture, several varieties of kestrels, eagles, goshawks and harriers.

If you are approaching the Serengeti from the southeast, **Lake Ndutu**, fringed by acacia woodland, lies southeast of the main road. Lake Ndutu is a soda lake, with a substantial quantity of mineral deposits around the shoreline. It is home to many birds, including flamingos. During the rainy season it offers excellent opportunities to see a large variety of animals including predators. Next you will reach the **Short Grass Plains**. The flat landscape is broken by the **Gol Mountains**, seen to the right, and by kopjes. The grass here remains short during both the wet and dry seasons. There is no permanent water supply in this region as a result of the nature of the soil. However, during the rains water collects in hollows and depressions until it dries up at the end of the wet season. It is then that the animals begin to move on.

Routes

The **Southern Plains** provide nutritious grasses for the wildebeest, and when the short rains come in November these mammals move south to feed. In February-March, 90% of female wildebeest give birth and the plains are filled with young calves.

Naabi Hill Gate marks the end of the Short Grass and beginning of the **Long Grass Plains**. Dotted across the plains are kopjes. These interesting geological formations are made up of ancient granite that has been left behind as the surrounding soil structures have been broken down by centuries of erosion and weathering. They play an important role in the ecology of the plains providing habitats for many different animals from rock hyraxes (a small rabbit-like creature whose closest relation is actually the elephant) to cheetahs.

A number of kopjes that you might visit include the **Moru Kopjes** in the south of the park to the left of the main road heading north. You may be lucky enough to see the Verreaux eagle, which sometimes nests here. The Moru Kopjes have a cave with Masai paintings on the wall and a rock called **Gong Rock** after the sound it makes when struck with a stone. There are also the **Simba Kopjes** located on the left of the road before reaching Seronera, which, as their name suggests, are often a hide-out of lions.

Passing through the Long Grass Plains in the wet season from around December to May is an incredible experience. All around, stretching into the distance, are huge numbers of wildebeest, Thompson's gazelle, zebra etc.

The village of **Seronera** is in the middle of the park set in the **Seronera Valley**. It forms an important transitionary zone between the southern grasslands and the northern woodlands. The area is criss-crossed by rivers, and as a result this is where you are most likely to spot game. It is reached by a gravel road, which is in fairly good condition. Seronara is the best area to visit if you can only manage a short safari. It has a visitor centre and the research institute is based here. It also contains a small museum noted for its giant stick insects – located near the lodge. In the approach to Seronera the number of trees increases, particularly the thorny Acacia trees. The valley itself is home to a large number of animals and is a popular viewing area. You can expect to see buffalo, impala, lion, hippo and elephant. If you are really lucky you might see leopard; however they are few and far between, are nocturnal and spend most of the day in trees, so the chances of seeing them are fairly remote.

About 5 km north of Seronera the track splits. To the right it goes up to Banagi and Lobo beyond, and to the left to the so-called Western Corridor, about 20 km north of Banagi Hill, which is home to both browsers and grazers. At its base is the **Retina Hippo Pool** located about 6 km off the main track at Banagi. Banagi was the site of the original Game Department Headquarters before it became a national park. North of here the land is mainly rolling plains of both grassland and woodland with a few hilly areas and rocky outcrops.

In the northeast section of the park is the **Lobo Northern Woodland**. Wildlife remain in this area throughout the year including during the dry season. The area is characterized by rocky hills and outcrops, where pythons sunbathe, and woodlands fringe the rivers, frequented by elephants. Lobo is the site of the **Lobo Lodge**, 75 km from Seronera. Further north is the Mara River with riverine forest bordering its banks. This is one of the rivers that claims many wildebeest lives every year during the migration. You will see both hippo and crocodile along the river banks.

If you take the left-hand track where the road splits north of Seronera you will follow the **Grumeti Western Corridor**. (This is also the route to take if you are heading for Mwanza.) The best time to follow this track is in the dry season (June-October) when the road is at its best and the migrating animals have reached this area. Part of the road follows, on your right, the Grumeti River, fringed by lush riverine forest, home to the black and white colobus monkey. On the banks of the river you will also see huge crocodiles basking in the sun. The Musabi and Ndoha Plains to the northwest and west of Seronera respectively can be viewed if you have a four-wheel drive vehicle. The latter plain is the breeding area of topi and large herds of up to 2,000 will often be found here. All but the main routes are poorly marked.

Sleeping

The Park Headquarters are at Seronera and there are airstrips at Seronera and Lobo

In the Western corridor of the Serengeti, 93 km west of *Seronera Lodge* and 50 km east of Lake Victoria, there is a luxurious permanent tented camp called the **L** *Grumeti River Camp*, which overlooks a tributary of the Grumeti River, that is teeming with hippo and crocodiles. The wildebeest migration also passes through this area. This is real African bush country and boasts an abundance of birdlife including Fisher's lovebird. Central bar/dining area, has 10 self-contained, custom-made tents with private shower and wc, solar power electricity minimizes noise and pollution, expensive at US$450 per person per night. Agents: *World Archipelago Ltd*, 6 Redgrave Rd, London SW15 1PX, UK, T020-8780 5838, F020-8780 9482, worldarc@ compuserve. com Arusha: PO Box 2174, T027-6079, F6475, Conservation Corporation Africa, Nairobi, PO Box 74947, T2-750928, F2-746821. **L** *Klein's Camp*, a sanctuary located on a private ranch on the northern-eastern boundary of the park just south of the Kenyan border. Named after the American big game hunter, Al Klein, who in 1926 built his base camp in this valley, the ranch is located between the Serengeti Park and farmland and makes it a natural buffer zone. There are 8 stone cottages with thatched roofs, each with en-suite facilities, dining and bar facilities are in separate rondavels with commanding views of the Grumeti River Valley, solar power electricity reduces pollution and noise – US$450 per person per night. Agents: *Archers Tours & Travel Ltd*, PO Box 40097, Nairobi, T254-2-331825, F254-2-212656, or *Conservation Corporation Africa*, PO Box 74957, Nairobi, T2-750928, F2-746826. **L** *Mashado Serengeti Kusini*, PO Box 14823, Arusha, T027-6585, 0741-510101 (mob), F2548020, Mashado@ habari.co.tz Located at the Hambi ya Mwaki-Nyeb Kopjes in the Southwest Serengeti, near the border with the Maswa game reserve, well off the usual tourist track, the camp is situated in a conchoidal outcrop of large boulders or kopjes, offering superb views, the camp is accessed by car from Arusha, and closes during the rainy season Apr-May (for UK agent, see page 318). **L** *Migration Camp*, bookings through *Halcyon Africa*, Private Bag X5, Norwood 2117, Johannesburg, South Africa, T+27-11-8030557, F8037044, res@halcyonhotels.com, or through *Redds African Grill House*, PO Box 1861, Arusha, T027-2544521, F2544374, sales@halcyontz.com, or juilet.halcyon@virgin.net (UK agent). The camp is built within the rocks of a kopje in the Ndassiata Hills near Lobo, overlooking the Grumeti River, giving excellent views of the migration masses to and from the Southern Plains. Managed by a friendly Australian couple, facilities include jacuzzi, swimming pool, restaurant, the camp has many secluded vantage points linked by timber walkways, bridges and viewing platforms; resident game includes lion, leopard, elephant and buffalo. **L** *Serena Kirawira Camp*, Western Serengeti, central reservations: *Serena Hotels*, PO Box 2551, Arusha, T255-27-2544158, F2544058, reservations@serena.co.tz A luxuriously appointed all-inclusive tented camp 90 km from Seronera in the secluded Western corridor of the park, area famous for giant crocodiles, tree-climbing lions and the annual wildebeest migration. **L** *Serengeti Serena Lodge*, idyllic central location with superb views towards the western corridor. Set high overlooking the plains, this lodge is constructed to reflect the design of an African village. Central booking – see entry above for *Serena Kiriwira Camp*. **L** *Serengeti Sopa Lodge*, bookings through PO Box 1823, Arusha, T2502332, F2508245, info@sopalodges.com Luxury all-suite lodge with 75 suites in the previously protected area of Nyarboro Hills north of Moru Kopjes. Excellent views of the Serengeti plains through double-storey window walls in all public areas, multi-level restaurant and lounges and conference facilities, double swimming pool and satellite TV, way off the beaten track involving an extra 45-50-km drive over poor roads (one-way).

A *Lobo Wildlife Lodge*, PO Box 3100, Arusha, T3842. Book through the **Tanzanian Tourist Corporation** in Dar es Salaam (see page 337) or Arusha (see page 437), 50% discount from Easter to 30 Jun, 75 rooms, located northeast of Seronera Village, swimming pool, shop, also built overlooking the plains, good restaurant and bar. **A** *Ndutu Safari Lodge*, bookings through PO Box 6084, Arusha, T027-2506702, F2508310. Accommodates about 25 in rooms and about 40 in tented camp, located about 90 km from the Ngorongoro Crater near southern boundary of Serengeti National Park, wonderful view of Lake Ndutu and the plain beyond, excellent for service, food and welcome. **A** *Seronera Wildlife Lodge (TAHI)*, PO Box 3100, Arusha, T3842. Book through **Tanzanian Tourist Corporation** in Dar es Salaam (see page 337) or Arusha (see page 437), 50% discount from Easter to 30 Jun, 75 rooms. Fantastic building constructed on and around a kopje with wonderful views of the plains around, restaurant, shop, electricity mornings and evenings, bar and viewing platform at the top of the kopje (beware the monkeys), calm, efficient and friendly. Recommended.

Kijirishi Tented Camp, PO Box 190, Mwanza, T40139. *Balloon Safaris*, US$300 per person available at *Seronera Lodge*, 1-hr balloon flights, champagne breakfast and transport to and from your lodge (see page 317 for details).

Camping: be prepared to be totally self-sufficient and bring food with you as there is little available in Seronera Village. **C** *Special campsites* at Seronera, Lobo, Ndutu, Nabi Hill, Hembe Hill. **D** *Public campsites* at Lobo, Nabi Hill and Kirawira. **D** *campsites* at Seronera close to the *Seronera Wildlife Lodge*. **B** *Kijereshi Lodge* at the end of the Western corridor, partly luxury tents and bungalows, convenient if you want to pass through the corridor and visit the Grumeti River with hippos and crocodiles.

Tanzania

Lake Eyasi

Colour map 4, grid A4

There are few tourist facilities but in recent years it has been included in walking safaris by several companies

The lake, one of several lakes on the floor of the Rift Valley, is sometimes referred to as the 'forgotten lake'. It is larger than Lakes Manyara or Natron and is situated on the remote southern border of the Ngorongoro Conservation Area, at the foot of Mount Oldeani, at the base of the western wall of the Rift Valley's Eyasi Escarpment. The Mbula highlands tower to the east of the lake. Seasonal water level fluctuations vary greatly, and following the trend in the region the lake levels are falling, and salt brines have developed. This soda lake is relatively shallow even during the rainy season, but the size of the lake varies. Lake Eyasi mostly fills a graben, or elongated depression of the earth's crust, areas that are commonly the sites of volcanism and earthquake activity. The Mbari River runs through the swampy area to the northeast of the lake known locally as **Mangola Chin**i, which attracts much game.

Two ancient tribes inhabit this area. The **Hadzabe** people (also called the Watindiga) who live near the shore are hunter-gatherers, still live in nomadic groups, hunt with bows and arrows and gather tubers, roots and fruits. These people are believed to have origins in Botswana. It is estimated that they have lived in this region for 10,000 years. Their language resembles the click language associated with the Bushmen of the Kalahari Desert. Their hunting skills provide all their requirements – mostly eating small antelopes and primates. Their hunting bows are made with giraffe tendon 'strings', and they coat their spears and arrows with the poisonous sap of the desert rose.

Nearby there is a village of **Datoga** pastoral herdsmen, also known as the Barabaig or Il-Man'ati (meaning the 'strong enemy' in the Masai language). The Datoga are a tall, handsome people who tend their cattle in the region between Lake Eyasi and Mount Hanang. The Masai drove them south from Ngorongoro to Lake Eyasi about 150 years ago, and remain their foes. As with the Masai, cattle denote wealth. They live in homes constructed of sticks and mud, and their compounds are surrounded by thornbush to deter nocturnal predators. Like the Hadzabe, the Datoga speak a click language. They scarify themselves to form figure of eight patterns around their eyes in a series of raised nodules.

The north eastern region of the lake is a swampy area fringed by acacia and doum palm forests. Nearby are some freshwater springs, and a small reservoir with tilapia fish. These springs are believed to run underground from Oldeani to emerge by the lakeshore. There are several kopjes close by the lake. Wildlife includes a profusion of birdlife including flamingos, pelicans and storks. Leopards, various antelope, hippos and many small primates can be seen.

Archaeological excavations were undertaken in 1934 by Ludwig and Margit Kohl-Larsen, of the nearby **Mumba cave shelter**, and their discoveries included many fossilized hominoid remains on Eyasi's lakeshore. Their findings included a complete prehistoric skull, human molars, prehistoric tools including knives and thumbnail scrapers, types of animal remains including rhino, various antelope, zebra, hippo and catfish. The Mumba cave also contained ochre paintings. It is believed that the Mumba cave shelter was occupied over the years by various people, as demonstrated by the artefacts uncovered.

Sleeping There are now many private campsites along the lake shore with good facilities including toilets and showers.

Tour operators Several companies visit Lake Eyasi including *Klub Africo Safaris* as part of their educational trek, www.klubafrico.com, and *Roy Safaris*, who offer excellent value, www.roysafaris.com

Transport Access to Lake Eyasi is from the Kidatu-Ngorongoro road. The journey takes about 1½-2 hrs, driving southwest of Karate and the Ngorongoro Crater.

Tarangire National Park

Tarangire National Park is reached on the main Arusha-Dodoma road (see map of National Parks). From Arusha the road leaves the bustling town and enters the heavily cultivated countryside. You will pass maize, coffee and banana plantations. A few acacia trees start to appear and you will probably see groups of Masai grazing their herds along the road. About 85 km from Arusha at Makuyuni the main road up to the Serengeti and Ngorongoro branches off to the right. Continue along the Great North Road towards Tarangire, which is signposted – it is about 120 km from Arusha. The gate opens at 0630, although an earlier entrance is possible if you have paid the fee in advance.

Approach
3° 50'S, 35° 55' E
Colour map 4, grid A4
Altitude: 1,110 m

The Tarangire National Park, established in 1970, covers an area of 2,600 sq km and is named after the river that flows through the park throughout the year. The best time to visit is from July to September when, being the dry season, the animals gather in large numbers along the river. Although you may not see as many animals here as

Background

Tanzania

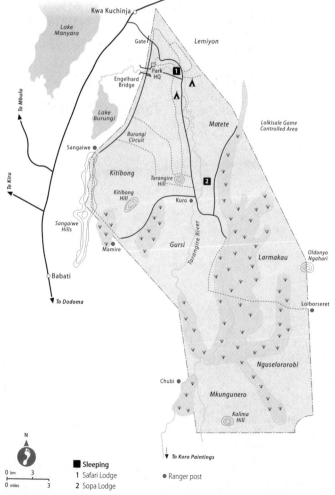

Tarangire National Park

To Arusha

Kwa Kuchinja

Lake Manyara

Gate — Lemiyon

To Mbulu

Park HQ — **1**

Engelhard Bridge

Lake Burungi

Matete

Lolkisale Game Controlled Area

Burungi Circuit

Sangaiwe

Kitibong

Tarangire Hill

Kitibong Hill

Kuro

2

To Kiru

Sangaiwe Hills

Mamire

Gursi

Tarangire River

Larmakau

Oldonyo Ngahari

Babati

Loiborseret

To Dodoma

Nguselororobi

Chubi

Mkungunero

Kalima Hill

N

0 km   3
0 miles   3

To Koro Paintings

■ **Sleeping**
1 Safari Lodge
2 Sopa Lodge

● Ranger post

Tanzania

in other places, Tarangire is a wonderful park. There are fewer people here than in Ngorongoro and that is very much part of the attraction.

One of the most noticeable things on entering the park are the baobab trees that rise up from the grass. With their massive trunks they are instantly recognizable. As the park includes within its boundaries a number of hills, as well as rivers and swamps, there is a variety of vegetation zones and habitats. The river rises in the Kondoa Highlands, which are located to the south, and flows north throughout the length of the park. It continues to flow during the dry season and so is a vital watering point for the animals of the park as well as those from surrounding areas.

Wildlife The Tarangire National Park forms a 'dry season retreat' for much of the wildlife of the southern Masailand. The ecosystem in this area involves more than just Tarangire National Park. Also included in the ecosystem are the Lake Manyara National Park to the north and a number of 'Game Controlled Areas'. The largest of these are the Lake Natron Game Controlled Area further north and the Simanjiro Plains Game Controlled Area towards Arusha. The Mto wa Mbu Game Controlled Area, the Lolkisale Game Controlled Area and Mkungunero Game Controlled Area are also included in the ecosystem. The key to the ecosystem is the river and the main animal movements begin from the river at the beginning of the short rains around October and November. The animals moving north during the wet season include wildebeest, zebra, Thompson's gazelles, buffalo, eland and hartebeest. The elephant population in this park was estimated at around 6,000 in 1987 but numbers are believed to have fallen since then due to poaching. At the height of the rainy season the animals are spread out over an area of over 20,000 sq km. When the wet season ends the animals begin their migration back south and spend the dry season (July-October) concentrated around the River Tarangire until the rains begin again.

The number of species of birds recorded in Tarangire National Park has been estimated at approximately 300. These include migrants that fly south to spend October-April away from the winter of the northern hemisphere. Here you may spot various species of herons, storks and ducks, vultures, buzzards, sparrowhawks, eagles, kites and falcons, as well as ostrich.

Part of the reason that this area was put over to national park status is that being a tsetse fly infested area it is not suitable for stock rearing (see box, page 475).

Routes The park is large enough for it not to feel crowded even when there are quite a few visitors. There are a number of routes or circuits that you can follow that take you to the major attractions.

Lake Burungi circuit Covering about 80 km, this circuit starts at the Engelhard Bridge and goes clockwise, along the river bank. Continue through the acacia trees until about 3 km before the Kuro Range Post where you will see a turning off to the right. Down this track you will pass through a section of Combretum-Dalergia woodland as you head towards the western boundary

Tarangire migrations

KENYA

Lake Natron

1

Wildebeest & Zebra
2

○ Arusha

3 Lake Manyara

Wildebeest & Zebra
4

5

Buffalo, Gazelle, Elephant, Kongoni, Eland & Oryx

Tarangire National Park

Wildebeest, Zebras, Buffalo & Eland
6

Buffa Gazel Elepha Kongo Eland Oryx

N

Not to scale

1 Lake Natron Game Controlled Area
2 Mto wa Mbu Game Controlled Area
3 Lake Manyara National Park
4 Lolkisale Game Controlled Area
5 Simanjiro Game Controlled Area & Pla
6 Mkungunero Game Controlled Area

Tsetse fly

The tsetse fly is a little larger than the house fly and is found over much of East Africa including Tanzania. Its presence is a serious threat to human habitation because it is a carrier of two diseases. The first is a human disease known as 'sleeping sickness' and the second is a disease affecting cattle called trypanosomiasis, known as nagana among the people of Tanzania. This disease can be deadly to cattle while leaving man uninfected or can affect both man and cattle. In the former areas people can live and can cultivate the land but cannot keep cattle, while in the latter areas the presence of the tsetse fly has meant that large areas of Tanzania are uninhabitable by human beings and are left to the wild animals. Interestingly the tsetse fly does not affect wild animals. When it was realised that humans would never be able to live in these areas, but that wild animals could, large areas were designated to be game reserves in the early colonial era.

There are eight different species of tsetse fly found in Tanzania of which four are most important. The different species are each suited to a different type of environment and vegetation. Unfortunately there is a species of fly for almost all conditions in East Africa. Areas where there are no tsetse include land over about 1,830 m, and areas with under 400 mm of rainfall. Tanzania is probably the worst affected by tsetse fly of all the countries of East Africa.

Since the colonial period great efforts have been made to control the movement of tsetse fly. This was done by moving people out of certain areas and clearing the bush. A 5-km wide belt is cleared of bush and people moved into this belt in a dense settlement. This belt provides a barrier that the tsetse cannot move across. Spraying has also been used. However a lapse in the efforts is all that is needed for the fly to return to areas that have been cleared.

Tanzania

---

of the park. The route continues around and the vegetation turns back to parkland with acacia trees and then back to Combretum as the road turns right and reaches a full circle at the Englehard Bridge. The lake water levels have fallen and Lake Burungi is almost dry. If you are very lucky you may see leopard and rhino in this area although the numbers of rhino have reportedly decreased.

Lemiyon area

This circuit covers the northern area of the park bound on each side by the eastern and western boundaries of the park and to the south by the river. This is where you will see the fascinating baobab trees with their large silvery trunks and gourd-like fruits. Their huge trunks enable the trees to survive through a number of rain failures and they are characteristic of this type of landscape. Also found here are acacia trees, which provide food for giraffe. Other animals that you expect to see are wildebeest, zebra, gazelles and elephant.

Kitibong Hill circuit

This track covers the west section of the park and is centred on Kitibong Hill. It includes acacia parkland in the east and Combretum-Dalbergia woodland in the west, the Gursi floodplains to the south and the foothills of Sangaiwe Hill, which are along the western boundary of the park. This area is home to a variety of plains animals including buffalo and elephant.

The Gursi & Lamarkau circuit

The grasslands found in the south of the park are home to many plain-grazing species. You are also likely to see ostrich here. During the wet season a large swamp forms in what is known as Larmakau – a corruption of the Masai word 'o'llakau', meaning hippo, which can be seen here.

Without a four-wheel drive vehicle you will not be able to see much of the southernmost section of the park and during the wet season it is often impassable to all vehicles. There are two areas in the south – Nguselororobi to the east and Mkungunero in the southwest corner. The former is mainly swamp, with some plains and woodland, and if you are lucky you might see cheetah here. Mkungunero has a number of freshwater pools that serve to attract many different species.

Sleeping **L** *Oliver's Camp* in the eastern part of Tarangire National Park offers a small luxury twin bedding camp, which accommodates 12 guests, carefully designed to blend into the Kikoti landscape, bookings c/o *Abercrombie & Kent*, PO Box 427, Arusha, T7803, F7003. **L** *Tarangire Sopa Lodge*, bookings through PO Box 1823, Arusha, T2502332, F2508245, info@sopalodges.com Luxury all-suite lodge with 75 suites, opened in 1995, opulent lounges, bars and restaurant, excellent food and barbecues, large landscaped swimming pool and conference facilities, probably Tanzania's most luxurious safari lodge. **L** *Tarangire Swala Camp*, Mashado Central Reservations, PO Box 14823, Arusha, T6585, F2548020, Mashado@habari.co.tz, camp accessed by air from Arusha. Located on the edge of the Gursi swamp, which makes the camp a first-class site for ornithologists, comprises 8 extremely comfortable guest tents, en-suite facilities, special activities at the camp include informal talks by a scientist involved in conservation-related research camp closed during the rainy season Apr-Jun, for UK agent see page 318. **L** *Tarangire Treetops*, just outside the park, bookings through *Halcyon Africa*, Private Bag X5, Norwood 2117, Johannesburg, South Africa, T+27-11-8030557, F8037044, res@halcyonhotels.com, or through *Redds African Grill House*, PO Box 1861, Arusha, T027-2544521, F2544374, sales@ halcyontz.com, or juilet.halcyon@virgin.net (UK agent). Large tree houses among baobab trees, reportedly excellent food and service, offer walking safaris, mountain biking, mobile camping and night drives.

B *Tarangire Safari Lodge*, bookings through *Serengeti Select Safaris*, PO Box 2703, Arusha, T/F7182, sss@habari.co.tz, direct to the lodge: T027-2531447/8, tarsaf@habari.co.tz Luxury tented camp with hot water, showers, toilets etc, sleeps 70, good restaurant and bar, swimming pool, overlooking the river – wonderful setting, this area is relatively free of tsetse flies, best tented location for game viewing. **Camping** **C** *Six special campsites*, enquire at Park HQ, water and firewood are provided. **D** *Two public campsites*.Kongoni Campsite, just off the main road, a few kilometres before the gate, is a good alternative to the camps inside the park, since you do not have to pay the daily park entrance fees.

Babati &
Mt Hanang
Colour map 4, grid A4

Mount Hanang is the ninth-highest peak in East Africa, with an altitude of 3,417 m, and a challenge for more adventurous trekkers. It lies to the southwest of Babati, a small town approximately 170 km southwest of Arusha on the road to Dodoma. *Kahembe's Trekking and Cultural Safaris*, PO Box 366, Babati, T027-2531088, fidebabati@hotmail.com, is a local company whose owner, the enterprising Joas Kahembe, has been the pioneer for tourism in this otherwise rarely visited but rewarding area. The company offers a gentle four-day trek up Mount Hanang using the easy Gendabi route for US$160 per person or a two-day trek along the steeper Katesh route for US$80 per person. They also have a number of imaginative local tours at US$40 per person per day (US$30 each for three or more people). These include 3-5-day walking safaris that explore the still largely intact traditional culture of the semi-nomadic pastoralist Barbaig people, and other longer cultural safaris, which have visits to and stays with several different local ethnic groups. Independent exploration of the area is possible but not common.

Sleeping In Babati there is accommodation at the old *Fig Tree Hotel*, which has a bar, dining-room and 3 detached rondovels for guests. It was run by Baron von Blixen and his second wife, Cockie, between 1928-32. The Prince of Wales was entertained to lunch there by the von Blixens during his safari in 1928. There are also several cheap and basic guesthouses. There are also several basic but clean guesthouses in Katesh including **E** *Colt Guest House*, just around the corner from the bus stand, which is secure and has mosquito nets.

Transport From Arusha there are several buses to Babati, while you could also travel on the Mtei bus to Katesh, the village at the base of the mountain, a journey of 3-4 hrs. A guide for climbing the mountain can be arranged from the petrol station in Katesh. The Katesh route can be completed in one day with a knowledgeable guide, the ascent and descent taking up to 12 hrs in total.

Lake Victoria and Environs

Dar es Salam

This area is a long way from the coast and transport links leave much to be desired. The road to Mwanza through central Tanzania is in a poor state, and better access is by train (albeit slow), or by air (can be erratic) or by road through Kenya (this will require either a multiple-entry visa or a second visa if you are coming from a location in Tanzania). Mwanza is a busy town, and there is much activity in exporting fish from Lake Victoria. Bukoba, on the west side of the lake, is in a very attractive setting. Haya men from this region are tall, and Haya women have a reputation for great beauty.

Lake Victoria, bordered by Kenya, Tanzania and Uganda, is the largest freshwater lake in Africa and the second largest in the world. Occupying a shallow depression at an altitude of 1,135 m, it covers 69,490 sq km and is the source of the White Nile.

Tanzania

Musoma

This small port is set on the east shores of Lake Victoria close to the border with Kenya. It is a bustling and friendly town, the capital of Mara Region, located on the south side of a bay, with many visitors who are on their way to or from Kenya. It is also close to the Western Corridor of Serengeti National Park and so should be one of the centres for safaris to the park. However, because the Kenyan border was closed for several years and its general inaccessibility, it has not developed as such. It has a climate of hot days and cool nights.

Electricity and water supplies can be erratic, and the small hotels will not have generators. None of the hotels currently take credit cards, only the banks will

1°50'S 34°30'E
Phone code: 028
Colour map 4, grid A3
Population: 100,000

Musoma

Map labels: To Islands, To Port, Harbour, Fish, Lake Victoria, Kusaga St, Government Hospital, Omega Health Centre, Library, Ghandi St, Air Tanzania, Manota Photo Shop, Fish Factory, Jubilee Insurance, Mukendo Rd, Fleb's Traders, Mukendo Hill, Eagle Air/ Precision Air, Clothes, Airstrip, Majita Rd, Makoko Rd, To Mwanza & Butiama, Penninsula Beach Complex

N — Not to scale

■ Sleeping
1 Afrilux
2 Busamba Guest House
3 Catholic Conference
4 Embassy Lodge
5 Orange Tree
6 Penninsula
7 Silver Sands
8 Stigma
9 Tembo Beach

● Eating
1 Freepark Bar
2 Mama Riziki's
3 Mamboleo Bar
4 Mara Dishes Frys

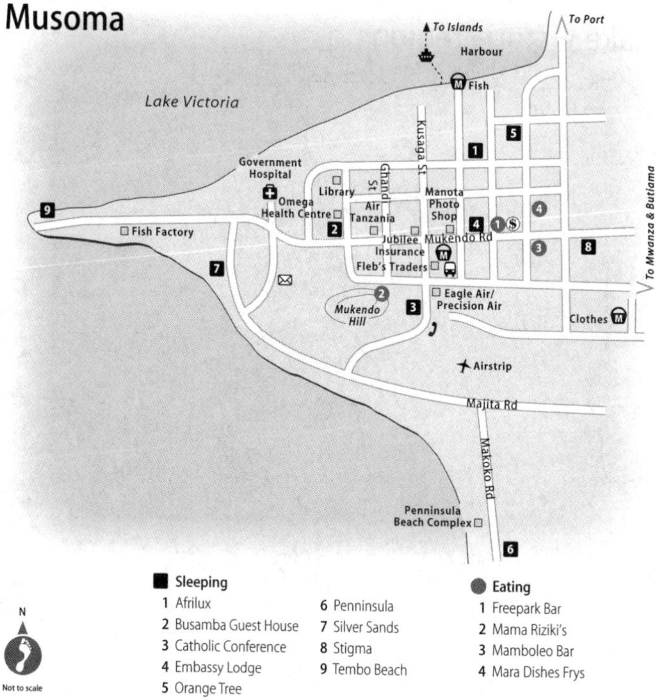

change travellers' cheques, and there are no internet cafés. Enquire at *New Space Entertainments*, opposite *Embassy Lodge* on Mukendo Road, for discos and performances by live bands.

Excursions **Butiama** The home village of Julius Nyerere (see box, page 586) is located 48 km from Musoma. The village has a museum that commemorates Nyerere's life and work (entrance US$2). Tanzania's first president was buried here, not far from the humble dwelling where he was born 77 years before. The bus ride is through pleasant scenery and costs US$1.

Lukuba Island takes several hours to reach by boat. It has a small tourist resort that allows camping (US$10), but is planning to develop as a more luxurious destination. *Flebs' Traders* on Kusaga Street can provide updated information.

Small boats can be taken across the bay and to the little islands nearby for around US$1 per person. They leave from the fish market and harbour on the north shore, not far from the *Afrilux Hotel*. It is a wise precaution to take food and drink if you are planning to make a day excursion.

Sleeping **C** *Penninsula*, 2 km south from town towards the pleasant suburb of Makoko. A/c, TV, hot water, fridges. Large restaurant, separate beach area with a swimming pool (not always open) and boats. **D** *Afrilux*, central, newly constructed and very good value, hot water, fans, restaurant and a large garden bar area. **D** *Orange Tree*, in town centre, good bar and restaurant. **D** *Stigma Hotel*, Mukendo Rd. Some rooms have en-suite bathroom (shower), bar and restaurant. **D** *Tembo Beach*, PO Box 736, T/F622887, hotel town office T622386. At Old Musoma Pier, 2 km west of town, private beach on a peninsula. Variety of accommodation from self-contained units with porches and hot water to camping. Good bar and restaurant facilities, a little dilapidated, but very peaceful, with wonderful views of the lake. Popular with overland trucks. **E** *Catholic Conference Centre*, town centre, secure and clean, bathrooms are shared. Good restaurant and bar, with a satellite TV. Recommended for value.

Bark cloth

Bark cloth is a product of the Lake Victoria region. It has been used in the past as a material for making ceremonial clothes and more recently it is seen for sale to tourists as table mats etc.

The preparation of the cloth is a long and complex process and making good quality bark cloth is a very real skill. The process begins with the scraping down of the outer bark. It is then slit from top to bottom and a cut made around the top and bottom of the tree trunk. Using a ladder, the bark is gradually removed beginning at the bottom and working upwards. It is removed from the entire circumference of the tree trunk, then rolled up and taken back to the house of the cutter. The next step in the process is to scorch the side of the bark that was closest to the tree. This 'melts' the sap and helps in the softening and stretching processes. The bark

is scorched by laying it on the ground, placing dry banana leaves on it, lighting them, then very quickly removing them so that the bark is not burnt too much. The bark is then rolled up in fresh banana leaves to prevent it from drying out and is left overnight.

The next day the process of pounding the bark begins. This is done in two stages using a special beater with ridges on it. As the bark is beaten it gradually gets thinner and wider. The process of stretching the bark is next and is usually undertaken by two or three people. The bark is alternatively beaten and stretched until it is stretched out and fixed with stones and left in the sun to dry. By this stage it is a thin and totally malleable piece of cloth. If it is good quality the bark cloth will be large and of a uniform thickness, however it is common for several pieces to be sewn together and for there to be the odd thin patch.

F *Busamba Guest House*, town centre, noisy, cheap, unwise to leave valuables in the rooms. **F** *Embassy Lodge*, central, houses a disco so very noisy, again unwise to leave valuables in the rooms. **F** *Silver Sands*, just west of town centre, a little run-down, with a big garden bar, but no food.

Camping F *Tembo Beach*, PO Box 736, T/F622887, hotel town office T622386. Situated at Old Musoma Pier, 1.5 km west of Musoma town.

Eating & bars

Cheap *Penninsula Hotel*, particularly recommended for Indian food. *Freepark*, open air, good atmosphere and excellent value food. *Mama Riziki's*, cheap local food, boiled drinking water, satellite TV. *Mara Dishes Frys*, good value, including Indian snack food, boiled water. *Mamboleo Bar*, central, on Mukendo Rd, has a lively atmosphere and pool tables.

Shopping

Flebs' Traders, Kusaga St, has a good range of imported items.

Transport

See Dar es Salaam transport, page 360, for further advice and contact details

Air *Air Tanzania* flights go to Mwanza, see page 483, although schedules are subject to frequent cancellations and alterations. Link to Musoma by road. Also, one direct flight leaves Dar es Salaam (DSM) at 0800 on Wed, takes 2 hrs, leaves soon after for Dodoma, and then arrives back in DSM at 1425. *Eagle Air* has 2 flights per week on the route DSM-Arusha-Musoma-Mwanza. The service

Tanzania (side tab)

is erratic and liable to be cancelled without warning. Flights from DSM via Kilimanjaro on Mon and Fri. Depart DSM 0830, then Kilimanjaro at 1010, arrive Musoma at 1120. Flights continue to Mwanza (arrival 1210), then back to Kilimanjaro (1350) and DSM (1530). Their office in Mwanza is on Kusaga St, near the bus station. *Air Excel* (Arusha: PO Box 12731, T2501597, F2548429, T0741-510857 (mob), airexcel@ark.eoltz.com) have a daily flight that leaves Arusha airport at 0800, stops off at Lake Manyara, Seronera and Grumeti airstrips and arrives in Musoma at 1025, returning by the same route to arrive in Arusha at 1305.

Boat Ferry: the ferry for Kisumu to Mwanza used to stop at Musoma, but this is not now the case.

Road Bus: Mwanza: the road is good, and there are regular buses leaving from the bus station, which is behind Kusaga St in the centre. The trip takes up to 5 hrs, and costs US$4. From Mwanza, *Takrim* and *Tawfiq* have big buses that leave Mwanza at around 1000. **Serengeti National Park**: take the Mwanza bus and ask to be dropped off at the Ndabaka Gate, 10-15 km south of Bunda on the main road. The park gate itself is about 5 mins' walk from the main road. The guards are not very helpful at the gate, and normally will not allow you to wait for a lift there, telling you to go back and get your own transport. It is possible to wait for lifts at the turn-off from the main road. Then you have to pay the park entry fee. The tracks in the park are bad, taking 5 hrs to reach the *Senonara Wildlife Lodge*. Negotiate a price for the lift – around US$8-10. **Arusha**: buses no longer go through the Serengeti and across the top of Lake Manyara Park. Public transport from Musoma to Arusha now goes via Nairobi, Kenya. From Mwanza there is a bus that travels painfully slowly over very difficult roads south of the Serengeti, taking an age to reach Arusha. Road travellers from **Dar es Salaam** say that the quickest road route is to Arusha, then across the border at Namanga to Nairobi, then Nakuru, Kericho, Kisii or Nakuru to Kisumu and back across the border. The roads are good all the way now that there is a new road from Musoma to the Kenyan border. Buses leave for Nairobi at 0700 and 2000 and take about 12 hrs, the fare is $US5.

Train The nearest station is at Mwanza. Train tickets can still be bought at the old ferry ticket station, although the ferry is now closed. See pages 328/329 for details of train services, timetables and fares.

Directory **Communications** Telephone: Telecoms on Kusaga St has international call facilities and will send faxes. **Medical services** Omega Health Centre, in the town centre, is recommended. Musoma Hospital is next to the market, T2622111. **Money** *Jubilee Insurance*, on Mukendo Rd, will change money and offers good rates.

Mwanza

2°30'S 32°58'E
Phone code: 028
Colour map 4, grid A2
Population: 400,000

Mwanza is the largest Tanzanian port on Lake Victoria and it is Tanzania's second-largest town. It lies on a peninsula that juts into the lake. It is surrounded by rocky hills and the land is dominated by granite outcrops some of which are very impressive and look as if they are about to topple. The road approach is spectacular, tunnelling through some of the great boulders on the route. As the railway terminus and major lake port, Mwanza is a bustling and lively town. The produce from the lake region is gathered here and is then transported to the coast by rail. The lake is dotted with islands of varying sizes from the smallest specks, unmarked on maps, to Ukerewe which is heavily populated. Fishing is a major commercial activity in this area, although coffee, tea and cotton are also important. Recently the town has received a major economic boost with the South African takeover of the Mwanza Brewery, and the substantial mining developments in Shinyanga and around Geita.

Sights The colonial centre of Mwanza was around the port on the west side of the town. Among the historic buildings in this area are the **Primary Court**, dating from the

German period, and the **Mahatma Ghandi Memorial Hall** from the British period. The **Clocktower** has a plaque recording that on 3 August 1858, on Isamilo Hill, a mile away, John Hanning Speke first saw the main water of Lake Victoria, which he later proved to be the source of the Nile.

The colonial residences spread over Capri Point and social life centred on the **Mwanza Club** and its golf course and the **Yacht Club**. One of the celebrated sights is **Bismark Rock**, which appears precariously balanced, located just south of the main port. An unusual sight is the **Pile Driver Office**, which has been built in an abandoned section of Caterpillar heavy-plant machinery on Station Road, opposite the Mwanza Institute, and which houses the officials of a timber yard.

Saa Nane Island This wildlife sanctuary is not far from Mwanza, in the lake. It has hippo, zebra and wildebeest, as well as various caged animals, including some very unhappy looking hyenas, although it is reported that the number of animals has fallen. It gets very busy at the weekends, but it's a pleasant place to spend an afternoon, with rocky outcrops appearing out of a grassy landscape. ■ *Boats from Mwanza depart from the jetty 1 km south of the centre off Station Rd, at 1100, 1300, 1400, 1500 and 1600. US$0.50. Combined boat and entry fee about US$1.50.*

Excursions

Tanzania

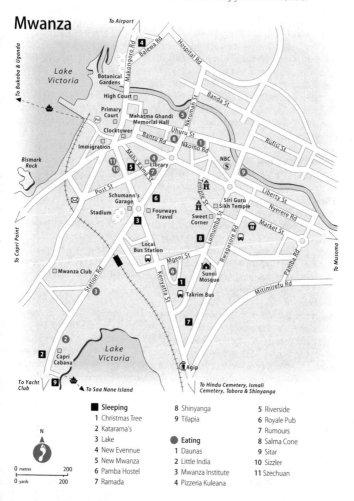

Mwanza

Sleeping	8 Shinyanga	5 Riverside
1 Christmas Tree	9 Tilapia	6 Royale Pub
2 Katarama's		7 Rumours
3 Lake	● **Eating**	8 Salma Cone
4 New Evennue	1 Daunas	9 Sitar
5 New Mwanza	2 Little India	10 Sizzler
6 Pamba Hostel	3 Mwanza Institute	11 Szechuan
7 Ramada	4 Pizzeria Kuleana	

N

0 metres 200
0 yards 200

Tanzania

Bujora Sukuma Village Museum Originally set up by missionaries from Quebec in 1952, the museum celebrates the traditions and culture of the Sukuma who make up one of the largest tribal groups in Tanzania. Exhibits include an unusual two-storey royal pavilion in the shape of the royal stool, shrines, and traditional instruments, including a drum collection. Traditional dances are held when the museum is busy, usually on a Saturday, and include the impressive Sukuma snake dance or *Bugobogobo*. It is best to be shown around by a guide, cost US$1.25. ■ *18 km from Mwanza on the Musoma road, reached by taking a local bus from the bus station near the market in Mwanza to Kisessa, then walking the remaining 2 km.*

Ukerewe, Kome and Maisome Islands These three islands are very pretty, but there is little else to attract the tourist. **Ukerewe Island** to the north of Mwanza can be reached by ferry, taking about three hours, leaving Mwanza at 0900 and Nansio, the main town on Ukerewe, at 1330. It is also possible to go by road – east round the lake to Bunda and then west along the north shore of Speke Gulf, crossing by ferry to Ukerewe Island. There are no regular buses on the last leg of this route so it is necessary to hitch. There are some small hotels and a number of cheap restaurants.

Kome and **Maisome** islands are served by the ferries to Myamirembe, which leave Mwanza on Monday (0800) and Thursday (2100). Kome takes about three hours to reach and Maisome about seven hours. Ferries return from Nyamirembe on Tuesday (0800) and Friday (1900).

Sleeping **A-B** *New Mwanza*, PO Box 25, T2501070, F2503202, central, on Post St. Restaurant, bar, a/c, pleasant and convenient. Has recently undergone a major refurbishment, which has introduced plenty of marble and gilt. **A-B** *Tilapia*, on Station Rd near ferry to Saa Nane Island, 1 km southwest of town, PO Box 82, T2500517, F2500141, tilapia@mbio.net Chalet-style accommodation, s/c, a/c or fans, TV, fridge, swimming pool. Has Indian, Thai and Japanese restaurants and a decking bar overlooking the lake. Fax and internet services, pleasant and comfortable, can arrange car hire. A vintage box-body Ford has been restored and is on display in the foyer area. There is also some accommodation on a boat moored on the lake by the hotel. **D** *Christmas Tree*, just off Mgeni St, modern block, s/c, hot water, restaurant with well-prepared, tasty food, good value. **D** *Lake*, PO Box 910, T2500658, off Station Rd close to stadium. Restaurant, outdoor bar, parking space, noisy and busy, fans, nets, s/c, good value. **E** *New Evennue*, Balewa Rd, north of port, not s/c, hot water, extremely well run, and good value. **E** *Pamba Hostel*, on Station Rd near roundabout. Central location, shared facilities, squat WCs, noisy, especially at the weekends, serves a continental breakfast, restaurant, bar. **E** *Ramada Hotel*, PO Box 6338, Rwegasore Rd, T40237, fans, continental breakfast, reasonable value. **E** *Raterama's Hotel*, Station Rd, opposite ferry to Saa Nane, some rooms are s/c, restaurant, good location. **F** *Shinyanga*, Lumumba St. Just off centre, rather run-down, no restaurant or bar. **Camping** Available at the *Sukuma Museum*. The *New Blue Campsite*, Capri Point Rd, US$1.75 per night. *Yacht Club*, US$2.50.

Eating **Mid-range** *Kidepo Grill*, in *New Mwanza Hotel*. Live music at weekends and occasionally other nights, note that quoted prices exclude VAT, the menu doesn't mention this and some travellers have been caught out. *Kuleana Pizzeria*, Post St, near the *New Mwanza Takeaway Service*. Cappuccino US$1, excellent pizza US$2-US$5, ice cream US$1, excellent value, they support street kids. *Lake Hotel*, off Station Rd, close to Stadium, varied menu, reasonable value, owner will prepare a special meal if ordered in advance for a group, lacks atmosphere. *Little India*, Station Rd towards the *Yacht Club*. Serves north Indian food, outside barbecue and bar, good location overlooking the lake. *Sitar*, corner of Liberty St and Lumumba St. Rather dreary interior, Indian food, slow service but food excellent, also has Chinese food. *Sizzler*, PO Box 247, T41978, Kenyatta St. Serves international, Chinese and Indian food. Good quality, but perhaps a little pricey. *Szechuan*, Kenyatta St, reasonable quality Chinese food. *Tilapia*, Station Rd. Near ferry to Saa Nane, nice location overlooking part of lake. Good standard and popular, restaurants inside in basement and outside on roof, Chinese, Japanese and Indian food. **Cheap** *Yacht Club*, Station Rd, south end. The *Kingfisher Restaurant* serves

Indian and Italian food, very good value, pleasant views. US$0.50 entrance fee for non-members. **Seriously cheap** *Daunos*, Nkomo St, snacks, samosas. *Salma Cone*, corner of Barti St and Nkrumah St. Serves coffee, snacks and ice cream.

Rumours, Station Rd, new bar with a modern interior, satellite TV and big screen, pool tables, **Bars** very popular. *Riverside*, Nkrumah Rd, bar with pool tables, darts and barbecued food. *Royale Pub*, just off Mgeni St, is a big outdoor bar under a large canopy, where the barbecued meals are very popular. *Pamba Hostel*, Station Rd, near the centre, is a very popular bar. *Mwanza Institute*, Station Rd, is a popular outside bar, formerly the club for African government employees. Has a good location overlooking the lake.

Disco *Capri Cobana*, Station Rd towards *Yacht Club*, is especially lively over the weekends.

There is an excellent supermarket on the site of the previous *U Turn Restaurant*, corner of **Shopping** Nkrumah and Hospital St. This sells frozen meat, toiletries, canned drinks including Diet Coke, English biscuits and chocolate bars, English choc ices, fairly expensive but has an impressive range of products.

Yacht Club, Station Rd, southern end offers sailing on the lake. Well-appointed premises **Sport** with restaurant, bar and a billiards table. US$0.50 entrance fee payable for non-members. *Mwanza Club*, located just off the southern end of Station Rd, rather run-down although there are still books in the library. It has 3 tennis courts, a tennis practice wall, snooker table but the swimming pool is currently closed. Daily membership US$1.00, tennis court fee US$2.00. The golf course ran southwest from the club – since this closed, the international community has moved on to the *Yacht Club*.

Dolphin Tours & Safaris, Kenyatta St/Post St corner, PO Box 336, T2500096. *Fourways Travel* **Tour operators** *Service*, PO Box 990, T2502273. Very helpful travel agency, managed by Sharad J Shah. *Masumin Tours & Safaris Ltd*, Kenyatta St, PO Box 1884, T2500192, T0742-550786 (mob), F2500373, masumins@mbio.net, also offers car hire. *Serengeti Services & Tours Ltd*, PO Box 308, T2500061, F2500446, serengeti@mbio.net

Air There is an airport at Mwanza served by *Air Tanzania*. There is one scheduled flight from **Transport** Dar es Salaam (DSM) on Tue, Fri and Sat, all leaving between 0700 and 0800, taking approx *See Dar es Salaam* 90 mins. On Mon, Tue and Thu flights from DSM go via **Kilimanjaro**. On Wed an early morn- *transport, page 360,* ing flight from DSM to **Entebbe** in Uganda stops in Mwanza at 0725, the return flight calling *for further advice* at Mwanza at 1015 and arriving back in DSM at 1220. A flight that leaves DSM at 1400 for **Nai-** *and contact details* robi calls at Mwanza at 1525 and returns on the same route, leaving Mwanza at 1935, arriving in DSM at 2100. On Mon there is a flight from DSM via **Dodoma**, leaving DSM at 0800 and Dodoma at 0930; from Mwanza it goes to **Bukoba** before returning to DSM. Other flights from Mwanza to Bukoba leave at 1030 on Thu and Sat, and start the return journey at 1140. However it is not uncommon to turn up at the airport with a valid and confirmed ticket and be turned away due to overbooking. Fare from DSM is around US$100, but half that for residents. *Air Tanzania* also have scheduled flights. *Precisionair* and *Eagle Air* also serve Mwanza – again, the service can be erratic and schedules change from time to time. The *Precisionair* office is at *New Mwanza Hotel*, T2560027. There are flights that leave DSM at 0730 on Mon, Thu, Sat and Sun going via Shinyanga.

On Tue and Fri, a flight leaves **Zanzibar** at 1040 to Arusha, from where the plane departs at 1215 for Mwanza. The plane leaves at 1350, heading for Arusha, then Zanzibar and finally DSM. The fare to Zanzibar is US$205.

Eagle Air flights are scheduled to serve several routes each week. Flights to Mwanza from DSM go via **Kilimanjaro** and **Musoma** on Mon and Fri, via **Shinyanga** on Tue, Thu and Sat, and via **Dodoma** on Wed. All flights leave DSM at 0830 or 0900 and return to DSM the same day. There are also 2 return flights from Bukoba on Mon, Tue and Thu, and flights serving Mwanza, Bukoba, Tabora and/or Dodoma on Wed, Sat or Sun.

Tanzania

Lake Ferry: this is easily the most reliable and comfortable way to travel on to the town of **Bukoba**. The boats, though old, have recently been refitted. There is a ferry each day (but not Wed from Mwanza, nor Thu from Bukoba), leaving at 2100 taking 8-11 hrs depending on the ports of call. Fares are US$16, US$13 and US$9. 1st class provides a berth in a 2-person cabin, 2nd in a 4-person cabin. Earplugs can be boon. **Nyamirembe** is served by 2 ferries a week, from Mwanza at 0800 on Mon and 2100 on Thu and from Nyamirembe at 0800 on Tue and 1900 on Fri. The journey takes 10 hrs. Its ferries call at **Kome** and **Miasome Islands** and cost US$5 (2nd class) and US$3 (3rd). **Ukerewe Island** has a daily ferry, leaving Mwanza at 0900 and returning around 1300. The trip is 3 hrs and costs US$1.50. There were ferries to and from **Kisumu** in Kenya until the border closed in 1977. Although it reopened in 1983, the ferries have not returned. However there have recently been co-operation initiatives between Kenya and Tanzania, and hopes are high that the ferry will resume.

Services to Port Bell (Kampala) for Uganda were restarted in Feb 1999 on the *MV Victoria*, but have now been discontinued. According to the Tourist Information centre near the Parliament building, there are still cargo ships that take passengers, although it is an uncomfortable journey.

Road Arusha buses no longer go through the Serengeti and across the top of Lake Manyara Park. However, it is possible to travel from Mwanza to Arusha via Shinyanga and Singida. The buses do not run every day. Road travellers from **Dar es Salaam** say that the quickest road route is to Arusha, then across the border at Namanga to Nairobi, then Nakuru, Kericho, Kisii (or Nakuru to Kisumu) and back across the border and south through Musoma. Be aware, however, that if you are a visitor, you may need visas (depending on your nationality) to enter Kenya and to re-enter Tanzania. The roads are good all the way and the stretch from the border to Musoma has a brand new highway. *Tawfiq* and *Takrim* run large buses on this route, costing $US30 and taking 30 hrs. For Dar es Salaam, buses leave Mwanza for Musoma and all destinations beyond at 1000 from the Buzuruga bus station. There is at least 1 bus a day to Kisumu in Kenya, leaving at around 0700. The bus journey from Mwanza to Musoma takes about 4 hrs. *Takrim Bus*, Lumumba St, PO Box 10172, T400358, T0741-640157 (mob).

Train The railway line, built in the 1920s during the British administration, was completed in 1928. It forms the extension of the Central Line and was considered vital for the development of the northwest area. See pages 328/329 for details of train services, timetables and fares. The train from **Dodoma/Mwanza** takes approximately 26 hrs.

Directory **Banks** *Standard Chartered Bank* on Makongoro Rd, north of the Clocktower, has an ATM that accepts Visa cards. *Stanbic Bank* is on Nyerere Rd. **Communications** Internet: Internet café on Bantu Rd, US$1 for 30 mins. **Post**: post office on Post St. The quickest and cheapest place to send a fax is across the road from the post office at the *Fax Centre*. **Medical services** The Bugando Hospital, T40610-5, built in the 1970s with Israeli support, is located on a hill about 1 km southwest of town. **Useful addresses** Immigration office: on the road leading off from the Clocktower towards the lake.

Rubondo Island National Park
2° 30' S, 31° 45' E
Colour map 4, grid A2

Rubondo National Park is an island located northwest of Mwanza. It has an area of about 240 sq km that includes the main island and a number of smaller ones. The best time to visit is November-February.

There are a number of different vegetation types on the island providing differing habitats for a variety of animals.

Rubondo Island National Park

With a high water table the island is able to support dense forest. Other vegetation includes more open woodland, savannah grassland and swamps. There is little 'big game' on the island although some has been introduced, including giraffe, elephant and rhino. Other animals include crocodile, hippo, bushbuck, sitatunga (a swamp-dwelling antelope only found here and in Selous), vervet monkeys and mongeese. The park has wonderful birdlife. You are likely to spot fish eagle, martial eagle, sacred ibis, saddle billed stork, kingfishers, water fowl, cuckoos, bee eaters and sunbirds. There are animal hides from where you can view the wildlife.

There are camping facilities on the island but they are very basic so you are advised to take all your own equipment. All food supplies must be taken with you. The park headquarters are located at Kageye. No vehicles are allowed on the island although there is a lorry that can be hired to drive visitors around. Boats and camping should be booked in advance through the Park Warden, Rubondo Island National Park, PO Box 11, Geita, or send a message through the National Parks radios, or through the *Schumann's Garage* (T40037) in Mwanza.

Transport The quickest and easiest access is by air (there is an airstrip suitable for light aircraft). Other cheaper ways are by hiring a boat directly from Mwanza. Alternatively you can drive the 6-7 hrs to Nungwe (300 km via Gieta) from where it is a 2-hr boat journey or you can drive the 10 hrs to Nyamirembe (via Gieta) from where the boat journey is about 30 mins. It is wise to check on availability of boats at *Schumann's Garage* (T40037) in Mwanza before departing.

Bukoba

Bukoba is now the main urban area west of the lake, but for several centuries, until Bukoba was established at the end of the 19th century, **Karagwe**, some 100 km inland, was the principal centre. The Bahinda, a cattle herding people from the

1°20'S 31°59'E
Phone code: 028
Colour map 4, grid A2

Bukoba

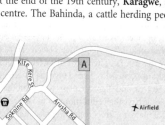

■ Sleeping
1 Coffee Tree Inn
2 Lake View
3 Lutheran Centre
4 Upenda Lodge

Not to scale

Related map
A Bukoba centre,
page 487

The Hen and the Hawk: a Bukoba Fable

Once upon a time a hen and a hawk who were friends lived together in the same hut. One day, during a great famine the hen went off in search of food. She was successful for she met a man who had some bananas. As she was carrying her load home she met the hawk who asked her how she had got the bananas. The hen, standing on one leg and hiding the other in her feathers, replied that she had paid for them with her foot. The hen told the hawk that he must also buy some food with his foot.

The hawk agreed that this was indeed fair and went off in search of some food. He met a man and offered his leg in return for some food. The man agreed, cut off the hawk's leg and then gave him some food. The hawk had great difficulty walking home with only one leg, trying to balance the load.

When the hawk eventually reached home he saw the hen standing on two legs. He was extremely angry with the hen, saying that although the hen was supposed to be his friend she had cheated him. The hawk told the hen that he could not forgive her and would kill her. The hen replied that he would never succeed in killing her for she would run away. Sure enough the hen ran away and lived with man, while the hawk and all his descendants remain determined to kill the hen and its offspring. This is why the hawk will always try to kill any hen that it sees.

interior, operated a feudal system where chiefs took tributes from their subjects. The wealth of the area was based on cattle that were raised successfully despite problems with tsetse flies (see box, page 475). Bukoba, set in a bay between lush hills is Tanzania's second largest lake port, with a population of 47,000 and a university. However it receives few visitors. It was founded for the Germans in 1890 by Emin Pasha. It is a lovely part of Tanzania – green and fertile and with a very relaxed way of life. The major food crop here (as in much of the area around the lake) is *matoke*. This is the green banana you will see grown everywhere. It is peeled, wrapped in banana leaves and cooked very slowly by steaming. The major commercial crop is coffee, which has contributed significantly to the wealth of the area. There is a coffee factory near the jetty. Unfortunately the world price has fallen in recent years with notable effects on the people of this district. There are quite a few aid projects in this area so a number of expatriate aid workers live here. Huge deposits of nickel and cobalt have been discovered in the area, and there are plans to exploit these.

The Haya people have high educational standards and, together with the Chagga from around Kilimanjaro, are strongly represented in academic life, government service and business. This feature of Tanzania has been attributed to climate. Both Kilimanjaro and Kagera (West Lake) are at high altitude and are cool, thus proving to be attractive locations for early missionaries from Europe. Both Catholic and Protestant mission activities were particularly strong, and competition between the two groups led to superior educational facilities being offered to attract converts.

Sights Near the lake shore is a group of buildings from the German period. *Duka Kubwa*, the first general store in the town and the first stone building in Bukoba, is on the corner of Jamhuri Road and Aerodrome Road. Originally the market was in this area – during the British period it was moved about a kilometre inland. When the British took the town in 1914 during the First World War, in their excitement they blew up the German Boma (which was on the site of Trinity Church) and the German Post Office (set under the heliograph – a device for sending messages by mirrors – along the lake shore, of which only the concrete feet still remain). Later the British regretted their impetuosity – they had no administrative centre, and they used the German Hospital (now called the Old Boma, and currently housing part of the University of Bukoba). Across the road from the *Lake View Hotel* is a German cemetery. Further west is the area with European housing up in the hills. Beyond the aerodrome runway to the east is Nyamukazi fishing village. Between **Lake View Hotel** and the lake shore is the former Gymkana Club where there was a cricket pitch, a golf course and tennis courts, now called the *Bukoba Club*.

Tanzania

The centre of town has many Asian style buildings, now very shabby.

The **Mater Mesericordia Cathedral** (Roman Catholic) is an extraordinary building on a huge scale in spectacular style. When it was originally constructed the dome began to subside. All the cladding was removed, new foundations inserted under the building, and the whole shebang was raised 3 m on hydraulic jacks. The levitation was done a millimetre at a time and took 2½ months.

The **Lutheran cathedral** is an altogether more modest and practical construction in modern style.

Coffee has long been the economic mainstay of the region and there is a coffee factory on the lake shore by the wharf, south of the administrative centre, and it is usually possible to be shown round. Continuing southwest from the wharf is the **Bunena Roman Catholic Mission** buildings with a spire, gardens and a cemetery.

Sleeping

D *Lutheran Centre*, PO Box 98, T2220027, F2220954. Very comfortable accommodation, simple but excellent food, hot water, **D** *Coffee Tree Inn*, PO Box 5, T2220412, town centre, near the stadium, 14 rooms, bar and restaurant. Very run down. **D** *Edan Hotel*, corner of Borongo St and Karume Rd, new construction, well run, has a restaurant and bar. **D** *Lake*, PO Box 66, T2220232. Imposing building on the lake shore, comfortable accommodation, some rooms s/c. Moderate food, hotel has bureau de change, open daily. Has recently been refurbished. **D** *New Banana*, PO Box 311, Zam Zam St, east of the Market, T2220861. Restaurant, central and well run, outside area with tables, quite popular. **D** *Spice Beach Motel*, on the lake shore, on the lower road to the port, modern bungalow. **D** *Upenda Lodge*, off Jamhuri St to the southwest of *Coffee Tree Inn*, courtyard with bar. Popular. **E** *Bunena Mission*, about 5 km from town centre along Shore Rd. Dormitory accommodation. **E** *Kahawa Guest House*, PO Box 1263, Arusha Rd, T578. Cheap and reasonable. **E** *Kolping House*, Arusha Rd, Private Bag, Bunena, T21289. Small, very clean, well run, good value. **E** *Lwa Bizi*, on the corner of Nyara Rd and Kashaza. Rather simple **E** *New Highway*, PO Box 1319, Hamugembe, on Uganda Rd, T2223014. Basic, but very cheap. **E** *Rukindo Guest House*, Hamugembe, on Uganda Rd, T2221140. Simple accommodation. **E** *Sukira Guest House*, PO Box 1756, Hamugembe area, on Uganda Rd. Simple and inexpensive. **F** *International Mtiga Guest House*, PO Box 92, Hamugembe area, on Uganda Rd. Has a bar, no frills. **F** *Lily Villa Guest House*, next door to the *Kahawa Guest House*, very clean, owner speaks good English.

Bukoba centre

■ **Sleeping**
1 Edan
2 Kahawa Guest House
3 Kolping Guest House
4 Lwa Bizi
5 New Banana
6 New World
7 Sunrise Inn

● **Eating**
1 Pizza
2 Soft Rock Café
3 West End Café

N
Not to scale

Related map
Bukoba, page 485

Tanzania

Recommended. **F** *New World*, PO Box 954, T303. Very simple, central location. **F** *Rukindo Guest House*, Hamugembe, on Uganda Rd, T2221140. Simple accommodation. **F** *Super Star Guest House*, PO Box 870, Hamugembe, on Uganda Rd. Shared bathrooms.

Camping possible at the *Lake Hotel*, US$3.50 per person per night.

Eating   Reasonable if a bit uninspired. **Cheap**: *Lake Hotel*, moderate food at present, management has sent the chef away for training, we await the results. *New Banana*, food a bit above average. *Pizza Restaurant*, just off Jamhuri St in commercial centre, small restaurant with very good pizzas, samosas and juices. Only open at lunch times, and not all lunch times at that. *Soft Rock Café*, off Karume St on Kashai Rd, established by a German guy working in Bukoba as a sports bar with an outside patio bar. Serves grilled chicken and fish. Has changed hands and has been closed temporarily. *Spice Beach*, Lower Port Rd on the lake. Probably the best place to eat – grills and kebabs in demand, if you order the day before they will lay on an Indian meal. *West End Café* on roundabout at northwest end of town, serves mostly simple grills, and is quite popular. **Bars**   Best places are the verandah terrace at the *Lake Hotel*, with excellent barbequed kebabs, and *Spice Beach*, which is on the sandy lake shore and particularly charming at night when ferry boats are docked at the port. *Coffee Tree Hotel*, disco on Sat. *Garden View Bar*, disco on Fri and Sat, US$1, located in Hamugembe, on road to Uganda, about 1 km. *NBC Club*, just to west of Jamhuri St. Disco Fri and Sat.

Transport   **Air**   Transport to and from Bukoba is fitful. Buses, ferries and flights are all rescheduled on a
See Dar es Salaam   regular basis, depending on demand, and you must check before you travel. With *Air Tanza-
transport, page 360,   *nia* the usual problems apply of unreliability and overbooking. Many travellers fly to Mwanza
for further advice and   from Dar (which has a daily *Air Tanzania* flight) and then take the ferry. *Precisionair* fly here –
contact details   flights tend to be overbooked but travellers report good service. *Eagle Air* have several flights a week between Mwanza and Bukoba, including flights that also go to Tabora on Sun, Tabora and Dodoma on Wed, and Dodoma on Sat.

Road   Two bus companies, Tawfiq and Takrim (booking offices at the bus station) run through services to Kampala. At one stage there were daily departures at 0700hr, taking 5-7 hrs, costing $12, but as demand has fallen the service has been reduced. It is possible to do the trip in a series of short journeys by minibus, costing about the same, but usually taking up to 10 hrs. Local buses west to Bugene and Kaisho US$4 and south to Biharamulo US$9.

Lake Ferry: this is easily the most reliable and comfortable way to travel to **Mwanza**. The boats, though old, have recently been refitted. There is a ferry on Mon, Wed and Fri from Bukoba and Sun, Tue and Thu from Mwanza leaving at between 2000 and 2100 and arriving next morning at around 0800. Fares are US$9, US$6 and US$3. A US$5 port tax may be levied on visitors. 1st class provides a berth in a 2-person cabin, 2nd in a 4-person cabin.

The lake ferry service to Port Bell, Uganda restarted in Feb 1999 but stopped in 2000. There are no plans to resume the service at present.

Karagwe   Located inland, this was an important centre until Bukoba came to prominence with
2°0s, 31°0'E   the introduction of access by steamer across Lake Victoria to Mwanza and the rail
Colour map 4, grid A2   link to the coast. The surrounding area is rich and fertile and cattle thrive particularly well. In the past few years Karagwe has served as a base for the non-government organizations coping with the exodus of refugees from Rwanda. The refugee camps are to the west of the border, but supplies come through Bukoba and then Karagwe. There are several small hotels charging less than US$5 per night. They are very basic, with shared bathrooms and no running water. ■ Getting there: *Buses from Bukoba take about 4 hrs to cover the distance of about 100 km, and cost around US$2.50.*

AIDS

With one in six people suffering from HIV or AIDS, the Kagera region west of Lake Victoria is one of the worst hit places anywhere in Tanzania yet it is possible to come to this part of Africa and not really be aware of the extent of the problem. People who have contracted the disease prefer to stay at home in the last stages of their illness, nursed by their families. It is partly shame, partly a desire not to be a financial burden on their relatives by being in hospital, partly a feeling that their plight is hopeless and that medical resources can be better used on those with curable diseases, and partly a desire to be surrounded by family and friends at the end.

The feature of HIV that seems so interesting in Africa is that it is primarily a heterosexually contracted disease. One problem highlighted early on was the presence of other sexually transmitted diseases leading to open sores and lesions on the penis through which the virus could enter from vaginal fluids.

Some unusual sexual practices might account for the high incidence of HIV among the Haya, the main people in the Kagera region. There are cases where straw and soil are introduced into the vagina to increase friction, causing cuts and blisters to the penis. There is another practice, known as katarero, where the man and woman sit cross-legged and entwined and the man beats the woman's vagina and clitoris with his erect penis. Bruising and minor local trauma of the penis follow and the practise is believed to increase the risk of transmission of the virus. Additionally, as Haya males do not circumcize, their foreskins are prone to split under the stresses of erection and sexual intercourse. Lesions of the penis result, allowing the virus to enter the bloodstream.

The Haya have another unusual practice known as sexual networking. A male is allowed to have sex with his wife's younger sisters. Families in rural areas are large, and it is not unusual for a wife to have four or five younger sisters. There is usually some quid pro quo such as help with school fees or finding employment. If the husband dies, his brother is expected to take the wife as an extra spouse. As the most likely cause of early death is AIDS, HIV will probably be transmitted to the brother, and his wives.

Finally, there is a resistance to using condoms on the grounds that they diminish male pleasure. Women in possession of condoms are accused of being prostitutes, and even if there is an inclination to use them, quite often there are no condoms available in Bukoba at all, or only the expensive ones.

Tanzania

South from Bukoba

Kemondo Bay port is about 18 km south of Bukoba. On the ferry you don't get a chance to appreciate the attractiveness of the bay entrance to the port as it is usually dark when the boat docks and departs. The quayside is a grand sight when the lake steamers, en route from Bukoba and Mwanza, are in – bags of charcoal and coffee being loaded, great bunches of bananas are piled on deck, joyful reunions at homecomings and tearful partings as relatives and work mates come to bid travellers farewell.

Continuing south from Muleba, skirting the edge of the game reserve (not much wild-life visible from the road), is **Biharamulo**, a well laid out town that served as an administrative centre during the German period. There are some fine buildings from the German period, and the entrance to the town is through a tree-lined avenue. The **Old Boma** has been restored. At present the town houses government offices, is a market for the surrounding area, and is the nearest town to the Biharamulo Game Reserve (see page 490). Large market, bank and post office with telephones and fax.

Biharamulo
2° 25' S, 31° 25' E
Colour map 4, grid A2

Sleeping E *Sunset Inn*, opposite the bus stand. Spartan rooms with communal bathrooms, serves food all day.

Transport Buses from **Bukoba**, leave when full, usually around 1100, takes about 6 hrs to cover about 200 km, and costs around US$5. The road is unsealed and in poor shape. Also buses to **Mwanza**, about 3 hrs and US$3.

Biharamulo, Burugi & other northwest game reserves

2° 30', 31° 30° E
Colour map 4, grid A2

Adjacent to Rubondo Island National Park on the mainland (see map, page 478) is the **Biharamulo Game Reserve** (1,300 sq km). This is located to the south of Bukoba on the main Mwanza to Bukoba road but has no facilities and receives very few visitors. Because of the proximity of the large numbers of displaced Rwandan refugees in the Ngara District of northwestern Tanzania the flora and fauna of the game reserve have been greatly depleted. Trees have been felled for firewood and land cleared for cultivation.

The reserve borders Lake Victoria, at an altitude of between 1250-2000 m, and is contiguous with the Burigi Game Reserve to the west. There are north/south ridges and valleys, and much of it is swampy with a healthy, thriving mosquito population. Most of the larger mammals numbers have been decimated by poaching. Animals that formerly lived in the reserve include hippo, elephant and zebra. A small population of sitatunga antelope lived here. Primates included the red colobus monkey. The birds are believed to have been less adversely affected by human encroachment. They include saddle billed storks, the rufous-bellied heron, several varieties of starlings, sunbirds and weavers, the grey kestrel and the fish eagle.

It is possible to hunt in Biharamulo – see page 318 for Hunting Safari agents. There are no visitor facilities and the old guesthouse has fallen into disrepair.

The **Burigi Game Reserve** (2,200 sq km) is contiguous with Biharamulo Game Reserve to the west. Following the huge influx of refugees from Rwanda in the aftermath of the civil unrest, many large camps were set up on the edge of the game reserve. The result was that many of the animals were poached, trees were cut down for fuel and large tracts of land were cleared for the cultivation of crops.

Other game reserves in northwest Tanzania were also adversely affected including **Moyowosi Game Reserve**, **Ibanda Game Reserve** and **Rumanyika Game Reserve**. The Kagera Kigoma Game Reserve Rehabilitation Project (KKGRRP) is seeking to reverse the extensive damage done to these game reserves, which cover a total area of 14,500 sq km. It is estimated that the mammal population decreased by 90% after the arrival of the refugees. There are plans to rehabilitate the roads and coordinate anti-poaching enforcement strategies.

Dar es Salaam

Central: Morogoro, Dodoma, Tabora, Kigoma

The central route from Dar es Salaam to Kigoma in the far west passes through a number of different landscapes and vegetational zones. The distance between the towns is large and much of this route is sparsely populated. The major towns that you pass through are Morogoro, Dodoma and finally Tabora before reaching Kigoma. The Central Railway line is the focus of this route, and it follows the old slave and caravan trail from the coast to Lake Tanganyika. The road is good only as far as Dodoma, just over a third of the distance to Kigoma.

Chalinze
Colour map 4, grid B5

Chalinze lies 100 km to the west of Dar es Salaam. A small town, essentially a truckstop, the main fuelling centre for travellers to north and south Tanzania out of Dar es Salaam. There are six fuel stations, hundreds of little bars, everyone accommodated for. It is also a big HIV centre. Chalinze is a buzzing place in the evenings, and a good place to break a journey for 30 minutes.

Morogoro

Morogoro is based at the foot of the Uluguru Mountains, which reach a height of 2,138 m. The mountains provide a spectacular backdrop to the town, and the peaks are often obscured by dramatic, swirling mists. It was here that Smuts was confident he would confront and destroy the forces of von Lettow in the First World War – only to be bitterly disappointed (see page 581).

6°50'S 37°40'E
Phone code: 023
Colour map 4, grid B5
Population: 120,000
Altitude: 500 m

Morogoro has been particularly unlucky in that the two main enterprises that were expected to provide substantial employment in the area, the Groundnut Plantation at Kongwa on the route to Dodoma (see page 502) and the state-owned Morogoro shoe factory, have been failures.

The countryside is green and fertile, and large sisal plantations predominate. The town is an important agricultural marketing centre, and fruit and vegetables from here are transported the 195 km to Dar es Salaam. The market is probably the largest in the country; it is busy, bustling and worth visiting to soak up the atmosphere.

Mikumi National Park is 100 km further down the road. Morogoro is also the largest town nearest the **Selous Game Reserve**, which lies to the south of Mikumi National Park, along the most frequently used road route. It was en route to Morogoro that Edward Sokoine, the Prime Minister, widely expected to be Nyerere's successor, was killed in a road accident in October 1984. The Agricultural University in Morogoro has been named after him.

The old German **Boma** is located to the south of the town in the foothills of the Uluguru Mountains, along Boma Road. The Ulugurus dominate Morogoro, with a range of impressive summits rising over 2,132 m. The lower slopes are densely cultivated, and the terracing is quite a feature. Higher up it is forested and there are some splintered rock bastions. Further back they rise to over 2,438 m. There are three birds endemic to the Ulugurus, the Loveridge sunbird, the black cap shrike and Mrs Moreau's warbler. The **Railway Station**, a rather utilitarian two-storey building with a bay of colonnades at the front, is not one of the most attractive German buildings. The *Savoy Hotel* was formerly the *Banhof Hotel*, also dating from the German period, but also not particularly distinguished.

Sights

At the top of Kingalu Road there is a **rock garden**, laid out around a mountain stream. It is very pretty, and there is a café.

The **War Cemetery**, south on Boma Road and then turn west, is interesting in that it records the deaths in both the German and the British and Empire Forces. There are two graves of Germans from before 1914, a postal officer and a train driver. Also here is the grave of Kannanpara John, born in Kerala, India, and the first Asian priest of the Diocese of Central Tanganyika. The involvement of the British Empire in the First World War is apparent with 49 graves for troops and support service personnel of regiments from South Africa, Gold Coast, West Africa and the British West Indies, as well as East Africa. There is a special plinth to the 'Hindus, Mohammedans and Sikhs' who died in Imperial Service. These troops were accompanied by 'followers', including their families, traders and craftsmen, and three of these – 'Jim', 'Aaron' and 'Harr' – are recorded as having died in the fighting around Morogoro. The plinth for the Germans records about 180 dead, a mixture of German officers and African soldiers of the Schuztruppe (see box page 494). The cemetery is well preserved and maintained and there are beds of pink flowers as well as an array of flamboyant orange trees.

Further along Boma Road, well into the Ulugurus, is **Morningside**. It is one of the summits above Morogoro and a relatively popular climb. The area is reminiscent of Switzerland with pretty valleys and good fishing in the mountain streams. A villa, with an ornate façade and a verandah, formerly a hotel, is situated just below the forest line. There is a road up and a communications mast at the top. Morningside is almost 10 km from the centre of Morogoro, and it is necessary for Europeans to obtain permission to visit from the District Commissioner's Office on Dar es Salaam Road, just opposite the *Acropole Hotel*.

Tanzania

Excursion to Mgeta

Colour map 4, grid B6

By *dala-dala* one can do a nice three-hour trip to Mgeta, located in the Uluguru Mountains. The road leading there is very rough, and you have to walk from time to time, but it offers excellent countryside views. However, it is advisable not to take this trip during the long rainy season as the vehicles are prone to get stuck. Mgeta is a small town where people are friendly. There is a pleasant 10-km hike to the village of **Bunduki** through a farming area. Bunduki is a hill station, surrounded by eucalyptus trees, and has trout fishing. Alternative access is via Mikumi. **Sleeping** *Mgeita Guest House*, centre of Mgeta, 200 m from the Matutu stop, US$2, rarely has water, mosquito nets, clean, one of two buildings in town with electricity, regular video shows on offer. **Eating** No restaurants, foodstalls offer chips and meat, daily market has fruit, some shops offer soft drinks and tinned food. For longer stays bring your own food from Morogoro.

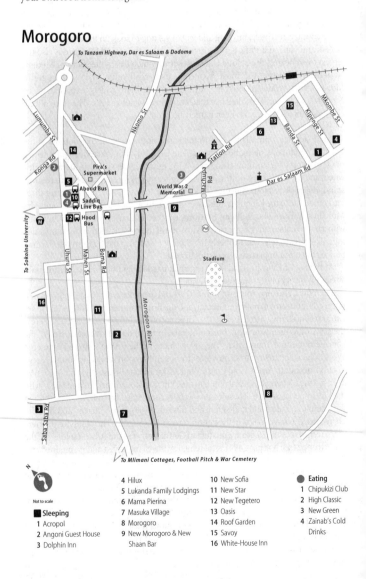

Morogoro

To Tanzam Highway, Dar es Salaam & Dodoma

Lumumba St
Nkomo St
Mkombe St
Kipenge St
Banda St
Konga Rd
Pira's Supermarket
Machupa Station Rd
Dar es Salaam Rd
Aboud Bus
World War 2 Memorial
Saddiq Line Bus
Hood Bus
To Sokoina University
Uhuru St
Mahen St
Boma Rd
Morogoro River
Stadium
Saba Saba Rd

To Mlimani Cottages, Football Pitch & War Cemetery

Not to scale

Sleeping
1 Acropol
2 Angoni Guest House
3 Dolphin Inn
4 Hilux
5 Lukanda Family Lodgings
6 Mama Pierina
7 Masuka Village
8 Morogoro
9 New Morogoro & New Shaan Bar
10 New Sofia
11 New Star
12 New Tegetero
13 Oasis
14 Roof Garden
15 Savoy
16 White-House Inn

Eating
1 Chipukizi Club
2 High Classic
3 New Green
4 Zainab's Cold Drinks

B *Acropol*, PO Box 78, Old Dar es Salaam Rd, T2603403. Bar, Greek restaurant, family-run. Is rather over-priced. **B** *Morogoro* (Bushtrekker Hotels), PO Box 1144, T2603270, 1 km from town. Comfortable accommodataion in chalet-style rooms, main buildings were previously thatched, but now the roofing has been replaced with corrugated iron sheeting, restaurant, bar, swimming pool (currently not in service), conference centre. **C** *Hilux*, along Old Dar es Salaam Rd going out of town on the left, PO Box 1915, T2603946, F2603956. Comfortable, pleasant outside beer garden at the back, restaurant, bar. **C** *Hotel Oasis*, Station Rd, PO Box 624, T2603535, F2604830, sited on the road to the station, this is the newest and smartest hotel in town, s/c, a/c, hot water, satellite TV, covered patio bar and a restaurant serving Indian, Chinese and western dishes. The price includes breakfast. **C** *Savoy*, PO Box 1086, T2603304, just opposite the railway station. This was the former *Banhof Hotel* constructed in the German period and the scene of an elaborate prank by von Lettow in the First World War (see page 581), it is now rather shabby and run by the government. Rooms are s/c with hot water and a/c but there is no restaurant or bar. **D** *Kola Hill Hotel*, PO Box 1767, T2603707, F2604394. One of the nicest hotels in rural Tanzania, set on a hill overlooking the city 3 km away, breathtaking views, well maintained, mosquito nets, hot and cold water, private bathrooms, nice restaurant serving local and international food, exceptional value. Highly recommended. **D** *Milimani Cottages*, PO Box 950, T2604873, located off the Boma Rd to the south of the town. S/c, hot water, fans, nets, comfortable rooms with bedside lamps, patio bar area has alcoves. Has satellite TV and a small general store. **D** *New Sofia*, PO Box 921, T2604847. Has a variety of rooms, some s/c, some with TV. Western toilets. Price includes continental breakfast. Good value, comfortable, small, gloomy restaurant to the rear and small patio bar at the front. **E** *Dolphin Inn*, PO Box 194, T2600004, located west of Boma Road, offers s/c rooms with squat toilets, hot water, fans, nets and a bar. The restaurant serves mostly grills and local food. **E** *Mama Pierina*, PO Box 338, T2602172, on Station Rd next to *Hotel Oasis*. This is best known for its good food, also has some comfortable cottage-style rooms, s/c, hot water, nets and fans. Recommended. **E** *Masuka Village*, PO Box 930, T2604430, on Boma Rd. The rooms are arranged in two circular courtyards, s/c, with hot water, fans, nets, restaurant and bar. Is very good value – recommended. **E** *New Tegetero*, PO Box 382, T2600195, on the main road. Has s/c rooms and a simple restaurant. **E** *Roof Garden Hotel*, PO Box 352, T2603189, T0741-530 325 (mob), sited on the road leading out of town, modern structure with balconies, s/c, hot water, western WCs, and has a restaurant with a bar through to the rear. **E** *White House Inn* PO Box 1704, T2603248. Has s/c rooms, hot water, fans, nets with breakfast included in the price. Restaurant has satellite TV, bar with banda shelters, and offers secure parking. **F** *Angoni Guest House*, PO Box 1409, T2604414, on Boma Rd. Shared rooms, squat toilets, cold water but very cheap. **F** *Lukanda Family Lodgings*, central location just off the main road. Some rooms are s/c, is rather gloomy but otherwise OK. **F** *New Morogoro*, PO Box 382, T2600195. On the site of the *Shaan Cinema*, 3rd floor, price includes breakfast. Rooms not s/c, hot water and has western toilets. **F** *New Star*, PO Box 714, situated on the Boma Rd. Has shared rooms, with no hot water, squat toilets but is very cheap.

Sleeping

Mid-range *Hotel Oasis*, on the road to the station has probably the best food in Morogoro. It has Indian, Chinese and western dishes, as well as a buffet at weekends. *Mama Pierina*, on Station Rd, is located next to *Hotel Oasis*. Comfortable establishment, that has a nice outside verandah on which to eat and drink, and quality food with a good choice on the menu. *Morogoro Hotel*, has reasonable restaurant, if perhaps a bit uninspired. *New Green*, on Station Rd, has been closed recently due to a bereavement but is expected to re-open. Indian food, good standard. 1 High Classic, PO Box 1821, T2604721. Fairly central, bright and well maintained, has satellite TV, grills, chips, omelettes, pilau and local dishes. Good value.

Cheap *Sofia Hotel*, uncomplicated but sound, cosy atmosphere. *Zainab's Cold Drinks*, centrally located, menu includes grills, snacks and, no surprise, the eponymous! Well maintained and is strongly recommended.

Eating

There are 2 **cinemas** – *Shaan* and *Sapna*. A film here, either Indian or martial arts, is an experience. There is also a **disco** or live band each Sat at the *Morogoro Hotel*, and a disco at the *Luna Hotel*. The *Hilux Hotel* shows **videos** in the garden bar. *New Shaan Bar* at the site of the

Entertainment

Tanzania

Harvest dance of the Turu

The Turu are found in central Tanzania and each year put on a dance, which is one of the most colourful and elaborate of all dances in East Africa. The dance is held to celebrate the gathering of the harvest and usually lasts about three weeks. The men and youths paint their faces and bodies and wear elaborate head-dresses. The women play only a minor role in the dance and they do not dress themselves especially for it, wearing only their normal clothes.

It is only the men and youths who actually partake in the dancing. They gather into small groups and there is competition between the groups for the best performance. A group of about a dozen individuals stand shoulder-to-shoulder facing in the same direction. To begin with there is

comparatively little movement – just a slow and rhythmic rising on their toes and contortions of the body. They all hold bows or staves, which they strike together in unison. The dance gradually builds up in intensity. At various stages of the dance groups of women and girls (about the same number as the corresponding group of men and youths) line up opposite the men and youths for a few minutes. However they do not stay long before they retire to the sidelines to be spectators throughout the rest of the dance. At intervals leaders of the groups separate themselves from the group and dance alone nearby. These leaders are usually more elaborately dressed and decorated and their dances will usually be of greater intensity than those of the groups.

Shaan Cinema, through a rather dingy arcade, is an open-air bar with bandas, and has a dart board. *Chipukizi Club*, central location, a likely local bar with a pool table, satellite TV, and barbecued food.

Shopping There is an excellent German shop in Morogoro, selling pastries, cheese cake and ice cream
There is strict of international standard. Next door there is a magnificent meat shop, stocking smoked
adherence to opening hams and cheeses. These shops are located close to the cathedral on the Dar es Salaam Rd.
times and the shops The building is easily identified as it is an all white multi-storeyed building. There is an
are closed on Sun unmade road alongside the cathedral and both shops are about 50 m down there on the left.
and Mon There may be a business connection with the church. They are open from 0930-1200 and
1400-1700 Tue-Fri, 0930-1230 Sat. *Para's Supermarket*, PO Box 61, T2604594. Central position on Lumumba St offers a wide range of items.

Transport **Air** Morogoro has an airstrip, but there are no regular flights. **Road** The 196-km road to
See pages 328 and Morogoro from **Dar es Salaam** is tarmac. There are numerous buses making the trip, and the
329 for details of train fare is around US$3. Buses leave from several locations – by the *Sofia Hotel* just of Madaraka
services, timetables St, from the bus stand on the corner of Boma and Madaraka, and on the road out of town
and fares towards Dar es Salaam. There is a good choice of buses, and it is safest (the road is busy and notorious for accidents) and most comfortable to opt for a large coach rather than a minibus. At Morogoro the road divides northwest to Dodoma and southwest to Mikumi National Park, Selous Game Reserve and then on to Iringa and, ultimately, the Zambian border.

Mikumi National Park

7°26'S 37°0'E Mikumi National Park is popular with weekend visitors as it only takes about four
Colour map 4, grid B5 hours on a good road to drive the 300 km from Dar es Salaam. From Morogoro the
Altitude: 549 m main Tanzania-Zambia road travels through well-populated cultivated land for about 100 km before reaching the boundary of the park. The national park is on both sides of the road so drive with care. The southern boundary is close to Selous Game Reserve. There is an airstrip near the park headquarters suitable for light aircraft; a flight from Dar es Salaam will take approximately 45 mins.

The park is about 10 km north of the small village of Mikumi, which has a number of cheap hotels and guesthouses. It is possible to visit the park one afternoon, stay overnight in Mikumi village and return to the park the following morning, paying the National Park entry fee of US$15 per 24 hours once. The hill station **Bunduki**, amid stands of eucalyptus, with trout fishing, can be accessed via Mikumi.

Established in 1964, Mikumi National Park is set in a horseshoe of towering mountains – the Uluguru range, which rises to 2,750 m – and covers an area of 3,230 sq km. It lies between the villages of Doma and Mikumi from which it takes its name. 'Mikumi' is the Kiswahili name for the borassus palm, a variety of palm tree found in the area. The park has an important role as an educational centre for students of ecology and conservation.

Background
The best time to visit is Sep-Dec

There is a lot of wildlife to be seen in this park including elephant, buffalo, giraffe, the famous tree-climbing lions, leopard, zebra, many sorts of antelope and over 400 bird species. Birdlife is abundant in Mikumi, and many of the birds are infrequently seen in the game parks of northern Tanzania. They include the violet turaco and the pale-billed hornbill, along with various species of storks, pelicans, herons, ibis, kestrels, kites and eagles.

Wildlife

It is well worth taking a guide for a short time when you first arrive. This isn't expensive (about US$10) compared to the other costs involved and can greatly improve chances of seeing the rarer types of game.

From the park gate the road leads to the floodplain of the Mkata River, which is particularly important for the wildlife. To the north the floodplain remains swampy throughout the year, while in the south water channels drain to the Mkata River. Here you will see, among other animals, elephant, buffalo and hippo.

Routes

About 15 km northwest of the park gate there are some hippo pools where there are almost always a number of hippos wallowing in the mud.

Other areas worth visiting are the Choga Wale area and Mwanambogo area – the latter can only be reached in the dry season. The track is to the east of the flood plain and heads north towards the Mwanambogo Dam. The Kisingura circuit is another popular drive, as is the Kikoboga area where you are likely to see elephant, particularly during December and January.

Mikumi National Park

To Morogoro

Mwanambogo Dam

Chamgore

Mkata Flood Plain

Mgeta River

Visada Circuit

Kisingura Circuit

Kikoboga

HQ
Gate
Gate

Ikoya Loop

Mkata River

To Iringa

Mikumi

N

0 km   3
0 miles   3

■ **Sleeping**
1 Mikumi Wildlife Tented Camp   ◦ Waterholes
2 Mikumi Wildlife Lodge

Tanzania

The road that goes along the river is a good one to take for viewing. It passes through a patch of woodland and some swampy areas before coming on to the grasslands of the Chamgore. Chamgore means 'place of the python' and here there are two waterholes that are always ideal for spotting game. Hill Drive leads up the foothills of the Uluguru Mountains and from here you will get wonderful views all around. The vegetation is miombo woodland and the ebony tree grows here.

To get to the south part of the park take the track that branches off opposite the park entrance, which heads towards an area called Ikoya. Here you will see sausage trees, *Kigelia africana*, with their distinctive pods hanging down. This is also where you may see leopard.

Sleeping **L** *Kikoboga*, bookings through *Oysterbay Hotel*, PO Box 2261, Dar es Salaam, T2600352-4, F2600347, oysterbay-hotel@twiga.com Formerly called *Mikumi Wildlife Camp*, 300 m off the main road, near the park headquarters. 12 thatched stone bandas, each with verandah and en-suite bathroom, some can accommodate up to 8 people, bar, restaurant, raised viewing platform, small swimming pool, games room and library, full board, game drives extra. **L** *Mikumi Safari Camp*, Foxtreks, PO Box 10270, Dar es Salaam, T2440194, T0741-237422 (mob), F0741-327706, fox@twiga.com Luxury tented camp, en-suite bathrooms, likely to become a permanent camp soon, thatched tents and a swimming pool will then follow. **L** *Mikumi Wildlife Tented Camp*, about 300 m off the main road to the right, near the park headquarters. Very comfortable, accommodates about 10 people, bar and restaurant, booking through *Oysterbay Hotel* (see *Kikoboga* above). **L** *Vuma Hill Tented Camp*, book through *Tusker Safari Ltd*, PO Box 179, Mikumi, T0741-338892 (mob), T2031650, F2031651, vuma@mail.station12.com Luxury tents with en-suite bathrooms, swimming pool.

B *Mikumi Wildlife Lodge*, book through *Blueline Enterprises*, PO Box 6550, Dar es Salaam, T0742-780330 (mob). Located down a left turning off the main road about half-way across the park, discount of 50% between Easter and end-Jun. Built of local materials on a hill 500-600 m from a waterhole, restaurant, bar, swimming pool, shop and petrol station, bathrooms need renovation. **D** *Youth Hostel*, located at park headquarters. Bookings through Chief Park Warden, Mikumi National Park, PO Box 62, Morogoro, sleeps 48 people, basic. **D** *Campsite*, about 4 km from park entrance gate. Water and firewood usually available, otherwise very basic. **E** *Genesis Hotel*, Mikumi village, rooms, camping, restaurant, secure. **E** *Mikumi Medical Centre Guest Cottages*, excellent place to stay, run by a Dutch organization who have funded the building of the guest cottages as a continuing source of income for the medical centre. Facilities include fully equipped kitchen, shower room with hot water, lounge/dining room and a number of bedrooms with fans and nets. Medical centre can be found by driving from the park entrance to Mikumi – keep going until you cross the railway and it is on the left a few hundred metres on (there are Hospital road signs by the entrance).

Camping also available at the *Southern Highland Estate*, 28 km from Mikumi.

Selous Game Reserve

Background
9° S, 38° E
Colour map 4, grid B5

This enormous reserve in south Tanzania, first established in 1922, is the largest park in Africa and the second largest in the world, covering an area of 45,000 sq km. This makes it about twice the size of Denmark. However, the size of the park is misleading in that visitors are restricted to the area north of the Rufiji River. South of the Rufiji is completely undeveloped, much heavily forested, with series of steep cliffs and forbidden to visitors. The landscape is largely open grassland and acacia woodland, cut across by slivers of riverine forest and patches of miombo woodland. The density of animals in the park is lower than that of other parks. Being here gives you the feeling of being somewhere where little has changed for hundreds of years. During a game drive you are unlikely to see any other vehicles.

Wildlife of East and Southern Africa

"Well, make up your mind", said the Ethiopian, "because I'd hate to go hunting without you, but I must if you insist on looking like a sunflower against a tarred fence."

"I'll take spots, then," said the Leopard; "but don't make 'em too vulgar-big. I wouldn't look like Giraffe – not for ever so."

"I'll make 'em with the tips of my fingers," said the Ethiopian. "There's plenty of black left on my skin still. Stand over!"

Then the Ethiopian put his five fingers close together (there was plenty of black left on his new skin still) and pressed them all over the Leopard, and wherever the five fingers touched they left five little black marks, all close together. You can see them on any leopard's skin you like, Best Beloved. Sometimes the fingers slipped and the marks got a little blurred; but if you look closely at any Leopard now you will see that there are always five spots—off five fat black finger-tips.

"Now you are a beauty!" said the Ethiopian. "You can lie out on the bare ground and look like a heap of pebbles. You can lie on the naked rocks and look like a piece of pudding-stone. You can lie out on a leafy branch and look like sunshine sifting through the leaves; and you can lie right across the centre of a path and look like nothing in particular. Think of that and purr!"

How the Leopard got his spots
Just So Stories, Rudyard Kipling

Wildlife of East and Southern Africa
Text: adapted from original version by Margaret Carswell with additional material from Sebastian Ballard. Photographs: BBC Natural History Unit Picture Library, Bruce Coleman Collection, gettyone Stone Images, Gus Malcolm.

Contents

The big nine

It is fortunate that many of the large and spectacular animals of Africa are also, on the whole, fairly common. They are often known as the "Big Five". This term was originally coined by hunters who wanted to take home trophies of their safari. Thus it was, that, in hunting parlance, the Big Five were Elephant, Black Rhino, Buffalo, Lion and Leopard. Nowadays the Hippopotamus is usually considered one of the Big Five for those who shoot with their cameras, whereas the Buffalo is far less of a 'trophy'. Also equally photogenic and worthy of being included are the Zebra, Giraffe and Cheetah. But whether they are the Big Five or the Big Nine, these are the animals that most people come to Africa to see and with the possible exception of the Leopard and the Black Rhino, you have an excellent chance of seeing them all.

■ **Common/Masai Giraffe** *Giraffa camelopardis* (top). Yellowish-buff with patchwork of brownish marks and jagged edges, usually two horns, sometimes three. Found throughout Africa in several differing subspecies. ■ **Reticulated Giraffe** *Giraffa reticulata* (right). Reddish brown coat and a network of distinct, pale, narrow lines. Found from the Tana River, Kenya, north and east into Somalia and Ethiopia. Giraffes found in East Africa have darker coloured legs and their spots are dark and of an irregular shape with a jagged outline. In southern Africa the patches tend to be much larger and have well defined outlines, although giraffes found in the desert margins of Namibia are very pale in colour and less tall – probably due to a poor diet lacking in minerals. ■ **Buffalo** *Syncerus caffer* (above). Were considered by hunters to be the most dangerous of the big game and the most difficult to track and, therefore, the biggest 'trophy'. Generally found on open plains but also at home in dense forest, they occur in most African national parks, but like the elephant, they need a large area to roam in, so they are not usually found in the smaller parks.

■ **Cheetah** *Acinonyx jubatus* (left). Often seen in family groups walking across plains or resting in the shade. The black 'tear' mark is usually obvious through binoculars. Can reach speeds of 90km per hour over short distances. Found in open, semi-arid savannah, never in forested country. Endangered in some parts of Africa but in Namibia there is believed to be the largest free-roaming population left in Africa. More commonly seen than the leopard, they are not as widespread as the lion. ■ **Lion** *Panthera leo* (below). Nearly always seen in a group and found in parks all over East and Southern Africa. ■ **Leopard** *Panthera pardus* (bottom). Found in varied habitats ranging from forest to open savannah. They are generally nocturnal, hunting at night or before the sun comes up to avoid the heat. You may see them resting during the day in the lower branches of trees.

Wildlife of East and Southern Africa

■ **Black Rhinoceros** *Syncerus caffer* (right). Long, hooked upper lip distinguishes it from White Rhino. Prefers dry bush and thorn scrub habitat and in the past they were found in mountain uplands such as the slopes of Mount Kenya. Males usually solitary. Females seen in small groups with their calves (very rarely more than four), sometimes with two generations. Mother always walks in front of offspring, unlike the White Rhino, where the mother walks behind, guiding calf with her horn. The distribution of this animal has been massively reduced by poaching and work continues to save both the Black and the White Rhino from extinction. You might be lucky and see the Black Rhino in: Etosha NP, Namibia; Ngorongoro crater, Tanzania; Masai Mara, Kenya; Kruger, Shamwari and Pilansberg NPs and private reserves like Mala Mala and Londolozi, South Africa.

■ **White Rhinoceros** *Diceros simus* (right). Square muzzle and bulkier than the Black Rhino, they are grazers rather than browsers, hence the different lip. Found in open grassland, they are more sociable and can be seen in groups of five or more. More common in Southern Africa due to a successful breeding programme in Hluhluwe/Umfolozi NP, South Africa. The park now stocks other parks in the region. ■ **Elephant** *Loxodonta africana* (above). Commonly seen, even on short safaris, throughout East and Southern Africa, though they have suffered from the activities of war and from ivory poachers. It is no longer possible to see herds of 500 or more animals but in Southern Africa there are problems of over population and culling programmes have been introduced.

Wildlife of East and Southern Africa

■ Hippopotamus *Hippopotamus amphibius* (top). Prefer shallow water, graze at night and have a strong sense of territory, which they protect aggressively. Live in large family groups known as "schools". ■ Mountain zebra *Equus zebra zebra* (above). Smallest of the three zebras shown here, with a short mane and broad stripes, it is only found in the western cape region of South Africa on hills and stony mountains. ■ Common Zebra (Burchell's) *Equus burchelli* (left). Generally, broad stripes (some with lighter shadow stripes next to the dark ones), which cross the top of the hind leg in unbroken lines. The true species is probably extinct but there are many varying subspecies found in different locations across Africa, including: Grants (found in East Africa) Selous (Malawi, Zimbabwe and Mozambique) and Chapman's (Etosha NP, Namibia, east across Southern Africa to Kruger NP). ■ Grevy's Zebra *Equus grevyi*, (bottom left) larger than the Burchell's Zebra, with narrower stripes that meet in star above hind leg, generally found north of the equator. Lives in small herds.

Wildlife of East and Southern Africa

Larger antelopes

On safari the first animals that will be seen are almost certainly antelope, on the plains. Although there are many different species, it is not difficult to distinguish between them. For identification purposes they can be divided into the larger ones which stand about 120 cm or more at the shoulder, and the smaller ones about 90 cm or less.

■ **Common** *Kobus ellipsiprymnus* and **Defassa** *Kobus defassa* **Waterbuck** 122-137cm (right). Very similar with shaggy coats and white marking on buttocks. On the Common variety, this is a clear half ring on rump and round tails; on Defassa, the ring is a filled in solid white area. Both species occur in small herds in grassy areas, often near water. Common found in East and Southern Africa, Defassa only in East.

■ **Nyala** *Tragelaphus angasi* 110cm (above). Slender frame, shaggy, dark brown coat with mauve tinge (males). Horns (male only) single open curve. As the picture shows, the female is a very different chestnut colour. Like dense bush and found close to water. Gather in herds of up to 30 but smaller groups more likely. Found across Zimbabwe and Malawi.
■ **Eland** *Taurotragus oryx* 175-183cm (right). Noticeable dewlap and shortish spiral horns (both sexes). Greyish to fawn, sometimes with rufous tinge and narrow white stripes down side of body. Occurs in groups of up to 30 in both East and Southern Africa in grassy habitats.

■ **Sable antelope** *Hippotragus niger* 140-145cm (left) and **Roan antelope** *Hippotragus equinus* 127-137cm (bottom left). Both similar shape, with ringed horns curving backwards (both sexes), longer in the Sable. Female Sables are reddish brown and can be mistaken for the Roan. Males are very dark with a white underbelly. The Roan has distinct tufts of hair at the tips of its long ears. Found in East and southern Africa (although the Sable is not found naturally in East Africa, there is a small herd in the Shimba Hills game reserve). Sable prefers wooded areas and the Roan is generally only seen near water. Both species live in herds. ■ **Gemsbok** *Oryx gazella* 122cm (below). Unmistakable, with black line down spine and black stripe between coloured body and white underparts. Horns (both sexes) straight, long and look v-shaped (seen face-on). Only found in Southern Africa, in arid, semi-desert country. Beisa Oryx occurs in East Africa.

■ **Greater Kudu** *Tragelaphus strepsiceros* 140-153cm (above). Colour varies from greyish to fawn with several white stripes on sides of the body. Horns long and spreading, with two or three twists (male only). Distinctive thick fringe of hair running from the chin down the neck. Found in fairly thick bush, sometimes in quite dry areas. Usually live in family groups of up to six, but occasionally larger herds of up to about 30. ■ **The Lesser Kudu** *Tragelaphus imberis* 99-102cm is considerably smaller, looks similar but lacks the throat fringe of the bigger animal. Has two conspicuous white patches on underside of neck. Not seen south of Tanzania.

Wildlife of East and Southern Africa

Wildlife of East and Southern Africa

■ **Brindled or Blue Wildebeest** or **Gnu** *Connochaetes tauri- nus* (right)132cm. Often seen grazing with Zebra. Found only in Southern Africa. ■ **The White bearded Wildebeest** *Connochaetes taurinus albojubatus* is generally found between central Tanzania and central Kenya and is distinguished by its white 'beard'.

■ **Hartebeest**, 3 sub-species, (right) and **Topi** (above). In the Hartebeest the horns arise from boney protuberance on the top of head and curve outwards and backwards. **Coke's Hartebeest** *Alcephalus buselaphus* 122cm, also called the **Kongoni** in Kenya, is a drab pale brown with a paler rump. **Lichtenstein's Hartebeest** *Alcephalus lichtensteinii* 127-132cm, is also fawn in general colouration, with a rufous wash over the back, dark marks on the front of the legs and often a dark patch near shoulder. The **Red Hartebeest** *Alcephalus caama* is another subspecies that occurs throughout Southern Africa, although not in Kruger NP. **Topi** *Damaliscus korrigum* 122-127cm. Very rich dark rufous, with dark patches on the tops of the legs and more ordinary looking, lyre-shaped horns.

Smaller antelopes

Wildlife of East and Southern Africa

■ **Impala** *Aepyceros melampus* 92-107cm (left). Bright rufous in colour with a white abdomen. From behind, white rump with black lines on each side is characteristic. Long lyre-shaped horns (male only). Above the heels of the hind legs is a tuft of thick black bristles (unique to Impala), easy to see as the animal runs. Black mark on the side of abdomen, just in front of the back leg. Found in herds of 15 to 20 in both East and Southern Africa.

■ **Thomson's Gazelle** *Gazella thomsonii*, 64-69cm (left) and **Grant's Gazelle** *Gazella granti* 81-99cm (above). Superficially similar Grant's, the larger of the two, has slightly longer horns (carried by both sexes in both species). Colour of both varies from bright to sandy rufous. Thomson's Gazelle can usually be distinguished by the broad black band along the side between the upperparts and abdomen, but some forms of Grant's also have this dark lateral stripe. Look for the white area on the buttocks which extends above the tail on to the rump in Grant's, but does not extend above the tail in Thomson's. Thomson's occur commonly on plains of Kenya and Tanzania in large herds. Grant's Gazelle occur on rather dry grass plains, in various forms, from Ethiopia and Somalia to Tanzania.

Wildlife of East and Southern Africa

■ **Vaal Rhebuck** *Pelea capreolus* 75cm (right). Sometimes confused with the Mountain Reedbuck where the two species coexist. The Rhebuck has a long, slender neck and a woolly coat and narrow, pointed ears. Brownish grey in colour, its underparts and the tip of its short bushy tail are slightly paler. The horns (male only) are quite distinctive: they are vertical, straight and almost parallel to each other. It lives in family groups of up to 30. They are usually found in mountainous or hilly regions where there are patches of open grasslands. ■ **Springbuck** *Antidorcas marsupialis* or Springbok, 76–84cm (below). The upper part of the body is fawn, and is separated from the white underparts by a dark brown lateral stripe. A distinguishing feature is a reddish brown stripe which runs between the base of the horns and the mouth, passing through the eye. The only gazelle found south of the Zambezi River. You no longer see giant herds, but you will see Springbuck along the roadside as you drive between Cape Town and Bloemfontein in South Africa.

■ **Steenbok** *Raphicerus campestris* 58cm (right). An even, rufous brown colour with clean white underside and white ring around eye. Small dark patch at the tip of the nose and long broad ears. The horns (male only) are slightly longer than the ears: they are sharp, have a smooth surface and curve slightly forward. Generally seen alone, prefers open plains, often found in more arid regions. A slight creature which usually runs off very quickly on being spotted. Common resident throughout Southern Africa, Tanzania and parts of Southern Kenya. ■ **Sharpe's Grysbok** *Raphicerus sharpei* 52cm (bottom). Similar in appearance to the Steenbok, but with a white speckled rufous coat. Nose dark brown, white belly. Horns (male only) are very short and sharp, rising vertically from the forehead. Prefers stony and hilly country, often seen amongst kopjies, could be confused with the klipspringer. Lives alone except during the breeding season. Often seen under low bushes, which they browse upon, looking for new shoots and any small fruits. Limited distribution in East Africa, but common along the mountainous areas of the rift valley. In South Africa you are likely to see the **Cape Grysbok**.

■ Oribi *Ourebia ourebi* 61cm (left). Slender and delicate looking with a longish neck, sandy to brownish fawn coat. Oval-shaped ears, short, straight horns with a few rings at their base (male only). Like the Reedbuck it has a patch of bare skin just below each ear. Live in small groups or as a pair. Never far from water. Found in East and Southern Africa. ■ Kirk's Dikdik, *Rhynchotragus kirkii* 36-41cm (below). So small it cannot be mistaken, it is greyish brown, often washed with rufous. Legs are thin and stick-like. Slightly elongated snout and a conspicuous tuft of hair on the top of the head. Straight, small horns (male only). Found in bush country, singly or in pairs, East Africa only.

Wildlife of East and Southern Africa

■ Bohor Reedbuck *Redunca redunca* 71-76cm (above). Horns (males only) sharply hooked forwards at the tip, distinguishing them from the Oribi (top). Reddish fawn with white underparts and short bushy tail. Live in pairs or small family groups, in East and Southern Africa. Often seen with Oribi, in bushed grassland and always near water. ■ Suni *Nesotragus moschatus* 37cm (left). Dark chestnut to grey fawn in colour with slight speckles along the back. Head and neck slightly paler with a white throat. Distinct bushy tail with a white tip. Longish horns (male only), thick, ribbed and sloping back. One of the smallest antelope, they live alone and prefer dense bush cover and reed beds in East and Southern Africa.

Wildlife of East and Southern Africa

■ **Gerenuk** *Litocranius walleri* 90-105cm (right). Disinct long neck, often stands on hind legs to browse from thorn bushes. Likes arid, semi-desert conditions. Only found in Kenya and possibly Uganda.

■ **Bushbuck** *Tragelaphus scriptus* 76-92cm (below). Shaggy coat with variable pattern of white spots and stripes on the side and back and 2 white, crescent-shaped marks on front of neck. Short horns (male only) slightly spiral. High rump gives characteristic crouch. White underside of tail is noticeable when running. Occurs in thick bush, especially near water. Either seen in pairs or singly in East and Southern Africa.

■ **Klipspringer** *Oreotragus oreotragus* 56cm (bottom right). Brownish-yellow with grey speckles. White chin and underparts, short tail. Distinctive, blunt hoof tips. Short horns (male only). Likes dry, stony hills and mountains. Found only in Southern Africa.

■ **Common (Grimm's) Duiker** *Sylvicapra grimmia* 58cm (above). Grey fawn colour with darker rump and pale colour on the underside. Dark muzzle. Prominent ears divided by straight, upright, narrow pointed horns. This particular species is the only duiker found in open grasslands. The duiker is more commonly associated with a forested environment. Common throughout Southern and East Africa, but difficult to see – it is shy and will quickly disappear into the bush.

Other mammals

Although the antelopes are undoubtedly the most numerous animals to be seen on the plains, there are many other fascinating mammals worth keeing an eye out for. The following are some of the more common mammals that you may see in East and Southern Africa.

■ **Warthog** *Phacochoerus aethiopicus* (left). Almost hairless and grey with a very large head, tusks and wart-like growths on face. Frequently occurs in family parties and when startled will run at speed with their tails held straight up in the air. Often seen near water caking themselves in the thick mud which helps to keep them both cool and free of ticks and flies. Found in both East and southern Africa.

Wildlife of East and Southern Africa

■ **African Wild Dog** or **Hunting Dog** *Lycaon pictus* (above). Easy to identify since they have all the features of a large mongrel dog: a large head and slender body. Their coat is a mixed pattern of dark shapes and white and yellow patches, no two dogs are quite alike. Very rarely seen, they are seriously threatened with extinction. Found on the open plains around dead animals, but not a scavenger. They are in fact very effective hunters, frequently working in packs. ■ **Dassie** (left, above Rock hyrax, left below Tree hyrax) *Dendrohyrax arboreus*. There are three main groups of this small, guinea-pig-like rodent: the rock hyrax, the yellow spotted hyrax and the tree hyrax. Tree hyraxes are nocturnal and feed in trees at night. They have longer fur than the rock hyrax. The rock hyrax, also nocturnal, lives in colonies amongst boulders and on rocky hillsides, protecting themselves from predators like eagle, caracal and leopard by darting into the rock crevices if alarmed. Found only in Southern Africa.

■ **Bat-eared fox** *Otocyon megalotis* (right). Distinctive large ears (used for listening for prey underneath the surface of the ground) and very short snout are unmistakeable. Greyish-brown coat with black markings on legs, ears and face. They are mainly nocturnal, but can be seen lying in the sun near their burrows during the day. Found in East and southern Africa.

■ **Civet** *Viverra civetta* (right). Yellowish-grey coarse coat with black and white markings and black rings around eyes. Nocturnal animal rarely seen and quite shy. Found in woody areas or thick bush. ■ **Black-backed Jackal** *Canis mesomelas* 45cm (bottom). Foxy reddish fawn in colour with a noticeable black area on its back. This black part is sprinkled with a silvery white which can make the back look silver in some lights. Often seen near a lion kill, they are timid creatures which can be seen by day or night.

■ **Serval** *Felis serval* 50cm (left). Narrow frame and long legs, with a small head and disproportionately large ears. Similar colouring to a cheetah, but the spots are more spread out. Generally nocturnal, they are sometimes seen in bushy areas, near rivers or marshes. Found in both East and Southern Africa. ■ **Spotted Hyena** *Crocuta crocuta* 69-91cm (below). ■ **Brown Hyena** *Hyaena brunnea* (opposite page, centre). High shoulders and low back give characteristic appearance. Spotted variety is larger, brownish with dark spots, a large head and rounded ears. The brown hyena, slightly smaller, has pointed ears and a shaggy coat, more nocturnal. Found in both East and Southern Africa.

Wildlife of East and Southern Africa

■ **Caracal** *Felis caracal* (left). Also known as the African lynx, it is twice the weight of a domestic cat, with reddish sandy colour fur and paler underparts. Distinctive black stripe from eye to nose and tufts on ears. Generally nocturnal and with similar habits to the leopard. They are not commonly seen, but are found in hilly country, sometimes in trees, in both East and Southern Africa.

Apes

Baboons

■ **Chacma** *Papio ursinus* (top). Adult male slender and can weigh 40kg. General colour is a brownish grey, with lighter undersides. Usually seen in trees, but rocks can provide sufficient protection from predators. Occur in large family troops, have a reputation for being aggressive where they have become used to man's presence. Found in East and Southern Africa. ■ **Hamadryas** *Papio hamadryas* (right). Very different from the other two species, the male being mainly ashy grey with a massive cape-like mane. The face and buttocks are bright pink, and the tail does not appear broken. Females lack the mane and are brownish in colour. ■ **Olive Baboon** *Papio anubis* (top, opposite page). A large, heavily built animal, olive brown or greyish in colour. Adult males have a well-developed mane. In the eastern part of Kenya and Tanzania, including the coast, the Olive Baboon is replaced by the Yellow Baboon *Papio cynocephalus*, smaller and lighter, with longer legs and almost no mane in adult males. The tail in both species looks as if it is broken and hangs down in a loop.

■ **Vervet** or **Green Monkey** *Cercopithicus mitis* (above). Appearance varies, most commonly has a black face framed with white across the forehead and cheeks. General colour is greyish tinged with a varying amount of yellow. Feet, hands and tip of tail are black. They live in savannah and woodlands but have proved to be highly adaptable. You might think the Vervet Monkey cute: it is not, it is vermin and in many places treated as such. They can do widespread damage to orchards and other crops. On no account encourage these creatures, they can make off with your whole picnic, including the beers, in a matter of seconds. Found in East and Southern Africa. ■ **Chimpanzee** *Pan troglodytes* (left) and the **Gorilla** *Gorilla gorilla* (centre, page 16) are not animals you will see casually in passing, you have to go and look for them. They occur only in the forests in the west of the region in Uganda, Rwanda and Zaire. In addition there are some Chimpanzee in western Tanzania.

Reptiles

■ **Blue-headed Agama** *Agama atricollis* (opposite page, top) and **Orange-headed Agama** *Agama agama* (right) up to 20cms long. Only the males have the brightly coloured head and tail. They run along walls and rocks and are frequently seen doing 'press-ups'. You will notice them around your lodge or camp site. They make lovely photos, but are not easy to approach. The Blue-headed is the most common and more widespread of the two.

■ **Monitor lizard** *Varanus niloticus* (centre and right) up to 200cm long, about half this being tail. Greyish brown in colour, with lighter markings. It stands fairly high on its legs and constantly flickers its tongue. It is fairly common and you have a good chance of seeing one, especially near water. Found in both East and Southern Africa.

■ **Crocodile** *Crocodilus niloticus* (above, hatchling). Particularly common on the Nile in Uganda, but also occurs elsewhere in East and Southern Africa. Though you might expect to find it in Lakes Edward and George, it does not occur here, but is plentiful in the other large nearby lake – Lake Albert.

■ **Green Chameleon** *Chamaeleo gracilis* (below). Well-known and colourful reptiles, there are several species of Chameleon, but this is the most common and is fairly widespread. ■ **Tree Frogs** *Hylidae*, (bottom). There are many different sorts of tree frog. They are all small amphibians which are not often seen, but occasionally one can be found half way up a door post or window frame which it has mistaken for a tree. They are usually bright green or yellow, often with pretty markings.

Water and waterside birds

Wildlife of East and Southern Africa

Africa is one of the richest bird areas in the world and you could spot over 100 species in a single day. The birds shown here are the common ones and with a little careful observation can all be identified, even though they may appear totally strange and exotic. To make identification easier, they have been grouped by habitat. Unless otherwise stated, they occur both in East and Southern Africa.

■ **Greater Flamingo** (96) *Phoenicopterus ruber* 142cms (right). The larger and paler bird of the two species found in Africa has a pink bill with a black tip. ■ **Lesser Flamingo** (97) *Phoenicopterus minor* 101cms, deeper pink all over and has a deep carmine bill with a black tip. Both occur in large numbers in the soda lakes of western Kenya.

■ **Hammerkop** (81) *Scopus umbretta* 58cms (top left). Dull brown in colour with a stout, moderately long bill. Distinctive large crest which projects straight backwards and is said to look like a hammer. A solitary bird usually seen on the ground near water – even roadside puddles. Builds an enormous nest in trees, large and strong enough to support the weight of a man. ■ **Pied Kingfisher** (428) *Ceryle rudis* 25cms (above). The only black and white kingfisher. Common all round the large lakes and also turns up at quite small bodies of water. Hovers over the water before plunging in to capture its prey. ■ **Blacksmith Plover** (258) *Vanellus armatus* 30 cms (right). Strongly contrasting black, white and grey plumage. White crown, red eye, black legs. Common resident found around the margins of lakes, both freshwater and alkaline, also close to rivers and cultivated lands. Distinct, high-pitched call which it utters when it that feels its nest or young are threatened.

■ **NB** The number in brackets after the birds' names refers to the species' 'Roberts' number, which is used for identification purposes in Southern Africa. This code is not used in East Africa, but it can still help in cases where the same species has a different local name.

■**Fish Eagle** (148) *Haliaeetus vocifer* 76cms (left). This magnificent bird has a very distinctive colour pattern. It often perches on the tops of trees, where its dazzling white head and chest are easily seen. In flight this white and the white tail contrast with the black wings. It has a wild yelping call which is usually uttered in flight. Watch the bird throwing back its head as it calls. ■**Goliath Heron** (64) *Ardea goliath* 144cms (below). Usually seen singly on mud banks and shores, both inland and on the coast. Its very large size is enough to distinguish it, but the smaller **Purple Heron** (65) *Ardea purpurea* 80cms, which frequents similar habitat and is also widespread, may be mistaken for it at a distance. If in doubt, the colour on the top of the head (rufous in the Goliath and black in the Purple) will clinch it.

Wildlife of East and Southern Africa

■**African Jacana** (240) *Actophilornis africana* 25cms (left). This is a mainly chestnut bird, almost invariably seen walking on floating leaves. Its toes are greatly elongated to allow it to do this. Its legs dangle down distinctively when in flight. Found in quiet backwaters with lily pads and other floating vegetation.

■ **Paradise Flycatcher** *Terpsiphone viridis* male 33cm, female 20cm (right). Easily identified by its very long tail and bright chestnut plumage. The head is black and bears a crest. The tail of the female is much shorter, but otherwise the sexes are similar. It is seen in wooded areas, including gardens and is usually in pairs. In certain parts, notably eastern Kenya, its plumage is often white, but it still has the black head. Sometimes birds are seen with partly white and partly chestnut plumage. ■ **Egyptian goose** (102) *Alopochen aegyptiaca* (below) 65cm. Brown to grey-brown plumage. Distinct chestnut patch around the eye and on the centre of the breast; wings appear white in flight. Red/pink legs and feet. This is a common resident found throughout the region except in arid areas. Occurs in small flocks and pairs. Most likely to be seen around the margins of inland waters, lakes, rivers, marshes, pans and cultivated fields.

■ **Crowned Crane** (208) *Balearica pavonina* 100cms (right). It cannot really be mistaken for anything else when seen on the ground. In flight the legs trail behind and the neck is extended, but the head droops down from the vertical. Overhead flocks fly in loose V-shaped formation. Not a water bird, but quite common near Lake Victoria, it also occurs in much of the rest of East Africa as well.

Birds of the open plains

■ **Ground Hornbill** (463) *Bucorvus cafer* 107cm (left). Looks very like a turkey from a distance, but close up it is very distinctive and cannot really be mistaken for anything else. They are very often seen in pairs and the male has bare red skin around the eye and on the throat. In the female this skin is red and blue. Found in open grassland.

Wildlife of East and Southern Africa

■ **Bateleur** (146) *Terathopius ecaudatus* 61cm (above). A magnificent and strange looking eagle. It is rarely seen perched, but is quite commonly seen soaring very high overhead. Its tail is so short that it sometimes appears tailless. This, its buoyant flight and the black and white pattern of its underparts make it easy to identify. ■ **Secretary Bird** (118) *Sagittarius serpentarius* 101cm (left). So called because the long plumes of its crest are supposed to resemble the old time secretaries who carried their quill pens tucked behind their ears. Often seen in pairs hunting for snakes, its main source of food.

■ **Ostrich** (1) *Struthio camelus* 2m (right). Male birds are predominantly black, while the females are usually a dusty dark brown. Found both in national parks and on open farm land. The original wild variety has been interbred with subspecies in order to improve feather quality. In South Africa the region known as the Little Karoo was once the centre of a boom during which millions of birds were kept in captivity. The Ostrich is sometimes seen singly, but also in family groups.

Wildlife of East and Southern Africa

■ **Kori Bustard** (230) *Otis kori* 80cm (top left). Like the Secretary Bird, it quarters the plains looking for snakes. Quite a different shape, however, and can be distinguished by the thick looking grey neck, caused by the loose feathers on its neck. Particularly common in Serengeti National Park and in the Mara. ■ **Red-billed Oxpecker** (772) *Buphagus erythrorhynchus* 18cm (above). Members of the starling family, they associate with game animals and cattle, spending their time clinging to the animals while they hunt for ticks. ■ **Cattle Egret, Forktailed** (71) *Bubulcus ibis* 51cm (right). Follows herds and feeds on the grasshoppers and other insects disturbed by the passing of the animals. Occasionally too, the Cattle Egret will perch on the back of a large animal, but this is quite different from the behaviour of Oxpeckers. Cattle Egrets are long legged and long billed white birds which are most often seen in small flocks. In the breeding season they develop long buff feathers on the head, chest and back.

Woodland birds

■ **Superb Starling** *Spreo superbus* 18cm (left) and **Golden-breasted Starling** *Cosmopsarus regius* 32cms (below). Both are common, but the Superb Starling is the more widespread and is seen near habitation as well as in thorn bush country. Tsavo East is probably the best place to see the Golden-breasted Starling. Look out for the long tail of the Golden-breasted Starling, and the white under tail and white breast band of the Superb Starling. Both are usually seen hopping about on the ground.

■ **Little bee-eater** (444) *Merops pusillus* 16cm (above). Bright green with a yellow throat, conspicuous black eye stripe and black tip to a square tail, lacks the elongated tail feathers found in many other species of bee-eater. Solitary by day, but at night often seen bunched in a row. Favours open woodlands, streams and areas where there are scattered bushes which can act as perches. Look out for Carmine bee-eater colonies in sandbanks along rivers. This beautiful bird is an intra-African migrant. ■ **Drongo** (541) *Dicrurus adsimilis* 24cm (left). An all black bird. It is easily identified by its forked tail, which is 'fish-tailed' at the end. Often seen sitting on bare branches, it is usually solitary.

■ **Red Bishop** (824) *Euplectes orix* 13cm (right). Brown wings and tail and noticeable scarlet feathers on its rump. Seen in long grass and cultivated areas, and often, but not invariably, near water. Almost equally brilliant is the **Blackwinged Bishop** *Euplectes hordeaceus* 14cm. Distinguished by black wings and tail and obvious red rump.
■ **Red-cheeked Cordon-bleu** *Uraeginthus benegalus* 13cm (below). Brown back and bright red cheek patches. They are seen in pairs or family parties and the females and young are somewhat duller in colour than the males. They are quite tame and you often see them round the game lodges, particularly in Kenya and parts of Uganda and Tanzania but not in Southern Africa.

■ **Red-billed Hornbill** (458) *Tockus erythrorhynchus* 45cm (above). Blackish-brown back, with a white stripe down between the wings. The wings themselves are spotted with white. The underparts are white and the bill is long, curved and mainly red. Use the tops of thorn trees as observation perches. ■ **White-crowned Shrike** (756) *Eurocephalus rueppelli* 23cm (right). Black wings, tail and eye stripe, brown back. Throat and breast white, with a distinct white crown. Always seen in small parties, making short direct flights from one vantage point to the next. Walks confidently on the ground amongst debris in the dry bush country they tend to favour. Look out for them in 'feeding parties' in acacia woodlands. Similar in appearance to the White-headed Buffalo Weaver *Dinemellia dinemelli* 23cm, though not related.

■ **Helmeted Guinea Fowl** (203) *Numida meleagris* 55cm (left). Slaty grey with white speckles throughout, bare around the head which is blue and red with a distinct horny 'casque' – the helmet. A common resident in most countries, found close to cultivated lands and open grasslands. Highly gregarious, during the day the flocks tend to forage on the ground for food; rarely do they take to flying and even then it is usually only for a short distance. At night the birds roost communally, making a tremendous din when they come together at dusk. Look out for them near water, they tend to approach the source in single file.

■ **Red-billed Francolin** (194) *Francolinus adspersu* 35cm (below). Medium sized brown bird, finely barred all over. Legs and feet red to orange, yellow eye with bare skin around it. This particular species is found throughout central and northern Namibia, Botswana and western Zimbabwe. Other similar species with only minor variations are found throughout East and Southern Africa. An annoying bird which makes itself known at dawn around campsites with a harsh cry that speeds up and then suddenly stops.

■ **D'Arnaud's Barbet** *Trachyphonus darnaudii* 15cm (above). Quite common in the dry bush country. A very spotted bird, dark with pale spots above, and pale with dark spots below. It has rather a long dark tail which is also heavily spotted. Its call and behaviour is very distinctive. A pair will sit facing each other with their tails raised over their backs and wagging from side to side and bob at each other in a duet. All the while they utter a four note call over and over again. "Do-do dee-dok". They look just like a pair of clockwork toys.

■ **Lilac-breasted Roller** (447) *Coracias caudata* 41cm (left). The brilliant blue on its wings, head and underparts is very eye-catching. Its throat and breast are a deep lilac and its tail has two elongated streamers. It is quite common in open bush country and easy to see as it perches on telegraph poles or wires, or on bare branches.

Wildlife of East and Southern Africa

Urban birds

The first birds you will see on arrival in any big city will almost certainly be the large numbers soaring overhead. Early in the morning there are few, but as the temperature rises, more and more can be seen circling high above the buildings. The following (with the possible exception of the Quelea) are often seen in either in towns or near human habitation, although you may see them elsewhere, such as arable farmland, as well.

■ **Black-headed Weaver** *Ploceus cucullatus* 18cm (right). Male has a mainly black head and throat, but the back of the head is chestnut. The underparts are bright yellow and the back and wings mottled black and greenish yellow. When the bird is perched, and seen from behind, the markings on the back form a V-shape. Often builds its colonies in bamboo clumps.

■ **Marabou Stork** (89) *Leptoptilos crumeniferus* 152cm (above, with fish eagle devouring a flamingo). Overhead, its large size, long and noticeable bill and trailing legs make it easy to identify. Although this bird is a stork it behaves like a vulture, in that it lives by scavenging.

■ **Hooded Vulture** (212) *Neophron monachus* 66cm (right). Medium size vulture, dark brown, pink head. This is one of the smallest of the vultures and is unable to compete with other vultures at a carcass. Often solitary, feeding on small scraps of carrion as well as insects and offal.

■ **Red-billed quelea** (821) *Quelea quelea* 13cm (left and below). Similar colour and markings to a common sparrow, black face and a distinct thick red bill. Widespread throughout tropical Africa, a quiet bird when alone or in pairs. Best known for their destructive abilities around harvest time. They gather into flocks of several hundreds of thousands and can wipe out a seed crop in a single day. When they reach plague proportions they are treated as such and destroyed.

■ **Scarlet-chested Sunbird** *Nectarinia senegalensis* 15cm (above). Male is a dark velvety brown colour with scarlet chest. Top of the head and the throat are iridescent green. The tail is short. One member of a large family of birds which are confusingly similar (particularly the females), rather like the weavers. Often perches on overhead wires and in parks and gardens, especially among flowers, allowing you to get a good look at it.

■ **African Pied Wagtail** (711) *Motacilla aguimp* 20cm (left). Black and white with a white band over the eye, black legs. Common where resident throughout the region. Associated with human habitation, sports fields, city parks and drains, also seen on sand bars along river beds. A very tame bird which you may be able to approach in some hotel gardens.

Wildlife of East and Southern Africa

Ins and outs

There are a number of approaches to the park. **Air** The most convenient is certainly by air and there are airstrips at all the camps – see Transport below for details. **Road** If you have your own vehicle take the Dar es Salaam-Kibiti-Mkongo road. The road to Kibiti (145 km from Dar) is tarmac for about one-third of the distance, after that the road is very poor. There are plans to tarmac the road all the way to Kibiti. Kibiti is the last place you will be able to get petrol. It is then 30 km from Kibiti to Mkongo, where a west turning will take you on to the final 75 km to **Mtemere Gate**. It will take about 7-8 hrs by road from Dar. The other road you can take is the Dar es Salaam-Morogoro-Matombo-Kisaki road, which will take you into the north section of the park – from Kisaki it is 20 km to **Matambwe Gate**. This route is a total of 350 km and will take 8-9 hrs. The road from Morogoro is rough, should only be attempted in the dry season and will require a 4WD vehicle. **Train** Take the TAZARA railway as far as Fuga, 1st class approximately US$9. From here, by prior arrangement, someone from the lodges will collect you. This may be expensive unless you get a group together to share the costs.

The best time to visit is Jul-Oct. The camps and lodges are closed at the peak of the wet season from Apr-Jun when the rains render many of the roads impassable, but check as they may stay open in drier years. Beho Beho Camp stays open all year.

The park is named after Captain Frederick Selous who was killed in action in January 1917 while scouting in the area (see box, page 499). His grave is near Beho Beho.

The game reserve has an interesting history. In the days of the slave trade the caravan routes passed through the park. It is said that the occasional mango groves that can be seen grew from the mango stones discarded from the caravans on their way to

Getting there
There are no buses to Selous and hitching is almost impossible. Because of the problem of accessibility most people go to Selous on organized safaris from Dar es Salaam, see page 358 for companies to contact

Climate

History

Tanzania

Selous Game Reserve

Related map
Selous Game Reserve
– Beho Beho,
page 500

the coast. In the early 20th century during German colonial rule some of this area was designated into game reserves but in those days big game hunting was the most significant activity. In 1910 Kaiser Wilhelm gave part of the reserve to his Kaiserin as an anniversary gift. This is how the nickname 'Shamba la Bibi', meaning 'The Woman's Field', came to be. During the First World War the area was the location of confrontation as described in William Boyd's novel *An Ice-cream War*.

Wildlife There are supposed to be over a million animals in the park, which is probably best known for its large numbers of elephant. However poaching has been an enormous problem in the past and the numbers have been reduced substantially in recent years. A very disturbing report that came out in 1988 estimated that the elephant population had fallen by 80% in Selous in just 10 years from 1977 (census estimated population at 22,852) to 1987 (population estimated at 3,673). However, more recent estimates of the numbers of elephant show an increase. Rhino have also been seriously affected and their population in Selous is estimated to have fallen from 2,500 in 1976 to fewer than 50 in 1986. Numbers are still low but thought to be increasing slowly. Other animals you may see include lions, buffalo, hippo, African wild dogs and crocodile, while over 400 species of birds have been recorded. The overall population of African wild dogs is greatly depleted in East Africa. The canines living in the Selous Game Reserve and Mikumi National Park are one of the largest-remaining, viable wild dog populations in Africa. The proximity of areas for trophy hunters exacerbates the difficulty of viewing the animals. Part of the reason for the lack of human habitation in this area is that it is infested with the tsetse (see box, page 475). For this reason using insect repellent on any exposed areas of your body is a good idea. Although sleeping sickness is rare, the flies do have a nasty bite.

Routes Much of this enormous park is without tracks and in the wet season is completely inaccessible. The best-explored area is to the north where the lodges and camps are located.

Great Rufiji River Central to the park is the Great Rufiji River. This river and its associated water system has the largest catchment area of any river in East Africa and is probably the most significant feature of the park. It rises from the south and becomes the Rufiji where the Luwegu and Mbarangandu join together. Other rivers join it and further north it swings east before it is forced through Stiegler's Gorge. At its delta, opposite Mafia Island, millions of tonnes of silt are deposited every year during the wet season. During this season it swells to such an extent that it renders much of the park inaccessible. During the dry season it subsides and the sand banks are revealed.

Stiegler's Gorge Found in the north of the reserve at the junction of the Rufiji and Ruaha rivers, Stiegler's Gorge is a 40-km, two-hour drive from Matambwe (see Beho Beho map, page 500). It is a bottleneck as the water from this huge catchment area is forced through the narrow gorge. The gorge is named after a German explorer who was killed here by an elephant in 1907. The gorge is about 7 km long, 100 m wide and deep and if you have a head for heights there is a cable car that spans it. There was a plan to build a hydro-electric dam here. This project was to be undertaken by the Rufiji Basin Development Authority (RUBADA) with Norwegian funds. However it has been put on hold and the Stiegler Gorge Safari Camp is made up of what were to be the housing facilities for the expatriate workers on the project.

Beyond the gorge the river widens out again and splits to form a number of lakes – Tagalala, Manze, Nzerakera, Siwando and Mzizima. This swampy area is home to many animals that congregate there especially when water is scarce during the dry season. In particular elephant, buffalo and, of course, hippo gather here, sometimes in large numbers. Birds that can be seen in the park are similar to those in Mikumi National Park and include herons, fish eagles, kingfishers, various waterfowl and birds of prey.

Other attractions in the park include the hot springs known simply as **Maji Moto** (hot water in Kiswahili). These are located on the eastern slopes of Kipalala Hill and

Frederick C Selous: Greatest of the White Hunters

Born in 1852 in London, the young Selous went to Rugby school. An early expedition saw Selous trek to a lake 25 km from Rugby, strip off, swim through the icy water to a small island and shin up a tree to collect eight blue heron's eggs. On returning to school he was rewarded by being made to copy out 63 lines of Virgil for each egg. Inspired by the writings of Livingstone, Selous determined to visit Africa. After toying with the idea of becoming a doctor, he travelled to South Africa in 1871, and rapidly established himself as a supreme tracker and hunter.

Hunting was tough. The rifles were heavy muzzle-loaders, and powder was carried loose in one pocket, ignition caps in another and a supply of four ounces of lead bullets in a pouch. It was not uncommon for a hunter to be knocked out of the saddle by the gun's recoil and accidents were common.

Selous killed numerous game in his early years, partly for trophies in the case of lion and rhinoceros, for ivory in the case of elephants, and anything else as meat for his party. Later he was to become more restrained, virtually giving up trophy hunting. His skills were based on absorbing the skills of African hunters and trackers, and in 1881 he published the first of a series of highly successful books on his methods and exploits, A Hunter's Wanderings in Africa. In 1887 he began a career of paid work leading safaris for wealthy clients, which culminated in a huge expedition organised for President Roosevelt in 1909. A young British diplomat in South Africa, H. Rider Haggard, based his

character Allan Quatermain on Selous and his adventures in his novel King Solomon's Mines, published in 1895.

During one visit to England, Selous took delivery of a new .450 rifle at his hotel an hour before he was due to catch the boat train from Waterloo to return to Africa. There was no time to test the sights and alignment on a rifle range, so Selous ordered a cab to stand by, flung open his bedroom window, squeezed off five shots at a chimney stack, checked that the grouping was satisfactory with his binoculars, swiftly packed the rifle and skipped down to the cab, forcing his way through a throng in the lobby, pausing only to remark that he had heard some shots on his floor, and the manager had better look into it.

By 1914, Selous, now married, had retired to Surrey and busied himself with running his own natural history museum. At the outbreak of war, despite being 63, he was determined to serve in East Africa, where he felt his skills would be useful. He joined the Legion of Frontiersmen, a colourful outfit that included French Legionnaires, a Honduran general, a handful of Texan cowboys, Russian émigrés, some music hall acrobats and a lighthouse keeper.

In January 1917, scouting in the campaign against General von Lettow Vorbeck (see page 581), he was killed by a German sniper at Behobeho on the Rufiji River. Behobeho Camp is now part of the Selous Game Reserve. In 1985, the Rugby School Natural History Society was renamed the Selous Society.

Tanzania

---

the water flows down into Lake Tagalala. You get to them by walking (with a ranger at all times) up the ravine. The water is heated deep in the earth by thermal activity and emits the strong smell of sulphur. The highest springs are the hottest, while further down they are sufficiently cool for you to be able to swim in them.

Apart from seeing Selous by road, the other popular ways are by foot and by boat. This is one of the few national parks where you are allowed to walk. All the camps can arrange a walking safari. You will normally set off early in order to avoid the worst of the midday sun when most of the animals retire for a siesta. You must be accompanied by a ranger. Animal sightings tend to be rarer on walking safaris as the animals frequently shy away from humans. However, it is very pleasant to be able to stretch your legs and get a different perspective of the country. Trekking safaris of several days are also a possibility.

Walking & boating safaris

Rufiji and Mbuyu Safari Camps can both arrange boat trips up the river Rufiji. Boat trips are a wonderful way of seeing this park.

Essentials

Sleeping

The camps, except
Beho Beho which
remains open all year,
close from Easter until
the beginning of June
because of the rains.
Selous Safari Camp
may remain closed for
longer because of its
location on the
floodplain. The
cheapest camp is
US$110 per night,
excluding park fees

L *Beho Beho*, bookings through *Oysterbay Hotel*, PO Box 2261, Dar es Salaam, T2600352-4, F2600347, oysterbay-hotel@twiga.com, or *Bay Travel*, Sovereign Court, 631 Sipson Rd, Heathrow, UB7 0JE, UK, T020-8897 9991, F8564 9867, baytravel@btinternet.com Confusingly, *Beho Beho* used to be called *Selous Safari Camp*, while the former *Mbuyuni Tented Camp* is now called *Selous Safari Camp* (see below). Expensive (US$250 per person sharing) resort on hillside overlooking the river and lakes, includes full board accommodation, and all activities – game drives and boat and walking safaris. Children under 12 years not allowed. 10 thatched stone cottages with flush toilets and open-air showers, some cottages a/c, lounge and verandah area, swimming pool. Guests of the lodge have the option of travelling to Selous in the Beho Beho Express, a private train that leaves Dar es Salaam around noon, stops to see animals along the way, and arrives at Fuga Halt towards dusk. **L** *Rufiji River Camp*, bookings through *Hippotours & Safaris Ltd*, PO Box 13824, Dar es Salaam, T2128662, T0744-267706 (mob), F2128661, hippo@twiga.com, radio call HF 5189.00 LSB. Overlooking the Rufiji River, tented camp with WCs and showers within the tents, electricity, nets, restaurant and bar, a swimming pool is planned. There are 20 tents, most have twin beds, some have doubles. Rates (US$295 single, US$470 for 2 people) are inclusive of park fees, full board accommodation and 2 excursions per day, from a choice of fishing, boat safaris, game drives or walking safaris. **L** *Sand Rivers*, just 8 cottages offering comfortable but expensive accommodation, overlooking the Sand Rivers, which is teeming with hippo and crocodiles, contact *Abercrombie & Kent*, PO Box 427, Arusha, T7803, F7003. **L** *Sable Mountain Lodge*, bookings through *A Tent with a View Safaris*, PO Box 40525, Dar es Salaam, T/F2151106, T0741-323318 (mob), tentview@intafrica Located just outside the reserve, 10 km along the road from Kisaki village, a 20-min drive from the airstrip at Matembwe. 8 stone cottages, en-suite bathrooms, solar powered lighting, full board. Swimming pool and treehouse overlooking a waterhole

Selous Game Reserve - Beho Beho

Related map
Selous Game Reserve,
page 497

Sleeping	3 Rufiji River Camp
1 Beho Beho	4 Stiegler Gorge
2 Mbuyu Safari Camp	Safari Camp
	● Ranger post

were due to be constructed in 2000, offer game drives and foot safaris. **L** ***Selous Mbega Camp***, bookings through *Baobab Village Co Ltd*, PO Box 23443, Dar es Salaam, T022-2650250, F2650251, zapoco@afsat.com, www.baobabvillage.com New tented camp just outside Mtemere Gate, full board, good varied menu and excellent service, offer game drives and half-day boat safaris and walks. **A** ***Selous Safari Camp*** (previously *Mbuyuni Tented Camp*), a luxury development with view overlooking the lakes, individual huts, WCs, showers, solar electricity and swimming pool, bookings through *Selous Safari Co*, PO Box 1192, Dar es Salaam, T2134802, F2112794, selous@twiga.com Animals wander freely in the camp during the night; the wildlife is excellent and camp visitors include elephant and hippo. Boats and fishing equipment available. **A** ***Mbuyu Safari Camp***, T022-2124897, F2111139, www.mbuyu.eastafrica.net Bookings through *Southern Tanganyika Game Safaris and Tours Ltd*, PO Box 2341, Dar es Salaam, T0742-781971 (mob) (ask for Mbuyu), F2116413 or 0741-324662, stgs@twiga.com Named after the large baobab tree that the camp is sited around, accommodates about 30 people, located on a high bank overlooking the Rufiji, luxury tented camp, all tents with hot water and shower, lovely setting, restaurant and bar. Fishing equipment, boats and Land Rovers for hire. Boat safaris, fishing excursions, walking safaris, all provided with an armed ranger and experienced guide, can be arranged from here. Specialize in overnight camps off road in the bush. **C** ***Hidden Paradise***, bookings through *Family Travel & Tour Services Ltd*, PO Box 456, Dar es Salaam, T2772215, T0744-280028 (mob), ftts@raha.com In the village of Mloka, about 7 km from Mtemere Gate, sleep on mattress in basic tent, restaurant, can organize game drives and boat safaris, US$30 each; future plans for a permanent lodge with swimming pool.

Tanzania

Camping allowed beside the bridge over the Beho Beho River a few kilometres northwest of Beho Beho itself, and at a site beside Lake Tagalala. No facilities apart from a pit latrine, so visitors need to bring everything with them, although small fires made with dead wood are permissible and rainwater can be collected nearby. Camping fees must be paid in advance at one of the gates. Further information from Chief Warden, Selous Game Reserve, PO Box 25295, Dar es Salaam, T2866064, F2861007, selousgamereserve@cats-net.com

Transport

Air There are airstrips at all the camps. The flight takes about 45 mins from Dar es Salaam (DSM), cost about US$130. *Coastal Travels Ltd* (DSM: T2117959, F2118647) have daily flights from **Zanzibar** (depart 1400) via DSM (depart 1430), leaving at 1515 for the return. On Mon, Thu and Sat a flight leaves Zanzibar at 0800 and DSM at 0830, departing at 0915 for the return via Ruaha. They can arrange flights to link with other airstrips including Mtememe (Rufiji River Camp), Siwandu (Selous Safari Camp), Beho Beho and Kiba (Sand Rivers). Some travellers have reported that the service can be chaotic, running hours late. *Zan Air Ltd* (Zanzibar: T2233768, T0742-750478 (mob), T/F2233670; DSM airport: T0742-605230 (mob)) are also meant to have scheduled flights to Selous.

Dodoma

6°8'S 35°45'E
Phone code: 026
Colour map 4, grid B4
Population: 150,000
Altitude: 1,113 m

Dodoma, the offficial capital of Tanzania, is a dry, windy and some say desolate place to choose for a capital, lying at an altitude that gives it warm days and cool nights. It is located 453 km west of Dar es Salaam.

Dodoma was formerly a small settlement of the semi-pastoral Gogo people. Caravan traders passed through the plateau and it developed into a small trading centre. It owes its growth to the Central Railway as the Germans hoped to take advantage of Dodoma as a trading and commercial centre. During the First World War Dodoma was important as a supply base and transit point. In the years after the war, two famines struck the area and an outbreak of rinderpest followed. The British administration was less keen than the Germans to develop Dodoma as the administrative centre, for its only real advantages were its central position and location on the railway line. From 1932, Cape to London flights touched down here and Dodoma received all Dar es Salaam's mail, which was then transferred by rail.

As it is located in the very centre of the country, Dodoma was designated the new capital by the former president Nyerere. However the process of transfer has never fully taken off and today only one government ministry has its permanent base in Dodoma. The area's water shortage and poor road network are important contributory factors, and thus the city functions as a capital only when parliamentary sessions are held. Besides this, and being the CCM party political headquarters, the most notable things about Dodoma are probably that it is the only wine-producing area in the country. It is also an important beef producing area and delicious roasted meat can be found in the many open bars scattered around town. A cattle market (*mnada*) takes place each Saturday on Kondoa Road, 5 km from the centre. It is an important event for many locals and is an interesting spectacle. Dodoma is a peaceful town surrounded by a large number of missions. Few tourists stay long here, although as the designated administrative centre the city is becoming fairly important for foreign businesses.

There is a ranch of 33,500 ha at nearby Kongwa, which produces beef and high quality breeding cattle. It was originally a site for the ill-fated Groundnut Scheme (see page 584). A cattle crossbreed was developed here, known as *Mpwapwa Sahiwal*. However it has not been an enormous success and has been registered as an endangered species.

Excursions
Colour map 4, grid B4

The **Kondoa Irangi Rock Paintings** These are the nearest attraction to Dodoma and are among the finest rock paintings in the world. They are located about 180 km down the Great North Road to Arusha in the Great Rift Valley. The rock paintings are a fine example of ancient art and a further reminder of the existence of ancient humanity in this part of Africa. The rock shelters were used in the later Stone Age by the Bushmanoid tribes who were mainly hunters. Many of the shelters have fantastic views over the plains for miles around. The paintings vary in quality, size, style and colour. The most important are from the pre-agriculturalist period, red pigment outlines in streaky and silhouette styles more than 3,000 years old. There are patterned designs, human and animal figures, mainly giraffe, eland and elephant, and

Dodoma

Sleeping
1 Christian Council of Tanzania Guest House
2 DM
3 Dodoma
4 Horombo Malazi Guest House
5 Ujiji Guest House

Eating
1 Aladdin's Cave
2 Food Junction

Not to scale

hunting scenes. 'Late whites' from a later period are mostly abstract finger paintings. More than 100 sites were described by Mary Leakey in the 1950s but only recently have efforts been made to preserve and promote them, and they are currently nominated for designation on the World Heritage List. At Kolowhere interesting paintings are most accessible; guides must be hired from the visitors' centre office. Other sites include Kinyasi, Pahl, Swera and Tumbelo. The closest accommodation is in Kondoa, a small town five hours by bus from Dodoma or nine hours from Arusha. The best guesthouse is **E** *New Planet*, near the bus stand, which has clean single and double rooms with basic private bathrooms.

Mount Hanang, sometimes called the forgotten mountain, East Africa's ninth highest, rising some 1,828 m above the Mangati Plain, is accessed off the road from Dodoma to Arusha, southwest of the town of Babati, northwest of Singida. See page 476.

C *Dodoma Inn*, PO Box 411, T2323204. **D** *DM Hotel*, PO Box 1326, T2321001/2, F2320416. New, comfortable hotel just off Hospital St, opposite Independence Sq. Clean rooms each with bathroom (and hot shower), TV, fan and telephone, restaurant serves European food. **D** *Dodoma*, PO Box 239, T2322991, F2324911. Double s/c rooms, old German Hotel, now extended, close to the railway station, bar, a little run down, no hot water, convenient location, very loud disco at the weekends, however the hotel has recently changed management to a private hotel company from Mwanza. **D** *Nam Hotel*, PO Box 1868, Dodoma, T2352255, F2352263. Comfortable 3-storey hotel, cold running water, private bathroom, mosquito nets and optional TV, clean restaurant serving predominantly European food, bar and restaurant are noisy at weekends, appears safe, good value. North of the centre, on the road to the airport. **D** *National Vocational Training Centre*, T2342181, F2342781. Single and double rooms with bathrooms, recently built Scandinavian style, training centre for chefs and waiters, best place to eat, has a good bar, excellent meeting rooms, fax, phones and photocopiers, own water well and hot water, 15-min walk past from the train station, next to new parliament building. **E** *Christian Council of Tanzania Guest House*, PO Box 372, T2321682, F2324352, on Fifth St, next to the cathedral. Canteen, cold showers, water supply are petrol barrels, refilled every 3-4 days, toilets very off-putting, mosquito nets, extremely basic, food not recommended. **E** *Horombo Malazi Guest House*, central and simple. **E** *Ujiji Guest House*, near the bus station.

Sleeping
The town can be very busy when parliament is in session or there is a CCM meeting, and it is wise to book ahead

All hotels serve meals to non-residents. It might have been expected that the transfer of the seat of government would have seen the emergence of some reasonable restaurants. This doesn't appear to have been the case. Tanzanians do not eat out extensively, and the diplomatic community has remained in Dar es Salaam. **Seriously cheap** *Food Junction*, new and excellent Indian restaurant, also has some western food, located just off Tandamti St. *Aladdin's Cave*, on Market St near the corner with Lindi Av. Serves delicious ice cream. Only opens in the late afternoon until evening.

Eating

NK Disco, Tembo Av. Good music with a room upstairs where you can watch kung-fu movies all night.

Entertainment

Air There is an airport at Dodoma and theoretically there are flights by *Air Tanzania*. Scheduled flights are on Mon, depart Dar es Salaam (DSM) at 0800, takes 1 hr, flight continues to Mwanza, Bukoba and then DSM. However cancellations, delays and rescheduling are a real problem. Fare is about US$100 one-way. Now that the National Assembly meets at Dodoma, the flights are often full with VIPs. On Wed there is a service from Musoma (this plane having arrived as a flight from DSM), departs 1030, arrives 1250, then continues to DSM. *Eagle Air* have a flight from DSM on Wed, departing at 0900, which then flies on to Mwanza and Bukoba. On the same day they have a late afternoon flight from Mwanza, and on Sat there is a flight from Bukoba (0900) via Mwanza, arriving at 1145. *Air Excel* (Arusha: PO Box 12731, T2501597, F2548429, T0741-510857 (mob), airexcel@ark.eoltz.com) fly from Arusha airport on Mon and Thu. Flight departs 1400, arrives 1510, continues to Ruaha and back to Dodoma, leaving again at 1725 for Arusha.

Transport
See Dar es Salaam transport, page 360, for further advice and contact details

See pages 328 and 329 for details of train services, timetables and fares

Road Bus: buses go to **Arusha** via Chalinze daily taking 12-15 hrs. They can fill up so it's advisable to book a seat a day in advance. Costs US$11. A journey to Arusha via Konoa takes 2 days on a largely unsurfaced road. The road to **Dar es Salaam** is surfaced all the way. Buses go daily, take about 7 hrs and cost about US$8. Car journey time is about 6 hrs.

Tabora

5°25'S 32°50'E
Phone code: 026
Colour map 4, grid B2
Population: 100,000

The railway continues along the old caravan trading route reaching Tabora, which was founded in 1820 by Arab slave traders and is of enormous historical interest. From 1852 Tabora was the Arab's slaving capital ('Kazeh') in Unyanyembe, the Nyamwezi Kingdom (Tanzania's second-largest tribe) with famous chieftains Mirambo and Isike. Ivory and humans were bartered in exchange for guns, beads and cloth. Its heyday was in the 1860s when 500,000 caravan porters annually passed through the town. Many trade routes converged at Tabora. The Germans realized this and constructed a fort. Isike later fought the Germans here in 1892, and the Germans captured the town in 1893.

The building of Mittelland Bahn (the Central Railway) in 1912 increased the town's importance. It fell to Belgian forces from the Congo after 10 days' fighting on 11 September 1916. Tabora was a 'railway town' by the time the British took over. Tabora School 1925 was important for nurturing future leaders including Nyerere. The explorers Burton, Speke, Livingstone and Stanley all used the town as an important base for their journeys into more remote areas. It is here that the railway divides, one line going on to Kigoma, the other north to Mwanza. For this reason people often stay a night in order to change trains.

Sights Tabora is dominated by the **Fort** (or Boma) on a hill overlooking the town built by the Germans at the turn of the century. This is southeast of the town centre along Boma Road at the junction of Boma Road and School Street. Do not take pictures as it is a military building.

Kwihara Museum This is probably one of the major attractions of Tabora. It is located about 10 km outside the town and is dedicated to Dr Livingstone. The museum is in the house that Livingstone occupied for about 10 months before setting off on the final leg of the journey in 1872 that was to be his last. He died less than

Tabora

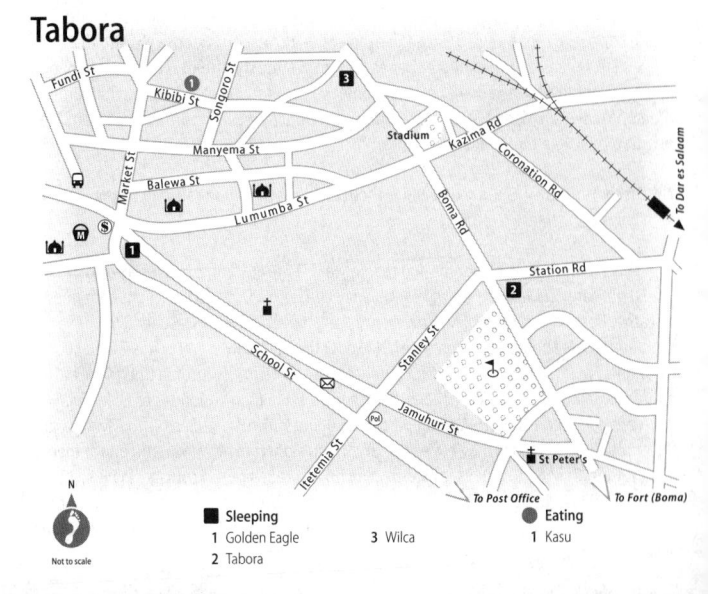

N
Not to scale

■ **Sleeping**
1 Golden Eagle
2 Tabora
3 Wilca

● **Eating**
1 Kasu

The Miombo Woodland of Tanzania

A type of woodland called miombo is found in large parts of the south, central and western part of Tanzania. One of the major towns in the heart of miombo country is Tabora. At a glance these areas appear to be ideally suited for agricultural and other development. However this area is infected with the tsetse fly (see page 475), which is a serious hindrance to settlement and so parts of it are very thinly populated.

If you are visiting miombo country around the rains it is a very colourful sight – all hues of reds, pinks and browns – and plenty of shade. However in the dry season all the leaves fall and bush fires are common. There is little shade and the slate grey bark of the trees seems to shimmer in the heat. One of the most successful economic activities in areas of miombo is the cultivation of tobacco. This has been introduced in the Urambo area and is ideal as tsetse fly make the area unsuitable for livestock.

a year later at Chitambo, Zambia. The museum, although run down, is interesting and contains various letters, maps, pictures etc associated with Livingstone, as well as other early missionaries and explorers.

B *Rafiki*, PO Box 310, T2482, town centre. **C** *Tabora* (*Railway Hotel*), PO Box 147, T2172, town centre. Hot water, bar, restaurant. **D** *Golden Eagle*, Songeya Rd, central. Reasonable value. **D** *Wilca*, Boma Rd. Comfortable and well run. **E** *The Moravian Guest House*, friendly and pleasant. **E** *YMCA*, hostel accommodation, spartan.

Sleeping

Cheap *Wilca*, simple menu but food is well prepared. **Seriously cheap** *The Mayor Hotel*, PO Box 1191, T3411, behind Market St, behind the *National Bank of Commerce*. Excellent breakfasts available.

Eating

Air There is an airport at Tabora and theoretically there are regular flights by *Air Tanzania* and *Precisionair* on the Wed and Sun DSM-Tabora-Kigoma-DSM route (see Kigoma, page 510). Fare is about US$150 one-way. *Eagle Air* have one flight that departs DSM at 0830 on Wed and Sun, arrives 1040, it returns to Tabora after going to Kigoma, and leaves at 1420 for DSM. On Wed and Sun there are also flights on the Bukoba, Mwanza, Tabora, Mwanza route. **Train** The Kigoma and Mwanza trains stop at Tabora. The railway station is 3 km outside the town. A taxi there costs US$1-2. **Road** There are no direct buses to **Mwanza**. Take the daily bus to Shinyanga and change buses there for the onward journey, but the roads are poor. Buses to **Dodoma** are scheduled daily, but a more reliable route is via Ngeza and Singida. There is a twice-weekly bus to **Mbeya**, taking roughly 24 hrs over very poor roads. The road from Tabora west to **Kigoma** is impassable in places during the rainy seasons.

Transport
See Dar es Salaam transport, page 360, for further advice and contact details See pages 328 and 329 for train timetables

The Ugalla River Game Reserve, located to the west of Tabora, is approximately 5,000 sq km. Its inaccessibility and lack of facilities mean that is rarely visited by tourists. It is located between Tabora and Lake Rukwa, approximately 100 km north east of Mpanda, well off the beaten track. It consists of miomba woodlands, and is home to the rare Sable antelope, lion, leopard and cheetah, elephant, buffalo and waterbuck. West of the Ugalla River there are chimpanzees living in the riverine forests. There is abundant birdlife with over 300 different species recorded, including the pygmy goose, various herons and the glossy ibis. If you do manage to get there be aware that there are no tourist facilities and visitors must bring all their own supplies and be prepared to be totally self-sufficient.

Ugalla River Game Reserve
6° 30′ S, 32° E
Colour map 4, grid B2

Tanzania

Shinyanga

3°45'S 33°27'E
Phone code: 028
Colour map 4, grid A3

Mosquitos are a major problem here – the region is known for having drug-resistant malaria strains. Report unusual symptoms to a doctor immediately

Shinyanga is a large, sprawling town with buildings and roads in poor condition, mostly built in the 1940s and 1950s when the area was thriving on gold, diamonds and cotton. During that time a large number of Europeans lived here and many vets from the UK were employed at a research station involved in eradicating rinderpest.

The region is known for its cattle production and African dew-lapped cows can be seen everywhere. Some gold is found in the area and mined in open-cast pits with the ore broken in large mortar and pestles. Much cotton grows in the region and is brought to the area's ginneries for processing. Rice is also grown and just outside town are several large, circular covered stores where the surplus is kept to be distributed in the event of crop failure. The area has been deforested, the timber being used for firewood and now the region is hot, dry and dusty.

The inhabitants are very friendly and there is no problem walking around, especially in the day time. Education has always been very important in Shinyanga and now there is a large college on the road to Kamborage Stadium. There is a sizeable Indian community and also many Africans of Arab descent, hence the large number of Muslims.

There are no large shops, but a great number of stores selling only a few items, many with a dressmaker and sewing machine outside. Every day there is a busy market selling just about everything.

Electricity and water supply is unreliable and when there is water (not every day) it is so muddy it has to be filtered as well as boiled. The water treatment works built by the Germans in the mid-1980s is no longer in use.

Shinyanga has a large number of Marabou storks and during the breeding season these huge birds have nests on most of the acacia trees in town. During the heat of the day the adult birds shade the young with their vast wings. Kites frequently swoop down to pick something off the road, and Shinyanga has many other birds of all types and sizes.

Sights

Kamborage Stadium is where soccer matches are played – football is a very popular pastime in Shinyanga with more pitches in the town.

Further along the road to Mwanza can be seen a large white meat processing factory that has never been used and cattle are still transported live by rail to Dar es Salaam. There is a left turning, which takes you through a sisal lined village of thatched mud huts towards a large kopje (a hill) and the remains of a **zoo,** the only inhabitant left is a huge crocodile. The café and bar are now no longer used, but this area makes a most attractive place to walk particularly when the many flamboyant trees are in flower – here also can be seen small ebony trees, the wood used for cooking before they get much chance to grow.

Beside the zoo is the reservoir serving the region, **Lake Ningwa,** and local lads can often be seen catching small fish. It is also a popular place for migrating waterfowl.

Another 15-20 minutes along the road to the southeast of Shinyanga, on the right you come to a turning for **Mwadui Mine,** where there is a tree lined road leading up to the compound. In the 1960s it was a flourishing diamond mine with its own hospital, churches, supermarket and schools, and a considerable number of Europeans were employed. A Dakota flew weekly to Nairobi from the on-site airstrip for

Shinyanga

To Old Shinyanga
To Mwanza
Catholic
Cinema
Kamborage Stadium
African Inland
To Nzega

N

0 metres 50
0 yards 50

■ Sleeping
1 Butiama
2 Shinyanga

Shinyanga witches

In the two-year period up to October 1999 it was reported that 168 women and 17 men had been killed after being accused of witchcraft. Most of these had been elderly people.

Some of the killings have been attributed to polygamous males moving on to younger wives and using accusations of witchcraft to incite vigilantes to kill their elderly spouses. Sometimes the motive is acquisition of property owned by the elderly. Finally, there are the irresponsible activities of soothsayers. Consultations ask for the soothsayers to identify enemies, who are accused of perpetrating evil spells against the client. Over half the population of Shinyanga follow traditional religions that recognize witchcraft and condone the killings.

The situation is complicated by the activities of a local enforcement group known as SunguSungu. Their founder decreed that they should go about their work bare-chested, and this rules out the participation of women. SunguSungu claim to apprehend the perpetrators of witchcraft killings, extracting confessions by beatings. When SunguSungu thugs are handed over to the police, it has been difficult to secure prosecutions because people are unwilling to testify as they fear reprisals from the witch-killers and their families.

The police say that more secure dwellings need to be provided for the elderly and that they should live with their families and not alone, as has been the custom in Shinyanga region.

shopping trips. The same Dakota still flies to Dar es Salaam and onward to South Africa, with diamonds.

The Mwadui diamondiferous kimberlite pipe was one of the largest in the world. A combination of flooding and exhaustion of the ore reserves have led to a reduction in the output. The most famous stone mined here was the 'Williamson pink' diamond found in October 1947, given to Princess Elizabeth as a wedding gift. It weighed 23.6 carats after cutting and polishing, and was a beautiful rose colour.

The Williamson diamond mine is part-owned by the Tanzanian Government (30%) and De Beers (70%), who are refurbishing the mine, but only industrial diamonds are now found. The mine covers a huge area and sometimes it is possible to get a permit to look around. During the mine's heyday there was a **Yacht Club** a few miles away on the other side of the main road; it is still a most attractive red-tiled clubhouse set in lovely shrubbed gardens, but all is now neglected. The small area of water on which the club is located, **Lake Songwa**, no longer has sailing boats.

Shinyanga has attracted an unenviable reputation for its appalling treatment of elderly women in the district. Years of cooking over cow dung open fires have caused many of the women to develop red, inflamed eyes. This feature has been interpreted as a sign that the elderly person is a witch, allegedly responsible for all manner of ills from crop failures, ill-health or other misfortunes. In recent years, many elderly women have been killed, usually by machete blows to their heads, but their possessions left untouched.

Many people dig up their own land in areas close to the Mwadui Mine in the hope of discovering the precious stones. The Sukuma people of this region have always strongly believed in the power of witchcraft. Offerings of grain and domestic animals are made on the advice of the witch doctors to enhance their chances of successful prospecting. Another theory is that the reason these poor women are killed is as human sacrifices, offered up to bring good luck to people prospecting for diamonds and gold.

Leaving Shinyanga going south to Nzega, across the railway lines, you shortly come to a brightly painted **Catholic church** and small hospital on the right. This road has a lot of use, with lorries bringing cattle and cotton to Shinyanga station and many heavy vehicles and car transporters travelling onward to Dar es Salaam via Nzega. It is deep sand during the dry season and becomes very sticky with the rains.

Within a few kilometres houses give way to plains and baobab trees, to the left is a vast open area and the smoke of the engine at **Manonga Ginnery** in Chomachankula village can be seen way off in the distance with large blue hazy hills behind. Large eagles can be seen on the plains around here; they feed on some of the many snakes. Further along the main road is a strange sight – an **oasis** with a group of palms providing Shinyanga with a good supply of dates. The baobabs have a crop of heavy seed pods, which the children harvest to sell in the market. They are popular, with a taste similar to sherbet.

Further on is a large area used as paddy fields during the rains and often oxen can be seen here working. Away to the left on the plains is the main **gold region** where settlements have sprung up, having the atmosphere of gold rush towns.

Sleeping **B** *Mwoleka*, en-suite facilities, it is clean, has quite good food and a locked compound for vehicles. **C** *Shinyanga* is being refurbished and may now be serving food, bedrooms are en suite, noisy as close to railway. **C** *Three Stars*, rooms en-suite and passable food, vehicle parking is in the street but beside the railway and so quite noisy. **D** *Butiama*, north of the post office. Bar, serves food. **D** *Safari*, fairly central, modest standard.

Eating **Cheap** *Green View Bar*, on road to Mwanza. Serves charcoaled chicken in the evening and
Poor water – use is a most attractive place with lots of shrubs, seating is in thatched rondavels, Masoi, the
boiled water even owner, makes customers welcome, to one side of the road leading to the bar there is a foot-
for cleaning teeth ball pitch used by the locals and most evenings the teams of shirts versus no-shirts can be seen playing. *Mama Shitta's Café*, in the centre of town. Serves the best African food to be found anywhere, especially if a booking is made in advance, local dishes cooked over charcoal – beef, roast potatoes with crispy onions, rice, many vegetables, wonderful value, cold sodas are available and the staff will bring back cold beer from the nearby bar.

Transport **Air** A grass airstrip is a few kilometres out of town toward Mwanza. When the cows are
See Dar es Salaam shooed off, a joint *Air Tanzania/Precisionair* flight departs Dar es Salaam (DSM) 0730 and
transport, page 360, lands at 0920. *Precisionair* also fly from Shinyanga at 1230 on Sun to Kilimanjaro International
for further advice Airport, taking 90 mins; the return flight departs at 1425. *Eagle Air* are scheduled to fly here
and contact details from DSM, depart 0830, arrive 1030, continues to Mwanza and eventually back to DSM at 1420. More commonly a plane lands to bring missionaries to or from nearby *Kolondoto Hospital* and sometimes it is possible to get a seat to Mwanza or Nairobi. It is also occasionally possible to get a seat on the Mwadui Mine plane to DSM. **Road** Shinyanga is 162 km from Mwanza, but as the roads are so bad in this region most people speak of time taken for a journey and not distance. When the road has been graded Shinyanga/Mwanza can be driven by car in just over 2½ hrs but 4 more hours can be added to this time during the rains. There are a great number of buses in every direction daily. **Train** The rolling stock is in poor condition, the concertina between carriages long gone and the external doors swing open and shut disconcertingly during journeys. The staff are polite and helpful. Much freight, cotton bales and cows are loaded at Shinyanga station. See pages 328 and 329 for train services, timetables and fares.

Directory **Medical services** On the main Shinyanga/Mwanza road about 20 mins out of town is **Kalandoto Hospital**, run by the African Inland Church, T28627. Several American doctors and nurses work here, some for over 30 years. It is the best place to go if taken ill in the region. The state-run **Shinyanga Hospital** is in the centre of town, T2235/6.

Kigoma

4°55′S 29°36′E Kigoma is a small, sleepy town on the edge of Lake Tanganyika 1,254 km west of Dar
Phone code: 028 es Salaam. It has one main road that is tree-lined. Most people come here on their
Colour map 4, grid B1 way to Burundi or Zambia across the lake on the steamer *MV Liemba* or else on their
Population: 80,000 way to **Gombe Stream National Park** (see page 512). The **Mahale Mountains**
Altitude: 800 m **National Park**, also famous for chimpanzees, lies to the south of Kigoma but is very remote and is accessed most easily by boat on Lake Tanganyika (see page 514).

The **railway station**, the terminal point of the line from Dar es Salaam, has been marked by the German colonialists by a very imposing building. While here, it is well

The graveyard at Kigoma

At the graveyard at the top of the hill at Kigoma there are three gravestones dating back to the late 19th century. Two of them belong to members of the London Missionary Society (LMS) – Rev J B Thompson and Rev A W Dodgshun.

The LMS had sent an expedition of four ministers and two laymen to establish a mission on the shores of Lake Tanganyika under the leadership of Rev Roger Price. Following the death of the bullocks used to carry their equipment inland – they were struck down by tsetse fly – Price returned to the coast to try to persuade the missionary authorities to establish a string of mission stations along the road heading into the interior. The expedition that continued on to the Lake divided into two, with Thompson – who had had seven years' experience as a missionary in Matabaleland – taking the forward party and Dodgshun, who had only recently left training, following on behind.

The advance party reached Ujiji on 23 August 1878. Thompson, who had been seriously ill during the early part of the journey, again fell ill and he died on 22 September. Meanwhile Dodgshun was having many problems of his own and did not reach Ujiji until 27 March 1879, by which time he was very unwell. He died just one week later on 3 April.

A third gravestone belongs to Michel Alexandre de Baize (known as Abbe de Baize), who had gone out to Africa under the auspices of the French government. He was a young man, with no experience of Africa or of exploration. He had been generously equipped with a large sum of money by the French government and had a huge array of supplies and equipment, including such things as rockets, fireworks, coats of armour and a barrel organ. He planned to travel across Africa from east to west and set off from Bagamoyo with a small army of about 800 men. However, he was beset by troubles. He was attacked at night, many of his porters deserted, leading to much of his equipment having to be abandoned, and many of his supplies were stolen.

When he reached Ujiji he apparently became upset that the White Fathers failed to come out to greet him. He is said to have paraded Ujiji firing his revolver. He received assistance from the LMS before setting off for the north shores of Lake Tanganyika. During that stretch of the journey he offended a local chief and set fire to a number of huts and had to be rescued by the LMS at Ugaha. He then fell ill and the LMS again came to his aid. When he was well enough he returned to Ujiji where he again fell ill. He died on 12 December 1879.

The LMS finally abandoned their station at Ujiji in 1884. The graveyard has fallen into disrepair. It is difficult to find. Walk in the direction of Ujiji, after the CCM building turn to the right.

Tanzania

worth making a trip to **Ujiji**, which is 10 km south of Kigoma (see page 512). The major industry is fishing. This is mostly done by night with pressurized paraffin lamps mounted on the rear of the boat over the water to attract the fish. The sight of hundreds of flickering lamps bobbing up and down and reflected in the lake waters is really quite a spectacle. There are a large number of refugee camps close to Kigoma following the unrest in RD Congo, Burundi and Rwanda. The **fishing villages** south of the town are charming and merit a visit (half-day walk).

Kitwe Point Sanctuary, 5 km south of Kigoma on a small peninsula, is a small chimpanzee sanctuary established in 1995 to accommodate six orphaned primates that were living in a cage behind the *Aqua Lodge Hotel*. Not all the chimps survived the move, but their welfare is being monitored by workers from the Gombe Stream National Park.

Fossilized fish remains in the extensive sedimentary deposits of Lake Tanganyika are currently being examined as part of the **Nyanza Project** in Kigoma. Lake Tanganyika is considered to be an evolutionary 'hot spot' due to its lengthy, complex geological history. Over 1,500 species of animals and plants have been identified in this biologically diverse lake. Cichlid fish, gastropods and crustaceans account for most of the endemic species.

Tanzania

☞ MV Liemba

The steamer Liemba, originally named Gotzen, was built in Germany in 1913 and transported at great expense to Kigoma where it was reconstructed. Its first trial runs took place in June 1915 and average speeds of around 8 knots were reached. It was the flagship of the German flotilla on Lake Tanganyika and was used during the First World War as armed transport, particularly to carry troops down the lake from Kigoma to Kasanga. The Gotzen was the largest ship on the lake at this time and could carry about 900 men in a quarter of the time that it took the dhows to do the same journey. In June

1916 the Gotzen was attacked by Belgian aeroplanes but was not too seriously damaged. In July of the same year, when the railway to Kigoma was captured, the Germans scuttled her.

After the war, the Gotzen was raised from the deeps and refitted. On 16 May 1927 the ship was rechristened Liemba, the name by which Lake Tanganyika had originally been known by local people, and in trials that month managed an average speed of 8.5 knots – not bad for a ship that had spent from 26 July 1916 to 16 March 1924 at the bottom of the lake. It is still in operation today!

Sleeping **B** *Kigoma Hilltop Hotel*, PO Box 1160, Kigoma, T2804435-7, F2804434, or through Dar es Salaam: PO Box 19746, T2337181, F2113518, www.kigoma.com Luxurious resort on headland overlooking the lake. 30 a/c cottages with colonial-style furnishings, en-suite bathroom, TV, fridge and balcony, suites also available, restaurant and buffet restaurant, swimming pool, gym, tennis, watersports facilities for jet-skiing, water-skiing, snorkelling, parasailing and fishing. Also operate as a tour company: 3-8-day tours to Gombe Stream (at least US$250 per person) and Mahale Mountains (from US$1000) NPs by speedboat. **C** *Aqua Lodge*, on lake shore. Comfortable. **D** *Lake Tanganyika View Hotel* (previously called the *Railway Hotel*), T64, accepts payment in TSh, overlooking the lake, beautiful views, very clean, 24-hr water, toilet and shower in room, price includes breakfast, has a bar and restaurant, will arrange private boat trips to Gombe Stream or Mahale Mountains NPs, nice lake-shore walk road south, past the power station and local prison that resembles a medieval fort, hotel holds a disco on Sat. **E** *Mwanga Guest House*, PO Box 57, T88, town centre. **F** *Community Hostel*, near the post office, basic, friendly and helpful, particularly if you want to get to Gombe Stream NP. **F** *Kigoma*, town centre. Spacious rooms, good value, bucket shower, laundry facilities, no mosquito nets, serves reasonable food and has a noisy bar, very basic, suspect mattresses. **F** *Lake View*, town centre. Boasts a working shower and toilet system. **F** *Mapinduzi*, very basic, doubles only.

Eating

Lots of restaurants opposite the station serve cheap local food

Mid-range *Lake Tanganyika View Hotel*, previously called the *Railway Hotel*, good. **Cheap** *Kigoma Hotel*, adequate, if a little uninspired. *Lake View*, simple but good value meals. **Seriously cheap** *Ally's*, along Ujiji Rd going east. Quite reasonable. Closed during the month of Ramadan.

Transport

See Dar es Salaam transport, page 360, for further advice and contact details
See pages 328/329 for details of train services, timetables and fares

Air Flights to Kigoma from Dar es Salaam (DSM) are costly at over US$200 one-way. Theoretically there are Wed and Sun flights by a joint *Air Tanzania/Precisionair* service that continue to Tabora and back to DSM. However cancellations, delays and rescheduling are common. *Air Tanzania* run a minibus from their office by the roundabout to the airport. *Precisionair* also operate a 0730 flight from DSM to Kigoma via Tabora, arriving in Kigoma at 1050, then returning to

Kigoma

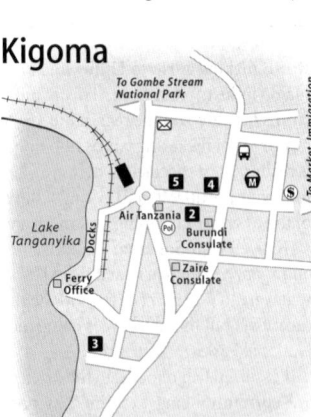

Sleeping
1 Aqua
2 Kigoma
3 Lake Tanganyika View
4 Lake View
5 Mapindezi

Not to scale

Dr Livingstone

David Livingstone was born on 19 March 1813 in Blantyre in Scotland. He had a strict Scottish upbringing, and his first job was in a factory. He studied during the evenings and at the age of 27 finally qualified as a doctor. In 1840 he joined the London Missionary Society, was ordained in the same year and set off for Africa. On the voyage out he learnt to use quadrants and other navigational and mapping instruments, which were to prove vital skills during his exploring of uncharted parts of Africa. In 1841 he arrived in South Africa and journeyed north from the mission in the search for converts.

In his first few years as a missionary Livingstone gained a reputation as a surveyor and scientist. His first major expedition into the African interior came in 1853, lasted three years, and included in 1855 the discovery of the Victoria Falls. When he returned to England in 1856 he was greeted as a national hero, was awarded a gold medal by the Royal Geographical Society, and made a Freeman of the City of London.

He returned to Africa in 1858 and began his quest for the source of the Nile in 1866. This trip was funded by a grant from the British government, which enabled Livingstone to be better equipped than during his previous expedition. During this journey little was heard of him and rumours reached Britain of his apparent death. Henry Morton Stanley, a newspaper reporter for the New York Herald, was sent by James Gordon Bennett, his publisher, to find Livingstone. On 1871 Stanley found Livingstone's camp at Ujiji, a small town on the shores of Lake Tanganyika, greeting him with the now legendary, 'Dr Livingstone, I presume?' At the time of the meeting Livingstone had run short of supplies, in particular quinine, which was vital in protecting him and his companions from malaria.

Livingstone set out on his last trip from near Tabora in Tanzania and continued his explorations until his death at Chitambo in what is now Zambia. His heart was buried at the spot where he died, his body embalmed and taken by Susi and Chumah, his two servants, to Bagamoyo (see page 372) from where it was shipped back to England. He was buried at Westminster Abbey and a memorial was erected at Chitambo.

DSM. *Eagle Air* have one flight from DSM (departs 0830) via Tabora on a Wed and Sun, while *Precisionair* do the same route on Tue, Thu and Sun. **Road** There are local buses to **Kasulu** and **Ujiji**, but no long-distance services. Buses leave from outside the railway station. **Train** The journey from Kigoma to Dar es Salaam is 1,254 km and it takes about 36 hrs although it may be worth getting off at Morogoro and doing the last stretch by road, saving a few hours. The difference between 1st and 2nd class is that in 1st class there are only 2 beds in the compartment. In 2nd class there are 6 beds, and men and women are separated unless you book the whole carriage. It is easy to buy fruit and small meals in the stations along the way. There is also a reasonable restaurant car, which offers beef or chicken with rice or chips for US$3, and warm drinks including beer; book ahead if at all possible. Local people fear theft on the train, especially at stations. The women frequently lock themselves inside their compartment and don't go out at night. Police ride on the train.

Lake **Ferry**: the ferry on Lake Tanganyika is the *MV Liemba*. The *MV Liemba* leaves at 1600 on Wed for **Mpulungu** (Zambia), arriving there on Fri morning. It stops at lots of small ports on the way. If travelling to **Mbeya**, and wanting to remain in Tanzania, it may be worth dis-embarking at **Kasanga**, at **Kipili** (journey time 24 hrs) or at the town of **Kirando** just north of Kipili. Kirando may be preferable to Kipili because you arrrive while there is still daylight, there is no port but small boats take passengers to the shore for approximately US$0.60. Buses to **Sumbawanga** will be waiting. The ferry reaches **Kasanga** the next morning. Kigoma-Kipili 1st class US$35, 2nd class US$30, 3rd class US$23; Kigoma-Kasanga 1st class US$50, 2nd class US$40, 3rd class US$31; Kigoma-Mpulunga (Zambia) 1st class US$50, 2nd class US$40, 3rd class US$35; Kigoma-Bujumbura (Burundi) 1st class US$25, 2nd class US$20, 3rd class US$15. Plus US$5 port tax. Journey described by travellers as 'quite a hairy affair', can be very crowded and rowdy at times. The return to Kigoma is at 1600 on Fri, arriving Sun morning in Kigoma, a 40-hr journey. 3rd class are benches or deck space, 2nd class cabins are small, hot and stuffy with 4 or 6 bunks. 1st class cabins have 2 bunks, a window, fan. Meals and drinks are available on the ferry and are paid for in Tanzanian shillings.

Gombe Stream National Park (see page 512) can be reached by lake taxis (small boats with an outboard motor), which are hired at Kigoma (ask around for the best price). The journey takes about 3 hrs. A passenger boat heads north from Kibirizi at around 1500 and a trip to Gombe will cost approximately US$1.25. The boat returns the next day, passing Gombe at about 0730. You can get to Kibirizi by walking north along the railway track from Kigoma; any hotel should be able to provide further details.

Directory **Banks** *National Commercial Bank* is next to the market. **Communications Post**: Post office is about 500 m to the north of the main roundabout past the *Caltex* station. **Embassies and consulates** The **Burundi Consulate** is just off the main street and the **RD Congo Consulate** is next door to the police station. **Medical services** Maweni Hospital, T2802671, is a kilometre or so down the road towards Ujiji. **Useful addresses** The **Mahale Mountains Wildlife Research Centre** has an office in Kigoma where you can ask about transport to the park and accommodation availability there.

Ujiji

This small market village 10 km south of Kigoma has a thriving boat-building industry. It used to be the terminus for the old caravan route from the coast and the resulting Arab influence is clear to see. The houses are typical of the coastal Swahili architecture and the population is mainly Muslim. It is however most famous for being the place where the words 'Dr Livingstone, I presume' were spoken by Henry Morton Stanley. The site where this is thought to have occurred is marked by a plaque, between the town and the shore, on Livingstone Street. There are also two mango trees that are supposed to have been grafted from the one under which they met.

The post office on Kigoma Road is a substantial structure dating from the German period. Further south on Kigoma Road, past the hospital, is the **White Fathers' Mission**.

Sleeping and eating **E** *Matanda Guest House* is plain and cheap. There are several other small guesthouses and eating places on Kigoma Rd between Livingstone St and the post office.

Transport **Bus**: regular buses to and from Kigoma. The bus station is next to the market on Mnazi Moja St.

Gombe Stream National Park

4°38'S 31°40'E
Colour map 4, grid B1

Gombe Stream National Park is about 16 km north from Kigoma and can only be reached by boat from there. The major attraction of the park are the chimpanzees that were made famous by Jane Goodall.

Ins & outs
The park can be visited all the year around

Getting there You can get a boat fairly easily. They normally leave Kigoma around 0800 and the trip takes about 3 hrs and costs about US$3. They return to Kigoma at around 1700. They do not run on Sunday. The boats continue to Banda, on the border of Burundi, so you can approach the park from both ways. A hired taxi boat from Kigoma will cost at least US$60 for the trip – be prepared to barter. However, the local taxis are reluctant or refuse to return to Kigoma from Gombe in the afternoon. You can also arrange a tour from *Kigoma Hilltop Hotel*, see page 510.

Park information The main purpose of the park is research rather than tourism and the facilities there are minimal. The park headquarters is located at Kasekela. The entrance fee is US$100 per person per 24-hour period. Obligatory guide US$10 per trip.

In 1960 Jane Goodall set up the area as a chimpanzee research station. She wrote a book on the findings of her research called *In the Shadow of Man*. Her work was later filmed by Hugo van Lawick, the wildlife photographer. This attracted much publicity to the reserve and in 1968 the Gombe Stream National Park was established. It covers an area of 52 sq km, making it the smallest park in Tanzania. It is made up of a narrow, mountainous strip of land about 16 km long and 5 km wide that borders Lake Tanganyika. The mountains, which rise steeply from the lake to a height of 681-1,500 m, are intersected by steep valleys, which have streams running in them and are covered in thick gallery forest (that is, the river banks are wooded, but beyond is open country).

Background
As chimpanzees can catch many of our diseases, you will not be allowed to visit Gombe if you have a cold or any other infectious illness

There are approximately 200 chimpanzees in the park divided into three family troupes. They each mark and guard their territory fiercely. One of the groups often goes down to the research station so you can observe them from there. Alternatively there are a number of observation points around the park and the wardens usually know where to go to see them. However there is no guarantee that you will see the chimpanzees during your visit. They are less visible here than at Kibale Forest in western Uganda. Other primates include red tailed and blue colobus monkeys. Birdlife is prolific in the park and includes various barbets, starlings, sunbirds, kingfishers, the palm-nut vulture and the Rufous-bellied heron.

Wildlife

Gombe Stream National Park

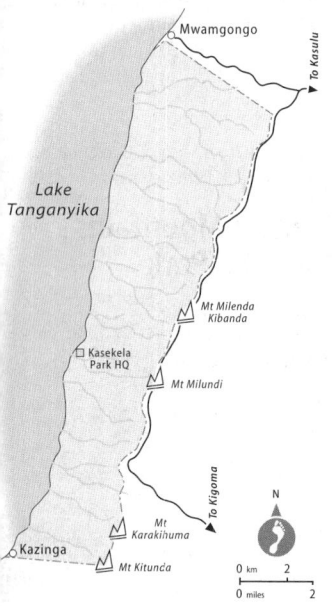

It is compulsory to take a guide with you into the forest. From the guesthouse there is a trail leading up to the research station about 2 km away and a lovely waterfall a bit further on. If there are no chimps at the station itself you will have to ask one of the guides to take you into the forest to try and track them down. It can be hard, slippery walking up and down the valleys through the forest. Another route you can take (which does not require a guide) is along the lake shore.

Routes

There is a *hostel* that sleeps about 15 people. It is advisable to book ahead in Kigoma. Beds and mattresses are provided but all cooking equipment and food should be brought with you from Kigoma. The Tanzania National Parks Authority (TANAPA) operate simple lodges and guesthouses, bookings: PO Box 3134, Arusha, T/F027-2548216, tanapa@habari.co.tz Camping is allowed with permission – in fact the park is becoming so popular that it is a good idea to have your own tent and stove.

Sleeping

Mahale Mountains National Park

Colour map 4, grid B1

This is another chimpanzee sanctuary established in 1985 as a national park covering an area of 1,577 sq km, and lying at an altitude of over 1,800 m. Mahale has five times the number of chimps of Gombe Stream. The highest peak reaches 2,460 m and the prevailing winds from over the lake, when forced up to this level, condense and ensure a high rainfall.

Ins & outs

The best time to visit is May-Sep during the drier months

Getting there There is no main road to the park although there is a track of sorts. The easiest way to get to the park is by boat from Kigoma, a distance of approximately 170 km. There are no roads in the park so you will have to walk. It is very remote and difficult to get to and for this reason is visited by few tourists. Entrance fee: US$100 per person per 24-hr period. Obligatory guide US$10 per trip.

Wildlife The park is largely made up of montane forests and grasslands and some alpine bamboo. The eastern side of the mountains is drier, being in the rain shadow, and the vegetation there is the drier miombo woodland (see box, page 505), which is found over much of west Tanzania and east RD Congo. The wildlife found in this park is more similar to that found in Western Africa than Eastern. It includes chimpanzee, porcupine, colobus monkeys (both red and the Angolan black and white), and elephant, although there are also giraffe, zebra, buffalo and roan antelope. The range and numbers of animals found here has increased since the *Ujaama* villagization programme of the 1970s. Indeed animals such as the leopard and lion have reappeared in the area. The park is probably best known for its chimpanzee population and they have been the focus of much research by scientists from around the world. There are an estimated 1,000 in the park divided into 20 family troupes of about 50 each. Birds seen here include the fish eagle, kestrels, kingfishers, barbets and starlings, similar to those found at Gombe Stream.

Sleeping **A** *Mahale Mountains Tented Camp*. Very expensive at US$400 per person. **E** *Guest House* at Kasiha village. Facilities are minimal, bring all food requirements from Kigoma.

Camping Allowed in designated areas. If possible take your own equipment although you may be able to hire it. Check at the MMWRC (Mahale Mountains Wildlife Research Centre) in Kigoma for current availability of accommodation and transport.

Transport **Sea Boat**: to get to the park, take the lake steamer (*MV Liemba* or *MV Mwongozo*) from Kigoma, see page 512. You get to Lagosa (also known as Mugambo) after about 6 hrs at about 0300 and will have to get a small boat to take you to the shore. From Lagosa you will have to hire another boat to take you the 3-hr journey to Kasoge. As you are relying on the lake steamer you will have to stay until the next ferry comes, which is usually in about a week although it is not very reliable. A package tour can be arranged through Kigoma Hilltop Hotel, see page 510, who have their own boats.

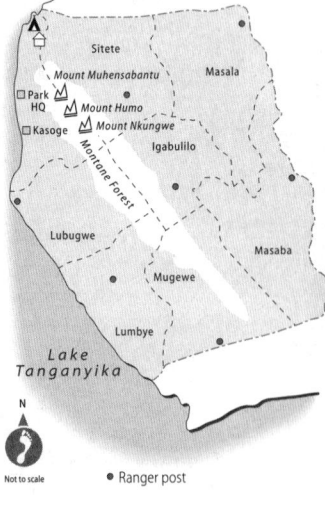

Mahale Mountains National Park

Sitete

Mount Muhensabantu — Masala

Park HQ — Mount Humo

Kasoge — Mount Nkungwe

Montane Forest

Igabulilo

Lubugwe

Masaba

Mugewe

Lumbye

Lake Tanganyika

N

Not to scale ● Ranger post

Tanzania

Kigoma to Mbeya

Approximately 80 km southeast of Kigoma on the road towards Mpanda and Sumbawanga are the ancient **salt mines** at Uvinza. Salt mining here dates from the early Stone Age, and local chieftains have traditionally traded salt across Lake Tanganyika – the trade continues to this day. The Germans have funded major rehabilitation works at the mine, and on completion it is expected that the mines will supply 50% of the region's salt requirements. There is only very basic accommodation available.

Uvinza

This small town, approximately 120 km east of Mahale Mountains National Park, is the closest town to the **Katavi National Park**, 40 km south of the town, and the adjacent **Rukwa Game Reserve** (4,100 sq km). There are no facilities in this little-visited reserve. The ecological balance of much of this area, including the infrequently visited **Ugalla Game Reserve** (see page 505), has been seriously threatened by human activity including tree clearance, tobacco cultivation and over fishing. *Africare* has been helping local communities to develop alternative income generation schemes. Nearby mineral exploratory studies by international mining companies at the Cu-Pb-Au field have found small quantities of gold.

Mpanda
Colour map 4, grid B2
There are a number of small basic hotels that have little to choose between them

Katavi National Park

Katavi National Park is located 40 km southeast of Mpanda town astride the main Mpanda-Sumbawanga road. It was upgraded to a national park in 1974, covering an area of 2,253 sq km, and expanded to 4,471 sq km in 1997. The park is characterized by miombo woodland (see box, page 505), acacia parkland as well as some water-logged grassland plains.

7° S, 31° E
Colour map 4, grid B2
Best time to visit is Jul-Oct

Travelling south from Mpanda or north from Tunduma (the border town of Tanzania and Zambia), the road passes through the park. However, like the Ugalla River Game Reserve, its isolation and lack of facilities has meant that it receives few visitors – annual visitor numbers are typically in double figures.

There is a large swampy area around the Katuma River, which joins the two lakes in the park – Lake Katavi and Lake Chada. The park is famous for its sable and roan antelope, rarely found in other Tanzanian parks. It also has a high density of crocodiles, *Defassa* water buck, topi, eland, hartebeest and greater kudu. Other large mammals seen here include hippo, crocodile, zebra, elephant, buffalo, various antelope as well as lion and, if you are lucky, leopard. Over 400 species of birds have been identified. The park has many waterbirds and birds of prey including the black heron, Dickinson's kestrel, bee-eaters, strikes, weavers, nightjars and the Go-away-bird.

Sleeping   The nearest hotels and other facilities are at Mpanda, which is 40 km away, except **L** *Katavi Tented Camp*, which is US$400 per person per night, and **A** *Katavi Safari Camp*, Foxtreks, PO Box 10270, Dar es Salaam, T2440194, T0741-237422 (mob), F0741-327706, fox@twiga.com, a temporary camp seeking permanent status. If you have your own camping equipment you can use the sites in the park.

Katavi National Park

Located on the shores of Lake Tanganyika, **Kipili** is one of the *MV Liemba*'s ports of call. Just a few kilometres north is a very pretty town called **Kirando**. **E** *Bahama Guest House* on the main road, near the bus stop. Very basic but cheap, no mosquito nets, cheap and tasty food available next door.

Kipili
Colour map 4, grid B2

Tanzania

To link to the road to Mbeya take a bus to **Sumbawanga**. The buses (cost about US$8) leave at 0700 and just after arrival of the ferry. The roads are poor and it is a very slow journey taking about 24 hours.

Sumbawanga

Phone code: 0637
Colour map 4, grid B2

This is a lovely large town with some impressive buildings, in particular the Roman Catholic church. There is a large market selling second-hand clothes, and a separate market selling a wide range of fruit, vegetables and fish. The town is very clean, with a newly laid tarmac road. The town's name is said to mean 'witch people'.

Sumbawanga attracted some notoriety in 1998 when the owner of a dog called 'Immigration' was given a six-month suspended sentence and ordered to kill the animal because the dog's name offended immigration officials at Kasanga.

The **Rukwa Rift Valley** is currently being investigated in several sites by archaeologists. Near Sumbawanga is the **Milanzi Rockshelter** dating from the Upper Palaeolithic period. It is still used today as an ancestor shrine. **Chamoto Hill**, north of the village of Igurusi, was discovered by E. Haldemann during the 1950s and many artefacts were identified. Northeast of Sumbawanga on the shores of Lake Rukwa is the village of **Mkamba**, identified as an **Early Iron Age site** where a virtually complete pot was found in the sediment in 1989 by researchers from the University of Alberta.

In October 2000 an earthquake destroyed several houses in Nkasi District, part of the Kipili-Sumbawanga area. One person was killed and several injured. This was the largest earthquake in this area since 1910.

Sleeping and eating F *Zanzibar Guest House*, behind the bus station. Clean, communal bath facilities, mosquito nets. *Upendo Hotel*. Recommended.

Transport Regular bus service to **Mbeya**. Be warned of serious competition from ticket sellers – there is room to bargain. Expect to pay around US$7. Buses leave at 0600 and arrive in Mbeya at 1300. In the morning several 4WDs leave from the petrol stations for the Zambian border or to Kasanga. The journey takes the best part of the day.

Nuzi &
Kasanga
Colour map 4, grid C2

Southwest of Sumbawanga on Lake Tanganyika is the charming, unspoilt village of **Nuzi**, which is surrounded by palm trees. Nuzi has no electricity or piped water and there is only one very basic hotel – bucket shower, no mosquito nets. However, there are lots of mosquitoes in this area. Transport by truck from Sumbawanga will cost US$5 and take eight hours on a very poor road.

Nuzi is a short walk away from the next, larger village of **Kasanga Bismarck** (5 km, sometimes called Kasanga). It is possible to arrange for a local fisherman to take you by boat from Nuzi to Kasanga. The trip takes about half-an-hour and costs about US$1 per person. The *MV Liemba* also calls here.

Shopping is very expensive in Kasanga. It is difficult to buy mineral water, toilet paper, fresh fruit and snacks. There are 2-3 local restaurants serving local food – the fish is cheap and very good. Kasanga has one guesthouse. If waiting to board the lake ferry one can visit the nearby ruins of the German Fort Bismarckburg.

Kalamba
waterfalls

Close by, near the border with Zambia, are the Kalamba waterfalls, which merit a visit despite the poor road. These falls are said to be the second highest in Africa and there are many crocodiles there. If you don't fancy riding in the back of a truck for several hours it is possible to organize a trip from *Upendo Hotel* in Sumbawanga. A car and driver will cost just under US$100 but it will still take five hours each way.

Southwest: Iringa and Mbeya

The southwest has much to offer in the form of huge untouched areas of great beauty and wildlife and has only recently been 'discovered' by many tourists. The parks in the southwest are increasingly popular, particularly with those who want to avoid the tourist trails. The area's isolation is as much a part of its attraction as a problem. The major towns in the southwest are Iringa and Mbeya. Road communications are good, and Mbeya is on the TAZARA railway.

Dar es Salaam

Beyond the Mikumi National Park the road climbs into the Kitonga Hills, which are part of the Udzungwa Mountains. It is quite a journey, with sharp bends, and dense forest all around. Part of the road runs alongside the Ruaha River gorge. Eventually the road levels out to the plateau on which Iringa is sited.

The southern highlands of Tanzania form one of the largest blocks of highland within East Africa. They mostly have a high rainfall and because of their altitude are cool. Like the rest of south Tanzania (and unlike the highlands to the north) they have one long wet season and one long dry season. As with most highlands areas in East Africa they are associated with the Rift Valley system and there has been much volcanic activity in the area over the years. It is probably their inaccessibility that is the most notable feature about the southern highlands.

Until the construction of the TAZARA railway Mbeya was 650 km from the nearest railway and this meant that development of the area was slow. However the high rainfall and rich soil have meant that this area is agriculturally productive in both food crops and some coffee and tea, which are the major cash crops in the area.

Ifakara

For those with a penchant for getting off the beaten track a visit to this isolated central Tanzanian town southeast of Iringa is recommended. Ifakara is a verdant, tree-dotted old trading station situated close to the Kilombero River in a highly fertile agricultural area. The most important crop of the local Pogoro people is rice and there is thriving trade in this commodity between Ifakara and Dar es Salaam. Tropical hardwoods (from the rainforests north of Ifakara) are also being sent from here to the coast for export. In the town itself there are no obvious sights, though the secondary school (built in the 1930s) and church are quite interesting, as are some of the Indian traders' shops along the main street, which were mostly constructed after the Second World War.

Colour map 4, grid B4

The countryside surrounding Ifakara is very attractive and being flat is ideal for cycling around (bikes can be hired from the town centre); it is also rich in birdlife. The Kilombero River flows past about 10 km to the south of the town. At Kivukoni there is a ferry crossing for the road to Mahenge. There are hippos in

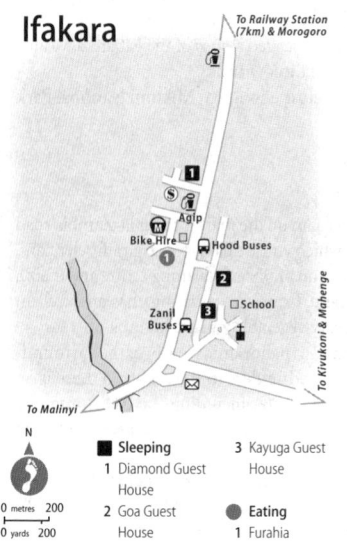

Ifakara

To Railway Station (7km) & Morogoro

Agip

Bike Hire

Hood Buses

School

Zanil Buses

To Kivukoni & Mahenge

To Malinyi

N

0 metres 200
0 yards 200

Sleeping
1 Diamond Guest House
2 Goa Guest House
3 Kayuga Guest House

Eating
1 Furahia

the river here and it is possible to arrange a trip in a dug-out canoe to see them. North of Ifakara the Udzungwa Mountains rise scenically from the Kilombero plain.

Sleeping   **E** *Goa Guest House* is the best of the local lodges; a clean, simple double (s/c). If it is full both the
& eating   **E** *Diamond Guest House* and the **E** *Kayuga Guest House* are similarly priced. Confusingly, there are two Diamond Guest Houses in Ifakara. The **Furahia Restaurant**, near the market, is the best of a bad bunch – try their baggia and egg chop for breakfast, you'll probably have difficulty finding anything else you'd want to eat at that time of day in Ifakara! It is perhaps advisable to have meals at the Mission (next to the church), which you can arrange in advance.

Transport   The best way to travel to Ifakara from **Dar es Salaam** is on the ordinary **TAZARA train**, not the
See pages 328 and   international train that arrives at 0100. The station is situated 11 km north of the town centre.
329 for details of train   Buses also go from Kariakoo to Ifakara daily. Leaving Ifakara, the trains depart at rather inconve-
services, timetables   nient times, however, there are several companies running **buses**. By far the best of these is
and fares   *Zanil's*, which has daily buses leaving at 1000 for **Morogoro** and **Dar es Salaam**. Book a seat on the left-hand side for good views of the Udzungwa Mountains. For the more adventurous there are also daily bus services to **Mahenge** and **Malinyi** (towns to the south and west of Ifakara).

Udzungwa Mountains National Park

7° 50′ S, 37° E   This has recently been been classified as a national park, where previously it was a
Colour map 4, grid B4   national forest reserve. The conservation team effort programme is designed to ben-
The best time to visit   efit the local people and improve their social amenities of health and education,
is from Sep-Dec   water supplies and transport to encourage them to fully co-operate in the conservation programme with the National Park Management. Funds raised by tourism will directly benefit the local people.

This is a forest area and covers an area of approximately 1,000 sq km lying between 300 and 2,800 m. Since the mountains are so steep there has been little development apart from at the foothills, where sugar is cultivated. There are no roads or tracks through the park but guided walks are available. The shortest walk takes you to the Prince Bernhard waterfalls. The **Mwanihani trail** can be walked in two days, climbing to a height of over 2,000 m. A tent, all food and water must accompany you as there are no fixed facilities. This great altitudinal range makes for a great diversity of vegetation and thus habitats for many different species. These include the Iringa-Uhehe red colobus monkey and the Sanje mangabey, as well as elephant, buffalo, lion and leopard. Birds found in the park include sunbirds, strikes and the Iringa akalat. To the south lies the green Kilombero Valley, with the jagged slopes of the Mbarika Mountains, 100 km away, clearly visible rising out of the lowlands.

As yet there are no facilities here but it is close enough to Mikumi National Park for those facilities to be used.

Iringa

7°48′S 35°43′E   The town of Iringa is 502 km from Dar es Salaam on the main Tanzania-Zambia road
Phone code: 026   beyond Mikumi National Park, a drive on which you are likely to see giraffe, elephant,
Colour map 4, grid B4   zebra and baboons close by. A fertile area, it is an important farming centre and maize,
Population: 90,000   vegetables, fruits and tobacco are grown here. Consequently Iringa has an excellent
Altitude: 1,635 m   market, where you can barter for almost every vegetable you could think of.

The town is safe and   The town itself, set on a plateau, commands a panoramic view over the surround-
welcoming and is also   ing countryside. The pleasant climate attracted settlers to the area and there is an
a good place to buy   impressive legacy of German colonial architecture, including the old **Boma**, the
traditional souvenirs   **Town Hall**, the **Hospital** and **Post Office**. The streets are lined with trees, all planted when Tanzania was German East Africa.

Next to the Assemblies of God church in town is the **Iringa Rockshelter** where artefacts have been identified from the Late Stone Age, or possibly even the Middle Stone Age period, by researchers from the University of Alberta.

Kalenga The area is of some historical interest for near Iringa, at Kalenga, is where Chief Mkwawa fought off the Germans in an uprising of 1894. He was finally defeated in 1898, but refusing to be captured by the Germans he committed suicide. His head was severed from his body and sent back to Germany, but in 1954 was returned and, together with a letter, is on display at the small museum at Kalenga. However it is often difficult to find anyone to unlock the museum and show you around. Near the museum is a shop selling good, cheap local crafts. There is a good local hotel that offers decent food and cold drinks, and bandas with en-suite showers and toilets, US$10. There is a daily bus service between Iringa and Kalenga. The town is within easy reach of Ruaha National Park (see below page 521).

Isimila Stone Age site This is considered to be one of the finest stone age sites in East Africa. The site was discovered in 1951 by a South African, D Maclennan, and excavated in 1957-58 by Dr Clark Howell and G Cole, sponsored by the University of Chicago. The site was once a shallow lake, now dried up. Soil erosion in a *korongo* (a watercourse, which is dry for most of the year) exposed a great number of Acheulian stone tools, including pear-shaped axes, cleavers and spherical stones, which had been artificially shaped. The lake beds are white in colour and consist of alternate layers of clay and sandstone. The clays were laid down in relatively deep waters and the sandstone was around the lake shore. The stone artefacts and fossilized animal remains were found extruding out of the lacustrine or lake deposits.

The tools found there are believed to date from 60,000 years ago. Also among the finds were fossilized animal bones, including those of now extinct forms of hippopotami (*H Gorgops*), whose eyes protruded like periscopes and a short-necked giraffe (*Sivatherium*). Other fossils include elephant, an extinct giant pig and antelope. It is believed that early hominoids used this area as both a watering place and to hunt the animals that came to drink there. A small museum was built on the site in 1969 and displays some of the tools, fossils and bones found during excavations.

Isimila Gully This is upstream from the Stone Age site and is a spectacular natural phenomenon. Erosion over the millennia has left standing several pillars that tower above you. ■ *Isimila is about 20 km from town and can be reached by buses going to Mbeya. There is then a walk to the site of about 2 km. A taxi from Iringa will cost US$20. Entry to museum US$2.*

A *Fox Farm Highland Lodge*, Mufindi, PO Box 10270, Dar es Salaam, T/F0741-327706 (mob), fox@bushlink.co.tz Above the Great Rift Valley, south of Iringa, are the scenic southern highlands. High on a hill among the tea plantations is Fox Farm, whose well-appointed log cabins command fine views across the valley. The cabins have en-suite bathrooms and private verandahs, while there is also a TV room with pool table, living room with large log fires, octagonal dining room for meals cooked using fresh produce from the farm. Full board accommodation, activities included: mountain biking, horseriding, bird-watching, walking, canoeing and swimming in dammed pools. Trout fishing and scenic drives (if with own transport) available at extra cost. The farm is off the sealed road to Mbeya. Go past Kisolanza Farm (see below) and turn off at Mafinga, the junction just past a Total petrol station (about 45 mins from Iringa). Head towards Sawala along this unsurfaced road for 30 km until a signposted turning to the left. Follow the signs for a further 11 km. There are buses to Sawala from Mafinga, pre-arrange for someone to meet you at the Fox Farm sign.

B *The Old Farm House*, Kisolanza Farm, PO Box 113, Iringa, F2505. Charming old farmhouse with new thatched roofed guest cottages, situated 50 km southwest of Iringa adjacent to the Dar es Salaam-Mbeya Rd, has been the home of the Ghaui family for over 60 years, pleasant climate at an altitude of over 1,600 m, large freshwater dam offers excellent swimming and fishing, nearby golf at Mufindi. A separate site for **campers** and overlanders is available in a secluded area away from the main house. The site has showers, WC, stone-built barbecue and plenty of shade. Fresh food, including bread, meat and eggs available from the farm. Very friendly management, beautiful site. Telephone messages can be left via the phone at

Iringa Stores, T255-642073. Personal callers can go to the farm. From Iringa (travelling towards Mbeya) pass by Ifunda (on your right), and when you reach Ulete Mission (again on your right) Kisolanza Farm will be found shortly afterwards on the left-hand side of the road.

C *Iringa* (*Railway Hotel*), PO Box 48, T2039, town centre, comfortable colonial hotel, built by the Germans in anticipation of the arrival of a railway line that never materialized. **C** *MR Hotel*, off Uhuru Av, near bus station, PO Box 431, T2702006, F2702661, mrhotels@costech.gn.apc.org Popular with expats and Japanese, best hotel in town, the spacious rooms have hot showers and TV, price includes breakfast, excellent restaurant, slow service, chef's cooking recommended. Many of the staff speak good English. There are executive suites, a conference centre and a shop. **D** *Hoteli ya Kati*, under new management. Friendly, basic, includes breakfast, nice garden, on Uhuru Av, past library. **D** *Huruma Baptist Conference Centre*, Mkwawa St, 1 km north of centre, PO Box 632, T2700182, F2700172, hbcc@maf.org Very good value, very clean, good food, price includes breakfast, dormitory beds also available, may be possible to camp here. Can arrange transport to Ruaha and Mikumi national parks, and located here is a Swahili language school. **D** *Isimila*, Box 216, Uhuru Av, T2605, secure parking. **E** *Staff Inn 1*, behind the bus station, comfortable rooms with own bathrooms. **E** *Staff Inn 2* is located behind the local bus stand further south and offers similar facilities. **E** *Tembo*, Pangani St, simple but reasonable. **F** *Taj Lodge*, central, on Uhuru St close to Uheme St. Modest but comfortable and very clean, friendly staff. Interior resembles an American diner.

Camping At *The Old Farm House* (see above) and at *Riverside Campsite*, PO Box 934, T2725280, rvphillips@maf.org Located at an attractive site on the Little Ruaha River, 15 km southeast of Iringa, 2 km off the road to Dar es Salaam (the Tanzam Highway). Friendly, hot showers, toilets, cold drinks, barbecue under a large tree, fresh farm produce and other food supplies if requested in advance, separate area for overlanders, US$3 per person. Horse-riding can be arranged at the nearby farm, mountain bikes for hire on request, bird-watching, cold but refreshing swimming in the river. There are regular *dala-dalas* along the Tanzam Highway to Iringa, while a taxi from town may cost up to US$7.

Eating **Cheap** *Bottoms Up*, Majumba St, Chinese, Indian and local dishes, including seafood, good value, friendly service, generous portions, also bar with good selection of imported drinks, closed Mon. *Iringa Hotel*, solid fare and reasonable value. *MR Hotel*, off Uhuru Av, near bus station. American diner-style interior, excellent food when the chef is on duty, and unusually offers a separate vegetarian menu. *Taj Lodge*, recommended, international and Indian food, safe

Iringa

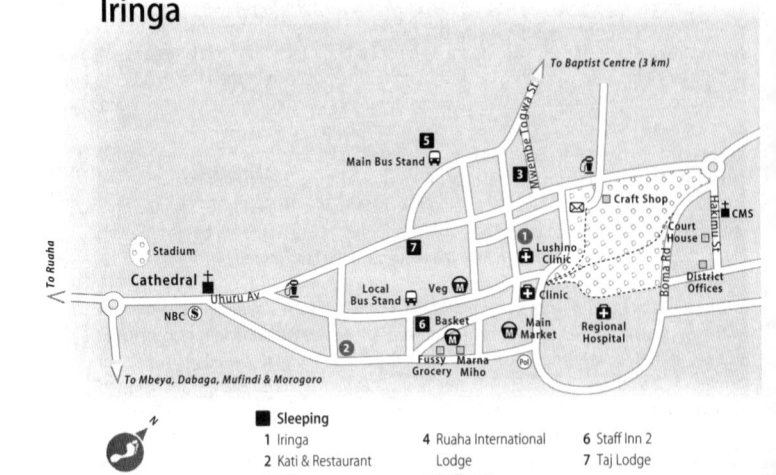

Sleeping

1 Iringa
2 Kati & Restaurant
3 MR
4 Ruaha International Lodge
5 Staff Inn 1
6 Staff Inn 2
7 Taj Lodge

Not to scale

parking for motorcycles. **Seriously cheap** *Aashiana*, central, between Uhuru Av and the market, snacks and light lunches. *Hasty Tasty*, on Majumbu St, simple but reasonable. *Hasty Tasty Too*, Uhuru Av, opposite *Hoteli ya Kati*, good milkshakes, simple, tasty food, some Indian. *Hoteli Ya Kati*, good value. *Lulu's*, Dodoma Rd, pleasant place for a simple lunch or evening meal, good service and nice ice cream. *Staff Inn 2*, Store St, near the market, good for snacks.

Air *Precisionair* (Iringa office: PO Box 755, T2702652, F2725090) have scheduled flights between **Dar es Salaam** (DSM) and Mbeya, with a stop in Iringa; they leave DSM 0930 on Tue, Thu and Sun. **Road** This is really the only feasible mode. Buses from Dar es Salaam leave from the Mnazi Moja bus stand. They take about 7 hrs and cost US$9. *Scandinavian Bus Services Ltd* serve this route and have an office in Iringa, T2702308, cost US$9.50. To **Mbeya** costs US$3 and takes 3 hrs. The main bus station in Iringa is just off Mkawa St; some local buses leave from the stand on Store St, near the market.

Transport
See Dar es Salaam transport, page 360, for further advice and contact details

Ruaha National Park and Rungwa Game Reserve

Ruaha National Park is located 130 km west of Iringa, a drive of about four hours. It is one of the most remote parks in Tanzania, and visitor numbers reflect that: 2,500 per annum to Ruaha, 45,000 to Tarangire and 150,000 to the Serengeti. Initially the road passes through densely populated countryside until the population gradually thins out. The vegetation becomes miombo woodland and about 60 km from Iringa the turning off to the right to the park is indicated. It is another 50 km down this road to the park boundary and from there about 10 km to Ibuguziwa where you pay the park entrance fees and cross the Ruaha River. About 1 km beyond the river there is a junction. To the right the track goes to Msembe and the park headquarters and to the left to Ruaha River camp. There is an airstrip at the park headquarters for light aircraft (see Transport below).

*6°55'S 33°32'E
Colour map 4,
grid B4 and B3*

Ruaha National Park was classified a national park in 1964. The area was a part of Sabia River Game Reserve, established by the German colonial government in 1911, and later renamed the Rungwa Game Reserve. It covers an area of 12,950 sq km and ranges from 750 m to 1,900 m above sea level. The park gets its name from the river that forms part of its boundary. The name *Ruaha* is from the word *Luvaha*, which means great in the Hehe language and the river certainly is this. It is vital to the economy of the country for it supplies much of Tanzania with electricity through hydro-electric power from the dam at Kidatu. Further downstream the Ruaha joins with the Ulanga to form the Rufiji River.

Background

Visiting is possible during both the dry 'yellow' season and the wet 'green' season, even in January when the rain is heaviest because the rains are short and most of the roads are all weather. However in the wet season the grass is long and game viewing is almost impossible, so the best time to visit is from July-December. The park's inaccessibility means that not many people visit it, although the Ruaha River camp is very popular.

A 2-hr foot safari with an armed ranger can be arranged at park headquarters. Recommended

There is a wide variety of wildlife in this park, largely due to the variety of vegetation types found here. Animals include elephant, lion, zebra, giraffe, ostrich,

Wildlife

To Isimila Hotel →

Uhuru Av
S CRDB
Benbella St
Dodoma Rd
Kenyatta Dr

● Eating
1 Aashiana Snack Bar   4 Lulu's
2 Bottoms Up
3 Hasty Tasty Too

Tanzania

greater and lesser kudu, gazelle, and other antelope and, in the river, hippo, packs of cape hunting dogs and crocodile. There are over 400 recorded species of bird in the park. It is a huge park and is largely underdeveloped and inaccessible. Unfortunately poaching in this park is a serious problem and the animal population has suffered enormously from this. In particular rhinos, which were once found here, are probably now extinct. Also the elephant population has fallen tremendously from over 22,000 in 1977 to under 4,000 in 1987. The 4,000 elephant still represents the largest number in any national park in Africa. Ruaha is unrivalled for buffalo and hippo too, and the bird count is unsurpassed in Tanzania, possibly all East Africa. The rare Eleonora's falcon may be sighted here, as well as the pale-billed hornbill and violet-crested turaco. Pel's fishing owls are also seen, as well as several species of bat. The fall in the number of elephant is probably the most dramatic decline in all the national parks of Tanzania. However efforts are being made to improve the situation and the Friends of Ruaha Society (PO Box 60, Mufindi, or PO Box 786, Dar es Salaam) is the motivating force behind this. They, together with the park's wardens, have improved the roads and signposting and thus the game drives have improved. They have also increased the anti-poaching patrolling.

Routes There are four major vegetation zones within this park: the river valleys; the open grassland; the miombo woodland (see box, page 505); and undulating countryside where baobabs dominate.

Around Msembe is bush country, with acacia and baobab trees, and elephants are often found here. Along the river, particularly during the dry season, many animals congregate and you may see confrontations between lions and buffalo. You can expect to see elephants, giraffe, baboons, wart-hogs, buffalo, zebra, all sorts of antelope and if you are lucky leopard and cheetah. In the river itself are both hippo and crocodile.

The Mwagusi Sand River joins the Ruaha about 10 km from Msembe. If you cross this river and follow the track you will get to Mwayembe Hill and the escarpment where there is a salt lick often frequented by elephant and buffalo.

Ruaha National Park south

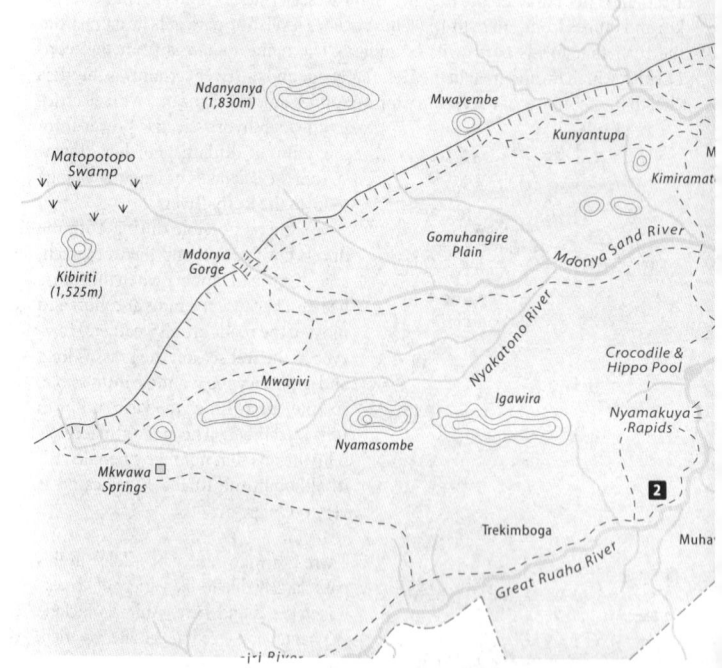

To Mzombe Ri

The Mdonya Sand River joins the Ruaha between the ferry and the park headquarters. From the ferry a drive southwest will take you past the Nyamakuyu Rapids and Trekimboga to where the Jongomero joins the Ruaha about 40 km upriver. This is a good place to see hippo and crocodile. Roan and sable antelopes can be seen, which are difficult to see elsewhere. There are supposed to be rhino in the western part of the park, but the location is kept secret.

Sleeping

L *Mwagusi Camp*, owned and run by Chris Fox (Foxtreks Ltd), PO Box 84, Mufindi, Tanzania and Foxtreks, PO Box 10270, Dar es Salaam, T2440149, T0741-2440194 (mob), F0741-327706. The site overlooks the Mwagusi Sands River, which does not dry up and so attracts all kinds of wildlife to drink there. It's a tented camp with en-suite showers, hot water in the morning, evening and on request, the site accommodates 16 people and is 30 mins away from the airstrip. As soon as you disembark from the plane you are among the wildlife – highly recommended if you want to see the wildlife and few other human beings. The owner will take you on game drives and is very experienced, alternatively short guided walking tours are available, giving you an opportunity to 'touch the wild'. Animals wander freely through the camps. All-inclusive rate, US$280 per person per night. **L** *Ruaha River Lodge* (Foxtreks, PO Box 10270, Dar es Salaam, T2440194, T0741-237422 (mob), F0741-327706, the direct telephone and fax booking number for *Ruaha River Lodge* is 255-741-327706). US$200 per person full board, banda accommodation in one of 3 sites, located 18 km south of Msembe on and around a kopje overlooking the Ruaha River, each camp has a restaurant (one recent traveller reported that the food was mediocre, another that it was very good) and bar, vehicle hire available, wonderful setting, excellent value, you will undoubtedly enjoy your stay here. Some bandas are on a hill, others overlook the river, the bandas have WC and shower, essential because many animals roam the campsite during the night, nearby there is a hippo pool – worth a visit. During the dry season (Oct) the animals remain in this vicinity.

C *Rondavels and campsite*, located at the park headquarters, bookings through Chief Warden, Ruaha National Park, PO Box 369, Iringa. Cold showers, pit latrines, bring your own food, camping US$10. There are two campsites inside the park, bring everything you need with you, US$10.

Transport

Air The scheduled air service by *Coastal Travels Ltd* in Dar es Salaam (T2117959, F2118647) costs US$300 each way. It departs Dar es Salaam at 0830 (having previously departed Zanzibar at 0800) on Mon, Thu and Sat, goes via Selous and arrives at 1140. The return to Dar es Salaam and Zanzibar departs only 5 minutes after arrival.

Iringa to Mbeya

The road from Iringa to Mbeya goes through mixed woodland and savannah as well as cultivated land. Gradually it opens up to more open savannah. There are various roads that you can take off the main road that will lead you into the Usangu Plains. About 25 km from Mbeya on the right-hand side of the road is the Mwambalisi River, which is fairly spectacular during the rainy season. At about 37 km from Mbeya is the Mlowo River and one of its waterfalls, Kimani Falls, can be seen.

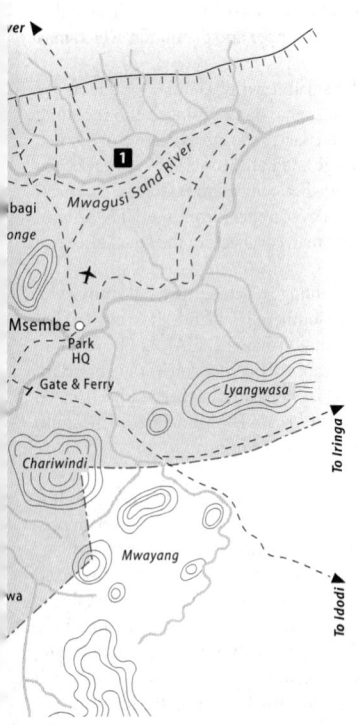

Tanzania

👉 **Poaching**

The estimated national elephant population fell from around 200,000 in 1977 to 89,000 in 1987 – a fall of some 55% in just 10 years. These figures give rise to the fully justified concern for the future survival of some of these species. It is important that the ivory trade is discouraged and every tourist can help in this by not buying any ivory of any description. This rule should extend beyond ivory to other living creatures. For example there was a time when on a trip to the coast you would be sure to see a great many extremely beautiful shells along the reef. As a result of the tourist trade you are now less likely to see them in the sea and more likely to see them being sold to tourists on the road side. Many people collect the brightly coloured starfish found on the reefs. However these quickly die and fade

once they are out of the water. Their population has undoubtedly been affected as a result of tourists collecting them. If you want these species to survive do not buy or collect any such souvenirs.

If you want to become involved in any conservation activities in Tanzania there are a number of societies and organizations you can contact. These include the Tanzania Wildlife Protection Fund, PO Box 1994, Dar es Salaam; The Wildlife Conservation Society of Tanzania, PO Box 70919, Dar es Salaam; African Wildlife Foundation, PO Box 48177, Nairobi, Kenya or 1717 Massachusetts Avenue NW, Washington DC, 20036, USA; Frontier Tanzania, PO Box 9473, Dar es Salaam or Studio 210, Thames House, 566 Cable Street, London, E1 9HB, England.

Mbeya

8°54'S 33°29'E
Phone code: 025
Colour map 4, grid C3
Population: 160,000
Altitude: 1,737 m

Set in the lush and fertile part of Tanzania, against the Mbeya Range, this town has a most scenic setting. The town was founded in the late 1920s when the gold mines at Lupa became active, and continued to grow after they shut down in 1956. However, recent international exploration of an 150 sq km area near the town of Makongolosi, to the north of the old **Lupa Goldfields**, have indicated that there are still significant deposits of gold, silver, copper and diamonds, which may prove economically viable to extract.

Between Mbeya and Lake Rukwa is the small town of **Galula**, located at the northern end of the Songwe River Valley. Galula has an imposing Catholic church built by the French White Fathers. Nearby are lake deposits indicative of a much larger lake in the past and evidence of **Iron Age** and **Late Stone Age** sites have been found on the river terraces. At **Mapogoro**, northeast of the Lupa Goldfields, volcanic **rock shelters** were identified in 1990 by researchers from the University of Alberta, close to the village of Njelenje where many artefacts of the Late Stone Age were identified, including scrapers.

Mbeya has developed into a bustling town, though of late seems a little run down, and is an ideal base from which to explore the Southern Highlands. It is only 114 km from the Zambian border being the last main station on the TAZARA railway before the border and is a popular overnight stop. Because of this location it is an important trading centre. However being 875 km from Dar es Salaam it has been rather isolated until the construction of the railway and the sealed road. The Mbozi area to the south of Mbeya is an important arabic coffee and maize growing area.

Excursions & activities

Chunya is an old gold-mining and tobacco market town 65 km to the north. It is rather inaccessible without your own transport. There are some small guesthouses and some faded buildings from its more prosperous era in the interwar period.

Mbozi Meteorite is a 12-tonne mass, believed to be the eighth largest in the world and to have landed over 1,000 years ago. The meteor is roughly rectangular in shape, approximately 5 m in diameter. There is evidence that many small samples have been removed for analysis judging from what appears to be saw indentations in several places. It is located 40 km southwest of Mbeya, along the road to Zambia, with the turn-off just after Mbowa. It is situated a good 10-15 km from the highway.

The **Ngozi Crater Lake**, 38 km south of Mbeya, is worth a visit but you will need a guide to get there – see entry on page 528.

Walking This is walking country and you will be able to get some really tremendous views of the surrounding countryside. The mountain to the north of the town is **Kaluwe** (otherwise known as Loleza Peak) and rises to 2,656 m. It can be reached in about two hours and is well worth it if you have a spare afternoon. Go about 150 m from the roundabout towards the water works, turning left down a gravel track before you reach them. You will pass a quarry and a few houses before getting to the path that climbs up the mountain where you will find the views merit the fairly steep climb. In the wet season the highland flowers are also impressive. Recent travellers report that there are security concerns for walkers, and that the environs of Mbeya are no longer considered to be safe for tourists unless accompanied by a guide.

Mbeya Peak, rising to 2,826 m, is the highest peak in the range and looms to the north above the town. There are two possible routes, one harder than the other. The first is down a track about 13 km down the Chunya Road. From the end of this track the climb will take about one hour, including a walk through eucalyptus forest and high grass. The second, and more difficult climb, is only recommended for those prepared for a steep climb and, in parts, a real scramble. This begins from the coffee farm at Luiji. There is very charming accommodation here at **C** *Utengele Country Resort*. At the top you can catch your breath and admire the view for miles around.

Another worthwhile, but energetic trek is to **Pungulume** (2,230 m) at the west end of the range. It is approached from the road at its base near Njerenji. Alternatively follow the ridge from Mbeya Peak. This particular trek should be avoided in the wet season.

Tanzania

Mbeya

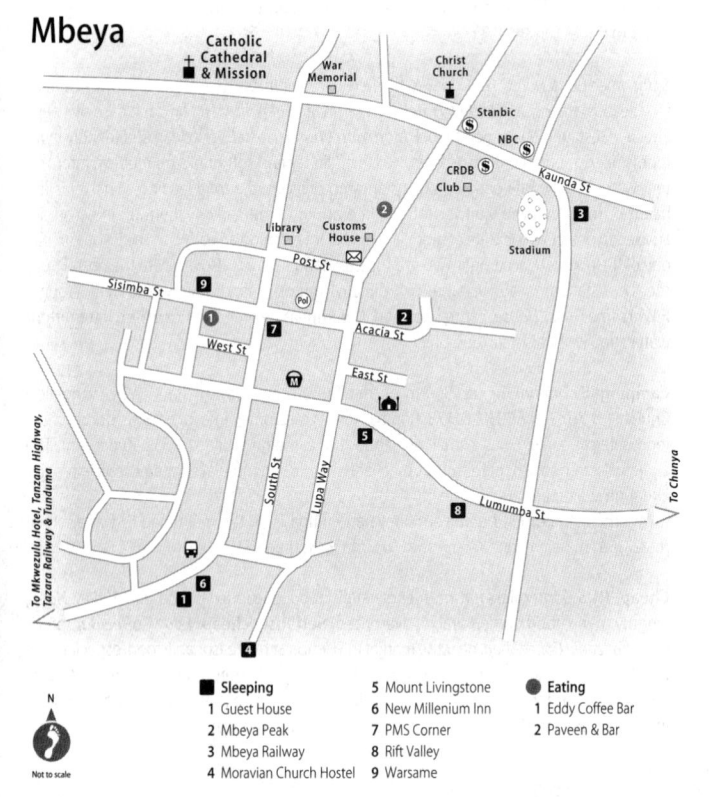

N
Not to scale

■ **Sleeping**
1 Guest House
2 Mbeya Peak
3 Mbeya Railway
4 Moravian Church Hostel

5 Mount Livingstone
6 New Millenium Inn
7 PMS Corner
8 Rift Valley
9 Warsame

● **Eating**
1 Eddy Coffee Bar
2 Paveen & Bar

Probably one of the best viewpoints in the area is known as **World's End**. From here you will see the Usangu Flats and the Rift Valley Escarpment; the view is really quite breathtaking. To get to it go about 20 km down the Chunya Road to a forest camp and take the track off to the right.

The **Poroto Mountains,** southeast of Mbeya, are home to a wide variety of birdlife, including Livingstone's turaco and the green barbet. There are also several species of kingfishers, woodpeckers and eagles.

Mbeya is the base of the Sisi Kwa Sisi Society, which is an affiliated partner of the Cultural Tourism Programmes of the north of Tanzania. Like those programmes, Sisi Kwa Sisi offer tours of the area and use profits to help the local community, in this case through agricultural projects. Tours offered include visits to all attractions in the Mbeya, Tukuyu and Matema areas, with the chance to also experience the traditional local cultures. The guides speak good English, and some speak French and German. The society has a small office in the centre of Mbeya, near the Rhino monument, and can be contacted by sisikwasisi@hotmail.com

Sleeping **B** *Utengule Country Hotel*, PO Box 139, T2560100, F2560089, utengule@twiga.com, located 20 km south of Mbeya beneath Mbeya Peak and 90 km from the Zambian border. Restaurant, bar, comfortable rooms. Has a swimming pool and tennis court, plus its own coffee estate. Under new management since 1997 and was refurbished in 1998. **C** *Mbeya Peak*, PO Box 822, town centre. **C** *Mkwezulu*, PO Box 995, southwest of centre, on road to Tazara railway. **C** *Mount Livingstone*, PO Box 1401, opposite mosque on Lumumba St, T3331. Noise from disco can be irritating, ask for a room away from it, beautiful gardens and good food. **C** *Rift Valley*, PO Box 1631, T3756, town centre. **C** *Tembo Tourist Resort*, 25 km on the road to Tunduma. **E** *New Millennium Inn* (formerly the *Central Tourist Lodge*), a reddish building on the hill opposite the bus stop, quite smart, it is extremely convenient for catching the early buses to Dar es Salaam.

E *Unnamed Guest House*, next door to the *New Millennium*. Clean and basic, also convenient for the bus station. **F** *Holiday Hotel*, central, near *Rift Valley Hotel*, doubles only, nets, attached restaurant has good food. **F** *Moravian Church Hostel*, very clean and friendly, twin rooms only, good security, breakfast available, dinner and soft drinks on request, intermittent water supply. Safe parking for cars and motorcycles, the road leading to hostel is the haunt of muggers who wait for tourists late at night and early in the morning. You are advised to get a taxi back late at night, and if you are catching an early bus see if you can pay one of the *askaris* to accompany you to the bus stand. There is also a way to the hostel from the bus station; head up the hill directly opposite and follow the path round. **F** *Warsame Guest House*, central position. Communal showers, no hot water, intermittent water supplies but is clean and quiet.

Camping **E** *Karibuni Centre*, 500 m off the Tanzam highway at the Mbalizi Evangelical Church, PO Box 144, T3035, F4178. Run by a Swiss missionary in a forest area, good simple food, safe car parking, has a small guesthouse or camping facilities, US$2.50 per tent. The church also runs a school for motor mechanics and is a good place for any vehicle repairs, although spare parts are not cheap.

Another campground between Mbeya and Iringa is on the main road to Dar approximately 50 km before Iringa – see *The Old Farmhouse*, page 519.

Eating **Cheap** *PMS Corner Restaurant*, friendly staff, good, cheap local food. *Rift Valley Hotel*, lengthy menu, food unmemorable, overpriced. **Seriously cheap** *Eddy Coffee Bar*, previously *Tanzania Coffee Shop*, near the market in Sisimba St has reasonable food, especially the fish. The chicken/rice dish is uninspiring. Excellent vegetarian fare. *Pavern Restaurant & Bar*, Lupa Way, near the Customs House. Popular local eating spot, very good choice of food including curries and steak and chips, excellent value for money.

Air *Precisionair* have scheduled flights between Dar es Salaam (DSM) and Mbeya via Iringa, leaving DSM 0930 on Tue, Thu and Sun. Fare is about US$150 one-way. Being so close to the Mbeya Range makes for a fairly spectacular, if dramatic, landing.

Transport
See Dar es Salaam transport, page 360

Road Buses are very regular to **Dar es Salaam**. Fare is around US$15 luxury, US$13 semi-luxury and US$9 ordinary, and journey takes 10-12 hrs. The best companies are *Fresh ya Shamba* (every other day), *Safina* but especially recommended is *Scandinavian Express Services*, T2504305; fixed departure times are 0630 and 0700. The road goes through the Mikumi National Park (see page 494). There are 2 buses a week to **Tabora**: the road is poor, they take about 24 hrs and cost around US$10. There are frequent small buses to the **Zambian border** at **Tunduma** and to **Kyela** close to Lake Nyasa (Lake Malawi) for the **Malawi border**, both taking 3-4 hrs and costing US$2.50. Few buses or minibuses from Mbeya travel all the way to the Malawi border, but transport is fairly easy to Kyela. Ask to be dropped off at the turn-off to the border before you reach the town of Kyela. From there it is about 5 km to the border and you should be able to get a lift. After Tanzanian immigration formalities you cross the bridge over the Songwe River to the Malawi immigration on the other side. It's a friendly border. Your yellow fever card may be checked. From the Malawi border there is one bus to Mbeya; it departs at 1200, costs US$2.50 and takes 4 hrs. Malawi is 1 hr behind Tanzanian time.

Take great care of your possessions at the railway and bus stations as local thieves target travellers, especially backpackers. Thieves and pickpockets also operate on the minibuses linking the stations

Buses for **Morogoro**: take the Dar es Salaam bus and get off at the junction outside Morogoro. Takes 8-9 hrs and costs US$10. The *Scandanavian* bus company is highly recommended, costing US$17, departing 0630 and 0700, and arriving in Dar at 1730 and 1800. Buses to **Songea**: there are 3 buses daily costing US$6.50 and taking 6-7 hrs. Buses to **Njombe** leave several times a day, costing US$5 and taking 3-4 hrs. Buses to **Iringa** cost US$5, take 4-5 hrs and leave several times a day. Buses to **Tunduma** are frequent, cost US$1.70 and take 1-2 hrs.

Train Trains are often full and booking in advance is essential through the Tanzanian-Zambia Railway Authority (Dar es Salaam: PO Box 2834, T2864191). The journey takes about 2 days. The TAZARA railway station is outside the town on the Tanzam highway – the main road linking Dar es Salaam to Zambia.

See pages 328 and 329 for details of train services, timetables and fares

Banks The best banks are all on Kaunda St. *National Bank of Commerce*, on the corner of Kaunda St, opposite the stadium, has reasonable rates and is the best place to cash TCs (no commission but you need to have the cheque receipts and passport) and the bank will change most major currencies, taking about 10 mins. Nearby is *CRDB*, which tends to offer slightly better rates for large dollar bills, $10 commission for TCs. *Stanbic Bank*, on the corner with Lupa Way, recently being rebuilt. There are no ATMs or cash advances on credit cards available. **Communications Post**: near the library. **Medical services** Mbeya Medical Centre, the main state hospital in the region, T3571/3351.

Directory

Tukuyu

This is a small town about 40 km south of Mbeya, on the road to Lake Nyasa (Lake Malawi). It was an administrative centre for the Germans and there is a group of colonial buildings to the southeast of the town. Tukuyu is a pretty dreary town; on the other hand it has a glorious location in the scenic **Poroto Mountains**. There's nothing to keep you in the town itself but a great deal to see in the surrounding countryside. Tukuyu is an important tea-growing area and the road to Kyela is lined with the picturesque fields of the mostly foreign-owned plantations.

9°17'S 33°35'E Phone code: 025 Colour map 4, grid C3 Altitude: 1,615 m

Tukuyu is a good centre for trekking. It is necessary to engage a guide, and the *Langiboss Hotel* can arrange one. Among the local attractions are **Mount Rungwe**, the most important mountain in this area, and at 2,961 m the highest mountain in southern Tanzania. The slopes of the mountain are vast and wild with over 100 sq km of uninhabited forest, upland scrub and rock terrain. It is accessed from Isangole, 10 km north of Tukuyu, and will take at least a full day to climb; **Masoko Crater Lake** 15 km to the southwest; Kapalogwe Falls, south of Tukuyu, the falls are spectacular, around 40 m high in an attractive lush setting. Half-way down there is a

Trekking

Tanzania

cave behind the falls, which it is possible to enter. There's good swimming at the bottom in the pool the falls cascade into. To reach them go about 6 km down the main road towards Kyela to the Ushirika village bus stop. From there it's about 2½ hours to walk or it's possible to hire a bicycle at the main road (with or without rider!). **Ngozi Crater Lake** about 20 km north of Tukuyu in the Poroto Mountains, is a beautiful lake lying in the collapsed crater of an extinct volcano the sides of which plunge down steeply from a rainforest covered rim. The forest is home to colonies of Colobus monkeys. Witch doctors are said to call upon ancestral powers here and local legend claims that there is an underwater snake-like monster hidden deep in the waters of the crater lake, causing the surface waters to change colour from time to time. To get there catch a *dala-dala* going to Mbeya up to Mchangani village (this takes 1-1½ hours). It's probably advisable to arrange for a guide at Mchangani to take you up to the lake as the route is by no means obvious. It's a two-hour walk from the main road to Ngozi. The second half of the walk entails a steep climb through rainforest before you emerge at the crater rim. From here the views across the lake are spectacular. You could camp at the top, in which case you would be there for sunset and dawn, which would be rather special. **Daraja la Mungu** (Bridge of God), also known as Kiwira Natural Bridge, is an unusual rock formation spanning a small river close to Tukuyu. To get there take a *dala-dala* going to Mbeya and get off a Kibwe (12 km north of Tukuyu). Here change to one of the Land Rovers waiting at the beginning of the road branching off to the left (ask for Daraja la Mungu). It's a further 12 km down this rough road. There are apparently also hot springs (*maji ya moto*) a little further on and nearby is Kijunga waterfall.

Sleeping **D** *Langiboss*, about 1 km from the town centre on the road to Masoko. Modest but well run, food available if you order in advance. The *Bombay Restaurant* offers cheaper fare of similar quality.

Transport **Road Bus**: there are regular buses running from Mbeya to **Kyela**. The buses to **Dar es Salaam** come early (around 0500-0600) and cost US$16.50. Journey time around 11 hrs.

Kyela

Colour map 4, grid C3 Kyela is a small commercial centre loated in a rich agricultural area to the northwest of Lake Nyasa. The countryside surrounding the town is verdant and fertile, abounding in banana plants, mango trees, maize, bamboo and also rice, which is particularly prized throughout Tanzania, much of it being transported to Dar es Salaam after harvest. Unfortunately the town itself doesn't match its attractive surroundings; it is dusty and characterless and on arrival you'll probably be keen to get out as soon as possible! However, if you're hoping to catch the ferry to Mbamba Bay or Nkhata Bay (in Malawi) at least one night in Kyela is necessary, as this is the access town for the ferries that leave from Itungi.

This corner of southwestern Tanzania, south of Mbeya, is home to Nyakyusa, who, along with the Chagga of Kilimanjaro and the Haya of Bukoba region, are one of the country's most prosperous and successful ethnic groups.

Sleeping Fortunately several good guesthouses have recently been built in Kyela, an indication of the increased trade and rising prosperity in the area. Best of all is the **D** *Pattaya Central*,

Kyela

■ Sleeping
1 Bikutuka Guest House
2 Kilimanjaro Guest House
3 Livingstone Cottage Guest House
4 Pattaya Central Guest House

● Eating
1 Bar
2 Hassan
3 New Steak Inn

To TRC Office & Itungi Port

0 metres 200
0 yards 200

which has spotless rooms. TVs in each room have been promised for a couple of years but still no sign of any. The only drawback, TV or not, may be the noise resulting from its central location. **E** *Bikutuka Guest House* is another good place; cheaper, shared bathroom, quieter due to its residential location. **E** *Kilimanjaro Guest House*, close to the market, has clean rooms with fans and nets but slightly smelly toilets, and is cheaper still. **E** *Livingstone Cottage* on the road to Mbeya is similar to the *Kilimanjaro Guest House*.

New Steak Inn is a fairly new and surprisingly plush restaurant for a Tanzanian town of this size, yet it has a run-down look already. It does good basic dishes. There is another Arab-run restaurant just down the road that serves all the Tanzanian regulars and is fine.

Eating

Road Bus: to **Dar es Salaam**, you have to be an early riser to catch a bus going to Dar es Salaam. They leave between 0440-0500 and pick up passengers at Tukuyu and sometimes Mbeya also. The most reliable (and safe) company is *Scandinavian Express Services* whose fare is US$17, journey time 13 hrs. To **Mbeya**: there are numerous minibuses going to Mbeya, which if you're very lucky will take 3 hrs, normally will take 4 hrs, and can take up to 6 hrs or more. Be prepared! It costs US$2.50. To **Tukuyu**: catch a bus going to Mbeya. It takes 2-3 hrs and costs US$1.20. To **Itungi (for the Nyasa ferry)**: takes 30 mins and costs US$0.60. If you're catching the Thu ferry then you'll need to get up very early. To **Matema**: very difficult to reach on public transport. See under Matema below. **To the border with Malawi**: some of the minibuses to Mbeya go via the border. There are also occasional Land Rovers. It costs US$0.60 and is about 30 mins away.

Transport

Warning Matema Beach coaches have rather a bad reputation. **Ferry** To Lake Nyasa, the boats are run by Tanzanian Railways Corporation (TRC). Tickets are best bought in the afternoon before departure from the TRC building, which is located 1 km down the road to Itungi on the right. A bus leaves the TRC office for Itungi at around 0500. See the timetable under Mbamba Bay.

Matema

The Lutheran Mission guesthouse at this beautifully located lakeside village is justifiably a favourite among expatriate workers in Tanzania. It is situated at the foot of the Livingstone mountains on a magnificent beach that sweeps around the northern tip of Lake Nyasa.

Colour map 4, grid C3

The Kisi, one of the peoples who make up the population of the surrounding area, are well known throughout Tanzania for their pottery skills. There is a market to the south of Matema that can be reached by dug-out and in the centre of Matema village itself large piles of Kisi pots can be seen bound up awaiting transportation to Mbeya, Iringa and even as far away as Dar es Salaam.

There are supposed to be hippos and crocodiles in the river that flows into the lake about two miles or so west of the guesthouse. It is a pleasant walk anyway, along the beach and then returning on a path slightly inland.

Dug-outs can be hired, which take you across to the far shore where there is good snorkelling (you need to have your own equipment). It's not as good as some spots further south in Malawi though. Dug-outs can also take you to the Kisi pottery market. Beach safe for swimming, reportedly clear of bilharzia.

On the northeastern side of Lake Nyasa are found the **Livingstone Mountains**, which are among the most spectacular in all Tanzania –vertiginous rock, meadows and waterfalls plunging into the calm waters of Lake Nyasa. These mountains were formed by the uplifted shoulder of the Lake Malawi Rift, and rise to over 1500 m above the lake, but just 2 km offshore the depth of the lake waters exceed 400 m.

The old German mission stations of Milo and Perimiho are a major feature of this area. They were later converted to UMCA stations.

The choice of accommodation is very limited. **E** *Lutheran Guest House*, which with its superb location and good rooms is all you could ask for, some rooms have up to 5 beds in them and

Sleeping & eating

Tanzania

Tanzania

are ideal for families, has good value accommodation in bandas and is well recommended, simple and spotlessly clean. It is possible to camp. Another mission, just west of the *Lutheran Guest House*, was recently nearing completion and should offer comfortable rooms for guests. The guesthouse does good breakfasts (which are included in the price of the room) and very reasonable school dinner-type lunches and dinners for US$2.50.

Transport The only way I can account for Matema being so little visited is the difficulty in getting there by public transport. Buses to Matema are painfully slow, uncomfortable and extraordinarily overcrowded. A traveller reports that recently part of the road was impassable and a walk of 20 mins was necessary to continue the journey. If you are lucky you'll catch a direct bus from Kyela to Matema. The distance is 35 km and it costs US$0.65. If you're not lucky then you'll get a bus to Ipinda and change there (after a considerable wait); if you're unlucky then you might have to spend the night at Ipinda (there's a basic but reasonable guesthouse there) and hope to get a bus on to Matema the following morning. Leaving Matema: however you get to Matema you're going to want to spend a few days there if only to put off the return journey! There are buses leaving daily early in the morning to Kyela, and occasionally to Mbeya via Tukuyu. Alternatively, a fellow guest with their own transport may assist you. Unfortunately the Lake Nyasa Ferry no longer stops at Matema.

Liuli is a small impoverished village on the eastern shores of Lake Nyasa in the shadow of the Livingstone Mountains. German missionaries built a hospital here in colonial times and it still provides excellent service to the region today. The ferry calls here before travelling on to Mbamba Bay. Liuli is also famed as being where the British Navy destroyed the armed German steamer *Hermann Von Wissmann* by shellfire in May 1915. The steamer had been docked there having been damaged by the steamer *Gwendolyn* the previous year. This was one of the first British naval victories of the First World War.

Mbamba Bay

11°13'S 34°49'E
Colour map 4, grid C4

This is mainly a transit point for travellers en route for Songea. The route from Songea to Mbamba Bay is very scenic, passing up, down and around the green hills and mountains surrounding Mbinga before descending to Lake Nyasa. The road is bad, however, and the journey is pretty awful in the rainy season. Mbinga has become an important centre for the growing of Arabica coffee.

Mbamba Bay (known in the German colonial period as Sphinxhaven) is a modest village located on a glorious bay surrounded by hills on the eastern shore of Lake Nyasa (to Malawians, Lake Malawi). Most people coming to Mbamba Bay will be here to connect with (or arriving on) the ferries (Swahili – 'ëmeli') going north to Itungi or across the lake to Nkhata Bay and will probably only stay overnight. The scenic surroundings of Mbamba Bay, however, may well entice you into waiting for a later ferry. Many of the houses here are made in the traditional style with sun-dried, baked bricks, topped with thatch made from a long grass called *nyasi*. There's nothing much to do here, but what a setting for doing nothing! If Mbamba Bay was in Malawi the place would be heaving with tourists, as it is you're likely to have the place to yourself.

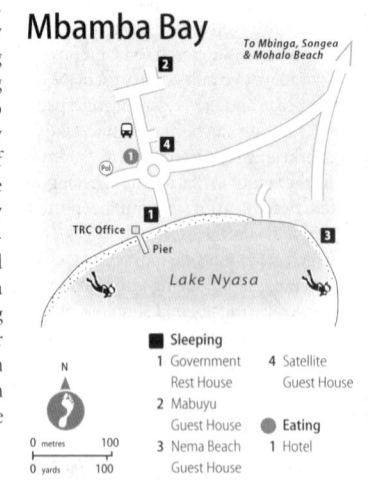

Mbamba Bay

To Mbinga, Songea & Mohalo Beach

TRC Office
Pier
Lake Nyasa

N
0 metres 100
0 yards 100

■ **Sleeping**
1 Government Rest House
2 Mabuyu Guest House
3 Nema Beach Guest House
4 Satellite Guest House

● **Eating**
1 Hotel

Sailing schedule for MV Songea				
	Arrive		**Leave**	
Mbamba Bay	Tuesday	0500	Tuesday	1400
Itungi	Wednesday	0900	Thursday	0800
Mbamba Bay	Friday	0500	Friday	1100
Nkhata Bay (Malawi)	Friday	1300	Friday	1800
Mbamba Bay	Friday	2100	Friday	2400
Itungi	Saturday	1700	Monday	0800

Sailing schedule for MV Ilala				
	Arrive		**Leave**	
Mbamba Bay	Tuesday	0430	Tuesday	0730
Nkhata Bay (Malawi)	Tuesday	1100	Tuesday	1300
Monkty Bay (Malawi)	Thursday	0600	Sunday	1130

NB The boats are subject to delays from time to time

Tanzania

The magnificent Mohalo Beach, reportedly over 20 km in length, lies 4-5 km south of Mbamba Bay. It can be reached by walking along the road to Mbinga and taking a right at the junction after 1.5 km or so, or alternatively by hiring a dug-out canoe to take you around the headland (this takes about 45 minutes). It is an ideal place for camping. There is another long beach to the north of the village.

Sleeping & eating E *Nema Beach Guest House* is the best place for longer stays but inconvenient for overnights. It is located on its own beach about a mile from the centre of the village. Very good rooms, clean, s/c. E *The Government Rest House*, a signless pink building next to the ferry, has basic s/c rooms, it has an excellent location on the beach. If you want to stay in the village there are the E *Satellite* and the E *Mabuyu Guest Houses*, which both have clean doubles without toilet/shower. Limited places to eat. There is a simple hotel on the roundabout. The restaurant at the *Nema* isn't bad, but it's inconvenient if you're not staying there.

Transport **Road** **Bus**: for buses to Songea, see Songea below. The road to Songea is very rough in parts and the bridges are occasionally severely damaged. The last bridge into town has collapsed and until repairs are carried out you will have to walk the last leg of the journey into the town of Mbamba Bay. **Boat** The ferry journey up the lake to Itungi, cruising along the eastern shore of Lake Nyasa with the impressive Livingstone Mountains looming at the background. Highly recommended. 1st class cabins are for 2 people and small but comfortable. Try to get a cabin facing the lake-shore for the view. The ship's clerk on board the boat allocates the cabins. In 3rd class you get a wooden bench and plenty of company. 2nd class seems to have disappeared! Fares for non-residents are US$16 plus US$5 port tax for 1st class and US$6 plus US$5 port tax for 3rd. Food is available on board.

Songea

This town, located northeast of Mbamba Bay, was comparatively isolated until the construction of the sealed road from the Iringa-Mbeya highway.

10°40'S 35°40'E
Phone code: 025
Colour map 4, grid C4
Altitude: 4,000 ft

The journey from Tunduru to Songea is tough going and not particularly scenic, undulating miombo scrub mostly, until you begin to ascend the hills approaching Songea, by which time you'll probably be too knackered to appreciate the scenery anyway!

Songea is the provincial headquarters of Southern Province. It was named after the Ngoni chief of the same name. It's a pleasant enough place, although there is little to keep you in the town itself. On the other hand, it is surrounded by attractive rolling countryside and hills, which are good for walking. Matogoro peak is within easy reach to the southeast of the town – take one of the tracks leading off the road to

Tanzania

👉 Matengo farming

Between Mbamba Bay and Songea is the Mbinga district of Ruvuma region in southern Tanzania, home to the Matengo people. They live in mountainous highlands ranging from 1,400-2,000 m. The flora was originally montane forest, which has largely been cleared for farming. The area is cultivated using a unique system called ngoro or the Matengo pit system. This allows for intensive production, using crop rotation and protects against soil erosion. The grass is cut and laid in rows forming a grid pattern. Then the square sections between the grass are hoed and the excavated earth – to a depth of up to 30 cm – is placed on top of the grass. Crops of beans, maize and wheat are planted in rotation along these rows of earth on grass. The fields bear a resemblance to honeycombs.

After a couple of years, new earth banks are built up over the previous pits, which are filled with any of the grass remnants and soil, plus any crop residue. New pits are dug at the intersections of the previous ridges, grass is cut and placed on the new ridges, and fresh soil from the new pits laid on top ready for planting.

This technique has enabled the Marengo people to achieve very high yields, needed as the area is densely populated. This method, which is thought to have been in use for over 100 years, has proved to be very effective at improving soil fertility, conserving moisture and reducing soil erosion.

Tunduru. It is situated in part of the **Matogoro forest reserve** most of which stretches to the east of the peak itself. There are fine views from the top.

Songea and the surrounding area is home to the **Ngoni**, a group descended from an offshoot of the Zulus who came from South Africa in the mid-19th century fleeing the rule of King Chaka in about 1840. The Ngoni had to fight several tribes who lived in the area to establish a foothold. They were hunters and farmers and later on strongly resisted the German colonial settlement. From 1905-1907, there was an extensive two-year insurgence against the Germans, triggered by the harsh working conditions in the cotton plantations. It was known as the **Maji Maji Rebellion**, led by a witch-doctor named Kinjekitile, who led his followers to believe that they would

Songea

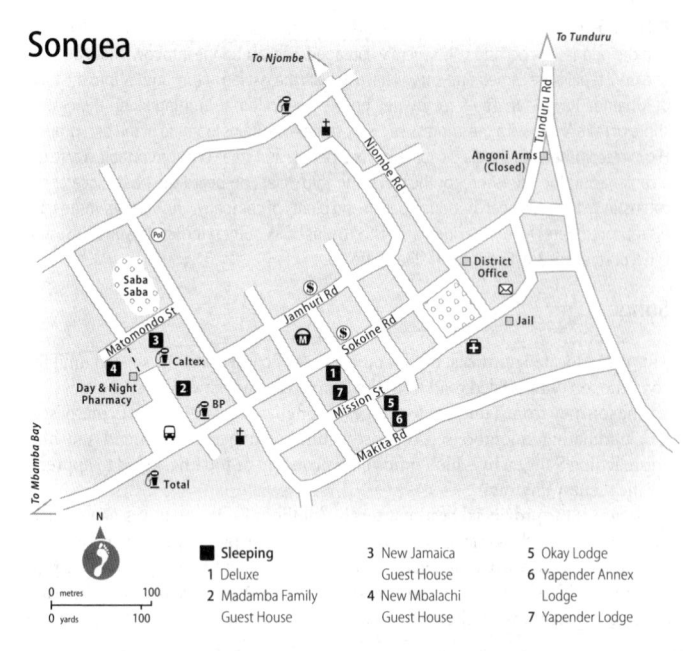

Sleeping
1 Deluxe
2 Madamba Family Guest House
3 New Jamaica Guest House
4 New Mbalachi Guest House
5 Okay Lodge
6 Yapender Annex Lodge
7 Yapender Lodge

be invincible after drinking or being sprinkled with his magic liquid potion, which his disciples were convinced had the power to transform bullets into water. The magic potion is reputed to have contained water, ground maize and sorghum seeds. Warriers shouted '*maji maji*' (meaning 'water water'), while going into battle armed only with swords, pangas and clubs, convinced that in doing so they would disable the German arms. The rebellion was finally suppressed locally when the Ngoni chiefs were all hanged in Songea by the Germans in 1907. The tree used to execute the local chieftains survives, close to a small museum built nearby.

Tobacco is the main cash crop in the area, although Mbinga, to the south, is an important centre for coffee growing.

Sleeping & eating

If you have your own transport it is worth staying at a Roman Catholic Mission, including a well-equipped hospital, run by German nuns and brothers called **D** *Peremiho*, a few kilometres outside town towards Lake Malawi, which has very good facilities for guests. The **D** *Yapender Annex Lodge* has spotless, spacious s/c double rooms. Just down the road the **D** *Okay Lodge*, PO Box 282, T2602640, also has good s/c doubles. The rooms at the **D** *Yapender Lodge* are the same price as those at the Annex but not as good value. Best budget hotel is the **F** *New Mbalachi Guest House*, which has the added advantage of being very close to the bus stand. Very clean, rooms have mosquito nets. To reach it go to the back of the station and walk down the passageway between the Caltex pumps and the Day & Night dispensary. Actually located at the bus stand is the **F** *Madamba Family Guest House* where rooms are very cheap but noisy. **F** *The New Jamaica Guest House* on Matomondo St, has cheap, basic rooms. **F** *The Deluxe Hotel* on Sokoine Rd, has cheap and not so cheerful rooms. There are few culinary highlights in Songea. All the hotels have small restaurants but the best bet is probably the restaurant at the *Okay Lodge*, which does decent simple meals such as fish and chips or *ugali* and stew.

Transport

Road Bus: there are several buses leaving daily to Dar es Salaam all leaving early. Best company is Kiswele Bus. The journey takes around 12 hrs and costs US$12.50. Three buses a day go to Mbeya costing around US$6.50 and taking 6-7 hrs. Buses to Njombe are numerous, costing US$4.50 for the 3-4 hr ride. To Mbamba Bay (outside the rainy season) there are two daily buses leaving between 0600-0700. The journey takes 8-10 hrs, US$10. Book a seat the day before. There is at least one bus leaving Songea for Tunduru leaving early every other morning. Costs US$10. Try to book a seat in front of the back axle in view of the appalling state of the roads.

Njombe

Set among attractive green rolling highlands Njombe is another undistinguished Tanzanian town in a wonderful location. The surrounding hills are excellent walking country and are easily accessible from the town. Being 1,859 m above sea level the climate here is cool all year round. There are several wattle and tea plantations in Njombe district, some of which can be seen on the road to Iringa and Mbeya.

9°20'S 34°50'E
Phone code: 026
Colour map 4, grid C4

The town was set up in rich farming country of the Southern Highlands, possibly because of the aerodrome, an early refuelling point en route to South Africa. Nearby is a **spectacular waterfall**, within an easy walking distance north on the road to Makambako where you can picnic, and wattle estates and tanning factory on the hill opposite (Kibena). The UMCA Diocesan HQ, Bishop's House and cathedral are worth a visit. Njombe is very much the centre of missionary activity and the old hotel was bought by the mission. Single high street, usual stores included at one time Sachadena's Fancy Stores. The town is a safe place provided the usual common-sense precautions are taken. This is on the route from Songea to the Mbeya-Iringa highway. There are frequent buses between Mbeya and Songea that pass through Njombe. There is a Roman Catholic Mission at **Uwemba** run by German nuns and brothers, located in the countryside after a 40-minute drive along the road to Songea. There is a guesthouse, and visitors can tour the farm, school and medical facility, and also try some horse-riding.

Sleeping　**D** *Chani*, 5-7 mins' walk north of the centre, T2782357. 8 double and 4 single rooms with en suite showers and toilets, some rooms are carpeted, regularly used by Peace Corps volunteers, recommended. Bar and good restaurant, but there is often a long wait for the food, an hour or more, even if you pre-order. **E** *Africa Guest House* is comfortable. **E** *Annex Guest House*, near the market in the centre of town. Basic, clean rooms, some are s/c, hot water provided in a bucket, the lack of TV in the bar makes for a relaxed, quieter atmosphere than is found elsewhere, restaurant serves good local meals. **E** *Mbalache Guest House* is the best value in town, good rooms available with or without showers and toilets. **E** *Milimani Hotel*, near the post office, T2782408. 20 spacious double rooms, some a little larger than others, each has own bathroom with hot shower, excellent value. Seating in the bar is arranged like a cinema, facing a satellite TV screen, popular with locals especially when football is showing. The restaurant serves tasty, generously portioned meals but you should pre-order, otherwise you may have to wait for up to an hour for the food. **E** *New Magazeti Guest House*, T2782108. Same price and standard as the Annex Guest House. The rooms are arranged in typical Tanzanian style where all rooms lead off from an inner atrium. Some rooms have en-suite facilities of shower and toilet and hot water is available. The cosy bar is a good place for a drink, and the restaurant offers tasty, generous meals.

Eating　For a town of its size Njombe is particularly poorly served for restaurants – but then you won't have come here for the cuisine! Good simple meals are available from the attached restaurants of the hotels mentioned above. **Seriously cheap** *Sangamela Restaurant*, a few minutes' walk south of the centre, is a small restaurant that has very good freshly prepared meals, simple and cheap.

Transport　**Road Bus**: to **Dar es Salaam**, two direct buses daily leaving 0500-0600, journey time 9-10 hrs. Fare US$15. To **Arusha**: Hood Transport runs buses twice weekly on Mon and Fri, leaving at 0800 and arriving 2200. Fare US$21.50. To **Songea, Iringa and Mbeya**: there are numerous buses daily, they all take around 3-4 hrs and costs around US$4.50. There are also 4WD (*gari ndogo*) going to Ludewa on Lake Nyasa (where you could link up with the ferry) for US$7.50. It will probably be fairly tough going though.

Makambako

Colour map 4, grid C4　A town approximately half-way between Iringa and Mbeya, it developed because of its station on the Tanzania-Zambia Railway, and because it is a stop for road traffic and truckers passing through from Zambia. It is also at the intersection with the road to Njombe and Songea. Not a pleasant place to stay, the much more friendly and amenable Njombe is only 50 km away on a good surfaced road. If you do stay, there are several cheap hotels and a Lutheran church hostel, but only the comfortable *Uplands Hotel* offers a good degree of safety. Uplands serves OK meals, the railway canteen offers good food during the day, and there are many cheap local restaurants.

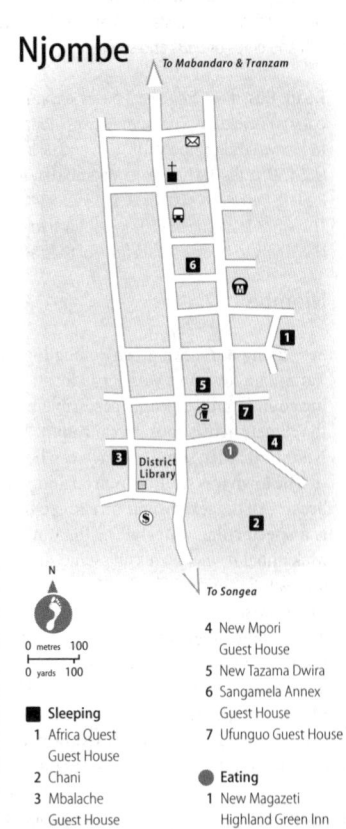

Njombe

To Mabandaro & Tranzam

To Songea

■ **Sleeping**
1 Africa Quest Guest House
2 Chani
3 Mbalache Guest House
4 New Mpori Guest House
5 New Tazama Dwira
6 Sangamela Annex Guest House
7 Ufunguo Guest House

● **Eating**
1 New Magazeti Highland Green Inn

District Library

0 metres 100
0 yards 100

Zanzibar and Pemba

Dar es Salam

The very name Zanzibar conjures up exotic and romantic images. There are two main islands making up Zanzibar, Unguja and Pemba. Zanzibar Town is on Unguja Island, but Unguja Island is popularly referred to as Zanzibar. The town is steeped in history, is full of atmosphere and immensely attractive. There are excellent beaches on the east coast. The island is about 96 km long, has an area of about 3,350 sq km and is separated from the mainland by a channel 35 km wide. The main rains are from March to May, and the best time to visit is from June to October.

6°12'S 39°12'E
Phone code: 024
Colour map 4, grid B6

Tanzania

Tourist facilities and prices of accommodation, tours and excursions have all increased rapidly over the past couple of years. Prices quoted may therefore be inaccurate at times. Zanzibar has a relaxed and sympathetic attitude to visitors. However, the islands are predominantly Muslim and although Zanzibaris are too polite to raise the issue, they feel uncomfortable with some western dress styles. In the towns and villages (that is, outside the beach hotels and resorts) it is courteous for women to dress modestly, covering the upper arms and body, with dresses to below the knee. Wearing bikinis, cropped tops or shorts cause offence. For men there is no restriction beyond what is considered decent in the west.

Ins & outs

Zanzibar is perhaps most famous for once being the home of the slave trade, and an important trading post for spices and cloves. Once Zanzibar was the world's most important supplier of cloves but it has now been overtaken by producers in the Far East. Cloves do remain the most important export of the island, while tourism is now the largest source of foreign currency. On the western part of the island there are clove plantations with trees 10-20 m tall.

Background

The island has been a stopping-off point for traders going up and down the coast for many years and as a result has seen many different travellers including Greeks, Egyptians, Persians and Chinese. European explorers and missionaries also visited the island and it was used as a starting point for their travels inland. The legacy of these early visitors is shown in the people, architecture and culture.

Since 1964, when the rule of the Sultans ended, Zanzibar has neglected its heritage. In a union with the mainland, Zanzibar sought to progress by socialist policies and a modernizing philosophy. The relics of this period are to be seen in the brutal concrete blocks constructed to the east of Creek Road in Zanzibar Town. Fortunately much of the glorious old Stone Town escaped unscathed and, with a change of heart towards the past, is now being restored.

History

The origin of the name Zanzibar is disputed. The Omani Arabs believe it came from Zayn Zal Barr, which means 'Fair is the Island'. The alternative origin is in two parts – the early inhabitants of the island were from the mainland and were given the name *Zenj*, a Persian word that is a corruption of *Zangh* meaning negro. The word *bar* that means coast was added to this to give 'Negro Coast'.

The earliest visitors were Arab traders who brought with them Islam, which has remained the dominant religion on the island. They are believed to have arrived in the eighth century. The earliest building that remains is the mosque at Kazimkazi that dates from about 1100.

For centuries the Arabs had sailed with the monsoons down from Muscat and Oman in the Gulf to trade in ivory, slaves, spices, hides and wrought-iron. The two main islands, both of roughly similar size, Unguja (usually known as Zanzibar Island) and Pemba, provided an ideal base, being relatively small islands and thus easy to defend. From here it was possible to control 1,500 km of the mainland coast from present day Mozambique up to Somalia. A consequence of their being the first arrivals was that the Arabs became the main landowners.

In 1832 Sultan Seyyid Said, of the Al Busaid dynasty that had emerged in Oman in 1744, moved his palace from Muscat to Zanzibar. Said and his descendants were to rule there for 134 years. In 1822, the Omanis signed the Moresby Treaty that made it illegal for them to sell slaves to Christian powers in their dominions. To monitor this agreement, the United States in 1836 and the British in 1840 established diplomatic relations with Zanzibar, and sent resident Consuls to the islands. The slaving restrictions were not effective and the trade continued to flourish. Caravans set out from Bagamoyo on the mainland coast, travelling up to 1,500 km on foot as far as Lake

Zanzibar Island

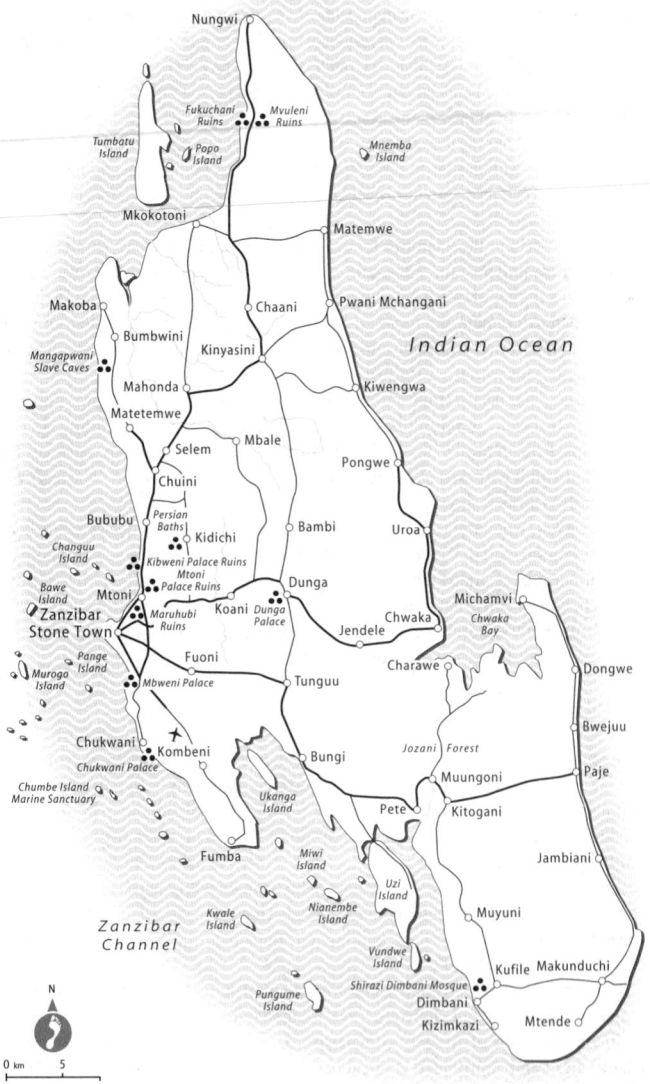

Tanzania

★

Things to do in Zanzibar

There is no shortage of attractions in Zanzibar. Here are some that particularly appeal to your Editor:

- Take an evening meal at **Emerson and Green's** rooftop restaurant, looking out over Stone Town (essential to look in to book the day before).
- Hire a bicycle on Creek Road and **cycle** north of Zanzibar Town to the ruined palaces of the Sultans at Muhurubi, Mtoni, and Kibweri and then on to the Mangapwani Slave Caves.
- Take a **Spice Tour** with a swim and a lunch in one of the villages on Zanzibar Island.
- Book a trip for a day at **Chunguu Island**, with lunch, a swim and some ancient and huge tortoises.
- Take a day trip to **Jozani Forest** where there is a well laid out nature trail.
- In the evening dine casually on the sumptuous food offered by the numerous outdoor grills and stalls in **Jamituri Gardens**.

Tanzania

Tanganyika, purchasing slaves from local rulers on the way, or, more cheaply, simply capturing them. The slaves, chained together, carried ivory back to Bagamoyo. The name Bagamoyo means 'lay down your heart' for it was here that the slaves would abandon hope of ever seeing their homeland again. They were shipped to the slave market in Zanzibar Town, bought by intermediary traders, who in turn sold them on without any restrictions.

All the main racial groups were involved in the slave trade. Europeans used slaves in the plantations in the Indian Ocean islands, Arabs were the main capturers and traders, and African rulers sold the prisoners taken in battle to the traders. Alas, being sold into slavery was not the worst fate that could befall a captive. If a prolonged conflict led to a glut, the Doe tribe from just north of Bagamoyo would run down excess stocks of prisoners by the simple expedient of eating them. Nevertheless, it is the perception of the African population that the Arabs were mainly responsible.

Cloves had been introduced from Southeast Asia, probably Indonesia, prior to the advent of Sultan Seyyid Said. They flourished in the tropical climate on the fertile and well-watered soils on the western areas of both Zanzibar and Pemba islands. Slaves did the cultivation and harvesting and the Sultan occupied plots, such that by his death in 1856 he had 45 plantations. Other plantations were acquired by his many children, as well as by numerous concubines and eunuchs from the royal harem. In due course cinnamon, nutmeg, black pepper, cumin, ginger and cardamom were all established, their fragrances were everywhere and Zanzibar became known as the 'Spice Islands'. Slaves, spices and ivory provided the basis of considerable prosperity, mostly in the hands of the Arab community, who were the main landowners, and who kept themselves to themselves and did not intermarry with the Africans.

This was not true of a second group that came from the Middle East to settle on the East African coast. In AD 975 Abi Ben Sultan Hasan of Shiraz in Persia (now Iran) is said to have had a dream in which a rat with iron jaws devoured the foundations of his house. He took this as a sign that his community was to be destroyed. Other members of the court in Shiraz poured scorn on the notion, but Sultan Hasan, his family and some followers decided to migrate. They set out in seven dhows from the nearby port of Bushehr and sailed through the mouth of the Persian Gulf into the Indian Ocean. Here they were caught in a great storm, separated, and made landfalls at seven separate places along the East African coast, one of which was Zanzibar, and established settlements. Intermarriage between Shirazis and Africans gave rise to a coastal community with distinctive features, and a language derived in part from Arabic. This became known as Swahili. In Zanzibar the descendants of this group were known as the Afro-Shirazis. They were not greatly involved in the lucrative slave, spice and ivory trades. They cultivated coconuts, fished and became

Tanzania

Zanzibar of the Sultans

Salme Said was the daughter of one of the concubines of Sultan Said, who ruled from 1804 to 1856. Later known as Emily Ruete, she described her life in Memoirs of an Arabian Princess from Zanzibar *(Princeton: Markus Wiener), from which the following extracts were distilled:*

On life at Mtoni Palace

The Palace buildings were arranged round a large courtyard in which roamed a variety of exotic wildlife – peacocks, gazelles, geese, flamingoes and ostriches. One side of the courtyard contained 12 bathhouses, each with two baths 15 ft by 12 ft by 4 ft deep. Platforms, either side of the baths, covered with mats served for rest and prayer areas. The baths were in continual use during waking hours. The older children had riding lessons, twice a day, in the morning and evening. When they were sufficiently competent, each boy was given a horse, and each girl a white donkey. A regular diversion for these children was a ride in the country.

The Sultan's wife occupied the rooms overlooking the sea. The Sultan only spent four nights a week at Mtoni, the rest at the Palace by the promenade in Stone Town. Other palace rooms were occupied by concubines and their children, while the outbuildings housed slaves and eunuchs. In all there were estimated to be about 1,000 people living in and around the palace. On the shore side was a tower with a vaulted roof and balcony that caught the breeze. Coffee was taken and a telescope offered sightings of approaching vessels and a view of Stone Town to the south. A flagpole on the shore was used to run up messages for the Sultan's ships at anchor in the bay.

On a typical day at the palace in Stone Town

The first set of prayers would begin some time between 0400 and 0530. After these prayers sleep would be resumed until around 0800 when there would be a massage from a slave followed by a bath. At 0900, the children all went to greet their father after which the Sultan would preside over breakfast attended by his wife, relatives and children, but not the concubines. After breakfast small children would play, older children attend lessons, the women engage in conversation or embroidery. Slaves were dispatched to arrange evening visits.

The Sultan would repair to the audience chamber on the first floor. A rather grand entrance was made with an African guard followed by a detail of eunuchs then the Sultan, followed by his sons. All senior notables were expected to attend and the company rose as the Sultan's party entered. Disputes, requests and complaints were dealt with, the Sultan delegating minor matters to his ministers, judges or the senior eunuchs. The business was all transacted verbally and the senior eunuchs recorded the decisions.

At 1300, the second prayers took place, followed by siestas, perhaps a visit to the bathhouse, while fruit and cake were partaken.

Third prayers were at 1600 and were followed by the evening meal, with much the same food being served as for breakfast. During the meal there would usually be organ music or some Taraab.

Fingers were used for eating, and rinsed in bowls of scented water. Sherbet water and coffee were available after the meal. The assembly sat on the floor and ate in silence round a long, low table with the Sultan at the

agricultural labourers. Those Shirazis who did not intermarry retained their identity as a separate group.

Two smaller communities were also established. Indian traders arrived in connection with the spice and ivory trade, and, as elsewhere in East Africa, settled as shopkeepers, traders, skilled artisans, money-lenders, lawyers, doctors and accountants. The British became involved in missionary and trading activities in East Africa, and had exercised themselves in attempting to suppress the slave trade. Germans had begun trading on the mainland opposite Zanzibar. Things needed to be sorted out with the Sultan of Zanzibar, who controlled the 10-mile coastal strip that ran for 1,500 km from Mozambique to Somalia. Germany bought their strip of the coast from the Sultan for £200,000. The British East African Company had been paying the Sultan £11,000 a year for operating in the Kenyan portion. In 1890,

head. A variety of rice dishes, meat and fresh breads and sweetmeats were served onto small dishes.

The fourth prayers were said at 1900 after which the Sultan would conduct a second audience session at which coffee would be served. This was also the time for womenfolk to visit each other, and for men to do likewise, proceeding through the narrow streets of Stone Town accompanied by slaves carrying lanterns. The day concluded with the fifth prayers before bed at around 2200.

On the education of women

School (madresse) for the children of the affluent began at the age of six and continued to 12 or so. Usually all the children of the household would be taught privately by a female teacher in a room in the house, sitting on the floor, on matting. There were a few schools for the children of poorer parents. Children often brought their personal slaves to class with them, and they sat at the back.

The only book would be the Koran, open on a folding wooden book holder. As a result, the Koran would more-or-less all be learnt by heart, but there would be no discussion of the text or its interpretation, which was regarded as irreverent. The girls would be taught the Arabic alphabet first and then reading from sections of the Koran. Except in a few cases, only the boys learned to write. Quill pens and washable ink were used to copy sections of the Koran onto smooth tablets made from a camel's scapula (shoulder-blade). After use the tablets could be scrubbed clean and used again. A little arithmetic was taught, mostly simple addition and subtraction. Classes started at 0700, breakfast was at 0900 and school finished at noon. Discipline was strict, and the teacher used a bamboo cane to punish pupils. Girls learned sewing, embroidery and lace-making from their mothers.

On the role of women

Women in society, as long as they were not concubines or slaves, had equal rights with men. Dress conventions demanded that a woman must be completely veiled except for the eyes when meeting with any male who was not a relative or a slave. Furthermore, a woman was forbidden to speak with a male stranger. This made life very difficult for single women, particularly as this restriction prevented discussions with employees or officials.

Although Islamic law allowed four formal wives, in Zanzibar it was unusual for a man to have more than one wife. There was no restriction on the number of concubines or slaves, which were purchased. Children born to concubines were free, and in the event of the master's death, the concubines, too, became free.

Marriages were arranged. The girl was not allowed to meet with her intended husband, but endeavoured to find out as much as possible about him from relatives. Normally the girl was required to agree to the match, although occasionally the match went ahead against her wishes. Brides tended to be youthful, sometimes as young as nine.

Prior to the wedding, the bride-to-be was required to spend eight days in a darkened room. The marriage ceremony took place in the bride's house. The bride would not be present but would be represented by a male relative.

Tanzania

Germany allowed Britain to establish a protectorate over Zanzibar in return for Heligoland, a tiny barren island occupied by the British, but strategically placed opposite the mouth of the River Elbe, 50 km from the German coast. In 1895 Britain took over responsibility for its section of the mainland from the British East African Company and agreed to continue to pay the £11,000 a year to the Sultan. The British mainland territory (later to become Kenya), was administered by a Governor, to whom the British representative in Zanzibar, the Resident, was accountable.

The distinctive feature of Zanzibar as a protectorate (Kenya had become a colony in 1920) was recognized in 1926 when the British Resident was made directly responsible to the Colonial Secretary in London. Germany had by this stage lost control of its section of the mainland when, as a result of its defeat in the First World War, the territory was transferred to British control to become Tanganyika.

The colonial period Further legislation in 1873 had made the slave trade illegal, the slave market in Zanzibar was closed and the Protestant cathedral erected on the site. But slavery lingered on. The trade was illegal, but the institution of slavery existed openly until Britain took over the mainland from the Germans in 1918, and covertly, it is argued, for many years thereafter. Many former slaves found that their conditions had changed but little. They were now employed as labourers at low wage rates in the clove plantations. Zanzibar continued to prosper with the expansion of trade in cloves and other spices. The fine buildings that make Zanzibar Stone Town such a glorious place were constructed to a high standard by wealthy Arab slavers and clove traders, British administrators and prosperous Indian businessmen and professionals. These structures were so soundly built they have survived for the most part without repairs, maintenance and redecoration from 1964 to the present.

The wealth of the successive Sultans was considerable. They built palaces in the Stone Town and around Zanzibar Island. Islamic law allowed them to have up to four wives, and their wealth enabled them to exercise this privilege and raise numerous children. Until 1911 it was the practice of the Sultan to maintain a harem of around 100 concubines, with attendant eunuchs. The routine was established whereby the Sultan slept with five concubines a night, in strict rotation. The concubines had children, and these were supported by the Sultan.

Social practices changed with the succession of Khalifa bin Harab, at the age of 32, as Sultan in 1911. He was to reign until his death, in 1960, at the age of 81. The harem and concubines were discontinued – apart from anything else, this proved a major economy measure. Gradual political reforms were introduced, with successively more democratic representation until the Sultan was a constitutional monarch with no significant legislative or executive powers. With the influences from Oman and Shiraz, Zanzibar is overwhelmingly Islamic (97%) – the remaining 3% are Hindus, Christians and Sikhs. Moreover, the practice of Islam was tolerant and relaxed. Social pressures on non-Muslims are minimal. A member of the British High Commission tells of being on the verandah of the palace at sundown with Sultan Khalifa bin Harab. They scanned the skies, as Ramadan would begin officially when the Sultan glimpsed the moon. They drew blank, and the visitor was offered a whisky and soda. The next night there was a sliver of silver low down on the horizon, and the Sultan apologized for the fact that he felt he was not able to be so hospitable.

The office of the Sultan was held in considerable awe. As the Sultan drove each day to spend the afternoon a few kilometres away at his palace on the shore, his subjects would prostrate themselves as he passed. In 1959, when it was suggested that there should be elected members of the Legislative Councils, and Ministers appointed to deal with day-to-day matters of state, the Sultan received numerous delegations saying change was unnecessary and the Sultan should retain absolute power. The present Sultan is still addressed as 'Your Highness' when Zanzibaris visit him. British protocol decreed that the Sultan should qualify for a 19-gun salute on ceremonial occasions. This placed Zanzibar on an equal footing with Tonga. At the coronation of Queen Elizabeth in 1953, the diminutive and reserved Sultan was consigned to share a carriage with the formidable physical presence of Queen Salote of Tonga, who insisted on driving through the pouring rain with the hood down so she could wave to the crowds. As they passed, a bystander asked Noël Coward if he knew who was sharing the carriage with Queen Salote. 'Her lunch', was the reply. It says much for the Sultan's sense of humour that this was the first item of news about the coronation that he recounted to the British Consulate staff on his arrival back in Zanzibar.

British American Tobacco had several plantations on the mainland. One of the tasks assigned to new trainees from Britain was to sail to Zanzibar with a consignment of cigarettes, each stamped in gold with the Sultan's monograph. The trainee then had to go through the palace, taking the stale contents out of the cigarette boxes in each room and replenishing them with new cigarettes. It was not possible to give the old cigarettes away as local people refused them when they saw the monogram. They were taken down to the beach and burnt.

David Reed, writing for *Readers' Digest* in 1962, described Zanzibar as the "laziest place on earth – once a Zanzibari has caught a couple of fish, he quits for the day, to retire to his bed, or the heavenly chatter of the coffee house". He developed his theme – "Once a clove has been planted, its lethargic owner has only to sit in the shade and watch as its tiny green buds grow into handsome pounds sterling. Even when the market is in the doldrums, a good tree may produce as much as £6 worth of cloves a year for its owner. In better times, it simply rains money on those who sleep below."

Despite these impressions of tropical torpor under a benevolent ruler, there were significant tensions. Several small Arab Associations combined to form the Zanzibar National Party (ZNP) in 1955. The leader was Sheikh Ali Muhsin, educated at Makerere University in Uganda with a degree in agriculture. The leadership of the party was Arab, and their main objective was to press for independence from the British without delay. Two African associations, active with small landless farmers and agricultural labourers, formed the Afro-Shirazi Party (ASP) in 1957. The leader was Sheikh Abeid Karume, at one time a school teacher, a popular and charismatic personality, with great humorous skills that he exercised to the full at public meetings.

Although the ZNP tried to embrace all races, the fact was that they were seen as an Arab party, while the ASP represented African interests. Arabs comprised 20% of the population, with Africans over 75%. Elections to the Legislative Council in 1955 were organized on the basis of communal rolls – that is, so many seats were allocated to Arabs, so many to Africans, and so on. This infuriated the ZNP who wanted a common electoral roll so that they could contest all seats. They boycotted the Legislative Council. When a ZNP member broke ranks, he was assassinated, and an Arab was executed for his murder. The next elections, in 1957, were held on the basis of a common roll, and the ZNP did not win a single one of the six seats that were contested. ASP took five and the Muslim League one. More damaging, Ali Muhsin insisted on a head-to-head with Karume in the Ngambo constituency, and was soundly beaten, polling less than 25% of the votes cast. ZNP's confidence that they could draw broad-based support was very badly dented. In the next four years, the ZNP greatly increased its efforts with youth and women's organizations, and published five daily papers. It was also felt that wealthy Arab land owners and employers flexed their economic muscles to encourage support for ZNP among Africans. ZNP was greatly assisted in 1959 by a split in the ASP. Sheikh Muhammed Shamte, a Shirazi veterinary surgeon with a large clove plantation in Pemba, formed the Zanzibar and Pemba People's Party (ZPPP). Two other ASP members of the Legislative Council joined Shamte, and the ASP was left in a minority with just two seats.

The dispute was a clash of personalities as much as anything, the more urbane Shamte finding it difficult to rub along with the rough and ready manner of Karume. A contributing factor was that ASP contested the 1957 elections on a pro-African platform, particularly playing to fears that ZNP would only allow Arabs to vote in future elections and would reintroduce slavery.

In the run-up to Independence, there were three more elections. In the first, in January 1961, ASP won 10 seats, ZNP took nine and ZPPP was successful in three. A farce ensued in which both ASP and ZNP wooed the three ZPPP members. One supported ASP and the remaining two supported ZNP, creating a deadlock with 11 apiece. In the event, ZNP and ASP formed a coalition caretaker government on the understanding that new elections be held as soon as possible.

For the June 1961 elections a new constituency was created, to make a total of 23 seats. ASP and ZNP won 10 each, and ZPPP three. However, ZPPP had committed itself to support ZNP, and this coalition duly formed a government. However, ASP had gained a majority of the popular vote (albeit narrowly at 50.6%) and this caused resentment. The improved performance of ZNP in the two elections after the debacle of 1957 was bewildering to ASP. There were serious outbreaks of violence, and these were clearly along racial lines and directed against Arabs. There were 68 deaths of which 64 were Arabs.

Tanzania

John Okello – drifter who destroyed a Dynasty

John Okello was born in Uganda in 1937. There is no record of him having had any early schooling. He left home at the age of 15 and did a variety of jobs while travelling, including work as a domestic servant, a tailor and as a building labourer. Eventually he worked as a mason in Nairobi and went to evening classes where he learnt to read and write. In 1957 he was given a two-year prison sentence for a sexual offence. On his release he travelled to Mombasa, and did some casual building jobs. In 1959 he crossed illegally, at night, in a dhow, to Pemba. While doing odd jobs he attended some ZNP political meetings. Later he began a stone-quarrying business, and joined ASP, campaigning for them in the three elections in the run-up to Independence.

After the third election, Okello moved to Zanzibar Island. The Shamte administration was anxious that the police force contained many African recruits from the mainland, and began to replace them with inexperienced Zanzibaris. It was in this context that John Okello began to form plans to overthrow the government, recruiting mainly from Africans who were not Zanzibaris (including some disaffected former policemen) and who feared that they may be expelled by a pro-Arab government. Okello warned his followers that after Independence all male African babies would be killed, Africans would be ruled as slaves, and 3,000 Africans would be slaughtered in

reprisal for the 64 Arabs killed in the 1961 disturbances. By November Okello was having visionary dreams and commanding his men to abstain from sex until after the revolution and not to wear other people's clothes, in order to keep strong. He designed a Field-Marshal's uniform and pennant for himself. Final battle instructions indicated who should be killed (males aged between 18 and 55) and who could be raped (no wives of men killed or detained, and no virgins). The Sultan and three specified politicians were to be killed and the remainder captured. Some of his followers thought that Independence Day, 10 December 1963, would be an appropriate day for the revolution, but Okello thought it would be a pity to spoil the celebrations for the many overseas visitors.

Okello led the crucial attack on Ziwani Police Station on 12 January 1964, which overthrew the government and resulted in the flight of the Sultan into exile. Following this coup Okello pronounced himself Field-Marshal, and for a while assumed the title of Leader of the Revolutionary Government. As a semblance of order was restored, it was clear that Okello was an embarrassment to the ASP Government, and by 11 March he was expelled, resuming his former career of wandering the mainland, taking casual employment, and languishing for spells in prison.

In 1962 a Constitutional Conference was held at Lancaster House in London, attended by the main figures of the three political parties. A framework was duly thrashed out and agreed, with the Sultan as the constitutional Head of State. The number of seats was increased to 31 and women were given the vote. Elections in 1963 saw ASP gain 13 seats, ZNP 12 and ZPPP six. A ZNP/ZPPP coalition government was formed under the leadership of Muhammed Shamte of ZPPP. Once again ASP had the majority of the popular vote with 54%. Independence was set for later that year, on 10 December.

The old Sultan had died in 1960 and was succeeded by his son Abdullah bin Khalifa, who was to reign for less than three years, dying of cancer in July 1963. His son, Jamshid Bin Abdullah, became Sultan at the age of 34.

The revolution   It has been described as 'the most unnecessary revolution in history'. At 0300 on the night of 12 January 1964, a motley group of Africans, armed with clubs, pangas (long implements with bent, curved blades, swished from side to side to cut grass), car springs, bows and arrows, converged on the Police Headquarters at Ziwani on the edge of Zanzibar Stone Town. There were two sentries on duty.

As the mob came into view one sentry managed to fire a couple of shots and kill two of the attackers. For a moment the assault was in the balance. John Okello (see box, page 542) was the leader of the attacking force. As his supporters faltered, Okello rushed forward, grappled with the sentry, seized his rifle and bayonetted him. The other sentry was hit by an iron-tipped arrow. The door was beaten in and Okello shot a policeman at the top of the stairs. Encouraged, the attackers stormed the building. In a matter of moments the police had fled, and the mob broke into the armoury. Thus armed, they moved on to support other attacks that had been planned to take place simultaneously at other key installations – the radio station, the army barracks, and the gaol. There was some brisk fighting, but the inexperienced defenders had little stomach for the fight against rebels intoxicated by their early success. By midday, most of the town was in the hands of Okello's forces.

As the skirmishes raged through the narrow cobbled streets of the historic Stone Town, the Sultan, his family and entourage (about 50 in all) were advised to flee by the Prime Minister and his Cabinet. Two government boats were at anchor off-shore. The Sultan's party was ferried to one of these, and it set off to the north-west to Mombasa, in nearby Kenya. The government there, having gained Independence itself only a month earlier, had no desire to get involved by acting in a way that might be interpreted as hostile by whatever body eventually took control on the island. The Sultan was refused permission to land, and the boat returned southwards down the coast to Dar es Salaam in Tanganyika. From there the party was flown to Manchester and exile in Britain.

Following the assault on the Ziwani Police Headquarters at 0300 on 12 January, all other strategic targets were swiftly captured and Okello began the business of government by proclaiming himself Field-Marshal, Leader of the Revolutionary Government, and Minister of Defence and Broadcasting. Members of the ASP were allocated other ministries, with Abeid Karume as Prime Minister. Meanwhile there was considerable mayhem throughout the islands, as old scores were settled and the African and Arab communities took revenge upon one another. Initial figures suggest that 12,000 Arabs and 1,000 Africans were killed before the violence ran its course.

The British kept themselves aloof, refusing military assistance to the Sultan and Shamte. A cruiser with troops was moored in the Pemba Channel, and the British High Commission sent Morse signals to it and was allowed to receive an envoy and some supplies each day. After a particularly hot day, a request was signalled for two bottles of calamine lotion. On arrival with the envoy, the consignment was seized and a member of staff of the High Commission was hauled out to explain to the Field-Marshal why bottles of high explosive had been requested. Okello waved one of the bottles, and pointed out that if he took the top off they would all be blown sky-high. The officer unscrewed the other bottle and dabbed a little lotion on his sun-burnt forehead.

A trickle of countries, mostly newly independent African states and Soviet regimes recognized the Karume regime fairly promptly. In February 1964 Karume expelled the British High Commissioner and the Acting US Chargé d'Affaires as their countries had not recognized his government.

Army mutinies in Kenya, Tanganyika and Uganda earlier in the year, the presence of British troops in the region and some ominous remarks by the US Ambassador in Nairobi about Communist threats to the mainland from Zanzibar, all served to make Karume anxious. He felt very vulnerable with no army he could count on, and what he saw as hostile developments all around. He needed some support to secure his position.

On 23 April, Karume and Julius Nyerere signed an Act of Union between Zanzibar and Tanganyika to form Tanzania. Later the mainland political party merged with ASP to form Chama Cha Mapinduzi (CCM), the only legal political party in Tanzania.

The union

The relationship between Zanzibar and the mainland is a mess. It is neither a proper federation nor a unitary state. Zanzibar retains its own President (up to 1995, *ex officio* one of the Vice-Presidents of the Union). It has a full set of ministries, its own Assembly, and keeps its own foreign exchange earnings. Mainlanders need a passport to go to Zanzibar, and cannot own property there. No such restrictions apply to Zanzibaris on the mainland. Despite comprising less than 5% of Tanzania's total population, Zanzibar has 30% of the seats in the Union Assembly. The practice of rotating the Union Presidency between Zanzibar and the mainland meant that from 1985-95 two of the occupants of the top three posts (the President and one of the two Vice-Presidents) come from Zanzibar. Zanzibar has not paid for electricity supplied by the mainland's hydro-electric power stations for over 15 years.

Despite all these privileges (which annoy the daylights out of many mainlanders) the Zanzibaris feel they have had a rough time since 1964. The socialist development strategy pursued by Tanzania after 1967 has seen living standards fall in Zanzibar. Where once the inhabitants of Zanzibar Town were noticeably better off than the urban dwellers in mainland Dar es Salaam, they now feel themselves decidedly poorer. They consider that if they had been able to utilize their historical and cultural links with oil-rich Oman they would have benefited from substantial investment and development assistance.

The legitimacy of the Act of Union has been called into question – it was a deal between two leaders (one of whom had come to power unconstitutionally) without any of the democratic consultation such a radical step might reasonably require.

Separatist movements have emerged, pamphletting sporadically from exile in Oman and Scandinavia, and suppressed by the Tanzanian government. A Chief Minister in Zanzibar, Seif Sharrif Hamad, was dismissed when it was thought he harboured separatist sympathies. Later he was detained for over two years on a charge of retaining confidential government documents at his home.

Multiparty elections were set for the end of October 1995. No one appears to have thought through what this would mean for Zanzibar.

When political parties were sanctioned again, a cluster of organizations applied to get themselves registered, including a group based on the old ASP in Zanzibar. One of the successes of Tanzania, on the mainland at any rate, has been the absence of any serious tribalism. The government was determined to ensure the new parties were broadly based and not merely representatives of a particular race, region or religion. This was to be achieved by requiring each party to obtain 200 members in each of at least 13 of Tanzania's 25 regions. The Registrar of Political Parties has had 2,600 names and addresses checked for each of Tanzania's 13 registered parties. This, it was felt, would scupper a group like the re-formed ASP, based on a region, and which might campaign in Zanzibar on a pro-separation ticket. In the event, the Zanzibaris appear to have bought an already registered party, the Civic United Front (CUF), off the shelf.

The former Chief Minister and detainee, Sharrif Hamad, was the CUF candidate for the Zanzibar Presidency. Support for CUF in the islands prior to the election was very strong. It was hard to find anyone in Zanzibar or Pemba, who wasn't actually a member of CCM, who said they weren't going to vote for CUF. In the event, it is thought that Hamad and CUF were victorious by a narrow margin in both the Presidential and Assembly elections. A recount was called, and independent observers claim that forged voting papers supporting CCM were introduced. In the event, the incumbent Salim Amour was declared President with 50.2% of the vote (Hamad had 49.8%) and with two constituencies changing hands at the recount, CCM formed the islands' administration with 26 seats (to CUF's 24). CUF and Hamad were incensed at the outcome, and CUF have boycotted the Zanzibar Assembly. The international community pressed for a re-run of the election under international monitoring and control – the 1995 election only had international observers, who were powerless to prevent the alleged fraud at the recount.

Jordan
Kyrgyzstan
Lebanon
Lombok
Libya
Madagascar
Mali
Malawi
Malaysia
Mexico
Morocco
Mozambique
Namibia
Nepal
New Zealand
N. Cyprus
Peru
South Africa
Spain
Sri Lanka
Syria
Tanzania
Thailand
Tibet
Turkey
Uganda
USA
Venezuela
Vietnam
Zambia
Zimbabwe

Discovery

If you're looking for adventure without too much physical exertion you're not alone. Thousands of people a year travel with us on escorted trips where culture, places and landscapes are the main focus and accommodation is in small, comfortable hotels. You could join a trip which explores the lively markets and historic Inca sites of Peru. Or a journey by boat, bus, rickshaw and train through Vietnam. There are ornately carved temples just waiting to be discovered in places like India or Mexico, ancient wonders in Egypt and Jordan, and ways of life that seem lost in time in Cuba, Bolivia, Libya, Mali, Japan…

Wildlife

Follow in the footsteps of Darwin on a cruise through the enchanted Galapagos Islands of Ecuador, a tiger safari in India, a gorilla search in Uganda, or on a journey into the rainforests of Costa Rica. Our safaris in Africa visit some of the world's finest reserves; like the Serengeti, the Ngorongoro Crater, Kruger, Etosha and the Okavango Delta. Our group leaders are assisted by local guides to bring out the best of nature's exuberance, as well as allowing time to explore local villages and perhaps walk local trails.

Walks & Treks

Easy day-walks, moderate hikes, challenging treks… Walk to remote villages in Andalucia or the Canary Islands, hike through stunning mountains in the Pyrenees or Corsica or snowshoe through pristine wilderness in Finland or Quebec. Join a classic trek in Nepal, hike through the Andes, visit tribal villages in Thailand or stay with the Berbers in Morocco's Atlas Mountains. All walks graded. No backpacking.

Tel: 01420 541007
travelbag-adventures.com

Trekking • Wildlife • Cultural Journeys • Wilderness • Activity • Cycling

AFFIX
STAMP
HERE

Travelbag Adventures (GFP)
15 Turk Street
ALTON
GU34 1AG

Zanzibar Stone Town

Even with a map it is surprisingly easy to get lost as the narrow winding alleys and over-hanging balconies mean it is difficult to maintain a sense of direction. Only bicycles, scooters and hand carts are able to use the narrow alleys. You must constantly make way for those with wheels – listen out for the tinkling of bells and the 'quack-quack' of horns. Once you are accustomed to the area you will be able to walk around confidently and enjoy the atmosphere as well as the architecture and lovely doors. The door to a house was built to reflect the wealth and social status of its owner. They were often elab-orately carved or decorated with brass studs.

Ins & outs

You could hire a guide who will show you all the sights. A local artist John da Silva (T2232123) gives walking tours that are particularly attractive if you are interested in the architecture of the island, cost US$25. *Emersons and Green* has a security man who will provide an all-day tour for US$10, although some of his information on buildings is suspect. As you wander around the streets you will notice that the ground floor of many of the buildings is taken up by shops and businesses, while above are the homes of the Zanzibaris. Exploring on foot during the day or night will give you a real feel of this wonderful town and its people. Walking around Zanzibar has previously been very safe, but recent incidents, would advocate more caution.

Tourist information

Tourist offices *Commission for Tourism*, PO Box 1410, Zanzibar, Amaan Rd, near the stadium, T2233485-7, F2233448, www.zanzibartourism.net *Tourist Information Centre*, Creek Rd, at the north end, T/F2233430. Sells map of island but otherwise not terribly helpful. *Recommended*, free quarterly publication available from some hotels and tour agencies, also from a few embassies and airline offices in Dar es Salaam. Lists hotels, restaurants, transport services etc, and also has a small map of Stone Town and the island. **Maps**: excellent colour *Map of Zanzibar* available with town map on one side and the Island map on the other. Includes hotels, beach resorts, flora and fish. *Zanzibar at Sea* illustrates the diving, snorkelling and game fishing facilities and Mnemba Atoll, by Giovanni Tombazzi, 1996, distributed by MACO Ltd, PO Box 322, Zanzibar, T/F2233778, US$5 each.

Sights

Greater Zanzibar

The area to the west of Creek Road is known as the old **Stone Town**, recently declared a World Heritage Site, and a tour will take at least a day. It is such a fascinating place that it is easy to spend a week wandering the narrow streets and still find new places of charm and interest.

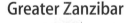

A good place to start the trip is from the **Central Market** located on Creek Road. This was opened in 1904 and remains a bustling, colourful and aromatic place. Here you will see Zanzibarian life carrying on as it has done for so many years – lively, busy and noisy. Outside are long, neat rows of bicycles carefully locked and guarded by their minder while people are buying and selling inside the market. Fruit, vegetables, meat and fish are all for sale here as well as household implements, many of them locally made, clothing and footwear. **NB** The chicken, fish and meat areas are not for the squeamish.

Creek Road

Sleeping
1 Bwawani
2 Fisherman's Resort

Related map
A Stone Town,
page 546

Stone Town

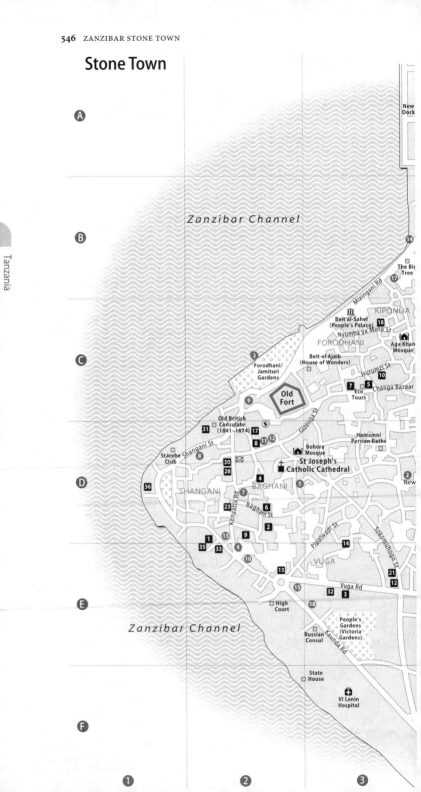

Tanzania

Zanzibar Channel

New Dock

The Big Tree

Mizingani Rd

KIPONDA

Beit al-Sahel (People's Palace)

Nyumba ya Moto St

FORODHANI

Aga Khan Mosque

3

Forodhani/ Jamituri Gardens

Beit-el Ajaib (House of Wonders)

Hurumzi St

10

7 **5** Eco Tours

Changa Bazaar

9

Old Fort

Gizenga St

Hamamni Persian Baths

Old British Consulate (1841–1874)

31 **17** **$**

8 **11** **12**

Bohora Mosque

St Joseph's Catholic Cathedral

Starehe Club

Shangani St

8

30

28

4

5

New

2

36

SHANGANI

7

BAGHANI

23

6

Kenyatta Rd

Baghani St

2

1

35 **33**

13

9

4

10

Pipalwadi St

14

VUGA

Sokomuhogo St

21

12

13

15

Vuga Rd

32 **3**

High Court

18

People's Gardens (Victoria Gardens)

Russian Consul

Kaunda Rd

Zanzibar Channel

State House

VI Lenin Hospital

N

| 0 | metres | 100 |
| 0 | yards | 100 |

Tanzania

■ **Sleeping**
1 Africa House
   & Africa Club Restaurant *D2*
2 Baghani House *D2*
3 Beit-al-Amaan *E3*
4 Blue Ocean *D2*
5 Bottoms Up *C3*
6 Chavda *D2*
7 Clove *C3*
8 Coco de Mer *D2*
9 Dhow Palace *D2*
10 Emersons & Green & Tower Top
   Restaurant *C4*
11 Flamingo Guest House *E4*
12 Florida Guest House *E3*
13 Garden Lodge Resthouse *E2*
14 Haven Guest House *E3*
15 Heart of Zanzibar *C4*
16 International *C4*
17 Karibu Inn *D2*
18 Kiponda *C3*
19 Kokoni *B4*
20 Malindi Guest House *A5*
21 Manch Lodge Vuga *E3*
22 Marine *A4*
23 Mazsons *D2*
24 Narrow Street Annexe I *C4*
25 Narrow Street Annexe II *B4*
26 Pyramid Guest House *B4*
27 St Monica's Guest House *D4*
28 Shangani *D2*
29 Spice Inn *C4*
30 Stone Town Inn *D2*
31 Tembo *D2*
32 Victoria Guest House *E3*
33 Vuga *E2*
34 Warere Guest House *A4*
35 Wazazi Guest House *E2*
36 Zanzibar Serena Inn *D1*

● **Eating**
1 Al Jabr *B5*
2 Baobab Tree *D3*
3 Blues *C2*
4 Camlurs *E2*
5 Chit Chat *D2*
6 Ciné Afrique Café *B4*
7 Dolphin *D2*
8 Fisherman *D2*
9 Le Bistrot
10 Le Spices Rendezvous *E2*
11 Luis Yoghurt Parlour *D2*
12 Luna Mare *D2*
13 Pagoda *D2*
14 Pitchy's Bar *B3*
15 Two Tables *E2*
16 Sinbad Sailors *B4*
17 Sea View Indian *B3*
18 Zi Bar *E3*

Related map
Greater Zanzibar,
page 545

Nearby, also on Creek Road, is the **Anglican Church of Christ**, which was built in 1887 to commemorate the end of the slave trade. The altar is on the actual site of the slave market's whipping post. The columns at the west end were put in upside down, while the bishop was on leave in the UK. Inside are impressive marble pillars and stained-glass windows. Other points of interest are the small wooden crucifix said to have been made from the wood of the tree under which Livingstone died in Chitambo in Zambia. If you can, try to go up the staircase of the church to the top of the tower from where you will get an excellent view of the town. It is sadly run down and needs all the funds it can get. Next door, under the St Monica restaurant, you can visit the underground slave pens. Also on Creek Road is the **City Hall** that is a wonderfully ornate building currently undergoing renovation.

Western tip **Mathews House** is located close to *Africa House Hotel*, just to the south of Ras Shangani at the western tip of the town. Before the First World War it was the residence, with characteristic overhanging balconies, of Lloyd Mathews (1850-1901). Mathews was a naval officer who was put in charge of the Sultan's army in 1877 (he was a mere Lieutenant of 27 at the time). Later he became Chief Minister, and was known as the 'Strong Man of Zanzibar'. The **Africa House Hotel** was once the British Club. Also in this area is **Tippu Tip's House**, named after the wealthy 19th century slave-trader, which has a splendid carved wooden door and black and white marble steps. Tippu Tip was the most notorious of all slavers and Livingstone's arch-enemy – the latter's report of the massacre at Nyangwe, in the Congo, where Tippu Tip had commercial hegemony, led ultimately to the abolition of the slave trade.

Also at the western tip of the town is the building known now as **Mambo Msiige**, which was once owned by a slave trader. It is said that he used to bury slaves alive within the walls of the building in accordance with an ancient custom. Since then the building has been used as the headquarters of the Universities Mission to Central Africa and later as the British Consulate.

Old Fort The Old Fort (also known as the Arab Fort or Ngome Kongwe) is located in the west of the town next to the House of Wonders. This huge structure was built in 1700 on the site of a Portuguese church, the remains of which can be seen incorporated into the fabric of the internal walls. Its tall walls are topped by castellated battlements. The fort was built by Omani Arabs to defend attacks from the Portuguese, who had occupied Zanzibar for almost two centuries. During the 19th century the fort was used as a prison and in the early 20th century it was used as a depot of the railway that ran from Stone Town to Bububu. It is possible to reach the top of the battlements on the west side and look at the towers. The central area is now used as an open air theatre, and renamed the Zanzibar Cultural Centre. On Friday at 1930 film nights are held, and on Tuesday, Thursday and Saturday there is a Zanzibar buffet barbecue with African dance and drums. The fort also houses an art gallery, several small shops selling crafts and spices, plus a tourist information desk. There is also a charming café, with tables in the shade of a couple of large trees.

On the south side of the fort you can take a walk down Gizenga Street (used to be Portuguese Street) with its busy bazaars. This will lead you to **St Joseph's Catholic Cathedral**, and on the opposite side of the road the **Bohora Mosque**.

Beit-el-Ajaib This is Zanzibar's tallest building and is located close to the fort opposite the **(House of** Jamituri Gardens. It was built in 1883 by Sultan Barghash and served as his palace. **Wonders)** The name House of Wonders came about because it was the first building on the island to have electricity and even a lift. It has fine examples of door carving. At the entrance are two Portuguese cannons, which date from about the 16th century. It is a four-storey building and is surrounded by verandahs. In 1896 in an attempt to persuade the Sultan to abdicate, the palace was subjected to a bombardment by the British navy. Inside the floors are of marble and there are various decorations that were imported from Europe, there are also exhibits from the struggle for independence.

The building served as the local headquarters of Tanzania's political party CCM, and has recently been opened to the public.

Beit al-Sahel (People's Palace)

The palace on Mizingani Road, north of the House of Wonders, is where the sultans and their families lived from the 1880s until their rule was finally overturned by the revolution of 1964. The building has now been opened as a museum. There are three floors of exhibits and it is well worth a visit. There is a wide variety of furniture including the Sultan's huge bed. Look out for the formica wardrobe with handles missing – obviously very fashionable at the time. Good views from the top floor. ■ *Tue-Sat 1000-1800, US$3.* The palace has grounds that can sometimes be viewed, containing the tombs of Sultan Seyyid Said and his two sons Khaled and Barghash.

Na Sur Nurmohamed Dispensary

Often called the Old Dispensary, this very ornate building – situated on Mizingani Road, between the House of Wonders and the Arab Fort – was donated to the community by a prominent Ismailian Indian Sir Tharia Topan. It has recently undergone renovations funded by the Aga Khan Cultural trust and now houses the Zanzibar Cultural Centre. Inside is a small tourist development with fixed priced shops, including a jeweller, curio and clothes boutique and a small, very pleasant **cheap** restaurant with a shady courtyard. There are cultural events with *Taarab*, Zanzibari traditional drummers in an open air stadium. ■ *US$12 including barbecue, US$5 for show only.*

Dhow harbour

Further up Mizingani Road is the **Dhow Harbour** which is a lively and bustling part of the Malindi quarter. It is at its busiest in the morning when the dhows arrive and unload their catches, and buyers bargain and haggle over the prices.

Livingstone House

Located on Malawi Road, now housing the offices of the Zanzibar Tourist Corporation, this was originally built for Sultan Majid in about 1860. In 1866 it was used by Livingstone as a base while he was staying on the island before what was to be his last journey into the interior. It was from Zanzibar that he arranged his trip inland, organizing porters, supplies and guide. The building was later used by some of the Indian community before it was purchased by the government in 1947 for use as a laboratory investigating diseases associated with clove production. ■ *Open to the public.*

Hamamni Persian Baths

Iin the centre of Stone Town, these baths were built by Sultan Barghash for use as public baths and have been declared a protected monument. If you want to have a look inside them ask for the caretaker, Hakim Wambi, who keeps the key and he will let you in and show you around. As there is no water there any more you have to use your imagination as to what it was like in the old days. ■ *US$1.* Hakim also runs the Zanzibar Orphans Trust from the building opposite the baths. He will show you around – donations are gratefully received.

Museum

The museum is located in two buildings and although fairly run down and shabby has some interesting exhibits relating to Zanzibar's history. It was built in 1925 and has relics and exhibits from the sultans, the slave traders and European explorers and missionaries. Livingstone's medicine chest is here and the story of the German battleship the *Königsberg*, sunk during the First World War in the Rufiji Delta, is documented. There are also displays of local arts and crafts. It is located near the junction of Creek Road with Nyerere and Kuanda Roads at the south end of the town. If you are 'out of season', it has a most interesting exhibition on clove production. There are giant tortoises in the grounds of the natural history museum next door. ■ *US$1 for both buildings.*

Tours

In order to maximize your time in Zanzibar it is worth considering going on a tour. This applies especially if you do not have the time to stay on the east coast and transport can be a problem. Most companies offer a range of tours:

Tanzania

Tanzania

Freddie Mercury

In 1946 Farokh Bulsara was born in Zanzibar to parents who were Parsees – followers of the Zoroastrian faith. The Zoroastrian Fire Temple in Zanzibar is located on Vuga Road to the east of Zanzibar Stone Town. His father worked as a civil servant for the British colonial government on the islands. The Parsees had a great affinity with the British, and Mr Bulsara senior was a cricket enthusiast, spending much of his leisure time at the ground at Mnazi Moja. The family lived in a house in the square behind the present Post Office. When he was nine, Farokh was sent to boarding school in India, and he never subsequently returned to the place of his birth.

In 1970, while studying graphics at Ealing College, he joined up with some students at London University's Imperial College of Science and Technology. He changed his name to Freddie Mercury and they formed the group Queen.

The influence of his Zanzibar background is expressed in the lyric of Queen's best-known song Bohemian Rhapsody with "Bismillah will you let him go". Bismillah means 'the word of God' in the Islamic faith, and it has become a rallying cry for Muslim groups pressing for Zanzibar to break away from Tanzania.

Freddie Mercury died in 1992, his body being cremated at a Zoroastrian funeral ceremony in London.

City tour   Half day: includes all the major sites of the Stone Town – market, national museum, cathedral, Beit al-Sahel and Hamamni baths. ■ *US$15.*

Spice tour   About four hours: includes pleasant stops at various villages to taste the freshly picked local fruits and herbs. The highly decorated Persian baths at the Kidichi are often included. You may be offered a swim on the west coast – however, the water is usually cloudy and useless for snorkelling. **NB** This tour is highly recommended, but only during the harvest – out of season you may get weary of looking at leaves that look very similar. ■ *US$20.*

An option besides going on an agency organized spice tour is to get a taxi driver to show you around. ■ *US$30 maximum price for 4 people in the car, which competes favourably with some of the organized agency tours.*

Alternatively visit the **Zanzibar Heritage Conservation Park** (Zaheco) in Jumbi, 12 km southeast of Stone Town. The park is a private enterprise, operated by the very knowledgeable Omar Suleiman, who will show you around the large garden of herbs, fruits and other plants, and also the small museum and aviary. ■ *Entrance under US$1, to get there ask a taxi driver to take you to Jumbi as the park is not widely known. There is a small sign on the left of the road as you approach the village.*

East Coast   Full day: the tour may include a visit to the **Jozani Forest** where the rare red colobus monkey is found (recommended). ■ *US$35 (US$15 if you only go to Jozani).*

North Coast   Full day: this can be combined with the spice tour and usually ends at the beach at Nungwi. The Mangapwani slave caves are sometimes also included. ■ *US$35.*

Dolphin tour   Dolphin tours are an increasingly promoted part of the tourist industry in Zanzibar. Wander along Forodhani Gardens or up Kenyatta Rd and you will be approached by men offering spice/dolphin tours. Prices vary a lot from US$10-75. The quality of the boats are also variable, from leaky wooden to fibreglass. Many of the small boats do not run to a timetable but wait to fill up, usually accommodating 6-8 tourists. More recently dolphin tours tend to involve transport by minibus to Kizimkazi, and transfer to a boat at the beach, a route that easily allows for a visit of Jozani Forest (see above). ■ *About US$25.*

The dolphins swim in pods off Kizimkazi Beach, on the southwest of the island, and are not always readily spotted. It takes about an hour for the boats to reach Kizimkazi Beach, and you are advised to leave early. Loud noises or splashy water entries will scare off the dolphins. If you see a school, do not chase them in the boat.

Get reasonably close and the helmsman will turn off the engine. Slide gently into the water, swim with your arms along your body and duck dive/spiral – do interesting things to attract their attention. Dolphins are curious mammals but they are wild. If you are lucky they will surround you and nudge you. Try not to touch them and do not feed them.

Swimming with the dolphins is not recommended if you are a nervous swimmer. The dolphins are found in the open sea, which frequently has a marked swell. Dolphins' idling speed equates with a reasonable swimmer's top speed aided by fins.

There is research being conducted into cetacean behaviour in relation to tourists, to ascertain whether this incredible experience from our point of view may pose long-term problems for the dolphins.

While at Kizimkazi Beach it would greatly benefit the local people if a donation was made for their library. There is a book that you can sign and a locked donation box in the rondavel of the guesthouse in Kizimkazi, which has basic food and cold beer available.

Safety Safety is becoming an increasing concern in Zanzibar. There have recently been several violent robberies, at knifepoint, of tourists even during daylight hours in Stone Town and its environs. There is speculation that the perpetrators are mainland Tanzanians, as Zanzibaris are noted for their honesty. More recent speculation suggests that these crimes are carried out by a native Zanzibari who has connections within the police force. Indeed, some travellers have reported that the police do not appear to be actively seeking out these gangs of robbers. Be careful walking after dark, especially in poorly lit areas. Avoid alleyways at night, particularly by the Big Tree on Mizingani Road. Valuables can usually be left at your hotel safe as an extra precaution. Use taxis to get back to the hotel. Exert caution on quiet beaches.

A drawback of wandering around Stone Town, especially near the *Africa House Hotel,* is the number of young men who tout for business to travellers, offering taxis, spice tours or trips to Prison Island. Some can be very aggressive and persistent. It is better to deal directly with one of the many tour companies for excursions. There will also be many touts near the port awaiting the arrival of the next batch of tourists. A polite no thankyou is rarely a successful method to rid yourself of their services. If you have just arrived you could tell the touts that you have already booked hotel accommodation from Dar es Salaam, and if you make your own way to a hotel insist that the management give no commission to any touts who may be following and will try to claim credit for your arrival. Other strategies for tout evasion include saying you have been on all the tours, and that you are leaving tomorrow and have already bought the ticket.

It is not uncommon for travellers to be stopped by the police while driving to one of the beaches. The police may say that they are thirsty or try to claim that your papers are not in order – basically they are looking for a small bribe to supplement their meagre incomes. If you ask for a receipt they will frequently wave you through.

A couple of recently published colour maps of Zanzibar Island, town and the sea (US$5 each) are highly recommended to help plan your stay (see Maps, page 545).

Essentials

All non-residents are expected to pay for hotel accommodation in US dollars even for somewhere very cheap. However the relaxation of currency controls and the introduction of foreign exchange bureaux has meant that local currency is becoming more generally accepted and paying the bill in TSh is invariably cheaper. A few hotels and restaurants now accept Visa credit cards, charges are very steep, at 15-20% commission in the £ or US$, plus a 20% worse exchange rate. Recent travellers have told us that it is possible to negotiate hotel rates, even in high season, by speaking to the manager and booking for several days' stay. The explosion of interest in Zanzibar has resulted in many houses being turned into hotels and guesthouses. Nevertheless it has been the case that the town has been full in Jun, Jul and Aug, and the overspill has been accommodated in tents on the beach. It is advisable to book. If you

Sleeping
■ *on map, page 546*
Price codes:
see inside front cover

Some hotels in Zanzibar are charging up to 8% 'commission' if you use TCs to pay your bill, far more than the forex bureau charges

don't want to stay in the heart of Stone Town, there are places to the north (Mtoni and Bububu) and the south (Mbweni) via the coast roads.

L *The Fisherman's Resort*, PO Box 2586, T2230208, F2230556, fishermans@zanzinet.com, Mazizini area, 10 mins south of Stone Town, situated in a secluded cove overlooking the nearby islands. Village layout with restaurants, bars, health club, conference rooms, diving and watersports centre, a/c, fridge, private safe, s/c bathrooms, private terraces. **L** *Zanzibar Reef Hotel*, just outside Zanzibar City, 10 mins south from Stone Town. Magnificent rooms with good bathrooms, fine swimming pool, lovely clean beach, bit shallow for swimming. **L** *Zanzibar Serena Inn*, Shangani St at Shangani Sq, PO Box 4171, T2233587, F2233019, 0741-333170, www.serenahotels.com One of the nicest hotels in East Africa, stunning restoration of two historic buildings in Stone Town funded by the Aga Khan Fund for Culture to provide a seafront hotel, with 52 luxury rooms and swimming pool. Restaurant has an excellent but pricey menu. Wonderful location with first-class service. Pool-side snack menu also recommended – delicious smoked sailfish. Central reservations: Kenya: Williamson House, 4th Ngong Av, PO Box 48690, Nairobi, T254-2-711077, F718103; Tanzania: 6th floor, AICC Ngorongoro Wing, PO Box 2551, Arusha, T255-27-2548175, F2544058, serena@habari.co.tz

A *Bwawani Hotel*, PO Box 670, T2230200, F2231840, located overlooking the Funguni Creek, follow Creek Rd north past the intersection with Malawi Rd. It's a dull and characterless modern concrete building, reportedly taken over by the government and free of guests for a while. When open guests can expect good facilities, a/c, tennis courts, restaurant and bar, previously there was a disco on Sat. **A** *Emersons and Green*, 236 Hurumzi St, PO Box 4317, T2230171, F2231038, emegre@zanzibar.org Sadly the original *Emersons* hotel has now closed. This hotel is owned by the same imaginative couple, also in Stone Town, behind the *House of Wonders*, lower floors have a/c, with a spectacular rooftop restaurant called *Tower Top* – open-sided, no shoes, sit on cushions, not cheap but worthwhile – a really magical experience, beautiful, individually themed rooms with old Zanzibari furniture and fittings. **A** *Tembo Hotel*, opposite the *Fisherman's Restaurant*, Forodhani St, PO Box 3974, T2233005, F2233777. Recommended, pool, has a terrace for sundowners, great location right on beach, food is good – no alcohol. Staff very friendly, reception willing to negotiate rates. One of the nicest hotels in Stone Town.

B *Chavda*, PO Box 540, T2232115, F2231931, newly renovated building in heart of Stone Town, off Kenyatta Rd. Nice large rooms, rooftop bar has cold drinks, good restaurant serves Chinese and western meals. **B** *Dhow Palace Hotel*, Stone Town, just off Kenyatta Rd, PO Box 3974, T2230304, F2233008. Large rooms with private bathroom, a/c variable effect, fans, fridge, phone, antique furniture and courtyard, rooftop restaurant rarely busy, minimal breakfast, Muslim hotel so no bacon or booze on premises. **B** *Heart of Zanzibar*, Kiponda St, just to the east of *Spice Inn*, PO Box 1912, T/F2231264, heartofzanzibar@hotmail.com Pleasant and small family-run hotel. **B** *Hotel Marine*, Malawi Rd, Malindi area, PO Box 2255, T2232088, F2233082, hotelmarine@africaonline.co.ke **B** *Inn by the Sea Hotel*, T2231755, on the way to Mbweni, good location. As its name suggests, near to the ruins of Kirk House (see page 562). **B** *International*, PO Box 3784, T2233182, F2230052. Part of the *Narrow Street Hotel Group*, comfortable, a/c, fridge, TV, phone, restaurant, bureau de change, near *Emerson's* and *Spice Inn*, approached through the market, which adds to the atmosphere. However some travellers have reported that standards have declined, that there is poor service, food and room conditions. **B** *Mazsons Hotel*, Kenyatta Rd, PO Box 3367, Stone Town, T2233694, T0741-320655 (mob), F2233695, mazsons@twiga.com A/c, fridge, TV, only charge US$1 commission on TCs used to pay the bill. **B** *Spice Inn*, located where Changa Bazaar meets Kiponda St, PO Box 1029, T2230728/9, F2230326. Used to be very popular, exudes atmosphere, the rooms vary so ask to take a look before you decide, price including breakfast, some rooms with a/c available, shared or private bathroom. **B** *Shangani Hotel*, PO Box 4222, T/F2233688, on Kenyatta Rd in Stone Town near the Old Post Office. Services include a/c, fridge, TV, some rooms s/c and bathroom, gift shop, rooftop restaurant, laundry service.

C *Baghani House*, one block south of Baghani St, next to closed *Zanzibar Hotel*, PO Box 609, T2235654, T0741-321058 (mob), F2235653, baghani@zanzinet.com Private house with 6

rooms, a/c, fans, TV, breakfast served in courtyard but no restaurant, *Livingstone's Bar*, slightly more expensive in the high seasons. **C** *Beit-al-Amaan*, Vuga Rd, opposite Victoria Gardens, T2239366, T0747-410410 (mob). 3 pleasantly furnished double rooms with private bathrooms, also shared kitchen and large living room, friendly and excellent value. Attached is the *Zi Bar and Restaurant*. **C** *Clove*, PO Box 1117, T2231785, F2232560, located on Hurumzi St, behind the *House of Wonders*. S/c with fridge and fan, hot water, good bar at rooftop level, cheap, basic food available. **C** *Coco de Mer Hotel*, PO Box 2363, Stone Town, T2230852, T0741-320045 (mob), F2233008. Including 10 rooms, restaurant, bar, fans, between Shangani St and Gizenga St, one block east of Kenyatta Rd. **C** *Golf Hotel*, T2233963, F2232560. Includes a/c, fans, TV, fridge. **C** *High Hill*, PO Box 907, T2230000, located on Nyerere Rd and is rather out of the way and difficult to get to. Modern, a/c rooms available, price including breakfast, hot water. **C** *Hotel Kiponda*, PO Box 3446, T2233052, F2233020, on Nyumba ya Moto St, behind the People's Palace, central location with good restaurant, sea views, fans. **C** *Island View Hotel*, Kilimani area, about 2 km south of Stone Town, PO Box 6, T2235222, F2234605, islandview@workmail.com A/c rooms with TVs. **C** *Mtoni Marine Centre*, 4 km north of Stone Town near the Maruhubi Palace ruins offers excellent facilities at a reasonable cost – see entry under North, page 563. **C** *St Monica's Guest House*, PO Box 5, New Mkunazini St, T2232484/22307673. Very clean and comfortable, own restaurant, price including breakfast. **C** *Tufaah Inn*, Stone Town, T2230326, F2230225. Some a/c, fans. **C** *Vuga Hotel*, PO Box 3904, T2233613, F2236532, near Africa House. 4 single, 4 double and 2 triple rooms, with a/c, most are s/c, includes breakfast, friendly and helpful.

D *Africa House*, PO Box 317, T2230708, F2231312, located just off Kenyatta Rd, on Suicide Alley. This used to be the British Club in the pre-independence days, became a very run down, rambling traditional building, had problems with its water supply, and the staff were fairly indifferent to guests, but during 2000 it was closed for major renovation work. By Jul 2001 little progress with the renovations was visible. It has a good terrace bar overlooking the sea, which has remained open throughout, and the bar remains popular. A visit is recommended for a cold beer, as it is worth having a 'sundowner' simply to see the milling tourists, and watch the setting sun. Annexe I in Narrow St, T2232620, Annexe II, T2233006. **D** *Blue Ocean Hotel*, Baghani St, PO Box 4052, T/F2233566. Good rooms, management fairly orthodox Muslims, male/female couples are expected to be married. **D** *Flamingo Guest House*, PO Box 4279, Mkunazini St, just north of junction with Sokomuhogo St, not far from Vuga Rd, T2232850, F2233144, good value. **D** *Florida Guest House*, off Vuga Rd, T2231828. Has been recommended by some travellers, can organize a full day spice tour including lunch and visit to a beach for US$10. **D** *The Haven Annexe* at Mtoni, T2232511 (previously the *Mtoni Sunset Beach Hotel*), about 4 km north of the town off the road to Bububu. Modest but extremely good value. **D** *The Haven Guest House*, PO Box 3746, T2232511, T0741-320204 (mob), located behind the *Cultural Musical Club* off Vuga Rd. Owned by Mr Hamed, who is also the proprietor of the Annexe, safe, secure place to stay, s/c, plenty of hot water, nets and fans, breakfast included in the price, spotlessly clean and very friendly. **D** *Karibu Inn*, Stone Town, next to *Coco de Mer Hotel*, T/F2233058. 15 rooms, fans, double rooms have fridges. **D** *Kids Play Guest House*, PO Box 2632, Mwembetanga, T/F2230475. S/c rooms, a/c, fridge and satellite TV, free pick-up service – at the edge of Mapem beani ground, excellent breakfasts. D *Kokoni Hotel*, PO Box 1256, T/F2231584, T0742-750232 (mob), located in the heart of Stonetown behind the BP Shell garage in Darajani, near the Tourist Information Centre. Offer a free pick-up service from the airport and the port, hotel very clean with en-suite bathroom, hot water, fans and nets and TV, some rooms have a/c. **D** *Lail-Noor Guest House*, PO Box 132, T2234343, T0742-750051 (mob), F2233089, Maisara, 5-min walk from Stone Town along Nyerere Rd, close to the beach. S/c bungalows, nets, restaurant and bar, transport to town. **D** *Malindi Annex*, near the main guesthouse, T/F2232359, very good rooms with nets, hot showers, friendly. **D** *Malindi Guest House*, PO Box 609, T2230165, F2233030, malindi@zanzinet.com Located on Malindi St at Funguni Bazaar – excellent value and a wonderful atmosphere, central courtyard with plants, plenty of space to relax, clean, prices including breakfast. Recent renovations have created a rooftop coffee shop with views of the harbour. **D** *Narrow Street Annexe II*, PO Box 3784, T2233006, F2230052,

Zanzibar under the British – the English Club

Although the English Club was formed some time before the turn of the 20th century, it was only in 1907 that it began to look seriously for substantial premises. A suitable building was located in Shangani just back from the shore, which is now the African House Hotel and, backed by a government loan, the club opened in 1908 on its new site with the restaurant, a committee room that doubled as a library, a bar and a billiards room.

In 1911 the club proposed taking over two rooms in an adjoining building to provide accommodation for out of town members visiting Zanzibar and members of other clubs with which its members had reciprocal rights. The government was approached to provide the capital to purchase a lease and to refit the rooms. It agreed on condition that the rooms would be made available to the government for officials and their wives, and other visitors needing accommodation in Stone Town.

The Secretary, EWP Thurston, reported that the constitution of the club did not allow Americans or Europeans, and that it was a 'Man's Club', and there were the "strongest social and sanitary reasons against ladies occupying rooms". The government reacted vigorously to the proposed exclusions. They challenged the notion that it was a 'Man's Club'.

Women were allowed in to use the library in the mornings and between 1800-2000 in the evenings. Women were also admitted to take lunch and dinner in the restaurant. As for the Committee's sanitary objections to women using the accommodation, these were dismissed by the government as the "merest bogies of their perfervid imaginations". In April 1912 the club gave way, and the two rooms were added. Later some garages were built on the shore site of the building, and more rooms for women were added above them.

In 1916 the club had plans to demolish a warehouse on the shore and build a swimming pool and squash courts. The war interfered with these plans and they never went ahead. The space was cleared, however, and became known as 'German Forodhani' (Forodhani means 'customs house' – the German Consulate was nearby) or 'Shagani Steps'. Coloured lights were strung from cast-iron telegraph poles (two can still be seen on the site), and on Tuesday evenings the Sultan's band played a selection of classical and popular music, for the benefit of locals who sat around on the grass and those taking sundowners in the club's verandah bar.

The British in Zanzibar (as everywhere) were profoundly insular, and in general reluctant to establish social relations with other communities. This was expressed in the formation of the English Club, which provoked every other significant community to establish its own club, thereby underscoring the religious and racial divisions in the society.

---

located on Kokoni St, off Creek Rd. Despite the rather unprepossessing exterior the rooms themselves are quite pleasant and all have baths, restaurant, friendly staff. **D** *Pearl Guest House*, T2232907, sited in the Stone Town, close to the Shia-Ithna Asheri Mosque. Rooftop views, 100-year-old building, if prearranged by phone, will arrange collection from port or airport at no extra cost, very helpful. **D** *Pyramid Guesthouse*, Kokoni St, PO Box 254, T2233000, 2230045, T0741-328460/1 (mob). Charming staff, modest, but well recommended. **D** *Stone Town Inn Hotel*, T/F2233658. A/c, fan. **D** *Victoria Guest House*, T2232861, F2233566. Located on Vuga Rd – good value, friendly staff. **D** *Wazazi Guest House*, next to *Africa House* on Suicide Alley, rather basic.

It seems that the authorities will no longer allow camping on beaches. **E** *Bottoms Up*, excellent location in the very centre of Stone Town, Changa Bazaar, near *Clove Hotel*, T2233189. Run down, very small breakfast, attracts international backpackers, fans and nets available, friendly, good terrace, attached bar currently closed because of neighbours' complaints about noise. **E** *Garden Lodge Resthouse*, Kaunda Rd, PO Box 3413, T2233298, located at Vuga opposite the National Library/High Court. Lovely gardens, peaceful and quiet with friendly staff. **E** *Manch Lodge Vuga*, Stone Town off Vuga Rd, PO Box 3060, T2231918. Friendly, clean, best rooms on top floor, includes huge breakfast. **E** *Riverman Hotel*,

Mkunazini St, PO Box 1805, T/F2233188, cheap and clean with good facilities. **E** *Warere Guest House*, including a large breakfast, clean, nets (but holes are appearing), fan, shared bathrooms, top floor should now be renovated. Located near the the entrance to the harbour, from the roundabout walk about 50 m in the direction of *Malindi Guest House*, it is one block back from the road on the right, livelier than the *Malindi*, can arrange cheap transport to east coast beaches.

There are a number of moderate standard eating places in Zanzibar and you will not usually need to reserve tables. Many of them have good, fresh seafood. During Ramadan it is difficult to get meals in the day time. It is not possible to purchase bottles of spirits in shops any more, only available in bars. Bring your own supply from the mainland if required.

Eating
● *on maps*
Price codes:
see inside front cover

Expensive The only first-rate restaurants are *Baharia*, T2231015, F0741-333170, an expensive à la carte restaurant in *Serena Inn*, and *Emersons and Green*, T2230171, where you can eat in wonderful surroundings in rooftop restaurants; if you are not staying there you need to book a day ahead as space on the roof is limited. *Hotel Kiponda*, T2233052. Another relaxing rooftop restaurant serving speciality seafood dishes. *Pagoda*, T2234688, T0747-411168 (mob), F2231758. Has really excellent spicy Chinese cuisine, generous portions, has relocated from Funguni to the Shangani area, and is now only a few paces away from *Africa House*.

Mid-range *Blues* (formerly the *Floating Restaurant*), T0741-328509 (mob), F2236211, blues@zanzinet.com Extensively upgraded by a South African company, lovely position, very professional staff. Recommended. On the dock in front of the old fort, which is a good place to watch the children somersaulting from the seawall into the water. *Camlurs*, Shangani St, PO Box 546, T2231919, 1-min walk from *Africa House*. Specializes in Goan cuisine, open evenings only. *Fisherman Restaurant*, PO Box 3530, T2233658, T0741-334872 (mob), F2233480. Located on Shangani St has good food but is very overpriced. *La Fenice*, on seafront just around the corner from the *Serena*. Does a good lunch as well as a good dinner. *La Lampara*, Vuga Rd, good Italian. *Le Spices Rendez-vous*, Kenyatta Rd, near the High Court, T2234241, T0747-413062 (mob), lespices.rdv@zitec.org Formerly the *Maharaja Restaurant*, retained is the excellent food, Indian meals and snacks, seafood, African music and dance on Tue evenings. Prices have risen steeply since the change of ownership. Recommended. *Sea View Indian Restaurant (Tomane Palace)*, Mizingani Rd, PO Box 666, T2232132, has a splendid location that overlooks the harbour. You can eat inside or out and there is a wide range of food on the menu, freshly cooked on order, but nevertheless service can be slow, and if you want to sit on the balcony you would be advised to book ahead.

Cheap *Baobab Tree*, New Mkunazini Rd, near the UMCA cathedral, large thatched roof constructed around the trunk of a baobab tree, open-sided seating area beneath, some meals, snacks, juices, bar. *Dolphin Restaurant*, Shangani St, PO Box 138, T2231987, is popular and sells mainly seafood plus some other dishes (nothing special). *Le Bistrot*, Stone Town, off Shangani St, signposted from behind the Old Fort. Simply decorated inexpensive restaurant with a small but groovy bar. Lots of reggae, delicious fresh fish, generous portions. Popular with backpackers/locals, cold beer. Very noisy. Sited close to the Old Orphanage, *Cultural Centre Restaurant*, at the Na Sur Nurmohamed Dispensary, Mizingani Rd, between the House of Wonders and the Arab Fort, hosts cultural events like *taarab*, Zanzibari traditional drummers in an open-air stadium, barbecued food. *Divers Restaurant*, in Old Town (opposite Eagle Bureau de Change). Serves good, cheap, local food. *Heart of Zanzibar*, Kiponda St, close to *International Hotel*, T2231264, heartofzanzibar@hotmail.com Formerly called *House of Spices* and *Zee Bar & Zee Pizza*, very good wood oven baked pizzas, also cocktail bar. *Luis Yoghurt Parlour*, Gizenga St, is very small and serves excellent local dishes including lassi yoghurt drinks, milk shakes, fresh fruit juices, spice tea, opens 1000-1400 and 1800-2200 Mon-Sat. Closes for long periods in off season while the owner goes on holiday. *Luna Mare*, Gizenga St, signposted from the Kenyatta Rd end, PO Box 3424, T2231922. Reasonably priced Indian food. The *Narrow Street Hotel* on Kokoni St has good food (but not to everyone's taste). If you want a seafood meal it's best to order in advance. *Pichy's Bar*,

Tanzania

situated on the seafront opposite the *Old Dispensary* on Mizingani Rd. Speciality is pizza, lively bar, live band on Thu. *Two Tables Restaurant* is very charming, on the verandah of a private house, local food and drink (non-alcoholic), situated very close to Victoria House – look out for the signs as no entrance from the street, reservations necessary, T2232861. *Zi Bar and Restaurant*, Vuga Rd, opposite Victoria Gardens, T2239366, T0747-410410 (mob). Pasta, good pizza, seafood, salads.

Seriously cheap Other good value places include the café at the *Ciné Afrique* and *Chit Chat*, Cathedral St, PO Box 4089, T2232548. Moderate prices, seats 36, serves snacks, refreshments and quick meals, also specializing in traditional Goan cuisine, open Tue-Sun evenings. Finally, from the early evening there are a large number of vendors with charcoal grills selling a variety of foods in the *Jamituri Gardens* (also known as *Forodhani*), between the fort and the sea. Here you can get excellent meat or prawn kebabs, lobster, corn on the cob, cassava and curries all very cheaply. It is very popular with tourists and fun to wander around even if you don't feel hungry. Some stalls are better than others. If you're thirsty, try some fresh coconut milk or freshly squeezed sugar cane juice from one of the local stalls. Try 'African Pizza' (*mantabali*) – well worth a try. Excellent foodstall next to the *Fisherman Restaurant*, very popular.

Entertainment The most popular bar in the town is that at the *Africa House Hotel* which looks out across the ocean. The beers are cold and plentiful although rather expensive, and it is a good place to meet people. Get there early if you want to watch the sun set: seats are quickly taken. Other bars include the *Wazazi Bar* next door to the *Africa House Hotel*. It is cheap, popular, and there is music (sometimes live) and it stays open fairly late. *Livingstone* and *Stanley Bars* in Baghani are open until 0200 where this is good music. Finally the *Starehe Bar*, located on Shangani St, overlooks the harbour and tends to be less crowded than the *Africa House Hotel*. It sometimes holds discos. There is a disco, the *Garage Club*, next to Fisherman's Restaurant on Shangani St, open Wed-Sun. The *Bwawani Hotel* has popular discos on Sat.

Scuba diving
See also Diving, page 40
Zanzibar is a great place to go diving. There are 2 scuba-diving schools in town that both offer good value. *Zanzibar Dive Centre-One Ocean*, PO Box 608, T/F2233686, T0742-750161 (mob), www.zanzibaroneocean.com, located behind/under *Africa House Hotel*. Italian owned, very friendly, motorized dhows and custom-built dive boats go to several coral reefs, PADI certificate course US$300 for open-water diving. If you have a scuba certificate, 1 dive including boat trip to the reef costs US$35 and 3 dives US$90, including equipment hire costs. The inexperienced are offered 'fun dives' for US$30, which includes 30 mins' instruction in the basics of scuba diving from an experienced instructor, plus a 6-m deep dive in the coral reef, snorkelling is US$15 a trip, safety highest priority, with fully trained dive masters/instructors. Recommended. *Dive Zanzibar* (previously known as *Indian Ocean Divers*), T0741-323096 (mob) Stone Town and T0741-326574 (mob), Paradise Beach, Nungwe, PO Box 2370, T/F2233860, located on Mizingani Rd beside the *Sea View Indian Restaurant*. They offer similar packages to *Zanzibar Dive Centre One Ocean* and have the same quality and experience but use only rigid inflatable boats. The PADI Open Water Diver course costs US$300, but you can keep the theory book. The coral reef near Zanzibar Town is well preserved. Depending on the season one can see a lot of coral fish, stingrays, scorpion fish, doctor fish and large shoals of sardines. The deepest possible dive is only 26 m. *The Zanzibar Dive Adventures*, PO Box 2282, Zanzibar, T/F2232503. For diving in the north and northeast. *Bahari Divers*, PO Box 204, T0742-750293 (mob), baharidivers@hotmail.com, www.zanzibar-diving.com Small shop next to the *National Bank of Commerce*, Shangani St at the northern end of Kenyatta Rd. Offer diving, PADI courses and snorkelling.

Shopping The Market Place off Creek Rd sells mainly fresh fruit and vegetables. However the shops nearby sell kikois and kangas, wooden chests and other souvenirs. Also try the small shops in the Old Fort, one shop sells only locally handcrafted wooden boxes, many made of fragrant rosewood. If you want batiks or paintings, a visit to the small art gallery above *St Monica's Guest House* is worth while. The *Rashid A Nograni Curio Shop* and the *Chanda Curio Shop*

Taarab music

The most distinctly Swahili of all the musical idioms found in Tanzania is Taarab, developed in Zanzibar in the 19th century out of Egyptian, Omani and local influences. It was first heard at weddings. Today's Taarab combos have largely replaced the Arab 'ud (a type of mandolin) and violins, with electric guitars and keyboards, but the scales used are still distinctly Middle Eastern. Taarab is still important at weddings. Most of the singers are women, and the themes of the songs have a bias towards female domestic topics, jealousy between wives being one of them:

Ninachokula ni changu,
Ukiwa unaonja acha …
[What I'm eating is mine,

If you were tasting it, leave it alone …]
Sometimes Taarab is performed as a contest, with the singers of two bands taking turns to fling poetically disguised insults at each other. In Zanzibar, Taarab performances can be seen at the Cultural Music Centre on Vugu Road.

In Dar es Salaam popular bands are TOT, Muungano Cultural Troupe and East African Melody, a Zanzibar outfit. Venues that host Taarab include Max's Bar in Ilala, the FM Club in Kinondoni, and Le Petit Prince in Magomeni. It's best to go to these venues in a group, or accompanied by a local person.

sell carvings, wooden boxes, brass and copper coffeepots and jewellery. You can pick up good reading material at **Masomo Bookshop** near the Old Empire Cinema just behind the Central Market, also has Tanzanian and Kenyan newspapers. **Stone Town Memories**, T/F2233300, T0742-750023 (mob), Gizenga St, deal in old artefacts and handicrafts. **The Gallery**, Gizenga St, behind the Old Fort, T/F2232244, T0741-320644 (mob), gallery@ swahilicoast.com, has an excellent range of new and secondhand books, and a huge range of curios. It also sells excellent postcards taken by the owner's son. Accepts credit cards. **Abeid Curio Shop**, T2233832, F2232004, Cathedral St, opposite St Joseph's Cathedral, sells old Zanzibari furniture, clocks, copper and brass ware. In the area near Mlandegi Bazaar there is a wide choice of kangas and kofias – the traditional Muslim head covering. Also available are bread baskets, woven flat trays from Pemba and Mafia, plus wooden artefacts. Zanzibar is a good place to buy film (mostly Konica) and tends to be cheaper than Kenya. Outside the **Hammamni Public Baths** there are ceramic bowls for sale, which the Zanzibarians use to decorate their homes. Originally Dutch in design. Visitors are advised not to buy products of rare and endangered species such as green turtle.

Tour operators *Mitu*. Contactable at the café next door to the *Ciné Afrique* early in the mornings or in the evenings. Get a group of 4 together, and Mitu, an elderly Indian (or one of the people he has trained), will take you on one of his own guided tours visiting the Marahubi Palace, 2 spice plantations, the Kidichi Baths and a 1-hr trip to relax on the beach. They are good value. However they have become very popular and you may find yourself in a large group. Cost US$10 per person including vegetarian lunch. Get there by 0900, depart 0930, return 1600. Mitu now also arranges Dolphin Tours for US$15 per person. Advance bookings in Dar es Salaam: *Coastal Travels Ltd*, PO Box 3052 Upanga Rd, Dar es Salaam, T022-2117957-9. Bookings are also taken at the office next to the Ciné Afrique from about 0800 on the day, PO Box 139, T2234636. **Adventure Afloat** organize **African Boat Safaris**, PO Box 4056, Zanzibar, T/F2230536, T2231832, T0741-320166 (mob), c/o *Mbweni Ruins Hotel*, Marine Channel 72 (156.625 MHz). Excursions to see the dolphins, game fishing and dhow trips available. UK office, 21 Linton St, London N1 7DU, T020-7354 0771. **Al Salaam Tours & Travel**, T2234596/7, F2234595, alsalaam@zitec.org **Anderson's African Adventure**, T2234833, T0742-402401 (mob), www.andersons-africa.com **Chema Bros Tours & Safaris**, PO Box 1865, Kenyatta Rd, at the roundabout with Kaunda Rd and Vuga Rd, T2235364, T0742-750158 (mob), F2233385, chemah@zanzinet.com **Classic Tours**, c/o Emerson's House, T2283629. **Coastal Travels**, at the airport, T/F2233112, T0741-324378 (mob). **Dolphin Tours**, PO Box 138, New Mukanazini Rd, T2233386. **Easy Travel & Tours**, Malawi Rd, opposite *Hotel Marine*, PO Box 4586, T2235372, T0744-260124 (mob), F2235571, easytravel@zanzinet.com **Eco Tours** .

Tanzania

Tanzania

Recommended for the Dolphin Tour US$25 per person including transport, guide, lunch, boat and snorkelling gear. *Equator Tours and Safaris*, PO Box 2096, Sokomohogo St, T/F2233799, T0741-771564 (mob), F2233882, eqt@zanlink.com *Faizin Tours & Travel Agency*, PO Box 702, T2232501. Also have a branch at Pemba. *Fisherman Tours & Travel*, Vuga Rd, PO Box 3537, T2233060, T0741-321441 (mob), T0812-750112/3, F2233060, fisherman@cctz.com *Giant Tours*, near the Old Fort, PO Box 2071, T0741-323285 (mob). *Jasfa Tours & Safaris*, PO Box 4203, Shangani Rd, T/F2230468, Res 2231457. Good reputation and will confirm flights, organize hotel bookings etc. *Kigaeni Travel & Tours*, PO Box 1741, T0742-740362 (mob), F2237327, for tours and car hire. *Kikuba Tours & Safaris*, PO Box 1887, T2233416, F2233020, kikuba@zanzinet.com *Links Tours & Travel*, at the port, PO Box 812, T0741-606799 (mob). *Marlin Tours & Safaris*, Kenyatta Rd, Shangani, PO Box 3435, T2232378, T0741-327073 (mob), F2232378, marlin@zanzinet.com *Orbit Travel & Tours*, PO Box 719, T0741-328812. *Mreh Tours & Safaris*, PO Box 3769, T/F2233476, F2230344, mrehtours@zanzinet.com *Old Town Tours & Travels*, PO Box 4164, T/F2232096, T0742-750000 (mob), oldtown@zitec.org *Orient Expeditions*, opposite New Happy Bar near *Africa House*, T2233299, T0741-339682 (mob). *Rainbow Tours & Travel*, T2233469, F2233701. Car and bike hire, tours, hotel bookings, flight confirmations. Recommended. *Ras Tours & Safaris*, T2231078. *Sama Tours*, PO Box 2276, Changa Bazaar St, T2233543. *Sun and Fun Safari Tours*, PO Box 666, Shangani Rd, T2232132. *Target Tours & Travel*, PO Box 3349, Sonara Building, Darajani area, T2230257. *Tima Tours & Safaris*, PO Box 4194, Mizingani Rd, T2237278/9, F2231298, timatours@zanzibar.net. *Triple M Tours Africa House Club*, T2230708/2230709. *Tropical Tours & Travel*, Kenyatta Rd, Shangani, T/F2230868. Good, reliable agency. *World Travel Adventure*, PO Box 1, 193 Hurumzi St, T/F2235631, T0742-750043 (mob). *Zan Tours*, PO Box 2560, Malindi St, T/F2233116, T0741-335832 (mob), zantours@zanzinet.com *Zanea Tours*, PO Box 620, Shangani Rd, T2230413. *Zanzibar Aviation Services & Travel*, PO Box 1981, Vuga Rd and Airport, T2231819, F2237536, zat@zanzinet.com *Zanzibar Safari Tours*, PO Box 4052, Kenyatta Rd, T2231463. *Zanzibar Tourist Corporation*, Creek Rd, PO Box 216, T2232344. Incompetent. *Zanzique*, Creek Rd, PO Box 152, T/F2231287, F2233030. *Zenith Tours & Travel*, PO Box 3648, behind the Old Fort, T0741-339286, F2232320, zenithznz@cats-net.com *Zenj Tours*, PO Box 3355, T2231894.

Transport **Local** You can hire **minivans** seating 8 passengers through one of the tour agencies to get around the island. It will cost about US$40 for the van. At the southern end of Jamituri Gardens it is possible to hire 4WDs that are parked there for US$30 a day. If hiring a vehicle make sure all the paperwork is in order as you can be stopped several times by traffic police. Hiring a taxi to take you across the island is cheaper if negotiated directly, rather than through a tour agent. Pickup vans (known as *dala-dalas*) with wooden benches in the back are the cheapest way of getting around the island. It will cost about US$2 per person to the east coast, and is a hot, dusty and not very comfortable journey. You can hire **bicycles** (there is a shop close to the Tourist Bureau on Creek Rd) for US$5 a day and there is a US$50 deposit. **Motorbikes** can be hired for US$20 per day from behind the tax office close to Jamituri Gardens. Vespas can be hired for US$25 and Honda 125ccs for US$30 per day (rates negotiable). Left side of Post Office (recommended) and opposite Post Office. Most **buses** go from the bus station on Creek Rd opposite the market. Buses with lettered codes serve routes in and around Zanzibar Town. Numbered buses go further afield, and tend to leave once a day around noon, returning early the next morning. Bus number 9 goes to Paje, Jambiani (3 hrs) and Bwejuu (4½ hrs), costing US$2.50-3. There is a bus that returns from the East Coast to Stone Town leaving at 0630. However, this means that you need to get your baggage to the bus stop under your own steam. Other buses from Creek Rd go to Pwani Mchangani and Matemwe (bus number 1), Mangapwani (bus 2), Fumba (bus 7), Makunduchi and Kizimkazi (bus 10), Nungwi (bus 16), and Kiwengwa (bus 17). There is another bus station, Mwembe Ladu, one block north of the new Post Office about 1½ km east of Stone Town. Bus number 6 from here goes to Chakwa (1½ hrs), Uroa and Pongwe.

Travellers have reported that trips may be offered by unscrupulous touts to remote parts of the island at an agreed price, eg to Jambiani by minibus/4WD. However, on arrival, the travellers are forced to pay 3 times the agreed original price. The return trip cost 4 times the original one-way quote.

Long-distance Air Several companies have scheduled services to and from Zanzibar airport. Bear in mind that the airline industry is highly changeable, so the following timetables are also subject to change. *Air Tanzania* (PO Box 773, T2230297, T/F2230213) has a rather irregular schedule of flights between Dar es Salaam (DSM) and Zanzibar. There are flights from DSM on Mon (depart 1430) and Thu (depart 0750), and flights in the opposite direction on Tue (depart 1445), Wed (depart 1925) and Thu (depart 1930), journey time 20 mins. There are also flights to DSM on Wed (depart 0940), Sat (depart 1955) and Sun (depart 1610). These are the continuation of flights from Kilimanjaro International Airport, from where flights depart 0815 on Wed, 1830 Sat and 1445 Sun, they take 45 mins and cost US$130.

There are buses between the airport and the town for US$0.50. Alternatively you can get a taxi for about US$6-10. Zanzibar Airport, T+24-2230213

The following services between DSM, Zanzibar and Mombasa are operated in conjunction with *Precisionair*. Flights depart DSM at 0800 on Mon, Tue, Wed, Fri, Sat and Sun, then depart Zanzibar at 0845, taking 50 mins to reach Mombasa. On the return, the flights depart Mombasa at 1015 for Zanzibar, and leave Zanzibar at 1125 for DSM. There is a second service on the same route on Wed, Sat and Sun, depart DSM 1700, depart Zanzibar 1745, depart Mombasa 1910, and depart Zanzibar for DSM at 2030. Flights between DSM and Zanzibar cost US$45 and take about 20 mins. The *Air Tanzania* office is at the Majestic Cinema on Vuga Rd and closes for lunch (1230-1400), T2230297.

Precisionair also have services between Zanzibar, DSM, Arusha and Mwanza. On Mon, Thu and Sat flights leave DSM at 1310 and go to Zanzibar, US$55. From Zanzibar they depart at 1350, taking 70 mins to Arusha. From Arusha, departing at 1525, the plane returns to Zanzibar, and from here leaves at 1655 for Zanzibar. On Tue and Fri flights to Zanzibar depart DSM at 1000, then leave Zanzibar at 1040 to Arusha and on to Mwanza. On return to Arusha, they depart at 1525 for Zanzibar, and then leave Zanzibar at 1655 to return to DSM. On Wed and Sun there are 1525 flights from Arusha, which then depart Zanzibar for DSM at 1655. Zanzibar-Arusha US$170 one way, Zanzibar-Mwanza US$205 one way. Precisionair used to have once weekly flights to Mafia but it appears that these are no longer in operation. The Precisionair office in Zanzibar is at *Mazsons Hotel*, T2234520, T0741-511717 (mob), F2234520. For flights to Arusha it is usually necessary to book in advance; occasionally these flights are overbooked.

Coastal Travels Ltd, T/F2233112, have daily flights from DSM to Zanzibar at 0900 and 1645, and at 1400 and 1715 from Zanzibar to DSM, cost US$55 one way. The 1400 from Zanzibar continues to Selous (cost from Zanzibar US$130), while there are also daily return flights to Arusha, which depart Zanzibar at 0930 and Arusha at 1215, take approximately 2 hrs and cost US$175 one way. In addition, on Mon, Thu and Sat flights to Zanzibar from DSM leave at 0730. They leave for DSM again at 0800, continuing to Selous and Ruaha (cost from Zanzibar US$300), on return departing DSM for Zanzibar at 1330.

Eagle Air fly from DSM at 0900 and 1145 on Fri and 0700 on Sun, from Arusha at 1445 on Fri (taking 90 mins), 1615 on Sat and 1300 on Sun, and from Mafia at 1700 on Sun (45 mins). There are no direct flights to Mafia, so you would have to go from DSM. From Zanzibar there are flights to DSM at 1705 on Fri, 1815 on Sat, and 1500 and 1815 on Sun. There are also flights to Pemba at 0940 on Fri (30 mins), to Arusha at 1245 on Fri, and to Seronera at 0800 on Sun (2 hrs).

Air Excel (Arusha: PO Box 12731, T2501597, F2548429, T0741-510857 (mob), airexcel@ark.eoltz.com) have daily flights between Zanzibar, Arusha and DSM. They leave Arusha at 1330, arrive in Zanzibar 2 hrs later, leave Zanzibar for DSM at 1515, leave DSM for Zanzibar at 1550, then depart Zanzibar for Arusha at 1625.

Zan Air Ltd, Malawi Rd, Malindi area, PO Box 2113, T2233768, T0742-750478 (mob), 0747-410077, T/F2233670, zanair@zitec.org, Dar es Salaam Airport: T0742-605230 (mob), have scheduled flights to Pemba, Selous and Kilimanjaro. Charter flights are available from *Coastal Travels Ltd*, *Precisionair* and *Zan Air*, and also *Air Zanzibar*, PO Box 1784, T2232512, F2232512, air@zanzibar.net, *Skyland Safaris & Travel*, PO Box 518, T2232652, and *Twin Wings Air Ltd*, PO Box 3379, T/F2230747.

You can fly to Zanzibar from **Nairobi** on *Kenya Airways*, who have daily flights in each direction, leaving Nairobi at 1030, and Zanzibar at 1240, journey time approximately 75 mins. The *Kenya Airways* office is opposite the Ijumaa Mosque, just off Mizingani Rd, PO Box 3840, Zanzibar, T2232041-3.

Tanzania

Tanzania

Sea Ferries to Zanzibar			
Name of ferry boat	**Schedule**	**Fare** **TSh**	**Duration**
Sea Express *T255-51-137049* *F255-51-116723* *zpd@catsnet.com*	*DSM Depart:* *1000* *1515*	*Residents* *1st class 15,000* *2nd class:12,500*	*70 minutes*
	ZNZ Depart: *0700* *1200*	*Non resident* *1st class US$40* *2nd class US$35*	
MS Sepideh *N T0811-326414*	*DSM Depart:* *Daily except Sun and Thu* *0730*	*Resident* *15,000*	*90 minutes*
	ZNZ Depart: *Daily except Sun and Thu* *1600*	*Non resident* *Salon US$35* *VIP US$40*	
Sea Star Service *T0812-789393 or* *781500*	*DSM Depart:* *0730, 1145* *1400, 1615*	*Resident* *Economy 12,500* *1st class 15,000*	*90 minutes*
	ZNZ Depart: *0815, 1015* *1415, 1615*	*Non resident* *Economy US$35* *1st class US$40*	
Flying Horse *T255-51-124504*	*DSM Depart:* *1230*	*Resident* *1st class 9,500* *2nd class 9,000*	*2 hours*
	ZNZ Depart: *2000* *arrive DSM 0600*	*3rd class 8,500* *VIP class 10,500*	
		Non resident *US$25*	
Sea Bus	*DSM Depart:* *1400* *1600*	*Residents* *1st class 15,000* *2nd class:12,500*	*105 minutes*
	ZNZ Depart: *1000* *1300*	*Non resident* *1st class US$40* *2nd class US$35*	
Port tax US$5			

Gulf Air also have direct flights from Europe, PO Box 3179, Zanzibar, T2233772, F2233083, the office is in front of Ijumaa Mosque, on Mizingani Rd. As always book in advance as this is a popular route. It is possible to get a *Gulf Air* flight from Zanzibar to DSM on Thu and Sat at around 1500, the flights originally coming from Muscat.

If you are returning from Zanzibar to DSM, you could try and get a seat on the plane that brings the daily newspapers over. Tickets are sold from the *Masomo Bookshop* (T2232652) and cost $40.

Sea Dows: a cheaper alternative from **Dar es Salaam** is by motorized dhow (nicknamed *yongo*, which is Swahili for millipede). These go each way most days leaving early in the morning (about 0600), costing about US$3 and taking up to 8 hrs. It is hot and there is no food or water on board so take your own. To get back to Dar es Salaam book from the Malindi Sports Club opposite Sinbad Sailors Restaurant 1 day in advance. This is strictly speaking illegal as there have been some restrictions on non-Tanzanians travelling by dhow. You can also get a dhow to **Pemba** and **Mombasa**. For Pemba book at the Malindi Sports Club. For Mombasa they go once or twice a week. Ask for details at the Institute of Marine Science on Mizingani Rd. It costs about US$3 and takes about 6 hrs to Pemba, to Mombasa US$10 and takes about 24 hrs.

The *Zanzibar Shipping Corporation* runs a weekly service between Dar es Salaam, Pemba and Zanzibar. The Zanzibar booking office is at the wharf, and the fare is about US$2-3. It's an unreliable service and not recommended unless you're on a very tight budget with time to spare. The booking offices of the ferry companies are on the approach road to the harbour.

For further details of ferry services see Dar es Salaam, page 362, and Pemba, page 575

Directory

Banks The chaotic *People's Bank of Zanzibar*,T2211138/9, F2231121, is located behind the fort on Gizenga St. There is also a branch at the Airport Terminal, T221118/9, F2231121. Close by is the *Tanzania Commercial Bank*. However banks often give an inferior rate compared with the foreign exchange bureaux, which are also open for longer hours. There is a foreign exchange bureau opposite the Tourist Bureau at north end of Creek Rd. *Malindi Exchange* on Malawi Rd, opposite Ciné Afrique, next to Zanair offer good rates reputed to be the best in town, T2230903, F2230052. *Icon Bureau de Change* on the Mchangani St, off Creek Rd, T2234820. Near the Post Office is the efficient and friendly *Shangani Bureau de Change*, T2231660, F2233688. *The Forex Bureau* around the corner from *Mazsons Hotel* is reported to offer excellent exchange rates. Western Union money transfer is available from the Tananian Postal Bank on Malawi Rd, Malindi area, open 0830-1800 Mon-Sat. There is a *Visa and Mastercard Assistance Point* in Shangani, next to Serena Inn, open 0830-1730 Mon-Sat. Here you can withdraw cash against your credit card. There are no ATM facilities in Zanzibar.

Communications Post: the new Post Office is located out of Stone Town, in Kijangwani area just over 1 km east of the Karume Monument. Bus A or M from the market will take you there. Poste restante and faxes are held there. The poste restante charge is US$0.15 per letter held for collection. Ask to see all letters if you are expecting mail as the local sorting and filing can be erratic. The old Post Office is on Kenyatta Rd in the Shangani area, there is a fax machine and they should be able to help with poste restante. Worldwide delivery services available from DHL, opposite Serena Inn, and TNT, Kenyatta Rd, T2233592, T0741-334412 (mob), F2231140. **Internet**: services are particularly good in Zanzibar, with fast connections and reasonable prices. *Shangani Internet Café*, Kenyatta Rd, opposite the *Dolphin* restaurant. *Zanzibar Cyber Café*, Changa Bazar St, in the Hurumzi area of Stone Town, near *Eco Tours*, T2237644, F2237645, macrosoft@zanzinet.com Internet surfing, email, colour and laser printing. *Zanzibar Computer & Communications Services*, 150 m from the harbour towards *Malindi Guest House*, look for a 'Zanzibar Capital Zoo' sign. *Zanzinet*, Kenyatta Rd, Shangani, T2239014, T0747-411114 (mob), info@zanzinet.com *ZiTec*, behind the Majestic Cinema, Vuga Rd, T2237480, F2237482, info@zitec.org Fast access, US$1.25 for 15 mins.

Medical services There is a state hospital (Mnazi Mmoja) on Kaunda Rd, T2231071-3. Also private clinic – *Mkunazini Hospital*, near to the market. British trained doctor. Pay fee to register, wait to see doctor then pay for any prescription necessary. Pay again when go to collect medicine: this may be at the clinic or in a nearby drug-store. An interesting way to pass a few hours if not too ill. A good clinic is *Zamedic*, PO Box 1043, near Majestic Cinema, off Vuga Rd, T/F2233113, T0742-750040 (mob). Ask for Dr Mario Mariani. *Dr Mehta's Hospital*, on Pipalwadi St, Vuga has a 24-hr casualty facility, T2230194, T0747-410009 (mob).

Changuu Island (Prison Island)

Also known as Prison Island (almost 5 km northwest of Stone Town), Changuu Island was once owned by an Arab who used it for 'rebellious' slaves. Some years later in 1893 it was sold to General Mathews, a Briton who converted it into a prison. However it has never actually been used as such and was later converted to serve as a quarantine station for East Africa in colonial times. The prison is still relatively intact and a few

Tanzania

Tanzania

Changuu tortoises

The earliest trade routes from Europe to India and the Far East, before the building of the Suez Canal in 1856, went down the west coast of Africa, round the Cape, and northeast through the Indian Ocean Islands. On such a long journey, ships put in to ports along the route to replenish water and victuals. On the Indian Ocean leg giant tortoises, turtles and dodos proved easy to catch for their meat that was salted and stored. Reunion, Rodrigues and Mauritius were the principle sources.

By 1750, the tortoises on Mauritius were facing extinction, and 30,000 tortoises were brought in from Diego Garcia 5,000 km to the west in the Indian Ocean. The new supply could not meet with demand, however, and by 1850 tortoises were extinct in Mauritius, Réunion and Rodrigues, as well as in the Farquar Islands in the Seychelles. In 1884, in an effort to make sure that some tortoises survived, tortoises were shipped from the Aldabra Islands in the Seychelles, and were used to establish protected colonies in Mauritius, the Chagos Islands near Diego Garcia, and on Changuu Island off Zanzibar. As tortoises can live for 150 years, some of the tortoises you can see on Changuu began their lives on Aldabra, 1,000 km to the southeast, more than 120 years ago.

remains of the hospital can be seen including the rusting boilers of the laundry. There is good snorkelling, wind surfing and sailing from the beautiful little beach. Jellyfish can sometimes spoil bathing and snorkelling however. The island is also home to giant tortoises, which are supposed to have been brought over from Aldabra (an atoll off the Seychelles) around the turn of the 20th century. The tortoises are no longer roaming freely over the island because many were stolen. Now they are kept in a large fenced area. You can buy leaves to feed the tortoises. There is a US$4 landing fee.

Grave Island is a nearby private island that has no facilities, but there is an interesting cemetery with headstones of British sailors and marines who lost their lives in the fight against slavery and in the First World War.

Sleeping   **C** *Changuu Island Resort*, PO Box 216, T2232344, F2233430. Simple and reasonable with cold beers, also has facilities for snorkelling, wind surfing and sailing, plans are afoot for a huge holiday complex to be built by Lonrho.

Transport   **Local**   You can get there through one of the tour agencies or a boat will take you across to the island and back for about US$5 per person, ask around on the beaches in front of the *Sea View Indian Restaurant* or *Tembo Hotel*.

Bawe Island   An island 5 km west of Stone Town, it receives fewer visitors than Changuu Island, although it is also widely offered by touts and boat owners on the beach in front of *Tembo Hotel*. One fisherman and his family live on the island, it has an idyllic small beach, but no facilities. There are rumours that a hotel is to be built on the island.

Kiungani, Mbweni & Chukwani   The route south of Zanzibar town will take you past Kiungani where there was once a hostel built in 1864 by Bishop Tozer for released slave boys. A little further on are the ruins of **Mbweni Settlement**, which was also established for rescued slaves. This was built in 1871 by the Universities Mission to Central Africa. In 1882 St John's Church was built in the same place for the use of the released slaves. There is a fine carved door and a tower.

Also at Mbweni is **Kirk House**, which was built by Seyyid Barghash in 1872. Kirk came to Zanzibar as the Medical Officer as part of Livingstone's expedition to the Zambezi. He played an important role in the fight to end the slave trade and in 1873 was appointed His Majesty's Agent and Consul General in Zanzibar. He was also a botanist, introducing a number of plants to the island said to have originated from Kew Gardens, including cinnamon, vanilla, mahogany and eucalyptus.

Further south at Chukwani are the **Mbweni Palace Ruins**. This was once a holiday resort of Sultan Seyyid Barghash and it had a wonderful position overlooking the sea. However it has been totally neglected and as a result is slowly crumbling away. The main palace has completely disappeared, although some of the other buildings do remain and may be toured. The ruins are located to the south of the town off the airport road.

Sleeping L-A (depending on the season) *Mbweni Ruins Hotel*, PO Box 2542, T2231832, F2230536, T0741-320855 (mob), www.mbweni.com Built between 1871-74 in the spacious grounds of the ruins of the first Anglican Christian missionary settlement in East Africa, seafront, pool, garden setting, art gallery, 13 suites with a/c and fans, 4-poster beds, nets, free shuttles to Stone Town 5 times a day.

Approximately 4 km off-shore southwest from Chukwani Palace ruins lies the **Chumbe Island Coral Park**. This is a wonderful reef with coral gardens that can be viewed from glass-bottomed boats. Snorkelling is available. There are nature trails through the forest of the island, the home of the rare roseate tern and coconut crab, the largest land crab in the world, and now a refuge for the shy Ader's duiker, introduced to the island with the assistance of the World Wide Fund for Nature. There is also an old mosque and a lighthouse, built in 1904, from the top of which is a good view of the island. A day trip can be booked directly with the park, PO Box 3203, T/F2231040, or through *Mbweni Ruins Hotel*, US$70 per person including transport, snorkelling equipment, nature trail guides and a picnic lunch. The island is a private conservation project and has an all-inclusive resort of the same name.

Chumbe Island

Sleeping L *Chumbe Island Coral Park*, T2236171, chumbe@zitec.org The utmost care has been taken to minimize the environmental impact of the resort, from the sustainably harvested local materials used in construction of the 7 luxury cottages and dining area, to the utilization of solar power and composting toilets, and the use of rainwater as the source of freshwater. Recognition of these efforts came when the resort was made the global winner of the British Airways Tourism for Tomorrow Awards 2000.

North to Ras Nungwe

These are located about 3 km to the north of the town. They were built in 1882 by Sultan Barghash for his harem of many (said to be 99) women. The palace was almost completely destroyed by a fire in 1899. All that remains are the pillars and aqueducts which brought water to the palace from the nearby springs. The site is very overgrown, and marble from the baths has long since been stolen.

Maruhubi Palace ruins

Between the ruined palace of Maruhubi and Mtoni to the north is Mtoni Marine Centre, PO Box 992, Zanzibar, T2232540, T0741-323226 (mob), F2286569, mmc@twiga.com There are two kinds of accommodation on offer, **B** *Mtoni Club*, a/c, self-contained rooms with verandahs, thatched roofs. The attached *Mtoni Marine Restaurant*, T2250117, T0742-740433 (mob), mmr@africaonline.co.tz, is an open air à la carte restaurant on the beach, barbecue buffets on Tuesdays and Sats. **C** *Mtoni Village*, simple, comfortable, self-contained rooms by the beach, and 2 or 3 bedroom villas, includes breakfast. There is a private jetty, safe moorings, all marine activities, closest beach to Stone Town, dhows trips can be arranged and excursions to Jozani Forest etc. Safe parking for motorcycles. Accommodation and watersports also to be found at **B** *Mtoni Beach Resort*, T2250133, T0744-274831 (mob), juria@zanzinet.com An alternative restaurant at Mtoni is **mid-range**: *Zanzifun*, on the road from Bububu, T/F2250264, zanzifun@zanzinet.com, which offers French cuisine and watersports facilities, with barbecue buffets on the beach on Sat.

Mtoni Marine Centre

Building began on this palace for Seyyid Said in 1847, but was left unfinished when he died. Some of the impressive stone arches can still be seen. The rest was used in

Beit-ell-Ras Palace Ruins

Tanzania

the construction of the Bububu Railway at the start of this century, which linked the centre of the town with the village. The line wasn't viable, and closed in the 1920s.

Fuji beach This can be easily reached from Bububu village, and is a great place to take a relaxing swim if you've been exploring the area. There is a disco on the beach every Friday.

Sleeping and eating B *Imani Beach Villa*, Bububu Beach, PO Box 3248, T/F2250050, www.imani.it, for reservations. Only 7 clean, comfortable rooms with a/c, own bathrooms and traditional-style furniture. Breakfast served in pleasant gardens that run down to the beach, other meals are a fusion of Mediterranean and African influences. Recommended. Another good place to stay is the **D** *Bububu Beach Guest House*, T/F2250110, bububu@zanzinet.com Rooms with en-suite bathrooms, hot water, nets, fans, also laundry, fax and email services available, offer free shuttles to and from Stone Town on request. Alternatively any *dala-dala* with the letter B from the main road will get you to Fuji beach. 5 km north of Fuji Beach, past Chuini Palace, is **Mawimbini** *Village Club*, Chuwini Village, PO Box 4281, T31163, offering watersports – diving, snorkelling, sailing, windsurfing and boat excursions. The **cheap** *Fuji Snackbar & Restaurant*, Bububu, serves snacks and quick meals. Ideal for travellers on the spice tours or for those going to Nungwi.

Persian Baths Built on the highest point of Zanzibar Island by Sultan Seyyid Said in 1850, they were for
at Kidichi his wife who was Persian, and are decorated in an ornamental stucco work that is in the Persian style. The remarkably preserved baths have a series of domed bathhouses with deep stone baths and massive seats. This is quite a contrast to the plain baths nearby at **Kizimbani**, which were built within Said's clove tree and coconut plantation.

Mangapwani Located about 20 km north of the town, these were used to hide slaves in the times
slave caves when the slave trade was illegal but in fact continued unofficially. One particular trader, Mohammed bin Nasser, built an underground chamber at Alwi that was used as well as the naturally formed cave. The cave itself is said to have been discovered when a young slave boy lost a goat that he was looking after. He followed its bleats, which led it to the cave containing a freshwater stream. The discovery of the cave (although it was used to hide slaves and thus helped the slave trade continue illegally), was actually a blessing in disguise, as the freshwater stream was a boon to the confined slaves. You may well see women carrying water from this very same stream today. ■ *US$1. If you want to get there independently the caves can be reached by taking bus number 2 from Creek Rd opposite the market.*

Eating Expensive: *Mangapwani Seafood Grill and Watersports*, T2233567, F0741-333170. Part of the Serena chain, dinner by reservation only, also snorkelling, boat rides, dhow trips and fishing available, there are 2 free shuttle buses from *Serena Inn* in the mornings.

Tumbatu Located northwest of Zanzibar, Tumbatu Island contains Shirazi ruins of a large
Island ancient town dating from the 12th century. There are about 40 stone houses remaining. The Mvuleni ruins are in the north of the island and are the remains of the Portuguese attempt to colonize Zanzibar.

Nungwi

At the north tip of the island is Nungwi, located about 56 km from Zanzibar town. The population numbers about 5,000, mostly fishermen. Down on the beach, local men are often working in groups to build dhows. Boat enthusiasts can observe how dhows are constructed. Tourist minibuses go from Stone Town throughout the day, take approximately one hour, and cost US$2.50 (return US$3.50), ask from any hotel or guesthouse. There are also local *dala-dala* and the number 16 bus from Creek Road. These take about two hours and cost less than US$1 each way. If using *dala-dala* on the way back to Stone Town ask to be let off near the port, otherwise you may be taken a couple of kilometres to the east of the tourist area.

Nungwi is a pleasant fishing village, and has a number of good, white, beach-side bungalows. There are several good beaches and it is a good place for snorkelling and diving. Snorkelling equipment can be hired from local shops. A number of places organize 'sunset cruises' on traditional dhows for US$15 per person. The name of this resort is derived from the Swahili word *mnara* meaning lighthouse. Built in 1886 by Chance and Brothers, this 70-ft lighthouse was operated by a kerosene burner for its first 40 years, when it was converted to an automatic system. It flashes for half a second every five seconds. Currently the lighthouse is in a restricted area, with access permitted only by special request. Photographing the lighthouse is prohibited. Nungwi has arguably the best beaches, with little seaweed and the water is a little cooler than the east side. The tide does not go out for miles either. As in other parts of the island beach robberies have been reported.

However, it is developing fast. Remember to respect local custom if you go in to the village. Women should cover their arms, shoulders and thighs. Men are expected to cover up too.

Maviko ya Makumbi: As you walk along the beach there are mounds of what look like stones, known locally as 'Heaps of Stones', which are in fact deposits of coconut husks. These are made into coir and may be used to make ropes, matting and decorations. Each Heap of Stones belongs to a family or sometimes an individual, and some are 60 years old, passed down from one generation to the next. The coconuts are buried in the mud for 3-6 months, which accelerates the decay of unwanted parts of the coconut, leaving the coir. The sea water helps to prevent insect infestation. The coir is hammered, which helps to separate it from other vegetable matter. It is recommended that if you see a group of women working on the Maviko ya Makumbi, that you request permission before taking a photograph.

Boat building has been a traditional skill for generations using historic tools and a 12-m boat takes approximately six months to build. Goats are slaughtered when certain milestones are reached, eg raising the mast, and verses and prayers are read from the Koran. Upon completion a big ceremony is organized, with all villagers invited. Before the launch the boat builder hammers the boat three times in a naming ceremony.

You can buy basics at the small shops along the beach front but it is much cheaper to go into the village where water, bread and other items are available. There are two natural aquariums near the lighthouse at the northern tip of the island. **Mnarani Aquarium** was established in 1993 by a local resident in an attempt to help restore the local turtle population, which had been rapidly declining in recent years. Turtles in optimum conditions have a life expectancy of over 150 years. Four varieties of turtle are endemic to Zanzibar; the hawksbill (Ng'amba); the green turtle (Kasakasa); the leather back turtle (Msumeno) and the longer head turtle (Mtumbi). In the aquarium are five green turtles, which have a light grey/yellowish shell and two hawksbill turtles, which have a yellowish/red shell. Their diet is seaweed and the hawksbill also eats fish. Any turtles hatched at the aquarium are released into the sea. It is possible to hand feed these protected turtles with seaweed. Wild vervet monkeys live in the trees surrounding the rockpool. ■ *US$2.* Visitors are advised not to buy any turtle products on offer, to discourage this illicit trade.

Sleeping A *Nungwi Village Beach Resort*, T0741-606701/2 (mob), nungwi@nungwivillage.com, for online reservations. Rooms furnished with traditional-style Zanzibari wooden decor, en-suite bathrooms, premium rooms have a/c, restaurant speciality is seafood, facilities for watersports including diving. **A** *Ras Nungwi Beach Hotel*, Zanzibar, PO Box 1784, T2233767, F2233098, rasnungwi@zanzibar.net 68 km from Stone Town near Nungwi (north). 19 lodge rooms and 36 beach chalets, all with en-suite bathrooms, fans and balconies. All major credit cards accepted, excellent dive centre with good diving on the reef, deep-sea fishing. The hotel is closed for a few weeks in low season Apr-Jun. Mastercard and Visa attract a 10% surcharge.

B *Mnarani Beach Cottages*, PO Box 3361, Zanzibar, T/F2240496, T0741-334062 (mob), mnarani@cctz.com, www.lighthousezanzibar.com 12 s/c cottages, located right by the sea,

Tanzania

next to the beach, friendly management, clean, comfortable and well maintained, great service and a good atmosphere, reductions can be negotiated in low season, caters for middle budget tourist/traveller, sited up near the lighthouse, 20-min walk from the main strip. Breakfast included, full and half-board accommodation available, service includes bar, seafront restaurant, international cuisine, laundry facilities, hot water, snorkelling, fishing and diving trips, accept major credit cards.

C *Amaans Bungalows*, PO Box 132, T2231086, T0741-327747 (mob), F0741-337453. Clean, basic, s/c or shared bathrooms, no fans, has a restaurant too, transport by minibus can be arranged from hotels in Zanzibar Stone Town, situated right on the beach, breakfast included, 3 bars and restaurant on site serve good quality food. Scuba diving centre.
C *Paradise Beach Club*, T0741-326574 (mob), run by *Indian Ocean Divers*, has pleasant bar/restaurant. If you wish to sleep out under the stars try out 1 of the 2 bandas next to the Baraka Bungalows on the beach at US$5 per person, breakfast not included in the price.
C *Saleh's Beach Bungalows*, located very close to the *Ras Nungwi* complex. Sea-facing bungalows and summer houses set in gardens. The restaurant serves local and western food. The bar offers wonderful ocean views.

D *Baraka Guesthouse*, simple bungalows close to Nungwi Village, including breakfast, communal showers, cheap restaurant with generous portions, close to the beach, mosquito nets, clean. **E** *Ikibala Guest House*, in the middle of the village. Simple, clean accommodation. **E** *Jambo Brothers*, close to the beach. Basic, budget accommodation. **E** *Kigoma Guest House*, PO Box 1496. No phone, slightly more basic than *Baraka* and *Amaan* but quieter, popular with budget travellers, very friendly staff, nets, fans and en-suites. **E** *Morning Star Guesthouse*, PO Box 7092, in the village. New, very clean, friendly staff, including breakfast, own

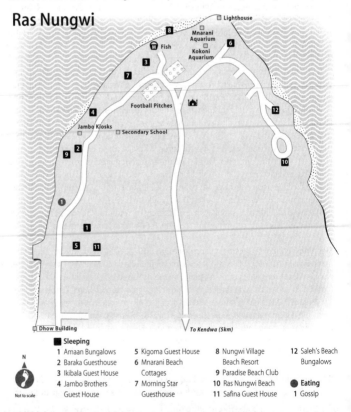

Ras Nungwi

Sleeping ■

N
Not to scale

1	Amaan Bungalows	5	Kigoma Guest House	8	Nungwi Village	12	Saleh's Beach
2	Baraka Guesthouse	6	Mnarani Beach		Beach Resort		Bungalows
3	Ikibala Guest House		Cottages	9	Paradise Beach Club		
4	Jambo Brothers	7	Morning Star	10	Ras Nungwi Beach		**Eating** ●
	Guest House		Guesthouse	11	Safina Guest House	1	Gossip

bathroom and shower, 6 rooms. **E** *Safina Guest House*, PO Box 2050. No phone, self-contained, fan, breakfast, has 11 rooms, soon to have 14.

Eating The cheapest and tastiest place to eat is the *Gossip Restaurant* between Paradise and Amaan guesthouses. Set menu, usually coconut rice with coconut sauce, tuna steak or king fish, calamares or octupus, sweet potatoes and chapattis. There are several other restaurants and 2 bars at prices that range from US$3 to US$7.

Diving Diving is good, 2 dive shops, both with representatives in Stone Town, *Dive Zanzibar* (previously known as *Indian Ocean Divers* and *Dive Africa Watersports*), at Paradise Beach Club, T0741-326574 (mob), and *Zanzibar Dive Centre-One Ocean Divers* – see information on page 556.

South of Nungwi, about 20 minutes/3 km along the beach, is the small resort, Kendwa Rocks. It is reached by a boat that is free for residents at the two hotels at Kendwa Rocks and leaves at 0930 daily. **E** *Kendwa Rocks Hotel* and the nearby similar **E** *White Sands Hotel*, PO Box 1933, T2232854, T0741-337462 (mob). There are bandas and a campsite, basic food available. It is reported that next door there is also a fancy resort costing US$30 a night. Boat rides to Tumbatu Island can be organized. Snorkel and kayaks can be hired. *Getting there:* Their Land Rover meets the minibuses, which bring tourists from Stone Town to Nungwi daily.

Kendwa Rocks

There are many new developments catering for diving and deep-sea fishing on the north, northeast and west coast. These include: **L** *Mnemba Island Lodge*. Mnemba Island lies 15 minutes by boat from northeast Zanzibar, private island resort, 10 s/c cottages, full board accommodation, includes most watersports, big game fishing, 'Barefoot luxury', bookings via Archers Tours, Nairobi, PO Box 40097, T254-2-331825, F254-2-212656. Very expensive, costs over $500 per person per night. **A** *Mapenzi Beach Resort*, located about 2 km south of Pwani Mchangani village, T0741-325985, F0741-325986. Marine sports centre, good food, friendly staff, hotel has an excellent relationship with the local village residents. **B-C** *Mtoni Marine Centre* (north of Zanzibar Town), T/F2232540/2250140. Watersports, adjacent to ruins, seafront, restaurant and bar. **B** *Mawimbini Hotel Village*, T/F2231163, Italian hospitality in a club setting. **D** *Makunduchi Beach Bungalows*, T2232344, F2233430. Government-run beach house at the far southeast of the island.

Mnemba Island

The east part of the island is not too difficult to get to but has a remote, 'get away from it all' feel, which is part of its attraction. Recently the road to Paje has been sealed – the trip there by minibus takes just over an hour. Cost there US$2 per person, back US$3. Here you will see the fishermen go out in their dhows, while the women sit in the shade and plait coconut fibre, which they then make into everything from fishing nets to beds.

East coast

Communications with the east coast are poor. For the most part it is necessary to book through an agent in Zanzibar or in Dar es Salaam – or take a chance on getting a room when you arrive. This is particularly risky from June to September. However, the number of places offering accommodation are increasing significantly. It is reported that licence applications had been made for a further 200 hotels in Zanzibar.

Central and northeast Zanzibar

This route takes you across the centre of the island. Just over 20 km down the road are the ruins of the Dunga Palace, which was built by Chief Mwinyi Mkuu Ahmed bin Mohamed Hassan. Unfortunately there is little left of the palace today beside a few arches and bits of wall, and the area has been taken over by a plantation. At the end of this route you will reach Chwaka Bay. Also on the east coast to the north of Chwaka is Uroa, another beach resort. Heading this way you will pass the small

Dunga & Chwaka to Matemwe

Tanzania

Ufufuma Forest, a home for Zanzibar red colobus monkey, impala and many bird species, and also the site of several caves. The forest has been actively conserved since 1995, and tourists are welcome, although there are no facilities at present. For more information contact the Environmental Protection of Ufufuma Jendele (EPUJE), T2223690, himajue@yahoo.com ■ *Getting there: Bus number 6 from the Mwembe Ladu station in Zanzibar Town goes to Chakwa (1½ hrs), Uroa and Pongwe, cost approximately US$0.60.*

Chwaka   Popular beach located 32 km from Zanzibar town. Has one of the island's main fish markets. It was also popular as a holiday resort with slave traders and their families in the 19th century. The beach is lovely and the fishing is said to be good. Swimming is impractical at low tide – long walk out.

Sleeping B *Chwaka Bay Hotel*, T2233943, F2230406.Curio shop, bar, relaxing atmosphere, good food. **D** *Chwaka Beach Bungalows* (2), run by the Tourist Office at Chakwa, T2232344, F2233430. **D** *East Coast Guest House* and restaurant, cheap with basic facilities, friendly, good food. **D** *Kichipwi Guest House*, book through Ali Khamis, PO Box 25, Zanzibar.

Uroa   Lovely, unspoilt fishing village located 10 km to the north of Chwaka, Uroa is close to the Dongwe Channel. It offers suitable diving for novices.

Sleeping L *Uroa Bay Village Resort*, PO Box 3389, T2232552, F2233504 or c/o *Coastal Travels*, PO Box 3052, Upanga Rd, Dar es Salaam, T2117957-9. Italian-run establishment, high standard, swimming pool, tennis courts, watersports, selective game fishing, water-skiing and diving school – SSI and PADI. **A** *Tamarind Beach Hotel*, T2233041/60, F2233041/2. Dive centre offering fishing, snorkelling, game fishing, sailing, surfing and parasailing, *Buddies Divebase*, located between Uroa and Chwaka, European-run, no pool, pleasant restaurant and open-air bar. **C** *Sun and Sand Beach Bungalows*, Stone Town office, T2232449. Comfortable accommodation. **C** *Uroa Bay Hotel*, T2232552, F2233584. **D** *Blue Sea Guest House*, near *Uroa Bay Hotel*, cheap, basic accommodation.

Pongwe   Five kilometres north of Uroa. **D** *Pongwe Beach Hotel*, nice beach bungalows, small, comfortable, good beach, T0741-338687 (mob), F0741-339296. Book through *Fisherman's Tours* in Stone Town, see page 558.

Kiwengwa   Ten kilometres north of Uroa, unsealed road from Pongwe. The number 17 bus from the Creek Road station in Stone Town goes along the better roads to Kiwengwa via Mahonda, cost US$0.60. A taxi from Stone Town or the airport might cost US$30 after some bargaining. The beach here is very good.

Sleeping L *Kiwengwa Club Village (Francorossa)*. Luxury development, beautiful, good diving, *Orca Diving Centre*, c/o Kiwengwa Club Village, PO Box 4095, T0741-326205, F0741-325304, professional diving centre offers PADI courses. **A** *Bluebay Beach Resort*, PO Box 3276, T2240240-4, T0741-338170 (mob), F2240245, bluebay@twiga.com, www.bluebayzanzibar.com Opened 1999, 88 rooms with sea views, 4 poster beds, a/c, nets, en-suite bathrooms, satellite TV and minibar, 2 restaurants, disco, swimming pool, fitness centre, tennis court, children's club, watersports, *One Ocean Diving* have a base here. **A/C** *Shooting Star Inn*, on headland at the north end of the beach, a 15-min walk along the road or beach from the village, PO Box 3076, T/F2232926, T0741-335835 (mob), star@zanzibar.org, www.zanzibar.org/star 6 luxury bungalows with Zanzibari-style beds and verandahs overlooking the ocean. Also lodge rooms overlooking the garden and budget makuti bandas. All have mosquito nets, the bungalows and lodge rooms have fans and en suite bathrooms. Open-air bar and restaurant, seafood, grills, traditional Zanzibari cuisine, selection of vegetarian meals, breakfast included, full and half board accommodation also available, have bicycles for hire, accept credit cards. **C** *Reef View*, PO Box 3215, T0747-413294 (mob), bandas and bungalows, bar and restaurant, south of the village.

Small village 45 km from Stone Town and 15 km north of Kiwenga.   **Matemwe**

Sleeping A *Matemwe Bungalows*, PO Box 3275, T2231342, F2236536, matemwe-znz@
zanzinet.com, www.matemwe.com To the north of the village, offers simple accommodation. Recommended. The 16 bandas are built from local materials, coral stone walls and dried
palm leaf roofs and all the bandas are surrounded by colourful flowers and have an ocean
view. Most bandas are s/c and have solar powered lighting and hot water, 4 of the bandas
have shared facilities with cold water, all have verandahs and mosquito nets. The food is the
fresh fish catch of the day and meat dishes are also available. The area is unspoilt with white
sandy beaches and excellent snorkelling is possible at the nearby coral reef. The Mlanga diving centre operates from here.

Southeast Zanzibar

There is a small nature reserve, **Jozani Forest**, located about 40 km to the southeast   **Bwejuu,**
of Zanzibar town, which is home to roughly one third of the remaining endemic   **Makunduchi,**
Zanzibar red colobus monkeys, one of Africa's rarest primates. Only 1,500 are   **Kizimkazi**
believed to have survived. In Zanzibar the Kiswahili name for the red colobus monkey is *Kima Punju* – 'Poison Monkey'. It has associations with the kind of poisons
used by evil doers. Local people believe that when the monkeys have fed in an area,
the trees and crops die, and dogs will lose their hair if they eat the colobus. Although
legally protected the colobus remain highly endangered. Their choice of food brings
them into conflict with the farmers, and their habitat is being destroyed due to
demands for farmland, fuel, wood and charcoal. The monkeys appear oblivious to
tourists, swinging above the trees in troups of about 40, babies to adults. They are
endearing, naughty and totally absorbing. There is a visitor centre where you pay
US$8 per person for a guide, some of which goes to the people of Pete and Jozani vil-
lages. There are a series of nature trail walks in Jozani Forest. Stout shoes are recommended as there are some venomous snakes. The rare Zanzibar leopard can
occasionally be sighted. Lizards, civets, mongooses and Ader's duiker are more
plentiful and easier to see. Unless you state otherwise you are unlikely to be taken
into the reserve at all as the best place to get close to the monkeys is an area adjacent
to farmland to the south of the road. Most people visit the reserve as part of a tour,
usually combined with a dolphin tour, but you can get here independently by
dala-dala and either bus 9 or 10 from Creek Rd in Stone Town.

Jozani-Chwaka Bay is also an excellent place to spot birds, including spotted fly-
catchers, greenbuls, kingfishers and cattle egrets.

About 1 km south of the Jozani Forest Visitor Centre there is the **Pete-Jozani
Mangrove Boardwalk**. From the visitor centre the walk takes you through coral
forest to an old tamarind tree, which marks the beginning of the boardwalk. The
transition from coral forest to mangroves is abrupt. The boardwalk, which is horseshoe shaped, takes you through the mangrove swamp – the forest in the sea. Mangroves anchor the shifting mud and sands of the shore and help prevent coastal
erosion. There are 18,000 ha of mangrove forests along the muddy costs and inlets of
Zanzibar. When the tide is out the stilt-like roots of the trees are visible. Crabs and
fish are plentiful and easily seen from the boardwalk.

The **Jozani-Chwaka Bay Conservation Project** is a partnership between the
Commission for Natural Resources, Zanzibar and CARE Tanzania, and is funded by
the government of Austria. The construction costs of the boardwalk were paid for by
the government of The Netherlands, with local communities providing labour. Part
of the profits made from tourists are returned directly to the local villagers. Going
there by taxi will cost around US$25 (for four people inside one car), which is com-
petitive with agency tours.

The road continues south to the village of Kitogani, and just south is located **ZALA
Park,** which is primarily a small educational facility set up in conjunction with the
University of Dar es Salaam for Zanzibari children to help them learn about and help

Tanzania

conserve the island's fauna. ZALA stands for Zanzibar Land Animals and the park is run by the energetic and hard-working founder, a local teacher, Mr Mohammed Ajoub Haji. Entry is free to local children if unable to pay, subsidized by the tourists' entry fee. The aim is to make it a self-funding enterprise in time. There is a small class-room where the children are taught. The adjacent **zoo** has a number of reptiles includ-ing lizards, chameleons and indolent rock pythons weighing up to 40 kg, eastern tree hyrax, *Dendrohyrax validus*, as well as suni antelopes, *Neotragus m. moschatus*, an endemic Zanzabari subspecies. There are plans to extend the venture to include an aviary. Donations to support this worthwhile enterprise are appreciated.

From here you can take a road across to the coastal village of Paje on the east coast about 50 km from Zanzibar town. Also on this coast is the resort of **Bwejuu** (see below). There are a series of other villages on the coast as you head south before you reach **Kizimkazi**, the southernmost village. There is little of significance in this small fishing village apart from the ancient (12th century) mosque, which is still in use. Entrance costs less than US$1, although further contributions are welcomed, and women are allowed to enter. However this was once the site of a town built by King Kizi and his mason Kazi from whom the name Kizimkazi originates. The beach is attractive, and there is a restaurant where those on dolphin tours from Stone Town are often taken to have a meal. Limited choice of food and quite expensive (when not paid for already as part of the tour), but tasty. There is a dolphin tour from Kizimkazi for US$13. ■ *Getting there: Bus number 10 from Creek Rd in Stone Town comes here via Makunduchi.*

Shirazi
Dimbani
Mosque ruins

Found near Kizimkazi in the south of the island this mosque contains the oldest inscription found in East Africa – from AD 1107. The mosque has been given a tin roof and is still used. However its significance should not be underestimated for it may well mark the beginnings of the Muslim religion in East Africa. It was built by Sheikh Abu bin Mussa Lon Mohammed and archaeologists believe that it stands on the site of an even older mosque.

Paje

Small village on the east coast mainly relying on fishing. There is a low rectangular mausoleum in the village, inset with old plates and dishes. This design is believed to be Persian in origin. Excellent palm-fringed beach. *Paje East Coast Diving* are based here. ■ *Getting there: Bus number 9 from the Creek Rd station in Stone Town reaches here, and continues to Jambiani and Bwejuu.*

Sleeping D *Hotel Bizarre/Paje by Night*, PO Box 1714, T2230840, hotelpbn@yahoo.com, www.zanzibar-hotel.com Very rustic verging on ethnic, run by 2 Germans, 20 s/c thatched bungalows, bar and restaurant with local and international food. **D** *Ndame Guest House*, PO Box 229, T2231065, reasonable. **D** *Paje Ndame Village*, PO Box 3781, T/F2231065. Very quiet and relaxing, food OK, rather unspoilt. **D** *Paradise Beach Bungalows*, PO Box 2346, T2231387, T0747-414129 (mob), saori@cats-net.com 8 s/c bungalows run by a Japanese woman, attached restaurant food is excellent but fairly expensive, has to be ordered in advance.

Bwejuu

This is considered to be the best of the eastern beaches. White sandy beaches extend for kilometres with lovely palm trees and good swimming areas. Sixty-five kilometres from Stone Town. Excellent snorkelling at low water in the lagoon at the end of the jetty, 15 minutes along the beach by bike. Hire bicycles to get there from *Dere Guest House*, see below. It is possible to book a tour to see and swim with the dolphins from Jambiani. Cost US$13 per person including mask and snorkel. Important to bring flippers in order to follow the dolphins. Nice experience. Recommended.

Sleeping A-B (depending on the season) *Breezes Beach Club*, PO Box 1361, T2233098, T0741-326595 (mob), F0741-333151, breezes@africaonline.co.tz, www.breezes-zanzibar.com, or through Tour Africa Safaris Ltd, Nairobi, T254-2-720835, bookings@tourafrica.co.ke Opened 1998, 1.5 km north of *Sunrise Hotel*, well-appointed club. All rooms have a/c, fans and en-suite bathrooms, there are standard, deluxe and superior deluxe rooms, the latter have sea views. Shopping arcade, conference facilities, restaurants, bars, large swimming pool, fitness centre, watersports centre, tennis courts and disco. The *Rising Sun Dive Centre* is based here. **B** *Sunrise Guest House*, PO Box 3967, T/F0741-320206, sunrise@cats-net.com, 2 km north of the village. All rooms s/c with fans and nets, bungalow rooms all face towards the sea, French seafood cuisine in garden, Belgian chef/owner. Recommended. Best quality place to stay in this part of the island, try the chocolate mousse while supplies of Belgian chocolate hold out, also famed for its spiced pudding. **C** *Palm Beach Inn*, T2233597, F2232387. This is simple and basic, some bungalows have been added, there is no running water or electricity, just buckets and paraffin lamps, for many adding to the charm, the food is fresh and good and the staff friendly, if you want to drink while you are there, take your own alcohol. **C** *Bwejuu Beach Hotel*, another simple place and popular with budget travellers, all rooms and bathrooms are shared, there is a bar here and beers are usually cold, good swimming when the tide is high in the afternoon. **D** *Bwejuu Beach Bungalows*, T2232344, F2233430. Government-run beach hotel. **D** *Bwejuu Dere Beach Resort*, PO Box 278, T2231047. Offer s/c or shared bathroom, excellent value, safe parking for motorcycle, restaurant food unremarkable. **D** *Dere Guest House*, T2231017. Simple facilities and good, straightforward food, hires out bikes and snorkelling equipment. **D** *Twisted Palm*. Simple accommodation on the beach, 5 rooms, very relaxing. You can get a simple but excellent meal at *Jamal's Restaurant*.

North of Bwejuu, about 3 km before Michamvi, is Karafuu village and **B** *Karafuu Hotel*, PO Box 71, T0741-325157 (mob), F0741-325670. This is a large but quiet hotel, excellent food, swimming pool, diving, the beach is good although there is very sharp coral close offshore.

Situated on the southeast coast of the island. Great white sharks are found offshore **Jambiani** beyond the coral reef. The Zanzibar Village Tourism Programme, PO Box 1390, Zanzibar, based at Mandes Co-op Souvenir Shop near Visitors Inn, offers an interesting half-day bicycle tour around the Jambiani area. The tour takes you to see seaweed farms, agricultural crops and fruit trees growing in coral ground, coral caves inland where the village used to be, and to see a traditional herbalist. The tour costs US$5, part of which is used for community development projects.

Sleeping **C** *Jambiani Beach Hotel*, run by the very friendly and helpful Mr Abu, bookings through PO Box 229, Zanzibar, T2233597. **C** *Oyster Hotel*, PO Box 4199, Mobile/F0741 333125, town office 2231560. Brand new hotel, very congenial, Tanzanian owned, good food, closer to the beach than Sau Inn. Staff mostly locals, rooms clean, light, good mosquito screens, bike rental, sea sports. Recommended. **C** *Sau Inn*, PO Box 1656, T2222215, Mobile/F0741 340039/337440, sau-inn@cats-net.com Best guesthouse on the beach. Recommended. Thatched cottages with fans and mosquito nets, bar and good seafood restaurant, sports facilities, volley ball, tennis, snorkelling and diving. **D** *Gomani Guest House*, most beautiful in Jambiani, uncomplicated but comfortable, T2231471. **D** *Horizontal Inn*, owned by local Zanzibaris, simple and good value. **D** *Imani Beach Lodge Annex*, T2233476, F2231329. Small lodge caters for up to 14 people, bar and restaurant, bike hire available. **D** *Jambiani Beach Bungalows*, T2232344, F2233430. Government-run beach house. **D** *Manufaa Guest House*, PO Box 278, T2231017, small rooms but clean, price drops by US$1 the second night, friendly, breakfast included. **D** *Shehe Guest House*, T2233949, good value bungalows. **D** *Visitors Inn*, T2232283, T0741-33430 (mob), good value bungalows.

Tanzania

Pemba Island

5°0'S 39°45'E
Colour map 4, grid B6

The island is much
hillier than Zanzibar
and the higher rainfall
ensures that the
vegetation flourishes

The island of Pemba is located about 60 km to the northeast of Zanzibar and is about 70 km long and 23 km wide. It has not, so far, been much developed as a holiday spot and so is much less touristy. There is however an airport on the island and there are plenty of attractions.

Zanzibar is connected to the African continent by a shallow submerged shelf. Pemba, however, is separated from the mainland by depths of over 1,000 m. During September and March the visibility around Pemba has been known to extend to a depth of 50 m. Scuba diving is better from Pemba than Zanzibar (Unguja) and underwater photographers will enjoy the sharks, tuna and barracuda. Diving is available from John Denny's *in Mkoani,* Swahili Divers *in Chake Chake (see page 575) and* Manta Reef Lodge *at Ras Kigomasha (see page 576).*

Numerous fine, deserted beaches are dotted round the coast and there are 27 islands, most with good sandy beaches. The shores are fringed by mangrove forests. The coral reefs are excellent for snorkelling and diving. In deeper waters there are great game fish such as marlin and barracuda, and the Pemba Channel, between Pemba and the mainland, is one of the world's great game fishing waters. There are some important ruins with historical sites, towns with handsome Arab architecture and charming Swahili villages.

Ins & outs

Getting there See Chake Chake, page 575, for flights to/from Dubai, Dar es Salaam and Zanzibar, and Mkoani, page 575, for ferries.

Getting around There is one bumpy main road in Pemba running from Msuka in the north to Mkoani on the south, which is served by public transport. Although the *dala-dala* themselves are not the most comfortable they do provide a fairly good service. From Chake Chake the No 6 goes to Wete and the No 3 to Mkoani. From Chake Chake to Wete takes about 45 mins and costs US$0.30. Besides this, it is very difficult to get around.

Tourist offices and information There is a tourist information office next to the *Hoteli ya Chake Chake*, T2452121, but it has no maps and little information. An excellent map can be obtained from the Ministry of Lands and Environment situated behind the Esso station near *Hoteli ya Chake Chake*.

Climate There are long rains from Mar to mid-Jun and short rains in Nov and Dec. The timing of the rains is thought to be more erratic than in the past, and they can often vary by a month or so, and sometimes the short rains hardly seem to occur at all. The hottest period is after the short rains, running from Dec-Feb, with temperatures up to 34°C at midday. The period just before the long rains, in Feb, can be particularly oppressive, with high humidity. The most comfortable time of year is Jun-Oct, with lower temperatures, little rain and plenty of sun, made bearable by the cooling Trade Winds from the southeast, known as the *Kusi* or the Southeast Monsoons.

Pemba Island

Clove production

It has been estimated that there are about 6,000,000 clove trees on the islands of Zanzibar and Pemba and they cover about one-tenth of the land area. The plantations are found mainly in the west and northwest of the islands where the soil is deeper and the landscape hillier. To the east the soil is less deep and fertile and is known as 'coral landscape'.

Cloves were at one time only grown in the Far East and they were greatly prized. On his first trip back from the East, Vasco da Gama took a cargo back to Portugal and they were later introduced by the French to Mauritius and then to Zanzibar by Sayyid Said who was the first Arab sultan. At this time all the work was done by slaves who enabled the plantations to be established and clove production to become so important to the economy of the islands. When the slaves were released and labour was no longer free, some of the plantations found it impossible to survive although production did continue

and Zanzibar remained at the head of the world production of cloves.

Cloves are actually the unopened buds of the clove tree. They grow in clusters and must be picked when the buds are full but before they actually open. They are collected in sprays and the buds are then picked off before being spread on the ground to dry out. They are spread out on mats made from woven coconut palm fronds for about five days, turned over regularly so that they dry evenly – the quicker they dry the better quality the product.

There may be many clove trees on Zanzibar now – but there were even more in the past. In 1872 a great hurricane passed over the island destroying many of the trees and it was after this that Pemba took over from Zanzibar as the largest producer. Zanzibar however has retained the role of chief seller and exporter of cloves so the Pemba cloves first go to Zanzibar before being sold on.

Tanzania

From Oct-Mar the winds change, blowing from the northeast, and they are known as the *Kaskazi* or the Northeast Monsoons.

The island is perhaps most famous for its clove production. In addition there are coconut palms, mango trees and bananas. Much of the island was covered in vegetation until clove cultivation began at the beginning of the 19th century, and great swathes were cleared for clove trees and other cultivation. Three small areas of forest remain: **Ras Kiuyu Forest** is at the north tip of the Ngezi peninsular in the northeast, an area of about 210 ha; **Msitu Kuu Forest** is just south of Wingwi in the northeast and covers an area of about 130 ha; and **Ngezi Forest** is west of Konde in the north. Msitu Kuu has antelope and monkeys, while the Pemba flying fox inhabits the Ngezi Forest. Ngezi Forest Reserve covers 1,440 ha. Despite its coastal location it contains tree species that occur on the East African mainland from lowland mountain forests, eg *Quassia undulata*. Other trees with Madagascan links are also present, eg *Musa acuminata, Typhanodorun lindleyanum*. Ngezi has its own plant species and subspecies that are unique to this area. Half the reserve is covered by lush moist forest containing thick undergrowth. Several bird species, some endemic to Pemba, live in the reserve, including hadada, the African goshawk, the palm-nut vulture, Scops owl, the malachite kingfisher and the Pemba white eye.

Wildlife & vegetation

The narrow coastal strip of the Forest Reserve is covered with thick vegetation. The ground is ancient coral rag, often sharp edged, containing pockets of soil. Mangrove forests grow on the tidal coastal creeks and the incoming tide sees seawater running deep up streams forming brackish swampy areas.

The central reserve area contains heather dominated heathland where the soil is leached sand. The heather, *Philippia mafiensis*, is only found on Pemba and Mafia Islands.

Pemba's flying fox a large fruit-eating bat, is found in Ngezi. Tree mammals include the Pemba vervet monkey and the Zanzibar red colobus monkey. Indolent-looking Hyrax can also be seen climbing in the trees eating leaves. The Pemba blue duiker, an antelope about the size of a hare, is also found in Ngezi Forest Reserve. However, it is very shy and is rarely spotted. Feral pigs, introduced long ago by the Portuguese, can be found along with the Javan civet cat, which was probably brought to the island by Southeast Asian traders for the production of musk for perfume. The only endemic carnivore in Ngezi is the marsh mongoose, which normally lives by ponds and streams.

The major income for islanders is from cloves – the clove production of this island is actually about three times that of Zanzibar – and it is the mainstay of the island's economy. Also, unlike Zanzibar, production is largely by individual small-scale farmers who own anything from 10 to 50 trees each. Most of the trees have been in the family for generations. They were first introduced to the island at the beginning of the 19th century from Indonesia. The production is very much a family affair especially during the harvest when everyone joins in the picking. Harvest occurs about every five months and everything is geared towards it and even the schools close. The cloves are then laid out in the sun to dry and their distinctive fragrance fills the air.

Background The island is overwhelmingly Muslim, with more than 95% of the population following Islam. It is tolerant of other cultures, and alcohol is available at hotels, some guesthouses and in the police messes (where visitors are welcome). Local inhabitants do, however, like to observe modest dress and behaviour and it is a courtesy not to appear in swimwear or shorts in the streets, and for women to wear long skirts or trousers.

An unusual feature is the bull-fighting that takes place in October and November at the end of the cool season. It is thought that bull-fighting was introduced by the Portuguese during the 16th and 17th centuries when they established forts and settlements in the Indian Ocean, most notably at Mombasa, Lamu and Zanzibar. Why the practice endured in Pemba and not elsewhere remains a mystery. It is a genuinely sporting event in that there is sparring between the bull and the fighter, but the bull is not weakened with lances or killed at the end – the pragmatic Pembans consider the animal too valuable to sacrifice in this way. Two villages where fights are staged are Wingwi in the northeast and Kengeja in the south.

At Tumbe in the north, at the end of the cool season in October, there is a boat race. Teams of men compete, paddling dug-out canoes and the day is completed with a feast provided for contestants and onlookers.

Chake Chake

5°15'S 39°45'E
Phone code: 024
Colour map 4, grid B6

This is Pemba's main town located on the west coast of the island. The town sits on a hill overlooking a creek and is fairly small. **Nanzim Fort**, on the hill, dates from the 18th century but construction of the old hospital destroyed all but the eastern corner

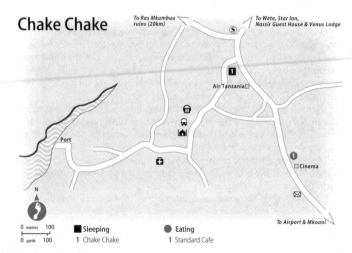

Chake Chake

To Ras Mkumbuu ruins (20km)

To Wete, Star Inn, Nassir Guest House & Venus Lodge

Air Tanzania

Port

Cinema

To Airport & Mkoani

N

| 0 metres | 100 |
| 0 yards | 100 |

■ **Sleeping**
1 Chake Chake

● **Eating**
1 Standard Cafe

and tower. It now houses the Ministry of Women and Children. A battery, dating from the same period, overlooked the bay to the west, but only two cannons remain to mark the site. There are some handsome administrative buildings near the fort in Moorish style with verandahs, and a **clock tower**. A sports stadium has also recently been built. The market and bus stand are both located in the centre of town close to the mosque. There have been some strikes and riots since the multi-party elections. Pemba is the stronghold of the CUF opposition party, who dispute the outcome of the elections.

Sleeping & eating

There is currently very little hotel choice in town. One (*Chake Chake*) is fairly central – most others are a 15-min walk on the road to Wete. **C** *Hoteli ya Chake Chake*, PO Box 18, Chake Chake, T2452069, F2433430. It is government owned, all rooms have bathrooms and a fan – it is a clean and friendly place, the hotel has a restaurant with a fairly limited menu, and a bar. **C** *Nassir Guest House*, PO Box 385, Zanzibar, T2452882. No restaurant or bar. **C** *The Star Inn*, PO Box 109, Zanzibar, T2452190. Has 7 rooms, restaurant and a bar. **C** *Venus Lodge*, PO Box 183, Zanzibar, T2452293/4. Restaurant but no bar. **D/E** *Swahili Divers Lodge*, PO Box 146, Chake Chake, T2452786, F2452768, swahilidivers@intafrica.com, www.swahilidivers.com, 200 m north of *Hoteli ya Chake Chake*. Probably the best budget accommodation on Pemba, renovated old Quaker mission house on small hill, friendly, 7 simple rooms with fans and tra-ditional Zanzibar-style beds, some rooms are a/c and have own bathrooms, also dormitory accommodation, very good food, with notice they will pick you up from the ferry port at Mkoani. PADI instructors, diving from a dhow and rigid inflatable boats, although 4 km from the nearest beach, can arrange dhow trips. Alternative places to eat are **Cheap**: *Balloon Bros*, just south of mosque on main street, charcoal grill, cold drinks, pleasant patio with thatched bandas; *Best Colours*, PO Box 62, T2452383, opposite *Hoteli ya Chake Chake*. Small but smart, friendly and good value; and the *Standard Café* by the cinema.

Tour operators

Partnership Travel, PO Box 192, T2452278. Located opposite *Hoteli ya Chake Chake*. *Hamisa Touristers*, PO Box 389, T2452343. Near People's Bank of Zanzibar, ferry bookings.

Transport

Air The airport, T2452357, serving the island is located about 5 km out of town. The airport departure tax is about US$1 but you do not have to change money on arrival. Public trans-port to and from the airport only operates when there is a flight due. The daily Gulf Air flight from Dubai brings in tourists to Pemba direct. Precisionair (Stone Town, Zanzibar: T2234520, T0741-511717 (mob), F2234520; Dar es Salaam: T2130800, T0742-781420 (mob), F2113036, precision-dar@twiga.com) have flights from Dar es Salaam at 0830 on Mon and 0900 on Wed and Fri. They take about 75 mins, and return to Dar es Salaam soon after arrival. There are also return flights from Zanzibar at 0950 on Wed and Fri, taking 25 mins. Eagle Air (Dar es Salaam: PO Box 5794, T2127411/2/7, F2127415, eagleair@africaonline.co.tz) have a flight from Dar es Salaam at 0830 on Tue. It takes 45 mins and leaves at 0935 for the return to Dar es Salaam. There is a flight from Zanzibar at 0940 on Fri, taking 30 mins, that then departs at 1030 for Dar es Salaam. **Road** There are buses or *dala-dalas* between Chake Chake, Wete and Mkoani, but these tend to operate in the mornings only. Also from Wete to Tumbe and Michiweni in the north of the Island. It is possible to hire vehicles at around US$35 a day by asking at the hotels. Similarly with bicycles at US$10 a day. **Sea** The *Sepideh* boat operates a normal scheduled service between Dar es Salaam, Zanzibar and Pemba on Mon, Wed, Fri and Sun, see Mkoani, page 578. There is also a dhow service to Tanga.

Directory

Airline offices *Air Tanzania*, PO Box 92, Zanzibar, T2452162 (town), T2452357 (airport). Situated on the road to Mkoani, opposite the National Bank of Commerce. **Banks** *People's Bank of Zanzibar*, PO Box 135, Zanzibar, T2452351/2452367, F2452139. Open 0830-1530 Mon-Fri and 0830-1200 Sat, the only bank on the island to change TCs. *Pemba Bureau de Change*, PO Box 283, T2528058, opposite *Hoteli ya Chake Chake*, accept TCs.

Around Pemba island

Ruins at Ras Mkumbuu About 20 km west of Chake Chake, these are probably Pemba's most important ruins and are believed to date back about 1,200 years, the site of a settlement originating in the Shirazi period (see page 383). The ruins include stone houses and pillar tombs and the remains of a 14th-century mosque. Access is best by boat, which can be hired informally at the shore. Zanzibar Tourist Corporation Office at the *Hoteli ya Chake Chake* has a boat for hire at about US$70 for the day for a party of six, and from Ras Mkumbuu it is possible to go on to **Mesali Island** where the marine life on the reef is excellent for snorkelling and there is a fine beach.

Ruins at Pujini About 10 km southeast of Chake Chake, this settlement is thought to date back to the 15th century. There was a fortified enclosure and rampart surrounded by a moat, the only known early fortification on the East Africa coast. It is believed to have been built by a particularly unpleasant character, nicknamed Mkame Ndume, which means 'a milker of men', because he worked his subjects so hard. The memory remains and local people believe that the ruins are haunted. The settlement and the palace of Mkame Ndume were destroyed by the Portuguese when they arrived on the island in about 1520. It is best to visit by hiring a bicycle (ask at the hotel).

Tumbe Tumbe is at the north end of Pemba and is a busy fishing village. Local fishermen contract to provide catches for firms, which chill the fish and export it from the mainland. Tumbe can be reached by bus from Chake Chake.

Ras Kigomasha The authorities are apparently sensitive about the lighthouse at Ras Kigomasha, the far northwestern tip of the island, so photography is not advised. The Manta Reef Lodge is an excellent place for scuba-diving.

Sleeping A-C *Manta Reef Lodge*, PO Box 22, Wete, T0741-320025 (mob), mantareef@ twiga.com, or though *One Earth Safaris*, PO Box 82234, Mombasa, T+254-11-471771. Quiet location on cliff overlooking private beach. Excellent location for scuba diving, well equipped, US$35 per dive but negotiable, more suitable for experienced divers. Large central area with terrace, verandah, lounge and snooker room, 11 wooden bungalows on stilts for up to 20 guests, with en-suite bathrooms. Also dormitories, US$15 per person, actually 2 chalets with good rooms, only 1 or 2 beds in each, shared bathroom with hot water. The dormitories are excellent value, and few people stay in them so you may get the whole chalet to yourself, but note that the meals are not budget priced. To reach Manta Lodge is either expensive or slow. A 4WD taxi from Chake Chake will cost US$50-60. *Dala-dala* to Konde from Chake Chake run throughout the day, US$1, the remaining 14 km is a very rough track; one *dala-dala* leaves from the centre of the village when full, usually early afternoon, US$0.60.

Wete This town is located on the northwest coast of Pemba and serves as a port for the clove trade. It is a pleasant town on a hill overlooking the port. Clustered close to the dock area is a pleasant group of colonial era buildings. On the north side of the market is a craftsman making very fine carved doors.

From Wete travel to the north of the island to **Vumawimbi beach** or to **Panga ya Watoro beach** on the other side of the northwest headland. North of the latter beach is a big hotel, near a manta reef, which specializes in scuba diving, where you can buy a wholesome if expensive lunch. The best way to get to the beaches from Wete is to hire a motorcycle – enquire at the Sharooq Guesthouse. It is possible to cycle there but the terrain is hilly. The last *dala-dala* leaves from Wete at around 1300.

Sleeping C *Hoteli ya Wete*, PO Box 66, Zanzibar, T2454301, F2433430. Government-owned, it has a restaurant and bar. **D** *Sharooq Guest House*, PO Box 117, Zanzibar, T2454386. Located just near the market and bus stand, it is good value and has a restaurant with the best food in town. If you are just visiting Wete you can leave luggage here for the day while you explore for about US$0.25. Food can be provided if pre-ordered. Own generator. Can arrange trips to local islands, or bicycle hire.

Eating Other places to eat besides the hotel include: **Seriously cheap**: *Garden Café*, next to the hospital. Pleasant outdoor eating area; *Laki Supisa*, near *Sharooq Guest House*; *New 4-Ways Restaurant*; and *Pop-In Restaurant*, which are both located opposite *Hoteli ya Wete*. *Salim Café*, on the main road near the post office, sells coffee, milk, ice cream, etc.

Bars Located at *Hoteli ya Wete* and at the *Police Mess*, down toward the docks, where guests are welcome.

Directory Banks *People's Bank of Zanzibar* on the main road and *Wete Bureau de Change*, PO Box 258, T2454072, close to the post office. **Useful addresses** Also on the main road is the **post office** and the **police station**. The market and matatu stand are located in the centre of town.

Mkoani

This town is located to the southwest of the island and is the principal port. If you come to Pemba from Zanzibar by boat this is where you will arrive. It is a little town of some charm on a verdant hill rising up from the shore. Just back from the dock are the offices of Azam Marine and Zanzibar Ferries and a small café. Nearby is a **traditional bakery** with a large earthenware vessel, surrounded by a wattle and mud cylinder, with a charcoal fire underneath. Pieces of dough are slapped on the inside of the vessel and levered off with a wooden spatula when they are cooked, and sold for US$0.10.

South of the dock there are steep steps down to the **market** by the shore, where small boats leave for Makoongwe Island.

Following the winding road to Chake Chake, which runs up the hill inland from the port, the old colonial **District Commissioners Office** is on the right. There is a bandstand in front of the compound. On the left is **Ibazi Mosque**, with a fine carved door.

Sleeping L *Fundu Lagoon*, north of Mkoani across the bay close to the village of Wambaa, T2232926, www.fundulagoon.com Luxury British development opened in 2000. Very stylish, with bottle green tents under thatched roofs. The 20 tent rooms on stilts are llinked to the communal areas by decking walkways. All variety of water sports are available including diving. Restaurant, bar, dive centre and satellite TV available.**A** *Kiweni Marine Resort*, Kiweni Island, T0741-325367, F0741-325368. Also tent accommodation. **C** *Hoteli ya Mkoani*, T2456271, F2433430. Restaurant and bar. **C** *Star Inn* (Jodeni Annex), PO Box 109, T2452190.

Wete

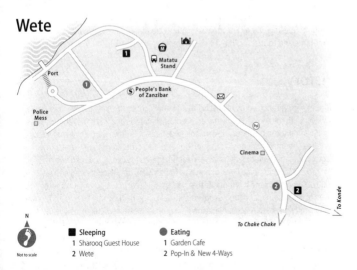

N
Not to scale

■ **Sleeping**
1 Sharooq Guest House
2 Wete

● **Eating**
1 Garden Cafe
2 Pop-In & New 4-Ways

Tanzania

A short walk (10 mins) north along the shore, nicely located on a bluff overlooking the sea, simple restaurant. Recommended.

Eating Apart from the hotels, **Seriously cheap**: *Koani*, PO Box 64, T60304/6002, further along the main road, before the hospital, simple fare; *Nguru*, close to hospital, opposite CCM office.

Other services *Ali Atem Photocare*, PO Box 31, T2456248. Sells film and will develop photos.

Transport   Rental Motorcycles and bicycles can be rented at the hotels – negotiation is necessary as ever. The motorcycle is the most comfortable form of transport on the island, more so than cars, as pot holes are more readily avoided. Car rental can be arranged with the government hotels costing from US$35 a day with a driver.

Sea There are frequent ferry services between Zanzibar and Pemba. Sea Express (Dar es Salaam: T2137049/2110217, F2116723; Zanzibar: T2233002) operate M/S *Sepidea*, which serves Pemba on Mon, Wed, Fri and Sun. It departs Dar es Salaam at 0730, and then Zanzibar at 1000, arriving in Mkoani at around midday. The return journey from Pemba begins at 1300. Fare from Dar es Salaam US$65, from Zanzibar US$35. Azam Marine (Zanzibar: T2231655, T0741-334884 (mob)) run a high speed service on Tue to Fri, departs Zanzibar 1000, departs Pemba 1300, journey time 70 mins. Otherwise, from Zanzibar, **dhows** arrive at Mkoani and from Tanga they arrive at Wete. Bookings from Zanzibar (which is easier and more reliable) can be made at the Malindi Sports Club in Zanzibar and the trip takes 6-8 hrs. You can also get a dhow to **Mombasa**. Departures are from Wete, and take about 12 hrs for a motorized dhow, and 24 hrs for a sailing vessel.

Background

Present-day Tanzania comprises a union between the former mainland Tanganyika and the islands of Zanzibar. Its modern history has involved three profound changes of direction from colonialism to socialism to capitalism. Like a traveller uncertain of the way, these diversions have slowed progress. As a result Tanzania has not developed as rapidly as its northern neighbour, Kenya. Its cities have few modern buildings, living standards have remained more-or-less unchanged since independence in 1961, and the considerable mineral, agricultural and tourist resources of the country have been only partially exploited.

In the past few years, however, there have been significant improvements. Roads have been repaired, foreign investment has increased rapidly, new businesses are springing up everywhere. For the visitor, there are many new hotels, lodges, restaurants and tourist facilities.

History

Earliest times Without any written records, relatively little is known about the early history of Tanzania. However, with the use of oral history, archaeology, linguistic analysis and anthropology, a certain amount can be deduced. Archaeological finds at Olduvai Gorge have provided evidence of human evolution. At this site bones of two types from the Australopithecine stage of human development have been found. These are *Zinjanthropus*, known as Nutcracker Man and *Homo habilis*, known as Handy Man. They lived together about 2,000,000 years ago and it is thought that *Homo habilis*, capable of using tools, is the ancestor of modern man – *Homo sapiens*. Olduvai Gorge has become known as the cradle of mankind. The era of Australopithecine man probably lasted several million years.

By about 500,000 years ago the *Homo erectus* stage came into being, which was somewhere between Australopithecine and *Homo sapiens*. The brain was larger and the hands more nimble and therefore better at making tools. The development of tool-making is clearly seen at Olduvai Gorge. The different layers of rock contain tools of different ages, which show the development from crude tools to more efficient and sharper implements. Another collection of such tools can be found at Isimila near Iringa (see page 519).

The Middle Stone Age saw the further development of tools, advances in human ingenuity and craftsmanship and the use of fire. Progress accelerated in the Late Stone Age, which began about 100,000 years ago. There are a number of sites from the Late Stone Age in Tanzania, which are particularly well known as they are the locations of rock painting. The hunter-gatherers were probably related linguistically and racially to the Bushmen and Hottentots of South Africa. Interestingly the Sandawe who now live in the area of the rock paintings speak a form of the Khoisan or 'click' language, which otherwise is not spoken in East Africa and which is characteristic of the Bushmen.

The virtual disappearance of these people was a result of the migration and expansion of other people who were more numerous and more advanced. The most significant factor about these migrating people was that instead of being hunter-gatherers they were food producers – either by agriculture or by keeping livestock. They spoke the language of the Cushitic group (legendary biblical descendants of the Cush in Ethiopia, Somalia and north Sudan) and came from the north from around 1,000 BC onwards. They did not have iron-working skills and this meant that the efficiency of their agriculture was limited.

Later still, during the past 1,000-2,000 years, two other groups migrated into the area. These were both Negroid but were of different linguistic groups – the Bantu from the west and the Nilo-Hamite pastoralists from the north. A process of ethnic assimilation followed and the Cushitic intermarried with the newcomers and adopted their languages. The Bantu possessed important iron-processing skills, which greatly improved agricultural efficiency and this enabled population growth. There was not one single migration but a series of waves of various groups, expanding and contracting, assimilating and adapting. The present ethnic mix is as a result of this process over many centuries. **Bantu migration**

The most recent of the Nilotic migrations was by the Masai. By about the year 1800 they had reached the area around Dodoma where their advance was stopped by the Gogo and the Hehe (see page 596). Their reputation as a warrior tribe meant that the north part of Tanzania was largely avoided by slave traders and caravan routes.

As a result of these migrations north and central Tanzania has great ethnic diversity. In this part of the country there are Khoisan, Cushitic, Nilotic and Bantu speaking peoples. The rest of the country is entirely Bantu speaking; indeed about 95% of Tanzanians born today are born into a family speaking one of the Bantu dialects. Swahili itself is a Bantu tongue and this has developed into the national language and as such is a significant unifying force.

Initially Swahili was a coastal language and developed as the language of trade. The earliest visitors to Tanzania were Arab traders who arrived on the coast, and the influence of these traders can be seen in the coastal settlements such as Kilwa. These coastal towns were very much orientated to sea-going trade and away from the interior and until the beginning of the 16th century the coast and the interior had very little contact with each other. However the development of long-distance trade led to the integration of the two. Caravan routes went from the coast to the Congo and Buganda. By the 13th century there was a bustling trade on the coast with the gold and ivory trades becoming particularly important. Initially the trade was dominated by the Persians, Arabs, Egyptians, Indians and Chinese. The Arab influence increased and with it the spread of Islam. The major trading objects were gold, ivory and rhino horns, in exchange for guns, textiles and beads. **Arab traders**

By the mid 15th century the Portuguese had arrived on the scene. Vasco da Gama noted the beauty of the town of Kilwa, and attempted to take control of the gold trade from the interior. The Portuguese were later expelled by the Arabs and the influence of the Arabs increased again. A period of reduced trading activity followed until the latter half of the 18th century when trade flourished again and the commodity traded was slaves. Around 1776 the only trading route inland went southwest from Kilwa to the area around Lake **Portuguese seafarers**

Tanzania

Nyasa and this became increasingly important through the slave trade. During the 18th century Kilwa became East Africa's major slave-trading port, drawing first on the peoples of southeast Tanganyika and then on the Lake Nyasa area.

During the 19th century the trade pattern shifted. This was as a result of the changes in the supply of ivory. During the first half of the 19th century, most of the ivory came from within what was to become Tanganyika. However as Tanganyika's elephants were destroyed, so the price of ivory rose rapidly. Prices at Tabora are reported to have increased tenfold between 1846 and 1858. Thus the hunters looked further afield and eventually left Tanganyika altogether. As the hunters moved away the chiefs in these areas lost their major source of revenue. It was this that led some of them to look to the new trade in slaves.

The slave trade Caravan routes into the interior developed by the 19th century and trade centres developed at places such as Ujiji and Tabora. Humans and ivory were exchanged for guns, beads and cloth. The slaves were largely obtained by bartering with the local chiefs rather than by force. Some of the more militarized tribes raided their neighbours and 'prisoners of war' were then sold on to the Arabs as slaves. Convicted criminals were often sold as slaves and this penalty was sometimes extended to include their families.

The size of the slave trade remains speculative. However it has been estimated that approximately 1,500,000 slaves from the interior reached the coast and 10 times that number died en route. Bagamoyo was a terminus of the trade and from there they were taken to Zanzibar, which developed into an important trading centre. The slaves were either put to work in the plantations of Pemba and Zanzibar or were shipped to the Middle East.

By the 1830s Zanzibar had become sufficiently prosperous from slaves and spices for the Omani Sultan Seyyid Said to move his capital from Muscat to Zanzibar itself. For some time Britain tried to suppress the slave trade by signing various agreements with the Omani Sultans. However it was not until 1873 that the slave trade was officially abolished when an agreement was signed with Sultan Barghash (Seyyid Said's successor) that forbade the seaborne trade. However this prohibition was implemented only slowly and the practice continued in the mainland for some years. By the 1880s the internal market for slaves had become more important than the external.

The first Europeans The first Europeans in this part of Africa were missionaries and explorers. In 1844 John Krapf, a German missionary working for the Church Missionary Society of London arrived in Zanzibar. He was joined by John Rebmann who was to become the first European to set eyes on Mt Kilimanjaro in 1848. The two British explorers Burton and Speke, sent by the Royal Geographical Society, arrived in Zanzibar in 1856 and journeyed along the caravan routes into the interior. In 1858 Speke came across the huge expanse of water, which he named Lake Victoria. Dr Livingstone (see box, page 511) was perhaps the most celebrated of all the missionaries, being found, after no news of him for several years, by HM Stanley, a newspaper reporter.

By the 1880s numbers of Europeans were arriving in East Africa as missionaries, big game hunters, traders and adventurers. There were some with political ambitions including two Germans, Carl Peters and HH Johnson, who wanted to see this part of Africa under the control of Germany. They formed the Society for German Colonization from which emerged the German East Africa Society. Emissaries of the Society signed 'protective treaties' with unsuspecting and often illiterate chiefs from the interior. These so-called treaties of friendship were then used by the German East Africa Company to exploit the areas that they covered with the apparent agreement of local authorities.

Both Germany and Britain made claims over East Africa, which were resolved by a series of agreements between the two countries. The Berlin Conference of November 1884 to February 1885 was convened by Bismarck and was important in demarcating European spheres of influence in Africa. This saw the recognition of the German 'protective treaties' and by early 1885 several chiefdoms were formally placed under the control of the German East Africa Company. Three years later the Germans were shaken by an uprising of both

Arabs and Africans and the German government took control in 1891. The Anglo-German Agreement of November 1886 defined the north boundary from the coast inland to Lake Victoria. A month later another agreement saw the defining of the boundary with Mozambique. These and various other treaties saw Zanzibar, Pemba and a 16-km coastal strip go to the Sultan under British Protectorate rule in 1890, while what is now mainland Tanzania, Rwanda and Burundi became German East Africa. It was not until 1898 that German rule was secured and consolidated with the death of Mkwawa, chief of the Hehe who had resisted German domination.

While Germany and Britain were deciding the north boundary, Kaiser William I insisted that Mount Kilimanjaro should be German because it had been discovered by a German, John Rebmann. Queen Victoria generously 'gave' the mountain to her grandson, the future Kaiser William II, on his birthday in 1886. Although no official record exists the Queen is supposed to have explained, by way of justification for her royal 'gift', that 'William likes everything that is high and big'. The boundary was thus moved so that Kilimanjaro is now found within Tanzania. As can be seen on the present map, instead of marking the boundary by pencilling it in with a ruler from the coast to Lake Victoria in one go, a freehand detour was made when the ruler hit the mountain, before carrying on again with the ruler and pencil on the far side.

Mount Kilimanjaro

There were a number of phases of German colonial rule. The first around the turn of the century saw attempts at establishing a settler economy. This was to be based in the north highlands and agriculture was to be the basis of the economy. However this was initially not a great success. Revolts occurred in Bagamoyo, Pangani and Tanga, which were all crushed. The best-known uprising was the Maji Maji rebellion (*maji* means water in Swahili), which occurred in the south of the country from 1905 to 1906. Discontent was initially aroused over a cotton scheme that benefited the Africans little although they were obliged to provide all the manual labour. The uprising was unique in eastern Africa for it was cross-tribal and included a large area – almost the whole of the country south of Dar es Salaam. With only spears and arrows, but believing themselves to be protected by sacred water (hence Maji Maji), the rebels were pitted against German troops equipped with rifles.

The German colonial period

The uprising led to a major reappraisal of German colonial policy. The administrators realized that development would be almost impossible without a contented local population. This period saw the building of the railway to Tabora to open up the area to commerce, and crops such as coffee and groundnuts were encouraged. Economic activity increased and a world boom led to the re-emergence of a settler cash crop economy as the most significant part of colonial policy. In particular the boom saw prices of sisal and rubber soar. Most farming took place along the coast and on the slopes of Mount Kilimanjaro and Mount Meru. Inland the threat of the tsetse fly hindered development as domestic animals could not be raised in affected areas. Missionary activity led to the growth of clinics and schools.

With the outbreak of hostilities in Europe, the German commander General Paul von Lettow Vorbeck realized that his meagre forces could not defeat the British. He resolved to aid Germany's efforts in the European theatre of war by tying up as many British military resources as possible. Von Lettow, his German officers and African troops conducted an astonishing rearguard campaign, retreating from Kenya through what is now Tanzania and Mozambique, being undefeated when Germany surrendered in Europe.

The First World War

Paul von Lettow had arrived in Dar es Salaam at the start of 1914 to take command of the German forces. He was 44 years old, son of a general, a professional soldier and experienced in bush warfare from service in German South West Africa (now Namibia).

His forces consisted of around 2,500 Schutztruppe (see box, page 583) *askaris* in 14 field companies, and he promptly signalled his intentions by capturing Taveta across the border in Kenya. The British assembled a force of 5,000 mainly British, South African and Indian troops and von Lettow withdrew to begin his epic, 4,000-km, four-year campaign. When

Central and northern railways

The first railway to be constructed in Tanganyika was the Tanga (Northern) line which began when the German authorities decided in 1891 that a metre-gauge line should be built from Tanga to Muheza, and then on to Korogwe. Eventually this line would be continued on to Moshi and Arusha. A small port was built at Tanga to land equipment and material and the construction of the line began in 1893. Labour was scarce and at times had to be imported from Mozambique making progress slow. It took two years for the laying of just 40 km as far as Muheza. Financial difficulties caused the construction to be halted periodically and the line finally reached Korogwe in 1902 and Moshi in 1911. Unfortunately much of this line, built at great expense over a long period of time, was destroyed by the Germans as they retreated in 1914.

Meanwhile the central route of the old slave trail to Lake Tanganyika was receiving attention. Dar es Salaam had been made the capital of the German protectorate in 1891 and talk of the construction of a railway began soon after. However, delays again ensued and it was not until 1905 that construction began on a line from Dar es Salaam to Morogoro. This was to be built by a private company with a grant from the Imperial German Government. The Maji Maji rebellion created problems with the supply of labour, but the line reached Morogoro in December 1907. By 1914 the line had been extended as far as Kigoma although it was clear that this line had little commercial value and traffic was extremely light.

Planning continued for other lines but the First World War intervened and much of the work already carried out was destroyed. Most of the bridges between Dar es Salaam and Kigoma were blown up, and the rolling stock destroyed. A line was built during the war, linking the Tanga line to the Kenya railway system which facilitated the advance and occupation of Tanga by the British.

Following the war many repairs were carried out so that the goods traffic on the railways increased. However the problems returned with the depression of the 1930s which severely affected revenues. The non-metre gauge lines were closed and about 40% of the staff were laid off. The Second World War saw an increase in the activities of the Railways, and following the war the 'Groundnut Scheme' (see box, page 584), involved the hasty construction of a branch line from Lindi on the coast to Nachingwea, one of the areas where groundnuts were to be grown. However the scheme was a monumental failure, the expected traffic never materialized, and the line was abandoned.

In 1948 the railway and port services in Tanganyika were amalgamated with the Kenya and Uganda railways under the East Africa High Commission. A regional authority, East African Railways & Harbours (EAR&H), ran the railways until 1977 when the East African Community collapsed, severing the rail link through Taveta to Kenya, with Tanzania assuming responsibility for its own network.

Friends of Railway Heritage are currently restoring steam locomotives. Contact Andreas Huber at Tanzania Railway Corporation, PO Box 468, Dar es Salaam.

---

faced by overwhelming odds von Lettow fell back, but at defendable positions, although always hopelessly out-numbered, he inflicted fearful losses on his adversaries, most notably at Tanga and Kibata (see page 377).

The British fared better when commanded by the South African, Jan Christian Smuts, for 11 months in 1916. A rare combination of intellectual, politician and soldier, Smuts was later to be Prime Minister of South Africa. Smuts found himself pursuing an infuriatingly elusive, and surprisingly humorous, foe. He was convinced that he would trap and destroy von Lettow's troops in Morogoro, where retreat to the south was blocked by the Ulunguru Mountains. But as his forces marched into the town they heard a mechanical piano playing *Deutschland Uber Alles* in the *Bahnhof Hotel* and, in the empty Schutztruppe barracks, on every item of furniture, was a piece of human excrement.

Never defeated, at the end of the campaign von Lettow and his force numbered 155 Germans 1,156 Schutztruppe *askaris* and about 3,000 camp-followers made up of porters and *askari* wives and children, many of the latter born during the campaign. Over 250,000

The Schutztruppe – an African fighting elite

It was recognized by the Germans from the start that white troops in East Africa would be nothing more than a 'walking hospital'.

Under German officers, an African fighting force of askaris was recruited, thoroughly drilled, trained, disciplined and well paid – 30 rupees a month for privates (about US$80 in present-day values) and 150 rupees for non-commissioned officers.

The Shutztruppe became an élite. The uniform was a khaki jacket, trousers and puttees and a black leather belt with ammunition pouches. Head gear was a kepi – rather like a khaki fez with a chin-strap and a gold Imperial eagle on the front. The non-commissioned officers decorated their kepis with feathers. Each soldier had his own servant (an askari-boy). When travelling, a

Schutztruppe private would send his askari boy ahead to a village with a cartridge. This was an order to the local headman to have ready four beds (one for the askari, one for his rifle, one for his ammunition pouch and one for his uniform) – and some 'blankets' – a selection of the village girls.

Tough, resilient, and brave, around 150 askaris made up a field company that included two machine-gun teams. With several hundred porters carrying food and ammunition, it was highly mobile. During the First World War, the British were contemptuous of these African troops, considering they would collapse when faced with European and Indian forces. In the event, the Schutztruppe was never defeated, and inflicted fearful losses on the British and their allies.

Allied troops had been thrown against them at one time or another during the four years.

Von Lettow returned to Germany, in 1920 entered politics and for 10 years was a Deputy in the Reichstag. In 1929 he was guest of honour in London, with Smuts, at the anniversary dinner of the British East African Expeditionary Force. In 1930 he resigned from the Reichstag and in 1935 Hitler suggested he become Ambassador to Britain. Von Lettow declined. It is said he told Hitler to 'go fuck himself', but von Lettow subsequently denied he had ever been that polite.

In 1958, at the age of 88, von Lettow returned to Dar es Salaam. He was met at the dockside by a crowd of elderly Schutztruppe *askaris* who carried him shoulder-high to an official reception at Government House.

In 1964 the German Bundestag finally voted the funds to settle the back-pay owing to the Schutztruppe at the surrender in 1918. Over 300 veterans, some in faded and patched uniforms presented themselves at Mwanza. Only a handful had their discharge papers. Those who didn't were handed a broom and taken through arms drill, with the orders given in German. Not one man failed the test. The same year, at the age of 94, von Lettow died.

With defeat in the First World War the Germans lost control of German East Africa. The northwest, now Rwanda and Burundi, went to the Belgians. The rest was renamed Tanganyika, and the British were allocated a League of Nations mandate.

The British period

From 1921 Britain introduced the policy of Indirect Rule, which had proved effective in other parts of colonial Africa. This involved giving a degree of political responsibility to local chiefs and ruling through them. Economic development between the wars was negligible. Tanganyika had few exportable products. Unlike Uganda, there was no major cash crop such as cotton suited to production by small African farmers. The most significant export was sisal, a spiky plant that yields fibres that can be made into ropes and twine, but this required long-term, large-scale, capital-intensive investment and was not suitable for small-scale African production. It was produced almost entirely by British and Asian companies with a local workforce. The most successful African cash crop was coffee grown by the Chagga on the slopes of Mount Kilimanjaro, and by the Haya west of Lake Victoria. Coffee growing was extended to Africans by the British in 1922. Previously only settlers were allowed to grow coffee on estates established by the Germans from 1910.

Most British settlers went to Kenya where there was already a sizeable settler community and the highlands provided an attractive climate. Moreover the British

The Groundnut Scheme

Immediately after the Second World War there was an attempt by the British Labour government to grow groundnuts on an enormous scale. Three sites were chosen in the south, near Lindi at Nachingwea; just north of Morogoro at Kongwa; and at Urambo west of Tabora on the Central Railway line. The scheme aimed to alleviate the world-wide shortage of edible oils following the war. The operation was to be capital-intensive, with a military style approach to planning, and there was immense enthusiasm among the British who went out to run the programme and became known as 'groundnutters'. It was thought that with modern methods and enough machinery it would be impossible for the scheme to fail. However, it was a complete disaster. When finally abandoned a total of £36.5 mn was written off. This huge sum was equal to a little less than the entire Tanganyikan government expenditure from 1946-50.

The reasons for failure were numerous and included inadequate planning, which meant the environmental and climatic problems were not properly considered; unsuitable machinery; and failure to test the scheme by way of a pilot project. Other difficulties included insufficient rain in the areas to support the groundnuts and inadequate capacity in the transport system to keep the tractors supplied with fuel. Although it was supposed to be a capital-intensive project the inappropriateness of the machinery meant that it was actually more efficient to clear the land by hand. The project is held up as an example of everything that was wrong with attempting to impose European agricultural techniques without adequate consideration of local African conditions.

Kongwa is now a ranch, Urambo has been given over to tobacco, and at Nachingwea, oilseeds and cereals are grown.

presence seemed more secure in Kenya, which was a colony. The League of Nations mandate required Britain to prepare Tanganyika for eventual self-government, and the British kept expenditure on administration, infrastructure and education to a minimum.

The 1920s saw the emergence of the first African political groups. In 1922 the African Civil Servants Association of Tanganyika Territory was formed in Tanga, and in 1929 the Tanganyika African Association (TAA). Throughout the 1930s and 1940s, unions and agricultural cooperatives developed. These were not primarily political associations although their formation obviously led to an increased political awareness.

The major issues upon which attention was focused were land-use policies, aimed in particular at soil conservation, and the eviction of Africans to make way for white settlers. The African population in 1950 was about 8,000,000, compared to an Asian population of 55,000 and European population of 17,000. However Europeans and Asians dominated in local government councils even in areas that were almost exclusively African. These were issues upon which the TAA focused. In 1953 Julius Nyerere became the leader of the TAA and the movement towards independence developed momentum. In July 1954, at a meeting of all political elements, the Tanganyika African National Union (TANU) was created with the slogan *Uhuru na Umoja* (Freedom and Unity).

There were two major strengths of this movement as against similar movements in other parts of Africa. Firstly there was no dominating tribal group, and secondly Swahili had developed into the major language, encouraged by German colonial policy, and this served as an important unifying force. A further point of relevance in the run-up to independence was that after the Second World War Tanganyika was given UN Trustee status in place of the mandate. Both the mandatory system and the trusteeship system were very important as they meant that controversial issues could be referred to the UN Council unlike in other colonial territories. In December 1956 Nyerere addressed the UN General Assembly's Fourth (Trusteeship) Committee. This gave Nyerere a platform to present the views of Tanganyikans to the outside world.

The first elections were held in two phases, in September 1958 and February 1959, and TANU won a sweeping majority. These were multiracial elections but even the European and Asian candidates owed their success to TANU. Tanganyika attained Independence on 9 December 1961 with Nyerere as the first Prime Minister. The constitution was subsequently changed, Tanzania becoming a republic with Nyerere as President.

In 1964 Zanzibar and Tanganyika merged to form Tanzania (see page 543). An awkward union has resulted in which Zanzibar has retained its own President, Parliament, a full range of Ministries and handles most of its own finances. The President of Zanzibar was, *ex officio*, one of the two Vice-Presidents of Tanzania until the multiparty elections in 1995. Despite having a population that is less than 5% of the total, Zanzibar has almost a third of the seats in the Tanzanian Assembly. **Post-Independence Tanzania**

   After independence there was pressure to replace Europeans with Africans in administration and the business sector. There was also considerable demand for basic education and health services. Although economic progress was significant in these early years, there was an impatience at the slow pace of development, and Nyerere made plans for a bold, radical change.

   This culminated in the 1967 Arusha Declaration. It was a programme of socialist development accepted by TANU and which was then amplified in a number of pamphlets by Nyerere. The two main themes of this programme were egalitarianism and self-reliance and it was broadly based on the Chinese communist model. It has been said that Tanzania took the Chinese model, mistakes and all and then added a few mistakes of its own. Politicians were subject to a leadership code, which required that they had no private sources of income, and no more than one house or car. Banks, plantations and all major industries were nationalized. The cornerstone of the programme was the villagization and agricultural collectivization programme known as *Ujamaa* (see below). This, and efforts in the rest of the economy, would, it was hoped, lead to the development of a just and prosperous society. Education was considered to be one of the most important aims of the programme and as a result Tanzania achieved some of the highest literacy rates in Africa. In the initial years there was success, too, in extending basic health care in the rural areas.

An important element in post-independence Tanzanian philosophy was *Ujamaa*, a programme for advancement in the rural areas. This was supposed to be the voluntary movement of people into villages with a major objective being to raise output through collectivization and large-scale agricultural production. Emphasis was also on the social benefits – the provision of services such as piped water, electricity, schools and clinics. Self-reliance was the key and the villages were meant to be set up and run by the villagers themselves. **Ujamaa**

   There were three phases of villagization in the decade from 1967. The first was voluntary movement on a locally selective basis combined with compulsory movement in Rufiji and Handeni, which were areas worst affected by drought and flood. From 1970 to 1973 this was replaced by a 'frontal approach' whereby incentives were given for people to move to villages, which included financial and technical assistance. The reluctance of people to move on their own accord meant the targets were not reached and so after 1973 these methods were replaced by a willingness to use force in support of rapid villagization. The results were dramatic. In 1970 the villagized population stood at about 500,000, or less than 5% of the population. After the first year of compulsory movement Nyerere claimed that there were over 9,000,000 people – or about 60% of the mainland population, living in villages. Force was justified on the grounds that people could not always see what was best for them and had to be shown the way. As it is easier to provide amenities such as piped water and electricity to people grouped in villages, the *Ujamaa* did provide some benefits.

   However attempts to farm collectively were disastrous and agricultural output fell. The programme was vigorously resisted in the major coffee-growing areas of Kagera (west of Lake Victoria) and in Kilimanjaro region. By 1977 the *Ujamaa* programme was effectively abandoned, although considerable villagization remains.

   In 1973 it was decided to move the capital city from Dar es Salaam on the coast to Dodoma in the centre. The position of this city is suitable in so far as it is on communication networks and is located in the centre of the country about 320 km inland. However it is also a dry and desolate area. The major problem with the plan has been the cost of moving. A Presidential official residence, the Prime Minister's office, and a National

Julius Nyerere

Julius Kambarage Nyerere was born in 1922 in Butiama, east of Lake Victoria. He was the Roman Catholic son of a Zanaki chief. His father died having reportedly had 26 children by 18 wives. The name Nyerere means 'caterpillar' in the Zanaki language and was supposed to have been given to Nyerere's father because at the time of his birth (around 1860) the countryside was infested with these creatures. Nyerere attended a boarding school in Musoma and, from 1937, the Tabora Government Secondary School. He was baptized in 1943 into the Catholic Church and the same year he entered Makerere College, Uganda. After Makerere he returned to Tabora where he taught history and biology at St Mary's Catholic Boys School operated by the White Fathers. In 1949 he went to Edinburgh University and in 1952 obtained his Master of Arts. In 1953 he married Maria Gabriel Magigo who was also a Catholic of the Msinditi tribe and was to become its first woman teacher. He paid the traditional bride price of six head of cattle for her and they have seven children.

Nyerere subsequently took a teaching post at the Catholic Secondary School of St Francis at Pugu a few kilometres west of Dar es Salaam and it was from here that he became involved in politics. In 1954 he became president of the Tanzania African Association and was instrumental in converting this into the political organization TANU. He was appointed a temporary member of the Tanganyika Legislative Council in 1954, and a full member of the Legislative Assembly in 1958 where he remained until his assumption of the Presidency in 1962. He resigned as President in 1985. Nyerere has become known as 'Mwalimu', which means teacher and he is undoubtedly one of Africa's greatest statesmen, admired for his integrity, modest lifestyle and devotion to equality and human rights.

Assembly building have all been established there. The cost of relocation has forced the rest of central government to remain in Dar es Salaam for the time being.

In 1975 a law was passed that gave legal supremacy to TANU as the national political party, and in 1977 TANU and the Afro-Shirazi party (which had taken control in Zanzibar after the revolution) merged to form *Chama Cha Mapinduzi* (CCM) the 'party of the Nation'.

The 1970s saw the gradual disintegration of the East Africa Community (EAC), which involved Kenya, Tanzania and Uganda in a customs union and provision of common services. Tanzania and Kenya had different ideological perspectives, and the three countries could not agree on the distribution of the costs and services of the EAC. Things came to a head over East African Airways. The failure of Tanzania and Uganda to remit funds to Kenya caused Kenya to 'ground' the airline (conveniently when all the planes were sitting on the tarmac in Kenya) and Tanzania reacted by closing the border with Kenya in February 1977. The border was only reopened in 1983 after the ownership of the assets of the EAC was finally agreed.

In 1978 Tanzania's relations with neighbouring Uganda worsened and skirmishes on the border were followed by an announcement by Idi Amin that Uganda had annexed the Kagera salient. This is an area of about 1,800 sq km of Tanzanian territory west of Lake Victoria. The OAU applied pressure, which caused Uganda to withdraw, but fighting continued. In January 1979 a Tanzanian force of over 20,000 invaded Uganda, Amin's army capitulated and the Tanzanians rapidly took control of the southern part of the country. The invading force had withdrawn by 1981 having spent the interim period in Uganda overseeing the election of Milton Obote for the second time. A remarkable feature of this episode is that, despite being the only African country ever to win a war in the 20th century, this event is not celebrated in Tanzania. The only monument is a small pyramid on columns, located on the road from Bukoba to Masaka, just south of the border. It is dedicated to the 16 Tanzanian soldiers who died in the war.

In 1985 Nyerere decided to step down as President of Tanzania (the first President in post-independence Africa to retire voluntarily). He remained as Chairman of the party (CCM) before formally retiring from politics in 1990. Vice-President Sokoine, who had been widely thought of as Nyerere's successor, was killed in a car crash in October 1984. Ali

Hassan Mwinyi, who was then President of Zanzibar, was nominated to be the sole candidate for President and was elected in October 1985.

Throughout the early 1980s Tanzania was put under pressure to accept economic reforms suggested by the World Bank and International Monetary Fund. These financial institutions, as well as western governments, aid donors and foreign investors argued that the socialist development strategy had led to a crisis involving falling incomes, decaying infrastructure, deteriorating health and educational provision, and a climate of petty corruption. For many years Tanzania resisted changes, but eventually the climate of opinion changed and in 1986, under Mwinyi, a market economy strategy was adopted, and Tanzania began an economic recovery.

In 1993, Tanzania allowed political parties other than CCM to form. In October 1995 there were elections in which CCM won a substantial majority of seats in the Union Assembly. The Presidency was won by the CCM candidate, Benjamin Mkapa, Mwinyi having retired after two terms in office. Mkapa and CCM were returned again in the 2000 elections.

In 1995, the main opposition in Zanzibar, the Civic United Front (CUF) ran CCM very close in both the Zanzibar Assembly and in the race for the Zanzibar Presidency. There were allegations of election fraud, supported by evidence from international observers. Nonetheless, CCM formed the administration in Zanzibar, and Salim Amour was installed as Zanzibar's President. In 2000, there were again allegations of election irregularities and administrative incompetence at the polls, but once more CCM were returned, and CCM's Amani Karume (son of Zanzibar's first President) secured the Presidency.

Modern Tanzania

Politics

Since independence in 1961 to 1995, Tanzania had single party rule. Julius Nyerere was President until 1985, followed by Ali Hassan Mwinyi until 1995 when Benjamin Mkapa won the multiparty elections. There has been negligible internal unrest since the revolution in Zanzibar in 1964 (see box, page 542), closely followed by a suppressed army mutiny on the mainland. The invasion of Uganda in 1979, and a subsequent period of peace-keeping occupation, although costly, had minimal disrupting effect on the economy.

The current situation in Zanzibar is a cause for concern. It is argued that the Union, created in 1964, although following constitutional procedures, has no political legitimacy as the Zanzibar party to the agreement seized power undemocratically after the 1964 revolution (see page 542). In addition, there are the cultural and religious differences with the mainland stemming from the population of Zanzibar being overwhelmingly Islamic. Zanzibaris feel the Union with the mainland has held back their development, and that they would have benefited in terms of aid and foreign investment if they had been able to forge stronger ties with Islamic states, particularly in the Gulf, where they have strong historical links (see page 535).

The structure of the Union is awkward. It is not a proper federation as Zanzibar has its own President, Assembly and Ministries, while the mainland does not. Until the 1995 elections, the Zanzibar President was *ex officio* one of the Vice-Presidents of the Union. Despite having a population that is under 5% of the Union, Zanzibar has 30% of the seats in the *Bunge*, the Tanzanian National Assembly.

In 1994, a group of mainland MPs pressed for the creation of a Tanganyika Assembly, and the reorganization of the Union into a proper federation. Though there was logic behind this move, the extra cost of another bureaucratic layer was a considerable drawback, and the proposal was dropped when the former President, Julius Nyerere, expressed his disapproval.

Various Zanzibari separatist groups have formed in exile, some wishing merely for independence, others pressing for an independent Islamic state. The splits within the separatist movement have enabled the government to contain the problem to date. A

Tanzanian satire

Tanzanians have an excellent sense of humour. Much amusement has come from making fun of their economic predicament, characterized by shortages, endless bureaucracy and inefficient state-run enterprises.

When neighbouring capitalist Kenya's dynamic, competitive society was criticised as a 'man eat man' society, the locals retorted that this was all very well, but Tanzania was a 'man eat nothing' society.

A Tanzanian arrives at the Zurich headquarters of a Swiss Bank. He explains that he is from the Central Bank of Tanzania and that he wishes to see the statements for all Tanzanian citizens with accounts at the bank. The official explains that this is not possible – customer information is confidential. The Tanzanian produces a letter from the Governor of the Bank of Tanzania authorizing him to collect the information. The official politely explains that he is still unable to help. The Tanzanian pulls out a gun. The bank official is unmoved.

"Shoot me if you must, sir, but I cannot release the information".

"Excellent", exclaims the Tanzanian, pulling out a wad of dollars. "Open me an account".

When President Nyerere died he was told by St Peter that Heaven was full and he'd have to go down to Hell for a while, but if he managed to survive for a year he could come up to Heaven. One consolation, St Peter said, was that he could offer Nyerere a choice of a capitalist Hell or a socialist Hell. Nyerere said he'd opt for the socialist Hell.

"I see you're a romantic" says St Peter.

"No, it's not that", replies the former President. "It's a matter of survival. You see, in a capitalist Hell there's plenty of firewood and matches and the fellow who lights the bonfire is on piece-rates, so you get burnt pretty quick. But in a socialist Hell there's always a shortage of firewood, the matches keep breaking and anyway the bonfire man is always away at a party meeting".

The Water Ministers from Kenya, Tanzania and Uganda are meeting in Kampala to discuss management of Lake Victoria, which they all border. They break for the weekend, and the Ugandan Minister invites his colleagues to his country home. The Tanzanian Minister is very impressed with the Ugandan's extensive residence, and asks how the Minister can afford such a palatial residence on his modest ministerial salary.

"Look out of the window", says the Ugandan. "Do you see the dam in the valley?" The Tanzanian nods.

"Well", says the Ugandan, "ten percent".

The next meeting of the Ministers is in Kenya, and the Kenyan Minister reciprocates by inviting the group to his home for the weekend. It is much bigger and more opulent than the Ugandan Minister's country house.

"My goodness", says the Tanzanian, "I was impressed by our Ugandan colleague's home, but this is a palace! What's the secret?"

"Look out of the window", says the Kenyan, "do you see a dam in the valley?"

"Er, no".

"Exactly. One hundred percent!"

---

former Chief Minister of Zanzibar, Shariff Hamad, who was suspected of sympathy to the separatist cause, was removed from office and detained.

In 1994 Zanzibar joined the Organization of Islamic States (OIS), which, although unconstitutional as Zanzibar is not an independent state, appeared to be tolerated by the government. However, Nyerere, whose liberal and egalitarian philosophy is uncompromisingly secular, denounced the move, and Zanzibar was forced to withdraw.

For the multiparty elections in October 1995 13 opposition parties were formed. The strongest was NCCR-Maguezi led by a former Interior Minister from CCM, Augustine Mrema, who has considerable popular appeal. CUF, in which Shariff Hamad, the dismissed former CCM Chief Minister on the Isles, is the driving force, had little support on the mainland, but was very strong in Zanzibar.

Prior to the election there was a good prospect that Zanzibar would elect a CUF president, and have a majority of seats in the Zanzibar Assembly. The Assembly could then instigate a referendum on the separation issue, and most observers judged that this would be carried. Given the commitment of Tanzania to democratic self-determination in the past, it would be difficult to resist the break-up of the union. Indeed Tanzanians seemed to be preparing themselves to face up to such an eventuality – "let us end the Union, if that is what the Zanzibaris want, while we are all still smiling" – was a sentiment frequently heard on the mainland. Former President Nyerere, architect of the original Act of Union, observed that he felt Zanzibar would always be a headache, and that if he could have towed it away from the Tanzanian coast to the centre of the Indian Ocean, he would have done so.

The CCM Presidential candidate was Benjamin Mkapa, from the south, a former journalist, diplomat, Foreign Minister, and latterly Minister for Science, Technology and Higher Education. The opposition parties failed to unite behind a single candidate, and NCCR-Maguezi fielded Augustine Mrema (also supported by CHADEMA, a party strong in the north); CUF put up Professor Ibrahim Lipumba, a pro-market economist; and the United Democratic Party (UDP) were represented by John Cheyo, a businessman. Mkapa won comfortably with 62% of the vote, over Mrema with 28%. The practice of having two Vice-Presidents (with one being the President of Zanzibar) was discontinued. The Vice-President is now the chosen running mate of the successful Presidential candidate.

In the Union Assembly elections, run on a first-past-the-post-basis, CCM got 219 seats, NCCR-Maguezi 19, CUF 28 (mostly from Zanzibar), CHADEMA four, and UDP four. Some irregularities were reported, but the general impression of observers was that the election was a reasonable reflection of the nation's political preferences.

By contrast, the elections for the Zanzibar Assembly and President were a disaster as far as both credibility and the medium-term future of the Islands were concerned. The initial outcomes of both sets of elections indicated narrow victories for Shariff Hamad and CUF over the incumbents, Salim Amour and CCM. Recounts were demanded, and pro-CCM ballot papers appear to have been smuggled into the count. Finally Salim Amour was declared President with 50.2% of the vote (to Hamad's 49.8%), and with two constituencies changing hands at the recount, CCM took 26 seats and CUF 24 (which included all the seats in Pemba).

CUF boycotted the Zanzibar Assembly, and the donor community exerted pressure for a re-run of the election under international control. Norway and Sweden and the EU suspended aid to Zanzibar.

The Mkapa presidency began well with a determined stance over corruption. Three ministers (the Finance Minister, the Deputy Finance Minister and the Minister for Wildlife and Tourism) were forced to resign because of corruption allegations.

The opposition fared less well. The major success was that the NCCR-Maguezi Presidential candidate, Augustine Mrema, won a by-election in a Dar es Salaam constituency. However, this was followed by an apparent split between the party General Secretary, Mabere Marondo and Mrema. Constitutional reform has emerged as a key issue, with the opposition unhappy at the power of the central executive to appoint Regional Commissioners and members of the Electoral Commission.

The 2000 election was fought by fewer parties, but the opposition was still divided, and CCM and Mkapa had comfortable victories.

In Zanzibar the incumbent President, Salmin Amour, having completed two terms, was prevented from running again. His successor as CCM candidate for the Presidency was Amani Karume, son of the former President. On election day there was chaos at the polls, and elections in 16 constituencies had to be re-run. Despite opposition claims of electoral fraud, the outcome was a victory for CCM and Karume.

In August 1998 there was a bomb blast at the American Embassy on the main road through an ocean-side residential suburb. The outrage, which killed 10 people and coincided with a similar bomb blast in Kenya, was attributed to an Islamic extremist group in Afghanistan led by Saudi-born/Osama bin Ladin. This incident is seen as a one-off – there is no terrorist group active and resident in Tanzania.

Overall, Tanzania's stability has remained excellent. The government has remained secure in a period that has seen the advent of multiparty democracy and economic policies that have changed from socialism to capitalism.

Tanzania

Economy

Economic strategy underwent a profound change in 1967 when financial and business enterprises were taken into public ownership and a major reorganization of the agricultural sector was introduced, involving collective production and relocating the population into villages. By 1977, the collectivization of agriculture had virtually been abandoned. In 1986 Tanzania signed an agreement with the IMF, which heralded the beginnings of a reversal of economic strategy to more encouragement for the private sector and reliance on market forces, rather than on planning and central control.

Economic structure In terms of both population and geographical area, Tanzania is a large country in the African context. The population has been growing rapidly at 2.8% a year, and in 2001 the population was estimated at 34,800,000 people. This gives a population density of 3.5 persons per sq km, rather higher than the African average. However, the distribution of the population is very uneven, with the areas around Mount Kilimanjaro and west of Lake Victoria heavily populated, while in the south and southwest there is much uncultivated fertile land. Urbanization is not as advanced as elsewhere in the continent, and only 23% live in the towns.

Despite its large area and population, Tanzania produces only a modest output of around US$8 bn of GDP, converted to US$ using the exchange rate. This gives a level of income per head of US$240. Using a purchasing power parity conversion, GNP per head is US$490 a year. Both these measures put Tanzania among the very poorest countries in the world.

Agriculture is the most important sector, producing 49% of GDP and, more importantly, providing the livelihood of 85% of the population. Maize and plantains (green cooking bananas) are the main staples with cassava and rice also grown. Wheat and barley (the latter for brewing) are grown in the highlands of Kilimanjaro, Arusha and Mbeya regions. The industry sector is small at 17% of GDP, employing only 5% of the workforce. The services sector is relatively small too, at 35% of GDP, generating 10% of employment. Both industry and services are relatively high-income sectors, with incomes three times the average.

A large proportion of income goes on consumption (83%), as is to be expected in a low-income economy where the main activity is subsistence agriculture. Investment is 18% of GDP. Government consumption is low at 8% of GDP, and this reflects inability to raise revenue through taxation, combined with spending limits to curtail inflation.

Export dependence is 16% of GDP. The main commodity sources of export income are manufactures (31%), coffee (21%), cotton (18%), minerals (17%) and cashews (13%). New export crops include beans, green beans and cut flowers grown around Mount Kilimanjaro and shipped by air to Europe. Tourism is a major service sector earner. Imports are the equivalent of 26% of GDP, and this high level is only possible as a result of donor assistance. The main imports are manufactures and transport equipment (43%), consumer goods (32%), building materials (10%) and fuel (8%).

Economic performance GDP growth is averaging around 7% a year, and this is faster than the rate of population expansion (2.8% a year) allowing living standards to show an improvement of more than 4% a year.

Agriculture has been growing at around 5% a year, aided by reforms in marketing arrangements and improvements in transport. Industry has been growing at more than 10% a year. Mining has been an important factor in the industrial sector, with a series of new gold mines coming on stream, and gold export earnings set to rise above US$300 mn a year by 2002. Services have also picked up to grow at more than 10% a year, driven by strong expansion in tourism, which is booming, with receipts rising at 25% a year, and visitors tripling since 1992.

Export volumes have recovered, and together with revenues from aid have allowed imports to rise steadily.

There has been slow but steady improvement in inflation performance in recent years and, in 2000, the rate was 6% a year.

Aid receipts at US$31 per head are a little below the African average, and total aid receipts are around US$1.3 bn a year.

In June of 1986, the Tanzanian government reached agreement with the IMF, after resisting IMF terms since 1979. Subsequently, there has been steady economic reform with considerable privatization taking place, with more in prospect. Now that the economy appears to have achieved steady growth, the emphasis of the government and the donor community is focusing on poverty alleviation. In the last major survey undertaken in 1991, 51% of the population were estimated to be below the poverty line.

As well as poverty alleviation, aid programmes have continued to support infrastructural improvements, particularly roads and ports.

The exchange rate has continued to depreciate. It stood at TSh17.50=US$1 in mid 1985 and by 2001 had fallen to TSh800=US$1. The exchange rate is now reasonably stable, and the value of the Tanzanian shilling is depreciating at about 6% a year against the US dollar.

Recent economic developments

Assuming that Tanzania maintains its record of political stability, and perseveres with a steady programme of liberalizing economic reforms, general prospects are good.

Economic outlook

In 1998 adult literacy was estimated at around 70%. Although this followed a widespread literacy campaign, it is widely thought to have been an over-estimate. Certainly literacy rates have slipped in recent years, and a more realistic estimate is thought to be around 60%.

Social conditions

It will prove difficult to maintain even this literacy level with primary enrolment at 48%. Secondary education has received very low priority and at 5% is well below the African average of 14%. Tertiary education enrolment rates are under one-half of 1%.

Life expectancy, at 48 years, is about the African average, and provision of medical care, indicated by numbers of doctors per head, is slightly better than the average elsewhere on the continent. However, infant mortality rates are high, and are a reflection of the concentration of medical services in the urban areas and comparative neglect of the majority of the population in the countryside.

Despite being a fertile country with unused agricultural land, nutrition levels leave something to be desired with average daily calorie supply about 10% below the recommended daily minimum.

A big effort has been made to improve the status of women in recent years, and enrolment levels for females are only slightly below the rate for males at the primary level. However, at the secondary level, a quarter fewer women are enrolled. Low income levels lead to many women needing to work outside the home (mostly on the family farm), and 87% are so engaged, compared to 60% in the rest of Africa. The burden of home-care and work are compounded by high fertility rates of close to six children per female. Only 10% of women are using contraceptives, and this rate of uptake is about half the African average.

In the latter part of the colonial era (1960/61) a waiter in a good hotel would earn TSh150 (US$10 per month) at a time when a bottle of beer cost TSh2.50 (US$0.20). In other words one day's pay was the equivalent of the price of two bottles of beer. In 2001 the same waiter would expect to earn TSh 30,000 (US$38 per month) while a bottle of beer now costs TSh500 (US$0.63). A day's pay continues to equate to the price of two bottles of beer.

Tanzania has a large area of forest, about 35% of its total land area. However, a fast expanding population has led to demands for more agricultural land. Poor provision of electricity, and inadequate income levels to allow purchase of bottled gas have led to a high demand for fuelwood. As a result the forest area has been declining at 1% a year, significantly higher than the African average.

Environment

In general there is adequate rainfall in Tanzania, although uneven distribution can lead to pockets of drought. Domestic usage per head is very low, and commercial usages are modest, and there is little strain on overall water availability, with only 0.6% of annual renewable freshwater supplies being utilized.

Tanzania

Culture

Art and architecture

There are five main styles of buildings in Tanzania. The most common are traditional African dwellings constructed variously of poles, mud, straw, cattle-dung and thatch. The styles of these traditional dwellings vary from one region to another. The second style, found on the coast and in Zanzibar, shows strong Arabic and Islamic influence and these buildings date from the earliest arrivals of these peoples. During the German colonial period, a substantial number of impressive public buildings were constructed with a distinctive design adapted to the tropical conditions. The British introduced mainly bungalow-style dwellings along lines developed in India. The Indian community constructed commercial and residential buildings in tenement style, but often with elaborate eastern decorations. Finally there are the concrete office-blocks of the modern era.

Traditional African dwellings
Among the main ethnic groups with distinctive building styles are: the **Nyaleylusa**, from the south between Mbeya and Lake Malawi with *isyenge* dwellings of bamboo walls and thatched roofs; the **Nyamwesi** from between Mwanza and Tawith *msonge* dwellings of thatched roofs and timber and mud walls; the **Masai** from the north border with Kenya, west of Arusha, with *manyatta* half-sphere dwellings of a timber frame entirely covered with mud reinforced with cow-dung; the **Makua** from the coast to the south near Mtwara with dwellings of mud-covered timber walls and thatch; the **Zaramo** from around Dar es Salaam with *msonge* dwellings all of thatch; the **Ha/Rundi** of west Tanzania region inhabiting grass-thatch *msonge* dwellings; the **Haya** from west of Lake Victoria with *msonge* elephant grass huts; the **Ngashi** from around Songea in the south with fairly extensive dwellings in *msonge* style; the **Fiba** from west of Lake Rukwa in the south with conical *msonge* dwellings; the **Gogo** from Tabora in central Tanzania with *tembe* dwellings, which feature a dried mud-covered roof; and the **Hele** from Winga to the south with *tembe* dwellings.

The **Swahili**, the Arabic/Bantu group from along the coastal strip, have *banda* with coral walls and lime mortar made from burnt coral with mangrove pole and clay tile roofs, ornately carved doors and usually a verandah. Later dwellings have corrugated iron roofs. Typically there is a central corridor with rooms off each side on solid coral and mortar floors. A stone slab in the front, shaped like a couch, is for sitting outside in the evenings.

Arabic period
Construction was typically of coral, bound together with lime mortar. The ground floor would be solid coral and mortar, while upper floors were coral and mortar on mangrove rafters (mangrove contains a chemical that discourages termites). The buildings have thick walls and are cool. Decorations often involved crenellations on towers, and carved doors. Examples include the Fort in Zanzibar and the Old Boma in Dar es Salaam.

German period
The German colonists constructed durable buildings, with high ceilings to keep rooms as cool as possible, invariably of two storeys with the upper floor designed to catch any breezes through open arches. Construction was in stone often on a steel frame. Steel girders (often railway rails) were used to support floors and verandahs. Roofs were tile or corrugated iron coated with red-oxide paint. The use of steel allowed the construction to be strong, yet not as heavy in appearence as the Arabic buildings. Crenellations, fort-like towers and Islamic arches were incorporated, giving the buildings a distinctive style. In almost all Tanzanian towns, the German-built, hotel, hospital and administration building (Boma) will still exist, and if the town is on the railway line, there will be a station.

British period
The British were not inclined to embark on an ambitious programme of public buildings as Tanzania was a protectorate (not a colony) destined for eventual self-determination. Government buildings were single-storey bungalows with over-hanging galvanized-iron roofs to provide an awning giving shade, supported by slender iron poles. Residential dwellings had clay-tiled roofs, again mostly single-storey. Some two-storey dwellings would have tile awnings over the lower windows to give shade, and to throw rainwater

away from the house, preventing it spattering in through the window. Examples of government buildings are the newer wards to the rear of the old German hospital in Dar es Salaam. Also in Dar es Salaam, British colonial bungalows are dotted throughout the Oyster Bay area and two-storey dwellings are grouped along Ali Hassan Mwinyi Road.

The temples and mosques of the Indian community are constructed in traditional style. The Hindu and Ismaili buildings are often several stories high with elaborate arches and columns. The commercial and residential buildings also tend to have two or three floors, decorated with inscriptions marking the owners and the date of construction, and with the upper storeys embellished with elaborate, arches, columns and façades. The centres of all main towns contain examples.

Indian architecture

Some bold attempts to introduce interwar suburban architecture took place, most notably the *Selander Bridge Police Post* (previously a hotel) in Dar es Salaam, with curved windows at the corners. Nearby *Palm Beach Hotel* is another example. There was wide experimentation with forms and materials. Reinforced concrete and the use of plank shuttering allowed the construction of external features such as cantilevered fire-escapes, prominent lift shafts, and projecting stair wells, while the use of coral, terrazzo and mosaic added to the richness and variety of texture. Style and creativity were exhibited by the use of glass-paned louvres, flat roofs and anodized aluminium fittings. Unfortunately, a lack of maintenance has had a deleterious effect on many of these modern buildings. Otherwise concrete construction for office buildings and large Mediterranean-style residential houses with arches and tiled roofs have been the order of the day. There are numerous examples of the latter on Msasani Peninsular, and along the road to Bagamoyo between Mwenge and Kunduchi Beach.

Modern era

Tanzania

People

The population is made up of largely mixed Bantu groups, the largest being the Sukuma and the Nyamwezi, but there are 129 recognized tribes. Swahili is the official language, but English is widely spoken. The country is sparsely populated. The majority of the population is concentrated in the north. The fertile lower slopes of Mount Kilimanjaro have population densities as high as 250 persons per sq km, causing severe land shortage, whereas the average density is 31 persons per sq km.

East Africans are frequently divided into 'tribes'; but exactly what makes a tribe is often difficult to define. A tribe usually refers to a group of people with a common language and culture. They possess a common name and recognize themselves to be distinct from their neighbours. Sometimes the group may be fairly distinctive and easy to define – but in other cases the divisions are much less clear. There are some observers who believe that the concept of 'tribe' is largely an artificial one imposed during the colonial period. The colonialists wanted identifiable groups with leaders through whom they could rule indirectly, and they were inclined to create such structures if they did not exist. Certainly there are some 'groups' who only attained full identity and unity after the arrival of Europeans. Putting this debate to one side, the term 'tribe' is used frequently and the people of Tanzania have been classified into such groups.

The 129 different tribal groups that have been distinguished in Tanzania vary from groups of over 1,000,000 people to tribes of just a few hundred. It is obviously impractical to look at all these groups here so only the most important are examined. The largest ethnic groups are the Sukuma and the Nyamwezi, although no group makes up more than 15% of the population. About a dozen of the largest groups make up about 50% of the population. Most of these groups are of Bantu origin (although there are some Nilotic groups as well) and about 95% of the population is Bantu-speaking – the most important Bantu language is Swahili, a language which is the mother tongue of the people of Zanzibar and Pemba as well as some coastal people. Swahili became a *lingua franca* before the colonial period in some areas and this was encouraged by both the Germans and the British. It is very widely spoken and in 1963 it became Tanzania's national language.

👉 ## Traditional alcoholic beverages

A variety of grains is used in the making of the traditional beer in Tanzania, known in Swahili as pombe. *The procedure followed varies in different parts of the country.*

In many parts, including Dar es Salaam, millet is used. It is allowed to germinate for three days before being sun-dried – it is then called kimea. *The* kimea *is ground and mixed together with ungerminated flour before being added to hot water and left to stand for a while before being boiled. The liquid is then left to cool and mixed with a suspension of* kimea *and cold water. Fermentation begins and more flour may be added. The whole mixture is then shaken up and roughly filtered. The pombe is left overnight and the next day is ready to drink. The whole process takes several days and is a skilled job often undertaken by women. The stage at which yeast is added varies – indeed in some cases no yeast is added at all and instead the sprouted millet provides wild yeasts. The alcoholic strength of pombe is 9-11% proof – double the strength of European beers.*

Another local brew is tembo, *which is made from part of the coconut palm. However its preparation and consumption have dropped off over the years. At the turn of the 20th-century everywhere that could grow the palms did and very large quantities of* tembo *were drunk. The flower head of the palm is used. The top is cut off and the juice within it allowed to collect in a gourd overnight. The next morning a further section of the flower head is sliced off and the juice again allowed to collect. Collections are made about three times during the day until the whole of the flower head has been used. This liquid that has been collected ferments quickly and spontaneously. The alcoholic content of* tembo *is higher than that of* pombe *and increases with time before it goes sour. The strength is 14-16% proof. Once it has gone sour the liquid can be used as a sort of vinegar.*

Tembo is not the strongest of the locally made 'traditional' drinks in Tanzania – a spirit called moshi, *which is also known as* brandi, *can be up to 90% proof. It is made using a still that traditionally would have been constructed of gourds. Nowadays however it is more likely that an old petrol tin (*debe*) will be used. The exact method varies, but it is based on a brew of* pombe *or* tembo, *which is successively distilled.*

Sukuma This is Tanzania's largest ethnic group and makes up between 10 and 13% of the population. The name means 'people of the north' and the group lives just to the south of Lake Victoria. The ethnic consciousness of this group is fairly recent and is not entirely pervasive. In the pre-colonial period they were organized into a large number of small chiefdoms. They practise mixed agriculture, with both cattle-herding and cultivation. This is also an important cotton growing area.

Nyamwezi The Nyamwezi people are found to the south of the Sukuma people in north Tanzania and in many ways are similar to the Sukuma. Like the Sukuma they were formerly made up of a large number of very small chiefdoms. Some of these chiefs tried later to dominate wider areas. Their identity is fairly recent and rather fragile. They are primarily a cultivating people and have established a reputation as traders.

Makonde These people are located in the southeast part of the country and are fairly isolated, being on the Makonde Plateau. Although they are one of the five largest groups the Makonde have been little affected by colonial and post-colonial developments. They are renowned for being a conservative people who are determined to defend their way of life. This is facilitated by the difficulty in reaching this part of Tanzania. Even today communications with the southeast are poor, particularly during the wet season. The Makonde are perhaps most famous for their beautifully crafted woodcarvings that are sold all over Tanzania. Makonde people are also found in Mozambique.

Chagga The Chagga (or Chaga) people are found around the south slopes of Mount Kilimanjaro and constitute the third largest group in Tanzania. They are greatly advantaged by living in a fertile and well-watered region, which is ideally suited to the production of coffee. They were also one of the first groups to be affected by the Christian missionaries, in particular the Roman Catholics and Lutherans, and this meant that the initial provision of education in the area was ahead of many other areas. The high level of education and opportunity of cash-cropping have resulted in a comparatively high level of income, and also a relatively high level of involvement in community activity. One example of the form that this has taken is through cooperative action in the production and marketing of coffee.

Chagga customs and beliefs The Chagga believe that the god they called Ruwa was greater than all the other gods that they worshipped. They believed all men had their origin in him and that, as he did not trouble them with petty demands, unlike some other gods he must love men. He is believed to live in a place in the skies that they called *nginenyi*, which means blue skies. Sacrifices would be made to Ruwa when someone was ill or when there was a famine or epidemic. Usually prayers would be said and then a goat would be slaughtered. The goat should be a male of uniform colour without any spots, and it should not have had its tail docked. Sacrifices would also be offered to the spirits of the dead. When a person dies it is believed that they would live in the new world but in a different form. The spirits of the dead would be able to return to the world to demand what is due to them from their relatives. Their physical presence would not be noticed but they would be seen in dreams or through the noises made by animals.

The Haya people are different from most other ethnic groups in Tanzania. They are located in the far northwest of Tanzania, to the west of the shores of Lake Victoria. Culturally and linguistically they are more closely related to the interlacustrine Bantu who are found to the north and west of the Haya. Like the interlacustrine Bantu they are organized into a few centralized states. Although the Haya have common traditions, social system, culture and language as well as territorial identity, they are divided into several chiefdoms, which suggests that in this case political unity is not an essential part of tribal identity. The Haya are cultivators, growing coffee and plantains, and live in densely populated villages. Exactly similar to the situation in Kilimanjaro region, the high altitude of west of Lake Victoria provided a pleasant climate for missionaries. The Catholics and Protestants competed for converts by providing education, and this, combined with the production of coffee, has had a significant beneficial effect on the economy of the area. **Haya**

Haya pregnancy and childbirth What follows is a description of some of the traditions originally recorded in the late 1950s by a Dr Moller who was the District Medical Officer in the area at the time. There is little doubt that some aspects will have changed since then, particularly with the increase of births in clinics and hospitals.

A Haya woman is usually married at about 17 or 18 years old and once married would be kept in seclusion until the birth of her first child. She is known during this period as *omu-gule*, and is not allowed to leave the house during the day. She is kept in a special part of the house and is under the watchful eye of her mother-in-law.

Once a woman discovers that she is pregnant the first person that she must tell is her mother-in-law or, if she is not available, another senior member of her husband's family. Only then can she inform her mother and her husband. There are a number of taboos imposed during pregnancy, including one that the mother must not walk through any entrance backwards or the labour will be difficult, and another that she must chew all her food very carefully and eat very slowly. This is because it is thought that the child may be hurt by the food falling on it, and if the mother eats too quickly the child, who is also eating, may choke. There are various food taboos that apply and the mother is also given a variety of herbal medicines throughout her pregnancy.

When labour begins a midwife is sent for. These are usually elderly women who have learnt their trade from their mothers and will in turn pass it on to their daughters. As labour progresses the midwife will check that no clothing on or belonging to the mother has a knot in it as it is thought that this will adversely affect the labour. The woman is allowed to drink during labour, but not to eat. When the waters break the woman is made to lie down. Herbal drugs are sometimes given to try to speed up the labour. It was believed by a doctor who observed numerous labours that many of these drugs were actually harmful and did little good to the mother or child.

The placenta is sometimes called the 'brother' or 'dead brother' of the child born. This may lead to women saying that they had two children, when in fact only one was born and the other was the placenta. The placenta is treated like a corpse and is disposed of in the same way. It is wrapped in bark cloth and is buried inside or near a hut. There are a number of taboos relating to the placenta and its disposal and the violation of these taboos was thought to be punished by various skin diseases.

The umbilical cord is tied with a piece of string made from a kind of tough grass, and traditionally it was cut using a sharpened slice of reed. There is a belief that any blood that is lost during delivery can be used for witchcraft and this will cause barrenness of the woman from whom the blood originated.

Finally it is believed that the man who first has intercourse with a woman is the father of her first child. The traditional belief is that the first intercourse did cause pregnancy but it 'broke off' and the child was 'hiding in the back' to be born later. This is called a long pregnancy or *bisisi* and the child is known as a '*bisisi*-child'. Thus if a couple marry but fail to produce children and later separate, the first child born to the woman belongs to the first husband – even if the child is born many years later. This means that any man who can prove that he has had the first intercourse with a woman can justly claim the first child of that woman as his. This is of considerable legal, social and economic importance to this district. Also from the time of the first birth, until the baby's cord has dropped, the woman returns to her 'virginal status' – thus any man who has intercourse with her during this time can claim the next child of the woman as his. For this reason a newly-delivered woman is guarded very carefully during this time by her husband's family. To make things even more complicated, it seems that 'real' intercourse is not necessarily essential – sometimes 'symbolic' intercourse is all that is needed.

Hehe The Hehe people live in the central south region of Tanzania around Iringa. They have a strong sense of being Hehe, and have their own more or less distinctive social system and culture with a unifying political system. However within this group there are differences in the way of life and social systems between those who live in the drier eastern parts of the region and those who live in the wetter uplands to the west. These are caused by environmental factors as well as the effects of distance. Despite this, one observer has suggested that there is a greater unity and identity among the Hehe than there is with any other group of people.

Masai The Masai inhabit the north border area with Kenya, but are found as far south as Morogoro and Tabora. They are a spectacular group of tall, slender cattle-herders, living off milk, blood and meat. Young men leave to become *moran* before returning to begin family life. As *moran* they carry spears, wear distinctive red garments and have elaborately decorated faces, bodies and hair. The women have shaven heads and often wear many coils of beads on their necks and shoulders.

Shirazi The Shirazi is the name given to people who are a mixture of Africans and people who are said to have come at a very early time from the Shiraz area of Iran. They are divided into three 'tribes' called the Hadimu, Tumbatu and Pemba. The Africans are descendants of mainlanders who came to the islands of Zanzibar and Pemba, often as slaves although later on of their own accord. Descendants of the Shirazis have intermixed with other Swahili people and have become more African in race, speech and culture.

Swahili This is the general term given to the coastal people who have a Muslim-oriented culture. They are the descendants of generations of mixing of slaves, migrant labourers and Afro-Arabs.

Other African groups The **Hi** people are a very small group of click-speakers. They are hunter-gatherers and live on the southwest shores of Lake Eyasi, which is found in the central north part of Tanzania.

Other click speakers found in Tanzania include the **Hadzapi** and the **Sandawe**. The Hadzapi live in the same area as the Hi and the groups are believed to be closely related. The Sandawe live in the interior central region of Tanzania to the north of Dodoma. The **Dorobo** are a small group of hunter-gatherers who are found throughout Masailand and are also found in Kenya.

Non-Africans

This group makes up under 1% of the population of Tanzania and comprises Europeans, Asians and Arabs. In the mid 1970s it was estimated that there were 1,500 European citizens (compared to 23,000 in 1961 at the time of independence, and 17,000 in 1967), and about 40,000 Asians (compared to 75,000 in 1967). A recent figure for the number of Arabs is not known, although there were about 30,000 in 1967 living on the mainland. Until the 1964 revolution Arabs were the dominant group in Zanzibar although they constituted only about 20% of the population.

Land and environment

Geography

Tanzania, in the East Africa region, is a large coastal country (approximately 945,000 sq km) which lies just below the Equator and includes the islands of Pemba and Zanzibar between 1° S and 11° S latitude and 30° to 40° E longitude. It is bounded by Kenya and Uganda to the north, Rwanda, Burundi and RD Congo to the west, Zambia, Malawi and Mozambique to the south. Temperatures range from tropical to temperate moderated by altitude. Most of the country consists of high plateaux but there is a wide variety of terrain including mangrove swamps, coral reefs, plains, low hill ranges, uplands, volcanic peaks and high mountains, as well as depressions such as the Rift Valley and lakes. Dar es Salaam is the main port and there are hydro-electric schemes on the Rufiji and Pangani rivers. Mineral deposits include diamonds, gold, gemstones (tanzanite, ruby, emerald, green garnet, sapphire), graphite, gypsum, kaolin and tin.

Climate

There is a long dry season, June to October, followed by short rains in November and December. January to March can be very hot, and are followed by heavy rains in April and May. The timing of the rains has been less regular in recent years and the volume also varies from year to year, and from region to region. Short rains have tended to spread from November to May with a drier spell in January and February. In northeast Tanzania, the long rains are in March to June. A quarter of the country receives an annual average of 750 mm of rain, but in some areas it can be as high as 1,250 mm. The central area of the country is dry with less than 500 mm per annum. In many areas two harvests can be grown each year.

Books

History

Millar, C *Battle for the Bundu*. Superbly readable account of the First World War in German East Africa. Hibbert, C (1982) *Africa explored: Europeans in the Dark Continent*, London: Penguin. Fascinating detail on the early visitors and their motivations. Packenham, T(1991) *The Scramble for Africa*, London: Weidenfeld and Nicholson. The events that laid the foundations for the modern history of Tanzania.

Natural history

Grzimek, B (1959) *Serengeti Shall Not Die*, London: Collins. Classic account of the unique character of this world-famous park. Douglas-Hamilton, I (1978) *Among the Elephants*, London: Collins. Interesting perspective on elephant conservation in Lake Manyara. Goodall, J (1971) *In the Shadow of Man*, London: Collins. Gives something of the flavour of what is involved in making a life's work of studying a particular species, in this case chimpanzees.

Field guides

Dorst, J and Dandelot, PA (1970) *Field Guide to the Larger Mammals of Africa*, London: Collins. Williams, J and Arlott, NA (1980) *Field Guide to the Birds of East Africa*, London: Collins.

Tanzania

☞ **Blessing the year**

This ceremony has been observed among the Rangi and Wasi peoples living in the Mbulu District near Lake Manyara in the north. Three groups of men take part in the ceremony: they are the elders and grandfathers, the adult men (from initiation upwards) and the boys (the uninitiated). No women or people from other tribes are allowed to take part. Special dress is not worn at the ceremony. The participants gather around a sacrificial tree and the ceremony involves the chanting and singing of various songs followed by the sacrificing of a lamb. One of the men then whisks or agitates a liquid in a gourd which quickly generates a large quantity of foam. When the foam overflows on to the ground it is scattered around while the man calls out "Howa! Howa!". A number of the other men repeat the process of whisking the liquid and scattering the foam. Meanwhile the lamb is skinned and the juices of the stomach contents squeezed into a half gourd, which is then hung from a branch of

the tree using strips of the lam's skin. Beer is then distributed amongst the men. A young girl is brought to sit at the base of the tree with a gourd containing seeds from all the plants grown in the area and some beer. This will later be carried around the boundaries before being returned to the tree. The seeds will then be divided up between all the participants who will mix them with seeds when planting the next year's crops.

The 'bound-beating' party then sets off with the half gourd containing the liquid which is scattered using twigs from the tree. The party contains two leaders, hornblowers and all the other participants except the elders. As the party goes around the area to be blessed they are given local beer at the houses that they pass. Large quantities of beer are consumed and the ceremony continues late into the day. The elders meanwhile roast the remains of the lamb using firewood from the sacrificial tree. They then eat the meat and drink the beer.

Larcassam, R (1971) *Hand guide to the Butterflies of East Africa*, London: Collins. Blundell, MA (1987) *Field Guide to the Wild Flowers of East Africa*, London: Collins. Hedges, NR (1983) *Reptiles and Amphibians of East Africa*, Narobi: Kenya Literature Bureau.

Travellers' tales Waugh, E (1960) *A Tourist in Africa*, London: Chapman & Hall. A trip through Tanzania just prior to independence. Dahl, R (1986) *Going Solo*, London: Penguin. Impressions of a young man sent out to work in the colonies.

Fiction Boyd, W (1982) *An Ice-cream War*, London: Penguin. Neatly observed, humorous and sensitive tale set against the First World War campaign in East Africa. Boyd, W *Brazzaville Beach*, London: Penguin. Although written as a West African story, clearly based on Jane Goodall and the chimps of Gombe Stream.

Other guides Jafferji, J and Rees, B (1996) *Images of Zanzibar*, London: HSP Publications. Superb photographs, good introduction to, and souvenir of, Zanzibar. Spectrum (1992) *Guide to Tanzania and Pemba*, Nairobi: Camerapix. Quite glorious photographs that serve to capture the special flavour of Tanzania and Zanzibar.

Uganda

5

Uganda

Uganda, straddling the equator high on the central African plateau and perched on the northern shore of Lake Victoria, is marketing itself hard as the ultimate eco-destination. Its gorillas represent perhaps the most powerful eco-image of them all. However, few tourists seem willing to make the journey and this is a shame as Uganda deserves better: it has a fantastic climate, an ever-changing landscape, and people who are honest, polite and genuinely pleased to help. Perhaps Uganda has suffered by being too honest – the negatives always seem to be widely reported in the foreign press while the positives never appear.

There are lots of positives and this becomes apparent as soon as you step off the plane. Well-maintained roads with immaculately clean verges immediately give a good impression. A huge array of greens, mixed with the terracotta red of the soil, is easy on the eye and, if you are looking for personal service in relaxed surroundings, then Uganda could well be for you. Above all, Uganda works: it is well organized and efficient. True, there are security problems, but Uganda has made a tremendous recovery under President Museveni. The economy is booming, facilities for tourists are as good as anywhere in East Africa, law and order has been restored and, apart from some parts of the north, northeast and southwest, it is once again a secure country for travellers.

Essentials

Planning your trip

Where to go

Most travellers visit Uganda for two reasons: gorillas and whitewater rafting. Neither is particularly cheap with gorilla permits now US$250 per person and whitewater rafting around US$65-95 per person, depending on the operator. Both are highly recommended though.

There is lots more to the country although, in all honesty, the wildlife can be a bit disappointing. The one animal that you will be guaranteed to see is the Ugandan kob, which is everywhere. Many animals were killed during the war years but numbers are now rapidly recovering. The problem is that no single national park has the same number of species of animals as you would get in the Masai Mara. This, however, can be seen as an advantage as, with patience, it becomes much more of a game tracking experience – there are no animals by appointment here and a distinct lack of zebra-camouflaged Toyota vans. To overcome this, the Uganda Tourist Board has developed the **Uganda Trail**. The aim is to let you see the bio-diversity of the country by visiting seven national parks on a 12-day trip. The itinerary is: **Day 1** at **Lake Mburo National Park** (impala, eland, klipspringer, waterbuck and zebra); **Day 2 Lake Bunyonyi** (birding); **Days 3 and 4 Bwindi** (gorilla tracking); **Day 5 Queen Elizabeth National Park** (hippos, lions, elephants and buffalo); **Day 6 Maramagambo Forest** (chimp tracking, black and white colubus monkeys and other forest creatures); **Day 7 Queen Elizabeth National Park crater lake area**; **Days 8 and 9 Kibale Forest** (chimps) and Semliki Wildlife Reserve (shoebill stork, Uganda kob, buffalo, forest elephants, birding and leopard); **Days 10 and 11 Murchison Falls National Park** (hippos, elephants, lion, giraffe and species of antelope); **Day 12** return to **Kampala**. It is true that this is an excellent way of seeing what Uganda has to offer but there is a lot of travelling involved – most days 3-4 hours and some days as much as six hours. This can be very tiring with only limited periods for relaxation. It does, however, offer you the chance to experience the Ugandan countryside and, although it may be a cliché, this really does seem to change around every corner. Some of it is absolutely stunning and only rarely is it boring. Shorter trips are available and all are documented on the UTB website (see below). It is pitched at the upmarket traveller and is consequently quite expensive if you are staying at the top end lodges. However, with the exception of the day spent at Semliki, it would be possible to go around on a low budget staying at the campsite within the national parks. Often these have comfortable bandas attached.

Uganda scores heavily with birders. Because of the topography, habitats change quickly inside a short distance and consequently the number of species in a particular area can be huge. Practically every lodge claims that there are around 400 species in the countryside around it. Indeed, several claim that you will be able to spot over 300 species in a day. Many are endemic to East Africa as a whole but there are maybe 100 or so that are only found in Uganda, the most famous of which is the shoebill stork. There are plans to introduce bird-watching trips by canoe down the Nile at Jinja, and possibly above the Murchison Falls.

There is some excellent sport fishing on the Nile (especially at Murchison Falls), where huge Nile perch are regularly caught. Several lodges are attempting to moor boats on the river and capitalize on this market. The annual fishing championship has been recently reintroduced. Fishing is also good in lakes Victoria and Albert. This is especially true now that the problem of the water hyacinth (see page 720) has been largely overcome.

Cultural walks are also on the increase and are being encouraged by the tourist board. These are cheap and often give a fascinating insight into Ugandan village life. Guides will show you the many different plants and how they are used for medicine as well as for food. Often they finish with a traditional village meal of *matoke*, peanut stew and plantains.

Climbing and trekking have come back on to the list of options. Mount Elgon with its caldera is quite popular and Rwenzori National Park reopened in July 2001 after four years. This offers some exceptional walking and it is possible to climb above 5,000 m. Ugandan troops have been stationed in the area to prevent actions by the rebel ADF. Permits are required and cost about US$350 per person.

There is not a huge amount to see in the towns outside of Kampala. Most of what there is revolves around the burial grounds of the kings of the various kingdoms. The towns themselves have largely grown up in colonial times and are pleasant enough to wander around and usually have interesting markets.

When to go

The heavy rainy season is March to May, and there are lighter rains in November and December. Generally there is some sunshine each day, even in the rainy seasons. From a practical point of view, it is probably best to try to avoid March-May, as the murram roads can become bogged (with lorries having to be dug out) and so journey times are extended. Gorilla tracking can become difficult as the jungle trails are very steep and it is difficult to keep your footing on the slippery slopes.

Tours and tour operators

There are a number of tour operators in Uganda. Many of them are concessionaires for the lodges within the national parks. Their main business, though, tends to be running safaris. The Uganda Tourist Board publishes a list of the members of the Uganda tour operators in its brochure. Recommended operators are: *Abercrombie & Kent*, *Afri Tours and Travel*, *African Pearl Safaris* and *Green Wilderness Group*. If you are on a very limited budget contact *Nile River Explorers* who will be able to give you an up-to-date overview of travel around the country, book you into other backpacking establishments, and arrange gorilla permits. Also recommended are *Adrift* (UK representative), Safari Drive Ltd, Wessex House, 127 High St, Hungerford, Berkshire RG17 0DL, T01488-684509, F685055, www.adrift.co.uk (whitewater rafting specialists) and *Volcanoes Safaris*, PO Box 16345, London Sw1X OZD, UK, T0870-8708480, F0870-8708481, www.volcanoessafaris.com

For tour companies in Uganda, see Kampala, page 637; Kasese, page 700 and Fort Portal, page 710

Finding out more

There are a number of quite good websites that offer information on Uganda. Among these are the Uganda Tourist Board site, **www.visituganda.com**, which has information on the Uganda Trail as well as the latest tourist information and press releases. Another site in the same vein is **www.uganda.co.ug**, which has a good overview of the country as well as information on cultural items such as dance. Sports fans will get a good idea of what is going on by looking at **www.sport.co.ug** News stories from around the region can be found at **ug.orientation.com**, together with some background material. Both of the national dailies have sites: the *New Vision* at **www.newvision.co.ug** and the *Monitor* at **www.monitor.co.ug**

Ugandan Embassies and High Commissions around the world have a tourism attaché who will advise (see page 604). The main *Uganda Tourist Board* is at IPS Building, Parliament Av 14, PO Box 7211, T342196/7, F342188. Other sources are: *Mountain Clubs of Uganda*, PO Box 4692, Kampala; *Safari Uganda Association*, PO Box 3530, Kampala, T233566, F235770; *Uganda Tourist Association*, PO Box 5011, T286353; *Wildlife Clubs of Uganda*, PO Box 4596, T534485; *Uganda Wildlife Authority*, Plot 3 Kintu Rd, PO Box 3530, Kampala, T346287.

Language

The official language is English, and it is widely spoken, although for most Ugandans it is their second language. However, as there are well over 50 dialects it does provide a unifying language. Swahili is also spoken (see box, page 320), but not as widely as in Kenya and Tanzania. Many Ugandans also speak Luganda.

Uganda

Embassies and consulates

For overseas representation in Uganda, see page 640

Canada, 231 Coburg St, Ottawa, T7897797, F2326689.
Ethiopia,* PO Box 5644, Addis Ababa, T513088, F514355.
France, 13 Av Raymond Poincaré, 7116 Paris, T47274680, F47559394.
Germany, Düerenstr. 44, 5300 Bonn 2, T228-355027, F228-351692.
Italy, Via 9 Pisanelli 1, Rome 00196, T63605211, F63225220, F330970.
Kenya, PO Box 60853, Phoenix House, Kenyatta Av, Nairobi, T2-330801.

RD Congo, 17 Av Tombalbaye/Av de Travailure, BP 1086, Kinshasha, T243-227740
Rwanda, Av de la Paix, Kigali. BP 656, T76495.
Tanzania, Extelcom Building, Floor 7, Samora Av, Dar es Salaam, PO Box 6237, T022-231004
United Kingdom, Uganda House, Trafalgar Square, London WC2 5DX, T0171-8395783, F0171-8398925.
USA, 5909 16th St, NW, Washington DC 20011, T7260416, F7261727, also New York.

* office does not issue visas.

Disabled travellers

There are some hotels such as the *Sheraton* in Kampala and *Paraa Lodge* in Murchison Falls National Park that cater for disabled travellers in wheelchairs. The Uganda Tourist Board will be able to advise further.

Working in the country

There is a vast amount of foreign aid being ploughed into Uganda and with it there are opportunities to work within the country as an expatriate. Several companies are offering 'gap year' projects but, because there are few tourists around at the moment, casual work is hard to get. *Nile River Explorers* are working closely with the local community to paint and help with maintenance projects. They have an arrangement with several overland companies that overlanders will do a day or two of voluntary work. Its good fun and rewarding. Email Hannah on rafting@starcom.co.ug if you are interested, or check out her website www.softpowerexpeditions.com

Before you travel

Getting in

Visas   List of countries whose nationals do **not** require a visa to enter Uganda: Angola, Antigua, Bahamas, Barbados, Belize, Burundi, Comoros, Cyprus, Eritrea, Fiji, Gambia, Grenada, Italy (Diplomatic Passport holders only), Jamaica, Kenya, Lesotho, Malawi, Malta, Mauritius, Madagascar, Rwanda, Seychelles, Sierra Leone, Singapore, Solomon Islands, St Vincent and Grenadine, Swaziland, Tanzania, Tonga, Vanuatu, Zambia and Zimbabwe.

Nationals of countries not listed above have to obtain a visa prior to their travel to Uganda. The only exemption is if you are in transit and remaining inside the airport. Should you be in doubt as to whether or not you require a visa, consult your nearest Uganda Diplomatic or Consular Mission. In Spring 2001, it was possible to obtain visas at Entebbe airport and other border crossings providing you had the correct documentation. The process was very quick and easy.

A visa application must include a valid passport for at least six months; a completed application form; two passport-size photographs; the appropriate fee; letter of invitation or introduction if travelling on business; a registered, stamped, self-addressed envelope if applying by post. Visa applications are processed in one to two working days. Visas are issued by the Ugandan representatives (listed on page 604).

Visa Fees US$15 Transit visa (valid for 24 hours); US$20 Student visa (valid for three months from date of issue); US$30 Single-entry visa (valid for three months from date of issue); US$80 Multiple entry (valid for six months from date of issue); US$160 Multiple entry (valid for one year from date of issue).

Transit Visa Applicants are required to have obtained entry visa for the country of destination. A valid airline air-ticket to country of destination has to be produced on application.

Journalists are required to notify, in advance, and obtain accreditation and clearance from the Director of Information, Ministry of Information and Broadcasting, PO Box 7142, Kampala, T254410, F256888.

Customs

Duty-free Cigarettes and tobacco 250 g; wines and spirits 1 litre; toilet water and perfume 0.5 litre (perfume 0.25 litre max). Equipment for personal use. **Pets** require permit in advance from Ministry of Agriculture, Animal Industry and Fisheries, PO Box 102, Entebbe, T20981/9. **Game Trophies** Permit required from Chief Game Warden, The Ministry of Tourism, Wildlife and Antiquities, PO Box 4241, 1 Parliament Av, T232971/2, F242247.

Vaccinations

A certificate indicating vaccination against yellow fever is required.

Money

Currency

The Ugandan shilling floats against other currencies, and the exchange rate can be expected to depreciate steadily as prices have been rising faster in Uganda than in the rest of the world. Best exchange rates are offered on US$50 or US$100 notes. The rates can be up to 5-10% better in Kampala. It can be difficult to change both cash and travellers' cheques away from Kampala, for instance in Fort Portal, where the rates are particularly low.

ATMs

It is possible to get money out on most credit cards at *Barclays* on Kampala Rd (but there can be long queues at weekends). This costs an additional US$3 for checking your card with Nairobi! Other banks' ATMs usually only accept local cards. The *Nile Bank* is the local agent for *Western Union*. Asian hoteliers and traders will occasionally exchange US dollars for cash at reasonable rates – however, such transactions may be illegal.

Banks

Money can be exchanged in banks or in the foreign exchange bureaux that have recently been established. The bureaux tend to offer better rates than the banks and to stay open longer hours. However some of the commission rates charged are steep. Money can be changed in the larger hotels 24 hours a day (although this is often restricted to their guests and they may not have sufficient cash before lunch). There is now no effective black market, and persons approaching visitors in the street and offering implausibly favourable rates of exchange are invariably engaged in some exercise designed to cheat the traveller.

Currently most transactions are carried out with Ugandan shilling notes although there is a coinage. Notes are in the following dominations: 1,000, 5,000, 10,000 and 20,000. When changing money you will normally be given high denomination notes. These can be difficult to change so make sure that you have an adequate supply of 1,000 and 5,000 shilling notes. Coins are 50, 100, 200, and 500 shillings. These have replaced the 5, 10, 50, 100, 200 and 500 shilling notes that were withdrawn on 31 December 2000 by the Bank of Uganda.

US dollars are the best form of cash to carry. It is helpful to have some US currency in small denomination notes to avoid changing too much at an unfavourable rate when that is the only option, and for last minute transactions when leaving. However it is difficult to exchange or spend bills of denominations of less than US$20.

Credit cards

Credit cards are accepted by the large hotels, airlines, main car hire firms, tour operators and travel agents. American Express is the most widely accepted card, with Visa, Diners and Mastercard also taken by some establishments.

Uganda

NB Dollar bills with the slightest mark or tear will be rejected – even if they pass the 'electronic counterfeit detectors' that are in use everywhere. Take notes issued after 1990 with the security strip.

Cost of living On a strict budget, it is possible to stay in backpacker accommodation, travel and eat for US$20 a day. If you go for a slightly better hotel prices start to escalate markedly. To eat well and travel in reasonable comfort allow US$50-60 per person a day. However, if you are going on a safari with an upmarket travel company you can at least double this figure. In addition you will pay US$150-200 for a car and driver. Finally do not forget to allow for national park fees, rafting and gorilla and chimp-tracking permits. These could easily amount to US$400 per person if you go to a number of parks.

Getting there

Air

Specialist agencies for discounted fares, see page 31

Direct flights are only available from three cities in **Europe** – *British Airways* London; *Air France* Paris; and *Lufthansa* Frankfurt. There are no direct flights from America.

The only direct flights between Uganda and other **African countries** are: *Ethiopian Airlines* Addis Ababa; *EgyptAir* Cairo; *Air Zambia* Lusaka; *Sudan Airways* Khartoum; *Kenya Airways* Nairobi; and, since December 2000, *South African Airways* have been flying direct to Johannesburg three times a week.

For all other points of departure, connecting flights are necessary. Deals are often available at Kampala travel agents and these can sometimes be much better value than those on offer in Nairobi. If you are only entering Uganda for a short trip (to see the gorillas for instance), it may pay you to check this out. An economical way to access Uganda is to obtain a cheap excursion flight to Nairobi and then to travel overland or take a local connecting flight with *Kenya Airways*.

Road

Kenya There are buses that run from Nairobi to Kampala, crossing at **Malaba** and **Tororo**, taking about 15 hours and costing around US$15. There is a variety of standards of service. *Akamba* seem to be one of the best. They leave Kampala at 0700 and 1500 daily and have their offices on De Winton Road close to the National Theatre. It is possible to do the journey in stages in minibuses or Peugeot taxis, but buses are more comfortable and safer.

There are also border crossings at **Busia**, no through buses, but convenient for Kisumu; and at **Suam** to the north of Mount Elgon.

Tanzania The route is south from Masaka to Bukoba. The road is not very good and this crossing is not used very much, although traffic is increasing. There are *matatus* (minibuses) from Masaka that go as far as Kyotera and from there you will have to get a lift to the border, crossing at **Mutukula**, with one of the trucks going across – this is not usually a problem. If you get to the border shortly before dark you may want to stay at the small guesthouse on the Uganda side of the border – there is nothing on the Tanzania side until you get to Bukoba. For crossing the border you will need to have patience as you go through rather a long drawn-out process. The road on the Tanzania side is worse than the Uganda road but there are four-wheel drive vehicles operating on the route. They go when full.

Rwanda In normal times, there are frequent daily minibuses between Kabale in Uganda and the **Katuna** border post, the trip taking an hour. There are frequent minibuses to Kigali from Katuna until mid afternoon and they take about two hours. Check locally.

The other crossing is from Kisoro in Uganda to Ruhengeri in Rwanda via **Kyanika**. This route is not as busy and it may be harder to get a ride from here. There is an hour time difference between Uganda and Rwanda, Uganda being one hour ahead.

Touching down

Electricity *220 volts. You will encounter a variety of sockets, particularly in the older hotels, and an adaptor is advisable.*
IDD *256. Ringing tones are either a double ring repeated regularly or long equal tones separated with long pauses. Equal tones with equal pauses indicate engaged.*

Hours of business *Business and offices Monday-Friday 0800-1245 and 1400-1700.* **Banks** *Monday-Friday 0830-1400. Saturday 0900-1200.* **Post Offices** *Monday-Friday 0830-1700.* **Shops** *Generally 0800-1700 or 1800 Monday-Saturday.*
Official time *Three hours ahead of GMT.*

RD Congo The most reliable crossing is **Kisoro** to Rutshuru. Minibuses from Kisoro to the border, about 10 km and costing US$0.50, and on the RD Congo side a motor-taxi (motorbike) to Rutshuru.

Alternatively Kasese to Beni via **Kasindi** There is infrequent public transport along this route. Some minibuses from Kasese to the border at Kasindi. The leg from Kasindi to Beni can be awkward. There are some minibuses, but a motor-taxi (motorbike) is probably the best possibility. There are small hotels on both the Uganda and RD Congo sides of the border in case you are stuck there late at night.

Finally, it is possible to cross the border from Kasese to Rutshuru, the border post being at **Ishasha**. There are infrequent minibuses on this route and hitching is possible.

The crossing to the north of Lake Albert at **Arua**, although possible, is extremely difficult to access and security is less certain.

Sudan The current impossible political situation in Southern Sudan rules out the routes from Juba to Gulu, which in normal times allow crossings at **Moyo** and **Nimule** to the west and east of the Nile respectively.

Vehicle entry If you are driving into Uganda, you must be registered in your home country, with registration plates, log book, and insurance against third party risks. A 30-day licence will cost between US$20 (2,000 kg vehicle) and US$100 (10,000 kg).

Train

In 1997 the passenger rail service in Uganda was discontinued. There has only been a freight service since then.

Touching down

Airport information

Uganda's international airport is at Entebbe, 30 km from the capital, Kampala. It is an efficient, modern airport with a wide range of facilities including some excellent and good value duty free shops. **Transport to town** A taxi to Entebbe costs US$3 and then a *matatu* (minibus) to Kampala US$1. Taxi from airport to Kampala US$20. *Thomas Cook International Timetable* – Table 3295 lists a limited Public Bus Service, and *Sophies Motel* in Entebbe and the *Sheraton Hotel* in Kampala run a courtesy bus to and from the airport (see page 638). It takes about 30 minutes.

There is a **departure tax** of US$20 on leaving Uganda by air, although this is now included in the cost of your air ticket. **Airport tax**

The **Uganda Tourist Board** has an office in Kampala, T256 41-342196, and gives out good, impartial information. They will also advise on the security situation. It has to be said that they can be a little 'economical' with their advice and so it is best to check with your consular official **Tourist information**

Uganda

Uganda

in Kampala if you are worried about this. They also regularly inspect hotels to make sure that standards are kept high. Up country there is little in the way of tourist offices. Instead an informal network exists to help travellers and most travel agents can quite easily find out information for you. The backpackers' network seems to be particularly efficient in this respect.

If you are going on safari, you may well want to take a good map. The Nelles map of Uganda at a scale of 1:700,000 is particularly clear and fairly accurate. The Macmillan Uganda Travellers map is at a smaller scale of 1:1,350,000 but has the advantage of having a number of national parks and a large map of Kampala centre on the reverse. These can be difficult to find and it is worth looking in the airport shop in Nairobi for them if you fly via Kenya.

Local customs and laws

As in much of Africa, it is considered a courtesy and a mark of respect to dress neatly and smartly. If you have an appointment with a senior government official or member of the business community, men should wear a collar and tie or safari suit; women should be conservatively dressed with a medium length skirt.

It may come as a surprise that a considerable number of Ugandans are Muslim. This is a result of Idi Amin's policies in the 1960s when he tried to outlaw Christianity. Most towns have mosques and Muslim schools. If entering a religious site (including the tombs of the kings), you will be asked to remove your shoes. Churches are often overfull on the big religious occasions such as Easter and it is quite normal for services to be broadcast to those on the street outside.

Tipping It is customary to give waiters and porters a small tip. More of a problem is what to do about national park guides, as you may have perhaps six or seven people accompanying you when you go gorilla tracking. The best guide is to remember that many will earn no more than USh40,000 per month. Tips can therefore be quite small, maybe USh1,000 per person, and should be given to the head guide who will distribute them.

Prohibitions Be careful about accepting any wildlife object from villagers and guides. They should be left where found. Your bags may be searched when you leave Entebbe airport and, if you are found with any bones, this can be awkward and may lead to some form of fine.

Safety

Overall, Uganda is very safe, with far less petty crime than is found in Kenya. Bag snatching remains uncommon. Lack of tourists means that there are virtually no beggars or hawkers and there is no real problem about wandering around the streets and market areas *provided* you take sensible precautions – don't carry huge amounts of money or flash your camera around. Every shop, store, restaurant, hotel and even the hospital has armed guards, which may alarm you at first, but you quickly get used to the sight of guns. It is wise to take taxis at night outside the centre of towns; not to walk about in dark or deserted areas; and to be careful about your belongings in crowded areas.

Because of Uganda's history, much has been made in the foreign press of rebel activity. There is no doubt that this does exist. However, it is easy to get it out of proportion. The government has cracked down hard on the LRA in the north and the ADF in the southwest to the extent that rebel numbers are now very small in both areas. In addition, all lodges and campsites have army outposts stationed nearby and you will be accompanied by soldiers when gorilla tracking. The best advice before travelling up country is to consult the resident consular official (British High Commission in Kampala, T257054) as well as the tour operators, most of whom will give good, unbiased advice. You are advised to check with your External Affairs Ministry before visiting these potential hotspots.

Where to stay

The most luxurious hotels used by business travellers and upmarket tourists have prices set in dollar terms, and are similar in cost and value to those in Kenya. On the other hand, devaluation of the Ugandan currency has made most other accommodation, particularly that used by ordinary Ugandans, good value. The price of hotel accommodation in local currency tends not to change too often in Uganda. The prices in this guide are given in US$, and, because the value of the Ugandan shilling has depreciated against the dollar by about 20% over the last 18 months, the effect is that many of the prices quoted (correct at the time of research) have now become significantly cheaper as a result of the favourable exchange rate. There is plenty of budget accommodation at less than US$10 a night, and reasonably comfortable lodgings can be had for between US$20 and US$30. Accommodation in the parks is good value if you camp or stay in the park bandas. However, the best lodges are expensive at around US$150 for a double room on full board, see Sleeping classification, page 36. One of their charms is that they often have no electricity and you will be entertained as the guest of the owner or manager. Meals are taken around a large table with other guests and are usually very simple (with no choice) but are delicious. Make sure that you inform them of any special dietary requirements (including if you are a vegetarian) when you check in. Avoid drinking wine at these establishments; it is very expensive.

Hotels
*For price codes:
see inside front cover*

Getting around

Most travel in Uganda is by bus, car or plane. Trains are no longer an option as, since 1997, the Uganda Rail Network has only operated a freight service. Steamers, ferries and small cargo boats sail between ports on the shore of Lake Victoria and the Ssese Islands.

Air

Several companies now offer flights internally, including Eagle Airlines, United and CEI Aviation (see page 639). Flying can be a real option if there are four or five of you, especially if you are on a tight schedule, as driving times on unsealed roads can be very long particularly during the wet season. It is also possible to charter light aircraft to fly to airstrips around the country (see Kampala page 639). These are located in **East** Tororo and Moroto; **North** Soroti, Lira, Gulu, Chobe, West Kasese; and **Southwest** Mbarara and Kisoro. The closest airfields to the National Parks are Pakuba – a 2,000-m grass runway – and the 800-m grass strip at Paraa for Murchison Falls National Park. Apoka has an 1,100-m grass strip adjacent to the Kidepo Valley National Park facilities. Myeya has a 770-m grass strip, the Kasese airstrip is a 1,570-m grass runway and Ishasha has a 900-m grass strip, and these are the closest airfields for the Queen Elizabeth National Park. Semliki Game Reserve has a 1,300-m grass runway 10 minutes away from the Lodge. Mount Elgon National Park is served by the 1,860 m sealed runway at Soroti. The Bwindi Impenetrable National Park has a small airfield at Kayonza with a 740 m grass strip. Mgahinga National Park is served by the sealed 550-m airstrip at Kisoro.

Road

There are good roads on the main routes, and travel is comfortable and swift. Care is needed though as accidents are waiting to happen, with overloaded charcoal lorries often tangling with speeding *matatus*. Further hazards are bicycles carrying *matoke* (green bananas) to market – each one usually has three 'stems' and it is clearly back-breaking work to push them uphill. Each district is obliged to keep the verges clean, free from rubbish and the grass cut. This is done even in the most isolated of places and the result creates an excellent impression. Away from the main roads, the roads are constructed from murram. This is generally well maintained although there are some notorious stretches where travel is very slow, bumpy and generally pretty uncomfortable. In the dry season dust is a big problem, while in the wet

Uganda

Uganda

lorries often get bogged down and, as the roads are usually only single tracked, this can cause real problems.

Buses are a safer and cheaper way to travel. Bus travel is roughly US$0.02 per km. Most buses and *matatus* wait until they are full before departure. That can take a long time on Sun and holidays. However a few bus companies adhere strictly to listed departure times, so avoid being late. Post office buses are generally safely driven and well maintained (see page 638).

Matatus are minibuses or converted pick-up trucks or cars or station wagons carrying passengers. They are privately owned, and operate on the basis of departing from the terminus when full. Minibuses are fine for short journeys; a Peugeot station wagon is more comfortable and safer for a longer journey. Costs are roughly US$0.04 per km. *Matatus* in Uganda tend to be better than in Kenya. Nissans with individual (rather than bench) seats are frequently used.

Taxis are generally available in large towns. Always advisable to agree the fare before departure. In small towns 'taxi' mopeds and bicycles are common. These can be useful for travel where public transport is scarce, for example Entebbe/Kasenyi (for Ssese Islands) or Sanga/Lake Mburu National Park. Bicycle taxis are called ***boda-bodas***.

Car hire There is a wide choice of tariffs and some extra charges you might not expect (for example 'up country driving'). Prices are often quoted in US$, but have to be paid in local currency, converted at a rate determined by the local operative. Drivers are an asset in case of a breakdown, but some can be obstructive and morose. Self-drive saloon US$50-60 per day, plus US$0.40-.50 per km per day over 100 km, plus tax (15%). Toyota landcruiser, including driver, US$150 per day, plus US$0.60 per km after 100 km per day, including fuel. Take great care when hiring vehicles as they are not always well maintained.

Train

There has been no passenger rail service in Uganda since 1997. The network is now used only for freight transportation.

Keeping in touch

Communications

Internet Internet is really only a viable option in Kampala, where there are several excellent outlets that provide quick access. Connection rates vary but you should expect to pay about US$4 for a half-hour connection. There are often special deals at weekends and holidays. There are other outlets around the country in the bigger towns but the line charges are so prohibitive that they mostly do not offer an internet service. They will send and receive specific emails, but this is on a 'batched' basis. You will need to call in the following day to see if you have a reply and you are unlikely to be able to pick up messages in your hotmail folder. These are usually charged at about US$0.75 per message. No doubt in an emergency, they would be persuadable (if the price was right!).

Post Services are reliable and letters take about 10 days airmail from Europe. There is a Poste Restante service in Kampala (Poste Restante, GPO, Kampala Rd, Kampala). Most post offices offer a fax service – cost US$2 per page outgoing overseas, US$0.50 for an incoming fax. Postcards and letters cost US$0.50.

International calls can be made from the GPO office on Kampala Rd in Kampala. Phonecards are required – offered by Uganda Telecom and private companies. Newly privatized services are also available using pre-paid phone cards. Some, like MTN, offer half-price international calls at the weekends. There has recently been an explosion of mobile phones and it is certainly worth checking before you leave home whether your own mobile will work in Uganda. There are currently three networks: UTL Telecel, Mango and MTN. Coverage around the country is pretty good and a signal can even be obtained in a number of national parks. This can be problematic though, as some of the magic of observing the animals is destroyed if your driver is having a telephone conversation! It is possible to hire a mobile from the airport or other outlets such as the *Sheraton Hotel*. The deposit (refundable) is around US$130 and there is a service fee of US$47. A one-day rental costs US$4, seven days US$24 and 30 days US$46. Call charges within Uganda are about US$0.20 per minute, to Europe about US$1 per minute and US$1.40 to North America.

Telephone
*Country code: 256
Access to Celtel
network 075;
MTN network 077*

2- and 3-digit phone numbers need to be connected by the operator as they are part of the older network

Media

The main newspaper is *New Vision*, published in English. Although it is government-owned it has considerable editorial freedom but carries no advertising. It contains good listings of upcoming events in Uganda. Its rival, *The Monitor*, is independent, carries advertising and is widely available in Kampala as well as up country. Both have some coverage of international news and sport. Most Ugandans seem to buy both papers!

Newspapers

Radio broadcasts mainly in English, but some in Swahili and Luganda. **BBC World Service** is broadcast to Uganda, and can be received on a short waveband radio, see guide, page 38.

Radio & television

There is a colour television service run by the government and broadcasting for about six hours every evening, mostly in English. Satellite is widely available now and a number of hotels and bars have widescreen televisions for watching big sporting events.

Food and drink

Simple meals are good value, but the range and variety of food is limited. The food in the larger hotels is often a buffet. If there are not too many guests, this can stand around for a little while with the obvious health implications. There is usually a choice of chicken, fish (tilapia is very good) and steak (which is often goat). Breakfast is usually quite large and you will be asked how you like your eggs. Spanish omelettes are very popular in this respect. Most hotels and lodges will prepare a packed lunch if you are travelling. Packed breakfasts (for an early morning game drive) can be interesting! Local food includes *posho* (known as *ugali* in other parts of East Africa), which is maize ground and boiled to form a stiff dough: and *matoke*, which is boiled plantains (cooking bananas). Indian additions to the menu include *chapatti*, a flat bread, and *pilau*, which is rice and meat together with a vegetable curry, see restaurant classification page 39.

Uganda produces a range of soft drinks and beers that are quite acceptable and good value compared with the imported alternatives. There are two main breweries, Bell and Nile (which are based in Jinja), both of which produce a range of lagers that are sold in 500-ml bottles. Bell also produces a draught beer that is quite widely available in Kampala. Nile is more widely distributed up country with their Club brand being especially popular. This has won several brewing prizes internationally. Imported wines, spirits and beers are widely available but very expensive.

Uganda

National park by-laws

- *Camping and camp fires permitted at official sites only.*
- *Off-road driving prohibited.*
- *Driving between 1915 and 0630 is forbidden.*
- *Blowing of motor horns is prohibited.*

- *A speed limit of 40 kph should be observed.*
- *Carrying of arms or ammunition is forbidden.*
- *Dogs are not allowed in the parks.*
- *Littering in the parks is an offence.*

Shopping

With so few tourists around, there is not a very highly developed craft market, and you will certainly not be hassled wandering around the streets. Outside of Kampala, the lodges usually have a shop of some sort in which crafts are displayed, but the best option by far is to head for the African Crafts Village in Kampala (see page 621). Here you will find a range of goods, many of which are imported from Kenya and the Congo. If you want something authentically Ugandan, look out for the nicely woven pots and mats. These can also be found on the road to Mbarara at the equator, as well as at Kinoni. Drums can also be bought on this road at Mpigi. Some bargaining is possible. There are craft shops in Kampala where you can find really nice pieces of Congolese carving. You do need to know what you are looking for though: try to get some local knowledge as to whose work is reputable.

Entertainment and nightlife

This varies from the sublime to the ridiculous. In Kampala and larger towns, discos are very much the order of the day especially on Friday and Saturday nights. In theory the style of music varies from night to night – house one night and African the next. In practice it tends to merge! It is extremely loud and goes on until dawn. No hotels in the centre of Kampala are immune. As one expat said "You either learn to dance or move out!" Once out of the towns, there is virtually no nightlife. Occasionally the manager of a lodge will arrange for a local dance group to put on an entertainment. As there are very few guests around, they are difficult to avoid. The best advice is to listen and watch for an hour or so and then gracefully depart for bed. This will not cause offence and the dancers and drummers will continue to perform for the staff! Otherwise you will be left to gaze at the stars, which are truly spectacular: you won't believe how milky the Milky Way really is.

Holidays and festivals

1 January *New Year's Day*; 26 January *NRM Day*; March/April (variable) *Good Friday*; March/April (variable) *Easter Monday*; 1 May *International Labour Day*; 3 June *Uganda Martyrs' Day*; 9 June *National Heroes Day*; 9 October *Independence Day*; 25 December *Christmas Day*; 26 December *Boxing Day*; (variable) *Idd-el-Fitr*; (variable) *Iddi Adhuha*.

National parks and reserves

The national parks covered in this guide are in the west and northwest Queen Elizabeth National Park, page 691; Rwenzori Mountains National Park, page 701; Kibale Forest National Park, page 717; Semliki National Park, page 713; Murchison Falls National Park, page 679; Kidepo Valley National Park is in northern Uganda, page 669; Mount Elgon National Park in eastern Uganda, abuts the Kenyan border, page 662; Lake Mburo National Park is located in central southern Uganda, page 730; Bwindi (Impenetrable) Forest National Park is located in the far southwest of

Uganda, page 743; **Mgahinga Gorilla National Park**, page 748, located south of Bwindi, offers both gorillas and volcanoes; and **Katonga Wildlife Reserve**, page 687, has an unusual wetlands canal trail by canoe.

Then there are the tropical rainforest reserves – **Mabira**, page 628, **Mpanga**, page 723, **Budongo**, page 677, **Kalinzu**, page 689, and **Kasyoha Kitomi**, page 689, where tourist facilities have recently been developed. The **Ssese Islands Reserve**, page 727, are a lovely group of islands on northwest Lake Victoria. **Semliki Wildlife Reserve**, page 713, previously called the Toro Game Reserve (not to be confused with the national park of the same name), is located in the west. Other designated parks or reserves (see map) do not have any facilities and are, at present, unpromising to visit.

For up-to-date information on the parks, and to buy a gorilla tracking permit, you should visit the *Uganda Wildlife Authority*, Kintu Rd, Kampala, 300 m past the main entrance of the *Sheraton Hotel*, PO Box 3530, T041-346290, F346291, www.visituganda.com

Uganda national parks & game reserves

◆	National parks & game reserves	9	Mount Elgon NP	17	Ssese Islands
1	Kidepo Valley NP	10	Semliki Forest NP	18	Lake Mburo NP
2	Ajai GR	11	Rwenzori Mountains NP	19	Bwindi NP
3	Achwa Lolim GR	12	Semliki Valley NP	20	Mgahinga Gorilla NP
4	Matheniko GR	13	Kibale Forest NP	21	Mabira Forest Reserve
5	Murchison Falls NP	14	Katonga Wildlife Reserve	22	Mpanga Forest Reserve
6	Bokora Corridor GR	15	Queen Elizabeth NP		
7	Pian Upe GR	16	Chambura River Gorge		
8	Budongo Forest Reserve				

0 km 50
0 miles 50

Uganda

Ugandan park fees

Prices are per person and subject to change

Category A *(entrance per day)*
Murchison Falls, Queen Elizabeth,
Bwindi Impenetrable and
Mgahinga Gorilla national parks

Adult	US$15
Youth 5-18 years	US$8
Children under 5 years	Free

Category B
All other protected areas in the UWA system

Adult	US$7
Youth 5-18 years	US$3
Children under 5 years	Free

Ranger guide fees

Per half day	US$10

Accommodation

	Single	Double	Triple	Extra person
Category A: en-suite	20,000/-	30,000/-	40,000/-	5,000/-
Category B: basic/traditional	10,000/-	15,000/-	20,000/-	3,000/-

NB *Advanced booking requires a 50% non-refundable advance payment.*
Prices are per person unless otherwise stated

Do-it-yourself camping

Per person per night	US$10

Vehicle entry fees
Only for Murchison, Queen Elizabeth, Kidepo, Lake Mburo national parks and all wildlife reserves

Motorcycles	US$20
Minibuses, cars and pick-ups	US$30
Rescue fees	US$10

NB *Foreign-registered vehicles carrying tourists are allowed in the country as long as the driver has an international driving licence and buys at the point of entry a temporary vehicle licence, which is determined by the Uganda Revenue Authority based on the capacity, purpose of use and duration of stay. The minimal sum is US$50*

Gorilla tracking
Bwindi Impenetrable National Park*
US$250 plus park entry fee advance booking
US$150 stand-by
*US$30 non-refundable booking fee for advance booking 6 months to 1 year
Mgahinga Gorilla National Park* US$175
*US$50 deposit fee for 2 months' advance booking

Chimpanzee tracking

Kyambura Gorge	US$30

Primate walk

Kibale National Park	US$10

Launch cruise/boat trip	US$20
Queen Elizabeth National Park *(2 hours)*	
Minimum charge per cruise US$120	
Murchison Falls National Park *(3 hours)*	
Minimum charge per cruise US$150	
Lake Mburo National Park *(2 hours)*	
	US$40 per trip

Guided nature walk
All protected areas

	Half day (up to 5 hours)	Full day (over 5 hours)
Adult	US$5	US$7.50
Youth	US$2.50	US$3

Mountaineering*

	Up to 5 days	Up to 10 days
Rwenzori Mountains National Park		
	US$250	US$350
Mount Elgon National Park		
	US$90	
	US$10 per every extra day	

*Includes park visitation fee

Virunga volcano climb
Magahinga Gorilla National Park US$30
Includes park visitation fees

Sport

There are regular football matches in the main towns, and hockey and cricket in Kampala. League football matches are often played on Sunday, and fans with scarves streaming from *matatu* windows are a common sight along the main roads. The national Mandela Stadium, is located at Kireka, about half an hour out of Kampala on the Jinja road. Football internationals are played here on a fairly regular basis.

Health

It is not uncommon for travellers, particularly those visiting the country for the first time, to have some form of **stomach upset**, often caused by food from hotel buffets that has been standing around for too long. Plenty of fluids are advised, and a rehydration preparation such as *Dioralyte* can be invaluable.

For more details see page 58

Still-water pools and lakes present a risk of **bilharzia**, and it is wise to ask local advice before taking a swim. Swimming in chlorinated pools is the safest option.

Malaria is a serious risk, and the appropriate prevention tablets, sleeping under a treated net and the use of insect repellents after dark are essential.

It is not safe to drink local **water**. It should be boiled or treated with sterilization tablets. The local soft drinks and bottled water, which is very widely available, are quite safe (provided the seals are intact).

Uganda has a high prevalence of **HIV** and **AIDS**.

Uganda

Kampala

0°20'N 32°30'E
Population: 1,500,000
Altitude: 1,230 m
Phone code: 41
Colour map 3, grid B2

The capital of Uganda, Kampala, with its seven hills, is a surprisingly modern city. Over the last few years the centre has been transformed and is now dominated by skyscrapers – the latest addition being the social security building, a huge, blue-glassed edifice. These have interrupted the views somewhat, although the three religions, Catholic, Protestant and Muslim, with their cathedrals and mosques, can still keep a wary eye on each other. The city centre is largely made up of government buildings and is neatly bisected by the Kampala-Jinja road. Uphill, all is calm with pleasant colonial-style buildings and pretty streets lined with jacaranda trees and flamboyants. Most of the buildings, if not government offices or embassies, have been turned into apartments. Downhill all is bustle with a huge street market surrounding the chaotic matatu station and Nakivubo Stadium. The city has always been known for its greenery, although in recent times much of this has been lost. But even today, with many of the valleys built over, the impression is still an extremely pleasant one, a mixture of blue sky, green open spaces and red roofs. Kampala is a friendly city and in the last few years security has improved dramatically so that the nightlife is lively again.

Ins and outs

Getting there The city centre is located about 7 km to the north of Port Bell on the shores of Lake Victoria and the average height above sea level is 1,230 m. It is about 30 km from the airport at Entebbe (see page 638 for transport details). If arriving by bus from Nairobi, you will enter along the Jinja Rd and will need to take a *matatu* to get to the backpackers hostels, which are all about 3 km out of the centre.

Getting around The city centre is very compact and easy to walk around. However, quite a number of hotels and restaurants, as well as some of the sights such as the National Museum, cathedrals, palace and Kisubi tombs, are away from the centre. Public transport runs from about 0500 to midnight. There are a number of taxi ranks around the centre and *matatus* patrol the streets trying to drum up business. The taxi and *matatu* park are to be found near the Nakivubo Stadium below Kampala Rd (just keep heading downhill). A convenient and cheap way of travelling about town is to use a 'motor-taxi'– motorbikes known as *boda-bodas* or *piki-pikis*. They are available on Kampala Rd and any cruising bike can usually be hailed and hired.

Safety
Be especially vigilant at night

Generally speaking Kampala is safe to walk around and fairly hassle-free. There are certain parts of town where you are likely to be hassled by people asking for money, or find you are being followed. The beggars, who often claim to be Rwandan or Congolese refugees, will usually desist with a polite refusal. It is very rare for tourists to be attacked. The worst areas include Speke Rd between the post office and the *Grand Imperial*, around the back entrance of the *Sheraton* (Nile Av), on Jinja Rd between *Nando's* and *City Bar/Bakery*, and around the taxi park. You are advised to keep a close eye on your possessions and hide your jewellery and cameras. The most common crimes are pick-pocketing/purse-snatching and thefts from vehicles. Unaccompanied women are at particular risk of assault. Opening zippers on rucksacks of unwary travellers is common.

At night the area between the *Cineplex* and the taxi park is best avoided. Car hijacking is a problem on the Mulago Hill Rd (going to Kisimenti) and going towards the *Hotel Equatoria*. There have also been reports in the local press of similar offences on the road to Entebbe. However, it is nothing like the problem in Nairobi. Thieves are often treated with severity in Uganda, and stoning is not unknown. Do not accept any food or drink from strangers as it may be drugged and used to facilitate a robbery.

★

Things to do in and around Kampala

- Visit the Kasubi Tombs on the outskirts of Kampala where the Kabakas are laid to rest (take a taxi).
- Go rafting for a day on the Nile at Jinja, one of the best stretches of whitewater anywhere.
- Take in a weekend cricket match at Lugogo, or watch a football match at Nakivubo Stadium.
- Go on a day trip to Entebbe, tour the colonial-period buildings and visit the famous Botanical Gardens on the shore of Lake Victoria.
- Visit the Kampala Museum in the outskirts of the city for a fine collection of historical items, and displays of traditional art.
- Go for an evening meal at *Carnivore* in Kabalega, maybe take in a live band at nearby *Half London*, or look in at the lively *Al's Bar*.

The *Uganda Tourist Board* staff are very helpful. It may be advisable to cross-check their **Tourist** advice with your embassy. The office is situated at Impala House, Kimathi Av, T342196/7, **offices** F342188, www.visituganda.com *The Uganda Wildlife Authority*, PO Box 3530, Headquarters, Plot 3, Kintu Rd, Nakasero, T346287, F346291, uwa-vsd@infocom.co.ug, is in charge of all Uganda's national parks and game reserves. The main office is close to the *Sheraton Hotel* on the Kintu Rd (300 m) and is open 0800-1300 and 1400-1700 Mon-Fri and 0900-1300 Sat. Arrange to pay for and collect permits to see the gorillas from here. Alternatively, the *Backpackers Hostel and Campsite* is an excellent source of up-to-date information about Uganda. The visitors' book is a compilation of many travellers' experiences.

History

The name Kampala came from the Bantu word *Mpala* meaning a type of antelope, **Early days** which, it is said, the Buganda chiefs used to keep on the slope of a hill near Mengo Palace. The name 'Hill of the Mpala' was given specifically to the hill on which Captain Fredrick Lord Lugard, a British Administrator, established his fort in December 1890. At the fort, which was also an administrative post, Lugard hoisted the Imperial British East African Company flag in 1890, which in 1893 was replaced by the Union Jack. The Fort at Kampala Hill, as it became known (now known as Old Kampala Hill), attracted several hundred people and a small township developed.

As time went on traders erected shops at the base of the hill, and by 1900 the confines of the fort had become too small for administrative purposes and it was decided that the Colonial Offices and government residences that were in Kampala (at this time most offices were at Entebbe) should be moved to Nakesero Hill. The shops and other commercial premises followed.

Kampala grew and the town spread, like Rome, over the surrounding seven hills. These historical hills are Rubaga, Namirembe (Mengo), Makerere, Kololo, Kibuli, Kampala (Old Kampala) and Mulago. On top of three of these hills, Rubaga, Namirembe and Kibuli, places of worship were built – Catholic, Protestant and Muslim respectively.

In 1906 Kampala was declared a township, and the railway joining it with the coast reached Kampala in 1915. In 1949 it was raised to municipality status, in 1962 it became a city and, in October of the same year, it was declared the capital. The city has continued to grow and now covers 23 hills over an area of nearly 200 sq km.

Like the rest of Uganda, Kampala has suffered enormously in the post-Independence upheavals. Prior to these years Kampala had developed into a green city – it was spacious and well laid out and had evolved into the cultural and educational centre of Eastern Africa. During the Amin period the most dramatic changes to Kampala came with the expulsion of the Asian community. By the early to mid-1980s there were

Uganda

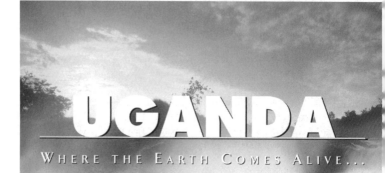

many business premises and blocks of flats that had not been touched for over a decade and had become very dilapidated. Many of these are in fact Asian properties that have since been returned to their original owners as part of Museveni's attempts to attract investment to the country. Other buildings have also been renovated and the roads repaired, and Kampala is gradually smartening itself up and looks like a modern capital with a number of imaginatively designed skyscrapers dominating the skyline.

Visitors to Kampala often comment on the greenness of the city and its number of trees (many of them inhabited by marabou storks who make an awful mess on the pavements – and on you if you aren't careful). Many of these trees have been lost in the last few years. This is due to two factors. First, there has been a massive building boom since 1986 in Kampala, and this has led to previously empty areas being divided up and built upon. One example of this is Kitante Valley (running from the golf course to the museum), which a few years ago was public land, on which pupils at Kitante School used to go cross-country running. It has now been built up almost entirely. Secondly, the bricks used for building are made locally, being baked in wood-fuelled furnaces. As you drive into Kampala you may notice these furnaces dotted all over the countryside, trying to keep up with the tremendous demand for bricks, and in the process decimating Kampala's trees.

Sights

Kampala is small enough for you not to have to worry about taking a tour. It is a pleasant city to wander around, although, if you are going to visit the sights away from the city centre, you will need to arrange transport. *Pearl of Africa* run tours every Saturday which take in the Uganda Musuem, Nommo Gallery, Kasubi Tombs, Bahai Temple, Owino Market, Kabaka's Lake, Kibuli Mosque, Makerere University, Namirembe Cathedral and the Craft Centre. ■ *US$30, T340533* (reservations).

City centre

A pleasant way to spend a day would be to walk around the centre of Kampala. Start at the Parliament building and go east along Parliament Avenue to the National Theatre and African Craft Village behind it. Walk back along De Winton Road and turn left down Siad Barre Avenue (watch out for the elephant fountain at the bottom). Turn west on to Jinja Road until you see the Railway Station. Jinja Road now turns into Kampala Road; both have lots of shops, restaurants and places to have a cooling drink and something to eat. There is a great view of the Kibuli mosque looking back down Jinja Road, with its three green and white minarets. Turn north up Colville Street and west again along Kimanthi Avenue at Christ the King Church. You will then see the Sheraton Gardens at the end of this road. Walk round them along Speke Road (going underneath a bridge), and turn right up Ternan Avenue. You can make a detour here along Victoria Avenue to the Nommo Gallery, otherwise walk past the entrance to the *Sheraton Hotel* to see the Kampala Club. Retrace your steps and walk through the Sheraton Gardens to the Speke Gate and stop at the *Speke Hotel* for a beer or cup of tea. Turn east on to Nile Avenue until you once more reach Siad Barre Avenue. You are then back at the National Theatre. An easy detour takes you on to Hannington Road where you can finish your walk at the Tulifanya Gallery.

The Parliament buildings complex is located on Parliament Avenue (the road that **Parliament** has undergone the most name changes in Kampala – it has been Obote Avenue twice **buildings** and this is the third time it has been Parliament Avenue) and is the seat of the Uganda Government. It is lined with lovely umbrella trees. The archway at the entrance is the symbol of Uganda's Independence (declared on 9 October 1962) and here are often perched what must be one of the world's most sinister birds – the

The Parliament building in Kampala

Uganda's parliamentary building is in the shape of a 'T' – the cross stroke forms the administrative offices and the down stroke the Council Chamber. Entering under the large gate you walk up the drive and through the doors to the large entrance hall, 15 m square and 14 m high. Here, if Parliament is sitting, you are likely to see a gathering of people waiting to petition their representative. Fall into conversation with them and you may learn a little of the lives of many Ugandans – typical issues being petitioned are for help with school fees, entrance to university and land disputes.

The wooden screen that separates the entrance hall from the Council Chamber is a large decorative relief which uses timbers from all over Uganda to depict a symbolic map of Uganda.

Along the base of the screen are papyrus plants and various birds that might be found by the lakeshore and in the swamps. Above this and to the left are more scenes from lakeshore life – a crocodile and a canoe. In the centre and lower half of the screen are other features representative of life – local musical instruments and banana trees. Further up on the left-hand side are images that represent the Western province – you may recognize the terraced hillsides, rainforests and clumps of bamboo, as well as the Virunga volcanoes of the far southwest of Uganda.

Across the top of the screen are the Rwenzoris – and you will see a copper drill symbolizing the Kilembe copper mines. Below the mountains are animals representative of those found at Lake Albert and Murchison Falls, including a rhino that, nowadays, is quite rare. Here the Murchison Falls themselves are shown, with the Nile meandering down the screen to the Owen Falls Dam at the source. To the right of the screen you will see Tororo Rock. Notice also the drums and the Ankole cattle.

The screen is made up of separate panels that are fitted together. Much of it was actually made in the UK – wood from Uganda was shipped over to be treated, carved and polished, before being sent back to be slotted together. A number of different woods were used: mvule, a teak-like hardwood that darkens with age, makes up the background timber; munyama, a type of mahogany; mumuli, a fine-grained yellowish timber; abura, a walnut-like timber; elgon olive, with a copper colour, and podo, a soft light-coloured timber.

---

marabou stork. The archway has now been completely renovated. On the metal gates at the entrance are the emblems of the original districts of Uganda. Here too a sign has been erected by the Rotary Club. The four-way test asks: 1. Is it true? 2. Is it fair to all concerned? 3. Will it build goodwill and better friendship? 4. Will it be beneficial to all concerned? Inside, at the entrance to the main Chambers (which is far as visitors can go), there are engravings representing the different modes of life in all the districts. A skyscraper, the Crested Towers, is being renovated at the rear of the main Parliament building, to house several government departments that are currently located in temporary office accommodation around the city. The white building with the clocktower further up the hill is the Kampala City Council building. A pleasant garden separates the two. The British High Commission is also located in Parliament Avenue.

National Theatre The National Theatre is located on De Winton RoadStreet at the eastern end of Parliament Avenue. It took three years to build and was opened on 2 December 1959 by the then Governor Sir Frederick Crawford. It is a curious building and is faced with a whole series of interconnected concrete circles. There is something presented most weekends – dances, drama and music. There is a notice board outside that announces the events planned. The British Council shows films once a month, and the Alliance Française conducts French classes. Occasionally there are visiting musicians from around the world – they are usually advertised in the main daily paper *New Vision* and on posters around town. ■ *Box office Mon-Fri 0830-1230, 1400-1645 and Sat 0830-1200. It is also open ½ hr before each performance. T344490, afk'la@imul.com*

This is a compound of over 36 small shops and kiosks built in a semicircle behind the National Theatre. Batiks, prints, carved folding chairs, wooden sculptures, bark-cloth, jewellery, antique masks are all reasonably priced and bargaining is possible especially if trade is slow. ■ *In theory it is open 0900-1700 Mon-Sat and 1000-1600 on Sun. Note though that not all the stalls are open all of the time, especially on bank holidays.*

African Crafts Village

South of centre, the solid, colonial-style railway station was completed in 1928 (see box page 226). The final stretch of line, west to Kasese, was opened in 1956, and the ceremonial copper fish-plates and bolts are on display. Today, with no passenger trains running, the building with the Ugandan and Ugandan Railways flags fluttering limply in the breeze, and a clock with no hands, is rather sad and seems to be locked in a colonial time warp. The booking hall still has its office and nostalgic platform ticket machine. If it is locked (as is most likely), you can glimpse the copper bolts in a case under the 'Telephone' sign. The façade looks directly across the grass square up the hill, King George VI Way, to the Parliament building and white City Hall behind it – a strongly symbolic link of colonial power.

Railway Station

This small building on Princess Avenue is Uganda's National Art Gallery, where artwork by local artists, as well from other parts of East Africa, are displayed. Exhibitions are advertised in the local press, but there is invariably something on display, including interesting banana-leaf pictures. There is also a shop attached with both artworks and crafts available. Well worth a visit, many banana-leaf pictures for sale. It was once a private house and is set in spacious grounds. ■ *0900-1700 on weekdays, and from 0900-1500 at weekends. Free entry.*

Nommo Gallery

These used to be known as the **Jubilee Gardens** but are now kept – in superb condition – by the *Sheraton Hotel*. They originally commemorated George V's jubilee and there is a bust of the king in the gardens. They are extensively used, especially at weekends when newly married couples arrive with their bridesmaids to have their photographs taken. There are lots of freelance photographers waiting to oblige. The Speke Gate connects the gardens with Nile Avenue opposite the *Speke Hotel*. This is closed at dusk and also on Sundays. There is a complex of craft shops in the Gardens but they are not always open. Just outside the gardens, opposite the *Imperial Hotel* at the top of Speke Road, is an impressive statue of a mother and child. Sculpted by Gregory Maloba, *Independence* depicts a mother with bandages around her legs and waist lifting a child with arms held aloft.

Sheraton Gardens

This small but charming art gallery in Hannington Road is run by Maria Fischer. It features African artists. There's a pleasant café in the gardens. ■ *PO Box 926, T254183.*

Tulifanya Gallery

In the town centre close to the *matatu* park are two temples – one Hindu and one Sikh. One of these was used as a school for some years but has now been returned to its original use. Just to the north of them lies Nakasero Market. There are some fine examples of old colonial stores with spacious balconies. They are rather neglected now, with peeling paint and rusting roofs. A little further west, the area around the taxi park and bus station and Nakivubo Stadium is known as Owino Market. It has outgrown its designated area and most of the pavements in the streets surrounding it are covered in all manner of trade goods. It's an absolute hive of activity as shoppers race to catch their *matatus* clutching their purchases.

Sikh & Hindu temples & market area

Uganda

West of centre

Kampala Old Fort

These sights are all about 3 km from the centre

This is a block house on a small hill to the southwest of the centre of Kampala. The whole area is being built over with a new mosque. Unfortunately work has had to be stopped while the architects and engineers try to work out how to straighten the huge, slender, concrete minaret. This is visible from many parts of the city and the top third is clearly out of alignment. It is difficult to know if the Old Fort still exists, or whether it was demolished to make way for the mosque. Entry, in principle, is through a gate on the west side of the hill, just next to the abandoned Aga Khan Sports Club, but access is restricted. The area around the fort was known as Old

Greater Kampala

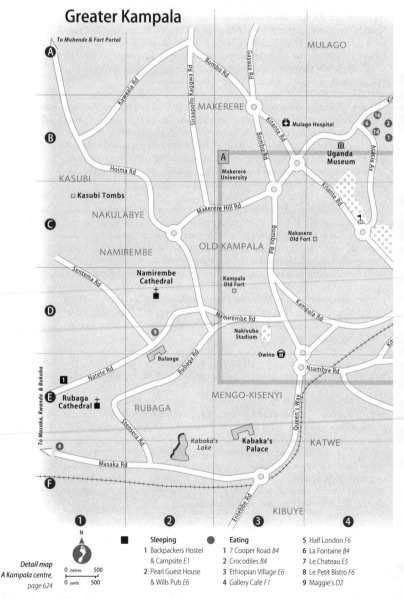

To Mubende & Fort Portal

A

MULAGO

Kawaala Rd

Sir Apollo Kaggwa Rd

Bombo Rd

Gayaza Rd

MAKERERE

Kitante Rd

Mulago Hospital

B

Hoima Rd

Bombo Rd

6 16 2
14   1

A

Makerere University

Uganda Museum

KASUBI

☐ **Kasubi Tombs**

NAKULABYE

Makerere Hill Rd

Kitante Rd

C

NAMIREMBE

OLD KAMPALA

Nakasero Old Fort ☐

Sentema Rd

Namirembe Cathedral †

Kampala Old Fort ☐

D

Namirembe Rd

Kampala Rd

9

Nakivubo Stadium

Rubaga Rd

Bulange

Owino 🚇

Natete Rd

Nsambya Rd

1

E

Rubaga Cathedral †

RUBAGA

MENGO-KISENYI

Queen's Way

Stensera Rd

Kabaka's Lake

Kabaka's Palace

KATWE

To Masaka, Rwanda & Bukoba

4

Masaka Rd

F

Entebbe Rd

KIBUYE

To Masaka, Rwanda & Bukoba

①   **②**   **③**   **④**

N

Detail map A Kampala centre, page 624

0 metres   500
0 yards   500

■ **Sleeping**
1 Backpackers Hostel & Campsite *E1*
2 Pearl Guest House & Wills Pub *E6*

● **Eating**
1 7 Cooper Road *B4*
2 Crocodiles *B4*
3 Ethiopian Village *E6*
4 Gallery Café *F1*

5 Half London *F6*
6 La Fontaine *B4*
7 Le Chateau *E5*
8 Le Petit Bistro *F6*
9 Maggie's *D2*

Uganda

Kampala and was where the Asian population used to live before they were expelled by Amin. Some of the buildings are still badly neglected.

Kasubi Tombs

These tombs are situated a few kilometres out of town on Nabulagala Hill, off the Kampala-Hoima Road. They are the site of the burial place of the kings known as the Kabakas of Buganda and are constructed reflecting the typical Ganda architectural style of a large circular house, topped by a domed, thatched roof. There are several buildings of similar construction in the surrounding area, the largest of which houses the tombs. Many of the artefacts of the kings, including spears, drums, furniture and a stuffed pet leopard reputed to have been owned by Muteesa I, are on display. The site contains the tombs of Muteesa I (1856-84), Mwanga II (1884-97), Sir Daudi Chwa (1897-1939), and Edward Muteesa II (1939-66). Mwanga II was exiled to the Seychelles in 1899; he died there in 1903 and his body was returned to Uganda and buried at Kasubi in 1910. Muteesa II was removed from his position soon after Independence during the Obote I regime and died three years later in 1969 in London. His body was returned to Uganda in 1971 and buried at Kasubi in an attempt by Amin to appease the Baganda. During Museveni's rule Muteesa II's son has been allowed to return to Uganda and in July 1993 he was crowned as the Kabaka at Budo.

There is a two-doored house, *Bujjabukula*, which you pass through as you enter the main enclosure, as well as the drum house *Ndoga-Obukaba*. There are also a number of smaller buildings of similar design around the outside, within the inner enclosure, which were for the royal wives. Originally there was an outer fence that enclosed the whole of the area, which held over 500 houses – over 6 km in length – but only the inner wall remains.

The largest building, which is the tomb house, is called *Muzibu-Azaala-Mpanga*. It is a large thatched round house which, although it can be said to reflect traditional Ganda architecture, is actually a modern structure built during the colonial period by a British company of architects. The thatch is supported by 50 rings, each made by a different tribe. Only the three topmost rings are thought to be from the original structure. They look much blacker than the rest.

To Kabira Club & Blue Mango

Bukoto Rd

MAGURA

a Rd

KATALE

Lugogo By-pass

KOLOLO

Lugogo Sports Centre

Lugogo Indoor Stadium □

Jinja Rd

To Jinja, Mount Elgon & Kenya

Spring Rd

⑫ ⑮

Old Port Bell Rd

To Bugolobi, Red Chilli Hideaway, Port Bell, Palais Dacha & Silver Spring Hotel

ⅈ Rd

KIBULI

Kibuli Mosque

Mboga Rd

Kisugu Rd

Gaba Rd

⑦

⑩ ❷

⑬ ❸

To Hotel Diplomate, Hotel International, Muyenga Club, Ethiopia Village & Laughing Lobster Restaurant

⑪

⑤ ⑧

❺ ❻

Uganda

10 Seventh Happiness *E6*

● **Bars & clubs**

11 Al's *F6*

12 Ange Noir *C6*

13 Capital *E6*

14 Just Kicking *B4*

15 Silks *C6*

16 Wagadugu *B4*

Visitors remove their shoes and enter to sit in the cool, dark interior on mats. There are pictures of the different Kabakas and some of their belongings – including a large number of spears and a stuffed leopard. Interestingly there are also a couple of chairs and an oil lamp, which were presented to Muteesa I by the earliest missionaries. The main hut is divided into two by a bark-cloth curtain behind which are the tombs, in an area closed to visitors, called the *Kibira*. Each of the

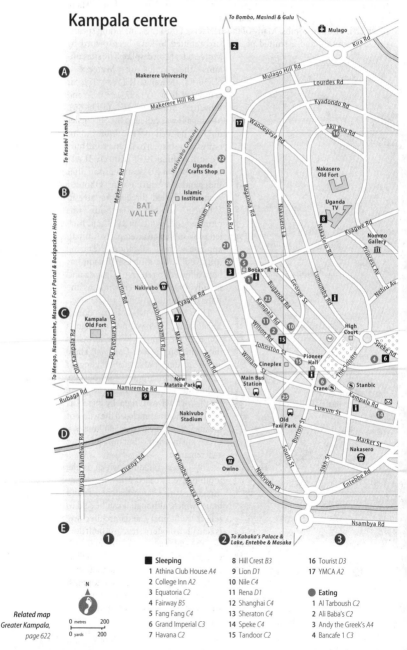

Kampala centre

Related map
Greater Kampala,
page 622

■ Sleeping	8 Hill Crest *B3*	16 Tourist *D3*
1 Athina Club House *A4*	9 Lion *D1*	17 YMCA *A2*
2 College Inn *A2*	10 Nile *C4*	
3 Equatoria *C2*	11 Rena *D1*	● Eating
4 Fairway *B5*	12 Shanghai *C4*	1 Al Tarboush *C2*
5 Fang Fang *C4*	13 Sheraton *C4*	2 Ali Baba's *C2*
6 Grand Imperial *C3*	14 Speke *C4*	3 Andy the Greek's *A4*
7 Havana *C2*	15 Tandoor *C2*	4 Bancafe 1 *C3*

graves has a corresponding platform just outside the *Kibira*. The medals are those won by Sir Daudi Chwa during the First World War.

The descendants of the wives of the Kabakas live in huts around the main tomb and look after it – they are usually sitting inside making mats. The duty that they perform is called *Ejisanja* – looking after the house and making mats.

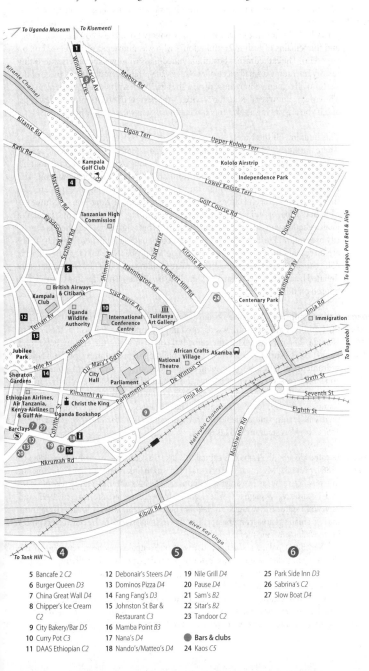

Uganda

■ *0900-1800 daily. USh3,000, includes a very knowledgeable guide. If the wives are in residence you will be expected to leave a tip for them (around US$3) in the bowls provided. There's a small shop where you can have a look at the plans for the building. They sell a guidebook, as well as a variety of souvenirs.*

Namirembe Cathedral This brick-red Anglican Cathedral, with its impressive dome, is visible from much of Kampala and is located at the top of Mengo. Particularly interesting is the graveyard which includes the graves of both the Cooks (who established Mengo Hospital) and the remains of Bishop Hannington – who was murdered in 1885 (see box on page 655). The cathedral has beautiful stained-glass windows, and a very interesting history, including a small piece of St Paul's Cathedral in London and a piece of the Berlin Wall cemented into the wall near the altar. Well worth a visit; guide available. The congregation is called to the service by the beating of drums instead of by bells, and if you are staying at *Namirembe Guesthouse* you will certainly hear them.

Bulange This building off the Natete Road is passed on the way to Rubaga Cathedral. It is where the king meets his council and serves as an assembly and administrative centre for the Buganda. One of the conditions of the king's return in 1993 was that his role would be purely ceremonial and cultural, without any political function. The Bulange is an imposing building with two little spires and a large central one. All three have very graceful curves. There is a large statue of King Ronald Muwenda Mutebi II. Most of the land around this building belongs to the king. You can ask the guard whether you can look around the gardens but you may be searched as a security precaution. Further down the road in a blue building is Libateroi church. There are three giant tortoises in the grounds. You will probably be told that the oldest is 450 years old whilst the youngest is a mere stripling of 300! They were apparently donated by a Swedish gentleman. A small tip is in order. The Supreme Court is also housed on this road.

Rubaga Cathedral of the Sacred Heart Rather confusingly a number of signs refer to this building as Lubaga Cathedral. It is the Catholic Cathedral and was restored in preparation for the visit of the Pope to Uganda. The garden next to the cathedral commemorates the visit by Pope John Paul II on 9 February 1993. It is a huge building with sculptures of the heads of prominent Catholics above the main door. There is an illuminated cross outside and you look across to a fenced area that is the Kabaka's land. Inside the cathedral are the remains of the first African Catholic Bishop and the first African Archbishop of Kampala Diocese, Joseph Kiwanuka. There is a desk inside the door and usually there will be someone available to show you around. You can buy snacks and drinks at *St George's* restaurant and takeaway.

The Kabaka's lake & palace Located close to the Kabaka's capital this lake was constructed from about 1885 to 1888 by Kabaka Mwanga. The original plan was to link it up with Lake Victoria but this was not to be, as Mwanga was deposed. The lake got into a fairly terrible state and became very stagnant. The Kabaka-to-be reopened the lake in 1993 and unveiled a statue to Mwanga. The lake is a pleasant scenic stretch, formed by damming two small streams from the north, with two small islands in the centre. It is possible to walk round most of the lake shore.

The hilltop palace at Mengo, just west of Kampala, has been returned to the Kabaka. The palace was once the pride of Buganda, with its high walls, beautiful gardens and lake. It is a handsome building with a cupola in Classical style, and it faces across the valley north toward the *Bulange* building.

A group of Ugandan royalists worked to prepare the palace for the return of the Kabaka. By tradition the king is forbidden to enter the palace until he has been anointed by witch doctors, soothsayers and healers.

North and east of centre

About 1½ km from the centre, Nakasero Hill is dominated by the Ugandan Television building. The Old Fort lies just behind it and overlooks the Kitante Valley where the golf course has been built. It is of brick construction, with concrete-rendered perimeter walls, and rifle slits. It now houses the Police Quartermaster's Depot, and access is restricted.

Nakasero Old Fort

Founded in 1908 on the site of the Old Fort on Old Kampala Hill, the Uganda Museum moved to the present site in 1954. Most of the displays have been renovated and the rest are in the process of being restored. Many of the items were looted between 1970 and 1986 and efforts are being made to return the museum to its former standard. Displays include a number of artefacts from archaeological sites from around the country, with exhibitions of Stone and Iron Age finds, and fossil materials from the Albertine Region; models of dwellings, settlements and hunting scenes; wood-carvings, metal-work and leather-craft, pottery, weapons; a collection of musical instruments including many drums and a large and impressive canoe. Uganda's first printing press, used to print the Bible, is also on view. Every so often the museum hosts afternoon concerts of live traditional music. The museum is home to the Uganda Society, the Historic Buildings Society, and the Uganda Food and Drink Society. ■ *1000-1300, 1400-1800 except Sun/public holidays 1500-1900. US$1.50. T244061. Located out of the town centre on 5-7 Kira Rd.*

Uganda Museum

You can carry on past the museum along Kira Road. The very pleasant drive down Acacia Avenue takes you to the golf course. There are a number of restaurants in this area, which is known as Kololo.

The Bahá'í Temple is situated about 4 km out of Kampala on Kikaya Hill, off the Gayaza Road. It is the only temple of the Bahai religion to be found in Africa. This religion believes that every religious manifestation forms a successive chapter in one great and continuous revelation of God. People of all faiths are therefore welcome to visit this temple for prayer and meditation at any time. A wonderful view of the temple can be seen from the end of Kira Road in Kampala, just beyond the museum to the left. From the temple itself there are excellent views of Kampala and the surrounding countryside. ■ *Services are held here on Sun at 1030.*

Bahá'í Temple

This is the oldest university in East Africa and for many years had a fine international reputation. However, it suffered greatly in the 1970-80s and is now struggling to return to its former high standards. Despite the rather shabby look at present, the original impressive appearance is unmistakable. The main campus contains the administrative buildings, the academic faculties, the library, seven halls of residence, the guesthouse and staff residences, as well as recreational facilities including the Student Guild and a swimming pool.

Makerere University

Within the Faculty of Fine Art there is a gallery which hosts exhibitions of students' works. The building dates from 1923, and there is a permanent display of sculptures. In the basement is a Victorian art printing press bearing the Royal Arms, with handsome cast-iron feet and the maker's name: Payne & Sons, Otley, Yorkshire, England. ■ *1000-1800 Mon-Sat.*

On Kibuli Hill is the mosque, which, as a result of recent cutting down of trees, is now visible from Kampala town centre. Prayers are held here five times a day. Guided tours can be arranged for a donation, and there are spectacular views of Kampala from the minaret.

Kibuli Mosque

Excursions

Namugongo Shrine

The Namugongo Martyrs' Shrine is located about 12 km out of Kampala off the Jinja Road. This is the site where 22 Ugandan Christian converts were burnt to death on the orders of Kabaka Mwanga in 1886. On the visit of Pope Paul VI to Uganda in 1969, the victims were canonized and since then the shrine has been an important site for Ugandan Christians. On the site there are two churches – one built by the Roman Catholic Church, and the other by the Church of Uganda. The steel structure, built in traditional style, has artistic work on its interiors depicting scenes from this episode and, in the centre, preserved in glass, are some of the remains of one of the martyrs, Kaloli-Lwanga. Nearby is an artificial lake that is believed to have been formed from a well that belonged to one of the Kabaka's soldiers who was staying in the area. There is a public holiday every year on 3 June in remembrance of the martyrs.

Pleasant daytrips, either in your own vehicle or by public transport, can be made to **Entebbe** (see page 640), **Mabira Forest Reserve** (see page 628), **Jinja** (see page 647) and the **Mpanga Forest Reserve** (see page 723).

Essentials

Sleeping

A very informative free quarterly publication called *The Eye* lists what's on in Kampala. It is available from tour operators, the tourist board, UWA office. It lists accommodation, restaurants, services, embassies. Occasionally, listed telephone numbers are incorrect.

■ on maps,
pages 622 and 624
Price codes:
see inside front cover

L *Sheraton*, PO Box 7041, Ternan Av, PO Box 7041, T344590/6, F256696, www.sheraton.com/kampala Located in the centre of Kampala this 245-room hotel is ideally set within the 4 ha of the Sheraton Gardens (which are beautifully maintained by the hotel and open to the public). It has meeting rooms to cater for conferences from 400-500 people, a complete recreation centre with a swimming pool, squash courts, tennis court and health club open to hotel guests and members only; in the foyer there is a good coffee bar which is a perfect meeting place; email services and internet access are offered in the business centre. All rooms have balconies (not wide enough to sit out on). The *Barbeque* restaurant offers good value for money buffets for lunch and dinner daily; the *Rhino Pub* with large TV screens showing satellite sports and music channels, has draught beer, pool tables, darts, serves Sun brunches and a snack menu is available. It suffers badly from the noise of discos at weekends and as such is overpriced. The hotel offers airport transfers for hotel guests and is a 45-minute drive from Entebbe Airport.

A *Equatoria*, Junction of Bombo Rd and Kyagwe Rd, T259571/4, F234160, equator@swiftuganda.com This is a newly refurbished, Indian-owned hotel, with 3 restaurants including the excellent *Chopsticks* with Chinese cuisine, *Haandi* (Indian) and *Trattoria* (Italian), which are all good value for money. It also offers a swimming pool, sauna and fitness room/gym. Live music on Fri and Sat. **A** *Grand Imperial Hotel*, PO Box 9211, Plot 6, Nile Av, T250681, F250605/6. Pleasant conversion of a colonial building, very central, a/c, 3 restaurants, 4 bars, ballroom, pool, saunas, jacuzzis, steam and spa baths, massage, shopping mall, satellite TV. Outgoing international telephone charges are exorbitant. **A** *Nile Hotel International*, PO Box 7057, 32 Nile Av, T258080, F259130. Luxury 4-star fully a/c hotel, aimed at business traveller. Has an international conference centre connected to the hotel, with a capacity of 1,550, shopping centre, duty free shop, Art Gallery, Bank Forex Bureau and postal services, airport shuttle service, several bars, cafeteria and restaurants, set in 7 ha of grounds, with a swimming pool.

Uganda

B *Hotel Diplomate*, PO Box 3583, Tank Hill, T267625, F267655, diplomate@spacenetuganda.com Out of the hustle and noise of the city centre but awkwardly placed if you are without transport, relatively expensive, although it does have some of the best views of Kampala. Restaurant, bar, airport shuttle service and business centre. Excellent barbecue on the terrace – all you can eat for US$10 per person. **B** *Fairway*, PO Box 4595, 1-2 Kafu Rd, T259571/4, F234160, fairway@starcom.co.ug Located opposite the golf course close to the Kampala Club this is a pleasant hotel with nice grounds, swimming pool and health club, it is also one of the more friendly hotels in Kampala. **B** *Havana Hotel*, PO Box 2251, 28 Mackay Rd, T250762, F343533, havana@starcom.co.ug Located close to the new taxi park. Good Indian restaurant, adequate facilities, safe parking, some rooms have a/c. **B** *Hotel Africana*, PO Box 10218, Plot 2-4 Wampewo Av, T348080/6, F348090, africana@starcom, www.hotelafricana.co.ug Located in the pleasant lower Kololo area. Modern hotel, 115 rooms with a/c, satellite TV, health club, sauna, gym, free temporary membership to golf course next door, business centre, shops, bar, restaurant. Free airport and city shuttle service. **B** *Kabira Club*, PO Box 1936, Old Kira Rd, Bukoto, T543481, F541257, kabira@starcom.co.ug A members' club that has reciprocal membership arrangements with other clubs, approx 5 km from city centre. Offers 2/3-bedroom cottages, some en suite. Set in pleasant gardens. Club House, lounge, bar, terrace restaurant, swimming pool, tennis and games room. Also has a business centre with email and fax. **B-C** *Palais Dacha Guest House*, PO Box 24520, Muntungo Hill, T/F223827. Located 3 km southeast of the city centre, 1 km from Port Bell harbour. Spacious gardens, airport transport by prior arrangement, own generator, satellite TV. Offers long-term and whole-villa rental rates for up to 10 people. Self-catering available by negotiation otherwise traditional cuisine/bar. **B** *Speke*, PO Box 7036, 7-9 Nile Av, T259221, F235345, speke@swiftuganda.com One of the oldest hotels in town and recently renovated. With 50 rooms, it is very attractive with striking murals and portraits of John Manning Speke. Although there are 5 restaurants and a bar, be aware that they are all franchise operations owned by different operators so nothing can be charged to your room – cash payments only taken. **B** *Shanghai Hotel*, behind the *Sheraton* in the grounds of the *Kampala Club*. Very clean. Free laundry service, breakfast in room, other meals in restaurant, no bar. Recommended. **B-C** *Tourist*, PO Box 7036, Market St, T251471/2, F251473, tourist@swiftuganda.com Very centrally located right in the middle of town, overlooking Nakasero. Recently reopened after a major upgrade. All rooms are furnished to a very high standard with en-suite facilities. Spacious and offers excellent value for money. Restaurant serves continental food. Safe neighbourhood, close to the taxi stands.

C *Antler's Inn*, Bat Valley, opposite *Uganda Crafts*. Nicer than it looks from the outside, catering mainly for businessmen. If you are planning to be in town for a fairly long time you can usually negotiate a reduction in the price. The staff are very helpful and friendly and it is good value. Restaurant does breakfast only. **C** *Athina Club House*, Windsor Crescent, T341428, F236089, athina@afsat.com Located by north end of the golf course in Kololo. Very comfortable, Mediterranean atmosphere, pleasant restaurant under awning, with lunchtime buffet. **C** *Colline*, PO Box 7, T290212, located in Mukono about 20 km to the east of Kampala, signposted on the left of the road. There is traditional music and drumming most Sun afternoons. **C** *Hotel Fang Fang*, Ssezibwa Rd, Nakasero, T235828, F233620, fangfang@swiftuganda.com **C** *Hotel International*, PO Box 4037, Tank Hill Rd, Muyenga, T266924, T077-483156 (mob), F269916, hotelint@imul.com Nice views from here, but it is a little dilapidated. Swimming pool not always clean. Hot water supplies erratic. **C** *Lion*, PO Box 6751, Namirembe Rd, T243490. Clean and comfortable, hot water, good value. **C** *Muyenga Club*, PO Box 2255, Plot 1792 Kisugu Rd, T267080, T077-483156 (mob), F230521. Bit run down for this price bracket. Swimming pool, restaurant, bar and pool table. **C** *Reste Corner*, PO Box 9153, 31 Tank Hill, outside the city centre, T267910, F267938. Hotel rooms or cottages available, conference facilities, fairly modern. **C** *Silver Spring*, on the Port Bell Rd. There are either small cottages, or cheaper bandas which are particularly popular. Reported to have become rather shabby, with slow service. There is a swimming pool that is free to guests, a gym, sauna, restaurant and bar, poor value. **C** *Tandoor*, PO Box 12034, Kampala Rd. Small, rather cramped, but well run and good value. Renovation work may still be in progress.

D *College Inn*, Wandegaya, close to the university campus. A friendly place and clean, although rather basic. **D** *Hill Crest*, PO Box 4037, Nakasero Rd, T343624, F269616. Good area, west of city centre, peaceful atmosphere, gardens, bar (jazz on Fri). Restaurant serves excellent French, Italian and Congolese food. Lovely gardens, camping in grounds. **D** *Kidikuru Economic Hotel*, Portal Av, T257192. Sound value. **D** *Luwero Guesthouse and Restaurant* on Nakivubo Place, near bus station, next to stadium. Basic and clean. **D** *Makerere University Guest House*, University campus. T077-462311 (mob). Biggest problem with it is the noise from the Student Guild which has loud music until late at night, rooms facing away from the Guild are quieter. Food (both European and African) is available, breakfast is included. **D** *Namirembe Guest House*, PO Box 14127, Mengo, T272071, close to Mengo hospital, situated high on Namirembe Hill with a 'million dollar view', just below the cathedral. Run by Church of Uganda Christians. There is a range of rooms – singles, triples and dormitories – in the original building and in the new extension.The extension has hot water showers and is generally nicer, but more expensive, some dormitory accommodation. Clean facilities, friendly and helpful staff offer a high level of customer satisfaction. Samll shop, 'million-dollar view'. **D** *Noble*, has moved from Nakivubo Rd to William St on the block east of Bombo Rd. Renovations under way to include a restaurant. Basic single rooms, friendly helpful service including breakfast delivered to the room, noisy on Sat nights. **D** *Pearl Guesthouse & Will's Pub*, very nice guesthouse, clean self-contained rooms, some with TV. Restaurant and bar just opened. Near Kabalagala (close to *Al's Bar*). Nice area in which to stay. Tank Hill Parade is further up. Great variety of eating places locally including lots of cheap street food. **D** *Rena*, Namirembe Rd, on way up to cathedral. Shared bathrooms, bar and restaurant, very good value.

E *Backpackers Hostel and Campsite* (previously *Natate Backpackers Hostel*), PO Box 6121, T344417, T077-430587 (mob), F272012, www.traveluganda.com 3 km from city centre, *Backpackers Hostel* is situated on Kikandwa Hill just past Mengo. There is a choice of bandas, double rooms, dormitory, floor space or camping space, bar, restaurant or you can cook your own food. There is a good notice board with lots of travel information/advice. Has internet and email facilities. Can get noisy and crowded with overlanders' trucks. Laundry facilities and hot showers. Tent US$2per person, dormitory US$3 per person, double US$7-US$14, food US$2-5, breakfast from US$1. Nile rafting can be arranged from here with a New Zealand company called *Adrift*. A one-day trip costs US$95 including lunch. They will arrange a pick-up in Kampala or Jinja. To get to Natate take a *matatu* from the centre of town from the *Matatu* station opposite Nakivubo Stadium, US$0.40 out, US$0.20 back. Look for a pole with an attached sign 'Backpackers' at the new taxi park in Kampala. **E** *Blue Mango Lodge*, Old Kira Rd, Bukoto, T542245, T077-701757 (mob), go2bluemango@hotmail.com Situated between Kisimenti and Ntinda in Bukoto – coming from Ntinda take 1st right turn, and then 1st right before Kabira Club; coming from Lugogo bypass take 1st left turn and then 1st right after the Kabira Club. Opened in Jan 2001 – new backpackers' place, very nicely fitted out. Offers camping, fee US$1.50 per person; dorm US$3.50 per person with nets; cottages and rooms with shared facilities US$9-11, with en-suite bathroom US$14. Wonderful atmosphere, big bar, relaxed seating area, TV and games room, pool table, sometimes has a DJ who plays music (house/rave). Highly recommended for either staying there or just chilling out, having a drink. Takes Visa/Mastercard. **E** *Red Chilli Hideaway Hostel and Campsite*, T223903, T077-509150 (mob), www.redchillihideaway.com Situated in Bugolobi, off Old Port Bell Rd, in lovely surroundings with good security. Camping US$2 per person, 40 dormitory beds US$4.50, small double room US$9.50, large double room US$12 or en-suite US$19, self-catering cottages from US$30. Very clean and has a nice atmosphere. Sun BBQs, Fri night 'Happy Hour'. Bar, good restaurant (open 0730-2130) offers big food portions at very reasonable prices. Has satellite TV, video, internet and email facilities, pool table, book swap, hot showers, western toilets, laundry facilities – hand or machine. Access from town by *matatu* going towards Bugolobi, Luzira or Port Bell. Get off opposite *Silver Springs Hotel* and follow signpost to the left. Take 2nd left turn – approx distance is 500 m. **E** *YMCA*, Bat Valley. Popular with campers and backpackers and probably the cheapest place in town, but very basic – you have the choice of the floor (with a mattress if they haven't run out) or camping outside. The main problem is that during the day it acts as a school – so you have to pack up and move out by 0700. If you have a tent you can camp in the grounds, although being on the main road you have little privacy and security is poor. Despite the drawbacks, the staff are very friendly.

Hostelling & camping

Uganda

Eating

City centre
● on maps,
pages 622 and 624
Price codes:
see inside front cover

Expensive *Chopsticks*, *Equatoria Hotel*, William St, T250781. Excellent Chinese restaurant. *China Great Wall*, Kampala Rd near the Diamond Trust building. Chinese cuisine. Generous portions and reasonable standard. *Fang Fang's*, 3rd floor, Greenland Towers, Kampala Rd T344806(opposite the post office). Popular Chinese restaurant, wide range of dishes from various regions, live piano music. Open daily. The *Lion Restaurant* at the *Sheraton* does a very popular buffet lunch. There are other restaurants and snack bars at the *Sheraton* – they are rather expensive but the quality of the food is excellent. *Maharajah*, *Speke Hotel*, Nile Av. Good-quality Indian cuisine, pleasant setting with a rock garden, cream tablecloths, large parchment parasols and, in their flowering season, a carpet of blue jacaranda petals. *Sam's Restaurant*, Farmer's Choice Alley, 78 Kampala Rd, T251694, next to *Sabrina's*. Excellent food and service. Offers game such as crocodile, roebuck and antelope as well as tandoori and continental. Very nice atmosphere. *Shanghai*, Ternan Rd, T250336, behind the *Sheraton* in the grounds of the Kampala Club. Excellent Chinese food.

Mid-range *Ali Baba's*, Kampala Rd, T244149. Sound Indian cuisine. *Al Tarboush*, Park Royal Shopping Arcade, 76 Bombo Rd, Lebanese restaurant. Décor rather tacky but offers generous portions with very friendly service. No alcohol served. *Bancafe* There are two branches, the one near the *Grand Imperial* is nicer than the Kyagwe Rd one. Great coffee, capucino, chocolate brownies, fruit juices and toasted sandwiches. Only open at lunchtime. Nicely decorated. Has a supply of daily newspapers for customers to read. *Burger Queen*, Kampala Rd opposite City Square, upstairs. There are seats inside as well as outside on the cool balcony, international and African food with a good selection of hamburgers, steaks and fish. The fish fingers are rather different from the *Bird's Eye* variety. Good standard and value. *Chadenel Restaurant*, near the *Grand Imperial Hotel*. Serves a good variety of grilled fish and meat dishes. *DAAS Ethiopian Restaurant*, Kampala Rd. Interesting food. *Debonair's Steers*, T231623/4, T077-770011 (mob), corner of Kampala Rd/Entebbe Rd. South African version of *Pizza Hut/Burger King*. Fast food (very fast in Ugandan terms), no atmosphere but good value for money. *Golden China Restaurant*, Jinja Rd. Good Chinese food. *Le Petit Bistro*, Gaba Rd, Kansanga. Very cute place with outdoor seating. Nice starters and excellent steaks. Service is slow, but it's good value for money. *Mama Mia* at the *Speke Hotel*, Nile Av, has excellent Italian food including pasta, pizzas and ice-creams. Portions are very generous. *Matteo's*, Kampala Rd. Situated behind *Nando's*, one floor up, recently opened. Part of the same chain. Serves good food, relatively cheap for the quality and size of the portions. Very friendly staff. Bit noisy because of the low ceiling and the lighting is rather dazzling. Also has a cocktail bar. *Nando's*, T340840, Cargen House Food Court, Kampala Rd. Nicer than *Debonair's* because you can sit outside, more choice and a bit cheaper. Pizza, salads, Portuguese piri piri, nice ice-cream and excellent bakery (French bread, cakes and pies, even ciabatta). Cargen House Food Court also has *Vasili's Bakery*, *Creamy Ice-Cream*, *Pizza Inn* and *Chicken Inn*. *Nile Grill*, Uganda House, Kampala Rd. This popular drinking spot also does some food, relatively expensive for the size of the portions, but a useful meeting place. Live bands perform regularly in the evenings, when it is packed to overflowing. *Pause Café*, Metropole Arcade, 8-10 Entebbe Rd, T349921. Excellent for lunch, quiet with outdoor seating. Popular with locals, different menu every day. Great milkshakes/Belgian salads/pastrami sandwiches. *Swagat Restaurant*, junction of Kampala Rd/Kyagwe Rd. Indian food catering for European tastes. *Tandoor Restaurant*, Kampala Rd (Bombo Rd end), formerly the Odeon cinema. Downstairs is *Fido Dido*, which serves ice-cream and snacks, very clean and modern, excellent ice cream.

Cheap *Antonio's* (previously *Sikoni Restaurant*), Pioneer Mall, Kampala Rd, serves nice fajitas with chicken and guacamole, fish and chips, omelettes, spaghetti, curries, club sandwiches, ice-cream. No real atmosphere, more a fast food outlet. *Chippers Ice-Cream*, T254512, across from *Hotel Equatoria*, Bombo Rd, just past Books 'R' It. Currently the best ice-cream parlour in Kampala. *CityBar/City Bakery*, 11 Kampala Rd. Oddly, lists both names on its frontage. Serves Ugandan/western/Indian food at very reasonable prices. Very relaxed

Uganda

atmosphere, big comfortable chairs or outdoor seating. *Curry Pot*, Kampala Rd, Bat Valley end. It has a rather limited menu but the food is all right. *Hot Loaf Bakery*, next to UCB. Very good cakes. *House of Foods*, Plot 26 Luwum St, next to Barclays. Local dishes, snacks, pizzas, friendly service. *Johnston St Bar and Restaurant*, Johnston St. Indian food, kebabs, grills, snacks. *Munchies*, American-style fast food: burgers and pizza, good quality and cheap, relaxed atmosphere. Located at Kampala Rd/Kyagwe intersection. *Nana's*, Kampala Rd, close to the *Nile Grill* in the Uganda House complex. Although not as popular as the *Nile* it is just as pleasant, with seats outside, good service and good fruit juices and snacks.

Expensive *Sitar's*, quite a long way out on Bomba Rd, Bat Valley. Indian restaurant, gener- **West side** ally considered to be the best in town, the menu is extensive, the food is excellent and there is a nice atmosphere. **Mid-range** *Gallery Café*, Masaka (opposite the Railway Corp), T272021. 2 km from Makindye roundabout. Verandah to sit on and enjoy the art. Small but varied menu. *Maggie's Bar*, close to Namirembe Cathedral at junction of Sentema and Natete roads. Sells good Ugandan food, busy until about 2300. Lively place, incompetent service, little English spoken. Lots of street food sold near by. **Seriously cheap** Good local food at the night market in Natate, US$0.50 per head.

Expensive *Andy the Greek's*, 30 Windsor Crescent in Kololo, T231074, T075-744018 (mob), **Kololo** near *Athina Club House*. Popular, with a lively Hellenic atmosphere but somewhat over- priced, with very small portions. Closed Sun. *7 Cooper Road*, Kisementi, T235134, T075-777747 (mob). Nice décor, friendly atmosphere, choice of world cuisine, western/Mex- ican/Italian. Has seating indoors or out on the terrace. Next door to *Just Kicking* (same owner). Closed Sun. *Krua Thai*, Windsor Crescent, Kololo, T075-777 433 (mob). Delicious, fresh, deli- cately spiced Thai food. Closed Sun. *La Fontaine*, 6 Bukuku Rd, Kololo, T077-406197 (mob) . Quite sophisticated French cuisine. Expensive but good value. Seating in and outdoors. *Mamba Point*, 22A Akii Bua Rd, T343225. Very good Italian food, really friendly service, steaks are really good. Indoor and outdoor seating. **Expensive-mid-range** *Crocodiles*, 21 Cooper Rd, Kisementi, T254593, T075-721717 (mob). Western menu, atmospheric, nicely decorated restaurant with good food and service. Friendly Belgian owner will advise you about the 'special menu'. Including excellent baguette sandwiches. Seating in or outdoors in the small courtyard. **Mid-range** Closed Mon. *Pearl Gardens*, 4 Victoria Av, Nakasero, T234475, is an excellent outdoor café.

Expensive *Laughing Lobster*, Tank Hill Parade, Muyenga, T266794, T077-401912 (mob). **Kabalagala** Specializes in fish/seafood. **Mid-range** *Café Roma*, T077-200086 (mob), in Tank Hill Shopping Mall. Serves good-quality pizzas. *Ethiopian Village*, Tank Hill. Nice Ethiopian food in an atmospheric setting. *Le Chateau*, Gaba Rd opposite *Pulsations*. French cuisine and great steaks. *Kampala Carnivore* at *Half London*, T077-506562 (mob). Similar to the famous Nairobi restaurant. *Seventh Happiness*, 160 Tank Hill Rd, T267341. Chinese food, nice roof terrace. Not the best Chinese in town but cheaper than *Fang Fang's* or *Chopsticks*.

Bars and nightclubs

City centre *Grand Imperial Hotel*, Nile Av, Upper Deck Bar, jazz band by the pool, piano in **Bars** coffee lounge. Recommended. *Slow Boat*, next to the *China Great Wall*. Comfortable bar. *Park Side Inn*, 45 Ben Kiwanuka St. Rooftop bar, quite seedy, pool tables. Typical African bar with 2 balconies for a superb view over the taxi park. *Sabrina's Pub and live music*, 76 Kampala Rd, Nakasero, US$1.25 entrance fee. Live band or karaoke. Has an English-style pub at the front. Music outside on the terrace.

Kabalagala This is one of the areas on the outskirts of Kampala that established themselves as night spots when it was not safe to drive across town. Originally there were mainly shops with just a couple of bars serving warm beers – now it is lively with bars, restaurants and well-stocked shops. The bars have chairs outside on the pavement and include the *Tex Bar* (one of the oldest) and the *Afrianex*. *Half London*, Gaba Rd beyond the turning for Tank Hill.

Part of it has changed into an eating place called *Kampala Carnivore*, similar to the famous one in Nairobi. Thriving and popular place for eating and drinking. There is often a live band here and it can be too noisy to talk. However there is a good atmosphere and the service is fairly good. There is food available – steak, fish, chips and excellent pizzas.

East side *Kaos Bar*, Kitante Rd near the golf course, nightclub and bakery, with a large outdoor area. Huge place, popular with both Ugandans and *muzungus*. Fri nights there is African music, with everybody dancing. *Wagadugu*, Kisimenti. Very spacious rooftop bar with splendid views over Kampala. Space at the back to sit and chill out; in the front, people tend to stand and chat. No food served. Clientele mostly Ugandan, but the occasional expat or visitor walks over from *Crocodiles* or *Just Kicking*. *Matteo's*, Kampala Rd. Situated behind *Nando's*, one floor up, recently opened. Only cocktail bar in town! Extensive cocktail menu, beautiful bar with a nice view over the Jinja Rd. Also serves good food. *Just Kicking*, next to 7 *Cooper Road* in Kololo (same owners). Sports bar, popular with expats and visitors, especially on Fri when it is very crowded. Good dance music but nobody really dances. Terrace. Sun afternoon is good for rugby and football matches. Strap line 'No hookers allowed, but locks and props are fine'.

Nightclubs *Al's Bar*, on the Gaba Rd, southwest of centre (take a taxi). Great atmosphere, very popular, disco (no entrance charge). *Ange Noir*, Plot 77A Jinja Rd and 1st St, T230190, industrial area. Open Wed-Sun. Currently one of the hottest nightspots in town. Dress smartly – no flip flops. They also have a large notice at the entrance saying 'No Firearms Allowed'. At time of writing they have different music on each night of the week – for example Fri is 'oldies', Sat is disco, Sun is African – but in practice by the end of the evening there is little difference. This is the only club in Kampala that has fluorescent lights, nets on the ceiling, even a smoke machine. Mostly the young smart set. *Blue Note*, on Gaba Rd, close to *Al's Bar*. Quieter than its neighbours. *Capital*, Tank Hill Rd, southwest of centre (take taxi). Seedy place with horrendously dirty toilets. Good for late nights and heavy drinking. Very loud music, bar, food. *Club Silk*, 15/17 First St, T345362, has 2 nightclubs open on Tue and Fri-Sun. Offers a variety of music on different nights including karaoke, theme nights, R&B, techno and soul. Sat is groove night and has a happy hour. *Half London*, on Gaba Rd (next to *Al's Bar*). Excellent live music on Wed and Sat, bar and restaurant. *Little Flowers*, Bombo Rd, Bat Valley. Part of the Uganda Crafts/UNICEF/ Sitar restaurant complex. Not as popular as it used to be, but still blasts its music across Bat Valley. *Starlight*, close to Nakasero Market on the Kampala Rd side. From the outside it looks very unimpressive and a bit of a dive. Inside, the bar and dance floor are actually outdoors, in a sort of courtyard. Very popular with local people. Foreigners and travellers here are relatively rare, although it is very friendly. *Silks*, off Jinja Rd, near industrial area. Unexceptional disco. *Viper Room*, *Hotel Equatoria*. Rather gloomy atmosphere.

Entertainment

Cinemas *Cine Afrique*, 70 Kampala Rd, T236379. *Cineplex*, 10 Wilson Rd (near Pioneer Mall), T347713, www.africanwebs.com/cineplex   Good quality and fairly recent releases (half price on Tue).

Gambling *Kampala Casino*, 1st floor, Pan Africa House, 3 Kimathi Av, T343628/30. Blackjack, pontoon, roulette, punto banco, stud poker, slot machines. Bar and restaurant open from 1200, casino from 1400-0500 daily. *Casino International*, at *Hotel International*, Tank Hill, T266924, F234265, open from 0800-2300 daily. *Equatoria Hotel*, corner Bombo Rd and Kyagwe Rd. Newly established casino.

Music See the *New Vision* for announcements of where the local bands are playing. Particularly popular are *Big Five Band*, *Afrigo*, *De Joe's Band*, *Super Rocket Band*, *New Generation Band*. *Nile Grill*, Kampala Rd. One of the most popular places in town, particularly for the wealthier section of the Kampala community. *Simba Sounds*, Fri, Sat. Members of the audience will often get up on the stage and join the musicians. *Nile Hotel*, Nile Av, *Nile Quintet Band*, Wed. *Little Flowers*, Bombo Rd, *Big Five Band*, Sat. *Hotel Equatoria*, Bombo Rd, *De Joe's Band*, Sun.

Uganda

Slow Boat, Kampala Rd, *Super Rocket Band*, Wed, Thu, Fri. *Fairway Hotel*, Kitante Rd, *Afrigo Band* with *Moses Matovu*, Fri. *Roof View Bar*, between Nakivubo Stadium and BZ Matata Park, open 0900-midnight, beer US$1.50, live Congolese music 7 nights a week. *Hill Crest Hotel*, Nakasero Rd. Live jazz and blues on Fri at 2200.

Canoe racing Annual event, the date of which has varied (most recently in July). At Munyonyo on Lake Victoria (see box, page 636). **Cricket** *Lugogo*, on Jinja Rd. Exceptional location in a natural amphitheatre that was originally a quarry set in the side of a hill. Regular games between local clubs. Europeans, Indians and Africans all participate. **Football** The most popular sport in Uganda. Matches at the Nakivubo War Memorial Stadium near the taxi park. As well as international matches for the Africa Cup, there are also league matches. Supporters are extremely loyal. Even if you are not a great football fan you will find the occasion fun. **Tennis** *Lugogo* on the Jinja Rd. Clay courts with occasional tournaments. The show court is well appointed, with seating in stands. **Tennis, cricket and hockey** *Kololo Indoor Stadium*, near Lugogo on Jinja Rd.

Spectator sports

Shopping

A very interesting selection of old photographs, postcards, engravings, books, stamps, coins and paper money can be purchased at *Roberto Andreetta's Antiques*, PO Box 9407, Colline Shopping Mall (ground floor), 4 Pilkington Rd – next to the Mukono Bookshop, T254759, F250128. *Antiques and knicknacks*, *Sheraton Hotel*. Antique brass and copper measures, cut-glass lamps, polished oil-lamps, padlocks, saxophones, trumpets.

Antiques

Books 'R' It, 87 Kampala Rd. Large selection of imported books, fiction, adventure, romance, etc, takes shillings and hard currency, western-orientated shop, reasonable collection of history books on Uganda. *Pauline Book Shop* Kampala Rd near *Curry Pot* restaurant. Has an outstanding selection of worldwide religious books. *Aristoc Booklex* on corner of Kampala Rd and Colville St. Highly recommended, excellent selection of African literature, Ugandan history, politics and economics, physics, geography, also stocks text books and stationery. *Uganda Bookshop*, Colville St just past the Blacklines building, off Kampala Rd. One of the best bookshops in town but even here the stock is fairly limited. Other bookshops around Kampala tend to mainly sell stationery and text books.

Bookshops

Pioneer Mall, on Kampala Rd/City Sq intersection. Modern indoor/outdoor mall with food, ice-cream, clothing shops, video rental, gift shops, travel bureau, etc, in a relaxed atmosphere. *Minimarket*, Kampala Rd, located in the new shopping centre opposite City Square. This supermarket is run by a European and caters largely for the expatriate community. Prices are high and most of the goods are imported. *Tank Hill Shopping Mall Family Shop*, run by an Austrian, has a good selection of sausages, cheeses and home-made bread. *Quality Cut*, a Belgian-owned butchers with recommended meat and sausages. *Hot Loaf Bakery*, Kampala Rd, next door to the *Nile Grill*. Actual bakery is out on the Jinja Rd. Many different breads as well as lovely pastries, pizzas and croissants. *Beaton's Cookies*, Kampala Rd, just round the corner from *Hot Loaf*, in the same shopping complex. Small shop that specializes in cookies. Expensive by Ugandan standards – but very good.

General

African Village behind the National Theatre, see page 620, Derwinton Rd. Has a wide selection of local goods. Goods have marked prices but can be negotiated. *Banana Boat Gift Shop*, Plot 23 Cooper Rd, Kisementi, T232885. Sells a selection of African textiles, jewellery and paintings. *Cassava Republic*, Plot 8 Bukoto St, opposite Kisementi, Kamwokya, T075-630244 (mob), is a gallery/studio/craft shop selling ceramics, soft furnishings and cards inspired by African Art. *Uganda Crafts*, on the Bombo Rd, just north of the junction with William St, is the largest craft shop in Uganda and has a wide range of products from all over East Africa. The goods are made by the disabled. There is also a Uganda Crafts Village on the Entebbe Rd. Prices are fixed and the quality generally good.

Handicrafts

Uganda

Uganda

Canoe regatta at Munyonyo

Munyonyo is a small landing site on Lake Victoria, which is located down the Gaba Road. Normally a matatu goes as far as the turning off the main road and then there is a walk to the shore, but on the day of the regatta you will have no problems getting public transport all the way.

It was in 1871 that Kabaka Muteesa I fell in love with Munyonyo and a hunting lodge was built for him where he could indulge in some of his favourite pastimes – canoeing on the lake and hunting for hippos.

Muteesa was succeeded as Kabaka by his 17-year-old son, Mwanga Basammula. He also used the lodge at Munyonyo, especially when his palace at Mengo was undergoing repairs following a fire.

Muteesa's grandson, Kabaka Daudi Chwa, was the first of the Kabakas to hold an organized canoe race and the tradition was passed down the generations.

In 1986, when peace began to return to Uganda, a group of Baganda royalists got together and organized a canoe race to mark the centenary of the Uganda martyrs. One year later the event was repeated in the presence of Prince Ronnie Mutebi. Since then it has become an annual event.

Food and drink are available at the regatta – mainly roasted meat and grilled maize. On the day of the races a festive mood descends on the area and thousands of Baganda arrive for a day out. The men are dressed up in the traditional white kanzus, the women in brightly coloured busutis, many wearing hats to show which clan they support.

Once the guests of honour have arrived and taken their places the teams set off. There are a number of races. In the first the teams race to the nearby island and back. The major race of the day is also the longest and follows a course all the way around the nearby island. During much of the race the teams are out of sight and dancers and musicians entertain the crowds. It is also possible, on payment of a small fee, to go for a trip in one of the motor canoes that follow the racing canoes during the contest. As the race nears its end the cheering begins and if it's neck and neck the crowds go wild.

Markets   *Nakasero Market*, town centre. The largest and best fruit and vegetable market in the town centre. The prices are slightly high because it caters mainly for expatriates. It is divided into two, and all around the edge are small shops. In the lower market (built in 1929) there are stalls with a wonderful range of unusual spices. As you approach the market you will be inundated by offers from boys to carry your bag. *Owino Market*, a huge and bustling market by the Nakivubo Stadium, sells everything from pots and pans to sheets, bags and clothes. As with all similar markets you should be prepared to bargain. There is also a large second-hand clothes section where selective shoppers may find designer labels from the west going very cheap here. Any repairs or alterations can be done for you while you wait. The market stays open until 2300, with stalls lit by small kerosene lamps. This area is due to be redeveloped soon. *Shauri Yako Market*, by the Nakivubo Stadium is particularly good for second-hand clothes from Europe. The quality is usually very good and you will almost invariably pick up a bargain.

Sport

Climbing, trekking & walking   *Mountain Club of Uganda*, PO Box 4692. Climbers and walkers meet on the second Thu of the month at 1730 at the Athina Club, Windsor Av. Lectures and slide evenings are also organized. *Nature Uganda,* T540719, F533528, organize monthly nature walks. Meet at 0700 at the Makerere Faculty of Science car park. No charge.

Golf   Located on Kitante Rd opposite the *Fairway Hotel*, the 18-hole *Uganda Golf Course* opened in 1909, and the club trophy, the Wilson Cup, has been competed for every year since 1926 (except 1979-81). Pleasant bar and patio café. Visitors can play for US$30 a round. Club Secretary, PO Box 624, Kampala, T257345.

Mountain biking   Contact *Uganda Mountain Bike Association*, PO Box 30287, T341664. *Lake Kitandara Tours and Travel*, F255288, Kitanda@infocom.co.ug, are a specialist tour company.

One day's rafting on the River Nile, US$95 per person with a New Zealand company for **Rafting** *Adrift*, T268670, T075-707668 (mob), F341245, www.adrift.co.nz Transport from the *Sheraton Hotel* and (Natate) *Backpackers Hostel*. Jinja-based *Nile River Explorers (NRE)* offers a cheaper rafting package at US$65 per person (see page 637 for details).

Lugogo on Jinja Rd. *Sheraton Hotel* in the city centre. *American Recreation Association* **Tennis** *(ARA)*, 59 Makindye Hill Rd, T267033, T075-767033 (mob). Restricted eligibility. Excellent sports facilities.

Tour operators and travel agents

Abercrombie & Kent, Tank Hill, PO Box 7799, T242495/9, F242490. Long-established company offering upmarket tours to see Uganda's major tourist sights including the gorillas. *Adrift*, PO Box 8643, T/F041-268670, T075-707668 (mob), adrift@starcom.co.ug *African Pearl Safaris*, PO Box 4562, Embassy House, Parliament Av, T233566, F235770. An Australian/Ugandan partnership organizing trips to the gorillas as well as to most other parts of Uganda. *Afri Tours and Travel Ltd* specialize in safari planning, domestic air charters, hotel and lodge bookings and conference planning, and is the concessionary for *Sambiya River Lodge and Tented Camp*. *Delmira*, PO Box 9098, T235499, F231927, delmira@imul.com Acts as the agents for Far Out Camp. *Green Wilderness Group*, 22 Acacia Av, PO Box 23825, T077-489497 (mob). The concessionary for Semliki Safari Lodge in the Semliki Valley Wildlife Reserve and also offers bespoke safaris with very experienced guides. Highly recommended if you are in the medium to upmarket price range. *Nile River Explorers*, PO Box 2155, Plot 41 Wilson Av, T043-120236, T077-422373 (mob), F121322, www.raftafrica.com Whitewater rafting specialists. Their subsidiary company, *Sebek expeditions*, T77-643398, www.canoeafrica.com, is localized at the same address, and specializes in canoeing trips on the Nile and Lake Victoria. *Nile Safaris*, PO Box 12135, Farmers House, Parliament Av,

Uganda

T245092, F245093. Tours ranging from 1-19 days. *Rwenzori Mountain Tours and Travel*, PO Box 10549, Impala House, T321290, F241754. *Volcanoes Safaris*, PO Box 22818, T346464/5, T075-741718 F341718, www.volcanoessafaris.com Tour company offering upmarket safaris. It has tented camps at Sipi Falls, Bwindi and Mgahinga which it is keen to promote.

Transport

Local Unless you are staying outside the centre of town you probably will not need to use public transport much as most places are within easy walking distance. The **post bus** is well driven with some luggage space and it runs to a fixed timetable. Post buses depart from the front yard of the main post office on Kampala Rd. Runs include Kampala/Lira via Jinja/Tororo/Mbale. There are other routes, one of which is to Mbarara, leaving at 0800. The fares are similar to other buses (Kampala/Mbale US$6). the stops to load and unload mail don't add much to the journey time.

Bus: cheaper than *matatus* but less regular, with fewer routes and extremely crowded. They have the advantage of going across town so on some routes you do not have to change buses. They stop around City Square and are usually marked by their destination. The bus leaves Kampala at around 1400 for the border town to Tanzania, Mutukula. There are 2 bus services to **Kigali**, Rwanda from Kampala: Komesa and Kibungo, cost US$15, leaves at 0800 from big bus area in Namirembe Rd. There is also a special terminal for buses to Kenya on Burton St.

Car hire: *City Cars*, T232335, F232338. Take care with hired cars and mopeds, as vehicle maintenance can be very poor.

Matatu: *matatus* are minibuses running along the main routes and only leaving the terminus when full. They are the cheapest way of travelling between the centre and the suburbs. At the *matatu* park very few of the vehicles are marked, and there is no system of route numbering, but the *matatus* all have regular stations in the park. Keep an eye on your belongings and put any jewellery or smart watches out of sight – particularly in the evenings. Most *matatus* stop running at about 2200; some run later, although they usually charge more. The fare to most places in town is US$0.30; to Entebbe it is US$1. There are two *matatu* parks, one opposite the stadium in Namiremba Rd, the second in Kiwanuka St some 400 m away.

Taxis: if you have a lot of luggage or miss the last *matatu* you can get a private hire – this may be a *matatu* or a taxi. You will have to bargain the fare – from Kampala city centre to one of the suburbs will cost around US$3.

Long-distance **Air** The main international airport is at Entebbe, 37 km from Kampala. Many of the larger airlines are starting to use Entebbe after many years of absence – including British Airways, which now flies in twice a week. A service has operated from Entebbe to Kisoro since 1998. The return flight costs about US$100. There are plenty of *matatus* shuttling up and down to Entebbe town, though getting to and from the airport itself is not so easy. Having arrived at the airport you can of course take a taxi (US$30) all the way to Kampala, although there is a tendency to overcharge new arrivals. If you are trying to save your money, the best thing to do is try to persuade a taxi driver to take you to Entebbe town, and from there take a *matatu*, which will only cost you US$1. However, drivers may refuse to do this in the hope that you will go with them all the way to Kampala. The *Sheraton*'s free bus shuttle connects with most of the incoming and outbound international flights. You do not have to stay at the *Sheraton* to use it.

Boat There is no ferry service leaving from Port Bell at present.

Road The most common approach to Kampala from Kenya is by road. If you have your own transport then you can choose whether to cross the border at **Busia** or **Malaba**. If you are planning on using public transport you can travel all the way from **Nairobi** on an overnight bus. There is now more than one company that goes direct – meaning it is no longer necessary to change buses at the border. *Akamba* was the first company to offer this service but there is now competition. All the buses leave Kampala at 1500. The Akamba office is on Lagos St in Nairobi and a number of buses go each day at 0700, getting in at about 1000 the next morning. The Kampala

Bus and *matutu* fares from Kampala

From Kampala to	Bus	Matutu	Timing	Departs
Burogota (Bwindi)	15,000/-	n/a	11 hours	0630
Fort Portal	10,000/-	12,000/-	6 hours	several during mornings
Kabale	12,000/-	15,000/-	6 hours	several
Kisoro	15,000/-	18,000/-	9 hours	0630
Masaka	2,500/-		2 hours	all day
Mbale	7,500/-		3 hours	all day
Mbarara	7,000/-	7,000/-	4 hours	up to mid-afternoon
Masindi	7,000/-		3 hours	all day
Queen Elizabeth (gate)	12,000/-		6 hours	several during mornings
Wanseko	12,000/-		6 hours	mornings
From Kabale to				
Kisoro	5,000/-		3 hours	several during mornings

office is on Dewinton St near the National Theatre. Buses return to Nairobi at 1500 – book a day in advance to be sure to get a seat. The bus stops at about 0200 in the morning at Kericho (where there is little to eat there) and gets in to Nairobi at about 0530 the next morning.

Directory

International Air Tanzania, Airline House, United Assurance Bldg, 1 Kimathi Av, T234631. **Airline offices** *British Airways*, Kampala Rd, behind the Kampala Club, T256695. *CEI Aviation*, Metropole House, 8-10 Entebbe Rd, Kampala, T255825, F236097. *Eagle Airlines*, Box 312, Kampala, T042-20513 ext 3020. *Egypt Air*, Metropole House, 8-10 Entebbe Rd, T241276. *Ethiopian Airlines*, Airline House, 1 Kimathi Av, T254796/7. *Kenya Airways*, Airline House, 1 Kimathi Av, T233068. *Sabena*, *Sheraton Hotel* Arcade, T259880. *Zambia Airlines*, 1 Kimathi Av, T244082. **Domestic and charter:** Anyone hoping to see more of Uganda, particularly the north, who is short of time and wants some comfort, is likely to use one of the charter airlines. *Bel Air Ltd*, Spear House, T242733. *Speedbird Aviation Services*, PO Box 10101, Kampala, T231290, 1st Floor, *Sheraton Hotel* Arcade or *National Insurance Building*. Airport office, T042-20689 (Entebbe).

The relaxation of regulations has meant that there are now a large number of foreign exchange bureaux **Banks** all over town. These offer a quick and efficient service 5 days a week, and on Sat mornings. The rates around town may vary by a few shillings but not by an enormous amount. Money may also be changed at banks, but it takes longer, and they are only open in the mornings. Changing TCs can present a problem at some of the banks as there have been a number of forged TCs in circulation. You may be asked to produce the original sale receipt for the cheques. Barclays Bank in Luwum St won't cash TCs – you have to go to the Head Office. *Barclays*, PO Box 2971, Kampala Rd, T232597. *Crane Bank*, Kampala Rd, near the Speke, are reported to offer excellent rates without surcharges. Open all day Mon-Fri and Sat mornings. *Sheraton Hotel Forex Bureau* will exchange TCs without seeing the original receipt. *Stanbic*, Kampala Rd, T231151, are reported to offer good rates for TCs, with no commission and an unusually easy procedure. *Standard Chartered Bank*, PO Box 7111, Speke Rd, T258211.

Internet There are several email and internet facilities in Kampala. The *Sheraton Hotel Bureau*, **Communica-** T344590, charges US$10 an hr online. A much better bet is the *Web City Café*, on Kimathi Av, T347080, **tions** which is open from 0800-2200 Mon-Sat and 1000-2000 on Sun and holidays, and charges about US$4 per hr. It is very comfortable with a/c and connections are quite fast.

Post office The main post office is situated in the centre of town on Kampala Rd and is open from 0830 to 1700. The post is expensive – to Australia a 3 kg parcel costs US$80 airmail or US$25 by sea and takes 6-7 months to arrive. Most post offices offer a fax service, US$2 overseas, US$0.50 for an incoming fax. **DHL**, Blacklines House, Clement Hill Rd, T251608, offer a reliable service.

Telephone International telephone calls can be made from the card phones outside the post office. There is a telephone booth at the *Backpackers Hostel* where you can ask your contact to return your call.

Uganda

YMCA also offers cheap phone calls. Most international calls made from the hotels are at exorbitant rates, which are often only apparent when you check out.

Cultural centres *British Council*, Parliament Av, PO Box 7070, Kampala, T257054. Has films, concerts and talks, library and all UK newspapers, excellent facilities. All British Councils offer email facilities and for a small fee they will send and receive messages. *Ugandan-German Cultural Society*, PO Box 11778, T259617, F251648, Nakasero Rd, 1000-1900 Mon-Fri, 1400-1900 Sat.

Embassies, high commissions & consulates *Algeria*, 6 Acacia Av, T232689. *Austria*, Crusader House, Portal Av, T235103/179. *Belgium* (E), UDC Building, Parliament Av, T230659, F250307. *Burundi* (E), Plot 7, Bandali Rise, in Bugolobi area, T233674, F250990, has moved from Nakasero area, serves non-Ugandans. Visa for Burundi US$20, 2 photos, issued in 24 hrs. *Canada*, IPS Building, 14 Parliament Av, T258141, F234518. *RD Congo*, 20 Philip Rd, Kololo, T232021. *Denmark* (E), 17/19 Hannington Rd or 3 Lumumba Av, T256783. *Ethiopia* (E), 7 Hse 7A Okurut Close, near Uganda Museum, Kira Rd, T341885. Visas for Ethiopia cost US$63 and are issued in 24 hrs. *France* (E), PO Box 7218, Embassy House, 9/11 Parliament Av, T342120/176. *Sheraton* Hotel Bldg, T347223. *Germany* (E), PO Box 7294, 15 Philip Rd, F3412520. *Ireland*, 12 Acacia Av, T344344. *Italy* (E), 11 Lourdel Rd, Nakasero, T341786, F250448. *Japan*, EADB Building, 4 Nile Av, T349542/3, F349547. *Kenya*, 41 Nakasero Rd, T258235/6. *Netherlands*, 4th Fl, Kixozi Complex, Nakasero Ln, T231859, F231861. *Nigeria* (HC), 33 Nakasero Rd, T254943, F344631. *Norway* (E), Crusader House, 3 Portal Av, T343621, F343936. *Rwanda* (E), PO Box 2468, Plot 2 Nakayima Rd, T344045, F258547, opposite Uganda Museum, Kira Rd. Visas for Rwanda, single entry US$20, multiple entries US$30, 2 passport photos, valid 3 months, immediate issue. 3 Bandali Rise, T221816. *South Africa*, 8 Kisozi Complex, Kyagwe Rd, T231007. *Spain*, 9th Fl, Uganda House, 10 Kampala Rd, T344331. *Sweden*, Impala House, Kimathi Av, T236031, F341393. *Switzerland* (C), PO Box 4187, T67305. *Tanzania* (HC), PO Box 5750, 6 Kagera Rd, T236245. *UK* (HC), PO Box 7070, 10/12 Parliament Av, T257054/5. *USA* (E), PO Box 7007, British High Commission Building, 10/12 Parliament Av, T259791/3, F259794. The following countries handle diplomatic affairs for Uganda from their Nairobi Embassies or High Commissions (see page 113): *Australia*, *Austria*, *Canada*, *Greece*, *Japan*, *Zambia*, *Zimbabwe*.

Medical services There are several hospitals but the quality of care varies. *Nsambya*, PO Box 7161, T268016. A private Catholic Mission hospital that was undoubtedly the best through the difficult years, although its superiority is now less marked. *Mulago*, adjoining Makerere University, PO Box 7161, T268016, has had an enormous amount of foreign aid invested in it. The infrastructure has recently much improved (there is running water, etc), and there are doctors available. Many of the staff suffer from apathy (not really surprising considering their wages) and it is often necessary to pay to get attention. You will also have to buy drugs at local pharmacies. At the *International Health Centre*, in the Pentecostal Church building, T341291, an excellent medical service is available. A malarial blood testing service takes 20 mins and malaria treatments are in stock.

Entebbe

0°4'N 32°28'E
Phone code: 041
Colour map 3, grid B2

Entebbe is situated on the shores of Lake Victoria, about 30 km from Kampala, and until 1962 was the administrative capital of the country. Very quiet compared with bustling Kampala, it is rather a pretty town, built on lots of little hills that slope down to the shores affording almost constant views of the lake.

Ins and outs

The country's main airport is just outside Entebbe. A taxi into town costs about US$3. Frequent minibuses make the 1-hr journey from Kampala.

Sights

There is a lot of new house-building on the road from Kampala to Entebbe as it has become a popular area for middle-class Ugandans to set up home. Consequently, travel to and from the capital can be very busy indeed in the rush hour. On the drive down to Entebbe you will pass a signpost for the **Kajansi Fish Farm**, which used to be home to a number of huge crocodiles. It is a very good bird-watching spot.

Entebbe is the home of Uganda's international airport and became famous in 1976 when an Air France plane from Israel was hijacked and forced to land there. The Jewish passengers were held hostage as demands were made for the release of prisoners held in Israeli jails. All but one of the prisoners were rescued when Israeli paratroopers stormed the airport building. The raid actually took place in an old part of the airport that is no longer used. You can see the control tower of this building on the drive to the new terminal. The plane from the hijack was converted into a beach bar near the airport.

At the turn of the 19th century the colonialists built their administrative centre at Entebbe and some government offices are still located here, including the Ministry of Works, Ministry of Agriculture and Ministry of Health. State House, the official residence of the Head of State, has recently moved to Entebbe.

One relic from former times is the **cannon** in the square in front of the Entebbe Club, captured from the Germans during the First World War (see page 581). It bears the maker's number, name and date: 103, Krupp of Essen, 1917. The square was renovated in December 2000 by an Arab company. The gun now sits on a plinth and is surrounded by fountains (not always working). Standing alongside the gun are the statues of two modern camouflaged soldiers peering through binoculars across Lake Victoria.

Walking along the criss-cross of lanes between the main road and the lake shore, there are a number of beautiful old buildings to be seen. Most of these were built when Entebbe was the capital of the Uganda Protectorate – they have painted red roofs and wide verandahs and are used mainly by government departments and ministries. Particularly attractive is the Ministry of Agriculture building which dates from the 1920s. It can be clearly seen from the *Imperial Botanical Beach Hotel*.

Colonial Entebbe

Uganda

Entebbe

To Kampala

Cinema

Kampala Rd
Portal Rd

Entebbe Bay

Botanical Gardens

Entrance to Garden

Prime Minister's Office

Department of Lands & Surveys

Hill Rd

Apollo Square

Department of Agriculture

Pier

Geological Museum (Closed)

Wildlife Education Centre

Wilson Rd

Taxis

Lugard Av

Children's Playground

State House
Court House

Cannon

Nakiwogo Rd

Entebbe Council

Entebbe Club

St John's

Lake Victoria

Church Rd
Mugwanya Rd

Airport Taxis

To Entebbe Resort, Sophie's Motel, Peninsular Hotel & Sacred Heart Church

To Kidepo Hotel, Bus Station & Airport

N

0 metres 200
0 yards 200

■ **Sleeping**
1 Entebbe Backpackers Tourist Campsite & Hostel
2 Entebbe Flight Motel
3 Imperial Botanical Beach
4 Stay 'N' Save
5 Windsor Lake Victoria

● **Eating**
1 Esso
2 New Africa Village

Mugala's chair

The word entebbe *means chair and there is a legend attached to this name. Mugala was the head of the Mamba (or lungfish) Clan. Apparently Mugala used to command his domain from a royal enclosure not far from the present Entebbe Airport, seated in a chair carved out of the rock. Eventually his seat was submerged by the lake but the area continued to be known as Entebbe.*

Botanical Gardens
The Johnny Weismuller 'Tarzan' films were shot here

The Botanical Gardens were established around the turn of the last century by the Protectorate government, and the first curator was a Mr Whyte. This was originally a natural forest and the gardens were used as a research ground for the introduction of various exotic fruits and ornamental plants to Uganda. There are species in the gardens from all over the world, including cocoa trees, and rubber plants, which were introduced to see how well they would thrive in Uganda's climate and soils.

Some of the trees have died a natural death and have not been replaced. Many still have their metal labels on them, and there is a small patch of virgin forest down close to the lake shore. Walking through this on the well-maintained paths you will experience lots of different noises and smells, and it is worth remembering that large areas of Uganda were once forested like this patch. Watch out for the dragon spiders (so named because they catch dragonflies, which are pretty big and weave enormous webs. There is a troupe of black and white colubus monkeys here, as well as green vervet, which can be seen playing on the grass in the early morning as well as at dusk. For people spending longer in Uganda, there is also a very good plant nursery. Take some fruit to feed the very tame vervet monkeys Young boys will act as guides and show you the vines as well as swing on them. It is a popular picnic and swimming spot at weekends and holidays; these times are best avoided as there is usually lots of noise from overloud ghettoblasters.

■ *To get there from Kampala, take a* matatu – *they go every few mins and take about 45 mins, costing US$1. Stay on until the turning off to the right to Entebbe town, just after a Shell petrol station. Walk down Portal Rd (which heads towards the Lake Victoria Hotel and the airport) for about 100 yd, until you see Lugard Avenue forking off to your left. Turn left again at the Department of Agriculture building. Follow on past the compound until you see the sign for the Botanical Gardens on your right. There is an entry charge of USh1,000 and a charge for using a camera or video recorder, but there is not always anyone there to collect it. There is no café or snack bar, so take a drink on a hot day.*

Entebbe Wildlife Education Centre

The zoo at Entebbe was originally established as an animal orphanage and gradually developed into a zoo with a wide range of species. Until fairly recently it was a miserable sight, and a place to avoid. However it has been renamed the Entebbe Wildlife Education Centre and attempts have been made to improve the conditions. Large amounts of aid money are being spent on the rehabilitation. The master plan was designed by experts from the New York Zoological Society, and it incorporates an educational centre as well as dormitories for school children and other visitors. There are regular talks by the keepers throughout the day. The proposals for the centre itself include replicating some of the country's ecological zones, such as savannah, wetlands and tropical forest. The main features will be a forested reserve for primates and an island surrounded by moats for chimpanzees. The effort is paying off and, although there is still much to do, many of the enclosures are now occupied and most of the worst cages have been demolished. It is worth visiting just to support the efforts of the staff. There are a pair of shoebill storks here if you are not able to visit either the Semliki Wildlife Valley Reserve or Murchison Falls National Park. In November 2001 a pair of southern white rhino were relocated to the centre. The project is supported by the World Bank and is the first step towards reintroducing these herbivores into Uganda. ■ *Lugard Av, just* *past the Imperial Botanical Beach Hotel. US$1. There are refreshments and a small gift shop.*

Located about 5 km off the Airport Road is the place where the first Catholic Missionaries to Uganda, Rev Fr Simon Lourdel and Brother Amans of the Society of White Fathers, landed, on 17 February 1879. There is a small brick church marking the spot and a memorial plaque. There is a small fishing village near by. **Kigungu Landing**

This fishing village is located 6 km off the Entebbe to Kampala road. Both traditional and more modern fishing techniques are used today, and many fishermen have a canoe with an outboard motor attached. Nile perch and tilapia are among a number of species caught. You will be able to see fishermen mending their nets and boats and it is possible to arrange a trip to some of the nearby islands. Local boats also go to the Ssese Islands. Boats leave for all the islands at about 1500, US$7.50. **Kasenyi fishing village**

Essentials

L *Windsor Lake Victoria*, PO Box 15, Circular Rd, T20644, F20404. Newly refurbished hotel, described as the best in Uganda. The facilities are excellent and include a swimming pool and the nearby golf course, swimming for non-residents at US$7, snacks and drinks available and hot showers. The wine list is reported to be rather expensive and somewhat limited. If you are flying out of Entebbe on the early-morning *British Airways* flight, you can get a discount to stay here and you will be provided with transport to the airport the next morning. Ask for details at the *British Airways* office in Kampala. **A** *Imperial Botanical Beach Hotel*, off Lugard Av just after turning for the Botanical Gardens, PO Box 90, T20800. Fairly modern, with bars, restaurant (food and service not very good), comfortable and quiet, free transfer to airport, very loud disco on Sat, lovely gardens. Extensive conference facilities and claims to be able to cater for weddings with 5,000 guests! Bill Clinton stayed here when he attended the Entebbe conference. Rather bizarrely it has the largest indoor swimming pool in the country. The restaurant is located down a flight of stairs on to the lake shore, with magnificent views. **Sleeping**

B *Entebbe Resort Beach*, PO Box 380, T20934, F21028. Turn left after the *Entebbe Club* and go through the golf course towards the lake. Banda accommodation. There is a beach but, as with all of Lake Victoria, remember that swimming here involves the risks of contracting bilharzia. **B** *Peninsular Hotel*, south of centre, PO Box 390, T20391. Restaurant and bar, good standard, small (8 rooms). **C** *Sophie's Motel*, Plot 3 Alice Reef Rd, south of centre, PO Box 6186, Kampala, T321370, T075-645471/2 (mob), F321384. Range of rooms, pleasant location, quite small, 6 rooms, 3 in the main building and 3 chalets, more rooms are being added, courtesy bus to and from the airport. Only accepts payment in US$.

C *Stay 'n' Save*, corner of Kampala Rd and Wilson Rd, PO Box 7666, Kampala, T21044. Quite central, but not particularly good value. **D** *The Entebbe Flight Motel*, new mid-range accommodation, conveniently sited for the airport. **E** *Entebbe Backpackers Tourist Campsite and Hostel*, Plot 29/31 Church Rd, T320380, T077-482877 (mob), entebbebackpackers@ hotmail.com Newly established hostel situated just behind the *Lake Victoria Hotel*. They currently have 2 dorms and a double room but the owner, Barnabus, hopes to expand in the future. Nice garden for camping in. Meals available as well as kitchen. Fully stocked bar. **E** *Kidepo*, beyond the *Lake Victoria Hotel* on the airport road. Rather basic and not particularly good value, but convenient if you cannot get to Kampala, or have an early flight.

Camping at *Entebbe Resorteach*, excellent facilities. Highly recommended. US$10 per person.

Cheap Apart from the hotels the best place to eat is the *Entebbe Club*, which is very pleasant, with tables outside and a fairly limited menu – including steak, fish and chips and such like. This was the club for colonial officials. No food served in the evenings. **Eating & drinking**

Uganda

Seriously cheap *China Garden*, Kampala Rd, near *Stay 'n' Save*. Newly opened, good service. *Esso Restaurant*, Kampala Rd. Simple fare. *New Africa Village*, Kampala Rd. Pleasant garden bar.

Entertainment & sport

Golf *Entebbe Club*, US$10 for 18 holes. **Cricket** Played in the middle of the golf course, very pleasant, spectators can watch from the *Entebbe Club*.

Shopping

Entebbe has a range of small shops including a supermarket and pharmacy as well as a spice and fruit market

Crafts On the road down to Entebbe there are a number of stalls selling everything from pottery, mats and baskets to a huge range of fruit and vegetables. Prices are not as cheap as you might expect – the sellers are obviously used to people buying on their way to and from the airport. The wares include brightly coloured woven baskets made by Nubian women. Generations of Nubians have lived close to Entebbe, but have maintained their cultural identity.

Maps The Department of Surveys and Mapping has its office in Entebbe – turn left opposite the playground and walk down the road. This is also a good source of Kenyan maps, which are not available in Nairobi for security reasons. The staff are very helpful and will do their best to dig out the maps that you want (although many are out of stock; the department is in the process of reprinting many of the old series.

Transport

Road Minibus from the *matatu* park in **Kampala**. They go every few mins and take about 1 hr, costing US$1. A taxi from the airport to Entebbe town should cost about US$3.

Directory

Banks *Bank of Uganda* has a branch in Entebbe.

East to Jinja, Tororo and Mount Elgon

Compared to the west of Uganda, the east receives relatively few visitors apart from those passing through on their way to and from Kenya. Jinja is a very popular stopping point, however, as it offers some of the best whitewater rafting in Africa on the Victoria Nile. Interest in climbing Mount Elgon from the Uganda side is once again increasing.

There is an excellent paved road from Kampala to Jinja and it takes not much more than an hour to cover the 82 km. After leaving the Kampala suburbs, you will pass the 60,000-seater Mandela Stadium at Namiryango. All Uganda football internationals are played here. Shortly afterwards is **Mukono**, the district headquarters town of the Mukono district (**C** *Colline Hotel*), and the market town of **Lugazi**. The road then crosses through the Mabira Forest Reserve with the village of **Najjembe** being the main access point. There are towering trees lining the road, but you really only get a small idea of the size of the forest as the road emerges after only a few kilometres to pass through sugar cane fields and tea plantations on the hillsides. There are lots of trails through the forest and it is well worth spending a day here (see below). The Nile Brewery is situated at Njeru and shortly afterwards the road crosses the Owen Falls dam before entering Jinja.

Mabira Forest Reserve Both guided and self-guided walking trails wander through both primary and secondary forest teeming with butterflies, birds and monkeys. Go for a half-hour, go for four hours – there is something for everyone. If you are out to see the monkeys, it's best to go in the morning or during the late afternoon when the heat of the day has

East to Jinja, Tororo & Mount Elgon

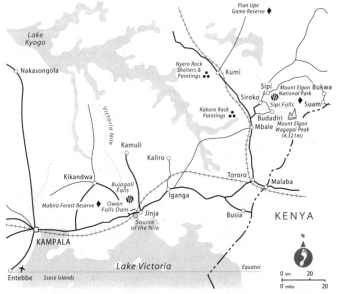

passed. A community tourism centre established by the Forest Department in 1994, operates at the forest reserve. All guides are trained and knowledgeable. Facilities are simple but comfortable. The cost of a day permit to the forest for both walking and cycle trails is US$0.60 for Ugandans, US$2.80 for foreign residents, and US$3.50 for foreign visitors. All prices include a guide.

Walking and cycling trails are the main attraction at the forest centre. If you're a keen cyclist, mountain bike trails will take you through a wide variety of landscapes – through the local communities, sugar cane and tea plantations, past waterfalls and through the rainforest. It's best to bring your own bike though, until the centre has purchased new ones.

Mabira, technically a moist semi-deciduous forest, covers 306 sq km and ranges in height from 1,070-1,340 m. Much is secondary forest, having been heavily influenced by human activity until the late 1980s. There are more than 300 species of **trees** and shrubs recorded in the forest. Several species occur in the forest outside their altitudinal range. Nine restricted species and one unique species (*Caesalpicia volkensii*) grow in the forest. *Ficus nantalensis*, the famous 'strangler fig,' is widely present in the forest and is the source of the fibre for the bark-cloth that is traditional to central Uganda.

Red-tailed monkeys are fairly common and seen more often than the elusive black and white colobus. There are more than 20 species of shrews and rodents.

The large moth fauna here is quite typical of a large forest on the Victoria Lake crescent. The forest is home to approximately 100 species of large moths, including seven range-restricted, three hawkmoth and four rare forest silkmoth species. Indeed, it's considered a high-ranking site for silkmoths. Mabira has extremely rich butterfly fauna and supports species seldom found in Uganda, including several species with 'novel' distribution patterns and limited ranges. Despite the heavy historical influence of humans, the butterfly populations have shown marked resilience. Approximately 200 species have been recorded with more than 75% of them being forest-dependent.

The **bird** community at Mabira Forest is especially rich with rare and threatened species present and a lot of conservation work being undertaken. There are over 300 species present in the forest, more than 50 of which can be viewed just from the picnic area. Almost half the species found in the forest are strictly forest-dependent. Many rare birds have been recorded at Mabira forest, including: the *Blue swallow*, the *Papyrus gonolek* and the *Nahan francolin*. Other species present and seldom seen elsewhere in Uganda are the *Tit hylia*, *Purple-throated cuckoo shrike* and the *Grey apalis*. Mabira is especially valuable for its lowland species as well, for example the *Whitebellied kingfisher* and the *Blue-crested flycatcher*.

Sleeping Both banda and camping accommodation is available. Single bandas are about US$4, with one double banda available at US$5.50. Camping (own equipment) is US$1.50. No electricity is available, but water and lanterns are, on request from the staff.

Eating Picnicking facilities in traditional umbrella-thatched shelters are available at no cost. Both local and more western-style foods are available at good prices. There are a variety of options. A local cook can prepare food for visitors at reasonable rates, however you must order well ahead of time. You can bring your own food and have it prepared for you while you relax. Or you can go up to the roadside market for fried chicken, goat or cow. Sodas, beer and local food including chapattis and gonja are also available at the roadside. The price, quality and variety of fruits and vegetables are fantastic. The roadside market is considered the best along the Kampala-Jinja highway, so be sure to stop.

Transport To visit Mabira Forest, take a *matatu* taxi from either the old or new taxi park in Kampala, heading towards Jinja. Get off at Najjembe village, only 55 km along the highway. If you are on Kampala Rd, catch a taxi from the Caltex gas station near *Nando's*. It should cost you US$1.40 from the taxi parks and US$1.10 from Kampala Rd. If you are coming from Jinja, take a taxi heading for Kampala from the taxi park by the market or by the Caltex on Main St (US$0.55) and get off at Najjembe, about 26 km out of Jinja. Taxis are frequent in both Jinja and Kampala and run all day, every day at unscheduled times. At Najjembe Village, on the north side of the highway, follow the path by the 'Mabira Forest' sign for about 500 m to the forest centre where trained local staff can help you.

Jinja

Jinja would probably be a fairly nondescript town if it were not for its location. It is at the head of Napoleon Gulf, on the northern end of Lake Victoria, and lies on the east bank of the Victoria Nile. The town is perhaps best known for being the source of the Nile. Even as it leaves the lake, it is a surprisingly large river and it's a bit spooky to think of it wandering north for 4,000 miles until it reaches the Mediterranean Sea. Practically everything to do with the town is connected to the river: electricity production, brewing and now tourism being its main sources of income. It suffered severely during the bad times but it is now a pretty and vibrant place. The shops in the main street are well maintained and, as you walk through the town, you will see the old colonial and Asian bungalows in their spacious gardens, many of which have been renovated. Some of the back streets are fairly desolate and it's a little depressing to see quite so many maribou storks strutting over the open spaces. Soon, however, it will be crawling with consultants and engineers, as the plans to build a second dam at the Itanda rapids are now well advanced. The resulting lake will mean that some of the best whitewater rafting in East Africa will be lost for ever – visit while you can.

0°25'N 33°12'E
Phone code: 43
Colour map 3, grid B3

Uganda

Ins and outs

The journey from Kampala to Jinja takes between 1 and 2 hrs by bus or *matatu*. If you want to explore the area more independently, it is much cheaper to hire a 4WD here than in Kampala. Contact Walter Egger, T121314.

Getting there & getting away

The **Tourist Centre**, opposite the *Total* garage on Main St, T120924, will be happy to help with any queries, and assist with bookings for many of the activities.

Sights

The source of the Nile was actually at the site of the Rippon Falls. These were submerged during the construction of the Owen Falls Dam, although ripples can still be seen from the picnic area. It is lovely to sit on the lawn in the shade listening to the birds and watching the swirling river below. The islets and rocks recorded by Speke (see box, page 649) also disappeared with the building of the Owen Falls Dam. There is a plaque marking the spot from which the Nile begins its journey through Uganda, Sudan and Egypt.

Source of the Nile

On the Jinja side stands the **Bell Memorial**, popular with Ugandans, and often swarming with secondary school children. To get to it you can either walk or take a bicycle taxi from the town centre – you will have no problems finding someone to take you. If you are walking, go along Bell Avenue out beyond the Sports Club and then turn left along Cliff Road. ■ *US$1.50.*

Many consider the setting on the west bank to be much more atmospheric. Here you will find the Speke Memorial, a small rock with a plaque indicating the spot where Speke stood when he first sighted the source of the Nile, on 28 July 1862, naming it the Rippon Falls. There is no public transport access but the site can be reached by *boda-boda* from town (about US$1), over the dam wall towards Kampala, then ask for directions from locals.

Owen Falls Dam

Because of the dam's strategic and economic importance, you are not allowed to take photographs

The Owen Falls Dam was built in 1954 and it supplies most of Uganda, and a good part of Kenya, with electricity. During the turmoil of the Amin period a group of dedicated engineers managed to keep the generators going almost without interruption. The falls themselves were hidden during construction of the dam, but the dam and the new falls that it creates are impressive in themselves. The main road from Kampala to the east crosses the dam, so if you are travelling by bus or *matatu*, try and get a seat on the appropriate side (left if you are heading east) in order to get a good view.

Booze cruise

A popular choice has recently been a booze cruise on Lake Victoria, which gives the opportunity to watch the sunset over the water, and see the fishing boats lit up by paraffin lamps at dusk. These cruises can by organized by *Speke's Camp and Sporting*

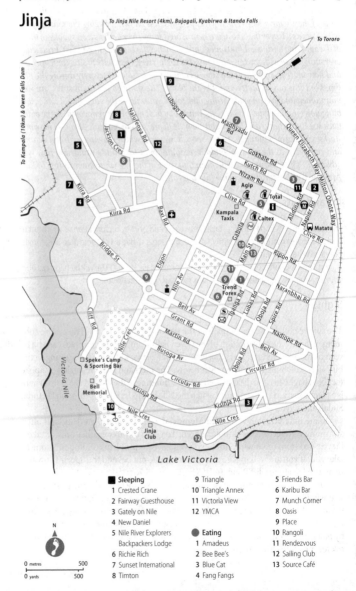

Jinja

■ Sleeping	**9** Triangle	**5** Friends Bar
1 Crested Crane	**10** Triangle Annex	**6** Karibu Bar
2 Fairway Guesthouse	**11** Victoria View	**7** Munch Corner
3 Gately on Nile	**12** YMCA	**8** Oasis
4 New Daniel		**9** Place
5 Nile River Explorers	**● Eating**	**10** Rangoli
Backpackers Lodge	**1** Amadeus	**11** Rendezvous
6 Richie Rich	**2** Bee Bee's	**12** Sailing Club
7 Sunset International	**3** Blue Cat	**13** Source Café
8 Timton	**4** Fang Fangs	

Speke and the source of the Nile

During his 1860-63 journey with Grant from Zanzibar to Khartoum via the west shore of Lake Victoria Speke was the first European to see the source of the Nile, in 1862, from the other side of the inlet to the present picnic area. He recorded the moment thus:

"Most beautiful was the scene, nothing could surpass it! It was the very perfection of the kind of effect aimed at in a

highly-kept park; with a magnificent stream from 600 to 700 yards wide, dotted with islets and rocks, the former occupied by fishermens' huts, the latter by terns and crocodiles basking in the sun, flowing between fine high grassy banks, with rich trees and plantains in the background. The expedition had now performed its functions; old Father Nile without any doubt rises in the Victoria Nyanza."

Bar, T077-401508/9 (mob), at a price, or can be negotiated with locals in the small trading centre next to the Sailing Club. The latter set off in a local fishing boat with crates of drinks purchased by the clients. *Speke's Camp* cruise is on a pontoon and costs US$25 per person (minimum of five people) and includes all drinks plus some snacks and a fruit platter.

Jinja Market This very relaxed market is definitely worth a look, with occasional great clothing 'finds'. More adventurous travellers may wish to try the fried grasshoppers and white ants.

Nile Brewery tours These complimentary tours include a free beer and are run on Tuesdays and Thursdays according to demand. It is an entertaining way to spend the afternoon during the rainy season, and interesting to see how Ugandans operate a brewery. There is a small souvenir shop on site.

Essentials

Sleeping Two places have recently opened in Jinja and offer a very high standard of accommodation. **A-B** *Jinja Nile Resort*, PO Box 1553, T122190/1, F122581, www.madahotels.com Located 4 km up the Bujagali Rd. All the rooms are in cottages and have private balconies facing the Nile (try for a downriver outlook, otherwise the dam spoils the view). Facilities include restaurants (mostly buffets), 2 bars, swimming pool, sauna, gym, tennis, squash, pool, 'chip & putt' golf, plus conference and business centres. The pool and gardens are very pleasant and there is a spectacular view across the river. Popular with locals for the swimming pool. Local excursions can be arranged. **B** *Gately on Nile*, Nile Crescent or 34b Kisinja Rd, PO Box 1300, T/F122400, T077-469636 (mob). An exclusive B&B on the shores of Lake Victoria, opened in 2000 by an Australian, Merryde Loosemore, a beautiful old colonial house set in stunning grounds. Restaurant, laundry and dry-cleaning facilities. Telephone and email available. There is a health salon offering Swedish massage, facials and reflexology. These services are also available to non-residents. It is very popular so booking is advisable. Bookings for local activities can be organized from here. There are simpler (and cheaper) rooms in the annexe. **B** *Crested Crane Hotel*, PO Box 444, 4-6 Hannington Square, T120891/2. Sometimes referred to as the *CC* or *Hotel for Tourism Training Institute*. Largely used by conference groups. Small restaurant, bar and satellite TV.

C *Hotel Triangle*, PO Box 515, 5 Lubogo Rd, T122090/1, T077-500874 (mob), F122090. Good standard, with en-suite rooms, an excellent restaurant with a varied menu and bar. **C** *Hotel Triangle Annex*, Nile Crescent, T122098/9, T077-490340 (mob), F120885, has stunning views over the lake. The double rooms have private balconies. Each room has a telephone. Pool table and laundry facilities. The restaurant provides a buffet for US$4.50. **C** *New Daniel Hotel*, Kiira Rd, T121633, is over-priced and is not recommended. **C** *Sunset Hotel International*, Plot 17 Kiira Rd, PO Box 156, T120115, F121322. Fine location

Uganda

with lovely gardens, beautiful views over the lake and brewery. There is a Chinese restaurant and local food is also available. Rooms are clean and include en-suite and fan. Boat trips and fishing can be arranged. **C-D** *Timton*, Jackson Crescent, T120278. Clean rooms with en-suite. Has a restaurant and small bar.

E *Fairway Guesthouse*, T121784, near the market and taxi park. Clean but lacks atmosphere, uninviting surroundings. Cheap restaurant downstairs. **E** *Richie Rich*, most often used for its restaurant facilities, has basic single/double rooms for US$8.50 and a bar and pool room. **E** *Victoria View*, T121363, also close to market and taxi park, clean but basic. **E** *YMCA*, PO Box 1223, T20365, provides accommodation ranging from basic dormitory beds at US$4 to more expensive private rooms. They have tennis courts, a sauna, gym and a pool table.

Camping D-E *Nile River Explorers Backpackers Lodge*, PO Box 2155, Plot 41 Wilson Av, T120236, T077-422373 (mob), F121322, camping US$3 per person, dorm bed US$5 per person, double room US$15 per person, food (order in advance), bar, free pool table, internet access and email facilities, satellite TV, hot showers, western toilets and laundry facilities. *NRE* can help with organizing gorilla permits and other bookings, eg Chimp Island, and vehicle hire. Credit cards and travellers cheques accepted. Highly recommended. *Timton Hotel* also offers cheap camping, with basic shared facilities including the use of a hot shower, US$2.50 per person.

Eating   **Mid-range** There are a few places in town worth trying besides those attached to hotels. The *Sailing Club*, off Nile Crescent on the shores of Lake Victoria, has a delightful setting. There haven't been any boats there for years but it is a relaxed, mellow place with pleasant views. They do a very good buffet on Sun for US$5.50 and an average main course costs US$4. All seating is outside during the day, but from 1900 food is served inside. The menu

Whitewater rafting

Most people stop off in Jinja to go rafting. Shooting the rapids is described in the publicity material as an 'adrenaline-pumping experience' and it's certainly not for the faint-hearted. It is tremendous fun but physically quite demanding. Although it's often seen as a young person's sport, really anyone older than about 14 can take part in it. The Nile is a deep river and consequently pretty safe, with few rocks to worry about. Its exact depth depends on the Owen Falls Dam, as the water level can vary by around a metre or so depending how much is flowing through the dam. Note that you will need an extension to your insurance policy to take part, as it is normally excluded as a dangerous sport. Watch out for sunburn: the combination of water and the equatorial sun is lethal. Even with Factor 30, most people are rather red and sore at the end of the day.

Two companies currently offer rafting on the Nile and there is some debate about which is the better. Adrift reckon that they take in four 'true' grade 5s stretches and are therefore even more 'adrenaline-pumping' than Nile River Explorers. Frankly, unless you are an experienced rafter, you will be

hard put to notice the difference. The main difference is that NRE start further upriver, just below the dam wall, giving everyone the chance to practise safety drills and enjoy some smaller rapids before running the grade 4s and 5s further downstream. The other big advantage is that, if it's really not for you, you can get out before hitting the big stuff. Adrift, on the other hand, start at Bujagali, which is a true baptism of fire. For many, the experience of jumping from the raft and letting the current take you down the river is almost as big a thrill as hitting the G spot. At least you have time to appreciate the experience! All the rapids are named to heighten the anticipation: for instance 'Total Gunga', 'Silverback', 'Rib Cage' and 'Surf City'.

Plans to build another dam at Itanda Falls (Silverback) are at an advanced stage. This will probably be complete by 2004/5, providing the environment impact study is approved. Quite how the two operators react to this will be interesting as a number of the grade 5 rapids will no longer exist.

For details of the two companies, see *page 652.*

Uganda

---

includes Indian and Italian. **Gately on Nile**, T/F122400, T077-469636 (mob), also has a restaurant open to the public. The gardens overlook Lake Victoria and the atmosphere is quiet and relaxed. The food is of excellent quality and reasonable value. Lunch is US$3.50, a 3-course dinner costs US$7.75 and afternoon tea is served for around US$2. Booking advisable.

Cheap *Fang Fangs*, 30/32 Kyabazinga Way, Shell Ambercourt Station, T21588. Sister restaurant of the Kampala Chinese restaurant of the same name, offering a variety of dishes from different provinces. Situated outside the town centre, near the roundabout to Kampala. The restaurant is not particularly attractive, but the food is definitely worth it. *Oasis* does excellent pizzas. *Munch Corner* is very popular for its spicy Indian food.

Seriously cheap *Bee Bee's* on Main St does good lunches and snacks but is only open from 1200-1400. *Source Café* does chips and snacks in a very pleasant environment, and is also a gift shop selling cards and batiks. Main St has lots of local eating houses, all in the price range, and the best are: *Friends Bar*, *Rendezvous* and *The Place*. Local meals cost about US$1.40. *Rangoli Restaurant* on Main St does the best chips in town. *Richie Rich* serves excellent value chicken and chips for US$1.10. *Karibu Bar* and *Blue Cat* also do cheap food but are often out of most items on the menu and are frequented more as bars. Austrian-run *Amadeus* serves reasonable cheap food but has very pricey drinks.

Nile Art and Crafts Gallery, 4-6b Main St, T075-653141 (mob), sells quite a wide range including interestingly designed batik, made on the premises. **Shopping**

Canoeing *Sebek Expeditions* launched their canoeing trips in 2001 at US$50 a day. These **Sport** start below the last major rapid (about 35 km from Jinja) and will concentrate on bird-watching, fishing, swimming as well as cultural interaction. It is run with *Nile River Explorers* and you can combine rafting and canoeing. For example, 2 days' rafting and 3 days' canoeing will cost around US$300. Contact *NRE*, T43-120236, T077-422373 (mob), F121322, www.raftafrica.com, for futher information.

Golf *Jinja Club* has a 9-hole golf course which costs US$5.60 for 2 rounds plus US$1.50 caddie fees.

Speedboat rides These can be organized at the *Sailing Club*. Short excursions cost US$1.75 per person (minimum of 3). To Samuka, Kisima or private hire (30 mins) costs US$22.25 per person.

Swimming The obvious choice for a swim would be the river. Avoid the lake due to risk of bilharzia, but anywhere where the water is flowing should be fine. It is possible to swim from the Bujagali campsites in beautiful surroundings. There is a swimming pool at *Jinja Nile Resort* (complete with pool bar) and at the *Jinja Club* (water a bit green!). Both cost US$3.50 per person.

Tennis and squash are on offer at the *Jinja Club* at US$1.75 per session.

Tubing (sitting on an inflatable tube and being carried along by the currents) flat water only costs US$5.50 for 15 mins. **Fishing**, at US$15 per session, can be arranged at *Speke's Camp and Sporting Bar* T077-401508/9 (mob).

Whitewater rafting Two companies offer this: *Nile River Explorers* (NRE) and *Adrift*. *NRE*, T120236, T077-422373 (mob), F121322, its based in Jinja and provides a free night's accommodation either at its *Backpackers Hostel* in Jinja or at the Bujagali campsite. Its package, at US$65, follows a slightly different rafting route, 18 km long including 8 rapids. Many consider that *NRE* runs a more personal day than *Adrift* – all the guides and staff live locally and after the day's rafting will spend the evening with the clients. *NRE* has recently introduced river-boarding – surfing the standing waves on the Nile – which is physically very demanding (previous surfing experience is an asset). The package offered is much the same as with the rafting and costs US$65. The cost includes transport from Jinja to the river and back, a light lunch of fruit and sodas, and the day is rounded off with a BBQ, beers and sodas. 2-day rafting trips are also available with *NRE*, as are river-boarding and rafting combination packages. *NRE* also operate a kayak school tailored to individual clients.

Adrift is based in Ggaba, Kampala, T041-268670, T075-707 668 (mob), www.adrift.co.nz Transport pick-up from the *Sheraton Hotel* and (Natate) *Backpackers Hostel*. No experience is necessary and they offer the option of paddling as a team or riding in an oar raft, with the guide rowing. 1- and 2-day trips down the Nile, starting from Bujagali Falls. Cost US$95 per person includes transport from Kampala, 1 day's rafting and a BBQ. Video footage of every trip is available from both companies and makes an excellent memento.

Bus Jinja to Kampala, 1½ hrs, US$1.50. *Matatu* Jinja to Busia, US$3. From Kampala to Jinja by **Transport** *matatu* takes 1-2 hrs and costs US$1.50. There is one taxi park in Jinja, but if travelling into Kampala taxis can be caught from a side-road off Clive Rd (see map) to avoid the scrum!

Banks The best rates are at *Allied Bank*, *Crane Bank* and *Trend Forex Bureau*, all on Main St. If you arrive **Directory** at the weekend when these facilities are closed the manager of *Fang Fang's* may be able to help. No credit cards accepted. *Forex bureaux* usually give better rates and quicker service than banks. **Communications** **Internet:** The most frequently used facility is at the *Source Café* on Main St. They have a newly established cyber-café and charge US$0.05 per min at weekends and US$0.10 during the week. The **post office** also offers email, as does the **tourist centre**, but they do not have internet access.

Excursions down the Nile

Downstream from the Owen Falls Dam are the Bujagali Falls. These can be reached **Bujagali Falls** by crossing the Owen Falls Dam (if you are coming from Kampala) and turning northwards at the Kyabazinga roundabout. The Bujagali Falls are approximately 8 km from Jinja (two-hour walk) – go straight on from Clive Road, past the round-about, continue for a further 7 km. It is a spectacular area with about 1 km of raging water. Local legend has it that a man called Mr Bujagali sometimes sits on the river on a bark-cloth mat. Even if you don't want to stay, Bujagali is worth a visit. It costs US$1 by *piki-piki* (motorbike taxi). For a small fee locals will offer to 'swim' over the falls whilst holding on to a jerry-can. This is a thoroughly stupid thing to do, and some have even drowned in the process, so it is not a good idea to encourage them by paying for this 'entertainment'. ■ *Entry to the falls, US$2.*

Sleeping and eating There are two campsites at Bujagali, one owned by *Nile River Explorers* and the other by Kampala-based *Speke's Camp*. The latter is not to be confused with *Speke's Camp and Sporting Bar* at the Source of the Nile in Jinja. Both campsites provide camping and banda accommodation, have a bar and serve food to order. In addition, *Speke's Camp* has dormitory bandas and is situated close to the water, just metres from Bujagali Falls. The *NRE camp* is sited overlooking the expanse of the river, with beautiful views and it pro-vides a fantastic spot to watch the sun set. There is a rustic bar, volleyball court, secluded showers, toilets, laundry facilities and full-time security. Both campsites have a friendly, infor-mal atmosphere. Prices are the same at both campsites: camping US$2 per person, bandas US$15 per person, dormitory bandas US$5 per person. Good security. ■ *To visit* Speke's Camp *there is a charge of US$1.25 per person.*

This is another set of rapids covered by both rafting companies (see page 652). There **Kyabirwa** is a shady, secluded campsite with latrines and bucket showers on request. **Camping** costs US$3 per person. There are no facilities and the owners would probably be sur-prised if you ask to stay as it is unusual, but they would make you very welcome. The camp can be found 9 km from Jinja on the Bujagali road. You can catch a *matatu* or get a *piki-piki*. There is a large red sign on the left to the camp. Either walk the last 2 km or try to get a *boda-boda*. ■ *Entry to the site, US$0.75.*

These falls are even further from town but are probably the most spectacular of all **Itanda** and well worth a visit. There are no facilities. **Camping** is permitted but the cost would have to be negotiated with the locals. The view is truly fantastic. To get there get a *matatu* to Kibibi and then ask for directions from the locals. Your best bet would be to hitch to the falls as public transport is scarce this far out. Locals will be able to direct you. If you prefer, get a *piki-piki* from town and ask them to take you all the way. The cost will be about US$5.60. ■ *Entrance fee to the falls, US$0.75.*

Samuka Island Samuka Island in Lake Victoria is a 4-ha island, about an hour's boat ride from Jinja. There are four self-contained cottages, all with en-suite facilities and solar-powered hot water. There is a bar and restaurant for the use of residents and day visitors (buffet US$15 per person, menu US$10 per person). There is also a campsite with shared water and toilet facilities. It has a very quiet and idyllic atmosphere, is rarely full, and is the perfect place to unwind and relax. There are a number of packages available. Canoe boat (powered) US$8.50 including meal plus US$4.50 transport costs. Pontoon (including transport, buffet, drinks and boat ride) US$15 per person (for 10 people or more) or US$25 per person (if less than 10 people, minimum of 5).

Sleeping C *Sunset Cottages*, B&B and full board available. Special rates Mon-Wed of around 15-20% discount on a double room (less on a single). Prices include transport, accommodation and a day at Jinja Golf Club (and a free key chain for the ladies!). To book, either visit *Speke's Camp and Sporting Bar* or phone T077-401508/9 (mob).

The road to Kenya

From Jinja the road to Kenya continues first northeast and then swings east. About 20 km from Jinja the road goes through the small market town of Magamaga and then, after another 5 km or so, there is a road off to the right. Here is the little village of Buluba, where Bishop Hannington was murdered in 1885 (see box page 655). After another 15 km, you will pass through the town of Iganga, the district headquarters.

Iganga
Phone code: 43 This sleepy little town has wide streets bordered by shops and houses with broad verandahs. Most people just pass through in transit and there are no tourist facilities at all, but Iganga offers a fine opportunity to experience real African town life. South of the town is Nenda Hill, a viewpoint for the surrounding plains. It contains the shrine of the *Bazungu* (white people) and is a 10-15 minute taxi ride from town.

Sleeping D *Mwaana Highway Hotel* is a new place, clean with a nice lobby and very friendly staff. It has a restaurant, satellite TV, hot water, self-contained rooms, breakfast included in the price. On Wed, Fri and Sat, the bar next door plays loud music until midnight. **E** *East View Guesthouse*, 77 Old Market St, T2172, bit run-down but still fairly clean. Restaurant, self-contained rooms and hot water (intermittently). **E** *Tip Top Hotel*, is marginally better than the *East View* in terms of level of service and facilities. **E** *Holiday Inn*, is rated as slightly worse than the other **E**-grade hotels, although there is little to choose between them.

Eating Mid-range *Mwaana Restaurant* offers the most varied menu in Iganga, including western dishes like pizzas and cheeseburgers – however these often need to be ordered several hours in advance to allow time to buy the ingredients. **Cheap** *Najja*, serves nice fish,

Iganga

To Jinja
To Tororo
Old Market St
Tweyambe Women's Handicraft Shop
Main St
Private Car Taxis
Oboja Dr
Saza Rd
Taxis/Bus Park
To Nenda Hill Viewpoint & Bazungu Shrine

N
Not to scale

■ **Sleeping**
1 East View Guesthouse
2 Holiday Inn
3 Mwaana Highway
4 Tip Top

● **Eating**
1 Accra Kent
2 Najja

Bishop Hannington

Coming from Kampala, a little beyond Jinja on the right, is Buluba, where Bishop Hannington, consecrated in 1884 as the first Bishop of the Diocese of Eastern Equatorial Africa, met his death. Hannington kept a detailed diary during his journeys and it is through this, and stories from the survivors, that we know what happened.

James Hannington had first visited East Africa in 1882 as the leader of a party of reinforcements for the Victoria Nyanza Mission in Uganda. He had suffered severely from dysentery and had been forced to return to Britain. However, after being made Bishop, he began to plan his return to Africa. At this time the route into Uganda was from Zanzibar, through what is now Tanzania, to the south of Lake Victoria. In 1883 a new route was tried, through Kenya, via Busoga, to the north of the lake. This route through Masai country was more direct and climatic conditions were not as harsh.

Arriving on the East African coast in January 1885, Hannington made plans to use the Masai route. On hearing this, the missionaries in Buganda wrote to inform him that the current political situation in Buganda was such that entering by the 'back door', through Busoga, was extremely dangerous. However, the warning arrived about two weeks after Hannington had set off.

Hannington's only real mistake was that he did not stick to his plans as set out in a letter to the missionaries in Buganda. He told them that he would go overland as far as Kavirondo on Lake Victoria, where the mission boat would meet him, and that he would enter Buganda by boat. This would mean he would avoid entering Uganda through Busoga, which was so sensitive. Mwanga, the son of King Mutesa I, had been told that those entering Buganda from the east (that is, Busoga) would destroy the Kingdom of Buganda and the missionaries in Buganda had assured Mwanga that the Bishop would not enter via that route. So when he did, it appeared as a calculated deceit.

On 21 October Hannington reached the headquarters of Luba, the chief of the area of Busoga. He was imprisoned and, on the orders of messengers from Buganda, speared to death and his porters were massacred.

In March 1890 a boy who had been with Hannington arrived in the camp of Jackson, another missionary who was on his way to Uganda. The boy had with him a skull (its lower jaw bone missing), identified as belonging to Hannington by its gold teeth. He also had the soles of Hannington's boots, a rubber hot water bottle and the lid of an Army and Navy canteen.

The remains eventually found their way to Kampala and on 31 December 1892 they were buried on Namirembe Hill.

Uganda

---

chicken and chips and the best African food in town. Lovely outdoor seating, separated from the traffic of the busy road by a protective fence. On Wed, Fri and Sat a drama group performs simple mimes and *busoga* dancing from the region. Afterwards the audience is able to join in with the dancing to more modern music. It is the only real 'nightlife' in Iganga and shouldn't be missed. *Accra Kent* serves African food of good quality. In addition, there are many cheap African eating houses along the main road that serve good lunches.

Shopping The *Tweyambe Women's Handicraft Shop* offers a variety of locally produced goods of reasonable quality.

Tororo

Situated in the far east of Uganda this is close to the border with Kenya and many people pass through on the way to and from the border crossing at Malaba. Its major claim to fame is the rock named after it, which can be seen from miles around. Built during the colonial period in the late 1940s, the Tororo Cement Works made an important contribution to the development of Uganda as it took away the necessity of importing cement from Kenya. It functioned well until Amin's time. As everything in Uganda began to fall apart so did the cement works, its roof eventually collapsing under the weight of the cement dust. Now, however, the operation is up and running again.

0°45'N 34°12'E
Phone code: 45
Colour map 3, grid B3

The road to the border is fairly good, but has the usual pot-hole problems and you will pass through fairly typical Ugandan scenery – clusters of small huts surrounded by farmland, as well as areas of verdant bush and elephant grass with the occasional anthill sticking up. There are stretches of hills separated by marshy swamps. There are also many mango trees in this part of Uganda and during the season their fruit can be bought on the roadside. As you approach the border you can either continue straight on to Tororo for the Malaba crossing or take a right turning to Busia. The road block at this turning is there to stop smugglers, but it seems to do little more than collect bribes. From about this point you should be able to see the Tororo Rock sticking up in the distance. The **Hindu temple** is only open for services at 1800. Tourists are not welcome.

Tororo Rock is a volcanic plug that rises to about 1,800 m above sea level. It is possible to climb and the views from the top are fantastic. There are steps and ladders to help you get to the summit, and the climb takes about an hour. Tours of the rock can be organized from both the *Rock* and *Sunrise Hotels*. Contrary to some reports, Lake Victoria cannot be seen from the top of the rock.

Sleeping **C-D** *Rock*, 70 Malaba Rd, T44654/5, F44458. Set in gardens, situated behind the golf course, outside the town centre. All rooms (doubles) are self-contained. Prices include breakfast. The *Terrace Snackbar* serves samosas, chips and chapattis US$2. The restaurant meals of fish or steak and chips cost US$3. Breakfast (non-residents' rate) costs US$2.75. **D** *Sunrise*, Plot 2 Torgue Av/ Malaka Rd, 1 km out of town, T077-449405 (mob). Fresh, new, very clean hotel in a lovely setting. Gardens with the bar outside in a marquee. The Rotary Club meets there every Wed at 1900. Comfortable lounge with TV/video, dining room also has a TV for Sat viewing, bar selling wine at US$14 a bottle, plus a pool table. 6 self-contained double rooms. Restaurant

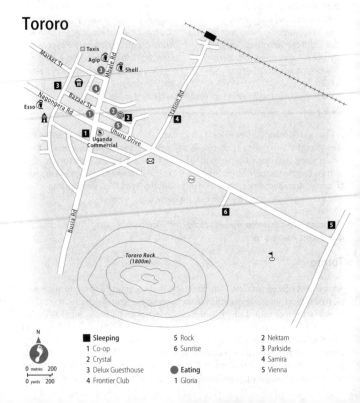

Tororo

Tororo Rock
(1800m)

N
0 metres 200
0 yards 200

■ **Sleeping**
1 Co-op
2 Crystal
3 Delux Guesthouse
4 Frontier Club

5 Rock
6 Sunrise

● **Eating**
1 Gloria

2 Nektam
3 Parkside
4 Samira
5 Vienna

serves sandwiches US$1 and local food, *matoke*, rice, chicken, chips at around US$1.25. **D** *Crystal*, 22 Bazaar St, PO Box 778, T44081, T077-499556 (mob). Manager: Mrs Joanita Okoroi. Has views of the Tororo Rock. Simple, clean, self-contained rooms all have balconies. Offers good value, with restaurant and bar facilities. **E** *Frontier Club*, Plot 2 Station Rd, T44474. All rooms have fans and nets, clean, self-contained. Nice atmosphere. Breakfast not included in the price but at around US$1.10 you can enjoy coffee, tea, chapatti, toast, egg, etc. Restaurant is cheap, and offers good local food at around US$1. The dining room has a TV. Surrounded by gardens, fairly close to the town centre but away from the worst of the noise. **E** *Co-op*, central, noisy, cheap but not particularly cheerful. **E** *Delux Guesthouse*, Plot 10 Market St, T44986. Above a shop and hairdresser, music playing loudly until 2200 (allegedly). Lively area. Simple, cheap, basic accommodation in self-contained rooms. No food.

NB The *Tororo Christian Guest House* only caters for long-term lets of 1 month or more, not for hotel use. Currently under renovation.

Seriously cheap *Nektam* is a very large restaurant, resembling a hall, with 2 different settings, as though 2 restaurants had merged, with a European appearance. Serves African food but is also the hang-out for the local youth, with a very relaxed atmosphere. On Sat there is dancing, both during daytime and at night. *Vienna*, opposite the *Crystal Hotel*, is a recently started enterprise, serving local food. Just 2 tables in rather bare surroundings. *Gloria*, situated opposite the Ugandan Commercial Bank at the roundabout in a little courtyard behind the shops, serves snacks such as eggs, chicken or fish with chips, and local food – *matoke* (steamed banana), rice, *posho* (milled maize cooked to a stiff porridge consistency), potatoes combined with beans, fish or chicken. *Samira* is a busy large restaurant with many tables. Serves African and Indian food eg samosas and chapattis US$1.10. *Parkside*, has a little terrace, as well as tables indoors. Nice atmosphere, pleasant waitresses. Serves local food. *Frontier Club* serves tasty local food. *Golf Course Clubhouse* serves snacks and local food. Nice views, relaxed ambience with outdoor seating.

Eating

Road Tororo is 217 km from **Kampala**, about 3½ hrs by *matatu* or bus. They go frequently. However, if you are heading for Kenya there is little reason to stop over at Tororo now that *Akamba Bus* offers a direct service from Kampala to Nairobi. From taxi park, fares to **Mbale** US$1.50, **Busia** US$1.2, **Iganga** US$2.25, **Jinja** US$3 and **Kampala** US$4.

Transport

Internet Email facilities are available in a small shop between *Crystal Hotel* and *Nektam*. With just 1 computer it charges US$5 per ½ hr, but only US$0.05 for sending per page if ready on a disk. Printing US$0.55 per page.

Directory

Mbale

This town is in the eastern part of Uganda in the foothills of Mount Elgon, giving it a pleasant climate. Mbale shows clearly the Asian influence on towns in Uganda – in particular, many of the buildings have the distinctive verandah that is seen all over East Africa. It is a pleasant, safe, bustling market town where tourists rarely hear taunts of *muzungo*. For many years it was possible to buy all sorts of things in Mbale that were unobtainable in Kampala thanks to smuggling from Kenya. During the colonial years eucalyptus plantations were planted all around Mbale as an anti-mosquito measure. Over the past 25 years the trees have gradually been cut down and malaria, which was once eradicated from the area, has returned. The roads are much better than in Kampala. There is a large **Commonwealth War Graves Cemetery**. Mbale is also the home of the **Islamic University**, founded in 1988 and one of only a few such institutions in Africa.

1°8'N 34°12'E
Phone code: 45
Colour map 3, grid B3

Not far from Mbale is a large rock called Nkokonjeru (also known locally as Wanale), which means 'the white rock'. Idi Amin once planned to build a huge international hotel and conference centre here. The building began with the construction of the road – almost a motorway – up to the top of the rock. That was as far

Nkokonjeru

Uganda

as it got and the complex itself was never begun. There are wonderful views and it is sometimes possible to see the peregrine falcons that live on the rock.

Imbalu dances If you happen to be in this area during even-numbered years you may manage to see some of the local festivities of the Imbalu people, as well as the mass circumcision ceremonies of the Bugisu and Sebei people (see box, page 661). The official first day of the circumcision season is on 1 August, when there is a celebration at the cultural centre just outside Mbale. There is a signposted turning to the east about 1 km south of Mbale on the Tororo-Mbale road. Anyone is welcome. The festivities reach a climax during December and involve singing, dancing, drumming and general merrymaking.

Kakoro rock paintings These paintings, about 20 km from Mbale, are to be found in the Pallisa district, behind the local schools. The paintings themselves, in red and white pigments, are not that impressive, and are being worn away by local children and by animals moving to graze. There are two sites with red paintings, including some concentric circles on the south and west sides of a rock pillar at the southern end of the hill. On the underside of a rock ledge there is a third example of rock art in white pigment, but the subject matter is unidentifiable. The paintings are thought to be the work of hunter-gatherers who lived in this region 2,000 years ago. There is a fairly spectacular ancient gong near the paintings that is balanced precariously some 10 m in the air, and a rock-slide near by. The rock paintings are in an area of scrub-land surrounded by plantations of sweet-potato and cassava. There is no accommodation but the local people are happy to talk to visitors about the rock paintings. Further north are the more spectacular **Nyero rock paintings** near the town of Kumi (see page 667). ■ *The site can be reached by travelling north from Mbale towards Kumi to the village of Nakaloke, then turning west to the village of Kabwangasi, from which there is a track to the paintings. A matatu from Mbale-Nakatoke costs about US$0.25, then by boda-boda or piki-piki to Kakoro costs around US$1. Alternatively, it is possible to drive all the way to the site in a 4WD.*

Mbale

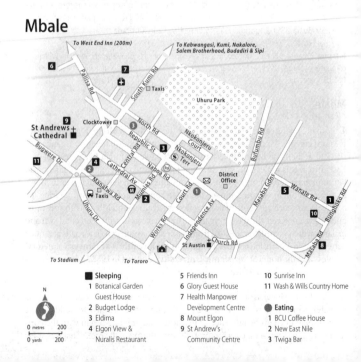

■ Sleeping
1 Botanical Garden Guest House
2 Budget Lodge
3 Eldima
4 Elgon View & Nuralis Restaurant
5 Friends Inn
6 Glory Guest House
7 Health Manpower Development Centre
8 Mount Elgon
9 St Andrew's Community Centre
10 Sunrise Inn
11 Wash & Wills Country Home

● Eating
1 BCU Coffee House
2 New East Nile
3 Twiga Bar

C *Mount Elgon*, 30 Masaba Rd, PO Box 670, T33454, F33891. A little way out of town just past the National Park Offices. Now privately owned. The communal areas are a little run-down, bedrooms large and clean. Extensive gardens are being developed. Restaurant, TV, en-suite bathrooms, nets, fans, laundry services and parking with good security. Has commanding views of Wanale Rock. Food reported to be a little uninspired and to taste of chip fat. Small shop. **C** *Sunrise Inn*, Plot 45 Nakhupa Rd, PO Box 2607, T33090, F33863. Opened in 1996, about 500 m past *Mount Elgon Hotel* on the Masaba Rd. Sited in a pleasant area. Lovely garden, good, clean, attractive accommodation with TV, video. Easy ½-hr walk or take a *boda-boda* ride. Price includes breakfast. *Sunrise Inn Restaurant* is very popular and needs to be booked well in advance. Serves very good meals – probably the best in Mbale. **C** *Wash and Wills Country Home*, Plot No 37 Mbiro Rd, Maluku PO Box 1327, T35264, F34173. Brand new developing hotel (2001). Excellent accommodation, lovely garden with bar. Swimming pool under construction. Access 5 mins by *boda-boda* from town centre. Price includes breakfast. TV, video, pool table, sauna, gym, and restaurant serving African, Indian, Chinese and western food. Nets, fans, parking with good security. Offers a shuttle bus service to Entebbe. **C** *West End Inn*, 97 Mbale (U) Plot 5 Kasamu Jamall Rd, Pallisa Rd, T34626, T077-525624 (mob), F33891. Good clean accommodation off the main road from Kampala opposite the Lions Playground (signposted), about 10 min *boda-boda* ride from town. Clean and well run. Snacks available. Evening meals rather limited. Price includes breakfast. En-suite, nets, fans, laundry services and parking with good security.

D *Botanical Garden Guest House*, Plot 7 Bunghoko Rd, PO Box 484, T33185, F33891. Out of town beyond the *Sunrise Inn*. Good clean accommodation in a pleasant location with lovely gardens. Restaurant serves western and local food. TV, en-suite bathrooms, hot water, western-style toilets, laundry service, fans and secure parking. **D** *Friends Inn*, 49 Wanale Rd, PO Box 2000, T34437. Developing family hotel with extensive grounds/gardens. Renovations and extension in progress. Price includes breakfast. Bar, en-suite bathrooms, hot water, nets, fans, laundry service and secure parking. Offers good views of Wanale Rock. **D** *Hotel Eldima*, 35 Republic St, PO Box 957, T35225. Recently opened, in the middle of town, with attractive clean rooms. Price includes breakfast. Restaurant serves local and western food. Hot water, bucket showers, western toilets, nets, fans, laundry services and secure parking. **D-E** *Salem Brotherhood Mbale*, PO Box 1558, T/F33368. Salem Brotherhood is a Christian NGO providing medical care and community support. It is partly funded by the SB in Germany but also raises funds through income generating projects such as a conference centre, the guesthouses and sale of handicrafts. All profits made go towards the running of the health centre and children's home. There is a variety of accommodation from self-contained to camping facilities. Fresh home-grown food is available. Highly recommended. Located northwest of the town on the road to Kolonyi.

E *Budget Lodge*, PO Box 157. Sited at the junction of Cathedral Av and Mumias Rd. Very cheap, basic, clean accommodation, situated close to the market on the edge of town. No food. Hot water, nets and laundry service. **E** *Elgon View*, PO Box 967, T077-445562 (mob). Basic, clean accommodation, with roof-top eating area and bar serving local, Indian, Chinese and western food. Centrally located above *Nuralis Restaurant*. Has a Forex, hot water, nets, fans, laundry service, extra charge for parking. **E** *Glory Guest House*, Plot 4 Mugishu Hill, Walker Lane, Industrial Division, PO Box 2446, T35262, T077-481272 (mob). Basic, clean hotel within walking distance of town off the Pallisa Rd. Price includes breakfast. Evening meals served on request. En-suite bathrooms, hot water, western toilets, showers, laundry service and parking available. **E** *Health Manpower Development Centre*, T33723. Run mainly as a workshop/conference centre but worth trying for a simple room at very low cost, centrally located close to the hospital. **E** *St Andrew's Community Centre*, Plot 12 Pallisa Rd, PO Box 614, T33650. Good, basic, friendly budget accommodation. Breakfast not included in price. Central location. Evening meals can be ordered from the dining hall. Has bucket showers, hot water, shared toilets, nets, laundry service and secure parking.

Eating	**Cheap** *Nuralis Restaurant*, on the ground floor of the same building as *Elgon View Hotel*
Food is available at the larger hotels	(but unrelated), is a good place to eat in town, serving tasty local, Indian, Chinese and west-ern food at reasonable prices. *Sunrise Inn*, a short distance from town in a pleasant location serves a good range of food at reasonable prices. Lovely outdoor eating area. *Hotel Eldima*. Newly opened, attractive restaurant, centrally located, offers an assortment of mostly local food. Well worth trying. Inexpensive. *Twiga Bar*, another local option, serves African food, clean, good service. **New East Nile Restaurant**, centrally located on South Kumi Rd, serves cheap, edible local food. Good range of cakes and snacks. There are numerous other cheap local eating places in town. **Cheap-seriously cheap** *BCU Coffee House and Restaurant*, Republic St, opposite the post office, is very popular with a fair range of good local and west-ern food. Inexpensive. Good service. Recommended as one of the best eating places in Mbale. Less plush than *Nuralis*.

Entertainment   There is only one nightclub in Mbale, the *Club Oasis* on Cathedral Av, but the town is a bus-tling, lively place at night.

Shopping   There are 4 small supermarkets close to the clocktower, as well as the market. The *Blue Bakery* offers the freshest bread in town, but is otherwise unremarkable. It is located close to *Wimpy*, along Naboa Rd.

Tourist office   There is a tourist office in Mbale, PO Box 135, Mbale, T33720, located just before the *Mount Elgon Hotel*, which provides information about climbing Mt Elgon. The tourist office also stocks camping equipment, the informative leaflet and map of the Mount Elgon Forest Exploration Centre, and can confirm accommodation availability there. There are maps as well as up-to-date advice, and anyone planning to climb the mountain is advised to visit the office before travelling to Budadiri.

Transport   **Road**   Mbale is 272 km from Kampala, about 3 hrs or less via the new tarmac road from Iganga on the Jinja-Tororo road. It is 1½ hrs from Busia on the Kenyan border. *Matatus* leave from the old taxi park in Kampala for Mbale throughout the day and cost US$4.50. If travel-ling independently watch out for the turning once you pass through Iganga. A sign indicates a left turn on the new road to Mbale, whilst the old, bad road continues towards Tororo. *Matatus* will drop you near the clocktower in Mbale in the town centre. Parking is not usually a problem in Mbale, either on the roadside or in the new car park just past the clocktower. There are two taxi parks in Mbale. The Kumi Rd taxis will take you out east to **Kumi**, **Soroti**, **Kapchorwa**, **Sipi** and **Budadiri**, while taxis from the Manafwa Rd park will take you to **Kampala**, **Jinja**, **Iganga**, **Tororo** and places south.

There is also a bus park just behind the taxi park (see map), buses leaving at regular inter-vals during the day. Fare to **Kampala** is US$4.50. Another option is the post bus, which leaves Mbale for Kampala on time each morning at 0800.

The *Akamba* bus travels daily to **Nairobi**. It leaves from Bulambuli House, Mumias Rd, near the junction with Pallisa and Kumi Rd at 1700. The fare is US$10. Connections can be made in Nairobi for Moshi, Arusha and Mombasa. A bus also leaves Mbale for Dar es Salaam.

Car hire   *Elgon Tours*, Plot 8 Manafwa Rd, PO Box 1513, T35018, opposite the taxi park. Very helpful owner.

Directory   **Banks**   *Mount Elgon Forex Bureau*, on Republic St, is halfway between the clocktower and the police station, but it does not change TCs. *Standard Chartered Bank* will change currency ($ and £) but not TCs. **Communications**   **Internet**: there are as yet no internet cafés in Mbale but a number of small firms offer email access on their computers. The post office offers this service for US$0.20 per min. **Faxes** can be sent and received at the Mbale post office, F33891. **Telephone**: There is now a good telephone communication service in Mbale, with MTN, Celtex having the monopoly. International calls are relatively straightforward from here.

Bugisu circumcision

The Bugisu have a strong belief in their rites and the ceremony of circumcision is very much an important part of the life cycle. All men must undergo circumcision, and males who die before this has been done will be circumcized before they are buried, in order to complete their life on earth.

Circumcision takes place every other year and is performed on young men aged between 14 and 25. The circumcision season is said to be marked by the appearance of a strange bird whose singing marks the beginning of the preparations. The elders gather under the clan tree, which is said to be older than the memory of man itself. They then begin training the candidates for the rituals, which last three days.

On the first day the young man is smeared with sorghum paste all over the body. He wears the traditional dress of animal skins and a head dress, puts three heavy bangles on each leg and then visits his relatives, singing and dancing. The songs he sings are mainly praising his forefathers and the gods. Every so often he stops and leaps high in the air.

On the second day his hair is cut and he is allowed to bathe – the last opportunity before the ceremony proper begins. This symbolizes the death of the past and of what he has been, and a new beginning. The white

sorghum paste is again smeared on his body. The singing and dancing continues and this evening is one of great celebration amongst the people of the village.

On the morning of the circumcision the young man wakes at first light and is again smeared with sorghum paste. He then sets off to visit his maternal uncles, who give him gifts of cows or goats, which are part of the bride price paid by his father. Later in the day he is taken down to the river by the men who wash him thoroughly from the waist to the knees. He is then brought at a slow pace to the ground that is traditionally used for these ceremonies. On the ground is a Y-shaped stick, which he picks up and holds behind his head. The circumcision itself is over fairly quickly and a whistle is blown to announce that the candidate has been successful. Occasionally it happens that a man will try to run away, but this is looked upon as the epitome of disgrace and cowardice.

Traditionally, once a man has been circumcized he can sit in on tribal meetings and participate in decision-making, and is also allowed to marry. Only once he has been through what is known as the pain of the knife can he be called a man, and it is said that, just like birth and death, it can only be done once in a lifetime.

Uganda

The village of Budadiri can be reached by taking the road north and then taking the **Budadiri** right-hand fork towards Siroka and Moroto after about 5 km, and then a right-turn after another 5 km, passing through the villages of Bulwalasi and Bugusege. There is an alternative route from the Mbale-Moroto road, which is to continue until you reach the right-hand turn just after Siroka. The latter route is a little longer, but the track is better. A *matatu* from the Kumi Road taxi park in Mbale costs US$1. Budadiri, a small trading centre about 30 km from Mbale, is the site of the Mount Elgon National Park office, where porters and guides can be arranged for climbers and walkers setting out on the main trail to the peak.

Sleeping and eating There are 2 simple but decent places to stay if you are making Budadiri a staging post for the climb. **E** *Rose's Last Chance* has 7 rooms and also offers camping. Breakfast included, meals and cold drinks available, and secure parking – vehicles can be left here for a small fee whilst climbing. **E** *Mere's Hotel*, just next to the Mt Elgon Park Office, offers sound accommodation, with good sanitation, as well as snacks and drinks. **Seriously cheap**: *Nabunubi's*, located near the taxi park, offers good meals at reasonable prices. It does not offer accommodation.

Mount Elgon National Park

To climb Mount Elgon from Kenya, see page 194

Near Mbale is an extinct volcano, believed to have had its last major eruption about 10 million years ago, located on the border of Uganda and Kenya. It has gradual slopes up to the peaks on the crater rim, which means that even non-mountaineers can climb it. At 4,321 m, **Wagagai** is the highest peak, and the fourth-highest East African mountain. The foothills around the base of Mount Elgon, known to the locals as 'Masaba', an excellent hiking area, very beautiful and virtually untouched by tourists. There are caves to visit as well as Sipi Falls.

Endemic flora includes the giant lobelia, giant heather and giant groundsel and wild flowers abound. Mammals include tree hyrax, bushpig and buffalo, blue monkey, baboon and black and white colobus monkeys. There are frequent sightings of casqued hornbill, the crowned eagle, Ross' touraco and the lammergeier. This area is well known for its high-quality Arabica coffee and you are likely to see coffee plantations. They are mostly small-scale farms using family labour.

Access There are essentially no tourist facilities outside Mbale, Sipi and Budadiri, yet anyone who is reasonably adventurous can explore the foothills of Mount Elgon with the help of *matatus*. These serve surprisingly wide and apparently remote areas from Mbale, possibly due to the high population density in this region. However, travel in the area is inevitably fairly slow. It is advisable first to buy a map of Mount Elgon National Park from the Department of Surveys and Mapping in Entebbe. To get to one recommended starting area, travel along the road to the border village of Suam. The national park office advises that it takes about 45 minutes from Mbale to Budadiri, 2½ hours from Mbale to Sipi Falls (with another half-hour to the Forest Exploration Centre), and three hours from Mbale to Kapkwata Visitor Centre, which is close to the border with Kenya.

It is also worthwhile exploring the area southeast of Mbale, leaving the tourist trail and heading towards places like Busano, a village in the shadow of **Nkokonjeru**, also called Wanale, Bududa (good views of Mount Elgon from this area nestled amidst small hills) and Bupoto/Buwabwala (an attractive and remote area adjacent to a peak called **Namisindwa**, which, although it doesn't look it, is not much lower than Nkokonjeru). All of these places are the final destinations of *matatus* from Mbale, of which there are several daily (especially to Bududa), so it should not be too difficult to find the right one. You will be ensured of a memorable journey, not least because you are likely to find yourself cramped by another 20 or so people, plus a goat/chickens in a minibus built for 14. There are no hotels in these areas but the people are very helpful and friendly – ask for permission to pitch a tent, or if stuck they may put

Climbing Mount Elgon

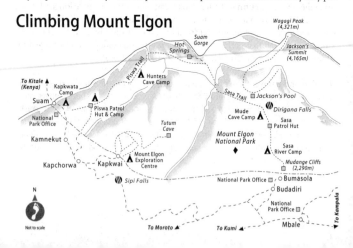

Uganda (side margin)

you up for the night, if you ask. The major problem you are likely to encounter is the very poor standard of English in these rural areas – it would be wise to find a school (there are many primary schools) and talk to one of the teachers. You shouldn't go hungry though, as small local *hotelis* (eating places) are to be found everywhere, usually serving tea, chapatti, *mandazi, posho* and beans. There are also tiny shops selling an amazing array of goods.

Encompassing the largest surface area of any extinct volcano in the world, Mount Elgon rises through a series of gradual slopes punctuated by steep cliffs to a height of 4,321 m above sea level. Volcanic foothills, cliffs, caves, gorges and waterfalls combine with panoramic views across wide plains to create some of the most spectacular scenery in Uganda. Elgon's upper slopes are cloaked in tropical montane forest while above this lies a vast tract of Afro-Alpine moorland. This unique vegetation extends over the caldera – a collapsed crater covering over 40 sq km at the top of the mountain.

Climbing Mount Elgon
Facilities continue to improve on the Ugandan side, making this a viable alterative to tackling the mountain from Kenya

The period to avoid is during the long rains, which are in April and May. Climbers should first head for the village of Budadiri where the climb begins. The Mount Elgon National Park office can arrange the climb for you – guides, porters, food etc. If you plan to get to the top expect the climb to last four days. There are two main trails: the Sasa Trail, accessed from Budadiri is quite steep in places with a climb of 1600 m on the first day; the Piswa Trail, starting from Kapkwata near Suam is gentler. However, if you are less ambitious there are many alternative walks, ranging from easy hikes to hard climbs.

Numagabwe Cave is within walking distance of Budadiri (see under Caves of Mount Elgon, below). The Tourist Office in Budadiri or in Mbale can give you maps and make suggestions to suit your requirements.

The climb itself is straightforward and can be accomplished easily by non-mountaineers. The trail is steep in places but it is possible to reach the caldera and return to the roadhead within three days of setting off walking at a comfortable pace. With an extra two days you could also reach Jackson's Summit on the highest point, Wagagai, or visit the hot springs at the head of the Suam Gorge.

A new trail to the summit of Mount Elgon is currently being made and should be in use shortly. There are four walks from the centre, ranging from 3 -11 km. The first is a circular walk via some of the falls, a cave and viewpoint, which takes about three hours. Two shorter walks of about 30 minutes are also available. A fourth trail leads to the enormous **Tutum Cave**, 14 km away.

There are numerous caves on Elgon and one of the most interesting and most readily accessible is situated within the spur on which Bulago Camp stands. Its impressive entrance is some 9 m wide and 3 m tall, and in wet weather it is partially hidden in spray from a small waterfall, which drops down banks of ferns that almost block the mouth. Just inside the main chamber are flat ledges cut into the rock, which are believed to have been used at one time, as sleeping berths by Bugisu people hiding from their enemies. The size of the main chamber is approximately 18 m by 45 m in depth, with a height of over 4.5 m.

Caves of Mount Elgon

According to native legend, the tunnel at the far end of the cave to the left leads to another much larger cavern. This is supposed to be full of water to a considerable depth. Whether this is true or not is unknown, but water can certainly be seen trickling from the tunnel.

The main cavern has no stalactites or stalagmites, nor any rock paintings. There are instead a number of garnet-like stones, embedded in a nest of a fine scintillating material resembling spiders' webs. The floor of the cave is flat and soft and littered with the droppings of bats. Looking out towards the entrance of the cave, especially when the sun is shining through the waterfall, giving off rainbows, is a lovely sight.

Numagabwe Cave, approximately 8 km from Budadiri, is traditionally a shrine where local people go to perform their rituals during the year of circumcision (see

Uganda

box page 661). The entrance to the cave is very narrow and leads into a large chamber inhabited by bats and small birds. Guided walks can be arranged at *Rose's Last Chance* in Budadiri. **Tutum Cave** can be reached following a 14-km hike with guides from the Mount Elgon Exploration Centre at Kapkwai.

There is a well-known cave opposite Sipi Camp, but it is not comparable either in size or interest with the one described above.

Rock climbing   Rock climbing with seven bolted routes is available at **Nagudi Rock**, located roughly halfway between Mbale and Budadiri. ■ *Cost US$1. Climbers must bring their own equipment. Directions available from the Park Information Office.*

Mount Elgon Exploration Centre   The Mount Elgon Exploration Centre is on the lower slopes of Mount Elgon at 2,057 m at Kapkwai, around a two-hour, 4-km guided walk across the undulating terrain from Sipi village. It is also possible to drive there from the village (approximately 12 km). ■ *The centre marks the boundary of Mt Elgon NP and charges US$15 NP entry fee. There appears to be some confusion over guide fees. If a Crow's Nest guide has brought you up to the camp you can pay the centre a fee of US$1.20 to remain with that guide, or employ one from the centre, though they are rarely there. The main office for bookings is in Mbale, T045-33720, or at Uganda Wildlife Authority, T041-346287.*

Sleeping and eating There is a small campsite and dormitory, both of which charge US$4.25 per person. Food can be provided if ordered in advance (US$2.25 dinner and US$1 breakfast) and drinks are available, provided someone is prepared to fetch them for you from the nearby trading centre. Guests are welcome to use the cooking facilities and cater for themselves. There are long-drops and bucket showers. The camp is very quiet, as guests rarely stay, probably because of the long hike to get there!

Sipi Falls   Sipi Falls offers stunning views of Mount Elgon and the plains of eastern and northern Uganda. The falls themselves are described as perhaps the most romantic in Africa. There are a large number of falls, not just the one featured in most of the promotional pictures. These are accessible via a network of well-maintained local trails, but the walking is not easy and a reasonable level of fitness is required. The resort's guides tend to offer only the short walk around the falls beneath the village, but can arrange longer walks if requested.

Sipi Falls are situated on the lower slopes of Mount Elgon at an altitude of 1,750 m, close to the village of Sipi, 60 km and a drive of about 2½-3 hours from Mbale on the Kapchorwa road, depending on the weather conditions. A four-wheel-drive is recommended. The waterfall and the surrounding area are very pretty and it is a pleasant place to spend a few days unwinding.

Sleeping   **A-B** *Sipi Falls Rest Camp* run by *Volcanoes Tours*, PO Box 22818, Kampala, T041-346464/5, F341718, sales@ volcanoessafaris.com, is the top-of-the-range resort at Sipi, in a prime position overlooking the main falls and the plains. The *Sipi Falls Rest Camp* is built around a small cottage with just 2 rooms – originally built as a

Sipi Falls

Mount Elgon Exploration Centre

♦ *Mount Elgon National Park*

3 km

To Kapchorwa

Sipi Secondary School

Sipi Falls

Sipi Village

N
Not to scale

■ **Sleeping**
1 Crow's Nest

● **Eating**
1 Go Down Bar

2 Elgon Masai Lodge
3 Moses' Campsite
4 Sipi Falls Rest Camp

1 To Mbale

holiday house for the Governor and officials during the colonial period – and has greatly expanded. Prices range from US$96 for a single room in the old house to US$54 per person for a triple banda, and US$72 for a double banda. All bandas have en-suite facilities, fans and nets. These prices are for full board including a 3-course lunch and dinner. Dinner for day visitors is US$5.50. There is a bar and games room on site, which non-residents are welcome to visit. Day visitors are charged a US$2.50 entry fee. Booking is recommended. Climbing expeditions to Mt Elgon can be organized from here.

E *The Crow's Nest*, PO Box 867, Mbale, thecrowsnest@e-architect.com (no phone on site, but email is checked weekly at the post office in Mbale). This is fast becoming the most popular choice and has spectacular views across to the main falls, as well as views of two smaller falls. Food is good and very cheap. The camp is run very efficiently by Ugandans, and has a laid-back, quiet atmosphere. In the dry season occasional overland trucks stay, and things get rowdier then. There is a famous swing perched on top of a sheer drop overlooking the falls, which has quite a reputation in Uganda and is something of a photo-spot. There are hot showers in the evening, western-style toilets and you either bring your own tent or rent their camping gear, sited under permanent shelters with mattresses. The dormitory bandas are very well equipped, with bedside lamps and a balcony overlooking the falls. Laundry facilities are available. The bar has no fridge but is fairly well stocked with drinks and snacks. If you choose to take an early walk (the guides recommend this, to avoid snakes and the midday heat) there is no breakfast available, so stock up on chapattis the night before. All the walking guides have been trained and are very helpful and knowledgeable. Most visitors arrive without having made a prior reservation, but it is recommended you book for large groups or during holiday periods. Cabin 1-decker bed/double bed US$12-15, 4-bed dorm US$5, camping US$2 per person. Tent and sleeping bag rental available. Offers guided walks at US$1.50-3 per person. *The Crow's Nest* is signposted with a left turn just before Sipi Trading Centre – the gate is approximately 200 m from the main road.

E *Moses' Campsite* (previously called *Elgon Sipi Falls View Campsite and Backpackers)* is very cheap at US$2 per person and also has two small bandas for US$3 per person. The staff are friendly but they do not have trained guides. There are long-drops and bucket showers. There is no bar or restaurant though occasionally Moses' mother will cook for guests. The popularity of this camp seems to be declining as facilities at *The Crow's Nest* develop, its simplicity may appeal to those who find the latter too 'westernized'. **E** *Elgon Masai Lodge*, located in the heart of Sipi village, is very basic and not particularly clean. Charges are US$3.75 single, US$5.50 double, though people have negotiated much lower rates for a shared single room. There is no hot water but they do have a western-style toilet and water for bathing is provided.

Eating There are a few eating houses in Sipi village. **Seriously cheap** *Go Down Bar* is the locals' favourite, also serving cold beers and sodas. Alternatively, try *The Crow's Nest* or *Sipi Falls Rest Camp*.

Transport Sipi is 60 km from **Mbale** on the Kapchorwa road. Follow the Kumi road for 6 km, then turn right on to the road to Moroto. Turn right at the fork in the road towards Kapchorwa (after 25 km). This is all clearly signposted, particularly by the *Volcanoes Rest Camp*. On public transport take the *matatu* from Kumi Rd taxi park in Mbale. This can take a couple of hours to fill up so be prepared for a wait. The price varies according to the weather, from US$2 in fine conditions to US$3 when it's raining. There is a new road under construction, which should improve things significantly; at the moment the journey is somewhat hair-raising.

Getting back to Mbale can be something of a mission as *matatus* are infrequent. Generally people hitch on the back of a truck down to the main road near Kamu market for US$0.30, and then catch a *matatu* from there, fare US$1.50. This is a well-established practice and no hassle at all.

Uganda

North to Soroti and Gulu

The north of Uganda can be divided into the northwest, north and northeast. The northwest covers what is known as West Nile – that is, anything beyond Murchison Falls, and including Pakwach, Nebbi, Arua and Moyo. The north includes Lira, Gulu and Kitgum. The main towns in the northeast are Soroti, Karamoja, Moroto and Kotido. There are conflicting reports as to how safe it is to travel here. Attacks on travellers in Gulu and surrounding areas do occur intermittently.

The northeast of Uganda, bordering on Sudan to the north and Kenya to the east, is an area of beautiful scenery, ranging from mountains to vast, flat, empty plains. It is a magnificent part of Uganda and totally different from the south of the country.

The inaccessibility of the north of Uganda, as well as its relative insecurity compared to the rest of the country, discourages visitors. However, some European residents have indicated that the security concerns have been overstated. Although security in the north has improved dramatically in the last five years, this part of Uganda does still suffer from being one of the most heavily armed. The most noticeable threat to date has been the Lord's Resistance Army (LRA), although their numbers are now very small. In an effort to increase the safety of people travelling to the north, the government has set up army posts in isolated areas, particularly in the national parks, and operates travel curfews.

A main feature of travel into the north is not so much the beauty of its scenery, which is quite breathtaking at times, but more the fact that it gives the visitor a glimpse of the history of the country, from the Arab slave traders of centuries ago, through the colonial era, to the turmoil in Uganda from the 1970s to 1986. The current presence of tens of thousands of refugees from southern Sudan, together with the activities of the international aid agencies, has made the area around Arua an important trading zone.

All the main churches have missions in the north and their representatives in Kampala are reliable sources of information on the current situation. For example,

North to Soroti & Gulu

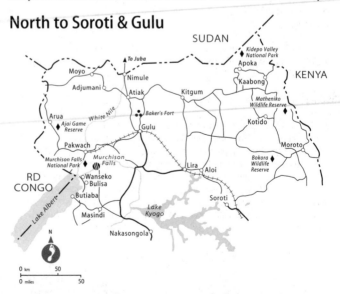

The Karamajong

The Karamajong (also spelt Karamojong and Karimojong) are one of the tribes inhabiting the more southerly part of the district of Karamoja, which is situated in the northeast corner of Uganda. Their language is Nga Karamajong.

The marriage system is polygamous, the number of wives being limited solely by financial circumstances. No boy is allowed to marry until he has been admitted by the elders to the status of manhood. Up to this time a boy must pluck out all his pubic hair. When the time comes (usually one group is presented at the same time) his father gives him a bull, which the boy kills and shares with his male relatives. He smears himself with the dung from the entrails and gives his mother the head, neck, hump, stomach and ribs. His hair is cut by an adult male friend, leaving a tuft at the back to which a short string is attached. Traditionally when the hair grows back he moulds it into two buns, one on top of the head and one at the back, with coloured clay.

When a youth has attained manhood he may seek a wife. It is usual that he will already have at least one lover and, if his father approves, his lover may be taken as his wife.

When a woman is about to give birth she is assisted by her female relatives. The umbilical cord is tied with fibre and cut near to the body. If the baby is a boy the cord is cut with the arrow used for bleeding cattle but if it is a girl a knife is used. The cord is buried in the cattle enclosure.

When someone dies the body is wrapped up in a hide and buried in a goat enclosure. If the person is a pauper without friends the body is simply thrown outside the kraal and left to the wild animals.

When a husband dies the widow passes into the possession of his principal brother. He will bring a sheep to her door, which he will then kill, and they will smear themselves with dung from its entrails. From this time onwards she belongs to him. If there is no brother then she will pass to the son of a co-wife.

Uganda

---

at certain times it is considered prudent to drive only in convoy. Don't let this put you off completely – but be aware of the situation.

Nyero rock paintings

These are located in the Kumi district on the Kumi-Ngora road in the village of Nyero, approximately 8 km from the outskirts of the town of Kumi. The dry rocky scenery of the area is attractive. The Nyero rock paintings consist of three painted shelters close to each other. Paintings are in red and white pigment and are mainly of geometric shapes. They are believed to be between 300 and 1,000 years old and are regarded as being among the best rock paintings in Eastern Africa. **Nyero site No 1** is a small shelter formed by an overhanging rock. The white-pigmented drawings are of concentric circles, plus some elongated shapes, sometimes described as acacia pods. At the main site, **Nyero 2**, a vertical rock face with an overhang that has helped to preserve the paintings from the elements. Concentric circles dominate in varying shades of red pigment. Linear motifs, again thought to resemble acacia pods or possibly a boat containing a couple of people, can also be identified. At the top of the rock face are some very weathered marks, said to resemble zebras. **Nyero 3** is a short distance away behind the other sites. It contains the painting which has been described as looking like an enormous star or a sunburst, and is best viewed by lying down underneath it. This white-pigmented painting is a series of concentric circles with lines drawn at right angles to the external circle. This pattern is repeated near by with red pigment but it is much fainter.

The surrounding area is covered with smooth boulders, many adorned by sunbathing monkeys. Occasionally, reptiles can also be seen basking on the rocks, mostly during the afternoons. Paving stones form a path between the sites, but care should be taken in wet weather, when they become extremely slippery. It is possible to climb some of the surrounding rocks for lovely views of low-lying hills to the west past Ngora. The cool breeze is pleasant and tall trees offer welcome shade. The local people water their animals near by and also fetch water from the rock pools. ■ *To get there, if you do not have your own transport, rent a motorbike taxi from Kumi. It is possible to walk there although the intense sun and heat in the area does not encourage this long return trek. Entry fee US$2.*

Karamajong phrases

The Karamajong language is one of the Nilotic languages and is complicated and subtle. Here are some words and phrases that you might find useful:		*Response*	Ejok *or* Ejok Noo
		Did you sleep well?	Iperi ejok a?
		Yes	Aye *(pronounced* Eeh*)*
		No	Mam
Formal greeting	Imaata!	*Please and thank you*	Alakara
General greeting	Ejoka	*Where is the office?*	Aye ayai apis?

Nine kilometres west of the Nyero Rock Paintings, near the town of Ngora, is another rock painting known as **Tank Rock**. A few groups of concentric circles in red pigment can be seen. However, this site was vandalized in the 1960s with red paint.

Sleeping D *Green Top*, PO Box 138, T71119. Opened in June 2000, with 20 rooms, including singles and en-suite, fans, nets, laundry service, fairly reliable lighting system. Less noisy than other local hotels and overall this offers the best accommodation in Kumi. **E** *Stay Free (Kumi) Hotel and Lodge*, PO Box 40, T71097, on the Korirot Rd. Very clean hotel with 11 rooms, basic facilities only. Full board not available. Quieter than some of the other hotels. Small restaurant serves local food, meat, chicken, vegetables including rice, *posho*, *matoke* and potatoes. **E** *Moonlight*, T711124, on the Korirot Rd, has 10 rooms, hot and cold water, good hygiene. Also offers a variety of western alcoholic drinks. **Camping** is available at the Nyero campsite at the base of the Nyero site No 1 (at your own risk), on a relatively flat piece of ground. The caretaker uses a small banda as an office. Drop toilets. Food and drinks have to be brought from Kumi. The surrounding fence is not very secure, but the place appears to be very peaceful.

Other attractions in the area include the possibily of viewing and climbing **Moru Apeso Rock** and the **River Awoja**, where there is a campsite.

Soroti
1°43'N 33°35'E
Phone code: 045
Colour map 3, grid B3

Although not that far north, there is something about Soroti that gives it a northerly feeling. It is a hot and airless town with a frontier atmosphere. It is the site of the **Soroti Flying School**, set up to train pilots for the whole East African region.

Sleeping C-D *Soroti Hotel*, T61269, offers clean, basic accommodation.

Transport Air *CEI Aviation*, Metropole House, 8-10 Entebbe Rd, Kampala, T255825, F236097. Return flights to Soroti for US$380. *Eagle Airlines* and *United* offer flights at similar prices and fly daily. **Road** Soroti is a drive of about 5 hrs from **Kampala** – a distance of about 385 km. It is 128 km from Lira, 113 km from **Mbale** and about 200 km from **Moroto**. Kampala-Moroto is less than 600 km, via Soroti, and the journey can be done in 1 day. There are now several buses between Kampala and Moroto.

Soroti to Moroto

The drive from Soroti to Moroto is mainly through acacia thorn bush. Every so often you will see a herd of scrawny goats being looked after by a couple of young boys, or perhaps some cattle with some Karamajong guarding them. Most of the time it is very hot and dusty but at certain times of the year there are the most fantastic thunderstorms. On this road, as you pass from Teso into Karamoja, you go between two hills called **Akisim** and **Napak**. They are quite impressive and can be seen for some miles around standing up above the plains. They mark the boundary into Karamoja.

Moroto
2°28'N 34°42'E
Colour map 3, grid B3

In the northeast of the country lie the vast open spaces of Karamoja. Here, rocky mountains interrupt the plains, making it an arid land of great scenic beauty. Mount Moroto, which reaches a height of about 3,400 m above sea level, offers challenging climbing to the enthusiast. It is the traditional area of the pastoralist Karamajong people (see box, page 667).

Labwor and **Nangeya** hills to the northwest of Moroto are noted for their giant inselbergs, volcanic plugs that have remained after the erosion of the cones. **Matheniko**, **Pian Upe** and **Bokora** are all designated game reserves in the area around Moroto, stretching from north of Mount Elgon up to Kotido. However the title 'game reserve' is somewhat inappropriate, as there appears to be little or no game left – the result of local firearm availability.

Sleeping **C** *Mount Moroto*, PO Box 54, T97, run by *Uganda Hotels*. Frequent water shortages.

Transport **Air** The easiest way to reach Moroto. Charter flights go fairly regularly from Entebbe. **Road** Kampala to Moroto is a distance of some 840 km so is not for the feeble-hearted. **Bus** from Moroto to Mbale/Kampala or Tororo leaves at about 0900 daily.

This small town 40 km west of Moroto and 4 km off the main road, has a busy hospital with Belgian doctors and a small market. **Sleeping** **D** Large comfortable guesthouse (unnamed) with s/c rooms. From here it takes five hours by road to Mbale or the Kidepo Valley.

Matany

Kidepo Valley National Park

Kidepo is one of the most spectacular national parks in Uganda but, being the most isolated, it is also one of the hardest to visit. While it may not have the animals of many of the national parks, it is one of the few remaining places in the world where you get a real feeling of wilderness.

Kidepo Valley National Park is located in the far northeast of Uganda on the border of Sudan and close to the border with Kenya (see map, page 613). The area adjacent to the national park is inhabited by the Ik people, hunters and farmers, who are described unflatteringly in Colin Turnbull's 1972 book *The Mountain People*. It is about 840 km from Kampala, and is an area of about 1,334 sq km with an altitude ranging between 1,350 m and 2,750 m. The Napore Nyangea mountain range is located to the west of the camp and the Natera hills to the east. In the distance to the north you will be able to see the peak of Mount Lotukei. The vegetation is typical savannah with some acacia woodland.

3°N 32°E
The northern section of the park is currently closed due to insecurity in Sudan

Uganda

Kidepo Valley National Park

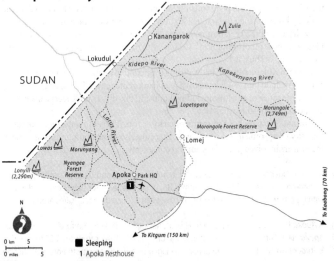

N

0 km   5
0 miles   5

■ **Sleeping**
1 Apoka Resthouse

Karamajong cattle

In Karamoja it is considered desirable to mutilate the horns of favoured cows so that they are twisted downwards. At first it may seem to be a natural malformation, but in fact it is deliberately brought about. Exactly how it is achieved and whether it hurts the animal in any way is unclear. The particular attributes of these short-horned, small to medium-size cattle, with cervico-thoracic humps, are believed to result from the interbreeding of zebu and Hamitic long-horn and/or short-horn strains. Over the years zebu cattle have developed some resistance to rinderpest and have survived outbreaks of the disease. The Karamajong people are known for cattle rustling, frequently carried out to pay a bride price or to replace cattle dying of sickness or lost in other ways. Raids during the past 15 years by the heavily armed Karamajong on their neighbours in eastern Gulu and Kitgum has reduced the livestock numbers in those regions from an estimated 285,000 to just 5,000 head of cattle – less than 2% of the previous stock.

One problem that Kidepo Valley National Park suffers from more than the other national parks in Uganda is that of water supply although the plants and animals of the area have adapted themselves well to this hardship. Low rainfall and a long and severe dry season of almost six months is characteristic of Karamoja as a whole. The effects of this are best appreciated between October and March when the national park is progressively baked, bleached and burnt by sun and, often by fire. Every scrap of moisture, except that which manages to survive in a few waterholes and dams, turns to dust under the scorching breath of the tireless northeast wind. Unattractive as this might sound, it is in fact perhaps the best time to visit as it creates conditions that are good for game-viewing. Animals are more tied to the available water sources, and there tends to be a concentration of animals around Apoka, the park headquarters, at the height of the dry season. The animals leave Kidepo Valley, which dries out very rapidly once the rains have ceased, and head for the comparatively lush savannahs and woodlands of Narus valley where there is enough water to see them through until the rain breaks again in March or April. Once the rains begin the animals drift back to the Kidepo Valley, and from April to October, when the grass is shorter, this is probably the best viewing area.

The **Kanangarok Hot Springs** that cross the Kidepo River are also worth a visit. The Kidepo River is a sand river, which only flows visibly for a few days of the year. However, below the sand, at depths that vary from a few centimetres to a few metres, there is water – depth depends on how far into the dry season it is. The animals of the park dig holes to reach the water. This also explains why on the banks of an apparently dry river the vegetation is often more green and lush than elsewhere in the park. Kidepo is an ornithologist's delight, with over 460 bird species, including the ostrich and kori bustard.

Game in Kidepo suffered badly during the period of turmoil and lawlessness. The animals include lion, buffalo, ostrich, elephant, zebra, cheetah, leopard, bushbaby and a wide range of antelope including kudu and dik-dik. Land Rovers can be hired at Apoka park headquarters US$2 per km.

The national park has a **museum** open to visitors. There are some pieces of skeletons as well as some insect specimens. There are also some photographs of some of the rangers involved in earlier efforts at conservation.

Security Northern Uganda has been subject to intermittent unrest and bandits are by no means uncommon. The Lord's Resistance Army (LRA) or Kony rebels have been active in this area, with reports that children and teenagers have been abducted from the area around Gulu.

Sleeping & eating
■ on map page 669

A Apoka Resthouse 16 chalets with 32 beds, nets, generally very comfortable. The nearby Apoka Rest Camp has several double bandas, US$22 daily, campsites US$10 per day. **E** Student Hostel, 15 renovated bandas managed by the park administration, with support from some Germans working for the Game Department. The standard is good, with warm showers, helpful staff, comfortable beds and mosquito nets. Bring your own food, including fresh fruit and vegetables. Basic foodstuffs can be bought on the way in Kaabong or Kotido.

Camping There are 4 sites close to Apoka.

Delmira, based in Kampala, T256-41-235499, F231927, delmira@imul.com, operates tours into the park. **Tour operators**

Air You can charter a light aircraft from Kampala, which will take about 2-3 hrs, and will cost somewhere in the region of US$1,000 per person for a 2-day and 1-night all-inclusive stay. Contact *Bel Air* (see page 639). **Transport**

Road The drive up to Kidepo should not be undertaken lightly. Before embarking on the trip speak to people who can give you up-to-date information, such as *Bel Air* (see page 639). This part of the world is heavily armed and when you arrive you will notice the high percentage of Karamajong men who carry guns. There have been periods when, because of the bandits, it has not been safe to travel in this area and it may therefore be advisable to drive up in a convoy. The drive to Kidepo is a 2-day journey by 4WD from Kampala via Moroto, but road conditions need to be checked before departure.

Uganda

Towns of the northwest

Situated in the north, 352 km from Kampala, the town of Lira has a park with fine trees and a bandstand. Lira Spinning Mill, the main source of income in the town, has recently been renovated. **Sleeping D** *Lira*, PO Box 350, T24 (via the operator). Scandinavian construction, water in bowls, candles and oil lamps, laundered clothes pressed with a charcoal iron. **Transport** *Matatus* from Gulu are not particularly frequent.

Lira
2°17'N 32°57'E
Phone code: 473
Colour map 3, grid B2

Gulu

Gulu, the largest town in northern Uganda, is located on the northern edge of the Murchison Falls National Park, and many people pass through it on the way to either the Murchison Falls or Kidepo Valley National Park. In October 2000 Gulu District was the centre of an outbreak of ebola haemorrhagic fever which affected over 400 people and claimed 160 lives. Most of the cases occurred in Gulu District but others were also confirmed in Mbarara (another army town) and Masindi. Fifteen health workers were among the deceased. The strain of ebola in this outbreak was identified as ebola Sudan, one of three strains that can affect humans. It was last detected in neighbouring Sudan in 1979.

2°48'N 32°17'E
Colour map 3, grid B2
Phone code: 471

The handicrafts made in the area around Gulu range from baskets to earthenware, as well as ironwork

If you have the time while you are passing through Gulu you might want to see **Bakers Fort**, which is located at Patiko, about 30 km north of Gulu. This was founded by Sir Samuel Baker in 1872 when he was Governor of Equatoria Province. It was built as a base from which to crush the slave trade and was later occupied by Gordon and Emin Pasha. There are said to be rock paintings at Samuel Baker's camp.

C *Acholi Inn*, PO Box 239, Gulu, T108. Run by *Uganda Hotels* and offering fairly good services. **D** *Hotel Roma*, 16 Coronation Rd, 250 m from the bus park. Very friendly but rather slow service, basic but clean. Self-contained rooms with fan but no nets. Breakfast available. Has a bar, satellite TV and a very noisy disco on Wed. Recommended. **E** *Church of Uganda Guesthouse*, simple but sound. **E** *Luxor Lodge*, opposite the lorry park. Fairly basic. **Sleeping**

Air There is an airstrip at Gulu, which is used by small aircraft. There are no scheduled flights to Gulu but there are charter flights from Entebbe. **Transport**

Road Gulu is 328 km from Kampala and is accessible via **Lira** from the east and **Masindi** from the west. The roads are worse than in many other areas of the country. The bitumen road stops at Karuma where you can go straight for Gulu or left for Pakwach and Arua. From here onwards you are travelling on roads that do not appear to have been touched for decades and the going is extremely slow, particularly after the rains. If you drive you must remember to buy enough petrol where you can as there are only service stations in the more developed towns of Gulu, Pakwach and Arua. It is not wise to drive after dark because of the possibility of being stopped by guerrilla fighters or bandits. Indeed, you are not able to drive through the national park after dark, and before entering you have to register your vehicle with soldiers at the checkpoint on the edge of the park as a safety measure. **Bus** There are daily buses to Gulu. All traffic north passes through Masindi.

Pakwach
2°28'N 31°27'E
Colour map 3, grid B2

Pakwach is a tiny town on the western edge of the Murchison Falls National Park. It is little more than one street but has everything a traveller is likely to need. Despite its primitive conditions (there appears to be no sanitation in town, though there is electricity), it is a very pleasant place to stay. Being on the edge of the river, its environment is green and fertile and it is a restful place where the people are very friendly.

The main reasons for being here are either to visit the park or to stop by the Nile, or to cross into RD Congo. Pakwach is only a few kilometres from the border and it is easy to cross at the northern tip of Lake George. However, the notorious corruption of Congolese officials, including customs officers, means an expensive crossing, particularly if you want to take your vehicle with you.

Sleeping and eating There are a number of small hotels. A popular venue is the **E** *Training Centre* at the end of the town. Turn left down a murram road towards the lake. The facilities for training purposes, but they can be used by the general public. The rooms are clean and equipped with mosquito nets. There are toilets and sinks in each room but the sanitation system does not yet operate. Water is brought to you daily. The rooms cost less than US$5 per night. You can also order food here – substantial local cooking at around US$3-5 per meal. There are several other small restaurants. The only place that seems to sell cold drinks is on the right-hand side at the western end of the town. It has no name but is easily identified by its garish electric lights and loud music. Beers and sodas are the same price as in all rural areas of Uganda.

Arua
3°1'N 30°58'E
Colour map 3, grid B2

This small town in the northwest is located close to the border with RD Congo about 500 km from Kampala. Sudanese-backed rebel terrorist activities occur from time to time, and the area is probably best avoided.

Sleeping and eating C *White Rhino*, PO Box 359, T157. Water from well in garden, oil lamps and candles. *The Grid*, good-value restaurant and bar frequented by aid workers, so called because it is exactly on 3° latitude north and 31° longitude east.

Transport Air Irregular flights, charter (see page 639) or with an aid agency. **Road** *Matatus* and **buses** from Bombo Rd in Kampala take about 6 hrs and cost US$12. Leave at 0300 to avoid travel in the heat. The route is popular, so it is necessary to book in advance. Travellers carry lots of luggage and merchandise, so it is wise to arrive well before departure (1 hr) to ensure there is room for you and your luggage.

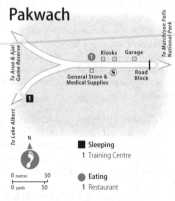

Pakwach

To Arua & Ajai Game Reserve

To Murchison Falls National Park

Kiosks
Garage
General Store & Medical Supplies
Road Block

To Lake Albert

N

0 metres 50
0 yards 50

■ **Sleeping**
1 Training Centre

● **Eating**
1 Restaurant

Moyo and Adjumani

This is one of the northernmost administrative centres in Uganda, on the border with Sudan. It is the headquarters of West Moyo, East Moyo and Obongi. It is actually on the border and is one of the major crossing points between the two countries.

3°20'N 31°50'E
Colour map 3, grid A2

This is a beautiful part of Uganda and the mountains of southern Sudan can be seen in the distance standing out against the rather flat landscape all around. Deforestation was rife in these parts as it has been host to waves of refugees from Uganda and southern Sudan since the 1960s. In some ways it adds to the beauty of the place as you can see for miles and at night the deep inky blackness of the landscape with bright stars above is lovely, though it has obviously had a rather negative impact on the environment and on people's livelihoods.

Moyo town itself looks much like all the other towns in the north. Before independence, much of this area was devoted to the cultivation of cotton and therefore there were good roads, a reasonable telephone and electricity system and thriving trade centres. The cotton industry collapsed so, too, did the wealth, commerce and trade of the area. The area has suffered terribly from Uganda's troubled history. Amin came from the neighbouring district to the west and, following his fall and the retreat of many of his soldiers through this area, the bulk of the population were forced to flee into Sudan. Subsequent waves of people fled to and from the area until 1986 when the NRM came to power and the majority of the Ugandans returned. Moyo is only 7 km from the border with Sudan, and bombing and shelling can be heard daily from across the border. There are also occasional raids on NGO compounds by armed men trying to steal supplies.

The history of Sudan has also played its part in this area, and the lengthy civil war in that country has caused tens of thousands of refugees to seek safety in northern Uganda. The insecurity and isolation of the area is apparent in the appalling roads, a non-existent telephone system (although the poles still stand along the roadside) and an electricity system relies on generators and is intermittent. However, Moyo can usually rely on an electricity supply between 1900-2230 daily. There have been some recent improvements. Electricity came to nearby Adjumani in late 1994 and is expected to make its way to other areas over the next few years.

An irony in this bleak picture is that you can buy coffee, whisky, international brands of cigarettes and other luxury items, or shop in the market near Adjumani, which is now a substantial trading area. This is because of the presence of the Sudanese refugees who now outnumber the local population and who are supported by a number of NGOs and UN agencies. Apart from this, you can buy most things in Moyo – basic food, newspapers, toiletries – and there is a good market. There is a hospital in town with limited supplies, staffed by an Austrian doctor.

Sleeping
Take plenty of insect repellent, as mosquitoes are prevalent in the area

A-B *Arra Fishing Lodge*, near Adjumani. T041-342926, F342995. Self-contained tents on the banks of the (Albert) Nile, 30-min drive from the small airfield at Adjumani, this is a small upmarket facility for serious fishermen. **D** *Wrakitura* has single and double rooms, running water, flushing toilets, although not pristine. The hotel has satellite TV, a bar and a darts board! There are 3 other basic guesthouses in Moyo, mostly used by locals who have come to sell produce at market. They are very cheap, but also not particularly secure and conditions are very poor.

Transport

Air There are daily flights from Entebbe to UNHCR-maintained airfields at Adjumani, Arua and Moyo. Flights are organized by the Ministry of Agriculture and Fisheries in Kampala. **Road** The best route is to Gulu continuing north to Adjumani, the administrative centre of the Moyo district and on to Moyo. This route takes you through Pakele and Dziapi, both small towns with nothing of interest to look at, but useful places to stop for a soda or roasted meat. There is petrol in Pakele. An alternative is via Pakwach if visiting the Murchison Park then to Arua. There is public transport to Arua and Adjumani. Parts of the route between Gulu and Adjumani have been very unsafe of late. UNHCR in Kampala can provide security assessments of the route by road.

Northwest to Murchison Falls National Park

For details of transport and routes to the national park, see page 683
For details on security in the area, see page 679

There is a fast road from Kampala to Masindi and consequently a long weekend away from the capital in the Murchison Falls National Park is very popular. The park is divided in two by the Victoria Nile, and the falls – where the river is squeezed through a gap only 7 m wide – are truly spectacular. There has been occasional trouble on the north bank from the Lord's Resistance Army (LRA, see page 758) but the south bank is safe. Murchison has some of Uganda's best game-viewing and it is one of the few places in the country where giraffe can be seen. Close by is the Budongo Forest Reserve (with chimpanzee tracking) and it is a pleasant drive down the east bank of Lake Albert and up the side of the Rift Valley to Hoima, which is about halfway between Murchison Falls and Fort Portal. There are some great views across the lake to the Blue Mountains, which are in the RD Congo, on the far shore.

Kampala to Masindi

The road to Masindi leaves Kampala heading north (starting at the Wandegeya roundabout near Makerere University) and passes through Bombo and Luwero, before swinging westwards. It takes about three hours from Kampala. About 30 km out of Kampala you cross into the Luwero district and quickly reach **Bombo** – very much an army town with row upon row of barracks. It began as an army town at the beginning of the 20th century with the Sudanese Volunteers in the King's African Rifles – they were always known as the Nubians. The area became known as the Luwero Triangle and was severely affected during the Obote II regime when army atrocities resulted in the killing of many thousands of people. Houses were looted and then burnt to the ground, along with the surrounding *shambas*. It did not take long for the vegetation to grow up again so there is now not much evidence apart from a couple of burnt-out tanks left to rust on the roadside. As a result of the events in the area Luwero has received considerable attention from aid workers and foreign governments.

The road is not very interesting, although it does go through quite varied countryside and at times there are some fine open vistas. Although it is not visible from the road there is a big lake system just to the north as the Victoria Nile flows first through Lake Kyoga and then Lake Kwania before reaching first the Karuma Falls and then the Murchison Falls before eventually flowing into Lake Albert. As a result the countryside for miles around is low-lying and therefore rather swampy. The road seems quite deserted, as there are no towns of any size after Luwero, until it reaches **Masindi Port**. This is different from Masindi itself, and is about 40 km to the east. It is located on the Victoria Nile at the western end of Lake Kyoga, which extends across much of central Uganda. In the days when steamers on the Nile were an important form of transport, the two sets of falls in the Murchison Falls National Park were major obstacles to travelling up the river. Coming from Lake Victoria, the steamers went up the Victoria Nile and into Lake Kyoga. Passengers and goods then disembarked at Masindi port and travelled overland to Butiaba on Lake Albert. From here they continued their journey north. Masindi port has since declined in importance, and is now mainly a market town.

The tarmac road carries on to Karuma where it crosses the Nile allowing access to Gulu, Pakwach (where it again crosses the river), Arua and, eventually, the RD Congo. To travel to Paraa, the best route is through Masindi. Watch out for the turning just after the Kafu river is crossed at Kibangya. Here the tarmac finishes and the final 40 km is along a good murram road.

Masindi

Many people pass through Masindi on the way to the Murchison Falls National Park. Apart from the park there are a few things near Masindi that you may want to do. It is a pleasant town with lots of flowers and greenery, although the main street (Masindi Port Road) is typical of the area – rather dry and dusty. The overnight population is estimated at 20,000, but this number swells by 5,000 during the day, because of Masindi's lively market, which lies just behind the main street.

1°43'N 32°2'E
Phone code: 465
Colour map 3, grid B2

A couple of kilometres out of town on Kihande Hill is **Kihande Palace**, the palace of the Omukama, Solomon Gafabusa Iguru, the King of Bunyoro. The Bunyoro Kingdom and its kingship was one of those abolished in 1967 during the Obote I regime. President Museveni restored the kingdoms and gave them their ceremonial powers back in 1993. Although Omukama Solomon normally resides in his palace in Hoima, there are plans to renovate the old palace.

Excursions to **Lake Albert** can be made from Masindi. Head for the town of **Butiaba Port** on Lake Albert – a distance of about 70 km. The drive on the escarpment to the Rift Valley is an experience in itself. Once you get to Butiaba ask the local fishermen and you should be able to hire a boat for the day.

C *Masindi*, PO Box 11, Butiaba Rd, T23, past the police post on the road to Hoima, 1 km out of town. The stylish exterior of this old colonial hotel is rather misleading. Usually has lots of vacancies, so the rate can be negotiated down. Has a bar and restaurant. **C** *Court View*, T20461, Nyanga Rd, 200 m from the Masindi post office. Has 15 comfortable round cottages and a restaurant and bar. Friendly and fast service. The most pleasant place to stay in Masindi.

Sleeping

D *Alinda Guest House*, on the main Masindi Port Rd. In the town centre, clean rooms with mosquito nets, verandah at the front of the guesthouse. **D** *Buma*, Commercial St. Big hotel opposite the market. Clean but lacking atmosphere. **D** *Kopling House*, new on Ntuha Rd, T077-463203 (mob). Quiet place, a bit out of town. Service not very friendly. **E** *Aribus*, T27472, next to *Alinda GH*, has 20 rooms, clean with cold showers. **E** *Executive Kyaterekera*,

Masindi

To Court View Hotel, Police Post, Masindi Hotel, Hoima & Murchison Falls

Murchison Falls
Tourist Centre

Football
Pitch

Town Council

Masindi
Hospital

Hospital Rd

Tongue St

Persse St

Kijumbwa Rd

Town Council

Ntuha Rd

Caltex

Davis Plaza

Masindi Port Rd

Western Rift
Valley Tours

Market St

Commercial St

Tongue St

Persse St

Taxis

Bikunya Rd

To Kampala

N

0 metres 50
0 yards 50

■ Sleeping	3 Buma	● Eating
1 Alinda Guest House	4 Executive Kyaterekera	1 Traveller's Corner
2 Aribus	5 Kopling House	

Uganda

Tongue St, cheap place between the taxi park and the market. Mosquito nets, friendly service. Basic rooms, check the toilet and shower before you enter.

Eating **Cheap** *Traveller's Corner*, on the main road next to the post office. Nice wooden verandah, bar and cosy restaurant. Good food, friendly and helpful staff. A good place to stop before tackling the 2-hr drive to Paraa. *Court View Hotel* and *Masindi Hotel* both offer an international menu.

Sport **Tennis** Courts available for temporary membership. **Football** There is a sports stadium in Masindi and matches are held there on a regular basis.

Tourist information The information centre for Murchison Falls NP signposted north from the main road, opposite the town council buildings, 50 m west of the post office. The sign directs you to the *Murchison Falls Conservation Area*, PO Box 455, Masindi, T/F20428, mfcamsd@ infocom.co.ug The staff are extremely helpful and can also give you information about Budongo Forest. *Western Rift Valley Tours*, PO Box 213, Masindi Port Rd, T077-637493 (mob), F20411, is a new enterprise that organizes trips to Murchison Falls and Budongo Forest. Run by Keith Bitamazire and Boniface Baruzalire, they have a 4WD, advisable during rainy weather for game drives. Cost US$85 for 1st day, US$45 per day thereafter. A 2WD costs US$55 for 1st day, US$30 for subsequent days. Prices are negotiable, especially in low season.

Transport **Road** The post bus from Masindi to Kampala leaves at 0730 from the post office and costs US$4. Bus to Kampala leaves at 0600, US$4 with a journey time of 5 hrs. Regular *matatus* to Kampala cost US$5. Frequent *matatus* travel from Masindi to Hoima along the unmade road, which is in good condition. Cost US$2, journey time 1 hr.

The road to Murchison Falls

It is a two-hour drive of 88 km from Masindi to Murchison Falls, Paraa and the ferry. This is the direct road that enters the park through the Wairingo Gate (take this road if you are staying at the *Sambiya River Lodge*). Take a right turn just after the *Court View Hotel* in Masindi. There is a large barracks on the hill. After 7 km take a left turn to the park at Kyema. Shortly after the road goes through an avenue of termite mounds before reaching Kaniyo-Pabidi (see below). A four-wheel-drive vehicle is generally advisable for this stretch during the rainy season. Staff at the *Murchison Falls Conservation Area* (see above) may be able to arrange a lift – there is no public transport directly into the national park. The alternative is to take a *matatu* from Masindi to Wanseko and Bulisa, but onward travel from these small settlements is limited to motorbike taxi or bicycle. It is recommended that you negotiate the motorbike hire from Wanseko rather than from Bulisa (see page 678). It is a longer route but allows for a visit to the Budongo Forest Reserve and is a rather more attractive drive. The road from Bulisa to Paraa enters the park at Bugungu Gate. It is only half an hour from here to the ferry.

Kaniyo-Pabidi Kaniyo-Pabidi has recently been incorporated into the Murchison Falls National Park – a park fee of US$15 is now payable. It has a visitor centre selling refreshments, two bandas, a campsite with a cooking area, covered area for cooking/eating, water and firewood, showers (cold) and pit latrines. A cook is available to prepare meals – food visitors need to supply their own can be bought in Masindi.

Highlights of the park include the mighty mahogany and ironwood trees. Occasionally lions, leopards and buffalo can be seen, and Pabidi Hill offers views over Murchison Falls Park, Lake Albert and RD Congo. The River Waiga runs through the site and there are many salt-licks to attract wild animals, as well as a bird-watching trail and chimpanzee tracking (best in the early morning, so an overnight stay is a good idea).

Transport Like Busingiro (see below), Kaniyo-Pabidi is accessed from Masindi. The site is 29 km from Masindi on the road north to Paraa. There is no public transport, but it is possible to hire a vehicle in Masindi from MATODA (PO Box 189, F0465-20411) at US$36 for a day return.

Budongo Forest Reserve

The reserve is the largest area of unexploited mahogany forest in East Africa, with huge trees growing up to 60 m high. About 700 chimpanzees live in the forest, and five groups have been habituated by the research station, and can be viewed up close. Other primates are black and white colobus, red-tailed monkeys, blue monkeys, potto, baboons and vervet monkeys. Birdlife is excellent with 366 species recorded, and there are spectacular views from Butiaba over Lake Albert and the Blue Mountains of RD Congo on the western shore of the lake. Two eco-tourism sites have been established, at **Busingiro** and **Kaniyo-Pabidi**, with nature trails, special-interest walks, chimpanzee tracking and a range of inexpensive bandas and camping facilities. Both are very attractive sites within the rainforest, with the main attraction being the guided walks to see the chimpanzees. As with all chimpanzee tracking there is no guarantee that you will see the chimps – there is an estimated 50% chance here. ■ *General information on the reserve can be obtained from Nyabyeya Forestry College, Private Bag, Masindi, F0465-20411.*

Busingiro has a visitor reception centre with information, snacks and drinks available, and an education centre for schools. There are two bandas, one with two beds, the other with four, simple and pleasant with good mosquito nets, and a campsite with water and cooking facilities, covered area for cooking/eating, hot and cold showers and pit latrines. The cost of the bandas works out as little more than camping, which makes them a better option if there is availability because, as in all rainforests, conditions are often very wet. A local cook will prepare your meals if you supply the food – provisions can be bought in Masindi. Officially two days' notice is required, but if you are prepared to eat simple food, such as *matoke* with beans or aubergine (eggplant), the staff will arrange something, even if you ask on the same day. Busingiro Eco-tourism site is outside the Murchison Falls Conservation Area, so it is a cheaper option than Kaniyo-Pabidi (recently incorporated into the national park) for chimp tracking as there are no national park fees payable. Mini packages – accommodation only, morning or afternoon guided walks only and combinations of all three – work out as being 75% of the separate prices. Morning guided walks cost US$8, afternoon US$6, camping US$6 per

Busingiro

Uganda

Budongo Forest Reserve

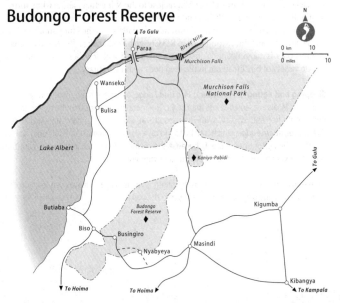

person per night, and bandas US$8 per person per night. Longer stays are relatively cheaper.

The 'Royal Mile' is a wide avenue of trees with abundant birdlife, 15 km away from the centre, so called because it was a favourite location of King Kabalega (see page 720). Near by at the forest edge is Lake Kanyege, with water birds and clouds of butterflies. Chimpanzees in habituated groups can generally be located by the guides, and the best time is at first light, so an overnight stay is a good idea. A historic Polish church stands near by.

Sleeping and eating Visiting the centre requires an entry permit – US$4 a day for foreign tourists. Guides cost around US$3, and camping US$2 a night. These charges are paid in Ugandan shillings, and charges are a bit less for Ugandans and residents.

Transport Busingiro is 42 km from Masindi on the road west to Butiaba, lying between Masindi and Lake Albert. *Matatus* from Masindi heading for Butiaba (on Lake Albert) and Wanseko (at the entry of the Nile into Lake Albert) pass by the site, taking about 1 hr and costing US$2. The entrance for the chimp tracking is clearly signposted on the left-hand side of the road, a few kilometres beyond the turning for the Nyabyeya Forestry College. A *private hire* is available from MATODA (PO Box 189, Masindi, F0465 20411) and a return for the day will cost US$55. It is very difficult to get transport from Busingero towards Bulisa and Wanseko in the afternoon.

Bulisa
Colour map 3, grid B2

There are many tsetse flies in the area

From the small village of Bulisa it is 18 km to the park gate, and 23 km to the Paraa ferry. **Sleeping and eating** There is only one simple lodge, **E** *Bulisa Corner Guest House*, which has very basic facilities and friendly staff. The food served is mostly *matoke* and *ugali* (*posho*). *One African Place*, the restaurant opposite the hotel, also serves mostly local food.

Transport It is possible to go by public transport from Masindi as far as Bulisa, but it is difficult to get transport from Bulisa to enter Murchison Falls National Park. You usually have to arrange your own transport in Masindi although bikes can be hired for US$8. It is cheaper to hire motorcycle taxis in Wanseko. A US$15 park entrance fee is payable at the gate.

Wanseko
Colour map 3, grid B2

Wanseko lies on the shore of Lake Albert close to the Nile estuary about 6 km northwest of Bulisa. It is extremely hot and plagued with huge numbers of mosquitoes at night. The sight of women drying thousands of small fish on the sandy shore against the backdrop of the Blue Mountains in RD Congo beyond Lake Albert, and its small fishing boats, is magnificent. Wanseko is a small town with few facilities, but there is a wide variety of birdlife living in the reed beds near the estuary.

Sleeping and eating **E** *Paramount Pub and Lodge*, along the main road, is very cheap and basic. Meals are served at less than US$1. The metal roof means that the rooms can be horrifyingly hot and sweaty, with little respite at night. Of a similar standard is the **E** *New Blue Room Lodge*, which is to be found on a side road (almost the only one). This is probably the better option, if only because the *matatus* don't park in the yard, with the accompanying noise and shouting in the early morning.

Transport The bus to Masindi stops overnight at Wanseko, and leaves very early in the morning. See page 676 for details of entry into the park.

Murchison Falls National Park

The Murchison Falls National Park is the largest national park in Uganda, covering   *2°15'N 31°30'E*
an area of nearly 4,000 sq km, and offering some of the most spectacular scenery in the
country. The park was briefly known as Kabalega Falls National Park in the early
1970s, having been renamed by President Amin after the King of Bunyoro, famous
for resisting attempts to colonize his kingdom. Until about 40 years ago, the waters of
the Nile were forced through a narrow gap in the rocks to fall through a series of foam-
ing, roaring cascades down a drop of about 50 m, creating one of the world's most
spectacular waterfalls. However, in 1961, a year of particularly heavy rains and
floods in Uganda, the waterfall broke through another gap in the rocks and there are
now two breaches.

Ins and outs

There is an airstrip at Pakuba and charter flights arrive here from Entebbe. The short grass   **Getting there**
airstrip near Paraa is not often used nowadays. Murchison Falls (Paraa) can be reached by   *For transport and*
road from Kampala via Masindi. It takes about 4-5 hrs (2 hrs on tarmac and 2½ -3 hrs on   *route details, see*
murram road).   *page 683*

Security on the north bank has been a problem because of repeated raids by the LRA, see   **Safety**
page 758. These have often been hijackings of lorries traversing the park on their way to and
from RD Congo. Rarely has there been a problem with tourists. The river is a major barrier to
the LRA and so the south bank is generally regarded as being completely safe. Even so, you
are advised to take local advice from the Park Authority Security Officer (currently Eddison).
He will be happy to provide an escort or even take you around himself if he is free. Telephone
the park office at Paraa for information.

Uganda

Murchison Falls National Park

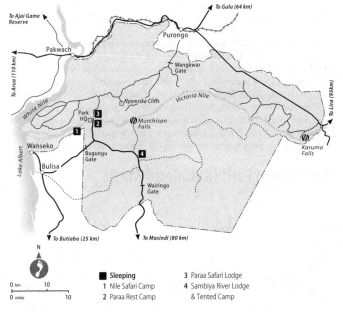

N

| 0 km | 10 |
| 0 miles | 10 |

■ **Sleeping**
1 Nile Safari Camp
2 Paraa Rest Camp
3 Paraa Safari Lodge
4 Sambiya River Lodge
& Tented Camp

Prehistory

The area around Chobe in the eastern part of the Murchison Falls National Park has been a popular habitat for man from early times for a number of reasons. First it has good animal and vegetable resources; it also had a good agricultural potential, and latterly iron ore suitable for primitive smelting technology became apparent in the area.

The earliest artefacts found in the area of Chobe date from the Middle Stone Age, when the banks of the Nile were peopled by small groups of hunters and gatherers, who may also have done some fishing. Some rough pebble tools, large flakes, some picks and a handaxe all have been found dating from this period, when it is believed that the Nile was flowing at a higher level than at present.

Throughout the Middle and Late Stone Age, agriculture and the domestication of animals were not known to the riverbank dwellers – they continued to eke out an existence based on hunting and gathering. However, over the years the manufacture of stone tools became more sophisticated and some new types of tool appeared for the first time. The abundance of flakes and chippings in places along the eroded banks of the river suggests that these may have been places where tools were made, rather than actual settlements.

Pottery fragments, ironware and iron slag have been collected, along the banks dating back as much as 2,000 years. Most of the finds, however, are much more recent, dating from the last 200 years. The settlers who are thought to have first introduced iron technology to this part of Africa left behind a very distinctive type of pottery known as dimple-based ware. This is characterized by bevelled rims and incised cross-hatched or grooved decoration, and is to be found over much of the Lake Victoria basin. Related pottery types occur over most of the sub-continent; but the most northerly occurrence of this archaeological complex so far is at Chobe.

Most of the pottery fragments found in recent years carry decorative motifs identical to those used by the people who live in the area around the national park today. They consist of concentric circles, raised bosses and zigzag chevrons all applied to the wet clay with a carved wooden roulette or a knotted cord.

Sights

The park is not in the risky area of the north, and is worth visiting more for the variation in its scenery than for its wildlife. It covers about 3,900 sq km and the further north you travel, the more savanna-like the terrain becomes. The south of the park is green and lush with many small settlements and banana or *matoke* (like plantain) cultivation everywhere. The further north you travel the drier and hotter it becomes, and the more infrequent the human settlements. Some parts are quite extraordinary, with long, wide alleys of palm trees and other exotic plants stretching from left to right to the horizon. The date palms were apparently planted by Arab slave traders centuries ago, to mark their route into and out of inland black Africa.

Murchison Falls (Kabalega Falls)

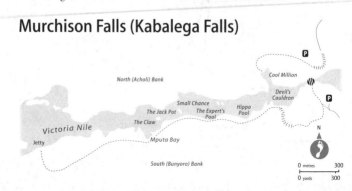

Many animals and birds still live in the park including Ugandan kobs, buffaloes, hippos, baboons and crocodiles. Lions, elephants and antelope are rarer. Prior to the civil war and the later effects of rampant poaching, elephants were plentiful in this part of Uganda, and it was common to see herds of up to 500. Even today herds of 200-300 can often be seen.

Everyone who visits Murchison Falls National Park is recommended to go on this **Launch trip** trip. It is operated by Uganda National Parks from Paraa, south of the river, to the falls themselves. If you happen to be on the north side of the river, a small boat can take you over. The cost is US$100 for up to 10 people – so if you can gather a group together it is not too expensive, but there is a minimum charge of US$10 per additional person. There is also the US$15 national park entrance fee on top of this. During the boat ride you are guaranteed to see hippos (there are reported to be 4,000 in this stretch of the river) and some huge Nile crocodiles. There is also a good chance of viewing elephants, red-tailed monkeys and black and white colobus monkeys, as well as some magnificent birdlife at close quarters. Other game found at Murchison Falls includes buffalo, giraffe and a range of antelopes. ■ *The launch trip usually runs twice daily from Paraa, at 0900 and 1400. The round trip takes about 3 hrs.*

It is not possible to stop at the base of the falls to walk up the steep footpath to the top. **Top of** They are only accessible by road from the south bank of the River Nile. The drive **the falls** from Paraa takes about 45 minutes and is roughly 30 km. A visit here should form an integral part of any trip to the park. It is a unique and breathtaking natural spectacle, the most powerful rush of water anywhere in the world. There is a small campsite and ranger post at the falls, and this is the starting point for a short walk down the hill to the water's edge. Here it is possible to get within a few metres of the falls. The narrow gap and the volume of water that rages through it, vibrating the ancient rocks, can only truly be appreciated from this vantage point. Care is required as the surrounding area can be slippery underfoot. Although there are two breaches, you can in fact only see the original falls. There used to be a concrete bridge spanning the 7-m gap but this was washed away in the 1961-62 floods. Try to be here at sunset, when hundreds of bats fly over the falls chased by birds of prey. *Sambiya River Lodge* organizes sundowners (book in advance, see page 682).

For game-viewing you have to go to the north of the park – there are very few animals on the south bank apart from small herds of Ugandan kob. Getting to the north bank necessitates crossing the river by ferry if you have spent the night south of the river. There are ferry crossings at 0700, 0900, 1100, 1200, 1400, 1600 and 1800. For safari vehicles the crossing costs US$13 and for foot passengers US$1. Early mornings are unquestionably the best time to see and photograph animals. The Nile valley is one of the hottest places in Uganda and animals tend to look for shade and rest towards 1100. Many animals such as lion, leopard, hyena, buffalo and most of the smaller mammals such as civet cats, are most active between dusk and dawn. It is always advisable to take food and water with you on a game drive. Getting stuck in the mud is part of the adventure so travel in a four-wheel drive is recommended, with a ranger guide (US$7 for half a day).

The best route for viewing animals is the Buligi Circuit, which includes the Buligi, Victoria Nile, Queens and Albert Nile tracks. Depending on the time available, there are numerous ways to explore this area. It is recommended that at least four or five hours are set aside for a thorough safari (expect to cover between 120 and 170 km). During the game drive you can spot Rothschilds giraffe, lion, leopard, hyena, elephant, buffalo, Jackson's hartebeest, oribi, Uganda kob and a huge variety of bird species including the amazing shoebill stork.

Fishing for Nile perch and tiger fish attracts many anglers. The fast-flowing waters **Sport fishing** above and below the falls are probably the best places from which to cast off. There are no hire facilities locally for fishing equipment. Permits cost US$50 a day. Boat hire costs an additional US$120 and US$200 for a half- or full-day respectively, and is controlled by the park authority. There are plans to license private operators (although there is a degree of scepticism that this will ever happen). The problem caused by water hyacinth has largely been resolved (see page 720), although you will notice many small pieces floating amongst the spume. The annual fishing championship, abandoned for many years, was reintroduced in April 2001.

Essentials

Sleeping
■ *on map, page 679*

L *Paraa Safari Lodge*, under the new management of the Madhvani group. Luxurious lodge with a colonial theme (lots of pictures of the early explorers and other memorabilia), on the north bank. 54 bedrooms (including one with facilities for the disabled) and 2 suites, own balconies all with a splendid view overlooking the Nile. Outdoor swimming pool with bar. Excellent breakfast buffet for US$10. Marasa Central Reservation Office, PO Box 22827, Kampala; 6th Floor, Greenland Towers, 30 Kampala Rd, Kampala, T041-255992/3, T077-788880 (mob), F041-259399, Paraa@wiltel.co.ug

A *Nile Safari Camp* is situated outside the national park, 11 km off the main road coming from Bulisa along an extremely rough track (not ideal for early-morning game drives on the north bank of the river). 6 double tents with wooden bathrooms, a couple of 4-person similar wooden bandas, situated 5 km downstream from the ferry, wonderful views of the Nile (the swing over the river is particularly recommended for watching the herds of elephants often seen on the opposite bank), one of the most upmarket camps in Uganda. Book through *Inns of Uganda Ltd*, 1st Floor Impala House, Kimathi Av, PO Box 2288, Kampala, T041-258273, F233992, iou@africaonline.co.ug

B *Sambiya River Lodge and Tented Camp* is on the south bank, only 20 mins' drive from the top of the falls, about 40 km north of Kichumbanyobo Gate. This open-fronted lodge with a swimming pool has 20 nicely decorated thatched cottages with private bathroom and a verandah. Most cottages have 1 bedroom, some have 2. The lodge has a quiet and relaxing atmosphere with a nice bar and good homely cooking (try the fish). The surrounding area is a mixture of savannah plain and riverine forest. Gary and Angela, recently arrived from Zimbabwe, hope to expand into bird-watching and fishing trips on the river. Sundowners are organized for guests to enjoy the sunset at the top of the falls. Booking office: *Afritours and Travel Ltd*, T041 344855, afritour@swiftuganda.com **C** *Tented Camp from Sambiya Lodge* Straightforward accommodation in the tented camp includes the use of the facilities of the lodge. Booking office: *Afritours* as above.

D *Paraa Rest Camp* has basic accommodation in bandas available south of the river, close to the ferry. Built in about 1988, the bandas are simple (self-contained or shared facilities), are kept fairly clean, and have mosquito nets and bedding provided. The bandas can be booked through the *Uganda Wildlife Authority* (PO Box 3530, Kampala, T041-346287, director@uwahq.uu.imul.com). This is the cheapest place to stay in the park, and camping is possible at US$4.50 per person. There are western toilets and hot showers. Electricity is provided by a generator, which is switched on 3 times a day. The bandas can be booked

through the *Uganda Wildlife Authority*. You can order meals (cheap) in the camp's bar (ask in advance) or bring your own food and borrow a charcoal stove, cost US$24 per person per night. **D** *Rabongo Forest Cottage* is a wooden cabin with 2 bedrooms in the southeast of the park, 1½ hrs' drive from Paraa, in an area of riverine forest surrounded by savannah grassland. Meals are not available. The *Rabongo Forest Ecotourism Centre* staff can arrange guided walks through the forest where several primate species live.

Camping E There are campsites at the top of Murchison Falls, 1 hr from Paraa by 4WD, Paraa, Rabongo Forest and Kaniyo-Pakidi. Toilets/pit latrines and showers or bathing shelters are provided. There are also a couple of bandas at Kaniyo-Pakidi, from where you can track chimpanzees (see page 676).

From Masindi you can take the **direct route** into the park, 88 km to Paraa. This stretch of well-maintained dirt road will take you about 2 hrs. A 4WD is recommended in the rainy season. This road passes Kaniyo-Pakidi, *Sambiya River Lodge*, and the turn-off to the top of the falls (signposted).

Transport
Charter flights operate between Entebbe and Pakuba airstrip

The more beautiful route is the road via Bulisa. From Masindi you take the Butiaba road through the Budongo Forest Reserve (stopping off at Busingiro, see page 677). Before reaching Butiaba, on the shores of Lake Albert, you head north. This is a very attractive drive looking across the Rift Valley towards Lake Albert and across to the RD Congo on the other side. When you reach the village of Bulisa it is 18 km to the gate and 23 km to the Paraa ferry. The first part of this road is very good murram; in the latter part you will meet more potholes. A 4WD is recommended during the rainy season, or if you want to go for a game drive on the north side of the park.

From Hoima you can take a straight route towards Butiaba and Bulisa. An alternative route is to take the left turning to the **Kinyara Sugar Works** off the main road from Hoima to Masindi. You will pass through the sugar plantations and can even visit the sugar factory if you are interested (book in advance: T078-600280). After the sugar plantations this road meets up with the Masindi -Butiaba road. The road passes through the Budongo Forest Reserve, where you will be able to track chimpanzees outside the Murchison Falls National Park, at Busingiro, saving the NP fees.

Public transport There is no direct public transport into Murchison. One possibility is to travel by public transport to Masindi and from there arrange a trip with the Western Rift Valley Tours, T077-479569 (see under Masindi, page 676). Alternatively, it is possible to get as far as Bulisa or Wanseko by public transport, but difficult to travel onwards to enter Murchison Falls National Park. You will probably have to stay the night in the small town of Bulisa (see page 678). From Bulisa you can either try to hitch or, failing that, hire a **bicycle** from the *Bulisa Corner Guest House*, US$8. It is 23km to Paraa and it is mostly flat, apart from a steep descent shortly after the park entrance gate. The bike ride takes 2-2½ hrs, allowing time for getting off to walk over some sandy stretches. Start early if visiting the park as the ferry runs at 2-hourly intervals starting at 0700 (see Paraa, page 681). If you want to go to Murchison Falls NP by motorbike taxi (very few chances of hitching from Bulisa) hire it from Wanseko rather than from Bulisa as it is often possible to negotiate a better price (about US$20 one way). Furthermore, getting a **motorbike taxi** from Bulisa can involve waiting for some time after negotiations have been finalized – the motorbike may need filling up with petrol and they have to go over to Wanseko to do this!

Uganda

Kampala

West to Fort Portal, Queen Elizabeth National Park and the Rwenzoris

Fort Portal, splendidly located in tea country in the west of Uganda, gives easy access to the Semliki Valley Game Reserve at the southern end of Lake Albert. Hop over the northern spur of the Rwenzori mountains and you can experience the huge Central African rainforest which stretches for thousands of miles to the west in the Semliki National Park proper (sadly currently closed). Other attractions around Fort Portal are chimp tracking in the Kibale National Park or cycling around the extraordinary Bunyaruguru crater lakes. Most travellers to Fort Portal will go on the main road via Masaka and Mbarara which is sealed for all but around 30 km. The slow but direct route via Mubende allows for a visit to the Bwera archaeological sites as well as the little-visited Katonga and Kasyoha Kitoma Forest. Another option is to take the Mbarara-Kasese road that passes the Queen Elizabeth National Park. The road goes through the park and when crossing the Kazinga Channel neatly bisects Lake Edward and Lake George, Uganda's other two royal lakes. Kasese is the gateway to the Rwenzori Mountains, the fabled 'Mountains of the Moon' which have been opened once again after being closed for four years because of the security problems with RD Congo. The border between the two countries runs along the mountain peaks. A description of the Kampala-Mbarara road is covered in the southwest section (see page 722).

West to Fort Portal & Kasese

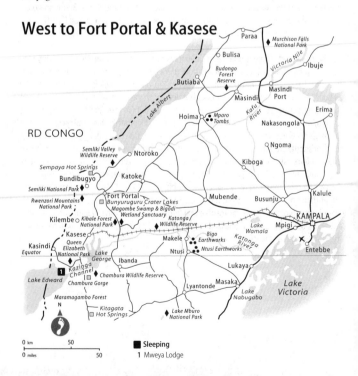

Sleeping
1 Mweya Lodge

Mubende and the Bwera archaeological sites

From Kampala to Mubende the road is tarmac, passing through swampy areas with graceful papyrus beds and woodlands scattered with acacia trees. Mubende is a small town, halfway between Kampala and Fort Portal, and vehicles tend to stop here for snacks and drinks – the barbecued chicken on wooden skewers is particularly good. You may wish to stay a night if you are visiting the Nakayima shrine or the archaeological sites at Bigo and Ntusi. The Bigo site is difficult to access, being 13 km from the main road, and you need to have a four-wheel-drive vehicle, or a lift on a motorcycle taxi. The Ntusi site is easier to visit, being quite close to the road, but rather less interesting.

Mubende
0°33'N 31°22'E
Phone code: 0464
Colour map 3, grid B2

Sleeping E *Nakayima Hotel*, T4053, Main St, clearly visible on the road from Kampala, among the shops, near the entrance to the barracks. It is Mubende's best hotel, good value and has a restaurant. There are some other **E** grade hotels, with flushing toilets, on the main road near the shops.

Nakayima Shrine, variously spelt Nyakaima, Nakaima or Nyakahuma, is an ancient 'witch tree', the base of which has large root buttresses forming nooks and fissures, sited on top of Mubende Hill about 4 km to the west of the town. The 213-m hill, with a flat tabletop where the ancient palace once stood, provides an excellent vista of Mubende town and the surrounding area. The shrine is visited by people paying homage to the matriarch Nakayima of the Bacwezi, a dynasty said to have supernatural powers, and who have passed into legend as demi-gods. Nakayima died in 1907.

At the tree you can make a wish by giving a coffee bean and a small donation which is placed into the nooks formed by the tree's roots – a local lady is on hand to explain the shrine. Local people with important wishes may offer chickens, sheep, goats and, reportedly, even cows.

This site in the Bwera region appears to have been a significant late Iron Age settlement. Radiocarbon dating suggests that it flourished at some time between AD 1300 and 1500, and was then abandoned in the latter half of the 16th century. There are very extensive earthworks, with substantial ditches clearly visible although overgrown with vegetation in places. Excavations at the site have yielded iron blades (most probably used for harvesting grain), pottery with simple decoration, cattle dung and post-holes for fencing.

Bigo earthworks
The descriptions of the Bigo earthworks (and Ntusi, later) are based on 'Ntusi and Bigo' by John Sutton in Azania, 1998, where more detailed accounts can be found

The inner ditches were probably developed first and, with strategic mounds, provided a fortified central site for the community. The large area contained by the outer ditches suggests it was extended to provide a secure area for cattle and possibly cultivation of grain such as millet. The nearby Katonga River would have supplied water for the community and its cattle. The northern side is protected by swamps and the Katonga River. The southern outer perimeter comprises about 5 km of ditches and these fortifications enclose more than 4 sq km.

A sophisticated social structure would have been required, first to establish such a settlement, comprising as it did extensive ditches, embankments, fences and gates, and then to man and maintain it for more than two centuries. There is little indication of the identity of the group ruling at Bigo, but is is likely that they were Hima cattle-herders in some sort of alliance with Iru cultivators.

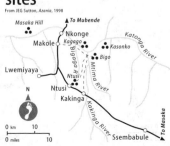

Bwera archaeological sites
From JEG Sutton, Azania, 1998

Uganda

In colonial times the site became known as *Bigo Bya Mugenyi*, which means 'Fort of Mugenyi'. This suggests a dynasty established by Mugenyi, with a royal residence in the inner area surrounded by a huge cattle kraal. Mugenyi would be from the *Bacwezi*, a people about whom little is known, but who have passed into legend as demi-gods. Some scholars have argued that association of the site with Mugenyi is a recent invention.

What precipitated the decline of Bigo is not known; its demise coincided with the rise of the cattle-herding Bunyoro to the north, the Ankole to the south, and the banana-cultivating Buganda to the east. The longer a dynasty endures, the greater the likelihood of it being destroyed by internal conflicts and disputes over inheritance. Expansion of herds and the population would tend to deplete grazing and wood supplies for fuel, and these were probably contributing factors. Today visitors are left to marvel at the sheer scale of the settlement, the outer ditches, ramparts, fences and gateways stretching 3 km from east to west, enclosing cattle and cultivation, and topped by a central compound 500 m wide with impressive thatched dwellings for the ruler and his entourage.

■ *There are 3 possible approaches to the Bigo site, all about 13 km from the main road. They can be negotiated by 4WD vehicles or motorcycle for most of the way, with a hike of about 3 km for the final approach. It is a good idea to engage a local person as guide when leaving the main road. Coming from Mubende, the first turn-off is at Makole where it is possible to strike east along a track towards the Katonga River and thence to the Bigo site. Further along the road from Mubende to Masaka is Ntusi, with a track leading north from just opposite the District Offices, the route following the Bigaga River and passing two dams. Finally at Bukiroga, about 8 km beyond Ntusi, is a track to the north, which follows the Kakinga River. Again two dams are passed on the way.*

The remains of two forts of considerably smaller dimensions can be found at **Kasonko**, 5 km northeast of Bigo and at **Kagago**, 3 km northwest. They consist of a rampart and a ditch sunk into the slopes of small hills and do not have inner fortifications. It is believed that the constructors of Bigo also built these as part of an all-round defensive system.

Ntusi archaeological settlement

Ntusi appears to have been the site of a substantial settlement of both cattle-herders and cultivators. Evidence from radiocarbon dating of fragments found at the site suggests it existed between the 11th and 13th centuries.

Near to the present-day Ntusi settlement are two substantial mounds, 4 m high, known as Ntusi 'Male' and Ntusi 'Female', surrounded by many smaller mounds. Excavations have yielded pottery, cattle bones and odd items such as ivory carvings,

Bigo settlements & earthworks

From JEG Sutton, *Azania*, 1998

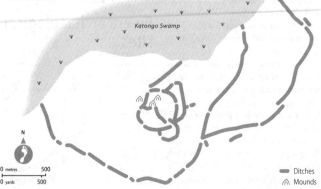

Katongo Swamp

N

0 metres 500
0 yards 500

● Ditches
⋀ Mounds

ostrich eggshell beads, glass beads and copper items. Archaeological interpretation is that these mounds were domestic rubbish heaps, and charred fragments suggest they were periodically burnt off to dispose of rotting material. To the north of the large mounds are a series of depressions, known as *bwogero*, which are thought to have been excavated to provide shallow ponds for watering cattle in dry periods.

Further to the north again is a hill on which signs of dwellings have been found. The dwellings appear to have been of timber frame and thatched roof construction, haphazardly grouped, with no signs of regular streets that would indicate a town. The pottery fragments have roulette decoration made by pressing a piece of toothed wood, or knotted fibre, into the clay. Kaolin (used as a type of plaster for walls) and slip (thinned clay for sealing and decorating) have also been found. The Ntusi Cylinder is an unusual clay object covered with protuberances and several holes, about 14 cm long and 8 cm in diameter. It was discovered at Ntusi in 1944, and is now housed in the Uganda (previously Kampala) Museum (see page 627). The function of the cylinder is not certain – holes at either end may have allowed wooden handles to be inserted, and the cylinder used as a roller for crushing or flattening.

Ntusi does not have defences like Bigo, and this has led to speculation that it may have been a satellite community ruled from Bigo, with Ntusi inhabitants retreating behind the Bigo battlements when under attack.

Katonga Wildlife Reserve The 207-sq-km Katonga Wildlife Reserve was gazetted in 1964 as a game reserve. It was a corridor for migrating wildlife in search of water prior to the civil unrest of the 1970-80s, and now much of the land is utilized by the nomadic hamites – Bahima – who graze their large herds of long-horned Ankole cattle there. The area is mixed savannah with acacia woodlands, and a few pockets of tropical and riverine forest. A large proportion of the reserve is wetlands – either permanent or seasonal. Katonga is one of the few places in Africa to have a large population of the extremely shy and reclusive Sitatunga antelope, whose favoured habitat is papyrus swamps. Other mammals include elephant, hippo, black and white colobus monkeys, olive baboon, Uganda kob, waterbuck, duiker and reedbuck. The wetlands support a population of river otter, along with various reptiles and amphibians. In addition there are over 150 species of birds recorded. The reserve does not have any roads at present, but three trails have been developed to allow visitors the opportunity to see the various ecosystems within Katonga. The early-morning walk along the **Sitatunga Trail** offers the best opportunity to spot the timid antelope. Other mammals are frequently seen as you walk through the savannah and later alongside the Katonga river. The **Kyeibale Trail** is a circular trek through the scrubland into the remnants of the forests, passing interesting rock formations and caves used for shelter by the animals. The **Kisharara Trail** traverses the savannah to the wetland canal, follows the Katonga River and continues up one of the tributaries through a variety of eco-systems, offering the visitor an opportunity to see the Sitatunga antelope and various primates as well as other mammals and birdlife. Uniquely, it is also possible to explore the reserve by canal. The **Wetlands Canal Trail** is a

Uganda

Ntusi archaeological sites

From JEG Sutton, Azania, 1998

To Bigo

North Hill

Bwogero

To Mubende

Ntusi 'Male' Mound

Ntusi 'Female' Mound

To Masaka

Shops & Stalls

Ntusi Administrative Offices

N

0 metres 200
0 yards 200

Mounds

2-km ride through the reed and papyrus swamp, guided by a local boat operator and accompanied by a ranger, allowing the best opportunity to spot wetland mammals such as the otter, and an abundance of birds including kingfishers and storks. It is also possible to organize an overnight trip into the undeveloped interior of the reserve, but not during the rainy season. This is really only an option for the very fit as there are no facilities and you will have to bring everything with you. Tents and sleeping bags can be hired from the visitor centre. ■ *Cost US$10. The costs of the guided walks vary from US$3-7.50 depending on the length/time of the trek. Contact the Uganda Wildlife Authority, T041 346287, director@uwahq.uu.imul.com or the Uganda Tourist Board, T041 342196.*

Sleeping is limited to **camping**, at US$3 per night plus the reserve entrance/visitation fee of US$7. The campsite is located on a hill overlooking the river valley. It has a small canteen, or you can order meals through a local women's group. Another option is to cross the Katonga River by canoe and stay in the small town of Kabarole, south of the railway.

Transport The most direct route is via the Kampala-Mubende-Fort Portal road, which is sealed as far as Mubende. Approximately 48 km past Mubende, at the small town of Kyegegwa, take the left turn in a southerly direction. This unmade road takes you through the villages of Mpara and Karwenyi before reaching the reserve headquarters close to the Katong River. Katonga is 42 km from Kyegegwa. A 4WD is needed during the rainy season. The journey time from Kampala is about 3 hrs. By public transport there are frequent *matatus* and buses to Kyegegwa. From here *matatus* run south, depending on road and weather conditions, as far as Karwenyi. From here walking is possible or hire a bicycle taxi. There is one taxi that will go direct to Katonga on request through Kyegegwa from Kampala's new taxi park.

An alternative route to Katonga Wildlife Reserve is to take the Kampala-Mbarara road. Shortly after Lyantonde, take the road north at Nakaiita to Kazo, passing through several small settlements (including Nyakashashara, Nsikisi, Rwensunga and Rushere) until you reach Kenshunga. Here, take the road north to Kazo and then follow the road northeast to Kabagole. From Kabagole it is just a short canoe trip across the Katonga River to the reserve. There is a bus service from Mbarara to Kabagole, or *matatus* via Lyantonde.

Kabarole can also be accessed from the Fort Portal-Mbarara road at Ruhoko, which is a short distance to Ibanda. From here, take the road east to Kazo via the small towns of Rwomuhoro, Kanoni and Kitongore. From Kazo take the road north to Kabarole.

Mbarara to Queen Elizabeth National Park

Bushenyi
0°35'S 30°10'E
Colour map 3, grid B1
Phone code: 0485

Bushenyi is accessed on the road to the southwest via Mbarara, which forks north to Queen Elizabeth National Park, Kasese and Fort Portal shortly after Mbarara. Bushenyi is the district centre and there is a hospital and a few small shops selling basic household merchandise. There are several hotels, a couple of cheap guesthouses, restaurants serving local food, a pub and two petrol stations. Bushenyi also has a bank and post office.

Bushenyi

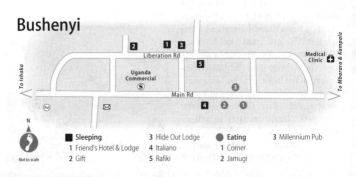

Sleeping	3 Hide Out Lodge	**Eating**	3 Millennium Pub
1 Friend's Hotel & Lodge	4 Italiano	1 Corner	
2 Gift	5 Rafiki	2 Jamugi	

Sleeping There are several low-priced places to stay, all much of a muchness, with simple facilities, adequate for a short stay. **E** *Italiano Hotel*, *Rafiki Hotel*, *Hide Out Lodge*, *Gift Hotel* and *Friend's Hotel and Lodge*.

    Eating There are two inexpensive places to eat, both serving local food and grills. **Cheap** *Jamugi Restaurant* and *Corner Restaurant*, or try the *Millennium Pub*.

The road from Bushenyi to Ishaka, a larger town 6 km west of Bushenyi, and then on   **Ishaka**
to Kasese is tarmac and in excellent condition, courtesy of a western government.
There are very good pineapples for sale on the road opposite Ishaka's Seventh Day
Adventist Hospital, with surely the most surly salesmen in East Africa.

Sleeping **E** *Homeland Hotel*, T42226, clean, basic accommodation.

If you are visiting the southern sector of the Queen Elizabeth National Park, a much   **Ishasha**
shorter alternative if coming from Kampala is to go via Ishaka to Rukungiri. It is not a   **& Queen**
very well-signposted route – Ishaka is on the main Kasese-Bushenyi-Mbarara road,   **Elizabeth**
about 6 km west of Bushenyi. From Ishaka take the road south to Rwashamaire and   **National Park**
then west to Rukungiri. If you are travelling independently there are *matatus* from   **(south)**
Ishaka to Rukungiri. From Rukungiri head for Ishasha village and a few kilometres
before you reach it the road joins the main road from Katunguru. Turn up this road
and follow it for 7 km to the entrance gate. If you do not have your own vehicle you will
have to get off at this junction and walk it or try to hitch a lift to the entrance gate. Once
at the gate it is another 7 km to the camp. It is usually possible at a cost of about US$12
to get a park vehicle to come and collect you, provided it is roadworthy at the time
when you visit. For details of the southern sector, see page 697.

Kalinzu Forest Reserve is situated 10 km northwest of Ishaka on the main   **Kalinzu Forest**
Mbarara-Kasese road. Guided walks along the scenic Rift Valley escarpment are avail-   **Reserve**
able. The eco-tourism site contains a campsite within the forest with basic facilities,
but you need to be self-sufficient. Basic supplies can be bought at Butare Trading Centre, 9 km from the campsite on the Mbarara-Kasese road. Four forest trails have been
developed. The **River Trail**, a 2½-km circular trail, takes one hour to complete, past
the Kajojo ('elephant') River, so called because it used to be a favoured bathing place.
There are nine primate species here, including chimpanzees. The **Palm Trail** is a 5-km
trail, which takes approximately two hours to complete. There is a fine example of a
'flame tree' and a spectacular 'dragon tree'. The **Valley Trail** is a 3½-km walk taking
two hours with a wonderful view overlooking a valley. The trek includes a ridge walk
and gives visitors a chance to see the 'viagra tree', *Mutragyne rubrostipuleta*. The
Waterfall Trail is an 11-km trail over hilly terrain taking four or five hours. The waterfall 'kilyantama' is known locally as the 'sheep-eater'. There are many fig trees providing the bark-cloth that is used widely in the local craft industry. ■ *US$6.50. Guides:
day treks US$2.75, night treks US$3.40, camping US$1.50 per person.*

Kasyoha Kitomi Forest is about 35 km north of Ishaka. Set between two crater lakes   **Kasyoha**
the forest overlooks the Albertine Rift Valley. Kasyoha Kitomi Forest supports a large   **Kitomi Forest**
bio-diversity of forest flora and fauna. The forest is home to many chimpanzees, and a
project is in hand to habituate a group so that these primates can be viewed in their
natural habitat. The visitor centre and campsite overlook Chemo and Mweru crater
lakes. Further into the forest reserve is Lake Kamunzuku, the 'transparent' lake,
which, along with its nearby caves, offers excellent bird-watching, swimming, fishing
or local exploration. From Lake Kamunzuku, a 17-km trail explores the gorges and
waterfalls of the **Chambura** (also spelt Kyambura) **River**. Three forest trails have been
established, and a fourth is being developed to Rurama Hill, which will offer the best
opportunity of viewing chimpanzees when the habituation programme is completed.
    The trail head is 3½ km from the visitor centre, which is accessible by own vehicle,
boda-boda or by walking 1½ km along a murram track. The trails meander around

Uganda

the crater lakes and rivers of the forest reserve, and require a reasonable level of fitness and mobility as some of the terrain is hilly and involves clambering. The guides will be happy to advise you on the fitness level required for each of the trail walks. These walks are not suitable for young children.

The 3-km **Lakeside Trail** is a gentle one-hour trip around Lake Kamunzuku including access to two sedimentary rock caves formed during periods of volcanic activity, traditionally used by hunters and fishermen to shelter from the elements. There are two beaches allowing access for swimming or boat trips. The lake is rich in fish and waterfowl. The **Waterfall Trail** is 2 km north of the lake through the forest to a spectacular waterfall on the River Lubale. Red-tailed monkeys are frequently spotted in this part of the forest. This walk can be extended by being combined with the **Lakeside Trail**. The **River Trail** is a rather more serious trek, taking a full day, and penetrating deep into the forest where chimpanzees are to be found. The trail continues to the river gorge, with a chance to see spectacular waterfalls, rapids and rock islands, deposited here many years ago by heavy flooding. It is possible to cross the river if you are fit and a trifle foolhardy, using the rocks as stepping stones.

Sleeping and eating Campers need to be self-sufficient as there are few local facilities. Meals can be ordered in advance. There is a small trading centre 1½ km away on the main highway at Nyakasharu (also spelt Nyancasharu), where basic foodstuffs can be bought. Nyakasharu also has a small hotel **E**, simple, clean with 9 single beds or alternatively, 35 km away in Ishaka, is the **E** *Homeland Hotel*. Guided day hikes cost US$1.50. Camping at the visitor centre is US$1.50 and at Lake Kamunzuku US$2.50 plus an additional payment of US$1.50 for the guide fee.

Transport Access is along the Mbarara-Kasese road, 35 km west of Ishaka to the Nyakasharu trading centre. **Buses** from Mbarara to Kasese stop at the trading centre. The Kasyoha Kitomi Forest is signposted and is just 1½ km off the main road along a murram track. A *boda-boda* from the Nyakasharu trading centre to Kasyoha Kitomi Forest Visitor Centre costs US$0.30.

From Bushenyi to Kasese the landscape is very hilly and at first the road goes up and down through forested hills, before it reaches the escarpment down to the Rift Valley. Just before descending the escarpment you pass the trading centre of Kichwamba, where a signpost on the eastern side of the road directs you to the **Chambura Game Reserve** (also spelt Kyambura). This lovely area has recently become incorporated into the Queen Elizabeth National Park, and your entry ticket will get you into all the other parts of the national park as well. The knowledgeable rangers of the reserve will helpfully show you the best spots in their area, such as a crater lake visited by flamingoes. From Kichwamba, it is only a few hundred metres before you zigzag down the escarpment. As you descend you will be able to see ahead of you Lakes George and Edward. At the bottom of the escarpment is the entry track to the **Maramagambo Forest**, part of the Queen Elizabeth National Park, with a campsite and the *Jacana Safari Lodge* at your disposal. From the cooler heights you descend into the hotter, dustier floor of the Rift Valley which is crossed by the road, passing through the Queen Elizabeth National Park. The vegetation around is mainly acacia bush and the grass is sprinkled with the occasional ant-hill. On the floor of the valley, just 2 km further to the north, the track to Chambura Gorge is signposted to the right as 'Fig Tree Camp, 2 km'. This is again part of the Queen Elizabeth National Park and one of the best places in Uganda to see chimpanzees. The tarmac road continues atop a causeway, which crosses the Kazinga Channel at Katuguru – a natural channel that connects Lake George to Lake Edward.

Here you can turn left and enter the main part of the Queen Elizabeth National Park. The northernmost part of the park is the area of the crater lakes, some with fresh water, others alkaline.

A bit further along on the road to Kasese you cross from the southern to the northern hemisphere – on each side of the road there is a large round wheel marking the Equator. The countryside around is mixed bush and some cultivation, including cotton, for many years Uganda's most important cash crop.

Queen Elizabeth National Park

The Queen Elizabeth National Park lies across the equator in the southwest of Uganda. It is bordered to the southwest by Lake Edward and to the northeast by Lake George. The two lakes are joined together by the Kazinga Channel, 33-km-long. The park covers an area of 1,978 sq km, with mainly flat and gently undulating terrain that rises from the lakes to 1,390 m above sea level at the crater area to the north of the Kazinga Channel. To the northeast are the Rwenzori Mountains, often known as the 'Mountains of the Moon', which rise to over 5,000 m. On a clear day it is possible to see the Rwenzoris from the park.

Ins and outs

There are two bases for touring the park: *Mweya Lodge* in the north (see page 693), and *Ishasha River Camp* (see page 697) in the south. It is possible to fly (charter) from Kampala to *Mweya Lodge*, or to Kasese, 64 km away. From Kasese there are *matatus* to the park every morning

Uganda

Queen Elizabeth National Park

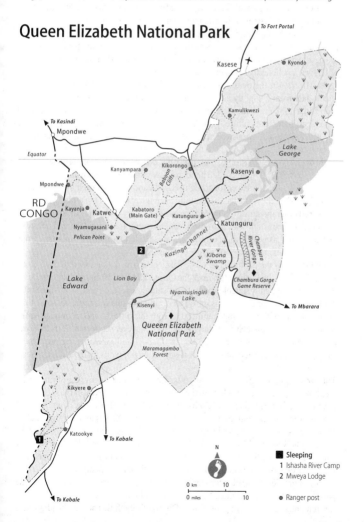

Sleeping
1 Ishasha River Camp
2 Mweya Lodge

● Ranger post

History

Uganda

Prehistory In the early 1930s Sir Vivian Fuchs discovered fossils from the Early Pleistocene Period along the Kazinga Channel, but it was not until some years later that prehistoric material was found. From the finds, and from work in Queen Elizabeth National Park, it is possible to indicate a little of the prehistory of this area. Fossils of water snails and other molluscs, crocodiles (which do not occur in Lakes George or Edward), hippos (including the pygmy variety), members of the pig family and various fish including Nile perch have all been found.

No tools belonging to the Early Pleistocene have been found in the fossiliferous ironstone bands, which are readily seen outcropping along the Kazinga Channel. Elsewhere in Africa this was an important period in human evolution, and in East Africa ape men of the Australopithecine family were beginning to make recognizable stone tools and become effective hunters rather than scavengers. Over a large area of the Queen Elizabeth National Park, and possibly as far north as Murchison Falls, transient lakes existed in the comparatively shallow trough of the Rift Valley. It seems that the early palaeolithic hunters lived around these lakes, hunting their prey; the bones of that prey are now often found in the ironstone bands.

Following the faulting in the Middle Pleistocene, the Rift Valley became more pronounced and the lakes more permanent. Stone tools found in the deposits from the period have been hand axes of quartz and quartzite, and pebble tools, which are water-worn pebbles flaked to give a sharp cutting edge.

At Mweya, on the peninsula of land leading to the present lodge, stone tools which date from a slightly later period have been found in gravels. The material found in a 1958 excavation consisted of all the types of tools of a fully developed Acheulean hand axe culture – hand axes, cleavers, round stone balls and waste flakes. Similar tools have also been found on the south bank of the Kazinga Channel.

The stone balls were thought to be wrapped in skin, attached to thongs and used to throw at animals. Hunting was probably conducted by making drives using wooden spears. The stone-bladed hand axe was a standard tool, an all-purpose cutting implement. The cleaver (or straight-edged hand axe) was used for skinning or chopping, while the waste flakes, resulting from the making of the tools, would have been used to scrape skin and sharpen spears. The tools were made quickly and had a short life. The constant search for food would account for the widespread nature of the stone tools as well as their profusion – it is likely that many temporary camps around the lakes and water holes were established.

Judging from the profusion of waste flakes of quartz dating from the Late Stone Age, right along the Kazinga Channel, the Queen Elizabeth National Park continued to be an area eminently suitable for hunting, fishing and fowling until recent times. It is not known when agriculture was introduced, although this was probably some time before the end of the first millennium AD. From this time the area became progressively pastoral. It is unlikely that a large population was ever supported. Surface collections of pottery indicate that the Kazinga Channel and lakeshore regions, where fishing supplemented agriculture, were always more populous than the drier plains.

Modern history The present depopulation of the park is largely a result of the ravages of rinderpest (see box, page 726) and smallpox in the 1890s and then the arrival of tsetse (see box, page 475) at the beginning of the 20th century. In 1910 the seriousness of the animal trypanosomiasis and human sleeping-sickness led the officials to move the inhabitants to areas free of the tsetse fly. In 1925 the Lake George Game Reserve was established, followed in 1930 by the Lake Edward Game Reserve. These were later enlarged to include the crater areas and the area south of the Kazinga Channel. The Kibale Forest Corridor Game Reserve, to the north of Lake George, was also established, to provide a corridor for elephants to pass to and from Kibale Forest. The park was renamed the Kazinga National Park and was gazetted in 1952. In 1954 it was renamed again following the visit by Queen Elizabeth II. The park headquarters

Elephant tusks

In the 1930s in Uganda large herds of elephants were common, and most of the adult pachyderms had tusks. Large tusks were believed to have evolved over the years as evidence of reproductive excellence, and were used by dominant bulls to fight competitors for a mate. Elephants that failed to grow tusks were considered to be a rare mutation, affecting less than 1% of the total number.

Elephants use tusks to dig for water and roots in the dry season, and to scrape for salt, as in the caves of Mount Elgon. Elephants have a dominant tusk, just as humans have a preferred hand, which can usually be identified as it is more worn and rounded at the tip. Nowadays, an elephant with large tusks is likely to be a relatively placid, older female that has avoided having her tusks broken during fights.

Over the last few decades poachers have decimated the elephant numbers in the Queen Elizabeth National Park, reducing them from an estimated 3,500 in the early 1960s to around 200, 30 years later. In the last 10 years elephant numbers have risen again, to around 1,200, but it is rare to find any with large tusks. An estimated 33% of elephants are now tuskless.

A mutation no longer seen nowadays is an elephant with three – or, even rarer, four – tusks. One photograph of an elephant with three perfectly formed tusks, each weighing an average 23 kg, dates back to the middle of the last century. It was taken by an American client, accompanied by the professional hunter John Northcote in the Kigezi region, close to the Uganda/RD Congo border. Several other sightings of elephants with three or four tusks were reported at the time.

were established in Mweya, and in 1960 the Nuffield Unit of Tropical Animal Ecology, later renamed the Institute of Ecology, was also developed there.

Ecology

The park lies in the area of Africa where two types of vegetation meet – the rainforest which stretches out to the west for thousands of kilometres to the shores of the Atlantic, and the Eastern and Southern Africa grassland. The park, like much of Uganda, gets two rainy seasons each year – from March to May and from September to November. However, there is often rain during the rest of the year and prolonged droughts are unusual. The temperature varies from a minimum of 18°C to a maximum of 28°C.

Animals found in the Queen Elizabeth National Park include hippos, lions (well known as tree-climbers), elephants, buffalo, Uganda kob, waterbuck, bushbuck and topi. Smaller animals that occur (although they are not necessarily easily seen) include warthog, hyenas, mongoose, red-tailed monkey, black and white colobus monkey, baboon, vervet monkey, and chimpanzees. Giant forest hogs live in the park ,too, and you are particularly likely to see them on the escarpment on the way up to Mweya, just outside the Maramagambo Forest. They look rather like large shaggy warthogs for which they can be easily mistaken. The park is famous for its wide range of birdlife – an estimated 540 species have been recorded. In marshy and waterside areas larger species such as cormorants, goliath herons, egrets, spoonbills and sacred ibis can be seen. Others include fisheagles and pied kingfishers.

Northern sector (Mweya Lodge)

The journey takes about two hours and you can expect to see plenty of hippos and a wide range of birdlife. For information ask at the desk at Mweya Lodge. The launch goes four times a day and costs US$20 per person. Minimum charge per cruise is US$200. The best chance of getting a group of 10 people together is during the weekend. You can also organize game drives through *Mweya Lodge* if you do not have your own transport. The orphaned chimpanzees that could previously be observed, have been moved from the small island in QENP to Ngamba island in Lake Victoria.

Launch trip on the Kazinga Channel
This is the most frequently visited part of QENP, with better access from Kampala and a wider choice of accommodation

Uganda

694 QUEEN ELIZABETH NATIONAL PARK

👉 ## Salt

The salt industry at Katwe is 700-800 years old and over many centuries has provided the local inhabitants with an important source of income. About 25 km from Butiaba, on the eastern shores of Lake Albert, is the village of Kibiro, where salt is produced in a process that appears to have changed little in over seven centuries. The only major change is that the containers used, formerly pottery, are now metal.

The first written reports of production came from Speke in 1863 and Grant in 1864, who described the product as perfectly pure in colour and taste.

The basis of the salt production are the hot springs, found here at the base of the western escarpment. One unusual aspect is that both the production and marketing of salt are done solely by women. The salt gardens are owned by women and ownership is by female inheritance. It is not possible to buy a salt 'garden', although recently it has become possible to hire one.

The main method of salt collection is by evaporation and the rate of production depends on the weather. First the salt garden is prepared, with an area of any size and shape being cleared of grass. In the second stage dry soil is scattered over the wet exposed surface.

The loose soil is left to dry, and as it does so, it draws salty moisture from below, which evaporated by the heat of the sun. This process increases and the salt content of the scattered soil at the end of the day is scraped together and heaped up so that if it rains the salt will not be lost. The spreading and drying process continues for a few days, depending on the weather and, as the salt content of the scattered soil increases, the colour changes to a greyish brown.

Once a sufficiently high concentration is reached, the third stage begins. This is a process whereby the soil impregnated with salt is leached with water so that all the salt dissolves into the water. To achieve this the loose soil is put in a container with holes in the bottom and water is poured through it and collected in a second container held underneath. The liquid collected is dark brown and has a very high salt content.

This liquid is then taken indoors to special buildings and boiled the solution to evaporate the water. Firewood is used and its supply is one of the major restrictions on the amount of salt that can be produced. As the brine boils, the water evaporates and after an hour or two the salt starts to form. By the final stages the salt is white and porridge-like and is poured on to a mud platform where it immediately solidifies. As more salt is ladled on, a salt cone grows until it is about 3-4 kg. The number of cones that a saltworker will be able to take to market will depend on how much firewood she can gather and how much brine she can prepare. These in turn depend on how many women are working at her gardens.

Channel track & north of the Kazinga Channel This area is perhaps the most popular for game drives and there is a network of roads that enable you to choose the length of drive that suits you. If you plan your route well there is no need to double back on yourself. Generally, the roads are passable, although after heavy rain patches of thick sticky mud may make some routes difficult. Hippo trails cross the road every so often – it has been observed that individual hippos tend to use the same route every night when they go inland to feed. If you do come across any hippos on land be sure to give them a wide berth and do not come between them and the water. There are hyenas, buffaloes, Uganda kob, and down by the Kazinga Channel are Nile monitor lizards. That most elusive of animals, the leopard, lives in this area, but is extremely difficult to spot.

Crater area There are seven crater lakes in this area, although only four of these are accessible on the existing roads: Katwe, Kikorongo, Munyanyange and Nyamunuka. They are all alkaline although to differing degrees. The name Nyamunuka literally translated means 'animal smell' and the lake is so named because of the strong smell of sulphur that is emitted from the water. Lake Katwe is known throughout Uganda as being an area of salt production (see box, page 694) and has been producing high-quality salt for many years.

Take the track opposite the main gate at Kabatoro to the Baboon Cliffs and follow it through the rolling grasslands. The road is generally good although after rain there may be some muddy patches suitable only for four-wheel-drive vehicles. The grasslands are torched regularly as the dominant plants are all species whose growth is encouraged by regular burnings. There is no permanent fresh water in this area so, apart from during the rainy season (March-June), you are unlikely to see many animals. During the rains, however, there are often herds of both buffalo and elephant. There are always plenty of birds (particularly grassland birds) and the area is especially popular with ornithologists.

The track to Baboon Cliffs is worth taking for the views alone. The road continues upwards, and thorn trees (*Acacia gerrardii*) become more common. About 12 km from Kabatoro the track ends at Baboon Cliffs, with a splendid view of the park and surrounding countryside. The crater of Kyemango is below and in the distance Lake George can be seen. To the north are the Rwenzoris and on a clear day you will be able to see the snowcaps.

To follow this route travelling west, take the right turning just after the main gate at Kabatoro and drive towards and then across the main Kasese road. The track continues towards Lake George and the fishing village of Kasenyi through open grassland. About 10 km from the main road look to your left and you should be able to see a Uganda kob lek (see page 696).

Lake George & Lake Kikorongo

Just before you reach Kasenyi you will see the small crater lake of Bunyampaka, which is also used for salt panning on a small scale. You can take the track around the rim of the crater lake from Kasenyi, which will also lead you to the channel. Alternatively you can return along the main track and turn right after 6 km. This leads you to the village of Hamukungu; turn left and you will pass through a large swamp and then pass the crater lake of Kikorongo before reaching the main Kasese road. On this latter route you may see elephant. In the swamp there is the possibility of sighting the shoebill, while there are sometimes flamingoes in Lake Kikorongo.

To get to Lake Katwe take the left turning just after the main gate and head for the now-abandoned village of Kabatoro. About 5 km from this is Katwe town and on your right are the crater lakes of Katwe and Munyanyange. These provide Katwe inhabitants with their main sources of income: salt panning and fishing. They are outside the park boundaries so it is possible to leave your car. You should be able to visit the salt works at Lake Katwe on payment of a small fee. You may be able to get a guide to show you around and explain the methods by which salt is evaporated and purified. As Lake Munyanyange is an alkaline lake it is sometimes the home of lesser flamingoes in varying numbers. It is possible to walk around the rim of the lake.

Lake Katwe & Pelican Point

Pelican Point is difficult to access by car, but there is a nice picnic spot by a former ranger's station, overlooking the Nyamagasani Delta

The tiny run-down town of **Katwe**, located just outside the boundary of QENP, appears to receive few visitors. Local children follow you everywhere you go within this strangely interesting place. Travellers on a tight budget might like to come here as there is no need to pay the daily park entrance fees as at Mbeya. However, there is only one place to stay, **E** *Express Hotel*, and it is hardly luxurious – bucket showers and pit latrine – although the mosquito nets are in surprisingly good condition. Cost US$2 per night. The front is a bar but meals are not available. It is on the main road coming from the national park. Simple local meals can be found at the typical small *hotelis* elsewhere – the one opposite serves particularly tasty food. Hitching along the road through QENP is not difficult even in low season, as long as you have a smidgen of patience, and it is very much cheaper than a private hire taxi from Katunguru.

The road beyond Katwe is not in very good condition and, if there has been recent rain, you would be advised to avoid this route unless you have a four-wheel drive. From the track you will be able to see the Nyamagasani Delta and the Kihabule Forest before you reach Pelican Point.

Uganda

Uganda kob

This is probably the most prevalent mammal in the Queen Elizabeth National Park with an estimated population of about 17,000. It prefers low-lying, open country without too much bush. Female kob and their young form loose herds of about 50. During the dry season they join up with males and with other groups to form herds of up to 1,000 in areas where green grass is still available.

Male Uganda kobs mate with females in permanent grounds known as leks. Within a lek there are a cluster of small, usually roughly circular, breeding territories. For a few days the males will defend their territory by *ritualized displays and by fighting when necessary. The females range freely within the lek and appear to favour males that hold territories in the centre of the lek. For this reason, most activity takes place within the central area, with these males constantly being challenged by other males.*

The leks can be recognized by the flattened grass that is the result of being trampled on over many years. They are usually located in open grassland near water. During a prolonged dry season leks are usually abandoned and the herds join together in search of food and water.

South of Kazinga Channel Take the main road and cross the Kazinga Channel. About 5 km south of the crossing turn right along the Ishasha road and follow it south. This route is mainly through grasslands, and about 8 km after the turning there is a kob lek on your left (see box above).

Lake Nyamusingiri & Maramagambo Forest This is one of the longer trips, taking a full day and requiring a four-wheel drive. Go back to the main Kasese road and turn east towards the Kichwamba escarpment. Cross the Katunguru bridge and continue along the road for about 12 km before turning right and starting to climb up the escarpment. The road takes you through both grasslands and acacia woodland. To your right you should be able to see the Kibona swamp, while ahead of you is the Maramagambo forest.

Lake Kasanduka and the start of the Maramagambo Forest are reached about 9 km along this track, and a further 3 km on is Lake Nyamusingiri. There are trails into the forest although you are advised to take a rancher who knows it. Chimpanzees live in the forest but are not habituated so you are unlikely to see them. Other primates that you may see are black and white colobus and red-tailed monkeys.

Chambura River Gorge The Chambura Gorge (also spelt Kyambura) and the former Chambura Game Reserve have been incorporated into the Queen Elizabeth National Park. The gorge was formed by a river that flows off the Kichwamba escarpment and into the Kazinga Channel at Katunguru. The gorge is 10 km long and supports dense forest, which is home to many different forest-living species, including chimpanzees. Tourists can visit these chimpanzees and tracking is organized by the Ugandan Wildlife Authority. The walk starts at 0730 and costs US$30 per person. You have to book in advance at the tourist information desk at *Mweya Lodge* or at the headquarters of the Ugandan Wildlife Authority in Kampala. It is not possible to buy a ticket at the Chambura Gorge. On each side of the gorge is savannah, and the view from the edge is spectacular. Walking along the top of the gorge and looking down on to the forest gives a wonderful view of the tops of the trees and any birds or animals that may be feeding off them.

The easiest way to get to the gorge is to take a park ranger with you, who will be able to advise you on up-to-date conditions locally. One possible route is to take the road from Katunguru for about 8 km towards the escarpment. There is a turning off to the left shortly before the road begins to climb the escarpment and from here it is about 2 km to the edge of the gorge. Once you get to the gorge it is possible to climb down the 200 m into it. This is a bit of a scramble as it is fairly steep. You pass from dry grasslands at the top to thick forest and the river at the bottom. *Mweya Lodge* should be able to organize a trip to Chambura River Gorge for a group.

Essentials

A *Jacana Safari Lodge,* located on the other side of the Kazinga Channel on the edge of Maramagambo Forest, not far from Lake Nyamusingiri, is an upmarket luxury camp run in conjunction with the Inns of Uganda, T041-258273, T075-714714 (mob), iou@swiftuganda.com Like the *Nile Safari Lodge*, its twin at Murchison Falls, it is difficult to get to, especially in the rainy season. Jacana's 7 cottages are arranged around the lake shore. The restaurant, positioned high over the lake, has average food and the service can be painfully slow but at least the view over the lake is pretty good and can be spectacular after rain at sunset. There is a swimming pool. **A** *Mweya Lodge*, PO Box 22, Kasese, T0483 44266, F259399, marasa@starcom.co.ug is managed by the Madvani Group. Located on the Mweya Peninsula on a bluff overlooking Katwe Bay, the original lodge was built in the mid-1950s but has recently been luxuriously rebuilt. Don't expect a sense of wildness though as the facilities are more fitting for a 5-star Kampala hotel. There is a superbly located bar, dining area and swimming pool. The rooms have a luxury atmosphere and not surprisingly the prices have increased markedly since the renovation. There's a good restaurant with lavish food, with a strong Indian influence. The lodge is rarely full, especially as it is a bit too far for Kampala residents to visit at weekends. Non-residents can eat at *Mweya Lodge*, breakfast is good value, US$6.50, dinner US$9-10. Very friendly staff. Will change travellers' cheques.

Sleeping & eating
■ *on map, page 691*

E *Institute of Ecology*, next to *Mweya Lodge*. Singles and doubles available, all with shared facilities, but no bed linen provided so it is pretty basic but is clean and comfortable, meals available. **E** *Student Hostel*, 1 km from the Ecology Institute. This is the cheapest place to stay, but it is very basic and not especially good value.

Camping   There are a number of campsites near *Mweya Lodge*. The most convenient if you want to use some of the *Mweya Lodge*'s facilities is the one on the south side of the peninsula overlooking the Kazinga Channel. Another 2 are located off the Channel Track – the first is 4 km from the lodge and the second is 6 km away. Each of the campsites has a pit latrine, water and firewood provided. It is also possible to camp at the *Student Hostel*, but you need to bring all equipment and food.

Air   Services can be chartered from Kampala to the airstrip at *Mweya Lodge* or alternatively to Kasese, which is 64 km from the park.

Transport

Road   From **Kasese** take a *matatu* going in the direction of Katwe on the north shore of Lake Edward – they go daily in the morning. Ask to be dropped off on the main road at the turning for the park entrance, which is 100 m down a track. From the gate it is about 6 km to *Mweya Lodge* – you can either try to hitch (this is not as difficult as it sounds), or ask the people at the gate to radio for a vehicle to be sent to pick you up. This collection service will cost you about US$10-15 and it is suspended from time to time, according to travellers who have visited recently.

It is 435 km from **Kampala**, via Mbarara, a journey that takes about 6 hrs. The Kazinga Channel is crossed on an iron bridge and then the road carries on to the small village of Katunguru. From Katunguru there are 2 different routes. You can either continue on the main road towards Kasese, turning left after 5 km and then a further 15 km to the main gate at Kabatoro, passing Lake Nyamunuka. From the main gate it is 8 km to the lodge. Alternatively you can turn left immediately after Katunguru and follow the road to the Katunguru Gate from where it is 20 km to the lodge along the Channel Track. The road from **Fort Portal** and **Kasese** in the north is sealed. The western route north from **Mahinga** and **Bwindi** parks is gravel and some sandy sections can be difficult when wet.

Southern sector (Ishasha River Camp)

Made up of mainly open partly wooded grasslands and heavily populated with animals, the southern part of the park is quite beautiful. It is less accessible than the northern part and so receives substantially fewer visitors. **Ishasha River Camp**, in

Uganda

the far southwestern corner of the park, close to the RD Congo border. There is simple accommodation available. The park sub-headquarters are at Ishasha, which is over 120 km south of Mweya. The 'tree-climbing' lions of Ishasha, which allegedly perch on savannah fig trees, are not easily spotted and some travellers have declared them to be mythical! However, the birdlife is excellent.

South Kigezi route The route covers a distance of about 14 km and begins at the bandas. Close to the bandas is a large hippo wallow, which, apart from being home to hippos, is also a watering point for various antelope and buffalo. The birdlife here is also fairly extensive, with herons, storks and ibises.

The famous tree-climbing lions live in the woodland in this southern area. They are rarer now and it has been suggested that their habit of climbing trees is less common. You may also see topi around here. These are splendid animals with beautiful coats. They are also found in Lake Mburo National Park in Uganda, and in a few national parks in Kenya and Tanzania.

North Kigezi route There are plans to renovate the roads in this rarely visited part of the park. It is an area of grassland with patches of woodland. The elephants in this area are the ones that move between Uganda and RD Congo; they are very shy. The northern route is reputed to be the best section of the national park for viewing the lions.

Sleeping At *Ishasha* the accommodation is in simple bandas with beds for up to 6 people. These were built during the colonial period and seem to have had little done to them since. For **camping** there are 3 very pleasant sites – located on the banks of the river, which is teeming with hippos, and in the riverine forest. The campsites have firewood and pit latrines provided but little else. There is no food available so you must come fully self-sufficient. Each site is very private and has a gazebo with a cement floor to shelter from the sun or rain. The charge is US$15 per person. You are not allowed to camp outside the park – even with a bribe.

Transport From *Mweya Lodge* take the main Kasese-Mbarara road south and turn off right at Katunguru. Although this is a route used by commercial traffic, it has not had any maintenance for many years and its condition deteriorates sharply during the rains making it impassable. The heavy trucks bound for RD Congo, Rwanda and Burundi frequently get stuck on this road, blocking all lighter traffic for hours – and occasionally days – on end. About 100 km after joining the road at Katunguru you will see a turning to the right with a sign to the Katookye Gate. From the entrance gate to the camp is a further 7 km. For the direct route from Kampala, see page 689.

Kasese

0°13'N 30°3'E
Phone code: 483
Colour map 3, grid B1

This industrial town was once infamous for its dusty 'Wild West' roads and it is still not a very pleasant place, perhaps because it is extremely hot and the mosquitoes are most troublesome at night. Factories, including a cotton ginnery, line the main road as it bypasses the town centre. It is not really worth a detour unless you need to stock up on supplies. It is the main base for expeditions into the Rwenzori Mountains (see below).

Trains from the East African Railways used to stop here, coming all the way from Mombasa, but the passenger train services between Kampala and Kasese have been suspended since 1997, and are unlikely to be resumed in the foreseeable future.

Kilembe Copper Mines, have closed, and Kilembe town, located 13 km to the west of Kasese, has lost all of its former glory. These mines were once an important source of foreign exchange for Uganda. In Kasese an Australian-financed foundry is now extracting considerable amounts of high-grade cobalt from the residual sludge of the copper mines. The plant is along the Kasese-Queen Elizabeth National Park road, a couple of kilometres out of Kasese. Many people confuse the old copper mines with the newly opened cobalt processing plant.

C *Margherita*, Kilembe Rd, PO Box 90, T44015, F44380. This former government hotel is set in beautiful surroundings, with the Rwenzori Mountains on one side and a golf course on the other. There is something magnificent about the vegetation in this area, especially when the trees are in flower. It is situated about 3 km down the road to Kilembe to the west of town and so not very accessible without your own transport. The rooms have been renovated but are overpriced for what you get, unless you want to pay for the nice setting. There is a restaurant.

D *Saad*, T44139. This hotel has been around for a long time. The rooms are not very nice and are off a long dark corridor. The restaurant is OK (although no alcohol is served on the premises as the owner is Muslim), and the *tilapia* (fish) is recommended. There are bicycles for hire and videos are screened. **E** *Mariana*, T077-493414 (mob). This brand-new hotel, on Stanley St, is very good value for money. Self-contained and rooms with shared facilities, with nets. There is a modern-looking bar, where they also serve snacks. **E** *Moonlight Lodge*, on Margherita St next to the *Shell* garage, is clean, with showers, mosquito nets and friendly staff. When it is hot go for the single rooms, as they are fresh and airy. **E** *Virina Garden*, T077-588161 (mob), has shared and self-contained (cold water) basic rondavels. It is also possible to put up your own tent. It is a bit far from the town centre and the taxi park. No food available. **E** *Paradise Lodge*, is a bit of a misnomer. Basic rooms with shared bathrooms.

Sleeping

Uganda

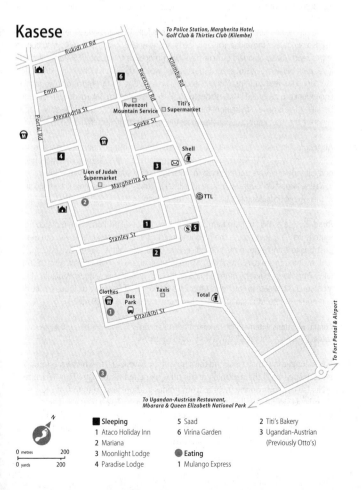

Kasese

To Police Station, Margherita Hotel,
Golf Club & Thirties Club (Kilembe)

Rukidi III Rd

Emin

Portal Rd

Alexandria St

Rwenzori Rd

Kilembe Rd

Rwenzori
Mountain Service

Titi's
Supermarket

Speke St

Shell

Lion of Judah
Supermarket

Margherita St

@TTL

Stanley St

Clothes

Bus
Park

Taxis

Total

Kitalikibi St

To Fort Portal & Airport

To Ugandan-Austrian Restaurant,
Mbarara & Queen Elizabeth National Park

0 metres   200
0 yards   200

N

■ **Sleeping**
1 Ataco Holiday Inn
2 Mariana
3 Moonlight Lodge
4 Paradise Lodge

5 Saad
6 Virina Garden

● **Eating**
1 Mulango Express

2 Titi's Bakery
3 Ugandan-Austrian
   (Previously Otto's)

Eating **Cheap** *Ugandan-Austrian Restaurant* (previously *Otto's Restaurant*), T077-500711 (mob), near the main road just south of Kasese, has Uganda's best bargain 3-course lunches and dinners, and a swimming pool too. Closed on Mon. **Seriously cheap** *Mulango Express* is a popular place for local food. You can eat outside under acacia trees. Go from the bus park towards the second-hand clothes market. *Mulango Express* is located to the rear of the market. The best chicken in town can be ordered in the bar next to the *Ataco Holiday Inn*. If you want to have a walk out of town, 2 km just off the road to Kilembe you will find the *Thirties Club*, with its nice verandah overlooking Kasese town, the mountains and the plains, and a disco on Wed and Sat nights. *Titi's Bakery* on Margherita St is famous for its salted bread, french bread, cakes, doughnuts, sausage rolls, etc. You can buy chilled drinks here too.

Shopping The best supermarkets are *Titi* on Rwenzori Rd, close to the post office, and the *Lion of Judah*, Margherita St. There are quite a few shops, close to the market where you can buy food suitable for hiking – such as dried soups imported from Kenya. At the market you can find some nice material from the Congo.

Tour operators When the national park was reopened in July 2001 after 4 years, 2 foreign firms *Afrik Alpine* and *Top Trekk* merged with the NGO *Rwenzori Mountain Services* (RMS) into one company called *ARTS*, PO Box 33, Alexandra Rd, Kasese, T493-259175. *ARTS* has the concession to provide accommodation, porters, guiding and rescue services, as well as marketing the national park. As a private company *ARTS* profits do not directly benefit the local community.

Part of the mountain trail has fallen into disrepair following landslides. The Mahoma River needs a bridge, and the bridge at Kyoho needs urgent repairs. Several of the huts need upgrading to reach 'basic' standards. There have been proposals to charge US$900 to climb the Rwenzoris, but as of November 2001 the cost for 1 week is US$350, and there are extra charges like park entry fees and tips. Climbers and trekkers need to bring all their own equipment. Equipment can be rented in Kasese but it is unlikely to be modern. Take good rain equipment because there is no real dry season. Take a stove – cooking over charcoal can be slow. Walking sticks are the most important equipment for the trip, along with waterproof boots.

Transport **Air** *Eagle Air* flies twice a week (Tue and Fri afternoon) from Entebbe to Kasese costing US$100 one way. T077-476184 (mob). There are plans to make Kasese an international airport, although they are not expected to reach fruition for some time. Charter flights also go to Kasese airport although, as they are usually taking tourists, they are more likely to go direct to the *Mweya Lodge* landing site in QENP (see page 696).

Road Kasese is 418 km from **Kampala** via Mubende and Fort Portal. The more common route is via Mbarara because the road is tarmacked all the way. At 0630 you can get the **post bus** to Kampala from the post office. Fare US$6, takes 8 hrs. Buses leave from the bus park, next to the taxi park. To Kabale costs US$5 and takes 6 hrs. To Kampala costs US$6 and takes 7 hrs. If you travel by *matatu* to Kampala you will have to change in Mbarara. Fare to Mbarara US$3. Kasese to Fort Portal takes 2 hrs costing US$2. There is a daily bus service from Fort Portal, Kasese, Mbarara to Kabale, departing at 0600 from Fort Portal.

Directory **Communications** Internet: Plot 72 Rwenzori Rd. **Telephones**: MTM phone boxes offer international calls at the weekend at half price. You will need to buy a phone card.

Nyakalengija Nyakalengija is a small village on the fringe of the Rwenzoris to which access may still be restricted until the national park is fully reopened to tourists. This agricultural area also depends on the income from guides and porters. Matatu from Kasese to Ibanda, US$1.50. Walking to Nyakalengija from Kasese takes about one hour. **Camping** Just opposite the RMS offices in Nyakalengija there is an **E-F** community campground with restaurant services. There are plans to build bandas but for the time being travellers must bring their own tents.

Rwenzori Mountains National Park

The Rwenzoris (Ruwenzoris) lie along the border of Uganda and RD Congo, rising to a height of about 5,100 m above sea level (see map, page 613). The range is about 100 km in length and about 50 km wide. It was formed from a block that was tilted and thrust up during the development of the Rift Valley. These beautiful, often mist-shrouded mountains are non-volcanic and offer mountaineers and walkers superb country and wonderful views.

"... you may be familiar with the Alps and the Caucasus, the Himalayas and the Rockies, but if you have not explored Rwenzori, you still have something wonderful to see." DW Freshfield (Explorer, 1906)

The Rwenzoris are also known as the 'Mountains of the Moon'. They were first described as such by Ptolemy because they were believed to be the Lunae Montes predicted by the ancient Greeks to be the source of the Nile.

A number of the mountain peaks are named after early explorers to Uganda and some of those in the centre of the range have permanent snow cover – these include Mounts Stanley (5,110 m), Speke (4,889 m), Baker (4,843 m), Gessi (4,797 m), Emin (4,791 m) and Luigi di Savoia (4,626 m). On Mount Stanley are the twin summits of Alexandra (5,044 m) and Margherita (5,110 m). There is some dispute about the actual heights of these peaks and some sources mark them as being significantly higher.

Ins and outs

It is possible to fly (charter) to Kasese. The Rwenzoris are approached from **Ibanda** in Mubuku Valley. On reaching Ibanda you will see a signpost for the Rwenzori Mountaineering Service on the right-hand side of the road and this is where you will need to go to organize guides, porters, etc.

For transport details see page 705

Geology

The Rwenzoris are relatively young mountains, at less than 10,000,000 years old. Until that time, the area was part of a huge plain that extended to the Atlantic coast to the west and rivers flowed to the west. A series of movements of the earth's crust resulted in major rifting and, in the Rwenzori area, an uplifting of the underlying rock. The Rwenzoris are made up of quartzite and gneiss.

Although not the highest, the Rwenzori range is certainly the largest and most important group of snow mountains in Africa. Mount Kilimanjaro (5,968 m) and Mount

Rwenzori Mountains

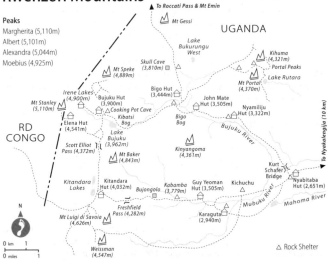

Peaks
Margherita (5,110m)
Albert (5,101m)
Alexandra (5,044m)
Moebius (4,925m)

Exploration of the Rwenzori Mountains

It is now generally accepted that Ptolemy (c AD 150), when writing of the 'Mountains of the Moon', the legendary source of the Nile, was referring to the Rwenzori massif. Interestingly, Speke, discovering the Virunga volcanoes in 1861, associated them with Ptolemy's description.

In the 19th century, Baker (1864) observed the Rwenzoris (and called them the 'Blue Mountains') but he failed to appreciate the importance of this natural feature. Sir Henry Stanley was the first to proclaim the existence of the Rwenzoris as Snow Mountains. In his book Darkest Africa he claims to have made the discovery himself, but in fact two members of his expedition Surgeon Parke and Mountenoy-Jephson had seen the snows a month before him, on 20 April 1888. The following year another member of the expedition, Lieutenant Stairs, ascended the mountains to a height of over 3,050 m.

It is to Stanley that we owe the name Rwenzori (often spelt Ruwenzori). The word means 'the place from where the rain comes'. No name appears to have been given to the mountains by the local residents – their custom was to name the rivers running off the mountains rather than the actual peaks.

In the summer of 1891 Emin Pasha's companion Dr F Stuhlmann climbed up the Butagu valley to a height of 4,062 m and had the first close glimpse of the snow. A few years later, in 1894-95, naturalist G F Scott Elliott also made a number of expeditions, which were of significant botanical importance. In 1900 an expedition by C S Moore proved the presence of glaciers, and shortly afterwards Sir Harry Johnston reached the Mobuku glacier at a height of 4,520 m. The first purely non-scientific climb, and the first by a woman, was in 1903 by the Reverend A B and Mrs Fisher. The twin peaks of Mount Stanley, Alexandra and Margherita, were climbed for the first time in June 1906 by an expedition led by the Duke of Abruzzi. This expedition produced important scientific results, and an excellent topographical survey of the range was completed with information on the areas of the glaciers. It was this expedition that named most of the main peaks. The duke chose to name the smallest, Luigi di Savoia, after himself.

Kenya (5,225 m) are both higher, but are single volcanic peaks. The Rwenzori, whose highest point is the Margherita Peak of Mount Stanley (5,110 m) is a massif composed of six separate mountains, all of which carry permanent snow and glaciers. The general axis of the range is north-south and the snow peaks, divided by lower snow-free passes, lie roughly along this axis in the middle of the range. Unlike all the other great mountains of Central Africa, Rwenzori is not of volcanic origin but is the result of an upthrust associated with the formation of the Western Rift Valley, in which it stands.

There are six separated glaciated groups and the glaciers are the equatorial type. That is, they are more truly ice caps than ice-rivers; movement is very slight as can be seen from the clearness of the streams and the absence of large moraines (accumulations of debris carried down by the glaciers). There have been times of much greater glaciation in earlier eras on the Rwenzoris, reaching thousands of metres below the current levels, and many of the valleys are characteristically shaped by ice erosion. The existing glaciers are in retreat.

Vegetation and wildlife

One of the most delightful aspects of the Rwenzoris is the diversity of plants and trees. Cultivation rarely extends above about 2,000 m around the base of the mountain, and in many places it is considerably lower. Ascending, the climber passes from the foothills, where most of the vegetation is elephant grass, up to about 1,800 m. From there is the montane or true forest, which is a mixture of trees, bracken and tree ferns. In this zone, which extends to about 2,500 m, it is possible to see orchids. Higher still is the bamboo zone, which continues up to about 3,000 m. The vegetation here also includes tree heather and, in moister patches, giant lobelias. The next fairly extensive zone is the heather forest, which extends from about 3,000 m up to about 3,800 m. The humid climate at this altitude causes vigorous development of mosses and lichens, which cover the ground and the trunks of living and fallen trees. At this level, on the better-drained slopes, tree groundsels and shrubby trees flourish, while the wetter parts are distinctly boggy. This zone also has brambles, orchids and ferns, all of which form a tangle that makes passage difficult. The highest vegetative zone, extending from about 3,800 m to the snowline, is alpine. From here most of the common herbaceous plants disappear, leaving tree heaths, giant lobelias and senecios. Reeds grow in the marshes and shrubby bushes with everlasting flowers (*Belichrysums*) are abundant. The rocks are covered with a loosely adhering carpet of moss. Above about 3,000 m there is little sign of life except hyrax and other small rodents. Birds are also fairly sparse.

People

Living on the Rwenzoris are the Bakonjo a Bantu tribe who speak Lukonjo, which is believed to be one of the earliest forms of Bantu speech. They are a short and sturdy people and frequently find work as guides and porters as many are excellent climbers. Apart from when they are acting as guides and porters, they rarely actually go high up into the mountain range, believing that a god called Kitasamba lives in the upper reaches of the mountains. On your ascent you may see small grass huts containing offerings to Kitasamba.

Climbing the Rwenzoris

On 2 July 2001, the mountains were once again opened for climbing. Permits are likely to be around US$350 per person. However, the situation may change and you should certainly contact the Uganda Wildlife Authority, T256 41 34287 or director@uwahq.uu.imul.com The *Rwenzori Mountains Services (RMS)*, PO Box 33, Alexander Road, Kasese, T493 259175, which maintains the huts and trails, has also reopened.

The Rwenzoris are suitable for almost all climbers and walkers who are reasonably fit. There are hiking routes in the foothills for those with no climbing experience – all that is needed is a little stamina and waterproof clothing. More demanding is the ascent of Mount Speke, which is a simple glacier requiring limited mountain experience. Most difficult are some of the routes on Mounts Stanley and Baker; only those with experience in rock, snow and ice climbing should attempt these.

The Rwenzoris have a reputation for being wet – and with good reason. The best times of the year to visit them are from the end of December to February and from mid-June to mid-August. The rest of the year there is often a lot of rain and, apart from making the walk or climb slippery, it also means that the views are not so good with mist sometimes shrouding the mountains, in particular the peaks.

Very roughly, the total price that you can expect to pay, for an eight-day trek will be in the region of US$400-500. This includes all fees, porters, guides, equipment hire and food. Most equipment that you may need can be hired from the *RMS* and food can be bought in Kasese. It is wet for much of the year and cold at night, so come well prepared, with waterproofs and plenty of warm clothing. Pack everything inside your rucksack in plastic bags.

It is obligatory to take porters and a guide. Porters carry loads of 22 kg excluding their own blankets and supplies. The headman does not carry a load although he is expected to relieve a tired member of the party. Guides are also necessary. Before departure, it is important to clarify what the charges are going to be – they depend on the number of days taken up on the trip and the stages covered.

You should take all the food that you will need. It is certainly worth taking a stove; apart from the environmental impact of cutting wood for cooking, the wood is almost always wet and difficult to light.

More serious climbers who intend to tackle the peaks should be sure that their guide is experienced. The best written work is Osmaston and Pasteur's *Guide to the Rwenzoris*,

Uganda

updated in 1997. This is not available in Uganda but can be obtained from *Stanfords Map and Travel Bookshop* (12-14 Long Acre, Covent Garden, London WC2E 9LP, England, T020 7836 1321). The other good guide with a detailed map is Wielochowski's *Rwenzori Map and Guide*, which is available from the author (32 Seamill Park Crescent, Worthing BN11 2NP, England), and also in some bookshops in Nairobi.

You should allow about 10 days for the trip and the most popular route (the Circuit, see below) should take you six to seven days. This is obviously just one possibility – you can break the route up with more frequent stops – for example Day 1 to Nyabitaba; Day 2 to Nyamiliju; Day 3 to Bigo; Day 4 to Lake Bujuku; Day 5 to Kitandara; Day 6 to Guy Yeoman and Day 7 back to Nyakalengija.

The Circuit

Day 1 Begin by heading for Nyakalengija (1,600 m), 5 km from Ibanda and 22 km from Kasese, where the trail begins and from there take the path to the Nyabitaba Hut (2,651 m), about 10 km. If you have made arrangements through the *RMS* they should be able to arrange transport to their office at Nyakalengija where you will pay your fees, etc. You can also park vehicles here fairly safely, and camp if you want to start the walk early the next day. From Nyakalengija head through a coffee plantation and a field and on into some elephant grass. The path gradually deteriorates as you enter the bush and the cultivation disappears and is replaced by elephant grass and nettles. The Mubuku River on your right contains trout that were introduced by the British. You descend to the edge of the river and then climb up and into the forest. Cross two streams and continue for several kilometres before crossing the Mahoma River. The final ascent is up a moraine ridge to Nyabitaba – before you get to the hut itself there is a small rock shelter. There is a larger rock shelter a little beyond the hut, used by many people in preference to the hut. Alternatively, you can camp in the clearing by the hut. The two-roomed Nyabitaba hut, built in 1987, sleeps up to 12 people. There is a water supply at the hut.

Day 2 **Nyabitaba (2,651 m) to John Mate Hut (3,505 m)**. You follow the ridge through
This is the most the forest and then fork down steeply to the left to the Mubuku River. This you cross
difficult day of the using the Kurt Schafer Bridge which was built in 1989 after the old one collapsed.
Circuit, and will take From here you climb up again on the other side – the path gradually gets harder,
you at least 7 hrs becoming a slippery scramble – and continue on to the bamboo forest. The walk through the bamboo forest is relatively easy but, before reaching Nyamiliju, there is a long hard climb upwards. It is here that you will start to go through the heather and groundsel towards Nyamiliju – in fact Nyamiliju actually means 'place of beards', a name that refers to the moss and lichen that hang from the trees. The old hut at Nyamiliju (3,322 m) is a round uniport with a wooden floor. It is not used much any longer as most people prefer to push on to John Mate Hut. But if you wish to go slower, it has a good water supply. There is also a nearby rock shelter, which some people prefer to use but which has no room for tents. If it is a clear day you should be able to see Mount Stanley and Mount Speke as well as the glaciers, and Nyamiliju can make a good lunchtime stop. From here it is a further two hours to John Mate Hut (3,505 m), climbing up through the giant heather and groundsel forest. The trail is much less clear – start by crossing the stream just below the rock shelter and carry on towards the river, but don't actually cross it. Continue from the heather forest until it opens out a bit, and up two fairly steep moraines before you reach the camp. The hut is in good condition and close to the Bujuku River, where you can collect water.

Day 3 **John Mate Hut (3,505 m) to Lake Bujuku (3,962 m)**. On the third day you go through the muddy bog of Bigo, past the Bigo Hut and on to the Bujuku Hut. Begin by crossing the river and then head for the left-hand edge of the valley, skirting around the bog. You will find it almost impossible to avoid getting muddy. Bigo Hut (3,444 m) sleeps 12 and is in fairly good condition and there is flowing water near by. There is also a rock shelter here, which the porters tend to use.

From Bigo Hut you can choose a number of different routes. You can go north to Roccati Pass, which runs between Mounts Gessi and Emin; or northeast to Bukurungu pass between Gessi and the Portal Peaks; or southwest to Lake Bujuku. The latter route is the most popular for Circuit users and is the one described below.

From Bigo (3,444 m) to Lake Bujuku (3,962 m) you cross the Kibatsi Bog to what is known as the Cooking Pot Cave and from there to Lake Bujuku Hut with its beautiful setting. Begin by following the route that swings southwestwards with Mount Stanley on your right (west) and Baker on your left (east). The path starts off rather steep but levels off as you round the southern spur. You will shortly reach the Kibatsi bog, which will take you 2-3 hours to cross and from the bog there is another steep climb. At the Cooking Pot Cave, the track splits into two. Take the right (northwest) route to the huts. The left fork leads to the Scott Elliot Pass and you will return here tomorrow to continue the Circuit. The Lake Bujuku Hut is actually two huts which sleep up to 14 people and are in fair condition. There is water available close by. It is one of the loveliest settings of all the huts on the routes, with Mount Stanley and an incredible ice cave in the Peke Glacier on Mount Speke both clearly visible.

Lake Bujuku Hut is the base for those planning to climb Mount Speke (4,889 m). Serious climbers hoping to reach the highest point on the range, Margherita Peak on Mount Stanley (5,110 m), should base themselves at Elena Hut (4,541 m). This is located about 2 km off the Circuit and is about three or four hours from Bujuku or Kitandara huts.

Lake Bujuku (3,962 m) to Kitandara Hut (4,032 m). This walk is a fairly light one, **Day 4** taking about half a day, and climbing to the highest point on the Circuit at the Scott Elliot Pass. Begin by returning to the Cooking Pot Cave and from there take the southerly path that leads to the Scott Elliot Pass (4,372 m). The track takes you through groundsel to a scree slope. At the head of this is a rock buttress and the pass is to the right. There is a cleft in the rocks to the left and from here the descent continues with the vertical cliffs of Mount Baker on your side. Before reaching Lake Kitandara the path rises then descends again. The two huts at Lake Kitandara are also in a wonderful setting, next to one of the two lakes and close to the foot of Elena glacier.

Lake Kitandara Hut (4,032 m) to the Kamamba rock shelter (3,779 m) or to **Day 5** **Guy Yeoman Hut.** If you go on to the Guy Yeoman Hut this is a walk of about five hours. The day begins with a steep climb to the Freshfield Pass (4,282 m), followed by a descent to a rock overhang called Bujongolo. This is where the first expedition to explore the mountains in 1906 based itself. A little further on is a second, larger rock shelter called Kabamba located close to a waterfall, where you can spend the night. Alternatively you can continue on to the Guy Yeoman Hut (3,505 m), one of the newer sites.

Guy Yeoman (3,505 m) to Nyabitaba Hut (2,651 m), or on to Nyakalengija **Day 6** **(1,600 m).** Continue your descent via Kichuchu where there is another rock shelter. From Kichuchu the descent continues through bog and bamboo forest and then across the Mubuku River. Having forded the river, follow the path along a ridge and down to the Nyabitaba Hut (2,651 m). Alternatively, you can go via Lake Mahoma where there is a hut, if you want to spend an extra night. From Nyabitaba Hut you then have to retrace your steps back to Nyakalengija, about another three-hour hike.

Air Chartered flights go to **Kasese** from where you can complete the journey by road. **Transport**

Road Ibanda can be reached from Kampala via Mbarara and Kasese from where it is a further 18 km.

Alternatively, from Kampala to Fort Portal and then 75 km on the Fort Portal-Kasese road before turning off for Ibanda. Coming from Kasese, about 10 km along the main Kasese-Fort Portal road, there is a turning off to Ibanda. Take this for about 12 km – it is a fairly good gravel road.

Uganda

Fort Portal

0°40'N 30°20'E
Phone code: 483
Colour map 3, grid B1

Heading to Fort Portal from Kasese is another beautiful drive. The road climbs out of the dry plain and gradually enters the hilly greenness that surrounds Fort Portal. Located a little over 300 km to the west of Kampala and 80 km north of Kasese at 1,600 m above sea level, Fort Portal is situated in the foothills of the Rwenzori Mountains. Small, quiet and refreshing, it is one of Uganda's most agreeable towns.

Ins & outs
For transport details, see page 710

Fort Portal is an 8-hr bus journey from Kampala and there are frequent *matatus* to and from Kasese and the nearest airport.

Tourist information

There are a number of tourist attractions accessible from Fort Portal (see below pages 710-718). You can get information from the *Kabarole Tourism Association*, which shares its office with *Kabarole Tours*, on Moledina St, behind the Caltex station. The staff are very friendly and helpful and have excellent tour guides. T22686, F22636, Ktours@ botex.africaonline.co.ug Local cycling tours are available.

Climate

Fort Portal is now the district headquarters for the Kabarole district. The town currently has a population of about 40,000 people and is the centre of the Toro Kingdom. It enjoys an excellent climate, almost temperate in nature, with moderate sunshine and heavy downpours

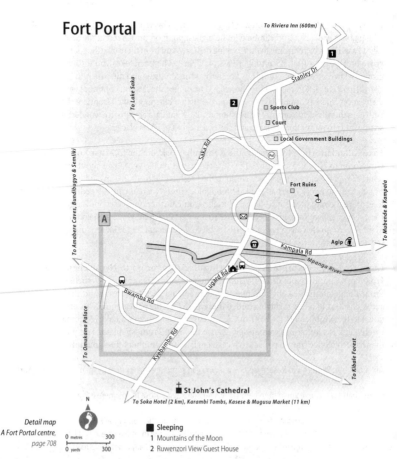

Fort Portal

To Riviera Inn (600m)

Stanley Dr

To Lake Saka

Saka Rd

□ Sports Club

□ Court

□ Local Government Buildings

Fort Ruins □

To Amabere Caves, Bundibugyo & Semliki

A

Kampala Rd

Agip

To Mubende & Kampala

Mpanga River

Bwamba Rd

Lugard Rd

To Omukama Palace

Kyebambe Rd

To Kibale Forest

✝ St John's Cathedral

To Soka Hotel (2 km), Karambi Tombs, Kasese & Mugusu Market (11 km)

*Detail map
A Fort Portal centre,
page 708*

N

0 metres 300
0 yards 300

■ **Sleeping**
1 Mountains of the Moon
2 Ruwenzori View Guest House

Uganda

Gerry's fort

Sir Gerald Portal was the British Consul General of Zanzibar who arrived in Uganda in late 1892 and died of malaria soon after his return to London in 1894. His statue in the centre of the roundabout, near the Uganda Commercial Bank in Fort Portal, shows him carrying a gun and describes him as a Major and an explorer. In fact he was a diplomat who held no army post. His weapon was a pen. Captain Lugard had left a string of forts with up to 4,000 Sudanese soldiers in the Toro area under the control of Captain de Winton. Originally Sir Gerald wanted these Sudanese troops to be withdrawn. De Winton died in 1892 and in 1893 Sir Gerald sent a young British officer, Major Roderick Owen, to discuss these plans with the Omukama (King Kasagama). On his return to Kampala, Owen managed to convince Sir Gerald that, instead of leaving Toro completely, only some of the Sudanese troops should be withdrawn and a new fort at Toro should be built. The fort was originally called Fort Gerry, but this seemed irreverent so in 1900 the name was changed to Fort Portal.

Sir Gerry's statue was repainted some time ago and he now has a particularly florid (bright yellow) complexion; his sword has also been broken, leaving a rather unfortunate protuberance!

during the rainy season. The main rains are from Mar-May and from Sep-Nov – although there are no real dry seasons. The annual temperatures are about 25-28° C. The climate is mainly influenced by the surrounding environment – particularly by the hills and mountains. The River Mpanga meanders through the municipality, its source being the tributaries from the Rwenzoris. It is this river that is the main source of water for the town.

History

Fort Portal was founded in 1893 under the name of Fort Gerry, and later renamed Fort Portal after Sir Gerald Portal (see box above). He never set foot in the town but contributed decisively to convincing the British Government of the benefits of Lugard's plan that these parts should become part of the British Empire, and was instrumental in the signing of agreements with the leaders of the kingdoms of Uganda that led to the formalizing of protectorate status for the country.

Fort Portal is in the centre of the Toro Kingdom and the town was a base from which British colonial power protected the then Omukama (or King) of Toro. In 1876 Toro was captured by the Banyoro King Kabalega, but the British expelled him in 1891 and replaced him with a new Toro King, Kasagama. In later years Catholic and Protestant missionaries followed the colonial administration in order to establish churches, schools and hospitals. By 1900 the town was expanding rapidly. Its development was helped by the booming trade in food and cash produce. In the 1930s Europeans and Indians came to set up large tea estates, and shops and residential premises were built. The growth of the town was also helped by the establishment in 1952 of the railway line from Mombasa as far as Kasese, for the transportation of copper from the mines at Kilembe. A cement factory was set up at Hima along the Fort Portal-Kasese road. As with the other kingdoms in Uganda, Toro was abolished in 1966 during Obote's first term of office. However, it was restored by Museveni in 1993.

Sights

Fort Portal's highest hill, Kabarole Hill, is the site of the former palace of the King of Toro (Omukama). It was built in the 1960s for the then Omukama, Rukidi III (son of Kasagama), but was looted during Amin's time (1979), and is now only a ruin. It is not a particularly attractive site but there are good views of the Rwenzoris from the top of the hill. A recent traveller has reported that written permission is needed to visit this site, and enforcement of this regulation is carried out by armed guards. **Toro Palace ruins**

Uganda

Next to the old palace a new mansion has been put up for the present Omukama, King Oyo. He was crowned king in 1995, when he was only three years old, after sudden death of his father (Omukama Kaboyo).

Fort ruins The fort after which the town is named is now the site of the town's golf course, and is little more than a collection of rocks. It is said that one of these rocks contains the footprints of General Gerald Portal's men.

Karambi tombs Located about 5 km out of Fort Portal on the main Fort Portal-Kasese road, on the right-hand side, these are the burial grounds for the Toro royal family, where Kasagama, Rukidi III and Kaboyo are buried. On display are personal artefacts of the kings, including drums and spears.

Excursions

From the town there is a beautiful view of the snow-capped Rwenzori Mountains – although cloud often covers the peaks. Some visitors base themselves at Fort Portal while organizing a trek up the Rwenzoris (see pages 703-705) but, although not so pleasant, Kasese is more convenient, as it is closer to the starting point at Ibanda.

The countryside surrounding Fort Portal is famous for its tea and in the old days this was an important export commodity for Uganda. During the colonial period many of the plantations were run by Europeans on land leased from the government (and rarely owned). Now the land is mostly owned by a few large companies, but smallholdings are encouraged. Labour is largely imported from the southwestern part of Uganda and this causes some social problems. Many of the original tea plantations had fallen into disrepair when the infrastructure of the country collapsed

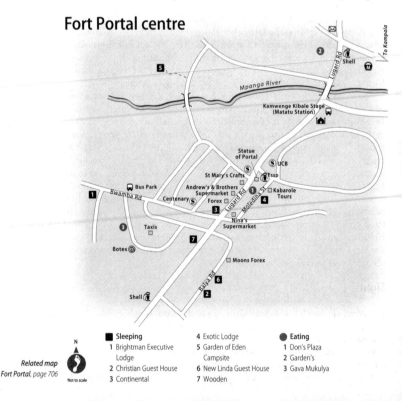

Fort Portal centre

	Sleeping	4 Exotic Lodge		Eating
	1 Brightman Executive Lodge	5 Garden of Eden Campsite		1 Don's Plaza
	2 Christian Guest House	6 New Linda Guest House		2 Garden's
	3 Continental	7 Wooden		3 Gava Mukulya

Related map
Fort Portal, page 706

Not to scale

between 1972 and 1986. Since then a massive rehabilitation **progra**mme has been very successful in restoring them to their former glory. If you leave Fort Portal early to go chimp tracking in the Kibale Forest, you will notice lots of 'squads' getting ready to head out to work in the fields.

Fort Portal is a base for trips to the Kibale Forest, Magombe Swamp, Bigodi, Bunyuruguru Crater Lake Fields, Semliki National Park and Sempaya Hot Springs, Semliki Valley Wildlife Reserve, hikes in the foothills of the Rwenzoris and Amabere Caves and Waterfall. You might also stop over here on the way to the Murchison Falls National Park (although it is a long day's travel to the north, along a notoriously bad road).

Essentials

C *Mountains of the Moon*, T077-494632 (mob), about 2½ km from the town centre. This is a lovely, but run-down old colonial hotel, set in beautiful grounds. The restaurant does good steak and chips, service variable. The water supply, both hot and cold, is reported to be unreliable recently. Ideal for a drink in the garden in the afternoon or in the bar during the evening. Recent travellers report that this hotel will not accept travellers' cheques in settlement of the bill. **C** *RuwenZori View Guest House*, PO Box 709, Fort Portal, Lower Kakiiza Rd, Plot 15 Boma, T22102, T077-722102 (mob), ruwview@africaonline.co.ug, sited about 500 m before the *Mountains of the Moon Hotel*. Well signposted. Excellent hotel (6 rooms), way above usual standards. Outstanding food served for dinner. Hosted by Ineke Jongerius and Maurice Barnes, a Dutch/English couple. Recommended by several travellers. **C** *Riviera Inn*, 3 km from town, past *Mountains of the Moon Hotel*. This double-storey house is transformed into a small comfortable guesthouse, with 4 rooms. Good restaurant (but first check what is available from the menu) and bar. It can be noisy at weekends. **D** *Soka*, 2 km out on the Fort Portal-Kasese road, T077-472330 (mob). Self-contained and rooms with shared facilities, clean but with no view. Snacks available, bar, pool table, sauna cabin and massage, can also be used by non-residents. **D-E** *Continental*, T077-484842 (mob). The most popular hotel if you want to stay in the town centre. Won the town prize in year 2000 for the cleanest building in Fort Portal. Additional charge for TV in the self-contained rooms. The rooms without a TV and with shared bathrooms are a lot cheaper.

E *Brightman Executive Lodge*, opposite the bus park, ideal if you need to catch the early bus. Simple straightforward rooms, no breakfast. **E** *Christian Guest House*, clean and simple, friendly place, food available. Shared rooms have 2, 3 or 4 beds. **E** *Exotic Lodge*, Moledina St next to *Kabarole Tours*. Simple and cheap, with the novelty of watching a tall container of water being heated over a charcoal stove early each evening for showers. **E** *New Linda Guest House*, T22937. Basic rooms with shared bathrooms, hot and cold water. Quieter rooms at the back. Friendly staff. Good restaurant for local food. **E** *Wooden*, T077-402770 (mob). Situated in the middle of town. Big hotel, 40 rooms. Popular with travellers, bar and restaurant, cold shower, hot water in buckets, TV in a bare lounge. Not a friendly atmosphere. Has a very noisy nightclub. Sleep impossible before 0200 except if there is a power cut. Expect to be woken again at 0600 by the shouting of touts at the *matatu* station.

Camping *Garden of Eden Campsite* lies on a river bank, close to the centre of town. Beautifully situated and friendly, but don't expect many facilities. Run by *Kabarole Tours*; check with them if you want to camp there.

Cheap *Don's Plaza*, on the main street in the centre. Popular bar with snacks and roasted chicken on the side. Currently the 'in place' where locals and expats meet for an evening beer, open at weekends until the last guest leaves. *Garden's Restaurant*, opposite the market, behind the Pepsi depot. For pepper steak and chips and local food. Nice outside bar, busy in the evenings. *Mountains of the Moon*, a bit out of town, but nice setting and varied international menu. Serves tilapia fish, steak and chicken in the basket. Good for Sun lunch in the garden. *Riviera Inn*, 3 km out of town, but nice chicken, pork and chips.

Sleeping
There are some excellent lodges and campsites in the area surrounding Fort Portal, see below for details

Eating
It is recommended that you check what is available before making your selection and ordering from the menu

Uganda

Seriously cheap *Gava Mukulya*, nice place with tasty local food at the taxi park. *New Linda Guest House*, friendly restaurant with high-quality local food. Recommended. *Jofa Restaurant*, next to *Exotic Lodge* on Moledina St, serves good local food.

Shopping A visit to the cloth market close to the post office is worthwhile. People who like markets should visit the big Wed morning Mugusu Market, 11 km from Fort Portal town on the road to Kasese. You can buy everything there, including a large selection of second-hand western clothes. *Andrew's & Brothers* and *Nina's* are two well-stocked supermarkets on the main Lugard Rd, where you can also find *Mary's Craft Shop* with locally made crafts and cards.

Sport The town has a 9-hole **golf** course that is open to members and those from affiliated clubs. Temporary membership is also available. The course is a 20-min walk up the road past the post office.

Tour operators *Kabarole Tours*, Moledina St, behind the Caltex station, T22686, F22636, ktours@ botex.africaonline.co.ug They are very helpful and have excellent tour guides. They share their offices with the *Kabarole Tourism Association*, who are very active in promoting eco-tourism in this part of Uganda. This *association* unites more than 80 local groups, and has done much work on developing eco-community tourism programmes lasting from half a day up to several days. You can visit local communities and learn about their life and cultural traditions, and visit farms and see what farmers plant for their own food, or to sell, such as coffee and tea. In the fragran tea-factory you can observe how tea is processed, from green leaf to black tea ready for auction in Mombasa. With local guides you can walk the community trails through local villages and forest, via crater lakes, waterfalls, hot springs, caves and mountains. For more detailed information about the programmes on offer contact the *Kabarole Tourism Association* office at Moledina St (see page 706).

Transport **Air** The nearest airport is Kasese. **Road** Fort Portal is accessible by road, by two alternative routes from **Kampala**. The first is 320 km through Mubende district but is only partly sealed; the other is through Masaka, Mbarara, Bushenyi and Kasese and is 430 km. By bus the journey takes about 8 hrs and goes through exceptionally beautiful countryside. *Matatus* run to and from **Kasese** taking about 2 hrs, cost US$2. Fort Portal to **Kampala**: bus leaves at 0600 but you must be there at 0500, takes 7-8 hrs, US$8 per person. *Matatus* to **Masindi/Hoima** (changing in Kagadi) cost US$10. It takes 7 hrs to reach Masindi. From Fort Portal there is a weekly bus that goes directly to Hoima. It runs on Sat, leaving at 0630 from Bwamba Rd. If it has rained recently, be prepared to get off the bus on uphill stretches and help push (male passengers only). **Bus** to **Kabale** takes 7-8 hrs and costs US$9. **Mbarara**: journey time 4-5 hrs cost US$4.50.

Directory **Banks** There are two banks in Fort Portal – the *Co-operative Bank* and the *Uganda Commercial Bank*. It is very difficult to cash ones as there have been a lot of forged TCs in circulation recently. You may be asked to produce your original receipt for the TCs. **Moon's Forex Bureau**, Kyebambe Rd, just past the junction with Bwamba Rd on the left-hand side (the road to Kasese), will change TCs at surprisingly good rates given the lack of competition. **Libraries** Public library at Fort Portal has an excellent selection of books. **Places of worship** Every religion is represented at Fort Portal: there are several mosques (including one under construction) and churches of Anglican, Roman Catholic, Pentecostal, Seventh Day Adventist and Church of Uganda denominations.

Changing money you may get anything up to 25% less than you would expect in Kampala (even for US$ bills and especially at weekends)

Around Fort Portal

Lake Saka **Amabere Caves and Waterfall** and three crater lakes lie west of Fort Portal off the Bundibugyo Road. After 8 km you branch off towards Nyakasura school, and follow the signs towards Amabere Caves and Waterfall – it's another 2 km till you get there. Don't expect anything too spectacular – the caves are small, almost like shallow openings in the rock, and moss-covered pillars half conceal the entrance. The first cave is dominated by the waterfall. There are stalagmites and stalactites (in the shape of a woman's breast, which is what the name Amabere means). The caves are dark, so bring a torch.

The local guide can tell interesting stories about the traditional history of the place. The area around the caves is very attractive and the walk to the nearby crater lakes is worthwhile. Guides from the Amabere Caves will be happy to show you the way. After a short steep climb there is a spectacular view over three crater lakes: Kigere, Nyabikere and Saka. Nyabikere means 'place of frogs', and amphibians are plentiful here. **Kigere** means 'footprint' in the local language. According to legend a footprint of a man was found in the stones of the caves after a volcanic eruption. The print has since disappeared but the lake and the story remain. You can walk from Fort Portal over the Saka Road towards **Lake Saka**, but it is not possible to swim in this lake unless you have the permission of the Catholic Seminary, which has its grounds on the lake side. Another local lake, **Lake Kiatabarogo**, meaning 'killer of witches', is where so-called 'bewitched' people were thrown. You cannot visit this lake because it is situated within the area of the army barracks.

Sleeping   It is possible to stay at the **E** *Amakoomi Campsite* near the caves, and about 1 km from the crater lakes. Pit latrines and shower enclosures US$3 per person. Tent hire also

Uganda

Fort Portal & around

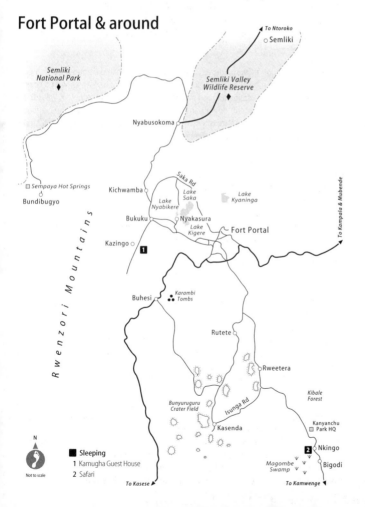

To Ntoroko
○ Semliki

Semliki
National Park
◆

Semliki Valley
Wildlife Reserve
◆

Nyabusokoma ○

□ Sempaya Hot Springs
Bundibugyo ○

Saka Rd
Kichwamba ○   Lake
                     Saka   Lake
         Lake   Kyaninga
         Nyabikere

R w e n z o r i   M o u n t a i n s

Bukuku ○   ○ Nyakasura
              Lake
Kazingo ○   Kigere   ○ Fort Portal
        1

To Kampala & Mubende

Buhesi ○   •• Karambi
                Tombs

Rutete ○

○ Rweetera

Kibale
Forest

Bunyuruguru
Crater Field   Kanyanchu
                   Isunga Rd   □ Park HQ

○ Kasenda

2 ○ Nkingo

Magombe ↓↓
Swamp ↓↓   ○ Bigodi

N
↑

Not to scale

■ Sleeping
1 Kamugha Guest House
2 Safari

To Kasese ▶   To Kamwenge ◀

available for US$3. A self-contained lodge with 2 rooms, each sleeping 2, is nearing completion. It will cost US$12 per person when fully operational. Beers and sodas available, but bring your own food. There are only basic facilities. The owner of the attractive campsite and nearby waterfall and caves is the very friendly Mr Rumombora.

Transport If you don't have your own transport, you can walk to the caves, hire a *boda-boda*, get a special hire taxi, or take a *matatu* and get off at Nyakasura stage. Alterna

tively, *Kabarole Tours* organizes 'bicycle safaris' to this area, providing a local bike similar to those used for bicycle taxis, but without the seat on the back, and a roughly drawn map – cost US$6.

Kazingo
■ *on map, page 711*

From *Kamugha Guest House* (see below), in Kazingo Trading Centre in the foothills of the Rwenzori Mountains, about 12½ km from Fort Portal town, Azoli Bahati organizes activities for tourists who are interested in local communities, customs, culture and environment. In this area there are two distinct tribes, the Batoro of the lowlands and the Bakonzo of the mountains. From the guesthouse you can take guided walks (US$5) in the foothills of the Rwenzoris, enjoy the scenic views, visit local communities, do some bird-watching, follow the waterfall trail and identify medicinal plants. It is also possible to visit a traditional witch doctor at his home (US$11 per visit). In the evenings you can watch traditional dancers (Batoro and Bakonzo) for US$11 per performance.

Sleeping E *Kamugha Guest House*, T077-621397 (mob), abahati@botex.africaonline.co, offers simple accommodation and local food, and organizes guided walks, with a cooked lunch served in the mountains. It is also possible to camp near the guesthouse. This experience is available as a day trip or with an overnight stay in *Kamugha Guest House*. Please phone or email as advance notice is required. It is expected that now the Rwenzori Mountains National Park has reopened, hikes will also be organized over the mountains to Bundibugyo and Semliki National Park.

Transport Take the Bundibugyo road and after 8 km branch off to the left at Bukuku for Kazingo. You can get a *matatu* up to Bukuku, and walk the remaining 3½ km to Kazingo. Alternatively you can hire a private taxi car.

Hot springs of Rwagimba

These springs can be visited off the main Fort Portal-Kasese road, on the border between the two districts. Be prepared for a lengthy guided walk, rewarded with a sauna bath in the hot springs, followed by a refreshing swim in the cool waters of the River Rwimi. For further details contact *Kabarole Tours* in Fort Portal (see also box on page 713.)

Northwest of Fort Portal: the Semliki Valley

Itwara Forest

Located to the northeast of Fort Portal this is another forest with a large number of small mammals as well as a great range of birdlife. Primates found include chimpanzees, black and white colobus, blue monkey, red-tailed monkey and red colobus. Also found are the African palm civet, the giant forest squirrel and the scaly-tailed flying squirrel. Tourist facilities have not been developed.

Towards Bundibugyo

The road northwest from Fort Portal to Bundibugyo offers many spectacular views. It skirts the northern spur of the Rwenzori Mountains and in clear weather provides good views of the Kijura Escarpment and Lake Albert to the north, and the Semliki River Valley to the northwest. As the road descends into the Rift Valley, it is astonishing to find that the scarp is heavily cultivated; incredibly narrow terracing on a 60° slope contains a patchwork of fields – a green quilt, laced with black soil and dimpled by the cassava plants. At **Nyabusokoma**, a depressing

The Spirit of Ndahura

Situated in Kisomoro, on the border between Kasese and Kabarole district, is a hot spring called Rwagimba, which, literally translated, means 'that which pushes or jets out'. The hot waters from the spring run into two rock pools, which lie, one below the other, within a few yards of the ice-cold waters of the Ruimi River.

The spring is widely known for the healing powers of its hot sulphurous waters, which are used both for washing and drinking, particularly by those suffering from skin diseases. The healing powers of the spring are supposed to be under the spiritual sway of Ndahura, a Muchwezi warrior whose career ended disastrously in defeat and smallpox. His name became so closely connected with smallpox that it actually became known as 'Ndahura's disease'.

The spring is jointly owned by two clans – the Bachwamba and the Basambu – and its keeper is always a Muchwamba man married to a Musambu woman. Although the man is the keeper he cannot exercise full powers, for it is the woman who is the actual priestess of the spring. From time to time, she may become possessed by the spirit of Ndahura. His spirit is not normally regarded as being imminent in the spring itself, but in the shrine that is maintained near to the keeper's house, where small offerings of food and beer are made. The spirit of Ndahura only becomes imminent in the spring when the waters are troubled. This seems to occur fairly rarely, and the rest of the time people seem happy to use the spring to bathe in and to help reduce aches and pains.

Uganda

collection of bandas for displaced people (see page 715), a road branches off to the fishing village of **Ntoroko** on the southern shore of Lake Albert, passing through the Semliki Valley Wildlife Reserve.

It is very easy to get confused over Semliki. There are two different parks: the privately run Semliki Valley Wildlife Reserve, run by the *Green Wilderness Group*, is always open; the **Semliki National Park** is over the spur of the Rwenzori Mountains and is often closed because of the security situation (see pages 713).

Semliki Valley Wildlife Reserve is the oldest protected area in Uganda and was previously known as the Toro Game Reserve. It is unique, gifted with geographic barriers that have formed a natural haven for wildlife. It is an area containing riverine forest, woodland and savannah, previously famous for its very high densities of wildlife including massive maned lions, buffalo, Jackson's hartebeest and forest elephants – known to the hunting fraternity as 'Semliki rats' and reputed to be very aggressive. Leopard, hippo, crocodiles and giant forest hogs were also common and the reserve had an estimated 10,000 Uganda kob. Chimpanzees and black and white colobus monkeys were frequently seen and there was also prolific birdlife. Apparently, as game was so plentiful in the Semliki Valley in the late 1960s, and the habitat was similar to that in India, a proposal was mooted to breed tigers in the valley, in the hope that, in 10 years or so, the numbers would have multiplied sufficiently to allow tiger hunts to be offered in Africa!

Most of the savannah game was decimated during the period of Amin and Obote's leadership, while the forest species were better equipped to survive the effects of the civil unrest and poachers. However, in the past few years Museveni has very successfully implemented measures to reduce the activities in this area of the rebels who terrorized the villagers and poached much of the wildlife. The lions and buffalo have returned and the number of Uganda kobs has multiplied and is now estimated to be over 8,000. The *Green Wilderness Group* holds the concession and is dedicated to rebuilding the game numbers. Poaching and rebel activity are no longer issues and the game is rapidly recovering. Within the next couple of years, it is estimated that the kob will have recovered to around 30,000. There are also plans to reintroduce Jackson hartebeest in the near future. Semliki is the only place in Uganda where you can go on night drives with a good chance of seeing leopard.

Semliki Valley Wildlife Reserve
Independent travellers are advised to check at Fort Portal for a current update before visiting this area

☞ Dwarf elephants

Recent biological findings indicate that the long-held belief that there are only two distinct species of elephants – the African and Asian – needs to be revised. Study of elephant DNA confirms that the African species can be sub-divided into two distinct groups, Loxodonta africana africana *and* Loxodonta africana cyclotis. *The former, commonly found in savannah grasslands is the largest living land mammal, averaging a shoulder height of over 3.2 m, weighing up to 7,500 kg, and with large ears. The latter is the forest elephant, a smaller and darker animal with thinner, straighter tusks, rounded ears, an average shoulder height of 2.5 m and weighing up to 6,000 kg. It has a different shaped skull and reputedly a more aggressive temperament. The genetic differences are reported to be about half as great as the variation between the African and Asian species. The genetic split is estimated to have begun over 2,500,000 years ago, and there is no evidence that the two species interbreed. There is a remnant of the distinctive sub-species* Loxodonta africana orleansi *previously found in northern Somalia and Ethiopia, but now confined to a small area close to Harar, in eastern Ethiopia. The war elephants used by the ancient Carthaginians and Romans in the area north of the Sahara are believed to have become extinct by the sixth century. There is controversial speculation over the existence of another elephant sub-species – the dark-skinned* Loxodonta pumilio – *the dwarf or pygmy elephant, said to live in swampy, dense jungle areas, measuring less than 2 m in height and with a reputation for very fierce, aggressive behaviour. According to reports it does not interbreed with the forest elephant. This elephant is said to be much more solitary than* Loxodonta africana africana. *In 1906 Professor Theodore Noark named and described* Loxodonta pumilio, *having studied a specimen in the Bronx Zoo. In 1982, the former West German Ambassador to the People's Republic of the Congo photographed a pygmy elephant herd in the Likouala region, with the tallest animal estimated to be less than 170 cm tall. Several other researchers including Edmond-White (1955), Haltenorth (1977) & Diller (1985) appear to have confirmed these findings. The dwarf or pygmy elephant shares the same jungle habitat as the forest elephant in Sierra Leone, RD Congo, Cameroon and Equatorial Guinea, and many experts believe that they are one and the same species. However, until genetic samples are obtained and analysed, the controversy is expected to continue.*

The original *Semliki Lodge*, designed by the Kampala architect Benito Larco, was destroyed by fire, but a new upmarket camp has been built near by. You can take guided walks to observe the wildlife, bird-watch or track chimpanzees, some of which are being habituated for research. Birdlife is still plentiful, with over 400 species recorded. This is the best place in Uganda to see the rare shoebill stork, most easily viewed from a hired boat on Lake Albert. Sport fishing for Nile perch, tiger fish and tilapia is excellent.

Sleeping **L** *Semliki Safari Lodge*, T/F41-259700, gwg@swiftuganda.com A luxury facility with 8 well-equipped tents, a dining and relaxation area plus swimming pool, run by the *Green Wilderness Group*. Exceptionally well managed, the lodge has something for everyone – swimming, birding, hiking or game drives (including night drives). The food is simple but well prepared and very tasty: try the aubergine chips as a snack. The guides are very knowledgeable. All in all a great place to chill out for a couple of days if you can afford it. Highly recommended.

Transport Take the road from Fort Portal to Bundibugyo. At Karugutu a road branches off to the fishing village of Ntoroko on the southern shore of Lake Albert and passes through the reserve. 4WD preferable as the road is poor and rocky 20 km after leaving Fort Portal. There are daily *matatus* going to Semliki and Bundibugyo. The Semliki Valley Wildlife Reserve has an airstrip.

The road from Fort Portal heads north to cross the northern tail of the Rwenzori **Semliki** range and then doubles back through Ntandi, Bundibugyo and Sempaya. Taking **National Park** the main road from Karagutu to Bundibugyo, the road loops around the northern edge of the Rwenzori Mountains and descends from 1,200 m to 720 m in a series of spectacular hairpin bends. At the bottom of the escarpment are the **Sempaya Hot Springs**, located by the Semliki National Park. Although the park is currently closed, it is still possible to visit the springs. Take local advice in Fort Portal before setting out, however.

Semliki (sometimes written Semuliki) National Park lies 52 km northwest of Fort Portal, located in the Bundibugyo District, on the far side of the northern tail of the Rwenzori Mountain range. It is mainly very dense tropical lowland forest, but with some grassland, wetland and bamboo forest. The terrain is quite flat, and the Rwenzori range forms a backdrop to the east. It rains a lot, and visitors should come prepared with waterproofs. The Semliki River defines the border with RD Congo, and several tributaries run through the park, providing watering places and good spots to observe animals. There are also some hot springs, and these attract birds and animals using the salt-licks. The various habitats attract a wide variety of wildlife, including elephants, buffaloes, leopards, civets, scaly-tailed flying squirrels and bushbabies. Primates are well represented, with eight species reported, and more than 400 bird species and 300 butterfly species have been observed. A trail round the park takes in the hot springs, and excursions to other areas can be arranged though the park headquarters at Ntandi, which is on the road from Fort Portal to Bundibugyo, situated just outside the park boundaries.

The pygmies who used to stand on the road near Ntandi village (5 km further along the road), who are still shown on tourist maps, have now disappeared. Instead, there are a series of camps of internally displaced people seeking safety from the activities of the ADF rebels, who have been causing problems in the region since 1977. The towns of Bundibugyo and Nyahuka are now several times their old size.

Camping The campsites, one inside the park near Ntandi and one outside at Sempaya, are **Sleeping** not currently operational due to rebel ADF activity in the area. In **Bundibugyo**, just outside the park, **E** *Picfare* and **E** *Moonlight*, on the main road, offer fairly basic alternatives to camping.

Although the road is fairly rough, access is possible by 4WD, or by a *matatu* from Fort Portal **Transport** to Bundibugyo, which will take 2-3 hrs to Ntandi. *Matatus* from Fort Portal stop at Semliki National Park, cost US$3, if you are willing to spend the night in Bundibugyo.

Bunyuruguru Crater Lake Field

This is a collection of crater lakes located about 30 km south of Fort Portal between the main Fort Portal-Kasese road and Kibale Forest. Crater lakes are formed by vulcanicity, with a violent eruption causing the top of a volcano to be blown off, leaving a crater. There are several lakes of varying size and character, and many have well-developed tourist facilities. Interesting features include a fascinating natural lava formation making a bridge under which water flows. The crater lakes are reputed to be bilharzia-free and therefore safe for swimming (however, there are leeches); they also offer good fishing and the opportunity to do some serious 'birding' with an estimated 300-400 species.

This beautiful small crater lake within the Bunyuruguru region is the only crater lake **Lake Nkurubu** remaining unspoilt by deforestation. It offers reportedly safe swimming, frequent *Maps are available for* sightings of black and white colobus monkeys, plus an occasional visit from *different trips/walks* Henrietta, a solitary nomadic hippo who travels between Lake Nkuruba and Lake Nyabikere. From here you can walk in the surroundings or hire a bicycle (with gears) for a trip around some of the nearby crater lakes or to the Mahoma Falls.

Uganda

Lake Nkuruba Nature Reserve Lake Nkuruba Nature Reserve is a community conservation project funds local education. There are three camping areas in tranquil settings and nice walks to the 'Top of the World', to neighbouring lakes, the Mahoma Falls and the explosion crater.

Sleeping and eating Accommodation ranges from campsites and a banda to the romantic lakeside house. Camping costs US$3 per person and tent hire costs US$1. Day visit charge US$1 and delicious evening meals with locally grown vegetables cost US$2. Vegetarian food is available and chapattis are baked fresh to order and served at the lakeshore.

Lake Nyinambuga South of Lake Nkuruba, this lake offers the only luxurious facilities in the crater lake field.

Sleeping A *Ndali Lodge*, T077-487673 (mob), F0483-22636, info@ndali.co.uk The well-appointed *Ndali Lodge* is set on a narrow ridge overlooking this blue-green lake 100 m below. There are stunning all-round views of the mountains to the west, the Rift Valley lakes to the south and the crater lakes to the east and north. Originally a tea planter's house, *Ndali* has 8 individual cottages set on the hillside in a nicely kept garden. No electricity but plenty of hot water heated by 'Tanganyika ovens'. Impeccable service and simple but beautifully

Bunyuruguru Crater Lakes

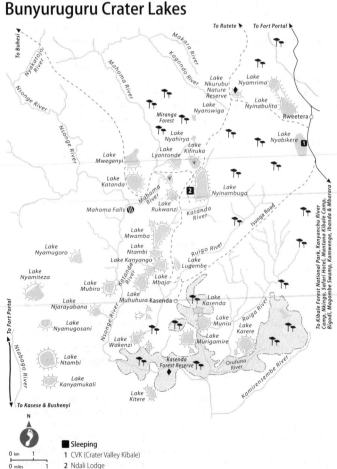

Sleeping
1 CVK (Crater Valley Kibale)
2 Ndali Lodge

0 km 1
0 miles 1

cooked meals make this a great place to stay for a couple of nights. Highly recommended. Boat trips can also be arranged by the lodge.

Lake Nyabikere, which means 'lake of frogs', is only 13 km or 30 minutes' drive from **Lake Nyabikere** Fort Portal on the Kamwenge Road, and just 100 m off the main road at the edge of Kibale Forest National Park. It is 10 km from the centre of Kibale Forest. It is possible to walk from *CVK* (Lake Nyabikere) to Lake Nkuruba via Lake Nynabulita and Lake Nyamirima. The route is shown on the map and part of it is negotiable by car. To make trips with local fishing boats, enquire at *CVK* (see below).

Sleeping D *CVK* (*Crater Valley Kibale*) T077-492274 (mob), F0483-22636, Kabopoza@   ■ *on map, page 716* starcom.co.ug, is beautifully located overlooking Lake Nyabikere from the east. It offers bandas, with options from sparsely to fully furnished accommodation. **Camping** is also possible at *CVK* and there is a restaurant and bar. Meals have to be ordered well in advance, but you can always get some chips and a soda or beer.

Most other lakes are difficult to reach or to enter. You can arrange a visit to Mahoma Falls in Kabata Village, near *Ndali Lodge*, or hire a bike with directions at Lake Nkuruba. Alternatively, *Kabarole Tours* organizes various crater lake tours, which can be personalized according to your wishes.

Despite various reports, *Rweetera Safari Campsite*, *Lake Lyantonde Campsite* and *Rwengo Lakeside Tourist Camp* are no longer operational. Kasende Forest Reserve has no tourist facilities.

Transport For Nkuruba take the *matatu* to Rwaihamba, cost US$1, journey time 40 mins. There is little traffic on the roads to the crater lakes but *matatus* go from Fort Portal to Rwaihamba, more frequently on Mon and Thu because it is market day. Cost is US$0.80 and it takes 40 mins. *Kabarole Tours* can also help to arrange transport. By **car** take the Kibale road from Fort Portal for 17 km and take the right fork, from which it is another 8 km to Lake Nkuruba (see page 717).

Kibale Forest National Park

Located south of Fort Portal, at an altitude of about 1,230 m above sea level, Kibale Forest provides a rich and unique habitat for more than 250 species of animal and over 300 types of bird. The animal species include 11 primates, including black and white colobus monkeys and chimpanzees. Monkeys can often be spotted from the road to the forest and the viewing of chimpanzees in their natural environment is the main tourist attraction.

Kibale Forest National Park covers an area of about 760 sq km (see map page 613) and is divided into seven zones for management purposes: research, natural reserve, civic-cultural, recreation, harvest, community and protection. There is an emphasis on conservation, sustainable utilization and non-consumptive use of the forest. Nature trails into the forest have been created and, quite apart from the chimps, the walks are wonderful. The forest is believed to contain the highest concentration of primate species in East Africa – these include chimpanzees, black and white colobus monkeys, red colobus monkeys, blue monkeys and baboons.

Tracking to the habituated chimp troops is conducted by trained guides who will also be able to tell you about the forest generally. The group of chimps in the Kanyanchu community is probably the largest in Kibale Forest, numbering about 45. Other animals found in the forest include elephants, buffaloes, bush pigs and duickers. However, many of these are very shy and you will be lucky to see them. There is also a huge range of birdlife and an estimated 140 species of butterfly.

The emblem of Kibale Forest is a black and white colobus monkey designed by Lysa Leland, a researcher and photographer who, with her husband Tom Struhsaker, worked in Kibale for many years, long before its popularity took off.

Uganda

Forest walks There are organized excursions to the chimps twice a day, leaving from Kanyanchu at 0800 and 1500. A maximum of three groups of six people can track the chimpanzees in a morning or afternoon. The morning walk is reported to offer a better opportunity to see the primates, usually to be found in the fig trees. The revenue from the Swamp Walk goes to the local community that is building a school nearby. A planned three-day hike will start on the Kampala-Fort Portal Road, which borders the forest, with two night forest camps; it should cost around US$100 all in, including food, porters and accommodation. Tourists are not allowed to walk in the forest unaccompanied and the knowledge of the guide will greatly increase your enjoyment of the walk. Costs: entry is US$5.50 plus US$7.75 for the 'guide'.

Sleeping **L** *Mantana Kibale Camp*, luxury well-appointed campsite run by Mantana Safaris T/F041-321552, T077-401 391 (mob), mantana@infocom.co.ug **E** *Safari Hotel*, located in Nkingo village on the main Fort Portal-Kamwenge road, just past the Kibale Forest and before the Magombe Swamp. Popular place with guest rooms or choice of private campsites. Has cooking grills, firewood and water, basic latrines, bush showers, restaurant and bar. Bring warm clothing for nights and rainwear; laundry services available. Excellent food, well spiced and delicious baked pineapple pie. **E** *Kanyanchu River Camp*, situated in Kibale Forest is about 35 km south of Fort Portal. It is on elevated grassland located within the forest itself and has a beautiful view of the Rwenzori Mountains. There are 5 covered camping sites – which are invaluable during very wet weather – as well as an open camping site. It is a wonderful setting, surrounded by thick forest and the design of the site has been well thought out. There are long drops, washing facilities, drinking water and firewood available. Bring your own food as the canteen is not always prepared for meals. Drinks are usually available for sale, and tents and paraffin lamps for rent. New shared bandas can be rented in the forest.

Bigodi Wetland Sanctuary & Magombe Swamp Bigodi Wetland Sanctuary and Magombe Swamp is managed by KAFRED (Kibale Association for Rural Development), a community-based organization that supports eco-tourism initiatives. The Magombe Swamp is situated 3 km past the Kibale Forest towards Bigodi. In the morning and late afternoon you can take a guided swamp walk along a trail with boardwalks. The swamp is rich with a variety of vegetation. The most common tree species are wild palms, polita figs and wild rubber trees. In addition there are ferns, water lilies, flowers such as those of the *Ipomea* species, fire lilies, wetland grasses, sedges and reeds. The dominant vegetation however is the papyrus. Primates such as the red colobus, black and white colobus and red-tailed monkey live in the swamp, along with over 138 bird species, including the great blue turaco, and a large number of butterflies. The money collected from the walk fees is used for local community projects like a school, health centre and the peanut butter project. The guides are knowledgeable about the Magombe Swamp and KAFRED. Make sure that you take precautions against red ants ascending your legs by wearing closed shoes or boots (avoid open-toed sandals)and tucking trousers into socks.

Transport **Road** **Car**: The *Kanyanchu River Camp* is located 35 km southeast of Fort Portal. From Fort Portal, Bigodi and the *Kanyanchu River Camp* are located off the Fort Portal-Kamwenge-Mbarara road. **Public transport**: Travellers without their own vehicles can get one of the *matatus* from Fort Portal that leave several times a day from Kamwenge stage, just near the bridge over Mpanga River, opposite the market on Kibale Rd, but not early in the morning. The road to Kibale Forest is gravel, but in good condition. *Matatus* to Kibale Forest/Bigodi cost US$2, leave throughout the day, but are more frequent in the afternoons. Journey time is 1½ hrs. If you want to track chimpanzees at 0800 you will have to arrange your own transport or stay the night in or near Kibale Forest, or arrange a trip with *Kabarole Tours* in Fort Portal. Coming back from Bigodi/Kibale Forest you will find regular *matatus* travelling to Fort Portal, but don't leave it too late. You could also try to hitch a lift, although this is difficult along this road. On a Tue there is a market at Rukunyu (a village between Bigodi and Kamwenge) so there is more traffic on the road. Alternatively, hire a *boda-boda* (motorcycle taxi) from Fort Portal.

Fort Portal to Hoima and Murchison Falls

Heading for Hoima and Masindi from Fort Portal, the first 50 km, to Kenyoyo, is tarmacked. Take a left turn here for the road to Hoima. This road has a bad reputation of sometimes being impassable but has been considerably improved recently. However, during heavy rains it can be very slippery. When you reach the halfway mark, at Kagadi, you have negotiated the worst part. If you have the time and a good four-wheel drive you will be rewarded by a trip through one of the most lovely parts of Uganda. For the first part of the journey the landscape is one of low cultivated hills, but as you proceed north it becomes mountainous and partly forested. Every so often the road reaches a spot where you can see for miles. It really is fantastically beautiful. The forest is interspersed with patches of cultivation but, being so cut off, this is one of the poorer parts of Uganda.

Hoima

The most direct route to Hoima from Kampala is on a poor road via **Kiboga** but the journey is an interesting one through the bush. After about 50 km the tar road becomes murram and gradually deteriorates. The landscape is hilly with a scattering of huge boulders amongst the farmland. The rather shabby and run-down town of Kiboga is about 120 km from Kampala and is strung out along the road.

1°40'N 31°30'E
Phone code: 465
Colour map 3, grid B2

Uganda

Soon after leaving Kiboga the road begins a gradual descent into the plain beyond which Hoima, the capital of Bunyoro, is located. The plain is punctuated by the occasional bare hill, and Hoima itself is spread across two such hills. Hoima can be seen from quite a distance, surrounded by eucalyptus trees that were planted as an anti-malarial measure during the colonial era. On entering the town you pass through the instantly recognizable old colonial part of town – bungalows with wide verandahs, set in large gardens, and fading government offices. The town centre sits overlooking a deep valley with a number of buildings, including one of the town's churches, on the opposite side.

Katasiha Fort is located about 3 km along the Butiaba road, which leads north out of town towards Lake Albert. The fort was established in 1894 by Colonel Colville when he was trying to subdue Kabalega, the King (known locally as the Omukama) of Bunyoro. All that survives of the fort are a rampart and a ditch.

Excursions

Hoima

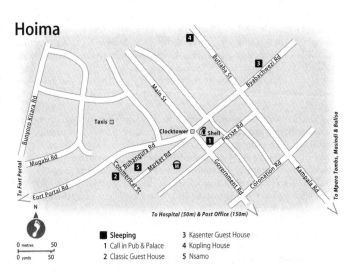

	Sleeping		
	1 Call in Pub & Palace	3	Kasenter Guest House
	2 Classic Guest House	4	Kopling House
		5	Nsamo

☞ ## Water hyacinth

For several years the attractive water hyacinth plant had been posing a serious threat to the ecology of Lake Victoria and to the 30 million people who rely on the waters of the lake for their livelihood. This fast-growing plant was rapidly choking the shores of the lake and its spread was phenomenal.

Numerous efforts were made to find a solution to the problem until, in 2001, it became clear that something miraculous had happened. The green weed has now gone and once again the lake shore is clearly visible with fishermen catching tilapia and pelicans flying lazily over the blue waters of the lake.

So what happened?

According to an article by Brad Collis in issue 34 of Kenya Airways' msafari inflight magazine, despite all efforts to clean the lake by chemicals and mechanical harvesting, it was clear that this was not the answer – not least as there was concern about the effect that chemicals could have on the Nile perch population. Instead, the Lake Victoria Environmental Management Project looked to the possibility of a bio-control solution based on the success of a group of Australian scientists in Papua New Guinea. The subsequent introduction of Brochi neochetina, a tiny weevil, had an immediate impact. Villagers were given training in how to grow the weevils before releasing them into the lake.

The weevil feeds on the hyacinth leaves, but crucially its larvae burrow into the stems of the plant which then rot as water seeps in.

The project has been astonishingly successful with over 80% of the hyacinth destroyed. The small clumps of the weed that remain are needed to maintain enough weevils to act as bio-control agents.

The **Mparo Tombs**, 3½ km from Hoima on the road to Masindi, are the burial places of the two most influential Bunyoro kings of modern times. Cwa II Kabalega was born in 1850. When his father King Kamasuri died, in 1869, there was a succession struggle. In 1870, at the battle of Buziba, Kabalega defeated his brother Kabigumire, forcing him to flee and giving himself the opportunity to bury his father and claim the throne. Establishing his palace at Mparo, Kabalega strengthened and consolidated his kingdom, and established a formidable military capability. In 1872, Sir Samuel Baker, Governor of Equatoria in southern Sudan, formally annexed Bunyoro. Kabalega began a hopeless struggle against the British, which culminated in his capture in 1899. Kabalega was exiled to the Seychelles, baptized as a Christian and, at the age of 49, taught to read and write. Six counties were transferred from Bunyoro to as a punishment for Bunyoro. In Kabalega's absence, the British installed his 12-year-old son, Prince Kitehimbwa, who ruled under the guidance of a series of regents. In 1902, Kitehimbwa was replaced by another of Kabalega's sons, Duhaga. In 1923, Duhaga requested that the British allow his father to return. Kabalega sailed back the next year, and was provided with a residence in Jinja, where he died two months later. He was buried at Mparo, having requested that only traditional roofing materials should be used to cover his tomb. In 1973 Murchison Falls National Park was renamed 'Kabalega Falls' by Amin (though it has now reverted to its original name).

Duhaga died the next year, and he was succeeded by Tito Winyi, yet another son of Kabalega, who had been educated at King's College, Budo. By cooperating with the British, Tito Winyi achieved considerable progress in the kingdom. He was knighted in 1934 and in 1964 negotiated the return of the six counties after a referendum. In 1967, Milton Obote abolished the traditional kingdoms (see page 754), and Sir Tito Winyi IV retired to Masindi. He died in 1971, and is buried at Mparo. In 1994, the kingdom was restored, and Tito Winyi's son Solomon Iguru was crowned at Hoima (see box, page 758).

As well as the two monarchs, several other members of the royal family are buried at Mparo. In keeping with his wishes, Kabalega's tomb has a thatched roof supported by a circular stone wall. Inside, the tomb is covered with a stretched cow hide and surrounded by a collection of the king's traditional personal belongings. Sir Tito

Winyi's tomb is similar. The site is surrounded by bark-cloth trees and a reed fence. Outside the compound is a memorial to Kabelaga and Emin Pasha.

D *Kopling House*, T40167, clean, pleasant hotel, set in a well-kept garden with smallish **Sleeping** rooms, private facilities and good mosquito nets, good restaurant, medium range, serves local and international dishes, friendly staff. Recommended. **D** *Call-in Pub/Palace Hotel*, T077-513489 (mob). Overpriced rooms with shared bathroom and a good breakfast. **E** *Classic Guest House*, T40341. New, clean, self-contained rooms, with bar and snacks, near taxi park on Commercial St. **E** *Kasenter Guest House*, clean rooms, shared bathrooms with cold shower, hot water provided on request, simple breakfast, quiet place. **E** *Nsamo Hotel*, close to taxi park on Buhangura Rd. Has a pleasant inner courtyard with flowers. A bargain at this price, offering soap and towels (like more expensive hotels), cool running water and reasonably intact mosquito nets. There is a choice of rooms – self-contained or, at approximately half the price, rooms with shared bathrooms.

Cheap *Call-In Pub*, good restaurant with quick service. Ask for the specialities of the day. **Eating** Have a drink and food in the garden. Popular bar, with pool table, stays open till the last customer leaves. *Kopling House*, restaurant and bar in pleasant garden. Local food and meat or fish and chips. **Seriously cheap** *Nsamo Inn*, unpretentious restaurant, with fairly plain food – usually *matoke* and chicken.

Road The town of Hoima is about 200 km from **Kampala** via Kiboga, a drive of about 3 hrs **Transport** on a poor road. As an alternative, it can be reached via **Masindi**, about 60 km away, making a total of about 260 km from Kampala, or from **Fort Portal**. Taking the latter route on public transport you will probably have to change vehicles at least once, usually at Kagadi. **Post bus** to Kampala via Masindi leaves Hoima post office at 0630, costs US$5. Regular *matatus* go to Masindi, US$2. Bus to Fort Portal leaves early mornings Mon-Wed-Fri. The journey takes 6 hrs in good weather costing US$5. Regular *matatus* leave for Kagadi, change there for a *matatu* to Fort Portal, cost US$4.

Money It is not possible to change money in Hoima, so it is important to bring sufficient Uganda **Directory** shillings with you. **Telephones** International calls can be made from the post office or from MTN telephone boxes. At weekends it is half price. Buy a phone card locally.

Uganda

Southwest to Kabale and Kisoro

The southwest region extends from Kampala to Kabale and Kisoro, and includes the Ssese Islands, which are the main tourist attraction in this area. Also in the region are Lake Mburo National Park and the less frequently visited Lake Nabugabo and Mpanga Forest Reserve. In the far southwest is the Bwindi Impenetrable Forest National Park and Mgahinga National Park, home of the mountain gorillas. The road leading out of Kampala through Masaka and on to the southwest of the country is one of the best in Uganda.

Kampala to Masaka

The road out of Kampala can be hectic, especially in the mornings as it passes through Nateete, with its endless trade stores (look out for the coffin makers) and *matatu* stops. It quickly becomes clearer though. The road is very fast and exciting as *matatus* swerve around the *matoke* bikes (always carrying three stems of bananas), which the men push for miles to market. Some 10 km out of Kampala, King's College, Budo is reached as well as the commercial flower-growing operation at the Dutch-owned Nsimbe Estate. You will pass through some swamps and small

Southwest to Kabale & Kisoro

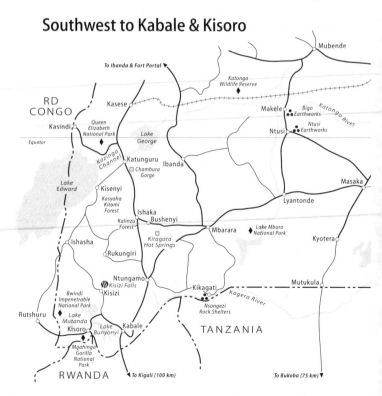

Twins in Buganda

The birth of twins is treated as something rather special in Buganda. Not only are they always given special names, but the names of the parents are also changed. When twins are born (it does not matter what sex they *are) the father changes his name to* Salongo *and the mother changes hers to* Nalongo. *If the twins are boys they will be named* Waswa *and* Kato, *while if they are girls they are* Nakato *and* Babyire.

patches of forest and the surrounding countryside seems fertile and well watered. About 40 km out of Kampala you will reach the village of **Mpigi** and, if you are hoping to buy any traditional musical instruments (particularly drums), this is the place to do so. You will see drum-makers and their stalls on the side of the road. Near here is the Mpanga Forest Reserve, which you might want to visit either on the way south or as an easy day trip from Kampala. Unlike the Mabira Forest on the Jinja road, only a very small patch is visible so watch out for the signs carefully.

Mpanga, a forest reserve – about an hour's drive from the capital – an excellent day trip. The entrance to the reserve is 5 km southwest of Mpigi on the road from Kampala to Masaka. It is well signposted, and there is a murram track from the highway to the reception centre, where there is a craft shop and secure parking (trail maps and guides are available). The main attractions are the mighty trees with their knotted roots, monkeys, birds and butterflies. Snakes can also be seen – if you are worried because a few of them are dangerous, tour the forest with a guide. The forest provides five types of timber used in the making of drums. The Royal Drum-Makers are located in the nearby village of Mpambire. There are camping and picnic areas, and some simple accommodation.

Mpanga Forest Reserve

Uganda

Three trails have been marked. The **Base Line Trail** traverses the forest to a papyrus swamp 3 km away on the west side. The trail crosses a couple of streams with drifts of butterflies to be seen in the clearings. The **Butterfly Loop** takes under half an hour to complete, and involves some scrambling over fallen trees and struggling through thick vegetation. Tracks of both bush-babies and leopards are reported but, alas, the mammals themselves are rarely seen. The **Hornbill Trail** follows a 5-km loop along streams with exotic fungi, butterflies, birds and monkeys all on view.

■ *Park entry fees are US$0.70 for Ugandans and US$2 for foreigners; guides are US$1.20.*

Sleeping and eating Camping and dormitory accommodation cost US$0.70 per head for Ugandans, US$2 for foreigners; bandas US$3.50 per person for Ugandans and US$7 for foreigners. There are camping, barbecue, picnic and latrine facilities near the reception centre, and another picnic site in a forest glade about 100 m from the start of the Base Line Trail. Water and firewood are available –

Drums of Buganda

There is a saying in Luganda that goes Tezirawa ngumba which means 'They are not beaten without a reason'. In modern times you are most likely to hear drums being played at traditional weddings, funerals, or occasions of celebration, particularly in rural areas. Drums are often played on occasions of celebration, too, such as the Kabaka's coronation (see box, page 758).

Although drums are frequently thought of as being merely musical instruments, they in fact have a wide range of uses. In the past there were literally hundreds of different beats for the drums and each rhythm was known and had a definite meaning – for example, a certain dance taking place, a call to war, a fire alarm, the news that a certain chief was passing. As a person heard the drum it was their duty to repeat the message so that within a few minutes the message could pass over many miles.

Traditionally, the drums belonged to the Kabaka and when he presented a chief with a position of office bestowed upon him a drum. This is why the playing of the drums was an important part of the ceremonies involved in the crowning of the Kabaka – once he had 'tuned' the drums no one else was allowed to play them.

Kiganda (as Buganda culture is known) has drums of two kinds – the first is made of a hollowed block of wood, tapering towards the base, with skins stretched over the head and base. The skins are laced with thongs of hide. They are named according to their size and use, and the important ones are also given names individually. The other type, seen more rarely nowadays, is known as ngalabi and exists in various sizes. Also made of hollowed-out wood, it is long and slender, tapering gradually and then widening out again to form the base on which the drum stands. The top is covered with a skin – usually that of a type of water lizard – which is pegged on. The bottom of the drum is left open. These drums are particularly attractive and large ones may be as much as 140 cm high.

In the past the ceremonies of the Baganda court were closely tied to the use of a large number of drums belonging to the Kabaka. Each drum or group of drums was named and men were specifically appointed to take up residence at the Lubiri (the Baganda palace) for the sole purpose of beating drums.

The range of drums used in the past was enormous – each was made slightly differently of varying sizes with different decorations. Each type served a distinct purpose and was played in a slightly different way, often by a specific clan. Examples of names include Nakawanguzu, which means the 'Conqueror'. This drum was played when the Kabaka had been successful in his attacks on surrounding tribes. The Kyejo was used when the Kabaka executed troublemakers as a warning to others. The Makumbi warned people to cultivate their banana gardens or risk having their hands cut off. The Va-mu-lugudo, meaning 'get out of the way', was used when the wives of the Kabaka were out walking – no one was allowed to be on the road in front of them, so the drummer went ahead to warn people to stand aside.

Drums are also associated with chieftainships, with each chief having his drum bestowed with his office by the Kabaka. The various clans of Baganda also had their own drums and particular drum beats. Selected clans were responsible for the making, beating, maintenance and safekeeping of the drums – different clans for each particular drum type.

There is a splendid collection of drums at the Uganda Museum in Kampala (see page 627). Drum-making can be seen in the Mpanga Forest Reserve (see page 723).

visitors should bring their own food and tents. Provisions can be purchased from nearby Mpigi. There are 2 twin bandas in a building with a thatched roof and a verandah, with bed linen, towels, nets, showers and oil lamps. There is also a dormitory with bunk beds, for which you need to provide bedding and nets. Hotel accommodation and restaurants are available in Mpigi.

Transport Public transport to the reserve from the new taxi park in Kampala to Mpigi is US$1, and then a *boda-boda* (motorcycle taxi) to the reserve is US$0.70. Or a *matatu* from Kampala bound for Masaka will drop you off at Mpanga for US$3.

The road along this section is never very far away from Lake Victoria. It is very marshy with a number of huts selling both fresh and smoked fish. About 75 km from Kampala just after Buwama, you cross the Equator, which is marked by a large concrete circle. Shops sell papyrus mats, trays and baskets. The Katonga River, which links Lake Victoria and Lake George, is also crossed. There is a checkpoint at Luyaka which looks like a motorway toll booth but there are no tolls. Taxis and *matatus* are checked though, and as a result there are lots of street vendors milling around. Masaka is quickly reached and is about two hours from Kampala.

Masaka

Masaka was extensively damaged during the Tanzanian invasion of 1979, and much of the destruction has not been repaired. Leaving the town to the west is the road to Tanzania – the route along which the Tanzanian troops advanced. Little of this is apparent as the main road now bypasses what appears to be a rather sleepy town. Nyendo, a suburb about 1 km to the west, is much busier. For all this, Masaka is a pretty town, built on the side of a hill. A huge radio mast dominates the skyline. It is also the stopping-off point for the Ssese Islands; make sure you get a *matatu* from Kampala that gets to Masaka by lunchtime if you are going to get to the islands the same day.

0°21'S 31°45'E
Phone code: 481
Colour map 3, grid B2

Uganda

Masaka

To Mbarara (146 km)
To Kampala (137 km)
Mutuba Gardens
Kampala Rd
Katwe Rd
Tropic Touch
Kalungu St
Agip
Bank of Uganda
Natubale St
Cooperative
Koki Rd
Total
Mawogla St
Folklands Club
Buddu St
Radio Mast
Greenland
Hobert St
Outspan Square
Kanasa Bookshop
Edward Av
Elgin Rd
Martyrs' Shrine
Victoria Rd
Ismaili Mosque
Jethabhal St
Kimaanya School
Yellow Knife Rd
Masaka Secondary School
Bwala Hill Rd
Kitovu Av
Muslim Cemetery
To Masaka Backpackers' Cottage & Campsite & Bukoba, Tanzania (169 km)
To Bukakata (39 km), for Ferry to Ssese Islands

N

0 metres   200
0 yards   200

■ Sleeping
1 La Nova
2 Laston
3 Victoria End Rest House

● Eating
1 Exotic Inn

Sleeping

D *La Nova*, not particularly good value, a fair step from the bus station near Jethabhal St/Bwala Hill Rd and often full, despite few creature comforts and frequent disruptions to the electrical power supply. D *Laston*, about 500 m from the bus station. Recent reports of this hotel have been less favourable. D *The Lodge*, situated on the corner near *La Nova*, has been recommended. Clean facilities with hot water. D *Victoria End Rest House*, in the town centre, is a very basic hotel with a range of rooms, probably one of the best places to stay.

E *Executive Lodge*, Plot 51 Hobert St, is somewhat shabby with basic accommodation. E *Masaka Backpackers' Cottage and Campsite*, PO Box 834, T21288, F20514, 4 km from Masaka, on the Bukoba-Kyotera road, in the village of Nyendo. Semi-rural hilly site. Cooking facilities, single rooms and dormitory. Taxi/minicab shuttle to Kirimya, disembark Kasanvu and follow the signs.

Eating

Cheap *Laston*, good value and reasonable standard. **Seriously cheap** *Elgin Inn and Restaurant*, basic, downstairs from *Victoria End Resthouse*. Good local food, friendly, US$1.50. *Exotic Inn*, simple fare.

Transport

Road There are frequent *matatus* and buses to Masaka from **Kampala**. Get to either one of the 2 bus stations in Kampala early in the morning as most leave soon after daybreak,

☞ ## Rinderpest

The first recorded outbreak of rinderpest in East Africa occurred in 1889 in what was then Somaliland. It is generally believed that the disease followed the introduction of cattle from India and Aden for use by the Italian army during the first expedition to Abyssinia. Once established, rinderpest spread like wildfire over the whole of East Africa, reaching Lake Tanzania by 1890.

The devastation resulting from the disease was terrible. Lugard was in Africa at this time and tells of the misery and suffering that the pastoral tribes, such as the Masai and the Bahima, endured as a result of this disease. Many were made destitute with cattle mortality rates generally over 90%. In some areas, not a single animal survived. It is believed that many people also perished along with their animals – often of malnutrition. Many species of game were almost exterminated – buffalo, eland, warthog and wild pig were particularly badly affected.

bus takes 2 hrs, cost US$2. The *matatus* continue later in the day. Masaka is 128 km from Kampala. Masaka is also where you change to pick up *matatus* to Bukakata for the Ssese Islands and for the overland journey to Mutukala on the Tanzanian border. Check the exchange rate before leaving Uganda and change leftover shillings at the border, as Uganda currency is not exchangeable elsewhere. Get your exit stamp before the Immigration Office closes, at 0500, because the only bus for Bukoba leaves Mutukula at 1700. The Immigration Office reopens at 0800. Hitching a lift to Bukoba could involve a very lengthy wait, as traffic is sparse.

Masaka to Tanzania (Bukoba)

From Masaka you can head for Tanzania – the only option until the ferry service is resumed is to travel by road. The road is not very good and this route is not much used, although traffic is increasing. There are *matatus* from Masaka that go as far as Kyotera and from there you will have to get a lift to the border crossing at Mutukala with one of the trucks going across – this is not usually a problem as pick-ups are often waiting for you in Kyotera (journey time about 6-8 hours). The road takes you through the district of Rakai infamous as a result of being devastated by AIDS epidemic. Evidence of it can be seen in the number of abandoned homesteads and *shambas*.

Possibly only 10-20 vehicles a day come this way. Theoretically this should mean a quick border crossing, but it doesn't. It takes between 30 minutes and two hours to get through the Ugandan-Tanzanian bureaucracy here and you require a letter from the government in Kampala confirming that the vehicle you are using is yours and not for sale. You need to pay US$100 for driving a vehicle into Tanzania. The reason for all this bureaucracy is said to be that many traders used to buy vehicles (new or second-hand) in Uganda and sell them in Tanzania, which affected the local market and reduced government revenue from sales tax on luxury items. If you can cope with the hassle the trip is well worth making as the scenery is lovely and there are many nice shady places to stop and have a soda en route.

If you get to the border shortly before dark you may want to stay at the small guesthouse on the Uganda side of the border – there is nothing on the Tanzania side until you get to Bukoba. **E** *Mutukula Safari Lodge* is highly recommended, clean, excellent value, meals available US$2 per person. The road on the Tanzania side is worse than the Uganda road but there are four-wheel-drive vehicles operating on the route. They go when full.

Lake Nabugabo This small oval lake, slightly less than 8 km in length and about 5 km wide, is located about 3 km from the western shore of Lake Victoria, from which it is separated by rough undulating country. Because of the mineral content of the lake, it is claimed that bilharzia does not occur here and this has made it popular for swimming. It is a very peaceful place to relax and to watch birds, either along the shores of the lake or from a small fishing boat.

Sleeping and eating D *Church of Uganda Guesthouse* at Lake Nabugabo, was built in 1926 as a holiday resort and conference centre for the missionaries of the church (which also runs the *Namirembe Guesthouse* in Kampala). There are 5 clean cottages for rent, with 1 or 2 bedrooms, sitting room and bathroom. The premises are very nicely situated and quiet. Hot water is provided in a jerry can. The generator gives power only from 1900-2100. It is occasionally full at weekends or during conferences. You can book via T077-433332 (mob) or check with the *Namirembe Guesthouse*, Mengo, close to Mengo Hospital, just below the cathedral in Kampala. **E** *Camping* is permitted but bring own equipment. Food (Cheap) is available in the restaurant if you order in advance, but no alcohol is served. However, you can buy plenty of beer next door, as indicated on the signboard of the **E** *Green View Site on the Lake*, a campsite with no facilities worth mentioning. **D** *Nabugabo Sand Beach*, just 1 km from the *Church of Uganda Guesthouse*, is the place to be if you want somewhere more lively. Although not a lot of sand is found on the lakeshores, it is a nice place to swim, especially for children, because the water gets deeper very gradually. There are 8 self-contained smallish double rooms. During the weekends and holidays it is a popular place for day visitors from Masaka. **E** *Camping* is available under thatched roofs which are built rather too close together. Chicken, fish and chips (Seriously cheap) are available and there is a well-stocked bar.

It is doubtful whether there are currently crocodiles in Lake Nabugabo – but you might want to check with local residents before you dive in...

Transport Lake Nabugabo is about 16 km from Masaka, 6 km off the Masaka-Bukakata road. Getting to it by public transport from Masaka is easiest if you happen to be in Masaka on a Mon, Wed or Fri, which is when a bus goes to Bukakata for the Ssese Islands. It leaves at about 1400 from the main Masaka bus station, and goes past the turning to Lake Nabugabo which is clearly signposted. Alternatively, if you are travelling from Kampala on the main road to Masaka, you can get off the bus 2 km before Masaka (or 2 km past Masaka if you are coming from Mbarara) at the *Total* petrol station near Nyendo town. From the petrol station it is 1 km to the Nyendo market where you can get a *matatu* to Bukakata, or you can take a special hire up to Lake Nabugabo for US$10, to save you walking the last 6 km. From Lake Nabugabo you can arrange transport back (US$5) to the Masaka-Bukakata road, from where you can proceed on your travels towards the Ssese Islands or towards Masaka.

Uganda

Ssese Islands

This collection of islands (sometimes spelt Sese) is situated in the northwestern part of Lake Victoria and is an increasingly popular tourist destination. There are 84 islands in the group, and they are very attractive. One resident of Kampala desibed them as a cross between the Hebrides and the Caribbean! Apart from having various species of monkey, and being a bird-watcher's and botanist's paradise, the islands are particularly suited to those keen on walking or sport fishing. Being cut off, they have retained an easy-going atmosphere. It's a wonderful place, with friendly people.

0°21'S 32°20'E
Phone code: 481
Colour map 3, grid B2

Ins and outs

The Entebbe-Kalangala ferry is only for foot passengers. The alternative is to go from the Masaka mainland by the Bukakata Ferry to Luku on Buggala Island.

Getting there & getting around
For transport details, see page 729

You are required to inform the police post of your arrival on the island. Recent travellers indicate that this formality to register with the police is not always adhered to, but it is probably best to check locally.

To get between the islands ask one of the **fishermen** and agree a price. There are *matatus* on the island of Buggala. Other than that the best way to see the islands is on foot.

Sights

There are beautiful walks around the island, through the forest, and you can visit the caves of bats, Speke's Fort (1862), pineapple and palm tree farms and fishing villages. You can also make a boat trip, with or without an engine, to see parts of the island that cannot be reached on foot, where birds can nest freely and otters roll in the water. It is now very rare to see either crocodiles or hippos, as the latter tend to avoid the inhabited islands, and have been frightened away to the more isolated areas of the lake. The islands are hilly and, in the uncultivated parts, are still forested. The most important crops are cassava, banana, sweet potato and coffee. It can be difficult to resist the water of Lake Victoria on a sunny day, but there is a risk of bilharzia.

The main island is **Buggala Island** (sometimes spelt Bugala), which is about 34 km long. Its main towns are Kalangala – also the name of the district and spelt Kalengala on some maps – and Luku. A bus and *matutus* link the main towns. The second largest island is **Bukasa Island**; **Bubeke** and **Bufumira** are also easy to visit.

Buggala Island
There are beautiful walks around the island

The island has about 50 km of road on it and really the best thing to do is simply to set off and explore – either on foot or by bicycle (hired from *Andronica's* at Kalangala). All around are wonderful views of the lake and of all the other islands – some forested, others cultivated and others a mixture of both. The forests contain a certain amount of wildlife, although nothing spectacular. There are various species of monkey and a profusion of birdlife. Mutambala Beach, off the Kalangala-Luku road, is popular.

Other islands

Although most visitors stick to Buggala Island there is no reason why you should not venture further afield. Provided you are flexible and not in any hurry, you can explore the other islands at your leisure. **Bukasa** is particularly attractive – it has a smaller population, is more forested and has a wider range of wildlife. There are two beautiful beaches on the island as well as a waterfall. For further information on how to get there, ask at *Agnes' Guest House*. **Bufumira Island** can be visited from Kalangala for the day, as can many of the uninhabited islands. Either talk to one of the fishermen or arrange it through *Andronica Lodge*.

Essentials

Sleeping & eating

Buggala Island Kalangala A *Islands Club*, T/F256-41231385, T077-504027 (mob). Has 3 luxury wooden chalets which can accommodate 18 people, on the lake side beneath a high forest canopy. Bargaining over the price is possible. An extra 4 beds are available in tents. Visitors are picked up from the ferry. Excellent meals (Expensive) are available, also caters for non residents. **A-B** *Ssese Palm Beach Resort*, T077-503315 (mob) or T041-254435. Managed by former air

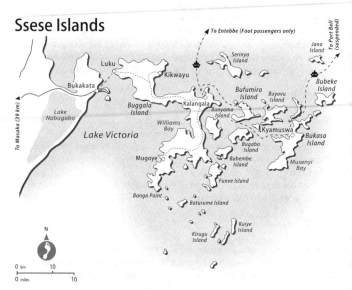

Ssese Islands

hostess Mrs Nina Muayanda Mutebi, whose husband is the representative of the Buganda King for the Ssese Islands. Situated at the top end of the island, you can see the beautifully constructed cottages from afar. There are 6 cottages in total; the Millennium Cottages are the newest and the most expensive. It is possible to negotiate the rates down. Hot water is provided in jerry cans. **E** *Camping* is possible for US$5 per person and you can sleep in a dormitory tent for US$10. Food (Mid-range) and drinks are available in an open-fronted restaurant, which has the atmosphere of a beach resort. In the evenings you can enjoy a drink round the campfire.

C *Ssese Islands Beach Hotel*, T041-220065, F220242, clinquip@infocom.co.ug, has recently opened, offering 3 suites. The main building is situated on top of a hill, quite some way from the beach, and on the lake shore in what looks like a separate house are 2 double rooms. In the main building one room has been turned into a dormitory with 5 overpriced beds (US$10). African dishes (Cheap), snacks and drinks are available in the main building. There are plans to open a food centre near the lake, dependent on the number of visitors attracted to this facility.

E *PTA Andronica Lodge* (previously known as *Malaanga Safari Lodge*) PO Box 1165, Kalangala, Masaka, T26. Run by the very friendly Mr Andronico Semakula (known to everyone as Mzee Andronico) and his daughter, this lodge provides food and lodging, it is the sort of place that some people love and others hate. Not many travellers are visiting the lodge these days, since the competition on the island is so fierce. Mzee Andronico tries to keep the standards up but there have been reports of poor hygiene. There is also a small library and bicycles are available for hire. Food is available at the lodge, but there are much cheaper, and equally good, places nearby. Mzee Andronico is a bit of a character – he is a retired teacher and likes to exercise his business skills so you may have to negotiate over the price of the room; he is full of stories and will be able to tell you all about the island.

E *Panorama Cottages/Panorama Camping Safari*, near the jetty in lower Kalangala. 14 self-contained and/or shared cottages with solar lights. A bit of a derelict place that has seen better days and more visitors. Some cottages are only half built. You can negotiate half-price tariffs if you stay in accommodation without a toilet. Plenty of notice is required if you want meals. Peaceful place with friendly staff. Food (cheap) and drinks are available and there is a small shop near the jetty. **Camping** **E** *Hornbill Campsite*, friendly but located 500 m down a steep track, near the lake with a private 'beach', also has a couple of very basic huts and a nice camping area. Cooking food takes a long time. The *Nsera Beach Resort* was a casualty of the 1998 El Niño, which caused the water level of Lake Victoria to rise by 2 m, and subsequently to destroy the campsite.

Bukasa Island **E** *Agnes' Guest House*, on the second-largest island, has a beautiful location overlooking the lake, it is a friendly place – there are both rooms and space for camping, a limited range of food is available.

Camping Apart from the places mentioned you can theoretically camp anywhere on the islands, although obviously you should ask if you are going to be anywhere near people's houses. It is meant to be very safe here, but it goes without saying that you should keep your valuables with you at all times and should not flaunt your wealth.

Ferry There are several ways of reaching the Sseses. The ferry from *Marine Craft Ltd* **Transport** between Entebbe and Kalangala is only for foot passengers. Booking office T041 235586 or T077-504027 (mob). The ferry leaves Entebbe from the pier near the Wildlife Education Centre, on Mon, Tue, Wed and Fri at 1500 and on Sat at 1200. It leaves Kalangala on Tue, Wed, Thu and Sat at 0800 and on Sun at 1500. The boat trip takes 3½-4 hrs and costs US$4.

The alternative is to go from the Masaka mainland by the Bukakata Ferry. (For transport to Bukakata, see transport to Lake Nabugabo.) This ferry goes to Luku on Buggala Island. The journey is shorter and it is possible to take a car if you are willing to squeeze it on, but remember the bus has priority. The ferry leaves Bukakata at 1500 on weekdays. On Sun you have to arrange your own transport, with the local fishermen. From Buggala Island back to the mainland the ferry leaves at 0900 during weekdays. No ferry on Sun. The *Port Bell* steamer sank in a storm in 1996, with the loss of around 100 people. A new ferry, paid for by Finnish aid, came into service in early 1999, but this is currently suspended until further notice.

Uganda

Bus The bus from Masaka via Bukakata and Luku arrives in Kalangala around 1900 and costs US$3. This 34-km stretch of road takes an unexpectedly long time since goods are offloaded at every stage. The bus stays in Kalangala town. If you want to go to one of the places down at the lake side, you need to arrange a *piki-piki* (motor taxi) or a special hire. You can also travel all the way from Masaka or Nyendo by *matatu*. This is faster and the *matatu* will bring you right down the beach.

Alternative routes are tough, even by African standards. Residents of Bukasa tend to sail directly to Kisenyi, rather than travel to the mainland via the other islands. The Kisenyi-Ssese Islands route is usually done in open boats. 5 hrs is a typical journey time, and it can be especially miserable in heavy rain and after dark. Travellers may find it cheaper to travel from Kalangala to Bukasa Island via Kisenyi (US$5 per leg of the journey).

West from Masaka

After leaving Masaka and heading west the countryside gradually gets drier and more hilly and the density of population falls as you move into Ankole, which is populated by pastoralists. About halfway between Masaka and Mbarara is the trading centre of Lyantonde. There is a turning to the right and 100 km to the north is **Ntusi** where there is an archaeological site. West of Ntusi is the **Katonga Wildlife Reserve** (see page 687). The main road once again crosses a marshy area: this is the Ksimbi swamp. After rain, pockets of marshland trapped between the undulating hills form mini lakes. Keep your eyes peeled, as zebra and other animals can often be seen mixing with the Ankole cattle. Lake Mburo National Park is on your left and is about 9 km from the Nshara Gate.

Lake Mburo National Park

Lake Mburo National Park is one of the newest of Uganda's national parks. A great attraction is that it is possible to walk around the park, rather than having to tour in a vehicle, and it is quite possible to get close to zebra, warthogs and impala. The landscape is of open plains, acacia grasslands and marshes. Around the lake itself is thicker riverine woodland while much of the rest of the park is acacia woodland. For

Lake Mburo National Park

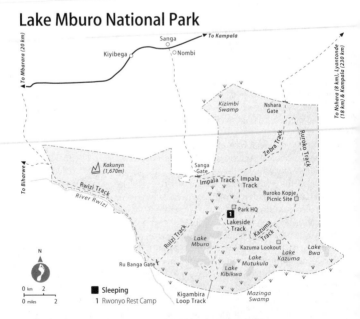

To Mbarara (20 km)
To Biharwe
To Nshara (8 km), Lyantonde (18 km) & Kampala (230 km)
To Kampala

Sanga
Kiyibega　Nombi

Kizimbi Swamp　Nshara Gate

Zebra Track　Ruroko Track

Kakunyn (1,670m)
Sanga Gate
Impala Track　Impala Track
Ruroko Kopje Picnic Site

Rwizi Track
River Rwizi

Park HQ
Lakeside Track
Kazuma Track

Lake Mburo
Kazuma Lookout
Lake Bwa
Ru Banga Gate
Lake Mutukula　Lake Kazuma
Lake Kibikwa

N

0 km　2
0 miles　2

■ **Sleeping**
1 Rwonyo Rest Camp

Kigambira Loop Track
Mazinga Swamp

Uganda

Mburo: what's in a name?

It is said that the two brothers, Kigarama and Mburo, once lived in the Ruizi (sometimes spelt Rwizi) River valley. One night Kigarama dreamed that they were in great danger, and urged his younger brother to take refuge with him up in the hills, but Mburo ignored the advice. The Ruizi flooded the valley, and Mburo was drowned. The lake is named after the drowned brother, while the hills bear the name of the brother who was saved.

The cassine tree is found in the area and it is called mboro *in the Ankole language. The tree is said to have aphrodisiac powers (coincidentally, the word* mboro *in Swahili is a vulgar term for penis). A cassine tree can be seen at the crossroads at the start of the Kigambira trail in the park – it shows signs of bark and branch loss, so it seems the local people believe in its powers.*

many years there has been a dispute between the use of this area by man as against game. For many years there has been a great deal of dispute between the use of this area which was declared to be a hunting ground for the Ankole royalty. After Independence it became a game reserve and in the early 1980s was finally gazetted as a national park. However, to establish the park it was necessary to resettle large numbers of people and their herds of cattle, and this is still a fairly controversial issue.

Animals found in Lake Mburo National Park include impala, zebra, topi, oribi, eland, klispringer, buffalo, waterbuck, reedbuck and warthog. Baboons and vervets are commonly seen and the lake contains hippos and crocodiles, while buffaloes can often be found in the marshes. Leopards are present but they are rare. Interesting birds include crested crane (Uganda's national emblem), saddlebill storks and Abyssinian ground hornbills. There is also a wide range of water birds.

Walks, accompanied by a ranger, cost about US$6 for a two-hour trip – the ranger is invaluable in locating wildlife, and a precaution in case you run into a leopard or a water buffalo. Early morning and evening are best. In addition to this you can also walk between the camp and the lake without a ranger – a distance of about 1 km. A game drive in the park vehicle can be arranged, but they are often unavailable at short notice. It is possible to hire a boat (US$22 for up to eight people) to go on to the lake, with good views of fish eagles, hippos and the odd crocodile.

Sleeping **A** *Mantana Camp Luxury Tented Camp*, located on a hill outside the park. It is run by two expatriates. Each tent is self-contained, and has a verandah facing west for views of the sunsets. Bar and restaurant built on stilts, with a great vista over 3 lakes. Mostly used by tour operators.

E *Rwonyo Rest Camp* Friendly and helpful staff. Double and single bandas as well as one 4-bed family banda, which are simple but comfortable, bedding, towels, a lantern, slippers and mosquito nets are provided. Showers are shared, and hot water is provided for these in the mornings and evenings. Toilets are clean. The bandas can be locked, and the camp is secure. Meals are available and are cheap and simple. Bandas cost US$9 per person per night.
E *Rwonyo Tented Camp*. About ½ km from the bandas, in a secluded area. The tents are permanent with wooden platform floors, everything provided as for the bandas, except showers which can be used at the main site. US$9 per person per night.

Camping There are 4 sites in the park, one by the Nshara Gate, and one beside the lake, this latter offering very good views. You will need to bring everything, equipment and food, with you. US$3 per tent.

Eating If you wish to have a bit more variety than is offered at the park restaurant, you can bring your own food, utensils, crockery and cutlery, and cook over one of the park campfires (wood provided). **Cheap** *Rwonyo Rest Camp* has a small restaurant, but it is important to order in advance. Breakfast is tea or coffee, bread and chapattis and an omelette. Other meals are fish and grills with beans and rice. Soft drinks and beers are not cold. *Lakeside* A restaurant and bar are currently being built, and will offer an excellent hippo-viewing area.

Transport The park can be reached from the main Kampala-Mbarara road. From Kampala it is 230 km, and the journey takes about 4 hrs. From Mbarara it is 47 km, and the journey takes less than 1 hr. There are 2 entrances. **Nshara Gate** Coming from Kampala, the turn-off to the left is 10 km past the Lyatonde trading centre. It is signposted (although according to recent reports the sign has been knocked down by a bus). The park gate is 8 km along an unsealed track. **Sanga Gate** Coming from Kampala, turn off left at the Sanga trading centre, about 33 km before Mbarara. There is a large blue and white sign announcing 'Lake Mburo NP'. The park gate is 13 km from the main road on a poor, unsealed track that is particularly difficult Sep-Jan, during the rains.

Vehicle hire The nearest place to rent a vehicle is Mbarara. Try *Crested Crane* on Main St in Mbarara or ask in *Mbarara Coffee Shop*. The use of a car for a day will cost US$30, and a 4WD will be US$40-60. **Public transport** Travelling by *matatu* from Kampala, ask to be set down at Lyatonde trading centre. From Mbarara, ask to get off at Sanga trading centre. It is then possible to hire a taxi for US$9, or a *boda-boda* for US$3 to take you to the park gate. If necessary, a park vehicle will take you from the gate to the park HQ and *Rwonyo Rest Camp*, for US$6.

Mbarara

0°35'S 30°40'E
Phone code: 485
Colour map 3, grid B2

The countryside becomes flatter towards Mbarara with more and more banana plantations as the acacia shrubs recede. There are lots of Ankole cattle grazing. Mbarara is a busy and rapidly developing town, which has greatly expanded in recent years. Since the Masaka bypass was built it is now the first major town you come to when travelling from Kampala. It is a lively town that receives many visitors and is a crossroads for travellers heading towards the Queen Elizabeth National Park, Lake Mburo, Rwenzori Mountains and Kabale in the southwest. There is a wide choice of places to stay and/or eat.

This area is renowned for Ankole cattle, and just before you enter the town centre you will see in the middle of a roundabout a statue of a steer with impressive horns. The huge Coca Cola bottling plant close by which makes for an interesting cultural juxtaposition. The town is home to one of Uganda's new universities and this, together with the regional offices and the *Bank of Uganda* regional building, tends to split the town into two. The town centre is in the east, where the central market and taxi and bus parks are located on William Street. Nearly 5 km to the east and beyond the university is another settlement. This is a very interesting suburb of the town, close to the River Rwizi, at the junction of the Fort Portal and Kabale roads. Called the 'Old Market' area or 'Rwizi Arch area', it is somewhat quieter than the bustling town centre. It has a traditional market, and is lively at night with many eating places and bars.

There is not much of interest although the **Library** on Main Street is an old colonial single-storey building, with a well-sheltered courtyard with foliage in front, which has unfortunately been allowed to deteriorate. The **Aga Khan School**, just on the eastern edge of town, is an impressive building combining neoclassical and Indian architectural styles. There are three arches at the front with double mock columns. Portico windows face the building and above the main entrance are crossed flags and the date of construction (1948).

Mbarara is the centre of the Kingdom of Ankole broken up soon after independence. As part of Museveni's policies all Uganda's kingdoms were offered the chance to have their kings back, on the understanding that they were to be cultural figures only, without any political role. The **Palace of the Omugabe** (King) of Ankole is located in Mbarara on a hill on the outskirts of town. The buildings have been taken over by the army and huts have sprung up all around the main structure, as accommodation for soldiers' wives and families. Although you will probably not be able to walk around the palace (which is in poor repair), you can drive past it. There is one main building and a few secondary ones. To the right of the main structure is the building that used to house the royal drums (see box, page 724). Three and a half kilometres west of Mbarara are the **Nkokonjeru Tombs** at Kakika, the burial place of the last two Omugabe of Ankole, Kahaya II and Gasyonga II.

Mbarara

To Lake Mburo National Park, Masaka & Kampala

Kampala Rd

Shell

Mbarara College

Ankole Steer Statue

Bus Park

Lucky Supermarket

High St

Nile MTN

Central

Taxis

Mercancing St

Mtagura St

William St

Clock

Buremba Rd

Cinema

Bushaya Supermarket

Ntare Rd

Shell

Computer Centre

Vision Empire Night Club

UC

Standard Chartered

Regional Council Office

Bank of Uganda

To River Rwizi

Kabale Rd

University

Esso/Total

Upet

Old Market Place

Petro

Bushenyi - Kasese Rd

Dairy

Total

RWIZI ARCH AREA

To Ntungamo, Kabale & Kasese

0 metres 500
0 yards 500

N

■ **Sleeping**
1 Africa Guest House
2 Agip Motel & Campsite
3 Andrews Inn
4 Church of Uganda Hostel
5 Classic
6 Entry View Guest House
7 Kikome Rest House
8 Lake View Regency
9 Mbiringa
10 Memory Lodge
11 New Safari
12 Oxford Inn
13 Pelican
14 Riheka Guest House
15 Rwizi Arch
16 Safariland Park
17 University Inn & Camping Area

● **Eating**
1 Friends Hoteli
2 Greenland Hoteli
3 Little Rock
4 Mbarara Coffee Shop
5 Muzuma Club
6 Western Hoteli

Excursions

Safariland Park, just outside Mbarara to the west, on the road to Kabale, is built in a rocky location and has little walkways and hidden nooks and crannies containing, among other things, a London Bus, a Wild West Garden and a Jungle Fever enclosure. It can be found by following the large triangular signposts. It is quite isolated and is on the other side of the Rwizi River from the rest of the town, which requires you to take a circular route behind the University to reach it. It takes about 15 minutes by car or *boda-boda*. Built to reflect 'unity in diversity', according to Banyankore tradition, it is a wooden structure of restaurants, bars, bedrooms with balconies overlooking the river and bandas – all linked together by complex and interesting walkways decorated in African style. There is also a stage where live music is played and a children's play area. It is built into the side of a hill overlooking the River Rwizi, and on a fine day is a very nice place to relax. It can also be reached via the river – a rowing boat service runs from behind the hospital going upriver to Safariland, a journey of approximately 30 minutes. To reach the boat-launching area take a *boda-boda* from the hospital down the unsealed road to the river. This road runs between the hospital and the police station. Despite having great potential and being very imaginative, Safariland has very few customers. This gives the place a rather ghostly air of desertion although it does get used quite a lots for functions such as office parties and weddings.

About 47 km east of Mbarara is **Lake Mburo National Park**, and about 40 km west on the Ishaka road are the **Kitagata Hot Springs**. These sulphur-rich springs are much utilized by local people suffering from rheumatism and arthritis.

The **Nsongezi Rock Shelters**, which overlook the Kagere River, are approximately 65 km due south of Mbarara, close to the small town of Kikagati, where tin used to be mined. Near by on the fast-flowing river that forms the boundary with Tanzania is **Kansyoke**

Uganda

Island. Both are important late Stone Age archaeological sites, where several artefacts have been discovered, which can be seen in the National Museum in Kampala. Kansyoke Island has also served as a place of refuge for the rulers of the Nkore Kingdom during times of conflict.

Sleeping

■ *on map, page 733*

In Mbarara **B** *Lake View Regency Hotel*, PO Box 165, T075-642025 (mob), T21398, F21399, lvh@infocom.co.ug This is the largest hotel in Mbarara, in very pleasant surroundings on the western outskirts of town and, as its name suggests, overlooking a lake. It has recently come under new management and new developments are planned. At the moment it offers swimming pool, tennis, gym, sauna, massage and beauty salon, tourist information and booking service, internet, restaurant, bar and conference facilities. Money and travellers cheques can be changed here. All rooms are en-suite and have TVs. International telephone calls can be made. Prices include breakfast. The lake is said to be the King of Ankole's lake and near by on top of a hill you will be able to see his palace. In front of the hotel is an interesting collection of concrete sculptures of traditional figures by S Rwemizhumbi. **B** *Safariland Park*, PO Box 1512, T21692, south of the road to Kabale, about 3 km from town, self-contained accommodation, hot water, European toilets, restaurant, bar, theme-park decor on a craggy site.

C *Agip Motel and Campsite*, PO Box 1191, T21615, F20575, on the Masaka highway from Kampala, on the left-hand side as you approach from Kampala. Modern and comfortable, with a conference centre, restaurant serving western and local food, satellite TV, phone and a bar that is popular with local businessmen. *Camping* is available at US$2 per person on a large flat camping area behind the hotel. It is securely enclosed by a wall, and has a BBQ area, as well as washing and toilet facilities. **C** *Hotel Classic*, PO Box 1152, T/F20609, T077-497758 (mob), centrally located on the High St opposite Nile Bank, is newly opened. All rooms have en-suite facilities, TV and telephone. Restaurant and bar plus secure parking. **C** *Oxford Inn*, next door to the *Pelican Hotel*. Opened in December 2000, the rooms at the front of the hotel have balconies overlooking the street. All 10 rooms are en-suite, with TV and fridge, and the ones at the back are darker than the front-facing rooms. Price includes breakfast. **C** *Pelican Hotel*, centrally located behind the main street, this popular hotel is often very busy. Rooms are comfortable but a little smaller than those of some of its competitors. The area is very lively and can be noisy at night and especially at the weekends. Breakfast included in price. **C** *Rwizi Arch*, PO Box 91, Fort Portal Rd, T20821, F20402. This is a recent addition to the town aiming at the mid-range to upmarket traveller. The hotel rooms are all en-suite, some with baths as well as showers, a/c, clean and modern with TV, restaurant, bar, conference centre, health club and laundry facilities.

D *Riheka Guest House* is set away from the town centre in quiet surroundings close to the golf course. The rooms are simple and comfortable, with en-suite showers. Breakfast included in price. **D** *University Inn*, PO Box 1410, T20334/5/7, situated close to the university in a pleasant wooded area. Simple, comfortable double rooms with bathrooms. The water supply is not terribly reliable but the surroundings make it worth staying here. Restaurant, bar. It also has a convenient **E** *Camping area*, often used by overland trucks. **E** *Africa GH*, PO Box 1378, T21712, F21304, main street. Shared ablutions, squat toilets, hot water. No bar or food, gate closes at midnight. **E** *Andrews Inn*, PO Box 1310, T20244, situated about 1 km off to the right just before you reach Mbarara. Unless you have your own vehicle it is rather out of the way. There is a range of self-contained rooms, hot water, restaurant and bar. **E** *Bunhorro*, located up to the right of the main road near the church, cheap and simple food available. **E** *Church of Uganda Hostel*, next to the bus station. Dormitory accommodation. **E** *Entry View GH*, PO Box 1252, north end of town. Shared ablutions, European toilets, hot water, local food, bar. **E** *Kikome Rest House*, PO Box 527, on the northern edge of town. Shared bathrooms, squat toilets, cold water, comfortable enough, but fairly simple. **E** *Mbiringi Hotel*, PO Box 843, T21162, north end of town. Shared squat toilets, hot water, bar (no food), good value. **E** *Memory Lodge*, PO Box 357, T20934. Central, hot water, shared ablutions, no food or bar. **E** *New Safari*, central. Very simple, shared squat toilets, no food or bar. **E** *Sabena Club*, located about 3 km out of town, down a turn-off roughly opposite the *Lake View Hotel*. Food available. **E** *Silver Inn*, PO Box 357, located off the main road to the right just after the *Motel Agip*. The rooms are basic but clean, hot water, shared European toilets, bar, good value. There are dozens of local lodges available in all areas

Uganda

of the town. The 'Old Market/Rwizi' area also has several choices, eg **E** *Travellers Rest*, which are very basic but usually spotlessly clean. The rooms are frequently arranged around a court-yard, share toilet/washing facilities. Prices are around US$2, not including breakfast.

Camping At *Agip Motel, University Inn, Safariland*, the *Sabena Club* and *Katatumba Resort Hotel*, below.

Outside Mbarara A-E *Katatumba Resort Hotel*, PO Box 1177, 99 Kabale Rd, T20152, F21300. Luxurious resort-style hotel with a fine variety of facilities – sauna, tennis courts, horse-riding, satellite TV and camel-riding – and a range of accommodation available: self-contained rooms (**A-C**), economy rooms (**D-E**) and, if you have equipment, camping for US$5. There is an excellent restaurant and bar run by the same people as the *Hotel Diplomate* on Tank Hill in Kampala. **B** *Pan Africa*, PO Box 1169, Mbarara. Resort-style hotel, located 40 km from Mbarara on the road to Kabale (loads of signs on the roadside saying '5,000-7,500-feet hillclimb'!). The staff are friendly and they will try very hard to persuade you to do one of their many activities, which include guided tours around coffee farms and banana plantations, and a trip to the hot springs at Kitagata.

Western food Expensive *Hotel Classic* serves a mixture of African/Indian/western food including good pizzas. **Expensive to mid-range** The *Lake View, Agip Motel, Rwizi Arch* hotels all serve excellent food in very well-maintained restaurants. The *Lake View and Rwizi* offer an eat-as-much-as-you-like buffet as well as an à la carte menu. A wide variety of meat, fish and vegetarian dishes are available, as well as wine and spirits. **Cheap** *Mbarara Coffee Shop*, Main St. Fish, local stews, grills, curries served with chips or rice, as well as spaghetti. **Seriously cheap** *Little Rock*, opposite the post office, is a pleasant place to sit and relax. It is called the 'Home of the Hamburger' but it does not sell this particular delicacy! Stews, fried chicken and chips are on offer as well as yogurt, fruit salad, buns, etc. Excellent value. *Muzuma Club*, located in the 'Old Market/Rwizi' area, serves very good fried tilapia (fish) or meat with chips or chapatti. Quite lively and interesting at night.

Eating

Ugandan-style food There are an enormous number of small eating places serving a very satisfying quantity of good-quality Ugandan food for about US$1. They normally offer beef, goat's meat, chicken or beans served with *matoke* (cooked green banana), rice, chapatti, or *posho* (maize flour). These places do not have a menu – they just have all the food there and you say what you want. The price is the same whatever you choose. The fol-lowing are particularly recommended. **Seriously cheap** *Western Hoteli*, in the heart of the town next to the cinema, is very popular among locals and visitors. Excellent service. Serves tilapia. *Friends Hoteli* opposite the *Western Hoteli*. *Paradise Hoteli* next to the *Western Hoteli*. *Greenland Hoteli* opposite *Rwizi Arch*.

Hoteli means 'eating place'

Pub Mercury, on the main through road, has a pleasant verandah.

Bars

Dancing Mbarara has one big nightclub, *The Vision Empire*. Discos take place on Wed, Fri, Sat and Sun. *The Vision Empire* is centrally located but it is recommended that you take a taxi rather than walk around late at night.

Entertainment

Sport *Mbarara Sports Club*, southwest of town centre has squash, tennis, golf. *Muscleflex Gym*, at the southern end of town, US$3 a day. The *Lake View Hotel* is a great place to visit during the day to make use of the facilities and enjoy the relaxed atmosphere. Swimming costs US$1 for non-residents. The pool is clean and of a reasonable size. There is a bar, a tennis court and in the same compound a sauna, gym and massage, all available for a moderate price. Aerobics/keep fit to music classes are held on Tue and Fri in the evening.

Air There is an airstrip at Mbarara but there are no scheduled flights any longer, only charter.

Transport

Road Car hire *Crested Crane,* on the High St near the Ankole bull monument. For private car hire, ask at the *Mbarara Coffee Shop* or *Little Rock* (may not conform to all legal niceties).

Mbarara is located nearly 300 km from **Kampala** and about 150 km from Kabale. The road is excellent – one of the best in the country. There are frequent buses to and from Kampala, at least 11 a day. They leave from the private bus station from 0600 when they are full, and cost US$5. Returning to Kampala there are also frequent buses. There are also *matatus* although many people choose to avoid them as they drive particularly fast on this road. It is also very easy to get a bus to Kabale from the bus park, or a *matatu* from the taxi park, or the Shell petrol station near the post office. Mbarara-Kabale costs US$4. There are also buses from Mbarara to **Kalshaka/Kasese** and **Fort Portal**, a distance of about 180 km on a newly improved road. Mbarara is a major crossroads and transport is plentiful. The main road to the west and southwest divides just west of Mbarara, with the northern fork going due west to Bushenyi and Ishaka, before turning north to QENP, Kasese and Fort Portal. The southern fork goes southwest, passing through Ntungamo, then on to Kabale and Kisoro.

Directory **Banks** *Uganda Commercial Bank*, opposite the post office, will change TCs at quite a good rate. *Nile Bank* is on the High St opposite the *Hotel Classic*. The *Standard Chartered Bank* is next door to the PO. All banks open 0830-1500. In addition they also open on the first and last Sat of the month from 0830 to 1100. None of these banks change TCs, but they can be changed at the *Lake View Hotel* and the *Rwizi Arch Hotel*. **Internet** Email service can be accessed from *Rwizi* or *Lake View* hotels. The *Computer Centre*, in a back courtyard near the post office, does not have internet access but you can send and receive emails by arrangement.

Ntungamo

0°50'S 30°15'E
Phone code: 485
Colour map 3, grid C1

Travelling on the southwest fork of the road that leaves Mbarara, the first town of any notable size is Ntungamo. The town is about 350 km from Kampala, and is the district headquarters. Travellers pressing on to Kabale will bypass the old town centre, but there are facilities for an overnight stay for more leisurely travellers. Lots of shops now line the bypass, and there are several simple lodgings, eating places, and a disco.

The town is situated in an undulating landscape with mixed vegetation and cultivated plots. Travelling 25 km southeast to Mirama, just before the borders with Rwanda and Tanzania, there are good views from Mirama Hill over the landscape and across to Rwanda.

Lake Nyabihoko, about 24 km from Ntungamo, offers boating, fishing and swimming (the lake is reputedly free of bilharzia), as well as a chance to see crocodiles and hippos and plenty of birdlife. Proceed north toward Ishaka and Kasese, and after 13 km, just past Kagamba, take the first left. After another 3 km turn left again, and after 8 km you will reach the lake. The road is sound and is possible without a four-wheel drive, even in the rainy season. A campsite is being constructed, with banda accommodation, but for the

Ntungamo

To Mbarara & Kampala

To Kabale

Uganda Commercial $

Health Clinic

New Kampala Rd

Old Kampala Rd

To Mirama Hill & Rwanda Border

Health Clinic

Discotheque

N

Not to scale

■ **Sleeping**
1 Corner Lodge
2 Park View
3 Salaama Lodge
4 Smart Lodge

● **Eating**
1 Karihura Milk Bar & Restaurant
2 Starlite Snack Bar

Chameleons

Anyone spending some time in East Africa is likely to see a chameleon. In Uganda, the Baganda call them nawolovu and most of them are terrified of these creatures and will not, with any amount of persuasion, touch them.

The best-known characteristic of the chameleon is perhaps its ability to change colour depending on its surroundings – but this is not its only peculiarity. Its tongue is long and worm-like and can be suddenly extended for a distance greater than the length of the creature's own body. Insects, particularly flies, which adhere to the sticky club-shaped tip of the chameleon's tongue are then drawn into its mouth. The eyes are set on prominent cones, which are covered with skin except for the little pupil openings at the end. Each eye moves independently so that while one eye is seeing where the next foothold is, the other is looking around for food. Its movements are slow and deliberate,

perhaps to help in the concealment that is attained by the change of colour to match the surroundings.

The eggs of the chameleon are laid in a hole in the ground. The female digs the hole during the day. She uses her front feet to collect up the earth, which is then pushed under her body towards the back limbs. When a small pile has collected under the middle of the animal the rear feet push the earth as far back as they can reach. This process is continued until the hole reaches about 7 ins deep – a process that takes about seven hours. The actual laying of eggs usually takes place at night and the hole is then covered up again.

One of the myths that surround the chameleon is that the female dies soon after giving birth. Another popular myth is that if you place a chameleon on a red surface it will burst – both these are in fact untrue.

moment it is possible to hire tents, or use your own. Entrance to the campsite is US$0.50 and boat hire is US$1.

There are several simple guesthouses, all in the **F** category, offering fairly basic facilities: *Park View*, *Salaama Lodge*, *Smart Lodge and Corner Lodge.* Both eating places offer cold drinks and menus of omelettes, fish, grills, chips, rice and beans. **Seriously cheap** *Starlite Snack Bar* and *Karihura Milk Bar and Restaurant* are both on the bypass (New Kampala Rd).

Sleeping & eating
■ *on map, page 736*

Kabale

The road from Mbarara to Kabale is good, passing through the pastoral areas – a mix of dry plains and some more undulating countryside. Some of the vistas are simply stunning: cattle grazing in hedged fields, with hills denuded of trees in the far distance. Shortly before you reach Kabale the terrain changes and becomes more hilly and greener. Before long the scenery becomes increasingly dramatic with very steep slopes. Very early in the morning the valleys are filled with mist.

Kabale is located in the southwestern corner of Uganda, an area characterized by great diversity of topography, landscape and vegetation. Parts of this area are densely forested while the rest is extremely heavily populated and intensively cultivated. During the colonial era some hillsides were terraced, to increase the cultivable area.

The old part of the town of Kabale is located up the hill. Here you will find the government offices and many buildings dating back to the early colonial period, such as the hospital, the church and the *White Horse Inn*. That other essential part of colonial life, the golf course, is also on the hill. Everything is spaciously laid out, with well-kept flower beds and mowed lawns in between. The newer part of the town is spread out along the main road, down in what used to be a swampy valley, with the buildings set back from the road. There are some nice colonnades marked with the years when the buildings were completed.

1°15'S 30°0'E
Phone code: 486
Colour map 3, grid C1

The area around Kabale is ideal for hikers – it is often described as the 'Little Switzerland' of Africa. There are tracks and paths through the hills, and local guides

Kabale is the town that you will pass through, and where you will probably stay a night or two, if you are planning a visit to the gorillas, which can be done in Uganda

Gorillas

Uganda

Kabale

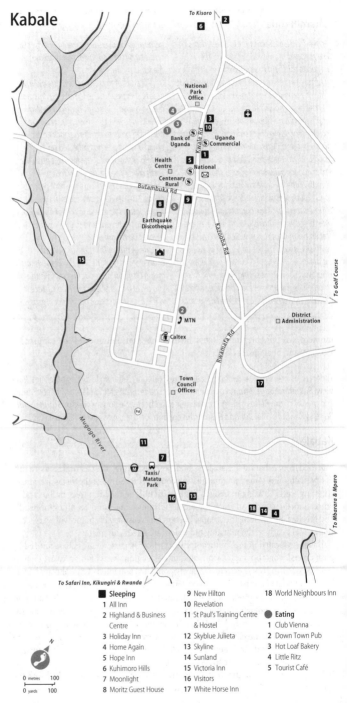

To Kisoro

6 **2**

National Park Office

4

1 **3**

Bank of Uganda

Uganda Commercial

3

10

Kvale Rd

Health Centre

5

1

National

Centenary Rural

Butambuka Rd

9

8

5

Earthquake Discotheque

15

Kazogha Rd

To Golf Course

2

MTN

Caltex

District Administration

Town Council Offices

Pol

Rwamafa Rd

17

Mugogo River

11

7

Taxis/Matatu Park

12

16 **13**

18 **14** **4**

To Mbarara & Mparo

To Safari Inn, Kikungiri & Rwanda

N

0 metres   100
0 yards   100

Sleeping		
1 All Inn	9 New Hilton	18 World Neighbours Inn
2 Highland & Business Centre	10 Revelation	
	11 St Paul's Training Centre & Hostel	Eating
3 Holiday Inn	12 Skyblue Julieta	1 Club Vienna
4 Home Again	13 Skyline	2 Down Town Pub
5 Hope Inn	14 Sunland	3 Hot Loaf Bakery
6 Kuhimoro Hills	15 Victoria Inn	4 Little Ritz
7 Moonlight	16 Visitors	5 Tourist Café
8 Moritz Guest House	17 White Horse Inn	

Uganda

(see page 743) or in RD Congo. The **Bwindi Impenetrable/Mgahinga Gorilla National Parks Information Office** (UWA), T24121, PO Box 723, Kabale, near the *Co-operative Bank* next to the *Hot Loaf Bakery*, helps tourists to get to the national parks, find possible places to stay and campsites, and provides information about places to visit in Kigezi Mountains. They also sell tourist maps, postcards and handicrafts. The standby permit system has been completely disbanded and the only way to get a permit for Bwindi is to book at the UWA office in Kampala. Tracking at Mgahinga is bookable only at the Kisoro office (not Kampala or Kabale offices, although these can be useful for information about whether gorillas are in the park and whether tracking places might be available). It is not advisable to turn up at either park hoping that someone will drop out due to illness, as this rarely happens. The strict 0830 deadline is not always adhered to and the exclusion of visitors with upper respiratory infections is lax, with people claiming that they are suffering from hayfever. If you want more information, try Ivan at the *Highland Business Centre* (the owner of the *Overlander*), who can tell you the latest information on permits and can sometimes arrange them.

Lake Bunyonyi is around 13 km away and is a popular day trip. See page 741 for further details.

There are some **hot springs** 10 km to the south of Kabale. You can either hire a bike or walk, although you may need a guide to find them. Many of the local people have traditionally used the hot springs for their ablutions and find the presence of tourists embarrassing. Before you set off, check that there are no problems – being so close to the Rwanda border this is a sensitive area.

The 27-m **Kisizi Waterfalls** are near the village of Kisizi, about 30 km from Kabale. *Matatus* leave Kabala about once an hour and take two hours. *Kisizi Hospital* has a small guesthouse with accommodation available for rent when not required by official hospital visitors. Unfortunately it is not possible to pre-book the rooms, but visitors are encouraged to check out this option as any money generated goes towards the cost of running the hospital.

B *White Horse Inn*, PO Box 11, 25-27 Rwamafa Rd, T23399, F23717. This is the best hotel in Kabale but the laurels are beginning to curl at the edge. Brick verandah off rather soulless dining room. High standards – in the past VS Naipaul was banned and Paul Theroux thrown out of the restaurant. Cottages with steep shingle roofs connected by walkways. Tennis court, pool table. Pleasant lounge, bar and restaurant. The wonderful log fire is welcome as it is quite cold at night. Set in wonderful gardens, food is good but somewhat overpriced, service is slow, offers great views but the access road is negotiable in the rain only with a 4WD. *Camping* possible. **C** *Victoria Inn*, PO Box 741, T22154, located in the southwestern part of town has about 20 very clean rooms all with their own bathrooms with running water. There is hot water available in buckets, and an electricity generator, wood fireplace, brick pathways, restaurant and bar, breakfast included.

D *Highland*, PO Box 95, T22175/9, F23742, highland@imul.com   At the north end of town on the road to Kisoro (see map). Guarded internal parking lot, running water, although there are only buckets of hot water. Also business centre, forex office, breakfast included. **E** *All-Inn*, PO Box 727, T24307, has shared facilities, hot water, European toilets. Restaurant and bar. **E** *Holiday Inn*, PO Box 866, T23550. Hot water, shared ablutions, squat toilets. Restaurant with grills and local food. Bar with billiards, darts, draughts, chess. **E** *Hope Inn*, PO Box 2234. Shared ablutions, hot water, squat toilets. Restaurant and bar. **E** *Hotel Revelation*, PO Box 752, T23292, F23290. Shared ablutions, European toilets, hot water, phones, TV. Restaurant with grills and local food, bar, good value. **E** *Kisizi Hospital Guest Accommodation*, PO Box 109, T271776, F34143. Due north of Kabale, about 30 km by road, turning off the road to Mbarara, just before Rwahi. Two cottages available. Kisizi Falls near by. Daily bus between Kisizi and Kabale Kabale, leaves Kabale at noon, Kisizi at 0700. **E** *Kuhimoro Hills Hotel*, PO Box 475, T22131. Simple style, shared squat toilets, hot water. **E** *Moonlight*, PO Box 822, T23317, near market. Shared bathrooms, squat toilets, simple

Excursions

Sleeping
■ on map, page 738
The accommodation at Kabale can be overcrowded due to foreign aid traffic for Rwanda and Burundi. NGO officials often stay in Uganda before venturing into less safe areas

Uganda

meals, bar. **E** *New Hilton*, Main St. Rather basic. Restaurant and bar. **E** *St Paul's Training Centre and Hostel*, take the left turning off the main road beyond the market and find it a little way down on the right, signposted. Cheapest of all the places in Kabale, with basic meals available. **E** *Skyblue Julieta* (PO Box and telephone same as *Victoria Inn* above), opposite the *matatu* stop. All rooms have common facilities, running water is intermittent but plenty of buckets of hot and cold water are provided. Safe parking for motorcycles. Run well by a very helpful manager called Elisa who will give you all sorts of useful advice. **E** *Skyline Hotel*, PO Box 78, T24071. Fairly basic. Shared bathrooms, European toilets, hot water. Restaurant with grills and local dishes. Bar. **E** *Sunland Hotel*, PO Box 617, south end of town on Mbarara Rd. Some self-contained rooms. Hot water, food and bar. **E** *Visitors* (sometimes spelt *Visitours*), PO Box 128, T22239. Next door to the *matatu* stop and usually sends someone to meet all the buses. It is very friendly and slightly cheaper than the *Skyblue*. The rooms are a bit shabbier but there is a lovely verandah, good meals, water at times. Rooms at the back are quieter than those at the front. Reasonably comfortable place to stay. **E** *World Neighbours Inn*, PO Box 664, south end of town on Mbarara Rd. Clean and simple. European toilets (shared). Bar but no restaurant. **E** *Safari Inn*, PO Box 431, on Katuna Rd, about 3 km from the main highway, self-contained rooms, secure parking and very quiet. **E** *Moritz Guest House*. Very simple, but cheap rooms, shared bucket water and African toilets. **E** *Home Again*, PO Box 549, T22151, Mbarara Rd. Shared showers with hot water, flushing toilets, snacks at the bar, extension under construction.

Camping Available at the *White Horse Inn*. There is a new *Golf Course Side* campsite located on the road to the right just before the *Highland Hotel* as you head north, with simple basic facilities.

Eating There are no separate restaurants, but all the hotels provide meals. **Mid-range** The *White Horse* is the most expensive, and quite reasonable quality. **Cheap** The popular *Little Ritz* serves European food of good quality. *Highland Hotel* does very acceptable food. *Visitors* and the central *Skyblue Julieta* do good-value food. **Seriously cheap** *Club Vienna* serves meats, including pork, with chips, and the standard is good. *Hot Loaf Bakery*, opposite Uganda Commercial Bank, sells excellent pizzas and pastry, and the best cakes in Uganda.

Entertainment *Earthquake Discotheque* has a bar and pool table, discos on Fri, Sat and Sun.

Sport Visitors can have a round of golf at the course to the northwest of town for around US$15.

Transport **Local** One of the features of flat Kabale is the bicycle taxi with a padded seat for the passenger behind the saddle. It is cheap and quick for travel about town.

Road Kabale is about 400 km from **Kampala**. There are daily buses direct in both directions. They leave Kampala (from the private bus station) around 0600 and arrive in Kabale sometime early in the afternoon, with an estimated journey time of 8 hrs, US$12. If you miss the bus you may want to get a *matatu*. The time of departure is not fixed and you wait until it is full. They are a bit cheaper, usually leave about mid-morning and take about an hour less than the buses. Return departs at 0600 – either go down to the bus station or else wait outside the central *Skyblue Julieta*, ready (preferably with a torch) to wave and whistle to be picked up. It is lovely to see the sun rise as you leave Kabale. Alternatively, the post bus runs between Kampala and Kabale (except Sun). Departs at 0645 from Kabale.

If you are heading for **Kasese** or **Fort Portal** take the bus as far as Mbarara and change there; it is possible in one day, but takes a lot of patience. There is one daily bus that goes all the way to Fort Portal, via Mbarara and Kasese. It is supposed to leave at 0600, but often leaves earlier, as it departs only when full.

For transport to Bwindi Impenetrable National Park ask at the National Parks Information Office. Best on Fri because there is a market in Buhoma on Sat.

There are 2 possible routes to **Rwanda**. The first is the border post of **Gatuna** (also known as Katuna) which is the more direct. Alternatively you can go via Kisoro to **Ruhengeri**; it is longer – about 3 hrs – but more scenic. Buses (*AMK Express*, *Horizon Express*) for Rwanda via

Matatus – a cautionary tale

The most reliable public transport from Kabale to Kisoro is definitely the bus, which goes every hour throughout the morning, stopping for a few minutes on the road outside the matatu *park (usually on the way from Kampala). Unusually for Uganda the buses cost a bit more than the* matatus *but they are worth every shilling. You can spend several hours waiting patiently for the* matatu *to fill up prior to departure. During this time the driver will be alerted that the next bus to Kisoro is about to arrive, so he starts up the vehicle, pretending the journey is about to begin. Instead, as soon as the bus has departed you will find yourself back in exactly the same spot in the* matatu *park as before. This charade is repeated hourly until the* matatus *are filled. Furthermore the* matatus *are in very poor condition, some of*

the worst in Uganda. Even if the windows are intact the tailgate is likely to be held in position by a piece of rope. Most travellers and their possessions get covered liberally with red dust.

A recent traveller reported waiting five hours, then walking over to the taxi rank where he was quoted US$36, then US$30, then US$22 on a shared basis. At this stage the matatu *driver came over and offered him the chance to pay for the 'empty' seats – US$16.60, which was further negotiated down to US$11.50. Loitering passengers were galvanized into action and they were off, thanks to a rich* muzungu *who needed to pick up his gorilla permit in Kisoro before the office closed at 1730. The single fare should be US$2.80. The journey takes two hours and offers spectacular views of the Virungas.*

Katuna stop at the Kiomesa office, south of town on the Mbarara Rd at around 1000-1100. Visas are available at the border US$20. *Matatus* to **Kisoro** go occasionally throughout the day. This is a wonderful journey through what some say is the most beautiful part of Uganda. Kabale to Bwindi pick-up, takes 4 hrs US$10 per person.

Money *National Bank*, Main St. 0830-1500 Mon-Fri, 0900-1300 Sat. *Highlands Forex Bureau*, *Highland Hotel*, 0800-2200. Also *Bank of Uganda, National Bank, Uganda Commercial Bank.* **Directory**

Lake Bunyonyi

Reputedly free of bilharzia, Lake Bunyonyi is fine for swimming and makes a popular day trip from Kabale, either on foot or by hired bike. Walking from Kabale takes about 2½ hours (13 km). On the road towards Kisoro and Kisizi there is a turn-off after 1 km, and a signpost to Lake Bunyonyi on the left-hand side. A taxi from Kabale will cost about US$5, and take about 20 minutes. *Overland Camp* and *Far Out Camp* (see below) will collect you if you give them a phone call and agree to stay with them. If you are cycling be prepared for a long hard slog up and a wonderful run down. It is sometimes possible to get a free lift from *Highland Hotel* in Kabale when they are taking supplies to *Bunyonyi Overland Camp* (without having to stay there). Ask at the hotel.

The lake itself is around 1,840 m above sea level and despite popular belief is not actually very deep, averaging about 40 m. What is true is that there are a number of sink holes on the Rwandan side, which have bubbling cold water welling to the surface. They are reported to be well over 200 m deep. Numerous plans to develop the lake have ranged from extensive watersports facilities including jet skis to a full-blown Disney-style theme park. To date none have materialized and the lake remains a haven of calm, with villagers paddling their canoes and visitors 'communing with nature'. On its southwest shores there are a number of villages. Pygmies walk over the mountains from Rwanda to sell their produce at the market at Hakekuba on Saturdays. Canoes can be hired from *Buyonyi Overland Camp*. There are lots of islands and a number of them have accommodation or campsites. At the head of the lake is Idi Amin's old villa, which is due to be redeveloped but in April 2001 was still a burnt-out wreck.

Sleeping *Karibuni Beach* is the site of a new campsite. Enquire at the *Visitors Hotel* for the local entrepreneur who rents dugout canoes. Prices – by negotiation – appear to vary considerably. *The Old Lodge* at the first hill on the lake shore offers camping. Cold beers and sodas available, but no food. *Bunyonyi Overland Camp*, T077-409510 (mob), www.bunyonyi.itgo.com, is a little further on and is used frequently by overlanders' trucks. It is a new development, ecologically built with local materials and several travellers have highly recommended. The staff are very helpful. Offers secure parking US$1 per car per night. Campsite well equipped with a variety of accommodation, always has hot showers, swimming and canoeing, bird-watching, volleyball, tortoise pond, biking and fishing. Restaurant serves locally caught crayfish. Fully stocked bar. Charges US$1.50 camping, furnished double tent US$12 or double-roomed cottage US$15. Emergency VHF radio contact. Car hire and transport can be arranged. Laundry facilities. Contact: Highland Business Centre, 1 Kazooba Rd, PO Box 710, Kabale, T0486-23743/1, F23742.

Crater Bay Cottages, PO Box 242, Kabale, T0486-22368, is a new development with 5 brick bandas, each self-contained, restaurant and games area, plenty of activities, US$10 single, US$15 double. Camping at US$2 per person with your own tent.

Far Out Camp, T0486-23741, T077-409510 (mob), F0486-23742. Swedish owner Niclas Jalkemo, a self-styled bushman, is a good authority on the district. The camp itself is on a 1-ha island more or less opposite the *Bunyonyi Overland Camp*: don't be put off if you are met by a couple of extremely fierce Alsatian dogs – the facilities are well worth it. There are 8 permanent tents, each with a shared bathroom, with verandahs giving good views across the lake. Excellent meals for about US$15 to include both lunch and dinner. Library, laundry, handicrafts. Trekking, canoeing, motorboat trips, mountain biking, swimming, fishing, golf at the course in Kabale. Luxurious, at US$55 for a single, less for sharing a tent, and much less (US$15) for East African citizens (buffet breakfast included).

Bushara Island C-D *Bushara Island Camp*, T/F0486 22447, T077-464 585 (mob), www.acts.ca/lbdc, on Bushara Island on Lake Bunyoni, has fully furnished tents. Managed by a Canadian, it is part of a project to minimize soil erosion and increase the agricultural yield of local farmers. The tourist revenues pay the salaries of agro-forestry workers who support the farmers. Excellent for bird-watching. Fully furnished tents (doubles) with wooden floors from US$11-16 per person, singles from US$8-14 per person and bandas US$19.50 per person. Full board (based on double occupancy) at US$33.50 with a single occupancy supplement of US$9.50. The full board price includes motor boat transportation, secure car parking, all meals, accommodation, hot showers, use of sail boat/windsurfer and dugout canoe, Bushara Island bird tour and night-time canoe tours. You can pitch your own tent for US$2. Landing fee for day visitors US$1. Booking office in Kabale at *Sky Blue Motel*.

Bamboo Tours Hotel is the only restaurant on the lake shore, serving very good crayfish with chips, and Congolese beer.

Bwama Island Once you get to Lake Bunyonyi you will almost certainly be offered a canoe trip across to Bwama Island (sometimes called **Itambira Island**), signposted at the lake shore. You can expect to pay US$1-2 per person to be rowed across. The island is a nice place for bird-watching and is the location for a school (originally it was a leper settlement), with pupils aged 5-17. The school is run by a social worker and a hard-working headmaster, Mgababa Jasper, PO Box 1114, Kabale. Jasper has done an excellent job with the school and the children, and welcomes visitors. *Jasper's Campsite* is also on the island.

Sleeping *Jasper's Campsite* is a small campsite and a nice little hut with a double bed and a bucket shower on an adjacent island. It is very quiet, with lots of birdlife and costs US$4 – proceeds go towards the running of the school. The school has a 'sponsor a child' programme costing US$11 for an entire year for travellers and volunteers. Again all proceeds go to help the school, costs US$2 per person per night. More information available at the *Visitors Hotel* in Kabale. The school children make craft items for sale to tourists and there is a shop on the island.

The far southwest: gorilla land

For many people, Uganda is synonymous with gorilla tracking. The gorillas are in the corner of the country where Uganda meets Rwanda and the RD Congo. It is very mountainous and the roads dip and dive over high ridges, with slopes now largely logged out, and deep fertile valleys. It comes as a shock to find fir trees growing nearly on the equator, but much of the time you will be travelling at over 2,000 m. The choice of park largely comes down to a question of permit availability. There is not really much point in visiting more than one of the national parks here. If you are unlucky with getting a Ugandan permit, you may be able to get a Rwandan one.

There are only three countries in which it is possible to visit mountain gorillas (*Gorilla beringei*): Uganda, Rwanda and RD Congo. With the continuing problems in RD Congo, visiting the gorillas there has been rendered impossible. The **Parc des Volcans** reopened to tourists in mid-1999 offering 32 permits daily. Since April 1993 it has been possible to visit the gorillas in Bwindi National Park. Booking is through the Uganda National Parks Headquarters (see page 613).

Mountain gorillas *Visiting the gorillas in RD Congo used to be possible although the political situation has made this option unwise*

It has been estimated that there are only about 630 remaining specimens of the mountain gorilla in the world, and about half of these are thought to be in Uganda. The vast majority of these are in Bwindi although there are a few in Mgahinga National Park, which is part of the Virunga volcano range that extends across Rwanda, Uganda and RD Congo. The development of gorilla tourism, and habituation of the gorillas, is proceeding with great care in order to avoid dangers such as the gorillas catching human diseases.

There are two ways of seeing the gorillas. The first is to go it alone by organizing transport, permits and camping equipment, etc, yourself. The alternative is much easier but prohibitively expensive for many; that is, paying a tour operator to organize the whole trip including transport, accommodation and permits. This can be arranged in the USA, Europe, Kenya or Kampala (see tour operators listed on page 637).

Good shoes and dirt-resistant clothes are essential as gorilla tracking is very muddy. It is also appreciated if tourists share their lavish lunches, as occasionally the porters and guides just have a banana. If you are not too fit, do consider taking a porter – especially if you are on one of the longer trips. They cost USh 10,000 per day. The question of tips may arise: it is sensible to agree an amount (say, USh 5,000 per head) and then give it to the ranger leading your trek. He will ensure that it is fairly divided between the rangers and guards.

Bwindi Impenetrable National Park

Bwindi Impenetrable National Park, in southwestern Uganda on the edge of the Western Rift Valley, covers an area of 321 sq km. The forest has had a number of names in the past including Bwindi, and **Kayonza**. In the local language *Bwindi* means 'a place of darkness' and the name refers to the thick vegetation. The other popular name is the Impenetrable Forest – a perfect description. It lies along the Uganda-RD Congo border in Kabale and Rukungiri districts, northwest of Kisoro and Kabale. Bwindi Forest was first gazetted to the status of a forest reserve in 1932, then in 1961 as an animal sanctuary. From 1961 it was under the joint management of the Forest and the Game Departments, until 1991, when it became a national park and was taken over by Uganda National Parks.

If you are relying on public transport and want to be sure not to miss your allocated day to see the gorillas, you should allow at least one spare day. There is plenty to do around the forest itself, and your park entrance fee lasts 4 days

The two gorilla groups that can be tracked at Bwindi are the **Mubere 'M' group**, 16 gorillas with one silverback, and the **Habinyanja 'H' group**, 23 gorillas with two silverbacks, which were habituated in 1998. There are plans to habituate a third group of gorillas in Bwindi, which may become available for tracking by 2002-03. Some recent scientific findings cast doubt on the Bwindi primates being true mountain gorillas. It is thought that the Bwindi gorillas may be a separate as yet unnamed sub-species more closely related to the eastern lowland gorilla *(Gorilla berengei graueri)*.

Ankole cattle

These very large cattle, with their horns, are famous throughout the country. Large horns are considered to be very beautiful and are highly prized. Some cattle have horns that are so large that they are unable to raise their heads, or their heads are constantly leaning to one side.

What is most striking when you arrive is the steepness of the valley's sides. It is easy to pick out the huge trees in the forest but they are completely dwarfed. It is a great topic of conversation among travellers as to which group they will be tracking. In 2001, the 'M' group was very near to Bwindi and groups were back by mid-morning. The 'H' group was about as far away as possible; many groups did not get back until around 1800 and some returned well after dark. It is very tiring going up and down the valley sides, so be prepared; take lots of water and don't worry about stopping to rest for a few minutes. Some slopes are so steep that you may well have to go on your hands and knees for part of the way. Although they were exhausted, many people in the 'H' group felt highly elated about getting to the gorillas (let alone seeing them), whilst those tracking the 'M' group felt slightly deflated. If you are going during the rainy season be prepared to get very wet and muddy. Your group is allocated when you book permits in Kampala; it is worth asking where the groups are and picking the easy or hard trek accordingly. The new group that is being habituated is reported as being a few hours away.

Before the Bwindi massacre there was great difficulty obtaining permits to track the mountain gorillas. However, since the tragic events of March 1999 when tourists and park rangers were murdered by guerrillas, there has been a huge decline in the number of gorilla tourists. Currently it is very easy to get a permit. Tourists are now better protected, with two armed rangers ('for the buffalo') and six soldiers accompanying every trek. There is a large army camp just inside the park gates and opposite the site where the tourists were killed. This has since been abandoned, but the track is guarded by an army tank that periodically trundles a few yards up and down the trail.

There are several guided walks of the forest available from Buhoma that can be started at any time from 0900-1415 (except the longer Ivy River Walk which has to be started at 0900)

The **Munyaga River Trail** is a short semi-circular walk which takes less than 30 minutes. The **Waterfall Trail** is a return walk taking approximately three hours, through the forest, leading to a series of three waterfalls. The **Muzabajiro Loop Trail** also takes around three hours to complete, through forest to the slopes of the Rukubira Hill, where a wildfire in 1992 created an open view across the forest towards the Virunga volcanoes. The **Rushara Hill Trail** is a three-hour trek to the top of the highest hill in the immediate area of Buhoma. The steep climb, to 1,915 m through fields and regenerating forest, can be strenuous, but is rewarded with views across the Western Rift Valley to the Virungas to the south, and as far north as the Rwenzori Mountains on a very clear day. The **Ivy River Walk** is a six-hour return walk along a route cleared in 1970 for a never-completed road to Kisoro. The path is an important route for the local people, and leads to the Ivy River at the southern boundary of the park.

There are also three trails from the much less-visited Ruhija in the southeast of the park, along the shorter but poorer road from Kabale to Buhoma. The **Guesthouse Nature Trail** is a short loop through the forest that takes about 30 minutes. The **Bamboo Trail** is a winding walk of at least six hours through bamboo to Rwamunyonyi Hill, the highest part of the park, which offers views as far as Lake Bunyonyi. The **Mubwindi Swamp Trail** is a four-hour walk that requires special arrangement with the management of the park or the director of the Institute of Tropical Forest Conservation – a muddy, swampy place of darkness (IFTC), which runs a guesthouse at Ruhija. This leads to a swamp of about 2 sq km, from which the forest is supposed to have got its name. It is home to many different animals.

The forest has been estimated to have at least 120 species of mammal, of which 10 are primates. There are chimpanzees, black and white colobus, red-tailed monkeys and vervets. Other species include giant forest hogs and bushbucks, although these

Bwindi gorilla visit

First thing in the morning we were introduced to our Ugandan guide for the day who explained some of the rules of the park such as no smoking, eating or drinking once we reached the gorillas. More disconcertingly, he then went on to explain what to do in the event of a silverback charging us. Above all, we were told, we must stay still, crouch down and keep our heads down. We should at all times follow his instructions while he and the two trackers would speak in gorilla language to reassure the boss of the group that we were friends not foes.

The first part of the walk was the easiest, along a sunlit path decorated by scores of dancing butterflies. About 45 minutes into the forest we turned off this path and the hard walking began. From here it was about two and a half hours up and down the steep valley sides – ascending, we pulled ourselves up with the help of nearby trees, and on the way down slid most of the way on our backsides. We traversed three valleys before we reached the place where the gorillas had spent the previous night. This spot is marked by the nests of branches and leaves that the gorillas make for themselves and huge piles of dung. From here the trackers hacked through the thick bush following the trail of the gorillas. Occasionally the pungent sweetness of jasmine descended. Everywhere cicadas hummed, punctuated occasionally by the haunting shrieks of chimps. We tried to spot them in the trees around – but in vain. Suddenly the trackers stopped – we are very close, they told us, so this was the last chance for a drink and a snack.

After this rest we walked on – the atmosphere changed as we realized we were so close. About 15 minutes later we suddenly heard a loud grunt – it sounded very close and my heart missed a beat but, peering through the bush, I could see nothing. The grunting continued – I would have sworn it was less than a metre away but the bush was so thick that still I could see nothing. Our guide started to reply to the gorilla, making a deep coughing noise, and we slowly crept around, keeping a fair distance away from the source of the grunting. Peering into deep green vegetation, I could see nothing. Suddenly I caught sight of an enormous hand reaching up from ground level to pluck a green shoot. At the end of the arm was the face of a female sitting with her young close by. She was staring at us but was remarkably unconcerned at our presence as she continued to eat her meal. As we watched our eyes were drawn upwards to the sounds of two infants playing in the trees – they were absolutely delightful as they clambered up the branches and pushed each other down again. We still hadn't seen the silverback, but knew where he was, as he was the source of the deep grunts. Slowly he emerged from the bushes, familiar from films and photographs, but in the flesh he was quite awe-inspiring. Everything about him was bigger than I'd imagined and as he moved through the undergrowth it collapsed around him.

We stayed with the family group for about an hour before returning to our camp, thoroughly delighted with the experience.

Grace Carswell

Uganda

are both rare and shy animals. An estimated 20 elephants have survived in the forest, although their population has been brought near to extinction over the past 20 years. The forest maintains a huge range of birdlife, with over 330 species. The plant and insect life is also phenomenal – there are about 150 tree species as well as a wide range of ferns, orchids, mosses and lichens.

Sleeping & eating At Bwindi (Buhoma) there is now a wide range of accommodation. **A** *Mantana Tented Camp*, T041 320152, mantana@africaonline.co.ug, is a simple camp sited in a rather damp forest patch. Very helpful staff. The camp is situated just outside the park boundary. **A** *Volcanoes Tented Camp*, PO Box 22818, Kampala, T041-346464/5, T075-741718 (mob), F041-341718, sales@volcanoessafaris.com Another simple camp that is just establishing itself although the tents seem to have seen better days. Very attentive staff and good wholesome food. **A-B** *Buhoma Homestead*, nice little houses, some self-contained, in a clearing inside the dense forest about 200 m from the park gate, opposite the National Parks Office. There are communal showers also used by those staying at the campsite. Feedback indicates that this company has occasionally charged visitors 'extra' costs after 'full payment' for bookings. Book via *African Pearl Safaris*, PO Box 4562, Lower Ground Floor, Impala House, Kimathi Av, Kampala, T041-233566/7, F235770, apsafari@swiftuganda.com **E** *Buhoma Community Campground* is a locally operated simple campsite with clean bandas, a small restaurant that serves breakfasts – other meals can be ordered in advance. In addition, there are 3 privately run campsites near by, each charging US$2 to camp. At Ruhija it is possible to use the guesthouse for a 'small fee' but you must bring your own food. Use of this facility should be booked in advance through the UWA in Kampala.

Transport **Road (public transport)** Buses leaving between 0600 and 0700 every morning from **Kampala** take 8-9 hrs to Kisoro via Kabale and cost US$12. *Matatus* leave when full – usually mid-morning – from Kampala, take about 8 hrs and cost US$11. From **Kabale** it is a journey of 3 hrs to the campsite at Buhoma – but transport links are difficult. Because you have to start tracking at 0830 in the morning it is strongly advised that you get to Buhoma the night before. If you are late you lose your booking and do not get any money back.

To get to the campsite you have a number of choices. *M/S Tour Operators*, PO Box 640, 147/149 Kabale Rd, Kabale, T22700, can arrange transport. But the cheapest alternative is to take a public pick-up as far as possible and then walk the rest of the way. The campsite is at Buhoma, and the pick-ups go part of the way, leaving from the Kabale *matatu* stand at about 0800. The nearest village is Butagota from where it is a 14-km hike. Using public transport shouldn't cost more than US$4 one way. **Butogota** has some simple accommodation (try the *Travellers Motel*) and many find that this is the easiest solution to spending an extra night at Buhoma. It is a pleasant village with wide green verges but quite spread out around the rim of the hill.

Kisoro

1°17'S 29°48'E
Phone code: 486
Colour map 3, grid C1

Kisoro is in the extreme southwestern corner of Uganda, about 510 km from Kampala, and just over 80 km from Kabale. At the moment the town is suffering rather from the lack of traffic through to Rwanda. The nearby **Mufumbiro Mountains** are made up of three extinct volcanoes: Mount Muhavura, 'the guide' (4,125 m), Mount Gahinga, 'small pile of stones' (3,474 m) and Mount Sabyinyo, sometimes spelt Sabinyo, meaning 'old man's teeth' (3,674 m). Located on the border of Uganda, RD Congo and Rwanda, they are also known as the Virunga Range. Physically fit hikers can trek these extinct volcanoes. Since the Bwindi massacre in 1999, you will be accompanied by an armed ranger ('for the buffalo') and six soldiers. Near to Kisoro to the north is **Lake Mutanda**. Ask around for a guide to take you there or else head back up the Kabale road for about 2 km and take the turn-off

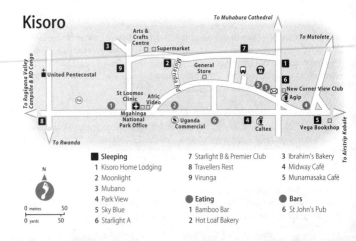

Kisoro

Sleeping	7 Starlight B & Premier Club	3 Ibrahim's Bakery
1 Kisoro Home Lodging	8 Travellers Rest	4 Midway Café
2 Moonlight	9 Virunga	5 Munamasaka Café
3 Mubano		
4 Park View	Eating	Bars
5 Sky Blue	1 Bamboo Bar	6 St John's Pub
6 Starlight A	2 Hot Loaf Bakery	

on your left. This lovely walk offers superb views over Lake Mutanda. It is easy to find your way using the 50,000:1 map available from the tourist office. On the northeast of the lake, on the Mushungero penisula approximately 14 km from Kisoro, is a new 'gorilla resort'.

Kisoro has a superb market on Monday and Thursday. This market used to take place on the Congolese-Ugandan border until the tense political situation prompted its move. It is very colourful and attracts traders from Uganda, RD Congo and Rwanda. Highly recommended.

The **Mgahinga Gorilla National Park Headquarters**, PO Box 124, T30098, can be accessed by road or boat for visitors wishing to track the mountain gorillas. Tracking in the park is currently booked only at this office. If you turn up at the park gate, the helpful officials will radio through to the office in Kisoro to make the booking for you. You then pay at the gate on the day of tracking. After tracking, on the same day, you have to go to the Kisoro office to sign the permit form (just to complete the formalities).

Boat/launch cruises on the lake are available. Book via Kampala office, PO Box 5326, T041-231218, T077-480192 (mob).

Sleeping

Many of the cheaper hotels have temporarily suspended business and a few may remain closed following the massacre in 1999. The listings may therefore be inaccurate

A *Mgahinga Safari Lodge*, PO Box 285, Kisoro, has 6 tented chalets on raised platforms and a lodge containing the lounge, bar and dining room. A boat launch is available for a cruise on Lake Mutanda. Book through *Travelust African Safaris*, PO Box 27943, Kampala, T/F41-231218, travel@africaonline.co.ug **A** *Travellers Rest*, T30021, is a well-known hotel among gorilla experts for it was once known as the unofficial gorilla headquarters. In the mid-1950s its owner, game warden Walter Baumgartel, was the self-styled 'King of the Gorillas'. He was one of the first people to take an interest in gorillas and their protection. Dian Fossey and George Schaller stayed here and it became a centre for primate experts from around the world. Baumgartel left Uganda in the late 1960s and the hotel was later taken over by the *Uganda Hotels Corporation* and renovated by *Volcanoes Tours*. Booking details: *Volcanoes Tours*, PO Box 22818, Kampala, T041-346464/5, T075-741718 (mob), F041-341718, sales@volcanoessafaris.com

D *Sky Blue*, PO Box 225, T76 (via operator). Shared bathrooms, hot water, simple but comfortable. **E** *Kisoro Home Lodging*, very basic, but cheap. **E** *Moonlight Hotel*, PO Box 282. Rather basic, shared bathrooms. **E** *Mubano*, PO Box 198. Doubles and triples only, all rooms have bathrooms and there is an excellent restaurant attached. **E** *Park View*, PO Box 92. Shared bathrooms, hot water, restaurant with good simple fare. **E** *Starlight 'A' and 'B'*, PO Box 89, T3001. Simple, shared bathrooms, hot water. *Starlight 'B'* has *Premier Club* bar attached. **E** *Virunga Hotel*, situated behind the park headquarters. Fairly basic, clean, friendly, good food, located just the other side of the fence of the *Mubano Hotel*. Shared showers and an outdoor sink. **E** *Village cooperative* bandas just outside the Mgahinga park entrance are recommended. New and clean. Good food.

Camping Available at *Virunga Hotel*, US$1.50 per person. *Rugigana Valley Campsite*, F0873 761610645, PO Box 4, 1½ km west out of Kisoro. Tents US$4, also lodge accommodation (**E**). Organizes hikes and hill-climbing.

Eating

Seriously cheap *Hot Loaf Bakery*, just past the Mgahinga NP booking office on the main road. *Ibrahim's Bakery*, close to market. Fresh bread, doughnuts, samosas. *Midway Café*, east end of town. Simple fare, grills and snacks. *Munamasaka Café*, near market. Basic snacks.

Bars

St John's Pub, busiest place in town. Disco on Fri and Sat. *Bamboo Bar*, *Premier Club*, *New Corner View Club*, all fairly simple bars.

Shopping

Markets held Mon and Thu – fresh fruit and vegetables available. *Art and Craft Centre* close to *Virunga Hotel*.

Uganda

Transport **Road** The Mgahinga NP is about 13 km from Kisoro. A *boda-boda* ride there is a cheap option although you may have to walk over some of the roughest parts of the route. The road is in atrocious condition, and is steep towards the end. The *Virunga Hotel* operates a shuttle service in the form of a pick-up, which costs the same whether or not you are staying at the hotel.

There are *matatus* to **Kabale** occasionally throughout the day. The *matatu* fare to Mgahinga NP is an extortionate US$11.50 'fixed price', which is more than the fare to Kampala (490 km). There are *matatus* to the Rwanda border to cross to **Ruhengeri**, taking about 3 hrs, a more scenic route through one of the most beautiful parts of Uganda.

Air Kisoro now has an airstrip close to the town opened in August 1998. Return flight from Entebbe to Kisoro costs around US$180.

Mgahinga Gorilla National Park

Gorilla tracking begins at 0830 sharp daily; late arrivals may lose their place

This, the smallest national park in Uganda at just 36 sq km, was established in 1991. It is in the far southwest of the country in Kisoro District, south of the town of Kisoro. It makes up the northeastern part of the Virunga volcano range which extends into RD Congo and Rwanda.

The protection of gorillas on the Ugandan side of the Virunga Volcanoes began in the mid-1950s when game warden Walter Baumgartel took an interest in them. Baumgartel left Uganda in the late 1960s and in the years that followed there was much encroachment into the forest, particularly along the lower slopes of Mounts Muhavura, Gahinga and Sabinyo. Poaching was also a threat and many of the gorillas retreated into better-protected areas in the neighbouring countries. It has been estimated that the gorilla population of the Mgahinga National Park declined by about 50% between 1960 and the early 1980s; it is currently believed to be 45.

It was not until 1989 that gorillas began to receive some protection under the Gorilla Game Reserve Conservation Project, which began to operate along the Virunga volcanoes on the Uganda side. This became the Mgahinga Gorilla National Park Project in 1991. Gorilla tracking tours are now established. It is not always possible to see gorillas in Mgahinga as they can move over to RD Congo, but recent travellers report that gorillas have been easier to see. Tourists should check in Kampala or the information office in Kabale to confirm the whereabouts of the gorillas first.

In Mgahinga Gorilla National Park there is still only one group of gorillas that can be visited – the **Nyakagezi group** (nine gorillas including two silverbacks). This group is usually in Uganda continuously from September until at least March, and at less predictable periods during other parts of the year.

There is a viewing platform about 1 km in from the Ntebeko Gate (the park entrance) but you have to pay the entrance fee to get there. This is definitely not worth it unless you have already paid the fee for doing something else that day. There is a better view from the entrance gate itself, and the wooden platform is rotting and needs replacing.

Other animals found in Mgahinga include a small number of elephants, buffaloes, giant forest hogs, the rare golden monkey and the uncommon blue monkey. The golden monkey is only found in the Virunga volcano range and two other forests in Central Africa. The monkey gets its name from the colour of its fur, which unfortunately puts it under threat from poachers. The project leader has adopted and tamed a young elephant which you will see around the camp.

Climbing The summit of **Mount Muhavura** is the highest point of the park at 4,127 m and has a small crater lake that tourists may want to visit. The view from the summit is frequently obscured by cloud. The vegetation in the park includes montane, alpine and sub-alpine flora at each of the different levels up the volcano, varying with altitude. The lowest vegetation zone of the mountain is mainly bamboo and this is the area where the gorillas are more likely to be found. The alpine zone is dominated by the impressive giant senecios and giant lobelias that are found at an altitude of between

3,600 and 4,200 m. It is possible to climb to the peaks of Gahinga, Sabyinyo and Muhavura, although the pace set by the ranger and armed escort may be exhausting unless you are fit. Climbs can be organized at the Mgahinga Gorilla National Park office in Kisoro, where they collect entrance fees, etc.

Mount Sabyinyo offers the opportunity of straddling Uganda, Rwanda and RD Congo simultaneously. There are three peaks to climb: **peak one** is reached along a ridge on the eastern side. Reaching **peak two** involves a traverse along the ridge with Rwanda on one side and Uganda on the other. Trekking to **peak three** involves the use of a series of ladders to help cover the terrain. These ladders to the summit are occasionally out of action – check before you start the trek. The **Mount Gahinga** climb includes a pleasant walk through bamboo forest, known locally as *rugano*, before the gradient increases up to the summit. There was a small crater lake at the summit but it has turned into a swamp over time. It can be cloudy on top, but it does offer the opportunity to step into Rwanda. The round trip takes about six hours.

■ *In addition to the park entrance fee you will be charged for a trip to the peaks (US$30 per person, including the ranger's fee). The hike takes around 6-8 hrs round trip, covering a distance of 12 km. Tipping the rangers after the climbs is not compulsory, is appreciated. Climbing and guided walks can be paid for in USh or US$ at the park gate, rather than in Kisoro, which is less convenient. Camping in the base camp of Muhavura costs US$10 per person in a tent. However this base camp has recently fallen into disrepair. You need to arrive at the park gates by 0630, to walk the 5 km approximately (led very quickly by armed soldiers), before you even start the Muhavura climb. Climbs of Gahinga and Sabyinyo start at 0700 at the park gates.*

Alternative, shorter walks include a visit to the enormous **Garama Cave**, which is over 340 m in length and 14 m deep. This was where the Batwa (Pygmies) warriors used to live during their long-running conflict with their neighbours, the Bantu, almost 100 years ago. The Bantu were unaware of the existence of the cave and had difficulty locating the Batwa after their periodic raids. The caves are currently occupied by bats. It is recommended to bring a torch. ■ *Cost US$13 per person, including the ranger fee, plus the park entrance fee of US$15. Other short walks within the park cost US$5 per person plus the ranger fee of US$10 (or US$5 for half a day) for the group.*

Camping

A *Mount Gahinga Rest Camp*, set in dramatic scenery in the shadow of the Virunga volcanoes, is a good base from which to see the gorillas, or to climb Mounts Muhavura and Gahinga. Run by *Volcanoes Tours*, PO Box 22818, Kampala, T041-346464/5, T075-741718 (mob), F041-341718, sales@volcanoessafaris.com **D-E** *Amanjambere Iwacu Community Campground* (bandas/campsite), PO Box 280, Kisoro, is a co-operative camp group owned by locals and sited next to the park HQ. The co-op has a gazebo dining area, attractive campsites, running water, bucket showers and a pit toilet, and 4 simple bandas, very clean, costing about US$6 per person. Highly recommended and worth supporting. Simple food, rice and chips, beans or omelette – tasty and filling – cheap, tasty and wholesome at US$3. The small canteen sells black tea and coffee, bottled water, biscuits, bread rolls, sodas, and a few postcards/T-shirts and little else. Ask for the water for your 'shower' to be heated, no matter how hot you feel – the water is absolutely freezing. It's worth considering staying here if you plan to spend more than 1 day in the NP as it will save you the expensive round-trip fare to Kisoro.

Hidden behind the community campground is a small canteen with a similar range of stock as described above but slightly cheaper. Opening times are less predictable. It also advertises that camping is available inside its grounds, at a cost a little below that of the community campground, but there is almost no room to put up a tent, and the shower enclosure is distinctly lacking in privacy. The community campground offers much more for only a little more money.

See travel to Kisoro, page 748.

Transport

Background

History

Before the arrival of the British there were as many as 30 different ethnic groups in the area that now forms modern Uganda, each with its own language, culture and social organization.

The political organization of these different states ranged from those with a highly developed centralized system of government, through small chiefdoms, to areas with no obvious system of government. **Buganda**, **Toro**, **Bunyoro** and **Nkore** were all of the first type, and all had a highly developed centralized system of government with a monarch in place. Around 1830 Toro broke away from Bunyoro when Prince Kaboyo rebelled against his father. For some time Bunyoro was the strongest and most powerful of the four, but from the second half of the 18th century it was overtaken by Buganda. In Nkore the system was rather different as the minority pastoral Bahima ruled over the majority agriculturalist Bairu.

Other areas had no obvious system of government and interpersonal relations were controlled by fear of spirits and the supernatural.

The first foreigners to arrive in the area were **Arab traders** in the 1840s. From about 1850 the first **Europeans** began to arrive. John Speke reached Buganda in 1860 and was the first European to locate the source of the Nile (see box, page 649).

The late 19th century was a period of instability in much of Uganda, and there were wars on a surprisingly large scale. In 1888 the **British East Africa Company** was given the Royal Charter and their control over the area was consolidated by a treaty with the Kabaka of Buganda (the central and most prominent kingdom) in 1891. However, the Company found the administration of the territory too much to manage, and in 1894 the British Government took over responsibility and Buganda was declared a protectorate. Similar status was given to Bunyoro, Toro and Ankole in 1896. During the following years the boundaries of the country were finalized, with a section of Uganda being transferred to Kenya as late as 1912.

Buganda Agreement of 1900 The so-called 'Buganda Question' goes back to the signing in 1900 of the Uganda Agreement (at this time, and until about 1906, the British referred to the District of Buganda as Uganda), which proved to be a watershed in the history of Buganda and, indeed, the whole of Uganda. It formalized the association between the British and the Buganda that had been developing since Speke's arrival in 1862.

One of the most important aspects of the agreement was that it secured a remarkably privileged position for Buganda in comparison with its neighbours. The constitutional relationship between the protectorate government and the government of the Kingdom of Buganda was set out at some length, and it emphasized Buganda's political identity while assuring it a greater measure of internal autonomy than the other districts enjoyed. Some of the other districts had their own agreements, but none were as comprehensive or as favourable as that accorded the Buganda.

The agreement led to important changes in land tenure. It won over the majority of the chiefs by giving them land grants known as *mailo*, and in doing so it recognized that land was a marketable commodity. The land not given to the Kabaka and chiefs became Crown land to be used for the benefit of the kingdom. The agreement thus created a landed class. It also gave, for the first time, recognition to the notion of indirect rule through the chiefs. The colonialists needed local allies to help them administer with the minimum expenditure, and to produce an economic surplus that could pay for the administration. In time the interests of the chiefs and the government became more closely interwoven. The chiefs collected regular salaries and promoted government policies, and in the public's mind they began to be associated with the protectorate administration.

The benefit of the agreement was in addition to the natural advantages that Buganda already had, with its fertile soils, regular rainfall, and a location on the shore of Lake

Victoria that ensured good transport links. Missionary activity in the area, stimulated by competition between the Protestants and Catholics, led to a greater concentration of hospitals, schools and other educational facilities. Britain encouraged the production of cotton, the major cash crop in the south, while parts of the remaining areas were discouraged from growing cash crops and were instead developed as a labour reserve. This served to accentuate further the differences between Buganda and the rest of the Protectorate, with the south producing cash crops and the north providing migrant labour. In keeping with this division, the north also provided soldiers to the army throughout the colonial period. Buganda's farmers benefited greatly from high coffee prices after the war, and in the early 1950s industrial and commercial development were concentrated in the south generally and in particular in Buganda with its locational and educational advantages.

Uganda – A Fairy Tale

"Uganda is a fairy tale. You climb up a railway instead of a beanstalk and at the top there is a wonderful new world. The scenery is different, the vegetation is different, the climate is different, and most of all the people are different from anything elsewhere to be seen in the whole range of Africa."
Sir Winston Churchill,
My African Journey, *1908*

The period of British rule in Uganda saw dramatic changes in the politics and economy of the country. Most of the wars and disputes were brought under control and the peace that grew up became known as **Pax Britannica**. The country was divided into districts headed by a District Commissioner, and the districts into counties (*saza*), sub-counties (*gombolola*), parishes (*miruka*) and sub-parishes (*bukungu* or *batongole*). A system of indirect rule was developed, with local people used at all these levels. In cases where a system of government was already in place the incumbents were used, but where this was absent other Ugandans – usually Baganda – were brought in. This meant that in many parts of Uganda in the early years of British administration, the British controlled large areas of Uganda through appointed Baganda chiefs.

While the south of the country developed into an agriculturally productive area producing, in particular, cotton and coffee, the north and southwest developed mainly as labour pools. Migration into the southern and central region became crucial to maintaining the high production in these areas. There was also a great deal of migration from outside Uganda to the central region. This was mainly from what was then known as Ruanda Urundi (later to be Rwanda and Burundi) but was also from Tanganyikya and the Congo. Migration was not just to large-scale government jobs, such as the building of the railway and the army, but also to work for individual cotton and coffee farmers in Buganda. There were some big European-owned farms and plantations in Uganda, but they were never as extensive as in Kenya and it was always planned that Uganda should be developed primarily for Africans. During the Depression of the late 1920s and early 1930s, the Uganda colonial government was not prepared to give the Europeans financial support to get them through the difficult times. Many went bust and left the country. A number of the plantations were later bought up by Asians and were developed into the sugar plantations that can be seen on the road from the Kenya border to Kampala.

The Christian missions arrived in Uganda early and their impact was enormous. Islam was also introduced into Uganda but never made the same impact. The first schools and hospitals were all mission-run; the Catholics and Protestants tried desperately to win the most converts, and the key was to provide superior education. The two Christian faiths divided the country up between their different groups so that, for example, the White Fathers went to Southern Uganda, the Mill Hill Fathers to Eastern Uganda and the Verona Fathers to the north. The Church Mission Society (CMS) is to be found across most of the country and its influence was significant.

Countries under colonial rule have usually achieved Independence when a growing nationalist movement has been successful, both in mobilizing a large section of the population and in extracting concessions from the colonial power. In Uganda however, it has been said that it was not nationalism that produced independence but rather the

Uganda

☞ **Cotton in Uganda**

In Uganda, for many years, the main base of economic development was small-farm agriculture, and during much of the colonial period the main cash crop produced was cotton. In 1902 the British Cotton Growers Association, wanting to reduce its dependence on the United States, supplied seed to the Uganda Company, which distributed it to the Baganda chiefs. From being introduced in 1904 as a commercial crop it expanded rapidly so that by 1918 it accounted for 78% of the value of all exports, and was worth £1 mn. From 1921 to 1945 it fluctuated but except for 1922 its value never fell to below £1 mn and in five years it was worth over £4 mn. In no year did it account for less than 75% of the value of Uganda's exports.

From 1921 there was increased administrative support for small-farm cotton production in the form of free seed and advice on planting and weeding. Improved communications and the effects of the government's agricultural policy were at least as important as market forces in influencing the output of cotton. The resilience of the farmers in the face of plummeting prices during the Depression, combined with the collapse of settler agriculture, explains why the government switched support from European to African agriculture. The main concern for the colonial government during the Depression was to protect its major sources of revenue, and it saw that this meant the African farmer.

In 1938 cotton represented 73% of the value of the exports, while coffee was only 7%. Cotton production never exceeded the level achieved in 1938 because the farmers found that other crops, in particular coffee, had become more profitable and gave better returns to labour than cotton, despite the fact that coffee prices fell throughout the 1930s. With the collapse of settler agriculture in 1921, coffee-growing by Africans was encouraged by the government. It was established in two areas of Uganda and while it had an impact on these areas it did not have such a great influence on Uganda as compared with cotton – until after the war, that is, when there was a phenomenal rise in coffee prices.

imminence of independence that produced nationalist parties. It was assumed that independence would be granted at some stage, and the focus was turned to the position and role that Buganda would take in an independent country. The Baganda did not wish for their role to be diminished after Independence. By the same token, the rest of the country had no wish to be dominated by the Baganda.

Kabaka Crisis of 1953-55 The issue of Baganda separatism came to a head when Sir Andrew Cohen was appointed Governor in 1952, and indicated that he was determined to push Uganda as quickly as possible along the road to self-government. A vital principle underlying his policies was that Uganda must develop as a unitary state in which no one part of the country should dominate any other. Thus a strong central government was required, in which all districts, including Buganda, would be represented on an equal footing. This challenged the privileged position that the Buganda had enjoyed since 1900.

The crisis of 1953-55 was sparked off by a chance remark in London by Sir Oliver Lyttleton, the Colonial Secretary, about the possibility of introducing a federal system in East Africa embracing the three British territories of Kenya, Uganda and Tanganyika. This was very unpopular with all Ugandans as it was feared that the federation would be dominated by the Europeans in Kenya. The Baganda were even more fearful that they would be unable to safeguard their privileged position in a wider union. Cohen responded to Lyttleton's remarks by giving public reassurances in the Legislative Council that there would be no imposition of a federation against public wishes. The Kabaka, Mutesa II, accepted these reassurances but took the opportunity to ask for the affairs of Buganda to be transferred from the Colonial Office to the Foreign Office, which would be a clear indication that Buganda was not just another colony, but had a more privileged position as a protected state whose monarch had invited British protection. He also asked for a timetable for independence to be drawn up.

The Kabaka then went a step further and rejected the policy of a unitary state and asked for the separation of Buganda from the rest of the country. Cohen demanded assurances in line with the 1900 agreement that the Kabaka would not publicly oppose the government's policies for Uganda's development. However the Kabaka refused, pleading that he first needed to consult the *Lukiko*, the Buganda council of elders. On 30 November 1953 Cohen signed a declaration withdrawing Britain's recognition of Mutesa as Native Ruler in Buganda, deported the Kabaka by air to Britain and declared a State of Emergency. Troops were deployed around Kampala but there was no outbreak of violence.

Following the Kabaka Crisis discussions to attempt to resolve the situation led to the Namirembe Conference of July-September 1954. In October 1955 the Kabaka returned to Uganda and signed the Buganda Agreement that was the outcome of the conference. The agreement declared that Buganda should continue to be an integral part of the Protectorate of Uganda, and recommended that the *Lukiko* should agree to elected Baganda participation in the Legislative Council, a step which, fearful of being submerged, it had consistently rejected. The Kabaka in theory returned as a constitutional monarch stripped of political power, but in reality the crisis had served to unite the various clans of the Baganda firmly behind the Kabaka, and thereby increase his political influence.

The crisis had a number of major effects. First, the question of federation with the rest of East Africa was ruled out. Second, the Buganda continued to have a special position and virtual internal self-government. Third, the Kabaka's personal power and popularity increased. Fourth, a statement was made in the British House of Commons that Uganda would be developed primarily as an African country, with proper safeguards for minorities. Fifth, non-Baganda members of the Legislative Council adopted an increasingly nationalist attitude and began to question the special treatment accorded to the Buganda, sowing the seeds of confrontation. And finally, now that Independence in Uganda was clearly just a matter of time, the major question was related to who would hold the power after independence, and to a definition of the future role of the Buganda and the Kabaka.

From the mid-1950s the first political parties were formed. The Democratic Party (DP), led by Benedicto Kiwanuka, had particular support among Catholics. They wanted a unitary state after independence and wanted to limit the powers of the Baganda – so initially they did not find much support in Buganda. The Uganda National Congress (UNC) was more nationally based and wanted greater African control of the economy in a federal independent state. In 1958 a splinter group broke off from the UNC and formed the Uganda People's Congress (UPC), led by Milton Obote. A political party called Kabaka Yekka (KY) – 'The King Alone' – also formed, representing the interests of the Baganda.

In the immediate run-up to independence the Baganda did not co-operate, fearing the loss of their political identity as part of a unitary state and becoming increasingly hostile towards the protectorate government. They refused to proceed with elections for Buganda's legislative councillors until Buganda's role in a future central government and the role of the Kabaka had been determined. On 31 December 1960 the Baganda declared themselves independent but this was a meaningless gesture as they did not have the power to make independence a reality.

In 1961 an inquiry was set up to look into the question of the relationship of the various parts of Uganda with the centre. It recognized that Buganda enjoyed what was virtually a federal relationship with the rest of the protectorate, and recommended that this should continue. Uganda should therefore become a single democratic state with a strong central government, with which Buganda would have a federal relationship.

The first elections were held in 1961 – the two main parties being UPC and DP. The Baganda boycotted the election so that only 3% of the Buganda electorate voted, allowing the DP to make a clean sweep in Buganda. Overall UPC won a majority of votes but DP's success in Buganda gave them the majority of the seats. Obote, as leader of the UPC opposition, and the Kabaka were both anxious to eject the DP from power in the 1962 elections, and so Obote agreed to support Buganda's demands – particularly for indirect elections to the National Assembly – in return for Buganda's return to the centre and acceptance of a single central government. Thus Buganda participated in the Constitutional Conference in London in September 1961.

Uganda

Independence: Obote I

At the 1961 conference the structure of the future government was agreed and the date of full Independence was set for 9 October 1962. Buganda obtained virtually everything that it had demanded. There would be a federal relationship with the centre, and the constitution would define all matters concerning the Kabakaship and traditional institutions. This opened the way for the Baganda to participate once again in central government, which they did through the Kabaka Yekka party, formed in 1961. They made an alliance with the UPC and the February 1962 elections in Buganda were really a fight between KY and DP; KY won 65 of the 68 seats. The KY victory determined the composition of the new government formed after the national, pre-Independence elections, in April 1962. Obote's UPC won a comfortable victory over DP outside Buganda, within it the KY-UPC alliance ensured a majority of seats for the alliance. In May 1962 Obote was sworn in as Prime Minister of the UPC-KY government and the Kabaka's role was that of constitutional monarch. On 9 October 1962, the day Uganda became an independent nation, Obote spoke of the joy felt by all in Uganda at the achievement of Uganda's independence, particularly as this had been reached in an atmosphere of peace and goodwill. He went on to speak of the need for a unity of purpose, mutual understanding and respect, and a resolve to place country above tribe, party and self.

However, the coalition between UPC and KY was fragile and by 1964 enough KY and DP members had crossed the floor to join the UPC so that the alliance was no longer necessary. Obote dismissed KY from the government.

In February 1966 Obote suspended the constitution, deposed the President and transferred all executive powers to himself. Shortly afterwards an interim constitution was imposed, which the parliament had neither read nor debated, withdrawing regional autonomy, and introducing an executive presidency – assumed by Obote who thus became Head of State with absolute power. This became known as the 'pigeon-hole constitution' because MPs were told to vote on it before they were allowed to read it – it was simply placed in their pigeon-holes for them to read afterwards. When the Baganda demanded the restoration of their autonomy, troops led by the second-in-command of the army, Colonel Idi Amin, seized the Kabaka's palace. The Kabaka fled to Britain, where he died in exile in a Bermondsey council flat – an ignominious end for a man who had once spent much of his time at Cambridge and would travel to the engineering works in Derby to supervise the carving of ivory from elephants he had shot to make the switches for the dashboard of his Rolls Royce.

Amin

The late 1960s saw the beginning of the years of trouble for which Uganda was later to became notorious. Detentions and armed repression became increasingly common. A 'Move to the Left' was introduced, which redistributed resources by way of nationalization and increased central power. Obote, who had used the army to prop up his own regime, was to be ousted by that same army under the command of Amin. The takeover occurred in January 1971 while Obote was out of the country at a Commonwealth Conference. Amin declared himself the new Head of State and promised that there would be a return to civilian government within five years. This however was not to be.

It is worth remembering that Amin was initially greeted with widespread support among the Ugandan population, particularly the Baganda, as well as in the western world. Not long into his regime, however, Amin suspended all political activity and most civil rights. The National Assembly was dissolved and Amin began to rule the country by capricious decree. In August 1972 he announced the expulsion of all non-citizen Asians. The directive was later expanded to all Asians, although under great pressure he did backtrack on this. However, in the event the atmosphere that had been established drove all but a handful of the 75,000 Asians to leave the country. Most went to Britain, while many others went to Canada and the United States. Britain cut off diplomatic relations and imposed a trade embargo. By the end of the year most other western countries had followed suit. The businesses that had been owned by Asians were Africanized, that is, given to various cronies of Amin. The expulsion of Asians and policy of Africanization was popular with the majority of the Ugandan population, many of whom had resented the success of the Asian businesses. However, many businesses collapsed and the sudden and dramatic loss of technical skills brought other enterprises to a standstill. Amin also attempted to gain the popularity of the Baganda by returning the body of the Kabaka for burial in the Kisubi Tombs outside Kampala.

Amin's administration was propped up by military aid from the Soviet Union and Libya, but the infrastructure – water supply, schools, hospitals, roads – collapsed. Many former cash-crop producers returned to subsistence production in an effort to survive. Unexplained disappearances increased, particularly among the Acholi and Langi people. There was conflict within the army.

In 1978, in an attempt to detract attention from the internal turmoil, Amin launched an attack on Tanzania. The Kagera Salient in southwest Uganda has, since the drawing of international boundaries, been rather a problematic area. Just to the west of Lake Victoria the international boundary is a straight line following the 10° latitude. However, the Kagera River forms a loop to the south of this. There is, therefore, an area of land that is part of Tanzania but, because of the river, has more contact with Uganda. One of the most important agreements that the Organization of African Unity (OAU) reached soon after its formation was that, however unfair or illogical the international boundaries drawn by the colonial powers, they should not be disputed. Amin's claim to the Kagera Salient was clearly in breach of this. Amin's undisciplined troops were no match for the Tanzanian army and the 1979 war led to massive destruction, as the army fled north pillaging and destroying as it went. Amin fled and went into exile, first in Libya, and later in Saudi Arabia.

Today His Excellency, self-styled Field Marshal and Life President of Uganda, Amin awaits the call to return once the 'misunderstanding' that led to his overthrow is cleared up. At his villa in Jeddah, he remains convinced that his people still love him. It is believed that the money he took with him from Uganda has gone, but the Saudi government grants him an allowance.

Following the war, the Tanzanian army remained in Uganda to maintain the peace. Meanwhile, on the political front, the Tanzanians arranged the Moshi Conference in March 1979. At this conference Dr Lule (who had formerly been Vice-Chancellor of Makerere) was chosen to be the leader of the National Consultative Committee of the Uganda National Liberation Front, which, together with a military commission, undertook the interim rule of Uganda. In April Lule was sworn in as President. However, in June he was voted out of office by the 30-strong National Consultative Committee, and former Attorney General Binaisa was put in his place. His length of office was to be only a year and in May 1980 the UNLF's military commission took over. This was headed by Paulo Mwanga and was supported by Museveni as vice-chairman. Elections were set for December 1980 and were contested by four political parties: UPC (headed by Obote) and DP (headed by Paul Ssemogerere), as well as a newer party, the Uganda Patriotic Movement (UPM), headed by Museveni, and the Conservative Party, largely a Buganda-based party derived from Kabaka Yekka.

Obote II

This election for which Uganda had such high hopes is widely believed to have been fixed – crowds had gathered in the streets of Kampala as the first results came out and word was that the DP had won. However, Mwanga announced that no further results of the election could be released before they had been approved by him. Needless to say, when the results were finally published – announcing a UPC victory – there was widespread belief that they had been falsified. The truth of the election result will probably never be known – but in the end the UPC had a majority of 20 seats, and Obote was proclaimed President with Mwanga as Vice-President. The election of the new government did not, however, bring peace and stability to the country. The policies that the UPC put forward were aimed at attracting World Bank and IMF-sponsored economic reconstruction, but rebuilding the country was not to be easy. On the security side the situation in many parts of the country deteriorated still further.

The dissatisfaction that resulted from the doubts over the elections led to a number of groups going into the bush from where they carried out a guerrilla war. These included the National Resistance Army (NRA), led by Museveni, who were based largely in the southern part of the country. The NRA was well organized and grew from a small collection of fighters into a powerful army. The atrocities perpetrated by the government in what became known as the Luwero Triangle, an area to the north of Kampala, were an attempt

The Ugandan National Anthem

Sung at the beginning of all major public events, and often at the beginning of films, plays and concerts. Be sure to stand up!

Oh Uganda! May God uphold thee,
We lay our future in thy hand
United free for Liberty
Together we always stand.

Oh Uganda! The land of freedom
Our love and labour we give,
And with neighbours all,
At our country's call
In peace and friendship we'll live.

Oh Uganda! The land that feeds us,
By sun and fertile soil grown,
For our own dear land
We shall always stand
The pearl of Africa's crown.

to rid the NRA of civilian supporters. Large numbers of people displaced by these atrocities joined up with the NRA, including children orphaned by the civil war.

Meanwhile there was also trouble within the UNLA – an ethnic division within the army, which was largely made up of Acholi and Langi, was to lead to another change in leadership in July 1985. This was led by the two Okellos (Tito and Basilio – not related). Obote fled to Kenya and from there to Zambia, and Tito Okello took over as President. The NRA did not join Okello but remained fighting and within a few months had taken over Fort Portal and Kasese in the west of the country. By the end of the year the NRA was within a few miles of Kampala. There were efforts at negotiation at a conference held in Nairobi, and in late December a peace treaty was signed. However, just three weeks after the signing, Museveni's troops advanced on Kampala.

Museveni Okello's troops fled north, Museveni was sworn in as President and formed a broad-based government with ministries being filled by members of all the main political factions. However, fighting continued in the north. By the late 1980s, under an amnesty offered to the rebels, almost 30,000 of them had surrendered.

Museveni, however, has not been without his critics. An Amnesty International report published in late 1991 accused the NRA of torturing and summarily executing prisoners during the operations against the rebels in the north. The criticism most commonly aimed at Museveni, particularly by the western donors, is his apparent avoidance of democratic elections. When he first came to power political parties were suspended and it was announced that there would be no elections for three years. In October 1989 the NRM extended the government's term of office to a further five years from January 1990, when their mandate was due to run out. Museveni argued that the time was not ready for political parties and that a new constitution had to be drawn up before elections could take place. In March 1990 the ban on political party activities was extended for five years. A new constitution was adopted in 1995, and Museveni was elected President in 1996, and re-elected in 2001.

Museveni allowed the Kabaka of Baganda to return to the country and to be crowned in a highly publicized ceremony in 1993. This was obviously immensely popular with the Baganda, although his role is purely ceremonial without any political function.

The Asian community have been encouraged to return, and the property they relinquished on their departure has now been restored. The Asians have been cautious, but they are once again filling positions in manufacturing, retailing, distribution and provision of skilled services.

People

The largest group in Uganda are the **Baganda**, with 16% of the total. Other main groups are the **Soga** with 8%; the **Nkole** with 8%; the **Teso** with 8%; the **Kiga** with 7%; the **Lango** with 6%; the **Gisu** with 5%; the **Acholi** with 4% and the **Alur** with 4%. The **Ik** are a small group of remote mountain people who inhabit a chain of volcanic mountains in the northeast of the country between the Timu Forest bordering Kenya and Kidepo Valley National Park. In all, there are 14 groups with more than 1% of the population. Prior to their expulsion in 1972 the **Asians** comprised about 2% of the total.

The basuti

The basuti *has become known as the traditional costume of Uganda and is seen across much of the country, although more commonly in the south. On Sundays in particular you will see many Ugandans dressed in their Sunday best – the basuti is usually made of bright materials and worn with grace. The sight of a group of women wearing them is a real feature of Uganda. The top half is fitted and has a square neck and very puffed sleeves, while the dress is made of yards of material wound round and round the waist. A brightly coloured sash is normally worn.*

Infact, the basuti *actually is of a relatively recent origin. It was designed by missionaries to be the school uniform for the first girls' school. This was located outside Kampala, and was to become Gayaza Girls' School. The design is said to have been based on the Victorian bustle as the square neck and puff sleeves were highly fashionable at that time.*

There is also a story that the basuti *was designed by a clever tailor and fabric supplier who realized that the demand for cloth would spiral if the costume became popular, because of the length of material needed.*

Modern Uganda

Although Museveni has remained in power since 1986, and brought political stability and economic recovery to the country, Uganda's appalling record makes him wary of a return to a multi-party political system. No new political structures appear to have emerged, and the parties waiting in the wings are based on the old groupings that fought the initial pre-independence election. Given that they failed on two previous occasions, Museveni has little confidence that they would succeed now. In addition there is the question of the restoration of the Kabaka and the possible re-emergence of pressure for the separation of Buganda. If boxed into a corner by the international community (and Uganda is the only country in the region not committed to a multi-party system) it is thought Museveni will launch his own party incorporating key figures from other political groupings.

Politics

Museveni has continued to argue that multi-party democracy is not suited to Uganda which needs instead what he calls 'no party democracy' or a 'movement' system with representatives of the main factions involved in government.

A significant event in 1994 was the setting up of the Constituent Assembly. As a result, the country's political system changed significantly to try to ensure greater representation of the people in political affairs and to decentralize certain elements of power. Each district has more decision-making ability on how to spend income raised locally through taxation. This will be good for areas where a cash economy is well established and taxation is possible, but will prove far harder in subsistence areas where revenue is likely to be low.

A cabinet reshuffle in November 1994, including the appointment of a woman, Dr Specioza Wandira Kazibwe to the vice-presidency, has ensured that Museveni is surrounded by anti-multi-party and pro-NRM decentralization people. Most political commentators agree that the reshuffle was an astute move as it removed some confrontational elements and increased public confidence.

In 1995 the Constituent Assembly endorsed a further five years of the current 'movement' system. In May 1996, presidential elections took place, the two main candidates being Museveni and Paul Ssemogerere. Ssemogerere is an experienced politician who ran with DP and UPC support (although the elections were formally non-party), and who served as a Deputy Prime Minister in Museveni's government before resigning in 1995. In a reasonably high turn-out (73%), Museveni received 76% and Ssemogerere 22% of the vote. The election was favourably viewed by observers, and only minor irregularities were reported. The question of a change to a multi-party system was settled by a referendum in June 2000. Political parties will be allowed to campaign in the run-up to the referendum, but the outcome was a 90% vote for a continuation of the movement system.

In the presidential elections in March 2001, Museveni was a comfortable winner against Kizza Besigye, a former minister in Museveni's government.

☞ Bunyoro Coronation

As part of the programme to restore traditional structures, as with the Buganda (see box, page 724), the monarchy was restored with the coronation of the 42-year-old, British-educated Solomon Iguru in 1994.

The previous king, Sir Tito Winyi IV, had been crowned in 1924, but deposed in 1967 when Obote abolished the monarchies (see page 754). It is the tradition that the king nominates his successor from among his heirs. There was a wide choice as King Winyi had several wives and 104 children. His choice of Solomon was disputed by another son, John, who claimed that, as the eldest son of the only wife to have been married in a Christian ceremony, he was the legitimate heir. The High Court of Uganda, however, decided in favour of Solomon.

The coronation took place on 11 June at Hoima where the king has a palace, a large, strong construction with two wings and a blue tiled roof, where the Rukerato, the Bunyoro parliament, is located. The ceremony was attended by President Museveni, the King and Queen of Toro and a representative

of the Kabaka of Uganda. As the previous coronation had been 70 years before, the procedures were uncertain. In the event it began with representatives of various religious denominations giving their blessing. A number of ceremonial objects were presented to the king: slippers to help him travel; a spear to kill anyone despising his people; a dagger for protection; a kaliruga, a club to beat anyone vexing him; a kujunju, a staff to punish offenders; an empese, a hoe symbolizing fathership of the people; a bow and quiver for fighting enemies; a leopardskin bag to assist in trading; a bamboo whistle to sound the war alarm; a kasisi, a vessel to ensure peace; and a second hoe to ensure good harvests.

The ceremony also included the presentation of 20th-century 'slippers' in the form of a Land Cruiser from President Museveni, and some centenary pottery from Leeds, where the new king had studied. Events were concluded with traditional music, drumming and dancing.

JJ Pearlman

The security situation in outlying parts continues to be a matter of concern for the government. Currently there are four areas where there are regular outbreaks of fighting. In the north, the Lord's Resistance Army (LRA), led by Joseph Kony, continues to mount attacks on communities around Gulu and Kitgum, abducting prisoners, including many children. The LRA is thought to be about 1,000 strong. It has received support from Sudan, and Uganda has retaliated by giving support in southern Sudan to the SPLA, which is fighting for seccession from the Islamic government in the north. In December 1999 Uganda and Sudan reached an agreement whereby each country would not offer refuge or support to the other country's rebels. Uganda followed this up with an offer of an amnesty to the LRA, held open for six months. There has been little response to these intitiatives, and the activities of the LRA continue.

In the east of Uganda there has been fighting between clans of the pastoralist Karamajong. During the Amin and Obote II periods firearms were acquired, and they are now used to try to settle disputes over cattle thefts. Several hundred people have been reported killed, and the government has become involved in trying to maintain law and order.

There is also rebel activity in the southwest of the country, around Kasese. A series of bomb attacks on buses and two serious assaults on Kasese have displaced some 70,000 people. It is thought that the groups forming the Allied Democratic Forces (ADF) are opportunistic rather than idealistic, and number only around 200 activists. Material support is said to come from Libya, Iran and the United Arab Emirates, and the ADF is believed to have a strong Islamic element. While the government has had some military success against the ADF, the nearby mountainous terrain of the Rwenzori Mountains provides a refuge that makes it difficult to imagine that the rebels can be easily defeated by military means.

In addition to the internal worries, Uganda has also become involved in the conflict in RD Congo. Uganda is concerned to secure its borders against incursions by armed groups formed mostly from Hutu displaced by the troubles in Rwanda and Burundi. In March 1999, eight tourists and four rangers were killed by Rwandan Hutu rebels in the Bwindi

Impenetrable Forest National Park. Museveni has responded by improving security for visitors in the area.

Uganda supported Laurent Kabila in overthrowing the rule of President Mobutu, in the hope that an ally in RD Congo would help in achieving secure borders. However, Uganda rapidly became disenchanted with Kabila, and with Rwanda began supporting the Rassemblement Congolais pour la Democratie against the RD Congo government. The RD Congo government is supported by Angola, Namibia and Zimbabwe. All five countries have committed troops, and it is said that there is a struggle for control of Zaire's mineral wealth. In 1999 there was a peace agreement signed in Lusaka, with the UN committing 500 observers and promising 5,000 peace-keepers after a ceasefire is established.

The assassination of Kabila in January 2001 saw the leadership of RD Congo pass to Joseph Kabila, the former president's son. There are hopes that the new regime will show a more sympathetic approach to an effective peace deal. Uganda would like to withdraw its troops from R D Congo, but only in circumstances where its borders are secure.

Although the various rebel activities have no prospect of overthrowing the Museveni government, they have closed the Semliki National Park, put large areas off limits for tourists, proved expensive for the government and made life a misery for local people in the affected areas.

Economy

Economic strategy has fluctuated, with Obote initially pledged to pursue a socialist development path, followed by the chaos of the Amin years which included the expulsion of the skilled Asian community. The restored Obote regime relied on market forces, but lack of security prevented any substantial progress. Museveni spent a while considering development options, but has now committed the government to an IMF-supported market-orientated strategy.

Economic structure

The population in 2001 is estimated at 22.7 million. The uplands in the east and west form the most densely populated areas, whereas the west has low population densities. The average population density is 94 persons per sq km, and this is well above the Africa average. Urban population, at 14% of the total, is low. Turmoil in recent years has led many to flee the towns to survive by subsistence production in the countryside. As urban employment opportunities have expanded only slowly, most people have been reluctant to return. The population growth rate at 3.5% a year is high despite the impact of AIDS, and this rate results from a high birth rate, with 6.6 children born, on average, to each woman.

GDP in 1999 was US$6.9 bn (exchange rate conversion) and US$24.5 (purchasing power parity conversion). In terms of economic size it is a medium-sized economy among the East African group. Income estimated by the exchange rate conversion method was US$320 per head, placing Uganda firmly in the low-income category. Estimated by purchasing power of the currency it is rather higher, at US$1,170 per head, but again this indicates low-income status.

Agriculture is the largest sector, providing 43% of GDP, and it is even more important in that it provides the livelihood of around 80% of the population. **Industry** is small, generating 18% of GDP, but incomes are high in this sector, as it comprises only 4% of total employment. Similarly services which contribute 39% of GDP, but make up only 10% of employment.

Most expenditure, as to be expected in a low-income economy, is in private consumption. Investment is slightly higher than the African average and is supported by donor contributions to rehabilitation of infastructure. Government spending is low, and reflects limited ability to raise revenue and to administer and monitor spending.

Exports make a very small contribution at 10% of GDP, although this probably underestimates export activity as the main crop, coffee, is easy to smuggle out through neighbouring states, where prices are often higher. Exports are 70% coffee, with gold at 8% and fish at 6%. Import dependence is 20% of GDP, and this level can only be sustained, in

Uganda

☞ Mweso, Bao or Mankala

Everyone who travels in Africa will, at some stage, come across a group gathered around a game played on a wooden board with round cups cut into it, dropping counters (or 'men'), made from stones or large dried seeds, into the cups. The board is rectangular and has four rows, each with eight cups. The game is known in Uganda as Mweso, *but has other names in different parts of Africa; in Kenya it is called* Bao.

In Uganda each player starts with 32 men. The aim of the game is to capture all your opponent's men, or to so reduce them that he cannot play. A central horizontal line divides the board into two halves so that each player has two rows of eight cups on his side.

Each player distributes his men anywhere in the 16 cups that make up his side of the board.

A move consists of picking up the men from one of your own cups (providing that there are two or more) and dropping them, one by one, in each of your own squares moving in an anti-clockwise direction. Dropping begins in the square next to the one that you picked up from and continues until the last man in your hand is dropped. If the last man drops into an empty square then your turn is finished. If he drops into an occupied square then all the men in that square are picked up and they are then dropped in each succeeding square in the same way. This process is repeated until the last man in your hand drops into an empty square.

When, during a move, the last man from a player's hand falls into a cup (containing one or more men) next to the central line, and immediately opposite two occupied cups on the opponent's side of the board, the opponent's men from those cups can be captured. The player continues his move with the captured men on his own side of the board. But instead of beginning, as you might expect, where he left off, the player starts from the cup next to the one last left empty

on his own side of the board. The player distributes the captured men in the same way as usual and may capture more men in one go – in fact a skilled player may go around the board quite a few times picking up his opponent's men each time. The player's move only ends when the last man in his hand falls into an empty cup.

Once the player's move has ended his opponent takes his turn and so it goes on until one of the players has captured all his opponent's men.

One final complication involves changing direction so that play moves clockwise. It is only permissible to move backwards by starting in one of the four cups at the far left of the board, and dependent on the move resulting immediately in the taking of some opponent's men. Having taken all the men possible by moving in a clockwise direction, the player continues his move in an anti-clockwise direction by starting to distribute the last lot of captured men from the cup on the anti-clockwise side of the empty cup.

Another way of winning is known as Nkutemye *which means "I have cut your head off!" and involves capturing in one turn, all your opponent's men from the cups at the end of each row of the board on your opponent's side (four cups in total).*

There are other versions of the game, known as Mankala *in English and more information can be found at www.elf.org/mankala/Mankala.html*

It is said that the sight of the game being played at Shinyanga in Tanzania (see page 506) using uncut diamonds as men first alerted travellers to the existence of diamonds in the area, leading to the establishment of the Williamson's Diamond Mine.

The handsomely carved game boards, sometimes with polished soapstone men, can make excellent gifts.

view of modest earnings from exports, by aid from the donor community. Imports are mostly machinery and transport equipment (47%) and fuel (21%).

Economic performance Given the state of the economy following the Amin period and its aftermath, Uganda has made an excellent recovery. GDP growth has averaged around 6% a year for the past five years and living standards have risen by 3% a year.

It is the resurgence of the industrial and services sectors, boosted by the return of the Asian community, that has spear headed the performance. Agriculture has kept pace with population growth at 4% a year, but industry has expanded at 11% a year, while services have grown at 8%.

Export growth has been good with volumes growing at 4% a year.

In recent years, the inflation has come under control, and is currently around 4% a year. As inflation has fallen so the excha nge rate has stabilized and there is currently an annual depreciation of around 10%.

Aid is clearly very important and comprises 13% of total income. Without this support, the level of imports could not be sustained, essential agricultural inputs of machinery and fuel would fall and economic progress would be impossible to maintain.

Recent economic developments

In May of 1987 President Museveni ended the period of indecision over Uganda's economic strategy when agreement was reached on a programme with the IMF on a return to a market-based economic strategy. The Kampala Stock Exchange opened for business in January 1988.

A privatization programme is under way, with 78 enterprises sold out of a total of 148. Progress has been slow as it has proved difficult to value assets and confirm trading records to present to potential buyers.

Tourism is recovering, reaching 160,000 visitors in 1998, almost 50% more than was anticipated but this has been set back by the killing of tourists in the Bwindi Impenetrable Forest National Park in March 1999.

Economic outlook

Future prospects depend on the maintenance of political stability and internal security. The problems in the north, the northeast and the southwest, and the hostile groups operating from RD Congo have dented Uganda's image. If these problems can be contained and gradually brought under control, confidence will increase and international business will be encouraged to expand investment. As things stand, Uganda can expect to enjoy rising living standards, and this modest pace of improvement will accelerate if tourism and mining can be restored to the levels of the 1960s.

Social conditions

Adult literacy is about 47%, below the African average. In former times literacy rates were better, but they have been adversely affected by the disruption of the Amin years and their aftermath. Primary and secondary enrolments have slipped in recent years. The priority is basic education, however, and numbers attending primary school are better than in Africa generally. Tertiary education enrolment is low. In common with much of Africa, the main responsibility for further education is being directed away from government provision and financing, and several new, private universities have been commissioned.

Life expectancy is low, at 42 years, the result of poor medical facilities, particularly in the rural areas. Infant mortality rates are among the highest in the world and are more than ten times the rates in the high-income western countries. About a quarter of children under five are malnourished.

Access of females to primary education in comparison to that of males is inferior by about 14%. The disparity is much greater in secondary education, with only 60% as many females as males enrolled. There is a high participation of women in work outside the home, caused by the heavy reliance on subsistence production and demands on women to contribute to household farm production. The burden on women is increased by high fertility rates and low access to contraception.

The banana and its uses

Apart from being an essential food across much of Uganda the banana has a number of other uses. The savoury matoke *(green banana) is cooked by steaming and is the staple carbohydrate in the southern part of the country. There are actually 14 varieties of* matoke *alone including* muvubo, musakala, nakitembe, kisubi, ssiira, nnambi *and* manwoge.

The sweet bananas eaten as fruit are known as ndizi *(the small ones) and* bbogoya *(larger). Another sweet type, known as* gonja, *is eaten cooked – either baked, roasted or fried – and can be dried and stored. Still other types,* kisubi, mbidde *and* kabula, *are used for making local alcoholic beverages (both beers and wines).*

The banana plant also has a wide range of uses. The banana tree consists of the juicy 'stem' surmounted by its canopy of broad green leaves and the fruit.

The juice from the stem can be used for a variety of purposes. It is traditionally given to young infants to supplement their food, and is sometimes used in the treatment of snakebites. The stem can be pulped and, when placed on heated stones, it releases steam that is said to help cure a cough or bad chest. Sections of the stem were traditionally used as a cleansing medium – a sort of soap and sponge, said to be very effective.

The dried outer coverings of the stem (known in Luganda as byai*) are used to make a strong pliable rope, either plaited or simply twisted. Untwisted it is used for thatching and has an advantage over grass in that it is less flammable. It is also used for making mats, baskets, plant pots, and food wrappings. A ring of banana fibre (called in Luganda* nkata*) is often used to help a carrier balance a pot on their head and it is also used by children to make footballs.*

The green leaf of the banana is used in the preparation of matoke: *the fruit is wrapped up in it to help in the long, slow steaming process. During a sudden downpour people will often run to a banana plantation to cut a leaf to serve as an umbrella. The leaves, as well as the skins of the fruit, are used as animal feed. It is also said that if you rub brown shoes with the skins, the leather colour will darken. And bananas themselves are often used as stoppers for petrol cans.*

Land and environment

In the last 15 years, Uganda has made a remarkable recovery. Peace has returned to the main parts of the country, although there are still some armed bands marauding in outlying areas. Many Asians and skilled Africans have returned, and the economy has begun to allow improved living standards. Many of the features that were so attractive to visitors before 1970 are there to be enjoyed again and Uganda offers excellent value in wildlife viewing and innovative tourism.

Geography   Uganda, in the East African region, is a medium-sized landlocked state bordered by Sudan, Kenya, Tanzania, Rwanda and DR Congo (formerly Zaïre). Uganda lies between latitude 4° North to 1° South and longitude 30° West to 33° East. It forms part of the Central African plateau, dropping to the White Nile Basin in the north. Lake Kyoga and Lake Albert lie in the Rift Valley and much of the territory to the south is swampy marsh. To the east is savannah and the western part of the country forms the margins of the Congo forests. Generally speaking, the south is agricultural and the north is pastoral.

There are hydroelectric schemes on the Owen Falls Dam. Mineral resources include copper, tin, bismuth, wolfram, colombo-tanalite, phosphates, limestone, gold and the gemstone beryl.

Climate   Temperatures vary little in an equatorial climate modified by altitude. Rainfall, greatest in the mountains and the Lake Victoria region, reaches an annual average of up to 200 cm. Elsewhere it averages 125 cm but the dry northeast and parts of the south receive less than 75 cm. The dry season lasts only one month in the centre and west, but three months (June, July and August) in the south. There are two dry seasons in the north and northeast, in October and from December to March, making two harvests possible.

Economic collapse invariably has an adverse effect on afforestation in low-income countries. There is increased demand for land and wood fuel for cooking, and in Uganda the forested area has been diminishing by about 1% a year.

Freshwater supplies are plentiful with adequate rainfall, resulting from the high altitude and location by Lake Victoria. Low industrial output means annual water usage per head is low, and only 0.3% of renewable freshwater supplies is used.

Environment

Books

Hansen B and Twaddle M (eds), 1988, *Uganda Now*, London: James Currey. An excellent series of essays on the political, economic and social problems that have plagued Uganda since Independence.

General

Miller C, *Lunatic Express*, weaves the history of East Africa round the story of the building of the Uganda Railway, from Mombasa to Kampala, well researched, engagingly written, and with a fine eye for the bizarre and amusing.
Moorehead A, 1960, *The White Nile*, London: Hamish Hamilton. Highly readable account of exploration to find the source of the Nile.

History

Blundell MA, 1987, *Field Guide to the Wild Flowers of East Africa*, London: Collins.
Dorst J and Dandelot PA, 1970, *Field Guide to the Larger Mammals of Africa*, London: Collins.
Hedges NR, 1983, *Reptiles and Amphibians of East Africa*, Narobi: Kenya Literature Bureau.
Larcassam R, 1971, *Handguide to the Butterflies of East Africa*, London: Collins.
Williams J and Arlott NA, 1980, *Field Guide to the Birds of East Africa*, London: Collins.

Natural history

Uganda

Uganda

Ethiopia

6

Ethiopia

Ethiopia is a large country both in terms of population and geographical area. It experienced no protracted period of colonial rule, although it was partly occupied by the Italians for six years from 1935. It has recently emerged from a disastrous revolutionary part-Marxist period under a military regime, 1974-91, which followed the fall of Haile Selassie. Visits to many parts of the country were not possible and permits, issued by an infuriatingly obstructive and inefficient bureaucracy, were required for travel outside the capital. Happily this is now all in the past, but the legacy is that tourist facilities have been neglected. Travellers seeing the countryside, people, culture, wildlife and historical sites for the first time are astonished by their richness and diversity. Prices have been rising, so do not be surprised if some of the rates quoted here have to be revised upwards.

At the end of the 1990s, relations with Eritrea deteriorated seriously as a result of a border dispute. There were bombing raids, the borders between the two countries were closed and, despite signing a peace accord, it is uncertain when they will reopen. Tourists are advised against visiting areas near the border with Eritrea until this dispute is fully resolved.

Essentials

Planning your trip

Where to go
Colourful spectacles
are provided by
Ethiopia's festivals,
some going on
for several days
(see page 778)

Ethiopia has a unique atmosphere. The people have a distinctive appearance, partly like their neighbours in the Middle East and partly like the rest of Africa. However, some 50% are Christian, and the influence of the church is considerable. Ethiopia has its own written language, Amharic, and traditions in literature, dress, dance and music that have flourished in the relative isolation provided by their mountainous territory.

Major attractions are the ancient cities of **Gondar**, **Axum**, and **Harar**, and these have all retained the atmosphere of their historical backgrounds. There are some extraordinary churches hewn from rock in **Lalibela**. The **Historic Route** (Bahar Dar, Gondar, Axum, Lalibela, Addis Ababa) is becoming popular with visitors and there are daily flights between the cities. The capital city, Addis Ababa, is friendly, and attractively located on a hilly site. It has a strong diplomatic community, and both the UN Economic Commission for Africa and the Organization of African Unity have their headquarters there.

Ethiopia has some fine wildlife, and all the major animals of Africa, except for rhinoceros, are present in the selection of relatively small but delightful parks scattered across the country. The birds are a particular attraction.

Ethiopia is bounded to the west by , to the south by Kenya and to the east and southeast by Somalia and Djibouti. Eritrea, which gained formal Independence from Ethiopia in May 1993, lies to the north, and Ethiopia is now landlocked. The country is divided into several regions and two chartered cities – Addis Ababa and Harar.

When to go It is best to avoid the rainy season from June to September because of mud and some difficulties in travel. The hot and dry months are April and May. However, if you do travel in the rainy season the countryside is very green, and the temperature is lower – it is usually obvious when it is going to rain; other times of day may be hot and sunny.

Tours & tour operators Special excursion fares for fixed dates of departure and return (around US$900 return London-Addis Ababa in high season in July, August and December; otherwise low season rates US$730) can be arranged through: *World Express*, 29 Great Pulteney St, Room 202, London W1R 3DD, T020-74372955, F020-77342550; *Willesden Travel Service* (*WTS*), 5 Walm Lane, London NW2 5SJ, T020-84517778, F020-84514727; *Ericommerce*, Robin House, 2A Iverson Rd, London NW6 2HE, T020-73727242, F020-76246716. See also page 900. For tours of the historic route, rock-hewn churches, bird-watching, trekking, mountainclimbing, horse-riding and fishing, contact *Experience Ethiopia*, PO Box 9354, Addis Ababa, T152336, F519982 or 211 Clapham Rd, London, SW9 0QH, UK, T020-7738 3197, F7738 3067, or *Travel Ethiopia*, PO Box 9438, Addis Ababa, T510168, F510200, Travelethiopia@telecom.net.et *Yumo Tours*, PO Box 5698, Addis Ababa, T518-878, F513451, or 4 Seymour House, 19 Hanson St, London, W1P 7IN, UK, T/F020-7631 5337, also specialize in bird-watching, trekking, fishing and mule trekking. *Discovery Expeditions*, Motcombe, Dorset, SP7 9PB, UK, T01747-855050, F855411, **organize expeditions on the Nile.**

Finding out more www.google.com/Top/Regional/Africa/Ethiopia/ The Google web directory offers a comprehensive overview of the rich cultural variety and diversity in Ethiopia, covering most topics traveller may wish to research. www.tourethio.com is well laid out, teeming with useful information. www.africaguide.com has also got much useful information

Language The official language is **Amharic**. It has its own unique alphabet (see box, page 769) and a wide and extensive vocabulary. There are about 80 other local languages and dialects.

English is widely spoken, and is the language of instruction in secondary schools and at university. French, Italian and Arabic are also spoken by some people.

The names of places and people are spelt in a variety of ways, reflecting periods of French, Italian and British influence. In translating the Amaharic characters into a European equivalent the phonetic sound of a word is sometimes the clearest guide.

Languages of Ethiopia

Amharic is widely spoken. Oromifaa is the language of the Oromo who live in central and southern Ethiopia. Tigrigna is the language of the Tigrayans in the north, and it is also spoken in Eritrea.

The first Amharic typewriter, with 236 characters, is on display at the National Museum in Addis, see page 788

Amharic basics

Thank you	*Amesegenalehu*	How are you?	*Akkam Jirtuu*
Excuse me	*Yekirta*	Goodbye	*Negaa-ti*
How are you?	*Tenastilign*	Yes	*Heya*
Goodbye	*Denaderu*	No	*Miti*
Yes	*Ow*	How much?	*Meega*
No	*Aydellem*	Water	*Bishaan*
How much?	*Sintinu*	Coffee	*Buna*
Water	*Wiha*	Tea	*Shaaye*
Coffee	*Buna*	Toilet	*Mana Fincaani*
Tea	*Shai*		
Toilet	*Shintibait*		

Tigrinya basics

Thank you	*Yekin yelly*
Excuse me	*Yekireta*
How are you?	*Kamelekhum*
Goodbye	*Dehankunu*
Yes	*Uwe*
No	*Aykonnen*
How much?	*Kindey*
Water	*Maih*
Coffee	*Bun*
Tea	*Shahi*
Toilet	*Shintibait*

Other useful words and phrases:

Ishee *The nearest English equivalent is the modern meaning of the word 'cheers'. That is, it can be anything from a greeting, to a farewell via a word of thanks or agreement.*

Yellem *Literally means 'there is none', but is quite a useful negative.*

Chigger yellem *No problem*

Oromifaa basics

Thank you	*Galtoomi*
Excuse me	*Dhiifama*

Few Ethiopian hotels have special facilities for disabled travellers. However many Ethiopians have sustained major injuries during the long-running war with Eritrea and people tend to be helpful towards the disabled.

Disabled travellers

Homosexuality is illegal in Ethiopia, as it is in many African countries, and transgressions are punishable by imprisonment. Extreme discretion is advocated.

Gay & lesbian travellers

Student reductions are restricted to Ethiopians and residents only. Overseas student travellers pay the full price.

Student travellers

Outside Addis there are few child-friendly hotels with cots or high chairs. Disposable nappies, formula milk powder and baby lotions/creams are only available in the more expensive supermarkets in Addis, and cost substantially more than at home. Children are more susceptible to gastro-intestinal upsets than adults, and care should be taken to avoid dehydration or sun damage. It is recommended you bring sugar/salt electrolyte replacement sachets and analgesics if travelling with children.

Travelling with children

Ethiopia is a relatively safe country. However it is advised that women dress modestly, take taxis after dark and avoid travelling alone if possible.

Women travellers

Before you travel

Visas are required by all visitors (with the exception of Kenyan nationals and citizens of Djibouti), and should be obtained before departure through an Ethiopian Embassy, see page 771. Tourist visas are usually valid for 30 days. Normal cost is US$63 (US$70 for a business visa). You may need to present a yellow fever certificate plus one photograph. It is possible to get an extended visa of 90 days (non-extendable) if it is obtained overseas in Europe or USA.

Visas

Ethiopia

The visas issued in neighbouring countries are limited to 30 days, which can be extended twice at the Immigration Office, Churchill Av, Addis Ababa, T553899.

In Cairo and Khartoum you are obliged to present an air-ticket to Ethiopia if applying for a visa. In Cairo overland travellers who do not wish to fly can get an air ticket to Addis Ababa for about $550 at any of the numerous travel agencies who will readily take the ticket back a few hours later for a small fee, allowing you to buy a same-day visa. However, in Khartoum getting your ticket refunded can be a lengthy process (up to two weeks), as you have to deal with the airline itself.

Entry points & borders

Djibouti If you are planning to visit Djibouti, you will require a multiple-entry visa (only available for **business visas**, which are for one month and can usually be obtained by an Ethiopian contact). A 72-hour **transit visa** can be granted on arrival. Transit visas will only be issued if the person holds confirmed onward booking and an entry visa for the destination country. It can be extended for up to seven days. You will be required to surrender your passport, and it costs around US$50. **Journalists** must obtain a permit from the Ministry of Information, PO Box 1020, Addis Ababa, T111124, and this can take up to three months to be granted.

Eritrea The border with Eritrea is currently closed, despite the peace agreement signed in December 2000.

Kenya Travellers with their own transport can now cross between Kenya and Ethiopia at **Lake Turkana**. Make sure you get your entry stamp there otherwise you will have to pay a fine when you try to get it in Addis Ababa. As with other remote areas there are intermittent flare-ups between conflicting groups that have an impact on the border crossings. For details of the border crossing at **Moyale**, see page 824.

Sudan The border at **Metema**, west of Gondar, is now open to travellers, but is very remote. Travellers have reported encountering difficulties with Sudanese visas. Their visa, purchased in Nairobi, was not accepted by the immigration officers at **Gallabat** (Ethiopia-Sudan border), who would only accept a visa issued in Addis Ababa. To get a Sudanese visa in Addis Ababa you need a letter of recommendation from your embassy; it costs US$60 and can take a week to be issued.

The Shahordi/Gondar bus fare should cost US$4 but it is common to try to charge tourists double that fare. There is always a big scramble for tickets so you need to be alert and prepared to join the mêlée. It is occasionally necessary to call for help from the police, especially if you want to travel from Shahordi to Gondar. You need to buy the ticket as soon as the bus pulls in from Gondar, so ensure that you are there in plenty of time. In Shahordi there are a couple of **F**-price hotels near the bus station. Onwards from Shahordi to Metema there is only a lorry, which takes about three hours, cost US$0.80, although they will try to charge you US$1.25. The border crossing is straightforward but extremely slow. One traveller reported that it took five hours for five people to cross! From Metema to Gederef, the first town in Sudan, the only transport is lorry or 4WD. Allow two days for the journey, more in the wet season.

Ethiopian embassies and consulates

Austria, *Freidrich Schmidt Platz 3/3,*
1080 Vienna, Austria, T4028410, F4029413.
Belgium, *B-1040 Brussels, T7333929, F7321816.*
Canada, *Suite 208, 112 Kent St, Ottawa.*
Côte d'Ivoire, *Immeuble Nour Al Hayat,*
4 eme Etage, PB 3712 Abidjian 01.
Egypt, *3 Ibrim Osman St Mohandessin Cairo,*
T3477805, F3477902.
France, *35 Av Charles Floquet, 75007 Paris,*
T47838395.
Germany, *Brentanostrasse 1, D-5300, Bonn 1,*
T233041, F233045.
Israel, *69 Bograshov St Tel Aviv 63429,*
T5250383, F5250428.
Italy, *Via Andrea Vesalio, 16-18, 00161 Rome,*
T4402602, F4403676.

Sweden, *Ostemalmsgatan 34, PO Box 26116,*
10041 Stockholm.
Switzerland, *56 Rue de Moillebeau,*
PO Box 204, 1211 Geneva 19.
Uganda, *nr Uganda Museum on Kira Rd,*
T241325, visas for Ethiopia cost US$63 and
are issued in 24 hours.
UK, *17 Princes Gate, London, SW7 1PZ,*
T020-75897212.
United States, *2134 Kalorama Rd Northwest,*
Washington DC 20008, T2342281, F3287950.
Zimbabwe, *PO Box 2745, Harare,*
T725823/720259.
Overseas representation in Ethiopia *See*
under Addis Ababa, page 804.

Customs

Under the Mengistu regime, there were comprehensive restrictions. These are now in the process of being relaxed, and many of the limitations listed below are no longer enforced. *Ethiopian Customs Office*, PO Box 4838, Addis Ababa, T153100.

Duty-free allowance of 200 cigarettes, 50 cigars, 250 g tobacco, 0.5 litres of spirits or two bottles of perfume, equipment for personal use. All duty-free goods must be declared. Souvenirs for export are limited to a value of around US$250 per person. Any specialized film, recording or video equipment requires a special permit from Ministry for Information and National Guidance, PO Box 1020, Addis Ababa, T121011.

Export of any antiquities requires a permit from the Antiquities Department of the National Museum, PO Box 76, Addis Ababa, T117150, for which there is a charge (see page 788). Sporting firearms and the export of any wildlife items require a permit from Wildlife Conservation Department, PO Box 386, Addis Ababa, T444417. Export and import of books, cassettes and records may require a permit from the Censorship Department, PO Box 1364, Addis Ababa, T115704.

Vaccinations

A yellow fever innoculation certificate is compulsory. Vaccination against cholera is only required if the visitor is coming from an affected area.

Money

Currency

The currency is the birr, which is divided into 100 cents. **Notes** come in denominations of 1, 5, 10, 50 and 100 birr, while **coins** are worth 1, 5, 10, 25 and 50 cents. The value of the currency was held fixed at birr 2.07 = US$1 from 1973 to October 1992, and in this period there was a black market in foreign exchange. The devaluation in 1992 set the exchange rate at birr 5 = US$1. The exchange rate is now set by foreign currency auctions.

It can be a major problem obtaining cash in Ethiopia. Hotels offer only limited supplies. Take sufficient supplies of US dollars rather than relying on travellers' cheques. It can be very difficult to change money out of Addis Ababa, in particular at Lalibela. Also on the Historic Route there are few banks, ATMs or opportunities to exchange travellers' cheques or use credit/debit cards – it is necessary to take sufficient cash with you.

The *Commercial Bank of Ethiopia* is state-owned, though there are now some private banks as well. It offers foreign exchange facilities, and is represented in all the major towns. It will exchange US, Canadian and Australian dollars, and major European currencies in every big town, but the service is slow. In Addis, bank hours are 0800-1400 Monday to Friday, and 0900-1200 on Saturday. Out of Addis the banks tend to have a prolonged lunch break. The larger hotels and the government-owned hotels operate **bureaux de change**, and some, such as the *Hilton* in Addis Ababa, offer a 24-hour service. In principle you can change birr

Ethiopia

back into US dollars on departure provided that you can show from your currency exchange receipts that you have spent US$30 a day.

Credit cards The large hotels and the main airlines (including *Ethiopian Airlines*) will accept cards. Outside Addis Ababa cards are only rarely accepted.

Cost of travelling Ethiopia is a very inexpensive country for travellers. Budget travellers who use the buses and eat local food can manage on US$10-15 a day including accommodation but excluding national park entry fees or admission charges to historic sites. Travellers staying in mid-range hotels and eating in more expensive restaurants should budget for US$45-55 a day. Travelling by bus is very cheap, time consuming and arduous. Long haul buses frequently leave at 0600, or earlier if full. Tickets can frequently be purchased the preceding day. Getting on to the buses is quite an interesting experience as you negotiate the scrum. Baggage is normally tied on the roof and incurs extra charges of about US$0.75 per piece. Internal air costs have risen substantially over the past few years and costs between US$42 Addis/Debre Markos to US$168 Addis/Gode. The fleet is small and there are no replacement aircraft when there are breakdowns, so adherence to the timetable is variable. The train service is cheap by western standards but again the trains do not run to the published timetable. Car hire is very expensive, reflecting the state of the roads and the scarcity of vehicles.

Getting there

Air The national carrier is *Ethiopian Airlines*. It is one of the more efficient airlines in Africa. It has offices in 54 cities around the world. In Addis Ababa, it has three offices in city centre: near National Theatre on Churchill Av, T447000; *Addis Ababa Hilton*, Menelik Av, T158400; in Piazza at southern end of Eden St. In the Horn of Africa region, *Ethiopian Airlines* flies twice a week (Tuesday and Thursday) to **Djibouti** from Addis Ababa. There are no flights currently to Somalia or Eritrea.

Flights to Djibouti can be included in special round-trip tickets taking in destinations in Ethiopia other than Addis Ababa

Ethiopian Airlines International flights: *Europe*: Athens, Berlin, Frankfurt, London, Moscow, and Rome. *Asia*: Beijing and Bombay. *Middle East*: Abu Dhabi, Aden, Dubai, Jeddah, Sanaa. *Africa*: Abidjian, Asmara, Cairo, Djibouti, Harare, Kinshasa, Johannesburg, Lagos and Nairobi.

Other carriers The following airlines have flights to and from their capitals and Addis Ababa. *Alitalia*, PO Box 3240, Addis Ababa, T154640. *Alyemda*, PO Box 40461, Addis Ababa, T441049. *Kenya Airways*, PO Box 3381, Addis Ababa, T443018. *Lufthansa*, PO Box 2484, Addis Ababa, T155961. *Yemenia*, PO Box 107, Addis Ababa, T445076. *Air France*, T159044, and *Air Tanzania Corporation*, T157533, both have offices in Addis Ababa. *Air Egypt* also flies from Europe via Cairo to Addis Ababa and Asmara.

Road In principle it is possible for non-Africans to enter Ethiopia overland. However, it is a lengthy journey, taking up to six days. Vehicles must travel in convoys, and this may incur a further delay. It is very difficult to make the journey during the rainy season. The main routes are from **Kenya**, crossing at Moyale (three days hiring a lift on a truck from Nairobi to Moyale, two days Moyale to Addis Ababa); from Malakal in **Sudan** to Gambela; from **Djibouti** to Galafi; and from Hargeisa in **Somalia** to Jijiga.

The political tension in 1998 between Ethiopia and **Eritrea** led to the closure of the border. A peace plan has been agreed and the situation is expected to improve. The routes from Eritrea, when the situation is fully resolved, are from Asmara to Adwa, and Assab to Debaysima. Travel via **Sudan** and **Somalia** is not really feasible as a result of restrictions and turmoil in these two countries.

There is relatively easy overland access to Ethiopia from **Kenya**. Moyale is the border town where most people make the crossing. It is also possible to cross the border further west at Lake Turkana. However, this border post is not always manned and you may have difficulties later on if your documents are not stamped.

The overland route from **Djibouti** to Ethiopia is open. There are no current border problems. Nevertheless, this part of the country is extremely hot and inhospitable, and some of the local people are unfriendly to strangers. With odd skirmishes between the Ethiopians

Touching down

Electricity 220 volts, 50 cycles AC. A variety of sockets are to be found around the country, and an adaptor is desirable.
Hours of business 0800-1200 and 1300-1600.
IDD 251. Equal tones with long pauses means it is ringing; equal tones with equal pauses means engaged.

Official time Three hours later than GMT. Local people use a 12-hour clock, which starts at 0600. Thus 0800 is 'hour two of the day'. At 1800 the night clock begins. Thus 0400 is 'hour ten of the night'.
Weights and measures Metric weights and measures are in use in the main towns and cities. In country areas, customs vary.

and Somalis, we tend to suggest catching the train from Djibouti to Dire Dawa, and changing there for the bus to Addis Ababa.

In the period when the rains make the River Baro navigable (June-September) it should be possible to enter by boat from Khartoum to Gambela. However, the current political situation in the south of Sudan makes this impossible.
    Since Eritrea became independent in 1993, Ethiopia has become land-locked. Access by sea is through Massawa and Assab in Eritrea, or through the port at Djibouti.

River & sea

A 782-km railway connects Addis with Djibouti on the Red Sea. It is primarily a freight service, but passengers are taken. The stretch of line running through the Awash National Park affords stunning views, making what can be an uncomfortable trip more than worthwhile. For further details see under Addis Ababa page 803.

Train

Ethiopia

Touching down

The main airport is Bole International Airport, some 5 km southeast of the city. There is a departure tax of US$20 only payable in US dollars. A taxi from Bole Airport to town is around US$8. A minibus is around US$0.50. There are several occasions (for example when arriving at the airport, and when cashing travellers' cheques) when you will be asked for a telephone number. It will facilitate things if you have a hotel number you can give. The airport, on Bole Rd, is accessed by minibus from Piazza (destination Bole, US$0.50). On arrival, the blue/white minibuses are to your right, a bit further on than the taxis. Yellow ones are more expensive. Major hotels have a shuttle bus. Taxi to and from airport is about US$8.

Airport information
Airport tax on departure US$20

Ethiopian Tourism Commission, Ras Mekonin Av, PO Box 2183, Addis Ababa, T447470, provides information for tourists, and promotes tourism overseas. *Ethiopian Airlines* offices are situated in 54 cities around the world. Invariably they have a staff member who takes responsibility for providing tourist information, and is a reliable source for information on any recent changes in visa regulations, health requirements, etc. **National Tour Operation** is the state-owned tourist organization. Main office near *Ghion Hotel* on Ras Mekonin Av, PO Box 5709, T512955, F517688. There's a branch in the *Hilton Hotel* and five regional offices, including one in Dire Dawa. It organizes sightseeing around Addis Ababa; excursions from Addis Ababa; visits to Omo, Gambela, Bahar Dar, Gondar, Lalibela, Harar; hiking tours; hunting safaris; fishing; birdwatching. Many new private travel and tour firms have set up since 1991 (see page 802).

Tourist information

Conduct It is customary for men to wear suits for business occasions, particularly when visiting government offices. Women would normally be expected to dress neatly on such occasions – it is regarded as a mark of respect for the persons you are meeting as much as anything else. When entering a church or mosque, it is necessary for shoes to be removed. Women are not normally allowed to enter mosques unless there is a special prayer room for women. When photographing local people, religious ceremonies or festivals, it is courteous to ask permission first.

Local customs & laws
Visitors are invariably offered a cup of tea or coffee, and it is a friendly gesture to accept

Accommodation sting

A couple travelling to Addis Ababa city centre from the airport may be asked by the driver if they are married. If they are not, the driver warns that they won't be able to stay in the same room in one of the large state-owned hotels – it is against the law. Even a married couple will need to show some documentary evidence, and this can be a problem – many passports do not show marital status. This puritanical attitude comes as something of a surprise seeing that Ethiopia takes pride in tracing its origins to an episode of casual adultery and group sex (see box, page 889).

However, the driver explains that he can fix things. The couple just need to stay in a private guesthouse where the restrictions do not apply. A farrago of a search then ensues with the driver clocking up unnecessary distance as unsavoury shacks round the outskirts are successively rejected. Sometimes the driver will persuade the couple to pay in advance for an unseen room that is turned down, but alas the money cannot be returned.

The final outcome is that the driver demands an exorbitant fare and the couple are stuck in an overpriced, miserable dive, miles from anywhere. Of course it is quite possible to stay without any of these restrictions in a non-state-owned hotel, of which there are now many in Addis.

Safety
Photographs of museums, art works, churches and mosques will often require permission

Ethiopia is a safe country, and it is possible to walk around with confidence although it is sensible to take taxis after dark. An exception can be Addis Ababa, especially at night in the Mercato area. Overall crime rates are very low although pickpockets operate in the Mercato and the Piazza areas. It is always wise to keep a close eye on your belongings, especially in crowded areas like bus stations, not just in Addis Ababa but all over the country.

There are restrictions on photographing tourist/historic sites, military installations, airports, bridges, civil engineering works, government buildings, military personnel and political gatherings. These rules have been more rigidly applied since the outbreak of hostilities between Ethiopia and Eritrea.

Begging There are many beggars almost everywhere in Ethiopia, especially in the towns, including Addis Ababa, Bahar Dar, Gondar, Hayk and Lalibela, where crowds of small children can be very persistent and occasionally aggressive. Persistent beggars, including children, may follow you for quite a long way asking for money. If you feel uneasy about handing coins over to beggars, an alternative is to buy meal vouchers *Hope Enterprises*, on Churchill Av in Addis Ababa.

Where to stay

Hotels
See inside front cover for details of price codes. Plenty of middle-range (B and C), privately owned hotels have opened in the last few years, and they represent the best value at present

Until the demise of Mengistu, tourists were officially only allowed to stay in the large hotels owned by the state and run by *Ethiopian Hotels and Spas Corporation (EHC)*. These hotels were grouped into five regional chains, each with a flagship hotel in Addis Ababa. The *Ghion Hotels* cover the north and the historic towns of Gondor and Axum. The *Ras Hotels* are in the east and include Dire Dawa and Harar. *Ethiopia Hotels* cover the west and in the south are the *Wabi Shabelle Hotels*. The *Filwoha Hotels* specialize in resorts and spas, with no regional concentration. It is difficult to recommend any hotel that charges fewer than 20 birr a night. Generally speaking these hotels will be dirty, many of them squalid. The sheets on the bed may be clean, but the blankets will not, and you may well share your bed with bedbugs (if you are suspicious, give yourself a dusting over with insecticide powder before you retire). The communal washing and toilet facilities are probably very poor, and water and electricity supplies intermittent. If it is at all possible go for a room with its own bathroom and toilet, as these will be a lot cleaner. In this context you will find a pair of flip flops are invaluable, as there will be bathroom floors you would rather not have to tread on, and the flip flops supplied look very doubtful.

There has been pressure to privatize these hotel chains, and in principle the government is in agreement with this policy, but the implementation has been slow.

There are smaller establishments all over the country that serve the needs of ordinary Ethiopians. They are very simple, but cheap, and the proprietors are invariably very welcoming to visitors. These vary in price and standard, but they all try to charge 'farangi' prices. This is the familiar practice of charging foreigners twice or more the rate paid by Ethiopians. This is also true of the government hotels. Two men or women sharing a room are invariably charged more than a couple. See Sleeping classification, page 36.

Getting around

Air

The national carrier is *Ethiopian Airlines*. In Addis Ababa, it has three offices in the city centre: near the National Theatre on Churchill Av, T01-517000, F01-611474; *Addis Ababa Hilton*, Menelik Av, T158400; in Piazza at southern end of Eden St.

There are daily flights to Bahar Dar, Gondar, Axum, Mekelle, Lalibela, Dessie and Dire Dawa. Special round-trips can be arranged – there is no cost saving but, as flights are always busy, booking the tour will avoid delays. The **Historic Route Airpass** covering (Addis Ababa – Bahar Dar – Gondar – Lalibela – Axum – Mekelle – Addis Ababa) requires a minimum of three people travelling together. The cost will vary depending on the number of stops. Fares on request through the reservation office.

Internal flights with *Ethiopian Airlines* are reasonably efficient, but changes to the published schedules are common, as the fleet is too small to replace aircraft taken out of service for maintenance. Sometimes internal flights do not offer refreshments. When delays occur due to cancellations, the situation is made worse by how difficult it is to ascertain when alternate flights will be laid on by *Ethiopian Airlines*. This leads to great frustration for travellers. Allow extra time for the almost inevitable delays when planning your trip.

When travelling north use the EA office at Gondar to book/confirm onward flights – it has computers. There's nothing computerized in either Axum or Lalibela. Flights to many of the northern towns were suspended because of the border conflict, although this is now returning to normal following the peace accord in 2000. There is no service at present to Awareh, Shakiso, Asosa, Mendi, Shedhi, Humera, Asmara or Assab.

Road

You do not require a carnet if driving into Ethiopia. A temporary import licence costs US$7

There are asphalt roads in Ethiopia, mostly linking Addis with the regional capitals. However, some of them are in poor repair, and in the rainy season (June-September) there will be delays. Elsewhere, roads are mostly unsealed. Bus and minibus transport is available on all main routes. As a rough guide, road transport costs around US$0.05 per km.

Outside Addis Ababa, bus conductors may try to overcharge for your luggage if it has to go on the roof. It should not be more than 25% of the fare, but check with other travellers. Recent travellers have indicated that the charge is US$0.75 a piece (that is a backpack).

Long-distance buses in Ethiopia have the drawback that they rarely display a timetable. The bus stations usually open at 0600, by which time many people will have gathered by the gate. The government buses tend in general to be in better condition than the private buses.

Ethiopia air routes

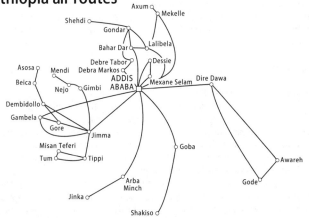

Ethiopia (side tab)

Aim to catch the early bus. There may be later buses but it's impossible to estimate their departure time. Sometimes tickets are sold in advance on the afternoon before travel. Other times you may pay at the bus station or on the bus. Again it is difficult to predict and information is very hard to collate. Having obtained your ticket, you join the scramble for seats – the front seats are more comfortable as the roads are bad. You have to put your luggage on the roof, where it is covered by canvas. The bus leaves when it's full. The whole loading procedure can take up to 1½ hours. Richer people pay someone to buy a ticket and reserve a seat for them, switching a few minutes before departure.

Car hire can be arranged through the *National Tour Operation*. The main office, PO Box 5709, T152955, is near *Ghion Hotel* on Ras Mekonin Av, and there's a branch in the *Hilton Hotel* as well as five regional offices, including one in Dire Dawa. This is an expensive option.

Train There is one train daily in each direction along the line from Addis Ababa to Djibouti. For further details see under Addis Ababa page 803.

Maps The Bartholomew map, *Sudan, Ethiopia, North East Africa*, is recommended.

Keeping in touch

Communications **Internet** Emails can be sent/received from the **British Council**, the **Business Centre** at the *Hilton Hotel* (non-guests have to buy cards valid for three months), the *Baro Hotel*, outside the main post office, and from several cafés along the street north of the post office. Charges are 1 birr per min for internet access, or 5 birr per sent email. The provision of email services is rapidly expanding here as elsewhere.

Post Post offices open 0800-1600. Mail is delivered only to PO Box numbers. **Poste restante** available at all post offices, no charge.

Country code: 251 **Telephone** Telecommunications everywhere are good, even from small towns. A deposit of around US$25 is usually required for international calls.

Media **Newspapers** *Ethiopian Herald*, published daily in English, is government-owned and covers only domestic issues. The *Monitor* is also published three times a week in English, but carries some international news. There are some independents like the *Sun* too. *Addis Tribune* is a weekly in English, with a section *Tribune d'Addis* in French. There is also an English-language quarterly, *Yekatit*. *Yezareyitu* is a weekly paper in Amharic, *Al Ahem* is a weekly Arabic newspaper, and *Berissa* is a weekly Oromo paper.

Radio *Radio Ethiopia* has a National Service and an International (External) Service. There are broadcasts in six Ethiopian languages each day. Broadcasts are in **Arabic** 1700-1800, **English** 1800-1900 and **French** 2000-2100. **BBC World Service** can be received in Ethiopia if you have a radio with short waveband reception. See guide, page 38.

Television There is one television channel, which broadcasts in colour, 1900-2300 Monday-Friday and on Sunday, and 1800-2400 on Saturday. About a third of the programmes are in English and two-thirds are in local languages, mostly Amharic. Satellite TV is now quite common in the more affluent areas or in hotels.

Food and drink

Food In Addis western-type food can be found, but if you eat in the smaller places and when you go out of town, you will normally be offered Ethiopian dishes. They are very palatable, even if they do get monotonous after a while. The carbohydrate staple, *injera*, is made from wheat, barley or maize, often mixed. It is said that the best *injera* is made from *teff*, a grain of fine grass seed grown in the highlands. In appearance it is grey, thin, flat and spongy. In simple restaurants it is spread flat on a large tin plate and various spicy sauces served with it. In more sophisticated places it will be rolled up like a carpet.

For restaurant classification, see page 39

The spicy sauces are known by the general term *wat* (or *wot*), and come in two basic forms: *kai wat* (red and peppery, with pieces of meat in a sauce), and *alicha wat* (yellowish and slightly greasy with meat). Other versions of the red and peppery *wat* include the following:

Ethiopia

Bayenetu is an interesting selection of vegetarian *wats*.

Doro fanta pronounced 'door-raw', includes egg (*doro*, 'chicken', but *fanta*, 'false', so the meat is probably mutton).

Doro wat contains chicken.

Kitfo contains minced meat – the meat can be raw or cooked, and you should specify which you want (the uncooked version is risky). *Ledleb* means the meat has been very lightly cooked.

Misto wat includes both *kai (or kay)* and *alicha,* and is not too peppery.

Misaire wat is considered to be a 'fasting food' (rather like fish in the western world). It is meatless and consists of a variety of vegetables such as lentils and spinach (usually only available on Wednesday and Friday, the fasting days of the Ethiopian church). Spaghetti, a legacy of the Italian occupation, is another fasting food.

Secundo a treat, not always available, and consists of a great variety of meat and vegetables.

Spestini contains potatoes.

Tibs (or *tibbs*) is made with roasted or fried pieces of meat, with green peppers and chilli. It is probably the most common Ethiopian dish, along with *kai wat and kitfo*.

All these are served with either *injera* or bread *(dahbo)*. Sometimes the only food available will be *tibs*. Vegetables are rarely available, although there are salads, but these, like all uncooked food, are best avoided. Whatever you eat you will be expected to use your fingers. All restaurants have somewhere where you can wash your hands, though the facilities are often less clean than you would wish.

Among Ethiopians chewing *chat* – sometimes called *ghat* or *qat* – is widespread as a social event, and groups of men are frequently seen sitting around tables talking and chewing. It is a mild and somewhat addictive stimulant, and is grown, especially in the east around Harar, as a cash crop. The green leaves are sold at the roadside in bunches, usually wrapped up in *ensete* (false banana) leaves.

Drink *Tella* is the local **beer** and *tej* a local type of **mead**. A local liqueur is *araki*. In the south there is a local beer made from sorghum or millet, called *chaka*. The most widely available bottled beers are *Bedele, Meta, Bati* and, in the east, *Harar Beera.* There are also draught beers available in many places. **Coffee** is served black in small cups, so, though delicious, is not thirst quenching. **Tea** is served in bigger cups, also with no milk, and varies enormously from the very refreshing tea with added spices such as cinnamon, to a tea bag hung over the edge of the cup. Both tea and coffee are apparently boiled during the making, so would seem to be safe to drink. **Soft drinks** (*Coca Cola* and *Fanta*) are widely available. The local bottled **spring water** comes in two types. In most of the country it is called *Ambo*, but in the east it is *Babille*. These are the names of the places where it is bottled. There is a subtle difference in the taste of the two varieties, but both seem to be safe to drink and are unbeatable if you have a raging thirst.

Much is made in tourist guides about the **Coffee Ceremony**, but there is nothing very ceremonial about it. It consists of a young woman roasting the beans over a charcoal fire, then grinding them in a mortar and making the coffee in a special coffee pot, which is heated over charcoal. This is usually done sitting on the floor and sometimes a stick of incense is burnt at the same time. This is a social occasion in much the same way that tea drinking is in England. The *Hilton Hotel* presents a coffee ceremony each week.

Shopping

Arts & crafts **Jewellery** is particularly fine, forged mostly from silver in a characteristic style, sometimes with amber decoration. Bracelets, necklaces, rings and pendants are all made. **Weaving** Traditional cloth, mostly from cotton, but sometimes from wool. Decoration is often by delicate embroidery, or in the rural areas by sewing on cowrie shells. **Leatherwork, hides and skins** Sheepskin capes are a speciality. Traditional curing of leather involves sun-drying the skin and then treating it with clotted milk and linseed oil. **Pottery** Pottery is made without use of a wheel by coiling ribbons of clay. Decoration is sometimes effected by smoking the clay, and polishing with a stone after open-pit firing. There are good examples of the large disc-shaped *injera* cooking plates, coffee pots and water carriers of varying sizes. **Horn** Horn is carved and polished to make drinking vessels, boxes and ornaments. Horn is fashioned into vessels by heating it until it is malleable. **Basketwork** Basketwork includes both woven items, and pieces made by coiling bundles of fibres. As well as containers, basketry techniques can be used to make brushes, brooms and umbrellas. **Woodcarving** Wood products are furniture, particularly three-legged stools and coffee tables. Vases, ashtrays, candle-sticks and musical instruments are also made.

It is often possible to watch craftsmen at work in co-operatives. Contact the *Handicrafts and Small-scale Industries Development Agency* near the *Wabe Shebelle Hotel*, T448809.

If you purchase a souvenir that is particularly old or rare, you will need to get a clearance from the National Museum in Addis Ababa (see page 788) before it can be exported. There is a small charge. You should always ensure you get a receipt for an antique item, and can produce it if challenged. Some travellers have been harassed, and have even spent time in jail for antiquities offences, so do take care.

Holidays and festivals

Celebrations in Ethiopia are great and colourful events, mostly religious, frequently taking place over several days, providing wonderful pageants

1 January *New Year's Day* (Julian Calendar). **7 January** *Genna* (Ethiopian Christmas: birth of Christ). **19 January** *Timkat* (Ethiopian Epiphany). This is an extremely colourful three-day festival commemorating Christ's baptism. The night before, priests take the Tabot (which symbolizes the Ark of the Covenant containing the Ten Commandments) from each church. Concealed by an ornamental cloth, it is taken to a tent, close to a consecrated pool or stream, accompanied by much ringing of bells, blowing of trumpets and the burning of incense. In Addis Ababa many tents are pitched at Jan Meda, to the northeast of the city centre. At 0200 there is a Mass, and crowds attend, with picnics lit by oil lamps. At dawn the priest extinguishes a candle burning on a pole set in a nearby river using a ceremonial cross. Some of the congregation leap into the river. The Tabots are then taken back to the churches in procession, accompanied by horsemen, while the festivities continue. **2 March** *Adwa Day* (commemorates the victory by Menelik II over Italy in 1896). **6 April** *Patriots' Day* (celebrates end of Italian occupation in 1941). **1 May** *International Labour Day*. **March/April/May** (variable) *Ethiopian Good Friday*. **March/April/May** (variable) *Fasika* (Ethiopian Easter Sunday). **20 May** *Downfall of the Derg*. **February/March** (variable) *Idd al Adha* (also spelt *Eid al-Adha* – a Muslim feast whose date changes according to the lunar calendar. **21 August** *Buhe* (Ethiopian feast connected with Virgin Mary's Assumption). Bands of small boys call at each house, singing and jostling until they are given some fresh dough (*buhe*), that is being prepared for baking. In the evening, bonfires are lit outside each home. **11 September** *Enkutatash* (Ethiopian New Year, also known as *Kiddus Yohannes*). This festival celebrates both the New Year and the Feast of John the Baptist. At the end of the long rains the season is spring, and the Highlands become covered in wild flowers. Children dressed in new clothes dance through the villages. In the evening residents of every house light a bonfire and there is singing and dancing. In Amharic, *enku* means jewels, and it is as though the country is bejewelled by the flowers of spring. **27 September** *Meskel* (or *Meskal*, Finding of the True Cross). Legend has it that the cross upon which Christ was crucified was discovered in the year 326 by Empress Helen, Mother of Constantine the Great. Unable to find the Holy Sepulchre, she prayed for help and was directed by the smoke of an incense burner to where the cross was buried.

In the Middle Ages, the Patriarch of Alexandria gave the Ethiopian Emperor Dawit half of the True Cross in return for the protection afforded to the Coptic Christians. A fragment of the True Cross is reputed to be held at the Gishen Marien monastery, which is about 70 km to the northwest of Dessie. *Meskel* means 'cross' in Amharic.

On the day of the festival, bright yellow Maskal daisies are tied to fronds, and piled high in town squares. Colourful processions carrying burning torches converge on to the square, where the brands are thrown onto the pyre. The bonfire burns and the celebrations continue until dawn. In Addis Ababa, the main celebrations take place in Maskal Square, to the south-east of the city centre.

28 December *Kullubi* (Feast of St Gabriel). St Gabriel is the patron saint who guards over homes and churches. There is a huge pilgrimage to St Gabriel's Church on Kulubi Hill, which is on the route from Addis Ababa eastwards, about 70 km before Dire Dawa. Many pilgrims carry heavy burdens as a penance, children are brought to be baptized, and offerings are made, to be distributed to the poor.

Variable *Idd al Fitr* (end of month of fasting for Ramadan).

Variable *Maulid* (birth of Prophet Mohammad, linked to the lunar cycle).

Ethiopia uses the Julian calendar, named after Julius Caesar, which is seven years and eight months behind the Gregorian (European) calendar – a result of differences of opinion over Christ's exact date of birth. The Julian calendar consists of 12 months of 30 days and a 13th month of five or six days. Hence the Ethiopians' claim that they enjoy 13 months of sunshine.

Calendar

National parks and sanctuaries

The parks are well run with helpful staff who try hard to make visitors welcome. All the major African animals are present, with the exception of the rhinoceros. The national parks include **Awash**, the very remote **Yangudi Rassa** in the northeast of the country, the **Babille Elephant Sanctuary** near Harar, the **Rift Valley National Park** encompassing lakes Abyata and Shala, **Nechisar National Park** incorporating lakes Abaya and Chamo, the remote **Mago** and **Omo** national parks in the far south and **Stephanie** near the Kenyan border. **Gambela National Park** is located in the west, close to the Sudanese border. To the north is the **Simien Mountains National Park**, and to the southeast are the **Bale Mountains**, readily accessible from Addis Ababa. Bale Mountains offers horse trekking, which is a splendid way to tour the park.

Tours are available and there is a wide variety of operators, as well as the state-owned service, see page 773. Until 1991, and more recently in the north of the country during the recent conflict with Eritrea, there have been daunting restrictions on visitors, and the tourist sector is only now beginning to get back to normal.

Health

Yellow fever inoculation is no longer compulsory. **Cholera** vaccination is only compulsory if the visitor is coming from an infected area. Inoculation against typhoid and hepatitis are strongly recommended. **Anti-malaria tablets** and general anti-mosquito measures, see page 63, are strongly recommended for visitors to the low-lying areas outside the capital. Addis Ababa is above the malarial zone. Acclimatization to the **altitude** normally takes about three days. Visitors with heart conditions or high blood pressure should take the precaution of seeking medical advice before they arrive. Swimming in lakes that have still water sometimes carries the risk of **bilharzia** – it is necessary to check locally. The alkaline lakes at Debre Zeit and Langano are safe.

For further advice see page 58

In Addis Ababa, **tap water** is usually safe to drink. Many people will, however, try to avoid even the smallest risk of a stomach upset by drinking only boiled, sterilized or bottled water. Tap water should not be drunk outside Addis Ababa although some travellers report no problems.

Ethiopia

Addis Ababa

9°2'N 38°42'E
Phone code: 1
Colour map 2, grid B3
Population: 2,084,600
at the 1994 census;
now estimated at
over 3,000,000.
Altitude: 2,400 m

Addis Ababa, meaning 'new flower' (the name reputedly coined by Empress Taytu, wife of Menellik II), is of fairly recent origin. Menelik II founded the city in 1887. Situated in the foothills of the Entoto Mountains and standing 2,400 m above sea level, it is the third highest capital in the world. Before moving to the present site, he had established temporary capitals at six different locations, each abandoned after fuel supplies had been exhausted. Addis itself was in danger of being abandoned until the introduction of fast-growing eucalyptus trees from Australia provided a regular source of fuel. The city is now large and sprawling and the municipal authorities are trying to introduce some logic and organization into its expansion. Bounded by mountains to the north, Addis is spreading south, and industrial and residential suburbs are expanding rapidly.

Ins and outs

Getting there
For Transport details, see page 803

Bole International Airport is 5 km from the city centre and is undergoing major extensions, with a new International Passenger Terminal under construction. **Taxis** and 'contract taxis' to and from the airport are run by the *National Tour Operation*. On a shared basis the fare is about US$8. However, it is possible to haggle this price down to about US$4 if you are obstinate enough (or even US$2.50 from the Piazza to the airport; taxi drivers at the airport are less amenable to negotiating with heavily laden tourists who have just stumbled out of the terminal on arrival). **Minibuses** charge US$0.25-0.50 and leave from the Piazza area. From the airport you may need to walk about 1 km towards the city. If you know where you're heading in Addis Ababa and if you have a manageable amount of luggage (a single rucksack, say) you can save money by taking a **line taxi** bound for the centre of town.

The 2 main **bus stations** in Addis are the **Autobus Terra** near Mercato, and the smaller terminal on **Ras Mekonin Av**, near the railway station. All national buses, with the exception of buses to Nazaret and Debre Zeit, leave from the Autobus Terra. Buses to Nazaret and Debre Zeit depart from the terminal in Ras Mekonin Av. (There is a second bus station in Mercato for the big (*Ambessa*) city buses, not to be confused with the Autobus Terra.)

Getting around

Very few streets in Addis Ababa have names, and if they do, they may not be known by the names shown on maps. The exception to this is **Churchill Av** which is the main thoroughfare and shopping street in Addis. This warning about street names cannot be over-emphasized. Some roads have one name on maps and another in general use. For example, Africa Av on the map is universally known as Bole Rd, and Ras Biru Av as Debre Zeit Rd. These generally used names often tell you where the road is going to. Be aware, for example, that 'Meskel Sq' is more commonly used nowadays than 'Abiot Sq'; the street linking Meskel Sq with Megenenya, which is home to a lot of upmarket hotels, has been renamed 'Haile G Selassie Rd' (or Av, both are in use), in honour of Ethiopia's latest superhero, the Olympic gold-medal-winning marathon runner. However, many maps in circulation refer to this road as 'Asmara Rd'. Even experienced officials working at the tourist offices are often bemused and bewildered by the names on the English-language maps of Addis Ababa. It is far better to navigate by using such landmarks as the **post office** (*posta bet*), **Abiot** (also known as **Meskel**), the station (*la gare*) and areas like **Piazza** and **Mercato**, which are shopping areas. With hotels, probably the most important thing to know is the neighbourhood your hotel is in (Kebane, Urael, Piazza, etc). Once you have found your way to that neighbourhood you can easily get directions to the hotel from people on the street.

Public transport in Addis is easy as there is a large and efficient network of blue and white minibuses which cover the whole town. Avoid travelling in the evening rush hour, as you will have great difficulty in elbowing your way on to the bus.

★

Things to do in and around Addis Ababa

- Find out about Ethiopia's historical heritage at the National Museum.
- Stroll round the massive Mercato market for an authentic introduction to Ethiopian life.
- Enjoy a day's entry to the hot Filwoha Springs at the New Filwoha Hotel.
- At weekends and on Thursdays, look in at a football match at the Addis Ababa Stadium on Demtew Street.
- Make a day trip to the 13th-century monastery of Debre Libanos on the edge of the spectacular Blue Nile Gorge.
- Climb Mount Zaquella for grand views over the Rift Valley, with the lakes on the valley floor clearly visible in the distance.
- Travel to Mangasha Park 35 km west of Addis, and climb through the forest to the crater valley of Wachacha.

Safety Safety is becoming an increasing concern in Addis. A number of tourists have been attacked and robbed in the Mercato area. There have also been reports of pickpocketing in the Piazza – in particular the pavement in front of the *Cinema Ethiopia* where a lot of line taxis and *Ambessa* buses stop. The area is always crowded and is a pickpocket's paradise. However, most of the trouble encountered in this area is after dark, and is frequently alcohol related. For Mercato and Piazza, probably the best rule is to maintain an area of 'personal space' around yourself. Don't let other people jostle against you. In Ethiopia, pedestrians seem to use the road as much as vehicles do, and in Mercato it may be advisable to walk along the side of the road rather than on the crowded and unsafe-looking pavements. Be especially careful walking after dark in poorly lit areas.

Tourist offices *Ethiopian Tourist Commission*, T517470, F513899, PO Box 2183, on Meskel Sq. Open daily, they have an excellent free brochure (sometimes out of print) about Lalibela, the Simeon Mts NP, Bale Mountains NP and other places, which is not always available elsewhere. *The Department of Natural Resources*, just off Africa Av (the road towards Bole), sells a range of information sheets and maps for many of the national parks, for just a nominal charge. *Trade, Industry and Tourism Bureau*, T157195, PO Box 101513, on King George St, is more an administrative centre, but they say they'll help any tourist who wanders in with questions. *National Tour Operation* (T514838, F517688, PO 5709, nto@telecom.net.et) at the very bottom of Churchill Av, also has branches at Piazza and in the *Hilton* and *Ghion* hotels. *Ethiopian Wildlife Conservation Organization*, T517922, F514190, PO Box 386, near Meskel Sq, is again, more an administrative centre, but they seem helpful enough if you come in off the street with questions. They organize monthly visits to interesting sites within easy reach of Addis Ababa.

Background Addis Ababa is an important administrative centre not only for Ethiopia but for the whole of Africa. Unlike many African capital cities it is located in the centre of the country, forming a hub. This bolsters its power as an administrative centre and also as a travel centre as, in order to get to virtually any part of Ethiopia, you usually have to go to Addis Ababa first.

The headquarters of the UN Economic Commission for Africa was established here in 1958. In 1963 the city hosted the African Heads of State Conference at which the charter of the Organization of African Unity (OAU) was signed by 30 independent African nations, and Addis Ababa was subsequently chosen as the site of the OAU's Secretariat.

Ethiopia

Sights

When going into many buildings such as government offices and sometimes banks, you will be asked if you have a camera, and your bag may be searched. If you do have a camera it will be taken away from you and you will be given a token with which to claim it back.

Filwoha An appropriate place to begin a sightseeing tour of Addis Ababa is Filwoha – Amharic for 'hot spring' – which can be justifiably described as the city's first attraction. After Menelik II had established a stronghold in the nearby Entoto Hills, the thermal waters surfacing at this spot came to the attention of his wife Taytu (also spelt Taitu). Having travelled down to visit Filwoha, she was so impressed by the spring and its surroundings that she persuaded her husband to begin building there, thus creating the nucleus of modern-day Addis Ababa. You can get to Filwoha by strolling down Menelik II Avenue from the *Hilton Hotel* and then turning west at the intersection with Yohanis Street. The original spring is now a murky pool but you can sample the water at the neighbouring *Filwoha* and *Finfine* hotels.

Africa Hall If you return to Menelik II Avenue and continue downhill, you will soon pass Africa Hall, an imposing building that symbolizes African independence and optimism. It forms the headquarters of the UN Economic Commission for Africa and hosted the meeting of the African Heads of State in 1963 responsible for the

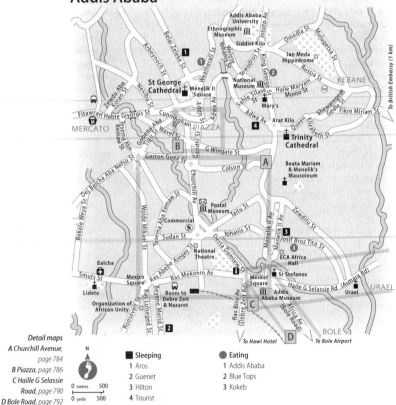

Addis Ababa

Detail maps
A Churchill Avenue,
  page 784
B Piazza, page 786
C Haille G Selassie
  Road, page 790
D Bole Road, page 792

N

0 metres   500
0 yards   500

■ **Sleeping**
1 Aros
2 Guenet
3 Hilton
4 Tourist

● **Eating**
1 Addis Ababa
2 Blue Tops
3 Kokeb

founding of the Organization of African Unity (OAU), which is still centred in Addis Ababa. Aesthetically, the interior of the building is more interesting than the exterior, for it contains majestic works in stained glass by Ethiopia's most celebrated artist, **Afewerk Tekle**, a man whose creations visitors will encounter again and again as they explore the sights of the capital. The huge windows depict the suffering of the people of Africa.

St Stephanos Church

South from Africa Hall, immediately past the bridge spanning the Bantiyiteku River and opposite the *National Hotel*, St Stephanos Church deserves a few minutes attention if only to see how the Orthodox religion exploited the possibilities of 20th-century architecture. A pale stone building shaped with no-nonsense right angles, flanked by an obelisk-like tower and riddled for some reason with square and cross-shaped holes, it is a striking departure from the traditional style of Ethiopian churches. However, the pleasant wooded grounds around it soften the impact of its modernist appearance.

Meskel Square

Past St Stephanos you quickly arrive at the huge amphitheatre of Meskel Square (also spelt Maskal and Meskal), previously known as **Abiot (Revolution) Square**. It is formed by both the natural contours of the area and by the convergence of several wide roads. Soon after sunrise, squads of young athletes and sportsmen take advantage of the early-morning quiet and use the square for jogging, exercises and games of soccer. Later in the day, however, the square is the scene of a different type of exertion, as simply trying to cross it and dodge the traffic that approaches from all sides requires physical effort and stamina. The square has a history of being used for parades and ceremonies. At the **Festival of Meskel** – or the 'Finding of the True Cross' as it is known in English – on 27 September, thousands of people assemble to witness the lighting of an enormous conical bonfire by the **Patriarch of the Orthodox Church**. Back in the years of the Marxist Dergue regime, on the other hand, rallies were staged every September to commemorate the 1974 Revolution, and portraits of Marx, Engels, Lenin and Comrade Mengistu used to adorn the square.

Ethiopia

Addis Ababa Museum

Up some stairs at the southern side of the square stands the Addis Ababa Museum, housed in a building with a flaking but still impressive wooden façade that was once the residence of Menelik II's War Minister, Ras Biru Wolde Gabriel. The museum was opened in 1986, the year of Addis Ababa's centenary, a fact that is reflected among the exhibits – some of them are gifts that were presented to the capital by organizations and other cities, both Ethiopian and foreign, to mark its 100th birthday. Other exhibits tell the story of the young Addis Ababa and its founders. The city's early history is shown in grainy old photographs of the original settlement in the Entoto Hills, of Filwoha, and then of the first post office, hotel, pharmacy, train, car, etc to appear in Addis Ababa proper. Meanwhile, portraits, ceremonial costumes, jewellery and other artefacts give some impression of the lives and characters of the couple responsible for the creation of the city, Menelik II and Taytu. In later rooms the museum focuses less on Addis Ababa and becomes slightly disorganized. Here, it devotes space to the Ethiopian patriots who resisted the Italian occupation, and various handicrafts and agricultural, household, religious and musical artefacts are displayed, as well as some sculptures and paintings, including a couple by Afewerk Tekle. It is a shame that the museum wanders a little in this manner but nevertheless it offers very good value for money. ■ *0830-1230, 1330-1730 Mon-Fri, 0830-1230 Sat and Sun. US$0.25, includes tour that lasts almost an hour.*

Churchill Avenue

Walk west from Meskel Square, past the **National Stadium,** and you will arrive at the city's main thoroughfare. Churchill Avenue climbs for a good 2½ km from the **railway station**, with its modest and picturesque and vaguely Mediterranean façade of small arches, columns and balconies, up to near the **City Hall**, which is distinctive because of its Axum-inspired tower. Regrettably the clock rarely seems to be working nowadays. More landmarks appear as you make your way up Churchill – the circular ***Commercial Bank of Ethiopia*** building, described euphemistically as resembling a 'giant flower', but more likely to remind you of a hovering flying saucer; the black stone statue of the **Lion of Judah** near the National Theatre, its crowned head squinting down from a long jagged-maned neck; and above that to the left, the **Tiglachin Monument** dedicated to the Ethiopians who perished in the 1977-78 conflict with Somalia.

Postal Museum Across from the Tiglachin Monument are the premises of Ethiopia's largest post office, in which you'll find Addis Ababa's Postal Museum. Don't be deterred if the glass doors at the end of the corridor leading to the museum are locked – ask in the offices left of the doors and you should find someone who can give you a tour inside. The enthusiasm of the staff here is infectious. Even if you arrive with the opinion that stamps rival train-spotting for dullness, you'll soon be converted. As your guide will explain, stamps have a massive educational value – their illustrations record the natural, historical, cultural and religious features of their countries – and the stamps that have adorned Ethiopian letters over the last century or so are an able demonstration of this. In the museum's archives you'll see stamps covering topics as diverse as Lalibela's churches, the country's first airplane, traditional ceremonial robes, freshwater fish, hairstyles, bracelets, the Meskel

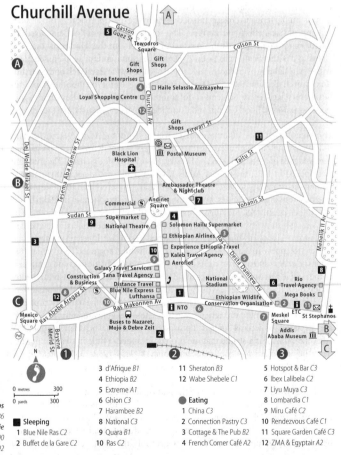

Churchill Avenue

Related maps
A Piazza, page 786
B Haille G Selassie Road, page 790
C Bole Road, page 792

0 metres 300
0 yards 300

■ **Sleeping**
1 Blue Nile Ras *C2*
2 Buffet de la Gare *C2*
3 d'Afrique *B1*
4 Ethiopia *B2*
5 Extreme *A1*
6 Ghion *C3*
7 Harambee *B2*
8 National *C3*
9 Quara *B1*
10 Ras *C2*

11 Sheraton *B3*
12 Wabe Shebele *C1*

● **Eating**
1 China *C3*
2 Connection Pastry *C3*
3 Cottage & The Pub *B2*
4 French Corner Café *A2*

5 Hotspot & Bar *C3*
6 Ibex Lalibela *C2*
7 Liyu Muya *C3*
8 Lombardia *C1*
9 Miru Café *C2*
10 Rendezvous Café *C1*
11 Square Garden Café *C3*
12 ZMA & Egyptair *A2*

festivities, and the Battle Adwa where Menelik II achieved perhaps his greatest feat and defeated an invading Italian army. Meanwhile, you don't need a history book to know what happened in Ethiopia in the early 1970s when you see how the stamps depicting an elderly Emperor Haile Selassie are replaced by ones bearing the hammer and sickle of the Dergue regime. ■ *0900-1215, 1330-1715, Mon-Fri. US$0.45. The Philatelic Services section of the adjacent post office sells an extensive, colourful catalogue of Ethiopian stamps for US$12.50.*

Mercato Closer to the top of Churchill Avenue you can turn west or east to visit two of Addis Ababa's liveliest neighbourhoods. Walk along Gaston Guez or Wavel streets and you will soon find yourself approaching Mercato, the largest market in Ethiopia and, according to some claims, in the whole of Africa. Mercato provides a taste of Addis Ababa at its best and worst. The shops, stalls and warehouses along its labyrinth of streets are stocked with a near-infinite variety of goods, while the dense crowds ensure that the opportunities for people-watching are as rich as the opportunities for shopping. The buzz in Mercato is exhilarating, especially on Saturdays when the area is at its busiest. On the other hand you will encounter in Mercato levels of hustle and hassle that you will not find elsewhere in Addis Ababa, and it has more than its fair share of pickpockets. Behind the shopping streets thousands of unfortunates have to live in squalid impoverished alleyways. A much-repeated and sensible piece of advice for tourists is to make two expeditions into Mercato. On your first visit carry as little money as possible and simply look around and decide what you would like to buy. The second time, when there is no need to loiter and deliberate (and attract unwanted attention), bring money and quickly buy the items you have decided upon.

Piazza Turning right where Churchill Avenue terminates at Cunningham Street, you will come to Piazza, an area that has some rough edges like its neighbour to the west, but is altogether less frantic in atmosphere. Piazza boasts a good selection shops, including giftshops, jewellers and silversmiths (see Shopping, page 800). The most sophisticated of these are contained in some new terraced buildings on Cunningham Street that look down the slope into the lower environs of southern Addis Ababa. There are also branches of the *Commercial Bank of Ethiopia*, the *National Tour Operator, Ethiopian Airlines*, two cinemas, some reasonably priced restaurants and cafés, one decidedly cheap-and-cheerful nightclub and a bewildering number of small pubs that attract large crowds after nightfall. For slickness and elegance, the shops, cuisine and nightlife of Piazza cannot compare with those offered by a more prestigious district like, say, the Bole Road, but if you want to save money, still have fun and feel that you have authentically experienced something of Ethiopia, Piazza is a good place to start.

Menelik II Square A short walk north from the top end of Churchill Avenue, above Piazza and the City Hall, brings you to Menelik II Square, where the dominant feature is a statue of the city's founder on horseback, in a war-like pose. At the side of the square stands **St George Cathedral** (Giorgis), which Menelik II built in 1896 in the traditional octagonal shape to commemorate his victory at the Battle of Adwa. Subsequent monarchs, including Zauditu in 1916 and Haile Selassie in 1930, were crowned here. The cathedral's name indicates the status given to St George in Ethiopia's pantheon of saints – visitors from England will be surprised at the degree of reverence that their country's patron saint receives here.

To learn something about the culture of Ethiopia's Orthodox Church , visit the small **museum** on the cathedral grounds which has a wide range of religious paraphernalia on display: tapestries, paintings, ceremonial robes, processional crosses, musical instruments, communion vessels, incense burners and prayer sticks. Of particular interest is a collection of religious books, handwritten – a process that often took two years – on a parchment made from sheep or goatskin and bound in

Ethiopia

wood and leather. The beautiful Ge'ez script is mainly in black ink but the most important words and sentences are transcribed in red. Also present are costumes, jewellery and portraits of Zauditu, who was something of a patron to the cathedral; and various depictions of St George, on canvas and wood and in ceramic, which have been given as gifts to the cathedral by visiting dignitaries. It seems a pity that no official visitor from England has had the foresight to bring a gift of this nature, given that the English and the Ethiopians accord such importance to the same saint. ■ *Museum open Tue-Sun 0900-1200 and 1400-1700. US$1.25.*

If the guide is feeling generous you may also be allowed to ascend the belltower above the museum – hold tight to the inside railing as there's nothing at the edge of the twisting staircase to prevent you from tumbling off. The bell hanging at the top was a present from Italy, but on display below is an older and bigger bell that came as a gift from pre-revolutionary Russia. You may also be permitted inside the cathedral itself. The interior has had to be painted twice, as the original murals were destroyed during the Italian occupation. The paintings that currently adorn the cathedral include depictions of the Madonna, the Day of Judgement, the Queen of Sheba and Haile Selassie's coronation; the most striking ones are the work of Afewerk Tekle.

Addis Ababa University Another neighbourhood worth visiting is that of the university, around the intersection known as **Siddist Kilo**, which can be reached by following Weatheral Street from the north side of Menelik II Square, across the Kechene River and up past the Yedkatit 12 Hospital. The university began life in 1950 as the University College of Addis Ababa, gradually expanded its number of faculties and mutated into Haile

Piazza

Related map
A Churchill
Avenue, page 784

● Eating		
■ **Sleeping**	1 Acapulco & Bar	4 Café Chaud
1 Baro	2 Arada	5 Castelli's
2 National	3 British Council	6 Cave Hotel
3 St George	Cafeteria	7 Continental Hotel
4 Taitu		8 GK
5 Tsigereda		9 Interlangano &
6 Wutma		Africans Bookshop
		10 Omar Khayyam
		11 Oroscope

4 Taitu
5 Tsigereda
6 Wutma

● Eating
1 Acapulco & Bar
2 Arada
3 British Council Cafeteria

4 Café Chaud
5 Castelli's
6 Cave Hotel
7 Continental Hotel
8 GK
9 Interlangano & Africans Bookshop
10 Omar Khayyam
11 Oroscope

12 Port Snack Bar
13 Shamrock
14 Soul Kid Pastry
15 Tsedey
16 Twins & Bar
17 Veronicas
18 Wing

B Refer to bars in text

Selassie University in 1961. It received its present name after the 1974 Revolution. The main campus can be entered at the north side of Siddist Kilo. It contains some uninspiring, blockish buildings that seem to bedevil college and university campuses the world over, but the grounds around them are green, wooded and extremely appealing. Bring your passport as the guards at the campus entrance need to see some identification before they can let you inside.

Lion of Judah's Lions

The Emperor Haile Selassie kept his own pride of lions at his palace in Addis Ababa. A lion would accompany him, on a lead, when official visitors were received. When touring Europe in 1924, Haile Selassie took six lions with him, giving four to the French and two to King George V.

One building there that certainly has style and antiquity is the **Gannata Le'ul**, designed in 1934 as a palace for Haile Selassie and now the university's administrative centre and also home to the **Institute of Ethiopian Studies**. Haile Selassie had only two years to enjoy his new palace: when the Italians invaded in 1936 and he fled the capital, it was first commandeered as a barracks for Italian troops, then turned into a headquarters for the second Italian Viceroy Rodolfo Graziani. In 1937 the palace became the flash point for one of the most traumatic episodes in modern Ethiopian history. Two Eritreans attempted to kill Graziani and his entourage there by throwing grenades at them. The assassination attempt failed but the Italians saw fit to slaughter several thousand innocent Ethiopian civilians during three days of reprisals. The tragedy is now commemorated by a sculpted obelisk at Siddist Kilo called **Yekatit 12** (the date in the Ethiopian calendar on which the assassination bid took place).

Another reminder of the fascist occupation stands next to the flagpole facing the palace. Fourteen stone steps rise in a column, with a statue of a lion sitting at the top. Built by the Italians in 1936, the steps represent the 14 years that had passed since Mussolini's march on Rome in 1922.

Inside the palace are two important facilities belonging to the Institute of Ethiopian Studies: a **library** with a huge collection of books, periodicals, microfilm and historical manuscripts including an extensive English-language book collection on Ethiopia, and the Ethnographic Museum on the first and second floors. This latter establishment is surely the best museum in Ethiopia. Its main exhibition – hundreds of artefacts relating to the various ethnic groups of the different regions of Ethiopia – is well organized, well labelled and well displayed in a large, handsome white hall with chandeliers. Among the most eye-catching items on view are some carved, one-piece wooden chairs from Illubador, a giant wooden container for *tella* (Ethiopian home-brewed beer) from Jimma, papyrus boats that used to navigate the waters of Lakes Ziway and Tana, and a replica of an Afar nomad's hut – an igloo-shaped structure called a *halalwa*, complete with a rifle suspended from the domed ceiling. Perhaps the strangest exhibits are a clutch of 'funeral statues' constructed for the funerals of Konso warriors. These are grotesque wooden effigies of the enemy warriors or animals that the deceased had slain during their lifetimes. The statues have sinister, staring eyes fashioned from ostrich eggshells, and fang-like teeth made of goat bones.

Ethnographic Museum

Away from this hall, another section of the museum commemorates the building's tenure as a royal palace, giving visitors a chance to see Haile Selassie's bedroom, dressing room and marbled bathroom. Also on display is a spectacular tapestry portrait of the emperor as well as his military uniform, medals and caps. A nearby room is devoted to Ethiopian money and contains examples of just about every form of currency that has been used in the country, from ancient Axumite coins to present-day birr. Among the more eccentric items used for buying and selling in Ethiopia were bars of salt, used in transactions from the 15th-19th centuries, and gun cartridges used in the latter part of the 19th century.

Ethiopia

The newest section of the museum, opened in May 2001, is an elegant set of rooms with subdued lighting on the second floor. Much of this section is devoted to Ethiopia's religious art. There are carved crosses, texts and manuscripts, diptychs and triptychs. The largest triptychs on display concern the life, crucifixion and resurrection of Christ, and St George's battle against the dragon and his martyrdom. They tell their stories scene by dramatic scene, almost like medieval comic strips. Another part of this new section deals with Ethiopian music and, as well as exhibiting examples of common indigenous instruments like the *druar* (a type of lyre) and *massinko* (a one-stringed lute played with a bow), there are also lesser-known Ethiopian variants on the drum, horn, flute, trumpet, bell and rattle. Some of them, including the long, ungainly *habaro* drum, are used only in religious ceremonies.

■ *0800-1200, 1330-1700 Tue-Thu; 0800-1130, 1330-1700 Fri; 1000-1800 Sat and Sun. US$2.50. The museum shop is on the way to the ticket desk.*

National Museum Further down King George Street, on the right, you'll see the entrance to the National Museum. Despite its good reputation, if you've just paid a visit to the Ethnographic Museum this institution may come as a slight disappointment. The choice of exhibits seems a bit scattershot at times and many items are displayed without any written information. It will certainly help your understanding and appreciation of the museum if there's a guide available when you arrive. If not, there are parts of the building where you'll simply have to look and wonder.

Without the services of a guide, the basement level, devoted to palaeontology, is probably the most enlightening as everything is labelled with helpful notes. Among the variety of bones and fossils you'll see a replica of the remains of **Lucy**, the 3,200,000-year-old 'Australopithecus' fossil discovered in northeast Ethiopia in 1974 and believed to be one of our earliest ancestors, if not a direct one. To Ethiopians Lucy is known as *Dinknesh*, which means 'you are wonderful' in Amharic. The ground floor contains an array of artefacts – again, with notes – relating to the pre-Axumite societies in Tigray and Eritrea, to the Axum civilization itself that existed during the first millennium AD, to the Islamic culture that sprang up around Harar, and to the Zagwe dynasty that was responsible for Lalibela's rock-hewn churches in the middle ages. These include skulls, hand-tools, pots and jars, stone seals, figurines and statues, jewellery, altars, crosses, even a fragment of a dice game and a wonderful oil lamp fashioned in representation of a dog hunting an ibex. There is a large collection of female stone statues, believed to be 2,500-year-old fertility symbols. There is also a collection of modern imperial robes and a selection of the more than 200 designs of crosses found in Ethiopia. Many of these crosses are decorative, but some have uses such as the one with a small spoon at the end, which was used for cleaning the wax from ears. At the centre of the ground floor there are also items belonging to the last members of Ethiopia's royalty, including the robes, crowns and saddle of Menelik II and the chair of his daughter Zauditu.

The first floor is more of a gallery, displaying religious paintings from medieval times, paintings of historical events and examples of 20th-century Ethiopian art. Unfortunately, only Afewerk Tekle's impressive work in oils, *African Heritage*, is presented with any background information. The second floor contains various handicrafts, pottery, weapons, religious artefacts, tools and utensils, costumes and jewellery, but these too are unlabelled.

■ *0830-1700. US$1.25. No photos allowed.*

Other sights At the next corner down from the National Museum, **Mary's Church** (Kidist Miriam) warrants a few minutes' investigation. The church itself is of a newish design but is enlivened by the splashes of yellow, red, blue and green on the windows and doors. Stone angels guard the entrance and above it rises an elaborate belltower with three pillared tiers.

A walk of a few minutes brings you down to **Arat Kilo** where there stands another commemorative obelisk, though marking a happier occasion than its counterpart at

Siddist Kilo (see above). This is the **Megabit 28 Monument**, built in memory of the day in 1941 when Addis Ababa was delivered back into Ethiopian hands.

Located a short distance east of Arat Kilo, on Queen Elizabeth Street, is the **Zoological Museum**, which, despite serious overcrowding and shortage of space, is worth checking out. The display of water birds – cranes, cormorants, flamingos, herons, pelicans, storks, ibis and so on – is impressively varied and the arrays of beautifully patterned butterflies a are a delight. As well as stuffed and preserved specimens there is a wealth of bones, fossils, heads, pelts and hoof-prints and these, along with the written and statistical information given about Ethiopia's national parks, make the museum a useful port of call for anyone planning to explore the country's wilderness areas.

The region south of Arat Kilo is home to two palaces, **Jubilee Palace** halfway down Menelik II Avenue and **Menelik Palace** in the walled-off grounds at the top of the avenue, but for security reasons both of these are out of bounds to tourists: Jubilee Palace serves as the official residence for the Ethiopian president while Menelik Palace is used as the government's headquarters. However, there is full public access to a couple of interesting churches in the same area. Below Queen Elizabeth Street stands **Trinity Cathedral**, completed in the early 1940s although it looks considerably older. Eight statues stand imposingly in front of its entrance doors, a pair of ornate towers flank its sides, and sections of stonework on the building itself have been sculpted with flair. Interred in the surrounding grounds are a number of Ethiopian patriots who lost their lives while resisting the Italian occupation, and you'll also see a memorial to the government ministers who were killed at the outset of the Dergue regime in 1974. The remains of the most famous victim of that regime arrived at Trinity Cathedral in the year 2000: in a large and emotional ceremony the bones of Emperor Haile Selassie were finally laid to rest here.

South from Trinity Cathedral, following the road that forms a loop at the top end of Menelik II Avenue, you'll find the entrance to **Beata Mariam Church**, which is also known as **Menelik's Mausoleum** on account of it being the resting place for the remains of Addis Ababa's founder. Built on the orders of his daughter Zauditu, the mausoleum is a majestic, grey-stone building topped by a large dome and with eight sculpted lions positioned like watchful sentries along the bases of its walls. **NB** You may be approached and asked if you wish to visit the 'museum' here. The vault beneath the building that houses the tombs of Menelik, Taytu and Zuaditu does also contain a few historical and religious artefacts, but the 15-minute tour in no way justifies the rip-off US8 you'll be charged for entry fee, obligatory donation to 'the church', and guide fee.

Essentials

Sleeping

The hotels range from the most expensive and prestigious that Ethiopia has to offer, to a few decidedly basic ones that might suit travellers on a tight budget. Addis Ababa now has a glut of fairly upmarket, very similar hotels, and finding something distinctive to say about each one can sometimes be difficult! International chains are here, such as the **L** *Addis Ababa Hilton*, Menelik II Av, PO Box 1164, T518400, F510064, hilton.addis@telecom.net.et, and the **L** *Sheraton Addis*, Taitu St, PO Box 6002, Woreda 14, Kebele 24, Addis Ababa, T171717, F172727. Reservations AddisEthiopia@luxurycollection.com

■ *on maps*
Price codes:
on inside front cover

A-B *Queen of Sheba*, PO Box 5090 T615400, F613174, QueenShebaHotel@telecom.net.et A hulking white hotel on the Haile G Selassie Rd opposite the Bulgarian Embassy. All rooms have a living room as well as a bedroom, bathroom, phone, satellite TV and fridge. Restaurant with buffet breakfasts plus buffet dinners on Sat. Terrace bar. Business services include internet access. **B** *Ghion*, PO Box 1643, Ras Desta Damtew Av, T513222, F510278. Accepts

Ethiopia

Ethiopia

most credit cards. Bungalows, suites and apartments and has an unusual glass-sided *tukul* with a connecting bridge linking it to the reception. Olympic-size swimming pool with natural hot-spring water (free to residents), tennis court, function rooms, cyber café/business centre, NTO taxi and tour desk, gift shop. 3 restaurants, poolside café, bars, 'nightclub and casino discotheque' extensive gardens, the Saba Rooms have ceiling paintings of the Queen of Sheba legend. *Travel Ethiopia*, T525478, has a base in the hotel grounds. **B** *Imperial*, PO Box 2966/2020, T293329, F293332, imperialhotel@telecom.net.et, on the road linking Megenenya roundabout with Bole Rd, on the right as you head north. Upmarket facilities, en-suite rooms, national and western food in restaurant, business centre offering computer and email services. *Imperial Travel*, on the premises, will arrange air tickets, car hire, bookings, tours and safaris. Also has a gym, with sauna, steam room and massage plus a nightclub. Convenient for the airport, but surroundings are barren and unappealing with lots of construction work nearby. **B-C** *Global*, PO Box 25245 code 1000, T664766, F664723, to the left if going south down Debre Zeit Rd, after the *Hawi* but before the *Concorde*. Brand new hotel, closer to the city centre than some of the other upmarket hotels on that road. Rooms with en-suite bathrooms, sauna, steam bath, *Omo Restaurant*, *Global Bar*, and *Bao Terrace*. Serves European dishes. Gym and nightclub are currently 'in the works'. Unfortunate luggage porter is dressed like a Great White Hunter in an old Tarzan movie. **B-C** *Hotel Ethiopia*, PO Box 1131, Yohannes Av, east of the intersection between Sudan St/Churchill Av, T517400-11, F510871. Located in business and commercial district. All rooms have TV, bathroom and phones. Restaurant serves European and Ethiopian food, has a lounge bar, terrace café called *Ethio Café*, souvenir shop and function rooms. **B-C** *Ibex*, PO Box 21429, T654400, F653737, unmarked street off the Bole Rd, not far from the airport. New, comfortable hotel, cocktail lounge, bar, restaurant, special buffets on Tue, Thu, Sat. Lots of facilities including nightclub, live music, gym, sauna, massage, indoor games and internet services. **B-C** *Ras Amba*, PO Box 34063, T556634/6, F551587, up on the slope on the left of Queen Elizabeth Rd heading from Arat Kilo. Blue-painted rooms with bathrooms, TVs and phones, singles have showers, doubles have baths. Bar, roof-top restaurant with magnificent city views and good food. Internet service. Majestic steps twist up from the roads to the front doors. **B-C** *Wabe Shebelle*, PO Box 3154, Ras Abebe Aregay St, which connects Mexico Sq with the main intersection on lower Churchill, T515187, F518477. Rooms have bath/shower, satellite TV, balconies, phones (no charge for local calls). Suites have fridges. Restaurants include the 11th-floor rooftop *Addis Seguenet* and bar. Post office, car rental, *Ethiopian Airlines* office etc, nearby. Confusingly the reception entrance is marked 'Restaurant'.

C *Airport Motel*, PO Box 100520, T610422, F610577, turn right off Bole Rd after leaving the airport. Single-storey, vaguely cubist appearance. Clean s/c rooms, bar, restaurant, local and international food, games room with pool and darts and a garden to the rear. **C** *Ararat*, PO Box 155, T461166, F461177, on the hillside above Megenenya, left of Fikre Maryam Aba Techam St if leaving town. Accommodation, food and view are good. **C** *Atlas*, PO Box 101471, T611610, F613661, on road running parallel to Bole Rd linking with Haile G Selassie

Haile G Selassie Road

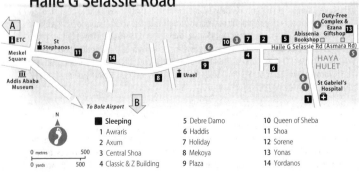

■ Sleeping
1 Awraris
2 Axum
3 Central Shoa
4 Classic & Z Building
5 Debre Damo
6 Haddis
7 Holiday
8 Mekoya
9 Plaza
10 Queen of Sheba
11 Shoa
12 Sorene
13 Yonas
14 Yordanos

Rd at Urael. Blockish exterior softened by trees and foliage, very friendly, helpful reception staff. En-suite rooms with TVs showers and phones, bar, 1st-floor restaurant serves national and European dishes. Wide selection of English-language papers available at reception. **C** *Axum*, PO Box 40318, Haile G Selassie Rd up from Meskel Sq, not far before Haya-hulet, T613916, F614265. Large white 5-storey building. Reception area has nice wood-carved panelling. Rooms have en-suite bathroom/toilet, hot water, TV and phone. Restaurant has lunch for US$3.60, 'candlelit' dinners on Thu, US$4.50 and buffet dinner on Sat, US$4.50, bar. Discounts for longer stays. **C** *Buffet de la Gare*, near station, PO Box 2381, T517888, F515959. Excellent value, ideal location, bungalow style, first-rate restaurant. All highly recommended. **C** *Central Shoa*, PO Box 21352, T611454, F610063. Left side of Haile G Selassie Rd as you approach Megenenya. En-suite rooms with TV, phone and fridge. Bar, restaurant – screened off from the main room serving western food. Tidy courtyard. 10% discount after 1 week. **C** *Concorde*, PO Box 3411, T654959, F653193, Debre Zeit Rd on the right after the *Hawi Hotel*. Upmarket hotel with usual facilities, but in addition has a piano bar, *Le Grand Café*, a night-club called *The Dome Club* and, best of all, a classy Chinese restaurant called the *China Paradise*. Worth visiting even if not staying there. **C** *Crown*, PO Box 101299, T341444, F341428, sited about 10 km down the Debre Zeit Rd. A well-known hotel but rather distant from city centre. The opening of the planned ring road should make it more accessible. Facilities include restaurant, bar, hairdresser, boutique, fax and computer services but its best-known feature is the coffee shop built like a giant coffee pot, and the traditional dancing shows. **C** *Desalegn*, around the corner from the *Atlas Hotel*, opposite the EU Building. Pleasant, prosperous neighbourhood, new hotel with en-suite facilities. Bar and terrace bar, plus restaurant offering national and western menu. Has a gym, sauna and steam bath and games room (pool and billiards). Live classical music accompanies the buffet lunch on Tue, Thu and Sat plus violin nights in the *Terrace Bar*. **C** *Filowaha Hotel*, PO Box 2450, T519100, F524344, corner of Yohanis St heading towards Churchill Av. Good value. Fuelled by the same springs as the *Finfine Hotel*. The steady stream of locals buying tickets for the baths make it feel more like a public amenity with hotel rooms attached than a hotel. Restaurant, bar, and sauna and massage. **C** *Harambee*, Yohanis St, PO Box 1131, T514000, F517533, near Churchill Av. Rooms have private bathroom, TV hire is US$1 extra. On the 1st floor is the *Harrar Restaurant* – European food – and the *Magala Lounge Bar*, decorated in the style of the old city of Harar. On the 2nd floor is *Fan-Fan Terrace*, a snack bar. **C** *Lalibela*, PO Box 7344, T614917, F615522, going down Bole Rd from the airport, follow the signposted turning on the left. Closest hotel to the airport. Rooms have TV, shower and phone and there's a bar, national and western restaurants, live music 2000-2400. Reception area handsomely decorated with wooden panelling. Discounts available with some travel agencies. Location is off-putting with a cluster of partially built edifices, non-sealed road, all windy and rubbish strewn. **C** *Meridian*, Bole Rd, PO Box 182160, T615050, F615092, meridian-hotel@telecom.net.et, from the airport on the right. Rooms are very spacious with bathroom, TV, large beds. Bar has big, comfortable armchairs. Restaurant does European-style meals. Internet access available. **C** *Plaza*, Haile G Selassie Rd, PO Box 4935, T612200, F613044, on the right past Urael Church. Rooms accommodate 2 people and have shower, TV and phone. Bar, restaurant serves national and western food. S/c, hot water. **C** *Semien*, Zeleke St, PO Box 7658, T550067, F551410, Simienhotel@telecom.net.et, to the right just past the *Aros Hotel* if heading north. North of city centre 20 mins' walk from Piazza or Siddist Kilo area. All very bright, posh and spacious with en-suite rooms, bar, restaurant (European food) gym, massage, sauna and souvenir shop. **C-D** *Classic*, PO Box 15294, T613598, F610946, opposite the *Holiday Hotel* on Haile G Selassie Rd at the side of the 'Z' Building. En-suite rooms with TVs, phones, bar and restaurant. In same

Ethiopia (vertical side text)

MEGENENYA

To Bole Airport

To Dessie & Debre Birhan

● **Eating**
1 Addis Peacock
2 La Terrazza
3 My Pub
4 Pride
5 Ras Snack
6 Saay Pastry
7 Tiru
8 Tukuls

Related maps
A Churchill
Avenue, page 784
B Bole Road, page 792

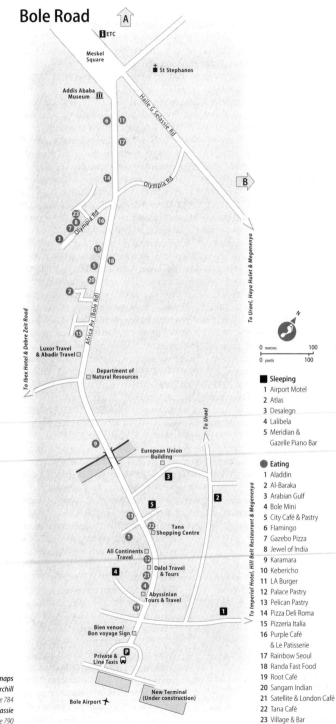

Bole Road

A

ⓘ ETC

Meskel
Square

✝ St Stephanos

Addis Ababa
Museum 🏛

Haile G Selassie Rd

⑥ ⑪

⑰

⑭

Olympia Rd

B

㉓
⑧
⑦
③

Olympia Rd

⑯

⑩
⑤ ⑱

⑳

② Africa Av (Bole Rd)

⑮

Luxor Travel
& Abadir Travel ☐

Department of
☐ Natural Resources

To Ibex Hotel & Debre Zeit Road

To Urael, Haya Hulet & Megenenya

N

| 0 metres | 100 |
| 0 yards | 100 |

⑨

European Union
Building

To Urael

❸

❺

⑬

㉒ Tana
☐ Shopping Centre

① All Continents ☐
Travel

⑫

❹ ☐ Dalol Travel
& Tours
㉑

④

☐ Abyssinian
Tours & Travel

⑲

Bien venue/
Bon voyage Sign ☐

❷

❶

To Imperial Hotel, Hill Belt Restaurant & Megenenya

Private &
Line Taxis 🅿

Bole Airport ✈

New Terminal
(Under construction)

■ Sleeping
1 Airport Motel
2 Atlas
3 Desalegn
4 Lalibela
5 Meridian &
   Gazelle Piano Bar

● Eating
1 Aladdin
2 Al-Baraka
3 Arabian Gulf
4 Bole Mini
5 City Café & Pastry
6 Flamingo
7 Gazebo Pizza
8 Jewel of India
9 Karamara
10 Kebericho
11 LA Burger
12 Palace Pastry
13 Pelican Pastry
14 Pizza Deli Roma
15 Pizzeria Italia
16 Purple Café
   & Le Patisserie
17 Rainbow Seoul
18 Randa Fast Food
19 Root Café
20 Sangarn Indian
21 Satellite & London Café
22 Tana Café
23 Village & Bar

Related maps
A Churchill
Avenue, page 784
B Haille G Sellassie
Road, page 790

Ethiopia

building are a couple of travel agents, a bank, photographic shop, a supermarket and a computer centre. **C-D** *Gedera*, PO Box 31452, T531900, F533893, off Queen Elizabeth Rd along the road leading to the Indian Chancellery. Rooms have bathrooms, TV and phones. Bar and restaurant serving local and international food. There is a buffet with live music every Thu. Fairly new hotel, with 2 sister hotels (same name) 10 km and 17 km out of central Addis Ababa. More appealing than many of its soulless competitors. **C-D** *Hotel d'Afrique*, Dej Wolde Mikael St, PO Box 1120, T517385. All rooms s/c, TV, phones. 2 restaurants, mosaic of Ethiopian folklore on wall of function room, lounge bar, terrace snack bar called *The Kunama*. The nightclub has been converted into a gym. **C-D** *Ras*, PO Box 1632, T517060. Near the bottom of Churchill Av just north of railway station, very popular, one of the oldest hotels in Addis, restaurants – European and national food and terrace café, bar, gardens. Has an international operator and can receive but not send faxes. The *Rocky Valley Safari Agency* is based in the hotel. Outside you run the gauntlet of a handful of 'chancers' ready to befriend/fleece you. **C-D** *Yordanos Hotel*, PO Box 1647, T515711, F516655, yordanoshotel@telecom.net.et, on a left turning on Haile G Selassie Rd, 10 mins' walk from Meskel Sq. Clean and friendly hotel, has about 30 rooms, no a/c, en-suite bathrooms, hot water/shower and flushing toilets, satellite TV bar, restaurant with Ethiopian and western cuisine, laundry and post facilities, not too noisy. Features an 'organ solo' at dinnertime in the main restaurant. Massage offered. Excellent value. Recommended.

D *Blue Nile Ras*, left-hand side of Ras Mekonin Av as you go east from Churchill Av, PO Box 1138, T511355. Regarded as the poor relation in the government chain that also includes the *Ras Hotel* and *Hotel d'Afrique*. Staff affable. Bar and restaurant serving Ethiopian and western food, a barber's shop and cybercafé in the front compound. Next to them is a 'garden-grill', an outdoor restaurant, with pleasant hedge-lined paths. **D** *Extreme*, Gaston Guez St, PO Box 6948, T553777, F551077, west of the roundabout near top of Churchill Av. Red-fronted, flat-roofed building in a beautiful location, quiet tree-lined road only minutes away from both Piazza and Mercato. Clean rooms, functional reception area with sofas and armchairs, bar, restaurant serving national and western food. Fully equipped gym, sauna although guests have to pay to use it. **D** *Finefare Adarash*, PO Box 2450, T514711, left side of Yohanis St going west from Menelik II Av. Lovely quaint, very atmospheric wooden hotel, gardened front terrace, rooms are in the verandahed wings either side. Ornate island bar past reception area. Above that, a restaurant serves national food. More gardens at back plus spa-style baths (non-residents pay 5.50birr). Barbers shop and video rental outlet on site. The décor was reputedly the work of Greek craftsmen. **D** *Guenet*, Beyene Metro St, south from Mexico Sq, PO Box 397 T518125. Resembles a rambling but spartan British boys boarding school that has seen better days – with several courtyards, hulking stone buildings with battered paintwork. Overpriced. Restaurant serves national and European food. 3 bars, tennis court, bowling alley and a children's playground, plus a gym (not functioning 'yet'). **D** *Hawi*, Debre Zeit Rd, right-hand side south of the city centre. Smart, pleasant, modern, well-run cosy hotel with just 10 rooms. Restaurant serves national and international food. Rather dwarfed by its neighbours the *Global and Concorde*. **D** *Holiday Hotel*, PO Box 258, T612081, F612627, Haile G Selassie Rd, between *Queen of Sheba and Axum Hotel*. Clean rooms with TV and phones, spacious and spotless bathroom, serve delicious Ethiopian and western food, friendly and helpful staff, sited close to a minibus stop, excellent value. **D** *Jerusalem*, Arbeynoch St, PO Box 16529, T551712, F550573, heading north from Piazza, near Ras Desta hospital. Situated about 2 km from the centre this offers very good value, its only disadvantage being its location. Has 2 bars and a restaurant, the food is cheaper and served faster in the bars. **D** *National Menelik II*, Av PO Box 100052, T515166, F513417. Lobby – adorned with the heads of various horned beasts – bar and restaurant on ground floor, offices on 1st floor and rooms on floors 2-7. Several tour/travel agencies have offices here: *Travel Ethiopia, Horizion Ethiopia Tours* and *Millennium Tour and Travel Agency*. Not to be confused with the *National Hotel* in the Piazza. **D** *Tourist*, PO Box 5518, T550122, right side of Adwa Av just before Arat Kilo, next to *Commercial Bank*. Resembles a relic of the Marxist years – no signs. Bare and functional, bar and restaurant passable, serves national and western food. **D-E** *Taitu*, middle of Piazza, T553244 (operator) or T560787 (reception), F552643. Built by Menelik II's wife, and is the oldest hotel in Addis. Used to be known as the *Awaris,* good meeting place. Plenty of rooms ranging from s/c with TV and phone in the main building to spartan rooms in the line of blocks at the back. Staff very friendly, service slow. Avoid the sandwiches. **D-E** *Yonas,* PO Box 110212, T184052, left of Haile G Selassie Rd, past Haya-Hulet, approaching Megenenya. Good value for money, spacious rooms, clean bathrooms, TV and phones in main rooms. Restaurant offers delicious food. Quite a distance from city centre.

E *Aros,* PO Box 22312, T553643, F553992, north of Piazza on Zeleke St to the right if going north. Seems happier as a bustling nightspot than a hotel, DJ nightly. Restaurant serves national and western food. A beauty salon and internet service are planned shortly. **E** *Baro,* Muniyem St, PO Box 23688, T559846, F551447, hotelbaro@telecom.net.et, facing the *Wutma Hotel,* off Queen Elizabeth St – often called 'English Rd' by locals – east of Churchill Av, Piazza area. Small bar and restaurant, pleasant leafy courtyard, passageways wind off to the rooms, internet access and fax, CNN on satellite TV, hot water, not very clean, some rooms have squat toilets and tiny private bathrooms. Friendly staff. You can organize a 4WD to Omo NP from here, and they offer left-luggage facilities. Prices have risen with fame – *Wutma* offers better value. **E** *Debre Damo,* Haile G Selassie Rd, PO Box 13139, T612630, F622920, on left just before Haya-Hulet. A pleasant red and grey brick building with a leafy compound at the back. Some small colourful murals on walls between the room doors. Hot showers. Staff very friendly, nice atmosphere. Recommended. Restaurant serves national and western food. Free taxi service to Bole Airport. **E** *Haddis,* PO Box 15972, T181493, down the side street opposite the *Axum Hotel* on Haile G Selassie Rd, turn left left past the school, well sign posted. Rooms OK, en suite, but over-priced for its location. **E** *National,* T551678, Piazza – same street as the *Taitu,* below Cunningham St. Some scope for self-catering in rooms with kitchenettes but the noisy, popular bar, may prove to be a drawback, restaurant, some upstairs rooms are small but clean, offering better value than the *Taitu.* The showers in the back courtyard are tiled with heated water. (There is another hotel with the same name.) **E** *Quara,* Sudan St, PO Box 40604, T158095, on the right if coming from Churchill Av. Pleasantly dilapidated hotel, restaurant serving national food and draught beer may be more of a draw that the s/c rooms. Sign is in Amharic but distinctive because of its blue and white corrugated-iron fence. **E** *St George,* next to *Wing Restaurant,* by Adwa Av, T119415. Easy to miss at the edge of the Piazza. Rooms surprisingly clean and well furnished – better than the nearby *Taitu Hotel.* Dubious communal toilets/showers. Cosy restaurant/bar with Ethiopian and western food with draught beer on tap. Hospitable staff. **E** *Wutma Hotel,* Muniyem St, central Piazza, PO Box 9919, T125360, near the *Baro Hotel.* Basic facilities, cheap, hot water, quiet, very clean. Cosy, comfortable lobby/bar/restaurant area. Serves good egg breakfast dishes, and pasta/fish dishes. Tables are candlelit at night. Great location. Luggage storage lockers available. The upstairs bathrooms suffer from poor water pressure with trickling showers only.

F *Ensaro,* off Queen Elizabeth Rd along the road leading to the Indian Chancellery. Almost in the shadow of the *Gedera Hotel.* Rooms are small, clean, sparsely furnished with own toilet and sink. No showers, not even communal ones. Main building has a bar but no restaurant. **F** *Mekoya,* T530710, on the right going up Haile G Selassie Rd from Meskel Sq, before Urael Church. Pretty rock-bottom with cell-like rooms, unglazed windows, wooden shutters. Quieter than similar places in Mercato or Piazza. However, it is very cheap US$1.50. **F** *Michael,* T161263, south down Debre Zeit Rd on a right turning. Possibly the cheapest en-suite rooms in Addis Ababa. Big beds, sink with small adjoining bathrooms with flush toilets. Clean. 20 mins' walk to the railway station. **F** *MG,* same road and beyond the *Michael Hotel.* Panelled bar at front has a shabby charm, back courtyard looks like a shanty town. 15 birr a night – only try here if the alternatives are full. **F** *Monaliza,* T125232, down the same road as the *Ensaro* off Queen Elizabeth Rd. Resembles a holiday camp attempt at being a hotel. Cell-like rooms reached down a pathway, window shutters but no glass. Rooms are fairly clean. No shower at all. Restaurant serves national food. **F** *Palm,* T155119, right side of Tito St going east from Menelik II Av. Windows have glass. Communal toilets unpleasant. Bustling bar at front, helpful friendly staff. **F** *Shoa,* T510016, a short distance up Haile G

Selassie Rd from Meskel Sq on the left. Even cheaper if you choose the room without a shower. Mainly of interest for its atmospheric traditional restaurant in the western-style building at the back. National food US$2 per person, live music/dancing. **F Sorene**, T189996, on the road from the Megenenya roundabout towards Bole Airport. White stone place, room with a bath, excellent value despite being some distance from the city centre. **F Tsigereda**, Piazza, T115534, next door to the *National Hotel*. A little further back than its neighbour, and a little quieter. The rooms are bare, but have very large beds. Communal facilities are poor. **F Warka**, T503346, heading south down Debre Zeit Rd on left side shortly after crossing the railway tracks. A survivable budget option within 15 mins' walk of railway station. Rooms are OK – glass in windows. The front bar area is fairly smart. Small restaurant. Along **Fatiwrari Habte Giyorgis St**, near the bus station, there are many basic hotels for less than US$3 a night, some do not have showers. Many bars also have cheap rooms at the back.

Eating

Blue Tops, King George St (which links Arat and Sidist Kilos), is very smart and clean and attracts tourists and wealthy Ethiopians. western menu, pasta, pizza and grills. Most expensive starter costs US$8, soup US$2, main dishes up to US$5. Security check before admission. Snack menu is cheaper. *Castelli's*, T111058, Gandhi St in Piazza area close to *Ethiopian Airways*. Local 18th- and 19th-century paintings, high standard, need to book at weekends. Speciality is spaghetti in gorgonzola sauce. Attracts well-healed tourists. *China Restaurant*, end of Desta Damtew St near entrance to *Ghion Hotel*. Well-regarded restaurant, wide variety of excellent Chinese dishes (the noodle dishes are especially good), well decorated in Oriental style with pristine toilets. *Finfine Adarash Hotel*, Atse Yohanis Av, near the *Hilton Hotel*. Ethiopian cuisine, leather stools and mats in one dining area, previously the home of a *Ras* (nobleman) who used Greek craftsmen to decorate and carve the wooden interior. *Kokeb*, behind Africa Hall on Menelik II Av on 10th floor. Decorated with horse-riding equipment and traditional jewellery. Expensive and fashionable, serving multi-course Ethiopian meals as well as western food. Difficult to locate on foot but most of the clientele are driven there anyway.

Expensive
● on maps
Price codes:
on inside front cover

Most of the hotels contain restaurants

Addis Ababa Restaurant, just north of Piazza, shown as 'Weatherall St' on some maps. Wonderful atmospheric old building, reputedly once the home of Queen Zauditu. Traditional Ethiopian food, in a circular dining room (*tukul*), with crimson walls and lots of carved woodwork. Smaller areas off the side provide extra dining space. Serves an excellent variety of *wat*, (see page 776) and *tej* – food is eaten the local way, without knives and forks. *Aladdin Restaurant*, right turning from Bole Rd past the bridge. Good Arabian food. For budget travellers it is possible to order several 'starters' to make up an excellent meal. *Al-Baraka Restaurant*, Bole Rd, towards airport between *Sangam* and *Pizzeria Italia* down a zig-zagging road. Well signposted. Smart restaurant specializing in Arabian food in an area with several Middle Eastern embassies. Main dishes include fish, lamb, chicken and kebabs and 'marinated baby lamb' for US$37.50. *Cottage Restaurant and Pub*, near the *Harambee Hotel* on Desta Demtew Av, offers Swiss food – cheese fondu – and Swiss chalet-style décor with wood panelling veering on the Gothic. International menu. Has a bar at the back called *The Pub*. *Flamingo Restaurant*, on corner of Bole Rd just up from Meskel Sq. Pleasant white, curved corner building. 1st-floor restaurant, posh in a whimsical way with troughs of plants and pink tablecloths. Food is good – Italian dishes, rice, lamb, beef, fish and chicken – portions are medium sized. *Ghion Hotel*, Menelik Av, T443170, north side of the National Stadium offers 3 restaurants – *Main*, *Unity* and *National* – that are open 1200-1500 and 1900-2200: *Main Restaurant*, housed in a narrow bridge that stretches over a roadway, connecting the main lobby to a glass-walled *tukul*. Offers a 'free' coffee ceremony at mealtimes and traditional music and dancing on Tue, Thu and Sun. *Unity*, garden restaurant with bar and terrace, flambé nights on Fri and Sat. *Harambee Hotel*, corner of Desta Damtew St and Yohanis St, T154000, offers the following: *Fanfan Tavern*, 2nd floor barbecue grill, traditional *masho* bead lamps, murals on walls. *Harar Restaurant* and *Magala Lounge*, both situated on the 1st floor are decorated in style of old city of Harar, Ethiopia's main Islamic city – international cuisine. *Hill Belt*, close to the *Imperial Hotel* on the link road between Bole Rd and Megenenya. A

Mid-range

posh bar and restaurant with a pleasant terrace. International dishes from tandoori to noodles to tempura, plus lots of soups and fish, steak and chicken dishes. *Jewel of India*, Bole Rd/Olympia Rd intersection. Posh, polite Indian restaurant, delicious food with lots of vegetarian options. Cheaper set lunch menu Mon-Fri. *Pizza Deli Roma*, right side of Bole Rd towards airport before Olympia Rd intersection. Small establishment offering good pizzas in 2 sizes. Adjoining compartment specializes in chicken dishes. *Rainbow Seoul*, left side of Bole Rd shortly after it leaves Meskel Sq. Korean, Chinese and Japanese dishes plus some western with the emphasis on seafood. Popular with ex-pats. *Sangarn Indian Restaurant*, Bole Rd on right side past *City Café*. Excellent Indian restaurant, offers curries, seafood and vegetarian dishes. Set dishes lunchtime Mon-Fri. *Satellite Restaurant*, among the new complex on Bole Rd near the airport. Unmissable – a restaurant contained in half an airliner protruding from the front of a building – unsettling in the post World Trade Centre era. Expensive and prestigious with fish dishes amongst the most pricey. Underneath is a place called *London Café* which sells coffee, ice cream, cakes and bottled beer. *Shanghai*, ground floor of the Omedad Olympia building on the left as you turn south on Debre Zeit Rd. Another classy Chinese restaurant but rather sparing with the prawns. *Taj Indian Restaurant*, at the back of the *Ibex Lalibela* building. Inexpensive Indian restaurant, pleasant owner, opens for dinner at 1900. Closed on Tue. Excellent food but the 'garlic butter nan' could do with more of the garlic butter. *Wabe Shebelle Hotel*, Ras Abebe Aragay St, T447187/90, has the *Seguenet Restaurant* Reasonably priced with rooftop views from the 11th floor. Efficient and functional. Good value especially when compared to other large hotels.

Cheap *Addis Peacock*, close to *Awraris Hotel*. Tropical theme bar plus restaurant overlooking a very pleasant, leafy, vined courtyard. Menu features both national and western dishes. The kebab is a specialty, served with lots of chips. *Arada Restaurant*, 1st floor of the big boutique building overlooking Cunningham St, next door to *Twins*. Serves western and Ethiopian food, bar serves European beers, good friendly service. *Arabian Gulf Restaurant*, right side Olympia Rd past *Jewel of India*. Clean pleasant Arabian-style restaurant offering both snacks, juices and meals. *Foule Special* overpriced. *Gazebo Pizza*, right side of Olympia Rd past the *Jewel of India*. Cheerful white-painted place, all pizzas cost US$2.75, cheaper than *Deli Roma* around the corner. Has a nice shaded courtyard at the front. *Gazelle Piano Bar*, left side of Bole Rd in same building as the *Meridian Hotel* down some steps. Small impossingly-furnished bar/restaurant offering salads and Italian dishes. *HeRa*, close to *Hawi Hotel* on Debre Zeit Rd. Rooftop bar and restaurant/fast-food venue with good food. Ground floor is an extensive café terrace. *In And Out*, Adwa Av towards Arat Kilo just beyond the bridge. Great pizza US$3 in plush surroundings – music very loud. Live music Thu-Sun when drink prices are doubled. *Hotspot Bar and Restaurant*, Desta Damtew St along from *The Cottage*. Pleasant white-painted building, partially roofed courtyard with fairy lights, wicker lampshades and potted plants. Has Ethiopian and western food including burgers, fish omelettes, spaghetti and draught beer. *Ibex Lalibela*, south side of stadium on Ras Menonin Av. Downstairs is a pastry, with a pizza section and a draught beer section. Upstairs the restaurant offers excellent value – seafood, pastas, soups, grills, pizzas and deserts. The carved wood-decorations reflect the style of the Lalibela rock-hewn churches. *Karamara Restaurant*, on Bole Rd before you reach the bridge going towards the airport. A huddle of *tukul* buildings with a walled terrace at the front. National dishes and dimpled draught beer. Entertainment from singers and musicians, popular with locals and foreigners. *La Terrazza*, on left-hand side of Haile G Selassie Rd as you approach Megenenya. It is a shame that this restaurant is such a hike from the city centre as it serves excellent Italian food. Restaurant is on 1st floor – downstairs is a less formal hamburger joint. *Liyu Muya Restaurant*, at the bottom of the *Semien Building* at the corner where Debre Zeit Rd begins. Decidedly knackered-looking building, but this place is a gem. Comfortable flowered-patterned chairs, light with large windows, plants, ornate wooden screens and well-stocked bar. Menus includes pizza, chicken, lamb, burgers, salads, pasta, fish and national food. *Lombardia*, on Ras Abebe Aregay Av, in the shadow of the *Wabi Shebele Hotel*. Italian food, fish, chicken and meat dishes. Coffee shop at the front. *Miru Café*, 1-min walk below *Ras Hotel* on Churchill Av. Coffee shop downstairs, restaurant. Courteous staff.

Good fish goulash. Popular with local office workers and gets very crowded lunchtime. *My Pub* Haile G Selassie Rd, near *Kasanches* – not to be confused with *Our Pub* around the corner. Basically an ex-pat-orientated approximation of a flashy tasteless British pub with pool table, dartboard and jukebox. Menu includes grills, salads, steak, chicken, hamburgers and ice cream. Bottled beer and overpriced coffee. *Pizzeria Italia* off on the right of the Bole Rd – look for the signpost near the Tonga Embassy. Menu includes pizzas and pasta. Popular with ex-pat. *Pride*, just north of the Haya-Hulet intersection on Haile G Selassie Rd – follow the VSO sign. Friendly cheerful staff serves national dishes, coffee, cakes and draught beer. Has a couple of tables set out at the front. *Randa Fast Food*, left side of Bole Rd past Kebericho. Pleasant front courtyard. Sells pizzas, burgers and kebabs. *Ras Snack*, Haile G Selassie Rd, opposite the *Yonas Hotel*. Generous portions, excellent fruit juices but the *foule special* is a bit bland. Many beggars in this area, so you may wish to eat inside rather than on the terrace. *Saay Pastry*, Haile G Selassie Rd, between Kasanches and Haya-Hulet on the 1st floor of *Bank of Abyssinia* building. Cheapish snack menu including pasta dishes, plus pastry with coffee and cakes. Position offers a contrast between bustling Haile G Selassie Rd in front and the shanty-town hovels to the rear. *Solo Restaurant Café*, just off Arat Kilo. Saloon-style swing doors, small terrace. Big painted mural of St George and the Dragon. National food, fish and *injera* on fasting days is particularly good. *Square Garden Café*, next to Ethiopian Tourism Commission on Meskel Sq. Looks like a big coffee shop but offers a snack menu of national dishes plus burgers, pasta and sandwiches, plus the usual 'pastry fare'. The slanting roof offers welcome shade. *Tiru Restaurant*, Haile G Selassie Rd, on the left just after leaving Meskel Sq opposite *Yordanis Hotel*. Pleasant courtyard bar/restaurant specializing in national food. *Tsedey*, Piazza around the corner from *Taitu Hotel*. Food very good apart from lumpen pizzas. National and western food. Roast chicken excellent. 4 large rooms with lots of seating. Serves draught beer. *Tukuls*, close to *Addis Peacock* on the right side. A trendy little place, much of the front courtyard is covered by a big *tukul*-style roof. Leafy plants add to the ambiance. National dishes, beef, fish and good vegetarian dishes, salad and rice available. *Village Bar and Restaurant*, down the alley before *Jewel of India* then turn right. The alley gives the appearance of doubling back on itself, and some parts resemble black, slimy quicksand. Clean, cosy and homely restaurant offering national foods, grills and pasta. Pleasant adjoining bar. *Zauditu Hotel*, south from Arat Kilo towards Parliament Congress Hall on the right. Excellent value for money, offering traditional dancing and live music but for a fraction of the cost at the *Crown Hotel*. Good cheap national food, draught beer. Recommended cultural experience for budget travellers. *ZMA*, upper Churchill Av, at the side of the building containing *Egyptair*. Smart basement restaurant serving Italian, veal and fish dishes. Spacious, pleasantly furnished, food is of a good standard.

Seriously cheap *Acapulco*, between *Castellis* and *Taitu Hotel,* serves local food and doubles up as a bar. *Bole Mini*, almost at the airport, sells burgers, juices, doughnuts and waffles. Somewhat overwhelmed by the construction work next door. *British Council Cafeteria*, gruelling climb to 4th floor of BC building, Adwa Av. Closes at 1800. Excellent place for a snack or coffee. Lunch menu has good pasta dishes, otherwise pizza is available. Satellite TV – BBC World, internet access and UK broadsheet newspapers (usually a week out of date). *Café Chaud*, Piazza below intersection Cunningham St/Adwa Av. A small innocuous doorway opens into a large pastry shop. Downstairs has a larger seating area. Excellent fresh juices, spicy 'quick' pizzas popular for breakfast amongst locals plus usual selection of cakes and biscuits. Trendily furnished with marble-topped tables and tall skeletal metal chairs. *Caffe Dolce Adwa*, Av between Piazza and Arat Kilo. Upmarket pastry, pleasant forecourt with tables and parasols. Delicious cakes, clean environment. *Cave Hotel*, on the Piazza between Arbegnoch and Cunningham streets. 1970s student-union-bar design, resembling a cave. Usual rations of cheap *kai-wat* and *tibs* plus draught beer with whacky music ranging from John Denver to Wham. Gruesome toilet. *City Café and Pastry*, Bole Rd opposite the *Randa*. Very clean and spacious, terrace at front. Some mouth-watering desserts, juices, coffee, ice-cream, cakes and biscuits.

College Café, King George St, to the left above Arat Kilo. A nicely furnished place serving tea, *makiato*, and later on draught beer as well as European beers. Cool shady ambiance assisted by the drawn curtains. **Continental Hotel**, Piazza at the corner near the *Taitu Hotel*. Ramshackle and teeming with bar girls. Only worth a mention because it serves local food after most other places have closed. **Connection Pastry**, Meskel Sq near *ETC*. Trendy appearance, black and white tiling. Serves good cappuccino, coffee, juices, pastries, cakes, excellent fruity desserts. Standing room only. **G K Restaurant**, Ghandi St. National food is very good here. Has good pizzas and salads too. **Dashen Sandwich**, close to *College Café*. Clean, charming narrow place, muted atmosphere, features big framed pictures of Emperor Haile Selassie. Sells eggburgers, cheeseburgers and hamburgers, but the famed *foule special* seems to be absent from the menu. **Dibab**, Entoto Av, across the road from main entrance to university. Green pavilion building with a *turul*-style room in the middle of extensive beautiful garden with lawns, flowerbeds, trees and hedges. Serves national dishes, sandwiches, hamburgers, pasta, rice, egg dishes, cakes, samosas, juice and draught beer – some items occasionally unavailable. **DJ's Café**, Adwa Av near Piazza. Large windows and glass door make you feel you are sitting in a giant aquarium but the mouth-watering cakes on display and the excellent fruit juices and *makiato* are a powerful draw. Fancy glass-topped tables and marble-like floor. **French Corner Café**, Churchill Av, in the 'gift shop' area. Cheap unspectacular, but makes a welcome resting spot if hiking up Churchill Av towards Piazza. Pool table in the adjoining room. **Interlangano**, Adwa Av opposite the British Council, on 1st floor of building containing *Africans Bookshop*. Entrance via alleyway, then into the compound on the right. Quaint, idyllic and charming place, with friendly staff – you can sit on the enclosed balcony overlooking the street, if you pass the bar and pool room. Service is supposedly provided when you press the button at the side of your seat. National dishes, the occasional fish dish and draught beer. **Kebericho**, on the right up Bole Rd past Olympia Rd intersection. Sandwiches, snacks and juices. **LA Burger**, Bole Rd opposite the *Flamingo*. Seems more popular as a recreational area than a food place. Pool table. Identifiable by the sign outside that it has been equipped with 'video games'. **Le Patisserie**, behind the *Purple Café* on Bole Rd, sells juice, hamburgers, pizza, croissants, bread, etc. **Mark Pastry**, Adwa Av next to *Caffe Dolce*. A good pastry but neither surroundings nor fare are up to the standard of its neighbour. **Master Sun Hotel**, Adwa Av, entrance up an alleyway shortly after crossing the bridge going towards Piazza. Not a hotel, but rather a bistro-like restaurant. Décor includes a carved wooden bar area with creamy-reddish walls. Mostly serves Ethiopian dishes, but also hamburgers and spagetti plus draught beer. Volume of music spoils the ambiance. **National Hotel Piazza**, same street as *Taitu Hotel*. Cheap bog-standard Piazza restaurant. Adjourning bar is bustling and good for socializing. **Omar Khayyam**, near *Taitu Hotel*, Arabic décor with partially covered courtyard at front. Has a good budget menu, offering kebabs, vegetarian dishes and wonderful bread – grills and kebabs recommended. **Oroscope**, off Churchill Rd across the road from the back of the *Taitu Hotel*. Quite atmospheric, Ethiopian bric-a-brac displayed on walls. Serves international food as well as pizza with unusual combinations – pork or 'Indian'. **Palace Pastry**, in new complex of buildings on the right just before the airport. Smart-looking pastry/coffee shop. **Pelican Pastry**, corner of *Aladdin/Meridian* hotels, Bole Rd. Offers burgers, milkshakes and juices. Roofed by a canopy of orange canvas. **Purple Café and Restaurant**, corner of Bole Rd/Olympia Rd. Purple exterior, pleasant terrace. Café serves pastries and ice-cream, restaurant not too busy, local food. **Rendezvous Café**, near *Construction and Business Bank*, Ras Mekonin Av. A great place to have lunch. *Neshef special* is excellent (spicy). **Root Café**, last coffee shop on the Bole Rd before the airport. **Seble**, next to *Solo Restaurant* on Adwa Av. Deceptively spacious inside, with a terrace and rooms on 2 floors. Generous hale and hearty fare, good fish on fasting days, draught beer available. Friendly staff but toilets run-down. **Sengatera Hotel**, Tesema Aba Kemaw, at around corner from *Wabi Shebele Hotel*. Not a hotel but a restaurant specializing in hearty Ethiopian meat dishes. Warren-like interior, with tables to the sides of the twisting passageway. **Shamrock**, Piazza along the street from *Ethiopian Airlines* in the direction of the *Taitu Hotel*. National food served in rather sombre surroundings. **Soul Kid Pastry**, Adwa Av, across from British Council. One of the best pastries in the area, serves cakes, biscuits, juices, delicious *makiato*. Gets very busy. **Tana Café**, in the Tana Shopping Complex on Bole Rd. Offers burgers, pastries, ice-cream, tea and coffee. **Veronicas**, north side of Piazza – go up the street from the traffic police box/mouth of Adwa Av. Appears a bit dark and cluttered, though there is additional seating space upstairs. Serves national food, pasta and fish dishes – the spicy fish goulash is particularly good. Draught beer available. *Wing*, located down alleyway on the right just after you enter Adwa Av from Piazza. Small pleasant restaurant serving burgers, pasta and fish.

Cheap snack bars are clustered around the Piazza and offer local food They include *Enricos* (Italian pastry/coffee shop), located half a block away from the *Baro Hotel* – down the hill, across the street and near the corner. Serve hot fresh brioche every morning for $0.15. *Port Snack Bar*, Piazza near *Taitu Hotel*. Serves hamburgers smothered in peanut butter, appealing at 0300 after several beers but less so during daytime. *Star Café Twins*, 1st floor of big boutique building on Cunningham St, Piazza. Speciality is *kitfo*. Cheap draught beer. Balcony seating affords wonderful sunset views. Also has a bar/pool room.

Snack bars

Bars and nightclubs

B1, below *Castelli's*, is a sleepy, rather shabby place, mostly frequented by old men. No bar-girls here. *B2* used to be a bog-standard pub but is currently being refurbished and smartened up to become a 'bar-restaurant'. *B3* and *B4* are tiny, pokey but cheerful places that rarely shut before 0400. *B5* is recommended for a quieter drink. It is set back from the street and up some stairs. *B6* is another 'back from the street, up some stairs' place. *B7,* a large lively bar that never seems to close, has a handy pool-table inside and a fast-food kiosk called *Roots Burger* out on the front terrace. *B8* is small dark bar with a rather sophisticated atmosphere. Tequila available here. *B9* A bit back from the street at the side of the *Venus*. True 'spit-and-sawdust' material. *B10* Very dark but comfortable. Currently giving Guinness the heavy sell.

Bars
There are lots of atmospheric bars around the Piazza, often noisy playing local music and many of them unnamed B=bar
See Piazza map, page 786

Other bars around Piazza are in the *Tigray* and the *Wegagen* hotels. These are acceptable, with front terraces, although they lack the atmosphere of the *National Hotel*. The sign has just been removed from the *Queen's Bar* (*B11* on map) and it has been given a tiled, garish façade, but the interior is unchanged. Used to have a reputation for a guaranteed nightly fight. *Florida Hotel* has a reputation for bad taste. Decorated with pink walls and staffed by mature staff this bar can be very lively. *Kenny Rogers*, nickname given to a bar that also operates as a popular breakfast place, offering the option of lasagna to start the day. Has a portrait of the Country and Western singer hanging on its wall.

The *Ambassador Nightclub* is next door to the Ambassador Theatre. The bar in the *Aros Hotel* on Dej Belay Zeleke St is very nightclubby and has a DJ every evening. *Dome Club*, in the *Concorde Hotel* on Debre Zeit Rd, is very popular. *Ghion Nightclub*, T443170, very central on Menelik Av, close to Revolution Sq. There is apparently a nightclub under construction at the new *Global Hotel* on the Debre Zeit Rd. The *Imperial Hotel* contains a nightclub. The *In And Out Restaurant* on Adwa Av often feels more like a nightclub than a restaurant (especially on Thu, Fri, Sat and Sun evenings as it regularly has live bands, a DJ, flashing lights and dancing. *Shala Bar*, Wabe Shebelle Hotel on Desta Damtew St to the west of Meskel Sq, T447187/90. From 2200, live band, Fri and Sat only. *The Tunnel*, on Churchill north of *Ras Hotel*. No T-shirts or tennis shoes allowed. *Memo*, just off Africa Av (Bole Rd) near the *Flamingo Restaurant*. Every night, good grill and bar outside, quite popular. The *Venus Hotel*, in Piazza, is a true budget option as there is no charge on the door and the draught beer costs only 1.50 birr. But the DJ's western record collection stops at *Another Brick In The Wall* and *Beat It*, and there are some light-fingered patrons thereabouts so hang on to your coats and bags.

Nightclubs
Nightlifers are advised to use taxis which gather in fleets around the venues; with a bit of haggling, you can travel from one venue to the next for 20 birr (US$2.50) at most

In addition to these relatively upmarket places there is a whole host of more local places in an area known locally as 'Kasantes', around Zewditu St and the old Asmara Rd, to the northeast of Stefanos Church. A bit further east is the *Mondial Club* also with live performers.

Entertainment

Mainly American, Indian and Arabic films. *Ambassador Theatre*, near *National Theatre* and *Harambee Hotel* on Atse Yohanis Av. *Cinema Ethiopia*, on Piazza. *Addis Katama* in Mercato. *Agar Fikhr* (Patriotic Association), close to Ras Mekonnen Terr, at the bridge on Adwa Av.

Cinema
See Ethiopian Herald for programmes

Ethiopia

Occasionally shows films. *National Theatre* on Churchill Rd, and *City Hall*, at the north end of Churchill Rd also show films from time to time. *Empire* is close to the Piazza. Cinemas in Ethiopia often show 2 films during the day and often the staff at the ticket booth aren't terribly clear about what film is showing at what time. So check and check again that you're paying to see the film you really want to see.

Spectator sport   **Horse-racing**: at Jan Meda, T112540. Northeast of the city centre off Mulugetsa St. **Soccer**: at Addis Ababa Stadium on Ras Desta Damtew Av. There are games on most Thu evenings and on Sat and Sun. See *Ethiopian Herald* for programmes.

Theatre
See Ethiopian Herald
for programmes

Traditional dance, music and classical western plays (Shakespeare is very popular, and has been translated into Amharic) at the *National Theatre* on Churchill Rd near the *Ethiopia Hotel*, and at *City Hall*, at the north end of Churchill Rd. *National Theatre* has regular traditional dance and music 1600-1800 on Thu. *Agar Fikr* (Patriotic Association), close to Piazza. Traditional dance and music 1600 on Tue.

The *Imperial Hotel* stages very occasional events, and the odd play is performed in the upstairs, gallery part of the *Taitu Hotel*.

Traditional
music &
dancing

Traditional music and dancing, meanwhile, can be enjoyed at the *Karamara* (Bole Rd), *Zauditu Hotel* (Arat Kilo), *Zendika* (top of Zewditu St, near where it joins Menelik II Av) and the *Crown Hotel* on the Debre Zeit Rd, a long way out from the centre of town

Shopping

Markets &
supermarkets
The high-quality
shopping area is along
Churchill Av. A useful
supermarket is
opposite the Ras Hotel
on Churchill Av. The
main hotels all have a
variety of shops

The area for bargains is **Mercato**, the city's main market to the west (it is about 1 km from Churchill Av, access is easy by taxi). Mercato has an enormous variety of wares on offer ranging from imported goods to typical Ethiopian-market items (fruit, vegetable spices, *teff, chat,* goats, chickens, etc) and clothes (both modern imports and traditional costumes). There are also many, many outlets for shoes and bags, electrical goods (there seems to be shop after noisy shop selling stereos) and handicrafts (baskets, pottery, pictures, crosses, etc). There are some covered sections at the Adrash market halls, which contain the imported goods and the traditional items. The other local shopping area is the Piazza, at the north end of Churchill Rd. The jewellery, gold and silverware is mainly concentrated here, as well as flower shops, ceramics and leather goods along Adwa Av. The jewellery shops extend along Adwa Av too, from Piazza.

If you're desperate for some western-style foodstuffs, then probably the biggest and best-stocked supermarket is *Bambi's* on the right side of Haile G Selassie Rd as you travel along from Meskel Sq before you reach Urael Church. But there are plenty of smaller but still useful supermarkets around, eg the *Loyal Shopping Centre* and *Solomon Hailu* on Churchill Av (the latter is opposite the *Ras Hotel*), *Twins*, on Haile G Selassie Rd (in the 'Z' Building beside the *Classic Hotel*), the *Tana Shopping Centre* and many others on Bole Rd, *Leonardo* on Zewditu St, and the *Iman* and *Abebe Abshir* on Awa Av. There are also a couple of useful little supermarkets near Arat Kilo, just after you turn north towards Siddist Kilo.

Bookshops   There is a bookshop by the *German Cultural Institute*, mid-way from the *National Museum* to Arat Kilo. It stocks a reasonable collection of non-fiction books about Ethiopia. The *Abissenia (sic) Bookshop*, at Haya-Hulet on Haile G Selassie Rd, is a tiny but *Tardis*-like shop with a lot of books crammed inside. The stock includes an unexpectedly high number of world-literature classics translated into English. The *African's Bookshop*, on Adwa Av opposite the British Council Building, stocks a lot of stuff about Ethiopia, though much of it seems a bit pricey. There are also a lot of second-hand English-language paperbacks available for about 15-40 birr. It is a good place to pick up some literary escapism if Ethiopia is beginning to get to you. It also sells postcards and tourism posters. *Bookworld* (first main turning on the right as you head down Churchill Av from Piazza, opposite Cathedral School) is probably the best-stocked English-language bookshop in Ethiopia. It has a lot of recent, or fairly recent, titles imported from Britain and America. Their range of books about Ethiopia is a bit disappointing. There are branches of the *Ethiopian Book Centre* on Adwa Av and near Arat Kilo. Like *Mega*, lots of academic titles, plus quite a few religious ones too. But again, you never quite know what you'll find there. The big official gift shops – especially the *Haile Selassie Alemayehu* (large selection) on Churchill Av and the *Ezana* (cheaper) at the duty-free complex on Haile G Selassie Rd – stock a range of books about Ethiopia, including guidebooks, coffee table volumes of arty photographs and academic titles. *Mega Books* have branches in Piazza, near Arat Kilo and near Meskel Sq. The majority of the stock consists of academic titles, but you may be able to find a (relatively) cheap book about Ethiopia there. You'll find a few books sitting around the gift shops in the big hotels. Here and there you'll find guys selling English-language books and magazines from makeshift stalls and displays laid out across the pavement. The ones in Piazza (in front of the *Dallas Music Shop*) seem well established, but deal mainly in rather old magazines – for example, issues of *Time* dating back to the heady days of Bill Clinton and Monica Lewinsky.

Crafts, souvenirs & jewellery

Most of the upmarket hotels now have some sort of shop on or beside their premises selling traditional and antique gift items. Needless to say, these places are particularly expensive, as is the gift shop at Arrivals in Bole airport. The gift shop beside the Ethiopian Tourism Commission offices on Meskel Sq seems a little cheaper. *Ethiopian Crafts and Antiques*, close to the *Ras Hotel* on Churchill Rd has a good selection of high-quality craftwork. *Addis Ababa City Gold* and the *Silversmith Co-operative Society* are particularly good sources for jewellery in the Piazza and there are more to be found along the western part of Adwa Av.

If you're prepared to haggle for more reasonable prices, there is of course the Mercato, and the upper end of Churchill Av boasts a cluster of little shops with names like *Salem*, *Lucy*, *Mursella Jobir*, *Abyssinia*, *Pharazee Family*, *Goobel*, *Rohobot* and *Yeta* which sell carvings, basket-work, jewellery, carpets, bags and so on.

At the roundabout on upper Churchill Av, the shops leave Churchill and straggle up the lower part of Gandhi St instead. You'll find similar gift shops clustering around Fitwari St, the turning off Churchill above the main post office. The usual advice is to aim at paying half of the original sum that the shopkeeper throws at you, so make your initial offer as low as his initial price is high and gradually work your ways up/down to that halfway sum. If you have neither the patience nor talent for haggling, the place to try is the *Haile Selassie Alemayehu*, also on upper Churchill Av. It has a big selection of goods – jewellery, baskets, injera tables, costumes, scarves, hats, horse-hair whips, books on Ethiopia, carvings, statues, old coins, crosses, prints, posters, triptychs, etc – and price-labels are provided, so you can be immediately sure of what you have to pay. Some prices are steep, but others are quite reasonable and there are some cheap 'nick-nacks' (simple bracelets for 5 birr, little carved masks for 10, small prints for 10 or 15). The *Ezana* gift-shop at the duty-free complex on Haile G Selassie Rd is similar in format, but has a smaller selection. However, they appear to be building a new, big gift-shop extension on the premises.

Newspapers

Foreign newspapers (*International Herald Tribune*, *Times*, *Washington Post*) are available at the airport. Foreign newspapers and magazines are also available at the *Hilton* and the *Sheraton* hotels. British newspapers (admittedly about a week old) and many periodicals are available for consultation in the reading rooms of the British Council building on Adwa Av. There's quite a range of small English-language newspapers printed in Addis Ababa – the *Ethiopian Herald, Monitor, Sun, Addis Tribune, Fortune* and *Capital* – and you'll find many of them on sale for 1-2 birr at the reception desks of the city's hotels.

Sport

Archery: at *Jan Meda*. Northeast of the city centre off Mulugetsa St. Call the race track, for information T112540. **Bowling**: at Emboy Mesk in Debre Zeit Rd. Also *Guenet Hotel*. **Canoeing and rafting**: International River Grade 2, but can reach 4 at high water flows in Sep on the River Omo (see entry on page 828). **Gym**: *YMCA* at Arat Kilo to the north of the city, going northeast from the Piazza along Adwa Av but you need a resident's card to be able to use its facilities. However, there are also plenty of hotels offering gyms and health clubs: the *Hilton, D'Afrique, Extreme, Desalegn, Imperial, Semien* and *Ibex*. New gyms are supposedly in the pipeline at the *Global* and *Geunet*. **Horse-riding**: at a site near the

Ethiopia

Victory Department Store along the old Airport Rd. **Sauna**: available at the *Sheraton*, *Hilton*, *Yordanos*, *Extreme*, *Filwaha*, *Imperial*, *Desalegn*, *Semien*, *Global*, *Ibex* and *Crown* hotels. **Squash**: There is a squash court at the *Hilton*. **Swimming**: at *Ghion Hotel*, US$2 (Olympic-size pool) the *Hilton* (US$4) and the *Sheraton* (US$4). **Tennis**: at *Ghion* , *Hilton* and *Guenet Hotel*.

Tour operators & travel agencies   The travel business has opened up dramatically since the collapse of the Mengistu regime, but the recent war with Eritrea has caused a setback. In addition to the state-owned *National Tour Operation*, there's a range of private tour and travel agencies offering their services. Many companies are based in the major hotels. The *Ethiopian Wildlife Conservation Organization* recommends the following companies for being the most respectful of the national parks, their staff and the animals: *Ghion Travel and Tours*, T505665, F505656, ghiontravel@telecom.net.et, *Hess Travel*, T156058, F512675, hestravel@telecom.net.et, *Travel Ethiopia*, T150036, F510200, travelethiopia@telecom.net.et

In addition the following are professional, well-established companies in Addis Ababa with offices, offering travel agency services: *All Continents Travel*, T620194, F620294. *Best Travel*, T513766. *Blue Nile Express*, PO Box 967, T151667, F514097. *Ethiographic Travel Agency*, T153315, F518422, PO Box 1350, ethio-graphic@telecom.net.et *Forship Travel Agency*, PO Box 30754, T552159, F553300, has a very good reputation and is recommended. *International Travel and Tour*, PO Box 2101, T151759, F712884. *Luxor Travel*, T157608, F534688. *Millennium Tour and Travel Agency*, T508868. *Olympic Travel Agency*, PO Box 17912, T613796, F620207, zidris@hotmail.com *Pioneer Ethio Aviation Travel Agency*, PO Box 16886, T519563, F517868. *Rio Travel Agency*, T510986. *Royal Travel and Tour*, T614699, F620976, PO Box 180024, Royal@telecom.net.et *Sheba Travel Service*, T513032/3, F651245, PO Box 3422. *Solast Travel and Tour Services*, T513423, F515200, PO Box 5390. *Tana Travel Agency*, T533835, F523719, tanatrvla@telecom.net.et

The following companies are among those that have been vetted and approved by the Ethiopian Tourism Commission: *Abadir Travel and Tours*, T534687, F534688. *Abay Travel and Tourism*, T614387, F612313, PO Box 502, code 1110, abay-travel@telecom.net.et *Abyssinian Tours and Travel*, T615740, F614260, PO Box 100359, abyssinian-tours@telecom.net.et *Active Airline Travel Agency*, T559984 , F551477. *Agelgel Tour and Travel*, T614398, F651811, PO Box 6807. *Alif Tour and Travel*, T762168, F137312, PO Box 4333. *Ark Tours and Safari*, T560108, F560109, PO Box 25396, ark@telecom.net.et *Bahir Dar Tour and Travel*, T550546, F553579, PO Box 5408. *Bekele Molla Tour and Travel*, T507565, F518223, Bekelemolla@telecom.net.et *Blen Ethiopia Travel*, T620887, F620888, PO Box 1749, gbd@telecom.net.et *Caravan Tour and Travel*, T562571, F553656, PO Box 1348, Caravan-tt@telecom.net.et *Dalol Travel and Tours*, T621142, F621088, PO Box 384, code 1110. *Discover Ethiopia Travel and Tour*, T713168, F713203. *Distance Travel Agency*, PO Box 8809, T151715, F515963. *Eastern Travel and Tourist Agency*, PO Box 1136, T511574, F511468, EASTERN-TRAVEL@telecom.net.et *Ecologies PLC*, T530419, F614223, PO Box 1269. *Ethio Fauna Safaris*, T505301, F505302, EthFauna@hotmail.com *Ethio-Fin Travel and Tours*, T504423, F504421. *Ethiopian Rift Valley Safaris*, PO Box 3658, T551127, F550298, ervs@telecom.net.et Organize fly-down safaris to the Omo Valley. Very experienced company with a river base camp and a permanent on-site 4WD. Can arrange game drives, river rafting and walking safaris. *Four Season Travel Agency*, PO Box 2856, T613121, F615500F, Fsta@telecom.net *Experience Ethiopia Travel*, (EET), PO Box 9354, Churchill Av, close to the National Theatre, T152336, F519982, eet@telecom.net.et Recommended reputable company. Well informed about less-visited parts of the country. *Galaxy Travel Services*, PO Box 8309, T510875, F511236, galaxyexpress@telecom.net.et *Lalibela Travel and Tour*, PO Box 2590, T514403, F510097, travellalibela@telecom.net.et *N.T.O.*, T514838, F517688, PO Box 5709, nto@telecom.net.et *Selam International Travel and Tourist Agency*, PO Box 30208, T626605, F551490. *Travel Ethiopia*, PO Box 9438, T510168, F510200, travelethiopia@telecom.net.et *Union of Nations Travel Agency*, PO Box 5261, T519550, F519550. *Yumo Tours*, PO Box 26240, T518400, F510064.

Transport

Bus Red and yellow *Ambessa* (lion) buses operate within the city, stopping at every red and yel- Local
low marking. There is a flat fare per person for a one-way trip. The *Ambessa* buses are not recommended for foreigners and with good reason: passengers are crammed in like sardines and they
provide happy hunting grounds for pickpockets. It's far better to stick to the line taxis, they cover
most areas of Addis Ababa, run from dawn to dusk and continue sporadically until 2000 or 2100.
Pickpocketing on line taxis is very rare. Minibuses (*wi yi yit*) are also available, running on set routes.

Minibus It takes a little time to tune in to the minibus system, as you need to be able to recognize the destinations shouted out by the conductors. They are so cheap that it is often simpler to take several minibuses if you are going on a long or complicated journey and change
buses at the large road junctions. Fares: **Piazza-Mercato** US$0.07; **Piazza-Kasanches**, **Arat
Kilo-Haya Hulet**, or **La Gare-Piazza** US$0.13; **Piazza-Haya Hulet**, **Haya Hulet-Mercato**
US$0.16; **Piazza-Megenenya** US$0.25. If several **line taxis** are heading for the destination
you want to go to, choose the vehicle which is fullest. Like all buses in Ethiopia, they operate
on a 'go when full' principle. You can waste a lot of time sitting on an empty line taxi while
others head for fuller vehicles that are likely to leave sooner.

Taxi Cream-coloured NTO (National Tour Operator) taxis operate at Bole International Airport costing between US$1.50-3 if you go directly to the drivers outside the airport. Brand
new yellow Hyundi taxis cost US$3 at the most. Taxis also operate from outside all the major
hotels. There is also a minibus service from the airport. The minibus can be found in the airport car parking area or 600 m away on the road towards town. Also, the private taxi service
operates in the smaller blue and white cars along set routes, often on a vehicle-sharing basis.

Air The national carrier *Ethiopian Airways* connects with many European destinations and Long-distance
with 23 African cities 5 European cities, 2 in the USA, 8 in the Middle East, 3 in the Indian
sub-continent and 2 in the rest of Asia. In addition there are direct flights by *Alitalia*,
Alyemda, *Lufthansa*, *Interflug*, *Yemenia* and *Kenya Airways*. For details about internal
flights, see Getting around page 780.

Road Many of the roads are in a poor condition, but the roads linking Addis Ababa with
Debre Zeit, Mojo, Nazaret, Shashemene and Awasa are among the best in the country. The
roads east of Awash and north of Weldiya are among the really poor ones. **Buses** to and from
the regions are frequent. The main bus terminal is at Mercato, while a second bus station
near the railway station on Ras Mekonin Av, has frequent services to nearby destinations
such as Debre Zeit, Mojo and Nazaret. It is actually possible to show up early on the morning
of departure and buy a ticket for destinations that are up to a day's journey away (Nekemte,
Dessie, Jimma, etc), but to be on the safe side you should buy your ticket the day before if the
destination is far away. These tickets are usually on sale at the bus station from mid-afternoon onwards. There is sometimes a secondary market in booked tickets at around double
the face value. Arrive for departure by 0600. There is an extra charge for a big luggage pack.

Train T517250 (Information). A 782-km railway connects Addis with Djibouti on the Red
Sea. Regrettably the scheduled service was greatly disrupted during the Ethiopia/Eritrea
conflict, and this rather unpredictable service continues. The whole system is in a state of
flux, and no doubt the details will be different next week, next month, and again next year.
There is currently no 1st-class service operating, only 2nd and 3rd classes; on some days (eg
Sun) there are only 3rd-class seats available, on other days only 2nd-class ones; the fares
from Addis Ababa to Dire Dawa are US$7 for 2nd class and US$5.15 for 3rd class. Departure
time is 1400, with arrival in Dire Dawa scheduled for 0500-0600 the next morning. Departures are frequently delayed. Details of tickets to Djibouti are currently unavailable.

   Although there have been incidents in the past where travellers have been attacked by
bandits on this train, security has much improved, and bars have been fitted to the train windows. Booking is at the railway station at the southern end of Churchill Av.

*It is necessary to buy
your ticket the day
before you travel as
the train is often full.
One aspect of rail
travel here is likely to
remain the same: you
will always have to
'fight' for your
allocated place*

Directory

Airline offices *Air Djibouti*, T157322. *Air France*, T519044. *Air Tanzania Corporation*, T157533. *Alitalia*, T514400, PO Box 3260. Located on Ras Desta Darntew Av (the street containing the Ambassador Theatre and *Harambee* and *Ghion* hotels). *Ethiopian Airlines* has 3 offices in city centre, near National Theatre on Churchill Av (use this office for internal flights, which have to be paid for in US\$ cash), T447000. The head office is at the airport T512222, F611474. *Addis Ababa Hilton*, Menelik Av, T158400, and in Piazza at southern end of Eden St. *Egyptair* is located in the Ayushashe Building on upper Churchill Av, T564493/94/95, F552203, gavanto@hotmail.com *Kenya Airways*, PO Box 3381, contact numbers are T513018/19 (reservations), T153339, F511548, addtokq@tyeb.sita.int However, they are in the process of moving their office into the *Hilton Hotel*, so this may change. *Lufthansa*, PO Box 3484, T515666, F512988, lhadd@telecom.net.et Located in the Ethiopian Insurance Corporation Building on lower Churchill Av, near the station. *Saudi Arabian Airways* which is located on Ras Desta Damtew Av, T614327 (Reservations) T512637 (office), F514399, PO Box 904/15. *Sudan Airlines*, T504724, F504725, PO Box 606, located on Ras Desta Damtew Av. *Yemenia*, PO Box 1079, T445076.

Banks There are now about 7 banks in the country, 2 government–run (the *Commercial Bank of Ethiopia* and the *Construction and Business Bank*) and 5 private (*Dashen*, *Awash*, *Wegagen*, *Hibret* and *Abyssinia*). For tourist-type transactions – eg cashing TCs – look for a bank sporting a yellow *Western Union* sign. The *Commercial Bank* branches at Arat Kilo, Piazza and in the circular building on Churchill Av should be able to cater for your needs. If you require the services of a bank at weekends, you could try the one on the premises of the *Sheraton Hotel*.

You will also find plenty of dodgy characters willing to change dollars for birr in Piazza, especially around the gift shops on Gandhi St, if you're willing to risk getting a not-very-accurate exchange rate and extravagant commission.

Communica- **Internet**: There is now a computer centre at the main post office on Churchill Av. A number of hotels –
tions the *Ghion, Ras Amba, Imperial, Meridian, Ibex, Baro, Queen of Sheba* – offer internet services and no doubt the list will grow rapidly over the next couple of years. Cybercafés are sprouting up in the city – the British Council Building has one on its 4th fl and there is another just north of Arat Kilo. **Post office**: Main post office on Churchill Av near Adwa Sq, open 0800-1600. There are also fairly reliable post offices at Arat Kilo, Piazza and Meskel Sq. **Telephone**: Calls can be made through the *Telecommunications Head Office* opposite *Holy Saviour Church*. Telegram and fax services are also available from here, and from the main post office on Churchill Rd. Collect (reverse charge) calls can be made. Most of the larger hotels have telex and telegram facilities. You can, of course, make international calls from the upmarket hotels, but these will be expensive. Fax prices operate on a flat rate from Ethiopia to Europe of about US\$2 (you'll be charged each time, even when the fax fails to get through). In addition commission may be payable on top of that.

Embassies & For any changes to information given here, contact the Protocal General Directorate, T251-1-51873.
consulates *Algeria*, PO Box 5740, T7113000, F712586. *Belgium*, Fikre Mariam Rd, T611813, F613636. *Burundi*, PO Box 3641, T651300. *Canada*, African Solidarity Insurance Building, 6th Fl, Churchill Av, PO Box 1130, T713022, F710333. *Djibouti*, PO Box 1022, off the Bole/Airport road T613006, F612504. *Eritrea*, the Eritrean Embassy is currently closed. *France*, PO Box 1464, T550066, F511180. *Germany*, PO Box 660, T550433, F551311. *Ireland*, PO Box 9585, T613361. *Israel*, PO Box 1266, T610999, F610608. *Italy*, PO Box 1105, T551565, F550218. *Japan*, Finfine Building, Revolution Sq, PO Box 5650, T511088, F511350. *Kenya*, Fikre Mariam Rd, PO Box 3301, T610033, F611433. *Malawi*, PO Box 2316, T712440, F710494. *Netherlands*, PO Box 1241, T711100, F711577. *Nigeria*, PO Box 1019, T120644. *Rwanda*, PO Box 5618, T610300, F610411. *Saudi Arabia*, PO Box 1104, T448010. *Spain*, Entoto St, PO Box 2312, T550222. *Sudan*, PO Box 1110, T516477, F518141. *Sweden*, PO Box 1029, T516699, F515830. *Switzerland*, Jimma Rd, PO Box 1106, T710577, F712805. *Tanzania*, PO Box 1077, T44064. *Uganda*, PO Box 5644, T551088, F514355. *UK*, Fikre Miriam St, PO Box 858, T612354, F610588. *USA*, Entoto St, PO Box 1014, T551002, F551166. *Zambia*, PO Box 1090, T711302. *Zimbabwe*, PO Box 5624, T183872.

Medical The Ethiopian Tourism Commission recommends 8 hospitals in the city of which the following may be
services most 'foreigner-friendly': *Black Lion Hospital*, PO 5657, on Churchill Av opposite the main post office and Ministry of Immigration, T511211/154079. Modern, good casualty department. *Balcha Hospital*, PO Box 94, on the road from Mexico Sq to Lideta Church, T515364/513205. *Ethio-Swedish Clinic*, T449933. *Hayat Hospital*, PO Box 15836, on the road connecting Meganagna and Bole,

T624488/620880. *St Gabriel Hospital*, PO 5634, on the road between Haya Hulet and Tek Medhant Alem, T184628/613622. The clinic at the *British Embassy*, PO 858, T624488, has a reputation for efficient – if brusque! – service, and tourists may want to get in touch to find out the terms under which they can receive treatment there.

Access to lavatories can be a problem in downtown Addis but things are improving. Every major road in the city now has a couple of upmarket hotels or cafés where the toilets are at least 'reasonable'. Carry your own toilet paper, as even the smartest toilest in the poshest hotels may not be equipped. The *Hilton* has lavatories you can use, but it is a little away from the centre. The *Harambee Hotel* is the most accommodating in the central area.

Public lavatories

Excursions from Addis Ababa

The **Entoto Hills**, the site that attracted Menelik II to this region in the first place, rise in a curving ridge north of the city to a height of 3,200 m. It was here in the early 1880s that Menelik established a military camp. Later, when building began, two of the structures to appear here were the **Church of Entoto Mariam**, in which Menelik was crowned emperor of Ethiopia in 1889, and the **Church of Entoto Raquel**. Both of these still stand today. However, though the hills were fine as a military capital – they were obviously easy to defend – as a civilian capital they suffered from their inaccessibility and their exposure to the elements. When the necessity for a civilian rather than a military capital became apparent, the site was abandoned in favour of the more hospitable territory of modern-day Addis Ababa, down below.

Entoto

In addition to the two churches there is a small museum in the area, **Entoto Museum**, which contains a few historical items such as the drum that initiated the march of the Ethiopian forces to the Battle of Adwa in 1896, the bed that Menelik had used earlier on when he was based in Ankober, and some ceremonial costumes worn by him and his wife.

To get to this area, you need to follow the road north of Sidist Kilo, past the American Embassy and up the forested slopes of Entoto for several kilometres beyond. The most practical means of travel is to use a private vehicle, though it should be possible to get on a line taxi at Siddist Kilo and take it as far up this road as it'll go, then cover the remaining distance on foot. As the road winds up and up through masses of eucalyptus trees, walkers will be treated to some breathtaking views of the landscape below. On the slopes they will also pass the legions of female wood carriers, local women who have the thankless task of ferrying loads of eucalyptus wood down from the high forests on their backs, all for a couple of birr a day (they'll be understandably curious about any unfamiliar faces they see during the drudgery of their work).

To reach this garden on the Debre Zeit Road southeast of Addis Ababa take a minibus from Abiot and get off opposite a large cemetery on your left. The entrance to Bihere Tsige is off to the right and about a 15-minute walk from the bus stop – follow the tarmac. During the week it is very quiet and only the gardeners will be there. It is a marvellous place for an introduction to Ethiopian birds and several of the endemic species are present. At the weekend it is a popular place for weddings.

Bihere Tsige

An hour's journey south of Addis brings you to Debre Zeit, which means Mount of Olives in Amharic, but is known as **Bishoftu** by the local Oromo people. It is a busy commercial centre tangled under a canopy of bougainvillea, flame trees and jacarandas, and it is also the base of the Ethiopian Air Force. Because of its proximity to Addis Ababa, Debre Zeit gets rather crowded at the weekends. Around town there are two-wheeled horse-drawn taxis called *garis*, which are recommended if you wish to visit all the lakes. The town is encircled by five crater lakes, and other lakes are

Debre Zeit & crater lakes
Colour map 2, grid B3

Ethiopia

located further afield. The most central and dramatic lake, Bishoftu, is a short walk off the main highway – a sheer wall plunging down to the dark green surface. **Lake Hora**, home to a stunning array of birdlife, including pelicans, storks and kingfishers. is 2 km north of town – follow the signposts to the *Hora Ras Hotel*, from where you can walk to the lake shore. One kilometre north of Lake Hora are another two crater lakes, **Lake Koriftu** – famous for its abundant fish – and just northwest of it, **Lake Bishoftu Guda**. Lake Chelelaka, 5 km northwest of Debre Zeit, is not a crater lake but a seasonal shallow wetland, home to a large variety of birdlife including flamingos. **Green Crater Lake**, 10 km south of Debre Zeit, is also renowned for flamingos. Fifteen kilometres north of town, the '**Cuban Lakes**', which are in fact dams, are worth a visit to see the huge numbers of birds.

Sleeping B *Hora Ras Hotel*, PO Box 126, T338666, perched on the rim of the crater beside Lake Hora. The *Lakeside Bar* is worth a visit for wonderful views over Lake Hora. Recent change of ownership, substantial improvements anticipated. **C** *Bishoftu Hotel*, near town centre, behind petrol station, fine views over Bishoftu Lake. Good value and recommended. **E** *Bekele Mola*, T338995, located southwest of the railway station with views of Lake Bishofta. Friendly but rather basic facilities which look somewhat careworn. **E** *Tourist Hotel*, close to bus stand in town. **F** *KB*, sited north of the town past the flour mill. Clean, some rooms have bathrooms. Good value. **F** *Terminal Hotel*, north of the bus station. Offers very basic, clean rooms some with showers.

Eating Cheap: *Warka Restaurant*, set in gardens with oleander and hibiscus, is a good place for a meal. It gets its name from a huge and magnificent ficus tree, which is called *warka* in Amharic. It is almost next door to the *AFH (Airforce Hotel)* and near the Telecom tower. Nearby is the *Main Grill*, which is highly recommended.

Transport It can be difficult to get a place on a bus going south or east as they are usually full coming from Addis Ababa. Take a bus to **Mojo**, where a connection can be made.

Debre Zeit

↑ To Addis Ababa

Lake Chelelaka

Flour Mill

4 KB

Lake Bishoftu

Lake Hora

Bars/ Cafés

→ To other lakes

→ To Mojo & Nazaret

N
Not to scale

■ Sleeping	
1 Bekele Mola	4 KB
2 Bishoftu	5 Terminal
3 Hora Ras	6 Tourist

● Eating
1 Main Grill

Rock of truth

In the 14th century, a recluse, Gabre Manfus, is said to have lived for 363 years, much of that time among his friends, the creatures of the wild on Mount Zaquella. He became Ethiopia's patron saint of animals.

On the feastday of Gabre Manfus, lovers travel to Mount Zaquella. High on the mountain is a split rock. As they pass through the cleft, they know that if their love is untrue,

the rock will close and crush them. Followers of Gabre Manfus, hermits in flowing yellow robes, continue to live on the mountain, existing on the fruits of the forest and sleeping in caves.

A painting of Gabre Manfus, surrounded by a lion, a leopard and a raven, is in St George Cathedral in Addis Ababa and many other churches.

Mount Zaquella

Known to local people as Mount Zuq'alla or Ziquala, this is an excursion off the main highway from Debre Zeit, which rises 600 m above the plain. An ancient monastery stands on the crater rim looking down at the lake. The monastery was built in honour of Kidus (Saint) Gebre Manfus Qeddus, or 'Abo', a hermit who lived in the vicinity for many years and reputedly made the area holy. He is regarded as a saint and is honoured every year by large crowds on the fifth day of Tikemt and Megabit (October and March). The water of the lake is believed to be holy. It is a stiff 2½-hour climb to the top, but majestic views looking south and east down the Rift Valley, the valley lakes glinting away in the distance, are the reward. Alternatively, it is possible to hire a local taxi to drive up most of the way. A little way beyond Debre Zeit, past the small transit town of Mojo, the road crosses the Awash River. Here the hot blue waters of thermal springs gush up from the molten interior of the rift and merge with the silty waters of the Awash. Lurking crocodiles prey on the fish here, and further downstream there's a hippo pool on **Lake Koka**. On through the bustling cattle town of Nazaret to the spa town of Sodere – three hours' drive from Addis and a favourite weekend resort. Here, the volcanic mineral springs constantly replenish swimming pools with clear blue, warm water. Giant shade trees cast a cool canopy around the pools, and when walking along the river bank you'll see baboons, hippos and crocodiles. **Sleeping B-C** *Sodere Filwoha Resort* is not recommended; it is better to camp.

Mangasha to Ambo

The **Gefersa reservoir**, which lies to the side of the Ambo road only a few kilometres from Addis Ababa, is a lake formed by damming the River Gefersa, which means buffalo in the local Orominya language. The reservoir, which supplies Addis Ababa, has a varied bird population of both indigenous birds and pelicans, cormorants and Egyptian geese. The peaks of two extinct volcanoes can be seen from here – **Mangasha** (Managasha) and **Wechacha** (Wonchi or Wenchi). The mountains can be reached by following a 15-km winding dirt road. The mountain slopes are covered with juniper forests and are host to the black and white colobus monkeys and the timid Menelik's bush buck and klipspringer. The **Mangasha Park** lies only 35 km west of Addis Ababa; a mountain forest sanctuary for birds and animals, and the climb through the forest to the beautiful crater valley of Wachacha is popular, although a guide is needed. The church of **Debre Tsion** at Addis Alem is worth a visit, and then on to **Hagere Heywot** (or Ambo), 125 km west of Addis Ababa on the same road. The spas here are good for swimming and 26 km away along a dirt track is the beautiful volcanic crater lake of Wonchi. **Sleeping B** *Ras Hotel*, located at Ambo.

Ethiopia

□ Addis
Ababa

West to Gambela

The Nilotic peoples – Anuak and Nuer – who inhabit the lowlands around Gambela are unique, as is the surrounding vegetation, landscape and climate. The western section of the central plateau comes to an abrupt end in the province of Illudador, around the picturesque town of Gore, and from here the land falls away to the Nilotic lowlands.

Descending from the highlands, where it is forced between steep-sided gorges, the **River Baro** loses momentum as it reaches the plain, spreading out to a broad river bed. Here, the Anuak settlements are interspersed between mango and banana plantations, while further downstream the vast grassland plains begin.

The southwest corner of Ethiopia is geographically part of the lowlands of Sudan, and has a very different feel to it compared to the rest of the country. It is much more the stereotypical Africa, with hot and humid weather, drums at night and fireflies flickering in the grass. The scenery too, is different. The road down the escarpment to Gambela is very dramatic, with passes through rugged mountains, and when the forest stops the landscape becomes bare and harsh looking. This border area is believed to be the location of the legendery ancient kingdom of Cush in Nubia, previously in northern Sudan. It was said to have flourished from the 11th century BC until the fourth century AD, when its capital, Merowe, fell to the Ethiopians. The hills gradually flatten out into rolling plains of tall elephant grass and occasionally swamps and forests. The people are of **Nuer** or **Anuak** origin and look very different from the highlanders. There are also many refugees from Sudan who have settled in the area. You will find no begging children here; indeed the children are more likely to run away and hide at the sight of you.

The road from Addis to Jimma passes across the high plateau. The scenery is pleasant, if not special. Look out for wattled cranes *(Bugeranus carunculatus)* as you go through the **Tefki marshes** about one hour from Addis Ababa. The vegetation changes slowly, especially after you have crossed the spectacular **Gibe River gorge**. The Jimma side of this gorge is much more like Central Africa, with its red soil and banana plantations. There are two banana-like plants to be seen. As well as the ordinary banana plant, *ensete* the so-called false banana is also grown. This is superficially very like the true banana, but the leaves are longer, broader and grow more upright. The leaves of the true banana curve downwards and, of course, produce the familiar fruit. The false banana does not produce fruit, but the root and part of the stem are cooked and eaten. Along this western road you may notice a green leaf being spread out on the tarmac verges to dry. This is *gesho (Rhamnus prinoides)*, which is used in brewing the local beer.

Jimma

7°40′N 36°47′E
Phone code: 7
Colour map 2, grid B2

Jimma (or Jima) is a pleasant, fairly large town, the biggest in western Ethiopia, approximately 330 km from Addis Ababa, and is sufficiently high to have a cool climate. It is the capital of the old province of Kaffa. This is a coffee growing region of Ethiopia and the villages along the road from Jimma to Gambela sell coffee beans and honey, which can be obtained quite cheaply. In this region the practice persists of mixing ground coffee beans with clarified butter (ghee), giving the drink a distinctive flavour. Jimma is a university town. Places of interest include the King Aba Jiffar's Palace and Jimma Museum, and further afield a day trip to the Seka Falls makes a pleasant break.

King Aba Jiffar (1859-1933) was the Muslim ruler of the area, with his capital centred in Jiren, for 55 years. He was well known and liked by his subjects. His palace, now a little ramshackle, still gives an idea of his influence. Set on a ridge, between two hills, it has commanding views over Jimma and the surrounding area and is noticeably cool after a hard climb on a sunny day. Aba had six wives and numerous children during his 74 years (it is widely promoted that the last is still living in the area). Look for the **lion**, hidden in the wooden carving above the main door, the **high balcony** surrounding a small courtyard where the king and his guests were entertained, and the **sentry post** on the roof with four viewing positions. This allowed communication between observation posts in the surrounding hills; signals of any approaching danger were usually communicated by drum. The crowning of Haile Sellassie ended the reign of this Oromo monarchy, and Aba was not succeeded after his death. Within months the Italians had entered Jimma, forming up to one-third of the population at their peak and the focus of power in the area shifted from Jiren and the palace into present-day Jimma. ■ *Mon and Wed 0900-1230; Tue, Thu and Fri 0900-1200 and 1400-1730; Sat and Sun 1400-1730. $1.25. Currently there are no English-speaking guides and photography is forbidden.*

To get to Aba Jiffar's Palace take a line taxi (blue and white minibus, 80 centimes) to the university, or further up the road to the teacher training college (TTC), knocking 10 minutes off the walk. From either of these points it may be possible to negotiate a contract taxi if the uphill walk looks too ominous. Jimma University and teaching hospital has a large campus on the right as you start up the second rise after the T-junction. It is around 3 km from Ferenj Arada. Try your luck at sweet-talking the *zebagnas* (guards) into letting you look around the campus; there are attractive gardens sprinkled with students reading and chatting. Take some simple ID – it may be asked for as a deposit. Alternatively, befriend a student at the excellent *Jiren Café* over the road. The road continues uphill to the TTC where the tarmac ends and it takes around one hour to reach the palace on foot. Water, sunscreen and a hat are

King Aba Jiffar's Palace

Ethiopia

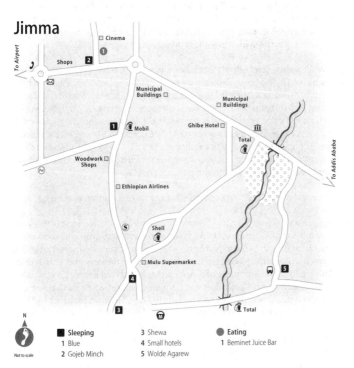

Jimma

Not to scale

■ **Sleeping**	3 Shewa	● **Eating**
1 Blue	4 Small hotels	1 Beminet Juice Bar
2 Gojeb Minch	5 Wolde Agarew	

recommended. The road makes a large left swinging turn before you enter **Jiren** village, identified by a large village green with football, and possibly volleyball posts. Turn left up a further rise and you will see the palace on the left.

After the tour you can walk around the area to see more of rural Ethiopian life. It is also possible, via a maze of haphazard paths, to wind your way back to Jimma through the forests. You will need a sense of direction and adventure, and allow at least two hours. If you return the way you came, consider pausing in one of Jiren village's *tej* (honey mead) or *tella* (local sour beer) *behts* (homes), marked by sticks with plastic bags on the end near the door. On the descent from the village, after about 1½ km, a grassed bank on the right marked by a solitary *beht* leads to the **Mosque of Aba Jiffar** and his burial place. You can see its bright green roof from the palace.

After this exertion you can try any of the cafés near the university for refreshment or, after turning right at the T-junction (at the bottom of the hill), walk a little further and visit the *Green Hotel* (well signed) which has good *tibs*, beers and atmosphere, and is popular with university and hospital staff.

Jimma Museum

Back in Jimma, and with time to kill, an hour could be spent at Jimma Museum, in the municipal buildings by the river opposite the *Ghibe Hotel*. The museum contains the vast majority of the furniture from Aba Jiffar's Palace and a selection of items typical of people of the region. The king received a number of gifts from his international friends including a rather ornate bed from Tanzania. Egyptian and other Arabic artefacts were also donated. Of particular interest is a small bottle of one of his wives' perfume, now 86 years old, a range of primitive forerunners to the flip flop and a massive table, 1.6 m in diameter and made from a single cross-section of tree. Also look out for uncomfortable looking traditional rural clothes, bibles made from goatskin, a framed single sheet containing the Koran, readable only by magnifying glass, and some frightening spears with multiple points. ■ *Mon and Wed 0900-1230; Tue, Thu and Fri 0900-1200 and 1400-1730; Sat and Sun 1400-1730. $1.25.*

A pleasant day trip from Jimma would be a visit to **Seka Falls**. Seka is around 25 minutes from Jimma on a bus heading for Bonga. Walk through to the end of the village and a turning on the right leads down a road to the falls. Ask locally for further directions. Seka town itself has little to offer.

Sleeping & eating
■ *on map*
For price codes: see inside front cover

D *Wolde Agarew Hotel*, behind the bus station. This 3-storey building gives no indication of being a hotel but is probably the best of the budgets in Jimma. Clean and has hot water, also a restaurant and bar. **E** *Blue Hotel*, blue-painted anonymous hotel opposite the *Mobil* petrol station, is said to be the best value in town, and it therefore fills up early. A bit run-down with off-hand staff, it does not have a proper restaurant, but the café downstairs is good for breakfast and snacks, and here the staff are very pleasant. **E** *Gojed Minch Hotel*, has a bar at ground level with upstairs lounges overlooking the bar area. Rooms are run-down, there is a choice of s/c bathrooms or communal showers. The *Shewa Hotel* has good food. The usual price difference between residents and tourists is enforced here.

Transport   *Ethiopian Airlines*, T07-11207, operate a service to Jimma (see Getting around, page 775).

Bonga
Population: 15,000
Colour map 2, grid B2

Bonga is a small town that straggles across a grassy hilltop in the middle of the Bonga Forest. This lush green area of Ethiopia is in stark contrast to the arid image of Ethiopia. Outside the dry season (November to February) it rains almost every day. The forest is well worth exploring and is very reminiscent of the forests in Central Africa. This area is the original home of coffee, and wild plants can be seen growing in the forest undergrowth. Bonga does not have much tourist accommodation except cheaper hotels, and it may be better to go on to Matu. The town has a Post and Telecommunications Office next to the *Commercial Bank*. In the same area there are shops and a market, which is only large on Saturdays. Bonga also has a Supak-S (Sustainable Poverty Alleviation Kafecho-Shekecho Zone – aid office) compound, primary and secondary schools and a prison, as well as Orthodox, Catholic and several Protestant churches. **Sleeping** F Either the *National Hotel* and *Misrak Hotel* are recommended as being the best of the local accommodation.

The stretch of road from Bonga to Matu goes through Misan Teferi and Tepi. It is almost unbroken forest, with a switchback ride up and down the sides of steep, forested valleys. There is also the **Wush Wush** tea plantation nearby just off the Mizan Tefari-Jimma road.

> **Misan Tefari**
> *Between Bonga and Matu there are several small villages, all of which have hotels, but none can be recommended*

From Bonga on the way to Adya Kaka-Durra on the right-hand side of the road, there is a marvellous walk descending to a natural bridge, over a tributary of the **Dynchiya River**. The walk takes approximately 45 minutes. A local guide is needed to take you on to an Orthodox church (which is on the left side of the main road). This walk takes you through a cool green valley inhabited by monkeys. After Misan Tefari, the road changes direction, going northwest to the small town of **Tepi** and then north through Gore and on to Matu.

Sleeping The best bet in Misan Tefari seems to be the **E** *Aden Hotel*, next to the town football field.

Gore, 25 km from Matu, is a place with an interesting and turbulent history. It was once a centre for the slave trade, and was also the capital of Ethiopia – for a brief 24 hours! Even today there are considerable political tensions. The surrounding scenery is extremely beautiful, including waterfalls and rainforest within 30 minutes' walk. There are occasional flights from the small airport, which was created 30 years ago by the Missionary Aviation Fellowship. The town itself is small but appealing. This is not a town to go out of your way to visit, but if you choose it as a stop-off point then there are several places to eat and some reasonable cheap hotels – with little to choose between them, but conveniently situated within a short distance from each other, so you can pick and choose with ease. The *Alif Cafeteria* does really quite good food, and it should also be noted that there is an excellent fruit market.

> **Gore**

> Ethiopia

Transport Air There is an *Ethiopian Airlines* service from Addis to Gore. Returning to Addis by air from Gore is fraught with difficulties, as the aircraft goes to Gambela first and preference is given to the passengers who board there. Reconfirming the flight from Gore to Addis requires great patience and persistence.

The **bus** trip costs US$6, takes 2 days, with an overnight stop in Jimma and is a more reliable form of transport.

Variously spelt Mattuu, Matuu, Mettu, Metu and Matu, this town is the capital of the zone of Illubabor. The variation in the spelling of the name reflects the difficulty in agreeing a phonetic approximation of the Cushitic pronunciation. Matu has a rapidly growing population, currently estimated at over 20,000. All things considered, Matu is not the most exciting of places – most travellers will probably only end up there for an afternoon and evening, as they travel by bus to or from Addis. It is friendly enough, quite scenic (although muddy in the rainy season) and has a busy and appealing feel to it. On Monday, Thursday and Saturday, there is a good outdoor **market** in town, to the right of the telecom building if coming from Gore.

> **Matu**
> *8°16'N 35°34'E*
> *Colour map 2, grid B2*

Sleeping There are several very cheap hotels near the bus station. The only hotel currently open, that does not appear to double up as a brothel, is the **F** *Matu Meganagna*, which provides a simple room with communal showers and toilet. The staff are friendly and helpful. Luckily, it is also the first hotel travellers will come to if walking into town from the bus station. **E** *Hotel Biftu Gada* has good basic facilities and an attached restaurant. **F** *Lusii Hotel*. This highly recommended hotel has temporarily closed due to financial difficulties, but is scheduled to re-open shortly. Here you will get a genuinely clean room with hot shower. **E** *Hotel Salaam* is also recommended. The restaurant is good, serving excellent *arosto* and *tibs*, with indoor and outdoor seating. This serves a particularly good breakfast of delicious bread and honey.

Eating Seriously cheap: There are 15 or so café/restaurants in the area covered by the map, but residents of Matu recommend only a few, including the *Harar Bar*. The service is good, and it is cheap at about US$1 per person for a main course and soft drink, but the food is unremarkable – the usual Ethiopian fare cooked by a very average chef. A truly dreadful meal at another of the eateries (*The Dashen*) revealed why the *Harar* is considered to be one of the best Matu has to offer. For carnivores, the *Bizuash Faantaa* might be a good choice. It serves pretty good *tibs*, but not much else (US$0.50).

Restaurant Mangoo is also recommended and is popular with residents, with a large variety of Ethiopian dishes, omelettes, salads and wonderful bread. It also serves good Ethiopian cuisine for the usual prices. *Restaurant Franca* offers good value for money. It's a family concern where the sons speak excellent English. The *Nesro Mohammed* bakery does good bread and nice cakes from 0600 to around 1600.

Transport   If you do not already have an onward ticket, you can escape Matu for US$2.50 to Jimma/Bedele or US$6.25 to Addis. Tickets are bought from the bus station one day in advance, the buses leave at 0600. Buses to Addis may be full, but asking the ticket man nicely could miraculously find you a seat. If you really get stuck, there are also buses daily to Bedele where there is a better chance of getting a connection through to Addis.

Gambela

8°14'N 34°38'E
Colour map 2, grid B1

Located about 777 km from Addis Ababa, Gambela has a strange history. From 1902 until it was captured by the Italians in the Second World War, it was administered by the British, the only part of Ethiopia to be so governed. The reason for this is that the British opened a port there on the wide Baro River, which during four months of the rainy season is navigable and provides direct access to the sea on the Nile via Khartoum. Ethiopian coffee was exported by this route, up to 1940. Now, alas, the port has fallen into disrepair, though remains of the warehouses and jetty can be seen. At its peak, up to 40 ships would be in dock at any one time.

Gambela makes a big impression on the traveller because it is just so different from the rest of Ethiopia. It comes as a shock to enter Gambela by road – dropping rapidly from cooler highland areas into the humid and lush lowlands. The tropical scenery and climate give it a very relaxed, laid-back feel. Visitors will probably be pleased to experience an almost total lack of attention and very few cries of '*Farenj*' or 'You'. This attitude is most certainly not unfriendliness, but is probably due more to the cultural diversity that exists in Gambela – different-looking people don't seem to be such a diversion.

If you wish to greet the Anuak or Nuer in their own language then you are guaranteed a suitably amazed reaction: 'Dirichott' for Anuak and 'Male' for Nuer

There are two indigenous peoples, the Anuak and Nuer, who are instantly recognisable by their height and very dark colouring. The population of 10,000 in Gambela town is divided roughly between the Anuak, Nuer and Ororno highlanders. Telling the two groups apart is sometimes problematical, but most Nuer men have tribal scarring on their foreheads in the form of four or five broad lines.

It is not advisable to visit Gambela during February-May, as this is the hottest time of the year, when the temperature can, and often does, rise to 48°C. Not only is the heat and humidity oppressive, but much of the surrounding greenery also dries up and dies, making the place markedly less attractive.

Gambela

To Dembi Dolo

Jejebe Hill

Mobil

Jejebe River

Total

Ethiopian Airlines

Baro River

To Ethiopia Hotel

N

Not to scale

■ Sleeping
1 Hotels

● Eating
1 KT Bar

Among Ethiopians, Gambela is sometimes referred to as 'a green desert'. The rest of the year sees an average daily temperature of around 35ºC plus high humidity.

The centre of Gambela has effectively moved as the town has grown in size. A nice way to spend a few hours is to take a walk down the **Jenina** area, or climb **Dejebe 'Mountain'**, actually only 67 m, but which nonetheless gives excellent views of the region. It is not too difficult to climb up around the back, especially in the cool of the morning. Travellers should be careful not to brandish their camera too openly near the Baro Bridge, as the no-photography rule is strictly enforced. Just 1 km downriver you can get good pictures of the numerous crocodiles basking on the rocks.

Sleeping

C-D *Ethiopia*, is the only tourist-class hotel. Most visitors will probably want to stay at this government-run hotel. It is set in very attractive grounds, the staff are unfailingly friendly and helpful and speak good English, the rooms are clean and have en-suite shower and toilet. Mosquito nets are available on request. Only place in Gambela that serves western-style food, and the standard is generally good. It is now also possible to stay in local **guesthouses** round the market area and the docks. Accommodation is a bit of a lottery in these establishments. There are about 10-15 budget hotels dotted around the town, with the main concentration just after the Dejebe Bridge area. Of these, the **F** *Total Hotel* offers a basic but clean room with a communal shower and toilet. **F** *Openo Hotel* costs about US$1 more than the *Total* and provides an en-suite toilet and shower and, unless the budget is severely restricted, is the best choice for those wishing to stay in cheaper accommodation. Travellers should bring their own mosquito net, as the hotels are unlikely to provide an intact, insecticide-impregnated net (or indeed one at all).

Eating

Seriously cheap *The KT Bar* is particularly good for Ethiopian food, and also has a very attractive shaded outside drinking area. For the local speciality *Godan tibs* (beef ribs), *Ojulu's Bar* is excellent (situated 10 mins' walk from the Baro Bridge). For just drinking, the large and shady outside area at the *Total* hotel is ideal and very popular, good service and live music on 3-4 nights a week. Unfortunately there are no restaurants serving Anuak or Nuer food.

Transport

Air *Ethiopian Airlines*, T07-510099, offer a service here – see Getting around, page 775. Schedules are subject to regular delays. As there are no taxis in Gambela, *Ethiopian Airlines* organize a service for the 17-km journey to the airport. See under Addis Ababa for flight details. **Bus** The bus to Gambela leaves from the bus stand on Addis Katema St, just to the west of Mercato in Addis Ababa, the fare is around US$7 one-way, and the journey takes at least 2½ days, but longer in the rainy season.

Directory

Malaria is a major problem in the Gambela region

Medical services Of the 4 private medical establishments, the *Selihon Clinic* is the best, open 24 hrs and offering an extremely efficient service. All the staff speak very good English. Anyone thinking of visiting the area during the rainy season (Jun-Oct) should take every sensible precaution against malaria, as Gambela is situated more or less in a swamp, and the mosquitoes rate among the most numerous and voracious anywhere in the world – they will bite through several layers of clothing. What makes this a serious problem for the traveller is that they will almost certainly be arriving from an area that is non-malarial, and may not be properly prepared.

If spending more than a week in the lowland regions of Ethiopia, it is strongly recommended to have a blood test prior to leaving for highland areas. Clinic staff in Gambela treat malaria regularly, and their expertise may provide a more accurate diagnosis than those unused to spotting the parasite in blood films.

Gambela National Park

Gambela gives access to the Gambela National Park. The undulating plains of high Sudanese grass offer excellent opportunities for wilderness exploration. All the elements of African safari used to be found here, including elephants, buffalo, lions, crocodiles and 100-kg Nile perch. However, during the past 30 years the numbers of elephant, giraffe and lion have dropped drastically, and few are within easy reach of the town. The occasional lion is seen, especially to the south of the town in the evenings, but if you come with the express intention of seeing large mammals you will almost certainly be disappointed. The olive baboon and vervet monkey, with its white whiskers, remain common, and hyenas can be heard whooping at night. Crocodiles are still plentiful and enormous. One of the best places to see them is 3-4 km upstream from the *Ethiopia Hotel*, after the river water levels have begun to fall (late November onwards). The birdlife in the national park appears to have fared more successfully, but is under threat as people cut down trees for firewood or construction purposes. Camping is allowed in the national park but a guide or scout is essential. Alternatively it is possible to stay in basic accommodation in Abobo.

To the Sudanese border

Beyond Gambela towards the Sudanese border, the Anuak cultivators give way to the nomadic Nuer. These pastoralists herd their long-horned cattle into huge camps when they stop for the night. There are occasional raids and skirmishes between the Anuak and Nuer people, but travellers are unlikely to be attacked. Onwards from Gambela, the towns of Abobo, Penudo, Bonga and Itang are well worth a visit. There are buses leaving for each of these towns from Gambela every morning at 0600. Tickets should be bought in the afternoon of the day prior to travel from the bus departure point, prices about US$1.25 return. There is a new direct road under construction from Gambela, south past Abobo and the huge Alwero Reservoir to Misan Teferi.

Abobo
If spending some time in the Gambela region, a day trip to Abobo would be very enjoyable

A fairly nondescript but extremely welcoming town, lying about 45 km southwest from Gambela town. The main feature of interest to the visitor would have to be the nearby Awash Dam and **Alwero Reservoir**, built during the Dergue period. This is a beautiful expanse of water, teeming with marine and birdlife and the occasional crocodile. In Abobo itself, *AlaMatu's Bar* is highly recommended, serving whole, freshly caught fish from the reservoir.

Penudo
Lying a further 40 km from Abobo, Penudo has an extremely remote feel to it

The drive takes you through some very beautiful woodland and is teeming with animal life: snakes, monkeys, birds and, during August, clouds of butterflies. It should be noted that during the rainy season the road might be impassable, even for a four-wheel drive vehicle. Much of the land around this region was an agricultural resettlement area for the Dergue. Adjacent to Penudo is a large Sudanese refugee camp (roughly 15,000 people), but you would need permission before trying to visit. A further reason to visit Penudo is that lions are being seen with increasing regularity on the road to Abobo. It is surprisingly large for somewhere so remote. There are several dollar-a-night hotels if you end up staying the night (bring your own mosquito net). There is one particularly good restaurant, unnamed, but easily recognized by the huge Coca-Cola sign outside the front door. The usual menu is on offer, the owners are extremely friendly, the servings generous and it is cheap even by small-town Ethiopian standards.

Itang

This small town 60 km west from Gambela is almost exclusively Anuak. It is an interesting road as the terrain changes, with good birdlife. Although not overtly welcoming it can make a nice change to be totally ignored. Itang itself does not have a huge amount to offer visitors, but the drive there and the surrounding scenery is some of the most beautiful in the whole of Ethiopia. It may be possible to get traditional Anuak food (porridge and ox blood) in Itang, but it can be difficult to track down. If you want to try some traditional Anuak or Nuer food the best bet may be to try and get an invitation to a home.

Nek'emte

Returning to Addis Ababa the daily Gambela-Addis Ababa bus travels on the northern loop via **Dembi Dolo** and **Gimbi** to Nek'emte. Dembi Dolo is an unremarkable town. A selection of basic hotels is 0available should you need to break your journey here. The route via Dembi Dolo is often impassable during the rainy season when the alternative route via Matu and Bedele is more commonly used.

Nek'emte is the capital of Welega province. It is a pretty town set among forests. The museum has a very large collection of Oromo artefacts, including woodcarvings, leatherwork and basketware. Northwest of Nek'emte on the road towards Mendi/Asosa, the road passes through the small town of **Nejo**, near which is said to be the oldest gold mine in the world. Local legend claims that this is the site of King Solomon's mines. Due south of Nek'emte is the small town of **Bedele**, which connects to Matu.

Bus links to Addis Ababa are via Bako. The scenery between Nek'emte and Hagere Heywot is dramatic, passing through forests and moorland and the highland area just before Guder. See page 807 for sights close to Hagere Heywot.

South to the Bale Mountains and Rift Valley Lakes

Addis
□ Ababa

The East African Rift Valley displays some of the most dramatic scenery in the world. The valley's passage through Ethiopia is marked by a string of lakes, seven in all, which dot the valley floor and are home to a fine array of flora and fauna. See also pages 805 and 807.

Nazaret

Further south is the small town of Nazaret (sometimes spelt Nazareth or Nazret), a weekend resort favoured by residents of the capital. Nazaret is unlikely to make it high up on any list of places with significant tourist attractions, but it deserves a few words because of its location and atmosphere. It is only two hours' bus journey from Addis Ababa, stands at the junction where the road from the Bale Mountains meets the road to Dire Dawa and Harar, and is close to Mojo where a third important route heads south to the Rift Valley and lakes area. It has a warm, sunny climate, an abundance of greenery and a confident, affluent feeling, sure to reduce stress-loads that travellers may have acquired elsewhere in the country. Beggars are relatively few in number and the new buildings are packed with cafés, restaurants, hairdressers, music shops and costly clothing boutiques, projecting a cosmopolitan air lacking in other Ethiopian towns of similar size. All in all, Nazaret makes an excellent spot for travellers to rest up for a couple of days between expeditions.

Colour map 2, grid B3
Phone code: 2
Population: 128,000

At Nazaret the road divides, one branch heading east towards Awash and Dire Dawa, and the other going south via Asela, Dodoja and Dinsho and on to Goba, a large town close to the Bale Mountains National Park.

The resort of **Sodere** (or Sodore), 20 km southeast of Nazaret, is famed for the volcanic springs that surface on the banks of the Awash River.

C-D *Adama Makonnen*, PO Box 2121, T02-11088, F114179, boasts up-to-the-moment computer services and an 'underground' nightclub. Rooms vary from a standard single room with a shower, to a 'first-class' room, a twin-bedded room, or a suite. The government-run **C-D** *Adama Ras Hotel* stands along the same road as the *Awash National* and *Adarna Makonnen*, but the rooms and bathrooms here have definitely seen better days and scarcely justify the prices. There is some compensation, however, in the hotel grounds, where large, leafy trees fan out over a long driveway and ground-level lamps give everything a cosy glow at night. Also attractive is the main courtyard that gives access to all the rooms. It contains a large swimming pool and surrounding that are 4 rows of trees with gorgeous multi-coloured blossoms. Single rooms with double beds and showers or suites are available.

D *Palace Hotel*, PO Box 560, T02-113800, stands opposite the entrance of the bus station and offers self-contained singles and doubles. The **D-F** *Bekele Molla Hotel*, T112312, offers a night's residency in a miniature bungalow equipped with bathroom, television and

Sleeping
■ *on map*
*For price codes:
see inside front cover
The town has a glut
of hotels of all shapes,
sizes and prices. At
the top end of the
spectrum are several
whose custom seems
to come as much from
wealthy business
people and important
conference delegates
as from well-heeled
tourists*

Ethiopia

refrigerator. This price also covers breakfast in the morning. If you are willing to forego these luxuries, there are also double rooms with toilets available for a quarter the price. **E** *Alief Hotel*, located on the same road as the *Bekele Molla Hotel*, is well established, offering reasonable value. **E** *Awash National Hotel*, PO Box 1151, T02-114478, out at the Addis Ababa end of town, has either single rooms with a communal shower or self-contained doubles. The lobby contains an attractive, looking bar area. Moving along the same road towards the town centre, the **E** *Garden Bedrooms Hotel* has double rooms with a shower or, for another US$1.25, a room with twin single beds. The rooms are clean, neat and spacious, and the bathrooms are in good condition with strong water pressure and working water heaters. Located in the 4th of the 5 boutique buildings as you head east, the **E** *Tinsae Hotel*, PO Box 5021, T114551, offers 1st-class single rooms with showers or 2nd-class ones costing US$2 less.

The **F**-graded *Canal*, *Organ* and *Sunshine* hotels are all in the area south of the bus station and all offer rooms with double beds and rather scruffy en-suite toilet/shower facilities. The water pressure can be erratic in these places and guests might have to contend with more than a few cockroaches. The *Canal* seems the best of the trio, with brighter rooms and tiled bathrooms, friendly staff, a lively bar dispensing draught beer and a room with a pool table. Those operating on a rock-bottom budget could try the even cheaper **F** *Unnamed hotel* with the Pepsi sign facing the entrance to the *Adama Ras*. The rooms are small and basic, with stained showers and seat-less and seemingly cistern-less toilets in the en-suite bathrooms, but cost just US$1.50 a night. And its female staff seem uncommonly jolly.

Eating
● *on map*
For price codes:
see inside front cover
Nazaret has no
shortage of good
eating places

Cheap *Yandano Zawditu Hotel* has a butcher's shop operating at one end of its premises, which explains the quality of its *kitfo special,* although this dish does seem unreasonably expensive. Also, their *zilzil tibs* is ridiculously tough. **Seriously cheap** Impressive dinner dishes at a reasonable price (less than US$2) can be found just around the corner in the *Tinsae Hotel's Restaurant,* up on its 4th floor, and in *Franco's Hotel* across the road. Both places serve truly excellent soups, though *Franco's* has the edge for providing slightly more generous portions – its fish cutlet is particularly good. Another strike against the *Tinsae* is that the 'Arabian, Japanese and Chinese food' promised recklessly on the sign outside does not appear on its menu. The *River Café* next to the *Adama Ras* serves up excellent egg dishes at breakfast time and dispenses sandwiches, cakes, biscuits and juice throughout the day.

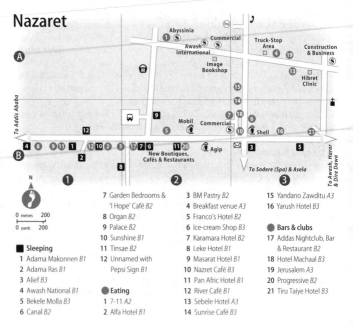

Nazaret

0 metres 200
0 yards 200

■ Sleeping
1 Adama Makonnen *B1*
2 Adama Ras *B1*
3 Alief *B3*
4 Awash National *B1*
5 Bekele Molla *B3*
6 Canal *B2*
7 Garden Bedrooms &
 'I Hope' Café *B2*
8 Organ *B2*
9 Palace *B2*
10 Sunshine *B1*
11 Tinsae *B2*
12 Unnamed with
 Pepsi Sign *B1*

● Eating
1 7-11 *A2*
2 Alfa Hotel *B1*
3 BM Pastry *B2*
4 Breakfast venue *A3*
5 Franco's Hotel *B2*
6 Ice-cream Shop *B3*
7 Karamara Hotel *B2*
8 Leke Hotel *B1*
9 Masarat Hotel *B1*
10 Nazret Café *B3*
11 Pan Afric Hotel *B1*
12 River Café *B1*
13 Sebele Hotel *A3*
14 Sunrise Café *B3*
15 Yandano Zawditu *A3*
16 Yarush Hotel *B3*

● Bars & clubs
17 Addas Nightclub, Bar
 & Restaurant *B2*
18 Hotel Machaal *B3*
19 Jerusalem *A3*
20 Progressive *B2*
21 Tiru Taiye Hotel *B3*

To Addis Ababa

To Awash, Harar
& Dire Dawa

To Sodere (Spa) & Asela

The nearby *BM Pastry* is also reliable for good cakes, juice and coffee, while hefty sandwiches can be obtained at the *Nazret Café* further up the road. Another *breakfast venue* worth trying is the one (unnamed) standing beside the truck-stop area, on the second major road running west-east in the town. Also worth considering are the *7-11 Restaurant*, the *I Hope Café* by the *Garden Bedrooms Hotel*, the *Sunrise Café* and the excellent *Ice-cream Shop* near the *Shell* garage. Other options include the *Leke Hotel*, *Masarat Hotel*, *Pan Afric Hotel*, *Alfa Hotel*, *Karamara Hotel*, *Yarush Hotel* and the *Sebele Hotel*.

Bars

Finally there is a plethora of cosy, relaxed drinking venues in Nazaret. If you need a beer after a gruelling bus ride you could do worse than try the bar on the right inside the *Addas Nightclub's* compound, a minute's walk from the bus station. The *Progressive Bar* on the 1st floor of one of the boutique buildings has a balcony where you can sit outside and view the town. The *Hotel Machaal*, near the *Yandano Zawditu*, is a down-to-earth pub with cheap draught beer and speedy service, but is given a faintly exotic air by the colourful murals on the walls. For a drink in secluded but neat and spacious surroundings, walk out to the *Tiru Taiye Hotel* at the corner, where the road past the main church meets the road to Dire Dawa and Harar. Its isolation doesn't seem to dampen the spirits of the barmaids there who go about their duties with a cackling heartiness. *The Jerusalem*, close to the truck-stop area, is also very lively.

Transport

Bus Nazaret's bus station contains a new building with offices and a café and is definitely a cut above most transport terminals in Ethiopia.There are regular buses from Nazaret to **Addis Ababa** for US$1.00, and early-morning ones depart for Dire Dawa/Harar costing US$5.50. Buses also head south for **Asela**, and **Awassa** can be reached by taking a US$0.40 bus ride to Mojo and then catching a bus on its way to the Rift Valley from the capital.

Adaba-Dodola area

Mountain trekking

The Adaba-Dodola area, located just north but outside of the Bale Mountains National Park, shares the same flora and fauna as the national park. Mountain trekking on foot or by horse is available. The **Integrated Forest Management Project Adaba-Dodola** (IFMP), an Ethio-German community-based eco-tourism project, aims at conserving the remnants of the Afro-montane forest by designing income-generating tourist initiatives, managed by and directly benefiting the local people. Forests can only be conserved if they can be shown to be as profitable as farming or herding. IFMP have established five forest camps at altitudes between 3,080 and 3,460 m, and donated them to the local community. The village administrators nominate camp keepers, who own the equipment but pay rent for the camp to the community. To maximize their returns, the camp keepers' interests are best served by using the camps to full capacity accommodating tourists. Payment to the keepers, guides and horsemen is made directly by the tourists.

The starting point for tours is Dodola. The area is malaria-free. On arrival at Dodola, an IFMP representative or the staff at the motel next to the *Mobil* petrol station will put you in touch with a guide to discuss your itinerary, which can range from two to five days. Hiring a guide is obligatory. To avoid sunburn a hat and sun block are imperative. It is necessary to bring warm clothing/ fleeces and waterproofs as night frosts are common at altitudes over 3,000 m. Sturdy trekking boots or shoes are also essential and a water bottle is needed. Pack horses carry bulky or heavy items.

Each camp can be reached from Dodola in half a day. Early morning starts are preferable to avoid the rain, which is more common in the afternoon, and is heavy and unavoidable during the rainy season (July and August). With increasing altitude it gets colder and wetter. The distance between camps varies from 5-18 km. Although trekking on foot is an option, at an altitude of 3,500 m many people find they rapidly become exhausted, so it is recommended to take along horses, chosen for their placid nature so that even inexperienced riders can cope. Regrettably recent forest fires have destroyed 30,000 ha in this area.

■ *Guide US$3.75 per day; riding or pack horse US$2.50 per day; horse-handling assistant US$2 per day; lodge accommodation charge US$3.25 per person per night; camping US$2 per person per night. All payments are made directly to the people who provide the service, but you may negotiate for your guide to handle it on your behalf. Contact TDS, PO Box 15246, Addis Ababa, T01-610086 (office), T610057 (residence), F621738, tds@telecom.net.et*

Sleeping & eating F *IFMP* (signposted) or F *Motel* (unnamed), next to the *Mobil* petrol station, both offer clean, basic accommodation and local food is available. The 5 basic lodges are located in different sites, and can each accommodate 8 visitors in 2 dormitories. Sheets, blankets, sleeping bags, towels and all kitchen and cooking equipment are provided. There are hot showers and western toilets, plus a fireplace and barbeque facilities. **Camping** with your own or a hired tent is another option. Only local food is available, but bring your own provisions if preferred. It is possible to arrange to have a sheep or goat slaughtered. Consult your guide for help in buying food and beverages in Dodolo. The camp keepers sell soft drinks and alcoholic beverages.

Transport Dodola is a 2-hr drive from the Bale Mountain NP headquarters, 320 km from Addis Ababa via Shashamene or 280 km via Asela. The direct bus from Addis Ababa to Dodolo and Goba via Shashamene leaves the Mercato Manharia bus station at 0800. The bus via Asela leaves the same bus station at 0700 to Dodolo. Goba is a 3-hr car journey from Dodola, a trip along the highest all-weather road in Africa.

Bale Mountains National Park

6°20'N 41°30'E
Colour map 2, grid B3

The Bale Mountains National Park is 400 km southwest of Addis Ababa, east of the town of **Shashamene** (see page 823). It covers an area of 2,470 sq km stretching right across the highest point of the Bale Mountain ranges, on the Sanetti Plateau between **Mount Batu** (4,300 m) and **Mount Bale** (3,340 m). The mountains are relatively recent, formed by lava flows in the Tertiary era, separated from the remainder of the Ethiopian highlands by the Rift Valley. Rocky magma outcrops remain, thrusting up like fists. In the foothills there is juniper and the African conifer *(Podocarpus falcatus)*. In the higher reaches, broad-leaved species become more common in woodlands. The bright yellow flowers of St John's wort *(Hypericum lanceolatum)* attract bees. Bamboo grows in the damper areas, especially close to the many swift-flowing mountain streams. In the sub-alpine zone above 3,200 m you'll find heather moorlands *(Erica)*, red-hot poker, helichrysum and St John's wort, which are usually seen elsewhere as small shrubs, but here attain huge dimensions. Further up, the climate becomes alpine, and the heathers decrease in size. The spectacular giant thistle and giant lobelia grow up to 4 m and 6 m respectively.

Garba Guracha (black lake) has particularly attractive surroundings. Several of the peaks are over 4,000 m, the highest being **Mount Tullu Deemtu** (red mountain) at 4,377 m.

The main feature of the park is that it houses three threatened endemic species: Menelik's bushbuck, the mountain nyala, and the rare Simien red fox with its black-tipped tail, sometimes called the Ethiopian wolf. The Simien red fox is unique among canines insofar as it does

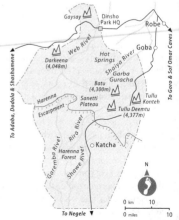

Bale Mountains National Park

not burrow, but lives outside, coping with diurnal temperature variations of up to 40°C. Only an estimated 700 of these handsome rust-coloured creatures remain, more common in the Bale Mountains than in the Simien National Park. Other wildlife includes leopards, black servals, lions, Anubus baboons, black and white colobus monkeys, olive baboons, Sykes monkeys, civet and the giant forest hog. There are several endemic rodents, including the giant mole rat, which burrows, leaving heaps of debris on the surface. Over 200 bird species are to be found, including the bearded vulture or lammergeyer, kestrels, falcons and several of Ethiopia's endemic birds including the blue-winged goose, the thick-billed raven, black-headed siskin, white-collared pigeon, black-headed forest oriole, wattled ibis, black-winged lovebird and Rouget's ralbus. The streams are famed for their plentiful rainbow and brown trout introduced from Kenya.

The people of the region are predominantly Oromo-speaking farmers and cattle herders who are skilful horsemen. In the forests are approximately 4,000 widely scattered homesteads. Bale Mountains National Park offers excellent fly-fishing opportunities (bring your own equipment), and dramatic high-altitude foot or horse-trekking routes.

■ *Entrance to the park costs US$6.50 for 48 hrs; camping fee is US$2.50 for 48 hrs; horse, mule or donkey (for riding or carrying luggage) US$1.50 per day; guide US$5 per day. It is best to schedule 6 days for a thorough tour. Stock up on provisions ideally before you reach Dinsho where the choice is limited. Nights at this altitude are very cold, and waterproof clothing is frequently needed.*

The park headquarters are in Dinsho. From there it is easy to visit the **hot springs** **Dinsho** that are to the east of the national park. ■ *US$0.50.* Ask at the bus station. It's a 30-minute bus trip (US$0.25), and a 15-minute walk at the other end.

D-E *Swedish Guest House*, self-catering, comfortable and popular. **E-F** *Dinsho Lodge* at the **Sleeping** park HQ. Self-catering dormitory accommodation. Alternatively, the towns of **Goba** and **Robe** are 30 km east of Dinsho, 14 kms apart. Goba, the old capital of the Bale region, is larger and offers a reasonable range of accommodation and places to eat. **Camping** is available behind the park HQ at Dinsho, and also at a site to the south of the escarpment at Katcha on the road from Goba to Mena that runs through the park.

Air *Ethiopian Airlines* offer a service to Goba – see Getting around, page 775. **Bus**: There are **Transport** two routes from Addis Ababa, the first via Shashamene or alternatively the shorter route via Asela. The direct bus from Addis Ababa to Dodolo and Goba via Shashamene leaves the Mercato Manharia bus station at 0800. The bus via Asela leaves the same bus station at 0700 to Dodolo. Then take a bus towards Goba, disembarking at Dinsho (US$2.50).

The town of **Goba** is the largest in this area; it has good facilities and is an excellent **Sof Omar caves** base from which to explore the region. About 120 km east of Goba are a series of *You'll need a powerful* enormous limestone caves extending several kilometres, formed by the Web River, *torch and a guide to* that has its source in the Bale Mountains. British speleologists surveyed the caves in *explore the caves* 1972, and in 1985 a Soviet team also studied the caves. The cave network is divided into three major sections. The upper section has large galleries adjoining the river to the left and right side of the river. The **Safari Straight** leads to the central section of the caves a distance of approximately 250 m after which the river winds around to the right. At the bend is the **Great Dome**, which reaches a height of 50 m in parts. After this landmark is the beginning of the middle section, with passages running off mainly on the left-hand side. Two large passages, old riverbeds, named **Railway Tunnel** and **Molossidae**, also run parallel to the river, rejoining the river at the impressive central hall called **Chamber of Columns**, which contains over 20 massive pillars supporting a high-arched roof, with the river encircling their pedestals, plus a gallery that offers an overview of this chamber. A maze of passages leads to other caves. After this is the **Shakehole-Collapse**, an area where a large sink has formed to the left of the river. There are rapids at this juncture, after which the lower section of the caves begins. To the left of the river is an area called the **Hulluqa**, a labyrinth of caves leading eventually to the exit, and to the right of the river is the **Claphem Series**, large passages and halls named after Kris Claphem who explored the cave in the 1960s.

These caves have been an important Muslim religious site since medieval times, and were named after the holy man Sheikh Sof Omar who, according to legend, took refuge here. The cave entrance was named after his daughter **Ayyo Mako**. Coleridge, author of the poem *Kubla Khan,* was greatly influenced by James Bruce's *Travels to discover the source of the Nile.* Coleridge's reference to 'Alph, the sacred river' running through 'caverns measureless to man', is claimed by some scholars to refer to the Sof Omar Caves.

Sleeping   Very basic accommodation is available in the nearby village of Sof Omar.

Transport   A round trip to the Sof Omar Caves is best arranged from Goba.

South to the Rift Valley

There are two routes south from Addis Ababa to Lake Ziway, the first being the national north-south road via Debre Zeit, Mojo and Meki. The alternative route to the west via Melka Awash and Butajira is slower but of greater appeal, as it passes within easy reach of several important archaeological sites, including Melka Kontoure and the stelae fields at Tiya and Silje.

Lake Ziway   If travelling via Debre Zeit, take the main road to the southwest at **Mojo**. After 25 km you will reach the **Koka Dam**, host to a huge variety of birds and waders. Continuing in a southwesterly direction, the next town of note is **Meki**, which is just to the northwest of Lake Ziway, 160 km from Addis Ababa. This is the most northerly of the Rift Valley lakes of Ethiopia, and at 26 km long and 18 km wide is also the largest of the northern group of Rift Valley lakes, dotted with islands and fringed with fig trees. Birds to be seen here include black egret, pelicans, marabou, ibises, herons and storks, black-headed orioles, jacanas and the handsome African fish eagle. To the north, the Meki River flows in to replenish the lake's waters, creating a wide bay where hippos gather. The island of **Tullo Guddo** is situated on Lake Ziway, clearly visible from the shoreline. According to legend the Ark of the Covenant was taken to Tullo Guddo for safe-keeping in the ninth century by refugee priests from Axum. Most Ziway people only visit the islands for religious ceremonies. An active monastery Debre Zion lies on the highest peak. The town of **Ziway** lies to the west of the lake. South of Lake Ziway, on the road to Lake Langano, are the ruins of an old fortress, towering over the village of Adami Tulu.

Sleeping and eating   **E** *Bekele Mola Hotel* offers great value, including local pricing for all visitors. Clean rooms, with hot water. Can organize boat hire to see the hippos from here but be prepared to haggle. Sited near the lake to the south of the town. **E** *Tourist Hotel* is rather more modern and the restaurant serves a variety of local and western food. **Seriously cheap**: *Brothers Hotel* has a justifiably popular restaurant.

For the alternative route to Lake Ziway via the secondary road, take the road from the capital southwest towards Jimma. At Alem Gena the road divides, here take the left fork via Boneya, and continue south to the small town of Melka Awash. The Awash River Gorge has a series of three waterfalls, with deep, swirling base pools. It is now difficult to visit the famous **Melka Kontoure** archaeological site nearby, excavated in the 1960s to reveal large deposits of Stone Age axes and tools, as

Rastafarians

The mixture of embattled Christianity in an unconquered independent Africa has for long been an appealing image to black people in the Caribbean and, as early as 1784, the Ethiopian Baptist Church was established in Jamaica. The defeat of the Italians at Adwa in 1896 by Emperor Menelik II was a particularly inspiring event.

The Rastafarian movement was founded by Leonard Howell, a Jamaican who had travelled to West Africa and fought with the Ashanti against the British. The focus was Ras Tafari, the eldest son of Ras Makonnen, Duke of Harar, who in 1930 became Emperor Haile Selassie of Ethiopia.

Once back in Kingston, Jamaica, Leonard interpreted the Book of Revelations to prophesy the advent of Haile Selassie, and sold pictures of the emperor as passports to Ethiopia. At a rally in 1933 he announced the six principles of the Rastafarian: black supremacy; hatred of whites; revenge on the whites; the overthrow of the constitution of Jamaica; the goal of a return to Africa; the recognition of Haile Selassie as the Supreme Being and the only ruler of black people. Howell was arrested and jailed. On his release he set up the Ethiopian Salvation Society in the hills in a community called Pinnacle, where he lived with his 13 wives. His followers cultivated bananas and ganja (marijuana), and grew their hair into dreadlocks, symbolizing defiance of white authority. Pinnacle was raided periodically and the community broken up, only for it to reform again later. In 1960, Howell died in Kingston Mental Hospital.

Ethiopia

permission must first be obtained in Addis Ababa. Nearby is the church of **Adadi Mariam**, the most southerly of the rock-hewn churches (see page 864). A three-quarter monolith, with 24 windows encircled by a wide, high tunnel, thought to date from the 12th century, the church was carved below ground level in a manner similar to the churches at Lalibela.

Monolithic stelae, upright stones or slabs used to mark a grave or as a commemorative tablet are widespread in southern Ethiopia. Some are undecorated, some have sculptured or engraved surfaces, stylized carved faces, limbs and/or ornaments, while others have engravings of swords or other weapons.

The most northernly of the southern Ethiopian stelae are found at **Tiya**. There are 36 stelae at the site (Soddo), 30 km south of Melka Awash, and now designated a **World Heritage Site**, that date from the 12th and 13th centuries. Joussaume and Anfray, French archaeologists, have discovered that many of these stelae mark the site of mass graves of predominantly young adults.

West of Lake Ziway, 25 km south of Butajira and close to a village called Kibet, there is another stelae field at **Silte** with intricately carved stones. They differ from the stelae at Tiya, although they are also of phallic and anthropoid design, but some are decorated with carvings and low reliefs. Silte is on the road to Hosaina and also has a beautiful crater lake. At Butajira there is a small road eastwards that brings you to Lake Ziway (see above).

Lake Langano

Lake Langano is set against a backdrop of the beautiful Arsi mountains, including Mount Kaka, which dominates the eastern horizon. It is a popular resort, especially at weekends when many people make the 210-km journey from the capital. There is a limited choice of hotels and camping accommodation. People swim in the lake as it is reputedly free of bilharzia, despite its unusual brown and copper-coloured waters. There are a number of hippos that are relatively easy to spot, but the crocodiles are more elusive. The lake shores teem with birds, including Hemprich's hornbill, butcher-birds, Helmet-strikes and fan-tailed ravens.

Colour map 2, grid B3

Boat trips can be arranged; enquire at the Bekele Mola Hotel

Sleeping
All the hotels around Lake Langano are situated at least 3 km off the main road, with no public transport

The hotels are known locally as 'Number One' (the northernmost, *Wabe Shebelle*), 'Number Two' (unnamed) and 'Number Three' (in the south, *Bekele Mola*).

C *Wabe Shebelle (Langano Resort)*, pleasing location on the shores of the lake, has bungalows that accommodate 4 people costing between US$35-50, bar, restaurant. Now very run-down, dirty, badly maintained and overpriced for the poor facilities. The restaurant is better than the rest of the resort. Disaffected staff. Camping available for US$3 per person. **C-E** *Bekele Mola* situated to the southwest of the lake, virtually opposite one of the Lake Abyata and Shala National Park entrances. Offers accommodation at a range of prices for bungalows, plus rooms at US$7.50 or camping US$2-3 per person. Alternatively, the town of **Arsi Negele**, southeast of Lake Shala, has a selection of very cheap accommodation and restaurants.

Camping is permitted by **Lake Abyata** (see below) at the official sites US$2.50 per person, or at 2 sites close to the **Ghike Hot Springs** near the national park entrance, or at the *Bekele Mola Hotel* on **Lake Langano**.

Transport
Any of the frequent buses on the main Addis Ababa-Shashemene road that runs between Lake Langano and the Rift Valley National Park (which encompasses Lake Abyata and Lake Shala) will drop you approximately 3 km away from the hotels. There is no public transport from the main road to the hotels, although it may be possible to hitch a lift at the weekends.

Rift Valley National Park

7° N, 38° E
Colour map 2, grid B3

About 200 km south of Addis Ababa, the park consists of two lakes, situated just west of Lake Langano. They are particularly attractive stretches of water, and each is very different in character to the other. The main interest stems from the extensive birdlife that the lakes attract, with over 400 species recorded. Despite national guidelines, a large number of people live within the national park boundaries.

Lake Abyata
Lake Abyata (also spelt Abiata, Abijata, Abiyata and Abyatta) is the more northern of the two, and measures about 20 km across. It is shallow and surrounded by grass-covered shores and acacia woodland. A soda lake, it has vast expanses of white shoreline and its surface is a carpet of pink flamingos. The birds can be seen circling the lake or soaring on the thermals that rise above it. Among the birds attracted to feed on the algae are greater and lesser flamingos and white pelicans, white-necked cormorants, herons, storks, spoonbills, ibises, gulls and terns. The pelicans nest in the adjacent Lake Shala, only flying here to feed. Also resident are fish eagles, and numerous species of duck. Surrounding woodland contains trogons, turacos and weaver birds. During the northern hemisphere winter, the lake is host to migratory ducks and waders from Europe and Asia. There are a few mammals on the shores, including Grant's gazelle, warthog and oribi.

Lake Shala
Lake Shala is a deep (260 m at maximum) crater lake surrounded by black peaks and cliffs. Shala is a pristine wilderness, surrounded by an aura of almost primeval splendour, the lakeside fringed with wild fig, euphorbia and acacia. There are two groups of **sulphurous hot springs** on the margins of the lake. One group is close to the park headquarters at Ghike, and the other is further round the lake on the southwestern shore near **Lake Chitu**. Lake Shala is also an important breeding ground for the birds. The lake is particularly famous for its colony of great white pelicans (about 15,000 pairs), ibises, Abdimi's storks and the white-necked cormorant. The pelicans use the early morning thermals to enable them to traverse the rocky barrier between the lakes in order to feed on Lake Abyata, as Lake Shala's high salinity has caused fish stocks to plummet. ■ *Entrance to the national park costs US$7 per person plus US$1.50 per car for 48 hrs. An armed guide is also advisable, cost US$7.*

For details of **sleeping** and **transport** in the area, see Lake Langano, page 822.

The busy, sprawling, crossroads town of Shashamene is where the main Addis Ababa-Moyale road intersects with the road east to the Bale Mountains National Park and west to Arba Minch via Sodo. North of Shashamene is **Jamaica**, a community of Rastafarians from the Caribbean (see box, page 821).

Sleeping and eating This busy town, teeming with people and modes of transport, has limited appeal. However, if you need to stay overnight, the **F** *Bekele Mola Hotel I* or **E** *Bekele Mola Hotel II* offer reasonable basic facilities and restaurants.

Transport Bus Shashamene is a major transport hub and there are frequent buses travelling in all directions. Several buses go daily to **Addis Ababa** and **Arba Minch**, starting at 0600. The long-haul buses tend to depart by 0600, so it is recommended that you arrive at the bus station by at least 0500. There is a very good road between Shashamene and Arba Minch, much better than the Addis-Awasa road. After Arba Minch there are no good roads, making travel almost impossible in the rainy season.

Shashamene
Colour map 2, grid B3
Phone code: 6

Twenty kilometres west of Shashamene near the village of **Aje**, where you take the road to the right, is **Lake Chitu** (not signposted), just to the southwest of Lake Shala. Hot springs and flamingos are found in this beautiful and peaceful place. Close by, the **Senkello Wildlife Sanctuary** is a small haven set up to conserve the endemic Swayne's hartebeest. The sanctuary lies south of the Rift Valley National Park (see page 822), and is administered by the staff based at Aje. Initially it was believed to contain about 2,000 of these hartebeest, but the numbers have sharply declined over the past few years as human settlement encroaches on the open acacia woodland.

In the **Arsi-Oromo** areas, especially between Lake Shala and Lake Awasa, there are **stone tombs** surrounded by engraved standing slabs. These show an affinity with tombs and statues found among other southern and southwestern Ethiopian people. Although frequently described as prehistoric, they are in fact thought to date from the 19th-20th century.

Senkello Wildlife Sanctuary

Ethiopia

The small town of Awasa (also spelt Awassa) is on the main north-south route from Kenya. Awasa, capital of the old Sidamo province and 270 km south of Addis Ababa, has developed quite rapidly into a pleasant, fair-sized town and offers a nice break from travelling. A short distance to the southwest is **Lake Awasa**, teeming with fish and generally considered the most beautiful of the valley lakes. A gentle chain of mountains and a low plateau surround the waters, opening to a wide bay in the south. The local fish is a speciality. You can hire a boat to spot hippos (price dependent on your bargaining skills), or go boating or fishing. There is a raised footpath on top of a grassy dyke, built to contain the rising water level, which begins about 1 km north of the *Wabe Shebelle No 1 Hotel*, follows the lake

Awasa

Awasa

To Shashamene & Addis Ababa

Lake Awasa

3

Boat Hire **2** **1**

S ♪ Garis

1

⊠ **2**

1

To Dila & Moyale

N

| 0 metres | 500 |
| 0 yards | 500 |

■ **Sleeping**
1 Louis
2 Unique Park
3 Wabe Shebelle No 1

● **Eating**
1 Pinna Pastry & Restaurant
2 Poste Rendezvous

shore south and is the best way of exploring the area. Birdlife abounds with crakes, cormorants, storks, herons, and several varieties of duck, geese, kingfishers, darters and plovers, all easily identified. The lake reaches a depth of 21 m, with a circumference of 62 km, and has several swampy bays offering ideal breeding conditions for waders along the shore line.

Sleeping D *Koko*, on main road next to Awash Bank. Good value, hot water all day. D *Louis Hotel*, modern, not far from the bus station, has good rooms with hot en-suite showers, plus a pool. Restaurant offers fine food, E *Kobeb Hotel*, clean, quiet, with s/c rooms. E *Unique Park*, near the lake shore. Clean and cheap.

Eating Cheap: *Pinna Pastry and Restaurant*, Awasa in the high street, PO Box 52, Awasa, T201231. Good food and juices, brand new 2-storey café, efficient service. Has good western food. *Poste Rendezvous* (next to the PO) serves good food including fish and is less expensive than *Pinna*.

Wendo Gennet Beyond the town of Shashamene, 17 km to the southeast, there is a beautiful wooded valley of ancient indigenous trees with natural hot springs at Wendo Gennet (or Genet). The forest glades are home to black and white colobus monkeys and teem with birds including the silvery-cheeked hornbill. The springs are very invigorating but western visitors should be aware that they will be an object of great local interest, carefully scrutinized, if pink skinned. There are two pools for swimming fed by the hot springs, the shallower one is known as 'Haile Selassie' (he was of modest stature). There are changing cabins and showers.

Sleeping C-E *Wabe Shebelle Hotel (Resort)*. This complex has been described by recent travellers as being very overpriced, charging up to US$9 for camping in the grounds. The rooms are at best basic, although the restaurant is good. The staff and management are reported to be both unhelpful and apathetic and the hotel suffers from poor maintenance and is generally unappealing despite the swimming pool. There are some cheaper local **guesthouses** round the station and marketplace, where there are also many small eating places.

Dila This small, quiet university town is on the main north-south route from Kenya. In a gorge at **Chabe**, 10 km west of Dila, travellers may be interested to see some very early examples of cave paintings (undated) with incised drawings and low reliefs of cattle. There are a few cheap places to stay and eat. Buses to Addis Ababa leave at 0600 – the journey taking 10 hours, US$3.50 passing through beautiful countryside.

Yabello Sanctuary
4° 50' N, 38° 8' E
Colour map 2, grid C3

This sanctuary is located about 600 km south of Addis Ababa, approximately halfway between Dila and Moyale, and 4 km west of the main Addis Ababa-Moyale road. The area was classified as a haven mainly to preserve four endemic bird species: Stresemann's bush crow, the Sidamo lark, the white-tailed swallow and the very rare Prince Ruspoli's turaco. It also contains lesser and greater kudu, gerenuk, Grevy's zebra, beisa oryx, dik-dik and giraffe.

There are some small hotels in nearby Yabello town. The nearest flights are to Arba Minch, about 150 km away (see under Addis Ababa, page 825).

Moyale
3°30'N 39°0'E
Colour map 2, grid B4

This southern town is adjacent to the Kenyan border on the national north-south road. Border crossings have been simplified since Immigration and Customs now share a building, provided you have a visa. The town straddles the border and, should you need to stay overnight, the Ethiopian side is preferable (accommodation and food are better and alcoholic beverages are only available in Ethiopia). Coming from Kenya, it is possible to cross into Ethiopian Moyale freely during the daylight hours to do some shopping, or even stay overnight, leaving the car behind on the Kenyan side, prior to completing the border formalities. Petrol and diesel are available here. Petrol is much cheaper in Ethiopia than in Kenya. Moyale (Ethiopia) supplies Moyale (Kenya) with water and in a recent dispute temporarily cut the supply, since when facilities on the Kenyan side have declined.

Border crossing The Ethiopian-Kenyan border crossing opens at 0600, but Immigration does not open until 0900. If you want to cross at 0600 you must obtain an exit stamp from Immigration on the previous day. There have been differing reports on the time at which the Kenyan side of the border currently closes, either at 1800 or 1600, so get there before 1600 to be sure. The Ethiopian border is closed all day Sun, and on public and religious holidays.

Sleeping and eating D *Port Hotel*, close to border checkpoint. Clean, self-contained rooms. **D** *Ysosadoyo Borena Moyale Hotel*, T93, close to the border checkpoint, located on the main road north to Addis Ababa, opposite the *Commercial Bank* and petrol station. Good value, friendly, clean, hot showers, good restaurant and safe parking. Well recommended. **E** *Abraham Hotel*, close to the bus station, on the main road. Offers basic, reasonable, standard accommodation. **E** *Brothers Hotel*, on the main road. Clean single rooms, has showers and toilets en suite in some of the rooms. **E** *Tewodros Hotel*, clean, s/c rooms, has bar and restaurant, friendly. The disadvantage is that it is a long walk along the main road, 1,500 m uphill from the border crossing.

Transport Buses going north to Addis Ababa leave at around 0500 so it is not possible to leave Moyale by bus on the day of entry. The bus northwards leaves from the *Brothers Hotel* courtyard. The journey to **Addis Ababa** takes 2 days from Moyale, which now has a sealed tarmac road. On the first day the bus goes to Dila for an overnight stop (journey time 11 hrs, US$5). Alternatively some buses stop overnight at **Shashamene** (US$6 Moyale-Shashamene). You need to arrive at the bus station no later than 0430. **Truck** convoys on the Kenyan side leave for **Marsabit** at 0800, but it is advisable to arrive early outside the police station to be guaranteed a lift. There is no regular bus service to Nairobi. Be prepared for an exhausting 48-hr journey, possibly on top of a cattle truck.

Southwest from Shashemene

From Shashemene (see page 823) the road southwest leads to the two southernmost lakes of Ethiopia's Rift Valley, Lake Abaya and Lake Chamo, partly encompassed by Nechisar National Park and the attractive town of Arba Minch, capital of the old Gamo-Gofa province. The road continues south to Konso, where it divides, east to Yabello Sanctuary, and west to Jinka, Mago National Park, and Omo National Park. Stephanie National Park lies to the south of Jinka, close to the border with Kenya.

On the bluff between Lake Abaya and Lake Chamo, known locally as the 'Bridge of **Arba Minch** Heaven' is Arba Minch, which means 'Forty Springs' in Amharic. The largest town in southern Ethiopia, Arba Minch – over 500 km south of Addis Ababa – has awe-inspiring panoramic views of the lakes. Looking west the **Guge** range of mountains provide a scenic backdrop. Arba Minch is divided into two main areas, **Secha** and **Sikela**, which are a short distance apart. It is very hot here, averaging 35-40°C in February and March. It cools down later in the year without too much rain. The town provides a good base from which to explore the area including nearby Nechisar National Park as the park headquarters are only 2 km from the Sikela roundabout. There are several fine walking possibilities around Arba Minch, including a stroll through the luxuriant forest below the *Bekele Mola Hotel* leading to the freshwater springs, which bubble up out of the ground.

Out of town going towards the airport, you can turn right down a muddy track, just past a rickety bridge over the River Keilfo, to the government-run **Crocodile Farm**. Crocodiles aged from three years upwards can be seen in pens. ■ *US$1.50. You'll need transport – bicycles can be hired at the Sikela roundabout for less than a dollar a day.*

It is a good idea to get a list of the local market days for the whole local area while in Arba Minch, as they are worth visiting. Generally things are cheap in Arba Minch.

Ethiopia

Sleeping **D** *Bekele Mola*, T810046. This is stylish and pleasantly located with good views of both lakes from the restaurant terrace, though it is a little dilapidated and is not known for its friendly service. Boat trips can be organized from here. **F** *Abaya*, T810181, located in Secha, costs about US$4 a night, good value and often full. Serves excellent fish – their Asa cutlet – fish fried in batter with a hot, spicy dip– is reported to be better prepared and tastier than elsewhere in Arba Minch. **F** *Roza's Restaurant* (see below) doubles up as a dollar-a-night hotel along with the **F** *Zebib*, *Tigistiferre* and *Meskeferra* in Sikela. All are fairly basic but clean. **F** *Kairo Hotel* is the best of the selection in Sikela, costing US$2-3 per night.

Eating *Roza's Restaurant* situated in the same street as the *Abaya*, is the best for fish, recommended for its Asa cutlet. *Roza's* also cooks a wide range of local foods, but travellers are charged at a higher rate than locals. The *Tigisteferre* and *Meskeferra* hotel restaurants in Sikela also offer good local food, with generous portions at bargain prices. *Zebib Pastry* sell nice fruit juices. You can get spaghetti and 'fasting food' on Wed and Fri only, or daily in the *Bekele Mola Hotel.*

Tourist information The Tourist Information Office, T810186, will help with local guided tours and boat trips to Lake Abaya and Lake Chamo, and to explore Nechisar National Park.

Transport **Air**: *Ethiopian Airlines* flies to Arba Minch (see Getting around, page 775). **Road Bus**: buses run regularly from Addis Ababa to Arba Minch. **Car hire**: is available. A 4WD costs US$100-200 per day. Trucks go at 0500 from the Agip petrol station at *Roza's* (Secha end of town); sun protection is advisable.

Lakes Abaya & Chamo
6°30'N 37°50'E
Colour map 2, grid C2

These are the two southernmost lakes of the Rift Valley chain, ringed by savannah plains and distant mountains. Lake Abaya, 1,160 sq km, and the crocodile-rich Lake Chamo, 551 sq km, are quite remote, but a trip here is rewarded with sightings of rich and varied wildlife in very lush vegetation. Birdlife flourishes with great white pelicans, hornbills, storks, ibis, cormorants, and black and white fish eagles frequently spotted, along with yellow weaver birds and brightly coloured kingfishers. The lakes teem with fish, including Nile perch, barbel, catfish, tilapia and tigerfish. Fishing is permitted but you will need to bring your own equipment. Hundreds of hippos can be seen at dusk when they emerge to graze on the grassy shores. One spot on the western shores of Lake Chamo is referred to locally as **'Crocodile Market'**

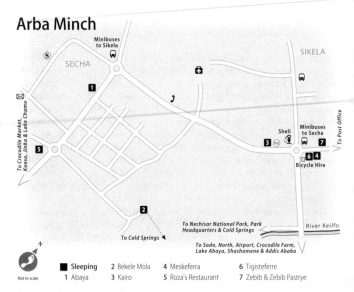

Arba Minch

Minibuses to Sikela

SIKELA

SECHA

To Crocodile Market, Konso, Jinka & Lake Chamo

Shell

Minibuses to Secha

To Post Office

Bicycle Hire

To Cold Springs

To Nechisar National Park, Park Headquarters & Cold Springs

River Keilfo

To Sodo, North, Airport, Crocodile Farm, Lake Abaya, Shashamene & Addis Ababa

Not to scale

■ **Sleeping**
1 Abaya
2 Bekele Mola
3 Kairo
4 Meskeferra
5 Roza's Restaurant
6 Tigisteferre
7 Zebib & Zebib Pastrye

because of the many crocodiles that congregate there, some reaching up to 7 m in length. To see the Crocodile Market you have to rent a boat. ■ *The boat trip on Lake Chamo costs US$47 for up to 5 people and takes approximately 5 hrs for the round trip. In addition it will cost about US$13 for transport to reach the park. You will also need to employ a guide to help identify the animals and birds. Guides cost US$8 per person per day on average. The trip can be arranged at the Bekele Mola Hotel. The entrance fee to the national park covers a 48-hr period, and camping is permissible.*

The islands and shores of Lakes Abaya and Chamo are home to the farming **Guji** and **Ganjule** people whose ancient traditions include hunting hippo. The Guji people are famed for their *ambatch* boats, with high prows similar to those depicted on ancient Egyptian tombs.

In the **Sidama** region, especially to the east of Lake Abaya, there are many stelae, mostly 3-4 m high, the tallest is 8 m, with phallic engravings, carved faces and ornaments.

Nechisar National Park
6°N, 37°E
Colour map 2, grid C2

The Nechisar National Park (also spelt Nechichar, Necht Sar and Necleser), meaning 'white grass' in Amharic, an area of 514 sq km, 2,000 m above sea level, encompasses the eastern shores of Lake Abaya and Lake Chamo and stretches eastwards over savannah plains. Although mainly open grassland, it contains areas of savannah woodland and highland forest. Northeast of **Mount Kalia** are **Shabe Carvings**. The park was established as a sanctuary for the rare endemic Swayne's hartebeest, but is also home to Grant's gazelle, Guenther's dik-dik, greater kudu, Burchell's zebra and olive baboons. Lion and leopard are reputed to live in this national park but are rarely seen. There are hot springs in the southeastern corner. The lakes are surrounded by heavy vegetation, and the waters contain Nile perch, tigerfish, hippos and crocodiles. The roads are difficult to drive on during the rainy season. Camping is allowed in the park (US$2.50) and there is a pleasant site by the Kulfi River, however, most people stay in Arba Minch. ■ *US$6.25 per person per 48 hrs, plus US$1.25 for vehicles.*

Chencha

Taking the road north just above Lake Abaya, there is good walking around the hills of **Sodo** and **Walaita** or up in the hills near the cool highland town of Chencha, in the Guge mountains, 36 km from Arba Minch. Swirling highland mists are common on this 4,000-m plateau. The **Dorze** people, once fearsome warriors, now live and farm in this region on well-maintained terraced slopes with irrigation channels. They are famed for their weaving skills, making the colourful *shammas* and *gabis*, similar to togas, worn throughout Ethiopia. The *shammas* are often smeared with butter for extra warmth and impermeability. The Dorze are also celebrated for their unique towering beehive-shaped houses up to 12 m high, with a nose-shaped reception area. These are covered with woven split bamboo (cut only on moonlit nights), then thatched with *ensete* (false banana), overlaid with grass to form a smooth convex dome and topped off with a spike of bamboo string. Each house has small garden/vegetable plot, and tobacco is grown for local consumption. The short drive from Arba Minch to Chencha involves an amazing transition, climbing from lush tropical lowland forests, through bamboo forests, up a switchback road to areas of juniper forest laced with Spanish moss. There are wonderful views over the Rift Valley but the road is impassable in wet weather. There is no public transport, but it is possible to organize a lift in a four-wheel drive.

Konso

Konso, 90 km south of Arba Minch, has a great market, with very friendly people. Slaughtering can be observed, with the blood being drunk out of pumpkins. The Konso people live in beautiful small stone houses, crowded together in compounds, their roofs almost touching. Entry to the house is via a short tunnel made of wood, meaning the visitor must arrive on all fours thus giving the occupant the opportunity to dispatch any foe. The towns and villages are enclosed by double stone walls, surrounded by woodland. Irrigation channels water the terraced slopes. The Konso people erected life-size wooden grave sculptures (*wuga*) after the death of brave

Ethiopia

hunters or warriors. The deceased is represented with a phallic symbol on his forehead, flanked by his wives and victims.

Sleeping There is plenty of basic accommodation in Konso at around US$1-3. **F** *Saint Mary's Hotel* is the most acceptable. **Camping** is available at the *Norwegian Mission*.

Transport There is a twice-weekly bus from Arba Minch to Jinka via Konso or trucks use this road, especially on market days.

Jinka Jinka, a town about 200 km by road from Arba Minch, is the gateway to the Lower Omo River Valley and Jinka is the main trading centre for the Omo region. The drive takes about eight hours, passing through the town of Konso and the Woita River Valley. Here you may see crocodiles and baboons.

Sleeping **F** *Arit*, **F** *Omo*, **F** *Amaluk*, both have restaurants but no hot water. The Natural Resources Office in Jinka can recommend safe **camping** areas.

Transport You can fly direct to Jinka from Addis Ababa (see Getting around, page 775). Jinka's airport is the soccer field. Onward transport from Jinka is limited to hitching.

Omo River

The Omo River rises in the highlands southwest of Addis Ababa, and travels south on a meandering course for 1,100 km before disgorging its waters into Lake Turkana. On its journey the Omo passes from an alpine environment to rainforest, then open savannah and finally through desert. This river is the sole feeder of Lake Turkana, East Africa's fourth largest lake, which straddles the Kenyan border. Over hundreds of years the river floodwaters have cut dramatic deep gorges. In the southern Omo valley the river marks the boundary between the **Kaffa** and **Gamo Gofa** regions. This region is very sparsely populated, but contains two remote national parks, one either side of the river. The valley is also rich in paleo-anthropological fossils; the latest hominid remains to be discovered date back over 4,000,000 years.

Little visited, this region is also home to some of the most colourful ethnic groups in Ethiopia. The **Hamar** people of the Gama Gofa region are noted for their very ornate, interesting hairstyles, which are retained in place for long periods by the use of neck rests when asleep; the women are bare breasted, and wear short goat-skin skirts. They are very friendly, in marked contrast to the Mursi. The **Mursi**, an ethnic group of the Kaffa area, are famous for the clay lip-plates and earlobe decorations of the women. The menfolk are decorated with tribal cicatrices, with deep incisions in their arms to show how many of the enemy they have killed. The Mursi have a reputation for being very aggressive and caution is advisable in their company. The **Surma** women who live west of the Omo National Park also wear lip-plates and earplugs made of wood or clay. The purpose of lip-plates is unknown, and theories range from making married women unattractive to other men, to the treatment of the effects of lock-jaw (tetanus) by keeping their airways patent.

Tours & tour operators **Whitewater rafting** is possible on the Omo River with the New Zealand company *Adrift*, which organizes (expensive) rafting trips on the upper and lower reaches of the Omo River. Prices can be negotiated as all-in packages from the UK or USA or locally for just the river run. Local rafting options include the Upper Omo run, the Lower Omo run or the African Queen for the combined trip. Contact *Adrift* on www.adrift.co.uk for pricing details. **Canoeing and rafting** For rafting and camping expeditions along the Omo River the people to contact are: Misgana Genanew, *Jacaranda Tours*, T628625 (Addis Ababa) or jacarandatours@ telecom.net.et, or Gary Lemmer, *Remote Rivers Expeditions*, T612081 (Addis Ababa), gary@remoterivers.com). **Guided trips** to the Omo region are better arranged as an organized safari. *Ethiopian Rift Valley Safaris*, PO Box 3658, Addis Ababa, T551127, F550298, are expensive but well recommended. This company has a permanent camp on the banks of the Omo River, and has many years of experience in this region.

The Mago National Park is located on the eastern side of the Omo River, in southwest Ethiopia, 700 km from Addis Ababa. Access is via the highway that runs through Jinka. Mago National Park was set up to help conserve the large number of plains mammals that abound in this region. The national park is mainly savannah with termite hills, and some forested areas near the rivers, which support a large number of hippo and crocodiles. There is negligible human habitation in the park, which is abundant in wildlife, including oryx, Burchell's zebra, Lelwel's hartebeest, buffalo, giraffe, waterbuck, kudu, lion, leopard and cheetah. The birdlife is varied, with hornbills, bustards, weavers, carmine bee-eater, starlings, kingfishers and herons that feed in and around the rivers. There are several camping sites in the park, but negligible facilities, and all equipment and provisions need to be taken. ■ *US$6.25 per person, tent US$2.50 and US$1.25 for vehicles. Access to the park is via Arba Minch, Konso and Jinka. There is no public transport here and few trucks travel this way.*

Mago National Park
6° N, 36°10' E
Colour map 2, grid C2

Further to the northwest, on the opposite bank of the Omo River, is the remote and little-visited Omo National Park. Virtually free from human habitation, except for a few nomadic people along the banks of the river, this is the largest national park in the country – 4,068 sq km – and is an area of true wilderness. Interspersed with acacia woodlands and grasslands this remote national park provides an ideal habitat for zebra, oryx, elephants, buffalo, giraffes, lions, leopards and cheetahs to roam in huge numbers. As in the Mago National Park the river has hippo and crocodile, and the birdlife is very varied. The park contains three areas with **hot springs** at **Sai**, **Ima** and **Liilibai**.

Omo National Park
6°25'N 36°E
Colour map 2, grid C2

Transport Omo National Park is even more difficult to access than Mago National Park. There are **flights** to Arba Minch, T06-810649. It is possible to charter a plane to visit Omo and Mago through NTO.
   Regular **buses** run along this route from Addis Ababa, going via Jinka. **Car hire** 4WD Landcruisers can be hired US$200 a day from *Bob Travel*, Jinka, although travellers have reported that it is possible to hire a battered 4WD locally for US$100 per day.

The national park surrounds **Lake Chew Bahir** (also known as Lake Stephanie) on the southern border with Kenya. The lake is seasonal, and for much of the year is marshland. There is a rich variety of birdlife, with black-tailed godwits and spotted redshanks to be seen. The nearest reasonable accommodation is at Arba Minch, 150 km away, see page 825.

Stephanie National Park
4° 40' N, 36° 50' E
Colour map 2, grid B3

East to Djibouti

Following the Assab (now part of Eritrea) highway east, 225 km from Addis Ababa is the spectacular Awash National Park – the oldest game reserve in Ethiopia. It stretches about 30 km from east to west and a little less from north to south, bounded on the south and east by the Awash River.

11°45'N 41°5'E
Colour map 2, grid C3

Awash National Park

The headquarters of the park are found near the dramatic **Awash Falls**, where the water cascades over the rocks in seven streams just before the river enters the enormous Awash Gorge. The terrain is covered with grassland and acacia woodland.
   The central feature is the **Fantalle Volcano** (2,007 m), now dormant, although steam can still be seen spurting from the fumaroles. The volcano is 25 km from the

park headquarters, negotiable only by four-wheel drive (two hours), or by horse or mule along a very rough road. A track leads part of the way up the volcano, and it is possible to climb the rest of the way to the crater edge. The caldera has a diameter of 3.5 km and is almost 500 m deep; the local Kereyu people graze their goats here. From the rim you can see the lammergeyers gliding on the thermal currents. A guide is essential as there are no signposts.

The **Awash River Gorge** runs along the southeastern edge of the park and there is a spectacular waterfall near the park headquarters. Although the river is substantial in the park, it does not reach the sea, but peters out in the Danakil Depression on the border with Djibouti, where the water evaporates off in a series of lakes.

To the north of the national park there are **hot springs** in deep, clear, blue pools at **Filwoha**, 43 km from the Awash Falls. This extensive area of hot springs is an oasis surrounded by tall green trees amidst the dry desert scrub. The superheated water emerges into translucent turquoise pools, quickly cooling to temperatures that are ideal for swimming. The area also contains unusual rock formations in the shape of blisters. This area is inhabited by the tall nomadic **Afar** people, who were much feared in the past for their rapacious and barbarous behaviour, which included castrating any male enemy killed or wounded in battle. The Afar men still wear a 40-cm curved double-bladed dagger, known as a *jile*, in their belts. A guide is mandatory if travelling to this part of the national park.

The main African wildlife of the plains are present with the exception of rhinos, giraffe and buffalo, although the animals are sparse compared with parks in Kenya. Most of the larger mammals are to be found in the **Illala Sala** plains in the southeast of the park. The main species to be seen are Beisa oryx and reedbuck, warthog and, less frequently, bush-buck, hippo, Soemmerring's gazelle, caracal, black and white colobus, green monkeys, Anubis and Hamadryas baboons, klipspringer, Grevy's zebra, the tiny dik-dik antelope, greater and lesser kudu, ardvaarks and bat-eared foxes.

One of the most beautiful areas is the **Kudu Valley** that takes its name from the large antelopes that inhabit it. Other game less commonly sighted include the big cats such as leopard, cheetah and the occasional lion. Over 400 species of bird are found within the 830 sq km park, including ostrich, the secretary bird and the

Awash National Park

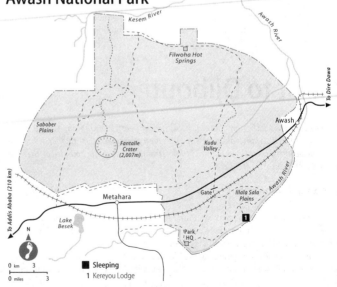

great ground hornbill. The birds are more plentiful in the dense riverine forest that abuts the Awash River, and here you may see coucals, barbets, hoopoes, bee-eaters, kingfishers and turacos. ■ *Entry to national park US$6.25 per 48 hrs plus US$1.25 for vehicles.*

C *Kereyou Lodge*, c/o EHC, Addis Ababa, T152700, located on the Awash River on the southern boundary of the park. It is a group of caravans, but reasonably comfortable. **Camping** Available at 6 sites, a couple of which are just outside the park boundary. Some of the campsites have rough tables and stoves and park staff can provide firewood. Basic local food is available at the *Lodge*, which has spectacular views from the verandah.

Sleeping & eating
Monkeys are efficient camp thieves so take care of your possessions

Regular buses and minibuses travel from Addis Ababa along the route through Debre Zeit to Awash, but to get around inside the national park you need your own 4WD vehicle.

Transport

Metahara is about 15 km east of the main gate of Awash National Park and is a short distance south of Fantelle, a dormant volcano that last erupted in 1820. The town is best known in Ethiopia for the large sugar plantation on its outskirts, but its biggest tourist attraction is sited on its western edge, where traffic on both the road and the railway line have to cross the **Beseke** crater lake. The lake is a good place for watching birds, trying to spot the crocodiles that supposedly reside there, and for exploring some extraordinary lava fields. The road and railway line share a causeway, built from black volcanic cinders, that slices the northern tip of the lake off from the main body of water. At times the water level looks alarmingly high against the railway side of the causeway and there have been reports of train passengers being loaded onto buses at Metahara because of flooded tracks. Just north of Metahara near the base of Fantalle are the ruins of the Muslim settlement of **Magala**, said to date from the period of Ahmad Gragn in the 16th century.

Metahara

Metahara is a ramshackle, fly-ridden but friendly place whose main social focus seems to be the verandah of the *Ergoshaa Hotel* beside the site where buses stop and depart. It is also a common place for finding a guide if you want to visit Awash National Park.

Sleeping F *Ergoshaa Hotel*, near the *Shell* petrol station, charges 20 birr a night for a room with its own cold water shower. It is a new hotel and, therefore, at the moment fairly clean, though that may change in the near future. **Eating** The *Ergoshaa's Restaurant* serves decent fish dishes (*asa lebleb*) and is a good venue to stop for food or drink if you've spent the morning travelling from Addis Ababa.

Awash lies just outside the national park boundary, on the road and railway line northeast of Metahara. A bus between the two settlements costs US$0.40 and takes about 45 minutes. This small town consists of an Afar settlement north of the railway line and a Somali one south of it. Foreign visitors will find Awash a dozy, sometimes sullen place but it has two redeeming features. Firstly, behind Awash Station, there is a wonderful view of the **Awash Gorge** and the area is a promising one for bird-watchers. Secondly, next to the station, stands the *Buffet D'Auche Hotel*.

Awash

Sleeping E *Buffet D'Auche Hotel* is a marvellous old French establishment built to service the railway. With fading whitewashed walls, verandahs hemmed in by unruly masses of vines and rubber plants, birds clattering across the awnings, lizards scampering up and down the woodwork and cats padding sleepily at ground level, it possesses a great deal of dilapidated charm. Good restaurant with satellite television, though the latter scarcely affects the timewarped-from-the-colonial-age atmosphere. Suites, a handful of en-suite rooms or a large bedroom with communal shower and toilet. The only drawback of staying there is the nocturnal noise from the train station. Light sleepers may prefer to check out the **E** *St George Hotel*, a presentable building on the town's main street with a rooftop terrace.

Ethiopia

Yangudi Rassa National Park

11°N, 41°E
Colour map 2, grid B4

The Yangudi Rassa National Park is about 500 km from Addis Ababa on the road north of Awash, and about 60 km after the small settlement of **Gewane** (which has petrol) on the road to Djibouti and Assab. It was primarily established to preserve a population of Somali wild ass. There are only a few other animals in the park, mainly Grevy's zebra, greater and lesser kudu, gerenuk and cheetah. The nearest reliable accommodation is at Awash, about 200 km away (see page 831).

Erta Ale Volcano

Lat.13·6°N,
Long. 40·67°E

Even further afield, the Erta Ale is a basaltic shield volcano situated in the **Danakil Depression** in the Afar Region, close to the Red Sea. It rises from 500 m below sea level to an elevation of 613 m. To the south of Erta Ale are the Alaita Lava Fields and Lake Afrera, and to the north is the border with Eritrea. It is very remote and infrequently visited but is of great interest to vulcanologists as it has two active lava lakes in its crater summits. Its local Afar name translates as '*the smoking mountain*'. There have been seven major eruptions since 1873, and since 1967 it has been erupting almost continuously. Following the cessation of hostilities between Ethiopia and Eritrea visits have been made to the volcano in 2000 and 2001, although difficulties were encountered from some hostile nomadic Afar people. There are plans to protect the area by creating a national park of the volcanoes.

The road to Dire Dawa

Beyond Awash the road continues to **Mieso**, where it parts company with the railway line and the Rift Valley and begins to climb into the **Arba Gugu Mountains**. By this time the road is mainly a dirt one, with only intermittent stretches of asphalt. Copious roadworks turn parts of it into a muddy assault course. The landscape changes, as do the birds and plants. The acacia of the Rift changes to prickly pear, which becomes the dominant plant. The camels give way to donkeys and sorghum is more commonly seen as you climb. The mountain road provides beautiful views, especially on clear days during or after the rainy season when everything is atypically green. Peaks with wooded summits and seemingly endless, sorghum-terraced sides rise around lush valleys. Far below, the corrugated-iron roofs of farmhouses glint like staples in a giant sheet of green felt. Buses travelling between Addis Ababa and Dire Dawa often break the journey in **Abse Tefari**, a narrow and muddy town in the lower reaches of the Arbu Gugu Mountains. Another common stop is the less claustrophobic and friendlier town of **Hirna**, about 60 km closer to Dire Dawa.

The town of **Kulubi** is 8 km from the junction with the road running between Harar and Dire Dawa. It is here that there was said to be divine intervention during the Italian invasion, and following the Italian defeat at Adwa, Ras Makonnen built the shrine to the Archangel Gabriel to give thanks. Even today, miracles are said to occur here. **St Gabriel's Church** is on a hilltop overlooking the town and is the scene of a bi-annual pilgrimage attracting up to 100,000 people. These massive influxes of pilgrims in late July and late December can seriously clog up the transport services – the well-to-do of Addis Ababa grab all the seats on flights to Dire Dawa, while everybody else piles onto the buses. Even without pilgrims Kulubi is a bustling place. On market days, buses attempting to pass through the narrow main street can measure their progress in centimetres thanks to the colourful throngs of shoppers and traders.

Dire Dawa

9°35'N 41°45'E
Phone code: 5
Colour map 2, grid B4
Population: 165,000

Roughly halfway along the Addis Ababa–Djibouti railway is Dire Dawa. It is 517 km east of the capital and has existed since the construction of the railway by French engineers in 1902. The French influence lingers on in Dire Dawa, and western visitors are as likely to be greeted by cries of 'Ça va?' as by cries of 'Hello'. Because of its key position on the road and railway it has expanded rapidly and is now the second largest settlement in Ethiopia. The climate here is warm and dry, with midday temperatures sometimes climbing to uncomfortably high levels, a reason why some offices in Dire Dawa don't resume business after lunch until 1500. Occasionally, welcome breezes dispel the heat a little.

Ins and outs

Ethiopian Airlines fly daily from the capital to Dire Dawa; buses leave early every morning and there are also daily trains. A popular arrangement is to take a train to Dire Dawa from Addis Ababa, and the bus back (see Safety, below). The bus and train take different routes and the bus trip is particularly attractive through the **Arbu Gugu Mountains**.

Getting there *For transport details, see page 835*

A dried-up seasonal waterway, known as the **Dechatu Wadi**, divides the town in two. The smarter side of the waterway contains the railway station, the main branch of the *Commercial Bank* (where travellers' cheques can be cashed) and most of the better hotels. It is distinguished by broad avenues, which are meshed around a number of roundabouts, with lines of trees adding shade along their edges. The other side of the waterway is more Muslim in character, bustling and atmospheric, but parts of it are decidedly scruffy.

Getting around

Dire Dawa's **Tourist Office**, PO Box 295, is in the administrative building next to the bus station, T112466, F112441.

There have been occasional attacks on travellers to this region, with some fatalities. Caution is also urged before using the train, which has been targeted by bandits in the past, although additional security measures have now been implemented. A more likely hazard on the train is one of petty and not-so-petty theft. There have been stories of thieves relieving sleeping passengers of their luggage, then tossing the luggage out of windows at points along the line where accomplices are waiting to collect it. Therefore, it is advisable to stay awake on the train and keep a firm grip of your bags.

Safety

Sights

The mood in Dire Dawa is relaxed and people are generally welcoming to foreigners, but the town has few features of interest. However, if you have to spend time in Dire Dawa itself, the market place has some appeal, with crowds of camel-herding Oromos, Somalis and Afars. The town also boasts the oldest market building in Ethiopia, if not the oldest market, and there are some pleasant though hardly spectacular churches and mosques. For entertainment, visitors can try the town's two cinemas and there are several decent hotels, bars and restaurants in which to eat, drink and socialize.

Dire Dawa

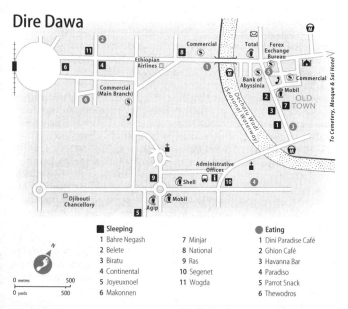

Sleeping		Eating
1 Bahre Negash	7 Minjar	1 Dini Paradise Café
2 Belete	8 National	2 Ghion Café
3 Biratu	9 Ras	3 Havanna Bar
4 Continental	10 Segenet	4 Paradiso
5 Joyeuxnoel	11 Wogda	5 Parrot Snack
6 Makonnen		6 Thewodros

Ethiopia

Dire Dawa is most useful as a starting point from which to explore the ancient city of **Harar**, only 54 km away – a spectacular journey up the escarpment of the Rift Valley. The road passes **Lake Adele** and its larger and prettier neighbour **Lake Alemaya**, the main reservoir for the area. It also goes by rich farmlands, where some of Ethiopia's finest coffee is cultivated. The local mildly narcotic leaf *chat* (or *khat*), is also widely grown here.

Dire Dawa's Caves

There are the caves in this region, some of which contain **prehistoric rock paintings** of cattle, antelopes, jackals and hyenas, estimated to be 3,500 years old, perhaps even older. **Porc Epic Cave** was excavated in 1929 and 1933 by French archaeologists, and further excavations were carried out by J Desmond Clark in 1974. It is located 2 km south of Dire Dawa, just below the top of a vertical cliff known as **Garad Erer**. A human jaw fragment with five teeth was uncovered, with Neanderthal features. It is believed that the cave, which is approximately 14 m wide and 3 m high, was used by early hominoids as a seasonal hunting cave, approximately 60,000-70,000 years ago.

The main concentration of prehistoric caves is in **Lega-Oda**, 36 km from the town. Information about these caves and their paintings, especially about where they are and how they can be reached, can be frustratingly difficult to find. It isn't possible to get to the caves by yourself but the tourist office staff in Dire Dawa are willing to arrange for a guide and a vehicle to take you there for a 'not so expensive' fee. The office would particularly welcome academic visitors as some of these caves and their contents have not yet been properly studied.

Sleeping

■ *on maps*
For price codes: see inside front cover
There are some cheap local guesthouses round the station and market place, where there are also many small eating places

The government-run **C-D** *Ras Hotel*, PO Box 83, T113255, about 10 mins' walk from the bus station, has an imposing high-ceilinged lobby, attractive wooded premises and what is reputedly the town's only swimming pool. The water looks a tad greenish but it certainly seems popular. In the same price league is the **D** *Sai Hotel*, PO Box 87, T112285, F111376, out near the Harar end of the town, offering self-contained singles and doubles. The hotel boasts a pleasant roofed terrace at the front, with a restaurant along to the left. The lobby contains the office for the *Sai Travel Agency*.

The **E** *Joyeuxnoel Hotel*, PO Box 1922, T111952, is a newish but secluded building on a lane across from the *Ras*, has large, pleasant rooms with a clean toilet and shower. Only the carpets look slightly the worse for wear. The proprietor is helpful and friendly and the bar in the lobby exudes a cosy, welcoming atmosphere. Near the railway station the **E-F** *National Hotel*, T113415, is a pleasantly rambling building with a restaurant in its central courtyard and rooms lining the sides of a second courtyard at the back. Some rooms have en-suite toilets and showers, and rooms with communal facilities cost half the price.

F *The Continental* is located along the street from the *National*, in the direction of the train station. It is small, functional but reasonably clean single rooms or doubles with shared toilets and showers. Opposite the *Continental*, the **F** *Wogda Hotel* has a cheerful proprietress and is fronted by a pretty little square of garden, but the rooms are poverty-row material and the communal shower looks like it was cobbled together from sheets of corrugated iron and pieces of piping about 5 mins earlier. Lovers of pub sports might appreciate the back room with a pool table, but that's about it. The *Wogda's* prices are especially laughable when you compare it with the **F** *Makonnen Hotel*, PO Box 301, T05-113348, around the corner in the central plaza, opposite the train station. The *Makonnen* has big, clean rooms with a ceiling fan, and a few rooms even have balconies. Admittedly the shower and toilet facilities are communal, but these are tiled and get a good wash down every day. Downstairs is a popular coffee shop with a large roofed terrace, its shade offering refuge for locals during the midday heat. Travellers facing an early-morning bus journey could do worse than consider the **F** *Segenet Hotel*, a minute's walk from the bus station, which has s/c rooms – not so big, but clean and acceptable. Rooftop terrace, an attractive courtyard, and inside the entrance gates a carcass-festooned butcher's shop ready to supply *tibs* and *kitfo*-lovers with the freshest of fresh cuts. The street that forks off to the right after you cross the bridge walking away from the railway station is home to a squad of cheap hotels like the **F** *Belete, Biratu, Minjar* and *Bahre Negash*.

Cheap *Paradiso Restaurant*, a posh establishment along from the turning leading to the bus station, which specializes in pasta. The quality of both the food and the service is impeccable.

Seriously cheap Around the corner from the *Paradiso*, a perfectly satisfactory plate of spaghetti can be had for a fraction of the cost at the *Segenet Hotel*. In the railway station area the best eating places are the *National* and *Makonnen* hotels. The restaurant in the *National* occupies a whole courtyard with a corrugated-iron roof erected above to protect diners from the weather – the clatter of rain on it during the wet season must be deafening. There are a number of tasty egg dishes available here for breakfast, which can be served up as snacks later in the day, though US$0.15 will be added to the price. The lunch/dinner menu in the *National* looks impressive but often many of the dishes are unavailable. Equally good breakfasts can be had at the *Makonnen* and its evening menu is more varied than most in the vicinity – the *tibs* are deliciously spicy and fat-free. Out by the bridge overlooking the waterway, the *Dini Paradise Café* is a relaxing spot to enjoy a fruit juice during the midday heat, provided you can stomach the sight of the monkeys and deer kept in cramped cages at the back of the children's playground area. Back towards the station, the *Thewodros Hotel* – not actually a hotel these days just a café – brews a potent cup of coffee. Other cheap eating places include *Ghion Café*, *Parrot Snack*, *Elga Café* and the *Havanna Bar*.

Cinemas There are 2 open-air cinemas in the town.

Sai Travel Agency, *Sai Hotel*, PO Box 87, T05-112285, F111376, will provide vehicles for US$80 a day, should any very wealthy people want to visit Harar but remain based in Dire Dawa.

Air *Ethiopian Airlines*, PO Box 176, T05-111147/05, flies daily to Dire Dawa (see Getting around, page 775). They offer morning and afternoon flights from Addis Ababa to Dire Dawa every day. Enquiries in Dire Dawa itself can be made at the new, plush offices of *Ethiopian Airlines* across the street from the *National Hotel*. A taxi ride between the airport and the centre of town should cost US$2.50-4, though there have been horror stories about much higher fares being demanded, especially of travellers trying to get away from the airport. **Road Buses**: every morning buses for Dire Dawa leave from the bus station on **Addis Katama St**, just to the west of Mercato in Addis Ababa, while a corresponding bus leaves Dire Dawa for the capital. The fare should be US$6-7 either way, with a journey time of a whole day – expect departure times of 0500-0530. Buses may not be able to cover the 500-odd km before nightfall, especially during the rainy season, and Addis Ababa-bound passengers may end up spending a night in Nazaret. There are also newer, faster and more comfortable buses plying the route between Addis Ababa and Dire Dawa/Harar, but charging higher fares. For further information see under Transport in Harar, page 841. **Train** See under Addis Ababa, page 803.

Eating
● *on map*
For price codes:
see inside front cover

Entertainment

Tours & tour operators

Transport

Ethiopia

Harar

Harar (sometimes spelt Harer) is a walled city of 123,000 people within the Oromiya Region, standing on the eastern wall of the Great Rift Valley, 526 km from Addis Ababa. The city's lofty situation gives wonderful views of the surrounding country – the vast Danakil desert to the north, the fertile mountains to the east and the cattle-rich Ogaden plains to the south. The whole town is surrounded by soaring mountains and fanned by cool, bracing air. The mountains around Harar produce some of the best coffee in Ethiopia.

Harar was a fiercely religious city from the early days of Islamic expansion into the Horn of Africa when it was a 'forbidden city' (closed to visitors), until 1887 when Menelik forced it into the Ethiopian Empire. The women of Harar are reputed to be the most beautiful in Africa, and Harar itself is famed for its silversmiths, with exquisite necklaces, bracelets and chains to be found in the market.

9°20'N 42°8'E
Population: 62,000
Phone code: 5
Colour map 2, grid B4

Ins & outs
For transport details, see page 841

Getting there Harar can be reached by train, road or air. **Getting around** Unlike most Ethiopian towns, Harar seems to rely more heavily on private taxis than on the minibus-type 'line' taxis, so be prepared to haggle with over-charging taxi drivers. The heart of the city is enclosed by a medieval wall and the ancient buildings and twisting alleyways within the wall are incredibly atmospheric. However, the more modern part of Harar, which has developed outside the main entrance to the Old City, is remarkably neat and handsome compared to most Ethiopian settlements and is worthy of investigation in its own right.

History

Harar has had a long trading history with the Middle East and India. It used to have a slave market, supplying slaves from all over East Africa, and also supplied eunuchs to harems in Arabia. It was here, in 1525, that Ahmad ibn Ibrahim, nicknamed 'Gragn' (left-handed), rallied together the Muslims of East Ethiopia and launched a *jihad* against the Christian highlands, choosing Lent as the time to attack as the Christians were weakened by fasting. Gragn conquered Shoa in 1529, Amhara in 1531 and Tigre in 1535, and gave Christian Ethiopians their most traumatic experience of defeat and subjugation until the Italian occupation four centuries later. Only in 1543, when Emperor Galawdewo enlisted the support of the Portuguese and defeated and slew Gragn at a battle in the Lake Tana area, was the Muslim tide turned. In the 1550s Gragn's nephew, Emir Nur, built Harar's most distinctive feature, the defensive wall known as the **Jugal**, which encircles the central part of the city and incorporates five major gates and 24 watch towers. Nur was able to give the city a more gruesome adornment in 1559, when his uncle's killer Emperor Galawdewo was himself slain and his severed head was put on display there.

Harar was a 'forbidden city', that is, closed to visitors, until the 19th century. In 1854 Richard Burton was supposedly the first European to set foot in the city. His stay in Harar was for only 10 days; a longer residency by a European visitor was that of the French poet Arthur Rimbaud, who lived in Harar during the 1880s and pursued several business activities, ranging from a photography service to

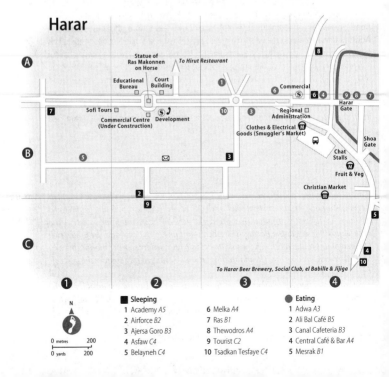

Harar

Sleeping
1 Academy *A5*
2 Airforce *B2*
3 Ajersa Goro *B3*
4 Asfaw *C4*
5 Belayneh *C4*
6 Melka *A4*
7 Ras *B1*
8 Thewodros *A4*
9 Tourist *C2*
10 Tsadkan Tesfaye *C4*

Eating
1 Adwa *A3*
2 Ali Bal Café *B5*
3 Canal Cafeteria *B3*
4 Central Café & Bar *A4*
5 Mesrak *B1*

gun-running for Menelik II. In fact, it was Menelik II who forced Harar into the Ethiopian Empire in 1887. He appointed as Governor of Harar and the surrounding province his friend and relative Ras Mekonin, who was the father of the future emperor Haile Selassie.

Even in the 20th century Harar was getting mentioned in the history books. During the latter part of 1977 the city came under siege by Somalian forces during the conflict over the Ogaden. Only when the Somalian troops ran out of supplies, and the Ethiopian army received massive amounts of training from the Cubans, and weaponry from the Soviets, was the onslaught driven back. Because of the many Cuban soldiers stationed there, in the late 1970s and early 1980s foreigners were called *Cuba Cuba*. These days, however, foreigners are more likely to be called *forengo*, said to be a corruption of the word 'French'.

Despite its history of slavery, *jihads* and sieges, Harar is an extremely friendly place and travellers arriving from other parts of Ethiopia will find it refreshingly free of hassle.

Sights

The setting is thrilling. The twisting alleyways and flat-roofed buildings are little changed from when Richard Burton arrived in the 19th century, and even the occasional satellite dish sprouting skywards cannot lessen the medieval atmosphere. Even after a few days, the labyrinth of little streets – which one enterprising tourist brochure has counted and totalled at 362 – will surprise you with their ability to lead you where you are not expecting. It is difficult to believe that such a warren can be crammed into an area of little more than 1 sq km. Local guides can be hired to help you discover the secrets of the town. They will ask for US$12.50 for a full morning and afternoon tour (be warned, though, that they might also expect you to buy them lunch into the bargain), or half that amount for a tour of a couple of hours. If you want to be sure that your guide is the authentic article, ask to see the official guide ID card given out by the town's tourist authority (see Tours and tour operators, page 841).

The Walled City

Ethiopia

To Hyena Man's Feeding Site

Jugal
Fallana Gate
Misrak Arbegnoch Hospital
Emir Nur's Tomb
Al-Jami Grand Mosque
Harari National Cultural Centre
Erer Gate
Medhane Alem
Ras Mekonin's Palace
Rimbaud's House
Jugal
Buda Gate
Secondary Hyena Feeding Ground
Sanga Gate

The city's bustling **market places** are regarded as among the most colourful in Ethiopia. The afternoons are frequently even busier because the **Droma traders** take some time to reach the city from the surrounding countryside. Particularly hectic are the markets in the Old City along from the central square towards **Sanga Gate** and on the road linking the square with **Fallana Gate** – the *chat* stalls in the second of these markets leave the ground carpeted with green leaves. Just outside **Shoa Gate** the road is lined with stalls selling more *chat*, fruit and vegetables, clothes and electrical appliances (often contraband that has been slipped in over Ethiopia's eastern borders). Additional stalls operate along the middle of the road, forcing shoppers and traffic to compete for the strips of remaining asphalt. Also worthy of investigation is the **Christian Market** along a lane across from Shoa Gate.

The encircling wall, the **Jugal**, can be walked along on the outside for most of its 3½ km. By the *Belayneh Hotel*, two lanes branch off from the main road: take the lane nearer the city centre. After a first, smelly few minutes, when the lane passes some open sewers and rubbish heaps, it brings you alongside the wall, with its gates and towers, and becomes charmingly scenic. On the **Erer Gate** side of the Old City there has been no urban development – as yet – and there is a beautiful and photogenic panorama of cultivated fields and distant mountains. This perimeter road doesn't quite encompass the whole city, unfortunately, and terminates at the **Fallana Gate**. If you try to walk around the wall on the road branching off to the left of **Harar Gate**, you'll be disappointed after a couple of minutes when it meets a dead end (see map).

Entering the Old City through Harar Gate – the three blank, whitewashed squares at the top entrance contained portraits of Marx, Lenin and Engels until 1991 – you walk along a thoroughfare with lanes of traffic and fairly modern shop-façades to the main square. Here the prime attraction is **Medhane Alem Cathedral** (Redeemer of the World), built at the end of the 19th century. Externally it is a beautiful structure with grey and pale mint-green walls, latticed brown woodwork above a verandah, and stone steps painted in the colours of the Ethiopian flag. Inside it contains excellent examples of traditional religious art.

If you continue in the same direction from Harar Gate and follow the street on the far side of the square, leading to Erer Gate, you soon pass the **Al-Jami Grand Mosque**, supposedly located at the exact centre of the walled city and dating back to 1216. Its pair of minarets and 58 thick pillars make it the most imposing of Harar's religious buildings. Incidentally, there are reportedly 82 mosques within the Jugal. Figures differ about how many mosques exist within the rest of Harar, so that calculations of the city's total range from the high 80s to nearly 100. Whatever the number, it is little wonder that Muslims consider the city the fourth holiest in the world, after Mecca, Medina and Jerusalem.

Before arriving at the Grand Mosque from the square, you can quickly visit the **Tomb of Emir Nur**. Turn down the alleyway on the left just before you reach the Misrak Arbegnoch Hospital, then go through the green door on the left side of the alleyway, and you'll emerge next to its compound. The tomb is shaped like a giant half-egg. Its surface bristles with stone studs and there are fragrant herbs growing around its base. Past the hospital and the mosque, another place to look out for is the **Harari National Cultural Centre**, which has a large room containing information on the city's mosques and on the Emirs who ruled from AD 969 until Menelik II's take-over in 1887, with copious displays of ornate pots, bowls, baskets and furniture, and a reproduction of a traditional Harari living room. ■ *US$0.40. The centre also has a small tourist office. Not a great deal of English is spoken there, but the staff are happy to let you browse through their few English-language brochures.*

Back in the square, if you follow the street snaking off on the other side of Medhane Alem, you can make your way to what was reputedly the **home of Arthur Rimbaud**. It is given the nickname of *'Rainbow House'* in the tourist literature on account of the blue, yellow and green panes in its windows, but is known to the locals by the less poetic title of **Rambo's House**. To get there, take the third alleyway branching off from the left side of the street as you descend from the square – the alleyway's entrance is flanked by two clothes merchants – and you will find the door of the house's compound on your left a minute later. Alternatively, ask a kid to lead you to Rambo's House. The building has an incongruously Oriental appearance, with multi-coloured windows, a jutting wooden façade, a handsome stone staircase and a verandah containing six wooden columns. The main doorway opens into a documentation centre whose shelves and glass cases contain bric-à-brac relating to Rimbaud and to Harar itself. This duality of theme – the poet and the city – is continued in the **museum** upstairs. In a large room with a circular balcony above and frescoed ceiling supposedly painted by Rimbaud himself, there are fascinating monochrome photographs detailing life in Harar in the late 19th and early 20th centuries. Up on the balcony hang panoramic photographs of Harar from the same era. You can compare them with the city as it is now, by looking out of the windows there, which give splendid views across the buildings to the countryside beyond. Rimbaud's life is described in a series of panels, written in French but with summaries in English, in a smaller room at the back. There are also extracts from his prose and poetry written in French, English and Amharic. Elsewhere in the museum you can find everything from paintings by modern Harari artists, to trophies won by the region's sporting teams, to examples of old books and manuscripts. All in all it is one of the best museums in Ethiopia and well worth the entrance fee. ■ *US$0.60* .

If you continue up the alleyway from Rimbaud's house to a T-junction, turn left and descend towards the main street again, you will find on your right the entrance to **Ras Mekonin's Palace** where Haile Selassie spent most of his childhood. The carved wooden door is still impressive but the building is now a decrepit, ramshackle mass of broken panes and faded green and yellow paint. The front courtyard is correspondingly squalid. However, you will warm to the sign advertising the business of the palace's current resident, a traditional healer. He claims to cure 'bronchial asthma, diabetes, paralysis, liver disease, haemorrhoids, cancer, gastritis, gynaecological diseases, mental diseases, STDs and epilepsy'!

The Hyena Man

One of the city's peculiarities/attractions is the so-called Hyena Man, who makes his living by collecting bones, offal and pieces of meat, summoning the wild hyenas that scavenge outside the walls after dark, and feeding them while spectators look on nervously. Tourist brochures usually talk about the Hyena Man in the singular, and feature pictures of the same, wizened hyena-feeder, suggesting that, like Santa Claus, there is only one legendary practitioner of the art. However, in fact, there seem to be several people working in the hyena-feeding business now that the region is more stable and tourism to Harar is on the increase.

One well-established group operates at the corner of a factory building a few hundred metres along the road from Fallana Gate, starting their shows just after nightfall and continuing for about an hour when there is enough meat. The dreadlocked feeder there is well known locally and is even the subject of a painting hanging in Rimbaud's House, so he must be as close to an 'official' Hyena Man as you can get. Another Hyena Man operates between the Erer and Sanga Gates. When you get a good show the spectacle is memorable. The creatures emerge cautiously from the darkness, their cries and the summoning calls of the Hyena Man making an eerie cacophony; torch beams and the headlights of taxis that have ferried in tourists weaving strange patterns of light and shadow around them. The hyenas are bigger than you expect; with their round ears they seem as much ursine as canine. Though they are cowardly and will scarper if an opportunistic dog darts forward to snap up a piece of meat, the crunching of bones between their jaws will give you an idea of what they are capable of doing. The Hyena Man dispenses the food by flicking it on to the ground, handing it to the hyenas directly and – the *coup de grâce* – passing it from his mouth to theirs. Brave tourists may even be invited to try feeding the beasts themselves. It is possible to walk up from Fallana Gate and simply drop in on a feeding session, but even if you arrive late or there is a meat shortage and you see the hyenas for just a few minutes, you will still be asked for the full viewing fee. You can try to haggle things down, of course, if you don't mind arguing with one or two men carrying large curved meat-knives.

■ *To arrange a viewing you can ask among the guides, taxi drivers or staff at the local hotels. A reasonable price is US$3 per head – this will be expected up front, to allow the Hyena Man to buy a sufficient quantity of meat, so obviously make sure that your middle-man is to be trusted. Alternatively, Sofi Tours advertise an afternoon sightseeing and shopping tour that climaxes with a visit to the Hyena Man's feeding ground.*

Ethiopia

The Harar Brewery

The locally brewed Harar beer is very popular in the east and south of Ethiopia, and is regarded by those in the know as the finest of the indigenous beers. Some 60,000,000 bottles are turned out by the city's brewery every year. Three varieties are produced, the regular lager, a stout called *Hakim*, and an alcohol-free malt drink called *Harar Sofi*. In recent years the brewery has acquired a reputation for its hospitality towards foreign visitors. Tourists showing up at the gates are given a tour of the premises and afterwards handed a sizeable carafe – or two, or three, or more – of beer and told to drink up. The staff appear to be delighted to be able to spread the word about their beer among the international community and will happily sit, drink and chat with you. However, one wonders if this practice can continue for much longer – nowadays groups of *farengoes* seem to trek up to the brewery every other day and there must surely come a point where the volume of visitors will interfere with the work done there. ■ *To arrange your visit in advance, contact the technical manager, T05-660718, F05-661555.* The walk to the brewery from the city centre is about 4 km. Go up the road past the *Belayneh, Asfaw* and *Tsadkan Tesfaye* hotels, turn right at the T-junction and continue until you see the brewery sign at the entrance of an avenue on the left.

Essentials

Sleeping
■ *on map page 836*
For price codes:
see inside front cover

C *Ras*, PO Box 45, T05- 660027. At the top of Harar's accommodation options is this 42-room hotel, one of the better establishments in the government-owned chain, 15-mins' walk from the Old City. It has rooms with communal showers and toilets; single and double rooms with hot showers or single and double rooms with baths. There's also a bar and restaurant with quite good food. Surrounding it are spacious and attractively wooded grounds.

More conveniently located is the **E** *Belayneh Hotel*, PO Box 72, T05-662030, a new, clean and bustling place, near the bus station by the Old City, offering a choice of rooms with either hot or cold showers. The rooms have balconies and there is a rooftop terrace providing great views across the city. Recommended. **E** *Thewodras Hotel*, T05-660217, is also a few mins' walk from the Old City. Try to secure a room on the upper floor of the building, as the en-suite bathrooms there are tiled, the corridor is less noisy and the windows let you see something of the city. The hotel is friendly and very popular with foreign tourists, though the check-out time of 0900 seems a bit brutal. Friendly, English-speaking staff and there's a good restaurant. Similar in price is the **E** *Tsadkan Tesfaye*, T661546, a little further up the road from the *Belayneh*, where the accommodation is contained in a new, 3-storey building at the rear. Enquire here if you fancy getting a fast bus to Addis Ababa, and don't mind paying extra, as the service seems to depart outside the hotel early in the morning.

For budget travellers the cheaper options are less appetising. There are some small private guesthouses, bars and atmospheric eating places near Feres Magala, the old horse market

F *Academy*, T660025, might be worth checking out if you are desperate for a location inside the Old City, in the main square near church, though be warned that the US$1.50 rooms are as bare as can be and there are no showers, not even communal ones. Squat toilets. The **F** *Airforce Hotel* is even more dubious than its neighbour the *Tourist Hotel*, asking US$1.50 for a scruffy room without shower or toilet. **F** *Ajersa Goro*, rooms upstairs, some with own toilet/shower. Only the severely financially challenged should consider the **F** *Asfaw Hotel*, not far from the *Belayneh*, which is basically a pub attached to a smelly alleyway of cell-like rooms. You can pay US$1 a night here if you don't mind sleeping in what is most likely a brothel. Another place offering showerless rooms for US$1.50 a night is the **F** *Melka Hotel*, T661996, just outside Harar Gate, but the rooms are at least clean-looking and the proprietor seems friendly. **F** *Tourist Hotel*, T660824, has its rooms located around a not-bad-looking, 2-storey courtyard with a reasonable restaurant on the bottom floor. However, there seems little point in paying for a room with a shower because the showers just don't work. Go for the cheaper rooms if you think you can stomach the fetid communal toilets. The bar in the *Tourist* is famed for its raucousness, and is decorated at night by a distinctive red light. The terrace outside is surrounded by what can only be described as a cage. Whether this is to keep troublemakers out or to keep them in is a matter of conjecture.

Cheap Vegetarians may find the choice of eating places in Harar a little limited, possibly because this largely Muslim city pays less attention to the fasting days and seasons in the Orthodox Christian calendar when meat is forbidden. However, there are salads available among the Ethiopian and western food on the *Ras Hotel's* menu. The *Mesrak Hotel* can serve up a good *beyenetu* (which is actually preferable to its sometimes-gristly meat dishes).

Carnivores will appreciate the restaurant in the *Thewodros Hotel*, where the roast chicken has acquired an excellent reputation. You can tuck into a whole chicken for US$3.75, though the US$2 half chicken is enough to satisfy most diners. Also recommended is the *Hirut Restaurant*, though it is something of a hike from the city centre. The posh-looking eating area attracts many western customers, though the back alleyway leading to the toilets definitely belongs to the developing world. The restaurant at the rear of the *Belayneh Hotel* lobby serves up ample portions, but the food is sometimes lukewarm and slightly greasy.

Seriously cheap *Adwa Restaurant* will prepare vegetarian dishes if asked in advance. For breakfast, the place to go to is the excellent *Central Café* next door to the *Melka Hotel*. Its scrambled egg and *foule special* are wonderful, and there are also fresh bread rolls, spicy samosas, pastries, juices, cakes, chocolate and biscuits. You can even buy bottled water here and it's generally a good place to stock up if you are planning to make a day trip out of Harar. Also worth investigating is the sociable bar next door. The food in the *Canal Cafeteria* on the other side of the road is less spectacular though there is a big selection of pastries, sweets and biscuits. Nearby, the *Towfik Sherif Recreation Centre*, a wooded park with a circular serving building in the middle, and around that a number of terraces for the customers, is popular with young Harari families. It's a pleasant place for a cake or a juice, though the loud public address system can be grating and the caged monkeys by the playground area are unsurprisingly miserable-looking. While touring the Old City, a good place to call at is the *Ali Bal Café* next to the entrance to *Medhane Alem*, stocked with the usual array of cakes, samosas and juices. There is a restaurant at the back and, in an adjoining room, a souvenir shop: the assistants here keep their distance and customers can browse among the gifts unmolested.

Harar has no shortage of pubs, though the apparent fondness for loud music, ghoulishly coloured fluorescent strips and flashing Christmas lights might deter those wanting a quiet drink. The road from Harar Gate to the centre of the Old City is packed with mini-discos – the *Hormmibea Africa*, *Hibret*, *Dimfaso*, *Samson*, etc – each trying to outdo its neighbour in noise and lurid lighting. Best of the bunch are the *Hibret*, a cosy enough venue during the day, which serves pint-sized glasses of draught beer, and the *Samson*, where some conversation is possible in the back room (though, disconcertingly, the tables in the room are tiled blocks of concrete that resemble truncated toilet walls). Beer enthusiasts may like to know that the indigenous *Hakim* stout is available on draught at two venues in the city: at the *Harar Brewery's Social Club*, just outside its gates, and at the *Medre Genet Hotel* on the boulevard running from *Harar Gate* towards the *Ras Hotel*.

If you're hunting for souvenirs, the city's stalls and shops provide a wide range of options: handmade baskets and other pieces of wicker-work, carved wooden bowls, cups made out of gourds, hand-woven cotton shawls, and beautiful silver necklaces, chains, bracelets, earrings and anklets.

Sofi Travel and Tourist Service, PO Box 575, T05-661088, arranges half-day tours of the city, incorporating sightseeing and shopping.

A minibus between Dire Dawa and Harar should cost about US$1 and take 1-2 hrs. There are some cars (though packed with bus-like concentrations of passengers and luggage) plying the same route for a similar fee. You'll see a couple of abandoned tanks on the roadside. **Buses** There now seem to be newer, faster and more comfortable buses plying the route between Addis Ababa and Dire Dawa/Harar, but charging higher fares – for instance, US$6.25 from Awash to Dire Dawa/Harar, US$10 from Harar to Addis Ababa. It should be possible to get information about these faster buses by asking at the *Tsadkan Tesfaye Hotel* in Harar outside which many of them begin and end their journey rather than use Harar Bus Station. **Train** See under Addis Ababa, page 803.

Eating
● *on map page 836*
*For price codes:
see inside front cover*

*Apart from the
full-scale chicken
experience at the
Thewodros, none of
these places should
charge more than
US$2.50 an item*

Bars

Shopping

**Tours & tour
operators**

Transport

Ethiopia

Excursions

The Valley of Marvels

To the southeast of Harar is the **Valley of Marvels**, an area notable for its many strange rock formations. The middle of the valley is a place called **Dakata**, sited about 5 km beyond the village of Babille on the Harar-Jijiga road. Dakata itself has no village, no signs and no vendors, but you will know where you are thanks to the famous **Dakata Balancing Rock** up on the mountainside to the north, which, quite frankly, resembles a massive walnut perched on a giant penis. There are other balancing rocks but their profiles are not so distinctive or suggestive. The valley itself can best be likened to a chaotic Giant's Causeway – on steroids. Huge boulders and slabs, many of them vertical, rear out of the undergrowth on the valley's sides and jut up from their skylines. There are trails winding up from the road but these tend to disappear when they encounter the bases of the larger rocks. To reach the summits be prepared to haul yourself over some formidable rocky obstacles and plough through some messy thickets of thorns and cacti. However, the scenery is impressive enough if you elect to stay on the road.

Transport **Buses** for Jijiga leave hourly from Harar Bus Station and you can get dropped off at Dakata, though the conductors may insist that you pay the full US$2 fare to Jijiga – an irritation considering that the fare to nearby Babille is only US$0.90. The drive should take just over 1 hr. Alternatively, it's possible to do the Harar-Babille part of the journey by bus and explore the Babille-Dakata part as a 10-km hike. The road out to the valley certainly makes a scenic walk.

Babille Elephant Sanctuary
9° N, 42° 30' E
Colour map 2, grid B4

This park covers an area of over 6,750 sq km and extends south from the village of Babille. It was created in the late 1970s as a shelter for a subspecies of elephant endemic to Ethiopia, the *Loxodonta africana orleansi*. However, the park is not well developed and it is not easy to sight the elephants. There are also problems with increased areas of cultivation by local farmers, and much of the bushland that used to cover the valley floors has now disappeared. The pressure on the environment has been increased by incursions of refugees from Somalia. The park is also reputedly home to black-maned lions, leopards, gazelle, oryx and dik-dik, though its most numerous inhabitants are its birds. A survey of birdlife there in 1995 recorded 106 species, including the rare Gillet's lark and scaly chatterer. It is also possible that the Salvadori seedeater (*Serinus xantholaema*), which has been sighted only a dozen times altogether, is found in the area. There are few visitors.

■ *Sofi Tours in Harar are willing to find a guide and arrange a tour of the Elephant Sanctuary. They say that past tours have cost about US$15 a day, but warn that price nowadays may be higher.*

Addis
Ababa

North to Tigray

The area to the north of Ethiopia contains some of the most interesting historical sites, including the ancient cities of Gondar and Axum, as well as the site of the extraordinary rock-hewn churches at Lalibela. Lake Tana has the spectacular Tisissat Falls on the Blue Nile, and between Gondar and Axum is the Simien Mountains National Park. To the north of Addis Ababa, the geographical centre of the country, the Historic Route leads to the marvels of Ethiopia's heritage. Two roads branch out from Addis, the road to Gondar going due north to Fiche and then continuing northwesterly through Debre Markos to Bahar Dar, Gondar, Debark and on to Axum. The other road travels initially in a northeasterly direction to Debre Birhan, Debra Sina and then due north to Dessie (Dese), Weldiya, Mekelle and on to Adigrat. The Historic Route is a circuit using both these roads.

Debre Libanos

The northern route leads to the beginning of the great gorges of the Blue Nile. Situated on the edge of a gorge, Debre Libanos is the site of a monastery, a church and the centre of a religious community, 103 km northwest of Addis Ababa, near the small town of **Fiche**. It is a place of enormous religious significance to Ethiopians. In fact, it is considered to be the most important monastery in southern Ethiopia. Two monasteries share the name Debre Libanos: this one founded in the 13th century by Abba Takla Haymanot (revered as an Ethiopian saint) in the Shoa district, and another founded near Shemezana, Tigray (Eritrea) in the sixth century.

Debre Libanos has an important **library**. Many Ethiopians make a pilgrimage here as the waters seeping through the rocky cliffs are attributed with healing powers and reputedly offer remission for sins. The rocky caves in the cliffs overlooking Debre Libanos have been used as burial sites for important persons.

Initially the monastery was known as Debre Asbo, later renamed Debre Libanos by **History** Emperor Zera Ya'qob (1434-68). **Takla Haymanot** is believed to have studied under Abba Iyesus Mo'a at Debre Hayk Estifanos for about 10 years, and then spent a further 10 years with Abba Yohanni of Debre Damo before coming here. He is credited with being a major force in the spread of Christianity in southern and western Ethiopia, and is also considered as being central to the transfer of power from the Zagwe Dynasty to the Solomonic Dynasty in 1270. The origins of most of the monastic communities in Ethiopia are derived from him, and are known collectively as the House of Takla-Haymanot.

Takla Haymanot was an ascete. One important Ethiopian monastic feature was the practice of self-imposed bodily torture, reflecting the belief that the body, which is temporal, is the enemy of the eternal soul. In order for the soul to be victorious over the body, it is necessary to torment the body by acts of penitence like fasting, standing in one position for long periods of time or by the exposure of the body to extreme heat or cold. There was a belief that when the ascete reached the extreme limit of self-torture he would develop wings. There are several manuscripts depicting Takla Haymanot with three sets of wings.

The monastery was devastated by pestilence and both Takla Haymanot and his successor Abba Elsa perished. However, those who survived went on to spread Christianity and establish other monasteries including Debre Besrat.

Several religious buildings have been erected at Debre Libanos over the centuries. There are no archaeological remains of the early monastery founded around 1284 by Takla Haymanot. The monastery and its ancient manuscripts were destroyed by fire in 1531 during the early part of the Islamic conquest. However, some of the monks escaped, taking the tabot of Takla Haymanot to Azezo for safekeeping.

In the 15th century there was great controversy over which day to celebrate the Sabbath. A decree had been issued to stop the practice of the Jewish custom of observing the Saturday Sabbath. Many monasteries resisted this decree. Emperor Zera Ya'qob instituted a compromise, whereby the Sabbath was celebrated on both Saturday and Sunday.

In the late 18th century there was dispute over the nature of Christ, which centred on whether the inseparable union of his divinity and humanity took place when he was conceived or when he was baptized. Debre Libanos formulated the doctrine of *Tsegga-Ledj* (three births), which was considered a heresy by the Orthodox Church. This dogma was relinquished by decree by Emperor Yohannis IV in 1878.

Emperor Menelik II built a church here, which took 12 years to complete (1881-93). Takla Haymanot's tabot was returned on Menelik's order in 1889. In 1909, **Empress T'aytu Betul** played a major role in persuading the monks to build a cloister for nuns, thereby re-establishing a community that had been disbanded 400 years before.

Later, in 1936, during the **Italian occupation** of Ethiopia, 425 monks and deacons at Debre Libanos were shot on Mussolini's orders as part of his policy of terror,

Ethiopia

to overcome Ethiopian resistance. And in the 1950s, **Haile Selassie** built an ornately decorated new church at Debre Libanos, completed in 1961.

The *abun*, spiritual head of the Ethiopian Orthodox Church, had to be a Copt ordained by the Patriarch of Alexandria, a tradition that lasted 16 centuries. The *abun* was usually a dignitary from one of the important monasteries, and this ecclesiastical office has been represented many times by the *Eccage* of Debre Libanos over the past 500 years. The *abun* acted as judge for clerical cases and liaised between church and state. In the 20th century the *abun's* role at the national level has diminished with the establishment of the *Beta Kehnat* (central church administration office). In 1957 the first Ethiopian bishop was appointed when the last Coptic *abun* died.

Sleeping There is basic, simple accommodation available at Fiche. **Transport** Frequent minibuses cover the 15-km trip from Fiche to Debre Libanos.

Blue Nile Gorge
Colour map 2, grid A2

Not long after Debre Libanos is the Blue Nile Gorge. The river begins its journey far to the north at Lake Tana, finally carving its way through a gorge that is 1½ km wide and almost as deep, and must be one of the most remarkable and breathtaking phenomena on earth, sometimes referred to as **Africa's Grand Canyon**. The road winds down over 1,000 m, a journey of over 45 minutes in a car, and at times the road, supported by Italian-built stanchions, actually leaps away from the side of the gorge ; it is an amazing engineering feat, absolutely terrifying at times. A modern single-span bridge crosses the river at the bottom before the ascent begins on the other side. It is possible to walk down the gorge, but it is forbidden to take photos of the bridge.

The gorge is easy to access by bus from Addis Ababa (fare about US$1.50, journey time 12 hours). If necessary, it is possible to stay at the village of **Dejen** just north of the gorge. Close to the turn-off to Debre Libanos, along a rocky track there is the 16th-century '**Portuguese Bridge**', which is still in use by the local people.

Debre Markos

A few kilometres north of Dejen the road divides into the direct route to Bahar Dar and the more circuitous route to the same destination via Debre Markos, the regional capital of Gojam. This town is 305 km from the capital, commonly used as an overnight stop for buses taking the two-day road journey between Addis Ababa and Bahar Dar, and so has a good selection of hotels and restaurants. The 19th-century church of Markos (St Mark) contains pale, beautiful paintings of religious and biblical history.

Sleeping and eating The following are all much of a muchness, fairly simple, shared bathrooms, reasonably secure and offer good value. **E** *Menkorere Hotel*, T712725; **E** *Nehase 30th Hotel*; **E** *Shebel Hotel*; **E** *Tekele Hakimanote Hotel*; **E** *Tourist Hotel*; **E** *Tseday Hotel*; **E** *Walia Hotel*. Food is available at *Saki Besake Bar*.

Bahar Dar

11°37'N 37°10'E
Phone code: 8
Colour map 2, grid A2

Travelling north about 280 km from the Blue Nile Gorge you come to the town of Bahar Dar (or Bahir Dar), situated at the southern end of **Lake Tana** (3,700 sq km). The Tana area is the traditional homeland of the Christian Amhara people, whose language was the national dialect of Ethiopia for many years. The southeast corner of the lake is the source of the Blue Nile. Hippos and crocodiles are often visible from the bridge that spans the river. Lake Tana contains 37 islands that house very old churches and monasteries, containing religious frescoes and artefacts. Many of the churches are closed to women. This exclusion is said to date from the ninth century when an evil Jewish/Falasha Queen Judith (also spelt Judit/Yodit) reigned over the Axumite Kingdom.

Within the compound of **St George's Church** in Bahar Dar is a two-storey building constructed by Pero Paes (see page 847).

Also worthwhile is the busy **Saturday market**, near the bus station, which has lots to buy including *shammas*, rugs, jewellery and honey. The **tourist office** is just a short walk from the centre, taking the turning by the *Commercial Bank*, T201112.

A *Tana*, on the lake shore. Good standard, pleasant location, excellent food. **B-D** *Ghion*, town centre, 5 mins from market and pier. Safe car and bike parking. Reported to have gone downhill of late. Flexible prices, open to negotiation. Nice grounds right on Lake Tana shore. Restaurant overlooks the lake (the best chance of seeing hippos is at dusk when they come up out of the water to graze), but the food is rated as only fair, although it does nice toast for breakfast. Unpleasant hassling has been reported by travellers to encourage them into paying exorbitant prices for tours. **C-D** *Dubambessa*, T08-201436, F201818, near the post office, costs less than the *Tana* and the rooms are clean and in far better condition than the *Ghion*, and the staff are superb. Recommended. However, the cost of Ethiopian food is relatively expensive in the restaurant. **C-D** *Inkutatash II*, 10 mins from the town centre past the *Ghion Hotel*, has nice, if slightly overpriced rooms and an excellent restaurant. **D** *Ethio-Star Hotel*, next door to the post office, has hot water, nets, laundry facilities and secure parking. Restaurant offers a good range of western and local foods.

Sleeping

■ *on map*
*For price codes:
see inside front cover*

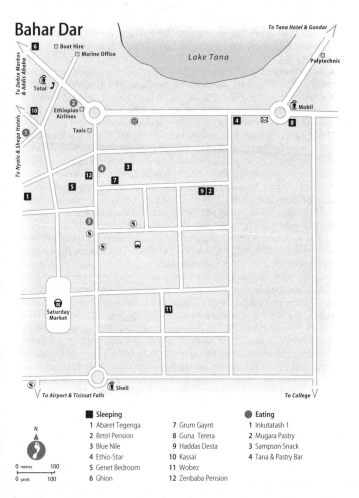

Bahar Dar

Lake Tana

To Tana Hotel & Gondar

To Debre Markos & Addis Abeba

Boat Hire
Marine Office
Total
Polytechnic
Ethiopian Airlines
Mobil
Taxis
To Nyala & Shega Hotels
Saturday Market
Shell
To Airport & Tisissat Falls
To College

Ethiopia

■ Sleeping
1 Abaret Tegenga
2 Betel Pension
3 Blue Nile
4 Ethio-Star
5 Genet Bedroom
6 Ghion
7 Grum Gaynt
8 Guna Terera
9 Haddas Desta
10 Kassai
11 Wobez
12 Zenbaba Pension

● Eating
1 Inkutatash 1
2 Mugara Pastry
3 Sampson Snack
4 Tana & Pastry Bar

0 metres 100
0 yards 100
N

E *Betel Pension*, T08-201488. Located past *Grum Gaynt Hotel*, follow road, hotel is on the right in front of *Nile Hotel*. Basic, clean and cheap, will provide a bucket of hot water. **E** *Genet Bedroom*, behind bus stand. Often full, shared bathrooms, clean and friendly. **E** *Grum Gaynt*, T08-200832. Take the 2nd turning left off the main road in town, turning before the *Melat Café*, restaurant serves local food, with laundry service and secure parking. **E** *Haddas Desta*, T08-200309, close to the *Betel Pension* is another basic hotel, with shared ablutions, restaurant, laundry service and secure parking. **E** *Wobez Hotel*, T08-204732. Go straight through bus station, turn left then take first right and this hotel is 20 m on the left. Simple, clean accommodation, shared toilets/cold shower. **E** *Zenbaba Pension*, main street opposite the *Tana Pastry* shop. Shared bathroom, laundry service. Among the better budget hotels are the **F** *Abaret Tegenga*, located behind the **F** *Genet Bedroom*, the **F** *Blue Nile*, behind the *Grum Gaynt*, the **F** *Guna Terera*, past the post office opposite the *Mobil* petrol station, and along with the **F** *Nyala* and **F** *Shega*, located on the same street as the **F** *Kassai*. These are all cheap, very basic hotels with shared cold showers/toilets. There are also several other **E-F** grade hotels near the bus station. **Camping** is available at *Tana Hotel,* US$6 per tent, including the use of one of the hotel bathrooms.

Eating

● *on map, page 845*

Mid-range *Inkutatash I Restaurant*, located behind the Telecom building. Slightly more expensive than the other restaurants, generous portions. Excellent fish for US$1.50. *Inkutatash II Restaurant*, located northwest of the *Ghion Hotel*, is even more expensive than *Inkutatash I*, but is an excellent restaurant for both western and local food.

Seriously cheap *Amanuel Restaurant*, T08-204501, first left after the *Dubambessa Hotel*, before the post office. Serves fish, chicken and meat stews, fried meat (*tibs*), fish cutlet and pasta with meat and tomato sauce. Has friendly staff, basic, clean interior with Ethiopian music. Toilets are clean. *Central Snack and Pastry Bar*, next to the bus station, T201782. Serves the usual range of snack foods. Charges foreigners approximately 100% over the local price. *ET Fruit Juice*, which looks like a tent on the main road, sells the best fruit juices in town. *Ethio-Espanol Lito Restaurant*, located on the same road as the *Nigist Saba*. Recommended for cheap, excellent local food, including fish and chicken stew, *tibs*, fish cutlets and fasting foods. Also serves cheap *gouda* (red) wine that has a very reasonable taste. *Kitfo Bet* serves excellent *tibs*. *Mango Park* and *Mugera Pastry*, located close to each other near the lake, are also good for snacks. *Nigist Saba*, T08-201407. Take 1st left at traffic lights on main town road, located 30 m past St George's Church on left side. Fish stew (*asa wat*), chicken stew (*doro wat*) and fried meat (*tibs*) cost US$1.00. Fasting foods (Wed/Fri), such as chickpea stew (*shiro wat*) cost US$0.50. Very friendly staff, has a traditional Ethiopian interior, eclectic music (Ethiopian and western). Toilets a little smelly. *Nile Hotel*, T08-200746. Located past *Amanuel Restaurant*, turn right at crossroads, and it is 30 m on the right. Menu includes fish stew, spicy mince (*minchet*) and chicken stew, plus fasting food (Wed/Fri) and salads. Friendly staff, interior grubby but toilets are clean. *Sampson Snack*, T08-200689, open all day, on the main road before *Wegagen Bank* and opposite *Melat Café*, serves excellent breakfast, for example *foule* (Ethiopia's answer to baked beans with chilli) and *nashif* (bread, butter, pepper, egg and yoghurt – nicer than it sounds). Also serves scrambled eggs, bean stew, fish and bean stew and spicy tomato stew. Family-run establishment, all staff very friendly and they sell draught beer, Ethiopian/western music, toilet new and clean. *Tana Restaurant and Pastry Bar* has a nice rooftop terrace. Does good hamburgers and sandwiches, plus cheap, tasty local foods. **Street food**: bread can be bought in numerous bakeries. Fruit is available (depending on season) at market or at fruit shops. *Sambosa* (like Indian samosas but filled with spicy lentils) are available near *Nile Hotel* and from vendors walking in the streets.

Transport

Air *Ethiopian Airlines*, T08-200020, flies daily to Bahar Dar (see Getting around, page 775). Contract taxi to/from airport is around US$6, but is usually shared, costing US$1.25-2 per person (max 4 people).

Road **Bus**: the bus station opens at 0600. Watch your bag; in the scramble to get a seat travelles' property has been stolen. It may be worth paying a child to run on board to claim a

Source of the Blue Nile

The first European to visit the source of the Blue Nile was a Spanish Jesuit, Pero Paes, in 1618. He was part of an expedition seeking to convert Ethiopia to Catholicism, and was travelling with Emperor Susneyos. Two springs at Gish, 130 km south of Lake Tana, were identified as the start of the great river. They come together to form a stream, Tinash Abbay (Little Nile), which flows into Lake Tana.

A Portuguese Jesuit, Jeronimo Lobo, visited the springs shortly after and gave a description of Tisissat (Smokefire) Falls. He also described the single-arch bridge at Alata over the Blue Nile (the Abbay), which was commissioned by Emperor Susneyos, and constructed by an Indian mason, Abdel Kerim.

The explorer who did most to publicize the Blue Nile and its origin was James Bruce, a Scotsman, who landed at Massawa in 1769.

After an extensive expedition he reached the source springs a year later. He also visited Tisissat Falls, and disputed Lobo's observation that it was possible to walk behind the cascading water. James Bruce became known as 'Bruce of Abyssinia' and his exploits are described in his five-volume Travels to Discover the Source of the Nile, *written in 1770. In it he describes the Tisissat Falls: "The river had been considerably increased by the rains, and fell in one sheet of water, without any interval, about half an English mile in breadth, with a force and noise that was truly terrible, and which stunned and made me, for a time, perfectly dizzy. A thick fume or haze, covered the fall all around, and hung over the course of the stream both above and below. It was one of the most magnificent, stupendous sights in creation."*

seat (1-2 birr tip), while you supervise your luggage being loaded on top of the bus. Unfortunately both Bahar Dar and Gondar bus stations have groups of thieves targeting tourists. The route south to **Addis Ababa** is via Debre Markos and the whole journey is 580 km. It is realistic to allow 2 days for this journey, with an overnight stop at Debre Markos. Travel is more difficult in Jun-Sep when the rains are heavy. There are regular buses running along this route, fare US$8.75 to/from Addis Ababa. An alternative route from Addis is on the Mota Rd, which is 35 km shorter, allowing you to visit the **Tisissat Falls** before reaching Bahar Dar. Bahar Dar to Mer Awi (30 km) costs US$0.75, taking 1½ hrs. Travelling north, Bahar Dar-**Gondar** (180 km) takes 5-6 hrs. The bus leaves at 0600. Buy tickets the night before, US$2. It is possible to leave later in the day and stay at Woreta.

Taxi: there are two types, line taxis (Ethiopian equivalent to a *matatu* in Kenya) and contract taxi. Line Taxis have 2 routes: hospital area to the market, or the market to the Blue Nile Bridge. Single fare is US$0.10. The contract taxi does the airport run – see above.

Bike hire: bicycles are available for hire at *Ghion Hotel* or in town costing US$0.75-2 per day, depending on your bartering skills.

Lake Tana Ferry It is possible to take a ferry across Lake Tana between Bahar Dar and **Gorgora**, south of Gondar, which is an excellent alternative to the bus. The boat leaves Bahar Dar every Sun at 0700. Tickets must be purchased the day before, costing US$15.75 for tourists. The boat heads first for **Degi Island** and then for some villages on the western shores of the lake. It stays overnight at one of these villages, **Kunzla** (or Quuzla), where there is a local hotel. Next morning you continue to the port of Gorgora arriving there in the early afternoon. The return ferry leaves Gorgora on Thu morning.

Excursions from Bahar Dar

Haile Selassie Palace is located 10 km from Bahar Dar, with good views of Lake Tana. The palace is currently closed to visitors, but can be viewed from the outside. A trip here by bicycle is manageable along a rather rough road to the palace, although opinion varies on whether it is worth the bone-shaking experience. Allow one hour each way for the ride. There is a steep hill on the approach to the palace, but you gain on the return downhill run. The views of Bahar Dar, Lake Tana and the Blue Nile River are good from here. Taxis from Bahar Dar charge approximately US$8.

Haile Selassie Palace

Ethiopia

Tisissat Falls   One feature of Lake Tana are the *tankwa* (boats) that can be seen on the shore. They are made from papyrus leaves bound together, and have been in use since time immemorial. These papyrus boats resemble the boats of Ancient Egypt.

Bahar Dar is the centre from which to explore the spectacular Tisissat Falls – more frequently called **Tis Abay**, 'Smoke of the Nile', by the locals – the largest waterfall on the Blue Nile River, which drains the lake just to the north. The falls are 30 km south of the town and are reached on foot from the nearby village of Tis Abay. There are excellent views if you continue walking for 20 minutes past the main viewpoint, then cross a small river that takes you to the base on the right side of the falls. There are great rainbows in the morning but the site is wet and muddy. Visitors will be offered trips to the falls by car, with guides, or in a papyrus boat, all of which are quite expensive compared with the local bus from Bahar Dar. Any number of young boys will offer to guide you from the village but are not really necessary. However, they can be very persistent, so if you don't want one make this clear; if you do, fix the price at the start. The most direct route, a 30-minute walk, is to proceed to the end of the village, turning right 50 m before the gate to the power station. Then take the path to the left towards the river, over the 17th-century **Portuguese bridge**, reputedly built from lime, eggs and milk. Turn left after the bridge; there are two viewpoints opposite the falls that offer a dramatic panorama. It is possible to follow the path all around so that you arrive at the bottom of the falls, where there is a pool you can swim in, or you can shower in the spray. Everywhere you walk you are standing in your own rainbow! The falls are best in November after the heavy rains, if visiting in September the area is awash with very muddy water, so the falls can be difficult to reach. Some hotels offer a shoe-cleaning service.

■ *Entrance to falls is US$2.50, US$1 student concession. A guide costs US$1. Check the return times for the bus before setting off as it fills up quickly. You are advised to allow a full day to view the Tisissat Falls because of the vagaries of the transport links. If you wish to do the trip in half a day take the 0600 bus to the falls and the 1100 bus back to Bahar Dar. Alternatively, hire a bicycle to get to the falls.*

Transport   The public bus leaves every morning at about 0600 from the station, but may also leave later at 0900, 1200 or 1500 (but not daily), or whenever it 'fills up'. It has the great advantage of being cheap (US$0.50). It takes about 1½ hours to get to the drop-off village.

Island monasteries

There are monasteries on many of the numerous islands that dot the southern end of the lake, most dating from the 14th century. Many were destroyed during the period of Muslim incursions led by Ahmad Gran in the 16th century, and were later rebuilt. The most accessible from Bahar Dar are Debre Kebran Gabriel and Ura Kidane Mehret, both less than an hour's boat journey away.

Tisissat Falls (Blue Nile Falls)

.... Footpath to falls

This monastery is situated within a stone-walled compound at the very top of the densely wooded island. Originally dated from the 14th century and rebuilt in 1687, during the reign of Emperor Iyasu I (1682-1706), this is one of the most beautiful and peaceful of the island monasteries. There is a large circular church with a thatched roof, built of the traditional materials of compacted mud and straw and decorated with frescoes.

Debre Kebran Gabriel
Entry forbidden to women

Situated on the Zege peninsula, this monastery is famous for its frescoes. A painting on the sanctuary door, *Gebre Menfes riding on a cock and surrounded by wild animals*, depicts the patron on the right wing. Dating from the same period and built in a style similar to Debre Kebran Gabriel, the Ura church has a huge conical thatched roof, but is more ornately decorated with biblical scenes. There is also a collection of crosses and crowns. ■ *US$2.50.*

Ura Kidane Mehret
Women are permitted to visit this monastery

First built in the 14th century on the summit of this lush, heavily wooded island, and then rebuilt in the 19th century after the original church was destroyed by fire, this monastery holds a priceless collection of icons and manuscripts, and silver filigreed royal crowns. It also contains a painting of the Madonna suckling the Christ Child, who is playing with a dove and is flanked by angels. The painting was commissioned by Zara Yaqob in the 15th century and, unusually, is signed by the artist – a monk called Fre Seyon. In addition, there are mummified remains of a number of Ethiopian emperors. Dega Estefanos lays claim to having been the temporary hiding place of Ethiopia's most important religious relic, the Ark of the Covenant, moved here, according to legend, from Axum during the Muslim occupation in the 16th century. The boat takes approximately 1½ hours to reach here.

Dega Estefanos
Women are denied access

Tana Cherkos monastery is located close to the eastern shore of the lake on a beautiful verdant island, covered with dense shrubs and cacti. According to legend the Ark of the Covenant remained on this island for 800 years prior to its transfer to Axum in the fourth century with the advent of Ethiopian Christianity. It is claimed that early Jewish settlers brought the Ark here. Close to the island's summit overlooking the lake are three stone pillars, hollowed out in a cup-shape at the top, said to be sacrificial altars. Oral tradition states that animal sacrifices were offered up here in the presence of the Ark. The church of St Cherkos is rather decrepit. The island also houses ancient manuscripts and books. The boat ride takes about 2½ hours.

Tana Cherkos
Access forbidden to women

North of Lake Tana on **Dek Island**, and not far from Gorgora, Narga Sellase was built in the Gondarene style by Empress Mentewab, wife of Emperor Bakaffa in 1747. It is well preserved, it has a dungeon under the compound wall and a two-storey gatehouse topped with a round dome. The church contains a striking picture depicting the empress reclining at the feet of the Madonna and child. Also on the north of this island is the remote church of **Debre Kota Mariam**. The inner sanctum is decorated with frescoes.

Narga Sellase

■ *Boats to islands to see the monasteries and the wildlife can be arranged from town or from the Ghion Hotel (see page 845). Boat trips on Lake Tana to see island monasteries (some not available to women), hippo colony and birdlife costs about US$25 for hire of boat, pilot and fuel. A trip to the closest island, which has a (non-famous) monastery will cost about US$12. The entrance fees to the monasteries are about US$2.50. Allow plenty of time to cope with the vagaries of local timekeeping.*

The surroundings of Gorgora are very pleasant. There are nearby hills offering great views over the lake. One of the hills, known locally as Mussolini, has an Italian war memorial. There are also several nearby islands with monasteries and the ruined castle of Fasilides' father, Emperor Susenyos, who reigned from 1607-32. This is thought to be the first of the Gondarene royal residences, built by Jesuits with Indian

Gorgora

Ethiopia

master builders. Before this, during the 15th and 16th centuries, the Ethiopian rulers had a peripatetic lifestyle, living in tents and moving their capitals from place to place. From Gorgora to Gondar there is a 0600 bus that takes three hours, cost US$1.

Sleeping Gorgora only has 2 hotels – the government complex (**B**) on the lake shore, situated in wonderfully lush gardens. The alternative is the local hotel at the entrance to the village, which ruthlessly exploits its de-facto monopoly and overcharges tourists.

Wanziya Wanziya, 35 km north of Bahar Dar, has rejuvenating hot springs. Take the sign-
& Woreta posted right turning and follow the road for about 9 km to reach the **Wanziya Hot Springs**. A few kilometres further along the Gondar road, Woreta, approximately 40 km (two hours) north of Bahar Dar, is a small town which is essentially a large bus and truck stop with many small hotels.

Sleeping In Wanziya: **E** *Wanziya Hot Springs Hotel*, single room, shared bathroom, bucket shower available, restaurant, only local food. Hire of a private bathroom at hot springs is available by the hour. In **Woreta**: **E** *Alemiya Hotel,* located on the right just after the bridge if coming from Bahar Dar, has clean, basic rooms, shared toilets, cold showers and good local food and pasta. **E** *Fassika Hotel* is of a similar standard and price and offers much the same choice of food.

Transport From Woreta, buses or trucks are available to **Gondar**, **Dessie**, **Weldiya** and **Lalibela**.

Gondar

12°39'N 37°30'E *Some 50 km north of Lake Tana, 748 km north of Addis Ababa and nestling in the foot-*
Phone code: 8 *hills of the Simien Mountains, the ancient city of Gondar (also spelt Gonder and*
Colour map 2, grid A2 *Gondor) is undoubtedly one of the most thrilling experiences that Ethiopia has to offer,*
Population: 64,000 *with its churches, castles and mountain scenery. Gondar was the capital of Ethiopia*
Altitude: 2,200 m *from the rise of Fasilades (1632-35) to the fall of Tewodros (1855-68), a status that is*
reflected in the many castles and palaces that grace the city. At first site the architecture
seems to reflect Moorish-European influence and, indeed, the presence of the Portu-
guese in the 16th century may have influenced the design of some of the fortresses, but
closer inspection reveals a continuity with the Axumite tradition.

Ins & outs **Getting there** *Ethiopian Airlines* fly daily to Gondar (see Getting around, page 775). By road
See page 854 for the route from Addis is via Bahar Dar and the whole journey is 740 km. Travel is difficult in
transport details Jun-Sep when the rains are heavy. It is realistic to allow 2-3 days for the journey there, with stops in Bahar Dar and Debre Markos or Dejen. **Getting around** Local transport is in the form of a line taxi (the Ethiopian equivalent to a *matatu* in Kenya), 'contract taxi' and *gari* (horse-drawn carts). A **Tourist Information Office**, T110022, has opened recently, and staff are very helpful (although opening hours during religious festivals are unreliable).

Sights

Royal The city's main imperial precinct, known as the Royal Enclosure, covers an area of
Enclosure 7.6 ha and contains five castles, raised walkways and connecting tunnels surrounded by high stone walls. The one or two-storey palaces have either square or rectangular ground plans, with roof terraces, battlements, square observation towers and round domed towers at the wall angles.

The oldest of these is the **Castle of Fasilades**. Built of stone and previously unused lime mortar in the mid-17th century, it reflects Axumite, Portuguese and Indian influences. The walls downstairs are decorated with a symbol that resembles the Star of David, later to become the Royal Ethiopian emblem. The upper storey offers panoramic views and Lake Tana is visible on a clear day. Fasilades' grandson,

The legend of Gondar

Archangel Raguel revealed to Emperor Lebna Dengel in a dream that Ethiopia would be blessed with a sacred capital, and that the name of the location would begin with the letter 'G'.

Nothing daunted, successive emperors began and worked their way doggedly down a list of places with names beginning with the designated consonant, dragging their entourage of 50,000 or so courtiers and camp-followers from site to site. Here and there they started some tentative civic construction, but never managed to establish anything that endured. Until, that is, Emperor Fasilades, hunting in the mid-17th century, stood to drink at a lake. As he raised his eyes, he saw a holy man rise up out of the waters. Fasilades was advised that he was in the paradise of Ezra and Enoch, and he was commanded to build his capital right there, at Gondar.

Iyasu the Great, who was considered one of Gondar's greatest leaders, built his own fantastic **'Saddle Castle'** – so called for the shape of the helm of its main tower – and decorated it with ivory, gold and precious stones. An earthquake in the early 18th century caused damage, a problem compounded by the British bombing of the Italian headquarters based in the Royal Enclosures during the Second World War. The **Reception Hall** used for lavish banquets by Emperor Bakaffa who reigned from 1721-30 is also well preserved. ■ *Entrance to the Royal Enclosure and the Bath of Fasilades (bring your ticket with you) is US$6.25. No student discount. Video recorder charge US$11.50.*

Palace of Ras Beit Other than the castles there is the Palace of Ras Beit, built in the 18th century as a private residence of the famous king maker, Ras Mikael Sehul, and in continuous occupation ever since. About 2 km away is the impressive **Bath of Fasilades**. The sunken pool is still in use for the Timkat Festival in January. Overlooking the pool there is a two-storey building, which is believed to have been Fasilades' second residence. It is 10 minutes by local minibus (1 birr). Ask to get off at Zobil, which is the stop closest to the pool.

The **Church of Debre Birhan Selassie** stands on raised ground to the northeast of the city. Built in 1682, during the reign of Iyasu the Great, it is well preserved, its ceiling and interior walls beautifully decorated with colourful religious paintings by the 17th-century artist Haile Meskel. It is probably the most famous church ceiling in Ethiopia. No flash photos are allowed; you are permitted to photograph it using a tripod and fast film. The Church of Debre Birhan Selassie has a special **festival** a few days before Timkat on 16 January, starting at around 0700. The tabot is carried around the church three times in a procession, to the cheers of the crowd. This has a very authentic atmosphere and the local people do not object to travellers observing the procession. ■ *US$2.50, US$1.50 student concession, guide recommended. Go early while prayers are being recited. The priests are very welcoming.*

Sadly, despite being a major attraction on the Historic Route, Gondar is fast gaining the reputation of being an overpriced tourist trap. The tourist information office is reputed to promote only the more expensive tours. It is better value to organize Simien Mountain treks from Debark. Visitors need to watch out for thieves, especially in the bus station.

Wolleka This **Falasha village** is 4 km north of the centre on the Debark Road. Almost all Falash (Ethiopian Jews) residents have moved to Israel now, but this village still prides itself on being the centre of Ethiopian Jewry. The village contains three former synagogues, which are used for other purposes now. Four families remain, and it is possible to look at one of the former synagogues, now a private home, which is well worth a visit. The **Gondar Pottery** is situated here. You can watch the pottery being made and there is a small shop. Small figurines of King Soloman and Queen of

Ethiopia

Sheba are on sale. It's a beautiful walk to the Falasha village (about 30 minutes). Alternatively, a taxi there and back costs US$4.50, or you can take a *gari* (horse and cart) for US$1.25. Make sure that the horse is in good condition, and ask the driver to wait for you at the pottery.

Outside the city in the direction of the airport, there's a very nice walk to the lovely **Quosquam Church**, situated on a hill with great views.■ *US$3.*

Essentials

Sleeping
■ *on map*
Overall, the sleeping options are fairly basic

C *Goha*, T08-110603, fine location on rise on the edge of town with magnificent views of both the town and the distant Simien Mountains. Good standard of food. Probably has the best accommodation in town. **D** *Circle Hotel*, T08-111991. Situated centrally just off the Piazza past the *Ethiopia Hotel*, follow the road towards Fasil's Pool for about 30 m. This brand-new hotel, opened in 2001, is circular as the name suggests, with excellent views from the rooftop bar of the piazza and surrounding areas. There's a pleasant restaurant, all rooms have en-suite facilities, hot water, laundry, car parking and good security. **D** *Fogera Hotel*, T110008, basic with spacious rooms. **D** *Misrak Pension*, Woreda 1, Kebeale 2, No 217, PO Box 391, T110069. Very clean rooms, nice garden, quiet, just a 5-min walk from the post office.

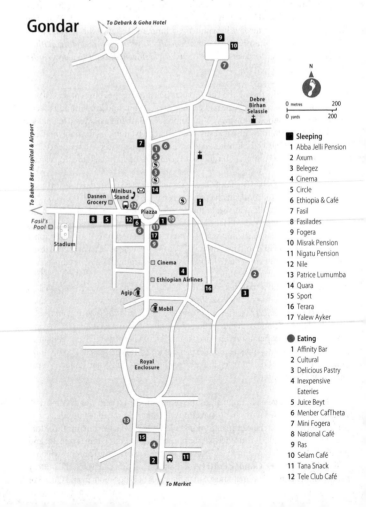

Gondar

Sleeping
1 Abba Jelli Pension
2 Axum
3 Belegez
4 Cinema
5 Circle
6 Ethiopia & Café
7 Fasil
8 Fasilades
9 Fogera
10 Misrak Pension
11 Nigatu Pension
12 Nile
13 Patrice Lumumba
14 Quara
15 Sport
16 Terara
17 Yalew Ayker

Eating
1 Affinity Bar
2 Cultural
3 Delicious Pastry
4 Inexpensive Eateries
5 Juice Beyt
6 Menber CafTheta
7 Mini Fogera
8 National Café
9 Ras
10 Selam Café
11 Tana Snack
12 Tele Club Café

Recommended. **D** *Nile Hotel*, close to the *Ethiopia Hotel*. Has a constant supply of hot water, a good restaurant and a pleasant terrace bar. **D** *Quara*, T110040, close to centre of town, in the Piazza. Disappointing with an unreliable water and electricity supply. Suffers from poor maintenance, overpriced, and has unhelpful staff. Restaurant is basic with a limited menu. The tourist accommodation price is 3 times the local rate. **D** *Terara Hotel*, T110008, Italian built, communal cold showers and bathrooms. Water supply is erratic. Spacious gardens, adjacent to the Imperial Precinct. Friendly, helpful staff, and has a good laundry service.

E *Abba Jelli Hotel*, clean, good value with views of the castles. **E** *Belegez Hotel* can be found behind the *Terara Hotel*; after the road bends to the left follow it for about 50 m. New, very clean hotel. A single room with en-suite hot shower costs US$7.50, or a single room with use of communal shower and toilet costs US$6.00. Lounge with satellite TV, laundry and safe car parking, very friendly staff and plenty of recommendations from travellers. **E** *Fasilades*, on the airport road. Clean and friendly, safe parking for vehicles and has a good restaurant. **E** *Patrice Lumumba*, close to the Piazza/telecommunications bldg (near the *Misrak*); the sign is in Amharic. You can barter over the price of the hotel, restaurant attached. **E** *Nigatu Pension*, location – near to bus station, if coming from the Royal Enclosure take left turning before the bus station. The hotel is some 50 m up the road. *Nigatu Pension* is sited within a large compound, with safe parking for vehicles and very friendly staff. Has hot water bucket showers and shared toilets. Laundry service is available. **E** *Sport Hotel* positioned near the bus station, look out for a small black and white sign outside. Doubles as a small cinema with movies shown every day and live football from satellite TV. Rooms are small and dark and the hotel is a little run down but the owners are very friendly. **E** *Yalew Ayker Hotel*, T111171, PO Box 438, is located just off the Piazza, close to the cinema. Restaurant, bucket showers/shared toilets, laundry facilities and is secure. **E** *Yimam*, is good value. Has a nice garden and bar, with a restaurant next door. Has safe parking for vehicles.

F *Axum Hotel* is almost straight across the road from the entrance to the bus station. The hotel looks a little run down and has water problems (like the whole of Gondar). Has a small restaurant, bucket showers, no hot water, shared toilets, laundry service and is secure. **F** *Cinema Hotel*, sited behind the cinema building, the shared toilets are smelly, bucket showers run down but it is secure and very cheap. **F** *Ethiopia*, T110203, is an old Italian building on the Piazza, across the road from the *Quara*. Slighty erratic water supply, but close by is a public shower with hot water and soap, popular with travellers. Clean, fair-sized rooms, basic toilets and cold showers and a very nice, bright bar. Good place to meet other travellers. Has friendly staff and is good value. Owner is Nege Kedame. There are many other **E** and **F** grade range hotels in the vicinity of the Piazza/telecom buildings.

Camping   It is possible to camp in the wonderful gardens of the *Terara Hotel*.

Eating
● *on map*

The best places to go for western food are the *Terera Hotel*, on the hill above the Piazza, and the *Fogera Hotel*, 5 mins from the Piazza in the direction of the bank (signposted from there). The *Goha* also serves western food, but the quality can vary and it is 30 mins' walk, or a 20-30 birr taxi ride. **Seriously cheap**   *Affinity Bar*, off the Piazza on the road going towards the bank, has a big, open courtyard, excellent food and very friendly staff. *Cultural Restaurant* (*Agar Bahil Megib Beyt*), near to *Belegez Hotel*, behind the *Terara Hotel*. Fish stew (*asa wat*), chicken stew (*doro wat*) and fried meat (*tibs*) cost US$1.00, fasting food (Wed/Fri) and chickpea stew (*shiro wat*) cost US$0.50. Serves *T'ej* (local honey mead drink, which is quite potent). The food is excellent. Very friendly staff, Ethiopian music played, toilets are a little smelly. *Delicious Pastry* is next to the *Quara Hotel*. Menu includes coffee, cakes, fruit juices and soft drinks. The closest place you'll get to an Addis Ababa pastry shop. Interior clean and staff friendly. *Ethiopia Café*, charming, old-fashioned, ground floor of hotel, packed all day, excellent coffee. There are many other cheap cafés in the city centre. Many of the cheap hotels also offer food. *Juice Beyt*, just up from the *Delicious Pastry*, has excellent fruit juices. *Menber CafTheta* is a 5-min walk from the Piazza. In Piazza face the *Quara Hotel*, turn left, past *Affinity Bar* until you come to a small roundabout. The *Menber CafTheta* is on the right.

Serves nice cakes and juice. **Mini Fogera**, across from the *Fogera Hotel* close to the *Misrak Pension*. Main dishes cost US$1, and include fish stew (*asa wat*), chicken stew (*doro wat*) and fried meat (*tibs*), and fasting foods (Wed/Fri) and chickpea stew (*shiro wat*) cost US$0.50. Nice, small eating cubicles hold 6-8 persons, but the staff are not the friendliest. The **Mintaub**, a small restaurant tucked away behind the palaces. Recommended. At the **National Café**, near *Ethiopia Hotel*, just off Piazza, the menu includes fish stew, spicy mince (*minchet*), chicken stew, fish cutlet, and pasta and sauce (meat and tomato) all costing US$0.75 and fasting food (Wed/Fri) for US$0.50. Staff friendly, clean interior, with acceptable toilets. **Ras Bar and Restaurant**, next to cinema. Main dishes cost US$0.75, including fish stew (*asa wat*), spicy mince (*minchet*), chicken stew (*doro wat*), fish cutlet, pasta with sauce (meat and tomato) and fasting foods (Wed/Fri), cost US$0.50. Friendly staff, interior nice but rather dark. Serves cold beers. **Selam Café**, at the Piazza across the square from the *Tele Club*. Menu includes scrambled eggs, spicy tomato stew, bean stew and fish/bean stew for US$0.30, or an egg sandwich for US$0.25. This is a basic, clean café with friendly staff. **Tana Snack**, next to cinema, serves very good, freshly cooked fish. Full menu includes fish stew, chicken stew, fried meat (*tibs*), fish cutlet, pasta with sauce (meat and tomato) and fasting foods (Wed/Fri), cost US$0.50 Friendly staff, basic interior. **Tele Club**, next to the stairs of the post office, serves coffee, bread and excellent breakfasts. The *foule* – a spicy bean dish with onions and chilli – is especially recommended ('special' *foule* comes with scrambled egg on top).

Entertainment **Gondar Cinema** is open 7 days a week; it shows a double bill in the afternoons for about US$0.30. Movies genres vary very little, predominately action, martial arts flicks are the favourites. Movies are frequently a little outdated but it is a nice way to relax if you have been travelling for a while. The cinema is situated in the centre of town. The toilets smell foul.

Shopping
Bread can be bought in numerous bakeries

Dashen Grocery (at Piazza) has everything foodwise that the Simien Mountain trekker will need. Fresh fruit, depending on season, is mainly available in Gondar during the mornings. Buy your supplies in Gondar as you'll find nothing in Debark, where fruit is virtually unavailable. The **Dashen Brewery** that opened in Gondar in July 2000 is the newest brewery in Ethiopia.

Tours & tour operators Guided 1- or 2-day trips to look at the Simien Mountains can be arranged at the NTO office in Gondar. However, this is a relatively expensive way to organize a trek. There are other freelance agents in Gondar who will help organize a trek, or you can easily arrange it yourself from Debark – where all the treks begin. It is preferable to allow 5-8 days for the more extensive trek.

An English-speaking guide called **Derbie Deksios** has been highly recommended by recent travellers, who described him as having an environmentally friendly attitude and not avaricious. **Seyoum Yigzaw**, T08-111917, F110705, has also been recommended as an excellent local guide. He is to be found at the airport in his *Hess Travel* van. Described as being funny, informative, polite and extremely knowledgeable. In addition to Gondar, he does extensive trekking in the Simien Mountains.

Transport **Local** The line taxi route goes from the Piazza area to Fasil's Pool, and on to Gondar College Hospital for a single fare of US$0.10. Contract taxis, which are usually shared, will drive to the airport at a cost of US$1.25 per person (max of 4 persons). Alternatively, from town to the airport, take a taxi or minibus as far as Azezo, US$0.30, then a horse taxi for the last 7 km.

Long-distance **Air**: *Ethiopian Airlines*, PO Box 130, T08-110129, flies daily to Gondar, (see Getting around, page 775).The airport is 17 km from town and a taxi is around US$6. You are recommended to book/confirm onward flights at the *Ethiopian Airlines* office in Gondar because the office has computers – there's nothing computerized in either Axum or Lalibela.

Ferry It is also possible to take a ferry across Lake Tana between Gorgora, south of Gondar, and Bahar Dar, which is an alternative to the bus if travelling south. See entry under Bahar Dar on page 847.

Road There are regular buses running along the route from Addis via Bahar Dar. To **Bahar Dar** the journey takes 5 hrs and costs US$2. There is now a direct bus service between Gondar and **Shire** (Inda Silase) leaving at 0630 from both Gondar and Shire (en route to Axum). The journey takes 10-11 hrs and costs US$3.50-4. Be aware however that if the bus fills up before the planned departure time, it leaves, so arrive by at least 0530, and buy your ticket on the day before travel. There is a stop at Debark. Buses from Gondar to **Debark** (for the Simien Mountain National Park) take 3-4 hrs, cost US$1.50.

For details about travel westwards to Sudan, see page 770

NB Take great care of your possessions in both Gondar and Bahar Dar bus stations, as there are gangs of thieves preying on tourists. The problem has become so acute that the police are now employing special agents to put you on to the bus safely, warning you to take care of your bags. Heed their advice.

Bank *The National Bank of Ethiopia* will change TCs and dollars/sterling. Opening hours are 0830-1100 and 1300-1500. The *Commercial Bank* in Gondar (both branches) are agents for *Western Union* if additional funds are needed rapidly.

Directory

To reach the border from Gondar takes at least two days on public transport. One bus a day leaves Gondar at 0600 and reaches the town of Shahordi (also spelt Shehedy), approximately 45 km before the Sudanese border, at around 1600, cost US$3.75. From Shahordi to the border costs US$0.80. Buy your ticket in advance. Here is where you have to obtain your exit/entry stamp at the Immigration buildings a little outside the town. There is no accommodation on the Sudanese side of the border, but you can (illegally) change your Ethiopian birr for Sudanese pounds with the customs officers. Public transport is unavailable in Gallabat but you can arrange something at the border.

Metema: border crossing
For visa information, see page 770

Debark is 100 km north, three or four hours by bus, from Gondar through attractive rolling hills. Alternatively, a taxi from Gondar to Debark will cost US$60-70, taking approximately two hours. If you wish to return by taxi, make arrangements with the driver to be collected, as there are no taxis for hire in Debark. Debark has a large **market**, with a reasonable range of supplies but more choice is available in Gondar or Axum.

Debark
All treks to the Simien Mountains National Park start here

The **Parks Office**, T16 (via the operator), about 10 minutes' walk from the *Simien Hotel*, is a green, corrugated-iron building set back off the left-hand side of the road at the beginning of Debark, coming from Gondar (faded sign on road). At the Parks Office, guides, armed scout, mules or pack horse and a horseman can be arranged. You have to bring your own food and camping gear and it is suggested that you allow extra for the guide, scouts and porters who frequently run out of supplies by day three. Expect to feed them despite what you are told beforehand. The hikes are about six hours a day, returning to your camp at around 1400.

Sleeping **F** *Simien Park Hotel*, on main road between bus stop and National Park Office (not to be confused with the *Simien Hotel*). Excellent value, good local food, hot communal bucket showers (only hot water available in Debark). Helpful staff can arrange hiking from here. Debark has other cheap, basic hotels too. Otherwise, see **Axum**, 2 days' travel by bus (change at Inda Silase/Shire, or Gondar).

Transport Travelling north from Debark it is 75 km to **Adi Arkay** (bus fare US$1.25) and the 2 towns are separated by a spectacular switchback road built by the Italians. The descent is over 1,000 m at the **Wolkefit Pass**. If returning to **Gondar** it is necessary to buy your bus ticket the day before travelling for the early morning departure at 0600. Cost US$2.50.

Simien Mountains National Park

North of Gondar are the Simien Mountains, designated by UNESCO as a **World Heritage Site**. The park is 100 km north of Gondar, east of the road to Axum. The park was recently inaccessible as a result of the fighting in the north, but it is now

13°N, 38°E
Colour map 2, grid A2

Ethiopia

possible to visit again. The park encompasses an area of 225 sq km, at an average altitude of 3,300 m, in the Afro-alpine zone. The rocky Simien Mountain massif is a broad plateau, truncated to the north and west by a single 60-km crag. Towards the south the tableland undulates to 2,200 m, divided by great gorges of more than 1,000 m depth, with fast-flowing streams. The Simien escarpments are frequently compared to the Grand Canyon in the USA. The jagged peaks of this volcanic range are so young that erosion has not yet softened their outline. The highest peak in Ethiopia is just to the southeast of the park, outside the national park, Mount Ras Dashen (sometimes spelt Deshen), and at 4,543 m is the fourth highest mountain in Africa.

Three endemic mammals are found in this spectacular setting, Ethiopia's rarest herbivore, the walia or Abyssinian ibex – a large mountain goat with a tufted beard and knotty horns, almost hunted to extinction and now estimated to number around 400-500; the Simien red fox (also known as the Ethiopian wolf) – the rarest of the world's 37 canine species – more frequently seen in the Bale Mountains National Park than here; and the striking-looking golden-maned gelada baboon (*Theropithecus gelada*) that is only found at altitudes between 2,000-4,500 m in the Ethiopian highlands. The gelada is one of five African baboons; the males weigh up to 20 kg and have a triangular patch of naked skin on their chest. The female's hairless chest area is bright red, with the nipples pointing inwards enabling the babies to suckle both nipples simultaneously. The herbivorous baboons live in harems or family groups, sleeping on the cliff face, and during the day they move to the ambas to find food (grasses and lobelias). The harems consist of a dominant male and several females and their offspring. Mutual grooming, including removal of fleas, is commonly seen. During confrontation the males have a rather harsh, barking call. Other mammals found here include the mountain nyala, klipspringer, jackel, bushbuck, rock hydras and the Hamadryas baboon.

The huge lammergeyers *(Gypaetus barbatus)*, known as 'bonebreakers', are spectacular bearded vultures with a wingspan of 2½-3 m, which drop the bones of animals killed by other predators on to rocks, to consume the marrow. They can be seen gliding over the escarpments catching the thermals and soaring upwards, along with the Auger buzzard, Verreaux's eagle, kestrel and Lanner falcon. Other birds spotted here include the white-billed starling, the thick-billed raven, the black-headed siskin, the wattled ibis and the spot-breasted plover.

In the Simien Mountains near Gich are found the Muslim descendants of Ahmad Gran (the Left Handed), a 16th-century Muslim rebel from southeast Ethiopia. He mounted a murderous campaign over 15 years to wipe out the Christians in this region and was killed by Portuguese-backed forces in 1543.

Trekking in the Simiens A trek in the Simiens is highly recommended. The national park offers a range of mountain trekking that can be handled by any reasonably fit walker who doesn't mind camping. There is a road to **Sankaber**, and all the way to **Chenek Camp**, and it extends another 100 km further east. You can hire transport for US$60 one way from Debark to Sankaber, 37 km by road, but only 23 km on the unsealed trail, which utilizes short cuts. The four-day trail crosses the road, but only occasionally follows it.

The landscape is very dramatic. The hike is relatively easy and the horse or mule can carry your packs. It gets very windy and extremely cold at night. Camps are at 4,000 m or so and frosts are common. Mietgogo Peak offers excellent panoramic views. The mountain huts at Sankaber, Gich and Chenek were destroyed in the war and the use of the repaired huts is now restricted to park employees only.

An armed ranger or guard is compulsory and the park rules also stipulate that all visitors must use a guide from the National Parks Office. The guides are not national park employees but are an organized group of trained guides, who speak English and take tourists into the park on a rotational basis and provide an excellent service. It is difficult to see much in less than four days. To climb Ras Dashen Mountain requires eight days.

Day 1: **Sankaber**, 23 km on trail from Debark (2,600 m) to Sankaber (3,200 m) (six hours), wonderful scenery and villages not visible from the road. Day 2: 21 km to next camp **Gich** (also spelt Geech) (3,600 m) with two long uphill climbs (five hours) short side trip to 500-m high waterfall. Day 3: 6 km to **Miet Gogo** (3,926 m) on edge of escarpment, great views and Saha, which also has magnificent views especially in the afternoon light. Then back 21 km to Sankaber. Day 4: 23 km back to Debark. A highly recommended alternative return route is that which leads down the escarpment and through the 'lowlands' with great landscapes and mountain scenery, rejoining the road at Adi Arkay. This trek (Debark-Gich-Chenek-Adi Arkay) takes seven days, or nine if you include a climb up Ras Dashen.

Suggested route

For those short of time and unable to do a 2-4 day trek to the Simien Mountains, just 5 km from Debark is **Lamalimu Camp**, which is on the edge of the escarpment within the Simien National Park. Hire a ranger, a guide and a mule at the National Park Office. This trip is highly recommended and offers the opportunity to see the wildlife too.

■ *US$8.75 per 48 hrs, campsite charge US$2.50 per 48 hrs. In the park it is occasionally possible to stay with villagers (US$3 per night) or hire a tent from a guide. Other costs: guide US$6.50 daily; ranger/guard US$4 daily; muleteer US$2.50 daily; mules US$2.50 daily; cook (a worthwhile investment) US$4 daily. In addition a tip is expected for each staff member usually amounting to 2 days' pay.*

Map The University of Berne, Switzerland published an invaluable 1:100,000 trekking map of the region in 1998, called *Simen Mountains, Ethiopia* (US$13).

Allow US$15-20 for 4 days' supply of food – it is worth asking your cook to buy supplies on your behalf. Stoves and tents can be hired for the walk – for details ask your guide or at the National Parks Office. Because of deforestation it is not recommended to cook over an open fire. At Gich Camp it is sometimes possible to buy a goat for US$10 – usually your team will prepare it for you in return for a share of the spoils. Water needs to be boiled for 20 mins or use purifying tablets. There is no malaria at this altitude.

Eating

Axum

A further 250 km northeast of Gondar lies the town of Axum (also spelt Aksum), site of Ethiopia's oldest city. Axum dates back some 2,000 years to when it was the hub of the Axumite Empire and the capital of one of the four world powers. It has been variously described as the throne of the King of Zion, the Mother of the whole country, the pride of the whole universe and the Jewel of the Kings. The half-buried ruins of palaces and fortresses make Axum one of Ethiopia's most important historical sites, and ongoing archaeological excavations and discoveries will help increase our understanding of its importance in the ancient world. The Queen of Sheba (called Makada in Ethiopia) made it her capital 1,000 years before Christ.

14°5'N 38°40'E
Phone code: 4
Colour map 2, grid A3

Getting there There are daily flights from Addis Ababa to Axum airport, 6 km from town. The journey by bus takes 3-4 days and access can be difficult Jun-Sep when the rains are heavy. **Getting around** Axum has line taxis (Ethiopian equivalent of a *matatu*) and contract taxis. Contract taxis to the airport charge US$1.25 per person, carrying a maximum of 4 passengers. They can be arranged from near the stelae field. It is also possible to hire bikes to visit nearby sights.

Ins & outs
For transport details,
see page 861

Sights

Evidence of past glories includes huge monolithic granite **obelisks** or **stelae** (pillars), some fallen and some still perpendicular. They are grouped together in the northeast of the town. The embellishment of the stelae shows a progression from crude stones to six monuments carved to represent multi-storey palaces, the latter believed to date from the third to the fifth century AD. Made of single blocks of granite, the tallest stood

Stelae field

Ethiopia

over 33 m high and weighs approximately 500 tons and is the largest monolith in the world. The four sides of this pillar are highly decorated and represent the front of a 12-storey building. The second tallest stela at 25 m was removed during the Italian occupation of Ethiopia (1936-41). It now stands in the Piazza di Porta Capena, in front of the headquarters of the United Nations, close to the Circus Maximus in Rome. The biggest still standing in its original site in Axum is 23 m high. The carving is both deep and precise, showing beams and windows representing a nine-storey building. It reflects a style of building still employed at Hadramaut in southern Yemen.

The stelae were probably quarried in the granite mountains close by, but the method of transportation and techniques used to erect them is open to speculation. Some scholars believe that the stelae were erected to honour the Sun God, who is symbolized by a metal disk, which was fastened in front of the 'patera' or half-moon-shaped top. The doorways sculpted on the faces of the monoliths symbolized the various heavens of the gods. It is also believed that blood sacrifices and offerings of wine, milk, bread, etc were offered up on the altars in front of the stelae – as in Egypt – at various times of the year.

■ *US$7 to the compound or to take photographs (even outside the fence). However, it is possible to see the stelae free of charge through the perimeter fencing. Free photographs can be taken if you climb the mountain next to the Yeha Hotel.*

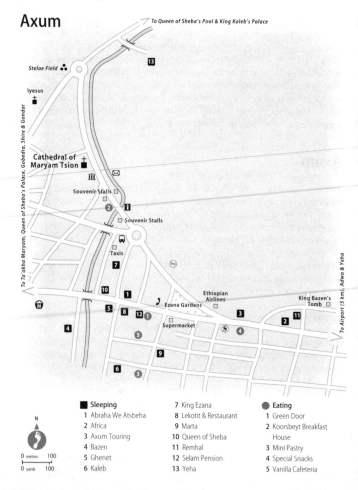

Axum

To Queen of Sheba's Pool & King Kaleb's Palace

Stelae Field

Iyesus

Cathedral of Maryam Tsion

Souvenir Stalls

Souvenir Stalls

Taxis

Ezana Gardens

Ethiopian Airlines

Supermarket

King Bazen's Tomb

To Ta'akha Maryam, Queen of Sheba's Palace, Gobedra, Shire & Gondar

To Airport (5 km), Adwa & Yeha

N

0 metres 100
0 yards 100

■ **Sleeping**
1 Abraha We Atsbeha
2 Africa
3 Axum Touring
4 Bazen
5 Ghenet
6 Kaleb

7 King Ezana
8 Lekotit & Restaurant
9 Marta
10 Queen of Sheba
11 Remhal
12 Selam Pension
13 Yeha

● **Eating**
1 Green Door
2 Koorsbeyt Breakfast House
3 Mini Pastry
4 Special Snacks
5 Vanilla Cafeteria

Ethiopia

The 16th-century Cathedral of Maryam Tsion (St Mary of Zion), recently renovated, was built by Emperor Fasilides in 1665 in the Gondarene style. This rectangular church is believed to have been built over the remains of a much older church, as the podium has the distinguishing features of Axumite architecture, with rebated walls furnished at the corners with hewn granite blocks. The church contains a fine painting of the Nine Saints.

Cathedral of Maryam Tsion
This is the holiest Christian sanctuary in Ethiopia

Women are forbidden to enter the church

The Ethiopian Orthodox Church was founded here in the fourth century and Axum remains the holiest city of the Ethiopian Orthodox Church and is an important pilgrimage site. Axum is also the centre of religious education in the Ethiopian Orthodox Church and students come here to study the Bible, as well as ancient Ge'ez manuscripts and poetry. Axum was not only the capital and the religious centre of the country, but also the place where the Ethiopian kings were crowned. King Zara Yaqob, who lived from 1434-68, was the first king who revived the old coronation ceremonies in Axum. The remains of the thrones used for the coronation of many Ethiopian rulers are in front of the gate to the compound. Nearby is a row of ancient stone seats, where sat the judges who counselled the monarchs. Next to the old church is a **museum** built by Haile Sellasie's wife, which contains collections of religious artefacts including ecclesiastical robes, crosses, manuscripts and jewelled crowns belonging to former kings. Two cannons captured by Emperor Yohannis IV from the Dervishes can also be seen in the compound.

The most important religious relic in Ethiopia is housed in the nearby Treasury. Ethiopians believe that the **Ark of the Covenant**, a sacred gold-covered chest from Old Testament times, containing the tablets on which Moses wrote the Ten Commandments, is housed here. According to legend, Menelik I, son of the Queen of Sheba and King Solomon, went to visit his father in Jerusalem, and on his return brought the Ark of the Covenant to Axum, along with 12,000 Jewish children. Another version of the legend claims that the Ark of the Covenant was brought to Axum by Azarias, the son of Zadok, before the sacking of the Temple in Jerusalem by Nebuchadnezzar, the King of Babylon, in 586 BC. Axum is therefore regarded by some Ethiopians to be the Second Jerusalem. Obviously the story is impossible to verify. However, the Treasury is closely guarded at all times by monks, and not even the president has sufficient authority to investigate further. Every Ethiopian church contains a replica of the Ark, used in every religious service.

The Treasury

Emperor Haile Sellasie built a rather ornate new cathedral in the compound, inaugurated during the visit of Queen Elizabeth II of Great Britain in 1965. Women are allowed to enter this church. ■ *US$7.50. The attached monastery is closed on Sun when only the museum with the crown jewels can be visited, US$3 (student rates available).*

Other historical sites include the **Grave of King Kaleb** (not worth a visit, according to one traveller, as "it's pitch-black and the guide just knocks on some hollow coffin and says 'so-and-so is buried there'"), and the newly excavated **Tomb of King Ramha** close to the stelae.

Other sights

Mai Shum, an enormous reservoir hewn out of rock covering an area of 1,400 sq m, is reputed to be the **Bath of the Queen of Sheba**. Although unappealing, this ancient major engineering feat supplies Axum's water, and is used for celebrating the Epiphany by the local priests.

Worth visiting is the **Axum Museum**, which contains many local artefacts including clay figurines, ancient Ge'ez inscriptions and a large collection of coins that mark the change from animist beliefs to Christianity. Axum was the only African state that minted its own money in antiquity. The minting of coins was an important instrument in the terms of propaganda, because it was able to show friends as well as enemies that it was a sovereign state. Moreover it helped to simplify its bartering system and proved to be a profitable business. It has been estimated that between the ninth and tenth centuries Axum had more than 500 types of coins. These coins are important for the reconstruction of Axumite history as they show half-length portraits of the kings, inscriptions and, up to the fourth-century, symbols of South Arabian gods. After that time the coins were no longer minted with the symbols of the sun and the moon, replaced instead with a cross. The museum contains a number of examples of Axumite coins, although many of the best examples are in Addis Ababa.

In central Axum, lying in a shelter within a park known as the Ezana Gardens, is the famous trilingual inscription of **King Ezana** (AD 320-40) on a stone tablet, in Sabba'ean (a language of South Arabia), Greek and Ge'ez, recording his military victories. There are numerous other inscriptions on stone slabs detailing military expeditions of the kings in a variety of locations in and around Axum.

The **Tomb of King Bazen**, who ruled at the time of the birth of Christ, is carved out of solid rock in contrast to the dressed stone blocks used in other royal tombs. This is believed to reflect its greater antiquity. Seventeen steps lead to an anteroom, with three adjoining chambers to the south. Other members of the royal family may also be buried in the nearby chambers. The subterranean tomb is accessed via a tunnel and nearby is a 6-m stelae.

The ruins of the vast Royal Palace **Ta'akha Maryam** were first excavated at the beginning of the 20th century. However, during their occupation in 1936, the Italians constructed the main road east to Gondar over the archaeological site, bisecting the remains. The palace is estimated to have contained over 50 rooms. New houses have been built over part of the remainder of the ruins.

About 3 km out of town to the north are the remains known as **Dongar (Palace of the Queen of Sheba)**. First excavated by French archaeologists in the 1950s, more recent diggings indicate that it dates from the seventh century, rather than over 2,000 years ago, as was believed. The entrance stairs and floor plan are intact and the palace had over 50 rooms. You can visit the Queen's bathroom, the throne room, a large kitchen with a brick oven, and there are remnants of stone flooring.

■ *To visit all the attractions and take photographs costs US$8.50, excluding the church. The entrance ticket to the sights of Axum allows only one entry to each site but visits may take place over several days.*

Excursions

Bring your own torch to view the tombs

To reach **King Kaleb's Palace**, 2 km from Axum, start from the square in front of the main stelae field, facing the stelae. Follow the asphalted road to your right. After a few hundred metres you reach Queen of Sheba's Pool. Follow the road uphill, leaving the stelae field behind you. After 1½ km the ruins of Kaleb are to be found at the right-hand side of an intersection, atop a small hill. When leaving the ruins, follow the path to your right. Beneath King Kaleb's Palace, underground chambers and galleries are reached by steep stone steps.(There are lots of bats inside.) Local belief is that this was the king's treasury, and the tomb of his son King Gabre.

After a pleasant walk of a few kilometres through fields and grasslands, you will reach **Pentaleon**, located at the top of a hill called **Debre Katin**. Women are not allowed to enter the church, but can go into the grounds and see the book and the cross. The setting is lovely, it's a very pleasant walk and offers an escape from the 'You! – Money!' shouting of enthusiastic locals. ■ *Entry to church US$2.50.*

It is also possible to explore the wider environs, including a visit to **Gobedra** (4 km west of Axum) where the stelae were quarried, and where there is also a lioness, over 2 m long, carved on rock.

Sleeping

■ *on map page 858*

Some of the hotel and restaurant names are only written in Amharic so ask one of the local boys to direct you

B-C *Yeha*, T750377. Part of the government-run *Ghion* chain. Offers a student discount, very beautiful hotel, overlooks the stelae and the dome of the Church of St Mary of Zion, good bar, restaurant and lounge. **B-C** *Remhal Hotel*, T04-751501, F750894. Located on the road to airport and Yeha, turn left before the *Mobil/Total* petrol station and continue for 50 m. The hotel is on your right-hand side. New, upmarket hotel, offers a range of accommodation from suites to budget rooms. All rooms come with en-suite hot showers, satellite TV and a refrigerator and there is a 200+ person meeting room. The hotel also has a restaurant (Cheap), which offers a varied range of good food, both western and local. As these prices are a bit steep for Axum you may be able to negotiate, especially in low season. **C** *Axum Touring Hotel*, T750205. Old Italian hotel, centrally located close to the *Ethiopian Airlines* office. Pleasant staff, restaurant/*tukul* has basic food only (see below). **D** *Africa*, close to bus stand. 14 hot showers, clean, safe parking for cars and motorcycles, has a bar and a cheap restaurant that serves good pasta and local food. **D** *Ghenet*, clean and comfortable, has a bar and restaurant. **E** *Abraha We Atsbeha*, next door to the school on the main street in town. Cheap and basic with bucket showers, shared ablutions and a laundry service. Food available. **E** *Bazen Hotel*, T750298. With the *Lekotit Hotel* to your left, take first left turning, the *Bazen* is on the right (50 m). Pleasant hotel with a bar and restaurant, has single and double rooms, shared bathrooms with hot water, laundry facilities and secure parking. **E** *Kaleb*,T750222, some rooms with own bath, very pleasant setting. **E** *Lekotit Hotel*, on main road in town opposite the school. Communal bathrooms with bucket showers/shared toilets and laundry facilities. Restaurant has excellent local food. **E** *Marta Hotel*, T750243. From the Telecom office, cross road, go past the *Green Door Restaurant*, continue for 50 m, on your left. Single rooms, bucket shower, shared toilets, restaurant, laundry service and secure parking. **E** *Queen of Sheba*, close to market. Basic and friendly, restaurant. **E** *Selam Pension*, on main road in town opposite the school. Offers single and double rooms, restaurant, communal toilets/bucket showers, laundry service, good security and parking. **E** *Shuferoch Hotel*, situated on main road in town opposite the school. Single rooms, shared ablutions, restaurant, laundry service, good security and parking facilities. **F** *King Ezana Hotel*, very cheap and basic accommodation.

Cheap *Remhal Hotel*, recent addition to Axum's eating possibilities. Serves excellent western and local food – varied menu. **Seriously cheap** *Axum Touring Hotel*, roasted meats (*tibs*) or steak cost US$1.50; spicy mince (*minchet*), chicken stew or pasta with sauce (meat and tomato) cost US$0.75; fasting food (Wed/Fri) and salads cost US$0.50. Staff friendly service a little slow, nice eating areas – *tukul*/restaurant. Clean toilets. *Green Door Restaurant* (sign in Amharic – no English name). Situated in front of the Telecom office. Menu includes chicken stew for US$1, *tibs* or pasta with sauce (meat and tomato) for US$0.75 and fasting foods (Wed/Fri), which cost US$0.50. Friendly staff, interior is basic. Toilets are OK. *Koorsbeyt Breakfast House*, serves excellent filling meals, tea, coffee and juices. *Lekotit Hotel*, on offer is chicken stew for US$1, *tibs* or pasta with sauce (meat and tomato) for US$0.75 and fasting foods (Wed/Fri) cost US$0.50. Has friendly staff, and is very popular with local people. OK toilets. *Mini Pastry*, located next door to the *Kaleb Hotel*. Menu includes scrambled eggs, bean stew and spicy tomato stew for US$0.30, egg sandwiches and fruit juices cost US$0.25 and pastries/cakes are a bargain at US$0.20. Very friendly staff, nice little courtyard at the back to sit and relax, but the toilets are a little smelly. *Special Snacks*, on main road almost opposite the *Africa Hotel*. Menu includes scrambled eggs, bean stew, fish/bean stew and spicy tomato stew at US$0.30; an egg sandwich will set you back US$0.25. All staff very friendly and the toilet is new and clean. *Vanilla Cafeteria* is on the road running parallel to the main road in town, close to the *Kaleb Hotel*. Chicken stew costs US$1, *tibs*, fish cutlet or pasta with sauce (meat and tomato) cost US$0.75, meat stew or fasting food (Wed/Fri) cost US$0.50. Friendly staff, basic, clean interior, toilets are passable. **Street food** There are many *ful* and *fata bets* in town. In addition bread can be bought in numerous bakeries. Fruit available (depending on season) at market or at fruit shops.

Eating
● *on map, page 858*

Galaxy Tours is based at the *Yeha Hotel*, and *Experience Ethiopia Tours* is based at the *Axum Hotel*.

Tour operators

Air *Ethiopian Airlines*, T03-750226, offer daily flights from Addis Ababa (see Getting around, page 775). The airport is 6 km from town.

Transport

Road The route to/from Addis via Gondar and Bahar Dar is 1,050 km. It is realistic to allow 3-4 days for the bus journey there, with stops in Gondar, Bahar Dar and Debre Markos. There are regular buses running along this route. From Gondar the journey takes 1½ days, US$3.50. Change buses at Shire/Inda Silase (usually an overnight stay in Shire is necessary, especially during the rains). The alternative route to Addis Ababa is via Adigrat, Mekelle and Dessie,

There is currently no bus service to Eritrea

Ethiopia

which takes 3 days. One bus goes all the way to/from Addis via Mekelle, Weldiya and Dessie, but does not run daily. Buy tickets in advance. The bus stand in Axum is right in the centre next to the Big Tree. The 120-km journey between Axum and Adigrat takes 4 hrs by bus. Buy tickets for the bus for Adigrat and Mekelle the night before. There is a good, sealed road to Adigrat. However, there are many places of interest en route, including the ancient ruins at Yeha, the tableland monastery of Debre Damo (see page 863) and the town of Adwa. There are frequent minibuses between Axum and Adwa.

South of Axum

Adwa Just south of the Axum-Yeha road is the site of the famous **Battle of Adwa** (sometimes spelt Adowa), one of the biggest battlefields of Africa where, on 1 March 1896 Menelik II defeated the Italians (see page 888). The historic Ethiopian victory over a well-prepared Italian army is considered nowadays by many people to be a symbol of triumph over aggression and foreign rule. The town of Adwa contains the handsome **Church of Medhane Alem**.

Yeha About 45 km northeast of Axum, Yeha is an ancient town thought to contain Ethiopia's oldest buildings. It is believed to have been the main Ethiopian capital during the pre-Axumatic period, and is located 5 km off the main Axum-Adigrat road to the northeast. Yeha is famous for its amazing rectangular stone **temple**, the oldest known sacred site in Ethiopia, located on a small hill with a mountain behind, believed to date from 500 BC. According to the German scholar, Heinrich Muller, this temple was built even earlier – possibly 700-800 BC. The temple base is 18.5 m x 15 m and 12 m high, consisting of only one long room. The roof (probably supported by timber) and west wall are missing. The temple is built of immense dressed sandstone blocks, some up to 3 m long, fitted together without mortar and which appear to have largely escaped destruction by erosion. The back of the temple has marble slabs and, according to legend, there is a tunnel that leads back to King Kaleb's Tomb in Axum. There is a small stela nearby, and the temple is in a compound surrounded by a more recent stone wall interspersed with gatehouses at intervals. The temple is still in relatively good condition because, according to Phillipson, it was probably used as a Christian church for a thousand years after its construction, in the sixth century AD. It is anticipated that other archaeological finds await discovery because the site has not yet been fully dug.

■ *US$2.50. The drive from Axum will take approximately 1½ hrs (each way) by 4WD. Take the road out past the airport, through Adi Abun Adwa and then Adwa. Look out for the 2 stone stelae on left-hand side of road. Turn here and follow the road for 5 km into the village of Yeha.*

Church of Close by is the Church of Abba Afse, named after one of the Nine Saints of the East-
Abba Afse ern Roman Empire who came to Ethiopia from Syria in the sixth century in order to teach the gospel. These monks founded numerous monasteries and churches in many parts of Tigray. The present rectangular church dates from the Middle Ages, and replaced the original church on the site. It is notable for a set of stone Ibex-Kopfen heads, which possibly came from the original building, set into the front wall. The ibex was a sacred animal in pre-Christian southern Arabia.

Adjacent to the church is an *Iqa-bet*, a two-storey stone storage building, which contains religious artefacts. The beautiful cross of Abba Afse, the founder of this church, can be seen here. There are some stone blocks with raised inscriptions in Sabba'ean, the ancient language of southern Arabia, as well as religious robes and fine silk umbrellas. The church **museum** also houses many beautifully illustrated manuscripts; drums; rattles with metal discs (*sistra*); and wooden objects (*meqwomeya*) rather like shooting-sticks on which the priests sit during long services.

There is a sixth-century monastery called Debre Damo near the small town of **Bizet**, a farming settlement, which lies on the road between Axum and Adigrat. Debre Damo is the oldest monastery of Ethiopia. It is situated 90 km northeast of Axum and 184 km northwest of Mekelle, the capital of Tigray. The monastery is situated on an amba or plateau approximately 2,800 m high, surrounded by steep cliffs. The plateau measures 1,000 x 500 m. To get to this monastery, you have to climb up using the 15-m plaited leather rope called a *jende*, which hangs down from the plateau. Visitors wishing to climb to the amba are offered an extra rope for additional security. It offers spectacular views but the climb excludes the less agile tourist.

The church was founded by Abun Aregawi, also known as Zemikael, who was one of the Nine (Syrian) Saints who came to Ethiopia during the sixth century to do missionary work. According to legend, Abun Aregawi climbed to the top of the mountain by a snake, which was sent by God. Nowadays the *jende* symbolizes this snake.

There are two churches on the mountain. According to legend, the main church that measures 20 x 9 m, was built by Emperor Gebre Meskal, who ruled over Ethiopia in the sixth century. The decoration of the walls is quite similar to the decoration of the stone pillars of Axum. In the nave you can see antique stone pillars and on the ceiling of the nave there are many animals carved in the wood, such as elephants, cows and water birds. The monastery at Debre Damo houses numerous treasures, including old manuscripts and crosses. Adjacent to the church are big cisterns or tanks for water storage.

Important religious figures associated with Debre Damo monastery include Abba Yohanni, one of the Nine Saints, who led an ascetic life here. Abba Iyesus Mo'a (revered as an Ethiopian saint) studied here under Abba Yohanni's mentorship, before founding the monastery at Debre Hayk Estifanos (St Stephen's) on Lake Hayk in 1248. Abba Takla Haymanot (also revered as an Ethiopian saint) studied at Debre Hayk Estifanos for about 10 years under Abba Iyesus Mo'a, then spent a further decade as a pupil of Abba Yohanni, prior to founding the monastery of Debre Asbo in the 13th century, later renamed Debre Libanos, the premier monastery in southern Ethiopia.

The monastery was used as a place of refuge several times by Ethiopian kings to escape persecution by enemies. Emperor Atse Lebne Dengle found refuge here in the 16th century when he was being pursued by the army of Ahmad Gragn. Despite the ban on women, his wife Empress Seble Wengel and daughters also sought refuge here in 1541. ■ *Entry to the monastery, US$4.*

Debre Damo
Women are forbidden to visit this monastery

Sleeping E *Axum Hotel*, in the village of Bizet, is clean and basic.

Transport There are buses from Axum to Adigrat, leaving at 0600 daily. Bizet is approximately 70 km from Axum – the bus fare is US$2 and the journey takes approximately 3 hrs. Alternatively take the bus to Adwa and change there for the bus to Adigrat, and get off at Bizet, journey time 4-5 hrs. Debre Damo is about 12-15 km from Bizet. Take the Axum road, and after approximately 1 hr you see a sign for Debre Damo. 400 m from the sign turn right on the path. Next to a stone building you come on to a road. Follow this for about half an hour. When descending from a small hill there are some white buildings and a shed – take the path to the right (white building on your left). Follow this path over a small hill. Cross the river in the valley and keep on

Debre Damo Monastery

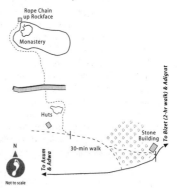

Rope Chain up Rockface

Monastery

Huts

Stone Building

30-min walk

To Axum & Adwa

To Bizet (2-hr walk) & Adigrat

N

Not to scale

Ethiopia

the path up the mountain (tableland). Climb the tableland, traverse it, going slightly around it to reach the chain (see map). Make sure that you carry sufficient water with you prior to setting off. It is difficult to get back to Axum the same day because public transport is not available in the afternoon. It is possible to hitch a ride on a lorry but it is slow. Taxi to Adwa costs about US$12.

Adigrat
14°20'N 39°26'E
Colour map 2, grid A3

Close to Adigrat the road climbs to over 3,000 m, offering spectacular views of the highest peak, **Alegua** (3,291 m), and the terraced slopes and cliffs of the Hista River gorge. Adigrat (also spelt Addigrat) lies at the junction of the Axum-Adigrat and Mekelle-Asmara roads. It is the second largest town in Tigray after Mekelle and an important regional centre. It is also renowned for the quality of its *t'ej* – mead or honey wine. Here you can try the local popular north Ethiopian bread call *ambasha*, made from wholemeal flour, pan baked and divided into triangular sections decorated with pricked patterns. **Chirkos Church**, adjacent to the market, is worth seeing. It contains wonderful paintings and offers good views of the area. There is a charge for going into the church but entry to the compound is free. Close to the stadium is a Catholic church. The market is south of the main roundabout.

Sleeping and eating E *Ethiopia Hotel*, central position, near main roundabout in town. E *Hiwunot Hotel*, just off the road west to Axum, near bus station. Clean, basic rooms, shower/toilets. E *Semian Hotel*, on road west to Axum, central but very noisy. E *Fasika Hotel* and E *Weldu Sebapadis Hotel* are close to one another on the road north, before the *Total* petrol station, offering clean, basic accommodation with shared showers/toilets. There are several restaurants and cafés. The *Sweet Cake Shop* on the road east to the stadium is recommended. Opposite the *Total* petrol station on the road north, the *Sweet Pastry* offers very good fruit juices and breakfast dishes. The *Breakfast Café*, opposite the *Ethiopia Hotel*, is also recommended.

The rock-hewn churches of Tigray

South of Adigrat towards Mekelle are rock-hewn churches scattered over the terrain stretching 70 km north to south and 100 km east to west. The date of construction of the rock churches of Tigray is uncertain, but the majority are estimated to date from about the 10th to the 15th centuries. There are local claims that some of the churches were built many centuries earlier. The churches are frequently hewn out of remote cliff faces or free-standing outcrops of rock, and are believed to pre-date those at Lalibela (see below, page 873). The architectural style may have evolved from burial chambers or hermits' caves. Some of the churches consist of simple rooms cut into the rock, possibly just modifications and enlargements of caves, others have one or more formed façades. Some are elaborately decorated with carvings and paintings on the pillars, walls and ceilings.

The churches are classified into groups or clusters reflecting their proximity to local towns or villages. The major groups are called the Gheralta, Tembien, Takatisfi and Atsebi clusters. Details of some of the churches are summarized below. Guides are essential as many of the churches are in remote, inaccessible locations with no public transport.

Further details can be obtained from the **Tigre Tourist Bureau**, PO Box 124, Mekelle, T03400769, who have a free leaflet, *Tigre: The Open Air Museum*, which includes a sketch map of the location of some of the churches on the back.

Recommended reading for more detailed information includes: Dr Tewelde Medhin Yoseph, *Monolithic Churches of Tigrai*; Ruth Plant, *The Architecture of the Tigre*; Georg Gerster, *Churches in Rock (Early Christian Art in Ethiopia)*; David Buxton, *The Rock-hewn and other Medieval Churches of Tigre Province, Ethiopia*; Paul Henze, *Ethiopian Journeys*; O Jager and Ivy Pearce, *Antiquities of North Ethiopia*.

The Gheralta cluster, northwest of Mekelle, contains the largest concentration of **The Gheralta**
churches. The landscape of Gheralta is mountainous. The churches are located **cluster**
west of the Mekelle-Adigrat road, between the town of Wukro (47 km north of
Mekelle) and Senkata (83 km north of Mekelle). The nearest villages are Degum,
Megab and Hawzien.

Debre Mariam Korkor is one of the biggest rock churches of Tigray, with interior dimensions of 17 m x 9.5 m x 6 m. There are six free-standing pillars, and wonderfully decorated arches, supporting the bas-relief carved ceiling. The walls and the
pillars of the church are decorated with scenes from the Old and New Testament,
and on one of the pillars there is a painting of an angel. The church also houses a big
collection of parchment, manuscripts and crosses. The west exterior frontage of the
church is painted white. This church is situated on one of the highest peaks of the
Gheralta region.

Daniel Korkor Church, located nearby, contains only two rooms. The ceiling of
the anteroom is decorated with primitive paintings.

Debre Tsion Abraham, named after its founder, the monk Abun Abraham, is
completely hewn out of the rock with a rectangular ground plan. It is believed to date
from the 14th century, although some scholars suggest that the paintings are from
the 15th century. The approximate dimensions of the church are 13 m x 8 m x 8 m.
There are magnificent wall paintings of saints and Apostles but water damage has
caused deterioration. The domed ceiling is supported by six pillars, decorated with
geometrical patterns. There is a ceremonial fan dating from the 15th century, measuring 1 m in diameter and containing 34 painted panels, each depicting an Apostle.

Abun Yemata (*bei Guh*) is another church famed for its difficult access and
colourful 15th-century wall murals illustrating the Old and New Testament. Ivy
Pearce, one of the first Europeans to visit this church, recorded the great difficulties
encountered climbing up the rock using only poorly defined steps. Nine of the 12
Apostles are illustrated on the dome and three other Apostles are painted on the
walls. The founder Abun Yemata is illustrated sitting on a horse. The church and
murals are thought to have survived the widespread destruction of the Islamic conquest of the 16th century because of their inaccessibility.

Yohannes Meakudi Church is situated on a plateau, reached by a narrow path
between two sandstone walls. Above the main door there is a large window carved
from the rock, which helps to light the church's interior. The ground plan of the
church is rectangular, measuring approximately 13 m x 10 m x 6 m. Four pillars support the ceiling. The church contains many early paintings in good condition,

Gheralta

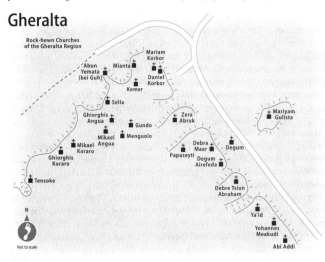

painted on non-porous stone, and the subjects include the Madonna and child, St John the Apostle and Adam and Eve plus serpent. There are two entrances, one for men and the other for women.

The Tembien cluster The Tembien cluster contains approximately 20 rock churches. Situated north of the town of Abbi Addi, the Tembien churches used to be in one of the most inaccessible places in Tigray, but the recently built Mekelle-Adwa road has aided access.

Gabriel Wukien, the most important church in this cluster, 16 km northwest of Abbi Addi, is surrounded by trees that, unless you stand right in front, screen the church from view. This church is believed to have been built during the reign of Atse Dawit (1382-1411). North of the church is a graveyard containing a set of stone bells. The church is compared to Medhane Alem of the Takatisfi cluster because of its detailed stone carvings. The church is 15 m long east-west and 15.5 m north-south. It contains eight 5-m free-standing pillars and a further nine wall pillars, of heights varying between 2.5 m and 3.4 m. Wooden doors lead from the south and east sides into the nave. The walls of the 'holy of holies' are decorated with arches in forms of half moons, similar to the obelisks of Axum. The domes are decorated with engraved crosses called *croix pâtées*. The eastern side of the church remains attached to the rock face and there are three rectangular windows allowing daylight into the church.

Abba Yohannes Church is 9 km north of Abbi Addi, close to the village of Menji. The white-painted façade makes it clearly visible from a great distance, 300 m up a steep rock face. Access is via the western approach over a bridge, built in the early 1970s. A dark, steep passageway leads to the church interior. The church contains a nave with two aisles. The twin domes are of differing heights, one approximately 7 m and the other 9 m. There are seven free-standing pillars and seven wall pillars in the cruciform church. A more recently built wall has paintings depicting the 12 Apostles.

Mariam Hibito Church design is believed to have been influenced by an older rock church like Medhane Alem of the Takatisfi cluster. According to the legend, this church was built during the reign of King Zara Yacob in the 15th century. The interior of the 13.9-m long church has six pillars on which arches are set to support the ceiling. It is quite dark and the floor is always damp. There are three doors, the central one leading into the nave. Above this door are three windows. On the west side of the church a narthex has been carved, leading from north to south of the church. On the ceiling of the narthex there is evidence of unsuccessful attempts to build domes.

The Takatisfi cluster The **Takatisfi** or **Teka Tesfay** cluster of rock-hewn churches are found just east of the Adigrat-Mekelle road, between Sinkata and Negash, 73 km north of Mekelle, close to a small village called Inda Teka Tesfay. The massif north of the famous mosque of Negash, named Tsaeda Imba (white mountains), is home to one of the highest parishes in Tigray where these rock-hewn churches are located.

Medhane Alem Adi Kasho (Saviour of the World) is one of the most important churches of the Tigray region, estimated to date from the late 10th or early 11th century. An unusual feature is the beautifully decorated narthex connecting the north and south of the church. Two doors lead to the interior of the church where the ceiling is supported by six huge square pillars. The ceiling is decorated with reliefs and geometrical patterns. Because of its immense height and massive pillars, this church resembles a cathedral. There are engravings on the walls and a *croix pâtée* on the right side of the back wall.

Petros and Paulos Church is carved into a steep cliff 2,770 m above sea level. This church is easily visible from below as the front is painted white, in contrast to the rocky background. The way up to the rock church is quite difficult. The sanctuary is carved from the rock with the remainder of the church built on a ledge. The church is constructed of a mixture of wood, stone and mortar. The ceiling is supported on two wooden columns. The architecture of this church is not very impressive, but its wall paintings are of high quality. A number of paintings depict Madonna with child, various angels and the Nine Saints. The church has not been used for several years because it is difficult to reach, and sadly the pictures are deteriorating.

'Haleka' Halefom Retta, a farmer from a nearby village, started building another church of the same name below the original in 1982. He reports having been inspired to build the church following a visit from the Holy Gabriel as he slept. The new **Petros and Paulos Church** is 10 m x 9 m x 3 m. There are four pillars and the front of the church is made of bricks. The internal rooms are not decorated. The church has been constructed so that it can house three replicas of the Ark of the Covenant.

Mikael Milhaizengi Church, dedicated to St Michael, is the third church in this cluster. Hewn out of a hillside at 2,760 m above sea level, the surrounding churchyard contains graves and gnarled trees. Stone church bells hang in one of the trees at the front of the churchyard. It is believed that this church was previously a cave. The main entrance is only 1.5 m high and less than 1 m wide, so that adults must bend down in order to gain entry. Its most remarkable characteristic is the beautifully decorated dome, which resembles a round *ambasha*, a kind of bread made only in this part of Tigray. In the centre of the dome is a Greek cross.

The Atsebi Dera cluster is on the way to Arho, east of the main road, towards the Danakil Depression, accessed either from Agula'e or Wukro, 35 km and 40 km north of Mekelle respectively. **The Atsebi Dera cluster**

Mikael Amba Church was built in the 10th century according to local belief, and scholars are in agreement that it predates the Lalibela churches. Sited on an amba or plateau at 2,329 m above sea level, 11 km south of Atsebi, the church is dedicated to Saint Michael. Described by Ruth Plant as "one of the great churches of Tigray", the large, cruciform church looks almost like a monolith, as three of its sides are completely hewn out of the rock. It measures 17 m x 9 m, has nine free-standing pillars and 16 wall pillars and the ceiling is approximately 6 m in height. The ceiling of the church includes geometrical patterns similar to the church in Wukro Cherkos plus a large bas-relief in the shape of a Greek cross. There is a delicately carved screen across the central nave. The walls are also decorated with many engravings. Mikael Amba was a wealthy church with many treasures and manuscripts (some fire damaged), and a rare 1.5-m black iron cross. Adjacent to the church are big cisterns or tanks for water storage, similar to those at Debre Damo.

Mikael Debre Selam Church is situated at 2,678 m in a cave in the side of an amba, on the crest of the Danakil escarpment. About 7½ km northwest of Atsebi and 36 km northeast of Wukro, this famous white-fronted church, with internal dimensions of 9 m x 7.5 m, is noted for its ridge paintings, although several are a bit faded. The architecture is unique, a combination of a front made of brick and the roof and walls made of rock. There is an internal wall constructed in the Axumitic 'sandwich style', where layers of wood alternate with layers of stone. The wooden frames of the doors and shutters are highly decorated with geometrical patterns, including swastika symbols. This cave church, described by Ivy Pearce as a church within a church, has the external arch of the sanctuary cut from solid rock, in contrast to the wooden arch more commonly used in Ethiopian medieval churches. There is a painting of Madonna and child on one of the shutters. Because this church is on the crest of the Danakil escarpment, and therefore on the edge of the old Ethiopian empire, it is believed that this helped it to escape the attention of the Muslim invaders.

Mikael Barka Church, 18 km east of Wukro, 7 km southwest of Atsebi, is set into a small amba and is relatively easy to access. The front of this fully excavated church is recent, dating to the 1960s. The base is square and the church includes 12 pillars, four of them free-standing. Mikael Barka is famous for its frescos and wall paintings,

Ethiopia

some of which are very faint, thought to date from the 16th century. There are fine ceiling reliefs in six of the nine bays. A picture on one of the pillars just inside the entrance shows St Michael with a cockerel sitting at the saint's feet. On other pillars are other faded paintings including the fine relief of a cross on a pillar to the right. According to legend, Queen Judith set this church on fire in the 10th century, however scholars believe the church dates to the 13th or 14th century.

Cherkos Agebo Church is sited on a ledge under a rock overhang, halfway up the face of an amba, 6 km east of Debre Selam Mikael. The church is built against the cliff face on the south side, and the east and north timber and stone walls have monkey-heads. A narthex, sanctuary arch and raised nave roof were added later according to Lepage. The ground plan is square, with a nave and sanctuary. The church contains a very fine Axumite frieze of carved panels, set into a wooden surround.

Inda Mariam Wukro Inda Mariam Wukro lies 6½ km northeast of the town of Nebelet in central Tigray, northwest of the Gheralta cluster. Access is difficult as you have to cross several rivers. The church is not fully separated from the rockface, and only the southern façade is visible from the exterior. The interior has richly decorated walls and ceilings. There are three doors, two of them leading directly into the nave and the third leading to the priests chamber, called a Kine Mahlet, measuring 9 m x 4.5 m x 5 m. This is highly decorated with stone bas-reliefs and relatively recent paintings. The western and southern parts of the ceiling have large, carved Greek crosses, and the northern and the central part of the ceiling have geometrically perfect domes. The ceiling is supported on two free-standing pillars. A special feature of the church is that the pillars are connected by double arches, and have no central pillar. A wooden door leads into the inner sanctum. The pillars divide the narthex and the passage into two naves. The interior measures 10 m x 9 m x 9 m. Four free-standing pillars with pilaster capitals on top, plus another 10 wall pillars support the ceiling. This church is similar to those churches of Lalibela and Debre Damo. Another chapel houses the Tabot, accessed by climbing up a wooden ladder.

Abraha Atsbeha Abraha Atsbeha Church is situated 50 km west of Wukro. Believed to be of very early origin, this cruciform church resembles the churches of Wukro Cherkos and Mikael Amba with 13 high pillars supporting the ceiling. The church measures 60 m x 13 m. Abraha Atsbeha is decorated with magnificent 17th-century paintings depicting saints and biblical scenes. The church contains many valuable masterpieces including the beautifully decorated prayer cross, said to have belonged to Frumentius, the first Bishop of Ethiopia, whose ecclesiastical name was Abba Salama, meaning the Father of Freedom. The church is dedicated to the famous twin kings of Axum who are credited with the introduction of Christianity into Ethiopia in the fourth century. Many Ethiopians believe that the bodies of Abraha and Atsbeha, also called Ezana and Saizana, are buried in the church. Local belief is that the church was built in the fourth century, however archaeological consensus dates the church from the 10th century. This is one of the most important churches in Ethiopia, with an estimated 10,000 people going there on **pilgrimage** each 14 October.

Wukro Cherkos Wukro Cherkos is another important cruciform rock church sited close to the half-Islamic and half-Christian town of Wukro, 47 km north of Mekelle. This large and easily accessible church is built of sandstone and is a three-quarters monolith. It resembles the churches of Abraha Atsbeha and Mikael Amba. The main entrance leads to a room containing a beautifully decorated 15th-century pillar with paintings depicting angels and saints. Line drawings cover the ceiling. On the west wall is an engraving of a *croix pâtée*. The 6-m high barrel ceiling is still blackened from a fire said to have occurred in the 10th century when Queen Judith reigned over the country.

Negash Negash is a small town 60 km north of Mekelle, on the main Mekelle-Adigrat road. It is situated on a flat mountain plateau with a wonderful view over the Gherelta

Mountains and it was one of the strongholds of the early Ethiopian Christians. The name Negash is believed to originate from the word *Neqash*, meaning king. Najashi is the Arabic version of this word. The history of Negash can be traced back to the seventh century AD. Followers of Mohammed were persecuted for practising their religion by the Quraysh tribe in Mecca. Mohammed sought a secure place for his followers, and the Negashi or Ethiopian King Armah granted the refugees asylum. Later a second group of refugees followed and it is said that King Armah refused to hand over the refugees to the Quraysh despite being offered substantial gifts. Negash is regarded as the second holiest place of the Muslim world. Many of the original refugees remained in Ethiopia until they died and were buried nearby.

The prophet Mohammed is said to have prayed for the king when he heard of his death. This led to the belief that the king had converted to the Islamic religion and was therefore the first Ethiopian Muslim, as claimed by some Ethiopian and Arabic scholars. This version of events is disputed by many Ethiopians, who claim that the king retained his Christian beliefs. The Najashi of the Habashat, as the Ethiopian king was called in the Arabic world, was reputedly buried in Negash in AD 630. Other scholars claim the king was buried 10 km away in Wukro. It is said that Ethiopia was left out of the Jihad, the Holy War of Islam, because of the hospitality and protection it gave to the Islamic world.

Nowadays Negash is famous for the ornate white Arab-style **tomb of Ahmed Negash**, and the recently built **mosque**, said to be on the site of the original mosque. An **ancient cemetery** has been uncovered, believed to contain the graves of those first Muslims refugees. There is an annual festival held at Negash, which attracts Muslim pilgrims from all over northern Ethiopia.

Mekelle

Continuing south, down the eastern flanks of the Simien Mountains, you will pass through Mekelle (variously spelt Mekele, Mek'ele, Makale or Makalle), the regional capital of Tigray, 777 km from Addis Ababa. Since the end of the war (see page 890) the town has grown and developed at a rate that has astonished the residents and prompted accusations of government favouritism. While the town has some way to go to catch up with or Awasa for their apparent prosperity, it is already a very pleasant place to be. There are no ancient sites to see in Mekelle but it is a very good place to ponder Ethiopia's more recent history.

Colour map 2, grid A3

The **Yohannes IV Museum**, formerly known as the Palace of Yohannes IV, was built by an Italian architect, Giacomo Naretti, in 1886. It has turrets and battlements, but the emperor is reported never to have inspected the fortifications as he refused to climb any stairs. Here you can see some of the regalia of the feudal lords who ruled Ethiopia up until the time of the Dergue. Visit the *Abraha Castle Hotel* and get an idea of the disparity between the lifestyles of the lords above and the peasants below.

Mekelle has an interesting **TPLF Monument**, which dominates the town. A miniature Eiffel Tower of marble-cased concrete, it rises 55 m, standing atop a hill at the edge of town. It is topped with a wheel of industry beneath a gold sphere. This impressive monument to the Tigrayan People's Liberation Front is not wonderfully proportioned perhaps, but the excellent sculpture sequence beneath it, with 20 large bronze statues depicting the misery of war, and showing how the Tigrean people rise from misery and subjection to march towards a brighter future, is genuinely moving. ■ *There is no cost to visit the monument but be a little careful taking photographs. Technically you're supposed to have a person somewhere in the frame or the film may be confiscated.*

Mekelle has a good range of shops, selling everything a traveller might need, from clothes and food, to a Walkman or computer software. The market area is enormous and exhilarating, and has none of the slightly threatening atmosphere of Addis Ababa's Mercato area, but it would be wise to watch your pockets anyway. There is

Ethiopia

plenty of nightlife in the city centre. Tigrean music is something of an acquired taste but the friendly atmosphere and good beer are appealing to all. From Mekelle, Afar nomads can be observed with their camel caravans carrying salt, climbing up from the Danakil Depression to market. The main **market day** is Monday.

The staff at the **Mekelle Tigre Tourist Bureau**, T400769, are very helpful and well informed about local historical sites. The war is still an emotive issue in Tigray, discussed with a mixture of pride and sadness.

Sleeping
■ *on map*
For price codes: see inside front cover

Mekelle has plenty of hotels at both ends of the market. There are also several very cheap places to stay. You'll find a reasonable room whatever your price range

B *Bubu Hills Hotel*, T404400. Wonderful views over the town from the terrace bar. Good food and drink. All rooms are large with en-suite bathrooms. Relaxed atmosphere, even has a swimming pool (although residents report that they have never seen any water in it). **B** *Axumite Hotel*. Vast and ostentatiously luxurious. All rooms have en-suite bathrooms. Good food. The place to be seen and to make deals in the business and NGO world. The huge lounge bar is worth a visit for those feeling cut off from civilization. **C** *Abraha Castle* is a lovely hotel converted from a real castle. The terrific terrace has wonderful views across town and of the TPLF Monument. Offers reasonable western food, and excellent Ethiopian food in an atmospheric *tukel* (a traditional round house). Generally friendly staff, has the comfortable feeling of fading elegance. "Best hotel in Ethiopia" according to a recent guest. **C** *Hawzen Hotel*, T404333, is like a more manageable version of the *Axumite*. **D** *Green Hotel* is the most convenient for the bus station. Large clean rooms with en-suite hot shower and small rooms above the bar with communal cold showers. Draught beer, and very good food. Nice garden drinking area with secluded booths. Generally friendly staff apart from irritating attempts to overcharge, so be prepared to bargain hard.

Eating
● *on map*
For price codes: see inside front cover

Mid-range *Jordano's Restaurant*. Best pizza and pasta outside Addis Ababa. **Seriously cheap** *Guna Sports and Social Club*. Best *foule* in Ethiopia, a must for breakfast time. The triangle connecting the 3 roundabouts has a plethora of excellent and **juice** and **pastry shops**; entire days can be spent drifting from one to the other. This area also has a number of shops selling biscuits, chocolate, jam, peanut butter, soy sauce – all those things you foolishly imagined you could live without.

Transport

Air *Ethiopia Airlines* offer a daily service to Mekelle – see Getting around, page 775. The *Ethiopian Airlines* office in the town centre is, as always, friendly and efficient. Mekelle airport is currently a dreary tin shack on a windy plateau but a new terminal building is under construction, which will be equal to Bole Airport in Addis Ababa.

Road The road heading towards Adigrat and Axum is one of the best in Ethiopia, but the road toward Addis is one of the worst. The road south is currently being improved and should be very much better as far as Adi Gudem within the lifetime of this guide. However, there are not, as far as I'm aware, any plans to improve the road from Adi Gudem to Maichew in the near future, significant as this is the worst section. The rocky

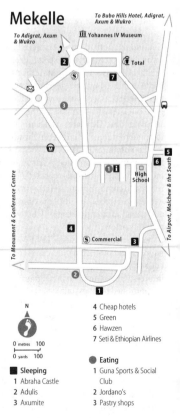

Mekelle

To Bubo Hills Hotel, Adigrat, Axum & Wukro

To Adigrat, Axum & Wukro

Yohannes IV Museum

Total

High School

To Airport, Maichew & the South

Commercial

To Monument & Conference Centre

N

0 metres 100
0 yards 100

■ **Sleeping**
1 Abraha Castle
2 Adulis
3 Axumite
4 Cheap hotels
5 Green
6 Hawzen
7 Seti & Ethiopian Airlines

● **Eating**
1 Guna Sports & Social Club
2 Jordano's
3 Pastry shops

Ethiopia

and dusty mountain roads twist and turn. Driving to Maichew, the halfway point (in terms of driving time) will be the village of **Adi Gura**, you would be well advised to stop here and have a strengthening glass of tea as the next couple of hours will be frankly terrifying. By car, the journey from Mekelle to Maichew should take 4-5 hrs.

Bus Mekelle bus station is enormous and confusing, but does not have much of a pickpocketing problem. While the vast majority of buses leave early in the morning (arrive at the bus station before 0600), there is a certain amount of traffic passing through during the day, and hitching is possible especially if you're not trying to go far. By bus, the journey from Mekelle to Maichew takes 6-7 hrs.

Maichew

Maichew is a mundane little town, which most travellers pass by without so much as a backward look; a shame as the town's beautiful surroundings and interesting history make it well worth a visit. The town is surrounded on three sides by gently rugged mountains, the fourth side drops sheer away to the plains far below. The name Maichew means 'salt water', nobody knows why, but given the many battles that have been taken place in this area the name is appropriate. Maichew was assured its place in history on 5 May 1936 when King Haile Selassie's army picked up their rifles and spears and took on the might of the Italian Air Force. The rout that resulted sealed the success of the Italian invasion and Haile Selassie fled. The battle started on the slopes of the mountain called Bukkara that sits at the southern end of town and the Ethiopians had retreated 22 km before the fighting ended. The battle finished at a small village between Maichew and Korem, which is now known as **Chinko Majo** – a corruption of the Italian *cinque maggio* – 5 May.

Colour map 2, grid A3

The best reason to visit Maichew is its beautiful surroundings

There is little to commemorate the battle now; a couple of nondescript monuments to the Italian and Ethiopian fighters are not really worth seeking out but a visit to the battleground (the sloping area behind the high school and the technical college) may be a moving experience for those with an imagination. More morbid sensibilities can be satisfied by visiting the Church of Mikael near the battle site, where a number of skulls have been kept in remembrance of the fight. It is said that the skulls are all of Ethiopian origin, not the 'inferior' Italian model. A search in the big **Saturday market** always produces fascinating items of militaria; go through the piles of scrap metal (close to the chicken and egg section of the market) and you may well find Dergue-era canteens, Italian bayonets, Ethiopian cap badges or buttons from the Haile Selassie era, along with a whole host of other strange things, such as a coffee grinder made from an old mortar shell, for example.

D *Ahadu Hotel* is the newest and most luxurious hotel in Maichew, most rooms are large and clean with en-suite toilets and hot showers, and excellent views. The food is generally good but unexceptional, and the western food is not worth bothering with. It occasionally has the only draught beer in town. **D** *Giorgis Hotel* lacks any atmosphere but the rooms are clean and have en-suite toilets. Only Ethiopian food is available. **F** *Abune Arragawi Hotel* is a typical Ethiopian cheap hotel, which is very convenient for the bus station and perhaps offers the best Ethiopian food in Maichew at a very cheap price. **F** *Yerakit Hotel* is a dive really, mostly used by bus and truck drivers. However, there is very good roast sheep on offer. **Mid-range** *Shewit Hotel*, offers food only, no accommodation. This is the only other contender for best Ethiopian food in Maichew; sitting out at the back of the hotel under the vines and eating excellent roast chicken is reminiscent of being in France.

Sleeping & eating

Road Diesel is available at 2 petrol stations, a *Shell* station at the north of town and a nondescript place near the post office. The road north to Mekelle has a terrible surface and loops back and forth on itself alarmingly – for experienced drivers only. The old road south clipped Lake Ashenge and passed through Korem, before heading down the most terrifying piece of road in Ethiopia, a roller-coaster ride called 'Gra Cassu'. Drivers can still take this route from Maichew to Alamata, with an average journey time of around 2 hrs. However, a new main

Transport

Ethiopia

road south was opened at Easter 2000 from Maichew to a very small town called **Mehony**, cutting as much as 2 hrs off the journey time and avoiding Gra Cassu. This new road is less scenic but far quicker and very much safer, allowing a 4WD to get to Alamata from Maichew in little over 1 hr.

Bus There is almost always a 0600 bus leaving for **Dessie** or **Addis Ababa** and **Mekelle**. Check at the bus station the night before; you might even be able to buy tickets and bag a place if the bus driver is around. To catch the early bus turn up by at least 0530 and find the person selling tickets for your bus. Throughout the day many trucks, buses and private vehicles pass through Maichew so you can ask a child to find you a place and settle down for a wait. Maichew-**Mekelle** usually takes 6-7 hrs and Maichew-**Alamata** takes about 2 hrs.

Tsebet Tsebet, Tigray's highest mountain, looms powerfully just outside the town. At just over 4,000 m, Tsebet is not on the scale of Ras Dashen, but is quite enough to put off the faint-hearted. There is no tourist industry at present in Maichew, so travellers wanting to explore the area will have the fun of finding their own routes. Local footpaths criss-cross the mountains and valleys – the challenge is finding the one path that goes exactly where you want. You are well advised to stick to the paths or to dry river beds for two reasons: firstly to avoid trampling young crops that often look like weeds; secondly, and more importantly, because some of the areas of the hillside may still carry the landmines left by the retreating Dergue army more than a decade ago. Whether this is fact or fiction is uncertain, but it is not worth the risk. There is little point in suggesting walks, as a curious traveller looking at this landscape will see a thousand places he or she wants to visit, and most of the nearby mountains can be tackled by any reasonably fit person in either a half-day or day; you will always be able to find and ask directions from a farmer or shepherd boy. The Tsebet is a more serious proposition, as it will take a fit person about six hours to climb and six hours to descend, so either start at first light or plan to spend the night at the top. The small village near the summit has been known to offer hospitality but you would be unwise to rely on this happy occurrence. Carry more than enough food and water, plus a warm sleeping-bag or blankets, and bring your warmest clothes as, at 4,000 m, the nights especially can be bitterly cold. Look out for the caves just beneath the summit. Although steep at times the journey to the summit involves no real climbing, and a path leads you right to the top.

Ashenge Hayk Within fairly easy reach of Maichew is a large placid lake called Ashenge Hayk. It is hardly on the scale of Lake Tana or the Rift Valley lakes, but after a few weeks in dry, dusty Tigre many people will be glad of some cooling water on which to rest their eyes. Since the main road was moved (see Transport, above) it has become harder to visit Ashenge, but it is still possible and well worth the effort. Wait at the 'truck stop' area by the *Ahadu Hotel* and find a minibus (or truck) heading for Korem; after about an hour and a half's journey you will see the lake. Get off the bus when the road dips near to the lake. It should be possible to walk round the lake in a day, although a couple of hours of rambling and soaking up the peaceful atmosphere, in the almost Scottish scenery, may be enough. Leave yourself time to hitch back to Maichew before dark, or you may have to spend the night in **Korem**, an unpleasant little town with little to recommend it, except the presence of fish on the menu.

Alamata Alamata sits on the plain but nestles against the mountains, it is hot and dusty and mosquito nets are advisable for the scorpions and cockroaches, although malaria is uncommon. Most travellers are just passing through. If heading south from Mekelle it would be a good idea to allow one day from Mekelle to Alamata before heading on to Dessie for a second night, reaching Addis Ababa late on the third day. There are pleasant walks in the Alamata area. The chief language used here is Amharic with only a little Tigrinya spoken. **Market day** is on Saturday but a few small stalls of vegetables can be found at the market area on any day of the week.

D *Tewodros Belay Hotel* is a huge concrete building with little character and less charm but has reasonably clean rooms, some of which have en-suite toilets and hot showers. It has very good food indeed. Draught beer is available. There is a tendency here to overcharge tourists, so be very sure of what you have asked for before you agree to pay for it. **D** *Raya Hotel* is almost the same standard as the *Tewodros Belay*, but the rooms are a little cheaper and the food is not as good. Avoid the cakes in the balcony pastry shop – some may have been there for a very long time. There are many other cheaper hotels in Alamata; a couple on the main road near to where the road from Maichew comes in are clean but basic.

Sleeping & eating

You will almost always find 0600 buses going north and south. It is rarely difficult to hitch a ride in either direction during the day. The road up to **Maichew** is reasonably good, the road south can be sticky in the rainy season but should never become impassable. **Mekelle**-Alamata takes 8-9 hrs, Alamata-**Dessie** is a 9-10-hr bus journey.

Transport

Lalibela

Lalibela, a listed UNESCO World Heritage Site 640 km from Addis Ababa, was built as the capital of a local king following the fall of Axum, and it became the centre of religious authority in Ethiopia. According to legend, in the 12th century Prince Lalibela, of the Zagwe Dynasty, was drugged by his brother the king, who feared he would be overthrown. During his drugged sleep angels brought him to heaven, where God instructed him to return home and build churches of a unique style. His brother later abdicated and Lalibela was crowned king. He gathered an army of craftsmen, who carved out the cliff face at Roha, fashioning 11 churches. It was said that the churches were completed so quickly because angels carried out the work at night. In fact the churches were sculpted out of the rock from the 13th to early 14th century. Four of them are monoliths, erected on stepped podia. They are tended by priests who guard their precious artistic and religious treasures and contain extravagant murals, crosses and manuscripts.

12°2′N 39°2′E
Phone code: 3
Colour map 2,
grid A3

Fleas can be a problem: ask at local pharmacy for treatment

Getting there Access is difficult Jun-Sep when the rains are heavy. It is realistic to allow at least 2 days for the journey there from Addis Ababa. There are daily flights from Addis Ababa to the new airport terminal, 12 km from town. **Getting around** There are no taxis or buses in town and the area is very hilly. **Best time to visit** The best time to visit is during *Timkat* (Epiphany) in Jan, but you need to book in advance (see page 778). The town is very dusty in the dry season.

Ins & outs
For transport details,
see page 875

Sights

There are six churches to the north and five churches to the south of the Jordan River, including the famous cross-shaped Beta Giorgis. The churches are linked by a series of hewn chancels and tunnels, similar to catacombs. Several of the churches are being renovated at present and are surrounded by scaffolding. It is recommended you use a guide otherwise you risk missing a lot as much is virtually hidden. The full tour takes three to four hours, and you need to start before 1500. It is advisable to tackle the two church groups at different times, maybe one before noon and the other after 1400. If you wish to use an English-speaking guide, make sure you fix the price in advance. Tours of Lalibela begin at the eastern cluster of churches. From the *Seven Olives Hotel* walk down the hill.

Flies are very annoying in and around Lalibela; insect repellent helps a little in the dry season

Beta Medhane Alem, 'House of the Saviour of the World', is located at the eastern end of this cluster of churches, and is the largest monolithic rock-hewn church in the world, almost 800 sq m in area, standing in a carved courtyard 6 m deep, accessed by a series of stone steps. The roof is supported by 36 external pillars, and another 36 internal pillars. The interior is reminiscent of a cathedral, with a five-aisled basilica and an ambulatory. This is believed to be a copy of the

Eastern cluster

Ethiopia

fourth-century cathedral of Maryam Seyon (the Virgin of Zion) in Axum, which is said to have been destroyed by Ahmad Gran during the 16th century. From the courtyard outside, a short tunnel leads to another courtyard that contains another three churches. The most imposing of these is **Beta Maryam**, dedicated to the Virgin Mary. It is much more ornately decorated than Beta Medhane Alem, with a richly decorated painted ceiling, windows in the shape of stelae, and it contains an Axumite frieze, extensive plaster decoration in geometric and plant patterns, and many fine carvings of animals and birds. Look out for bas-reliefs of the Star of David, the Lalibela Cross and St George fighting a dragon. A third courtyard grants access to another two churches, **Beta Golgota**, with its ornamental façade and **Beta Debre Sina** (also called **Beta Mikael**), where the remains of the King of Lalibela are rumoured to be buried. The king's prayer stick and personal hand cross are among the sacred relics held here.

Western cluster   The western cluster of churches includes the cruciform-shaped **Beta Giorgis**, which has been excavated to below ground level, including a sunken courtyard, all encompassed by steep vertical walls. Local legend claims that the holes visible in the wall are hoofprints of St George's horse, made as the saint rode the animal straight down the 6-m vertical walls. It has an unusual ground plan in the form of a Greek cross. **Bet Abba Libanos** is built around a cave in a vertical cliff face. The back and sides of the church have been carved to separate them from the cliff face but the roof is still part of the original rock. Legend has it that this church was built by King Lalibela's wife, with the help of angels. It is connected by a tunnel to a chapel, **Beta Lehem**, reputedly used by the king. **Beta Mercurios** is a cave church but the interior has partially collapsed. The entrance was renovated in the 1980s.

■ *Entry for the 11 churches is US$12.50 (excluding the monasteries outside the town). The ticket is valid to see the churches over several days. Official trained guides are quite knowledgeable and charge from US$7-17. Ask to see their certificate. Make sure their English is good before hiring one. Unofficial guides (usually boys) ask much less, as little as US$5 and often speak much better English. Some of the official guides have been reported to charge tourists exorbitant amounts for their services and for entry charges. At some times a priest may not be available to unlock a specific door, but you can always view the exteriors.*

Market   On Saturdays there is a local market that attracts hundreds of people. It caters mostly for local people and sells little in the way of tourist tat.

Excursions   There are several possible day excursions from Lalibela. **Inrahanna Kristos** is a church in a cave on Mount Abuna Josef. On the mountain above Lalibela there is a monastery and church visible from town. Guides will advise, but again, fix a price first. If you are fit it is possible to visit other rock-hewn monasteries at a fraction of the cost of the 11 well-known churches.

Asheton Monastery has very friendly priests and is an approximate two-hour hike up steep, rocky paths, with wet, slippery sections. It takes about 55 minutes to reach a lush plateau, with quiet villages. The next 30 minutes takes you through wet farmland and the last 30 minutes is a climb up a steep

Lalibela

♪ Shops

Church Ticket Office

Ethiopian Airlines

St George's (Beta Giorgis)   Western Cluster

Eastern Cluster

To Asheton Monastery

To Airport

Timkat Field   Football Field

N   Not to scale

■ **Sleeping**
1 Asheton   3 Lal
2 Government Roha   4 Private Roha
5 Seven Olives

mountain. It's very invigorating with fabulous views. The trails are unmarked and a guide would be helpful. ■ *US$3. Expect to pay a guide about US$3 for the round trip. Children often prove to be excellent guides. This hike is prohibitive for most people, but remains a cheap, viable alternative for fit travellers.*

It is possible to combine the walk to Asheton Monastery with a trip to **Na'akuto La'ab**, a monastery that appears glued to a rock. It is 7 km from Lalibela and 4 km from Asheton Monastery. There is a small, steep footpath between the two monasteries. You can also visit Asheton Monastery and Na'akuto La'ab or **Ganneta Mariam Church** by mule – allow a full day for the return trek.

B *Roha*, part of the government-run *Ghion* chain, has been refurbished and is exquisitely decorated, hot showers, a more reliable water supply, with a good selection of food in the restaurant and is the best hotel location for Timkat. Roha's disadvantage is that it is sited approximately 2 km from the town centre but it is a nicer place to stay than the other hotel in this price bracket. **B** *Seven Olives*, at top of village. Will change travellers' cheques and issue receipts, has been known to run out of cash, hot showers, the restaurant serves good western food. Good location for seeing churches and hiking to Asheton Monastery. The NTO office and *Ethiopian Airlines* office are on site. **C** *Hotel Asheton*, clean and cheap, central, 300 m from the *Seven Olives*. Recommended. Nice courtyard, restaurant, haggle over prices that tend to be variable. Restaurant serves good food, nice atmosphere. Safe parking for cars and motorcycles. **C** *Lal Hotel*, at the edge of the village, offers adequate accommodation, described by a recent traveller as "very good apart from the fleas". Water use restricted to limited hours but management will turn on the supply on request. Can supply an excellent guide to the churches for US$9.50 per person. **E** *Helen*, located just past the *Roha* on the main road. Cheap, reasonable. **E** *Kademt*, near the square where *Seven Olives* faces. Very cheap and basic. **E** *Lasta*, basic, communal showers. **E** *Hotel Private Roha*, at market entrance at bottom of village. Privately owned and popular, communal toilet, good beds, only 1 communal shower. **Camping** is available in the grounds of the *Seven Olives* (expensive) and Hotel Asheton.

Sleeping & eating

Timkat celebrations (see page 778) in Lalibela attract a lot of tourists, but it is still not commercialized. Make air and hotel reservations in advance. It starts at 1600 on **18 Jan** at the various churches, then a converging procession winds along the main road to a field across the *Roha Hotel* (2-km walk). There are prayers and celebrations at this site throughout the night. On **19 Jan** the major part of the celebration is held from 0900 to 1400. There is a very colourful and photogenic procession back to the churches. However, professional photographers jostle intrusively to get the best shots. On **20 Jan** a smaller celebration is held in honour of St Michael.

Locals say that Lalibela is the most famous place for *Genna* (the Eastern Orthodox Christmas, 7 Jan) and Gondar for Timkat. There is an early morning church service most days of the year in at least one church.

Festivals

Air *Ethiopian Airlines*, next to *Seven Olives Hotel*, up a long flight of steps, T000246 (via operator), flies daily to Lalibela (see Getting around, page 775). Reconfirm your onward flight the day before. There is a new airport terminal and a second runway has recently been built, which has improved access during the rainy season. The airport is some distance away (12 km) up a steep hill to town. Travellers have reported that it is cheaper to try to organize a private vehicle, certainly for the return journey. As there are very few private cars, the chances of hitching a ride are slim. Another transport option is an NTO, 4WD vehicle – cost US$12 for the round trip.

Transport

Road No petrol station. Diesel available in the *Shell* shop. Access is not easy overland. The route is via Dessie, which is 300 km to the northeast from Addis Ababa. Lalibela is a further 200 km from Dessie. A new road has recently been built via Weldiya, shortening the route by 200 km and has greatly reduced Lalibela's remoteness. The first leg to Dessie takes 12 hrs and costs US$4. Fill up with petrol here as there is sometimes no fuel until Debre Tabor. **Bus**: Leaving Lalibela by public bus is time consuming. The bus leaves at 0600 and reaches Weldiya at 1300, by which time the buses to other cities have left. It's worth trying to hitch a lift to Weldiya and get there earlier.

Ethiopia

Weldiya
11°50'N 39°34'E
Colour map 2, grid A3

Weldiya is worth a visit. It is a pleasant little town with lush vegetation situated among pretty rolling hills. Nice terrace cafés line the busy piazza. The **market** is held on Tuesdays. However, this is also a famine area. Average families can produce only three to six months' food supply and have to rely on aid. Weldiya is the centre of the aid agencies (FAO, SCF UK, Médicins Sans Frontières, etc).

Sleeping and eating D *Hotel Lal*, T367. Nice rooms, hot water, good restaurant. E *Kidane* is close to bus stand, but toilets and shower are poor. E *Lala Hotel*, near the roundabout, is clean, hot shower, has safe parking for cars and motorcycles. Good restaurant and meeting place in the evening for locals. There are several other small places of a similar standard.

Transport A relatively expensive government bus runs from Weldiya to Lalibela, US$3. This bus fills from 0600 but doesn't leave until 1100, once the Dessie bus has arrived and off-loaded passengers. It takes 6-7 hrs, arriving in Lalibela at 1730-1800. Excellent views, with mountain passes at altitudes of 3,000 m. The bus trip from Weldiya to Mekelle takes around 10 hrs. Buses to Asmara are currently suspended.

Lake Hayk

Hayk town
For Sleeping, Eating and Transport, see page 878

Hayk is approximately 30 km north of Dessie. It has to be said that Hayk, the town, has very little going for it. The town centre, where several lanes converge on the Weldiya-Dessie Road, is a nondescript and ramshackle place. The machine-gun-like cacophony of 'You! You! You! Farenji! Farenji! Farenji! Money! Money! Money!' from squads of children comes as a particular shock to the system if you are southward-bound and have just arrived from the relative calm of Tigre.

Debre Hayk Estifanos

Mercifully things quieten down when you follow the 5-km path that leads out of town to the lakeside and finally, to the monastery. There is some yelling from the occasional young cow-minder but most of the time you are alone with your thoughts. The path branches off from the town centre between the mosque and the asphalt road heading for Weldiya, and to get to the monastery you simply take the left turning at the only major fork you encounter. The way is signposted so it's almost impossible to get lost. The path meanders beside the lake, climbs for a stretch, then drops through superb scenery to the tear-shaped peninsula containing the monastery. A line of low hills screens everything off from the Weldiya-Dessie road, so that the symphonies of birds and insects and the murmur of water amid the rushes growing copiously along the shore are undisturbed by the noise of traffic. Papyrus boats glide across the water and while the slopes bordering on the lake are not as steep and spectacular as the mountains to the north, they form a very appealing backdrop.

Before entering the monastery you may want to check out the small church,

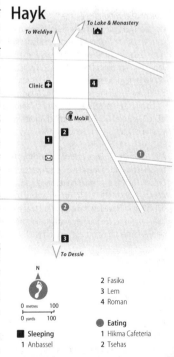

Hayk

To Weldiya
To Lake & Monastery
Clinic
Mobil
To Dessie

N
0 metres 100
0 yards 100

■ **Sleeping**
1 Anbassel
2 Fasika
3 Lem
4 Roman

● **Eating**
1 Hikma Cafeteria
2 Tsehas

Ethiopia

Georges, on the hillside overlooking the peninsula. It is a round, grey, stone building, simple in design, but quite affecting. Below Georges you pay the entry fee into the monastery grounds at a gate at the neck of the peninsula. Beyond the gate the peninsula is wooded, and there is so much bird-song and wing-flapping from the treetops you may feel you have walked into an aviary. An avenue lined with trees behind which the monks grow cereal crops and fruit, leads up to the central feature of the monastery, the **Church of Estifanos**. Crowned by a red roof, Estifanos has the same plain but effective design as Georges at the other end of the peninsula.

History In 1248, Abba Iyesus Mo'a founded the monastery at Debre Hayk Estifanos (St Stephen's) on Lake Hayk. Prior to starting the monastery, Iyesus Mo'a had studied under Abba Yohanni, one of the Nine Saints, who led an ascetic life at Debre Damo. Iyesus Mo'a, whose name means 'Jesus has won', is also a saint of the Ethiopian church.

Although monasteries were built in remote places, they were not just secluded places of worship for monks dedicated to a life of prayer and devotion. They were also centres of evangelical activity and education, where children as well as adults came to follow a traditional monastic education in literature, poetry, music and biblical studies, and translations of Christian texts into Ge'ez were produced.

Debre Hayk Estifanos rapidly became an important centre of education and pilgrimage, within Iyesus Mo'a's lifetime. Iyesus Mo'a's pupil, Yekuno Amlak (reputed not to be a name but a short sentence meaning 'There shall be to him sovereignty'), who restored the Solomonic dynasty in 1270, studied there before moving on to continue his studies in the south at Qawat and Tagwelat. Legend states that Iyesus Mo'a is credited with helping Yekuno Amlak to seize power from the Zagwe dynasty, although there is no historical verification of his involvement. In return for the support received in re-establishing the Solomonic dynasty, Yekuno Amlak is reputed to have bestowed great privileges on the monastery, many of which were later transferred to Debre Libanos in the 15th century. Yekuno Amlak granted the abbot of Debre Hayk Estifanos the title of Aqabe-Se'at, the administrative head of the Ethiopian church from that time onwards (until the rise of Debre Libanos), and appointed the Abbot to be the chief ecclesiastical representative at the Imperial court.

Iyesus Mo'a is said to have slept upright in a sitting position for his entire adult religious life, estimated to have been about 50 years – part of his practice of ascetic discipline of the body. A manuscript of the *Four Gospels* inscribed by Iyesus Mo'a can still be seen in the **library** at the monastery. Written reference also exists of visits by two Ethiopian monarchs to the monastery in the 13th and 14th centuries. The Ethiopian Church commemorates Iyesus Mo'a on 5 December (26 Hedar).

Many monks went on from Debre Hayk Estifanos to establish other monasteries. Another famous pupil of Iyesus Mo'a was Abba Takla Haymanot, who first studied at Debre Damo under Abba Yohanni, and later at Debre Hayk Estifanos, before returning south to start a monastery at Debre Asbo (later renamed Debre Libanos). The influence of the abbots of Debre Hayk Estifanos on the court continued until 1535, when Negede Iyesus, the last Aqabe-Se'at from this monastery, was executed by a Muslim general during the Islamic Conquest.

Down the bank behind the church an old mud-walled building serves as a **museum** for a small number of artefacts, including an altar stone from the ninth century, a grinding stone, cooking pot and stone cross from the 13th century, and wooden leg restraints used to punish monks who disturbed the peace of the monastery in the 15th and 16th centuries. One monk can give a brief commentary in broken but understandable English. Finally, at the tip of the peninsula, a clearing in the trees provides a beautiful view of the lake and the opposite hillsides.

■ *Entry to the monastery, $1.25. Women are forbidden to set foot on the premises. Colour pictures of Iyesus Mo'a are available for $0.25.*

Ethiopia

Sleeping Hayk is 1 hr by bus from Dessie and just over 2 hrs from Weldiya and, as the lake and monastery can be visited in a couple of hrs, there is no need to spend a night here. In fact, it is very difficult to get a full night's sleep here. Several long-distance buses use the town as an overnight stop and often resume their journeys at a bright-and-early 0400 the next morning. This means that from 0300 onwards the hotels are filled with the clamour of doors being banged, voices shouting and feet stomping as passengers rouse and ready themselves for the next leg of their journey. Even if you manage to sleep through that, you are unlikely to be able to doze when the call to prayer, via loud speakers, from the centrally located mosque begins 1 hr later.

If you do have to stay overnight in Hayk, try to get a room before mid-evening as the long-distance buses roll in and discharge their passengers at nightfall and then all the available hotel rooms are snapped up within minutes. Probably the best establishment is the unsignposted **F** *Roman Hotel*, in the new yellow building that dominates the town centre (no phone yet). The staff receive foreigners with friendly enthusiasm, there is a good restaurant serving western and Ethiopian food and at the back of the reception block, and a round tower-like building with a domed roof contains a pleasant bar. The rooms, housed in a 4-storey building behind the tower, have concrete floors and are bare and basic, but have comfortable beds and small en-suite showers and squat/flush toilets. The **F** *Fasika Hotel* at the side of the *Mobil* station offers rooms with communal toilets and showers. The rooms are scruffy and feel a bit claustrophobic but the proprietor seems affable enough. The **F** *Anbassel Hotel* is another basic alternative. The **F** *Lem Hotel*, down the Dessie road, brews a nice cup of tea and the female staff are very helpful. Avoid the *Selam Hotel*.

Eating The *Tsehas Restaurant*, near the *Lem Hotel* will never win any prizes for sophistication, but it has some good fish dishes from the lake. Ask for the *asa lebleb* if you fancy fish with a spicy tang. The *Hikma Cafeteria*, at the side of the *Selam Hotel*, is acceptable for coffee, cakes and juice.

Transport The bus fare from **Alimata** to **Hayk** is $2.50, the fare from **Weldiya** is about half that. It costs just $0.40 to travel the rest of the way to **Dessie**, journey time about 1 hr, and buses leave regularly from the centre of town.

Dessie

11° 5′ N, 39° 40′ E
Phone code: 3
Colour map 2, grid A3
Population: 120,000

Dessie (sometimes spelt Desé) is a beautiful, old, mainly Muslim town, situated picturesquely in a steep valley. It is the capital of South Wollo Zone and is situated 2,500 m above sea level in the Ethiopian Highlands, about 400 km north of Addis Ababa. Squeezed between the cliffs of Tossa and Azuoa, the town straggles along the Addis Ababa-Weldiya road for about 6 km. However, in spite of its size, the atmosphere in Dessie is palpably more parochial and less welcoming than that of towns like Kembolcha and Debre Birhan further down the road. Visually, Dessie is not particularly appealing either, with much of the town huddling under a decrepit canopy of rusting roofs. Still, as it is almost exactly a day's journey from the capital, and is the biggest settlement on the road up to Lalibela and Tigre, Dessie is a place where many travellers will end up staying for at least one night. Despite its crumbling appearance, the town has good facilities, including several decent hotels and shops, banks, government offices, health centres, a big, modern telecommunications building, a branch of *Mega Books* and a Cultural Centre that acts as a cinema, theatre and exhibition hall.

In addition, Dessie's geographical location is dramatic, with craggy peaks towering around it. Particularly impressive is **Mount Tossa** to the west (the mountain is the setting for various folk legends and is celebrated in a number of Amharic love songs). This may be connected with the local claim that the area's women are 'the most beautiful in Ethiopia'. (Mind you, Harar, Tigre and any number of other places make the same claim!)

The town also has a couple of features of cultural interest. On a hilltop overlooking the southern entrance to the town is a large hall called **Ayiteyef**. This was built in the early 20th century by King Michael, the ruler of Wollo, who established Dessie as

Dessie

To Weldiya

Zonal
Administrative
Offices

Red Cross

Cultural Centre

Hospital
(under construction)

Development

Shell

Total

Dashen

Mobil

Commercial

Mega
Books

Construction
& Business

Agip

N

0 metres 300
0 yards 300

Dessie
Museum

To Ayiteyef

To Kembolcha

■ **Sleeping**
1 Ambaras
2 Dessie
3 Ethiopia
4 Fasika
5 Fikreselam
6 Ghion Ambassel

7 Lalibela
8 Melaku
 Desalegn

● **Eating**
1 Café with
 Pepsi sign

2 Henok
3 Kibede
4 Shamrock
 Café

● **Bars & clubs**
5 Calypso Pub

the region's capital, and a place for royal feasts. The composition of the hall is unusual, with its blocks cemented together by a mixture of lime, egg-yolk and rye flour. However, the hilltop is now the site of a military installation and access to Ayiteyef is retricted.

Across from Ayiteyef, the hill beside the first roundabout at the southern end of Dessie (between the road arriving from Kembolcha and the road descending into the town) is the location of **Dessie Museum**. As you walk up the winding path from the roundabout, do not be deterred if the building looks shut. There should be a curator lurking somewhere who will unlock the premises and give you a tour inside. The rooms have an air of dilapidation, as do some of the exhibits – the stuffed animals and the models representing village life in feudal times are visibly decayed – but it's difficult to dislike a place with such an eclectic range of exhibits. The bones, fossils and ancient manuscripts; sculpted panels from the Workers' Revolution; artefacts belonging to King Michael, Menelik II and Haile Selassie; weapons captured from the Italians during the Battle of Adwa and more recent weapons supplied by the Soviets; farming tools, pottery, handicrafts and ethnic costumes on display can hardly be said to share a common theme, but most of the material is very interesting. ■ *$0.85. The curator will explain things in English and is present 0830-1200 and 1400-1730, except on Sat afternoons and Sun.*

The **Culture, Tourism and Information Department**, PO Box 69, T111086, located about 1 km north along the road from the bus station, can provide information about Dessie and South Wolle in general. They may not speak a great deal of English but they will try to find somebody on the premises who can help you.

Sleeping

The formerly government-run **C-D** *Ghion Ambassel*, PO Box 32, T111115, offers 1st, 2nd and 3rd-class rooms for 1 or 2 people. 1st-class rooms have showers and toilets, the others rely on communal facilities. Cosy rooms, if a bit antiquated. Do not let the rickety-looking corrugated-iron fence surrounding the grounds put you off – from inside, the

Ethiopia

fence is invisible behind a tall, sturdy hedge. Along the same road, the more modern **D** *Lalibela Hotel*, T116908, offers en-suite rooms, an appealing bar with satellite TV and ornate, wooden tables and chairs and a small but efficient dining room. Both these hotes are a little way from the busiest part of Dessie and can offer their residents peace and quiet. If you want to be at the very hub of the town the **E** *Ethiopia Hotel*, PO Box 114, T117056, stands at Dessie's main intersection. Beds and cupboards are expansive but the private bathrooms are a bit grubby. A bar, restaurant and the occasional wandering cockroach are to be found downstairs. **E** *Ambaras Hotel*, T118029, has rooms with showers and toilets. **F** *Fasika Hotel*, on the same road, T111271, might be slightly the worse for wear, but the rates are good and the rooms, overlooking a courtyard accessible through a doorway on a sidestreet, are big and clean, and bathrooms are equipped with sink and shower with functioning water heater and a toilet with a powerful flush. The **F** *Dessie Hotel*, T112310, nearby, charges the same price for its en-suite rooms, though the bathrooms are a bit cramped and the bedroom walls are rather weathered. Fairly clean, and the bar and restaurant downstairs do a good trade. For budget travellers the best option is the **F** *Fikreselam Hotel*, T111271. A back courtyard with a garden contains some clean rooms, fitted with sinks, communal showers and toilets. The entrance door opens into a big, old-fashioned-looking bar area with a wooden counter and a row of barstools that will fill soap-opera fans with nostalgic memories of the *Rover's Return*. The female staff have hardly a word of English between them but they are a friendly, helpful lot nonetheless. Alternatively, the **F** *Melaku Desalegn Hotel*, some way along the same road in the direction of Weldiya, has cheap rooms with communal facilities. The standard, however, is well below that of the *Fikreselam* and the communal shower, with its sawn-off water pipe protruding from the wall, looks very unhealthy.

Eating

There are some excellent fish dishes on offer in Dessie (the fish comes from Lake Hayk, 30 km to the north)

The restaurants in the *Lalibela*, *Fasika* and *Ambaras* hotels are all highly rated for their food and service, though people wanting a quiet meal in the *Ambaras* may be irritated by the volume of the TV in the adjoining bar. The *Fasika's* restaurant is especially recommended for its breakfasts, and the 'egg with meat' – a mixture of scrambled egg, minced meat, peppers and onions – is a treat. Reasonable breakfasts are also available at the **Stadium Café**, next door to the *Ambaras*, and at the **Henok Café** (*Hotel*) at the corner of the turning for the bus station. If you are looking for a good meat dish and don't object to a walk, try the **Kibede Restaurant** at the beginning of the road that forks off for Weldiya. There's a pleasant, roofed-over front courtyard with a butcher's shop at the side, ensuring that the *tibs*, *kaiwal* and *kitfo* are as fresh as can be. Before you get to the *Kibede*, the café occupying the triangle of ground in the middle of the fork (recognizable by the Pepsi sign above its entrance) is also worth investigating. Snacks and national dishes are served here in attractive, garden premises. Back in the main part of town, the **Shamrock Café**, opposite the bus station turning, stocks good fresh cakes and bread.

Bars

On the same side of the street as the *Shamrock*, between it and the *Fasika Hotel*, there are several **pubs** that will satisfy the most boisterous night-owls. They blast out such loud music and flash with so many lights that they resemble amusement arcades. A drink in equally cheap and cheerful, but considerably quieter surroundings can be enjoyed at the **Calypso Pub**, out beside the *Melaku Desalegn Hotel*.

Transport

Air *Ethiopia Airlines*, T112571, offer a daily service here – see Getting around page 775. **Road** From Dessie north to **Weldiya**, the bus leaves at 0600, and takes 4-5 hrs. The bus south to **Addis Ababa** also departs from Dessie at 0600 and covers the intervening 400 km in a day. It passes through Debre Birhan in the early afternoon and reaches the capital before nightfall. If you miss that, the alternative is to make a series of short bus trips between the towns that punctuate the same route. Minibuses run frequently from Dessie to Kembolcha, a small town 23 km to the southeast. The road between the 2 offers a stunning descent down vertiginous mountainsides and through eucalyptus forests where troupes of scampering monkeys are not an uncommon sight.

Kembolcha

A small town about 23 km southeast of Dessie, Kembolcha (or Kombolcha) stands at a junction where there is a choice between heading east to the towns of Mile and Serdo and, eventually, to Djibouti and Eritrea, and south to Addis Ababa. There isn't a great deal to do or see in Kembolcha, but the atmosphere is relaxed and friendly and it makes a therapeutic stopover after the hysteria of Hayk and the needling of Dessie.

Colour map 2, grid A3
Phone code: 03

In Ethiopia, Kembolcha's main claim to fame is as the home of the brewery that produces **Bati Beer**. In the town you will see quaint *garis* with crested wooden hoods scuttling along the streets, painted in the crimson colour and decorated with the distinctive lettering of the Bati bottle-labels. In addition, the **Kembolcha Brewery** churns out two more varieties of beer popular in Ethiopia, *Castell* and *St George*, and is now licensed to brew Guinness for the local market as well. Available only in bottled form this Guinness is worth a try, if only to find out how the flavour has been modified – in other words, lightened and sweetened – to suit Ethiopian tastes. Connoisseurs should not expect much resemblance to the stout produced in Dublin. The brewery is willing to arrange tours for visitors individually or in groups, but it needs to be informed by letter in advance about the visit. If you simply show up without warning you will be turned away. ■ *PO Box 290, T510283. To get there cross the Borkena River in the direction of Dessie and it's about a 1-km walk along the first major sideroad on the left.*

Sights

If you are interested in the Orthodox religion, the church dedicated to **Archangel Gabriel**, is well worth a visit. The building with eight walls and a three-tiered roof, reminiscent of a pagoda, is beautifully patterned in the red, green and yellow colours of the Ethiopian flag and sits serenely in the middle of a grassy compound. A track leading down towards the river at the back of the compound takes you alongside a number of graves which, in Ethiopian cultural style, actually look more like burial mounds. The church is easily reached by taking the dirt road that branches off at the side of the *Total* filling station a little way uphill from the bus station. At the crossroads past the church, you can resume your journey uphill by turning left and following a steep track that brings you back – at the quaintly named *James Bond 007 Boutique* – on to the main road near the town's hotels.

Near Kembolcha there is a large rock sculpture of a lion, believed to date from the Axumite period. The sculpture, known as the **Geta Lion**, is 4 km southwest of a

Ethiopia

Kembolcha

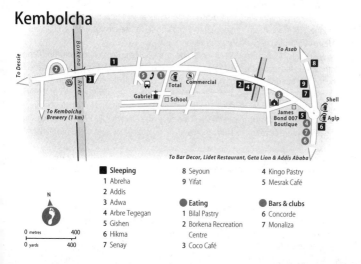

Sleeping	8 Seyoun	4 Kingo Pastry
1 Abreha	9 Yifat	5 Mesrak Café
2 Addis		
3 Adwa	**Eating**	**Bars & clubs**
4 Arbre Tegegan	1 Bilal Pastry	6 Concorde
5 Gishen	2 Borkena Recreation	7 Monaliza
6 Hikma	Centre	
7 Senay	3 Coco Café	

To Asab
To Dessie
Borkena River
Total
Commercial
Gabriel
School
To Kembolcha Brewery (1 km)
Shell
James Bond 007 Boutique
Agip
To Bar Decor, Lidet Restaurant, Geta Lion & Addis Ababa

N

0 metres 400
0 yards 400

place called **Chokorti**, which is itself 12 km down the Addis Ababa road from Kembolcha. The same area also contains the **Mosque of Geta**, which was founded by Haji Bushra Mohammed, a noted Islamic scholar, during the reign of Emperor Tewodros. It should not be difficult to find your way to Chokorti, since buses pass through it regularly on their way from Kembolcha to Kemise. Alternatively, there are sometimes vehicles available for hire on the *Hikma Hotel* side of the Kembolcha junction, and you may be able to arrange a trip to the Geta Lion using one of these.

Sleeping Kembolcha has several reasonable hotels in the **F** category. Best of all is the **F** *Hikma Hotel*, T510015, beside the junction, where there are large, clean rooms with spacious beds and cupboards, and tiled en-suite bathrooms with sinks, showers and fully operational flush-toilets and water heaters. The **F** *Senay Hotel*, T510357, a few mins' walk north from the *Hikma* and on the left, offers almost as good rooms for the same price. Only the somewhat shabbier en-suite bathrooms lower the standard slightly. Downstairs though there's an attractive little bar with satellite TV and draught beer and an equally pleasant-looking restaurant in the adjoining room. A third hotel in the junction area is the **F** *Gishen Hotel*, T510013. The rooms are a fair size and are equipped with wardrobes, but the toilets and showers are communal, and the place generally has the clean but bare feel of a well-scrubbed Victorian institution. There is a functional bar/restaurant room downstairs. In the same area of town there are several other hotels such as the **F** *Addis*, *Arbre Tegegn*, *Yifat* and *Seyoun* that may be options for travellers operating on a restricted budget.

If you have just climbed off the bus with a heavy load and don't like the look of the gradient, you can go downhill from the bus station to the nearby **F** *Abreha Hotel*, T510068. Though the lettering on the building claims there are two hotels inside, one is now closed and you should enter through the ground-floor bar below the *Abreha* sign. The rooms here are handsome with en-suite shower and toilet. They look out on an attractive courtyard at the rear of the building, and at the far end of that there's an 'organic' *tukul* – formed by a circle of bushes – containing a restaurant. The staff here are very cheerful too. Cheaper but less comfortable rooms, fitted with sinks, showers and toilets, are available at the **F** *Adwa Hotel*, T510018, further down the road. The hotel's name is signposted in Amharic only, but as it is the last hotel on the left-hand side before you reach the bridge it is not hard to find.

Eating **Seriously cheap** A good way to start the day in Kembolcha is to have breakfast on the big, roofed terrace of the *Hikma Hotel*, up a flight of steps, overlooking the Addis Ababa road. A wide range of savoury breakfast dishes – *foule special*, scrambled egg, *neshef* or sandwiches are available. The *Bilal Pastry* down near the bus station is the ideal place to keep your blood-sugar levels stoked up during the day, with doughnuts, cakes, biscuits, chocolate bars and *spreece* (an appealing fruit dessert with layers of sweetened banana, avocado and mango). The *Kingo Pastry* opposite the *Hikma* also serves ice-cream. The *Coco Bar* and the *Mesrak Café* also offer a reasonable menu).

For national food in attractive surroundings, try the *Borkena Recreation Centre and Restaurant*, across the road from the turning to the brewery. Its central building is a bit ramshackle, but it is surrounded by wooded grounds with hedged-in eating areas and gangly sunflowers. Decent meat dishes are available at the *Lidet Restaurant*, a few mins' walk down the Addis Ababa road from the *Hikma Hotel*. The décor is nothing special, but the butcher's shop next door guarantees that the meat is fresh off the bone. The *zilzil tibs* (US$1.25) is delicious. There are plenty more cafés and restaurants around the sidestreet that leads to the bus station.

Bars Those in search of raucous nightlife should note that there are several bars located along the road between the *Lidet* and the *Hikma* – the *Monaliza*, *Concorde* and *Decor* – where nobody seems to go to bed too early.

Transport From Kembolcha to **Debre Birhan** is 250 km. There is plenty of traffic on this major road, both long-haul buses and private transport. From Kembolcha you can take a proper bus for 50 km south to the town of **Kemise**, where there are minibuses continuing a further 100 km to another town, Robit.

The ride to Kemise offers little of note, except for some blobby, weirdly human-like **Kemise** specimens of cacti along the roadsides, but below Kemise things become more interesting. A few kilometres south of the town, the road snakes around a sizeable area of wetland that remains even during the dry season when rivers in the area have become rain-starved threads. Birdlife is profuse here, and storks are especially prominent among the long grass. Camels laden with bags of *teff* or bundles of firewood become a frequent sight, and Oromo and Afar men in long skirts with tartan-like patterns make striking figures.

Built in a low-lying area, Robit is an appealingly warm and (thanks to an extensive **Robit** local irrigation system) green place, and the bars, hotels and cafés whose verandahs overlook the road give it a lazy atmosphere. Those verandahs are an excellent place to relax and enjoy a drink. Although it is named Robit in most maps and guides, many locals, including bus-drivers, refer to the town as **Showrobit**.

After Robit, the one settlement of any size before you get to Debre Birhan is Debre **Debre Sina** Sina. This village deserves mention for the splendour of the surrounding countryside. It nestles below a mountain of more than 3,000 m, up which the road ascends in a series of torturous, hairpin bends before finally disappearing into the Tarmaber Pass Tunnel (also known in some western texts as the Mussolini Tunnel, which explains who its builders were). Provided it isn't obscured by low-hanging cloud, the view one gets climbing the road to the tunnel can be astonishing – the plains of the Rift Valley laid out below, mountain slopes forming a steep-sided cauldron around them, forests of eucalyptus, outcrops of rock and specklings of yellow flowers adding further decoration to the scene. Lammergeyers *(Gypaetus barbatus)* sail along the top of the escarpment. It is up here that there have been most sightings of troupes of gelada baboons and of that elusive endemic bird, the Ankober serin. At the bottom of the escarpment, lives the yellow-throated serin *(Serinus flavigula)*, yet another extremely localized Ethiopian endemic bird. The location is Debre Sina's only real attraction, as the village is a pretty run-down place. The main residential part of the village is a huddle of rusty iron roofs in a depression to the right of the road, as you travel south, with several tracks leading down to it. The road itself serves as the high street, though the shops, cafés and small hotels along it are actually set several yards back from its edges and the strips of dirt and stones in between can become unpleasantly muddy in wet weather. Buses heading both south and north stop along this section of road since there is no bus station. Dismounting there, you'll probably be mobbed by children trying to sell you oranges, bananas and small souvenir baskets, though they are friendly and helpful enough if you can speak to them in a few words of Amharic.

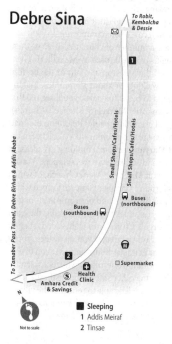

Debre Sina

To Robit,
Kembolcha
& Dessie

Small Shops/Cafés/Hotels

Small Shops/Cafés/Hotels

To Tamaber Pass Tunnel, Debre Birhan & Addis Ababa

Buses
(southbound)

Buses
(northbound)

Supermarket

Amhara Credit
& Savings

Health
Clinic

N

Not to scale

■ **Sleeping**
1 Addis Meiraf
2 Tinsae

Ethiopia

Sleeping Ask about accommodation and they'll invariably lead you to the F *Addis Meiraf Hotel*, which is Debre Sina's most imposing building. The rooms are spartan, with a private, ancient flush toilet and cold shower. The circular extension at the northern end of the hotel houses a small, functional restaurant, with a limited menu. The hotel is also frequented by bar girls and can become very noisy at times. If you have to spend a night in Debre Sina but find yourself longing for some creature comforts, the bar in **F Tinsae Hotel**, at the other end of the village, has cheap draught beer and MTV. It's a rather spartan hotel too, but its large windows do offer good views of the village and the surrounding landscape. There are several cafés in the vicinity of the bus stop.

Ankober

Colour map 2, grid B3 Ankober, 170 km north of Addis Ababa, 42 km east of Debre Birhan, and the Shoan capital in the 18th and 19th century, occupied a strategic position with views of the Danakil plains to the east. Ankober Hill was dominated by Sahle Selassie's palace, where he was reputed to have 300 concubines and 3,000 slaves. His son and successor, Haile Melekot, unable to resist the advances of Tewodros, attempted to destroy the palace, partially burning it down. Two years later Tewodros returned and his soldiers ransacked and totally destroyed Ankober. In 1865, Haile Melekot's son, the future Emperor Menelik II escaped from the mountain fortress of Magdala, where Tewodros had imprisoned him, and made his way to the ruined town where he was crowned as the Shoan king.

Travelling north out of Debre Birhan, take the turning right on to the untarred road just past the town's outskirts. In places this brings you along the edge of the escarpment with magnificent views of the landscapes far below. However, as with the Tannaber Tunnel, mists are frustratingly common here and can reduce visibility to a few metres. If you arrive in Ankober on an early morning bus, your first impressions may not be encouraging. The vehicle draws to a halt in the middle of a bizarre, oblong space in the middle of the village with a rough, rocky surface and ramshackle houses all around. Hordes of *gabbi*-clad figures immediately start scrambling on board for the ride back to Debre Birhan, and once you fight your way off the bus and clear of the scrum you then have to contend with squads of kids desperate to act as your guide. Don't panic – Ankober is actually a friendly place and the surrounding area is fascinating historically and breathtaking scenically. There is a small restaurant to the left of the bus-stop, which is a good place to duck into for breakfast (it serves a hot, filling scrambled egg) while you recover your composure.

Ankober's main historical attractions are a number of churches, three of them constructed by Sahle Selassie, and the remains of a castle used by Menelik II. These can be found by following the road beyond the bus stop and out of the bottom left-hand corner of the village centre. After walking for about 15 minutes, making numerous twists and turns and being treated to beautiful views, you'll see the first church up on a small rise on the left. This is **Ankober Mikael** (St Michael's Church), which though still intact is now derelict and crumbling badly. Rejoining the road after St Michael's, you almost immediately see a path branching off to the left. Follow this path for a distance and you come to **St Maryam**, a circular building in a pleasant grassy enclosure, which is well looked after and still receives worshippers. Walk a minute further along the path and you arrive at **Medhane Alem Church**, of which the only remnants now are five stone steps forming a circular platform topped with a tangle of bushes and shrubs. A house in a nearby compound performs the function of church on the site. From there the path continues to a fork. Taking the path branching off to the left, you get to **St George's Church**, an eight-sided, slightly scruffy-looking building. The path branching off right takes you up a steep, rocky slope to the ruins of the castle. Only the base of a circular house and a section of wall really remain of it, but its hilltop position is a beautiful one, offering further splendid views of the Ankober countryside. A path on the other side of the castle site leads back down to the road, and turning right there you'll be able to return to the village.

■ *To be sure of covering all these sights you can hire one of the local youths as a guide. They'll usually ask for US$1.25 (10 birr), though this can be haggled down.*

Accommodation in Ankober is basic and, once you've done your sightseeing, you might want to wangle a lift on one of the trucks occasionally leaving the village during the afternoon. A good policy is to promise your guide his full 10 birr if he can also ask around and secure a seat for you in an outgoing vehicle. Otherwise the **F** *Getachew T/Selassie Bar* above the village centre can offer a bed for less than US$1. The bedroom windows do not appear to be glazed and the ablution facilities seem to be limited to just a solitary toilet. It offers good local food (seriously cheap). Also **Seriously cheap**, the *'Seven-Up' Restaurant and Bar* opposite the bus stop, so-called because of the sign over the door, serves very good, hot and filling scrambled eggs. The *'kaiwat'* meat dish has been described as being horribly stringy. Hot tea is available, served from a vacuum flask, plus Ethiopian 'ouzo' from a selection of spirits behind the counter can be life savers, if exploring Ankober's historical sites in cold weather.

Sleeping & eating

The main problem with Ankober is transport. If you rely on buses to get around you might have trouble getting out of the village, because services between it and Debre Birhan (costing US$0.80) are sparse. A bus leaves Debre Birhan at 0600 – it's a good idea to be at the bus station at 0530 to be sure of getting a seat on this, because it is often packed out – and another goes at around 1000-1100, but only the first of these makes the return journey on the same day. The later bus doesn't go back to Debre Birhan until 0600 the next morning.

Transport

Debre Birhan

After a bumpy ride through the potholed Tannaber Pass Tunnel, it is another 57 km before you get to the pleasant highland town of Debre Birhan. The road here offers more ruggedly scenic countryside, though after the views on the northern side of the tunnel it's slightly anti-climactic. At 133 km northeast of Addis Ababa, and at an altitude of 3,000 m Debre Birhan enjoys some infamy as being the coldest place in Ethiopia, with the positive benefit that it is malaria free. The daytime here is often warm and sunny but at nightfall the temperature drops alarmingly, with the months at the start and the end of the western calendar being particularly cold nocturnally. The town's most famous products reflect its climate. Sheep can be seen roaming everywhere and a woollen goods factory stands on the eastern side of town, notable for its blankets, hats and traditionally patterned carpets. Some of these items can be bought at a factory shop next to the bus station. A large **market** is held every Saturday on a hillside at the town's northwestern outskirts but its wares – clothes, food, utensils – are for everyday use rather than for tourist consumption.

9°41'N 39°31'E
Colour map 2, grid B3

Ethiopia

Another Debre Birhan speciality is *araki*, a fierce, fiery spirit that does wonders for the drinker's body temperature. It is acceptable to drink *araki* in diluted form, and the town's *Akalu Hotel* offers quaint concoctions of mint *araki*, honey *araki* and, for true masochists, garlic *araki*.

The town is said to have been founded by Emperor Zara Yakob who was inspired by a mysterious light seen in the skies over the area – a phenomenon that many historians attribute now to Halley's comet, which would have been visible in 1456. Debre Birhan means ' place of light' and the emperor built a church and a palace here. The former was reputedly built in response to an epidemic that was laying waste to the local population, as it was believed that pestilence couldn't flourish in the vicinity of a holy building.

The palace was abandoned and then destroyed a long time ago, though the church, **Debre Birhan Selassie Church**, is still standing. It contains some interesting mural paintings, including one claimed to be, appropriately enough, of Halley's comet at the beginning of the 20th century.

Although the town has connections with other famous figures such as the Shoan King Sahle Selassie and modern Ethiopia's founding father, Emperor Menelik II, the church is the one building of any real historical note. The preponderance of traditional stone houses and a fairly spacious, tidy appearance do give Debre Birhan character, however. The town is near to but not on the edge of the escarpment overlooking the Rift Valley, so there are no views of the plains below from Debre Birhan itself. However, there is a deep gorge with a spectacular waterfall and towering rock formations 5 km west of town, which provides a pleasant afternoon's walk. To reach it, walk south from the town centre and market area, turn right after the church and then left after the track has descended a steep rocky slope, skirt the western perimeter wall of the local Teachers' Training Institute and strike out to the right again as you approach the river.

More adventurous walkers might like to enquire about finding a local guide who can take them the 8 km north from Debre Birhan to the religious community of **Debre Kirbe**. This can best be described as a sort of subterranean monastery, where 75 people live and worship in a series of caves, the longest being 150 m. It was founded only a few years ago by a man called Aba Gebre Kidan, who was supposedly influenced by a dream of divine origin. The community supports itself by growing vegetables and rearing livestock, and Aba Gebre Kidan's former profession as an electrician comes in useful in keeping its electrical generator running.

Being on the Dessie-Addis Ababa road, Debre Birhan is popular as a stopping-off place for light refreshments, meals or for a night's rest.

Sleeping   **D** *Haile Meskel*, T811124, a very clean, tidy but relatively expensive hotel, pleasant comfortable rooms and communal showers. In the forecourt the restaurant is to the left with a coffee shop to the right. The restaurant, recently renovated, serves good-quality food, especially for fasting foods (eg the *beyenetu*) but there is not much variety and, because the hotel is run by Protestants – the Ethiopian brand of Protestantism being extremely evangelical in character – no alcohol is served here. The coffee shop has become very quiet since the *Amanuel Pastry* opened up the road, but you can enjoy a peaceful snack sitting outside in the forecourt, the hotel wall keeping you safe from the unwanted attentions of the occasional drunk wandering outside. The gates close early, shortly after 2000. **E** *Akalu Hotel*, T871115, PO Box 57, is situated midway along the secondary road that leaves the main street before the central market place and rejoins it near the *Commercial Bank*. The hotel is in a guarded compound and has comfortable rooms with hot showers. The lady in charge is pleasant, and speaks good English and Spanish. The bar/restaurant is the most civilized in town serving both Ethiopian and western food including, a rarity in Debre Birhan, fish dishes. The fish cutlet is often overcooked but the *fish gored-gored* (a fish goulash) is very good if you like spicy foods. It serves very good *tibs*. Next to the bar is a little kiosk selling small souvenirs. The hotel also has a small function/party room. **F** *Helen Hotel*, situated within a gated compound at the north end of Debre Birhan, T811204, has a good reputation but is regularly booked up by lunch time. The staff are friendly but speak little English. The restaurant has only Ethiopian food and doesn't offer much variety. The **F** *Kebede*, an attractive Italian-built building and **F** *Sheneket* hotels are conspicuous along the main road and are well known locally, as both contain busy bars with dancing and deafening music; they should be regarded as nightlife spots only.

Debre Birhan

They are not recommended as accommodation – the description 'bar/restaurant/brothel' is more appropriate. Both serve food, usually just *kaiwat* or other staples.

Seriously cheap The *Green Zone Café*, which doubles up as a café and a bakery in the central market area, behind the ranks of seated shoe-shine boys, offers a sound breakfast and the traditional, spicy Ethiopian *foule special* is especially good. The scrambled egg is also recommended, and its proximity to the bus station makes it a good place to 'stoke up' before embarkation. Further south past the town's sports stadium, the new, plush and not quite so cheap *Amanuel Pastry*, on the left-hand side, has a good selection of hot and soft drinks and sweet snacks. With smart, glitzy furnishings it has become popular with travellers wanting just a snack and drink. Available are hot drinks, juices, cakes, biscuits and doughnuts, and pizzas on fasting days. For a meal, the *Tigist Restaurant*, across the road from the *Amanuel*, boasts both excellent food and friendly (occasionally boisterous) service. This restaurant's senior staff are Tigreans who engender a more jovial atmosphere than elsewhere in Debre Birhan, with music and dancing. There is not a huge variety – *kaiwat*, *tibs*, *kitfo* – but the food is very tasty. This restaurant remains open about 2 hrs later than most others in town, until 2200. In cold weather a charcoal burner can be requested, and positioned to take the chill off the diners.

Eating

Buses to Addis Ababa leave hourly as soon as Debre Birhan's bus station opens at 0530 and they continue until the mid-afternoon. Debre Birhan-bound buses from Addis Ababa's Mercato bus station follow a similar pattern. The fare either way is US$1.40. Going north from Debre Birhan, there is supposedly an early morning service for Dessie, but this can be erratic and you may have to make several shorter trips using Robit, Kemise and Kembolcha as stepping stones. Whether you go direct or break the journey up, the price from Debre Birhan to Dessie should be in the region of US$3.75.

Transport

Ethiopia

Background

History

Fossil remains discovered at a site on the Lower Awash River in northeast Ethiopia in 1974 by US palaeontologist Donald Johanson and named 'Lucy' have been identified as one of the earliest examples of an upright walking hominid. Dated at 3,500,000 years old, these remains constitute our oldest-known ancestors, and many now consider this region of Ethiopia to be the true cradle of mankind. A more recent find in early 1999 of a previously unidentified animal, dated 2,500,000 years old, is speculated to be the 'missing link'. The skull of a new hominid species, named *Australopithecus garhi*, with a brain capacity of 450 cc, as compared to 1,400 cc of modern man, was discovered near the small village of Bouri, northeast of Addis Ababa. Three independent discoveries were made in the vicinity of Bouri of a skull, and the arm and leg bones of a second individual, believed to have belonged to the same species and to have lived during the same period. Close to these humanoid remains were the bones of antelopes, horses and other animals, which showed clear evidence of having been cut with stone tools. Some of the animal boney remains had curved incision marks on them and the ends of the long bones had been crushed or broken off to enable the marrow to be extracted. This is the first evidence that stone tools were used for butchering. Anthropologists have theorized that eating fat-rich marrow enabled the dramatic increase in brain size. However, other scientists believe that the discovery of how to cook root vegetables to provide a source of disgestible carbohydrates would have been of greater significance.

Cradle of mankind

The early history of Ethiopia begins with the glorious but still only partly understood **Axumite Kingdom**, which grew up around Axum in the north highlands in the third

Early history

century BC and endured until the 10th century AD. The achievements of this early civilization are recorded today in the ruins of the old Axumite cities and towns, reservoirs, dams, temples and stone stelae (pillars) on which are recorded fragments of the history of the empire and dynasty. Legend records that Cush, son of Ham and grandson of Noah, came to Ethiopia from Mesopotamia (now Iraq). Other stories claim that Menelik I, the child born to the union of King Solomon and the Queen of Sheba (see box, page 889), settled in Axum, bringing with him the Ark of the Covenant from the Temple in Jerusulem and establishing a dynasty that ruled – with only brief interruptions – until the fall of Haile Selassie in 1974.

Ethiopia's historical importance stemmed partly from its favourable location and terrain. Lying on the edge of the Graeco-Roman world it was linked to both by the Red Sea and the Nile. Kinship, trade and culture also tied it strongly to the Persian Empire. Axumite commerce was based largely on the export of gold and ivory and trade links reached as far as Ceylon, although the strongest links were with Egypt and Greece.

Christianity reached Axum in the fourth century AD, during the reign of the Conqueror King Ezana. He was converted by a young Syrian named Frumentius who was shipwrecked off Adulis and who subsequently became the first Bishop of Axum (see box, page 889). Early coins from Ezana's reign show the traditionally worshipped symbols of the sun and moon, while later coins bear the sign of the cross.

The Axumite Empire reached its zenith in the sixth century when King Kaleb crossed the Red Sea to conquer parts of Saudi Arabia. However, the rise of **Islam** in the seventh century drove the Axumites back on to home territory and as Islam asserted itself in East Africa, the Ethiopian Christians became increasingly isolated.

The Axumite Kingdom, denied the trade routes which were its lifeblood, declined during the 10th century, after which the balance of political and religious power shifted south to Lasta and the new **Zagwe Dynasty**. Its most important ruler was King Lalibela, renowned for the rock-hewn churches he built at the capital that was later to bear his name.

The Zagwe were in turn overthrown in the late 12th century by Yekuno Amlak, who claimed descent from the rulers of Axum and thus restored the **Solomonic Dynasty**. This was a period of rule by chiefs and warlords who collected taxes and made war on each other, but who would submit themselves to the king of their province and through him to the King of Kings.

In 1531, as the Ottoman Empire began to expand, General Ibn Ibrahim, or Gragn (the left-handed), led a Muslim army into the Ethiopian Highlands. Emperor Labna Dengal appealed to Portugal for military assistance, which duly arrived in the form of Christopher de Gama (son of the explorer Vasco) and 400 men, and defeat was avoided. Subsequently, in 1571, the Pope sent the first of several Jesuit missions to Ethiopia in an attempt to introduce Roman Catholicism, but little headway was made and the Jesuits were banished in the mid-17th century.

Menelik II The monarchy of Gondar, which had become an important political and commercial centre in the early 17th century, lost its authority in the 18th century when the feudal lords became independent of central control. A hundred years of near anarchy ensued, giving way eventually to major attempts at reunification in the second half of the 19th century, moves which were given greater urgency as first France and Britain, and then Italy began to cast covetous eyes on Ethiopia. The main work of unification was left to Menelik II, an enterprising, vigorous and imaginative king from Shoa, who guided Ethiopia through the maelstrom of Europe's scramble for Africa. Menelik reigned as King of Shoa from 1865-89 and as Emperor of Ethiopia from that year until his death in 1913.

By fraudulent misrepresentation of the **Treaty of Wuchale**, which Italy concluded with Menelik, Italy laid claim to Ethiopia as its protectorate – a claim supported by Britain and France as they shared out the rest of eastern Africa between themselves. However, at the Battle of Adwa, on 1 March 1896, Menelik's forces routed the Italians, thus preserving Ethiopia's Independence throughout the colonial era. Menelik established most of Ethiopia's present frontiers. He also founded Addis Ababa and was a great modernizer, setting up schools and banks, a railway and a postal system.

King Solomon, the Queen of Sheba and the Lion of Judah Dynasty

On the last day of the visit of the Queen of Sheba to King Solomon in Jerusalem, the king asked if the queen would spend the night in his room. She consented, but took his invitation literally, making it a condition that Solomon should not force his attentions upon her. Taken aback, Solomon sought to save his dignity by demanding that the queen, in her turn, should respect both his person and his property. An agreement was struck and deviously, the king ordered a grand banquet of 10 courses, all highly spiced and salted. They settled for the night in separate beds, a vessel of water between them. A little peeved, the king made do with a maid from the queen's entourage, and the son she subsequently bore became the first king in the Zagwe Dynasty in Ethiopia.

During the night, the queen became thirsty, and drank some water from the vessel the king had placed between the beds. This allowed Solomon, somewhat ungallantly, to claim that the queen had broken the agreement, and that she must now replace the maid in his bed. The child of this union was Menelik I, the first Ethiopian king of the line that was to stretch down the centuries.

During the course of this modestly productive night, Solomon had a disturbing dream. He saw a glittering sun rise over Israel and then shift to shine on Axum. A second sun arose, illuminating all the world but casting its rays with special brilliance on Italy and Ethiopia.

The first sun is interpreted as the Ark of the Covenant, taken by Menelik I from the Temple in Jerusalem to St Mary's Church in Axum, where it is concealed in a secret chamber.

The second sun represented the teachings of Christ. In AD 330 a Syrian ship sailing up the Red Sea was boarded, and all but two boys from the crew were slain. The two were taken to the Imperial Court at Axum where one, Frumentius, so impressed with his wisdom, that a few years later he ruled for a while in place of Ezana, the young regent. When Ezana became emperor, Frumentius went to Alexandria where he was consecrated as the first Bishop of Axum. On his return to Ethiopia, he spread the word of Christ throughout the land.

This legend is recorded from oral sources in the 14th century in Kebra Nagast, the Ethiopian Book of the Glory of the Kings. The work was commissioned by St Tekla Haimanot, who pursued holy devotions for 27 years in a cave at Debre Libanos.

Italy still continued to have designs on Ethiopia, and although it became a member of the League of Nations after the First World War, this did not prevent Mussolini from overrunning the country in 1936. Italian forces remained in occupation for five years, despite pleas to the international community from the young emperor, Haile Selassie. Italy was forced out of Ethiopia by guerrilla and Allied forces during the Second World War and the country resumed its status as an independent nation. However, unrest continued in the north. After 11 years of British administration, Eritrea was federated to Ethiopia in 1952, but when in 1962 the federation was dissolved and the province was annexed by Haile Selassie, guerrilla warfare broke out and the subsequent struggle for Independence was to dominate Ethiopian history until the early 1990s.

Haile Selassie

Haile Selassie had established himself as a national hero during the campaigns against the Italians and had become a respected African statesman. He concentrated on international affairs, securing Addis Ababa as the headquarters of the Organization for African Unity (OAU) and the UN Economic Commission for Africa. A close ally of the US, he ensured that Ethiopia was a major recipient of US aid in the 1950s and 1960s. However, Haile Selassie governed Ethiopia like a medieval fiefdom, unable to understand or respond to agricultural stagnation, inequitable distribution of land and general lack of development. The continuing cost of revolt in Eritrea and drought and famine in Wollo 1972-74, with the death of 200,000 people, contrasted starkly with the accumulation of wealth by the nobility and the church. This caused a mass outbreak of resentment and on 12 September 1974, against a background of strikes, student demonstrations and army mutiny, Haile

Selassie was deposed. The monarchy was abolished the following year. The former emperor died in his palace, under armed guard, several months later. Haile Selassie's son, Crown Prince Asfa Wossen, lived in exile in London until he died in 1998.

Civil war & revolution

The imperial regime was replaced by a provisional military administrative council, known as the **Dergue**, which saw itself as the vanguard of the Ethiopian Revolution. It began to implement a programme of socialist, revolutionary reforms – nationalizing companies, implementing literacy campaigns and setting up over 30,000 local peasant/worker associations. After two years of infighting within the Dergue, Lt Colonel Mengistu Haile Miriam emerged at the head of the dictatorship – executing his rivals within the regime and launching an urban terror campaign against the Ethiopian People's Revolutionary Party, which argued for the immediate creation of civilian government. Tens of thousands were killed or tortured as Mengistu wiped out the opposition and imposed his own vision of Marxism-Leninism.

Military disarray in Addis prompted the Eritreans to step up their campaign, and in 1977 Somalia began encroaching into southeastern Ethiopia. The Dergue may well have collapsed at this time but for the intervention of the USSR and Cuba who re-equipped and trained the Ethiopian army. With this new weaponry and some 16,000 Cuban troops the army went back on the offensive, repulsing Somalia from occupied Ogaden and rolling back the gains, which the rival Eritrean People's Liberation Front (EPLF, predominantly Christian) and the Eritrean Liberation Front (ELF, predominantly Muslim) had made in Eritrea. The EPLF dug in around the remote northern town of Nacfa and over several years continued to inflict heavy losses on the Ethiopian army. In 1982 the EPLF, in alliance with the Tigrayan People's Liberation Front (TPLF), drove the ELF into Sudan where they disarmed and fragmented.

Mengistu was never able to achieve widespread support, largely due to his failure to solve the nationality problem, of which the struggle in Eritrea was the most obvious symptom. The revolution had raised expectations of regional autonomy among various nationalities such as the Oromos in the south and the Tigrayans in the north. The Oromo Liberation Front (OLF), advocating self-determination for Oromia and respect for its language and culture, gained support during the early 1980s from the rural base in the region that had benefited from reforms implemented in 1975. But the most serious threat came from the TPLF, established in 1975 to struggle for Tigrayan self-determination, receiving arms and training from the EPLF.

Mengistu's political and military responses to the nationalist movements were inadequate and the country was further weakened by the catastrophic famine of 1984-85. The international community's response to the disaster was slow, partly because of Ethiopia's close links with the Soviet Union and, when help did arrive, conflict ensured that many of the worst-hit rebel areas, especially in Tigray, were denied relief. The government's own relief measures consisted largely of an unpopular resettlement programme, in which 600,000 people were moved into the south and west of the country. At the same time the TPLF moved 200,000 Tigrayans into the Sudan.

The military situation deteriorated for Mengistu after 1988. While the EPLF continued to make gains in Eritrea, the TPLF now controlled all of Tigray and began to push south to Addis under the flag of the Ethiopian People's Revolutionary Democratic Front (EPRDF). Disillusionment grew in the army and Mengistu's refusal to seek a political solution was increasingly seen as a liability. By February 1990 the EPLF had captured the Red Sea port of Massawa, cutting off supply lines to the Ethiopian Army in Eritrea, and Mengistu was forced to make concessions. He abandoned Ethiopian socialism, invited opposition groups to participate in a unity party and built free market principles into economic planning. But this was insufficient and problems began to mount. The fall in the world price of coffee added to economic hardships and, with the collapse of the Eastern European regimes, Ethiopia lost most of its overseas alliances. As the opposition forces closed in on Addis Ababa in February 1991, Mengistu fled to Zimbabwe. On 28 May the EPRDF entered the capital and subsequently established an interim government.

Prester John

During the Middle Ages a recurrent story circulated over many years of a Christian priest-king, known as Prester John, claiming to be a direct descendent of the Magi, one of the three wise men who brought gifts to the infant Jesus. This legendary monarch was said to rule over a vast empire. A series of over 100 letters, reputedly written by the king, requested support from European Christians to repel the Barbarians. The first letter was addressed to Emmanual I, the Byzantine Emperor of Rome, describing the threatened kingdom as a crime-free land of milk and honey.

In 1177 Pope Alexander III sent an envoy, Magister Philippos, to find Prester John, but the quest failed. In succeeding years, several other expeditions followed, to places as far apart as India and the Far East, but all failed to find Prester John.

By the 14th century the search for Prester John moved from Asia to Africa when a letter was circulated indicating that this Christian kingdom was to be found in Abyssinia (now known as Ethiopia). Portugal responded by sending expeditions to rescue Prester John throughout the 15th century. At about this time the cartographers began to illustrate this fabulous kingdom on woodcuts and engravings and early maps of Africa.

Prester John was believed to have the power to divert and cut off the flow of the Nile to Egypt. Furthermore it was claimed that children in his kingdom were baptized in fire. Over time the letters became ever more extravagant, claiming that in the fabulously wealthy kingdom there were rivers of gold, precious stones so large that they were fashioned into plates and drinking vessels, and the land was the site of the Fountain of Youth. The search for the mysterious kingdom of Prester John continued until the 17th century. One view is that Genghis Khan was the source of the enduring legend, while others ascribe it to Ethiopian Christians.

A four-year transition period allowed the formulation of a new constitution. The first elections, in May 1995, for national and regional representatives, were won comfortably by the EPRDF.

Relations with Eritrea have been affected by the introduction of a new currency by Ethiopia's neighbour. This has complicated cross-border trade and made Ethiopia aware of the implications of the Independence of Eritrea in making Ethiopia land-locked. The border between the two countries is disputed, and in June 1998 this erupted into armed conflict and bombing raids, with all borders closed. In June/July 2000 a ceasefire was organized with the promise of UN peacekeepers on the border.

Modern Ethiopia

Politics

With the overthrow of the Dergue regime, the EPRDF drew up a national charter that allowed for the creation of an 87-seat council of representatives, representing some 32 political organizations and with the EPRDF occupying 32 of the seats. New internal boundaries were created, reflecting ethnicity and political power. Large, powerful and concentrated groups (Tigray and Oromo) appeared to gain fertile areas and relinquish desert, while weaker and dispersed groups (Amhara and Gurage) lost good land.

The intention is to allow Ethiopia's main ethnic groups to have self-determination within a federal structure. The EPRDF has found it difficult to maintain cohesion as there are now over 100 political groups based mostly on ethnic affiliations. The OLF and some other minor groups decided not to participate in the elections in 1992, and also withdrew from the government. An attempt by the OLF to revive guerrilla resistance has provided cause for concern, though not serious. The OLF is split into several factions, which limits its effectiveness.

The EPRDF dominated the 1992 elections, winning 890 out of 978 seats in Addis Ababa, and 81 out of 84 in the regions. Elections were postponed in two areas, it is said because the EPRDF had not got itself well enough organized.

By 1991, the EPLF had established a provisional government in Eritrea. In the process, more than 100,000 non-Eritreans were deported to Tigray. A referendum in April 1993 endorsed separation from Ethiopia, Eritrea became an independent state and joined the UN.

The new constitution was finally adopted at the end of 1994. It has a federal framework based on 14 regions, including the three city-sized regions of Addis, Dire Dawa and Harar. There are three legislative levels: regional state councils and a bi-cameral Federal Assembly. The chief executive is the Prime Minister, chosen by the elected Council of People's Representatives, one of the houses of the Federal Assembly. The President is to have a largely ceremonial role.

In 1995 the first elections under the new system resulted in an overwhelming victory for the EPRDF – however, the polls were boycotted by the main opposition groups. The Prime Minister is Meles Zenawi who was President in the transitional administration. The President is an Oromo, Negaso Gidada. The new constitution has reorganized the administration, and there are now nine regions and the metropolitan council of Addis Ababa. Most of the regions have a strong ethnic identity, raising the possibility of future tensions. Elections in 2000 saw parties opposed to the EPRDF gain a little ground.

Ethiopia's border with Somalia continues to present problems. The Somali *Al-Ihihad* militia has been involved in cross-border terrorist activity, and there have been clashes with Ethiopian government forces, including hot pursuit into Somalia.

In November 1997 Eritrea introduced its own currency, the nakfa, replacing the Ethiopian birr, which had previously been in use. This complicated trade relations, particularly goods in transit, now that Ethiopia is land-locked. Ethiopia retaliated by insisting that all transactions be undertaken in hard currency, a problem for Eritrea, which has limited foreign currency reserves.

Relations with Eritrea have been exacerbated by a dispute over the 1,500 km border between the two countries. Eritrea is claiming the territory marked by the Italian colonizers. These borders were amended when Eritrea was annexed by Ethiopia in 1962 and five small zones were allocated to Ethiopian provinces. Both sides have made efforts to occupy the disputed areas, all of no economic significance.

In May 1998 there were a series of air strikes and bombing raids on the airport in Asmara by the Ethiopians and on the airport and town of Mekelle by the Eritreans. It is not clear which side initiated the armed conflict, how it will be resolved or when the closed borders will re-open. The dispute seems utterly unnecessary and has aptly been described as "two bald men fighting over a comb".

After a lull in late 1988, when diplomatic intiatives to end the dispute were in progress, fighting resumed in the early part of 1999. The conflict is disastrous – transport links have been broken, both sides have expelled citizens and seized assets, with around 400,000 people now displaced. Agriculture has been disrupted, and the war effort has absorbed resources and increased government expenditure, thereby undermining structural reforms of the economy. In May 2000 Ethiopian army advances led to the ceasefire agreed in June.

Economics

The economy was badly affected by the repressive bureaucracy, capricious government interference and civil conflicts of the Mengistu period of 1974-91. Desperate shortages, decaying infrastructure and famine were the order of the day. In the past 10 years, however, with firm commitment to a market economy, Ethiopia has made a recovery.

**Economic &
social structure** The size of the population is now estimated at around 61,100,000 for 1999. This makes Ethiopia the most populous country in Africa, with the exception of Nigeria. The low level of development is reflected in the low level of urbanization, with only 13% living in the towns. Ethiopia is more densely populated than most of Africa – in fact the number of persons per sq km is more than double the African average. As with most other countries

in Africa, the population is growing fairly rapidly at 2.7% a year, and this rate implies an extra 1,500,000 persons each year.

Measured by production of output, the economy, with a GDP of US$5,694 m in 1998, is about average in size compared with the rest of Africa. However, the large population means that living standards are very low. Both methods of converting GDP to US dollars indicate that Ethiopia is one of the two or three poorest countries in the world. The exchange rate method gives GDP per head of US$100, and purchasing power parity US$450.

Low living standards lead to an emphasis on agriculture, mostly in small family farms producing output for household consumption, and agriculture generates 55% of GDP. Industry is very modest at 12% of GDP, as are services at 33%.

Most expenditure is on consumption, at 81% of GDP, while investment has improved to 16%. The government sector, hampered by inability to raise revenue, and the dislocation following the collapse of the Mengistu regime, undertakes a low proportion of overall spending (12%). Aid is equivalent to 23% of GDP, and this is above the African average.

Exports are low at only 15% of GDP, and comprise mostly coffee (44%) and hides and skins (13%). Ethiopia is the third largest coffee exporter in Africa after Uganda and Côte d'Ivoire. Imports are 26% of GDP, and are at this level as a result of aid receipts. The main imports are foodstuffs (23%), vehicles (13%), machinery (12%) and fuels (10%).

Social conditions

Adult literacy is estimated at 35%, and this is poor even by African standards. Only 23% of children in the appropriate age groups go to primary school, a very poor enrolment rate, and about a third of the African average. Secondary enrolments do not compare quite so unfavourably, but with 12% going to secondary school, there is hardly any education at this level for children outside the urban areas. Tertiary education levels are also low.

Life expectancy is 49 years. Almost half of children under five are malnourished. Infant mortality rates are among the highest in the world. Availability of doctors is a little better than in Africa generally, but they are almost all concentrated in the urban areas, and medical provision in the rural areas is woeful.

Primary education and secondary education both have lower enrolments for women. The disparity is less great at the secondary level, but again it must be remembered that secondary education is really only available in the towns, where there is a more enlightened attitude to the educational needs of females.

As with everywhere in Africa, there is pressure on women to help support their families by working outside the home, mostly by contributing to agricultural production, and two-thirds of women are so engaged. The burdens on women are compounded by an average fertility rate of almost seven births per woman, with only a small percentage of women using contraceptives.

Culture

There has never been a full census carried out in Ethiopia, but the population is estimated at over 61,000,000, with 85% working on the land. The Central Plateau is characterized by settled cultivation of cereals and pulses, while nomadic lifestyles persist at the desert margins.

People

There are over 80 languages and dialects. In Tigray region, around Axum, the Semitic language Tigrinya is spoken, while the heartland of Ethiopia is the home of Amharic, the official language. To the south and east are the Cushitic-speaking peoples, the Oromos, Afars and Somalis. Ethiopia's Nilotic peoples, the Nuer and the Anuak, are found to the far south and west. Living close to the border with Sudan, the Nuer and the Anuak are related to the people of southern Sudan. The Nuer are mainly a cattle-herding tribe, while the Anuak are fishermen living by the Baro River and adjacent swamplands. The Falasha, a few of whom live around Gondar, are linked to Ethiopia's early ties to Judaic Palestine, and thousands of Falasha were airlifted out of the country by Israel during the 1984-85 famine.

Amharas and Tigrays are predominantly Orthodox Christian, while Oromos, the largest ethnic group in the country, are more mixed, with communities following Christian, Muslim and traditional religions. Protestant and Catholic churches can be found in many parts of the highlands.

Land and environment

Geography Ethiopia lies between latitude 3° and 18° north and longitude 33° 48° east. Elevations range from over 4,000 m above sea level to 100 m below, the highest point in the country being Ras Dashan in the Simien Mountain Range, which rises to a height of 4,620 m northeast of Lake Tana. The southern part of Ethiopia is bisected by the East African Rift Valley, 40-60 km wide, and the valley floor is scattered with lakes. North of Addis, the western wall of the valley runs parallel to the Red Sea coast, creating a wide plain between the escarpment and the coastline. Further north, this plain narrows until the foothills of the escarpment run right down to the sea. To the west of the rift system, the gently dipping plateau runs down into Sudan, drained by the tributaries of the Nile, which have scarred deep canyons in the land. This part of the country is seriously denuded of top-soil, much of it having washed away to collect on the flood plains of Egypt.

The eastern wall of the Rift Valley runs due east from Addis, forming a steep escarpment that rises abruptly to over 1,000 m, commanding wide views over the Afar plains to the north.

The dominant feature of the country's topography is the high Central Plateau, generally between 2,000-3,000 m, and it is here that the majority of the population is concentrated. This plateau contains a number of river systems, the most significant of which is the Blue Nile (*Abbay*). The most fertile part of Ethiopia lies to the extreme south. Agricultural potential here is rich, and parts of the Sidamo Highlands, with rolling grassland and wooded hills, are in complete contrast to the image of Ethiopia as unrelentingly dry and arid.

The vegetation of the plateau is dominated by mountain grassland and settled agriculture. Population pressure has forced farmers into areas that are very marginal in rainfall and soil quality, particularly along the eastern escarpment, and this has exacerbated the drought and famine conditions that have characterized parts of Ethiopia since 1973. Coniferous forests have now largely disappeared from the highlands, although in the south, lower elevations and higher temperatures have produced broad-leaved forests, which, largely due to their inaccessibility, have not yet been subjected to extensive commercial exploitation.

The lowlands, depending on the amount of rainfall, have dry-zone vegetation, ranging from limited areas of desert to thorn scrub and savannah.

The forested area is about 13% of the total land area. Economic collapse invariably has an adverse effect on afforestation in low-income countries. There is increased demand for land and woodfuel for cooking, and in Ethiopia the forested area has been diminishing by 0.3% a year. Domestic water usage is very low at 6 cu m per person a year, and industrial and agricultural usage is comparatively low as well. As a result, Ethiopia puts little general strain on its renewable supplies of fresh water, utilizing only 2% of the total availability.

Climate Ethiopia's climate is determined by altitude and proximity to the Indian Ocean. Considerable variations in temperature are reflected in the traditional climate zone divisions: *dega*, the temperate plateau; *kolla*, hot lowlands; and the intermediate frost-free zone of the *woina dega*. Average annual temperatures vary over these zones from 16° to 26°C. Rainfall varies considerably too. In most parts of the central highlands the average is well over 1,000 mm per year, while the drier lowlands receive less than 500 mm. There are two principal seasons; rainy from June to October and relatively dry for the rest of the year, although some regions experience short February-March rains as well (the *belg*). The country is extremely vulnerable to drought conditions, particularly in the low-lying pastoral areas and along the eastern escarpment, where there is heavy dependence on the *belg* rains. A further set of rains (the *meher*) in October, November and December allow a second harvest in some places.

Vegetation and wildlife

Mammals

The wildlife of Ethiopia has suffered considerably in the last few decades and visitors should not expect to see the same abundance of animals that can be seen in the other East African parks. Various species of antelope are fairly widespread, if not numerous, in many of the game parks, and dik-dik, oribi, reedbuck, bushbuck and greater and lesser kudu can all be seen. Outside of the game parks two monkeys are quite common: the black and white colobus and the vervet. Compared with the animals of other parts of East Africa, both these monkeys occur in a slightly different form in Ethiopia. The colobus *(Colobus abyssinicus)*, usually known as the *guereza*, has a large and conspicuous white mantle extending downwards from the shoulders. The vervet *(Cercopithicus aethiops)* has very long and noticeable white whiskers. Baboons are also common. The olive baboon *(Papio anubis)* is usually known as the *anubis* in Ethiopia, where it is the commonest baboon. The endemic gelada baboon *(Papio gelada)* is often seen in parties in wild and rocky places (a species is said to be endemic to a certain place when it occurs in that place only, and nowhere else). The male gelada is an impressively large animal with a well-developed mane and bare red patches on its chest. Occasionally smaller mammals such as the Abyssinian hare *(Lepus habessinicus)* and some species of ground squirrel can be observed from the road. At night jackals are quite often seen, as is the spotted hyena *(Crocuta crocuta)*, though the latter is more often heard. Hyenas are often seen dead on the highways. They are scavengers and, especially on the edge of towns and villages, their eerie whooping is a characteristic sound of the Ethiopian night.

Birds

Although the animals in Ethiopia may not be as numerous as those elsewhere in East Africa, this is more than compensated for by the wonderful birdlife. There are more than 20 endemic species in Ethiopia and many of them can be seen around Addis Ababa. Furthermore, they are often large or colourful.

Endemics seen here include the white-billed starling *(Onychognathus albirostris)*, wattled ibis *(Bostrychia carunculata)*, white-collared pigeon *(Columba albitorques)*, black-winged lovebird *(Agapornis taranta)*, thick-billed raven *(Corvus crassirostris)*, Abyssinian longclaw *(Macronyx flavicollis)* and flocks of the black-headed siskin *(Serinus nigriceps)*.

Crops

Chickpeas are grown near Addis in small untidy-looking fields. They have a pretty blue flower and the peas are sold at the roadside still attached to the plant. Linseed, with its blue flower, is also a commonly grown crop. Teff, the staple grain crop of Ethiopia, grows in small fields and looks like a rather straggly grass. You will also see wheat, barley, millet, sorghum and many other crops.

Books

History

Haile Selassie I, 1975, *My Life and Ethiopia's Progress: the Autobiography of Emperor Haile Selassie*, Oxford: OUP. The man who ruled Ethiopia for 48 years, and whose demise brought to an end a dynasty reputedly stretching back to Solomon and Sheba. **Marcus, HG**, 1975, *The Life and Times of Menelick II*, Oxford: Clarendon Press. A thorough account of the career of the extraordinary emperor who defeated the Italians and created modern Ethiopia. **Marcus, HG**, 1994, *A History of Ethiopia*, Berkeley: University of California. **Ofcansky, TP and Berry, L** (eds), 1993, *Ethiopia: A Country Study*, Washington DC: US Govt Publications.

Ethiopia

Travellers' Tales Marsden-Smedley, P, 1990, *A Far Country: Travels in Ethiopia*, London: Arrow Books. An account of travels undertaken by an Ethiopia enthusiast in 1988, when the restrictions imposed by the Mengistu regime on tourists were a source of considerable frustration. **Murphy, D**, 1968, *In Ethiopia with a Mule*. Describes a mule-trek from Massawa to Addis Ababa, with good observations on local history, culture and customs. **Thesiger, W**, 1987, *The Life of my Choice*, London: Collins. Autobiographical reflections of an eccentric English explorer who spent his childhood in Abyssinia, later returning to travel across northeastern Ethiopia, land of the fearful Danakil (Afar) people.

Fiction **Waugh, E**, 1932, *Black Mischief*, London: Chapman & Hall. Based on material gathered by Waugh when he went to Addis Ababa in 1930 to report on the coronation of Haile Selassie for *The Times* newspaper.

Eritrea

7

Eritrea

SUDAN

Red Sea

YEMEN

Nakfa

ERITREA

*Dahlak
Islands*

Keren   Dongollo   Massawa   *Dahlak Kabir*

Ghinda   *Adulis*   *Bure Peninsula*

Agordat   Embatkalla   Zula

ASMARA   Nefasit

Dekamere

Barentu   *Qohaito*

Adi-Qayeh   Senafe

*Danakil
Depression*

ETHIOPIA

Assab

DJIBOUTI

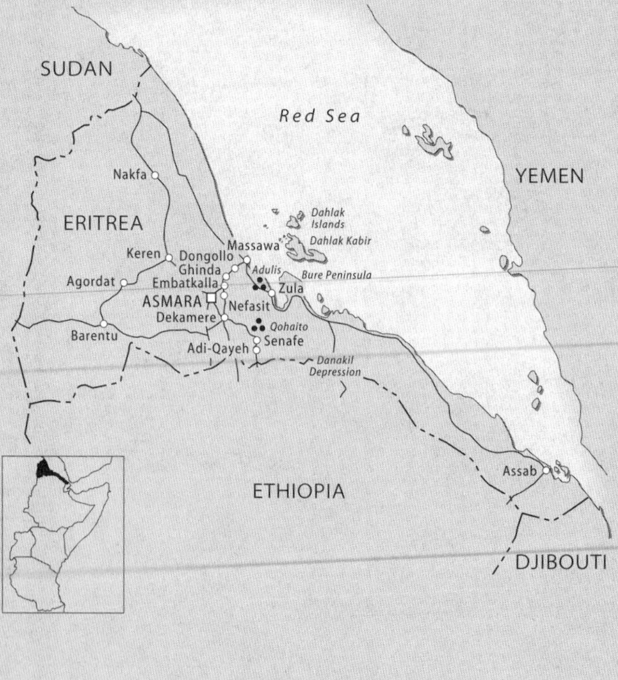

Eritrea is a friendly and relaxed country to visit, where you are soon made to feel at home. It has a great deal to offer – from Asmara, the capital, with its array of bars and cafés in wide, palm-lined streets, to the beautiful mountain scenery, miles of unspoilt white sandy beaches along the coast, the coral reefs and aquatic life at Dahlak Islands, and a number of historical sites dating back to the Axumite Kingdom. The emergence of Eritrea as an independent, self-reliant, working state is a testament to the resolution of the people of Eritrea and their considerable organizational skills. Their currency, introduced in November 1997 to replace the Ethiopian Birr, is named after the remote mountain retreat of Nakfa, the symbol of resistance to Ethiopian occupation, where the rebels survived 10 years of shelling from the Ethiopian army.

In May 1998 a border dispute with Ethiopia led to armed conflict and bombing raids. The two countries signed a peace agreement in December 2000 but the borders are still closed, and it is uncertain as to when they will be re-opened.

Essentials

Planning your trip

Where to go Eritrea is a compact country and its beautiful capital city Asmara sits atop the Eritrean highlands on the eastern edge of the Rift Valley escarpment. Asmara's 1930s Art Deco architecture merits exploration. Eritrea's other highlights include a visit to the ancient Monastery of Debre Bizen (only possible if you are male) near Nefasit. The ancient port of Massawa, where the Turkish, Egyptian and Italian architecture is currently being restored is sultry but evocative. Offshore the Dahlak Islands offer amazing unspoilt diving and snorkelling opportunities. If you are time limited it would be possible to visit these highlights within a week. Sadly the legacy of the recent conflict with Ethiopia is that many of the archaeological treasures in southern Eritrea and as well as visits to northern and western Eritrea are effectively off limits until mine clearing operations are completed.

When to go The main rainy season in the hinterland is July and August, the coast has rain in December to February, but the showers are short, and the rest of the day will be sunny. However if you do travel in the rainy season, the country is wonderfully green, the temperature is cooler and there are less tourists.

Finding out more The Eritrea Network Information Centre (ENIC) has an informative site on **www.eritrea.org** Ericommerce, Robin House, 2A Iverson Road, London, NW6 2HE, T020-7372 7242, F020-7624 6716, provide an up-to-date Eritrean travel information service. As tourism develops, guided tours of the major cities and sights organized before departure from Europe/USA are becoming available. Also www.asmera.nl and www.eriemb.se/tourismc

For a list of books see page 932

Language Tigrinya, Arabic and Amharic are most commonly spoken.

Before you travel

Visas A visa is required by anyone wishing to enter Eritrea. Visas are available from Eritrean embassies around the world and they cost about US$60 in European cities and are usually obtainable within 24-48 hours. A one-month, single entry visa costs US$25-30 if purchased in Africa. A transit entry visa costs US$15. If travelling by motorbike a carnet is not required, but you need to get a temporary import licence that costs US$14. You may be asked to provide proof of a return ticket or your next destination when applying for a visa. The dispute with Sudan (see page 928) has now been resolved. The border with Sudan is reported open, but the recent conflict with the Ethiopians in 1998-2000 has made much of western Eritrea unsafe for travellers as there are many uncleared landmine fields.

Vaccinations You will need a Yellow Fever vaccination certificate.

Money

See inside front cover for exchange rates

Since November 1997 the unit of **currency** is the Eritrean Nakfa. You will be best advised to get money exchanged in the capital, Asmara, as banking facilities in other parts of the country can be hard to find. Branches of the Commercial Bank of Eritrea are usually quick and efficient. The best currency to carry is the US dollar, though the English pound and Japanese yen are acceptable. You may have problems having any other currencies recognized. You should bring some cash, but the majority of your money should be in **travellers' cheques**. There is a modest black market at only marginally enhanced rates above the official rate, especially near the main post office in Asmara, which is best avoided as it is illegal.

Major cards are sometimes taken by large hotels in Asmara. Not generally acceptable outside Asmara.

Eritrea

Tigrinya

Tigrinya is the most widely spoken local language. It has a complicated alphabet, and there is no widely accepted transliteration of the phonetic language into the Roman alphabet. For those wanting to go further, Edward Paice's Guide to Eritrea *(Chalfont St Peter: Bradt) contains a wider selection of words and phrases (although transliterated slightly differently).*

Tigrinya Basics

Please	*Bedja*
Thank you	*Yekanielay*
Hello	*Salam*
Goodbye	*Salamat*
Yes	*Uway*

No	*No*
Good	*Tsebook*
Bad	*Hmark*
How much?	*Kenday*
Where is?	*Abay*
Why?	*Nementaree*
Water	*Maee*
Room	*Koosaree*
One	*Harde*
Two	*Kilte*
Three	*Seleste*
Four	*Arbarte*
Five	*Hamushte*
Ten	*Arsete*
Hundred	*Meti*
Thousand	*Shek*

Getting there

Air The international carriers to Eritrea are *Egyptair, Yemen Airways, Saudi Airlines, Sudan Airways* and *Lufthansa*. *Eritrean Airlines* operates flights to Middle Eastern countries and internally. Since the border dispute of 1998 *Ethiopian Airlines* no longer fly to Eritrea. *Lufthansa* operates two flights weekly to Asmara via Frankfurt.

Taxis to town cost US$5, buses operate from 0600 every half an hour costing US$0.10, departure tax of US$12 – payable only in US$.

Road It is not possible to get into Eritrea from Ethiopia by road at present due to the border dispute. The two routes were: from Addis Ababa to Asmara via Adigrat, or from Addis Ababa to Assab and then north along the coast. There is no regular public transport operating on this route. There has been a programme of road building with excellent new roads from the border (Adigrat/Ethiopia) to Asmara, from Asmara to Massawa and from Asmara to Keren. From Keren to Barentu the road has been upgraded and sealed.

Many of the recently improved roads were damaged during the 1998-2000 conflict

There are conflicting reports about whether it is possible to enter the country from Djibouti to Assab. There is no formal border crossing and you may experience later difficulties without the appropriate passport stamp. The route from Assab to Asmara is particularly uncomfortable and long (1,100 km) although it passes through some dramatic landscape. From Sudan the border crossing is between Kassala and Teseney, the distance between the two towns being 70 km. The border crossing can take up to a full day to complete entry formalities.

Sea There are two important ports in Eritrea: **Massawa** and **Assab**. Massawa is currently operational, though in disrepair, and many cargo ships dock here from other countries along the Red Sea. Every two weeks there is a cargo boat to Jeddah (Saudi Arabia), Port Sudan (Sudan) and Suez (Egypt). You may be able to get dhows to Assab on the Djibouti, Ethiopian, Eritrean border in the south.

Train Work has begun to repair the rail link between Asmara and Massawa destroyed in the protracted fighting. Over 70 km of track has been restored plus several steam trains.

Touching down

Tourist information The new tourist office is to be set up in Post Office Square, just to the north of Independence Avenue. **Travel and tour agents** The main carrier into Eritrea used to be *Ethiopian Airways*, with offices situated in 54 cities around the world. In Asmara, the Ethiopian Airlines

Eritrea

Eritrea

 ### Eritrea embassies and consulates

Several Etritrean embassies and consulates have been set up recently and include:

Australia, 26 Guilfoyle St, Yarralumla, ACT Canberra 2600, T6-2823489, F6-2825233.

Belgium, 382 Av Louise, 1050 Bruxelles, T2-5349563, F2-5393928.

Canada (consulate), ERRA in Canada IN, PO Box 2038 STND, Ottawa, Ontario KIP 5W3, T613-234-2181, F613-234-6123.

China, Ta Yuan Ran Gong Lou, 1-4-2, No 4 South Liang Maho Rd, Chao Yang District, Beijing PRC, T1-5326534, F1-5326532.

Djibouti, PO Box 1944, Djibouti, T355187, F351831.

Egypt, PO Box 2624, 87 Shahab St, Al Muhandesein, Cairo, T3030516, F3030517.

Ethiopia, PO Box 2571, Addis Ababa, T514302, F514911.

Germany, Markt Str 8, 50968, Köln, T221-3730168, F221-3404128.

Italy, Via Ferrucio 44/2, 00185 Rome, T06-70497908, F06-70497940.

Kenya, PO Box 38651, New Woumin House, 4th floor, West lanols, Nairobi, T443164, F443165.

Saudi Arabia, Ahmed Lary St, PO Box 770, Jeddah, T6612263, F6612014.

Sudan, PO Box 8129, Khartoum, T73165, F24911452256.

Sweden, Ostermalmsgatan 34, Box 26068, 100 41 Stockholm, T08201470, F08206606.

UAE, PO Box 2597, Abu Dhabi, T2331838.

UK (consulate) 96 White Lion St, London N1 9PF, T020-7713 0096, F020-7713 0161.

USA, 910 17th St, NW Ste 400, Washington DC 20006, T202-4291991, F202-4299004.

Yemen, PO Box 11040, T209422, F009671.

In other places information can be obtained from Ethiopian Embassies (see page 804).

Overseas representation in Eritrea

All the diplomatic representation is in Asmara (see page 911).

office was on Liberation Av, between the Catholic Cathedral and the Imperio Cinema. Invariably they have a staff member who takes responsibility for providing tourism information, and will cover developments in Eritrea, providing a reliable source for information on any recent changes in visa regulations, health requirements etc. This service has been suspended due to the 1998 border dispute.

Local customs & laws **Conduct** It is expected that **dress** will be sober for formal occasions, particularly when visiting government offices – it is regarded as a mark of respect for the persons you are meeting as much as anything else. It is recommended that both men and women cover their shoulders and skirts/shorts should extend to below knee length. Outside Asmara and Massawa if you dress skimpily or wear shorts you will be stared at and attract a lot of unwanted attention. The exception is on beach resorts. Visitors are often offered a cup of tea or coffee; it is considered a friendly gesture to accept. When entering a church or mosque, shoes should be removed. Women are not normally allowed to enter mosques unless there is a special prayer room set aside for them. Photographs of museums, art works, churches and mosques will often require permission. When photographing local people, religious ceremonies or festivals, it is courteous to ask permission first, and a small fee might be requested.

Religion The country is fairly equally divided between Muslims and Orthodox Christians, though there are some Roman Catholic and Protestant communities.

Safety Eritrea is a very safe country (though see below advice on landmines) and it is possible to walk about with confidence in the cities and towns even after dark. It is sensible to keep a close eye on belongings.

Although there are no restrictions on photography, military installations, airports, bridges, civil engineering works, government buildings, and military personnel should not be photographed. Charges may be made to take photos of ancient sites and buildings.

Landmines Caution A major problem is that many of the roads and pathways are mined and unexploded ordnance litters the countryside. It is advisable to travel only on well-utilized roads as infrequently travelled roads are potentially very dangerous.

Touching down

Hours of business *Banking hours are from Monday-Saturday 0700-1200.*
Official time *Three hours ahead of GMT.*
Language *French and Arabic are the official languages, and Afar and Somali*

are spoken locally. Some English is spoken in the capital.
IDD *253; there are no area codes. Equal tones with long pauses means it is ringing; equal tones with equal pauses means engaged.*

The areas identified as most at risk of unexploded mines include north and west of Keren, and a 40-km strip north of the Eritrean-Ethiopian border between the Mereb River to the south and the Setit River to the north. Massawa, Agordat and Ghinda have extensive minefields and the environs of town of Barentu has had several recent incidents of exploding mines. Other parts of Eritrea that are known to have extensive minefields include Nakfa, Teseney and Dekemhare.

The Eritrean government has started a mine-clearance programme, but there is concern that Eritrean Islamic Salvation (EIS), formerly the Eritrean Islamic Jihad, who are in conflict with the government, have relaid mines north and west of Keren and Barentu and north of Massawa. Although Eritrea and Sudan have re-established diplomatic relations overland travel westwards and northwards is ill-advised due to landmines and rebel insurgent activity.

Where to stay

The only place you are likely to find reasonable quality accommodation is in the capital, Asmara, as most facilities around the rest of the country were either destroyed during the war or have fallen into disrepair. However, you will be able to find modest places to stay in most towns as well as newer hotels built with money from Eritreans abroad or returnees.

Government hotels usually require payment in US dollars, while private hotels accept nakfa. It is advisable to ask whether the price is inclusive of 10% sales tax and another 10% service charge.

Camping is possible particularly on the coast, although there are no official campsites in the country as yet. See sleeping classification, page 36.

Getting around

Air Eritrea operates an internal service between Assab and Asmara every Tue, leaving **Air** Asmara at 0800, returning later in the evening. Asmara airport, T181891, can provide passenger air arrival and departure information.

Eritrea's transport infrastructure was severely damaged as a result of the war though the **Road** government is putting much of its financial and manpower resources into redeveloping the road system. There has been a huge road building programme during the past few years, and there are now excellent new roads from Adigrat/Ethiopia to Asmara, from Asmara to Massawa and from Asmara to Keren. From Keren to Barentu there is now a sealed road. However much of the road repair work in Eritrea was undone in the 1998-2000 conflict.

Otherwise there are few sealed roads and they are invariably in a bad state of repair. The way north is rough and difficult from Asmara up towards Sudan through the arid hills of Afabet and Nakfa.

There are daily buses between most of the smaller towns, several morning and afternoon buses between Asmara and Massawa and between Asmara and Keren. Buses do not run to a timetable. They usually wait until full before they will set out.

Car hire Hiring a car as a means of exploring Eritrea is not a cheap option, although this may change as the country begins to receive more visitors. If you only plan to travel from Asmara to Keren and other major towns, you can hire a vehicle for about US$50 a day. If you want to go to other areas, you will need a four-wheel drive vehicle, which can be hired for about US$80 a day, plus mileage.

It is possible to hire chauffeur-driven cars from Asmara (see page 910).

Train The railway between Massawa, Asmara, Keren and Agordat was dismantled during the war. A stretch of the track from Massawa inland to Ghinda has been reopened.

Keeping in touch

Media **Newspapers** *Hadas Eritrea* is published twice a week in Tigrinya and Arabic by the transitional government of Eritrea. There is also an English-language weekly paper first produced in 1994, called *Eritrea Profile*. At the moment it's only generally available in Asmara.

Television and radio *Voice of the Broad Masses of Eritrea* is a government-controlled radio station broadcasting in Arabic, Tigrinya, Afar and Kunama. *ERI-TV* was established in 1992 by the government and began broadcasting in 1993. Evening transmissions are limited to Asmara and are broadcast in Arabic and Tigrinya.

BBC World Service can be received in Eritrea with a radio that has short waveband reception.

Food and drink

Italian food has been absorbed into traditional Eritrean eating habits in the hotels and a standard menu will have pasta followed by a meat course and ice-cream or fruit. Fish is not often available outside Asmara, Massawa or the coastal resorts. Traditional Eritrean food is the large pancake made of fermented batter called *injera* that is served with a variety of meat or vegetable sauces. *Zigini* is the local name for Eritrean stew, which you will find in many places. Local cheeses, particularly those made from goats' milk, are well worth trying. Sweet black tea is the staple drink, which you may be offered at times as a gesture of welcome. Coffee 'bun' with ginger, and in some areas such as Nakfa with black pepper, is delicious and the coffee ceremony plays an large part in Eritrean culture – not to be missed!

You will be able to find most forms of alcohol – beer, whisky, wine – though they are expensive if imported. It is well worth trying Asmara lager (previously known as Melotti) a local beer or the spirit *araki*, a colourless aniseed drink both of which are available in most bars around the country. There are also quite reasonable Eritrean and Ethiopian wines/liquors of other kinds. Mes, a honey wine similar to mead, is delicious but can be very potent.

The water is reputedly safe to drink, though it is probably advisable not to drink it. Local bottled spring water is available throughout the country. See restaurant guide, page 39.

Holidays and festivals

As yet no official set of holidays and festivals has been declared. The following are days that will be observed by at least some sections of the Eritrean community:

New Year's Day 1 January. *Genna* (Ethiopian Christmas – Birth of Christ) Julian Calendar 7 January[2]. *Timket* (Ethiopian Epiphany – Baptism of Christ) 19 January[2]. *Fenkil* (liberation of Massawa, 1990) Mid February. *International Women's Day* 8 March. *International Labour Day* 1 May. *Liberation Day* 24 May. *Ethiopian Good Friday May (variable)*[1]. *Fasika* (Ethiopian Easter Sunday) May (variable)[2]. *Idd al Fitr* (End of month of fasting for Ramadan) May (variable)[1]. *Martyrs' Day* 20 June. *Id Al Adha Araja* Summer[1]. *Start of Armed Struggle* 1 September. *Id Mawlid-el-Nabi* (Prophets Birthday) Late Summer[1]. *Engutatsh* (Ethiopian New Year) 11 September. *Maskel* (Finding of the True Cross) 27 September[2]. [1] Date determined by lunar cycle. [2] Indicates an Orthodox holiday

Calendar When Eritrea was part of Ethiopia it used the Julian calendar, named after Julius Caesar, which is seven years and eight months behind the Gregorian (Western) calendar – a result of differences of opinion over Christ's exact date of birth. The Julian calender consists of 12 months of 30 days and a 13th month of five or six days. The Gregorian calendar is now officially used.

Health

Yellow fever inoculation is recommended and compulsory if coming from an affected area. Inoculation against typhoid and hepatitis A and B are strongly recommended prior to travel. Anti-malaria tablets and general anti-mosquito measures are strongly recommended in the coastal strip or at altitudes below 2,500 m as malaria and dengue fever are endemic. Asmara and other highland areas are too high and the nocturnal temperatures too low for the malarial parasite to reproduce successfully, and so are malaria free.

Although the water is reputed to be safe to drink, many people will try to avoid even the smallest risk of a stomach upset by drinking only boiled, sterilized or bottled water.

Staying healthy
For further advice see the section on Health, page 58

Asmara

Eritrea's capital city, Asmara (also spelt Asmera), is set in the centre of the country on the eastern edge of the high plateau. Its name, 'Forest of Flowers', is indicative of its feel – it is as friendly and relaxed as any small town, with an easygoing pace of life. Prior to the Italian occupation from 1889, Asmara was a small village and the home of Ras Alula, the then governor of the region. Contemporary Asmara was built as the capital of the Italian colony of Eritrea during the period 1890-1940. It has a mixture of Italian and Eritrean architecture. By the time of independence, it had become the second largest city in Ethiopia.

Ins and outs

Air Asmara is the only international airport in Eritrea so all incoming flights arrive here. The daily flight between Asmara and Addis Ababa costing about US$100 one-way has been suspended since the 1998 border dispute started. Taxis to town from the airport cost US$4-5; there is a half-hourly bus service which starts at 0600 and costs US$0.10. **Road** Road access between Ethiopia and Eritrea has been suspended since the 1998 hostilities. Major road building and repair works have been carried out within Eritrea since independence, but some of the repaired roads were damaged or mined in the 1998-2000 conflict. It is possible to reach Asmara from Assab on the Ethiopian border in the south but again the road is not good and the journey is long and exhausting. The scenery however is fantastic.

Getting there
There is a US$12 departure tax (not payable in Nakfa)

Unlike most African capital cities, Asmara's streets are clean and safe to stroll through, day or night. It is easy to get around on foot. The main bus station is north of the market, from where you can also get minibuses and taxis.

Getting around

The **Ministry of Tourism**, PO Box 1010, Asmara, T120073/123941, F126949, is on 3rd floor of the building in Liberation Av which houses the **Eritrean Shipping and Transit Agency**, east of the *Ethiopian Airlines* office. The **Eritrean Tour Service (ETS)**, PO Box 889, is located at 61 Liberation Av, Asmara, T124999, F126366. The *ETS* can arrange sightseeing tours of Asmara, trips to Massawa and car-hire services. *EriNine* Tour Operator PO Box 266, Asmara, T122271, eri.nine@mail.com, can help organize trips to the Dahlak Islands.

Another useful source of information, particularly about conditions outside Asmara, can be the numerous international development agencies which have set up in the capital such as **UNDP**, on the Airport Rd.

Tourist information

As Asmara is about 2,300 m above sea level, the temperature is comfortable, an average of 17°C. Rainfall is approximately 500 mm per year and comes mostly in Jul-Aug.

Climate

Eritrea

15°19'N 38°55'E
Colour map 1, grid B5
Population: 415,000
Altitude: 2,300 m

Asmara is said to date from 1508, founded by shepherds because of the good water supply. Its original name was Arbate Esmere – 'they (feminine) united the four.' According to legend the people of four neighbouring villages were feuding with one another until the womenfolk got together to collaborate on a plan to resolve the conflict.

There are surprisingly few signs that this city has been at war for over 20 years in that, except for the obvious neglect of buildings, there are few bullet scars or signs of bomb damage. However, Asmara was occupied by the Ethiopian Dergue and a legacy of this era is the prison at Mariam Gimbi where members of the Ethiopian army tortured EPLF sympathizers. The prison is now the Ministry of Water Supply and access to the public is prohibited. Also, there are hundreds of captured tanks and armoured vehicles waiting to be disposed of at Kagnew Station, a US communications centre in the time of the Emperor, now a military base on the edge of town and home to the EPLF.

Sights

Asmara is a beautiful Art Deco city, captured in a 1930s architectural time warp, a walk around which will be rewarded with evidence of the city's diverse heritage. The main market is a popular place to visit with its abundance of fruit, vegetables, spices and crafts and bustling atmosphere. During the Italian occupation of Asmara, the market area was the 'native' quarter of town. The main boulevard, Liberation Avenue, that runs east-west through the centre of Asmara is a pleasant palm-lined street with a number of open-air cafés that reflect a style of life established during the Italian period. If you want to soak up the atmosphere of Asmara, then this is the place to find it – sampling the bars, cafés and patisseries along the avenue.

Asmara

■ Sleeping			● Eating
1 Ambasoira	3 Hamasien	5 Nyala	1 Italian Club
2 Ambassador	4 Keren	6 Oasis Pension	2 Napoli Pizza

Not to scale

Things to do in Eritrea

★

- **Hike** the route of the old railway from Asmara to Nesfit.
- Hire a bike and **freewheel** 120 km downhill all the way from Asmara to Massawa (put the bike on the bus to go back).
- Visit the **Debre Bizen Monastery** dating from 1361 high in the clouds near Nesafit (women are not allowed to enter the monastery itself).
- Explore the ancient coastal port of **Massawa** where the historic buildings are being restored.
- Travel by **steam train** on the restored 70 km section of the railway from Massawa to Ghindi.
- Visit the **Dahlak Islands** for some of the best diving sites on earth.

The old **Imperial Palace**, built in neoclassical style with Corinthian columns, is at the western end of Liberation Avenue and is surrounded by pleasant gardens. The palace, now known as the **National Museum**, provides a useful introduction to Eritrea's history and its struggle for independence. There are scrolls in the ancient language, Ge'ez, and a particularly interesting ethnographic section demonstrating some of the traditions and customs of the nine tribes of Eritrean people. There are also archaeological and war sections, the latter with a collection of weaponry. ■ *0800-1100 and 1500-1700 daily. Note, however, that the museum was still closed pending completion of refurbishment at time of writing.* The **Opera House,** with its Romanesque portico built in the 1920s, designed by Cavagnari, is one of Asmara's most exquisite buildings.

The imposing **Catholic St Mary's Cathedral**, red brick with a distinctive narrow gothic bell tower, designed by an Italian architect, Scanavini, and built in 1922, lies about half-way along Liberation Avenue. This is believed to be one of the best examples of the Lombard-Romanesque style outside Italy. The cathedral, a Capuchin monastery, a nunnery and a primary school are in the same compound and are open to visitors. A sewing group in the back of the cathedral sells beautiful traditional embroidery. **St Mariam's (Mary's) Coptic Cathedral** was built in 1917 in a combination of Ethiopian and Italian styles. It has a brightly coloured mosaic front and a bell tower at each side. There is a traditional stone bell to the left of the main entrance. The open area in front of the cathedral is packed for religious festivals. It has a collection of religious artefacts including ancient biblical manuscripts, robes and crosses. The tower is a good landmark if you lose your bearings in the town. Other religious buildings are the **Kidane Mehret Orthodox Church** about 1 km north of Liberation Avenue, whose dome and minaret tower over the market; and the **Al Qurafi al Rashidin Mosque**, one of Eritrea's most sacred Islamic shrines designed by an Italian and built in 1937, is on Victory Street not far from the eastern end of Liberation Avenue. The Muslim quarter is situated behind the *Keren Hotel.* It contains spice markets, fabric shops, silversmiths and several mosques. The **Forto Baldissera**, an old Italian fort in the western part of the city, 1 km from the town centre, offers good views from the hill but entrance to the fort itself is prohibited. Unfortunately this view has recently been blighted by a new office block, built in the middle of the ruins.

On the outskirts of Asmara, en route to Massawa near the zoo, lies the **British War Cemetery**, dating from the time of the liberation from the Italians in 1941. There is also a sacred Hindu burial ground, resting place for Indian soldiers who served alongside the British at the time.

The **Tank Cemetery** – the graveyard of hundreds of rusting damaged military vehicles including tanks, armoured cars and other scrap military metal – is an unusual tourist sight. It is located on the road towards the airport.

Eritrea

Essentials

Sleeping

There are many small, privately owned pensions of good standard in the lower price ranges. All hotel accommodation has an additional 10% sales tax, on top of which a 10% service charge is usually added to the bill

L *Hotel Inter-Continental Asmara*, PO Box 5444, Deb Mie 04, Expo area, T150400, F150401, intercon@eol.com.er On the airport road opposite the Sembel Residential Complex, 2 km from the airport and 4 km from the city centre. A new luxury development opened in 1999 with 170 rooms with balconies. Restaurants, bars, coffee shop, swimming pool and conference facilities are all available on site. Close to the United Nations headquarters.

B-C *Ambasoira*, 32 Dejatch Hailu St, Kebebe T113222, F122596. One of the best hotels in town with 50 rooms, centrally located south of Liberation Av, next door to the *Hamasien Hotel*. **B-C** *Hamasien*, 30 Dejatch Hailu St, Kebebe T123 411, F122596. Similar to *Keren* in that it also was built during the colonial era in 1920 and has a certain charm after its recent refurbishment. It has 29 rooms and is located next door to the *Ambasoira*. It was the British officers headquarters during the period of military administration. **B-C** *Sunshine Hotel*, Hatsey Yohannes #76, T127880, F127866. Recently built with 26 rooms, near the British Council. **B-D** *Savanna International*, PO Box 3754, Chist Dagama Str #9, T116183/5, F202146. Outside the city centre, large hotel with 58 rooms offers a range of accommodation, all with TV.

To get to hotels in the Tiravolo district head down Martyrs' Av, turn right at the Clothing Factory – a taxi should cost about US$2

C *Ambassador*, 36 Liberation Av, T126544, F126365. The most centrally placed, another high-rise with 36 rooms. In the process of being refurbished and upgraded. Price includes a good breakfast. Accepts all major credit cards. **C** *Bologna Hotel*, Addis Abeba Av, in Tiravolo district, T181360, F182686. Has 34 rooms and a good restaurant. Advised to avoid the rooms above the restaurant, as the music and street noise continues until late. Accepts all major credit cards. **C** *Expo*, Addis Abeba Av, T181967, F182714, 5 mins out of the centre of town, in Tiravolo district. Reasonable standard private hotel with 65 rooms, with an Italian restaurant and shady terrace. **C** *Keren*, formerly the *Albergo Italia*, PO Box 181, 7 Victory St, T120740, a few blocks from Liberation Av. Built in the colonial era in 1899, this is the oldest hotel in Asmara and its interior of decorative urns and chandeliers reflects this. Currently closed for renovation. **C** *Nyala*, Semaetat Av, T123111, F121429. Slightly further out of town, a high-rise building with 67 rooms, the restaurant serves national dishes from a series of small tents – it's certainly different. **C** *Selam*, Dagmawi Menelik, T127244, F120662, past the National Museum. Conference centre, recently refurbished, this is mainly a business hotel with 47 rooms, restaurant. **C-D** *Stadium Hotel*, Churchill Street #2, T161173. Has 18 rooms and reasonable facilities. **C-D** *Top Five Hotel*, Serahtegnatat #8, T124922, F124931. Located a little way from the centre with 15 rooms, reasonable value.

D *Africa Pension*, T121436 (no PO Box number or street name). Built in the 1920s, previously an Italian villa with a walled garden that was later used as the high court by the Ethiopians during their period of occupation. Located one block from the *Hamasien Hotel*, opposite the Italian Embassy. Is a little run down but this is more than compensated for by its charm. **D-E** *Khartoum Hotel*, Ali Usman Buri #35, T119348, F121427. Opposite the *Imperio Cinema* just off Liberation Av on Nocra St, the hotel has 14 rooms and offers good value. Price includes breakfast. **D-E** *Shigey Hotel*, Desta W/ Yesus #6, T126562. Small, centrally located hotel with 12 rooms and a charming roof terrace.

E *Bristol Hotel*, T121688, a short walk off the road leading to the *Ambasoira Hotel* or *Hamasien Hotel*. Unexceptional 1930s hotel but has helpful and friendly staff. **E** *Capri*, located north of Liberation Av, close to *Ethiopian Airlines*. Shared bathrooms, large, comfortable rooms, very good value. **E** *Central Hotel*, behind the *Ambassador Hotel*, offers excellent value. It is very clean, with friendly staff, shared bathrooms, and there are hot showers on some floors. **E** *Legese Hotel*, Ras Beyene Beraki #42, T125054, F120446. Good central location, 46 rooms, own restaurant – a popular place offering very good value for money. **E** *Lion*, T126700, also in the Tiravolo district. Popular with locals as well as tourists, mainly because it serves tasty food at cheap prices. **E** *Green Island Pension*, central. Close to cathedral, friendly, basic. **E** *Pension Lalibela*, near the roundabout at the end of Liberation Av, near the petrol station. Safe parking for motorbikes, clean, hot showers. **E** *Oasis Pension*, just off Liberation

Av near the *Impero Cinema*. Cold bucket showers available. **E** *Impero Pension*, next door to the cinema. Basic, cheap pension. **E** *Pensione St Georg*, close to *Ethiopian Airlines*, just north of Liberation Av. Shared bathrooms. **E** *Red Sea Hotel*, on a side turning off Liberation Av near the roundabout. Clean basic facilities. **E** *Tsegareda ('Rose') Pension*, to the rear of the *Impero Cinema* block. Clean, friendly and quiet. Facilities for washing/drying clothes on the rooftop. **E** *Victory* or *Vittoria*, opposite cathedral on Liberation Av. Shared bathrooms, hot water.

Most hotels have their own restaurant, but the menus tend to be standard and a little unimaginative. Most restaurants are quite cheap, meals are unlikely to cost more than US$5 for supper. There is a great variety of cafés and bars, offering light meals and snacks, which are usually good value. 'Restaurants' tend to serve traditional dishes like *injera*. 'Snack bars' serve non-traditional food that is cheap and often authentically Eritrean – for example, *fatta* is like pizza except there is no crust. 'Cafés' serve tea, coffee, cappuccino and Italian pastries, and sometimes fruit juices.

Eating

Expensive *Cherhi Bar & Restaurant*, north of Menelik I St. Chinese, good but not cheap, located north of the covered market in a tall, rather curiously-designed building built in 1983 that resembles an air traffic control tower, situated at probably the highest point in Asmara, affording very impressive 360° views of the city. *Sembel Huts* (by the Sembel residential complex) opposite the *Hotel Inter-Continental* has a selection of restaurants offering a variety of menus. There is also a disco and live music twice weekly on Thu and Sat. **Expensive-mid-range** *China Star Restaurant*, Knowledge St, close to the *Nyala Hotel*. The Thu lunchtime buffet menu at $4.50 is especially good value. *Milano Restaurant* on Ras Alula St near the library offers a range of Italian dishes as would be expected. At the back of the restaurant there is a traditionally decorated National Restaurant serving Eritrean food at very reasonable prices.

Mid-range *San Giorgio*, Liberation Av. Italian cuisine, reasonable standard.

Cheap *Asmara*, Liberation Av, near post office. Serve *injira* and other Eritrean food as well as most of the popular Italian dishes, gets busy at lunch time. *Bar Vittoria*, near the British Council library. An old café but offers excellent delicacies, in interesting surrounds. *Bereket Fast Food* opposite the *Imperio Cinema*. This is a popular venue offering good local food, burgers, chips and juices. *Bologna Hotel Restaurant*, reasonable choice of dishes. *Café Alba*, run by an Italian family in a street running parallel to Liberation Av, serves a good breakfast and also serves pizza and Italian pastries. *Caravelle Bar and Restaurant*, Italian place serving good food, worth a visit for the weird and wonderful décor. *Castello*, another good Italian restaurant, close to the American Embassy. Indoor or outdoor shaded seating available. *Demera Pastry Shop*, Liberation Av, opposite the '*Bereket Fast Food*' towards the stadium. Has friendly welcoming staff and delicious pastries and juices. *Expo Hotel*, the restaurant is very popular. *Napoli Pizza*, 4 roads west of the cathedral, just above Liberation Av. Very good pizza, extremely popular among travellers. *Pizzeria Eritrea*, Gamela St, north of Liberation Av. *Sudan Restaurant*, 100 m from the *Cinema Impero* opposite the *Khartoum Hotel* offers excellent cheap Sudanese food. *Sudan Brothers'*, on a street behind the *Ambassador Hotel*. Offers a good range of Sudanese and Eritrean dishes.

Seriously cheap *Bar Royal*, previously called *Café Royal*, Liberation Av. Popular street café with seats outside, a/c, smoking prohibited near the cathedral. *Cathedral Bar*, on the main road opposite the cathedral, has excellent fruit juices. *Geneth Bar*, Haramat St. Good bar, very popular in the evenings. *Hollywood Stars Bar*, across from *Napoli Pizzeria*. Music non-stop. *Impero Bar*, on Liberation Av, 2 streets east of cathedral. Good ice-cream (next door to cinema). The *Italian Club* offers a comfortable respite serving lunch. *Modern Snack Bar*, 2 roads west of the cathedral. Serves light local dishes like *silsi*, *fool* and burgers. *Portico Snack*, Liberation Av, a few streets west of the Catholic cathedral. Offers milkshakes, burgers, fries etc, popular with good atmosphere, also has seats outside on the pavement. *Rino*, corner Ali Osman St and Liberation Av. Good value, main dishes. *Sesen Pastry*, described as having the best pastries in the Horn of Africa.

The Hard Rock Café now functions as a bar at the *The Ambassador Hotel*.

Eritrea

Entertainment Some of the hotels organize evening entertainment. The Italian community has set up a club at *Casa d'Italiano*, off Liberation Av, which apart from being an interesting place to visit can be a useful source of advice about how to get around the country, what to visit etc. *Caravelle*, not far from the *Nyala Hotel*, has a disco on Fri and Sat nights, 1100-0500, entrance fee US$5.50. The *Mocambo Club*, off Liberation Av, has live music each week. The other main disco is at the *Junior Club*. Entrance is about US$7. Venues are well advertised in hotels and shops, so check these for newly opened clubs.

Discos *Patamata's Night Club*, next to *Impero Cinema*, Liberation Av. Open Wed, Fri and Sat nights from 1130 to 0500, entry US$4.50 but free up to midnight, popular with Eritreans who have lived abroad, Afro-American rap included. *Delux Disco*, Massawa Rd, near the glass factory in Debezito section of town in the east end. Popular with teenagers on summer school holidays, closed during term time. *Lagetto Disco*, also in the east end of town. Open Fri and Sat nights. *Sembel Huts*, on the road to the airport. Very popular disco, entry US$7. *National Theatre Association*, across the street from *Impero Cinema*, Liberation Av. Has a bar which has a Fri/Sat night disco, extremely popular. The *Irish Nightclub* at *The Expo* is very popular on Fri nights.

Shopping **Bookshops** A good bookshop on the corner of Liberation Av and Martyrs Av is the *City Book Store*, containing many socio-politico historical books written in English about Eritrea. Next door to the cathedral there is a Catholic bookshop, *Friendship Bookstore*.

Curios and crafts Lack of tourists means there are few places specializing in curios and crafts. However, textiles, ceramics, woodwork, silverware and basketry are available in Asmara's main market, where you can also buy fruit and vegetables, pottery, spices, household essentials as well as second-hand clothes and shoes. Some of Eritrea's religious artefacts are very attractive and you will see a few shops around town specializing in old and new Orthodox Christian objects including distinctive Coptic crosses. *Haile Gebrehiwat*, at the end of Ras Mangesha St near the *Keren Hotel*, has craftwork and curios of a high standard.

Newspapers *Eritrea Profile* is an official government weekend newspaper published both in Tigrinya and English.

Transport **Road** **Bus**: buses are a cheap and reasonably reliable way of travelling, but not if you're on a
See also Ins and outs, tight schedule. They usually load with passengers between 0700 and 0900, and leave when
page 905 they are full. The main bus station is north of the market and in several sections near one another and there are fairly frequent buses. **Massawa** takes 5 hrs and costs US$2 (morning and afternoon departures); **Keren**, 3 hrs, US$1.50 (morning and afternoon departures); **Assab**, 4/5 days, US$15 (take plenty of water with you). The bus services to Ethiopia have been suspended. Most journeys only take a few hours' along reasonable roads. There are also minibuses/taxis available from the bus depot. **Car hire**: it is possible to rent chauffeur driven vehicles, either Fiat cars, Land Rovers or minibuses from *Africa Garage* at 29 Ras Wole Butul, T111755. *Leo Car Hire*, T125859, near Nakfa house and roundabout, also offers a range of services. **Cycle hire**: *Olympia* bicycles rent out mountain bikes for US$5 per day. To find *Olympia*, go down Liberation Av to Martyr's Av, over the first roundabout, then turn right between Nacja House and the Fiat garage. *Olympia* are 200 m down that road on your left.

Directory **Airline offices** *Ethiopian Airlines*, service currently suspended. *Eritrean Air*, 89 Liberation Av, T115500, flies from Asmara to Assab. *Saudi Airlines*, 97 Liberation Av, T120166. *Egypt Air*, T181461 (Egyptair), have offices on Liberation Av. *Lufthansa*, T182707.

Banks The main branch of the *Bank of Eritrea (Central Bank)*, PO Box 849, T123036, F123162, is on Liberation Av, where money can be exchanged. *Commercial Bank of Eritrea*, PO Box 235, T120350, F120401, on National Av, also changes money, hours 0800-1100 and 1400-1600. There are also lots of Forex offices with good rates of exchange. The main hotels will also change money. The black market rate is only marginally more than the official rate and travellers are advised against using this service.

Communications **Internet**: opposite the *Tsegareda Pension* (behind the *Impero Cinema*) there is an *Import/Export* company where you can email and receive faxes (T/F291-1-126667). **Post**: the post office is just off Liberation Av. **Telephone**: since telephone and fax numbers are likely to change as the service expands the directory enquiries number T97 could prove useful.

Eritrea

Embassies, high commissions and consulates China, PO Box 204, 6 Arbagugu St, T116988, F1572123 (satellite). **Djibouti**, Andinnet St, towards airport, PO Box 678, T182189, F181001. **Egypt**, 5 Deg Affwok St, T123603, F123294. **Denmark**, Ras Dashen St 11, PO Box 6300, T124346-8 F124343, dkemb@eol.com.er or asmamb@asmamb.um.dk **Ethiopia**, service currently suspended. **Germany**, T182901, on the airport road, 20 mins walk from the centre. **Israel**, Deg Fecrem Ariam St, T120137, F120187. **Italy**, 45 Shemelis Habte St, T120160, F121115. **Norway**, T127718, F121221. **Sudan**, PO Box 371, Deg Fecrem Ariam St, T124176, F120287. **UK**, PO Box 5584, 54 Emperor Yohannes Av, T120145, F120104. **USA**, PO Box 211, Franklin Roosevelt St, T120004, F127584. **Yemen**, PO Box 5566, 5 Lt Tesfalidet Idris St, T110208, F118962.

Libraries **British Council**, Rogu T Mariam St, off Liberation Av. Has good selection of books and newspapers. There is a **US Information Service** with a library in town, and an **Alliance Française**. The *Lufthansa* office has a supply of free German newspapers.

Places of worship The main Orthodox Church is *Kidane Mehret*, near the main market. The Catholic Cathedral, about half-way along Liberation Av, has an English language mass on Sat evenings at 1800. A number of mosques are scattered throughout the city.

Useful services **Public toilets**: access to lavatories can be a problem in Asmara. However, there are some public toilets very close to the *Ethiopian Airlines* office. It is best to use the restaurants/café toilets.

Asmara environs

Dekamere (also spelt Dek émháre) was once a beautiful small town to the southeast of Asmara developed by the Italians in their style. It is set in a fertile region that produced the best wine in the country. Unfortunately today it is almost destroyed as for some time it straddled the frontline of the war.

Dekamere
15°6'N 39°0'E
Colour map 1, grid B5

Although the town itself has little to recommend it except as a reminder of past glories, the surrounding countryside is spectacular and often a route for cycling races, a truly colonial inheritance. Travel west to Sudan is possible in theory, but not currently advised as the area was heavily mined in the recent conflict. The road from Dekamere through the hills of **Adi Qayeh** (also spelt Adik'eyih and Adi Keyeh) is particularly lovely. Along the route you can see the start of the rebuilding process underway in Eritrea with irrigation schemes in operation nurturing nurseries and market gardens. There are some small guesthouses and cafés near the market. Regular buses run from the bus stand near the market in Asmara.

North and west of Asmara

Keren is situated high up on a plateau in the midst of impressive mountain scenery, 105 km northwest of Asmara. It is a potentially productive agricultural area, with fertile soils and a temperate climate. The Eritreans controlled Keren briefly in 1977-78, and in retaliation some of the town was destroyed by the Ethiopian army upon recapture. Overlooked by a seemingly impregnable fortress, which still bristles with Ethiopian army cannon, the town itself boasts stylish public buildings and a Romanesque Catholic church. Today, Keren's community is largely Muslim. The pace is relaxed – here, you are more likely to see camels than cars.

Keren
15°45'N 38°28'E
Colour map 1, grid B5

The Sahel open-air **park** is a lovely place to visit. You can get a refreshing fruit juice here (mango and guava amongst others), as well as grilled and barbecued meats. It is also possible to purchase barbecued food at the station. Other places of interest are **St Mariam Dearit**, a shrine built into a baobab tree which is believed to have powers to influence fertility, a 20-30 minute walk out of town, with no shade on the way, past the Italian cemetery. Women wait outside to perform the coffee ceremony (which can take up to three hours) – the belief is that wishes are granted if the ceremony is performed there with a traveller or a foreigner.

Keren's old residential area has many beautiful Italian houses and villas. Near **Liberation Park**, 100 m from the main roundabout down by the Ciuf-Ciufit River, is the wood market in the dry river bed where camels unload timber brought from surrounding areas. Northeast of Keren is an old Turko-Egyptian fort at **Tigu**, built in the 19th century.

Eritrea

In 1941, at the height of the war in East Africa, Keren was the scene of some of the fiercest fighting between the Allies and Mussolini's troops. More than 1,000 soldiers were killed, and on the outskirts of the town towards Hagaz/Agordat lies the **British war cemetery**. Immaculately maintained, 400 British soldiers are buried there. In the town, the **Italian cemetery** for soldiers killed in the same battle is, likewise, beautifully maintained.

Monday is market day. Not only do the merchants bring their goods in on camels but there is also a **camel market**, where you can buy a ruminant with a three-chambered stomach for US$300. Vaccination is an additional US$0.50. A saddle is advisable. The market is past the Italian cemetery – follow the early morning crowd.

Sleeping and eating **C** *Keren*, the best of the basic accommodation available (rooms vary, so ask to see a few), located near the fruit and vegetable market. The hotel has a roof terrace with good views over the town, the bar is a popular drinking place in the early evening, the restaurant serves reasonable food, mostly Italian. **E** *Barka*, a Muslim hotel, with just 10 rooms. **E** *Eritrea*, Union Av. A small hotel with a bar which tends to get quite noisy in the evening. **E** *Sicilian*, next door to the *Eritrea*. Reportedly the oldest hotel in Keren, offering a range of rooms, which are clean and comfortable. Bucket showers, safe parking for motorcycles and friendly staff.

There are a number of restaurants around the market area, behind the *Keren Hotel*. There is a reasonable choice of cafés – look for those with shade, bougainvillaea, and a menu that includes Egyptian/Sudanese stewed beans called 'fool'. In Sahel Park, a 10-min walk uphill from the main plaza, vendors serve grilled and barbecued food.

Transport There are morning and afternoon buses to **Asmara**. The road between Keren and Asmara is sealed and in good condition.

Nakfa
16°40'N 38°32'E
Colour map 1, grid A1
Altitude: 2,700 m

Capital of Sahel province, Nakfa (sometimes spelt Nacfa) is about 150 km north of Keren. It holds a special significance for Eritreans, being home to the EPLF during the war. As a result, it was very heavily damaged with only a mosque surviving. It is planned to rebuild the town and reconstruction is already underway, but facilities are still very basic. Many young people doing their national service opt to spend part of it rebuilding Nakfa, planting trees to revive the blighted landscape. Despite its altitude, some windchill and the impoverished soil, the government plans to turn Nakfa into a regional centre. Most of the hotels or guesthouses are made of corrugated iron, some without shower or toilet. If you are interested in military history the trenches of **Denden** merit a visit – one hour's climb to the peak, which overlooks the Ethiopian frontline 500 m away. **Orota**, the EPLF's 'underground city' during the war years, lies northwest of Nakfa. About 20 km to the north of Nakfa is the **Tsabra underground hospital**, built into the mountainside, affording it protection during the lengthy conflict.

Transport There is only one bus daily to Nakfa from Keren. You need to book the day before and arrive at the bus station at 0400. It is a very rough journey along riverbeds for most of the way. Journey time is about 8 hrs.

Kerora in the far north of Sahel province has cave paintings. However access is difficult until the road is rebuilt.

Agordat
15°30'N 37°40'E
Colour map 1, grid B4
Population: 24,000

Also spelt Akordat, this small town in the Western Lowlands is 75 km from Keren. It was on the railway from Massawa that continued towards Teseney, but the line was dismantled during the war. The town can experience high temperatures, and sandstorms known as *haboob*. It is located on the river Barka, and the area is famous for its banana plantations. **D** *Barka Hotel* is an interesting meeting place. **D** *Oasis Hotel* has air conditioning when the electricity is on, usually only from 1000-2400. There are new hotels being built and there are some small guesthouses and basic cafés in the railway station area. A new open-air market complex is also under construction. There are regular buses from the centre and outside the railway station to Keren.

A further 65 km southwest of Agordat lies the provincial capital of Gash Setit. The
government **D** *Rest House*, high up on the hill overlooking the town, is the best place to stay. There's usually a pleasant breeze, and it is quieter than other places in the town. The **D** *Asmara Hotel* has a good restaurant. However, Barentu was ransacked and shelled in June 2000 by Ethiopian soldiers. Many businesses were abandoned during the recent conflict, so it is possible that the remaining facilities are very basic.

Asmara to Massawa

The journey down from Asmara to Massawa on the coast is a stunning one. The descent from about 2,500 m to sea level will take about three hours by car, or five hours if you take a bus. Alternatively, you can easily do the 120 km from Asmara to Massawa on a bicycle, since it is all downhill for six hours! Going back you put it on the roof of the bus, or pay US$1 for someone to do so on your behalf. *Olympia* bicycles in Asmara rent out mountain bikes for US$5 per day.

There is an early viewpoint, about 10 km out of Asmara, at the Bar Durfo, which is well worth a short stop.

Walk It is possible to walk along the old railway track from Asmara to Nefasit, a distance of roughly 25 km – beyond that to Ghihda the trackbed is possibly mined. This is a fantastic walk that takes six hours. Starting from Asmara, hitch or get a bus to the rubbish dump just past the zoo. Walk down the road until it bends sharply left. Clamber down to the trackbed below. There are tunnels so a torch is useful, though you have to scramble around a few of the tunnels that have collapsed and become blocked. Take plenty of water. You are likely to see baboons en route.

The first big town you pass on the winding road to Massawa is Nefasit, close to the
Debre Bizen Monastery, situated high up above the town at 2450 m, frequently wreathed in clouds. The monastery was built in 1361 and is home to an Orthodox religious community. Today, there are over 120 monks and students there. The tomb of its founder, Abuna Fileppos (St Philip), is in the grounds. Abuna Fileppos is reputed to have said that he would rather stare into the eyes of a wild lion than into a woman's eyes.

Abuna Fileppos, a follower of Ewostatewos, promoted the Jewish custom of observing the Sabbath on Saturday in addition to Sunday observance, and many of the religious communities in Ethiopia and present-day Eritrea resisted the royal decree in the 14th century to change to a Sunday Sabbath. One of the leaders of the opposition was Abuna Ewostatewos who left his monastery in Sarae and travelled to Egypt to seek the support of the patriarch Benjamin, which was not forthcoming. Abuna Ewostatewos died in Armenia and his Ethiopian followers left the church and set up their own communities, including the famous monastery of Absadi of Debre Maryam in Qohayyen. In 1450 the Council of Debre Metmaq accepted the Ewostatewosites back into the established church.

It is a two-hour climb up to Debre Bizen from Nefasit, which if you decide to do you will be suitably rewarded with 80 km views of the sea and Dahlak Islands in one direction on a clear day, and mountains in the other. There are three churches in the monastery compound, including a large round church containing many frescos and a recent church built in 1968 by the late Ethiopian Emperor Haile Selassie. There are also stone houses, some classrooms and many hermits or anchorites live in the surrounding area on ledges or in small caves chiselled out of the cliff face. They are reputed to survive only on a diet of acacia leaves, although it is said that the monks leave their food remains outside the monastery at night within reach of the hermits. There are collection troughs for rainwater – the only water source for the monastic community.

The monastery has a **library** that houses a collection of over 1000 illustrated ancient manuscripts in Ge'ez, including Coptic Bibles, the Lives of the Saints – one copy dating from 1361 when the monastery was founded – plus historical records of

☞ ## The railway

The line was built by the Italians and it was the first railway to be constructed in East Africa. Work began on the 95-cm gauge track from Massawa in 1887. The line was extended from Ghinda to Nefasit in 1910 and reached the capital Asmara in 1911. Its construction accelerated as gold was discovered at the turn of the 20th century on the outskirts of Asmara. The railway reached Keren by 1920 and its terminus – 280 km inland – at Biscia, close to Agordat, by 1932. Market towns sprung up around the various stations along the route, and it was vital to communications and the economy. It was envisaged that the line would eventually be extended west to Khartoum via a link with the Sudan Railway at Tesseney but this was never implemented.

Construction of the railway was a considerable engineering feat, considering the difficult terrain and the fact that it climbs to a high point of 2,128 m a few kilometres before the gentle descent into Asmara. There

are 65 bridges and 30 tunnels, the longest being 320 m, with most tunnels having to be bored through solid rock. The crossing at the Obel River is a 14-arch bridge, and there are viaducts before Nesfit, and just after Devil's Doors, the highest point on the line, where the track runs along the edge of a precipice. Between Mai Atal and Damas the gradient is so steep that trains have to be split and each half hauled up separately.

At its peak in 1965 the railway carried 446,000 passengers and 200,000 tonnes of freight. There was a daily service hauled by diesel locomotives between Asmara and the coast, and trains ran on alternate days from Asmara up-country to Agordat. It ceased operation during the war but is now being restored.

In addition to building the railway the Italians also built an aerial tramway called Le Teleferica Massaua-Asmara that extended over 100 km. Sadly it was destroyed in the Second World War by the British.

the Ethiopian Kings. Only the monks are allowed to read the books. There are also religious relics like crosses, incense burners, robes and crowns. The manuscripts and religious artefacts have been buried for safety during various turbulent periods of the monastery's history, eg during the Muslim and Italian invasions and to save the manuscripts from the edicts of the Ethiopian Dergue communist leaders, who instructed the monks to burn all religious artefacts. The Dergue regime used the monastery as a military base to oversee the surrounding region during the 30-year Eritrean independence war.

In 1520 Francisco Alvares, a Portuguese priest, landed nearby on the Eritrean coast. Alvares' accounts of his travels mentions 'a monastery in the clouds' believed to refer to Debre Bizen Monastery. There are the remains of three Portuguese sailors buried in a crypt, believed to have perished in an epidemic that affected the monastery at the time.

The monks make a rather bitter alcoholic brew called Sewa, which is a bit of an acquired taste.

■ *It is a fairly gruelling two-hour uphill walk from Nefasit, with ropes required for the final ascent. When you see a wooden cross and a stone bench you are almost there. With permission you may stay the night and attend early mass. There is one drawback in that women are not allowed to visit. In theory men need to have obtained permission to visit in advance, from the Orthodox Church in Asmara, but this regulation is not always enforced. It is recommended that you bring gifts of food and drink for the monks – coffee, sugar, honey, candles or wine are welcome – plus a plentiful supply of water for your journey.*

Sleeping in Nefasit   D *St George's Hotel,* a white building to be found near the entrance to the town. It has a small restaurant attached.

Embatkalla   Another 10 km on from Nefasit, you come to the pleasant town of Embatkalla, set
Colour map 1, grid B5   amidst lush green hillsides and dominated by a large, old Orthodox church.

Embatkalla was an Italian town in the colonial era. It is reputed to have the best climate in Eritrea, with fog settling and veiling the valleys. The hills are terraced and the moist atmosphere contributes towards excellent yields of fruit and vegetables, so it became a plantation area. Although Embatkalla is 84 km from the coast it was also the headquarters of the Italian navy, who were unable to bear the oppressive heat of Massawa where just a skeleton staff remained. The Eritrean Institute of Management (part of the University of Asmara) was initially housed in the buildings formerly occupied by the Italian navy. A few Italian villas and houses remain. There are few tourist facilities here, but there are a couple of basic hotels and restaurants serving local food.

Buses from Asmara to the coast usually stop for lunch at the pretty town of Ghinda where there are a few hotels and restaurants in the town centre. A local speciality is *capretto* (goat stew). Ghinda – whose name is derived from *ghinde*, the vegetable silk more commonly known as kapok – used to be very popular with the Italians. It also has a wonderful climate with good rainfall and is an extremely fertile, well-cultivated area. It is a major citrus fruit production area. Wild olive trees can be seen here.

Ghinda
Colour map 1, grid B5

The next town is Dongollo which, along with the nearby springs of **Sabarguma,** is famous for the production of Eritrean bottled mineral waters bearing the name.
    There is a fine Italian-built tripled-arched bridge spanning the Dongello River that bears the inscription in a dialect of Italy's northern Piedmont region *'Ca Custa Lon Ca Custa'*, translated as *'Let it cost whatever it costs'*, dedicated to the Italian General Menebrea. Below, camels wander alongside the pebbled riverbed. All 548 soldiers of the Italian squad led by Colonel De Cristoforis were killed by Ethiopian troops at the nearby **Battle of Dogali** on 26 January 1887, during the first Italian-Ethiopian War (1885-96). The Italians had secured a base at Massawa in 1885. Wishing to exploit more than the coastline area, the Italians made a pact with the chieftain of Shewa, later Emperor Menelik II, in 1889 and began to march inland. The Ethiopian forces, led by Emperor Yohannes (John), responded by surrounding the Italians, most of whom perished at the Battle of Dogali. Italy responded by sending an army of 20,000 men, garrisoning it near the coast, but little fighting ensued. In the following months most Italian deaths were caused by dysentery and malaria, which eventually prompted the army's recall. The peace treaty of Uccialli was signed by Menelik and the Italians in 1889. The Italians later interpreted the treaty as giving them protectorate status over Ethiopia, which Menelik rejected.

Dongollo
Colour map 1, grid B5

Eritrea

As you approach Massawa, about 10 km before the town centre, you will find the **EPLF Martyrs' Cemetery**. The **Italian Military Cemetery** at Otumlo is situated a few kilometres away.

Massawa and the Coast

Massawa was heavily damaged during Eritrea's struggle for independence. But it has managed to retain some of its atmosphere, and is likely to be of some significance to tourists as it is the gateway to the Dahlak islands. The Eritrean coastline, stretching more than 1,200 km along the Red Sea, is one of the least populated and developed coastlines in the world, inhabited by some of the poorest people worldwide. Between Massawa and the Sudanese border the narrow coastal plain has hundreds of isolated beaches, containing just a few coastal villages inhabited by fishermen, framed with dramatic mountains in the background. The region is also the home of the nomadic, tent-dwelling Rashaydas, who are renowned in the Middle East and North Africa for breeding racing camels. Eritrea has about 350 offshore islands including the Dahlak Archipelago.

Massawa

Massawa (also spelt Mitsiwa), known as the 'Pearl of the Red Sea', is 120 km from Asmara and consists of two islands and two causeways plus a strip of land on the mainland. It is Eritrea's main port (it used to be the headquarters of the Ethiopian navy) and access to the rest of the world and is being rehabilitated. The dockyard is back in operation and handling an impressive tonnage of merchandise. Much of Massawa remains somewhat dilapidated, although most of the hotels have now been repaired.

History

It can get extremely hot and humid, up to 40°C in Jun-Aug with little difference between day and night temperatures. The monsoon rains are in Dec-Feb

Massawa's early history is obscure but it is believed to have become an important port in the seventh century following the sacking and decline of the Axumite port of Adulis. The spread of Islam was rapid along the coastal strip, and by the 10th century the majority of the population were Muslim. The port was known to the Venetians in the 14th century and described by the Portuguese in the 16th century. It has long been settled and has the largest deep-water natural harbour on the Red Sea. The earliest signs of settlement here were when the **Ottoman Turks** invaded and occupied the island port in 1557. They retained the city for the next three centuries and their influence is still visible architecturally. The **Egyptians** were the next power to seize control of Massawa from 1846-85, only to be ousted by the **Italians** under a special arrangement until 1941, when the **British** regained control. The Turks, Egyptians and Italians built many fine buildings. A major fire in 1885 and the earthquakes of 1890 and 1921 caused substantial damage to the city, but the 30 year **struggle for Independence** and the 1998-2000 border conflict have caused even greater destruction with hardly a building left unaffected.

In addition to its fine sandy beaches Massawa was renowned for its mixture of Turko-Egyptian and Italian architecture. Unfortunately today there is little to see of its rich and varied history as it was fought over by both sides during the war and was devastated by the fighting. The great dome of the 19th-century Imperial Palace built on the site of the 16th-century palace of Ozdemir Pasha was cracked open. The former Banco d' Italia that previously dominated the harbour was reduced to little more than a skeleton. The colonial residences, the mosque, the waterfront and all major hotels were extensively damaged. At one time the yacht club and the nearby beaches and islands were popular places for weekends and vacations for the residents of Asmara. A famous craft of Massawa was the manufacture of mother-of-pearl buttons. A joint initiative by Unesco and the Eritrean Government is attempting to restore the city to its former glory. New buildings are restricted to three storeys, with the exception of some commercial buildings on Taulud Island.

Werner Munzinger (1832-75) – known as Pasha Munzinger – was a Swiss-born adventurer who at different times was the French Consular Agent to Massawa (1854), British Agent and political advisor to Lord Napier's expedition against Emperor Theodore at Magdala (1865) and the Egyptian-appointed Governor of Massawa (1872). He was instrumental in constructing the causeways linking the islands of Massawa and Taulud to the mainland as well as bringing fresh water into the old town via an aqueduct. Munzinger built the Imperial Palace in 1872 on the site of the 16th-century Turkish palace, later used by Haile Selassie as a winter palace.

Within the city limits Massawa is effectively divided into three zones: the island of Massawa known locally as Batsa/Batsi; the island of Taulud, called Twalet locally (the administrative area); and the mainland which is mainly residential, also known as Edaga. The **Edaga Berai Dam** visible from the causeway to Taulud Island supplies the city's water.

Massawa Island sights

The old town and the port are on Massawa Island, which is joined to Taulud by a causeway. The surviving architecture of the old town has great charm, reflecting the impact of Turkish and Egyptian rule during the 16th-19th centuries. Much of it is built out of coral blocks with carved stone lintels, with *roshans* – wooden windows – extending outwards over the streets. The narrow streets are laid out in a labyrinth pattern enclosing covered markets and mosques, including the 500 year old **Sheikh**

Hanafi Mosque with its elaborate stuccowork, containing an exquisite Murano chandelier. **Campo**, a large square lined on all sides by houses decorated by Turkish and Eygptian woodcarvers, have finely sculptured balconies, window shutters and doors, a glorious reminder of previous residents. Opposite the harbour is a 17th-century house made of coral blocks, also used in the Ottoman-style construction of the houses of **Abu Hamdum** and **Mammub Mohammed Nahari**. Most of the cafés, bars, coffee shops and restaurants are located on Massawa Island. Small boats can take your from Massawa Island southwest to **Sheikh Said Island (Green Island/Isola Verde)**, a favourite picnic spot, where there are excellent snorkelling opportunities.

Taulud Island is also a mixture of Turko-Egyptian and Italian architecture. The foundations of the **Imperial Palace** or Ghibi date from the 16th century, but the main building has been rebuilt many times during its history. It is located close to the causeway to Massawa Island. Taulud also has fine examples of Italian architecture. Opposite the Orthodox **Cathedral of St Mariam** is a monument of three burnt-out tanks, preserved where they stopped in 1990, commemorating the Eritrean struggle for independence. The **Port Club** complex contains sports facilities, a small library and museum and has a restaurant with indoor and outdoor seating. **Taulud Island sights**

Another causeway joins Taulud to the mainland. The airport and main market are on the mainland opposite the Taulud causeway. North of the causeway is the city's industrial area where the cement factory and salt flats are located. Past the airport at Hitumlo is the **Tomb of Hashim el Mirgani**. **Mainland sights**

There are beach facilities a few kilometres to the north of the city at **Gurgusum** (variously spelt including Gurgasam, Gergussum and Gurgussum) which has two hotels (minibus US$1, taxi US$4). From here it is fairly close to Emberemi where the **mausoleums of Sheikh el Amin and Muhammad Ibn Ali** are located. They are important Muslim pilgrimage sites. The salt works at Salina were damaged during the recent conflict and are under repair.

A new initiative to improve local employment and generate income is the **Seawater Farm**, near Massawa. This is a joint venture run by American and Eritreans where 600 ha of desert is being transformed into a shrimp farm. Seawater is piped to the 230 holding tanks stocked with the marine crustaceans that take 6-8 months to mature. The used water is then drained into the three artificial lakes stocked with tilapia and is used to irrigate crops of sea asparagus (Salicornia) which can be eaten as a vegetable, have oil extracted from its seeds or be used as fuel briquettes when dried. The water is next used to support 200,000 mangrove trees and other sea-grown crops and an artificial wetland has been created that attracts over 150 varieties of birds, many of them endangered, to feed on the waters rich with shrimp excrement. The water is then filtered before returning to sea. The post-larval shrimp were initially flown in from Mexico, but there are plans to build a hatchery and an ice factory.

Fishing along this part of the Red Sea is said to be particularly good as it has never been seriously exploited. The area is rich in tuna, barracuda, dolphin and mero.

Taulud Island B *Dahlak*, PO Box 21, T552818, F552782. Rooms with a/c, good restaurant, bar, best hotel with 45 rooms in Massawa, near the port. **B-C** *Red Sea Hotel*, PO Box 180, T552544. Recently reopened with 50 rooms, said to be built on the site of the old *CIAAO Hotel*, this luxurious hotel has many facilities including a swimming pool and private beach. **C** *Central*, PO Box 349, T552002, F552608, located on the waterfront. Recently refitted with 24 a/c rooms, has its own restaurant, with terrace. **D** *Corallo*, PO Box 158, T552406, close to *Dahlak Hotel*. Small, basic place on the waterfront with 25 rooms, some of which are self-contained with shower and a/c. **D** *Luna*, PO Box 91, T552272. 15 rooms some with en-suite bathrooms **Sleeping**

Massawa Island D *Savoya*, T552620. Clean, wooden stairways and a good bar, though you can hear the *Torino's* disco. **D** *Torino*, T552855. Popular hotel but very noisy. **E** *Massawa*, small place with only 10 rooms, own restaurant and a pleasant roof terrace. **E** *Hotel Ghenet*,

Eritrea

communal toilets/showers, reliable water supply, clean, some rooms have fans, outdoor sleeping allowed US$1.50 per night, safe parking for motorcyles. **E** *Yussef Hotel*, close to *Hotel Ghenet*. Cheap basic hotel.

Mainland coastal strip B-C *Gurgusum Beach Hotel*,PO Box 5354, T552911, F552872, 12 km north of Massawa. Beach hotel with 89 rooms, including 2-bedroomed cottages with sitting room and bathroom. Each room has a/c and is comfortable. Indoor restaurant or snacks like burgers or sandwiches served outside in a verandah area near the sea. The main view is the open horizon over the Red Sea but some beach views are marred by a cement factory. The white sandy beach has no shade but you can hire an umbrella and sun lounger. There are a few water activities like swimming and snorkelling. Camel rides offer a pleasant excursion. The hotel gets livelier at the weekend when Asmara residents come down to the coast. **D** *Hamasien Beach Hotel*, PO Box 225, T552725. Built on a smaller scale than *Gurgusum Beach* with 31 beds.

Eating

Along the harbour front you can get simple meals of fish at reasonable prices

Cheap *Dahlak Hotel*, good standard and reasonably priced. *Kidane Zeru Restaurant* on Massawa Island is highly recommended. *Eritrea*, located on Massawa Island, across from the *Massawa Hotel*. Lively place, serving tasty food, excellent fresh fish, generous portions. *Selam*, past *Adulis Sea Food Restaurant* (now closed) at the Mosque Square, turn right and it is on the next corner. Unbeatable fish for US$2. Highly recommended.

Beaches

It is difficult to get to the beaches without a car. Trips to **Green Island** can be arranged by Dolphin. Their boat is moored at the *Dahlak*, but it is better to arrange the trip the day before at the Dolphin's Club.

Transport

Road The 120 km road from Asmara to Massawa takes you through the breathtaking scenery of Semhar province, along twisting switchback roads offering glorious panoramic views down from the hills to the Red Sea. Regular buses to Massawa run from the bus depot near the market in Asmara. There are several buses daily, leaving when they fill up. Buses for Asmara and other destinations leave from Massawa Island in front of the Public Transport Office. A taxi from Massawa to Asmara takes 3-4 hrs and costs approximately US$45.

Sea Boat: there are cargo boats that carry passengers which go to **Port Sudan**, **Jeddah** and **Suez** every 2 weeks. Fare to Suez US$115.

If you plan to go to **Jeddah** by ship, go to the shipping agent's office behind the immigration building at the port (unmarked). Ask for the ship *Alra* sheet. Costs: US$80 per person, US$100 for a motorcycle and US$300 for a car, plus US$10 for the paperwork. Only the cost of the passenger ticket is payable in Nakfa, the remainder is payable in US dollars. You have to pay on board in dollars for the vehicle. In addition you have to give the captain a US$150 deposit per person for a hotel in Jeddah and US$75 for each person if you are in transit to Suez by ship. If you are in transit overland to Jordan, you do not have to give a deposit. However, you will have to pay US$30 in cash for the paperwork, which takes hours. It is not permitted to drive your vehicle in the harbour area, a port employee will do it for you. Allow plenty of time to process the paperwork. The cost of any damage to your vehicle while being driven by the port employee is likely to be borne by you, as reported by a recent traveller.

Surplus Nakfa cannot be changed into other currencies at the bank. Small quantities of Nakfa can be used up on board the ship. A black market operates in Massawa to redress this problem. World cruising yachts frequently dock at Massawa, following the winds and escaping the monsoons. You can easily get a lift in the right season, paying little or nothing in return for helping out on the boat.

See Box on page 914 for further details of the railway's history

Train The railway from Asmara to Massawa, destroyed in the independence struggle, is being rebuilt. The workers have laid reforged rails back towards Asmara. The metal detritus of war has been used to make the rails. Over 70 km of track has been replaced as far as Ghinda. The earthworks of the Ghinda-Embatkalla 11 km section have been completed, rails have been laid and the railway stations of Hutumlo, Mai-atal, Damas and Ghinda have been repaired. Several locomotives including two 1938 Italian steam engines have been restored to working order.

The Dahlak Islands

The Dahlak Islands lie between 15–100 km predominantly east and southeast of Massawa scattered over an area of approximately 15,500 sq km. The islands are relics of an ancient carbonate platform a few hundred metres thick that grew on evaporated salt deposits. Well developed reefs occur around the islands, which also support extensive mangroves. There are some 200 islands in all though few are inhabited and many are barren. Only four of the islands are inhabited, mostly because rainfall is very sparse. *15°50'N40°10'E Colour map 1, grid B5*

Over the centuries the islands have been ruled by successive external powers. The first visitors were probably Eygptian sailors who traded incense, gold and ivory. Islamic influences and the spread of Muslim beliefs throughout the Horn of Africa are believed to have started from Dahlak Kabir from the seventh century onwards. During a period of Arab unrest the Dahlak established its own Sultanate in the early ninth century. In the 13th century Dahlak Kabir came under the influence of the Byzantine Empire. Later on the Portuguese and the Ottoman Empire used the Dahlak Islands to gain supremacy of the Red Sea. In the 1870s the Egyptians ruled the islands. During the period of Turkish occupation the Dahlak Islands were used as a centre for slave trading and transportation, thriving after the construction of the Suez Canal. More recently Dahlak Kabir was used as a military base by the Ethiopians, upon which the Israelis have built an airstrip. **History**

The waters surrounding the Dahlak Islands provide a fascinating place to visit. The shallow waters and coral gardens house a great diversity of marine life including sharks, dolphins, barracuda, manta ray, the less common dugong (nicknamed the sea cow) and several turtle species, in addition to over a thousand different brightly coloured fish. On some of the islands the rare Arabian dragon, *Draco sinicus*, is found. It lives on a diet consisting mostly of fish and small rodents. On the islands you may be able to spot soot falcons, the brown booby, spoonbill, osprey and a number of other birds. Gazelles graze among the acacias. **Wildlife** *The Red Sea changes from blue/green to vermillion during growth periods of red algae, hence its name. It has the warmest and most saline seawater in the world*

The scuba diving and snorkelling is said to be among the best in the Red Sea. Diving is reported to be best near the islands of Shumma and Nokra or in the Dahlak Channel while Dessei and Madote are said to be the best islands for snorkelling. The water temperature ranges from 24°C in February to 35°C in August. However algae and sediment resuspension contribute to turbidity that can limit visibility during certain times of the year. **Diving**

Dahlak Kabir is the largest island, approximately 643 sq km, situated roughly 50 km (three hours) from Massawa. It has a permanent population of around 1500 people, who maintain a traditional living by fishing, herding goats and camels and by diving for pearls. On the south side of the island there is an ancient necropolis. The gravestones have inscriptions with Kufic characters. Close by are the famous monumental water-collecting cisterns cut out of the coral. These were mentioned in the writings of the 19th-century English travellers, James Bruce and Henry Salt, who described them as one of the wonders of the ancient world. **Dahlak Kabir** *Colour map 1, grid B5*

In 1995 a survey of a shipwreck site off Asarka Island, south of Dahlak Kabir, led by R Pedersen, found conical amphorae of three different shapes. The site was discovered by one of the team, Doi Malingri, while snorkelling. Amphorae similar to the Asarka amphorae have been found at various places around the Mediterranean, such as Spain and Carthage, in strata dating within the range from the fourth to seventh centuries. The ceramics appear to be of Byzantine-Egyptian origin. Coins are frequently found on shipwreck sites and help to date when the ship sank. Further excavations hope to yield this information.

Recent finds (2001) of fragments of sixth-century eastern Mediterranean wine amphorae in the far southwest of England in the ancient Celtic kingdom of

Eritrea

Dumnonia – present day Cornwall and Devon – indicate the previously unrecognized extent of the Byzantine wine trade. It is probable that the Celts sold locally mined tin in return for the wine.

Sleeping **B/D** *Luul Resort Hotel*, no telephone. The *Luul Resort* is the only hotel in the archipelago to date. It has 10 bungalows, with en-suite bathrooms and a/c. The complex includes a terrace and a restaurant serving excellent fish and western Italian influenced dishes. There is a sandy beach and visits to dive sites can be arranged from here. Fast boats can bring divers to the sites of Dur Ga'am, Isratu, Dur Gella, Nakuru, Madote and Dessei (called the 'Isle of Fire' because of its volcanic origin).

Transport Yacht trips to the smaller islands can be arranged from here or through the *Dahlak Hotel*. Boat trips to the islands can be arranged from Massawa, ideally arranged in advance. *Eritrean Shipping Lines*, T552629 (Taulud Island) or T124201 (Asmara), can arrange transport. Traditional fishing vessels called *sambuchi* can also be used to visit the islands. These vessels have a variable safety record as some are poorly constructed. Ensure you have sufficient water. Diving and snorkelling equipment can be hired from several places in Massawa.

Prior to visiting the Dahlak Islands a permit costing $30 for 3 days must be purchased from the *Eritrean Shipping Lines* office which is then verified at the Ministry of Tourism office. Tour operators normally do the paperwork on your behalf. The exception is for visits to Sheikh Said Island/Green Island/Isola Verde where no permit is required.

South of Massawa

Adulis
Colour map 1, grid B5

The coastal strip south of Massawa has numerous valleys carved out by seasonal rivers. The remains of the ancient port of Adulis are located 60 km south of Massawa, northeast of the small town of Zula.

In the early first millennium AD a new state, the kingdom of Axum that included most of Tigray and Eritrea arose on the Tigrean plateau. Its origins are unclear but by the fourth to sixth century Axum was one of the most powerful Christian kingdoms in the periphery of the Byzantine Empire. Axumite kings had their own coinage, and controlled the trade from the African hinterland to the Red Sea. Adulis was the wealthy main port of the Axumite kingdom attracting traders of ivory, spices and slaves from as far as Egypt to India. Adulis fell into ruin sometime in the seventh century. While the exact date of the city's demise is unknown, its decline is believed to have resulted from an attack by Islamic forces in AD 640. The Byzantines surrendered Egypt to the Arabs in AD 641, ending the Mediterranean connection with Axum, which in turn declined mainly due to the Islamic expansion along the Red Sea in the seventh century.

Archaeologists have uncovered the remains of Adulis 4 km from the shore, covering an area of 500 x 400 m. Buildings made of black volcanic stone, marble columns and walls several metres in height have been identified. The *Adulis amphorae*, believed to be of Byzantine origin, were excavated in the early 20th century and are now held in the National Museum in Asmara. This is believed to be the oldest archaeological site in Eritrea, little of which has been excavated.

Prehistoric stone tools Close to the village of **Abdur**, on the Gulf of Zula, ancient stone tools including Palaeolithic hand axes and obsidian flakes have been discovered in a fossil coral terrace. The age of the stone tools was estimated by radioactive dating of the fossil corals found closest to them. The once submerged 125,000 year-old coral barrier reef which extends for 10 km is now between 5-12 m above sea level. An international team including Eritreans, Canadians and Americans published their findings in May 2000. It is the earliest evidence to date for coastal marine occupation, possibly indicating how early humans migrated out of Africa. So far no hominoid remains have been found but the findings suggest that the early humans ate crabs, scallops and oysters. The migration of these people is believed to have been the result of climate change, when glacial cycles reduced the available fresh water in central Africa.

This remote area that lies east of the Gulf of Zula is renowned for volcanoes and wild- **The Bure** life. Gazelle, ostrich, jackels and hamadryas baboons are relatively common and the **Peninsula** rare wild ass can also occasionally be seen in the lowlands of the peninsula. Mangroves are found along the coastal strip, further inland the flora includes acacias and savannah. A wide variety of birds can be seen here.

South of Adulis is the Danakil Depression which lies 116 m below sea level and is one **Danakil** of the hottest and most inhospitable places on earth with the temperature reaching up **Depression** to 50°C. Vast plains of salt, relentless strong hot winds, volcanoes and unusual mineral *Colour map 1, grid B5* formations contribute to making this area unique. Danakil lies in the stretch of desert called **Denkalia**, the land of the hardy and ferocious Afar tribesmen. The majority of *Travellers into the* Denkalia lies within Ethiopia. This is not easy travelling territory, as it consists mainly *Danakil Depression* of volcanic rock and mountain. South of Mersa Fatuma, camel caravans travel weekly *need to use an* to a Sunday market in a small village called Badda. Nearby is found **Lake Badda**, a vol- *experienced guide* canic crater-lake with turquoise blue waters. *and bring sufficient*

quantities of water

In 1912 the Italians built a short railway next to the road from Baddo to Adaito, 42 km inland, where they were mining potash. It was a 600 mm narrow-gauge railway system known as Decauville, named after its inventor, a French engineer, that could be laid directly on the ground. Mostly used for yards or hand-pulled carts it could easily be dismantled and transported. When the potash mine was worked out the line was closed in 1929.

In 1997, a 1,000,000-year-old adult skull blending features associated with both **Buia man** *Homo erectus* and *Homo sapiens* was excavated by E Abbate working with an international group of paleo-anthropologists, near the village of Buia in the Afar region of Eritrea. The almost complete cranium, plus two teeth and fragments of the pelvis, were found in the sediment of an ancient lake. The skull is long and oval, pointed at the back, with massive brow ridges and a small brain capacity showing nascent modern human morphology. Found nearby in the same sediments were the remains of elephants, hippopotami and rhinoceroses. Prior to its discovery the oldest known fossils with modern human traits were the 600,000-year-old fossils known as *Homo heidelbergensis* from Bodo, Ethiopia.

Assab

Assab (also spelt Aseb) used to be Ethiopia's main port. Its geographical location *13°0'N 42°40'E* isolates it from the remainder of Eritrea, but it is of great economic importance. It is a *Colour map 1, grid B6* large, modern port, with an oil refinery built by the former Soviet Union. Assab is close to the border with Djibouti, and is best reached by air from Asmara. It also serves as a centre for scuba diving and deep-sea fishing.

The town centre is divided into two main parts – Assab Kebir and Assab Seghir (big and little Assab respectively). There are some pleasant uncrowded beaches. The town has a few hotels and restaurants, as well as a bank, post office, and even an open-air cinema. Inland there are large salt flats.

The weather is hot from June to September, usually 40°C. Even though there is a sea breeze, the temperature at night rarely falls below 20°C. For the rest of the year, the climate is more moderate.

A *The Port Club*, located down by the beach, T661114. Rooms are clean, with hot water and **Sleeping** a/c. **B** *Agip Motel*. Rather uninspired, but a reasonable standard and good restaurant. **C** *Albergo Assab*. Old colonial-style, bar, restaurant, some rooms a/c. **C-D** *Zerai Deres Hotel* near the port offers reasonable value. **D** *Nino's*, near the petrol station in town. **E** *Asmara*, on the opposite corner to the petrol station. This is a small place with communal showers.

Eating **Expensive** *The Port Club*, wide-ranging menu, from seafood to hamburgers, in pleasant surroundings. **Cheap** *Aurora*, down by the port. Good reputation for Italian dishes.

Transport **Air** All *Ethiopian Airways* services are suspended. *Air Eritrea* operates a weekly air service between Asmara and Assab on Tue. **Road** The distance between Asmara and Assab is considerable (1,100 km), the roads are in poor shape and transport is very meagre. **Bus**: There is a lengthy bus service to Massawa, prone to being cancelled at short notice. It is advisable to go well prepared with plenty of water and food. It is an amazing journey. There were regular buses from Addis Ababa, 750 km away, but these services are currently suspended.

South of Asmara

The southern highlands are the most densely populated region of Eritrea. From Asmara, there are two main routes heading south for Ethiopia.

*The first of these takes you through a number of villages, **Zigib**, 20 km south of the capital, in the forefront of **Mount Ad Hannes** (2,850 m). A further 30 km away, you pass through **Afelba**, notable for its two churches, Orthodox and Catholic.*

The town of Adi Qayeh, see below, was shelled in May 2000 and all the inhabitants were evacuated. From here to the border the countryside was occupied and ransacked during the recent fighting, and now forms part of the United Nations buffer zone. The extent of the damage to the historical sites has not been assessed, but visiting many of these ancient sites is currently suspended – uncleared land mines remain.

Adi-Qayeh

Adi Qayeh, also spelt Adik'eyih and Adi Keyeh, is the provincial capital, and from where you can visit significant archaeological sites, such as **Toconda** and **Qohaito**.

There are rock paintings at several locations in the area around Adi Qayeh. A guide is necessary to best explore the ruins and rock art, or negotiate permission to visit relics on private land from the local farmers, and is best arranged here. There are quite a few places to stay at Adi Qayeh, some more basic than others. If visiting the ancient sites bring plenty of water as well as sun protection cream/hat. Some of the ancient relics lie on cultivated land and permission should be sought from the farmer before visiting them.

Toconda **Toconda** (Takonda) There are about eight ancient columns carved in the Axumite style, both standing upright and lying on the ground, including some short segments, that are located in cultivated fields near the village of Toconda, 4 km south of Adi Qayeh. The pillars are thought to have supported the canopy of a royal throne. A lengthy Ge'ez inscription is carved into a nearby rock. As this site has not been excavated it is probable that many other relics lie buried. Nearby are rock paintings. There is no tourist accommodation here.

The plain of Qohaito, also known as Kohaito/Cohaito (that possibly contained the site of the city of Koloe/Coloe in ancient times), lies 12 km southeast of Adi Qayeh and 120 km south of Asmara. There are precipitous descents on either side and looking to the south affords views of the highest peak in Eritrea, Mount Ambasoira, 3,000 m. The descent can be made on foot or by camel for maximum impact.

The second most important city after Axum during the Axumite period, Qohaito was believed to be an important staging post between Axum and Adulis, the ancient Axumite port. Qohaito was three days trek inland from Adulis and it has been suggested that this was the route used by ivory traders in the fourth century, underpinning the wealth of the city where ancient royal rulers resided. Qohaito continued to thrive until between the 6th and 8th century AD, after which it was apparently abandoned. The small village of the same name contains some dwellings, a school, a new mosque and an Orthodox church.

Qohaito
Altitude: 2,700 m
Colour map 1, grid B5

The ancient ruins of Qohaito, measuring 15 km x 2½-3 km, some dating to pre-Axumite times, have not been fully excavated. It is estimated that only 20% of the ruins have been subjected to archaeological scrutiny. There are several standing columns, the ruined remains of several large buildings that were possibly palaces, temples or mausoleums. Four upright columns, one surmounted by a four-sided capital, mark the **Temple of Mariam Wakiro**, believed to be an early Christian church. This temple, built to a rectangular floor plan, possibly predated the Christian era. The surrounding area is strewn with columns, huge masonry blocks and rubble, the remains of several other temples.

Further north is the underground '**Egyptian Tomb**', so called because of its dimensions, hewn out of sandstone. The tomb was opened in 1894 and reportedly held the remains of over 80 people. It is a Christian tomb with a Coptic cross carved into the adjacent wall.

Safira's dam, alleged to have been the bathing place of the Queen of Sheba, is over 60 m long, constructed of beautifully dressed masonry blocks. It is believed to be more than 1000 years old and is still in use today. On one of the walls of the dam there is a lengthy inscription in the ancient religious language of Ge'ez. Ge'ez is believed to be akin to the Sabaean language brought to the area from Southern Arabia. The Ethiopian influence gained ascendancy over the structure and the result was the Ge'ez language, which is the ancestor of several of the modern Semitic languages of the region. Safira's dam, with its protruding headers and overall construction, is reminiscent of the great dam at Marib in the Yemen.

Rock paintings The cave of Adi Alauti houses some of the most spectacular rock art in this region. To reach there requires a guide and involves a walk from Qohaito along a pathway overlooking the gorge – best avoided if you have no head for heights. Among the inscriptions there is a long ochre and white pigment frieze of animals, measuring 5 x 2 m, depicting oxen, camels and gazelles. Another overhanging rock shelter near Qohaito contains over 100 painted figures of animals.

Transport Qohaito is not served by public transport. Take the bus south from Adi Qayeh for 11 km, from where it is another 10 km trek.

Kaskase (Cascase) is one of the most important pre-Axumite sites in Eritrea. There are four stelae (obelisks) believed to date from the third century approximately 250-300 m from the road in a cultivated field. One stele is intact, its upper edges smoothed off. The second stele is broken into three pieces, a third lies apart from the second, broken into five sections. It has a Ge'ez inscription. The remaining stele lies in seven segments. On this unexcavated site there are also many pottery remains.
■ *Kaskase lies south of Adi Qayeh, approximately 10 km north of Senafe. There is no tourist accommodation nearby.*

Kaskase

This is the last town on the Eritrean side of the border, the crossing being about 25 km further. The remains of the ancient Axumite city of **Metara** (also spelt Matara/Matera/Metera) can be seen about 1½ km southwest of the town of Senafe, 20 km from Qohaito and 136 km south of Asmara. Metara is the name of the village at the base of a mountain and on the surrounding plain are found archaeological

Senafe
Altitude: 2,400 m
Colour map 1, grid B5

Eritrea

remains covering an area of about 10 ha. The area has beautiful scenery and the ruins are known as *Zala Kaleb* (the ruins of King Kaleb) by the local people. There is a legend that the Emperor of Axum marched with his army to wreak vengeance on Metara's townspeople for their ill-treatment of a Tsadqan (saint). On seeing the approaching army the townsfolk fled. The king ordered a tunnel to be dug, and later destroyed the population of Belew Kalew. Two tunnel entrances in the towns can still be seen but the distance from Axum to Metara is approximately 100 km so the accuracy of the legend cannot be verified.

A 5-m stele stands beside the road at Metara, and at the top there is an inscription of a disc and a crescent dated to the third century. At eye level there is a four-line inscription in Ge'ez. The stele was moved from its original site on the hill and broke into two pieces at some stage, later to be repaired by the Italians with two unattractive metal staples. Recent excavations nearby by the Ethiopian Institute of Archaeology to the west of the stele have identified the remains of four edifices. These walls with alternating projecting and receding steps are in the classical Axumite architectural tradition. Excavations have also revealed evidence of a fairly large city of several districts, with 2 m high dry stone interspersed with slate foundation walls in many of the buildings, and evidence of several villas. Other findings of earlier civilizations include Roman-inspired jewellery and coins, as well as Persian-Sassanian pottery and Egyptian relics. In 1963 a bronze vase was found containing a remarkable group of gold *objet d'art* including a brooch, 3 chains, 14 Roman coins and 2 crosses, one of which had been gem encrusted. The bronze vase is on display at the Archaeological Museum in Addis Ababa.

In the present village of Metara at the foot of the mountain there is a baobab tree with 12 branches. Legend has it that only one branch of the tree flowers at any one time in rotation for about a month, while the other branches are denuded of leaves.

Debre Libanos monastery   To the south of Senafe is the village of **Hamm** and the monastery of **Debre Libanos** which is the oldest monastery in Eritrea (not to be confused with the 13th-century monastery near the Blue Nile Gorge with the same name). The site of the monastery at Shemezana was reputed to have been chosen by Abba Yem'ata of Guh, who was one of the Nine Saints, accredited with introducing Christianity to Eritrea and Ethiopia from Syria. The monastery, believed to date from the sixth century and still an important ecclesiastical site, lies in a steep valley which takes about 1-1½ hours to descend and 1½-2 hours to ascend. You need to be both fit and sure-footed to visit this monastery which also has an important library containing ancient religious scripts. The villagers from Hamm will be happy to act as guides to reach it. Nearby are a number of mummified bodies, believed to date from the fourth century. Further archaeological excavations are being carried out in this area.

NB This area is close to the disputed Eritrean-Ethiopian border where there was heavy fighting in the 1998-2000 conflict. It remains unclear whether any of the ancient sites were destroyed, and there is concern that many landmine fields were laid.

The second route south to the border takes you via **Mendefera** (previously known as Adi Ugri), provincial capital of Seraye. The most notable building in Mendefera is the enormous Roman Catholic Cathedral School. East of it is the very large Orthodox church of St Ghiorgis (George). There are a number of hotels to choose from if you are planning to stay overnight – the **E** *Semhar* is probably the best. The only other town of any significant size before the border is **Adi Qala**, also spelt Adikwala, where the plateau ends. The border crossing is at Ghundet, by the river Mareb.

Background

History

Eritrea's history is a long and splendid one. During the third and fourth centuries AD, it was part of the kingdom of Axum which spread from Meroe in Sudan right across the Red Sea to Yemen. The capital of Axum was in the highlands of Tigray (now a region in Ethiopia), and the main port was at Adulis (close to the present day port of Zula) in Eritrea. This kingdom was based on trade across the Red Sea and was founded by Semitic people originally from Arabia. Christianity became the predominant faith of Axum, introduced through contact with traders.

By the sixth century AD the Persian Empire expanded and with it came the expansion of Islam. In 710 AD Muslims destroyed Adulis and the ancient kingdom of Axum declined until it was reduced to a small Christian enclave. For the next few centuries, the region settled into being a remote, isolated community only re-emerging in the early 16th century as Abyssinia. The Abyssinian Kingdom covered the Ethiopian and Eritrean highlands ruled by kings and peopled by Christian Tigrinyans and remaining fairly isolated. This community had little or no contact with the lowlands of the region that was home to predominantly Muslim communities.

This period in Eritrea's history is highly contentious. The Ethiopians claimed Eritrea had been an integral part of historic Ethiopia but though there are some common practices and religious beliefs between Eritreans and Ethiopia, these ties do not extend throughout Eritrea. In fact, large parts of Eritrea, it would seem, were linked to other empires. The Ottoman Empire and Egypt had relations with the north and east part of the country, and various Sudanic Empires to the west and northwest have had their influence.

19th-century expansion

Abyssinia was subject to the expansionism of the Egyptians and some European powers (French, Italian, and British). In the early part of the 19th century, Ali Pasha invaded Sudan and gradually pushed on the Western Lowlands of present-day Eritrea. By mid-century, European interest in the area was also increasing. The British had a consulate in Massawa, and the French already had a presence. Italian missionaries were established in Keren.

Emperor Tewodros II, who ruled Abyssinia from 1855-68, also had to deal with rebel forces in Tigray with Ras Kassa as their ruler. Tewodros was defeated in 1868 after the British General Sir Robert Napier had landed in Zula to release the Consul and other prisoners held by the Emperor. After Tewodros's defeat, Ras Kassa was crowned Emperor Yohannes IV in 1872. Yohannes's forces won a significant battle against the Egyptians at Gura in 1875. From this victory, Yohannes's foremost General, Ras Alula, became governor of the province of Hamasien, and prince of Eritrea.

Italian influence

The first Italian mission in Abyssinia was at Adua in 1840, under Father Giuseppe Sapeto. He was the agent through which the Italian government bought up pieces of land near Assab, initially on behalf of the Rubattino Shipping Company. But as the European 'Scramble for Africa' gathered pace, the Italian government took over the area in 1882 and began to administer it directly. They also ousted the Egyptians from Massawa on the coast. However, expansion further inland soon led to clashes with Emperor Yohannes. In 1887, Ras Alula's forces inflicted a heavy defeat on the Italians at Dogali, forcing them to retreat.

This was a significant victory for Yohannes, who was also facing a number of other threats on different fronts at the same time – not only the Italians, but the Dervishes, and, in Shoa, Menelik, an increasingly disloyal general. Yohannes was eventually killed after being captured in battle against the Dervishes at Gallabat. Following his death, Ras Alula withdrew to Tigray. This allowed Menelik to be named Yohannes's successor in 1889 with substantial Italian backing, instead of the natural heir, Ras Mangasha.

Eritrea

The Italians then moved rapidly, taking Keren in July 1889 and Asmara one month later. Menelik had signed the Treaty of Uccialli with the Italians the same year, detailing the areas each controlled. Just four years later, Menelik renounced the treaty over a dispute arising from further Italian expansionist attempts. There were military clashes, including the historic battle of Adua in 1896, in which Menelik decisively defeated the Italian forces. However, in the face of sizeable Italian reinforcements, Menelik signed a peace treaty. Italy then began establishing colonial rule in the areas it controlled.

Colonial rule The Italians used a system of indirect rule through local chiefs at the beginning of the 20th century. The first decade or so concentrated on expropriation of land from indigenous owners. The colonial power also embarked on the construction of the railway from Massawa to Asmara. Fascist rule in the 1920s and the spirit of 'Pax Italiana' gave a significant boost to the number of Italians in Eritrea, adding further to loss of land by the local population.

In 1935, Italy succeeded in over-running much of Abyssinia, and decreed that Eritrea, Italian Somaliland and Abyssinia were to be known as Italian East Africa. The development of regional transport links at this time round Asmara, Assab and Addis produced a rapid but short-lived economic boom.

However, there began to be clashes between Italian and British forces in 1940. Under General Platt, the British captured Agordat in 1941, taking Keren and Asmara later the same year. As Britain did not have the capacity to take over the full running of the territory, they left some Italian officials in place. One of the most significant changes under the British was the lifting of the colour bar which the Italians had operated. Eritreans could now legally be employed as civil servants. In 1944, with changing fortunes in the Second World War, Britain withdrew most of its forces from Eritrea. The post-war years and economic recession led to comparatively high levels of urban unemployment and unrest.

Ethiopian rule Before the British withdrew in 1952 the fate of Eritrea was left in the balance. It was known that the British favoured partition – the north and west of Eritrea to Sudan, the rest to Ethiopia, which suited Haile Selassie. After initial presentations on the possible future of Eritrea, in 1949 the UN established a Commission of Enquiry with the task of finding out what Eritreans wanted for their own future. For a number of reasons, countries represented on the Commission could not agree on recommendations, but went along with the view that the Christian majority in Eritrea favoured unity with Ethiopia.

At the same time, Ethiopia had been strengthening its ties with the United States, even sending troops to fight with the Americans in the Korean War in 1950. In December that year, the UN finally declared Eritrea an autonomous unit federated to Ethiopia. Haile Selassie saw to it that the first three governors of the federated unit were related to him. In 1959, Tigrinya and Arabic were forbidden as teaching languages, and replaced with Amharic. Student protests and boycotts ensued, but were repressed.

For the next 40 years, Eritrea's plight was virtually ignored by the international community. Frustration at the lack of room for political manoeuvre finally resulted in the launch of an armed struggle in 1961. Ethiopia formally annexed Eritrea in 1962 as another 'province'.

The Eritrean Liberation Movement, one of the earliest opposition groupings, was formed mainly by exiles in Sudan. The founder members were all Muslims, but they gained some support from the Christian population too. However this group came into conflict with the Eritrean Liberation Front (ELF) based in Cairo. The latter, consisting of old leaders of the pro-independence opposition in the 1940s, gained more support from Eritreans despite being less well organized.

In 1965 the ELF restructured its forces into four command zones, adding a fifth zone, known as the 'Christian zone', one year later. The fifth zone covered the province of Hamasien, including Asmara.

There followed a period of bitter and destructive faction fighting, out of which resulted a coalition in 1972, comprising the Eritrean Liberation Force (another ELF) and the People's Liberation Front (PLF). At the start, they were only 500 strong. The three movements also clashed. In October 1974, the ELF fought the ELF-PLF while they were both launching an

Thief-seekers

In traditional areas of Eritrea, if someone discovers he has had possessions stolen, he will hire the services of a lieba shai. This is a boy thief-seeker, trained for the purpose and retained by a local elder. The thief-seeker fasts for a night, takes a draught of drugged milk, and smokes a pipe containing some special herbs. This potent cocktail, on an empty stomach, causes the boy to collapse, and the elder intones over the inert form until he recovers and reels away, sometimes in quite a frenzy. The elder follows, holding on to a sash round the boy's waist. Care is taken to avoid water, which will break the spell. The boy leads the elder to the stolen articles, and identifies the thief by breathing in great gasps, kneeing the culprit, and grasping him by the neck. The thief-seeker is then given

beer and bread to make him vomit and throw off the effects of the drugs.

A wrong-doer can thwart the thief-seeker by drenching himself in water, which makes him proof against the charm. Another ploy is to make as if to jump off a precipice, which the thief-seeker will copy unless the elder can manage to haul him back in time.

Sons of poor families are chosen to be thief-seekers and are trained by being drugged and set to find previously hidden goods. The powers disappear with the onset of puberty, but there are long-term effects such as 'weakness in the head'; ex-thief-seekers have reputations as 'drunkards and ravers', and alcohol induces wild staring eyes, a vacant expression and physical weakness.

---

attack on Asmara. After some negotiations, they fought together in a second attack in January 1975. Later that year, the PLF's leader entered into an alliance with the other ELF, although his forces did not support him. The fighters of the ELF-PLF coalition then renamed themselves as the EPLF. The different groups continued to clash for the next decade.

Despite these internal problems, the Eritrean guerrilla forces (estimated to number 20,000) managed to win considerable victories against the occupying Ethiopians. They were close to final victory in early 1978, but were thwarted by the Soviet Union's crucial intervention in the form of military aid for Mengistu's régime in Ethiopia.

The EPLF and ELF forces withdrew to the north. The EPLF held its first congress in 1977, and from that time on their ranks were strengthened by ELF fighters who had defected. By the end of the 1970s, the ELF was no longer a viable fighting force.

Through most of the war, Ethiopia occupied the southern part of Eritrea. The EPLF had to settle in the inhospitable northern hills towards the Sudanese border. These hills became a safe haven for the families of soldiers and the orphans and disabled. Consequently, much of the region around Afabet and Nakfa in Sahel province became home to makeshift homes, schools, orphanages, hospitals, factories, printers, and bakeries in an attempt to live life as normally as possible under extraordinary conditions. Most structures were built either into the ground or in caves to avoid being bombed by Ethiopian jets. Steep narrow areas were chosen as they were the hardest for the jets to negotiate.

The Ethiopian army under Haile Mariam Mengistu (an army officer who deposed Haile Selassie in 1974) intensified the war against Eritrea, but it was easily defeated in 1991 after Mengistu fell from power.

The war had a devastating effect on Eritrea. Around 60,000 people lost their lives, an estimated 50,000 children were orphaned, and 60,000 people were left handicapped. However, there is now great optimism with people pulling together to rebuild the country. The 100,000 strong army (without pay) helped with reconstruction and Eritreans who fled during the fighting are returned with their skills.

In May 1993, Eritrea separated from Ethiopia and became an independent sovereign state.

Tension with Ethiopia increased with the introduction of Eritrea's own currency, the Nakfa, in November 1997, and erupted, in May 1998 in territorial disputes, which developed into a full-scale war.

The war with Ethiopia has puzzled outsiders. The small area in dispute is of no economic significance, the communities on both sides directly involved are Tigrean, as are the presidents of both Eritrea and Ethiopia who collaborated so constructively over Eritrea's independence. The war finally ended with a ceasefire in May 2000 followed by a peace treaty in December. However, the war has done Eritrea enormous damage, with at least 19,000 Eritreans killed, and over US$ 3 bn of damage incurred through destruction and looting, particularly at Assab port in the south. Lost production through the disruption caused by the war cost at least US 100 mn, and the direct cost of the war probably another US$ 200 mn. The lucrative transit trade to Ethiopia through Assab is unlikely to resume as Ethiopia looks to Djibouti as a conduit for its exports and imports. Eritrea's international image as a pragmatic small nation reconstructing its economy and giving priority to peaceful development has suffered a severe setback.

Modern Eritrea

Politics The Eritrean Liberation Movement was founded in 1958 to liberate Eritrea from Ethiopian rule. It was succeeded by the Eritrean Liberation Front (ELF) in 1961. Clashes of ideology soon developed between its members who were from both the Christian highlands and the Muslim eastern lowland towns. A group left the ELF to set up what became known as the Eritrean People's Liberation Front (EPLF). Between 1972-74 a civil war developed. By the early 1980s the different factions came together to form a disciplined political and military organization.

Throughout the 1970s and 1980s new recruits joined the EPLF as Ethiopian forces terrorized resistance groups. By 1978 the EPLF had retreated into the hillsides of northern Eritrea with thousands of young supporters, both male and female. From then on, the EPLF steadily pushed back Ethiopian forces, capturing military equipment in the process. As they grew in numbers and military strength, so they turned from a guerrilla force into a regular army. In 1990 the EPLF captured the strategically important port of Massawa, and they entered Asmara, now the capital of Eritrea, in 1991.

At a conference held in London in 1991 the Ethiopian People's Revolutionary Democratic Front (EPRDF), who were now in control of Ethiopia having ousted Mengistu and were sympathetic to Eritrean nationalist aspirations, accepted the EPLF as the provisional government of Eritrea. So began the final process towards independence and international legitimation of Eritrea as a country in its own right.

In April 1993 a referendum was held in which 1,102,410 Eritreans voted; 99.8% endorsed national independence and on 28 May Eritrea became the 182nd member of the UN. Thus it is now eligible to receive international aid to help reconstruct and develop its shattered economy though it is very proud of its self-reliance. The Head of State is Isaias Afewerki, formerly secretary-general of the EPLF. Since establishing a provisional government in 1991, Eritrea has been a stable and peaceful political entity, with almost all political groups represented in the transitional government.

A new constitution was adopted in May 1997, with a 150 seat transitional National Assembly, with 75 seats allocated to the People's Front for Democracy and Justice (PFDJ), formerly the EPLF. 60 seats are to be filled by members of the Constituent Assembly, and 15 by Eritreans resident overseas. Tigrinya and Arabic are working languages, but there will be no official language. English is the language of instruction in secondary schools.

Regional relations, however, have not been so smooth. In particular, relations with neighbouring Sudan have become strained. Eritrea severed diplomatic ties with Sudan in December 1994, in response to allegations that the Sudanese government was backing the 'Eritrean Islamic Jihad', a rebel grouping which has been trying to destabilize the country. A number of minor incidents had been reported in the Western Lowlands region.

Sudan for its part, accused Eritrea of supporting a Sudanese opposition group in exile in Asmara. It seems clear that Eritrea is prepared to support Sudanese rebels fighting the National Islamic Front government in Khartoum. Complicating the issue are the 300,000 Eritrea refugees in Sudan. Eritrea is pressing for their return, which is being obstructed by Sudan, partly motivated by a desire to continue to benefit from the aid directed to the support of the refugees.

Eritrea has accused Sudan of an assassination plot, and it is reported that Libya is attempting to mediate.

In 1999 the Eritreans and Sudanese reached a diplomatic settlement and the Sudanese Embassy reopened in Asmara. Sudan took 70,000 Eritrean refugees who were fleeing the fighting around Barentu and the surrounding area in May 2000.

There has also been a dispute with Yemen over the uninhabited Zaquar-Hanish islands situated due north of Assab in the Red Sea. The dispute has gone to international arbitration. The islands are thought to have a strategic importance, and there is always the issue of any off-shore minerals.

An unusual gift

When contemplating matrimony, was the practice of the Afar, formerly known as the Danakil, to acquire an extra set of male genitals to present to their betrothed.

The most serious development has been the dispute with Ethiopia. The introduction in November 1997 of the Nakfa to replace the Ethiopian Birr, previously in use, has added complications to cross border trade. Ethiopia retaliated by demanding that all transactions be settled in hard currency, a problem for Eritrea which had limited foreign exchange reserves. More than anything, this has brought home to Ethiopia the implications of being landlocked now that Eritrea was independent.

The Italians established a border with the then Abyssinia when they colonized Eritrea after 1885. However, when Ethiopia annexed Eritrea in 1962, five small areas were reallocated from Eritrea to Ethiopian provinces. Eritrea wanted the Italian borders recognized, and both sides made efforts to occupy the disputed zone. Armed raids began in May 1998 and Ethiopia has bombed the airports at Asmara, Massawa and Assab and civilian targets in Barentu, Forto and Adi Qayeh, while Eritrea bombed the airport and civilian areas in Makale. After a lull in late 1998 when diplomatic initiatives were being pursued, fighting broke out again in early 1999. Ethiopia expelled citizens of Eritrean descent and seized their assets. Eritrea did likewise. The loss to Eritrea of income from goods in transit to Ethiopia through the port of Assab has been considerable. Ethiopia and Eritrea agreed a ceasefire agreement in June 2000 and signed a peace agreement in December 2000. The United Nations authorized sending a peace-keeping force to the Ethiopian-Eritrean border area in September 2000, and the first troops arrived in January 2001.

It is uncertain how the long-term relationship between the two countries will develop. Large numbers of Eritreans are internally displaced and a substantial area is out of bounds due to the formation of a buffer zone and the presence of land mines.

The contested zones are without any economic significance, and the dispute has aptly been described as 'two bald men fighting over a comb'.

Economy

As Eritrea is such a new nation, data is very sparse, and it will be a while before the necessary surveys are undertaken to give a more complete picture of economic life and performance.

Even such basic statistics as the level of population are not reliable – there were 2,700,000 people enumerated in the most recent Ethiopian census in 1984, but it is not clear what the overall impact of eventual independence and the recent border war have been. Many thousands of people have crossed the border. The natural rate of population increase has been around 3.1% a year Estimates suggest the population was around 4,100,000 in 2000. Urbanization at 10% is low by African standards, but this again has been affected by the war, with people fleeing the towns and reverting to subsistence production in the countryside. Population density at 30 persons per sq km is close to the African average, but needs to be assessed in the light of much of the southern coastal strip being arid.

The economy, with GDP estimated at US$ 755 mn in 1999, is small, with most activity being subsistence agriculture on small-scale family farms. Income per head is US$ 185, and this puts Eritrea firmly in the low income group of world economies. The low levels of income reflect the struggle for existence that successive wars have brought about.

Exports totalled US$ 95 mn in 1996 and comprised food (30%), minerals (35%) and manufactures (30%).

Imports were US$ 549 mn, and the gap between this and export receipts is covered by tourism earnings, aid, and remittances from Eritrean expatriates. Imports comprised food (22%), fuel (8%), machinery and transport equipment (36%).

Almost all the labour force is involved in agriculture in one form or another, as growing food has been the key to survival. The issue of land is being dealt with by the new Land Proclamation, which came into operation in 1996. This invests land ownership rights in the government, allowing for land to be allocated to Eritrean nationals for the span of their lifetime. The same land can also be passed on to their children.

Now the war with Ethiopia is over, Eritrea's future prospects are reasonably promising, and growth is expected to rebound to close to the levels being achieved before the war, despite the loss of most of the transit trade to Ethiopia. Prior to the war, growth averaged 4% a year 1996-98. The war caused a fall in GDP of 12% in 1999. The government is keen to encourage foreign investment, and there are inflows of capital from Eritreans overseas. Eritrea is in the enviable position of not being saddled with a massive external debt to service.

The government is committed to a market economy. Privatizations have taken place, comprising mostly small enterprises in furniture, timber, hotels and the like and further privatizations are being contemplated. Telecommunications and Eritrean Airlines are the most substantial of the planned privatizations.

International help is quite generous, and at US$50 per head, aid receipts are above the African average. Saudi Arabia has funded a US$35 mn electricity project. The Chinese have constructed a US$10 mn pharmaceutical factory. Several companies have taken up licences to prospect for minerals, mainly gold, copper and potash in the south and southwest highlands. Rift Resources of Canada is reported to have discovered gold at Adi Meshela. A US company is engaged on a US$29 mn oil exploration exercise. At Mount Adid, an extinct volcano about 100 km southwest of Massawa, there is a geothermal project to generate electricity. At present, all Eritrea's power comes from diesel generators.

There were some 200,000 arrivals in 1995, of which half are thought to be tourists and the other half returning Eritreans. Hotels are being refurbished and there is a US$300 mn casino project for the Dahlak Islands.

An independent currency, the Nakfa was introduced in November 1997, and has hampered trade with Ethiopia who have insisted on payments being settled in hard currency. The territorial dispute that erupted in June 1998 led to a cessation of trade with Ethiopia, and this will be an impediment to economic progress as well as a colossal waste of resources.

Over the past few years the government has asked all but six Aid providers to leave, including all religious organizations and Oxfam. This reflects President Afewerki's aim to avoid external reliance.

Culture

People

In 1984, the Ethiopian census put the population of Eritrea at 2,700,000, though the years of the independence struggle with Ethiopia have affected this figure. Around 60,000 people were believed to have been killed and at least 750,000 fled the country into neighbouring Sudan and Ethiopia prior to 1993. Significant Eritrean communities were established throughout Europe and North America, and some of these fugitives will have returned home. In addition it is difficult to gauge the overall impact of movements of Eritreans and Ethiopians back to their homelands as a result of the 1998-2000 war. Bearing all this in mind, best estimates put the population at 4,100,000 in 2000.

Eritrea was a creation of the colonial era whose boundaries were drawn up in the late 19th century with little consideration for the customs and cultures of different groups of people, consequently the country is home to nine different ethnic groups. There are two main groups, the Tigrinya making up about 50% of the population, and the Tigre who account for a further 34% of Eritreans. The two groups are closely associated, the language

Shamma

This is the dress worn widely in both Ethiopia and Eritrea by both men and women. It is made from handwoven cotten, and is very delicate in texture. Two pieces, one being about 1 sq m, and the other 2 m x 1 m, make up the garment. The borders of the fabric are decorated with bright borders, sometimes with linen and silk interleaved in the weave. The larger piece is wrapped round to make a dress, with the border making up the hemline. The smaller piece is used as a scarf or to make a hood over the head.

of both groups having originated from the ancient Ethiopian language of Ge'ez. The Tigrinya are mainly Christians (Orthodox or Roman Catholic) who live in the high plateau of the country. They have much in common with their neighbouring highlanders in the Tigray province of Ethiopia having similar language, faith and customs. The majority of Tigrinya are agriculturalists cultivating *tef* (a local type of grain), maize, wheat, millet and barley as well as a variety of different vegetables. Some people also herd animals as a supplementary form of income.

The Tigre are Muslims who live in the Western Lowlands, the northern hills and the coastal regions of the country. Their way of life is primarily as nomadic pastoralists. This group is made up of many different clans including the Beni Amer, the largest clan who have historical ties with the Beja of Sudan.

Eritrea's other Muslim peoples include the Danakil herdsmen who live in the desert regions in the south and who are closely associated with the Afar in Djibouti. There are also the Rashayda of Arabic origin and the Tukrir who are originally from Nigeria. The Tukrir set off from Nigeria on an overland pilgrimage to Mecca but came to Eritrea and decided to settle there. The smaller ethnic groups include the Afar, the Bilen, Hedareb, the Kunama, the Nara (or Baria), the Rashayda and the Saho.

Arabic and Tigrinya are the two working languages, but in total there are nine languages indigenous to Eritrea's nine nationalities – Afar, Arabic, Bilen, Kunama, Nara, Saho, Tigre, Tigrinya and ToBedawi. Italian is commonly spoken among the older generation. Arabic is widely spoken throughout the coastal areas of the country reflecting Eritrea's long trade associations with countries across the Red Sea.

Land and environment

Geography

Eritrea is 121,320 sq km in area, being narrow in the south and broadening out in the north. It is situated in the Horn of Africa bordered by Sudan to the west and north and Ethiopia and Djibouti to the south. It lies between 12° and 18° latitude north, and 36° and 44° longitude east. There are about 1,000 km of the country bordering onto the Red Sea opposite Saudi Arabia and Yemen. Its territory includes the Dahlak Islands which were formally used as a military base by the Ethiopians.

Eritrea consists of four main geographical regions. The first runs from Djibouti upwards and is little more than a long strip of desert. The central and northern part of the country – covering about 30% of the land mass – is made up of highlands and is an extension of the Ethiopian highlands, at an average height of 1,500 m (Asmara, the capital, is in this area). It is in this region that most cultivation takes place. Much of the forest that used to cover the hillsides has been cleared either for fuelwood or land and as a consequence, soil erosion is becoming an increasingly severe problem. West of the highlands spreading into Sudan lies the potentially fertile lowlands which are mainly flat. The fourth region is in the far north and comprises rugged hills which give way to lowlands going down to the coastal plain to the east where only pastoralism is possible. In 1995, the National Assembly reorganized Eritrea into six administrative regions or zones, namely Asmera (the preferred Eritrean spelling), Maakel, Semenawi Keyih Bahri, Gash Barka, Debub and Debuawi Keyih Bahri.

Eritrea

Eritrea's natural resources are to some extent still untapped. In prehistoric times there was evidence of iron ore, gold and copper ore being mined and it remains to be seen if these are still exploitable assets. Off the coast, some see pages of oil and offshore natural gas have been recorded and exploration for these resources is currently under way.

Climate

Given the diverse geographical make-up of the country, there are a number of different types of climate. The higher plateaux has an average temperature of 18°C with an annual rainfall of around 500 mm while the coast's average temperature is 30°C with rainfall of less than 200 mm each year. In coastal areas, the months from June to September can be extremely hot, at times reaching 50°C. The main rainy season throughout the country is between June and September. There are short rains between October and March along the northern coastal region, though these are unpredictable. December is generally the coolest month. During the rainy season or in the winter it can get chilly in the highlands, especially during the evenings and nights. A jacket or fleece/jumper is necessary.

National parks and reserves

Eritrea does not have any National Parks at present. An unfortunate result of the liberation struggle has been the destruction of much of Eritrea's flora and fauna. However, given the diversity of environments in Eritrea and the fact that it is so unspoilt, there is great potential for the country to develop national parks. The decades of fighting has scared the elephants and most of the larger mammals away. Elephants had returned to Tokombia but this area was in the centre of the fighting in May 2000. Prior to the war there were Reserves near Teseney in the west; just to the northeast of Keren; and in the north on the border with Sudan. The war has probably benefited the marine life as the fishing industry greatly contracted during the hostilities, and the fish population untroubled by marine pollution increased to a level where the waters are sometimes described as 'fish soup'. There are proposals to make some of the Dahlak Islands, eg Dessei and Shumma, into a Marine National Park.

Books

Parkyns, M (1868) *Life in Abyssinia* London: John Murray. An account of travels from Massawa west to Khartoum, which began in 1843, and took six years.

Tonkin, T (1972) *Ethiopia With Love*, London: Hodder and Stoughton. Contains descriptions of Massawa and Asmara during the time of Haile Selassie, with some excellent line drawings that evocatively capture the atmosphere of Eritrea.

Connell, D (1993) *Against All Odds* New Jersey: Red Sea Press. An account of the last 16 years of Eritrea's struggle for liberation, written by a journalist who travelled with the guerrilla armies. An insight into some of the characters and communities who fought for their freedom. There are several other Red Sea book publications including topics on women and the struggle period with photos, etc.

Murphy, D (1968) *In Ethiopia with a Mule*. A mule-trek from Massawa to Addis Ababa, with good observations on local history, culture and customs, although the section on Eritrea is fairly short.

Firebrace J & Holland S (1985) *Eritrea: Never kneel down* Red Sea Press.

Keneally T *Towards Asmara* (currently out of print).

Eritrea

Djibouti

8

Djibouti

One of Africa's smallest nations, strategically positioned at the mouth of the Red Sea, Djibouti is more expensive and less frequently visited than its neighbours. It offers great contrasts with spectacular diving and snorkelling among the unspoilt coral reefs or a chance to observe the infrequently spotted whale sharks in January. Inland the country is hot and inhospitable with dramatic but beautiful desert landscapes, active volcanoes and the great salt Lake Assal, 155 m below sea level, from where the nomadic Afars begin their long journey inland to Ethiopia to trade salt. In contrast with the dry interior there is a small remnant of verdant primeval forest – Foret du Day. Its recent international importance increased dramatically during both the Gulf War and the UN intervention in Somalia when it acted as a base for allied troops. The capital, Djibouti, houses over half the population of the country, acting as an international transit port and refuelling centre.

Djibouti

Essentials

Planning your trip

Where to go The adventurous might like to try land-yachting on the smooth sunken desert depressions known as the Grand Bara and Petit Bara. Lake Abbe in the south west offers a unique lunar landscape surrounded by dramatic needles extruding sulphurous gases.

When to go From June to August when the humidity is at its lowest.

Tours & tour operators
For a list of tour agents in Djibouti see page 941

Some European tour operators concentrate on watersports, others specialize in treks to the desert interior, and some offer a combination of both experiences. *Club Aventure*, 18 Rue/seguier, 75006 Paris, France, T1-4432-6944. Organize trips to the desert hinterland. *Explor'Action*, 11 Rue du Mont Blanc, Geneva, Switzerland, T22-7317026. Also arrange desert treks. *Intermedes*, 60 Rue de la Boetie, 750008 Paris, T1-4561-6939. *Terra Incognita* 36/37 Quai Arloing, 69 256 Lyon Cedex 09, www.terra-incognita.fr Specializes in trips accompanied by a geologist to the remote areas inhabited by the Afar people, including a visit to the famous lava lakes of the Erta Ale, an isolated active basaltic shield volcano in the Ethiopian section of the barren Danakil Depression (see page 921). *Zig Zag*, 54 Rue de Dunkerque, 75009 Paris, T1-42851393. Offer a range of tours.

Finding out more Tourism is not well developed in Djibouti and it can be difficult to obtain accurate advice. The best source is the excellent informative **ADEN** (Association Djibouti), Espace Nomade, 25 Av du Chateau, 94300 Vincennes, France, T01-4851-7156, F01-4398-9682, aden@club-internet.fr, where Dominique Lommatzsch has proved to be an extremely helpful source of information.

Language French and Arabic are the official languages although Afar and Somali are commonly spoken.

Gay & lesbian travellers Homosexuality is illegal in Djibouti. In Africa, generally, gay and lesbian travellers are poorly tolerated and great discretion is advisable.

Before you travel

Visas All people entering Djibouti now require visas, US$30, including French nationals. Visas are easily obtainable from Djibouti or French embassies around the world and are valid for 10 days. They can be renewed at the airport if necessary. Visas can also be obtained on arrival at the airport, but it has recently been reported that this involves a return to the airport the next morning.

A transit visa can be obtained on arrival at the airport for nationals of Belgium, Denmark, Finland, Germany, Italy, Japan, Luxembourg, Netherlands, Norway, Sweden, UK and USA. In order to get a transit visa you must have an onward ticket; if you do not, you will be forced to buy one before being granted a transit visa.

Vaccinations International certificates of vaccination against yellow fever and cholera are not required unless travelling from an affected area. It is wise to protect against malaria.

Money

Currency The currency is the Djibouti Franc divided into 100 centimes. There are no restrictions on the amount of local or foreign currency that can be taken into or out of the country. US dollars are widely accepted, and welcomed by the authorities. There are no money-changing facilities at the airport.

Djibouti embassies

There are very few Djibouti embassies: in Paris (France), New York (US), Cairo (Egypt), Djedda (Saudi Arabia), Addis Ababa (Ethiopia) and Mogadishu (Somalia). Visas can be obtained from French embassies in other parts of the world.

All overseas embassies and consulates are based in the capital city. For list see section under Djibouti city, see page 944.

Touching down

Hours of business Banking hours are from Monday-Saturday 0700-1200.
Official time Three hours ahead of GMT.
Language French and Arabic are the official languages, and Afar and Somali

are spoken locally. Some English is spoken in the capital.
IDD 253; there are no area codes. Equal tones with long pauses means it is ringing; equal tones with equal pauses means engaged.

Major cards are accepted only by large hotels, restaurants and travel agents. **Credit cards**

Getting there

If you intend to travel between Djibouti, Ethiopia or Somalia, it is best to check on access before making your travel plans.

All flights go to the capital, Djibouti City. For flight information, see page 942. **Air**

There is a sealed road from Addis Ababa to Djibouti. Buses go from Djibouti to Assab in **Road** Eritrea, but it is an awkward journey through Tadjoura and Obock, and the roads are poor from Obock on. There are normally road links with Somalia, with a mixture of bus and lorry transport to Hargeisa and Berbera. However, the current political situation will need to stabilize before this route becomes possible again.

The importance of Djibouti as a port means that many cargo ships dock here. In principle it **Sea** should be possible to travel by boat from Marseille and Aden. Djibouti has many dhows and it is possible to get to Berbera, Sudan, Karachi, Aden and the Persian Gulf this way. It is also possible to reach Djibouti by dhow from Al Mokha in North Yemen; it takes about 16 hours and you are even able to take a car or motorcycle with you.

The Djibouti-Ethiopian railway provides regular services from Addis Ababa and Dire Dawa to **Train** the capital. It is a long slow journey, but fairly comfortable, see page 944. In the past the train has been attacked by bandits in the Ethiopian segment. Recent reports suggest that only the line between Dire Dawa and Djibouti is safe, with security between Addis Ababa and Dire Dawa a serious problem. The buses between Addis and Dire Dawa are said to be safer.

Touching down

Tourist information is available in Djibouti City at *L'Office de Developpement du Tourism*, **Tourist** Place 27 June, BP 1938, T352800, F356322. **information**

Where to stay

There are a number of first-class hotels in the capital all of which are air conditioned and have **Hotels** restaurants, but they are expensive. There are also some cheaper hotels without a/c in the African quarter of town. In other parts of the country, accommodation for tourists or travellers is scanty. See hotel classifications, page 36.

Getting around

Djibouti Airlines, Place Legarde, T351006, F342429, fly daily to **Tadjoura** and **Obock**. Small **Air** planes can be chartered from the *Aero-Club*, T340824, sited next to the main airport.

Public transport is limited, although small buses run between the capital, Tadjoura, Randa, **Road** Diknil, Ali-Sabieh, Hol Hol and Arta. Hiring a car is a good option for travelling around the country by road. Over two-thirds of the roads are unsurfaced, and half are only usable by

Djibouti

lorries or four-wheel drive vehicles. There are now roads linking the capital, Djibouti City, with both the north and south of the country, and the road to the Ethiopian frontier is bitumen-surfaced.

Car hire can be arranged in Djibouti City (see page 943).

Sea Ferry boats for **Tadjoura** and Obock leave from L'Escale. For information on ferries to Obock and Tadjoura, **Societé du Bac le Goubet**, T352351.

Train The railway between Djibouti and Ethiopia makes stops in Djibouti at Gaubetto, Chebelle, Hol Hol, and Ali-Sabieh.

Keeping in touch

Media **Newspapers** There is only one local paper, *La Nation*, which is published weekly. There are also *L'Atout*, a twice-yearly paper published by the **Centre National de la Promotion Culturelle et Artistique**, and the *Carrefour Africain*, published fortnightly by the Roman Catholic mission.

Radio/TV Broadcasting is state controlled and operated from Djibouti City. There are programmes in French, Afar, Somali and Arabic. Radio transmission is 24 hrs and television 7 hrs daily. Djibouti is also a member of the Arab Satellite Communication Organisation which transmits both radio and television programmes. **BBC World Service** can be received in Djibouti if you have a radio with short waveband reception. See guide, page 38.

Food and drink

For restaurant classification, see page 39 There are restaurants to suit all tastes in both the capital and the main seaside resort of Arta with French, Vietnamese, Chinese and Arab cuisine. In other parts of the country simple local food (grills, stews and rice) are available.

Holidays and festivals

2 February *New Year*. February[1] *Lailat al-Miraji*. 1 May *Labour Day*. April[1] *Eid al-Fitr*. 27 June *National Day*. July[1] *Eid al-Adha*. 15 August *Assumption Day*. July[1] *Muslim New Year*. August[1] *Al-Ashura*. October[1] *Prophet's Birthday*. 1 November *All Saints Day*. 25 December *Christmas Day*.

[1] These dates marking Muslim holidays are approximate as they depend on the lunar year.

Health

See Health section, page 58 Remember to protect against malaria. It may be wise to take protections against prickly heat, and avoid becoming dehydrated. Clothing should be light and cotton; avoid synthetic fabrics. It is advisable to apply sunscreen creams liberally, protect your eyes from the bright light and desert sand with sunglasses and to cover your head. Tap water is not safe to drink. Mineral water is widely available.

Djibouti City

The city lies on a peninsula separating the Gulf of Tadjoura from the Gulf of Aden at the mouth of the Red Sea. More than half the population of the country live in Djibouti. The city is the centre of economic activity in the country as well as the administrative, political and legal centre. In recent years it has become of strategic importance to the UN and allied forces, firstly in the Gulf War and later as a base from which to go into Somalia. The city has an Arab flavour to it both in terms of its architecture and its culture. It is an expensive place to visit not geared to the needs of budget travellers.

11° 30' N, 43° 5' E
Colour map 2, grid A5

Tourist information L'Office National du Tourisme, Place du 27 Juin (previously called Place Menelik), PO Box 1938, T353790. Open 0730-1230 and 1630-1830. Closed Thu afternoons. A reasonable map of Djibouti City can be bought here. For railway information go to **Plateau-du-Serpent**, T350353. For information on ferries to Obock and Tadjoura, **Societé du Bac le Goubet**, T352351.

Ins & outs

The town centre of Djibouti is effectively divided into the two sectors – the *quartier Europeen* to the north and the *quartier Africain* to the south. There is a colourful and interesting market called **Les Caisses** in the centre of town near the mosque which retains elements of African, European and Arab culture. There are interesting guided tours of the town on offer by the local culture association IRIS (T354377), highlighting the architectural features of the old houses and arcades. The **Aquarium Tropical de Djibouti** offers a taste of Red Sea marine life. An evening guided walk to the northwest of town just before sunset past the **Presidential Palace** leads to **L'Escale** offering an opportunity to see the traditional dhows and skiffs in the marina. Just outside Djibouti (about 5 km) there are pleasant walks in the **Ambouli palm grove**. There are good beaches at **Dorale** (12 km) and **Khor Ambado** (15 km) though you will need a four-wheel drive to reach the latter.

Sights

Djibouti City

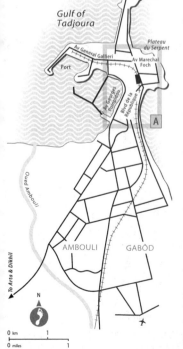

Ilot du Héron

Gulf of Tadjoura

Plateau du Serpent

Av General Gallieri

Port

Av Marechal Foch

Av Georges Pompidou

Blvd de la Republique

A

Oued Ambouli

AMBOULI   GABÒD

To Arra & Dikhil

N

0 km   1
0 miles   1

There are relatively few cheap places to stay in Djibouti, and they are all situated in the African quarter of town. Be warned that some of the cheaper hotels in the African quarter rent rooms by the hour and double up as pick-up joints.

Sleeping

L *Djibouti Sheraton*, Plateau de Serpent, PO Box 121, T350405, F355892. Casino, discotheque, tennis, beach with water sports, a/c, pool, restaurant, bars, pleasant gardens. **B** *Bellevue*, Blvd Bonhour, PO Box 1986, T358088, F352484. Good standard, some of the 28 rooms overlook the port. **B** *Continental*, Place de 27 Juin, PO Box 675, T350146,

Djibouti

F354682. A/c, bars, restaurant. **B** *Hotel Alia*, Av Lyautey, PO Box 1887, T358222, F358688. New comfortable hotel with good facilities. Located close to the *Sheraton*, whose swimming pool it is possible to use for a small fee. **B** *Hotel Residence de l'Europe*, Place de 27 Juin, PO Box 83, T355060, F356108. Large rooms with a/c, bars, restaurant. **B** *Menelike*, Place de 27 Juin, PO Box 1153, T351177, F354682. Good standard. **B** *Plein Ciel*, located at the junction of Place de 27 Juin and Av Cheik Osman, PO Box 1869, T353841, F356857. Pleasant location on west edge of commercial area, close to shore, a/c, bars, restaurant. **B** *Relais*. Close to the airport. **C** *Ali Sabieh*, Av Georges Clemenceau, PO Box 2059, T353059, F355084. Has 27 small rooms with a/c and is a little more reasonably priced than its competitors. Pizzeria on ground floor. **C** *Djibouti Palace*, Blvd General de Gaulle, PO Box 166, T350982. Eastern side of commercial centre, overlooks railway line and bay. Not highly recommended. **C** *Bienvenue*, Blvd du Bender, T354626, on the south edge of the commercial centre. **C** *Doraleh*, 10 km outside

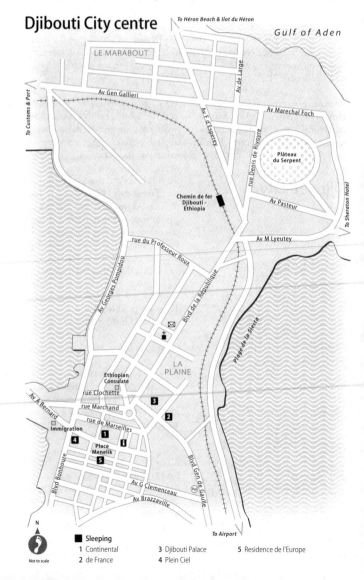

Djibouti City centre

To Héron Beach & Ilot du Héron

Gulf of Aden

LE MARABOUT

Av de Large

To Customs & Port

Av Gen Gallieri

Av Marechal Foch

Av F el Esperey

rue Denis de Rivoire

Plâteau du Serpent

Chemin de fer
Djibouti -
Ethiopia

Av Pasteur

Av M Lyeutey

rue du Professeur Roux

To Sheraton Hotel

Av Georges Pompidou

Blvd de la République

Plage de la Siesta

LA
PLAINE

Ethiopian
Consulate

rue Clochette

Av A Bernard

rue Marchand

3

rue de Marseilles

2

Immigration

1

4

Place
Menelik

i

5

Blvd Bonhoure

Blvd Gen de Gaulle

Av G Clemenceau

Av Brazzaville

To Airport

N

Not to scale

■ **Sleeping**
1 Continental
2 de France
3 Djibouti Palace
4 Plein Ciel
5 Residence de l'Europe

Djibouti

★

Things to do in and around Djibouti

- Take the train to **Ali Sabieh**, passing through three quaint French-built stations and view the iron viaduct at Hol Hol, before taking the bus back to Djibouti.
- Make an excursion to **Les Isles des Sept Freres** for some of the best snorkelling and diving anywhere.
- Go by boat (*navette*) to the picturesque port of **Tadjoura**, with its whitewashed dwellings and seven minaretted mosques.
- Spend an afternoon **land-yachting** (*char à voile*), or wind-surfing on wheels, at Grand Bara.
- Visit the **Aquarium Tropical de Djibouti** where the exotic and varied marine life of the Red Sea is on view.
- Make an excursion to the **Foret du Day National Park**, in a green and verdant valley near Randa, trekking to the Toha Waterfall and the Guedani Palm Plantation

the city. **C** *Dar Es Salam*, T353334. Has 22 rooms located close to *Cite Einguela*. **C** *Horsed*, Blvd de Gaulle, T352316. Small hotel with 10 rooms. **C** *Hotel de Djibouti*, Av 13, T356415. Court-yard rooms are the best option in this often noisy area. All 23 rooms have a/c, some have en-suite bathrooms. **C** *Hotel de France*, Blvd de Gaulle, T351843). Close to the Assemblé Nationale. Large clean rooms with fans, a/c and TV. **D** *Sekgabode*, Av 13, T351067. Small hotel with 12 clean rooms available.

Expensive *Chez Mamma Elena*. High quality Italian food. *Hanoi*. French-influenced Chinese and Vietnamese cuisine. *Restaurant Le Kintz*. French cuisine, high standard. **Mid-range** *Arta*, Rue de Paris, PO Box 1786, T358796. Seafood. *Bafena*, Route de l'Aviation, T355358, F355358. Ethiopian food. *Chez Therese*. Local Ethiopian food. *Drugstore*, Place de 27 Juin, PO Box 1115, T358014. French, local and fast food. *L'Etoile Kokeb*. Good quality Ethiopian dishes and entertaining traditional Ethiopian music and dance. *Figaro*, Administrateur Bernard, PO Box 1869, T353841, F356857. French and Italian cuisine. *Historil*, Place Menelik, T354422. Seafood. *Longchamp*, Av des Messageries, T353701, F351471. Excellent French cuisine, good value too, especially the option to try a little of everything on offer. Terrace overlooks the port. *Mickey*. High quality Italian food. *Petit Maxime*, 78 Routes de l'Aeroport, PO Box 6782, T341452. Ethiopian and French. *Pizzeria de 27 Juin*, Place de 27 Juin, PO Box 1786. Italian and American style pizzas. *Restaurant Palmier en Zinc*. Sound French fare. *Retro*, Rue Ras Makonnen, T350246, F325996. Coffee house. *Saba*, Av Lyautey, PO Box 2740, T354244. Yemeni dishes. *Vietnam*, Rue de Soileillet, T351708. Chinese and Vietnamese cuisine, friendly atmosphere.

Eating
Restaurants in the hotels tend to be expensive, but serve good European-style food

There are also a number of local restaurants serving cheap Arab and local dishes, some good ones are near the market past the Place Mahamoud Harbi. Along Rue George Clemenceau there are small seafood restaurants which serve tasty grilled or baked spicy fish.

Curios and crafts A good place to buy souvenirs is around the Place Menelik though they are expensive. **Bookshops** *Librairie Arnaud*, Place de 27 Juin, T351243. *Librairie Coleur Locale*, Rue de Paris, T352121. *Maison de la Presse*, Av Pierre Pascale, T350223.

Shopping

Aero Club, Aeroport d'Ambouli, T351514. Flying club that can also offer charter flights. *Club Cheminots*, Plateau de Serpent, T352974. Tennis, boules, bridge, gymnastics, judo and karate. *Djibouti Bowling*, Gabode, T354107. *Char a Voile*, T354695. Land yachting, more commonly known as wind-surfing on wheels locally. *Club Nautique*, Escale, T351514. Sailing and water-skiing.

Sport

Agence Dolphin, Rue de Dakar, PO Box 4476, T350313, F350380, dankali@hotmail.com Recently established by Frenchman Bruno Pardigon, has been highly recommended for scuba diving and boat trips (Oct-Jun) to the *Les Iles de Sept Freres* (Seven Brothers Islands) off

Tour operators

Djibouti

the northeast coast, an area considered to offer some of the best diving in the world. He also organizes expensive *sorties en brousse* – bush-walking trips, though using local guides would probably enhance the experience as they know the terrain better and are cheaper. *ATTA (Agence de Tourism et de Transport Aerien)*, Rue Marchand, PO Box 1181, T354848, F354288. Organize excursions, car hire and plane tickets. *Avecta*, PO Box 3451,T/F354695, Aecveta@hotmail.com Specialists in *char a voile* – land yachting. Between Djibouti and Ali-Sabieh are the depressions of Petit Bara and Grand Bara, dried up lakes that herds of antelope frequent. Grand Bara is a vast expanse of solid white clay, and with strong local winds throughout the year except summer, conditions are ideal for land yachting. Costs US$24 per hour. Also able to organize self-drive 4WD activities. *Caravane du Sel*, Place de 27 Juin, PO Box 2098, T356618, F353752, caravane@intnet.dj Organizes excursions to all parts of the country. They are probably the agency best able to reveal the 'real' Djibouti. Several excursions, of a varying number of days, to all Djibouti's major tourist attractions are available, including treks on foot/camel following the thousand-year-old route of the Afar nomadic traders whose camel caravans bring salt to Ethiopia from Lake Assal. *Le Goubet*, T354520, F351103, Av Saint-Laurent. Can organize airline tickets and trips to other nearby country destinations. Also offer a range of internal tourist services, including trekking singly or in groups and water sports.

The redoubtable *Jean-Michel Roux* owns an old Breton tuna-fishing boat, the *Breiz Izel*, which is fully equipped for diving. This skipper-diving instructor organizes cruises from Oct-Jun to *Les Iles de Sept Freres* (Seven Brothers Islands), where he is familiar with the best diving sites, and in Jan he organizes cruises to the Gulf of Ghoubbet El Kharab where the spectacular passage of whale-sharks can be observed. T253-354617, F254879, www.multimania.com/breizizel/

Caution: Before finalizing negotiations of underwater diving guide services, it is important to establish that the boat owners are licensed and insured to offer a diving service. There have been tragedies when boat owners have exceeded their capabilities and unfortunately decompression facilities are unavailable in Djibouti.

Transport **Air** *Air France*, Place de 27 Juin, PO Box 2484, T352010, has 3 flights weekly between **Paris**,
Taxis are widely **Amsterdam** and Djibouti (Sun, Wed and Fri). *Daallo*, Rue de Beme, PO Box 2565, T353401,
available in the city F351767. Serves a number of destinations in neighbouring countries including Addis Ababa.
and from the airport. Most flights change at Berbera in Somalia, but there are also direct services to Dubai and
Tariffs increase by Jeddah. *Ethiopian Airways*, T351007, flies daily between Djibouti and **Addis Ababa** , from
50% at night where there are flights to New York, Frankfurt, London, Bombay, Bankok, Beijing, and many airports around Africa. *Djibouti Airlines*, Place Legarde, T351006, F342429. Flies twice weekly between Dire Dawa in Ethiopia and Djibouti, and twice a week encompassing Borama and Hargueissa in Somalia, and Djibouti. They also fly daily to **Tadjoura** and **Obock**. *Yemenia*, Rue de Marchand, flies twice a week (Mon and Fri) between Paris and Djibouti, with a change at the Yemeni capital Sanaa. Other international destinations include Cairo, Jeddah, Khartoum and Bombay.

The *Regional Air Representative* (tickets from ATTA, PO Box 1181, T354848, F354288) serves the airports of Djibouti, Asmara (Eritrea), Bujumbura (Burundi), Entebbe (Uganda), Kigali (Rwanda) and Lusaka (Zambia).

There are no flights currently to Asmara, Eritrea.

Aero-Club, T340824, sited next to the main airport, can arrange charter flights. As there is no bus service from the airport to the city, which is 5 km south of the centre, you will need to get a taxi. There are no left-luggage facilities at the airport.

Driving is on the right **Road** The best roads are between Djibouti and Ethiopia, especially the road towards Assab
hand side of the road or west into Ethiopia via Dikhil. Most other roads are rough with many potholes but passable throughout the year. There is a good tarmac road between Addis Ababa in Ethiopia and Djibouti. There are many small **buses** that ply the routes between Djibouti City and Arta, Hol Hol, Ali Sabieh, Dikhil, Tadjoura and Randa, leaving when the bus fills up. This can involve a long wait at the bus station. The fares are very reasonable with a standard fare of $3 for most

Waugh in Djibouti

In 1930 the novelist Evelyn Waugh went from Djibouti to Addis Ababa by train. He was travelling to report on the coronation of Haile Selassie for The Times *newspaper.*

His first sight of the low coastline of French Somaliland, as Djibouti then was, came at dawn from the deck of the French steamship Azay le Rideau *from Marseille. A haggard couple in evening dress were dancing to a wind-up gramophone. Sleep was impossible as the retinue of the Egyptian delegation barked orders, dragging around numerous tin trunks of luggage and the massive crates which contained the Egyptian gift to the Emperor, a suite of bedroom furniture.*

It began to rain. Exhausted, the dancing couple slunk off to bed. Small boys hung around the deck, shivering and offering to dive for coins. Bags of coal were being hauled aboard over planks from barges. Ashore, they found the next train, in three days' time, was reserved in its entirety for the Duke of Gloucester. The next, in a further three days, was allocated to Prince Udine.

Waugh, a traveller morbidly obsessed by the impossibility of staying healthy in the tropics, repaired to the Hotel des Arcades. Run by a handsome Frenchwoman it had a fading stucco façade, a few first-floor bedrooms at the back facing onto a broad verandah, and hot water. In the courtyard a black monkey sat in a lemon-tree.

After lunch the rain subsided and Waugh toured the town in a one-horse cab churning through pools of steaming mud. The 'elegant and smiling boulevards' of the guidebook proved to be mere stretches of waste land between blocks of decaying buildings. A shower of stucco and bricks fell about them from one of the structures and a clutch of Indian clerks and Greek traders scampered into the street. It was an earthquake that they had not noticed due to the jolting of the cab.

The local people struck Waugh as a race of exceptional beauty, slender and tall, with delicate features and wide-set eyes. Most wore a strip of rag round the waist and a few coils of copper wire on their wrists and ankles. Heads shaven or dyed with yellow ochre. Half-a -dozen harlots besieged the cab. Naked children splashed through the mud screeching for money. Some warriors with spears spat contemptuously as they passed. At the edge of town, Waugh viewed the local dwellings which he likened to inverted birds' nests of mud, twigs, grass, rags and flattened tins with one low hole through which a man might crawl on his belly.

On returning to the hotel the travellers learned that places had been secured for them on a special train leaving that evening. Cheered up, Waugh bought a French novel with a lurid cover, some cheroots and changed some bank-notes for Marie Therese silver thalers, the massive coins minted in Vienna and the principle currency in Ethiopia. As darkness fell they chuffed and creaked slowly out of what Waugh described as 'the intolerable desolation of French Somaliland – a country of dust and boulders, utterly devoid of any sign of life'.

destinations. Otherwise you will need to either **hire a car** (though most of the interesting sites require a professional standard of 4WD driving skills) or rent a taxi with a chauffeur. The roads are poorly signposted, and visits to places like Lake Abbe, the *Foret du Day* or the volcanoes can only really be safely made in an organized excursion.

Car hire: it is not possible to hire a car in Djibouti from the airport. There are 3 car rental agencies: *Ets Frado*, T354930, next to the bowling alley; *Ets Marill*, Rue Marchand, PO Box 57, T351150, F355623; and *Roberto* garage, T352029, in the industrial zone. In addition, **Stophi**, T352494, rents out 4WD vehicles for trips into the interior of the country. It is advisable to take plenty of water and petrol on any expedition off the beaten track.

Sea Ferry boats serving routes between Djibouti City to Tadjoura and Obock leave from L'Escale port, T352351. However, these *navettes* run only once a day. For **Tadjoura** the boat leaves Djibouti at about 1100, returning from Tadjoura the next day at about 0630. Djibouti-Tadjoura US$6, Djibouti-Obock US$9. *Navettes* also run between the capital and Mucha and Maskali Islands, US$18.

Train A 782-km railway connects Djibouti with **Addis Ababa** on the Red Sea. This is a very picturesque experience not to be missed. The train rarely exceeds speeds of 40 kph, which is probably just as well when you examine the state of the old rails. However in recent years there have been incidents where travellers have been attacked by bandits on this train in the Ethiopian section. The trains leave at 0550 on Wed, Fri and Sun, arriving in Addis approximately 24 hrs later. Stops at Ali-Sabieh before the Ethiopian border and at Dire Dawa and Aouache in Ethiopia before going on to Addis Ababa. It is a long slow journey, but is fairly comfortable. Travellers to Ethiopia are advised to take the train as far as **Dire Dawa** before changing to the bus to avoid the security problems. The bus travels via the high plateau, a route that is much more beautiful than the train's which goes through the Awash Valley. If you want to break your journey it is only 54 km from Dire Dawa to the historic walled city of Harar.

The journey to Ali Sabieh takes 2-3 hrs depending on the number of breakdowns. The train stops at three charming small stations, Gaubetto, Chebelle and Hol Hol before reaching Ali Sabieh. Hol Hol is famous for its 19th-century engineering feat, a metal viaduct that crosses the *wadi*, or seasonal river, reputedly the work of Gustave Eiffel.

Booking is at the railway station at the north end of Blvd de la Republique. It is necessary to make a reservation as the train is often full. The fare to Addis Ababa is US$60 1st class (a sleeper on the overnight train); US$30 2nd class; US$16 3rd class. Djibouti to Dire Dawa, is approximately a 12 hr journey, US$23 1st class. Djibouti to Ali Sabieh costs US$7 1st class.

Djibouti-Ethiopian Railroad Company, T447250.

The Djibouti-Dire Dawa trip is an excursion in itself. It lasts about 12 hrs including about 4 hrs to cross the border. The train crosses the territory occupied by the Somali Issas who conduct all the commercial activities on the train. About half the passengers are Somalis who have no passport. A few kilometres before the border they get off the train having distributed their baggage to the remaining passengers. A caravan of people forms, which walks around the border and gets back on the train a few kilometres after crossing the border. Meanwhile at the border crossing the train is subjected to a meticulous search of every nook and cranny. Foreign travellers may occasionally be hassled by customs officers for their apparent excessive amount of luggage but the other travellers on board will defend you. It's a charming charade.

Directory   **Airline offices International**: A number of international airlines operate to Djibouti: *Air France*, *Yemen Airways*, *Ethiopian Airlines*, and *Somali Airways*. **Charter**: There is a small private airline from which it is possible to charter a plane. Contact the *Aero Club* at the airport. **Banks** There are several bureaux de change in the Place de 27 Juin. *Al Barakaad*, Rue d'Athene, T357024. *Bureau de Change*, Place de 27 Juin, T353719. *Western Union*, Place de 27 Juin. The main banks are: *Banque de Djibouti et de Moyen Orient*, PO Box 2471. *Banque Indosuez*, Place Lagarde, PO Box 88, T353016. *Banque pour le Commerce et l'Industrie*, Place Lagarde, T350857. *British Bank of the Middle East*, Place Lagarde, T353291. *Banque de Developement*, Av George Clemenceau, T353391. *Commercial Bank of Ethiopia*, T352101. **Chemists** in Djibouti City are well stocked. **Communications Post**: Main post office on Blvd de la Republique. **Embassies and consulates** Belgium, T350960. Egypt, PO Box 1989, T351231. Ethiopia, PO Box 230, T350718. France, 45 Blvd du Marechal Foch, PO Box 2039, T352503. Germany, T350507. Italy, T351162. Netherlands, T352022. Norway, T352351. Saudi Arabia, PO Box 1921, T351645. Somalia, Blvd del Republique, PO Box 549, T353521. Sudan, T351483. Sweden, T352022. Yemen Arab Republic, PO Box 194, T352975. USA, Villa Plateau du Serpent, Blvd Marechal Joffre, PO Box 185, T353995. **Places of worship** Almost the entire population is Muslim, consequently there are a large number of mosques throughout the city. There is a Roman Catholic Church on Blvd de la Republique, as well as a Greek Orthodox church and a Protestant church. **Useful addresses Police**: Av General de Gaulle, emergency number T17.

Outside Djibouti

There are a number of places which are interesting to visit around the country. At several of these there are newly established eco-tourism developments. These so-called camps typically offer simple accommodation in the form of traditional wooden huts. They are bases from which tourists are taken on an exploration of the local environment and the way of life of the nomadic peoples. Reservations are made, and more information can be found, at the travel agents in Djibouti City. Currently there are camps at **Lake Abbe**, **Sables Blancs**, *near Tadjoura, two sites in the* **Goda Mountains**, *and at* **Assamo** *near Ali Sabieh (see entries below).*

One of the major attractions of Djibouti is its coral reefs and clear seas, best explored by cruise boat.

Gulf of Tadjoura

The Gulf of Tadjoura to the north of Djibouti City is a haven for those interested in aquatic life. It is possible to go snorkelling, scuba diving or to do some underwater photography here as the area offers a wide variety of flora and fauna including many species of fish and different types of coral. Water-skiing and windsurfing can also be arranged. The best time for these activities is between September and May when the waters of the Red Sea are clearest. Several locations make for excellent diving including the reefs off the mangrove-fringed, white sandy beaches of **Moucha** and **Maskali Islands** in the centre of the gulf. Located 15 km north of Djibouti, a short boat ride away, there are beautiful coral reefs to explore. Camping is permitted.

The picturesque small white port of **Tadjoura** has seven mosques and is worth a visit for its beautiful mountain-backdrop setting. This town was very prosperous when the camel caravans travelled from here to Ethiopia before the coming of the railway. Encircled by mountains, the easiest approach is by sea. The minarets of the seven mosques can be seen above the whitewashed stone houses adding to the charm of this lovely town.

Tadjoura
Colour map 2, grid A4

A good place for diving and snorkelling is **Sable Blancs** beach where there is a simple campsite. Sable Blancs beach lies 7 km east of Tadjoura town.

The **Goda Mountains** just behind the town have a wealth of rare plants and there is a small remnant of a primeval forest – **Foret du Day** – that has been created into a national park. The Mount Goda massif (1,770 m) is home to the critically endangered endemic species *Francolinus ochropectus*, more commonly known as the Djibouti francolin, a bird related to the quail. Its population is estimated to be around 500-1,000 birds. The survival of this species is threatened by human encroachment for land use and by hunting.

Sleeping **C** *Hotel du Golf*, T424091, F424091, 2 km west of the town. Small bungalows with fans and a/c. **C** *Corto Maltese*, T426116. New hotel situated in the town centre.

Transport The boat to Tadjoura from Djibouti City leaves at 1100 returning the following morning at 0630.

Randa is located 35 km northwest of Tadjoura in a surprisingly green and lush valley at the edge of the Goda Mountains and can be reached by road. It is a high-altitude station in a magnificent green valley. Here is found Bankouale camp. Walks in the adjacent **Foret du Day National Park** will take you among ancient junipers, acacias, jujube trees and wild olives, the remnants of vegetation that once covered the

Randa
Colour map 2, grid A4

Djibouti

Saraha. The tiny remnant of primeval forest measures just over 3 sq km. From the summit of Day (1,800 m) it is a one-day walk to **Dittilou**, a cool and pleasant camp 800 m above sea level. From here it is possible to trek to the **Toha Waterfall** or visit the palm plantation at Guedani.

Sleeping *Centre Touristique de Randa*, T424031. Simple rooms. There is also a charming campsite at Dittilou and another at Bankouale.

Obock
Colour map 2, grid A5

Obock is located approximately 35 km from Djibouti City across the bay on the northeastern side of the Gulf of Tadjoura. The diving is excellent here. The distance from Tadjoura town to Obock is only 60 km but the road is very poor, with many dangerous potholes. Taking a fast *navette* boat is recommended as the best option for transport between Tadjoura and Obock. Obock is a fairly small town infrequently visited by tourists. Along with Tadjoura it was the traditional seat of the Afar Sultans, who sold settlement rights to the French colonialists. Obock was established by the French as their capital city from 1884 until 1888 when the water supplies proved inadequate for the town's requirements and they moved to Djibouti City. Much of Obock was destroyed during the political disturbances of the 1990s. To the north, prehistoric remains have been uncovered at Ras Sya.

Les Iles des Sept Freres (Seven Brothers Islands)

Located 100 km north of Djibouti City off the northeast coast in the Straits of Bab-el-Mandab, this group of islands extending southeast from the Ras Syan peninsula is considered by diving specialists to be one of the 'seven wonders' of the underwater diving world. The waters are rich in big fish like manta rays, scad, loach, barracuda and sharks.

Ghoubbet El Kharab
70 km west of Djibouti City

Linked to the west of the Gulf of Tadjoura by a narrow stretch of sea is a seawater loch, Ghoubbet El Kharab, known locally as 'the pit of demons'. This is an attractive bay, with some bays suitable for swimming. The water is estimated to be 200 m deep, with a very fast flowing current at the narrow channel that connects it to the Gulf of Tadjoura. Surrounded by steep volcanic mountains and 600 m towering black lava cliffs this separate handle of the Gulf of Tadjoura attracts divers and fishermen and was one of the areas that Jacques Cousteau studied. Large marine animals such as manta rays and sharks are found in the waters, together with extinct underwater volcanoes. Ghuinni Koma or Devil's Islands are two uninhabited islands formed by underwater volcanoes in the bay. Local belief is that these islands are haunted and many Djiboutians avoid them. In January the annual migration of whale-sharks can be observed.

Ardoukoba volcanic zone and Lake Assal

Colour map 2, grid A4

The region between Lake Assal and the sea is an active volcanic zone. A four-wheel drive vehicle will allow a trip to a viewing point called La Belvedere. From here can be appreciated the 7-km **Ardoukoba Rift** valley, a panorama of volcanoes, fault lines and lava bridges. From La Belvedere it is a two-hour walk to reach the Ardoukoba Volcano.

Earthquakes and vulcanicity are associated with the development of faults (cracks) in the earth's crust that result from collision between tectonic plates. On 7 November 1978 a series of weak earthquakes were detected in Djibouti and the following day the **Ardoukoba volcano** erupted. A new fissure opened, and produced a small cinder cone named Gira-le-Koma, approximately 30 m high x 200 m long x 25 m wide and lava flows that covered part of the rift floor. The volcanic activity continued for a week. The Ardoukoba Rift contains a number of lava flows thought to have erupted during the past 3,000 years that are more recent than the lake sediments in nearby Lake Assal, estimated to be 2,000 years older.

The birth of an ocean

The vulcanologist Haroun Tazief has described Djibouti as 'an open-air geology textbook' with its seismic activity, smoking fumaroles, and dramatic formations of basalt rock. The Ardoukoba Rift is located within the area known as the Afar Triangle that is of great interest to geologists as it lies at a triple junction between the African and Arabian tectonic plates. Three rift arms – the Red Sea, the Gulf of Aden and the section of the eastern Rift Valley that includes Ethiopia, Eritrea and Djibouti – are diverging from a centre southwest of Lake Abbe, the northern end of the Wonji Fault Belt that connects to

the main African Rift Zone. In time, estimated at several million years, this will lead to Arabia moving to the northeast, the break-up of the African continent separating eastwards along the East African Rift, and the formation of a new ocean. The Afar is a relatively low area and parts of it, such as the Danakil Depression, lie below sea level. It is thought that seawater will penetrate from the bay of Ghoubbet El Kharab westwards towards Lake Assal, eventually forming a link to the Mediterranean. Geological study of this region has been described as 'observing the birth of an ocean'.

Lake Assal is found beyond the Ardoukoba volcano, 100 km west of Djibouti City. At about 155 m below sea level this dead lake makes an interesting though somewhat eerie place to visit. Its surface area is about 60 sq km and its depth ranges between 60-80 m. The water in it has a salinity factor ten times greater than seawater (350 g per litre) due to the rapid rate of evaporation . The lake is surrounded by crystal banks of salt and startlingly white gypsum , giving a stark contrast with the cold dark waters and the landscape of black basalt lava fields encircled by both active and dormant volcanoes beyond. The colour of the lake changes frequently throughout the day, appearing almost fluorescent at times. There are many fumaroles and hot springs nearby. Although the salt banks can be reached by driving along the surfaced road, the lake is best visited by four-wheel drive. It is then possible to drive across the salt bank to the camp at the north side of the lake.

Lake Assal
Colour map 2, grid A4

From here traditionally the nomadic Afar camel drivers break off the salt and begin their long journey to Ethiopia, where the salt is exchanged for sorghum, charcoal and other goods. Several companies (see page 941) can arrange treks along this route, giving the traveller an insight into the nomadic way of life. It is also possible to fly over the salt banks, for which one is awarded a 'hypothalassic' flying certificate, recognizing the occasion of flight below sea level.

Volcanic activity sometimes results in the formation of precious stones and minerals. There are known gold deposits in the seismically active area around Lake Assal. A joint American-Djiboutian appraisal of the size of the gold prospects is currently being undertaken (2001).

The 1998-2000 Ethiopian-Eritrean conflict has resulted in much greater extraction of salt on an industrial scale from Lake Assal. Ethiopia previously bought most of its requirements from Eritrea. Many Djiboutians have been keen to meet the demand for 'white gold' and despite summer daytime temperatures of up to 57°C and appalling working conditions the lure of earning 2½ times the national average wage has brought them here. Five companies are licensed to extract the salt from designated areas, and large bulldozers are used to move the salt into piles. These are bagged up manually using shovels and picks and loaded on to lorries bound for Ethiopia. Approximately 100,000 tonnes of salt is being extracted every month. A settlement of approximately 2,000 people has grown up at the lakeside. There is concern that continuing salt extraction at this rate is unsustainable and will have a deleterious effect on this dramatic and beautiful region.

The Lake Assal depression is just one of many that continue into Ethiopia with the Danakil Depression. Not far from Lake Assal is **Sak Allol**, a distance that can be walked in one day, where there are three dried-up lakes where only a thin layer of sparkling salt remains in the folds of the black basalt. In one of the depressions the

Djibouti

salt was gradually replaced by sand, upon which a large palm grove developed. A large Afar community has lived here for centuries, making palm wine and trading with Ethiopia. Beyond Sak Allol, the track that continues northwards to Dorra is splendid, passing the volcano **Moussa Ali**, at 2,028 m the highest peak in Djibouti. A few remaining leopard are said to inhabit this mountain, but many members of the cat family, cheetah, serval and caracal, are believed to be close to extinction, killed by nomads who accuse them of eating goats. The peak of Moussa Ali is cloaked in a thin cloud cover and occasionally legionnaires of the French Foreign Legion can be seen climbing this rock-strewn mountain as part of a military exercise.

Also along this route are found many prehistoric settlement sites and cave paintings. Ongoing tectonic activity, such as is found in eastern Afar and Djibouti, is believed to have attracted the Palaeolithic hunters as the topography of the landscape with its basins and barriers curtailed the mobility of their prey.

The southwest

Arta
Colour map 2, grid A4

Arta is a small summer resort used by the expatriates, situated to the southwest in the mountains overlooking the Gulf of Tadjoura. It is about 40 km outside Djibouti on a sealed road. There is a good restaurant there that is part of a hotel school.

**Petit Bara &
Grand Bara**

The road to the southwest continues towards two sunken desert depressions known as the **Petit Bara** and the **Grand Bara**, approximately 70 km from Djibouti City. Herds of antelope frequent these dried-up lakes, as well as hyena and jackels. The Grand Bara is a vast expanse of solid white clay, as smooth as ceramic, and a thermal phenomenon results in strong local winds being present for 9 months out of 12, except June-August, and conditions are ideal for land yachting. Mirages are commonly seen here. At the eastern end of these salty desert plains there is a centre where you can organize land yachting or *char a voile* – windsurfing on wheels as it is known locally. Contact *Avecta*, PO Box 3451, Djibouti, T/F354695. The director of *Avecta* is Ali Liaquat, an ex-French Foreign Legionnaire, originally from Pakistan. It is great fun, even for inexperienced beginners. All the equipment is new and well maintained. The cost is $24 per person per hour. Buses heading for Ali Sabieh or Dikhil can drop you nearby on the edge of Grand Bara, or round trips can be arranged from Djibouti City

South of the Grand Bara the road divides, one branch going southwest to Dikhil, where it changes to a northwesterly direction towards the Ethiopian border via Yoboki. The other branch travels south towards Somalia to the town of Ali-Sabieh, which is also served by the railway.

Along the road to Lake Abbe is the town of **Dikhil**, an attractive small town perched on a rocky outcrop. The area around the town is home to many gazelle, antelope, hyenas, jackals and camels. Sleeping: **C** *Palmeraie*, T420164. Double rooms have a/c, singles without. Approximately 12 km west of Dikhil is the archaeological excavation site of Handoga.

Lake Abbe
Colour map 2, grid A4

Lake Abbe straddles the Ethiopian border in the far southwest of the country ,165 km from Djibouti City, and is the home of large flocks of flamingos, ibis and pelicans. This lake has an unearthly, moonlike appearance as its shores have bubbling pools of water, the result of fumaroles discharging steam continuously under low pressure emitting sulphurous gases. The lake is lined with jagged chimneys or needles of rock that also discharge vapour wisps of sulphurous gases. Unsurprisingly the whole area can be pretty foul-smelling – in the local language Lake Abbe means the stinking lake.

Before desertification occurred the water level of the lake was much higher. Lake Abbe used to be fed by the Awash River that travels down from the Ethiopian highlands never reaching the sea, but the course of the river was diverted northwards approximately 8000 years ago by seismic activity. As a result the water level fell and magma penetrating through the thin earth's crust (only 3 km thick) caused a chain reaction of events that resulted in dissolved limestone solidifying in the cool waters creating extraordinary sculptures. Now exposed, the oddly shaped needles, up to 50 m tall, are unique. It is estimated that these columnar formations continue for at least another 100 m underground. Upon close examination they contain fossilized animal and vegetable remains. Some of the columns can be climbed, offering a wonderful view of the lake and surrounding plains. After the infrequent rains the ground around the lake softens and many fossils of crocodiles, fish and birds are uncovered.

The only other place where these limestone chimneys are believed to exist is on the floor of the Atlantic and Pacific oceans where the great tectonic plates meet.

The best time to visit is at sunrise, and a guide is essential to take you away from dangerous hot quicksand along the lakeshore that can give you severe burns. The lake can only be reached by four-wheel drive and two days is needed for the trip. The nearest accommodation is the two nearby campsites at Kouta Bouyya and Gite d'Asboley that will enable you to see the needles shrouded in dawn mists, as well as the opportunity to see the flamingos feeding. Otherwise there is accommodation at As Ela that has a rest camp or at Dikhil.

Ali-Sabieh
Colour map 2, grid A4

The mountain town of Ali-Sabieh, located 97 km from Djibouti City, is the Issa capital and has a large flourishing market. It makes an interesting excursion from Djibouti by train and can also be reached by a surfaced road. A major stop for the train between Djibouti and Addis Ababa, the journey is slow (2-3 hours) but interesting, especially when crossing the impressive metal 100-m **Hol Hol viaduct**, reputedly built by Gustave Eiffel, that carries the train across the bed of the seasonal river or wadi. Exploration of the red sandstone mountains surrounding Ali-Sabieh requires a four-wheel drive vehicle. One tour takes in **Guestir** and **Assamo**, small fortresses perched high in the mountains like eagles' nests overlooking the borders with Ethiopia and Somalia.

Sleeping **C** *Palmeraie*, T426198. Doubles with a/c, singles without. There is a simple camp at Assamo.

Background

History

'The Land of Punt' is how Djibouti (and Eritrea) were known to the Egyptians in the ancient world. The area known as Djibouti was only sparsely populated by nomadic peoples, mainly the Afars and the Issas (see Culture and Life, page 954) who used it as grazing land. The discovery of precious incense and myrrh brought Arab traders to the area, building towns like Tadjoura and Zeila, and resulted in an expansion of Islam. The whole east coast then passed into the control of the Ottoman Empire, whereas inland pastoral societies began to develop, governed by local political and social organizations. In 1859, as work on the Suez Canal was beginning there was a massive influx of Europeans to the whole region, and the French became interested in the strategic value of Djibouti.

Earliest times

The initial interest by the French in the area was to counteract the British trading presence in Aden on the other side of the Babel-Mandeb Straits, stimulated by the desire of both countries to control the entrance to the Red Sea. In 1862 they established themselves in Obock on the coast and drew up a treaty with Afar leaders, the Sultans of Obock and Tadjoura, to legitimize their acquisition of the coastal region in the north. In 1888 the construction of Djibouti began. Treaties in 1884, 1885 and 1896 with the Afars, the Issas

Colonial period

and Emperor Menelik of Ethiopia eventually led to the establishment of the boundaries of French Somaliland (later to be known as the French Territory of the Afars and the Issas, before being named The Republic of Djibouti at independence). The establishment of the boundaries was made without any consideration to the ethnic links, language, trading patterns or even traditional grazing rights of the Afar or Issa people. The problems caused by these matters continue to dominate politics.

In a treaty in 1897, the French made an agreement with Emperor Menelik which designated Djibouti as the `official outlet of Ethiopian commerce' and led to the building of a railway from Djibouti to Addis Ababa which would act as the major trade route into Ethiopia. The railway was completed in 1915 and from this point on, the port of Djibouti and the trade route has become the mainstay of the Djibouti economy. The port of Djibouti expanded rapidly after the completion of the railway, which is of vital strategic and commercial importance to Ethiopia and it is for this reason that Ethiopia is hostile to the idea of a merger between Somalia and Djibouti.

The French had habitually supported the Issas in the region but the anti-colonial demonstrations, which started as early as 1949 by the Somalis and Issas, eventually meant that in the 1960's the French switched their support to the Afar, with their strong Ethiopian links, in order to counter Somali government claims to the territory. This also served to strengthen Emperor Haile Selassie in Ethiopia, who was seen as an ally. As a result of the switch of allegiance, the French placed the Afar, Ali Aref and his Afar colleagues in control of the local government council, displacing the previous Issa administration.

In 1967 a referendum was held to determine if the people of Djibouti wished to remain a colony of France. Electoral manipulation condoned by the French meant the country remained a French overseas territory with the Afar dominating local politics. The vote was achieved by arresting opposition leaders and by the massive expulsion of Somalis, many of whom went on to join the Somali Coast Liberation Front. In 1973 the Afar still dominated local politics and reaffirmed Djibouti's links with France but by the mid 1970's Issa opposition to Afar rule grew, culminating in an assassination attempt on the Afar leader, Ali Aref in 1975.

International pressure from the Arab League and the OAU, local unrest and the increasingly turbulent situation in the Horn of Africa eventually led to the French withdrawing from Djibouti in 1976. An independent referendum was held in which a predominantly Issa assembly was elected, headed by Hassan Ghouled, leader of the Ligue Populaire Africaine pour l'Independance (LPAI).

Independence   Self-determination did not bring harmony to the former colony and tensions between the Afar and Issa have been a feature of the last 15 years.

In 1981 the Rassemblement Populaire Pour le Progrès (RPP) replaced the LPAI and was declared the sole legal political party.

Hostilities broke out in the late 1980s after Aden Robleh Abwalleh, a former cabinet minister was expelled from the party for opposing Hassan Ghouled and the existing regime. Abwalleh fled the country and formed a new opposition party, the Mouvement National Djiboutien pour l'Instauration de la Démocratie (MNDID). Inter-tribal hostilities erupted in Djibouti city in 1989 and in the Afar town of Tadjoura. Security forces subsequently arrested several hundred people, some of whom were deported. From 1990-2 a number of opposition parties were formed to press for political reform. Among these was the Front Pour la Restauration de l'Unité et de la Democratie (FRUD), an Afar-based group committed to armed conflict. FRUD suffered a set-back from a determined government assault in July 1993, and retreated to the mountains in the north. FRUD was further weakened by an internal split, and the government began negotiations with one of the factions. As a result of the conflict, approximately 15,000 Afars fled to Ethiopia. In early 2000, negotiations began between FRUD and the government, which culminated in a peace treaty signed in May 2001.

A new constitution was drawn up in 1992 and a multi-party system has been introduced. Ghouled was re-elected as president and many opposition leaders have been released from custody. In the 1999 elections, President Ghouled stood down, and his

The White Train and the Black Arrow

Emperor Menelik II, the architect of modern Ethiopia, conceived the idea of a rail line from Djibouti to Addis Ababa. A pair of European engineers formed the Compagnie Imperiale des Chemins de Fer Ethiopiens, and bolstered by the Franco-Ethiopian Treaty of 1897, French financiers backed the project. Construction started the same year.

The terrain was difficult, mostly desert and mountains, and Addis Ababa is 2.5 km higher than Djibouti. Avoiding the most obstructive features added another 150 km to the line on its way up to the Ethiopian capital. Local labour was supremely uninterested in joining the work-camps building the line, and most of the labourers and all the skilled craftsmen were imported for the job. The nomads along the route gleefully took the iron rails, pins and fittings to fashion into spears, bracelets and necklaces. They grumbled about their cattle being killed by the locomotives, so the company agreed to compensate them for every animal lost. This was the signal for the pastoralists to round up every sick, halt and lame beast in the horn of Africa and lay fodder for them on the tracks.

By 1900, the line had got to Dire Dawa, and a watering post and repair workshops were established there. The traffic was limited on this stretch, and the company went bankrupt in 1907. A new company with loans guaranteed by the French goverment was formed in 1908, and a single line of 1-m gauge, 748 km long, finally reached Addis Ababa in 1917.

Two trains departed in each direction each day, and stopped at 32 stations along the line. Passengers were taken in the White Train which travelled only in the day and took two and a half days to make the whole journey. Freight went by the Black Arrow which took five days, at an average speed of under 7 kph.

Having a virtual monopoly of transport up to the capital of the Mountain Kingdom enabled the line to charge high rates, and the company was reported to be the most profitable in the entire history of railways. This was particularly the case in the period 1936-38 when the Italians were obliged to ship vast quantities of men and munitions up to Addis Ababa in their effort to subdue the country. So stung were the Italians by the charges that they built a road from Addis to the port of Assab in Eritrea (which they controlled), and imported 400 trucks to haul freight. So good was this road that the winner of the motorcycle race staged in 1938 to inaugurate the route won at an average speed of 85 kph. Competition from the road heralded the end of the highly profitable era for the line.

When the British captured Ethiopia from the Italians in 1941, they ran the line until 1946, when ownership was restored to the original French company. In 1959, the Ethiopian government took half ownership of the railway, by which time diesel locomotives had cut the travel time up to Addis to 24 hours.

Djibouti

successor as leader of the ruling party, Ismael Omar Guelleh was elected President with an emphatic majority over a combined opposition candidate.

After the Police Chief was dismissed in December 2000 there was a mutiny and an attempted coup, which was put down. Given Djibouti's close links with France and over 2,800 French troops stationed in the territory, a coup was never likely to succeed.

Modern Djibouti

Politics

Since independence, politics in Djibouti have been heavily influenced by events in the neighbouring countries of Somalia and Ethiopia reflecting the sympathies of the Issa to Somalia and Afar to Ethiopia. In 1977, just after independence, tension between the two groups was considerable over the Ogaden war between Ethiopia and Somalia (Somalia were trying to recapture the region which had strong ethnic links with its people), with the Issa supporting Somalian interests. President Hassan Ghouled used the initial Somali successes in the Ogaden war as an opportunity to remove Afars from key posts in the administration and security forces. As a result, Ethiopia reduced its trading activities through Djibouti which had negative effects on the country's economy.

The Ethiopian victory in the Ogaden war (won with Russian and Cuban support) highlighted the importance of Djibouti's links with that country and led to President Ghouled to try to reach a compromise between the interests of the Issa and the Afar. Thus, the majority of Afar prisoners were released and any Afar who had been removed from office was reinstated into the civil service and security forces. Also, efforts were made to develop the north Afar region of the territory.

A further source of political and economic discontent has been the substantial flow of refugees from the Eritrean and Ogaden conflicts in Ethiopia into Djibouti since the early 1980's. The United Nations High Commission for Refugees (UNHCR) has begun a programme to repatriate Ethiopian refugees, said to number about 35,000, but has only had limited success. This problem has been exacerbated by the number of immigrants flooding in from Somalia – by 1993 these were estimated to number 120,000. Djibouti has attempted to tighten its border controls and the checking of identity papers, but has not really succeeded in materially stemming the flow. The heavy influx of peoples not only places an economic burden on the country, but is also a source of insecurity as it affects the balance between the Issa and Afar.

Djibouti's geographical position, and limited natural resource base, has meant that good relations with its neighbours are essential. Since 1985, Djibouti has developed agreements with Ethiopia and Somalia for closer co-operation in transport, communication and trade. It has played an important role in developing diplomatic relations between Ethiopia and Somalia, firstly by promoting the creation of the Intergovernmental Authority on Drought and Development with a permanent secretariat in Djibouti, and secondly by bringing heads of state of the two countries to meet and agree to re-establish diplomatic relations and withdraw troops from their common borders.

In recent years the dissatisfaction among the Afars at their marginalization led to the formation of the Front Pour la Restauration de l'Unité et Democratic (FRUD) which has pursued a policy of armed conflict against the government.

At the election in 1991, the RPP gained all 65 seats in the Assembly. The main opposition, Parti pour le Renouveau Démocratique (PRD) polled 28% of the popular vote. Two other parties have been recognized, Groupe pour la Démocratie de la République (GDR), and Parti National Democratique (PND). The constitution, drawn up with French advice, allows only four parties.

A determined assault by government forces in 1993, reduced FRUD to carrying on its activities by cross-border raids. However, the army increased in size from 3,000 troops in 1991 to 18,000 by 1994. The government would like to demobilize half these troops, and is looking to raise US$15 mn from the donor community to make severance payments of US$1,500 per head.

A peace initiative in 1994 succeeded with one faction in FRUD, and two FRUD members were given cabinet posts. The other wing of FRUD, led from Paris by former Prime Minister Ahmed Dini, continued the armed struggle.

In the elections in December 1997, the alliance between RPP and FRUD won all 65 seats in the National Assembly.

In the April 1999 elections, the nephew of President Ghouled, Ismael Omar Guelleh, took over as leader of RPP. PND and PRD formed the Opposition Djiboutienne Unifiée to fight for the Presidency with Moussa Ahmed Idriss, a former RPP deputy as candidate. Guelleh took 74% of the vote, and with RPP holding all the seats in the assembly, leads a strong government.

In May 2001, a peace treaty was signed between the government and FRUD, and Dini was allowed to return from exile.

The border dispute conflict that erupted between Ethiopia and Eritrea in 1998 led to Djibouti breaking diplomatic relations with Eritrea. As Djibouti has gained enormously from the re-routing of Ethiopian freight through its port, it is hard to see this as anything other than cynical opportunism. The presence of French troops, however, continues to maintain stability (a police mutiny in December 2000 was crushed), and Djibouti City remains secure.

Economy

Economic data is sparse for Djibouti. Nevertheless, such information as is available is presented and gives a reasonable overall picture of economic conditions in the territory.

The best estimate of the population in 2000 is 550,000. It is thought that over 100,000 of these are refugees from Somalia, but it is difficult to be certain as to the exact numbers. The natural rate of growth of the population growth was 2.6% a year in 2000. About half of the population live in the town of Djibouti which has a population of over 300,000.

Economic structure

GDP in 1999 was estimated at US$ 550 mn. The level of income per head, , was estimated at US$ 1,200, and Djibouti was classified as a lower-middle income country.

The economy relies heavily on the port facilities it provides, and this is reflected in the structure of the economy with agriculture providing only 3% of GDP, industry 21% and services 76%.

The openness of the economy resulting from small size and specialized activities is reflected in 35% of GDP being generated by exports. Apart from the export of port services, there are exports of livestock, hides and skins to Somalia, Yemen, Saudi Arabia and Ethiopia. Expenditure on imports is equivalent to 68% of GDP. The gap is mainly covered by foreign assistance with France the main benefactor. In fact aid, at US$ 250 per head is many times greater than the Africa average of US$36.

Overall, Djibouti has a small economy with a high level of urbanization. The economy depends heavily on the supply of port services, and there is a substantial deficit on the current account of the balance of payments.

Economic performance has been erratic in recent years, and is much affected by political events in neighbouring countries as well as by domestic political events . Living standards are estimated to have fallen by 20% during the 1991-94 civil war, and unemployment rose to 50%. However, since the border dispute between Ethiopia and Eritrea erupted in 1998, Ethiopia has ceased using the Eritrean ports of Massawa and Assab, and has routed all its freight through Djibouti. This has been an enormous boost for Djibouti, with freight handling in some months more than ten times the normal level. In February 2001, Djibouti raised its port handling charges significantly – many rates trebled. Although the new charges were defended as fair, it is hard not to feel that Djibouti is taking advantage of Ethiopia's current rift with Eritrea.

Economic performance

Inflation is low, and is running at under 3% a year. The exchange rate has been very steady in recent years and was DFr 170 = US$1 in February 2001.

External debt is around US$280 mn, and debt service is quite manageable, taking up only 5.2% of export earnings.

Parastatal organizations have accumulated arrears, with the airport US$2.8 mn behind with payments to creditors on a US$22 mn upgrading programme. 19 parastatals in all, including water, electricity and the airport are scheduled for privatization. Air Djibouti with an accumulated deficit of US$4 mn has been liquidated but reformed under the private ownership of middle-east business interests.

Recent economic developments

Two geothermal drillings of a 4-well US$16.6 mn drilling programme have not yielded water of high enough temperature in the Hanle Gaggade region to make them commercially viable, but later drillings in the Goubet-Lac-Assal region appear more promising. It is hoped that the wells could meet Djibouti's electricity needs, and the programme is being funded by the International Development Association of the World Bank, Italy, the African Development Bank, the OPEC Fund for International Development and the UN Development Programme.

A major source of income is the use of Djibouti by the French as their main overseas military base. There has been a reduction in the number of tropps staitione in Djibouti, but there are still 2,800 troops stationed in the port, and the military community is more than 5,000, and contributes an estimated US$ 50 annually to the economy.

Economic outlook It is assumed that Djibouti's stability will remain good, with continuing French support and military presence. The settlement with FRUD should provide a major boost to the economy, reducing military expenditure and raising both foreign and domestic investment. Djibouti's outlook is particularly sensitive to the strength of economic recovery in Ethiopia, and progress in the Somaliland Republic. Recent expansion of the economy in Ethiopia and the dispute with Eritrea has caused a massive increase in port traffic. The coming years should see steady economic growth, although the refugee problem will continue to hamper improvements in living standards until the Somali situation is finally resolved.

Culture

The population of the country is thought to be anywhere between 450,000 and 650,000 in 2000. A figure of 550,000 is used by most agencies as a fairly realistic estimate. Although there is a trend toward more permanent settlement, the seasonal migrations of the nomadic peoples who make up about half the population of the country make any accurate population figures elusive. Djibouti City's population is estimated to be 350,000. There are also estimated to be about 60,000 people permanently living a nomadic lifestyle.

The indigenous population of Djibouti is evenly divided between the Issa who are of Somali origin and mainly occupy the south part of the country, and the Afar who live in the north part of the country. Both the Afar and the Issa are Muslim Cushitic-speaking peoples with a nomadic culture and close cultural affinities despite frequent rivalry. Both groups spill across the boundaries of Djibouti into neighbouring Somalia and Ethiopia. There are also many refugees, about 30,000, who have sought refuge in the country as a result of various wars in neighbouring Eritrea, Ethiopia, and Somalia. A small, yet significant, Arab community of Yemeni origin also resides in Djibouti City. Expatriates, mostly French, make up the rest of the population and are mainly in government employment or are members of the armed forces.

Religion   Largely Sunni Muslim (96%) though there are a small number of Christians (4%).

Social conditions

Adult literacy at 46% is poor, and well out of line with Djibouti's middle-income status. Primary and secondary enrolments are also low and below the Africa averages. There is little tertiary education in Djibouti, and most students have to seek higher education places overseas.

Life expectancy is 51 years, and infant mortality is high, both of these being worse than for Africa generally. Availability of doctors is very good, however almost ten times better than the rest of Africa. Clearly there is good medical provision for the elite, and very poor provision for others.

Females have significantly less access to both primary and secondary education compared with males, and Djibouti is less egalitarian in this respect than the rest of Africa. On average women bear 5.8 children, and this presents a formidable challenge in providing adequate nutrition, shelter and clothing in the poorer families.

Land and environment

Geography   'Part of the moon on the earth's crust', 'an image of chaos from the gestation of the planet', 'apocalyptic landscape', all are terms used to describe this constantly changing part of the world. The country covers an area of 23,000 sq km, most of which is volcanic rock-strewn desert wastes with occasional patches of arable land and spectacular salt lakes. It lies at 12° latitude north and 43° longitude east, located half-way between the equator and the Tropic of Cancer on the east coast of Africa, at the opening of the Red Sea and the Gulf of Aden. To the north lies Eritrea, a boundary is shared with Ethiopia to the west and south, and Somalia abuts to the southeast. The physical core consists of a triangular depression which is part of the East African rift system and is made up of a complex pattern of volcanic plateau, sunken plains and lakes (most of which are salty). Much of the territory is below sea level – millions of years ago this area was ocean floor but submarine volcanic activity caused rock and lava formations to develop. There are vast deposits of salt around the country that are mined, mainly by the Afar, and used throughout the region. To the north are found the *Massif du Goda* (the Goda Mountains) with summits reaching 2000 m in height. The south features parallel depressions with salt lakes and sunken plains alternating with a series of volcanic plateaux where nomadic people live. In the middle of the country the volcanic zone between Lake Assal and the bay of Ghoubbet El Kharab, a sea loch which extends westwards from the Gulf of Tadjoura, is a seismically unstable area of great interest to geologists as it lies at a triple junction between the African and Arabian tectonic plates where three rift arms converge. The thickness of earth's crust is estimated to be only 3 km thick in places and it is anticipated that in time the sea will break through the Ardoukoba Rift.

Vegetation in the country is spartan and seasonal and comprises mainly grasses, thorn trees and scattered palms. The only part of the country with continuous annual vegetation is the upper part of the basaltic range, north of the Gulf of Tadjoura where the altitude reaches more than 1,200 m above sea level. The poor quality of the soil and the arid climate prevents any large-scale crop production except under irrigation.

Climate

The climate is tropical with torrid temperatures and high humidity during the monsoon season. Average rainfall is less than 125 mm per annum, and temperatures can reach as high as 45°C. The country is particularly parched between June and August when temperatures are at their highest, and the dusty *khamsin* blows from the desert. It is cooler between October and April with occasional light rains.

Environment

Djibouti has negligible forest area, but what little exists is being maintained.

Despite being very arid, the population uses only 2% of renewable freshwater resources each year. This is because per capita utilization, at 30 cubic metres per person a year, is well below the African average of 120 cubic metres per person. Low utilization, results from the small size of the agriculture sector and low demand for water for irrigation.

Books

Thompson, V and Adloff, R (1968) *Djibouti and the Horn of Africa*, London: OUP. Thorough coverage of historical, political and economic issues prior to independence.

General

Waugh, E (1931) *Remote People*, London: Duckworth. Includes Waughs's impressions of Djibouti on the way to Addis Ababa in 1930, and on the way back.

Travellers' tales

Djibouti

Footnotes

9

958

Footnotes

Index

Advertisers

Things to do

Footnotes

Shorts

Maps

Animal location chart

	Aberdare	Amboseli	Marsabit	Masai Mara	Meru	Mt Kenya	Nairobi	Lake Nakuru	Sambur/Shaba	Shimba	Tsavo
Big Nine											
Lion		●	●	●	●		●	●	●	●	●
Leopard	●	●	●	●	●	●	●		●	●	●
Cheetah		●	●	●	●		●		●		●
Elephant	●	●	●	●	●	●			●	●	●
Buffalo	●	●	●	●	●	●	●	●	●	●	●
Black rhino				●							
Zebra		B	G	B	BG	B	B	B	BG		BG
Giraffe		M	R	M	R			M	Ro	R	M
Hippo		●		●	●		●	●	●		●
Larger antelopes											
Hartebeest		K		K	K	K					K
Gnu		●		●			●				
Topi				●							
Waterbuck	C	C		D	C		CD	D	C		C
Roan				●							
Sable											
Oryx			Bo		Bo				Bo		Fo
Kudu		GkLk	Lk		Lk					Lk	Lk
Eland	●	●		●	●		●	●	●		●
Smaller antelopes											
Oribi				●	●						
Reedbuck	●	●		●	●		●	●			●
Impala	●	●		●	●		●	●	●		●
Thomson's gazelle		●		●	●		●	●			
Grant's gazelle		●		●	●		●	●	●		●
Bushbuck	●	●		●	●		●	●	●		●
Dikdik		●		●	●		●	●	●		●

B = Burchell's zebra G = Grevy's zebra
M = Masai giraffe R = Reticulated giraffe
Ro = Rothchild's giraffe K = Kongoni (Coke's hartebeest)
J = Jackson's hartebeest L = Lichtenstein's hartebeest
C = Common waterbuck D = Defassa waterbuck
Bo = Beisa oryx Fo = Fringe-eared oryx
Gk = Greater kudu Lk = Lesser kudu

	TANZANIA									UGANDA			
	Arusha	Katavi	Kilimanjaro	Lake Manyara	Mikumi/Selous	Ngorongoro Crater	Ruaha/Rungwa	Serengeti	Tarangire	Kidepo Valley	Lake Mburo	Murchison Falls	Queen Elizabeth
		●		●	●	●	●	●	●	●	●	●	●
	●	●	●	●	●	●	●	●	●	●	●	●	●
						●	●	●	●	●	●	●	
	●	●	●	●	●	●	●	●	●			●	●
	●	●	●	●	●	●	●	●	●		●	●	●
						●							
	B	B		B	B	B	B	B	B	B	B		
	M			M	M	M	M	M	M	Ro		Ro	
	●	●		●	●	●	●	●			●	●	●
				K	L	K	L	K	K	J		J	
				●	●	●		●	●				
		●						●			●	●	●
		D		C	C	C	C	CD	C	D	D	D	D
		●						●			●		
					●		●						
								Fo	Fo				
					Gk		GkLk						
		●				●	●	●	●	●	●		
											●	●	
				●	●	●	●	●			●	●	●
				●	●	●	●	●			●	●	●
						●		●					
					●	●	●	●	●	●			
				●	●	●	●	●	●		●	●	●
						●		●	●	●	●		

Footnotes

Will you help us?

We try as hard as we can to make each Footprint Handbook as up-to-date and accurate as possible but, of course, things always change. Many people email or write to us – with corrections, new information, or simply comments. If you want to let us know about your experiences and adventures – be they good, bad or ugly – then don't delay; we're dying to hear from you. And please try to include all the relevant details. Your help will be greatly appreciated, especially by other travellers. In return we will send you details about our special guidebook offer.

email Footprint at:
eafr7_online@footprintbooks.com

or write to:

Elizabeth Taylor
Footprint Handbooks
6 Riverside Court
Lower Bristol Road
Bath
BA2 3DZ
UK

Footprint travel list

Footprint publish travel guides to over 120 countries worldwide. Each guide is packed with practical, concise and colourful information for everybody from first-time travellers to travel aficionados . The list is growing fast and current titles are noted below. For further information check out the website
www.footprintbooks.com

Andalucía Handbook
Argentina Handbook
Bali & the Eastern Isles Hbk
Bangkok & the Beaches Hbk
Barcelona Handbook
Bolivia Handbook
Brazil Handbook
Cambodia Handbook
Caribbean Islands Handbook
Central America & Mexico Hbk
Chile Handbook
Colombia Handbook
Costa Rica Handbook
Cuba Handbook
Cusco & the Sacred Valley Hbk
Dominican Republic Handbook
Dublin Handbook
East Africa Handbook
Ecuador & Galápagos Handbook
Edinburgh Handbook
Egypt Handbook
Goa Handbook
Guatemala Handbook
India Handbook
Indian Himalaya Handbook
Indonesia Handbook
Ireland Handbook
Israel Handbook
Jordan Handbook
Laos Handbook
Libya Handbook
London Handbook
Malaysia Handbook
Marrakech & the High Atlas Hbk
Myanmar Handbook
Mexico Handbook
Morocco Handbook

Namibia Handbook
Nepal Handbook
New Zealand Handbook
Nicaragua Handbook
Pakistan Handbook
Peru Handbook
Rajasthan & Gujarat Handbook
Rio de Janeiro Handbook
Scotland Handbook
Scotland Highlands & Islands Hbk
Singapore Handbook
South Africa Handbook
South American Handbook
South India Handbook
Sri Lanka Handbook
Sumatra Handbook
Syria & Lebanon Handbook
Thailand Handbook
Tibet Handbook
Tunisia Handbook
Turkey Handbook
Venezuela Handbook
Vietnam Handbook

Also available from Footprint
Traveller's Handbook
Traveller's Healthbook
Traveller's Internet Guide

Available at all good bookshops

www.footprintbooks.com
A new place to visit

THE LEGENDARY ADVENTURE CO

Traditional East African Safaris

For further information and reservations, contact:

THE LEGENDARY ADVENTURE CO

3025 47th Street, Suite 1
Boulder, CO 80301, USA

Toll Free: 800 924 9081 • Tel: 303 413 1182 • Fax: 303 413 1184
Email: legendary@tfcomp.com
Internet: www.legendaryadventure.com

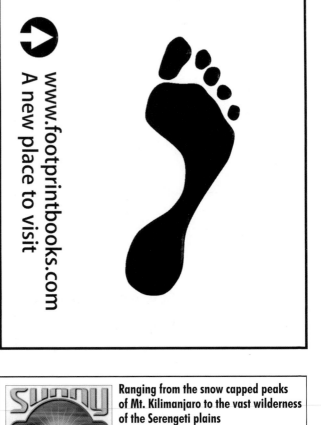

STAYING IN NAIROBI?

Try The Country Hotel In Town,
Set Within 5 Acres of Luxuriant Tranquil Gardens.
The Perfect Hotel for Business Travellers.

– The Fairview Hotel –

Spacious Reception – The Hub

A Comfortable Double Bedroom.

Fairview
THE COUNTRY HOTEL IN TOWN

Bishops Road, Nairobi Hill, P.O.Box 40842, Kenya, East Africa.
Tel: (254-2) 723211, 710090   Fax: (254-2) 721320   Email: reserv@fairviewkenya.com
www.fairviewkenya.com

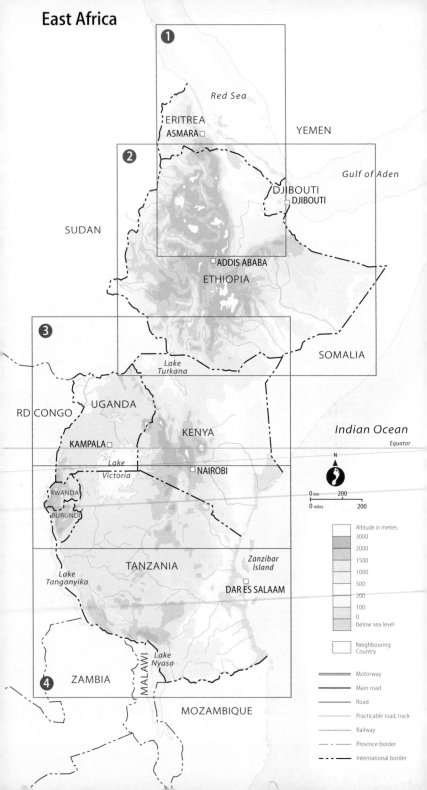

East Africa

①

Red Sea

ERITREA
ASMARA □

YEMEN

②

Gulf of Aden

DJIBOUTI
□ DJIBOUTI

SUDAN

□ ADDIS ABABA

ETHIOPIA

SOMALIA

③

Lake Turkana

RD CONGO

UGANDA

KENYA

Indian Ocean

Equator

KAMPALA □

Lake Victoria

□ NAIROBI

N

RWANDA

BURUNDI

0 km   200

0 miles   200

TANZANIA

Zanzibar Island

Lake Tanganyika

□ DAR ES SALAAM

Altitude in metres

3000
2000
1500
1000
500
200
100
0
below sea level

Neighbouring Country

④

ZAMBIA

Lake Nyasa

MALAWI

MOZAMBIQUE

═══ Motorway
─── Main road
─── Road
─── Practicable road, track
─── Railway
─·─· Province border
━·━· International border

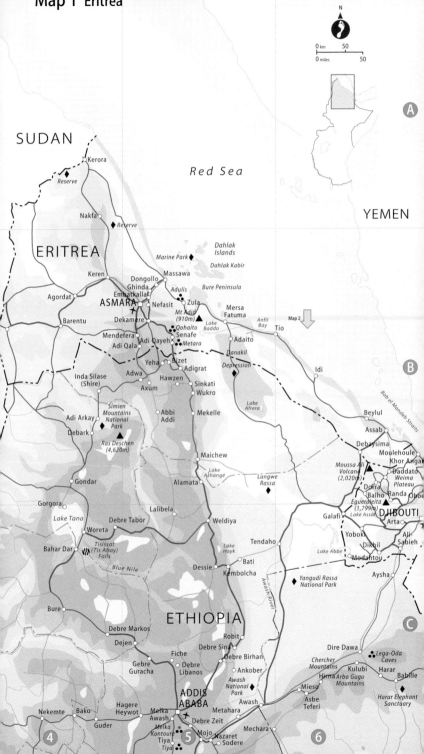

Map 1 Eritrea

N

0 km   50
0 miles   50

A

SUDAN

Red Sea

YEMEN

Kerora

Reserve

Nakfa   *Reserve*

ERITREA

Dahlak Islands

Keren   Dongollo   *Marine Park*   *Dahlak Kabir*

Ghinda

Massawa

Agordat   Embatkallal   *Adulis*   *Bure Peninsula*

ASMARA   Nefasit   Zula

Barentu   Dekamere   Mersa Fatuma

Mendefera   *Mt Adid*   *Anfil Bay*   Tio   Map 2

Adi Qayeh   *(910m)*   *Lake Baddo*

Adi Qala   *Qohaito*   Senafe   Adaito

Yeha   *Metara*   *Danakil Depression*   Idi

B

Bizet

Adigrat

Inda Silase   Adwa   Hawzen   Sinkati

(Shire)   Axum   Wukro   *Lake Afrera*   *Bab el Mandeb Straits*

Adi Arkay   Abbi Addi   Mekelle   Beylul

Simien Mountains National Park

Debark   Assab

Ras Deschen (4,620m)   Maichew   Debaysima

Moulehoule

Khor Anga

Gondar   *Lake Ashangè*   *Langwe Rassa*   *Moussa Ali Volcano (2,020m)*   Daddato

Alamata   Weima Plateau

Gorgora   Dorra   Balho   Randa   Oboc

Lake Tana   Lalibela   *Eguerdeita (1,799m)*   DJIBOUTI

Debre Tabor   Weldiya   Galafi   *Lake Assal*   Arta

Woreta

Bahar Dar   *Lake Hayk*   Tendaho   Yoboki   Ali-Sabieh

Tisissat (Tis Abay) Falls   *Lake Abbe*   Dikhil

Blue Nile   Bati   Modantou

Dessie   Aysha

Bure   Kembolcha

Awash River   *Yangudi Rassa National Park*

ETHIOPIA

C

Debre Markos   Robit   Dire Dawa   *Lega-Oda Caves*

Dejen   Debre Sina   *Chercher Mountains*   Kulubi   Harar

Fiche   Debre Birhan   Hirna   Babille

Gebre Guracha   Debre Libanos   Ankober   Mieso   *Arba Gugu Mountains*

ADDIS ABABA   *Awash National Park*   Asbe Teferi   *Harar Elephant Sanctuary*

Hagere Heywot   Melka Awash   Metahara

Nekemte   Bako   Debre Zeit   Awash   Mechara

Guder   Melka Kontoure   Mojo   Nazaret   Sodere

Tiya   *Tiya*

4   5   6

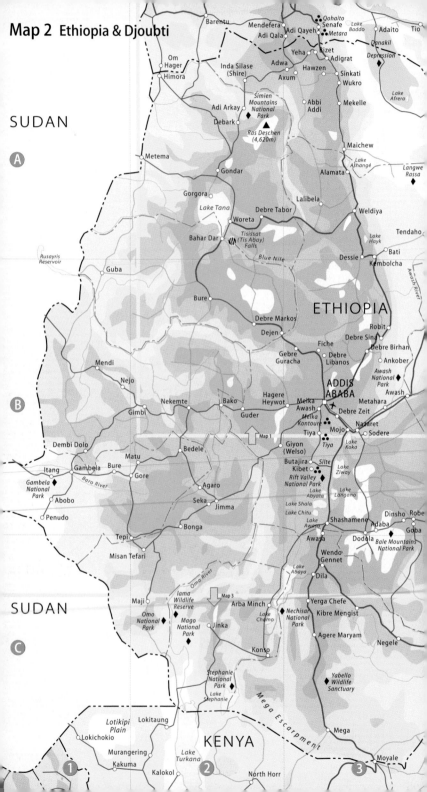

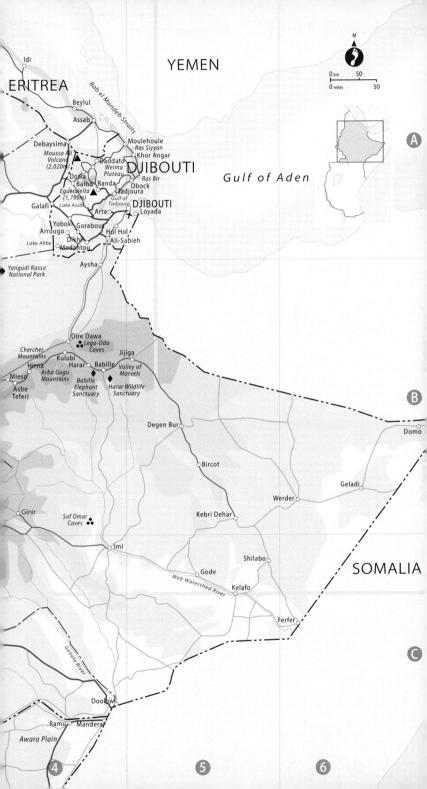

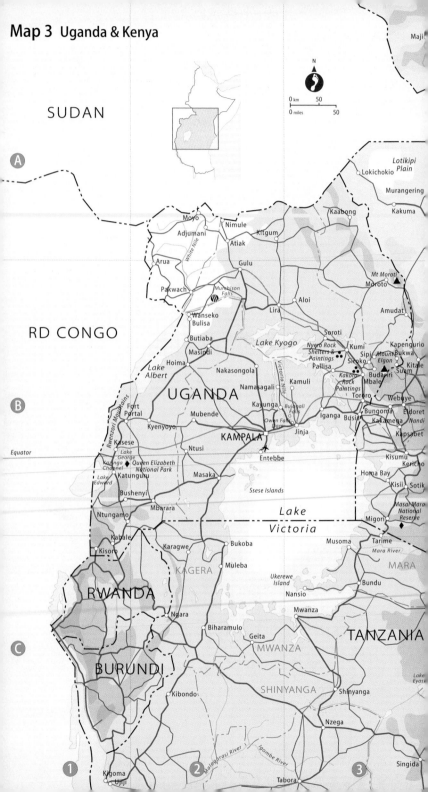

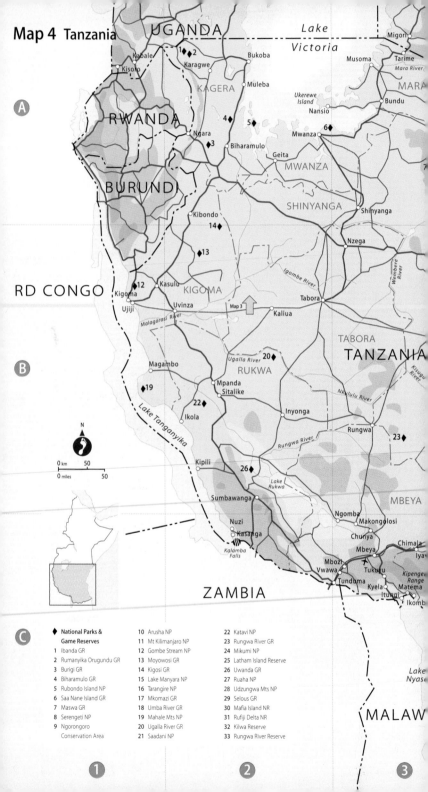

Map 4 Tanzania

♦ National Parks & Game Reserves
1 Ibanda GR
2 Rumanyika Orugundu GR
3 Burigi GR
4 Biharamulo GR
5 Rubondo Island NP
6 Saa Nane Island GR
7 Maswa GR
8 Serengeti NP
9 Ngorongoro Conservation Area
10 Arusha NP
11 Mt Kilimanjaro NP
12 Gombe Stream NP
13 Moyowosi GR
14 Kigosi GR
15 Lake Manyara NP
16 Tarangire NP
17 Mkomazi GR
18 Umba River GR
19 Mahale Mts NP
20 Ugalla River GR
21 Saadani NP
22 Katavi NP
23 Rungwa River GR
24 Mikumi NP
25 Latham Island Reserve
26 Uwanda GR
27 Ruaha NP
28 Udzungwa Mts NP
29 Selous GR
30 Mafia Island NR
31 Rufiji Delta NR
32 Kilwa Reserve
33 Rungwa River Reserve

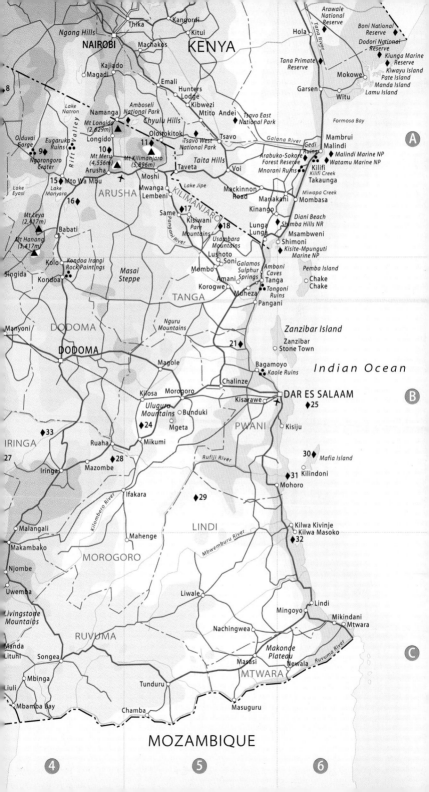

UNBEATABLE

THE CHEETAH. WITHOUT COMPARISON THE FASTEST ANIMAL ON LAND

Airkenya. The fastest way to experience a country known for its vast spaces, rugged beauty and wildlife.

Airkenya is the reliable, fast and comfortable mode of transport to help you fully appreciate Kenya's picturesque diversity.

We operate scheduled flights from Nairobi to Malindi, Lamu, Kiwayu, Amboseli, Samburu, Maasai Mara and Nanyuki.

We also provide charter flights throughout the East African region and cater for individual or group requirement

And because we operate from Wilso airport, only four kilometers from Nairol city centre, we are easily accessible.

We are renowned for our friendly an efficient service, half-hour check-i guaranteed seats, and a punctuali record second to none.

Call us or your travel agent an discover the unbeatable way t cover Kenya in comfort when you hav limited time.

AIRKENYA
The best way to fly.

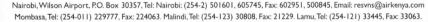

Nairobi, Wilson Airport, P.O. Box 30357, Tel: Nairobi: (254-2) 501601, 605745, Fax: 602951, 500845, Email: resvns@airkenya.com
Mombasa, Tel: (254-011) 229777, Fax: 224063. Malindi, Tel: (254-123) 30808, Fax: 21229. Lamu, Tel: (254-121) 33445, Fax: 33063.

Acknowledgements

Contributors
Margaret Carswell (Wildlife Guide), **David Snashall** (Health), **Grace Carswell** (Uganda and Kenya) and **Dan Collison** (Ethiopia and Eritrea), provided initial background research for the first edition. Since the last edition there has been a major up-date of the book using over 30 commissioned researchers, including **Mark Durham** and **Charlie Graham**, who have repeated what they did for *Footprint South Africa Handbook* by providing a special feature on diving in the region. My wife **Angela** helped to research and edit the book. **John Ellerker** was also an enormous help with the editing. Regrettably due to space restraints we are restricted to just listing the names of contributors.

We are very grateful to all our commissioned researchers, who provided excellent information:
Ethiopia: **Bill Derrett**, **John English**, **Ed Finch**, **Jody Henderson**, **Edith McCollam**, **Ewan McFarlane**, **Julia Parker**, **Sarah Wilson** and finally **Ian Smith** and **Gordon Winthrop** who deserve special mention and thanks.
Eritrea: **Alison Chapman** and her Eritrean colleagues reviewed the Eritrea entry.
Djibouti: **Dominique Lommatzsch** helped with the entire section, translated from the original French by the kind assistance of **Penelope** and **Claude Rosenfeld** (no relation).
Kenya: **Felix Hobson** and **Jack Hodd** (unfortunately related) updated 14 towns in Central and Western Kenya; **Sarah Thorowgood** provided information about the Kenya coast and Nairobi.
Uganda: **Jon Bosco**, **Krista Bradford**, **Marie Cates**, **Patrick Dawson**, **Ernst Frandsen**, **Ineke Jongerius** – a major contributor – **Annemarie van den Heuvel**, **Jennifer Vigano** and **Sarah Wicken**.
Tanzania: **Alex Becker**, **Felicitas Becker**, **Amy Coad**, **Debre Coupe**, **Rosie Hogg**, **Cheryl Oelsner**, **Tase Oputu**, **Estella Parkhill** and **Francesco Rovero**.

As always we have been delighted by the number of people who have written in with information.
John Ellerker, **Paul Miller**, **James Paterson**, **Manuelle Prunier**, **Thomas Schweiger**, **Heimon Smits** and **Dorine Wekking** all made major contributions, as did **Paul Bradbury**, **Rob** and **Dafne de Jong**, **Richard English**, **Vicki Hallam**, **Menno Harkema** and **Esther van Kemenade**, **Andre Hesselback**; **Steve Howard**, **Jenny** and **Jon Ison**, **Reverend Dom Bernard Kaboggdia**, **Jessica Lane**, **Jason McCaldin**, **Christine McNeal**, **Catherine Nesbit**, **Natalie Pearce** and **Craig Hilder, Bryan Pready**, the **Quinton family**, **Gerhard Rainer**, **Sarah** of *A Novel Idea*, Dar es Salaam, **Annie Sproston**, **Stefanie Stasse** and **Pascal Vervacke**.

Other useful information was provided by:
Ann Alton, Roberto Andreetta, Aline Baffalie, David V. V. Barnes, Michael Boller, Robert Carrelli, Ines Cattoor and Luc Stevens, Bengt Cederlund, Jon Dahl, Orlaith Gadsden, Maryann Gebauer, Ginny of Ukunda, Rolf Gloor, Peter Gower, Kathy Hanson, Deborah Harting, Steve Howard, Ally Ibrahim, Gabriel K Kago, Joas Kahembe, Mirjam Keijzer, Tony Kelly, Raphael Kessler, Dr Stefan Koeppen, Gavan Lim-Joon, Marie Lippens, Bridget Mc Ging, Michael McKean, Liz McKee, Pema Malmgren, Steven Nelson, Karsten Neuffer, Steve Nzau Nzivo, Steve Pasternack, Gemma Pitcher and Clare Edgington, Paula Post, Matz Lonnedal Risberg, Paula and Tracey Robinson, Dave Roscoe, Edward Scotcher, Mark Smith,

Richard Smith, Charles Szlapak, Mary Taylor, Robert van Seeters, Jo Verberckmoes, Aubin U Wilkens and Julie Wilson. We extend our thanks for your interest and help.

In addition we received help and assistance from:
Uganda Tourist Board staff in both Kampala and London; **Devota Karamaga** for the **Tanzania Tourist Board** was invaluable; **Kenya Wildlife Service** and **National Museums of Kenya** provided excellent information and **Marcel Leuzer** of the Netherlands helped with SNV initiatives.

We are grateful to **Philip Briggs** and **Bradt Travel Guides** for certain information and maps on Ethiopia, Uganda and Tanzania used in previous editions of this book.

Finally, we are grateful to the British Institute in East Africa for permission to use information and research undertaken by **John E G Sutton**, on Mubende, Bigo, and Ntusi in Uganda; and to **John Tuson** of Hove, UK, who proved to be a great resource on zoos in Tanzania.